1984	1985	1986	1987	1988	1989	1990	1991	1992	1993	1994	1995	1996	1997
236	238	241	243	245	247	250	253	255	258	261	263	265	268
74.7	74.7	74.7	74.9	74.9	75.1	75.4	75.5	75.8	75.5	75.7	75.8	75.9	—
3,902	4,181	4,422	4,692	5,050	5,439	5,744	5,917	6,244	6,558	6,947	7,265	7,636	8,083
5,778	5,984	6,168	6,350	6,593	6,814	6,897	6,834	7,019	7,182	7,431	7,578	7,788	8,083
24,446	25,093	25,632	26,154	26,907	27,549	27,595	27,049	27,484	27,828	28,514	28,811	29,338	30,173
3,841	4,020	4,180	4,308	4,478	4,581	4,657	4,628	4,756	4,896	5,056	5,179	5,313	5,489
865	855	843	853	860	896	846	766	820	896	1,013	1,029	1,110	1,238
1,165	1,236	1,299	1,334	1,351	1,389	1,431	1,439	1,446	1,433	1,433	1,433	1,439	1,454
−187	−217	−241	−230	−168	−122	−91	−33	−43	−103	−154	−145	−168	−209
3,342	3,472	3,588	3,732	3,883	3,948	4,026	3,994	4,097	4,178	4,291	4,397	4,515	4,703
1,343	1,371	1,364	1,428	1,529	1,561	1,560	1,506	1,512	1,590	1,689	1,770	1,864	1,854
4.6	3.8	3.7	4.9	6.0	5.0	4.0	2.4	0.8	2.8	5.4	5.7	6.0	—
7.5	7.2	7.0	6.2	5.5	5.3	5.6	6.8	7.5	6.9	6.1	5.6	5.4	4.9
105	107	110	112	115	117	119	118	118	120	123	125	127	130
35.2	34.9	34.8	34.8	34.7	34.6	34.5	34.3	34.4	34.5	34.7	34.5	34.4	34.6
12.97	12.92	12.99	12.86	12.79	12.71	12.51	12.39	12.33	12.29	12.31	12.29	12.36	12.54
64.7	67.0	68.3	70.8	73.7	77.3	81.4	84.9	87.4	90.0	92.3	95.0	97.8	100.0
4.3	3.6	1.9	3.6	4.1	4.8	5.4	4.2	3.0	3.0	2.6	2.8	3.0	2.3
9.6	7.5	6.0	5.8	6.7	8.1	7.5	5.4	3.5	3.0	4.3	5.5	5.0	5.1
1,261	1,355	1,382	1,359	1,390	1,433	1,505	1,530	1,553	1,543	1,563	1,581	1,592	1,601
987	1,051	1,073	1,156	1,187	1,242	1,239	1,218	1,227	1,264	1,346	1,410	1,482	1,579
−274	−304	−309	−203	−203	−191	−266	−311	−326	−279	−217	−171	−110	−22
22.3	23.1	22.6	21.8	21.5	21.4	22.0	22.6	22.5	21.8	21.4	21.1	20.7	20.1
17.5	17.9	17.6	18.6	18.4	18.5	18.2	18.0	17.8	17.8	18.4	18.8	19.3	19.8
−4.9	−5.2	−5.1	−3.3	−3.1	−2.8	−3.9	−4.6	−4.7	−3.9	−3.0	−2.3	−1.4	−0.3
1,797	1,877	1,947	1,995	2,027	2,080	2,163	2,194	2,321	2,351	2,369	2,422	2,466	2,511
1,694	1,774	1,832	1,934	1,981	2,057	2,073	2,056	2,103	2,172	2,272	2,347	2,461	—
−102	−103	−115	−61	−46	−23	−89	−139	−219	−179	−96	−74	−5	—
31.1	31.4	31.6	31.4	30.7	30.5	31.4	32.1	33.1	32.7	31.9	32.0	31.7	31.1
29.3	29.7	29.7	30.5	30.0	30.2	30.1	30.1	30.0	30.2	30.6	31.0	31.6	—
−1.8	−1.7	−1.9	−1.0	−0.7	−0.3	−1.3	−2.0	−3.1	−2.5	−1.3	−1.0	−0.1	—
111,830	105,935	109,509	114,337	117,440	122,090	126,893	125,331	128,344	132,228	134,196	138,186	132,121	—

*To Cindy, Gwendolyn,
Madeleine, and Rebecca*

Introduction To

ECONOMICS

② Second Edition

Alan C. Stockman

University of Rochester

THE DRYDEN PRESS
Harcourt Brace College Publishers

Fort Worth Philadelphia San Diego New York Austin Orlando San Antonio
Toronto Montreal London Sydney Tokyo

Executive Editor: Gary Nelson
Product Manager: Debbie Anderson
Developmental Editor: Amy Schmidt
Project Editor: Jim Patterson
Art Director: Bill Brammer
Production Manager: Eddie Dawson

Credits appear on page C-1, which constitutes a continuation of the copyright page.

ISBN: 0-03-022414-4
Library of Congress Catalog Card Number: 98-71885

Copyright © 1999, 1996 by The Dryden Press

All rights reserved. No part of this publication may be reproduced or transmitted in any form or by any means, electronic or mechanical, including photocopy, recording, or any information storage and retrieval system, without permission in writing from the publisher.

Requests for permission to make copies of any part of the work should be mailed to: Permissions Department, Harcourt Brace & Company, 6277 Sea Harbor Drive, Orlando, Florida 32887-6777.

Address for orders:
The Dryden Press
6277 Sea Harbor Drive
Orlando, FL 32887-6777
1-800-782-4479

Address for editorial correspondence:
The Dryden Press
301 Commerce Street, Suite 3700
Fort Worth, TX 76102

Web site address:
http://www.hbcollege.com

The Dryden Press, Dryden, and the Dryden Press logo are registered trademarks of Harcourt Brace & Company.

Printed in the United States of America

8 9 0 1 2 3 4 5 6 7   048   9 8 7 6 5 4 3 2 1

The Dryden Press
Harcourt Brace College Publishers

PREFACE

I'll confess: This book has a secret agenda. I wrote this book to teach students how to think like economists, but my ultimate motive for writing it was my own satisfaction—I seek the delight that arises in me when a student becomes enthusiastic about economics; when he proudly explains his new application of economic reasoning; when she decides to major in economics because of my course. These occasions generate feelings (with less intensity) similar to my immense joy in sharing some beautiful aspect of the world, such as the emotions of music or the pride of accomplishment, with my own children. The gratification of teaching occurs when students rekindle their natural curiosities to feed the appetite that curiosity creates.

Students who enroll in a principles of economics course seldom have more than the vaguest idea of its subject, let alone why they should care about it. Many of them expect economics to be boring and enroll in the course only to satisfy a requirement. They have no awareness of the market, let alone any sort of *awe* of the market. It has never occurred to them that our economy, without any central plan or direction, somehow coordinates the activities of millions of people to produce efficiently the goods and services that they want. Most students have never been exposed to the kinds of questions that economics answers. Although the results of those questions and answers profoundly affect their lives, they take them for granted.

Introduction to Economics inspires students not to take those results for granted but to think like economists instead. It does so by leading them on a path of inquiry and discovery, fostering the experience of its joys. Of course, the book does teach the substantive results of economics, such as the effects of an increase in demand on price, for example. More importantly, though, the book helps students acquire *new skills* that they can apply in their own lives. It teaches students the answers, but first and foremost, it helps them learn to formulate the questions. If this book accomplishes its goal, it will evoke in students an excitement of economics and appreciation for the power of economic analysis. They will share (with those of us who love economics) that "Aha!" feeling of new discovery, and their newfound abilities to think like economists will change their lives.

Information and Analysis

The relative price of facts and analysis has changed. Since the first edition of *Introduction to Economics*, the information revolution has swept our society, reducing the price of facts. Students can obtain data at a vastly lower time cost than ever before. But facts and analysis are complements. Without tools for analysis, students may drown in a sea of facts. The widening gulf between wages of unskilled workers and wages of skilled, "knowledge workers" is one outcome of the information revolution. The gulf may widen even further in coming decades as the information age continues to raise the marginal product of analysis.

This second edition of *Introduction to Economics* reflects these changes with a fresh focus on helping students learn how to *apply* economics to solve new problems and analyze new issues, ask new questions, formulate new ideas, and view old issues in new ways. It separates explanations and examples from main points. It employs examples as memory aids and develops applications to deepen understanding. The best way to learn how to think analytically and apply economics is to practice, and then to practice again.

Students learn by practicing applying concepts that relate to their own daily lives and to the greater world around them. This book provides that opportunity, and makes it both easier and fun. It helps students to venture beyond the description of economic models to the *uses* of those models. It encourages them to explore new vistas and supports their explorations by providing them with the maps and tools to do so.

A Personal Note

I expected to become a physicist or political scientist when I entered college in the fall of 1969. My interest in political science sprang from my fascination with political philosophy and broad social issues, but most political science courses appeared to focus more on the institutions of government than on fundamental questions. Meanwhile, outside reading led me to the works of Milton Friedman, Friedrich Hayek, and Ludwig von Mises, and inspired me to learn more economics. However, I found my introductory economics course dry and intellectually unsatisfying. The textbook required for the course never discussed (or even raised) the many fundamental questions to which economics applies. Rather than show me how to apply logical reasoning, the book implied that experts had already resolved most economic issues. It implied that these authorities armed with technical skills could manage government policies to correct the failures of markets and fine-tune the economy. How boring! Even if it were true (something I could not evaluate at the time), that approach to economics rejected the joy of discovery; the process of learning to think; the crucial ability to raise new questions.

Despite that experience, my outside reading (and some good professors in my classes at Ohio State University) sustained my interest in economics. When I decided to pursue economics in graduate school, I promised myself that someday I would write a better introductory economics textbook through which I could share with other people the fun and intellectual excitement I found in economics. After getting my Ph.D. at the University of Chicago and spending two years at UCLA, I found myself teaching a principles course at the University of Rochester in the fall of 1979. I have taught principles every year since then (two decades that have gone by very quickly!). The first edition of this book grew from my attempt to fulfill my promise to myself. The second edition, which you hold in your hands, grew from my desire to improve it. I hope you find that I have succeeded.

Applied-Price-Theory Approach

This book takes an applied-price-theory approach. Numerous examples help to clarify main points, illustrate the relevance of economics to important real-life issues, show the breadth of economic applications, and help students learn to apply their knowledge outside of class as they read news articles and participate in discussions about current events and public policies. Several chapters (particularly Chapter 6–8, but also more advanced chapters) apply the logical reasoning of supply and demand to a variety of topics including time prices, safety, bribery, lifestyles, speculation, international trade, discrimination, environmental issues, common resources, and government regulations. With its strong applications approach, the textbook contains separate chapters to explain and apply more advanced theoretical topics, including game theory, the economics of information, and the economic analysis of law and public choice.

Fundamental Issues and Everyday Applications

Discussions or questions about important social and political issues appear throughout the book, enticing students to broaden the set of questions that they ask about the world, to understand both sides of controversial issues, and to combine economic analysis with their own value judgments as they think about current events and fundamental social issues. The book also strives for a real-life flavor through the use of data, examples, applications of economics to personal and business decisions, and the extensive use of news clippings.

Chapter-by-Chapter Changes from the First Edition

Part 1: Issues and Methods

Chapter 1 Mysteries and Motives: What Economics Is About Chapter 1 has been rewritten to place students directly into the center of economic analysis. Consistent with this edition's enhanced focus on thinking skills, the chapter now opens with a simple but very important economic model of gains from trade. The implications of this model will surprise many students. Discussion of the model leads to a discussion of what economics is about, with key facts about the world economy presented in easily-digestible form and key issues of economic analysis appearing in clear examples.

Chapter 2 Solving Puzzles: The Methods of Economics This revised chapter contains a new discussion of economic models as artificial economies, similar to simulations in computer games. The new chapter also has more concise explanations and examples of logical fallacies.

Part 2: Fundamental Tools

Chapter 3 Let's Make a Deal: The Gains from Trade This substantially rewritten chapter now presents production possibility frontiers within the chapter rather than in an appendix. The two-student example of gains from trade in this chapter complements the shoe-store example of gains from trade from the beginning of Chapter 1, and it is thoroughly integrated with the discussion of production possibility frontiers.

Chapter 4 Supply and Demand This chapter has been streamlined for even easier reading and clarity than in the first edition. The chapter contains a new early section on the concept of price-taking behavior. Some more difficult material has been omitted from this edition. (All such omitted material will be available on the Web pages for the book for instructors who wish to cover those more advanced topics. However, the second edition focuses more strongly than ever on basic skills.)

Chapter 5 Elasticities of Demand and Supply This chapter now presents a simpler and more concise discussion of elasticities. It uses the usual formula for percentage changes and includes even more applications of critical-thinking skills.

Part 3: Applications of Supply and Demand

Chapter 6 Applied Price Theory This unique chapter has been reorganized in a way that groups together logical thinking skills. The first set of applications involves changes in conditions that shift demand or supply curves horizontally by a known distance. The second set of applications involves changes that shift demand or supply curves vertically by a known distance. The third set of applications involves chance events; the fourth set shows how to extend the range of economic analysis.

Chapter 7 International Trade, Arbitrage, and Speculation This streamlined chapter shows students how the same logical economic reasoning applies to a variety of topics—in this case, international trade, speculation, and arbitrage. Changes in this chapter enhance readability and place even greater emphasis on the common features of the logical thinking skills in each application.

Chapter 8 Price Controls and Taxes This revised chapter omits several of the more difficult sections from the first edition and focuses greater attention on the basic skills of logical thinking about price controls and taxes.

Chapter 9 Economic Efficiency and the Gains from Trade This chapter presents a new, unified discussion of consumer surplus (formerly in Chapter 9), producer surplus (formerly in Chapter 10), and economic efficiency (formerly in Chapter 11). New examples and explanations make the difficult topic of deadweight social loss more understandable than ever.

Part 4: Choices and Their Implications

Chapter 10 Choices and Demand Chapter 10 presents the basic logic of rational choice (formerly in Chapter 9). The chapter is significantly shorter and clearer than in the first edition, with more advanced topics, such as indifference curves, appearing in appendices.

Chapter 11 Business Decisions and Supply in the Long Run Chapters 11 and 12, newly reorganized for easier reading and comprehension, contain material from the old Chapter 12. Chapter 11 discusses long-run business decisions and supply (applying the logical thinking skills from Chapter 10). Discussions of profit and the distinction between accounting profit and economic profit, formerly in Chapter 13, now appear in this chapter for a more unified discussion.

Chapter 12 Business Decisions and Supply in the Short Run Chapter 12 discusses short-run business decisions and supply, which are more complicated than the long-run issues due to fixed costs. This chapter now contains a discussion of marginal productivity and diminishing returns (formerly in Chapter 16) and explains why these issues affect the short-run decisions of business firms.

Part 5: Competition and Strategic Interactions

Chapter 13 Perfect Competition This chapter on perfect competition (formerly Chapter 12) is now shorter and clearer with more difficult topics omitted.

Chapter 14 Monopoly This chapter on monopoly (formerly Chapter 13) is now shorter and clearer, with more difficult topics omitted.

Chapter 15 Monopolistic Competition Chapters 15 and 16 contain material from the old Chapter 15. This chapter focuses on monopolistic competition, with a stronger focus than ever on the basic ideas and applications.

Chapter 16 Oligopoly This chapter on oligopoly is shorter than the discussion in the previous edition. It focuses greater attention on basic ideas and thinking skills. This revised chapter omits sections on more advanced topics (which, like other omitted material, will appear as optional material on the Web pages for the book).

Chapter 17 Game Theory This unique chapter on game theory has been rewritten for greater clarity. The result is a short chapter accessible to all college students.

Part 6: Work and Wealth

Chapter 18 Labor Markets This chapter on labor economics has been substantially rewritten, reorganized, and shortened. Changes in emphasis provide more compelling discussion—for example, the section on job tournaments now places greater emphasis on their superstar features.

Chapter 19 Rich and Poor: Income Distribution, Poverty, and Discrimination This chapter on the distribution of income, poverty, and discrimination, now presents real-life data in easy-to-understand graphs (which replace many tables of numbers). Some advanced material has been cut, and the result is a shorter and clearer chapter, with stronger focus on both the main facts and key issues of analysis.

Part 7: Advanced Topics in Microeconomics

Chapter 20 Economics of Information This revised chapter on economics of search, moral hazard, and adverse selection is shorter and clearer.

Chapter 21 Environmental Economics and Public Goods This revised chapter places greater focus on the main ideas of externalities and omits sections on more advanced material. A stronger emphasis on property rights plays a central role in the new discussion.

Chapter 22 Government Regulations and Taxes This revised chapter on taxes and regulations better explains their connection and contains shorter and clearer explanations of key principles.

Chapter 23 Economics of Public Choice and Law The expanded section on public choice in this revised chapter clarifies the main issues better than in the first edition. The section on economic analysis of law is much shorter and substantially rewritten for greater focus on key ideas and issues.

Part 8: Macroeconomics: Mysteries, Measurement, and Models

Chapter 24 Macroeconomic Issues and Measurement This revised introduction to macroeconomics provides a shorter, yet more comprehensive introduction to main concepts and issues, with the same strong real-life focus present in the first edition. Growth rates, the rule of 72, the circular flow, and coverage of AS/AD have been moved to later chapters. This revised chapter has a stronger focus on macroeconomic questions and measurement of GDP, its components, the price level, employment, and unemployment.

Chapter 25 Simple Economic Models of GDP, Prices, and Employment This is an almost entirely new chapter that builds a basic macroeconomic model. The chapter focuses on models as logical stories, and the need for models to think about real-life economic issues.

The chapter begins with an essay from Professor Robert E. Lucas, Jr., "What Economists Do," which describes:

1. how economists think about the economy, and how

they answer "what-if" questions about the economy, by telling logical stories (constructing models)

2. the creation of a recession in an amusement park

Next, the chapter develops a story (model) of a Robinson Crusoe economy to examine the factors determining real GDP. This model illustrates:

1. production functions and diminishing returns to labor effort

2. factors that affect investment

3. real GDP as the sum of consumption and investment

Finally, the chapter extends the model to a large number of people, like Crusoe, who trade with each other. This extension adds two new features to the model:

1. money, with the circular flow to illustrate the equation of exchange

2. labor markets

The chapter includes new discussions of:

1. the neutrality of money

2. why money is *not* neutral in Lucas's amusement-park model

3. labor markets, employment, and unemployment

Part 9: Savings, Investment, and Growth

Chapter 26 Interest Rates, Savings, and Investment This chapter (formerly Chapters 24 and 25) contains an entirely reorganized discussion of interest rates, savings, and investment, with new, streamlined discussions of:

1. the distinction between real and nominal interest rates

2. investment decisions

3. connections between goods-market equilibrium and loan-market equilibrium

After summarizing the basic macroeconomic model, the chapter applies the model to answer "what-if" questions on the effects of changes in:

1. consumer patience (or confidence)

2. technology

3. taxes

Each discussion is newly rewritten and significantly shorter and easier.

New material includes greater emphasis on the supply-side (incentive) effects of changes in tax rates.

Chapter 27 Economic Growth This chapter has been rewritten for greater clarity and to emphasize use of the macroeconomic model developed in previous chapters. New material includes graphs of production functions to help illustrate the basic economic model of growth and the key issue of diminishing returns.

Part 10: Inflation, Money, and Banks

Chapter 28 Inflation This streamlined chapter now includes a focused discussion of the demand for money, and a new section on foreign exchange rates.

Chapter 29 Money and Financial Intermediaries This newly rewritten and reorganized chapter now begins with the advantages of monetary exchange over barter, followed by a streamlined discussion of the history of money. While maintaining coverage of basic issues such as the money supply, and the role of the banking system in the money multiplier, this edition places a new focus on the economics of financial intermediation. Recent financial crises in Asia illustrate the connections between the banking system and GDP, employment, and the exchange rate.

Part 11: Business Cycles

Chapter 30 Business Cycles 1: Aggregate Demand and Supply This first of two chapters on business cycles, substantially rewritten and shortened in this edition, introduces the AS-AD model and its applications.

Chapter 31 Business Cycles 2: Applications of Aggregate Demand and Supply This second chapter on the applications of the AS-AD model and the Phillips Curve is substantially rewritten and reorganized. Discussions of aggregate supply, the multiplier, and the Phillips Curve are easier to understand. The new chapter places greater emphasis on real-world applications and contains increased discussion of financial crises with applications to recent episodes in Latin America and Asia.

Part 12: Macroeconomic Policies

Chapter 32 Monetary Policy This shorter, streamlined chapter includes new material on the design of monetary systems and institutions, with applications to the new European currency and monetary institutions and to major monetary policy issues in Asia and elsewhere (connecting these monetary-policy issues to financial crises).

Chapter 33 Fiscal Policy This revised fiscal policy chapter contains new applications to issues such as the current Japanese recession, fiscal reform in Russia, and the issue of social security that looms over official U.S. government budget surpluses.

Part 13: Advanced Topics in Macroeconomics

Chapter 34 Financial Markets This shorter chapter on financial markets continues to introduce key facts and basic skills (such as reading financial news). However, this revised chapter also places a greater focus on *skills* of logical thinking about financial markets.

Chapter 35 International Trade This streamlined international trade chapter is reorganized for better comprehension and a stronger focus on the basic principles.

EXAMPLE

1. *Personal decisions on spending money*   Is it cheaper to buy or rent? Should you repair your old car or buy a new one?

IN THE NEWS

Since most teenagers are sensitive to the disincentive effects of high tobacco taxes, a tax hike could be deemed "economically efficient" on the grounds that it might prevent many from starting to smoke in the first place—something they would not have done if they were fully aware of the risks.

Source: Business Week

Does the government promote economic efficiency when it sets taxes to prevent decisions that it believes better-informed people would not have made?

PERSONAL DECISION MAKIN

Diversifying Risks

The key to diversifying risks is to choose inv returns move in opposite directions. An inve versified if some of that person's investmer returns in those situations where her other i vide low returns, and vice-versa. This mi ments protects the investor, rather like insur least some investments are likely to do we

Pedagogical Features

In-Chapter Examples and Exercises Paired with Explanations

This book maintains a reader-friendly organization that helps students by pairing main points with explanations and examples. This organization increases student understanding by "walking" readers step-by-step through the main concepts of economics. In addition, this delivery method helps students review material with less study time. Some sections deviate from this organization, but always for a reason.

Main Points to Understand and Thinking Skills to Develop Sections

New to this edition, "Main Points to Understand" and "Thinking Skills to Develop" sections now appear at the beginning of every chapter. Written in an outline format, these sections provide a quick walk-through of the chapter's core concepts, guiding students toward the important ideas about to be discussed.

News Clippings

The book makes extensive use of real news clippings to help students practice applying economic principles as they read about or listen to reports of current or historical events. The news clippings also increase student familiarity with news stories on economic topics, alleviating fears that such stories are beyond their comprehension and elevating their self-confidence not only to read but also to evaluate such stories. Chapter-by-chapter links to late-breaking news stories can be found on the Web site for this book.

Review Questions and Thinking Exercises

"Review Questions" and "Thinking Exercises" appear at the ends of sections, not just the ends of chapters. Some questions are mainly for review, while others require student analysis. This placement of the questions allows students to query themselves about the material in each section before continuing to the next. These questions and problems cover each level of learning, helping students learn to restate main points, to work through applications in the text and through genuinely *new* applications, and to apply economics to everyday life, current events, and broad social issues. Many problems help students learn to work with graphs (and some with numerical examples) and to state verbally the conclusions of the graphical analysis.

Decision-Making and Social and Economic Issues Boxes

Many chapters also contain boxes presenting the main arguments on both sides of important social and economic issues. The book's strong emphasis on how economics relates to major social issues and political debates stimulates student interest and ties economics to students' lives. Some chapters also have boxes applying economic analysis to business decision making or personal decision making, showing students how they can use economics to help achieve their own goals.

Marginal "Advice" and "Making Smart Decisions" Boxes

New boxes on "Advice" and "Making Smart Decisions" appear in the margins of this edition. The "Advice" boxes offer students helpful hints on economic reasoning and common pitfalls. "Making Smart Decisions" boxes show students how economics can help them in their daily lives. Marginal boxes provide students with information on how economics can help in making predictions, diversifying risks, and making strides toward personal improvement.

Internet References

Internet references available at the Web site for this book, http://www.dryden.com, and at the author's Web site, http://www.economics101.org, give students the opportunity to enhance their learning. Unlike many Internet resources that simply point to the latest data, Internet resources for this edition guide students on how to *use* the information and data. References to Internet sites that *apply* economic analysis supplement references to data from government agencies, think tanks, and private industry. This book's Internet resources include advanced topics and additional text-related explanations and examples.

Conclusion

The concluding sections of each chapter are organized by section, making it easier for students to identify sections that they need to reread. On a second reading, many students will find that they can skip explanation and example sections if they already understand the issues.

Inquiries for Further Thought

"Inquiries for Further Thought" are one of the most important features of the book. These distinctive inquires supplement other end-of-chapter questions and problems. They challenge students to use economic analysis to formulate positions on issues of fundamental social importance. The inquiries raise positive and normative questions on important public issues related to economics, teaching students (a) how to raise new questions and think about issues in new ways, (b) to distinguish between the positive and normative components of such questions, (c) that these positive and normative components are related to each other, (d) that economic analysis helps provide a logical way to approach many questions, and (e) that big-issue questions make economics interesting and important. The inquiries help students practice combining economic analysis with their own values and opinions about fundamental issues. Because most of the inquiries involve value judgments, they have no "correct" answers.

Supplements

Student Study Guide

Written by Dorothy Siden (Salem State College) and John Dodge (Indiana Wesleyan), the study guide utilizes numerous strategies for active learning and practice, thereby helping students improve their grades. Elements of this supplement include: learning goals, key-term quizzes, true-false questions, multiple-choice questions, fill-in-the-blank problems, priority lists of concepts, short-answer questions, and basic and advanced problems. All the problems have been checked for accuracy.

Web Sites

Located at http://www.dryden.com/econ, the Web site for the book has been newly reorganized on a chapter-by-chapter basis. This new organization makes the vast and sometimes overwhelming array of resources found on the Web intelligible. Each Web chapter provides a mini-learning module that students can learn from as they work their way chapter-by-chapter through the printed textbook. The new organization also enables professors to find more readily the material related to any particular chapter. The following are among the teaching and learning materials that can be found on the Web site:

Advice

Don't make the common mistake of thinking that competition always creates a winner and a loser. Remember that *both* sides win in a voluntary trade—as Lisa and Mitch did.

Inquiries for Further Thought

35. A person can buy the right to immigrate to some countries; sometimes, a person can buy citizenship in those countries. (Some of this trade involves illegal payments.) What factors determine the price of immigration rights? Do you think that the United States should sell rights to immigrate to the highest bidders?

For Instructors and Students:
Late-breaking news articles augmenting
  the textbook's "In the News" feature
Chapter-by-chapter links to economic
  Web sites
An economic URL database
Discussions of advanced topics

For Instructors:
Instructor's Manual
Overhead transparency masters
PowerPoint presentation slides

For Students:
Career listings
Chapter summaries
Chapter notes
Chapter-by-chapter, automatically
  graded, practice quizzes
Interactive learning graphs
"Cyber" problems
Glossary from the textbook

Additional resources for students are available at the author's online course at http://www.economics101.org.

Tutorial, Analytical, and Graphical (TAG) Software

Created by Andrew Foshee (McNeese State University) and Tod Porter and Teresa Riley (both of Youngstown University), this award-winning educational software for students consists of extensive chapter-by-chapter tutorials. Included are practice exams, hands-on graphic sections in which students are required to draw or adjust curves, "news" articles with word-substitution choices to evaluate their comprehension, and an "Econoquest" feature that requires them to solve economic problems by choosing among various economic data tools. TAG can be obtained at no additional charge with the purchase of the textbook from the publisher. Instructors can now customize TAG for their students, by requesting a copy of the TAG Editing System software. This software allows them to modify, add, and delete questions. The Dryden Press is also happy to grant permission to instructors wishing to use the software in a lab setting.

On-Line Course Management

The Dryden Press is proud to offer a new course offering and delivery software package that helps instructors build sophisticated Web-based learning environments for their students. This nontechnical software package can be used to create on-line courses or simply to post office hours or materials on-line that supplement the instructor's course. Instructors can design their own Web sites that provide a full array of educational tools including communication, testing, student tracking, access control, database collaboration tools, on-line searching and navigation tools and much more. Instructors interested in taking their courses to the Web can learn more about this important new resource by contacting their Dryden Press sales representative.

PowerPoint Presentation Software

Developed by Anthony Zambelli (Cuyamaca College), this easy-to-use, overhead lecture software has been vastly improved for the second edition, with the graphs now perfectly replicating those found in the textbook. Professors can now edit the graphs and the text to customize their presentations as they please. The PowerPoint presentation covers all of the essential materials found in the book. Colorful graphs, tables, lists, and concepts are developed sequentially at the click of the button.

Wall Street Journal Edition

Instructors can enhance the real-life applications in the text by using the special *Wall Street Journal* Edition. This special edition of the textbook is the same as the standard edition but includes a discounted ten-week subscription to the *Wall Street Journal*. The addition of the *Wall Street Journal* to the study program of students provides a nice tie-in with the "In the News" boxes found in the text, since new examples of economic principles can be found in each day's paper. Students can activate their subscriptions by simply completing and mailing the business reply card found in the back of the book. Instructors interested in finding out more about this program can contact their Dryden sales representative or simply call 1-800-782-4479 and reference the following ISBN: 0-03-022412-8.

Instructor's Manual

This supplement contains valuable outlines, teaching tips, and answers to all of the review questions, thinking exercises, and problems in the book. This information is also available on disk and the Web site, which allows instructors to customize their lecture notes.

Test Bank

Revised and organized by Dean Croushore (Federal Reserve Bank of Philadelphia), the test bank contains more than 3,500 multiple-choice and critical-thinking questions. Each question is graded by level of difficulty and all questions new to this edition are highlighted. All questions were checked for accuracy.

Computerized Test Bank

The test bank is available electronically in DOS, Windows and Macintosh versions. The ExaMaster system accompanying the computerized test banks makes it easy to create tests, print scrambled versions of the same test, modify questions, and reproduce any of the graphing questions.

Acknowledgments

How can I begin to thank all of the people who have directly or indirectly helped me create this book? I owe a great debt to my former teachers at the University of Chicago, particularly Milton Friedman, George Stigler, Gary Becker, Robert Barro, Jacob Frenkel, Robert E. Lucas, Jr., Tom Sargent, and my fellow students, particularly Tom MaCurdy and Dan Sumner. I also owe special debts of thanks to current and former colleagues, most notably Mark Bils, John Boyd, Mike Dotsey, Jim Kahn, Steve Landsburg, and Ken McLaughlin. I also am greatly indebted to Rao Aiyagari, Irasema Alonso, Jeff Banks, Karl Brunner, Jeff Campbell, Stan Engerman, Lauren Feinstone, Marvin Goodfriend, Jeremy Greenwood, Eric Hanushek, Ron Jones, Robert King, Per Krusell, Tony Kuprianov, Walter Oi, Charles Phelps, Sergio Rebelo, and Michael Wolkoff. I also owe special thanks to Jim Irwin, Andy Atkeson, Richard Rogerson, Masao Ogaki, Belton Fleisher, Peter Rupert, Lee Ohanian, and Craig Hakkio for their comments on parts of the book.

No successful principles of economics textbook could be written without the help of astute reviewers. I am very much indebted to the following people for their insightful recommendations, which helped me immensely to improve the second edition:

Michael P. Aarstol
University of Georgia

Michael J. Applegate
Oklahoma State University

Paul M. Comolli
University of Kansas

Harry Ellis, Jr.
University of North Texas

Soumen Ghosh
New Mexico State University

James D. Hamilton
University of California at San Diego

Charlotte Denise Hixson
Midlands Technical College

Beth F. Ingram
The University of Iowa

James R. Kearl
Brigham Young University

Benjamin J.C. Kim
University of Nebraska at Lincoln

Don R. Leet
California State University at Fresno

Larry T. McRae
Appalachian State University

Robert S. Rycroft
Mary Washington College

Donald J. Schilling
University of Missouri at Columbia

Tayyeb Shabbir
University of Pennsylvania

Stephen Shmanske
California State University at Hayward

Christopher J. Waller
Indiana University

The following people contributed greatly to the development of the first edition of the text, either as reviewers, class testers, or as focus-group participants: David Altig, *Cleveland State University;* Michael Anderson, *Washington and Lee University;* Richard Ballman, *Augustana College;* David Bivin, *Indiana University—Purdue University, Indianapolis;* David Black, *University of Toledo;* Robert T. Bray, *California State Polytechnic University, Pomona;* James A. Bryan, *North Harris Community College;* Tom Carr, *Middlebury College;* John Chilton, *University of South Carolina;* Daniel S. Christiansen, *Albion College;* Richard Claycombe, *Western Maryland College;* Kenneth A. Couch, *Syracuse University;* Mike Dowd, *University of Toledo;* Swarna D. Dutt, *Tulane University;* Catherine Eckel, *Virginia Polytechnic Institute and State University;* Sharon Erenburg, *Eastern Michigan University;* Paul Farnham, *Georgia State University;* David Gay, *University of Arkansas;* Lynn Gillette, *Northeast Missouri State University;* Gerhard Glomm, *Michigan State University;* Stephen F. Gohmann, *University of Louisville;* Philip J. Grossman, *Wayne State University;* Craig Hakkio, *Rockhurst College;* David L. Hammes, *University of Hawaii at Hilo;* Y. Horiba, *Tulane University;* William Hunter, *Marquette University;* Jim Irwin, *Central Michigan University;* Stephen L. Jackstadt, *University of Alaska at Anchorage;* Nasir Khilji, *Assumption College;* Janet Koscianski, *Shippensburg University;* Carston Kowalczyk, *Tufts University;* Stephen Lisle, *Western Kentucky University;* John Lunn, *Hope College;* Elaine S. McBeth, *College of William & Mary;* Catherine McDevitt, *Central Michigan University;* Michael Meurer, *Duke University;* Joanna Moss, *San Francisco State University;* Norman Obst, *Michigan State University;* Lee Ohanian, *University of Minnesota;* James A. Overdahl, *George Mason University;* Deborah J. Paige, *McHenry County College;* Jim Payne, *Kellogg Community College;* James Price, *Syracuse University;* Sunder Ramaswamy, *Middlebury College;* Kevin Rask, *Colgate University;* John Reid, *Memphis State University;* Christine Rider, *St. John's University;* Jose-Victor Rios-Rull, *University of Pennsylvania;* Peter Rupert, Federal Reserve Bank of Cleveland; Robert S. Rycroft, *Mary Washington College;* Michael D. Seelye, *San Joaquin Delta College;* Dorothy R. Siden, *Salem State College;* Larry Singell, *University of Oregon;* David L. Sollars, *Auburn University at Montgomery;* John C. Soper, *John Carroll University;* Todd P. Steen, *Hope College;* Michael Taussig, *Rutgers University;* Abdul M. Turay, *Radford University;* Ivan Weinel, *University of Missouri;* James N. Wetzel, *Virginia Commonwealth University;* Mark Wilkening, *Blinn College;* Edgar W. Wood, *University of Mississippi;* Kakkar Vikas, *Ohio State University;* Joseph A. Ziegler, *University of Arkansas.*

My deep gratitude goes out to the thousands of my students in introductory economics at the University of Rochester who have helped me with this project either directly (with comments on the manuscript) or indirectly, who have been experimental subjects in pedagogy, and who have helped me learn how to teach economics. I owe a great debt to all my former teaching assistants, who have taught me new ways to teach and showed me how to improve explanations and examples. I am also grateful to my former Ph.D. students at the University of Rochester, from whom I have learned more than they realize.

I have been extraordinarily fortunate to work with a number of outstanding people at The Dryden Press. I am indebted to a great team of professionals, including Gary Nelson, Acquisitions Editor, who encouraged me to use my own judgment in this revision. Special thanks go to Jim Patterson, Senior Project Editor; Eddie Dawson, Senior Production Manager; Bill Brammer, Senior Art Director; Linda Blundell, Picture & Rights Editor; Debbie Anderson, Product Manager; and Kimberly Powell, Manufacturing Coordinator. They all did a terrific job attending to each and every detail necessary to turn the manuscript into a book. The fine product before you is a testament to their expertise, ingenuity, and dedication. I am particularly indebted to my editor, Amy Schmidt, Associate Editor, for her outstanding professional work, superb advice, and sustained encouragement and support throughout the production and revision of this book. No author could wish for a better editor.

My greatest debt is to my wife, Cindy, and my children, Gwendolyn, Madeleine, and Rebecca, who sacrificed a lot of time with me and endured many burdens while I worked on this book.

Alan C. Stockman

About the Author

Alan C. Stockman is the Marie Curran Wilson and Joseph Chamberlain Wilson Professor of Economics at the University of Rochester, and Chairman of the Department of Economics. He also serves as Research Associate at the National Bureau of Economic Research and Consultant at the Federal Reserve Bank of Richmond. He has taught introductory economics for two decades and has been honored for his outstanding teaching of that course.

Professor Stockman received his Ph.D. at the University of Chicago in 1978, and has published widely in the leading professional journals, such as the *Journal of Political Economy, American Economic Review, Journal of Monetary Economics, Journal of International Economics,* and *Journal of Economic Theory.*

He specializes in macroeconomics and international economics, although his research also extends to other areas such as the economics of philosophy. He serves on editorial boards of several professional journals and presents frequent talks at universities and professional conferences around the world. In his spare time, he enjoys music, skiing, and spending time with wife and three daughters.

BRIEF CONTENTS

CONTENTS

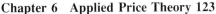

PART 1

ISSUES AND METHODS

How to Study Economics

Economics takes a little work to learn—but it can be *fun*—and it can help you achieve your goals in life and understand the world around you. You will do best if you follow this advice on studying economics:

1) *Don't memorize* the material in the chapter. Instead, think about the logic and the main points.

2) *Practice drawing graphs* without looking at the book.

3) *Explain* to yourself *out loud* the main points of each chapter and the meanings of the graphs. Research on learning suggests that you should repeat this two to three times per day for two to three days, then do it once more before an exam.

4) *Do the "Review Questions" and "Thinking Exercises"* at the end of each section before reading further. Try to do them *without looking* back at the chapter. If you need to look, that's okay, but do them again later without looking.

5) *Do the Problems.* This is the best way to learn to apply economics to real-life issues.

6) Discuss the *Inquiries for Further Thought* (at the end of each chapter) with your friends. Form your own opinions, and use economics to help you explain and support them.

7) *Read the newspaper clippings* in the book and identify the associated economic reasoning. Find your own news examples and *apply economics to your everyday life*. Ask yourself questions such as: "Why didn't the bookstore charge me $300 for this book? What affects the price and quality of food at my college? What makes college a good or bad investment? What are the costs and benefits of the way I spend my time each day?" Add your own questions and keep a list of them.

8) *Get on the Internet* site for this book at http://www.dryden.com/econ/stockman/ for additional learning help—explanations, examples, applications, problems, updates, and more. Also see the author's course web site at http://www.econ.rochester.edu/eco108/ for additional resources and help.

Many people believe that economics is only the study of business, stocks, and bonds. Follow the advice here and you will soon find that economics is much broader—and much more *fun*—than that.

CHAPTER 1

MYSTERIES AND MOTIVES: WHAT ECONOMICS IS ABOUT

In this Chapter...

Main Points to Understand

▶ People benefit from voluntary trades.

▶ Every action has a cost—an *opportunity cost*.

▶ People's material standard of living depends on what they produce.

Thinking Skills to Develop

▶ Recognize opportunity costs of your actions.

▶ Formulate your own questions about economic events in the world around you.

▶ Recognize gains from trade in everyday life.

W e live in the information age. The Internet has made facts and data easier to access than ever before. As a result, remembering facts is less important than ever before.

In contrast, *knowing how to think* and use facts, to analyze issues and solve problems, is *more* useful than ever before. That is why education has become increasingly valuable, and one reason why college-educated people now earn wages 40 percent higher on average than those of people with only a high-school education. It is one reason that wages of unskilled workers have stagnated for the last two decades while salaries of educated workers have risen.

A good way to learn how to think is to read a simple case study and then apply the reasoning and lessons of that case to new situations. This process of reasoning by analogy can help you to analyze new situations that you will encounter in the future, in your work, and in your everyday life. And so we begin . . .

Lisa and Mitch own a shoe store. Lisa runs the women's section and Mitch runs the men's section. Each year as shoe styles change, they rearrange their displays at the front of the store and count the shoes remaining in their inventory back in the storage room. Until a few years ago, Lisa did all the work in the women's section and Mitch did all the work in the men's section. One evening at dinner, they discovered a better way.

GAINS FROM TRADE: A THINKING EXAMPLE

Table 1 shows the number of hours Lisa takes to do each job in her section of the store. She spends 4 hours to take inventory and 3 hours to rearrange the display in the front of the store. She would take just as long to do each task in Mitch's section of the store—4 hours to take inventory and 3 hours to rearrange the display. As she pointed out to Mitch at dinner, it would take her 8 hours to take inventory in *both* sections of the store, or 6 hours to set up the new displays in both sections.

Table 1 also shows how long Mitch takes for those same tasks. Mitch needs 5 hours to count inventory in either section of the store, so it would take him 10 hours to inventory *both* sections. He would take 6 hours to rearrange the display in either section of the store, or 12 hours to rearrange the displays in *both* sections. As Lisa pointed out to Mitch at dinner, she works faster than Mitch does at *each* job; in that sense, she outperforms Mitch at both tasks.

Each year at this time, Lisa spent 7 hours working in her section of the store (4 hours on the inventory and 3 hours on the new display), and Mitch spent 11 hours working in his section (5 hours on the inventory and 6 hours on the new display). Then Mitch had an idea.

Lisa and Mitch decided to trade: Lisa would set up the displays in *both* sections of the store, and Mitch would take inventory in both sections. Now that they trade, Lisa finishes her work in 6 hours (3 hours in each section) and Mitch finishes his work in 10 hours (5 hours in each section). Lisa works 6 hours instead of 7; Mitch works 10 hours instead of 11. *They each* gain 1 hour of leisure time. Even though Lisa outperforms Mitch at *both* tasks, each partner gains from trade.

WHAT ECONOMICS IS ABOUT

Economics is largely about trades—how people produce, trade, and consume goods and services. Economists study the gains that people get from trading; who trades with whom and at what prices; which goods and services people produce, in what amounts, and by what methods (using which inputs and technologies); who consumes how much of each good; who invests how much in which new tools, skills, and ideas.

Table 1 | Lisa and Mitch Gain from Trade

	Hours of Work Required for	
TASK	Lisa	Mitch
Taking inventory in one section of the store	4 hours	5 hours
Setting up a new display in one section of the store	3 hours	6 hours
TOTAL TIME SPENT		
Without a trade	7 hours	11 hours
With the trade	6 hours	10 hours

THE TRADE

Mitch trades 5 hours of his time (taking inventory in the women's section) for 3 hours of Lisa's time (setting up the display in the men's section). Mitch pays 5 hours of his time for 3 hours of Lisa's time; Lisa pays 3 hours of her time for 5 hours of Mitch's time.

Lisa and Mitch both gain 1 hour of leisure time from the trade.

Economics is about the effects of scarcity:

> **Economics** is the study of people's choices and what happens to make everyone's choices compatible.

Because people's choices sometimes conflict with one another, something must happen to make their decisions compatible with one another. If Lisa and Mitch want to finish all the work at the store, *someone* must do each job—their choices must be compatible. They can make their choices compatible by talking with each other and deciding who will do each job.

Compatibility of the decisions of the 6 billion people on earth, or even a few thousand people in a small community, is much harder to achieve. Some people must choose to practice medicine, others to produce food, build houses, teach children, manufacture toys, push the frontiers of science, engineer new products, and entertain. People's career choices must fit together in a compatible way. Similarly, a construction crew building a house may need supplies of wood, bricks, mortar, glass, electrical wire, and other materials. The right kinds of materials, in the right sizes and quantities, must arrive at the construction site at the right times. Hundreds of people around the country work to produce and deliver these supplies. Individual people make their own choices, and these choices and activities must be compatible to construct the house. The compatibility of these individual choices results mainly from billions of voluntary trades.

The trade between Lisa and Mitch is only one of the many trades that people around the world make every day, in every culture, under every kind of conditions. Most involve exchanges of money for goods and services; some involve formal contracts written by lawyers; others involve simple promises between friends. People trade to improve their own situations in life.

Trades generate jobs, and they change the jobs that people do. The trade between Lisa and Mitch created an inventory job for Mitch and a display job for Lisa. Trades create incentives for people to improve their skills, their knowledge, and their tools. They provide the driving force behind increases in material standards of living. People today live in vastly better material conditions than did people 100, or 1,000, years ago because of the effects of voluntary trades.

WORLD: 6 billion people; Production of goods and services—$36 trillion; Average income—$6,000 per person. USA: 270 million people; Average income—$32,000 per person.

Today's average American is twice as rich as the average American 40 years ago (even *after* adjusting for price increases since then). If economic growth continues at this rate, by 2040, income per person in the United States will double again, to about $64,000 per person (higher than that if prices increase).

The logic of choices and trades applies to many types of questions. The following sections introduce a few important topics of economics.

Poverty, Wealth, and Growth

What makes our material standard of living rise over time? The average American today is twice as rich as 40 years ago. Total output of goods and services *per person* in the United States is currently about $32,000 per year. Will it double to about $64,000 over the next 40 years of your life? Can you expect to be much richer than your parents and grandparents?

Why do countries like the United States, Japan, and Germany produce so many more goods and services per person than countries like Bangladesh and Ethiopia? Why do 36 million people in the United States, including 14 million children, live below the government-defined poverty line (about $16,000 per year for a family of four)? Why does nearly one-fourth of all U.S. children under 6 years old live in families with incomes below that poverty line? What can governments do about poverty? Why do many highly educated and hard-working people earn below-average incomes, while some sports stars, entertainers, and business executives earn millions of dollars each year? How much will *you* earn and how will your future income depend on the choices you make starting today?

Production and Its Composition

What leads our economy to produce enough food and housing for us? Why do we produce millions of video games and several billion ounces of soft drinks? Why do we produce about $32,000 per person in goods and services rather than half that amount or twice that amount? Why do about 130 million Americans hold paid jobs outside the home? Why are 6 million unemployed? What goods or services will you provide in the economy?

Even average people in the United States and other rich countries have material standards of living vastly greater than those of the rich in previous centuries. Billions of people live in poor countries that produce, on average, only a few hundred dollars worth of goods and services per person each year.

The average Bangladeshi is only slightly richer now than 100 years ago. People in some countries, such as Ethiopia, Madagascar, Mozambique, and Zambia, are poorer today than they were several decades ago.

Income, Spending, and Their Composition

Who gets which of the goods and services worth $32,000 per person that are produced each year in the United States? Why? How does *production* of goods and services translate into people's *incomes?*

What affects the amount of money that you and other people spend on food, housing, and other goods and services? What happens when people decide to spend more money and save less, or to save more and spend less?

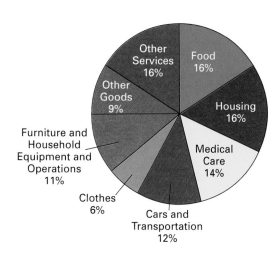

Other fast-growth countries in the last half of the 20th century include Hong Kong, South Korea, Singapore, and Taiwan.

Government Policies and World Conditions

How do government economic policies—taxes, regulations, and spending—affect your life? How about economic events in Russia, China, Japan, Mexico, and other countries? What can the government do about unemployment, poverty, the environment, and other economic problems? What *should* it do?

In the United States, a Typical ...	Earns about ...
Family with two married adults working for pay	$58,000 per year
Married couple with only one person working for pay	$34,000 per year
Adult male living alone	$24,000 per year
Adult female living alone	$15,000 per year

Review Questions

1. Define *economics.*

2. *Approximately* how large is the total annual output of goods and services per person in the United States? *Approximately* how many years ago was the average American only about half as rich as today?

3. List at least four questions about economic topics.

T h i n k i n g   E x e r c i s e s

4. Change the numbers in the example of gains from trade in the following way: Assume that Lisa takes *6 hours* (rather than 4 hours) to complete an inventory count. Then Table 1 changes to:

Hours of Work Required for:	Lisa	Mitch
Taking inventory in one section of the store	6 hrs	5 hrs
Setting up a new display in one section of the store	3 hrs	6 hrs

   (a) How much would Lisa and Mitch each gain from a trade in which Lisa sets up displays in both sections of the store and Mitch takes inventory in both sections?
   (b) How would your answer to part (a) change if Lisa took 10 hours to count inventory in one section of the store?

5. Change the numbers in the example of gains from trade in the following way: Assume that Mitch takes 2 hours (rather than 5 hours) to count inventory in one section of the store. Then Table 1 changes to:

Hours of Work Required for:	Lisa	Mitch
Taking inventory in one section of the store	4 hrs	2 hrs
Setting up a new display in one section of the store	3 hrs	6 hrs

   (a) How much would Lisa and Mitch each gain from a trade in which Lisa sets up displays in both sections of the store and Mitch takes inventory in both sections?
   (b) How would your answer to part (a) change if Mitch took 1 hour to count inventory in one section of the store?

6. Review your list of questions from Question 3, and explain how the answers to these questions could affect your life.

SCARCITY AND OPPORTUNITY COST

Most of the goods that people want are scarce. People face tradeoffs. They cannot have everything they want—they can have more of one thing only by accepting less of another. Economists say that a good is *scarce* (or *limited*) when people would like to have more than the total available quantity. Tangible products like videotapes, services like haircuts, natural resources like oil and human creativity, and more abstract goods like inner peace and friendship—all are scarce. Your time is scarce. Space on earth is scarce. Goods that are *not* scarce are free goods. Air is a free good, though *clean* air is sometimes scarce. Scarcity requires people to make choices. How will you spend your limited income? How will you spend your time today? How will you spend your life?

Before reading further, ask yourself "What would I do with my extra time if I decided not to read this book?" Whatever you would choose to do—whatever you sacrifice by spending your time to read this book—is your *opportunity cost* of reading this book.

> Your **opportunity cost** of something is the value of whatever you must sacrifice to obtain it.

Every scarce good or activity has an opportunity cost. This is a basic principle of economics: The cost of any action is its opportunity cost.

IN THE NEWS

Each week, millions of people nationwide carefully sort their trash, putting, say, cans in one container, bottles in another, newspapers in a third. Most people feel good about recycling, convinced that they are helping the planet, and their communities, by conserving resources and saving landfill space.

What they're also doing, though, is taking money away from health care and other basic services. As experts in municipal government and garbage disposal point out, the market value of those cans, bottles, and newspapers does not come close to meeting the costs of collecting and processing them.

"Recycling is a good thing, but it costs money," said David Gatton, the senior environmental adviser to the United States Conference of Mayors. "Money that could go for schools is being absorbed by increasing disposal costs."

Source: New York Times

The opportunity cost of money spent on the environment can be money spent on health and education.

Examples of Opportunity Costs

1. Your opportunity cost of buying a T-shirt might be buying a compact disc.

2. Your opportunity cost of 4 years in college might be 4 years at Disney World, where you could work part-time waiting tables, learn about the amusement-park industry without paying tuition, and have a good time.

3. A society can have a cleaner environment, but only by forgoing other values—producing fewer consumer goods that people want, reducing the use of automobiles, or adopting other measures that require people to sacrifice things they want.

Application: Recycling

Recycling often costs cities and towns more money than they would spend to dispose of the recycled materials in landfills. A few years ago, studies showed that recycling plastic, glass, aluminum cans, and paper costs about $20 more per ton than disposal would cost, not including the higher costs of collecting recyclables. Because local governments could have spent that money for other purposes such as health care and education, the opportunity cost of recycling is less government spending on these other services (or higher taxes to pay for them).

TWO TYPES OF ECONOMIC ISSUES

As the definition of *economics* suggests, economists study two types of closely related issues:

1. *Decisions*—factors that affect people's choices

2. *Markets*—how people's decisions fit together or *coordinate* with each other to become compatible.

IN THE NEWS

Increasingly, life and death issues become money matters

Medical care has always been a scarce resource, forcing decisions as to who will receive treatment and who will not. But the choices have come to seem more stark as public attention has been drawn to highly sophisticated techniques—treatments such as organ transplants and diagnostic methods such as nuclear magnetic resonance imaging—that are not available to everyone who needs them.

Source: New York Times

Scarcity of sophisticated equipment forces decisions about its use.

Decisions

Goods have opportunity costs because they are scarce, and these opportunity costs require you to make decisions. You must decide whether to watch more television or go to sleep, whether to eat dessert, whether and when to get married or have children, whether to put a hotel on Marvin Gardens or spend the cash for another house on Boardwalk, whether to keep what you have or trade it for what's behind the curtain, whether to major in economics or engineering, and whether to keep reading this book.

Opportunity costs affect people's incentives, and their incentives affect their decisions. One issue in economics involves the study of incentives and decisions—how people's tastes and opportunities affect their decisions.

EXAMPLES

1. *Personal decisions on spending money* Is it cheaper to buy or rent? Should you repair your old car or buy a new one?

2. *Personal decisions on spending time* Should you go directly from college to business school, or work for a few years first? Should you become a lawyer or an engineer?

3. *Business decisions* Should a business upgrade its equipment? Hire more workers? Cut prices to attract more customers?

4. *Government/social decisions* How do environmental regulations affect decisions of automakers? How do government welfare programs affect people's decisions to work? How do they affect decisions on having children?

Markets to Coordinate Decisions

Every day, people buy corn from Iowa, clothes from New Jersey made from cotton grown in Texas, and televisions from Japan. They make products using parts from distant countries, and they ship their finished products across the country and around the world. People seldom stop to think how amazing this activity is. Although no one directs the economy, the activities of billions of people—all making their own decisions—fit together.

What would life be like if you had to produce all of your own food, your own shelter, and all of the other goods you use? Even with access to every book ever published on modern technology, no single person could make many of the goods available in our economy. Millions of people would die if food, medical supplies, and energy for heat stopped flowing from around the world into the cities where they live. Few people ever pause to worry about this prospect, though. Most never doubt that stores will continue to offer goods for sale. Shoppers buy all kinds of goods without knowing who made them or how. Meanwhile, people around the world are working right now to produce goods for others they have never met, who speak different languages and practice different cultures in places they will never go. How do all these people know which goods to produce and how much? How do they know where to ship the goods? These questions lie at the heart of economics. Although the details of the answers vary across societies and situations, they almost always involve competition for scarce resources, usually based on the market process.

Competition

Not every team can win. Not everyone can be first in line, use the tennis court at noon, or live in a beachfront house. When people, businesses, or sports teams try to get something that not all of them can have, they compete. Scarcity inspires competition, the process by which people try to get scarce goods for themselves.

Competition takes many forms. Sports teams compete for a scarce good—victory. Students compete for grades and honors, and later for good jobs. Workers compete for promotions. Stores compete for customers. Cities compete for tourists and new businesses. People compete for attention and affection from others.

In a common form of competition, business firms compete for customers by trying to offer the most desirable goods and services on the best terms (such as the lowest price or most flexible payment schedule). Colleges, for example, compete for students by offering attractive campuses, strong academic programs, interesting features of nonacademic life for students, and scholarships that reduce costs for students who might not otherwise attend. Restaurants compete by offering enticing combinations of price, food quality, selection, service, atmosphere, and convenience.

When two sports teams compete, one wins and one loses. But the *process* of competition provides entertainment to people. When two business firms compete for your patronage, one firm may win your business while the other loses it. But the *process* of competition provides you with better goods at lower prices.

Advice
Don't make the common mistake of thinking that competition always creates a winner and a loser. Remember that *both* sides win in a voluntary trade—as Lisa and Mitch did.

Market Process

Economists use the term *market* for the activity of people buying and selling goods. For example, the real-estate market refers to the activities of people trying to buy and sell houses. The term *market process* refers to the coordination of people's economic activities.

Adam Smith, an 18th-century philosopher regarded as the founder of modern economics, pointed out two important features of the market process:

1. When people trade voluntarily, all parties expect to benefit.

2. Because people trade, each person's actions affect other people. Even selfish actions often help other people.

The first point observes that people expect to benefit from a trade, or else they would not trade. This point is obvious, but it is still important to remember.

Smith's second point is more subtle. Think of a baker who cares only about his own income. The baker can spend his time baking either bread or cakes, but which should he bake? If his customers want bread, it would be foolish to bake mostly cakes; he could earn more money by baking bread. Even though he cares only about his own income, he has an incentive to bake the goods that customers want most, measured by how much those customers are willing to pay. Though the baker acts from a selfish motive, the market process gives him an incentive to help his customers by producing the goods that those customers want most.

In his landmark book, *The Wealth of Nations,* published in 1776, Adam Smith explained:

> It is not from the benevolence of the butcher, the brewer, or the baker that we expect our dinner, but from their regard to their own interest. We address ourselves not to their humanity but to their self-love and never talk to them of our own necessities but of their advantages.

Through voluntary trades, each person helps others when he attempts to help himself. Even in acting selfishly, a person is often "led by an invisible hand to promote an end which was no part of his intention." That unintended end is to help other people. Smith pointed out that, "By pursuing his own interest he frequently promotes that of society more effectually than when he really intends to promote it."

The market process is an example of a *self-organizing system*. A self-organizing system creates a complex pattern from simple rules, without any central direction. Biologists have studied self-organizing systems of mutation and reproduction. Similar concepts apply to artificial intelligence, ecology, and traffic flows. Certain computer algorithms, called *genetic algorithms*, exploit the power of self-organizing systems. The Web page for this textbook can direct you to more information on self-organizing systems (and to sites where you can play the simulation game Life, which was at the forefront of the science of artificial life). This book concentrates on one such system—the market process. As economist Friedrich Hayek said, coordination by the market process creates a "spontaneous order" that is "the result of human action but not of human design."

The market process coordinates people's economic actions by providing them with incentives to do things that benefit others. A story written as the autobiography of a pencil demonstrates the remarkable coordination of activities that arises from the market process.[1] A pencil is a simple good, but making one from scratch would be difficult. Pencils are made because the market process coordinates the activities of many people, fitting them together for a purpose. Some people grow trees and cut them for wood. They use saws, axes, motors, and ropes made by others. They transport the cut logs to a mill using equipment made by a third group of people. Other people convert the logs into slats at the mill, and still others ship the slats to pencil companies. Meanwhile, people in another country mine the graphite (the "lead") for the center of the pencil, and other people transport it to the country where it will be sold. Another group of people mine zinc and copper to manufacture the brass collar that holds the eraser at the top of the pencil. Still other people manufacture that eraser.

People from around the world work together to make the pencil. They do not know one another; few even know that they helped to make a pencil. The pencil was not made because any one person planned the whole operation and directed it from start to finish; the pencil was made because the market process coordinated the activities of many people who live in different lands with different languages, cultures, and religions. They may not understand or like each other. Most of them work mainly to serve their own self-interests. Still, the market process provides them with incentives and coordinates their actions to produce a pencil. The same process operates to produce nearly every good or service you can name.

Adam Smith was thinking about this coordination of the activities of people who don't even know each other, let alone care about each other, when he wrote of an "invisible hand" in the market process.

Property Rights

People can trade only things that they own. As a result, property rights are necessary for the market process.

> **Ownership** means the right to make decisions about a scarce resource (whether and how to use it or to sell it); that resource is the owner's property.

Owners have property rights in all kinds of goods, including land, various products, their bodies, and sometimes their ideas. When people trade, they exchange property rights.

The results of competition depend on property rights. The following example shows one reason why.

Cookie-Jar Economics: A Thinking Example

Contrast two cases, in which four children want to eat cookies while they watch a video:

1. One big cookie jar contains 40 cookies. Each child can take as many as she wants, competing for cookies by grabbing them and eating them. Each child can bake more, but newly baked cookies must go into the common jar.

2. Each child has her own cookie jar with 10 cookies, and she can eat cookies only from her own jar. Each child can bake more cookies and put them into her own jar.

---

[1]Leonard E. Read, "I, Pencil: My Family Tree as Told to Leonard E. Read," *The Freeman*, December 1958.

In the first case, no single child *owns* the cookies. As a result, they are likely to eat all the cookies quickly. No child has an incentive to leave cookies in the jar to save for later, because she knows that any cookies she doesn't take and eat now will be eaten by the other children. If a child bakes more cookies, the other children are likely to eat most of them, leaving her with little incentive to bake more.

In the second case, each child *owns* her cookies. As a result, she has an incentive to eat the cookies slowly to make them last throughout the video. Further, any child who bakes more cookies gets them all, providing a stronger incentive to bake more. Ownership provides incentives to conserve resources, and to create more goods.

This simple example illustrates a principle that applies to competition everywhere. One important application concerns fishing. Because no one *owns* the fish in the oceans, competition gives people an incentive to overfish and deplete the waters. As the example shows, property rights provide incentives for people to maintain and conserve scarce resources. When no one owns a lake or stream, few people have sufficient incentives to prevent its pollution. In contrast, the owner of a lake or stream that is private property has an incentive to care for it to maintain its value. Water pollution has not been a serious problem in Scotland because people own streams there. Forests around the world have been destroyed because no one owned the trees that were cut, so no one had an incentive to balance the gains from maintaining the forests with the gains from harvesting the wood and replenishing the forests.

Laws and government regulations often limit property rights, restricting owners' choices about whether and how to use their property. Various laws limit property rights by prohibiting people from opening retail businesses (even on land they own) in certain areas, taking illegal drugs (into their own bodies), or selling medical advice (their own ideas) without licenses. Taxes on money that people earn also limit their property rights, because they cannot keep all the money for which they sell their labor services. To see the effects of this limitation, look back at the trade between Lisa and Mitch described at the beginning of this chapter. Suppose the government imposes a $10 tax on their trade: If Lisa and Mitch trade, they must *each* send a $5 tax payment to the government. Lisa and Mitch must now decide whether the trade is worthwhile. If they trade, each gains an hour of leisure time and loses $5. As a result, they may decide *not* to trade. They may prefer to sacrifice the gains from trade (and spend more time working) to avoid paying the tax. As you study this book, you will encounter many examples that show how property rights play an essential role in the market process.

Review Questions

7. What is an opportunity cost? Give an example.

8. Who wrote *The Wealth of Nations* and what important point did it make?

9. What was the point of the pencil story?

10. What was the point of the cookie-jar example?

Thinking Exercises

11. (a) What is your opportunity cost of attending this economics course?
    (b) What is your opportunity cost of attending college?
    (c) What was your opportunity cost of the last meal you ate?
    (d) What is society's opportunity cost of producing pizzas?

12. The beginning of this chapter discussed a trade between Lisa and Mitch. Look back at Table 1 and identify:
    (a) Lisa's opportunity cost of taking inventory in one section of the store
    (b) Lisa's opportunity cost of setting up a new display in one section of the store
    (c) Mitch's opportunity cost of taking inventory in one section of the store
    (d) Mitch's opportunity cost of setting up a new display in one section of the store

13. List five trades you have recently made. Explain your gains from the trades and the gains to the people with whom you traded.

Conclusion

Some important issues in economics include:

▶ What creates wealth, causes poverty, and leads to differences in people's incomes?

▶ What affects the prices of goods and services?

▶ What affects the amounts of money that people spend and save, how they spend money, and the quantities of goods and services that the economy produces?

▶ What affects business costs, business profits, and job opportunities for workers?

▶ How do government policies affect the economy?

Gains from Trade: A Thinking Example

People gain from trades, as Lisa and Mitch gain in the shoe-store example. They gain even when one person outperforms the other person at every task.

What Economics Is About

Economics studies people's choices and what happens to make everyone's choices compatible. What goods do people produce? How? How much do they produce? What do they trade and at what prices? How much do they gain from their trades? Who consumes how much of which goods?

These key questions lead to important issues of wealth and poverty, economic growth, and government policies.

Scarcity and Opportunity Cost

Every scarce good has an opportunity cost. Your opportunity cost of a good is the value of whatever you must sacrifice to obtain it.

Two Types of Economic Issues

Economics concerns two types of issues: decisions and their coordination. Opportunity costs affect people's incentives and decisions. Markets coordinate people's decisions through a process of competition and voluntary trades. That market process in turn affects opportunity costs, incentives, and decisions.

When people trade voluntarily, they expect to benefit. The market process can lead people pursuing only their own interests to do things that help others. Adam Smith described the market process in *The Wealth of Nations* with a metaphor: People acting in their own self-interest are "led by an invisible hand" to help others.

Because people can trade only things that they own, property rights are necessary for the market process to operate. Limits on property rights affect the outcomes of the market process.

Key Terms

economics	opportunity cost	ownership

Problems

14. Read the news article, "Clashing Priorities: Cancer Drug May Save Many Human Lives—At Cost of Rare Trees," and explain how its topic relates to scarcity and opportunity costs.

15. Comment on this statement: "The opportunity cost of AIDS research is cancer research."

16. What is the opportunity cost of:
    (a) Getting married
    (b) Freedom of speech
    (c) A law prohibiting college-age students from drinking alcohol
    (d) A policy to reduce global warming
    (e) The war on illegal drugs

I N   T H E   N E W S

Clashing priorities: Cancer drug may save many human lives—at cost of rare trees

That angers conservationists, who say taxol extraction endangers the prized yew

Right now, medical researchers say, the only way to produce quickly all the taxol that is needed for treatment and testing would be to chop down tens of thousands of yews. And conservationists are successfully opposing any large-scale sacrificing of the tree, which grows in the ancient forests that are refuge to the endangered Northern spotted owl and other wildlife.

"This is the ultimate confrontation between medicine and the environment," says Bruce Chabner of the National Cancer Institute, sponsor of the studies. "It's the spotted owl vs. people. I love the spotted owl, but I love people more."

Source: The Wall Street Journal

Opportunity costs can create political conflicts.

(f) Protecting children from pornography on the Internet

(g) Preventing terrorists from acquiring chemical, biological, or nuclear weapons

17. Explain how the market process can lead people who act out of selfish interests to do things that help others.

18. What is the "invisible hand" in economics?

19. Explain how limitations on property rights can lead people to waste scarce resources.

20. Explain how a tax can interfere with people's incentives to gain from a trade.

21. A baker is willing to bake a cake if he can sell it for at least $6 (to cover the costs of ingredients, the use of his oven, and his time and effort). A customer is willing to pay $10 for a cake.
   (a) Would some trade help both the baker and the customer? What trade?
   (b) How much do the baker and the customer gain from the trade you proposed in part (a)?
   (c) How would your answer to part (a) change if the government imposed a $2 tax on every cake sold?
   (d) How would your answer to part (a) change if the government imposed a $5 tax on every cake sold?

22. How can someone own a song? How can someone own an idea?

23. Comment on this claim: "People who say that the Gulf War [between the United Nations and Iraq in 1991] cost the United States billions of dollars are wrong. Most of those billions of dollars were spent on military equipment sold by American businesses. The arms manufacturers got money that would otherwise have gone to beer manufacturers, but the United States as a whole did not pay a big cost for the war." What was the United States' opportunity cost of the war?

Inquiries for Further Thought

24. Reread the news article from Problem 14. How do you think our society should make decisions on matters like this? Can you think of any general principles that would apply to all similar kinds of decisions?

25. Do people always benefit from voluntary trades?

Why might voluntary trades leave them worse off rather than better off?

26. Should the government prohibit people from trading some goods or services? Why or why not? Defend your answer.

CHAPTER 2

SOLVING PUZZLES: THE METHODS OF ECONOMICS

In this Chapter. . .

Main Points to Understand

▶ Positive statements are about what *is*. Normative statements are about what *should be*.

▶ Models represent logical thinking.

▶ Certain fallacies, which appear repeatedly in the media, create errors in logical arguments and interpretations of statistical evidence.

Thinking Skills to Develop

▶ Distinguish between positive and normative statements.

▶ Formulate models to help think about complex issues.

▶ Recognize logical fallacies in news articles and discussions.

A detective creates a logical story of how a crime took place, explaining a suspect's opportunity and motive. A court examines how well available evidence supports that story. A doctor examines a patient's symptoms for evidence to support a medical diagnosis and prescribe treatment. Late at night, a driver stops at the side of the road to look at a map. Where is he?

The detective, the doctor, and the driver have something in common. Each uses a *model*—logical thinking—and seeks evidence to judge the model. The detective's model involves an imaginary reenactment of the crime; the doctor's model involves the logic of biological processes in a human body; the driver's model is his interpretation of the map. Every model leaves something out—the detective's story ignores how long the suspect waited in hiding; the doctor's diagnosis omits the path by which the virus entered the body; the map leaves out the slopes of the roads together with the trees and driveways alongside. Evidence may support the models despite their imperfections. These imperfections may not affect the best course of justice, the best medical procedure, or the best direction to drive.

Economists use models and evidence, too. Like detective work, economics involves logical thinking to solve puzzles and evidence to support that logic.

POSITIVE AND NORMATIVE ECONOMICS

An economist recently told the U.S. Congress:

> Salaries of college graduates have increased, and wages of less-educated workers have stagnated, because of technological changes. Congress should act to curb this increasing inequality by raising subsidies to higher education.

Notice that the economist made two kinds of statements:

1. A statement of *fact:* Technological change has raised salaries of college graduates and kept wages of less-educated workers low.

2. A statement of *values:* Congress should raise subsidies to higher education.

The first statement is either a true or false assertion. It involves facts, not value judgments. It states what *is,* not what *should be.* The second statement is neither true nor false. It represents a person's opinion about what *should be,* so it involves that person's value judgments. Economics is mostly about statements of fact, though people's interest in those facts may arise from controversies over what *should be.*

> **Positive statements** are statements of fact, of what is or what would be if something else were to happen. Positive statements are either true or false.
>
> **Normative statements** express value judgments; they state what *should be.* Normative statements cannot be true or false.

EXAMPLES

Positive Statements	Normative Statements
Drugs can affect your health.	Laws should prohibit drugs.
If drugs were legal, then more people would take drugs.	The country needs a stronger antidrug policy.
A reduction in the corporate income tax would raise investment, but it would also raise the budget deficit.	Government should cut the corporate income tax.

Sometimes no one knows for sure whether a positive statement is true or false, and opinions on it differ. For example, consider this positive statement: Simple forms of life inhabit other planets in our solar system. No one knows (yet) whether this statement is true or false, and scientists have different opinions about it. Someday, perhaps, we will learn who is right. On the other hand, consider this normative statement: Classical music is better than popular music. It is neither true nor false. People disagree about it, but neither side is right or wrong.

Economics as a science involves positive statements about the economy. Knowledge about the economy gained by studying these positive statements can help people make intelligent decisions. For example, positive statements about the effects of international trade on the economy can help us decide whether the government should sign a new trade agreement.

Advice

Some statements in the media combine positive *and* normative components. Others are simply *ambiguous* claims, and need to be more precise to have any *meaning*. Beware of such statements.

You study almost any subject in two ways:

1. Think logically about it.

2. Gather evidence about it.

When economists think logically about an economic problem, they produce economic models:

> An **economic model** is a description of logical thinking about an economic issue. It may express its conclusions in words, graphs, or mathematical symbols.

Logical thinking by itself is not sufficient to reach reliable conclusions about economics; logic needs the support of evidence.

> Economic **evidence** is any set of facts that helps convince economists that some positive statement about the economy is true or false.

Many sciences gather evidence through controlled experiments. Sometimes scientists gather evidence simply by observing nature. Physicists learn about stars and galaxies by observing them and measuring their emissions of radiation; medical researchers learn about diseases by observing differences in their incidence in different societies and applying statistical analysis to draw inferences about those observations.

> **Statistical analysis** is the use of mathematical probability theory to draw inferences in situations of uncertainty.

Economists gather most of their evidence from observation followed by statistical analysis. An economist might examine inflation and interest rates in ten countries over the last 40 years (or the last century) to gather evidence about the connections between inflation and interest rates. This evidence could help the economist decide which of several economic models most effectively portrays the true relationships.

The rest of this chapter discusses economic models and evidence, logical fallacies and statistical fallacies, and how to interpret graphs. Much of the material in this chapter applies not only to economics but to other subjects as well.

Assumptions and Conclusions

Every economic model requires *assumptions* about how people behave. The model works from these assumptions to draw logical conclusions. These conclusions often take the form of "If . . . then . . . " statements that say what will happen *if* someone does something. These conclusions are the *predictions* of the model.[1]

Though you may not realize it, you use models in everyday life. Your models rely on assumptions, and you use them to make predictions. Here are some examples of simple models:

---

[1] A prediction, or the model that generated it, is sometimes called an *hypothesis*.

Figure 1 | Model of a Play in American Football

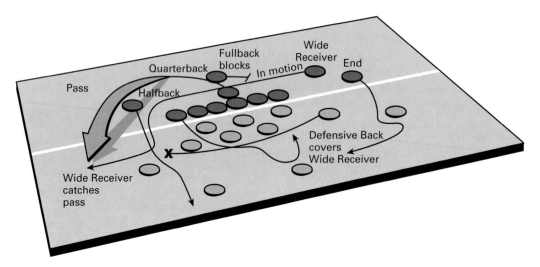

This diagram shows a model of a football play in which a wide receiver goes in motion across the field intending to fool the defensive back and break open to catch a pass.

EXAMPLES

1. "All the other people who interview for the job will *talk* about their experiences and qualifications, but this company wants to find someone different, with innovative ideas. If I prepare a *written summary* of my goals on this job and give it to them at the interview, I will impress them. Then I'll probably get the job offer."

2. "She would want me to kiss her if the time and place were right. She likes walks in the moonlight. If everything goes well tonight, I'll take her for a walk and then . . . "

Figure 1 shows a model of a play in American football. The lines show where players on the offensive team are supposed to go on the play, and where that team *assumes* that the defensive players will go. If these assumptions are correct, the quarterback can complete a pass to the wide receiver. This statement is the model's prediction. If the assumptions are wrong, then one of the defensive players may break up the play.

Each of these examples uses assumptions to derive a prediction or hypothesis. You can think of a model as a daydream based on logical reasoning.

Good and Bad Models

A model is good if it achieves its purpose. The models in the previous examples are good if the actions that they suggest raise the chances of getting the job, the kiss, or the completed pass.

You might think it is easy to find out whether a model is good or bad: simply do what the model says and see what happens. But the predictions of a bad model might turn out to be true (someone might get the job, the kiss, or the completed pass) simply by luck. Also, the predictions of a good model might be wrong by chance. (Perhaps the quarterback throws a bad pass or the intended receiver drops the ball.) No easy test can separate good and bad models. However, a good model is more likely than a bad model to lead to a successful outcome. Economists apply statistical analysis to control for luck and decide how good or bad their models are.

Purposes of Models

Economic models serve three purposes:

1. *Understanding.* A model simplifies an issue to help people understand it.

2. *Prediction.* A model helps people to predict, so they can answer questions like "What will happen . . . " and "What will happen *if* . . . " to resolve complicated, real-life issues.

3. *Interpretation.* A model helps people to interpret data as evidence about positive economic statements.

1. Models Simplify an Issue

Models are simpler than the real-life situations they represent. Many real-life situations are too complicated for the limited abilities of human minds to comprehend. Consequently, we create models—simplified versions of reality—to help think logically about real life.[2] A model assumes that some features of an issue are important to think about while other features are unimportant enough to ignore.

EXAMPLES

Imagine explaining to someone how a car works. You might give a general explanation of how the engine works and ignore details like the chemistry and physics of combustion. This simplified explanation, or model, may do the job. Similarly, suppose you are teaching a friend to play tennis. You cover the most important points about how to swing the racket, ignoring subtle details. Your *model* of tennis ignores these details to help focus your friend's attention on the most important aspects of the game; this model is useful because it helps your friend to understand the game and learn to play it.

2. Models Help Us to Predict

Economists may want to predict next year's inflation rate or the effect of a cut in military spending on unemployment. *Unconditional predictions* answer questions of the form, "What will happen?" *Conditional predictions* answer questions of the form, "What will happen *if* . . . ?" (For example, how would unemployment change if the government were to cut military spending by $20 billion?) Conditional predictions are particularly important because they help people to make good decisions: They tell people the likely results of alternative choices. Economists use models for both conditional and unconditional predictions.

EXPLANATION

If you want to predict your grade in a course, you need a model. Your model might say that because you are smart and motivated to study, you are likely to receive a good grade. (This is an unconditional prediction.) You may be confident that your model is good

Making Smart Decisions
Conditional predictions are necessary for good decisions. How much should you study for your courses? You need conditional predictions to make good decisions about this—to predict how your grades and future opportunities will change if you study more. To make these conditional predictions, you need a *model*. Your model might predict that your grade will rise by one letter, and your future salary by $1,000 per year, if you study an extra 30 minutes every day. You can use such conditional predictions to make good decisions on how much to study.

Economists use models to make conditional predictions about issues such as how employment would respond to a change in government policies. The predictions from these models can help the government make good policy decisions.

---

[2]Models help to economize on a scarce resource—our time and ability.

because you have received good grades in the past when you have been motivated to study.[3] Economists use models to make unconditional predictions about matters such as next year's inflation rate or foreign trade.

3. Models Help Us to Interpret Data as Evidence

Models can suggest which pieces of information to obtain as evidence—which statistical data are relevant for analysis of a particular economic issue. Models also indicate how to use data, clarifying questions like which numbers to add or multiply together to obtain a prediction. If a model makes accurate predictions, this accuracy is evidence that the model is a good representation of reality and that it gives reliable positive economic statements. Inaccurate predictions are evidence that the model is bad.

Evidence can prove that a theory is false by contradicting its predictions. Evidence that is consistent with such predictions can increase confidence in the truth of the theory, but evidence cannot conclusively prove a theory. No matter how much evidence supports a theory, a possibility always remains that new evidence will contradict it.

EXAMPLES

Why is a disease more common in one country than another? Medical researchers need a model to answer this question. Logical thinking about the disease can tell them which information is relevant (such as dietary intake of a particular substance) and which is not (such as exercise and sleep habits). In this way, the model helps researchers choose which data to collect and analyze. The model may also suggest how to analyze the data; perhaps the researchers should examine dietary intake above a threshold level. If the model accurately fits the data, scientific confidence in the model rises. If the model does not accurately fit the data, scientists search for ways to modify the model or construct alternative models.

Why is inflation lower in Argentina than in Brazil? Economists need a model to answer this question. Which economic data on Argentina and Brazil are relevant to explain inflation and which data are not? How should economists use those data? A model may tell the economist to:

1. Check the amount of new money each country's government has printed in the previous 2 years

2. Divide by the total amount of money in each country

3. Subtract the country's economic growth rate (the increase in its output of goods and services) over the last 2 years

These calculations would give the economist a number for each country. The model may predict that these numbers will roughly equal the inflation rates in the two countries. If data confirm the accuracy of this prediction, they provide evidence that the model is good; if not, the data indicate that economists need a better economic model to explain inflation.

Economists apply the "permanent income model" to explain how much money people spend and how much they save. The logical thinking in the model tells economists to collect data on a person's average income over many years to explain that person's spending in any particular month, say April 2001. The model says that two people of the same age, with the same education and average income over many years, will spend about the same amount of money in April 2001, even if one person earns more than the

---

[3]A different model might say that grades are completely random. Evidence from your past experience, showing that your grades are connected to your abilities and the amount of time you study, would be evidence against the random grade model.

Artificial Economies on Computers

Think of creating a computer simulation game—say Sim-Economy—that models the economy. Instead of building robots, the computer tells "virtual robots" how to behave—to work, produce, buy and sell goods, consume, invest, and so on. When these "virtual robots" interact, you have an artificial economy—an economic model. While no such game is currently available for home use, economists create such computer simulation "games" all the time. Economists use these artificial economies or *economic models* to analyze complex economic issues. By changing the computer programs, they can change the way that their "virtual robots" behave and analyze the consequences. See the Web site (www.dryden.com) for this book for more information.

other in *that* particular month. (The theory says that income in April 2001 is not very relevant to spending, but average income over many years before that month is relevant.)[4] Economists have found that the permanent income model gives reasonably accurate predictions, though certain inaccuracies have led economists to modify it slightly.

Models Are Artificial Economies

Imagine building 1,000 robots with computers inside them, programmed to direct the robots' behavior in various situations. You design each robot to produce a certain kind of toy, sell these toys to other robots, and spend the money to buy other kinds of toys from other robots. You could program each robot to respond to changes in the conditions it faces; for example, you might program a robot to buy a certain toy only if its price were sufficiently low. If you were to put the robots together in a room and let them interact, you could watch an entire artificial economy made up of robots.

You could change the way the robots behave by changing the computer program. In this way, you could see what happens to unemployment, wages, inflation, and interest rates in the robot economy, or what happens when you change taxes or government regulations. If the robot economy has features that are similar to our human economy, you might conclude that the robot economy is a good model of our real, human economy.

Building these robots would be expensive. Instead, you might use mathematics to describe the projected robot behavior and calculate what would happen in the robot economy. Economists do just that when they build models. Sometimes economists do the mathematical calculations by hand, and sometimes they use computers. The mathematical description of the robots' behavior and the results of their interactions is an economic model. Economic models are artificial economies that an economist invents and writes on paper or programs into a computer.[5]

---

[4]This summary oversimplifies the permanent income model a bit. The person who earns a higher income in April may also be more likely to earn a higher average income in future years, so that person would spend more in April.

[5]Scientists in other disciplines such as physics and biology use similar methods.

Models of Behavior

Economics deals with actions by real people, not robots, so economic models require assumptions about how people behave. Economists usually assume that people behave *rationally*. This term has a very specific meaning in economics.

> **Rational behavior** means that people do the best they can, *based on their own values and information,* under the circumstances they face.

In the words of the Nobel-prize-winning economist Gary Becker, people may be "selfish, altruistic, loyal, spiteful, or masochistic," but they "try as best they can to anticipate the uncertain consequences of their actions" and "maximize their own welfare *as they conceive it.*"[6]

People who dislike your values may call you *irrational,* but there are no "rational" or "irrational" values according to our definition of rational behavior. Even criminals and thoroughly disgusting people may behave rationally. Rational behavior refers to the actions people take to further their own goals, whatever those goals are. A rational person's values need not be materialistic; they may involve caring about family, friends, and poor or oppressed people around the world.

People must act based on limited information about the future results of their actions. How many times have you done something that seemed like a good idea at the time but that you later regretted? If you do what seems best to you at the time, based on your limited information, you are acting rationally, even if you later regret your actions.

People who behave rationally can make mistakes. Rational behavior does not preclude mistakes, but it implies that a person does not repeatedly make the same simple mistake; *rational behavior* means that people learn from past mistakes. It also means that their beliefs about the future reflect whatever information they have.

Most economic models assume that people behave rationally. Economists usually make this assumption with confidence because it has been successful in the past; it is a key part of many good economic models. Some economic models, however, assume *irrational* behavior, particularly in cases where evidence supports that assumption. Economists continually look for new ways to improve their models to make them better tools for understanding, predicting, and interpreting real-life economies.

Review Questions

1. What are positive statements? What are normative statements?

2. What is a model, and what purpose does it serve?

3. What do economists mean by the term *rational behavior?*

Thinking Exercises

4. Develop a model to explain the weather (such as why it rains some days and not others).
   (a) Discuss how your model simplifies the real-world situation to make it more understandable.

---

[6]Gary Becker, Nobel Lecture, "The Economic Way of Looking at Behavior," *Journal of Political Economy,* June 1993, pp. 385–409.

(**b**) What are some assumptions of your model?

(**c**) Discuss how your model can help you to predict the weather in various circumstances.

(**d**) Discuss how your model can help you to interpret data as evidence for or against the model.

COMMON LOGICAL FALLACIES

Most of this book discusses economic models. Because these models involve logical reasoning, you must understand common logical fallacies to apply the models effectively. Unfortunately, logical fallacies are common in popular economic discussions in the news media and elsewhere. Awareness of these fallacies will help you to identify invalid arguments when you hear them (and help you to improve your own reasoning).

Fallacy of Composition

> A **fallacy of composition** occurs when someone says that "what is true for one person must be true for the economy as a whole."

In fact, what is true for one person is *not* necessarily true for society as a whole.

EXAMPLES

Each of the following examples shows something that is true of an individual, but not true of a larger group:

1. When a professor grades exams on a curve, an individual student can increase her grade by studying more, but the class as a whole cannot increase its grades by studying more.

2. An individual at a sports event can see better by standing up than by remaining seated, but spectators as a whole cannot see better if everyone stands.

3. An individual can borrow money, but the world economy as a whole cannot borrow.

Advice
You can find more examples of each fallacy on the Web pages (www.dryden.com) for this book.

Post-Hoc Fallacy

> A **post-hoc fallacy** occurs when someone says that "one event happened before another, so the first event must have *caused* the second event."

In fact, there is no necessary relation between the timing of events and which event causes which.

EXAMPLES

1. Every year, Adrian sends Christmas cards to his friends before Christmas. He would commit the post-hoc fallacy if he concluded that his cards *caused* Christmas.

2. It always gets dark soon after the street lights begin to shine. Some street lights

have automatic timers that turn them on before dark. You commit the post-hoc fallacy if you conclude that it gets dark *because* the street lights shine.

3. Business firms often borrow money to expand their operations. A conclusion that increased borrowing *causes* business expansion would illustrate the post-hoc fallacy. Instead, the desire to expand causes business firms to borrow.

Other-Conditions Fallacy

> The **other-conditions fallacy** occurs when someone says that "if two events always occurred together in the past, they will always occur together in the future."

In fact, two events may occur together under some but not all conditions. When conditions change, incentives may change. When incentives change, past behavior is not necessarily a reliable guide to future behavior.

EXAMPLES

1. All season long, a football team punts on fourth down when it has more than one yard to go for a first down. It would be wrong to conclude that the team will always punt in this situation in the future, however, because conditions may change. If the team is losing by three points near the end of the championship game, it may pass the ball on fourth down with five yards to go. Why? Because conditions have changed: If it punts, it will lose the game, but if it passes the ball, it may win.

2. For many years, the government of a small country collected an extra billion dollars in tax revenue every time it raised the tax on business profits by 1 percent. Recently, the government increased the tax by 1 percent, but its tax revenue did not increase. Why? Because increases in world economic integration made it easier for business firms to move to other countries with lower taxes, and some firms responded to this tax increase by doing so.

STATISTICS

Economists use statistical analysis to draw inferences from economic data. The application of statistical analysis to economics is called *econometrics* or *empirical economics*.

You may have heard that people can lie with statistics. It is important to understand some basic statistical fallacies so that you can identify invalid arguments and correctly interpret statistical evidence.

Statistical Fallacies

Misleading Comparisons
One important statistical fallacy involves misleading comparisons:

> A **misleading comparison** occurs when someone compares two or more things in a way that does not reflect their true differences.

IMPORTANT EXAMPLE: FAILURE TO ADJUST FOR INFLATION

People sometimes compare dollar amounts in different years without adjusting for inflation. Someone may tell you "When I was your age back in 1950, I was happy to work hard for $1 an hour!" This statement may imply that you are lazy if you will not work for $5.25 an hour. But it may be a misleading comparison because of inflation: $1 in 1950 is equivalent to about $6.75 today. Similarly, politicians sometimes say a tax increase or tax cut is "the biggest in history"; this rhetoric is often misleading, because they fail to adjust for inflation.

Every few years, someone claims that a new movie is the highest-grossing movie of all time (the one that has earned the most money); this is usually misleading, because the person seldom adjusts for inflation. In fact, *Gone with the Wind* is the highest-grossing movie of all time after adjusting for inflation. When it was released in 1939, prices were much lower than they are today. After adjusting for inflation, *Gone with the Wind* has earned about $2.1 billion in today's dollars, more than twice the earnings of *Star Wars*, which occupies second place. The appendix to this chapter shows some misleading comparisons on graphs.

Selection Bias

A second important statistical fallacy is selection bias:

> **Selection bias** occurs when people use data that are not *typical*, but *selected* in a way that biases results.

EXAMPLES

1. Suppose you want to calculate the average income of rock musicians. If you use data on the average income of rock stars with hit videos on MTV, you would *not* get an accurate answer to your question. Your data would reflect only *successful* rock musicians with (on average) higher incomes. The data would not reflect the lower incomes of typical rock musicians without music videos on MTV. By looking only at the most successful performers, you cannot find out about the average income of all rock musicians.

2. Suppose you want to study the investment advice of stock analysts. You gather data on the results of investment advice given by all stock analysts who have been in business in your city for the last ten years. Did the analysts give good advice to their customers? You might find that the advice was good, on average: People who listened to these stock analysts may have earned more money on their investments (on average) than other people earned. Does this imply that stock analysts give good advice, on average? Not necessarily. The problem is selection bias: You probably lack data on stock analysts who went out of business because they gave less successful advice. Therefore, you would commit a fallacy if you draw conclusions about the average performance of investment advisors from your study.

Discussion An illegal business scheme may help you to understand selection bias. First, buy a large mailing list (a list of potential customers and their addresses) and divide it into two parts. Write to people on the first part telling them that you predict stock prices will *rise* next month. Write to the people on the second part of the list telling them that you predict stock prices will *fall* next month. Next month, throw away the part of your list reflecting an incorrect prediction and keep the part reflecting an accurate prediction. For example, if stock prices fall, throw away the first part of your list, and keep

IN THE NEWS

Data called misleading in rating contraceptives

Most methods can be effective, but bias clouds comparisons.

By Gina Kolata

The available data on the comparative effectiveness of different contraceptives is misleading and only marginally useful in helping people choose which method to use, according to a new study and a growing number of health experts.

Source: New York Times

'Selection Bias' Cited

A universal drawback of the contraception studies, the scientists said, is "selection bias." Women who are most anxious to avoid pregnancy will select methods they believe are most effective, so the group using pills, for example, is always more motivated to use the

method correctly than those using contraceptive foams. Even if the foam were just as effective as the pill, more women using foam would become pregnant.

This bias is a problem "because it cannot be corrected in the analysis stage," Dr. Trussell and Dr. Kost reported.

Sample selection bias can occur in any kind of research.

the second part. Divide that list in two parts and repeat. After several months, you will have a small mailing list of people who have seen your predictions come true several times in a row, with no mistakes. You are now ready to charge them a high price for advice (unless they understand selection bias)!

Correlations

When two variables (such as interest rates and inflation) tend to change together, economists say they are correlated.

> Two variables exhibit **positive correlation** if they tend to increase and decrease together. (They move in the same direction.) They exhibit **negative correlation** if one increases when the other decreases and vice versa. (They move in opposite directions.) The correlation of the variables is a number that measures how closely they are related.

EXAMPLES

Education level and income are positively correlated; people with more education tend to have higher incomes. (See Figures A4 and A5 in the appendix to this chapter.) Interest rates and inflation are positively correlated; they tend to rise and fall together. Automobile size and mileage per gallon of gasoline are negatively correlated; larger cars get fewer miles per gallon, on average.

Interpreting Correlations

Economists need models to interpret correlations. A correlation often allows several possible interpretations. For example, many studies have found that married men earn higher wages than single men of the same age and race with the same education and experience. One interpretation states that married men work harder than single men, because they are more motivated. Another interpretation states that employers discriminate against single men; perhaps employers view married men as more reliable employees. Either interpretation might lead a man to believe that he could earn more money by getting married. This move might raise his earnings by motivating him to work harder or by persuading employers of his reliability. But there is a third interpretation of the correlation: Perhaps women tend to marry men whose personal characteristics enable them to earn high wages. If the third interpretation is correct, then a man would not be able to increase his earnings by getting married. No one knows which interpretation is correct. Until more evidence becomes available about the best model to explain this correlation, room for disagreement remains.

Evidence in Economics

Economists work with two main types of data. *Time series* are data on a single person, business, industry, or country over some period of time. For example, data on the average starting salary of college graduates over the last 20 years would be time-series data. *Cross sections* are data on many people, businesses, industries, or countries at one particular time. For example, data on last year's average starting salary for college graduates in each state would be cross-section data. Time-series data provide evidence on which variables change together over time. Cross-section data provide evidence on how people or countries differ from one another at a moment in time.

Most evidence in economics comes from nonexperimental data: data gathered by observation rather than controlled experiments like those carried out in a science laboratory. Economics is not the only science that uses nonexperimental data. Scientists gather nonexperimental data when they study stars and galaxies through telescopes or the behavior of animals in their natural environments. If economists could experiment with the economy, they could change government policies to examine the results, perhaps changing one policy at a time to isolate the separate effects of each policy. Since economists cannot do this, they usually rely on statistical analysis of nonexperimental data to produce evidence for their economic models.[7]

Economists do not always agree with each other about economic issues. Disagreements arise for two reasons:

1. Economists may disagree about the truth of positive economic statements. Sometimes available evidence portrays mixed results for a model, with some evidence supporting the model and other evidence failing to support it. Sometimes there is simply not enough information, and the evidence is too weak to tell whether a model is a good reflection of reality. Economists are not alone; scientists in every field have such disagreements. Disagreements over positive statements can be resolved only by accumulating more evidence.

2. Economists, like other people, disagree about values. Even if they agree about the truth of positive economic statements, they may disagree about normative

WHY ECONOMISTS DISAGREE

---

[7]Some evidence in economics does come from experiments. Economists create small, artificial economies and study their operation. For example, they may pay a group of students to participate in an artificial stock market to examine the behavior of stock prices in the experiment. The economist can manipulate conditions in the artificial economy to see what happens.

IN THE NEWS

Impasse delays proposal to cut diet guidelines

By Robert Pear
Special to
The New York Times

WASHINGTON, Oct. 7— In an unusual move, the National Academy of Sciences announced today that some of the nation's most eminent scientists were in an irreconcilable conflict over proposals to alter the recommended levels of certain vitamins and minerals in the human diet.

Despite "exhaustive deliberation," Dr. Press said, the experts were unable to agree on the interpretation of scientific data and the recommended allowances for several nutrients.

Source: New York Times

In all sciences, experts disagree in some areas.

statements such as what the government *should* do. Economists, like everyone else, want to convince people that they are smart and that their views on normative issues are correct, so, economists who make public statements to the media are not always as honest as they should be. An economist who believes that the government should do something may exaggerate the evidence for positive economic statements that support this opinion. This exaggeration may be deliberate or unintentional, but it can create disagreements with economists who have other values.[8]

Review Questions

5. Explain and give examples of:
   (a) the fallacy of composition
   (b) the post-hoc fallacy
   (c) the other-conditions fallacy
   (d) a misleading comparison
   (e) selection bias

6. Why don't economists always agree with one another?

Thinking Exercises

7. Develop a simple model to explain the spread of influenza (the flu). Contrast the problem of predicting exactly who catches influenza and when each victim catches it with the problem of predicting the average number of influenza cases in a month.

8. By age 30, the average college graduate earns about $10,000 more per year than the average high-school graduate. Does this imply that a person who did not attend college could have earned that much more if he had done so?

A NOTE ON GRAPHS

Economists use many graphs, and you will need to use them to understand this book. The key point to remember is this: *Every graph answers a question.* If you are not completely familiar with the use of graphs, you should read the appendix to this chapter.

Conclusion

Positive and Normative Economics

Positive statements are assertions about facts; normative statements express value judgments.

Models and Evidence

Economic models describe logical thinking about economic issues: They are artificial economies written on

---

[8]Nobel laureate economist Robert Solow put the matter this way: Economists, he said, "feel an apparently irresistible urge to push their science farther than it will go, to answer questions more delicate than our limited understanding of a complicated economy will allow. Some of the pressure comes from the outside. Your friendly financial journalist is frequently on the phone, and nobody likes to say 'I don't know,' or even 'nobody can know.' Some of the pressure comes from the inner drive to push against the frontiers of knowledge, to find answers. When the answer is very faint, you can hear what you want to hear" (*New York Times*, December 29, 1985, p. 2F).

paper or programmed into computers. Evidence about economics consists of facts that help to convince economists that some positive statement is true or false. Statistical analysis uses mathematical probability theory to draw inferences in situations of uncertainty. Economic models can help with understanding, predicting, or interpreting. A model may simplify an economic issue to help us understand it, help us make unconditional or conditional predictions about the economy, or help us interpret data as evidence about positive economic statements.

Economic models require assumptions about behavior. Economists usually assume that people behave rationally, which means they do the best they can for themselves, based on their own values and information, under the circumstances they face.

Common Logical Fallacies

Someone commits the fallacy of composition if he reasons that what is true for one person must be true for the economy as a whole. Someone commits a post-hoc fallacy if she reasons that because one event happened before another, the first event must have caused the second. Someone commits the other-conditions fallacy if he reasons that two events must always be related in the future if they have been related in the past.

Statistics

Economists use statistical analysis to draw inferences from economic data. Positively correlated variables tend to change in the same direction. Negatively correlated variables tend to change in opposite directions. The correlation between them measures how closely the variables move together. Models are required to interpret correlations.

A misleading comparison occurs when someone compares two things in a way that does not reflect their true differences. A common misleading comparison involves comparing dollar amounts from different years without adjusting for inflation. Selection bias occurs when people use data that are not typical, but are selected in a way that biases the results.

Why Economists Disagree

Disagreements can arise among economists for two reasons. They may disagree about the truth of positive economic statements when they lack sufficient evidence to decide which of several economic models best portrays reality. They may also disagree about values, which can create disagreement about normative economic statements.

K e y   T e r m s

positive statement	statistical analysis	other-conditions fallacy	negative correlation
normative statement	rational behavior	misleading comparison	correlation
economic model	fallacy of composition	selection bias	
evidence	post-hoc fallacy	positive correlation	

P r o b l e m s

9. Are the following statements positive, normative, or a combination? Explain your answer.
   - (a) "College tuition is too high and needs to be cut."
   - (b) "The Yankees and Braves will probably be in the World Series."
   - (c) "The distribution of income has deteriorated in the last decade."
   - (d) "Foreign competition hurts American workers."
   - (e) "Government regulations make it harder for U.S. businesses to compete with foreign sellers."

10. According to the *Bill James Baseball Almanac*, professional baseball players lose ability to hit as they get older (batting averages peak at age 27), yet the batting averages of older players are no lower than those of younger players. Bill James says that this fact illustrates selection bias.[9] Explain why.

11. To start a business, you make up a wild story about how to control whether a newly conceived baby is male or female, and you sell this advice to prospective parents. All customers pay you in advance, but you offer a money-back guarantee: If your procedure does not work, you refund their money.
   - (a) How is your business related to selection bias?
   - (b) Does your reasoning apply to businesses that sell advice on lottery numbers or sports betting?

---

[9]Bill James, *Bill James Baseball Almanac* (New York: Villard Books, 1987), pp. 60–64.

12. Develop a model to explain the effects of diet on health. Why don't nutritionists always agree about the effects of vitamins and other nutrients on health?

13. Develop a model to explain:
    (a) How the classes that college students choose affect their future salaries
    (b) How the amounts of time that college students spend studying affect their future salaries

    (c) How levels of punishment for convicted criminals affect crime
    (d) How gun controls affect crime
    (e) The average birth rate in a country
    (f) How increased practice time affects performance in sports, music, or the arts. In each case, discuss how you could use statistical data as *evidence* about the quality of your model.

Inquiries for Further Thought

14. This chapter suggested several possible theories to explain why married men earn higher incomes than single men. How would you use statistical evidence to identify the correct theory? If you could perform experiments, what experiments would you choose and why?

15. Do people behave rationally? How would you obtain *evidence* for or against your view?

Appendix: How to Use Graphs in Logical Thinking

Every graph answers a question. You will understand a graph if you understand the question that it answers.

BASIC EXAMPLE

How much money has the average family in the United States earned in recent decades? The answer can be graphed, as in Figure A1.[10] To find the answer to the question, find a year on the graph's horizontal axis, say 1990. Go straight up until you reach the curve, then straight left until you reach the vertical axis. The number on the vertical axis shows how much money an average family earned in 1990: $41,224. You can do the same thing for other years.

Each point on the curve indicates two numbers, a year and an income. Point A in Figure A1 indicates 1990 and $41,224. The two numbers allow each point to answer the question for a particular year.

The year and the income level are variables.

> **Variables** are names for sets of numbers analyzed with a graph or with mathematics.

Every graph measures one variable along the horizontal axis and another variable along the vertical axis.

MISLEADING GRAPHS

Figure A1 shows incomes adjusted for inflation to indicate how much money a family made in each year, measured in 1995 dollars. Adjusting for inflation prevents a misleading comparison; it allows accurate comparisons of family incomes in different years.

---

[10]The graph shows *median family income,* meaning that half of all families earn more and half earn less than the indicated amounts. The numbers are adjusted for inflation by expressing all incomes in 1995 dollars.

Figure A1 | Median Family Income Adjusted for Inflation

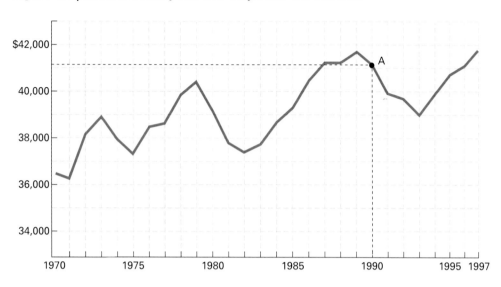

1. Find a year.
2. Go straight up until you hit the curve. Make a dot at that point (Point A).
3. Go left until you hit the *Y*-axis, indicating the average family income for that year: $41,224.

Source: Current Population Reports, Series P-60, No. 184, updated by author.

Figure A2 shows a graph that makes a misleading comparison among different years, because it does *not* adjust for inflation. Figure A3 shows that a typical good worth $10.00 in 1998 cost only about $8.15 in 1990, $5.14 in 1980, and only about $2.42 in 1970; prices have roughly quadrupled since 1970. Figure A2 misleads, because it fails to adjust for this inflation. Notice that the correct graph (Figure A1) conveys a very different impression than the misleading message of Figure A2.

A More Subtle Point

Figure A1 can mislead, as well, but for another, more subtle reason: The typical family of today includes fewer people than families did in the past. Median income *per person* has risen faster than Figure A1 suggests. If you remember to think critically about statistical evidence such as misleading graphs, you can protect yourself against mistakes in personal and business decisions, and you will improve your analysis of social and political issues.

Figure A2 | Median Family Income Not Adjusted for Inflation

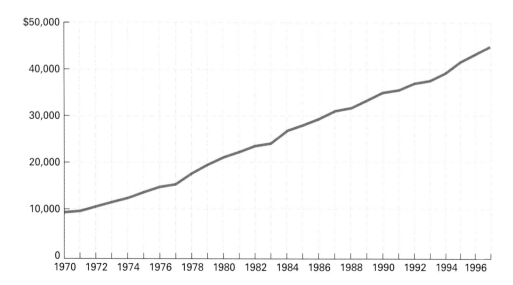

Average family income measured in dollars has risen over time, but this diagram illustrates a misleading comparison. Prices of goods have also risen over time, so families have not become as rich as quickly as the graph implies.

Source: Current Population Reports, Series P-60, No. 184, updated by author.

Figure A3 | Typical Price of a Good Worth $10 in 1998

A typical good that cost $10.00 in 1998 cost only about $8.15 in 1990, $5.14 in 1980, and only about $2.42 in 1970.

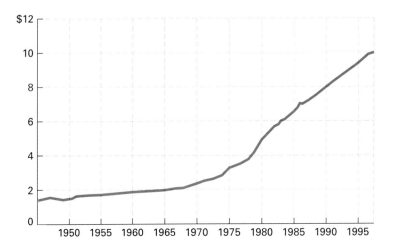

MANY CURVES ON THE SAME GRAPH

When more than one curve appears on a single graph, each curve answers a different question.

Figure A4 shows five curves. The highest curve answers the question, "How much money can an average person with some graduate school education expect to earn at different ages?" The second-highest curve answers the question, "How much money can an average college graduate expect to earn at different ages?" The other three curves repeat the

Figure A4 | Earnings of Full-Time Workers

Each curve tracks income for a certain level of education.

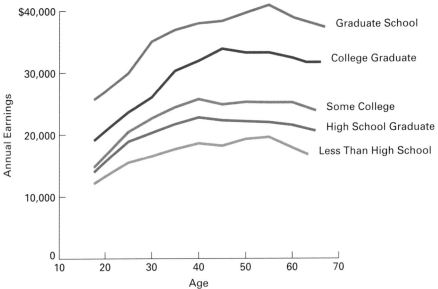

Figure A5(a) | Earnings of Males with Full-Time Jobs

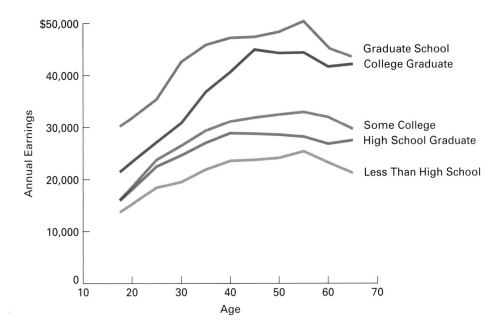

question for people with some college, high-school graduates, and people with less education. The horizontal axis measures age and the vertical axis measures income, in thousands of dollars. Figure A4 shows that a person with a college education can expect her income to rise until around age 50, after which it shows a slight decline. The average high-school graduate earns more each year until around age 40, and income falls slightly after that. This graph is adjusted for inflation; you can expect inflation to raise your future *dollar* income above the numbers in the graph.

Figures A5(a) and A5(b) show the same information separately for men and women. Compare these graphs to see that men earn, on average, more than women do.

Figure A5(b) | Earnings of Females with Full-Time Jobs

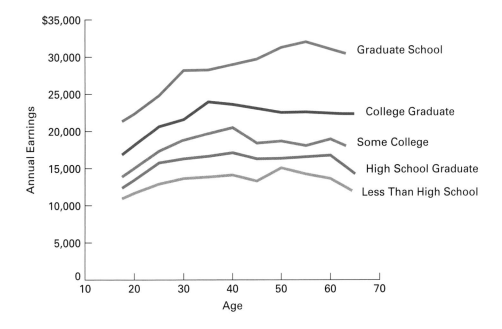

SHIFTING CURVES

Logical thinking with graphs often requires us to shift curves.

> A **shift** in a curve is a change in its position on a graph.

A curve on a graph shifts when a change in conditions changes the answer to the graph's question.

Figure A6 | The Earning Curve Shifts When a Student Goes to College

The arrow shows the shift in the curve.

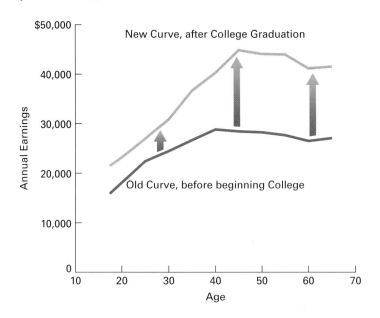

Figure A7 | Shifting a Curve: Reduced Sex Discrimination Raises the Earnings of Women

A fall in sex discrimination would shift the curve upward. (Both curves are drawn for a woman with a high-school education.)

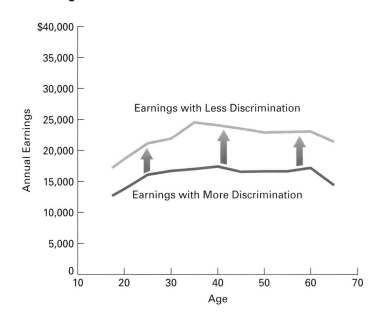

EXAMPLES

Consider a man who has just graduated from high school. The lower curve in Figure A6 shows the income that he can expect at various ages. Now suppose he goes to college. This decision raises his likely earnings at every age, so it shifts the curve in Figure A6. The curve shifts because a change in conditions (more education) changes the answer to the question, "What income can this man expect over his lifetime?"

Figures A5(a) and A5(b) showed that women earn less (on average) than men of the same age with the same education. Many people blame part of this difference on discrimination against women. If this is true, a fall in discrimination against women would shift the curves upward in Figure A5(b). Figure A7 shows the shift in one of these curves when a fall in discrimination changes the answer to the question, "How does the likely annual income of a female high-school graduate vary with her age?"

SLOPES OF CURVES

Figure A8 shows the answer to the question, "How does a change in time spent studying affect a typical student's grade on a biology exam?" The figure shows a positive correlation between the two variables, indicating that they move in the same direction. More time spent studying correlates with a higher grade. A curve with a positive slope shows the positive correlation between the two variables.

A **positive slope** refers to a shape that runs upward and to the right.

Figure A9 answers the question, "How does the time you have for watching television tonight depend on the amount of time you study?" The curve shows a negative correlation between the two variables, indicating that they move in opposite directions. A curve showing a negative correlation between two variables has a negative slope.

A **negative slope** refers to a shape that runs downward and to the right.

Figure A8 | Relation between Grade and Studying Time

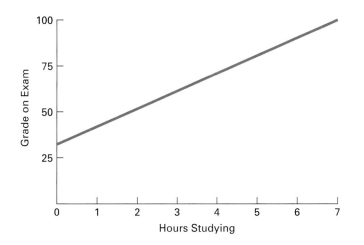

The line has a positive slope.

Figure A9 | More Studying Time Leaves Less Time for Television

The line has a negative slope. How would you choose to spend your time?

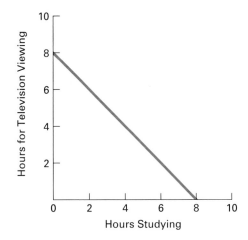

The slope of a curve is a number that measures its steepness:

> The **slope of a curve** is the distance by which the curve goes up or down as it moves 1 unit to the right.

The slope measures how much the variable along the vertical axis changes as the variable along the horizontal axis increases by 1 unit. If the curve rises as it moves to the right, the slope is a positive number; if it falls as it moves to the right, the slope is a negative number. Increasing numbers indicate ever steeper slopes.[11]

Figure A10 | Calculation of Slope

As you study one more hour, your likely grade rises by 2 points, so the slope of the line is 2.

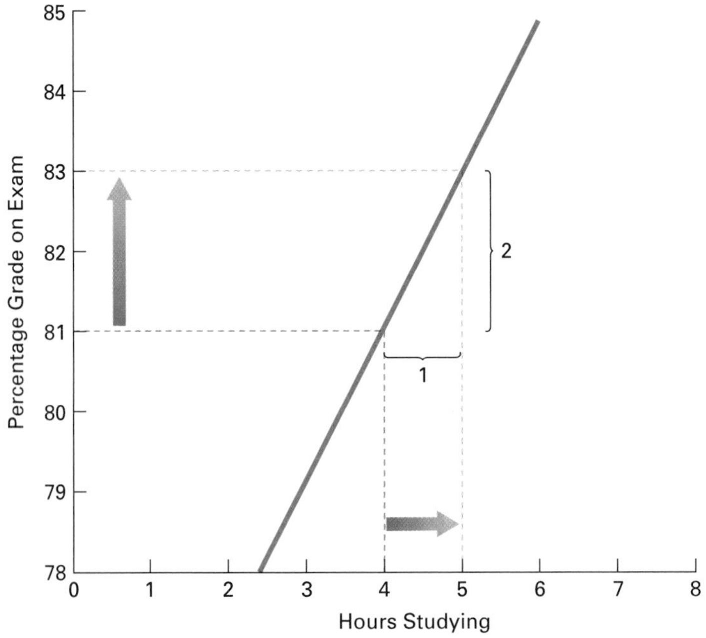

[11]Lines with slopes of 10 or −10 are steeper than lines with slopes of 3 or −3.

EXAMPLES

Figure A10 shows a line with a slope of 2; for every additional hour you study, your likely grade rises by 2 points. Figure A9 showed a line with a slope of −1; for every additional hour you spend studying, you lose an hour in front of the television.

The slopes of the curves in Figures A5(a) and A5(b) change at different ages. The curves are steeper for younger people than for older people. The slopes are positive at most ages: Increases in age usually lead to increases in earnings. The slopes are negative for older people, though; at advanced ages, further increases in age reduce earnings.

Logical thinking sometimes involves evaluating areas in regions of graphs.

AREAS

> An **area** of some region in a graph is a number that measures the size of that region.

Here are two formulas to calculate areas:

1. The area of a rectangle equals its base times its height. In Figure A11, the base of the shaded rectangle is 5 and the height is 6, so the area is 30 (5 times 6).

2. The area of a triangle is ½ the area of an associated rectangle. To calculate the area of a triangle, follow these steps:
    (a) Make a rectangle out of the triangle; one side of the triangle must become a side of the rectangle.
    (b) Calculate the area of the rectangle.
    (c) Divide by 2 to get the area of the triangle.

Figure A11 | Area of a Rectangle: The Base Times the Height

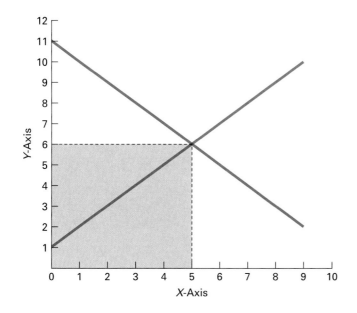

The base of the shaded rectangle is 5 and the height is 6, so the area is 5 times 6 or 30.

Figure A12 | Area of a Triangle

To calculate the area of Triangle A: *First,* make a rectangle out of Triangles A and B. *Second,* find the area of Rectangle AB. Its base is 5 and its height is 5, so its area is 5 times 5, or 25. *Third,* divide by 2 to get the area of Triangle A: 25/2 = 12½.

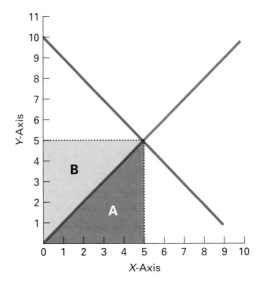

To find the area of Triangle B in Figure A12, form the rectangle with Areas A and B. This rectangle has a base of 5 and a height of 5, so the area of the rectangle is 25 (5 times 5). Dividing by 2 gives the answer 12½ for the area of Triangle B.

You will use these formulas later in this book for calculations such as how much money people pay in taxes and the losses in economic efficiency from restrictions on international trade.

Conclusion

Every graph answers a question. When a change in conditions changes that answer, the curve in the graph shifts. Curves with positive slopes show that variables move in the same direction. Curves with negative slopes show that variables move in opposite directions. Steeper curves have larger slopes (measured in absolute value). The area of a region in a graph measures the region's size.

Key Terms

variable   positive slope   slope
shift   negative slope   area

Problems

A1. Draw a graph to show the profits that U.S. manufacturing businesses earned after taxes on each dollar's worth of sales between 1973 and 1996.

A2. What makes a curve in a graph shift?

A3. Draw graphs of curves with:
   (a) Positive slope
   (b) Negative slope
   (c) Slope equal to 3
   (d) Slope equal to -2
   (e) Changing slope

A4. (Harder Problem) How might you use data to analyze how much the curve in Figure A7 would rise if discrimination against women were eliminated?

	Profit after Taxes per Dollar of Sales
1973	5.6 cents
1974	5.5
1975	4.6
1976	5.4
1977	5.3
1978	5.4
1979	5.7
1980	4.8
1981	4.7
1982	3.5
1983	4.1
1984	4.6
1985	3.8
1986	3.7
1987	4.9
1988	6.0
1989	5.0
1990	4.0
1991	2.4
1992	0.8
1993	2.8
1994	5.4
1995	5.7
1996	5.8
1997	5.7

FUNDAMENTAL TOOLS

LET'S MAKE A DEAL: THE GAINS FROM TRADE

In this Chapter. . .

Main Points to Understand

▶ The *production possibilities frontier* shows what the economy *can* produce.

▶ When people have different opportunity costs, they can gain from trade and consume amounts that would be impossible without trade.

▶ Different economically efficient situations are possible, with different distributions of income.

Thinking Skills to Develop

▶ Recognize limits to opportunities, and tradeoffs among opportunities; distinguish between limits and choices.

▶ Find trades in which all participants gain; recognize the gains from trade and how people share those gains.

▶ Understand why fairness is a subtle concept, and that people differ on its meaning.

Whatever you do, you face limits—constraints on your time, your spending ability, your opportunities. You can expand some of those limits. You can invest in skills that enable you to earn more money or save money to expand your future spending options. Almost everyone expands their limits, almost every day, through trade. You probably don't make your own clothes—you trade your work effort for money to buy them. You probably don't grow your own food, and you probably didn't build your own shelter. Like nearly everyone, you trade for these things. Your life would be very different without these trades. Trades vastly expand your limits and create new opportunities.

Whenever you voluntarily trade with someone, you expect to gain. The other person also expects to gain, of course. Some gains from trade are easy to understand: You have cookies and your friend has an apple, but you want the apple and your friend wants the cookies, so you trade. Other trades create much less obvious benefits, however, and this chapter explains them.

Some trades, like the cookie-apple trade, give people more of what they want by reshuffling goods that we already have. Other trades, as in the shoe-store example of Chapter 1, increase the total amounts of goods available.

Historically, standards of living rose when people started to trade, and today trade plays a larger economic role than ever before. People trade their services as carpenters, accountants, lawyers, teachers, or doctors for meal preparation and cleanup, child care, and other goods and services that people once provided mainly for themselves. If you are like most people in the United States, you spend more money on meals at restaurants than on meals at home. International trade involves a growing fraction of world output, as a single global economy develops. While the term *international trade* often evokes images of travel and excitement, its principles boil down to the basic ideas of this chapter.

LIMITS AND POSSIBILITIES

Everyone faces limits. Your time each day is limited; your budget is limited. The time you spend studying reduces the time you can spend on other activities. When you spend more on pizzas, you reduce the money you have available for other things.

Figure 1 shows a graph of your limited time. You have 24 hours every day, and every hour you spend studying leaves you with one hour less for other activities. Each point on the downward-sloping line shows one possible way to spend your time. You can choose Point A, at which you study for 2 hours and spend 22 hours on other activities. Or you can choose Point B (4 hours studying and 20 hours on other things), or Point C (8 hours studying and 16 hours on other things), or any other point on the line. But you cannot choose Point D, which indicates 8 hours of studying and 20 hours of other activities every day. Point D and other points above the line are impossible. The line shows all your possibilities.

Figure 2 shows a person's limited spending power on a graph. The graph applies to a person with $10 available to spend in a week, who can buy sodas for $1 each or rent videotapes for $2 each. Every dollar spent on one good leaves the person with $1 less for other goods. If the person spent all $10 on sodas, he could buy ten per week. (This is Point A in Figure 2.) If he spent all $10 on videotape rentals, he could rent five tapes per week. (This is Point B in Figure 2.) The person can choose any other point on the line in Figure 2, such as Point C (6 sodas and 2 videotapes per week). But the person cannot choose Point D, because he cannot afford six sodas and four videotape rentals per week. Point D and other points above the line are impossible. The line shows all the person's possibilities.

Figure 1
Your Limited Time

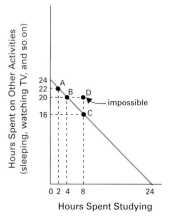

Figure 2
A Person's Limited Budget

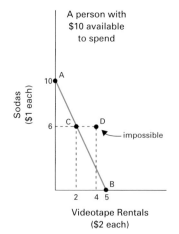

Production Possibilities Frontier

The economy as a whole also faces limits. The production possibilities frontier shows how many goods the economy can produce with its available inputs and technology.

> An economy's **production possibilities frontier,** or **PPF,** graphs the combinations of various goods that it can produce with its limited resources and technology.

Real economies produce millions of goods, and a computer can describe a PPF mathematically. To understand the PPF, imagine an economy that produces only two goods: videotapes and cars. Figure 3 shows its PPF. If the economy uses *all* its resources to produce videotapes, then it can produce 40 million videotapes and no cars. If it uses all its resources to produce cars, then it can produce 5 thousand cars and no videotapes. Alternatively, it can produce various combinations of videotapes and cars. Table 1 shows some of these possible combinations.

Main Facts about the PPF

1. *Scarcity:* The PPF shows the combinations of goods that an economy *can* produce with its current technology and resources—the economy's *possibilities*. Each point

Figure 3 | A Production Possibilities Frontier

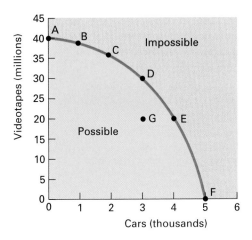

The production possibilities frontier shows the possible combinations of goods that the economy can produce if it uses its resources and technology efficiently. This combination depends on the resources and technology available to the economy, to the PPF shifts when resource availability or technology changes.

Table 1 | An Economy's Production Possibilities

Number of Videotapes Produced (millions)	Number of Cars Produced (thousands)	Point in Figure 3
40	0	Point A
39	1	Point B
36	2	Point C
30	3	Point D
20	4	Point E
0	5	Point F

on the PPF shows one possible combination of goods. All points under the PPF (such as Point G in Figure 3) are also possible. However, because resources are scarce, points above the PPF are *impossible*.

2. *Technical efficiency:* Points *on* the PPF are technically efficient combinations of output.

> **Technical efficiency** means that it is impossible to produce more of one good without producing less of another.

Technical efficiency means that the economy does not waste resources. Points A through F lie *on* the PPF, so each shows a technically efficient combination of outputs. On the other hand, Point G lies *below* the PPF, indicating a technically *in*efficient situation, because the economy could produce additional videotapes without reducing output of cars, or produce more cars without reducing output of videotapes.

1. *Decisions:* People's decisions and government policies determine which point on the graph shows the economy's *actual* output. In that sense, a society chooses some point on the PPF.

2. *Tradeoffs and opportunity costs:* The downward slope of the PPF shows the economy's tradeoff between producing cars and videotapes. The absolute value of the *slope* of the PPF shows how many videotapes the economy must sacrifice to expand production of cars. In other words, it shows the economy's opportunity cost of producing cars.

Everyone faces tradeoffs because of limited time.

Advice

If you don't yet understand why the absolute value of the slope of the PPF shows the economy's opportunity cost of cars, come back to this point after reading the two-student example below, or see the examples and explanations on the Internet site (www.dryden.com).

EXAMPLE

Suppose the economy is at Point D in Figure 3, producing 3,000 cars and 30 million videotapes. If the economy were to increase car production by 1,000 (to produce 4,000 cars altogether), it would have to produce 10 million fewer videotapes (20 million instead of 30 million). The economy would move from Point D to Point E. The slope of the PPF between Points D and E equals 10 million videotapes divided by 1,000 cars, or 10,000 videotapes per car. The economy's opportunity cost of producing a car is 10,000 videotapes.

General Point

The absolute value of the *slope* of the PPF shows the economy's opportunity cost of producing the good on the *X*-axis. In other words, it shows how many units of the good on the *Y*-axis the economy sacrifices when it produces a little more of the good on the *X*-axis.

Shifts in the PPF

The PPF shifts in response to any change in the economy's available resources or technology. The economy's resources include its available capital, labor, education and skills, and natural resources. Technical progress or an increase in resources shifts the PPF outward, as in Figure 4a. An economy's PPF shrinks inward, as in Figure 4b, if it loses resources or if its technology declines.

By expanding the economy's PPF, technical progress or accumulation of resources expands people's *consumption opportunities*. Growth in production increases the goods and services available for people to consume. As the PPF expands, people can consume more.

Application: Economic Growth

Economic growth refers to an increase in the economy's output of goods and services per person. A growing economy's PPF expands faster than its population grows. Economic growth can occur because the economy either gains new resources or discovers better technologies.

The U.S. economy has grown for both reasons. U.S. business capital (such as machines, tools, plants, and equipment) has roughly doubled since 1970 to about $6.3 trillion. (This number is already adjusted for inflation to avoid a misleading comparison with current conditions, as discussed in Chapter 2.) At the same time, U.S. technology has advanced (most visibly in computers, medicine and biotechnology, but also in thousands of other areas).

Figure 5 shows U.S. economic growth over the century from 1890 to 1990, with a prediction for 2010. The U.S. PPF for consumption and investment goods has expanded rapidly over time. Growth in total output of goods and services in the United States and western Europe averaged less than 0.2 percent per year in the years 1500 to 1750. Since that time, economic growth has increased dramatically:

▶ Growth rose to about 1.0 percent per year by 1850.

▶ It accelerated to between 1.0 and 1.5 percent per year between 1850 and 1950.

▶ Growth has continued at about 1.8 percent per year since 1950 (faster on average before 1973 and slower on average since then).

There is a huge difference between the 0.2 percent annual growth in the third quarter of the millennium and the more recent growth of 1.8 percent per year. When the economy grows at 1.8 percent per year, output doubles every 39 years. When the economy

Technological change contributes to economic growth.

Figure 4 | Shifts in a PPF

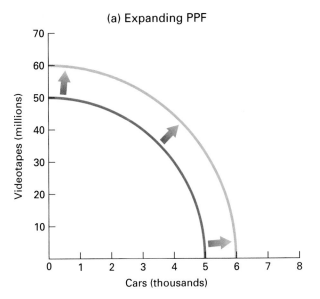

(a) Expanding PPF

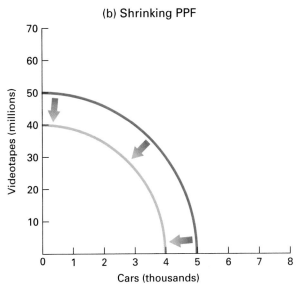

(b) Shrinking PPF

(a) This PPF expands as more resources become available to the economy or as technology improves.

(b) This PPF shrinks as the economy loses resources. This could occur if the economy failed to produce enough new machines and tools to replace those that became worn out. It could also result from an earthquake, a war, or another disaster that destroyed resources.

Figure 5 | Expansion of the U.S. PPF Since 1890

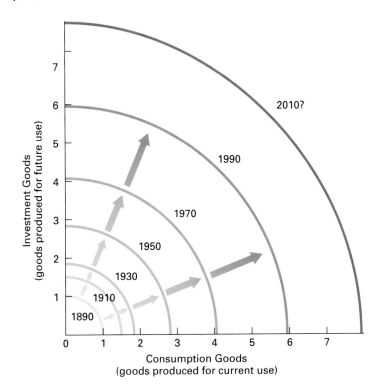

The shifts in the U.S. production possibilities frontier show the expansion of total output per person in the United States, adjusted for inflation. Each PPF represents a different year. Over each 20-year period, the United States has experienced economic growth, raising output to nearly six times the level of 100 years ago. It is now more than double the level of output in 1950, more than 50 percent larger than the level in 1970.

grows at 0.2 percent per year, output takes 350 years to double! Output per person in the United States (and most other developed countries) has more than doubled since 1950. Unfortunately, a few countries have experienced negative economic growth since 1950, with shrinking PPFs.

What happens to the extra goods and services that the economy produces when the PPF expands? Generally, people consume most of them: They wear the clothes, drive the cars, eat the food, and listen to the music. People also invest some of the extra goods they produce: They build new machines, tools, structures, and other new capital equipment.

Review Questions

1. Draw a graph like the one in Figure 2 to show your limited spending power if you have $10 to spend on tea and crumpets, and tea costs $0.50 per cup while crumpets cost $2.00 each.

2. How does a PPF show scarcity? Technical efficiency? Opportunity costs?

3. What causes a PPF to shift in?

Thinking Exercises

4. Explain why the absolute value of the slope of the line in Figure 2 shows the opportunity cost of buying videotapes.

5. Change the numbers in Table 1 so that the economy can produce twice as many cars. That is, change the numbers in the cars column from (0, 1, 2, 3, 4, 5) to (0, 2, 4, 6, 8, 10). Draw the new PPF. How does this change affect the opportunity cost of producing cars?

A FABLE WITH AN ECONOMIC MESSAGE

Once upon a time a brilliant businesswoman built a great factory by the sea, with high walls and tight security to protect the secrets of her new technological breakthrough.[1] Every month, she bought truckloads of grain from Midwestern farmers, and emptied the trucks inside her factory. Every month beautiful automobiles came out of her factory. "What marvelous technology has she discovered," people asked, "to make cars from grain?" Farmers were happy, because they sold more grain. Car buyers were delighted with their additional choices, and many chose the new "cars from grain." Competing car manufacturers resented the new competition, of course, but most people agreed that technological advance is generally good for society as a whole.

One day, government regulators investigated the factory and discovered the truth, which they promptly leaked to the nation's press. The "factory" was an empty shell. Behind its walls, workers exported the grain to foreign countries, using the proceeds to import cars. The miracle "technology" was simply international trade. Instead of putting grain into a machine that turned it into cars, workers put grain on ships, and

---

[1]Steve Landsburg tells a version of this well-known story in his book, *Fair Play: What Your Child Can Teach You about Economics, Values, and the Meaning of Life* (New York: Free Press, 1997), where he attributes it to Professor James Ingram of North Carolina State University.

the ships soon returned filled with cars. The moral: *Trade, like technological change, expands consumption opportunities.* The two-student example that follows will clarify this point.

International trade, like technological change, expands consumption opportunities.

TWO-STUDENT EXAMPLE: A KEY EXAMPLE OF GAINS FROM TRADE

Two students, Lauren and Steve, move into apartments next door to each other. The apartments are exactly alike, and each needs repairs to its walls and windows. The landlords provide all supplies, so the only cost of fixing the walls and windows is the time involved. Lauren and Steve do equally good work, and neither prefers one task to the other. Each has 12 hours to spend working.

Lauren can fix one wall in 3 hours; she can fix one window in 1 hour. Steve can fix a wall in 2 hours, but he takes 4 hours to fix one window. Table 2 shows the number of hours that Lauren and Steve need for each job.

Because Lauren can fix a wall in 3 hours, she could fix 4 walls in the 12 hours she has available. Alternatively, she could repair 12 windows in those 12 hours. Steve could fix 6 walls in 12 hours, or he could repair 3 windows in that same time. Table 3 shows the number of walls or windows that Lauren and Steve can repair in 12 hours.

Panels (a) and (b) of Figure 6 show Lauren's and Steve's PPFs, which are straight lines. Lauren could fix 12 windows and no walls, or she could fix 4 walls and no windows, or she could choose some combination (such as fixing 6 windows and 2 walls). Steve could fix 3 windows and no walls, or he could fix 6 walls and no windows, or he could choose some combination (such as fixing 2 windows and 2 walls).

A Trade

Without trade, Lauren may choose Point L on her PPF, fixing 2 walls and 6 windows. Steve may choose Point S on his PPF, fixing 2 walls and 2 windows. However, suppose that Lauren and Steve trade: Lauren fixes 3 windows for Steve, and Steve fixes 3 walls for Lauren. After Lauren spends 3 hours to fix 3 windows for Steve, she spends her other 9 working hours to fix 9 of her own windows. After Steve spends 6 hours to fix 3 walls for Lauren, he spends his other 6 working hours to fix 3 of his own walls. Figure 7 shows their trade.

Table 2 | Two-Student Example

Time Required to:	Lauren	Steve
Fix one wall	3 hours	2 hours
Fix one window	1 hour	4 hours

Table 3 | Productivity in 12 Hours

Work Done in 12 Hours	Lauren	Steve
Walls fixed	4 walls	6 walls
Windows fixed	12 windows	3 windows

Figure 6 | Production Possibilities Frontier for Steve and Lauren Together

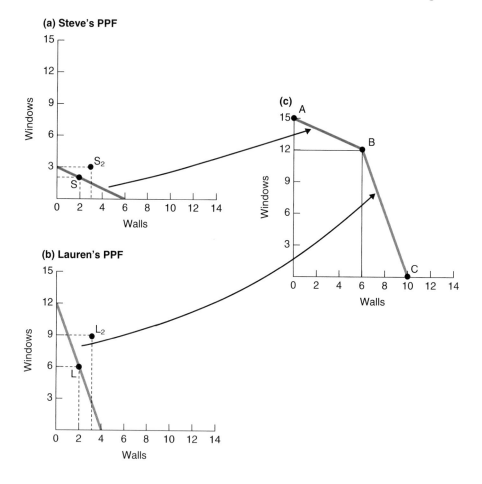

(a) Steve's PPF

(b) Lauren's PPF

(c)

Figure 7 | The Two Students Trade

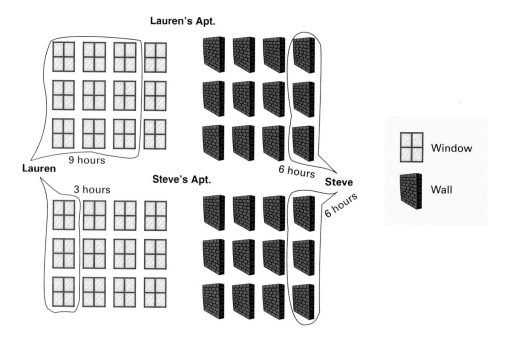

This trade places Lauren at Point L₂ in Figure 6b—she ends the day with 3 walls and 9 windows repaired. She could not possibly have reached this point on her own, without trading. Similarly, the trade places Steve at Point S₂ in Figure 6a—with 3 walls and 3 windows repaired. He could not have reached this point on his own. By trading, Lauren and Steve produce more (wall and window repairs) than they could without trading. Trade, like an improvement in technology, expands their possibilities.

Figure 6c shows the *combined* PPF for Steve and Lauren together. If they both work on windows, they repair 15 windows in a 12-hour day (Point A). If they both work on walls, they repair 10 in one day (Point C). If Lauren works only on windows while Steve works only on walls, they fix 12 windows *and* 6 walls in one day (Point B). The combined PPF also shows other possible combinations of repaired walls and windows when Lauren and Steve trade.

Gains from Trade

The trade just described moves Lauren to Point L₂ instead of Point L in Figure 6b. In other words, she gets 3 walls and 9 windows fixed, instead of 2 walls and 6 windows. Lauren's gain from the trade is 1 fixed wall and 3 fixed windows. Similarly, Steve reaches Point S₂ (3 walls and 3 windows fixed) instead of Point S (2 walls and 2 windows fixed), so he gains 1 fixed wall and 1 fixed window from the trade.

In the shoe-store example described at the beginning of Chapter 1, Lisa and Mitch share the gains from trade equally: They each gain one hour of free time from their trade. In contrast, Lauren gains more than Steve from the trade just described.

Trading Resembles Improved Technology
The fable about producing cars from grain made the point that *trade, like technological change, expands consumption opportunities*. The two-student example illustrates this point numerically. Trade allows Lauren and Steve to consume at Points L₂ and S₂, points outside their individual PPFs. This result would be *impossible* without trade or some improvement in technology that expands their PPFs as in Figures 4a and 5.

Opportunity Costs

In 3 hours, Lauren can fix a single wall. If, instead, she spent that time working on windows, she could fix 3 windows. Therefore, her *opportunity cost* of fixing a wall is fixing 3 windows. Similarly, in the time she takes to fix a window (1 hour), she could fix one-third of a wall. So Lauren's opportunity cost of fixing a window is fixing one-third of a wall.

In 4 hours, Steve can fix a single window. If, instead, he spent that time working on walls, he could fix 2 walls. His opportunity cost of fixing a window is fixing 2 walls. Similarly, in the time he would take to fix a wall (2 hours), he could fix one-half of a window. So Steve's opportunity cost of fixing a wall is fixing one-half of a window. Table 4 summarizes these opportunity costs.

Gains from the Trade
If Lauren fixes 3 windows for Steve, and Steve fixes 3 walls for Lauren, then:
▶ Lauren reaches Point L₂ instead of Point L. She gains 1 fixed wall and 3 fixed windows.
▶ Steve reaches Point S₂ instead of Point S. He gains 1 fixed wall and 1 fixed window.

Table 4 | Opportunity Costs in the Two-Student Example

Opportunity Cost of:	Lauren	Steve
Fixing one wall	Fixing 3 windows	Fixing ½ of a window
Fixing one window	Fixing ⅓ of a wall	Fixing 2 walls

Slopes of PPFs Show Opportunity Costs

Notice that the slope of Lauren's PPF in Figure 6 is −3. The absolute value of the slope, 3, is Lauren's opportunity cost of fixing one wall. Also notice that the slope of Steve's PPF in Figure 6 is −½. The absolute value of the slope, ½, is Steve's opportunity cost of fixing one wall. As noted earlier, the absolute value of the slope of a PPF shows the opportunity cost of producing the good measured along the *X*-axis (walls, in this case).

Notice that the combined PPF for Steve and Lauren in Figure 6c is not a straight line. Think of the two students together as a small economy. That economy's opportunity cost *changes* depending upon which combination of goods it produces. If the economy produces along the upper segment of its PPF, its opportunity costs are the same as Steve's. If it produces along the lower segment of its PPF, its opportunity costs match Lauren's. When an economy, like the U.S. economy, consists of *many* different people with different opportunity costs, its PPF looks like those in Figures 3 through 5. The curvature of the PPF shows that the economy's opportunity costs change as it changes the combination of goods that it produces. The appendix to this chapter explains this point in further detail.

Comparative Advantage and the Gains from Trade

The two-student example illustrates a general principle: People gain from trade whenever they differ in their *relative* abilities to produce different goods—that is, whenever they have *comparative advantages* at producing those goods.

> A person has a **comparative advantage** at producing a good if she can produce it at a lower opportunity cost than other people can.

In the example, Lauren has a comparative advantage at fixing windows, and Steve has a comparative advantage at fixing walls. In any situation like this, everyone has a comparative advantage at some task. This is true even when one person works more productively than others at every job—as in the shoe-store example in Chapter 1. (Also see Problem 21 at the end of this chapter.) You can gain from a trade that allows you to increase the time you spend in an activity at which you have a comparative advantage and decrease the time you spend on other tasks.

Case Study: Production Possibilities during World War II

During World War II, the U.S. government required the auto industry to convert from producing cars to producing military equipment. Figure 8 shows the automakers' production possibilities frontier between civilian automobiles and military equipment. In 1941, the auto industry produced and sold about 4 million cars and only a small amount of military equipment (Point A in the figure). During World War II, the U.S. government announced that the U.S. auto industry would convert to making military equipment. The government expected it to produce 117,000 tanks, 185,000 airplanes, and 28 million tons of merchant ships in 1942 and 1943 (Point G in Figure 8).

The government under-estimated the curvature of the industry's PPF, however, so Point G was impossible. Some conversion to military production was easy: Producing a small amount of military equipment required only a small cut in auto production. Massive conversion was more difficult, though. For example, most of the auto industry's machine tools were not easy to convert to produce military equipment. The curvature of the economy's PPF meant that instead of producing at Point G, the U.S. economy produced at Point B: 56,000 tanks, 134,000 airplanes, and 27 million tons of merchant ships.

Figure 8 | U.S. Production Possibilities Frontier during World War II

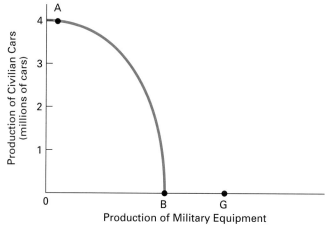

In 1941, the U.S. auto industry produced at Point A. The government expected the auto industry to move to Point G in 1942 and 1943. Because the PPF was curved, however, the industry could produce only at Point B.

Comparative Advantage in the Two-Student Example

Lauren has a comparative advantage at fixing windows. As Table 4 shows, her opportunity cost of fixing a window is fixing one-third of a wall. This is a lower cost than Steve's opportunity cost of fixing a window, which is fixing two walls. Because Lauren has a lower opportunity cost of fixing windows, that task gives her a comparative advantage.

Steve has a comparative advantage at fixing walls. As Table 4 shows, his opportunity cost of fixing a wall is fixing one-half of a window, lower than Lauren's opportunity cost of fixing a wall, which is fixing three windows. Because Steve has a lower opportunity cost of fixing walls, that task gives him a comparative advantage.

Everyone has a comparative advantage at some task. Within the two-student economy, determining that Lauren has a comparative advantage at windows immediately indicates that Steve has a comparative advantage at walls.

A Common Confusion: Comparative versus Absolute Advantage

As Table 3 showed, Lauren can fix more windows per day than Steve can, and Steve can fix more walls per day than Lauren can. Table 2 showed that Lauren can fix a window in less time than Steve would take, and Steve can fix a wall in less time than Lauren would take. Economists say that the more productive person has an *absolute advantage* at that task. Lauren has an absolute advantage at fixing windows, and Steve has an absolute advantage at fixing walls.

A common mistake is to think that Lauren and Steve gain from trade because Lauren has an absolute advantage at windows and Steve has an absolute advantage at walls. The correct statement is that Lauren and Steve gain from trade because they have different opportunity costs that give them comparative advantages. To see why, the next section changes the numbers in the two-student example. Before reading that section, though, look back at the shoe-store example at the beginning of Chapter 1. In that example, Lisa works more productively than Mitch at both jobs. (Lisa has an absolute advantage at both tasks.) Nevertheless, they gain from trade. The same logic holds in the modified two-student example.

Modified Two-Student Example

Table 5 changes Table 2 so that *Steve now takes twice as long* to do either job. He needs 4 hours (instead of 2 hours) to fix a wall and 8 hours (instead of 4) to fix a window. The numbers in Table 5 give Lauren an absolute advantage at both jobs. Nevertheless, Steve still has a comparative advantage at fixing walls. Steve's opportunity cost of fixing one wall is fixing one-half of a window. (In the 4 hours Steve takes to fix a wall, he could fix half of a window.) Lauren's opportunity cost of fixing a wall is fixing three windows. (In the 3 hours Lauren takes to fix a wall, she could fix three windows.) Because Steve's opportunity cost of fixing walls is lower than Lauren's, Steve still has a comparative advantage at fixing walls. Lauren still has a comparative advantage at fixing windows.

Lauren and Steve continue to gain from trade, even though Lauren has an absolute advantage at both jobs. Working for 12 hours *without* trading, Lauren may choose Point L on her PPF (as before), fixing two walls and six windows. Changing the numbers for Steve shrinks his opportunities and shifts his PPF inward to the one in Figure 9. Without trade, Steve may choose Point T on his new PPF, fixing one wall and one window.

Advice
Don't confuse *comparative advantage* (differences in opportunity cost) with *absolute advantage* (differences in productivity). The important concept is *comparative advantage*.

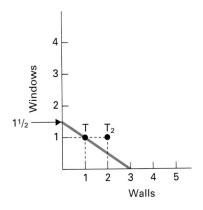

**Figure 9
Steve's PPF in the *Modified* Example**

Table 5 | Modified Example

Time Required to:	Lauren	Steve
Fix one wall	3 hours	4 hours
Fix one window	1 hour	8 hours

Now suppose that Lauren and Steve trade: Lauren fixes two windows for Steve, and Steve fixes two walls for Lauren. After Lauren spends 2 hours to fix two windows for Steve, she spends her other 10 working hours to fix ten of her own windows. After Steve spends 8 hours to fix two walls for Lauren, he spends his other 4 working hours to fix one of his own walls.

With this trade, Lauren ends the day with two walls and ten windows repaired. Steve ends the day with one wall and two windows repaired (Point T_2 in Figure 9). Lauren gains 4 extra repaired windows from the trade. Steve gains 1 extra repaired window.

Diversity and Values

The modified two-student example, like the shoe-store example from Chapter 1, shows that differences in opportunity costs create possibilities for gains from trade.

> People do not gain from trade because they are more or less productive than others. People gain from trade because of diversity in their opportunity costs.

Diversity of opportunity costs creates diversity in comparative advantage. If Lauren and Steve had the *same* opportunity costs, their PPFs would be parallel lines and they would not gain from trading with each other. Diversity is not merely the spice of life, but the source of gains from voluntary trade.

The modified two-student example measured the gains from trade in terms of the extra production (fixed walls and windows) that the trade created. The shoe-store example from Chapter 1 measured gains from trade in terms of the extra hours of leisure time that the trade created. As this comparison shows, gains from trade need not be materialistic. People can also gain leisure time or other values.

Review Questions

6. Explain why people can gain from voluntary trades.

7. What is comparative advantage? How does it differ from absolute advantage?

8. Define an economically efficient situation. Define an economically inefficient situation.

9. The cars-from-grain fable shows that trade resembles technological change. How does the two-student example illustrate this point?

Thinking Exercises

10. Suppose that Argentina can produce 14 bottles of wine or 40 pounds of beef in one day, while Chile can produce 12 bottles of wine or 30 pounds of beef in one day. Which country has a comparative advantage in wine and which in beef?

11. Discuss: "If a situation is economically inefficient, everyone involved has an incentive to change it."

12. Use Table 1 from Chapter 1, reproduced here, to answer these questions:
    (a) What is Lisa's opportunity cost of taking inventory? What is her opportunity cost of setting up the display?
    (b) What is Mitch's opportunity cost of taking inventory? What is his opportunity cost of setting up the display?
    (c) Who has a comparative advantage in taking inventory? In setting up the display?

Hours of Work Required for:	Lisa	Mitch
Taking inventory in one section of the store	6 hrs	5 hrs
Setting up a new display in one section of the store	3 hrs	6 hrs

EFFICIENCY AND THE GAINS FROM TRADE

Some people believe that whenever one person gets richer, another person must become poorer. They think the economy is like a pie; if one person gets a bigger piece, less remains for other people. Those ideas are false. *Everyone* involved can gain from a voluntary trade, as the two-student example shows.

> An environment in which one person's gain is another person's loss is called a **zero-sum game.**[2]

Dividing a cake between several people is a zero-sum game: a bigger piece for one person leaves less for someone else. Most economic situations are *not* zero-sum games, though. They are positive-sum games.

> An environment in which everyone can gain at the same time is called a **positive-sum game.**

People can all gain if they produce the same amount of goods with less effort or more goods with the same effort. They gain when each person produces goods at which he has a comparative advantage and then trades with others. The two-student example is a positive-sum game: Both students gain from the trade. The world economy consists of billions of people like those two students, though the details of their lives differ in countless ways. The world economy is a positive-sum game.

Economic Efficiency

The two-student example shows how people can gain from an increase in economic efficiency.

> A situation is **economically efficient** if there is no way to change it so that everyone gains, or so that some people gain while no one else loses.

An economically efficient situation leaves no unexploited opportunities that can benefit everyone; people have *already* made use of every such opportunity.

> A situation is **economically inefficient** if there is some way to change it so that everyone gains, or so that someone gains while no one else loses.

An economically inefficient situation leaves potential, *unrealized* gains from possible changes. It is economically inefficient to fail to exploit all the potential gains from trade.

---

[2]The term means that if some people enjoy positive gains, other people must suffer negative gains (i.e., losses) so that all the gains sum to zero.

EXAMPLES

1. Susie likes yogurt and Johnny likes peanut butter. If Susie has peanut butter and Johnny has yogurt, the situation is economically inefficient because a change could help them both: They could trade lunches. After the trade, Susie has yogurt and Johnny has peanut butter. That situation is economically efficient because any further change that would help one of them would hurt the other. (If Johnny takes some of Susie's yogurt, he gains and she loses.)

2. In the two-student example, it would be economically inefficient for Lauren and Steve not to trade. A change in the situation—choosing to trade after all—could help them both. When Lauren and Steve trade as described earlier in this chapter, the trade creates an economically efficient situation because no *further* change can help one person without hurting the other.

3. In the shoe-store example in Chapter 1, it is economically inefficient not to trade. When Lisa and Mitch trade, the situation becomes economically efficient.

Technical and Economic Efficiency

Technical efficiency and economic efficiency are different, but related concepts. Recall that technical efficiency means that the economy produces on its PPF, so that it cannot produce more of one good without producing less of another. *Every economically efficient situation is also technically efficient. However, not every technically efficient situation is economically efficient.*

EXPLANATION

1. **Every economically efficient situation is technically efficient.** If a situation were technically *in*efficient, then the economy could produce more of something without producing less of anything else. This change could help someone without hurting anyone, so a technically inefficient situation must also be economically inefficient.

2. **Some technically efficient situations are not economically efficient.** It would be technically efficient for the economy to produce only pizzas, as long as it produced as many pizzas as possible, given its PPF. However, this production choice would not be economically efficient because people would gain if the economy produced a few beverages and other goods rather than only pizzas. Similarly, it would be technically efficient to produce at Point A in Figure 3, producing only videotapes. However, people might gain if the economy produced at Point C or D instead of Point A. Point A would be technically efficient but not economically efficient.

Comparative Advantage and Efficiency

In an economically efficient situation, people tend to produce goods at which they have comparative advantages. In the two-student example, it is economically efficient for Steve to fix walls, at which he has a comparative advantage, while Lauren fixes windows, at which she has a comparative advantage.

Sometimes, however, it is economically efficient for someone to produce a good at which he does *not* have a comparative advantage. If the walls don't need repair, for example, it can be efficient for Lauren and Steve both to fix windows (even though Steve has a comparative advantage at walls). Similarly, it can be efficient for Lauren and Steve both to fix windows if they fixed all the walls yesterday, but some windows remain to be fixed. It would *not* be economically efficient for Steve to fix windows while Lauren fixed walls, though; they could both gain by switching jobs.

People have incentives to trade when the trade can create economic efficiency. They can share the gains from changing an inefficient situation into an efficient one. Voluntary trades produce economic efficiency without anyone else directing them.

SHARING THE GAINS FROM TRADE

Suppose Lauren and Steve each have *one* window and *one* wall in need of repair. Table 6 repeats the information from Table 2 for this case. If Lauren and Steve do not trade, Lauren works 4 hours in her apartment (3 hours to fix her wall and 1 hour to fix her window) and Steve works 6 hours in his apartment.

Now suppose Lauren and Steve trade one fixed wall for one fixed window: Lauren fixes Steve's window and Steve fixes Lauren's wall. Then Lauren works 2 hours (1 hour fixing the window in each apartment) and Steve works 4 hours (2 in each apartment). They each gain 2 hours of leisure time from this trade.

In this example, Lauren and Steve share the gains from trade equally. They could have made many other trades, however, any of which would have helped them both. In fact, there are *many* economically efficient situations. Each economically efficient situation has a different distribution of income; some situations give more goods to Lauren, while others give more to Steve.

EXAMPLE: HOUR-FOR-HOUR TRADE

In the trade discussed above, Lauren fixes Steve's window and Steve fixes Lauren's wall. While this trade leads to economic efficiency, notice that Steve spends 2 hours fixing Lauren's wall, while Lauren spends only 1 hour fixing Steve's window. In other words, Lauren trades 1 hour of her time for 2 hours of Steve's time.

Suppose, instead, that Steve and Lauren agree to trade their time on an hour-for-hour basis: Steve will spend 1 hour fixing Lauren's wall and she will spend 1 hour fixing his window. In that 1 hour, Lauren will finish fixing Steve's window, but Steve will not finish fixing Lauren's wall—the complete job would take 2 hours. Steve will get the wall *half done* in 1 hour, leaving the other half of the job for Lauren. Since Lauren can fix a wall in 3 hours, it will take her 1½ hours to finish the job. Table 7 summarizes the work the students do when each trades an hour's time.

Table 6 | Two-Student Example with One Wall and One Window to Repair

Time Required to:	Lauren	Steve
Fix one wall	3 hours	2 hours
Fix one window	1 hour	4 hours

When Lauren and Steve *each* have 1 wall and 1 window to fix:		
	Lauren works	Steve works
Without a trade	4 hours	6 hours
With the trade	2 hours	4 hours

Table 7 | Hour-for-Hour Trade

Lauren	Steve
Fixes her own window in 1 hour, completing the work	Fixes his own wall in 2 hours, completing the work
Fixes Steve's window in 1 hour, completing the work	Spends 1 hour fixing Lauren's wall, completing half of the work
Spends 90 minutes fixing her own wall after Steve leaves	
Total work time: 3½ hours	Total work time: 3 hours

With the hour-for-hour trade, Lauren works 3½ hours and Steve works 3 hours. Without any trade, Lauren would have worked 4 hours in her own apartment and Steve would have worked 6 hours in his. Each gains from the hour-for-hour trade; Lauren gains half an hour of leisure time, and Steve gains 3 hours. Although they do not share the gains from trade equally, the trade creates economically efficiency.

Comparison of the Two Trades

Table 8 compares these two trades. In the first trade, Lauren trades 1 hour of her work effort for 2 hours of Steve's. In other words, they trade one fixed window for one fixed wall. In the second, Lauren trades 1 hour of her work effort for 1 hour of Steve's. In other words, they trade one fixed window for *half* of a fixed wall. A comparison of the trades leads to four main conclusions:

1. Lauren benefits from either trade. So does Steve.

2. Each trade involves a different *price* at which fixed walls exchange for fixed windows.

3. The price affects how they share the gains from trade. Lauren gains more from the first trade; Steve gains more from the second trade.

4. Each trade leads to a different economically efficient situation.[3]

Lauren prefers the first trade because she gains 2 hours of leisure time, while she gains only 30 minutes from the second (hour-for-hour) trade. Steve prefers the second (hour-for-hour) trade because he gains 3 hours of leisure time, while he gains only 2 hours from the first trade.

Lauren and Steve could also choose many other trades that would help them both and that would lead to economically efficient situations. Each economically efficient situation has a different distribution of income—some are better for Lauren, and some are better for Steve.

Fairness, Equity, and Justice

Which trade is fairer? Any answer to this question requires criteria for fairness. It might seem fair for Lauren and Steve to share the gains from the trade equally, so the 1-hour-

---

[3]Both trades create economically efficient situations, even though the total amount of time spent working is larger in the hour-for-hour trade (6½ hours) than in the first trade (6 hours).

Table 8 | Comparison of the Two Trades

First Trade: One Hour for Two Hours	Second Trade: Hour for Hour	No Trade
Price: One fixed window for one fixed wall	Price: One fixed window for one-half of a fixed wall	Economically inefficient Lauren works 4 hours; Steve works 6 hours

Economically efficient
Lauren works 2 hours;
  Steve works 4 hours
	Economically efficient
	Lauren works 3½ hours;
	  Steve works 3 hours	

Compared with no trade:
  Lauren gains 2 hours of time;
  Steve gains 2 hours of time
	Compared with no trade:
	  Lauren gains ½ hour of time;
	  Steve gains 3 hours of time	

Lauren spends 1 hour working in Steve's apartment; Steve spends 2 hours working in Lauren's apartment	Lauren spends 1 hour working in Steve's apartment; Steve spends 1 hour working in Lauren's apartment	

for-2-hour trade might seem fair because Lauren and Steve each gain 2 hours of leisure time. Or it might also seem fair for Lauren to exchange 1 hour of her time for 1 hour of Steve's time, so the hour-for-hour trade might seem fair.[4] Alternatively, it might seem fair for Lauren and Steve to have equal amounts of leisure time, in which case they must spend equal time working. Each opinion would make a *different* trade seem fair.[5]

These three ideas of fairness conflict with each other. Each leads to a different conclusion about which trade is fair and which are unfair. Unfortunately, no definition of what is fair (or just or equitable) satisfies everyone. Many people use these words loosely without clear, precise ideas of what they mean. Even philosophers have failed to agree on criteria for fairness. Consider some different ideas of fairness:

▶ There should be an equal distribution of income.

▶ People who need high incomes for important purposes, such as medical expenses or to support large families, should have more income than others with less pressing needs.

▶ Incomes should not be equal, but no one should live in extreme poverty.

▶ People who work harder than others should have higher incomes.

▶ People should get whatever incomes they can earn by working.

▶ There is no such thing as a fair distribution of income. Fairness applies only to *rules* (such as laws).

Fairness and Rules

Among people who believe that fairness applies only to rules, some say that rules are fair if everyone would agree on them in advance, not knowing whether they will be lucky or unlucky, beautiful or ugly, smart or dumb, talented or not, or born into rich or poor

---

[4]Suppose that Lauren pays Steve $20 for his work and Steve pays Lauren $20 for her work. Then the hour-for-hour trade would give them equal wage rates.

[5]Lauren and Steve would work the same number of hours if Steve were to fix his own wall (which would take him 2 hours) and spend 1 hour and 12 minutes working on Lauren's wall. Since it would take Steve 2 hours to fix Lauren's wall, he would get 3/5 of the job done in 1 hour and 12 minutes. Lauren would fix the remaining 2/5 of her wall, which would take her (2/5)(3 hours), or 6/5 hours (1 hour and 12 minutes). She would also fix the windows in both apartments, which would take her 2 hours. Then Lauren and Steve would each work for 3 hours and 12 minutes. This situation is economically efficient. (Notice that in this situation, Steve spends 1 hour and 12 minutes working in Lauren's apartment, while Lauren spends only 1 hour working in Steve's.)

families. Before an American football game, for example, the teams accept the result of a coin toss to see who will receive the ball first. According to this view, it is neither fair nor unfair that one team wins the coin toss. Outcomes are not fair or unfair. Only the rules that produce those outcomes can be fair or unfair.[6] The rule requiring a coin toss may be fair (or, if the coin is weighted to come up heads most of the time, unfair). Some people who believe that fairness applies only to rules say that rules are fair if they allow each person to keep her own property and make any desired peaceful, voluntary trades.[7]

Economics deals with positive statements (statements of fact); it does not say anything about fairness.[8] However, economics can help people to understand the results of various laws, regulations, and government policies. This understanding helps people to apply their own ideas of fairness to decide what laws, regulations, and government policies they think are best.

COMPETITION AND THE GAINS FROM TRADE

Which trade would people like Lauren and Steve make in real life? When people can choose any one of several trades, their actual choices depend on their alternative opportunities. If one person has good opportunities for alternative trades, the other person faces strong competition for his services and bargains from a weak position. The trades people choose depend on their relative bargaining positions, which depend on their alternative opportunities for trading.

EXPLANATION

Table 8 compared two of the many possible trades that Lauren and Steve might have made. Each trade would lead to a different economically efficient situation, with a different distribution of income. Lauren prefers some trades and Steve prefers others. The trade that they actually choose depends on their alternative opportunities, which affect each party's bargaining power. Steve might convince Lauren to trade time on an hour-for-hour basis by telling her that if she refuses, he will trade with Linda instead, who *will* agree to his terms. In that sense, Lauren would face competition from other potential window-repair services. In the same way, Steve might agree to a trade that Lauren prefers because he faces competition from other potential wall-repair services.

IS ECONOMIC EFFICIENCY GOOD?

Economics deals with statements of fact, not value judgments. Still, economic efficiency is good in one sense, independently of individual values. In any economically inefficient situation, a change in the economy can create gains for everyone, or gains for some people without losses for anyone else. Economic efficiency is good in the sense that waste is bad; eliminating inefficiencies improves people's conditions according to their own values. In an economically inefficient situation, people usually have incentives to make changes to achieve efficiency and share the gains.

---

[6]In most real-life situations, we already know the outcomes: Some people are born to rich families, others to poor families. Some are smarter, more talented, and more beautiful than others. No one can say for sure what rules people would have accepted if they could have decided which were fair before knowing these outcomes. One can only guess. This approach to fairness was pioneered by economist John Harsanyi in 1953 and by Harvard philosopher John Rawls in his book, *A Theory of Justice* (Cambridge, Mass.: Harvard University Press, 1971). Most of Rawls's book discusses his guesses about which rules people would say are fair before knowing these outcomes.

[7]This position grows out of a long tradition in philosophy asserting that people have natural rights. (The U.S. Declaration of Independence was influenced by this tradition.) For one statement of this libertarian position, see Robert Nozick, *Anarchy, State, and Utopia* (New York: Basic Books, 1974).

[8]See Chapter 2 for a discussion of positive statements.

Many people believe that the government should redistribute income to some degree from the rich to the poor. With this view of fairness or equity, the economy faces a trade-off between equity and efficiency: To distribute income more equitably, according to this view, the government must often create economic inefficiencies. The government may tax people with high incomes and give the money to poorer people. The tax creates economic inefficiency by changing people's incentives to trade, as the next example will explain.

How Taxes Create Economic Inefficiency: An Example

Suppose that the government places a $5 tax on purchases of wall or window repairs. Anyone who buys repair services must pay $5 to the government. This tax can create an economically inefficient situation.

Economic efficiency implies that Steve should buy window-repair services from Lauren, and Lauren should buy wall-repair services from Steve. The tax may create economic inefficiency by causing them *not* to trade. If Lauren buys Steve's services, she gains leisure time at the cost of paying the $5 tax. She may decide that the extra leisure time is not worth paying the tax. Steve faces the same decision. If the tax prevents the trade, it creates an economically inefficient situation. In addition, if they do not trade, the government does not collect the tax revenue from them. The government collects tax revenue only from people who continue to buy repair services despite the tax.

An economic inefficiency usually creates incentives for people to find voluntary trades that change the situation and make it efficient. They can then share the gains from eliminating the inefficiency. Taxes change this result. Taxes alter incentives so that people do not always gain from eliminating inefficient situations. In this way, taxes create economic inefficiency.

A Tradeoff between Equity and Efficiency?

The government can use tax revenue to increase equity (at least according to some views of equity) at the cost of economic inefficiency. Economic inefficiency may be an opportunity cost of increasing equity (and vice versa). In other words, the economy may face a tradeoff between equity and economic efficiency. Many notions of equity, though not all, lead to conflicts with economic efficiency, at least in certain cases. It would be remarkable if a well-developed idea of fairness or equity never conflicted with economic efficiency.[9]

If economic efficiency and other values (including equity) conflict, people must choose whether to sacrifice equity or efficiency. Choosing involves value judgments about which people's opinions may differ, but it also involves economics. Economic analysis can help people to understand how much economic inefficiency they must accept to achieve some other goal, thereby helping them to evaluate tradeoffs and to make more intelligent decisions.

The two-student example showed how two people can each gain by trading. The same reasoning shows that nations can each gain from *international trades.* (Think, for instance, of two countries named Laurenland and Steveland producing cars and wheat

A NOTE ON INTERNATIONAL TRADE

---

[9]For an attempt to create such a theory, see Richard Posner, *The Economics of Justice* (Cambridge, Mass.: Harvard University Press, 1983).

rather than wall and window repairs.) By specializing in goods that it can produce at a comparative advantage and trading them with other countries, a nation can obtain more goods and services than it could produce on its own without trading. The reason is simple: Every trade between nations is really a trade between people living in those nations, so the lesson of the two-student example essentially applies to every trade. Some people compare international trade to a war, but that comparison misleads, because the world economy is a positive-sum game.

Review Questions

12. **(a)** Explain why every economically efficient situation is technically efficient.
    (b) Explain why a situation can be technically efficient but not economically efficient.

13. Briefly discuss alternative ideas of fairness.

14. In what sense is economic efficiency good?

15. Discuss this statement: "The economy faces a tradeoff between equity and economic efficiency."

Thinking Exercises

16. Explain why there are many economically efficient situations. How do they differ?

17. Discuss: "The hour-for-hour trade requires 6½ total hours of work from Steve and Lauren, while the original trade required only 6 hours of work, so the hour-for-hour trade is economically inefficient."

18. How do taxes cause economic inefficiency?

Conclusion

Limits and Possibilities

Everyone faces limits. The production possibilities frontier or PPF graphs the limits on the economy's production with its available inputs and technology. The PPF shows scarcity because it separates possible economic situations from impossible ones. The PPF shows technical efficiency (absence of waste) because only points *on* the PPF are technically efficient combinations of output. It shows the role for economic choices: People's decisions and government policies determine at which point in the graph the economy *actually* produces. It shows the economy's tradeoff between producing various goods: The absolute value of the *slope* of the PPF shows the economy's opportunity cost of producing the good on the X-axis. An economy's PPF shifts when its resources or technology change. Economic growth occurs when an economy's PPF expands faster than its population grows.

A Fable, and the Two-Student Example of Gains from Trade

The fable about producing cars from grain illustrates the point that trade, like technological change, expands consumption opportunities. The two-student example shows additional details of the gains from trade. Trade allows the students to consume at points *outside* their individual PPFs, which would be impossible without trade.

People can gain from trades by producing goods at which they have comparative advantages. A person has a comparative advantage at a task if his opportunity cost of that task is lower than other people's. Everyone has a comparative advantage at some task, even if they are less productive than others at *all* tasks. The modified two-student example and the shoe-store example of Chapter 1 illustrate why. People gain from trade *not* because they are more or less productive than others, but because they differ in their opportunity costs. Gains from trade can consist of increased production of material goods or enhancement of other values.

Efficiency and the Gains from Trade

In a zero-sum game, one person's gain is another person's loss. In contrast, a positive-sum game permits a win-win situation in which everyone gains. The economy is a positive-sum game: One person's gain is *not* another person's loss. Both participants gain in voluntary trades.

A situation is economically efficient if there is no way to change it so that everyone gains or some people gain while no one else loses. Economic efficiency leaves no unexploited opportunities that can benefit everyone, because people have already made use of all such opportunities. A situation is economically inefficient if there is some way to change it so that everyone gains or someone gains while no one else loses. The situation remains economically inefficient until that change actually occurs. In other words, an economically inefficient situation has potential but unrealized gains from a change.

Every economically efficient situation is technically efficient. However, not every technically efficient situation is economically efficient.

In an economically efficient situation, people tend to produce goods at which they have comparative advantages. Everyone can share the gains from changing an economically inefficient situation into an efficient one.

Sharing the Gains from Trade

There are many economically efficient situations, each with a different distribution of income. In an economically inefficient situation, people can usually choose from *many* mutually beneficial trades. Each involves a different price and a different division of the gains from trade.

People have many different and conflicting ideas about fairness. Economics deals with positive statements and does not say anything about fairness. Both economic analysis and value judgments are required for intelligent decisions on public policy.

Competition and the Gains from Trade

Alternative trading opportunities affect the trades that people choose. A person with better opportunities for alternative trades holds a stronger bargaining position. As a result, alternative opportunities affect the prices at which people trade and the way they share the gains from trade.

Is Economic Efficiency Good?

Economic efficiency is good in the sense that waste is bad. Eliminating inefficiencies benefits people according to their own values. Some ideas of equity imply an inverse relationship between equity and economic efficiency: The opportunity cost of greater equity is reduced economic efficiency, and the opportunity cost of greater economic efficiency is reduced equity. Taxes create economic inefficiency by changing people's incentives to trade.

A Note on International Trade

Nations gain from international trade just as individuals gain from trade. The world economy is a positive-sum game.

Key Terms

production possibilities frontier, or PPF	technical efficiency comparative advantage	zero-sum game positive-sum game	economically efficient economically inefficient

Problems

19. Explain why the economy is a positive-sum game.

20. Give an example of an economically inefficient situation, and explain how to make it efficient.

21. Consider the shoe-store example from Table 1 of Chapter 1. Change the numbers so that Lisa needs 8 hours (instead of 4) to take inventory. How does this change affect who has a comparative advantage at which task and the gains from trade?

22. You are the chief executive officer (CEO) of a major corporation. You face two urgent tasks: defending against product-liability lawsuits and finding tax loopholes for your company. You have two employees who can do these jobs. How will you choose to allocate these important tasks to them? Explain how the economic principles discussed in this chapter can help you, and illustrate your point with a numerical example.

23. (Harder Problem) Some people have suggested that the government should guarantee equal pay for workers at different jobs with "comparable worth," that is, jobs that are equally important or require similar levels of education and skill. Suppose that the government were to decide that

window and wall repair are jobs of comparable worth. Consider the two-student example in Table 6, when Lauren and Steve each have one wall and one window to fix. If Steve pays Lauren $10 to fix his window (which takes her 1 hour), and Lauren pays Steve $10 to fix her wall (which takes him 2 hours), Lauren's wage is $10 per hour and Steve's wage is $5 per hour. What alternative trade could the government suggest to Steve and Lauren? Can the government suggest a trade with equal hourly pay for Steve and Lauren that Lauren would approve? Explain.

Inquiries for Further Thought

24. Do you believe that the distribution of income in our economy is equitable or inequitable, fair or unfair? What could be done about it? What should be done? What would be the opportunity cost?

25. Describe your own view of fairness or equity in as much detail as you can.

Appendix: Changing Opportunity Cost along a Curved PPF

The chapter explained that an economy composed of many people with different opportunity costs has a curved PPF. The PPF for Lauren and Steve together, in Figure 6c, shows how this may happen.

More generally, think of an economy that produces food and computer software. If it produces a small amount of software and a large amount of food, then only the best programmers work on software, and others, who have a comparative advantage at food production, work on the farms. If the economy wants to produce more software and less food, it must recruit people less skilled at programming (and better at farming). This raises the opportunity cost of software as its production rises, creating curvature in the PPF.

A similar argument applies to other inputs, such as land and capital (equipment). Suppose that all the land in a country is equally good for housing, but some land is better than other land for farming. If the economy produces only a small amount of farm products, it can cultivate only the best farmland. To produce more farm products, the economy must bring some less fertile land into production. As the economy adds more acres of farmland, average output per acre falls because the economy begins using larger quantities of less productive land.

Figure A1 illustrates an economy that can produce 40 million houses and no food (Point A) or 39 million houses and 1 million tons of food (Point B). As the economy moves from Point A to Point B, it gains 1 million tons of food and loses 1 million houses, so the opportunity cost of 1 million tons of food is 1 million houses.

The opportunity cost changes along the PPF in Figure A1. If the economy moves from Point B to Point C, it raises output of food by 1 million tons per year (from 1 million to 2 million tons) while reducing output of houses by 2 million (from 39 million to 37 million). The opportunity cost of the additional 1 million tons of food is 2 million houses. If the economy moves from Point C to Point D, the opportunity cost of 1 million tons of food rises to 3 million houses; if it moves from Point D to Point E, the opportunity cost of food reaches 5 million houses. Opportunity cost changes along a curved PPF. The opportunity cost of food rises as the economy produces larger quantities of it.

Figure A1 | Production Possibilities Frontier

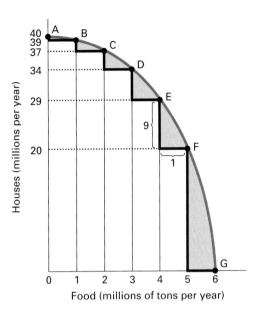

The base of the triangle between Points E and F shows an increase in food output of 1 million tons (from 4 million to 5 million). The height of the triangle shows a fall in house production of 9 million houses (from 29 million to 20 million). This is the opportunity cost of producing 1 million more tons of food.

The negative slope of the PPF shows that as the economy produces more food, it can produce fewer houses. The curvature of the PPF shows that the opportunity cost of food rises when food output increases.

P r o b l e m s

A1. Explain why the negative slope of a production possibilities frontier shows the opportunity cost of producing the good measured along the horizontal axis (*X*-axis). What is the opportunity cost of 1 million tons of food as the economy moves from Point F to Point G in Figure A1?

A2. An old machine powered by natural gas can produce either 4,000 backpacks or 2,000 bicycles in a month. A newer machine that runs on solar power can produce either 2,000 backpacks or 4,000 bicycles in a month. Table A1 shows the amount of each good that can be produced with a single machine of each type in a month.

  (a) Draw the production possibilities frontier for an economy with ten old, natural-gas-powered machines and no new, solar-powered machines. What is the opportunity cost of backpacks? Of bicycles?

  (b) Draw the production possibilities frontier for an economy with no old, natural-gas-powered machines and ten new, solar-powered machines. What is the opportunity cost of backpacks in this economy? Of bicycles?

  (c) Draw the production possibilities frontier for an economy with ten machines of each type. What is the opportunity cost of backpacks? Of bicycles?

  (d) Suppose that buyers want the same number of backpacks as bicycles. How many months of each year would an economy with one natural-gas-powered machine spend producing backpacks to produce an equal number of backpacks

Table A1 | Monthly Production from One Machine (thousands)

	Natural-Gas-Powered Machine	Solar-Powered Machine
Backpacks	4	2
Bicycles	2	4

and bicycles? How many backpacks per year would it produce? What if the economy had one solar-powered machine instead?

(e) Suppose that Country A has ten old, natural-gas-powered machines and no new, solar-powered machines, while Country B has ten new, solar-powered machines and no old, natural-gas-powered machines. People still want the same number of backpacks as bicycles. Explain why the two countries would gain from trade. (*Hint:* Calculate the number of backpacks and bicycles the world economy can produce with international trade and compare your answer to the number each country can produce alone without international trade.)

CHAPTER 4

SUPPLY AND DEMAND

In this Chapter...

Main Points to Understand

▸ *Demand curves* describe the behavior of buyers.

▸ *Supply curves* describe the behavior of sellers.

▸ Prices adjust to create equilibrium between supply and demand.

Thinking Skills to Develop

▸ Recognize forces that change the behavior of buyers (demand) and the behavior of sellers (supply).

▸ Understand how a market equilibrium coordinates buyers' and sellers' individual decisions.

▸ Recognize how changes in underlying conditions change a market equilibrium.

▸ Use graphs of supply and demand for logical thinking.

Why does a pair of shoes cost more than a compact disc? Why do entertainment stars earn more than mathematicians? Why do airline tickets cost more around holidays? Why have prices of personal computers and video equipment fallen?

What persuades farmers and manufacturers to produce all the food that people want to buy? What ensures that a city has enough apartments for people to rent? What prevents companies from making more computers than people want to buy?

Chapter 3 showed that people can gain from specialization and trade. This chapter explores which trades they choose and the prices they agree upon. The model of supply and demand presented in this chapter is among the most important models in economics.

As Chapter 3 explained, people can choose from many possible trades, and the trades they decide to make depend on their alternative opportunities. Everyone wants to make the best possible trades for herself. This chapter studies the trades that people make when their opportunities for trading are described by the *price-taking* model:

TRADING OPPORTUNITIES: THE PRICE-TAKING MODEL

1. Each buyer is a *price taker*—he can buy as much (or as little) of the good as he wants at some price, but he cannot affect that price.

2. Each seller is a *price taker*—she can sell as much (or as little) of the good as she wants at some price, but she cannot affect that price.

A price-taking consumer can buy as much of a product as she wants, without affecting its price.

For example, you can buy as many drinks as you want for 75 cents each, but no one will sell you a drink for less. You are a price taker in the market for drinks. A farmer can sell as much wheat as she wants at $5.24 per bushel, but no buyer will pay more than that amount. The farmer is a price taker in the market for wheat.

How does the price-taking model apply to the two-student example of Chapter 3? Suppose that Lauren could find *many* people like Steve, each of whom is willing to trade one repaired wall for one repaired window. No one is willing to give Lauren a better price—no one will repair more than one wall in return for one repaired window. Similarly, Steve can find *many* people like Lauren, each of whom is willing to trade one repaired window for one repaired wall. No one is willing to give Steve a better price—no one will repair more than one window in return for one repaired wall. In that case, Lauren and Steve are price takers. The price is one wall for one window, and neither Lauren nor Steve can get a better price from anyone. You might ask why the price is one window for one wall, rather than one window for *half* a wall (as in the hour-for-hour trade of Chapter 3), or some other price. That question is the topic of this chapter.

The price-taking model applies (at least approximately) to buyers of most products and to many sellers such as farms, retail stores, pizza parlors and fast-food restaurants, dry cleaners and laundromats, and gas stations. It does not apply as well to some traders, such as sellers of cable-television services or airline services. Competition among price takers is often called *perfect competition*. Competition among traders who are not price takers can take various forms: monopoly, monopolistic competition, or oligopoly. Later chapters will explore these issues. Because the price-taking model applies very accurately to many real-life situations (even when buyers and sellers are not exactly price takers), the associated model of *supply and demand*, which assumes that traders are price takers, lies at the center of economic analysis.

INTRODUCTION TO DEMAND

How many movies will you see this month? Your answer depends on many conditions, such as:

▶ The price—How much do movie tickets cost?

▶ Your tastes—How much do you like movies?

▶ Your income—Do you have enough money to pay for tickets?

▶ Prices of other goods—How much would you have to spend to rent videos or attend concerts?

Other conditions also influence the choice, such as whether you have a video recorder, how many parties you could attend, what your friends want to do, and how much studying you have to do. How many movie tickets would you buy this month if each ticket cost $1? What if it cost $3, $5, or $10? (In each case, you are a price taker; nothing you can do will change the price of a ticket.) Before you continue reading, briefly

Figure 1 | The Author's Demand Curve for Movie Tickets

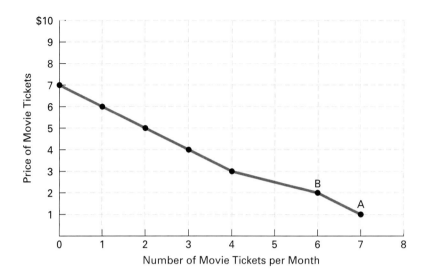

Each point is a row from Table 1.

Table 1
The Author's Demand Schedule for Tickets

Price of Tickets	Number I Would Buy
$1	7
2	6
3	4
4	3
5	2
6	1
7	0

answer these questions based on your own tastes and circumstances. Write your answers as in Table 1, which shows *my* answers.

The table you made is your demand schedule for movie tickets this month. Your demand schedule for a good lists the quantities you would buy at various possible prices. My demand schedule in Table 1 shows that my *quantity demanded* at a price of $1 is seven tickets, and my quantity demanded at a price of $2 is six tickets. Look at your demand schedule: What is your quantity demanded at a price of $1?

Figure 1 graphs my demand schedule for tickets. The vertical axis measures the price of a ticket, and the horizontal axis measures my quantity demanded at that price. If tickets cost $1 each, I would buy seven this month, placing me at Point A on the graph. If they cost $2 each, I would buy six, placing me at Point B. Each point on the graph shows a row from my demand schedule in Table 1. The curve that connects these points is my demand curve for tickets.

Now graph your demand schedule for tickets. Indicate various prices along the vertical axis. On the horizontal axis, mark your quantity demanded at each price. Each row of your demand schedule defines a point on your graph. Connect these points to draw your demand curve for movie tickets.

Every discussion of demand must specify a time period: Will we discuss demand over a week? A month? A year? Any time period will do, but we must specify it in advance. This chapter will discuss demand (and supply) during one month, unless otherwise indicated.

DEMAND

Roughly, a person's quantity demanded of some good is the amount she wants to buy.[1] More precisely:

> A person's **quantity demanded** of a good at some price is the amount she would buy at that price.

Notice that this definition involves hypothetical, "what if?" situations. It does not say what price buyers actually pay. Instead, it indicates how much a person *would* buy *if* the price were a certain level.[2]

A table (such as a spreadsheet on a computer) that lists various possible prices and quantities demanded is called a *demand schedule*. Table 1 shows an example of a demand schedule. Graphing a demand schedule gives a *demand curve*.

> A **demand curve** graphs the relation between the price of a good and the quantity demanded.

Figure 1 shows an example.

Market Demand

We can draw *one person's* demand curve for a good, or the demand curve by several people, or *all buyers* in the market. Chapter 1 explained that the term *market* refers to the activity of people buying and selling goods. Some markets, like the market for wheat, span worldwide networks of buyers and sellers; others, like the market for haircuts, cover local regions. Whatever the size of a particular market, the demand model can apply to that market.

> The **market quantity demanded** of a good at some price is the total amount that *all buyers* in the market would buy at that price.

To obtain the total amount that *all* buyers would buy, simply add together the amounts that individuals would buy.

A table (or spreadsheet) showing various possible prices and market quantities demanded is a *market demand schedule*. A graph of the market demand schedule is the *market demand curve*.

> A **market demand curve** graphs the relation between the price of a good and the market quantity demanded.

When economists talk about *the* demand curve for a good, they mean the market demand curve.

Straight Line or Curved?
Is a demand curve a straight line, or does it curve in some way? The answer is: it all depends! When you graphed your demand for movie tickets, did you get a straight line? The answer depends on how many tickets you would be willing to buy at various possible prices.

---

[1]Do not confuse the amount of a good you would like to *have* with quantity demanded (the amount you want to *buy*). You may want more of something, but you may be unwilling to pay the price. You may want more of almost everything, but this has nothing to do with your quantity demanded. Your quantity demanded shows the amount of a good you are willing to buy, given your limited budget.

[2]Because a person's demand schedule lists many hypothetical prices, that person may not know his demand schedule. For example, he may not know for sure how many shirts he would buy each year if shirts cost $1 each or $80 each. A person's quantity demanded at some price refers to the amount that the person would actually buy if the good were available at that price. Unless shirts actually cost $1 or $80 each, however, the person might not know how he would behave under those conditions.

EXAMPLE

Figure 2 shows how to sum individual demand curves to get a market demand curve. Panel (a) shows Archie's demand schedule and his demand curve for sodas. Panel (b) shows Veronica's demand schedule and her demand curve for sodas. Panel (c) shows the market demand schedule and demand curve for sodas, assuming that Archie and Veronica are the only possible buyers.

At a price of 80 cents, Archie wants to buy 20 sodas and Veronica wants to buy 10, so the total market quantity demanded is 30. At a price of 40 cents, Archie wants to buy 40 sodas and Veronica wants 50, so the market quantity demanded is 90. Notice that even if each *individual's* demand curve is a straight line, the market demand curve can develop kinks as in Panel (c). Also notice that the demand curves add *horizontally*—the market demand curve lies further to the right than either individual demand curve.

Conditions that Affect the Quantity Demanded

The amount of a good you choose to buy—your quantity demanded—depends on many conditions besides its price. It also depends on your tastes (what you like and dislike), the usefulness of the good (a coat is more useful in cold weather than in warm weather), your income and wealth, and prices of related goods. The *market* quantity demanded also depends on the number of potential buyers.

EXAMPLES

Four main conditions affect your demand for video rentals.

Your Demand for Video Rentals	
Your tastes	How much do you like watching videos?
Usefulness of the good	Do you have access to a VCR and television?
Your income and wealth	Do you have money to spend on videos?
Prices of related goods	How much does it cost to see a movie at a theater instead of renting a video?
	How much is pay-per-view on cable television? How much does a VCR cost?

The *market* demand for children's books depends not only on tastes (for books versus television) and the other factors listed above, but also on the number of people with children (which affects the number of potential buyers).

Law of Demand

An increase in the price of a good, with *no change in other conditions*, generally reduces the quantity demanded. Thousands of economic studies support a generalization about the behavior of buyers:

> *Law of Demand:* When the price of a good rises, holding constant other conditions, the quantity demanded falls.

Figure 2 | Individual Demands and Market Demand

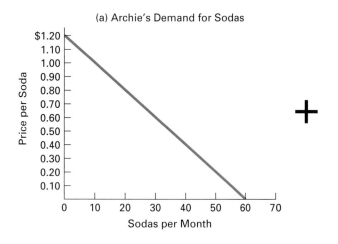

(a) Archie's Demand for Sodas

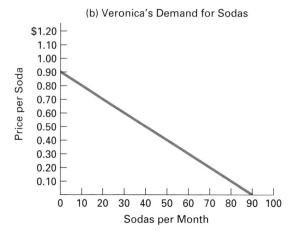

(b) Veronica's Demand for Sodas

Archie's Demand Schedule for Sodas (sodas per month)

Price per Soda	Quantity Demanded
$1.20	0
1.00	10
0.90	15
0.80	20
0.60	30
0.40	40
0.20	50
0.10	55

Veronica's Demand Schedule for Sodas (sodas per month)

Price per Soda	Quantity Demanded
$1.00	0
0.90	0
0.80	10
0.60	30
0.40	50
0.20	70
0.10	80

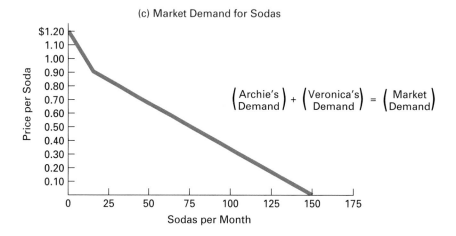

(c) Market Demand for Sodas

$$\left(\begin{array}{c}\text{Archie's}\\\text{Demand}\end{array}\right) + \left(\begin{array}{c}\text{Veronica's}\\\text{Demand}\end{array}\right) = \left(\begin{array}{c}\text{Market}\\\text{Demand}\end{array}\right)$$

Market Demand Schedule for Sodas (sodas per month)

Price per Soda	Market Quantity Demanded
$1.20	0 (= 0 + 0)
1.00	10 (= 10 + 0)
0.90	15 (= 15 + 0)
0.80	30 (= 20 + 10)
0.60	60 (= 30 + 30)
0.40	90 (= 40 + 50)
0.20	120 (= 50 + 70)
0.10	135 (= 55 + 80)

To state this another way:

> Demand curves have negative slopes.

Demand curves slope downward, as in Figure 1.[3]

EXAMPLES

1. Suppose the price of milk increases, with no change in your tastes, your income or wealth, or the prices of related goods such as other beverages or goods you might consume with milk (cookies, chocolate mix, etc.). You would be likely to buy less milk. Only rarely would anyone choose to buy *more*. If the price were to rise enough, everyone would certainly buy less.

2. Points A and B in Figure 1 both lie on my demand curve for movie tickets. My tastes (my likes and dislikes) are the same at Points A and B. I would buy more tickets at Point A than at Point B because the price is lower, not because my tastes are different. My income also remains the same at Points A and B. The only difference in conditions between these two points is the lower price at Point A, which raises my quantity demanded.

Why Demand Curves Slope Downward

Two separate logical reasons underlie the generalization that an increase in price (holding constant other conditions) reduces quantity demanded. First, buyers can replace that good with other, cheaper goods. If the price of corn rises, people tend to substitute broccoli and carrots for corn. The second reason is that people cannot afford to buy as much after a price increase. People must buy either less of the more expensive good or less of something else.[4] For both reasons, a price increase generally reduces the quantity demanded.

Review Questions

1. What is a demand curve? Why does it slope downward?
2. List conditions that affect a good's quantity demanded.

Thinking Exercises

3. Draw graphs to explain the difference between an increase in demand and an increase in the quantity demanded.
4. Draw a graph of your demand for leisure time. How can you buy more leisure time?
5. Comment on the following statement: "We lowered our price, which caused the demand for our pizzas to increase."

---

[3]Sometimes a price change does not affect the quantity demanded; then the demand curve is a vertical line.
[4]They could save less, but they would then buy fewer goods in the future.

CHANGES IN DEMAND

The quantity demanded of a good depends on its price and on *other* conditions such as people's tastes, the good's usefulness, people's income and wealth, prices of related goods, and (for the market quantity demanded) the number of buyers. Any change in one of these *other* conditions causes a change in demand.

> A **change in demand** means a change in the numbers in the demand schedule and a shift in the demand curve.

> An **increase (or rise) in demand** means an increase in the quantity demanded at a given price and a rightward shift in the demand curve, as in Figure 3 from D_1 to D_2.

Figure 3 | Increase in Demand

An increase in demand is a rise in the quantity demanded at each price. At each price, the new demand curve, D_2, shows a higher quantity demanded than the old demand curve, D_1.

Price	Old Quantity Demanded	New Quantity Demanded
$10	5	8
9	6	10
8	8	12
7	10	15
6	14	18
5	20	24

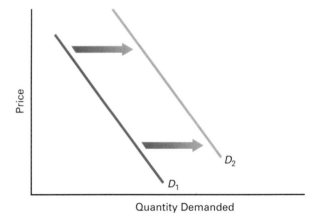

Figure 4 | Decrease in Demand

A decrease in demand is a fall in the quantity demanded at each price. At each price, the new demand curve, D_2, shows a lower quantity demanded than the old demand curve, D_1.

Price	Old Quantity Demanded	New Quantity Demanded
$10	5	2
9	6	3
8	8	4
7	10	6
6	14	9
5	20	15

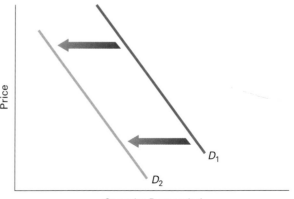

> An **decrease (or fall) in demand** means a decrease in the quantity demanded at a given price and a leftward shift in the demand curve, as in Figure 4 from D_1 to D_2.

When demand changes, the *horizontal* (leftward or rightward) shift in the demand curve shows the change in the quantity demanded. Figures 3 and 4 show changes in demand.

Changes in Quantity Demanded versus Changes in Demand

Economists distinguish between changes in the quantity demanded and changes in demand. A change in the quantity demanded occurs when the price changes, moving the economy from one row to another in the demand schedule. This appears as a movement along a demand curve, as from Point A to Point B in Figure 1.

> A **change in quantity demanded** means a movement *along* a demand curve due to a change in price.

The demand curve does *not* move when the quantity demanded changes, and the numbers in the demand schedule do *not* change. Buyers and sellers simply jump from one row of the demand schedule to another row. Figure 5 shows a change in the quantity demanded. When the price rises from $5 to $10, the quantity demanded falls from 20 to 10 units per month. In contrast, Figures 3 and 4 show changes in demand.

> A change in price changes the quantity demanded. It does not change demand. A change in conditions *other than the price of the good* can change the demand for that good.

Changes in Conditions that Cause Changes in Demand

Table 2 summarizes the changes in conditions that can change demand.

Figure 5 | Change in Quantity Demanded

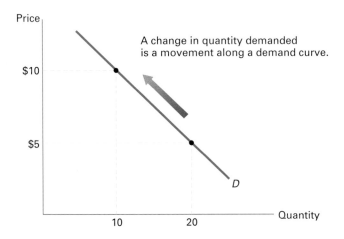

Table 2 | Effects on Demand of Changes in Conditions

Changes in Conditions That *Increase* Demand	Changes in Conditions That *Decrease* Demand
1. Change in tastes: people like the good more.	1. Change in tastes: people like the good less.
2. The good becomes more useful.	2. The good becomes less useful
3. For normal goods, buyers' incomes or wealth levels increase; for inferior goods, buyers' incomes or wealth levels decrease.	3. For normal goods, buyers' incomes or wealth levels decrease; for inferior goods, buyers' incomes or wealth levels increase.
4. The price of a substitute rises.	4. The price of a substitute falls.
5. The price of a complement falls.	5. The price of a complement rises.
6. The number of buyers grows.	6. The number of buyers diminishes.

IN THE NEWS

Putting it mildly, more consumers prefer only products that are "pure," "natural"

Shift in Behavior

The trend represents a significant shift in consumer behavior. For years, consumers were motivated mainly by manufacturers' claims of convenience, performance, or prestige. Now, many people are avoiding products that contain harsh or unnecessary chemicals, especially in their homes.

The growing allure of pure products is paying off for marketers. Sales of Tom's of Maine natural toothpaste in supermarkets and drugstores soared 55 percent to $12.1 million during the 12 months ended Feb. 28.

Source: The Wall Street Journal

Demand for "natural" products rises as consumers' tastes and beliefs about safety change.

Tastes

Tastes (or *preferences*) are people's underlying likes and dislikes. Economists do not explain why people develop certain tastes or what forces change them; those are subjects for psychologists. People's tastes affect their demands, though, and changes in tastes can cause changes in demand. For example, the demand for chocolate candy increased in the United States (as in Figure 3) after World War I: U.S. soldiers developed a taste for eating chocolate because the government gave them chocolate bars during the war.

Usefulness

People often use goods they buy to create (or produce at home) the products they really want. A good's usefulness is its benefit in creating the products people ultimately want. For example, the demand for coats rises at the beginning of winter not because people's tastes change (people always want to be comfortable) but because coats are more useful in the winter than in summer; in cold weather, they help people to create comfort (the really desirable product). Similarly, ground beef is more useful if you have a stove to cook it than if you don't.

Changes in usefulness cause changes in demand. The demand for Christmas cards rises in November (as in Figure 3) and falls in January (as in Figure 4). The demand for air conditioners rises each summer and falls afterward. The demand for low-fat foods increased when people learned that these foods could help them to produce good health.

Income and Wealth

Changes in buyers' income or wealth cause changes in demand.

> **Income** is the amount of money a person earns each year from working, interest on savings, and other sources such as gifts.

Economists always measure income in units of money per year (or some other time period). Increases in income raise the demand for most goods, such as restaurant meals and vacations.

> If a rise in income raises the demand for a good, as in Figure 3, economists call it a **normal good.** If a rise in income reduces the demand for a good, as in Figure 4, economists call it an **inferior good.**

Economists identify normal goods and inferior goods by statistical analysis. Normal goods include airline travel, big houses, and swimming pools. Long-distance bus travel and bologna are inferior goods. (When income rises, people tend to substitute other goods for bologna and bus travel.)

> **Wealth** is the accumulated value of a person's savings.

Wealth includes money in savings accounts, stocks and bonds, and the value of possessions like cars, houses, and record collections. Wealth also includes *human wealth:* the value of education and skills.[5] Economists measure wealth as a stock rather than a flow—as an amount of money, *not* money *per year.* Changes in wealth affect demand in the same way as changes in income: An increase in wealth raises demand for normal goods and reduces demand for inferior goods.

Prices of Related Goods

The demand for a particular good can change due to changes in the prices of related goods. These related goods fall into two categories: substitutes and complements.

Substitutes Goods are substitutes if they can be used in place of each other. Coke and Pepsi are substitutes, as are Fords and Chevys, or Wheaties and Cheerios. When the price of coffee rises, some people switch to tea or cocoa, so the demands for these substitutes rise. The general rule states:

> When the price of a good rises, the demands for its **substitutes** increase.

This rule defines the term *substitutes.* Similarly, demand decreases when the price of a substitute falls.

Complements Goods are complements if people tend to use them together. Cameras and film are complements, as are gasoline and cars, or compact disc players and compact discs.

> When the price of a good falls, the demands for its **complements** increase.

This rule defines the term *complements.* Of course, when the price of a good rises, the demands for its complements decrease.

Economists apply statistical analysis to identify pairs of goods that are substitutes, pairs that are complements, and pairs that are unrelated (neither substitutes or complements).

Number of Potential Buyers

A *market* demand curve shifts when the number of potential buyers changes. Demographic changes, such as the fractions of the population in various age groups, can cause changes in demand.

EXAMPLES

The U.S. Census Bureau projects that within the next 20 years, the fraction of the U.S. population over 55 years old will rise dramatically, and the fraction over 75 will roughly double. This change is likely to raise the demands for medical care, retirement

CD players and CDs are complements. A decrease in the price of one raises demand for the other.

IN THE NEWS

Some buyers were even shrewder.

Karen Mastin of Portland, Ore., eyed a Chevrolet pickup for eight months. "I knew the interest rates would come down. I waited it out," said Mastin, an apartment manager.

Intertemporal substitution (see box on page 80) leads car buyers to wait for interest rates on car loans to fall.

---

[5]Human wealth is the value of all future income that a person's education and skills will help to create.

Expectations of the Future Also Affect Demand

One substitute for buying a good now is to buy it later—a few days or a few months from now. You may postpone a vacation to take advantage of low, off-season prices, because a vacation later is a substitute for a vacation now. The current demand for a good falls when people expect its price to decline; they buy less now and plan to buy more later, after the price has fallen. Similarly, the current demand for a good increases when people expect its price to rise; they buy now before the price jumps. *Intertemporal substitution* (substitution over time) occurs when a change in the expected future price of a good causes a change in the current demand for that good. No one can predict future prices exactly, but people's guesses, or expectations, about future prices affect their demands.

Other expectations also affect demand. If you expect your income to rise, your demand for new clothes or a vacation may increase. When you buy a food that you have never tried, you may expect to like it. Of course, events sometimes confirm expectations and sometimes contradict them.

IN THE NEWS

Beef prices at record highs as cattle shortage continues

By Eben Shapiro

With barbecue season around the corner, a near 30-year low in the nation's cattle herd has resulted in the highest prices ever for steak, hamburger, and other cuts of beef.

Faced with the high meat prices, many grocers say they are promoting chicken breasts, which average $2.04 a pound, or less than half the price of a

Source: New York Times

T-bone steak, and that more and more shoppers are choosing chicken.

Growing Popularity of Chicken

Last year, for the first time, Americans consumed more poultry than beef, an Agriculture Department survey found.

"Forget about nutrition; it is just plain old economics," said William Roenigk, vice president of the Na-

tional Broiler Council in Washington.

Mr. Boehlje, the agriculture economist, said poultry would continue to gain market share at the expense of beef as meat prices rise. "The higher beef prices move, the more people are going to switch," he said. "We have seen substantial switching in the past and I think that is going to continue."

Chicken and beef are substitutes.

properties, old-age homes, and other services that satisfy the wants of elderly people more than young people. Increased international trade has raised the number of potential buyers for U.S. products and thereby raised market demands for those products.

Review Questions

6. What is a normal good? An inferior good?

7. What happens to the demand for a good if the price of a substitute for it rises?

8. What happens to the demand for a good if the price of a complement for it rises?

Thinking Exercise

9. Draw a graph of your demand curve for vacation days on a Caribbean beach. What conditions would affect your demand? How?

INTRODUCTION TO SUPPLY

Demand curves describe the behavior of buyers, summarizing the trades that buyers are willing to make. Similarly, supply curves summarize the behavior of sellers by describing the trades that they are willing to make.

Figure 6 | Supply Curve: Rebecca's Supply Curve for Painting Services

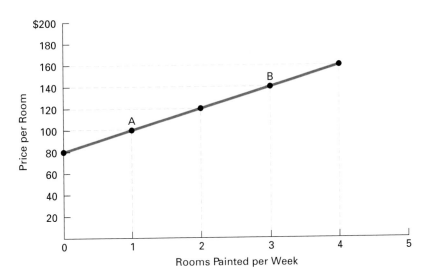

Each point is a row in Table 3.

Table 3
Rebecca's Painting Services Supplied

Price per Room	Rooms Painted per Week
$ 80	0
100	1
120	2
140	3
160	4

Suppose that your college offers you a job painting dormitory rooms next week for $100 per room, with the condition that you provide your own paint and brushes. You may choose how many rooms to paint. What choice would you make? How many rooms would you paint if the price were $80 per room, or $120, or $200? Your answer probably depends on conditions such as the cost of paint, your painting skills, how much you dislike painting, and how busy you are (the alternative uses of your time). Your answers form your supply schedule.

Table 3 shows Rebecca's supply schedule, that is, her quantity supplied of painting services at various prices. Rebecca is unwilling to paint at all for $80 per room. She will paint one room for a price of $100, two rooms for $120 each, three rooms for $140 each, or four rooms for $160 each. Figure 6 shows her supply curve of painting services. This curve graphs her supply schedule, measuring price along the vertical axis and her quantity supplied along the horizontal axis.

SUPPLY

Stated roughly, a seller's quantity supplied of a good is the amount she wants to sell. More precisely:

> A seller's **quantity supplied** of a good at some price is the amount she would sell at that price.

Notice that the quantity supplied describes the behavior of *sellers;* it is unrelated to the behavior of buyers. The definition involves hypothetical "what if?" situations. It does not say what price sellers actually receive. Instead, it indicates how much the person *would* sell *if* the price were at a certain level.

A table (such as a spreadsheet on a computer) that lists various possible prices and quantities supplied is a *supply schedule.* Table 3 shows an example of a supply schedule. Graphing a supply schedule gives a *supply curve.*

Straight Line or Curved?
Is a supply curve a straight line, or does it curve in some way? As in the case of demand curves, it all depends! In real life, some supply curves are straight lines, while many others curve. Chapters 11 and 12 will explain how technology affects the shapes of supply curves.

A **supply curve** graphs the relation between the price of a good and the quantity supplied.

Figure 6 shows an example.

Market Supply

A graph can display *one person's* supply curve for some good, or the supply curve by several people, or by *all sellers* in the market. Whatever the size of a particular market, the supply model can describe its sellers' choices.

The **market quantity supplied** of a good at some price is the total amount that *all sellers* in the market would sell at that price.

To obtain the total amount that *all* sellers would sell, simply add together the amounts that each individual would sell.

A table (or spreadsheet) showing various possible prices and market quantities supplied is a *market supply schedule*. A graph of a market supply schedule is a *market supply curve*.

A **market supply curve** graphs the relation between the price of a good and the market quantity supplied.

When economists talk about *the* supply curve for a good, they mean the market supply curve.

EXAMPLE

Figure 7 shows how to add individual supply curves to get a market supply curve. Supply curves, like demand curves, add horizontally. The figure shows how to add Papa's supply of pizzas to Mama's supply of pizzas to get the market supply curve, assuming that Papa and Mama are the only sellers in the market. The market quantity supplied is the total of the quantities supplied by the individual sellers.

Conditions That Affect the Quantity Supplied

Quantity supplied, like quantity demanded, depends on several conditions. The two main conditions are input prices and technology. The *market* quantity supplied also depends on the number of potential sellers.

An increase in the price of a good, with *no change in these other conditions*, generally raises the quantity supplied. A basic generalization about the behavior of sellers states:

> *Law of Supply*: When the price of a good rises, holding constant other conditions, the quantity supplied rises.

Later chapters will discuss exceptions to this law of supply, but it holds in most cases. To state this another way:

> Supply curves usually have positive slopes.

Figure 7 | Individual and Market Supplies

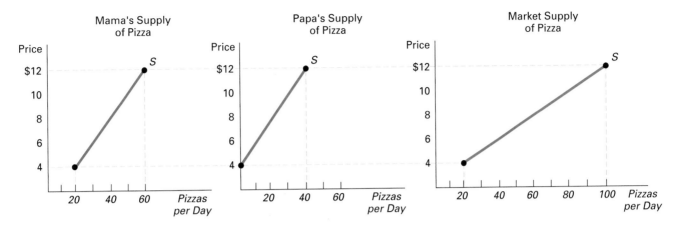

Price per Pizza	Mama's Quantity Supplied	Papa's Quantity Supplied	Market Quantity Supplied
$12	60	40	100
10	50	30	80
8	40	20	60
6	30	10	40
4	20	0	20

Supply curves usually slope upward, as in Figure 6, because an increase in price raises the incentive to produce and sell the good.

Market supply curves usually slope upward because individual sellers' supply curves slope upward and because more potential sellers become actual sellers when the price rises. For example, everyone with a ticket to a sold-out concert or football game is a potential seller—each could sell a ticket. Increasing numbers of these potential sellers become *actual* sellers as buyers offer to pay higher prices for the tickets. Consequently, the market supply curve for tickets sold outside the stadium slopes upward, even though each seller has only one ticket to sell.

CHANGES IN SUPPLY

The quantity supplied of a good depends on its price and on *other* conditions, specifically, input prices, technology, and (for the market quantity supplied) the number of potential sellers. A change in one of these *other* conditions causes a change in supply.

> A **change in supply** means a change in the numbers in the supply schedule and a shift in the supply curve.

> An **increase (or rise) in supply** increases the quantity supplied at each possible price, and the supply curve shifts to the right as in Figure 8, from S_1 to S_2.

Figure 8 | Increase in Supply

An increase in supply is a rise in the quantity supplied at each price. At each price, the new supply curve, S_2, shows a higher quantity supplied than the old supply curve, S_1.

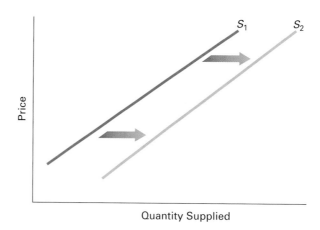

A **decrease (or fall) in supply** decreases the quantity supplied at each possible price, and the supply curve shifts to the left as in Figure 9, from S_1 to S_2.

When supply changes, the *horizontal* (leftward or rightward) shift in the supply curve shows the change in the quantity supplied. Figures 8 and 9 show changes in supply.

Changes in Quantity Supplied versus Changes in Supply

Economists distinguish between changes in the quantity supplied and changes in supply. A change in the quantity supplied occurs when the price changes, moving the economy from one row to another in the supply schedule. This change appears as a movement *along* a supply curve, as from Point A to Point B in Figure 6.

A **change in quantity supplied** means a movement *along* a supply curve due to a change in price.

When quantity supplied changes, the supply curve does *not* move and the numbers in the supply schedule do *not* change. The economy simply moves from one row to another in the supply schedule.

A change in price changes the quantity supplied; it does not change supply. A change in conditions *other than the price of the good* can change the supply for that good.

Changes in Conditions Causing Changes in Supply

Table 4 summarizes the changes in conditions that can change supply.

Prices of Inputs
Increases in the prices of inputs (such as materials, equipment, labor, energy, and natural resources) decrease supply as in Figure 9, by reducing the incentive to produce and sell the good. Similarly, a fall in input prices raises the incentive to produce and sell the good, increasing supply as in Figure 8.

IN THE NEWS

Rising rents threaten theater companies

Source: New York Times

Increases in the prices of inputs reduce supply.

Figure 9 | Decrease in Supply

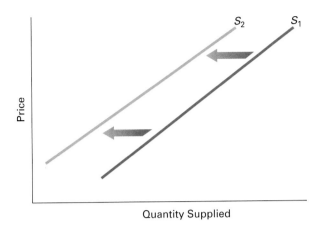

A decrease in supply is a fall in the quantity supplied at each price. At each price, the new supply curve, S_2, shows a lower quantity supplied than the old supply curve, S_1.

Technology

If an advance in technology lowers the cost of producing a good, it raises the incentive to produce and sell it. In this way, advances in technology can increase supply, as in Figure 8.

Number of Potential Sellers

Market supply increases with growth in the number of potential sellers. For example, the supply of workers increased when the baby-boom generation graduated from high school and college in the 1960s and 1970s. The supply of mail-delivery services fell in 1845 when the U.S. government prohibited anyone except the government-operated post office from delivering first-class mail; this edict reduced the number of potential sellers. The supply of telecommunications services increased dramatically in the last decade as the U.S. government deregulated the telecommunications industry, allowing new firms to enter the industry.

Expectations of the Future Also Affect Supply

One substitute for selling a good now is to wait and sell it in the future, when its price may be higher. *Intertemporal substitution* (substitution over time) affects supply when a change in the expected future price of a good causes a change in its current supply. The supply of a good falls if its expected future price increases. Freezing weather in Florida may kill orange trees and raise the expected future price of orange juice; this decreases the current supply of orange juice as producers hold already-made juice off the market, waiting to sell it in the future at a higher price.

Review Questions

10. What is a supply schedule? A market supply schedule?

11. What is a supply curve? Why does it usually slope upward?

Table 4 | Effects on Supply of Changes in Conditions

Changes in Conditions That *Increase* Supply	Changes in Conditions That *Decrease* Supply
1. Fall in the price of an input	1. Rise in the price of an input
2. Improvement in technology that lowers the cost of production	2. Decrease in available technology (e.g., a new law prohibits a certain technology)
3. Increase in the number of potential sellers	3. Decrease in the number of potential sellers

12. Draw graphs to explain the difference between a change in supply and a change in the quantity supplied.

EQUILIBRIUM OF SUPPLY AND DEMAND

Demand curves summarize the behavior of buyers. They also summarize the opportunities available to sellers by showing the trades that buyers are willing to make. Supply curves summarize the behavior of sellers. They also show the opportunities available to buyers because they show the trades that sellers are willing to make. These opportunities determine the trades that people really do make—the amounts they buy and sell and the prices they pay or receive.

This section combines supply and demand to examine these issues, beginning with a definition of *equilibrium:*

> An **equilibrium** occurs when quantity supplied equals quantity demanded.

> The price in an equilibrium is the **equilibrium price,** and the quantity is the **equilibrium quantity**.

A graph marks equilibrium at the point where the S (supply) and D (demand) curves intersect: Point A in Figure 10. The equilibrium price is P_1. The equilibrium quantity Q_1 shows the amount of the good bought and sold: the quantity traded. Buyers buy Q_1 units of the good from sellers, and pay P_1 dollars for each unit.[6]

Total spending on the good appears as the area of the shaded rectangle in Figure 10. This shaded area equals the quantity that people buy, Q_1, multiplied by the price per unit, P_1.[7] Of course, the area of this shaded rectangle also shows the total receipts of sellers, since they collect the money that buyers spend.

Why the Intersection of the Curves Shows Equilibrium

The demand curve in Figure 10 shows that at a price of P_1, the quantity demanded is Q_1. The supply curve shows that at a price of P_1, the quantity supplied is Q_1. At a price of P_1, the quantity demanded equals the quantity supplied, that is, the amount that buyers want to buy equals the amount that sellers want to sell. Equilibrium occurs at Point A, where the supply and demand curves intersect.

At any price other than P_1, however, the quantity demanded does not equal the quantity supplied, and the market is not in equilibrium.

> **Disequilibrium** is the opposite of equilibrium; it occurs when the quantity demanded does not equal the quantity supplied at the current price.

---

[6]The *X*-axis of the graph now measures both the quantity demanded and the quantity supplied, so its label reads simply *Quantity.*

[7]The area equals the base of the rectangle times its height, or Q_1 times P_1.

Figure 10 | Market Equilibrium

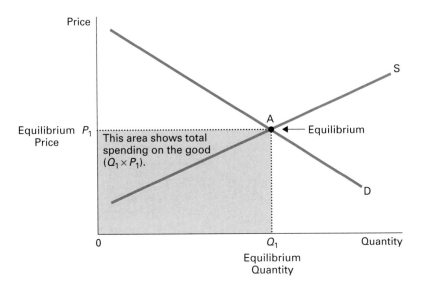

Market equilibrium is a situation in which the quantity supplied equals the quantity demanded. This occurs where the supply and demand curves intersect. Point A is the equilibrium, P_1 is the equilibrium price, and Q_1 is the equilibrium quantity traded. At price P_1, the quantity supplied and quantity demanded both equal Q_1.

A disequilibrium situation creates an inherent tendency for change. The price tends to change, and this change moves the economy toward equilibrium. To understand how, consider two kinds of disequilibrium situations: excess demand and excess supply.

Excess Demand

Suppose that the price is P_0, below the equilibrium price of P_1 in Figure 11. The supply curve shows that the quantity supplied at the price P_0 is Q_0^s units of the good. The demand curve shows that the quantity demanded at the price P_0 is Q_0^d units of the good. So the quantity demanded exceeds the quantity supplied; at price P_0, buyers want to buy more than sellers want to sell. There is a shortage of the good.

> **Excess demand,** or a **shortage,** is a situation in which the quantity demanded exceeds the quantity supplied.

A shortage occurs when the price of a good is below its equilibrium level. The size of the shortage, or the amount of excess demand, equals the quantity demanded minus the quantity supplied. At a price of P_0, Figure 11 shows a shortage of $Q_0^d - Q_0^s$.

A shortage creates pressure for the price to rise. Some buyers cannot buy the good, and stores run out of it. Sellers have an incentive to raise the price, because enough buyers are willing to pay the higher price. The price tends to rise until it reaches the equilibrium price P_1, where the quantity demanded equals the quantity supplied.

> A price below the equilibrium price creates a shortage, and the price tends to rise toward the equilibrium.

The shortage shrinks when the price rises. When the price reaches the equilibrium level, the shortage vanishes for two reasons. First, the quantity supplied increases when the price rises, helping to eliminate the shortage. Second, the quantity demanded falls when the price rises, also helping to eliminate the shortage.

At a price, P_0, below the equilibrium price, buyers want to buy Q_0^d units of the good, and sellers want to sell only Q_0^s units, so there is a shortage or excess demand equal to $Q_0^d - Q_0^s$.

Figure 11 | Excess Demand

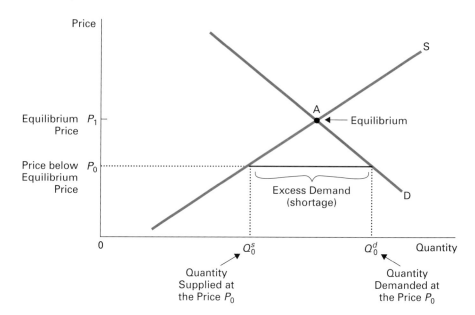

Excess Supply

The second type of disequilibrium involves excess supply. Suppose that the price is P_2, above the equilibrium price of P_1 in Figure 12. The quantity supplied at the price P_2 is Q_2^s units of the good. The quantity demanded at the price P_2 is Q_2^d units of the good. So, the quantity demanded is less than the quantity supplied at the price P_2; that is, buyers want to buy less than sellers want to sell, causing a surplus of the good.

> **Excess supply,** or a **surplus,** is a situation in which the quantity supplied exceeds the quantity demanded.

A surplus occurs when the price of a good exceeds its equilibrium price. The size of the surplus, or the amount of excess supply, equals the quantity supplied minus the quantity demanded. At a price of P_2 in Figure 12, the surplus equals $Q_2^s - Q_2^d$.

A surplus creates pressure for the price to fall. Sellers hold extra units that they cannot sell, and they would rather sell the goods at a lower price than not sell them at all. As sellers reduce the price to compete for customers, it tends to fall until it reaches the equilibrium price P_1, where the quantity supplied equals the quantity demanded.

> A price above the equilibrium price causes a surplus, and the price tends to fall toward the equilibrium.

A fall in the price of a good reduces a surplus in two ways: It decreases the quantity supplied and increases the quantity demanded. Sellers want to sell less while buyers want to buy more—both helping to eliminate the surplus.

Surpluses of automobiles show up as rising inventories at car dealers. The dealers respond by lowering car prices and sometimes by giving rebates, low-interest financing, or free options. Surpluses of clothing occur when people don't buy the styles that sellers expected them to buy. These surpluses lead stores to put the clothes on sale at reduced prices.

IN THE NEWS

Christmas sales are below expectations so far; price cuts possible in final days

"Things that aren't on sale are better," nine-year-old Sara Campbell believes. Sale items are "on sale because people want to get rid of them."

Source: The Wall Street Journal

Surpluses lead to price cuts.

Figure 12 | Excess Supply

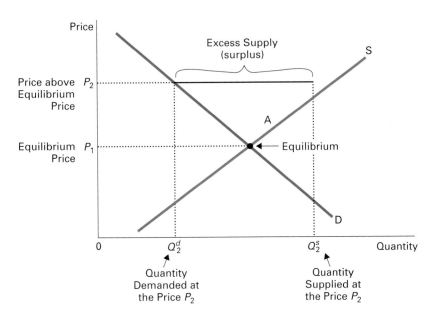

At a price, P_2, above the equilibrium price, buyers want to buy only Q_2^d units of the good, while sellers want to sell Q_2^s units, so there is a surplus or excess supply equal to $Q_2^s - Q_2^d$.

Summary of Equilibrium

At a price below the equilibrium price, a shortage occurs, and the price tends to rise. At a price above equilibrium, a surplus occurs, and the price tends to fall. At the equilibrium price, the quantity supplied equals the quantity demanded; without any shortage or surplus to disturb it, the price tends to remain constant unless supply or demand changes.

> At the equilibrium price, there is neither a shortage or a surplus, so the price shows no tendency to change unless demand or supply changes.

Changes in demand and supply cause changes in the equilibrium, as Figures 13a through 13d show. In each figure, the original equilibrium price and quantity (before the change in demand or supply) are P_1 and Q_1. The new equilibrium price and quantity (after the change) are P_2 and Q_2. Always remember the distinction between demand and supply: Demand describes buyer behavior, and supply describes seller behavior. Some changes in conditions cause changes in demand, while other changes in conditions cause changes in supply.

EFFECTS OF CHANGES IN DEMAND OR SUPPLY

Increase in Demand

An increase in demand raises the equilibrium price and the equilibrium quantity, as in Figure 13a. At the original equilibrium, Point A, the original demand curve D_1 intersects the supply curve at an original equilibrium price of P_1 and an original equilibrium quantity of Q_1. At the new equilibrium, Point B, the new demand curve D_2 intersects the unchanged supply curve at a new equilibrium price of P_2 and a new equilibrium quantity of Q_2. The increase in demand raises both the price and the quantity that people buy and sell.

IN THE NEWS

Gasoline prices rise as drivers flock to road

Source: The Wall Street Journal

An increase in demand raises the price.

Figure 13a | An Increase in Demand Raises Price and Quantity

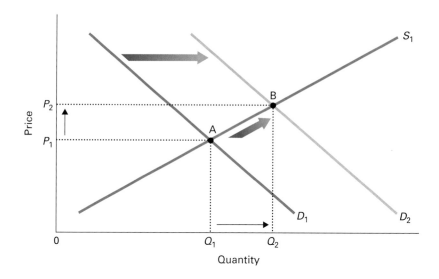

Source: The Far Side ©1987 Farworks, Inc. Distributed by Universal Press Syndicate. Reprinted with permission. All rights reserved.

Figure 13b | A Decrease in Demand Lowers Price and Quantity

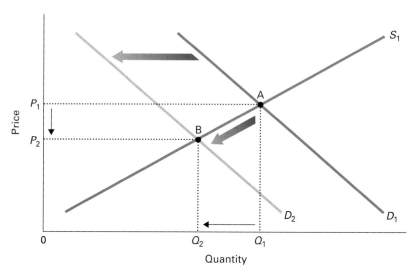

Notice that an increase in demand implies a shift in the demand curve *without* a shift in the supply curve. The supply curve stays at S_1. The quantity supplied rises, however, because the price increase from P_1 to P_2 causes movement along the supply curve from Point A to Point B.

Prices rise quickly sometimes; at other times they rise slowly. Stores may learn that demand for a product has increased and raise its price only after a shortage develops or inventories of the good decline. A seller may raise the price only after receiving more orders for a product than expected. Sellers may apply trial-and-error methods over time to find the new equilibrium price, but eventually the price will rise to P_2.

**Figure 13c | An Increase in Supply Lowers the Price and
Raises the Quantity**

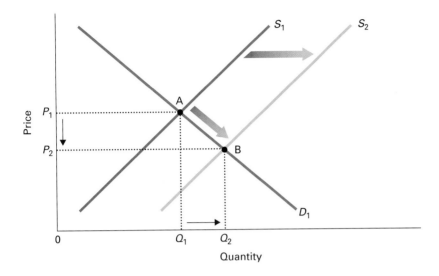

**Figure 13d | A Decrease in Supply Raises the Price and
Lowers the Quantity**

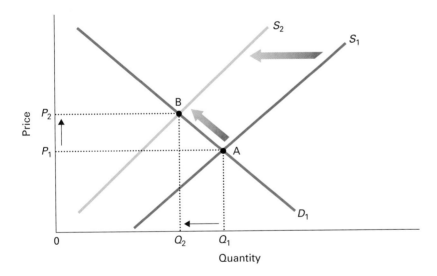

EXAMPLES

Concern over the spread of AIDS has increased the demand for both condoms and rubber gloves for health-care workers, leading to increases in quantities sold. The market demand for child-care centers increased when it became more common for both parents in families with children to work outside the home. This trend raised the number of child-care centers as well as the prices they charged.

Decrease in Demand

A decrease in demand lowers the equilibrium price and quantity, as in Figure 13b. The equilibrium point then moves from Point A to Point B. The equilibrium price falls from P_1 to P_2, and the equilibrium quantity traded falls from Q_1 to Q_2. The fall in price reduces the quantity supplied, causing movement along the supply curve from Point A to Point B.

IN THE NEWS

Fur industry shrinking with no end in sight

By John F. Burns

TORONTO, Feb. 25—These are bitter times for those involved in trapping, dressing, making, and selling furs. In a harshly symbolic blow to the industry, the Hudson's Bay Company of Canada announced recently that it was closing the last fur salons in its Bay department stores.

The company, which was synonymous with fur for centuries after it was founded in 1670 to pursue the trade under a royal charter, had been confronted by the relentless campaigning of animal rights advocates and plunging demand.

Source: New York Times

A decrease in demand reduces the price and the equilibrium quantity traded.

EXAMPLE

The demand for fur coats has decreased in recent decades because of increased sensitivity to animal-rights issues. This change reduced the prices of fur coats and the quantity bought and sold.

Increase in Supply

An increase in supply lowers the equilibrium price and raises the equilibrium quantity traded, as in Figure 13c. The increase in supply shifts the supply curve from S_1 to S_2 and moves the equilibrium from Point A to Point B. The equilibrium price falls from P_1 to P_2 and the equilibrium quantity rises from Q_1 to Q_2. Notice that an increase in supply means a shift in the supply curve *without* a shift in the demand curve, which stays at D_1. The fall in price from P_1 to P_2 raises the *quantity demanded;* that is, it causes movement along the demand curve from Point A to Point B.

EXAMPLE

An increase in the number of community recycling programs in the early 1990s increased the supplies of recyclable glass, plastic, and paper, reducing their prices.

Decrease in Supply

A decrease in supply raises the equilibrium price and lowers the equilibrium quantity traded, as in Figure 13d. The equilibrium moves from Point A to Point B as the equilibrium price rises from P_1 to P_2 and the equilibrium quantity falls from Q_1 to Q_2.

Market Process and Economic Coordination

Chapter 1 described the puzzle of market coordination. People buy goods from all over the world—goods that they could never produce by themselves, goods made by people they will never meet, sometimes in cultures they will never experience. No one directs all this activity of billions of people; the market coordinates decisions so that they all fit together. It provides enough soap, food, and footballs for those who want (and can afford) to buy these goods. Enough people become doctors, plumbers, and comedians. No one has to tell people, "Joe, you must become an accountant," and "Alison, you must become an engineer." People make their own decisions about which products to buy and how much to buy. People make their own decisions about occupations to choose, and what products their businesses should make. The market process provides the amazing coordination of activities to produce even a simple good like a pencil (see Chapter 1) through the operation of supply and demand, without any central direction.

IN THE NEWS

Maple sap is running, but fitfully in another 'off' year

It's driving up prices as much as $4 a quart

By Bob Bickel

CASTILE—When asked to perform, sugar maples can be as temperamental as opera singers. And recently,

they have been particularly recalcitrant about giving up their sap.

Throughout the Northeast, production is down for the second year in a row. . . .

At the retail level, consumers are now paying about $10 a quart for pure maple syrup—up $3–$4 [per] quart from prices two years ago.

Source: Rochester Democrat and Chronicle

A decrease in supply raises the price.

Prices influence all these decisions. What would happen if no one wanted to be a doctor? Wages of doctors would rise until people changed their minds. The cost of medical care would rise in the process, but the prospects of high incomes would induce people to produce medical services. What happens when many people want to become movie stars or musical performers? Wages of these occupations fall to low levels, except for the few who find success. Low wages induce people to choose other occupations instead, and pursue acting and music as hobbies rather than professions.

Prices play the key role in the market process. Whenever a good becomes increasingly scarce, the fall in supply raises its price. This price increase gives consumers an incentive to conserve the good—to use less of it and to substitute other, less scarce goods in its place. The price jump also gives producers an incentive to boost production as quickly as they can. No one needs to know why the good became scarce, and only a few people may know, but the market adjusts to the change. The price increase affects incentives and changes the quantities demanded and supplied. Similarly, an emergency that raises demand for a medicine in the Third World raises its price, giving people who live elsewhere an incentive to conserve it and to substitute alternatives. The price increase also gives people an incentive to transport the medicine quickly to locations where it is needed and to produce more. The operation of supply and demand described in this chapter underlies the insight of Adam Smith that, even in acting selfishly, a person is often "led by an invisible hand to promote an end which was no part of his intention."

IN THE NEWS

With mandatory recycling programs in place in many areas of the country, materials brokers said, glass, aluminum, and plastic containers continue to pour into collection centers, regardless of demand. With excess supply chasing inadequate demand, prices took a beating.

The price paid by brokers for aluminum cans fell from almost 30 cents a pound at the beginning of the year to barely more than 20 cents by the end, according to the survey. The value of clear polyethylene terepthalate, which is used in large soda bottles, fell from almost 7.0 cents a pound to 1.2 cents.

Source: New York Times

Review Questions

13. What is an equilibrium? What is a market equilibrium?

14. Why does excess demand tend to raise the price of a good, while excess supply reduces the price?

15. How does an increase in demand affect the equilibrium price and quantity traded? How does an increase in supply affect the equilibrium price and quantity traded?

An increase in supply lowers the price.

Thinking Exercises

16. Use demand and supply curves to predict changes in the price of a rental car in Florida at different times of the year (winter, spring break, summer, Labor Day, Christmas). Do the same analysis for motel rates at ski resorts in the Rocky Mountains.

17. Translate the following newspaper headlines into statements about supply and demand:
    (a) "Sweets Cost More Due to Sugar Price Rise"
    (b) "Pork Prices Rise as Farmers Cut Output"
    (c) "Profits from Popcorn Attract Farmers"

RELATIVE PRICES AND NOMINAL PRICES

Prices in the United States today are about twice as high as in 1980, on average, and about four times higher than prices in 1970. This rise in the average level of prices—inflation—makes it important to distinguish between two kinds of prices: nominal prices and relative prices.

> The **nominal price** of a good is its money price.

Everyone is familiar with nominal prices: If a hamburger costs $2.50, that is its nominal price. Inflation is an increase in the average level of nominal prices.

> The **relative price** of one good in terms of another good is its opportunity cost measured in units of that other good.

The rule to calculate the relative price between two goods is:

If the nominal price of one good is P_1 and the nominal price of another good is P_2, the relative price of the first good in terms of the second good is P_1/P_2.

The relative price of a sweater in terms of candy bars is the number of candy bars that you sacrifice each time you buy a sweater. Relative prices are important because they measure *opportunity costs*.

EXAMPLE

Suppose that a sweater costs $30.00 and a candy bar costs $0.50 (both nominal prices). The relative price of the sweater in terms of candy bars is 60 candy bars per sweater. You sacrifice 60 candy bars (and a monster stomach ache) when you buy the sweater.
    The relative price is the ratio of the nominal prices:

Relative price of a sweater   = Nominal price of a sweater/Nominal price of candy bar
    in terms of candy bars

= $30.00/$0.50 = 60 candy bars per sweater

Similarly, the relative price of a candy bar in terms of sweaters is 1/60 of a sweater per candy bar.

Which Price Is on the Graph?

When economists use the term *relative price* without saying "measured in terms of" some other good, they mean the relative price in terms of all other goods in the economy. When a good's nominal price rises faster than the average of the nominal prices of other goods, its relative price rises. For example, the relative price of wooden furniture has increased in recent years, while the relative prices of computers and home electronics equipment (video and audio components) have fallen. If all nominal prices rise by the same percentage, relative prices do not change.

Which price—the nominal price or the relative price—appears on the graph in a supply-and-demand diagram? It is the relative price.

The price on a graph of demand or supply is the good's relative price.

Demand is affected by the relative prices of substitutes and complements; supply is affected by the relative prices of inputs and other goods. Relative prices are inflation-adjusted prices. All analysis of demand and supply in this chapter applies to relative prices.

R e v i e w   Q u e s t i o n

18. Which kind of price—a nominal or relative price—appears on the vertical axis in a supply-and-demand graph?

T h i n k i n g   E x e r c i s e s

19. How is the relative price of tacos in terms of Frisbees related to the nominal prices of tacos and Frisbees?

20. If sneakers cost $30 and a hamburger costs $3, what is the relative price of sneakers in terms of hamburgers? What is the relative price of hamburgers in terms of sneakers?

C o n c l u s i o n

Trading Opportunities: The Price-Taking Model

The price-taking model describes trading opportunities. It states that each buyer and seller can buy or sell as much (or as little) of a good as desired at a given price, but no individual can affect that price. This price-taking model leads to the model of supply and demand, which works well in many real-life situations (even when buyers and sellers are not exactly price takers).

Demand

Demand models the behavior of buyers. A person's quantity demanded of a good at some price is the amount she would buy at that (hypothetical) price. A demand curve graphs the relation between the price of a good and the quantity demanded. The market quantity demanded and market demand curve are defined in the same way, but apply to all buyers in the market.

Four main factors besides price affect the quantity demanded: tastes, usefulness, income and wealth, and prices of related goods. The Law of Demand states that a rise in the price of a good, holding constant these other conditions, reduces the quantity demanded. This implies that demand curves slope downward.

Changes in Demand

A *change in demand* refers to a shift in the demand curve. A *change in quantity demanded* refers to a movement along a fixed demand curve due to a change in price.

Changes in demand result from changes in tastes, usefulness, income and wealth, and prices of related goods. Changes in market demand also result from changes in the number of potential buyers.

An increase in income raises demand for normal goods and reduces demand for inferior goods. Two goods are substitutes when a rise in the price of one increases demand for the other. Two goods are complements when a rise in the price of one decreases demand for the other.

Supply

Supply models the behavior of sellers. A seller's quantity supplied of a good at some price is the amount she would sell at that (hypothetical) price. A supply curve graphs the relation between the price of a good and the quantity supplied. The market quantity supplied and market supply curve are defined in the same way, but apply to all sellers in the market.

Two main factors besides price affect the quantity supplied: input prices and technology. The Law of Supply states that a rise in the price of a good, holding constant these other conditions, raises the quantity supplied. This implies that supply curves slope upward.

Changes in Supply

A *change in supply* refers to a shift in the supply curve. A *change in quantity supplied* refers to a movement along a fixed supply curve due to a change in price. Changes in supply result from changes in input prices and technology. Changes in market supply also result from changes in the number of potential sellers. An increase in the price of inputs decreases supply. An increase in technology that lowers the cost of producing a good raises supply.

Equilibrium of Supply and Demand

An equilibrium occurs when quantity supplied equals quantity demanded. That quantity is the equilibrium quantity, and the price is the equilibrium price. A graph marks equilibrium at the point where the supply and demand curves intersect.

If a price is *below* its equilibrium level, the resulting excess demand (shortage) causes the price to rise toward its equilibrium level. If a price is *above* its equilibrium level, the resulting excess supply (surplus) causes the price to fall toward its equilibrium level. In an equilibrium, there is no tendency for the price or quantity to change unless changes in underlying conditions cause demand or supply to change.

Effects of Changes in Demand or Supply

An increase in demand raises the equilibrium price and quantity. A decrease in demand lowers the equilibrium price and quantity. An increase in supply lowers the equilibrium price and raises the equilibrium quantity. A decrease in supply raises the equilibrium price and lowers the equilibrium quantity.

Relative Prices and Nominal Prices

The nominal price of a good is its money price. The relative price of a good in terms of another good is its opportunity cost measured in units of that other good. The relative price of a good is often expressed in terms of all goods produced in the economy. The price measured along the vertical axis of a supply or demand graph is a relative price.

Key Terms

quantity demanded	change in quantity demanded	supply curve	equilibrium quantity
demand curve	income	market quantity supplied	disequilibrium
market quantity demanded	normal good	market supply curve	excess demand (shortage)
market demand curve	inferior good	change (increase or decrease) in supply	excess supply (surplus)
change (increase or decrease) in demand	wealth	change in quantity supplied	nominal price
	substitute	equilibrium	relative price of one good in terms of another
	complement	equilibrium price	
	quantity supplied		

Problems

21. A national newspaper reported: "Increased retail demand for roasted and ground coffee because of lower prices . . . has contributed to a higher price for coffee." What's wrong with this reasoning?

22. Suppose that three companies sell lawnmowers. Their supply schedules appear in the following table.
   (a) Make a table of the market supply schedule.
   (b) Draw the supply curve for each company and the market supply curve.

If the Price Is	Alright Co. Wants to Sell	Better Co. Wants to Sell	Cut-It Co. Wants to Sell
$400	28	45	65
350	24	43	65
300	20	38	60
250	16	32	45
200	12	25	20
150	8	18	0
100	4	11	0
50	0	5	0

23. A change in the price of one good can affect demand and supply of other goods.
    (a) How is an increase in the price of bologna likely to affect the price of peanut butter and the amount of peanut butter that people buy?
    (b) How is an increase in the price of charcoal grills likely to affect the price of charcoal and the amount of charcoal that people buy?

24. Discuss this statement: "They're building too many hotels in this city. They think this town will become a big convention city. If they're wrong, we will have too many hotels and loads of empty rooms. It'll cost more to spend a night in a hotel here, because the hotels will charge more to make up for all the empty rooms."

25. How would the following changes affect demand curves, supply curves, and equilibrium prices and quantities? (Discuss as many economic implications of these changes as you can imagine.)
    (a) People learn about health benefits of cutting the amount of fat they eat.

    (b) Global warming raises the average world temperature by 5 degrees.
    (c) Scientists discover a cure for AIDS.
    (d) The NCAA allows college athletes to collect salaries.
    (e) A college improves its dormitories and enhances the desirability of dorm living.
    (f) California legalizes gambling.
    (g) Scientists perfect high-definition television (HDTV) and discover how to build a large-screen HDTV set for $300.

26. Suppose that a genetically engineered hormone were to raise the milk output of cows by 40 percent. How would this innovation affect the price of milk, the quantity of milk produced, and the number of dairy farmers?

27. Read the following news headlines and excerpts and interpret them in terms of supply and demand:
    (a) "Prices Soar as Everyone Wants Beanie Babies"
    (b) "Crude Oil, Petroleum Product Prices Rise after Explosion at Large Shell Refinery"
    (c) "Digital Camera Prices Fall as More People Buy, Contradicting the Law of Supply and Demand"
    (d) "Computer Prices Fall Again as Chip Technology Improves"
    (e) "Tuition Rises and College Enrollments Fall"
    (f) "Demand is increasing moderately, but with yields per acre rising, farmers have seen little change in prices."

28. If the average price of goods rises 5 percent and the price of tortillas rises 8 percent, what happens to the relative price of tortillas?

Inquiries for Further Thought

29. Which relative prices do you believe will rise over the next 20 years? Which relative prices will fall? Explain why. What conditions will cause the changes in demand or supply? Do your answers suggest that some types of businesses will become more profitable and expand, while others will become less profitable and shrink? How might you use these insights to make money?

30. How much money would you be willing to pay to become more physically attractive? Translate this into a demand curve for physical attractiveness. What products would rise in price if the demand for physical attractiveness were to increase?

31. How could you obtain evidence to support or refute the Law of Demand?

Appendix: Algebra of Equilibrium

Economists often express demand and supply curves as equations. If the demand curve is a straight line, it can be expressed as:

$$Q^d = a - bP \qquad\qquad \text{Example: } Q^d = 10 - 2P$$

where Q^d is the quantity demanded, P is the price of the good, and a and b are positive numbers that depend on buyers' tastes and incomes, the prices of complements and substitutes, and the other conditions that affect demand. For example, a might be 10 and b might be 2.

The equation for the supply curve, if it is a straight line, can be written as:

$$Q^s = c - dP \qquad\qquad \text{Example: } Q^s = -5 + 3P$$

where Q^s is the quantity supplied, P is the price, and c and d are numbers that depend on technology, input costs, and the other conditions that affect supply. The number d is generally positive, which means that the supply curve slopes upward. The number c can be positive or negative. For example, c might be -5 and d might be 3.

Graphs show the equilibrium price and quantity as the intersection of the supply and demand curves. At the equilibrium price, P_1, the quantity demanded equals the quantity supplied. In algebraic terms, that means:

$$Q^d = Q^s$$

Now substitute the two equations for Q^d and Q^s into this last equation (called the *equilibrium condition,* since it says that quantity supplied equals quantity demanded):

$$a - bP = c + dP \qquad\qquad \text{Example: } 10 - 2P = -5 + 3P$$

To solve for the equilibrium price, begin by adding bP to both sides:

$$a = c + dP + bP \qquad\qquad \text{Example: } 10 = -5 + 5P$$

Subtracting c from both sides:

$$a - c = dP + bP \qquad\qquad \text{Example: } 15 = 5P$$

Collect terms on the right-hand side:

$$a - c = (b + d)P$$

Divide both sides by the quantity $(b + d)$ and rearrange terms:

$$P_1 = (a - c)/(b + d) \qquad\qquad \text{Example: } P_1 = 3$$

To find Q_1, the equilibrium quantity, substitute the solution for P_1 into either the demand curve equation or the supply curve equation. After simplifying the algebra, either equation gives the same answer for Q_1. For example, substituting the equilibrium price P_1 into the demand curve equation gives:

$$Q_1^d = a - bP \qquad \text{Example: } Q_1^d = 10 - (2 \times 3)$$
$$\quad\;\; = a - b(a - c)/(b + d) \qquad \text{Example: } Q_1^d = 4$$

This is the formula for the equilibrium quantity.

Notice that changes in the numbers a, b, c, and d affect the equilibrium price and equilibrium quantity. Those numbers change in response to changes in tastes, technology, or other conditions that affect demand and supply.

Problems

A1. Suppose that the demand curve for rental cars is:

$$Q^d = 500 - 2P$$

and the supply curve is

$$Q^s = 100 + 6P$$

where Q^d is the quantity demanded (in cars per day), Q^s is the quantity supplied, and P is the rental price per day. Find the equilibrium price and quantity.

A2. Suppose that the demand curve for movie tickets is:

$$Q^d = 250 - 20P$$

and the supply curve is

$$Q^s = 50 + 30P$$

where Q^d is the quantity demanded, Q^s is the quantity supplied, and P is the price. Find the equilibrium price and quantity.

CHAPTER 5

ELASTICITIES OF DEMAND AND SUPPLY

In this Chapter . . .

Main Points to Understand

▸ Elasticity measures responsiveness of quantity demanded or supplied.

▸ Responsiveness of quantity demanded affects total spending when supply changes.

▸ For a given increase in supply, elasticity of demand determines the sizes of the changes in equilibrium price and quantity. For a given increase in demand, elasticity of supply determines the sizes of the changes in equilibrium price and quantity.

Thinking Skills to Develop

▸ Use elasticities to answer "what if?" questions about changes in supply and demand.

▸ Understand the factors that affect shapes of supply and demand curves.

How much less ice cream would you buy if its price increased by 10 percent? Would you buy 5 percent less? 10 percent less? 20 percent less? Your answer shows the responsiveness of your quantity demanded to a change in price. How many more (or fewer) hours would you want to work each week if your hourly wage were to rise by 20 percent? Your answer shows the responsiveness of your quantity supplied (of labor services) to a change in price.

Suppose that the government expands its war on illegal drugs, reducing the supply and raising the price. How would this affect total spending on illegal drugs? How would it affect the number of crimes, such as robberies, committed to finance spending on illegal drugs?

The Walt Disney Company restricts the number of videotapes of its classic animated films that it sells. Unlike most sellers, which produce as many units of their products as they can sell, Disney produces only strictly limited numbers of its videos, even when stores sell out all their available copies. Why might Disney's profits fall if it increased its sales of videos?

Evidence shows that countries adopt policies for cleaner environments as their incomes rise. At the same time, increases in income often raise the number of cars, creating more air pollution. How will world air pollution change in the coming years as incomes rise in less-developed countries?

Your student organization holds a car wash to raise money. If you raise the price by 25 percent, will your organization raise more money or less?

These examples, like many real-life issues, involve *quantitative* analysis of supply and demand. They deal with the *size* of the response in quantity demanded or supplied when the price changes, or some other condition changes.

ELASTICITY OF DEMAND

Responsiveness and Elasticity

Elasticity measures responsiveness to a change in conditions. The *elasticity of demand* measures responsiveness of quantity demanded to a change in price.

> The **elasticity of demand** equals the percentage change in the quantity demanded divided by the percentage change in price:
>
> $$\text{Elasticity of demand} \;=\; \frac{\text{Percentage change in quantity demanded}}{\text{Percentage change in price}}$$

Suppose that a rise in the price of pizzas from $8 to $10 leads you to reduce your purchases to two pizzas per month instead of four per month. The percentage change in the price of pizzas equals the change in price divided by the original price:

$$\text{Percentage change in price} \;=\; 100 \times \frac{(\$10 - \$8)}{\$8} \;=\; 25 \text{ percent}$$

The percentage change in your quantity demanded is:

$$\text{Percentage change in quantity demanded} \;=\; 100 \times \frac{(4 - 2)}{4} \;=\; 50 \text{ percent}$$

So your elasticity of demand for pizzas is:

$$\text{Elasticity of demand} \;=\; \frac{50 \text{ percent}}{25 \text{ percent}} \;=\; 2$$

Economists usually express the elasticity as a positive number—that is, as the absolute value of the number in the formula. This book will follow that convention. The *more responsive* quantity demanded is to price changes, the larger the elasticity of demand. For example, if your purchases were more responsive to the rise in the price of pizzas—if the price rise from $8 to $10 had led you to reduce your purchases to only one pizza per month—your quantity demanded would have fallen by 75 percent:

$$\text{Percentage change in quantity demanded} \;=\; 100 \times \frac{(4 - 1)}{4} \;=\; 75 \text{ percent}$$

so your elasticity of demand would be (75 percent)/(25 percent) = 3.

Elasticity versus Slope

Elasticity of demand describes the shape of a demand curve. But elasticity is *not* the same as slope. They differ in two ways:

1. Slope measures the rise or fall in a curve divided by its horizontal run, but elasticity measures the horizontal run divided by the rise or fall. As a demand curve becomes

Calculating Elasticities with Logarithms

The usual formula for percentage changes leads to an inconvenient result. When a variable first *rises* by 50 percent and then *falls* by 50 percent, it does not return to its original level. For example, if a price begins at $4 and then rises by 50 percent, it becomes $6. If it then falls by 50 percent, it drops from $6 to $3. This inconvenient result means that if we use the usual measure of percentage changes, the elasticity of demand differs depending on whether a price rises or falls.

For example, suppose that a 25 percent rise in the price of pizzas, from $8 to $10, leads you to buy two rather than four pizzas per month, a 50 percent change in quantity demanded. Your elasticity of demand for pizzas is (50 percent)/(25 percent) = 2. Now consider this price change in reverse. The price of pizzas *falls* from $10 to $8, a 20 percent change in price (instead of a 25 percent change). Your increase in quantity demanded from two to four pizzas per month amounts to

(continued)

steeper, its slope increases, but its elasticity decreases. A steep demand curve means that the quantity demanded does not change very much when price changes. As a demand curve becomes flatter, its slope decreases but its elasticity increases, indicating greater responsiveness of quantity demanded to a price change.

2. Elasticity is measured as a ratio of *percentages*, while slope is not.

Elasticities and Shapes of Demand Curves

Economists say that demand is *elastic* or *inelastic* depending on whether the elasticity is larger or smaller than 1.

Elastic demand means the elasticity of demand exceeds 1.

Inelastic demand means the elasticity of demand is less than 1.

When the elasticity equals 1, economists say that demand is *unit-elastic*.

Unit-elastic demand means the elasticity of demand equals 1.

Figure 1 shows examples of each case. It also shows the two extreme cases of perfectly inelastic and perfectly elastic demand curves.

A vertical demand curve is **perfectly inelastic**; its elasticity is zero.

Perfectly inelastic demand means that people want to buy the same amount of a good even if its price rises or falls (within some range).[1]

A horizontal demand curve is **perfectly elastic**; its elasticity is infinite.

Perfectly elastic demand means that the quantity demanded is *extremely* responsive to a change in price; even a small increase in price reduces quantity demanded to zero.

Explanation and Examples

Unit-Elastic Demand
Begin in the middle of Figure 1. Panel (c) shows a unit-elastic demand curve. Demand is unit-elastic if a 10 percent increase in price lowers the quantity demanded by 10 percent, so the elasticity of demand is 10/10 = 1. With unit-elastic demand, quantity demanded responds to a price change by an equal percentage amount.

Unit-elastic demand has a special property: Total spending on the good does not change when the price rises or falls. In Figure 1c, total spending stays at $160 whether the price is $8, $4, or $2. If the price is $8, the quantity demanded is 20 units, so total spending on the good equals $160. If the price is $4, quantity demanded is 40 units, so total spending again equals $160. Finally, if the price is $2, the quantity demanded is 80 units, so total spending equals $160. The change in quantity demanded exactly offsets the change in price, keeping total spending constant. (The elasticity of the demand curve

a 100 percent change in quantity demanded (instead of a 50-percent change). The formula for elasticity of demand would then give (100 percent)/(20 percent) = 5. When the price rises, the formula gives an elasticity of demand of 2, but when the price falls, it gives an elasticity of demand of 5.

Economists usually avoid this inconvenience by calculating percentage changes as:

Percentage change in price = 100 × (natural) *logarithm* of
$$\frac{\text{New price}}{\text{Old price}}$$

This equation is easy to calculate with a calculator or computer. Using the same method, the percentage change in quantity demanded is:

Percentage change in quantity demanded = 100 × (natural) *logarithm* of
$$\frac{\text{New quantity demanded}}{\text{Old quantity demanded}}$$

In the pizza example, this method says that both an increase from $10 to $12 and a decrease from $12 to $10 are changes of 18.2 percent. Both a decrease from four to two pizzas per month and an increase from two to four are changes of 69.3 percent. Therefore, this method gives the same elasticity of demand in both cases: 69.3/18.2 = 3.8.

The calculations in this chapter do *not* use logarithms, however. They use the more common method of calculating percentage change as the actual change divided by the original level.

[1]If the price rises far enough (say, to $5,000 per unit), people must buy less because they cannot afford as much as they would buy at a lower price. Consequently, the demand curve has a negative slope at some high price; demand can be perfectly inelastic only for a limited range of prices.

Figure 1 | Elasticities of Demand: Five Cases

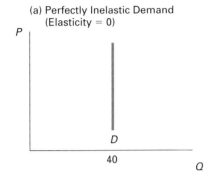

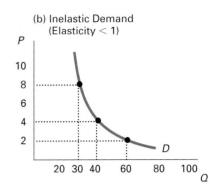

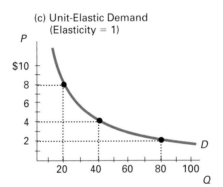

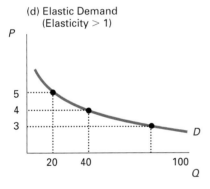

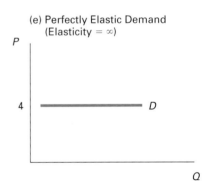

In Panel (c), note that total spending remains at $160, regardless of the price.

in Figure 1c equals 1 if you calculate the percentage changes using logarithms, as explained in the earlier box.) For example, a ski club may decide to spend $50.00 on beverages for its next party. It has a unit-elastic demand: If beverages cost $0.25 per can, the club will buy 200 cans; if the price is $0.50 per can, the club will buy 100 cans. Regardless of price, the club spends $50.00, so its demand is unit-elastic.

Unit-elastic demand plays a benchmark role: For elasticity less than 1, economists say demand is *inelastic* as in Figure 1b; for elasticity greater than 1, they say demand is *elastic* as in Figure 1d. Statistical evidence shows that demands for clothing, shoes, and electricity are roughly unit-elastic.

Inelastic Demand

If a change in price causes a smaller percentage change in quantity demanded, then demand is inelastic as in Figure 1b. For example, if a 100 percent increase in price (from $4 to $8, for example) lowers quantity demanded by only 25 percent (from 40 to 30 units), the elasticity of demand is $25/100 = 1/4$. In this case, quantity demanded is not very responsive to the price increase; people buy almost as much at the higher price as they did at the lower price. Statistical analyses find inelastic demands for water, funeral and burial services, and opera tickets.

Elastic Demand

If a change in price causes a larger percentage change in quantity demanded, then demand is elastic as in Figure 1d. For example, if a 25 percent increase in price (from $4 to $5, for example) reduces quantity demanded by 50 percent (from 40 units to 20), the elasticity of demand is $50/25 = 2$. In this case, quantity demanded is highly responsive to the price increase; people buy much less at a higher price than they would at a lower price. Statistical studies find elastic demands for Chevy trucks, ski-lift tickets, and restaurant meals.

Perfectly Inelastic and Perfectly Elastic Demand

Figure 1a shows a perfectly inelastic demand curve. It is a vertical line, showing that quantity demanded equals 40 units per month regardless of the price, within some range of prices. The elasticity equals zero because quantity demanded is totally unresponsive to the price. For example, Betsy's demand for the textbook required in her course is perfectly inelastic at prices below $75. She would buy one copy of the textbook regardless of its price (as long as the price does not exceed $75).

Figure 1e shows a perfectly elastic demand curve, which has an elasticity approaching infinity. It is a horizontal line, showing that quantity demanded is extremely (infinitely) responsive to price. Even a small change in price leads to a huge (infinite) change in quantity demanded. In other words, the quantity demanded at a price of $4.00 per unit is arbitrarily large, but the quantity demanded at even a slightly higher price, such as $4.01 per unit, is zero. The demand curve is horizontal at the $4.00 price. For example, Barney has a farm. He can sell as much wheat as he can grow at a price of $4.00 per bushel, but if he tries to charge more than $4.00, no one buys from him. (Instead, buyers get wheat from one of the other 2 million U.S. farmers or from farmers in other countries.) At prices above $4.00 per bushel, the quantity demanded of wheat from Barney's farm is zero. The demand for his wheat is perfectly elastic at the price of $4.00 per bushel.

A 1998 study on the demand for cigarettes by teenagers found that a 10 percent increase in the price of cigarettes from about $2.00 to $2.20 per pack would reduce purchases by teenagers by only about one-half of one percent. This result indicates that the teenage demand for cigarettes is inelastic, with an elasticity of only about 1/20.

Spending and Elasticity

When demand is unit-elastic, changes in quantity demanded offset changes in price to maintain constant total spending on the good. More generally, elasticity of demand shows how much total spending rises or falls when the price changes.

As Chapter 4 explained, total spending on a good (its price per unit multiplied by the quantity purchased) appears as the area of a rectangle in a supply-demand graph. The base of the rectangle is the number of units that people buy, and its height is the price per unit, so the area of the rectangle shows total spending on the good. In Figure 2a, supply is initially S_1, the price is $5, and the quantity purchased is 100 units per month. Total spending on the good is $500, the sum of the areas of Rectangles A and C.

The demand curve in Figure 2a is inelastic. When supply increases to S_2, the equilibrium price falls to $2 and the equilibrium quantity rises to 160 units. Total spending on the good is then $320, the sum of the areas of Rectangles B and C. With inelastic demand, an increase in supply lowers the price and reduces total spending.

> If demand is inelastic, buyers spend more on the good when its price is high and less when its price is low.

The demand curve in Figure 2b is elastic. When supply increases to S_2, the equilibrium price falls only to $4 and the equilibrium quantity rises to 240 units. Total

Figure 2 | Total Spending and the Shape of the Demand Curve

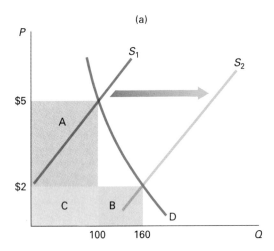

(a)

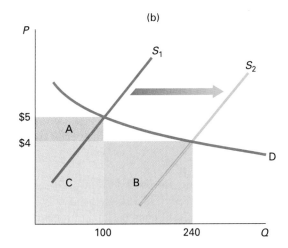

(b)

When supply is S_1, total spending on the good is the area of Rectangles A and C. The height of the total rectangle A + C shows the price that buyers pay for each unit, and its base shows the number of units they buy, so the sum of Areas A + C shows total spending on the good. In Panel (a), the steep demand curve indicates inelastic demand, and an increase in supply reduces total spending on the good from Area A + C to Area B + C. In Panel (b), the flat demand curve indicates elastic demand, and an increase in supply raises total spending on the good from Area A + C to Area B + C.

spending on the good is then $960, the sum of the areas of Rectangles B and C. With elastic demand, an increase in supply lowers the price and raises total spending.

> If demand is elastic, buyers spend less on the good when its price is high and more when its price is low.

Three Factors That Affect Elasticity of Demand

Three main factors affect elasticities of demand: the availability of substitutes, the fraction of their incomes that people spend on the good, and adjustment time.

Availability of Substitutes

Goods with close substitutes tend to have more elastic demands. If the price increases, buyers can easily switch to other products, making quantity demanded highly responsive to price (more elastic).

Goods with*out* close substitutes tend to have more *in*elastic demands. If the price increases, buyers cannot easily switch to other products, making quantity demanded fairly unresponsive to price (more inelastic).

Generally, narrower categories of goods have better substitutes and more elastic demands. People can usually find better substitutes for a narrowly defined good, such as chocolate fudge ice cream, than for a broadly defined good, such as food. Substitutes for chocolate fudge ice cream include other flavors of ice cream and other types of desserts. There are fewer substitutes for a more broadly defined good such as *food*. (There are *some* substitutes for food; after obtaining enough calories for survival, some people substitute chewing gum, smoking, and social activities for food.) Overall, the demand for chocolate fudge ice cream is more elastic than the demand for ice cream, which is more elastic than the demand for desserts, which is more elastic than the demand for food.

These two goods are substitutes. An increase in the price of one causes buyers to switch to the other.

Fraction of Income Spent on the Good

Demand tends to be more elastic for goods on which people spend larger fractions of their incomes. Chapter 4 mentioned two separate logical reasons for the law of demand. First, when the price of a good rises, buyers can replace that good with other goods. Second, a price increase reduces the amount that people can afford to buy, given the limitations of their budgets. (Figure 2 in Chapter 3 illustrated that limitation.) The second reason gains importance for goods on which people spend larger fractions of their incomes.

For example, doubling the price of salt would have only a small effect on your overall budget. You might buy less salt, but your response would likely be smaller than if the price of clothes doubled. You spend a larger fraction of your income on clothes than on salt, so a rise in the price of clothes tends to reduce your quantity of clothes demanded by more than a rise in the price of salt reduce your quantity of salt demanded. Stated another way, the demand for clothes tends to be more responsive to a price change—more elastic—than is the demand for salt.

Adjustment Time

Demand is more elastic when people have more time available to adjust to a change in price. When the price of heating oil rises, people with oil-burning furnaces turn back their thermostats to try to conserve on oil purchases in the short run. As time passes and they have more time to adjust, they may add insulation to their houses or replace oil-burning furnaces with gas-burning models, further reducing their quantities of oil demanded. As the time available for such adjustments expands, the responsiveness of quantity demanded grows. The demand becomes increasingly elastic as time passes.

Application to Disney Videos

The introduction to this chapter noted that the Walt Disney Company restricts output of videotapes of its classic animated films. Disney believes that additional sales of its videos would reduce their prices by enough to reduce total profits. This would happen if demand for the videotapes is inelastic, because an increase in supply would reduce total spending. If Disney were to boost its sales of videos, it would then lose profits in two ways: Total spending on the videos would fall, and Disney's costs would rise (since it would pay to produce more copies of the videotapes). With inelastic demand, Disney gains by selling fewer videos at higher prices, rather than more at lower prices.

IN THE NEWS

Everybody's getting pumped up for the holiday weekend—in spite of the price of gasoline.

That's not surprising to Craig Wakefield, a tourism marketing analyst for the state Bureau of Business Research and Statistics in Albany.

He said there is no reason to expect a decrease in travel because of the jump in the cost of fuel. "The increase is really not extraordinary. On a 500-mile trip, we're talking an extra $2.50 to $3.00. Is that a big deal?"

Source: Rochester Democrat and Chronicle

The demand for gasoline is inelastic, partly because most people spend small fractions of their incomes on it.

Review Questions

1. What is the formula for elasticity of demand?

2. How does elasticity of demand differ from the slope of the demand curve?

3. Draw elastic and inelastic demand curves and explain why they indicate different responses of buyers to a change in price. Draw perfectly elastic and perfectly inelastic demand curves and explain what they indicate about the behavior of buyers.

4. How is elasticity of demand related to total spending on a good?

5. What three main factors affect elasticity of demand? How and why?

Thinking Exercises

6. (a) If a 20 percent rise in the price of Frisbees reduces the quantity of Frisbees demanded by 10 percent, what is the elasticity of demand for Frisbees? (b) If a 10 percent fall in the price of pizzas reduces the quantity demanded by 30 percent, what is the elasticity of demand for pizzas?

7. (a) If the elasticity of demand for tortilla chips is 2, by how much would quantity demanded fall if the price were to rise by 10 percent? (b) If the elasticity of demand for virtual pets is 1/2, how much would the price have to increase to reduce quantity demanded by 10 percent?

8. Which is likely to have more *elastic* demand: Orange juice or fruit juice? College education or winter scarves?

ELASTICITY OF SUPPLY

Just as elasticity of demand measures responsiveness of quantity demanded to a change in price, the elasticity of supply measures the responsiveness of quantity supplied.

> The **elasticity of supply** is the percentage change in the quantity supplied divided by the percentage change in price:
>
> $$\text{Elasticity of supply} \quad = \quad \frac{\text{Percentage change in quantity supplied}}{\text{Percentage change in price}}$$

The elasticity of supply is usually positive because an increase in price usually raises the quantity supplied of a good. (Supply curves usually slope upward.) The definitions of other terms resemble those for elasticity of demand:

> Supply is **unit-elastic** if the elasticity of supply equals 1.

> Supply is **elastic** if the elasticity of supply exceeds 1.

> Supply is **inelastic** if the elasticity of supply is less than 1.

> A horizontal supply curve is **perfectly elastic:** its elasticity is infinite.

> A vertical supply curve is **perfectly inelastic:** its elasticity is zero.

Figure 3 shows a variety of supply curves with different elasticities. Panel (c) shows a unit-elastic supply curve; doubling the price from $4 to $8 doubles the quantity supplied from 40 to 80 units. Panel (b) shows an inelastic supply curve; a 100 percent increase in price (from $4 to $8) causes a smaller, 25 percent change in quantity supplied (from 40 to 50 units per month). Panel (d) shows an elastic supply curve; a 25 percent increase in price (from $4 to $5) causes a larger, 100 percent change in quantity supplied (from 40 to 80 units per month).

Panels (a) and (e) show perfectly inelastic (vertical) and perfectly elastic (horizontal) supply curves. A perfectly inelastic supply curve represents situation in which sellers offer a fixed quantity of a good for sale. In Panel (a), the quantity supplied is 40 units per month regardless of the price. The quantity supplied is totally unresponsive to price changes. In Panel (e), the quantity supplied is arbitrarily large at the price $4.00 per unit. However, at even a slightly lower price, such as $3.99, the quantity supplied is zero. The supply curve is horizontal at the price $4.00. With perfectly elastic supply, the quantity supplied is extremely (infinitely) responsive to a change in price.

Figure 3 | Elasticities of Supply: Five Cases

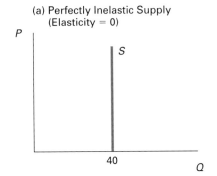

(a) Perfectly Inelastic Supply
(Elasticity = 0)

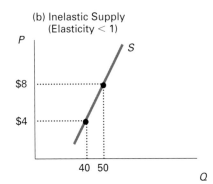

(b) Inelastic Supply
(Elasticity < 1)

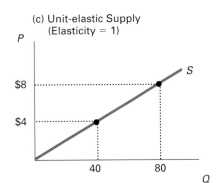

(c) Unit-elastic Supply
(Elasticity = 1)

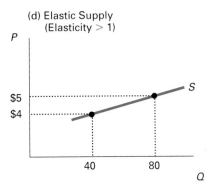

(d) Elastic Supply
(Elasticity > 1)

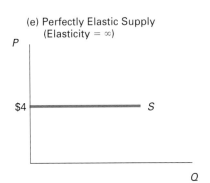

(e) Perfectly Elastic Supply
(Elasticity = ∞)

The supply of hotel rooms in a city is perfectly inelastic in the short run. (In the long run, hotels could expand and new hotels could open.) Similarly, in the short run, the supply of seats in a theater or on a bus is perfectly inelastic.

The supplies of *most* goods are perfectly elastic to *you,* or to any other *individual* buyer. That is what it means for a buyer to be a price-taker (as discussed in the first section of Chapter 4). The supply of coffee at Parisian cafes is perfectly elastic; a cafe will sell you as many cups as you want to buy for a few French francs per cup, but no cafe will sell coffee for less. Market supply curves for some goods, such as T-shirts, cookies, and light bulbs, are perfectly elastic in the *long run* (defined later in this chapter).

Two Factors That Affect Elasticity of Supply

Two main factors affect a good's elasticity of supply: the cost of producing additional units and adjustment time.

Cost of Producing Additional Units of a Good

If an increase in production of a good would require a large jump in costs, then that good's supply tends to have inelastic supply. For example, production of new land along a beach would entail a very high cost (to expand a lake or build a peninsula), so the supply of beachfront property is inelastic. In contrast, low costs of producing additional copies of videotapes, compact discs, or computer software make their supplies elastic.

Adjustment Time

An increase in the time available to adjust to a change in price raises the elasticity of supply. Production takes time. Companies spend months to build factories and offices. A forest takes 60 years to grow the trees used to make wooden baseball bats. Building new houses and apartments takes time, as does training new doctors and computer scientists. The elasticity of supply increases as suppliers have more time to adjust to any change in the price.

CHANGES IN DEMAND OR SUPPLY

Elasticities of demand and supply play important roles in determining how changes in demand and supply affect equilibrium. Recall that an increase in demand (or supply) means a rightward shift in the demand (or supply) curve.

> With perfectly elastic demand, an increase (or decrease) in demand means that the demand curve shifts upward (or downward).

Figure 4 shows an increase in demand when it is perfectly elastic. To understand why the demand curve shifts upward, draw a demand curve that is almost (but not quite) perfectly elastic. An increase in demand, which shifts any demand curve to the right, also shifts it upward. In the extreme case of perfectly elastic demand, it shifts *only* upward, indicating that buyers are willing to pay higher prices than before. Similarly, a decrease in demand means that the demand curve shifts downward, as in Figure 5.

Figure 6 shows an increase in supply when it is perfectly elastic. To understand why the supply curve shifts downward, draw a supply curve that is almost (but not quite) perfectly elastic. When that curve shifts to the right, it also shifts downward. In the extreme case of perfectly elastic supply, the curve shifts *only* downward indicating that sellers are willing to accept lower prices than before. Similarly, a decrease in supply means that the supply curve shifts upward, as in Figure 7.

> With perfectly elastic supply, an increase (or decrease) in supply means that the supply curve shifts downward (or upward).

Figure 4
Increase in Perfectly Elastic Demand

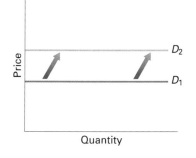

Elasticity and Changes in Equilibrium

Figures 8 and 9 show the effect on equilibrium of changes in demand and supply curves when one of the curves is perfectly inelastic. In each case, the old equilibrium occurs at Point A and the new equilibrium occurs at Point B. With perfectly inelastic demand, Figure 8 shows that an increase in supply reduces the equilibrium price without changing the equilibrium quantity bought and sold. The quantity remains the same, because buyers are totally unresponsive to a price change; they buy the same amount of the good regardless of its price. Similarly, with perfectly inelastic supply, as in Figure 9, an increase in demand raises the equilibrium price without affecting the equilibrium quantity, again because the quantity supplied is completely unresponsive to a price change. When one of the curves is perfectly inelastic, changes in the other curve do not affect the quantity traded.

Figure 5
Decrease in Perfectly Elastic Demand

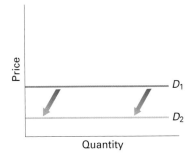

Figure 6
Increase in Perfectly Elastic Supply

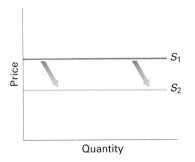

Figure 7
Decrease in Perfectly Elastic Supply

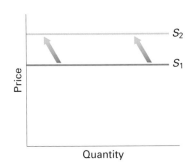

Figure 10 shows that with perfectly elastic demand, an increase in supply raises the equilibrium quantity without affecting the equilibrium price. Similarly, Figure 11 shows that with perfectly elastic supply, an increase in demand raises the equilibrium quantity, but not the equilibrium price. When one of the curves is perfectly elastic, changes in the other curve do not affect the equilibrium price.

The Drugs-and-Crime Example Revisited

Let's return to the example of the government's fight against illegal drugs. Suppose that crime rises and falls with total spending on drugs. A government program that reduces the supply of drugs increases crime (and spending on drugs) if users have inelastic demand for drugs; the program decreases crime if users have elastic demand for drugs. It leaves crime unchanged if the demand for drugs is unit-elastic.

Figure 8
Increase in Supply with Perfectly Inelastic Demand

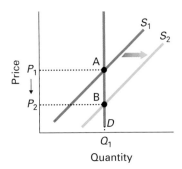

With perfectly inelastic demand, an increase in supply lowers the price from P_1 to P_2, but the quantity remains unchanged at Q_1.

Figure 9
Increase in Demand with Perfectly Inelastic Supply

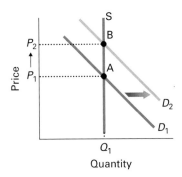

With perfectly inelastic supply, an increase in demand raises the price from P_1 to P_2, but the quantity remains unchanged at Q_1.

Figure 10
Increase in Supply with Perfectly Elastic Demand

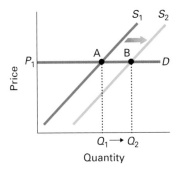

With perfectly elastic demand, an increase in supply raises the quantity from Q_1 to Q_2, but the price remains unchanged at P_1.

Figure 11
Increase in Demand with Perfectly Elastic Supply

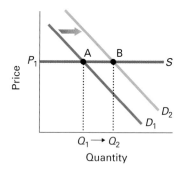

With perfectly elastic supply, an increase in demand raises the quantity from Q_1 to Q_2, but the price remains unchanged at P_1.

Statistical studies show that the elasticity of demand differs across cities. One study found inelastic demand for heroin in Detroit, so a fall in supply would raise total spending on heroin there. Another study found elastic demand for heroin in New York City, so a fall in the supply there would reduce total spending on heroin, and perhaps crime, as well. (An effective government program to reduce the *demand* for drugs would reduce spending on drugs regardless of elasticities.)

Review Questions

9. What is the formula for the elasticity of supply?

10. What two main factors affect elasticity of supply?

11. Draw perfectly elastic and inelastic supply curves and explain what they indicate about the behavior of sellers.

12. Draw graphs to show the effects on equilibrium of: (a) an increase in perfectly elastic supply; (b) an increase in perfectly elastic demand.

Thinking Exercises

13. Suppose that sellers have a perfectly elastic supply of bricks. What happens to the price of bricks and the quantity sold if the demand for bricks increases?

14. Suppose that buyers have a perfectly inelastic demand for combs. What happens to the price and quantity sold if the supply of combs increases?

15. How does an increase in the supply of computers affect total spending on computers if demand is elastic? What if demand were inelastic?

OTHER ELASTICITIES

The discussion so far has focused on the responsiveness of quantities demanded and supplied to changes in a good's price. Sometimes, however, economists want to know how much quantity demanded responds to changes in other conditions, such as buyers' incomes or prices of related goods. For example,

> How much more ice cream would you buy if your income were to rise by 10 percent?

> How much more would you buy if the price of cookies were to increase by 10 percent?

The first question involves responsiveness of quantity demanded to a change in income. The second involves responsiveness to a change in the price of a related good (a substitute or complement).

> **Income elasticity of demand** is the percentage change in quantity demanded divided by the percentage change in income.

> A **cross-price elasticity of demand (or supply)** is the percentage change in the quantity demanded (or supplied) divided by the percentage change in the price of a related good.

Income Elasticities of Demand

Restaurant meals	2.0
Newspapers	0.4
Potatoes	−0.1

Making Smart Decisions

A modern grocery store applies elasticities of demand every day in pricing decisions. Before deciding to put grapes "on sale," managers consider (from past experience) the elasticity of demand for grapes and try to predict how much more or less revenue the store will earn by lowering the price. They also calculate the cross-price elasticity between the demand for oranges and the price of grapes to predict how sales of oranges will change due to the special on grapes.

Store managers also realize that buyers often respond differently to temporary price changes than to permanent ones. (If you know that the price of soda is temporarily low, you may buy enough to last for months while you have the chance to buy it at a low price. If you know the price change is permanent, you have less incentive to buy a large amount now.) For this reason, modern grocers estimate separate elasticities for temporary and permanent price changes to aid their planning. Many other businesses also use data from their own experience—as well as data from associated stores or from stores willing to sell this kind of information—to improve their daily business decisions.

An increase in buyers' incomes raises demand for normal goods, and lowers demand for inferior goods. The income elasticity of demand measures the size of that response. An increase in the price of Cheerios may lead people to buy Wheaties and Corn Flakes instead. Cross-price elasticities of demand measure the sizes of those responses. If a 10 percent increase in the price of Cheerios leads people to buy 5 percent more Wheaties, then the cross-price elasticity of demand is (5 percent)/(10 percent) = ½.

SHORT-RUN AND LONG-RUN DEMAND AND SUPPLY

As an earlier section explained, demand becomes increasingly elastic as the time expands for people to adjust to a change in price. When the price of gasoline rises, the quantity of gasoline demanded immediately falls, and then it falls still further as people have time to get rid of cars with low fuel efficiency and buy higher-mileage cars. Economists call this a *long-run response* of demand.

> **Long run** means "after people have fully adjusted to a change."

Notice that *long run* does not refer to a specific period of time, like 2 years or 10 years; the time people need to adjust to changes varies from case to case. The term *long run* refers to the situation after all adjustments occur, regardless of calendar time.

> The **long-run demand** curve graphs the relation between the price of a good and quantity demanded after buyers have fully adjusted to a price change.

Figure 12a shows an example. From 1973 to 1974, the price of gasoline rose from 30 cents to 44 cents per gallon. (Adjusted for inflation, this corresponds to a rise from $1.00 to $1.35 per gallon today.) At first, people bought only slightly less gasoline than before. Many people owned big cars with poor gas mileage, and they could use less gasoline only by driving less. The short-run equilibrium moved from Point A to Point B along the short-run demand for gasoline, $D_{Short\ Run}$. Eventually, people began using more public transportation, walking or bicycling, carpooling, and vacationing closer to home.

In the long run, people will adopt other means of transportation in response to an increase in the price of gasoline.

As months and years passed, people bought cars with better gas mileage than before, further reducing their quantity of gasoline demanded. The increase in adjustment time increased the elasticity of demand; the demand curve *rotated* (around its original Point A) from $D_{\text{Short Run}}$ to $D_{\text{Long Run}}$.

Figure 12b shows that the decrease in supply from S_1 to S_2 moved the short-run equilibrium from Point A in 1973 to Point B in 1974. The price rose from 30 cents to 44 cents per gallon, and the equilibrium quantity fell 7 percent, from Q_0 to Q_1. In the

(a) When the price of a gallon of gasoline rose from 30¢ in 1973 to 44¢ in 1974, people immediately reduced their purchases of gasoline, moving from Point A to Point B along the short-run demand curve. As the adjustment time increased, people bought increasingly fuel-efficient cars and adjusted their habits in other ways. As a result, the long-run demand curve is more elastic than the short-run demand curve. (b) A fall in supply from S_1 to S_2 moved the short-run equilibrium from Point A to Point B. The price rose 47 percent from 30¢ to 44¢, and quantity sold fell 7 percent, from Q_0 to Q_1. As time passed, people adjusted to the higher price, moving the equilibrium from Point B to Point C. The price and the quantity sold both fell to a *long-run equilibrium* at Point C. The long-run effect of the decrease in supply was a 30 percent rise in the price from 30¢ to 39¢, and a 21 percent drop in the quantity sold. Notice that the price rose more in the short run than in the long run.

Figure 12 | Short-Run and Long-Run Equilibrium

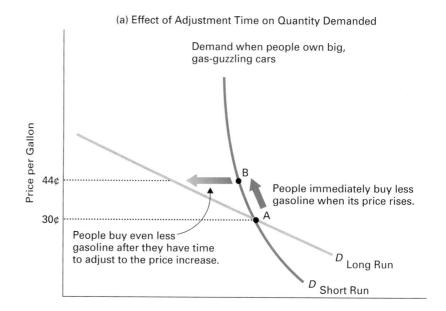

(a) Effect of Adjustment Time on Quantity Demanded

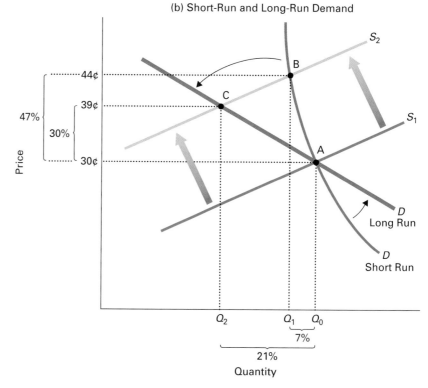

(b) Short-Run and Long-Run Demand

Table 1 | Some Short-Run and Long-Run Elasticities of Demand

Good	Elasticity of Demand	
	Short Run	Long Run
Food	About 0.0	0.7
Theater and opera tickets	0.2	0.3
Gasoline	0.2	1.0
Toilet articles	0.2	3.0
Child care outside the home	0.3	0.8
Jewelry and watches	0.4	0.7
Radio and television repair	0.5	3.8
Movies	0.9	3.7
China, glassware, and utensils	1.5	2.5

long run, after people had time to adjust, the equilibrium moved from Point B to Point C, where the *long-run* demand curve intersects the supply curve.[2] The price fell from 44 cents to 39 cents per gallon, and the quantity sold fell further to Q_2, 21 percent below Q_0. Notice that the short-run price response exceeds the long-run response.

Short-Run and Long-Run Elasticities of Demand

You can calculate long-run elasticities of demand just as you calculate short-run elasticities. Figure 12b shows that the price of gasoline rose 47 percent from 1973 to 1974, and the quantity demanded fell 7 percent (from Q_0 to Q_1). Accordingly, the short-run elasticity of gasoline demand was (7 percent)/(47 percent) = 0.15. The figure also shows that the price of gasoline rose 30 percent (from 30 cents to 39 cents per gallon) in the long run, and quantity demanded fell 21 percent (from Q_0 to Q_2). The long-run elasticity of gasoline demand was (21 percent)/(30 percent) = 0.70. Table 1 shows some short-run and long-run elasticities of demand.

Long-Run Supply

Many goods take time to produce, so a price increase has a larger effect on quantity supplied after producers have had time to adjust by expanding factories and hiring more workers than in the short run, when limited production capacity restricts quantity. Long-run supply curves show what happens after people complete these adjustments.

> The **long-run supply** curve graphs the relation between the price of a good and its quantity supplied after sellers have fully adjusted to a price change.

Long-run supply is more elastic than short-run supply. For example, the short-run supply of apartments in a city, at one point in time, may be almost perfectly inelastic as in Figure 13, but the long-run supply of apartments (after landlords have time to construct new buildings) may be very elastic, as in Figure 14. Many goods, such as pencils, videotapes, and pizzas, have perfectly elastic long-run supplies. When the per-unit cost of producing a good does not depend on the amount produced, that good has perfectly elastic long-run supply.

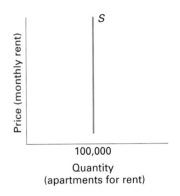

Figure 13
Short-Run Supply of Apartments

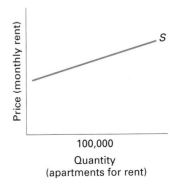

Figure 14
Long-Run Supply of Apartments

[2]To keep matters simple, consider S_1 and S_2 to be both short-run and long-run supply curves.

USING ELASTICITIES

IN THE NEWS

Dry days: Heat, drought hurt many farmers, firms; but others are helped

Some crops wither, but gain in prices raises profits
Farm Prices Up

The increase in prices at the farm level, coupled with the varying severity of the drought itself, is likely to result in big gains and big losses to individual farmers. Farmers in states such as Illinois and Iowa, where the heat hasn't been so deadly, and farmers with irrigation will gain handsomely.

Says Robert Kadrmas, a Dickinson, N. Dak., farmer who will lose thousands of dollars this year when he plows under 90 percent of his wheat crop: "I guess some farmers are really benefiting at the expense of others. There are attractive prices out there, but I don't have anything to sell."

Source: The Wall Street Journal

A drought creates both winners and losers.

Basic Calculations

When supply changes (the supply curve shifts), the elasticity of *demand* determines the responses of the equilibrium price and quantity. The equilibrium point *moves along* the demand curve, as in Figure 2. Given any two of the terms in the equation for the elasticity of demand,

$$\text{Elasticity of demand} \quad = \quad \frac{\text{Percentage change in quantity demanded}}{\text{Percentage change in price}}$$

you can find the third term. For example, if you operate a catering business and the elasticity of demand for your services is 2, then raising your price by 20 percent will reduce your sales by 2×20 percent $= 40$ percent. Similarly, if the elasticity of demand for sneakers is $\frac{1}{3}$ and an increase in supply raises the equilibrium quantity by 5 percent, then the price of sneakers falls by

$$\frac{5 \text{ percent}}{\frac{1}{3}} \quad = \quad 15 \text{ percent}$$

When demand changes, the elasticity of *supply* determines the responses of the equilibrium price and quantity. The equilibrium point *moves along* the supply curve. Again, given any two of the terms in the equation for the elasticity of supply,

$$\text{Elasticity of supply} \quad = \quad \frac{\text{Percentage change in quantity supplied}}{\text{Percentage change in price}}$$

you can find the third term. For example, if the elasticity of supply of golf balls is 4, then an increase in demand that raises golf ball purchases by 40 percent must raise the price by (40 percent)/4 $= 10$ percent. Business firms use calculations like these in their planning.

Application: Effects of a Drought

Suppose that a drought in the United States reduces the supply of wheat from American farms, leaving foreign farms unaffected. Because wheat trades on world markets, its equilibrium price is determined by total world supply and demand as in Figure 15. That figure shows three graphs that represent the supply of wheat from U.S. farmers, the supply from foreign farmers, and the world (market) supply of wheat.[3] The figure assumes a perfectly inelastic supply of wheat from farms in each country. The graph on the right also shows the world (market) demand for wheat. The world equilibrium occurs at Point A, with a price of $3 per bushel and world production of 400 bushels per month (the sum of American and foreign production).

When a drought reduces supply by American farmers by 100 bushels per month from S_1^{US} to S_2^{US}, the world market supply falls by 100 units per month from S_1^{W} to S_2^{W}. The new equilibrium occurs at Point B. The world price of wheat rises from $3 to $4, and world output falls from 400 to 300 bushels.

Foreign farmers sell as much wheat as before at a higher price, so the drought helps them. American farmers also sell wheat at a higher price, but they have less to sell. This example assumes unit-elastic world market demand for wheat, so total spending on wheat

---

[3]Adding the American and foreign supplies gives the world market supply; see Chapter 4.

Figure 15 | Effect of a U.S. Drought on the World Wheat Market

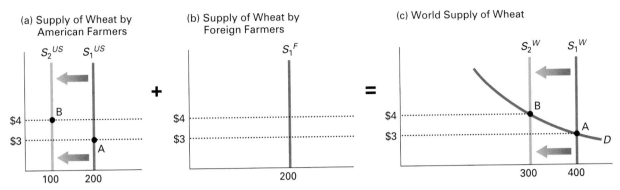

A drought in the United States lowers the U.S. supply to S_2^{US}, which lowers the world market supply to S_2^W. The original world equilibrium at Point A gives way to the new world equilibrium at Point B, so the price of wheat rises from $3 to $4 per bushel. American farmers sold 200 bushels at $3 per bushel before the drought. After the drought, they sell 100 bushels at $4 per bushel. Foreign farmers, who sell their 200 bushels at the higher price, gain from the American drought. American farmers lose unless demand is sufficiently inelastic. In this example, American farmers lose.

remains unchanged at $1,200 when supply changes. Before the drought, American farms sold 200 bushels for $3 each, earning $600. After the drought, they sell 100 bushels for $4 each, so they earn only $400. American farms lose $200 from the drought.

American farmers would gain from the drought if world demand were sufficiently inelastic. For example, if the elasticity of demand for wheat were ⅛, then the 25 percent fall in world supply from 400 to 300 bushels per year would raise the price by (25 percent)/(⅛) = 200 percent, from $3 to $9. After the drought, American farms would sell 100 bushels for $9 each, earning $900, which is $300 more than they earned before the drought. So whether American farms gain or lose from the drought depends on the elasticity of demand.

Similar analysis applies to other effects of a drought. Grains such as wheat are inputs into production of other goods, such as breakfast cereals, salad dressings, pet foods, beer, and rat poison. Higher grain prices reduce the supplies of those products and raise their prices. Economists estimate the sizes of these effects using elasticities of demand and supply.

Review Questions

16. What is the formula for income elasticity of demand?

17. What is the long run?

18. What does a long-run demand curve show?

19. Why is long-run supply more elastic than short-run supply?

Thinking Exercises

20. If a 10 percent increase in income raises the demand for airline tickets by 30 percent, what is the income elasticity of demand for airline tickets?

21. If a 30 percent fall in the price of DVD players lowers the quantity demanded of conventional CD players by 60 percent, what is the cross-price elasticity of demand?

22. (a) How does a 20 percent fall in the price of software affect the quantity demanded if the elasticity of demand is 2?

    (b) An increase in the supply of doughnuts raises the quantity sold by 30 percent. If the elasticity of demand is 2, what happens to the price of doughnuts?

    (c) An increase in the demand for a computer game raises the quantity sold by 50 percent. If the elasticity of supply is 5, what happens to the price?

Conclusion

Elasticity of Demand

Elasticity measures responsiveness to a change in conditions. The elasticity of demand (or supply) measures responsiveness of quantity demanded (or supplied) to a change in price. It describes the shape of a demand (or supply) curve.

The elasticity of demand (or supply) equals the percentage change in quantity demanded (or supplied) divided by the percentage change in price. Elasticity differs from the slope of the curve.

Elastic demand (or supply) means that the elasticity exceeds 1. Inelastic demand (or supply) means that the elasticity is less than 1. When the elasticity equals 1, demand (or supply) is unit-elastic. A vertical demand or supply curve is perfectly inelastic (with an elasticity equal to zero). A horizontal demand or supply curve is perfectly elastic (with an infinite elasticity).

With unit-elastic demand, a change in price does not affect total spending on the good. Total spending remains constant because changes in quantity demanded offset changes in price. A price increase raises spending on a good if its demand is inelastic and lowers spending if its demand is elastic.

Three main factors affect elasticities of demand. Goods with close substitutes tend to have relatively elastic demands. Demand tends to be relatively elastic for goods on which people spend large fractions of their incomes. Demand becomes more elastic as people have more time to adjust to a change in price.

Elasticity of Supply

Two main factors affect elasticities of supply. If an increase in production of a good would require a large jump in costs, then its supply tends to be inelastic. If the cost of producing another unit of a good is similar to the cost of producing previous units, then supply tends to be elastic. Supply is also more elastic when producers have more time available to adjust to a change in price.

Changes in Demand or Supply

With perfectly elastic demand, an increase in demand shifts the demand curve upward, and a decrease in demand shifts it downward. With perfectly elastic supply, an increase in supply shifts the supply curve downward and a decrease in supply shifts it upward. When either demand or supply is perfectly inelastic, changes in the other curve do not affect the quantity traded. When either demand or supply is perfectly elastic, changes in the other curve do not affect the equilibrium price.

Other Elasticities

Income elasticity of demand measures the responsiveness of quantity demanded to a change in income. A cross-price elasticity of demand measures responsiveness to a change in the price of a related good (a substitute or complement). Income elasticity of demand equals the percentage increase in quantity demanded divided by the percentage change in income. A cross-price elasticity of demand equals the percentage increase in quantity demanded divided by the percentage change in the price of a related good.

Short-Run and Long-Run Demand and Supply

The long-run response to a change refers to the response after people have fully adjusted to the new situation. The term *long run* refers to the new situation after all adjustments are complete, not to a specific period of calendar time. A long-run demand (or supply) curve graphs the relation between the price of a good and quantity demanded (or supplied) after buyers (or sellers) have fully adjusted to a price change. Long-run demand and supply are more elastic than short-run demand and supply.

Using Elasticities

When supply changes (the supply curve shifts), the elasticity of demand determines the responses of equilibrium price and quantity (as the equilibrium moves along the demand curve). When demand changes (the demand curve shifts), the elasticity of supply determines the responses of equilibrium price and quantity (as the equilibrium moves along the supply curve).

Key Terms

elasticity of demand (or supply)

inelastic demand (or supply)

elastic demand (or supply)

unit elastic demand (or supply)

perfectly inelastic demand (or supply)

perfectly elastic demand (or supply)

income elasticity of demand

cross-price elasticity of demand (or supply)

long-run

long-run demand (or supply)

Problems

23. **(a)** If the elasticity of demand for ice cream were ½, how much would quantity demanded fall if a decrease in supply raised the price by 10 percent?
    (b) If the income elasticity of demand for steak were 2, how much would the quantity demanded increase if buyers' incomes rose by 10 percent?

24. Which is likely to have a higher elasticity of demand:
    (a) Ice cream or chocolate ice cream?
    (b) Haircuts, or haircuts at the local Hair We Are outlet?

25. Your club is raising money by holding a car wash. If the elasticity of demand for your car wash is 3, by what percentage would quantity demanded rise if you were to reduce the price by 30 percent? Would your club earn more money or less?

26. Comment on this statement: "Toothpaste is a necessity. Everyone has to brush his or her teeth, so the demand for toothpaste must be perfectly inelastic."

27. Suppose that the elasticity of world market demand for wheat in Figure 15 were ¼ (rather than 1). Do American farmers gain or lose if a drought reduces their wheat supply (while leaving foreign supply unaffected)?

28. A walnut tree takes over 50 years to grow to a size at which it can provide a profitable harvest. The demand for wood from walnut trees has increased in recent years, causing the price of this wood to rise 20 percent. Use supply-and-demand analysis to show the effect of an increase in demand for walnut on its price and quantity sold in the short run and the long run.

29. Apply the elasticity formulas to answer these questions:
    (a) An increase in demand for carrots raises the equilibrium quantity sold by 30 percent. If the elasticity of demand for carrots is 2 and the elasticity of supply is 3, how much does the price of carrots increase?
    (b) An increase in the supply of cellular phones reduces their price by 20 percent. If the elasticity of demand for cellular phones is 2 and the elasticity of supply is 1, how much do sales of cellular phones increase?

30. **(a)** If the demand for a firm's product were inelastic, would a price increase raise or lower company profits?
    (b) If the demand for a firm's product were elastic, would a price increase raise or lower profits? What other information would you need to answer this question?

31. What information would you need about elasticity of demand in order to decide whether a college would gain or lose total revenue if it raised scholarships?

Inquiries for Further Thought

32. How would you try to measure the elasticity of demand for a good, such as pizzas or automobiles?

33. How can business firms use information about the elasticities of demand for their products?

Appendix: Elasticities and Slopes

The quantity demanded Q^d is a function of the price, so:

$$Q^d = f(P)$$

where P is the price. The function f describes the demand curve; an increase in the price P reduces the quantity demanded Q^d. Letting Δ denote a change, and $\%\Delta$ a percentage change, the elasticity of demand is:

$$\text{Elasticity} \quad = \quad \frac{\%\Delta Q^d}{\%\Delta P} \quad = \quad \frac{\Delta Q^d \times P^d}{\Delta P Q}$$

The slope differs from the elasticity. The slope of a demand curve is:

$$\text{Slope} \quad = \quad \frac{\Delta P}{\Delta Q^d}$$

PART 3

APPLICATIONS OF SUPPLY AND DEMAND

CHAPTER 6

APPLIED PRICE THEORY

In this Chapter . . .

Main Points to Understand

- ▶ Economic analysis gives insight into a variety of issues such as: government spending and borrowing, government farm policies, time costs, bribes, social pressures, lifestyles, crime, risk and safety, and the value of life.
- ▶ Government demand (or borrowing) affects private purchases (or borrowing).
- ▶ The cost of buying a good can differ from its price, and this cost can affect demand.
- ▶ Expected values affect decisions and equilibrium prices in situations involving chance.

Thinking Skills to Develop

- ▶ Distinguish changes in conditions that shift demand curves *horizontally* by given amounts from changes that shift demand curves *vertically* by given amounts, and understand the sizes of the shifts.
- ▶ Predict market responses to changes in underlying conditions.
- ▶ Apply the concepts of demand and supply to *chance events* (such as the risk of an accident).

Economic analysis applies to a wide range of subjects beyond buying and selling ordinary goods such as food, energy, and household products. Economic concepts give insight into health and safety, crime and punishment, marriage and divorce, family size and population growth, the legal system, fashions, and social norms.

This chapter will help you to develop thinking skills by working through these applications. Four sets of applications appear in this chapter. The first set involves changes in conditions that shift demand curves *horizontally* by certain distances. The second set of applications involves changes in conditions that shift demand curves *vertically* by certain distances. The third set of applications relates the supply-demand model to *chance events*. Finally, the fourth set of applications shows how to extend further the range of applications of economic analysis.

Each section of this chapter is independent of the others, so readers can cover them separately. Questions that follow each section pertain only to it. More difficult questions at the end of the chapter ask you to apply economic analysis to a few additional topics.

IN THE NEWS

Contractors must shrink with budgets

By David Craig
USA TODAY

The industry's problems can also be measured in human terms. McDonnell Douglas, which makes F-15 and F/A-18 fighter jets, slashed its workforce 17,000, to 118,000 people last year—a 13 percent cut that is high even in this period of staff reductions in all industries. Northrop has slashed its workforce 5,300, to 36,000—also a 13 percent cut. Grumman Corp., maker of the Navy's F-14 Tomcat and A-6E fighter jets, said in April that it will cut up to 1,900 of 25,600 jobs—a 7 percent decline.

Source: USA Today

A fall in government demand for defense products hurts their producers.

GOVERNMENT DEMAND OR SUPPLY

The first two sections of this chapter distinguish demand by the private sector of the economy from total market demand. Chapter 4 explained that market demand is the sum of all buyers' individual demands. When the government is one of the buyers, its demand is part of the market demand.

> **Private demand** refers to demand by the private sector, that is, people and businesses not owned or operated by the government.

> **Market demand** for a good refers to the sum of government demand and private demand.

Because government demand is one part of market demand, the direct effect of a change in government demand is to change market demand by the same amount. For example, a 100-unit increase in government demand for a good raises its market demand by 100 units. Sometimes a change in government demand also has *indirect* effects that change this answer, though. The next two sections, on Government Spending and Borrowing and Government Farm Policies, discuss these issues.

GOVERNMENT SPENDING AND BORROWING

Government spending on a good affects its price, its total production, and the amount that the private sector buys. Increases in government demand for a good drive up its price and reduce private purchases; decreases in government demand drive down a good's price and raise private purchases. The discussion here focuses on a fall in government demand; a problem at the end of this section asks you to discuss an increase in government demand.

Figure 1 shows the private demand, government demand, and market demand for airplanes.[1] Private demand includes purchases by airline companies, other business firms,

---

[1]The graph shows a perfectly inelastic government demand for planes to simplify the discussion. Readers can show that the same reasoning applies in the more realistic case.

Figure 1 | Decrease in Government Demand for Airplanes

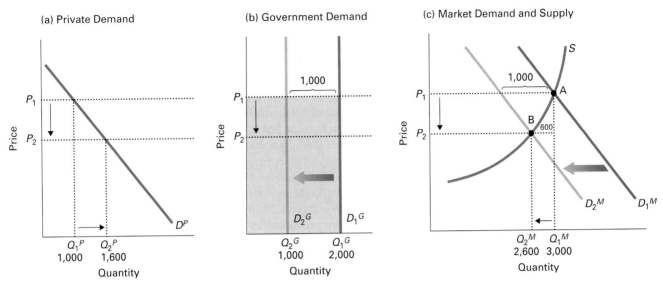

(a) When the price is P_1, the private sector buys Q_1^P planes. When the price falls, the private sector buys more. (b) A fall in government demand causes market demand to fall. (c) When demand is D_1^M, equilibrium occurs at Point A. When demand falls to D_2^M, the equilibrium moves to Point B, and both the price and the quantity traded fall.

and individuals. Figure 1c also shows the market supply curve for planes, labeled S. At the equilibrium (Point A in Panel c), the market demand and supply curves intersect. The equilibrium price is P_1 and the equilibrium quantity produced and sold is Q_1^M. (This analysis ignores differences among airplanes. A more sophisticated analysis allowing different types of airplanes would apply similar reasoning to reach similar conclusions.)

The graph in Figure 1a shows that the private sector buys Q_1^P planes (because the price is P_1). Figure 1b shows that the government buys Q_1^G planes. The area of the shaded rectangle shows government spending on planes. Total purchases of planes, Q_1^M, equal private purchases plus government purchases.

A Fall in Government Demand

If government demand for planes falls from D_1^G to D_2^G, market demand falls *by the same amount*—from D_1^M to D_2^M. The *horizontal distance* that the market demand curve shifts equals the decrease in government demand.

Point B marks the new equilibrium. Total production of planes falls from Q_1^M to Q_2^M planes and the price falls from P_1 to P_2. The private sector now buys more planes than before (Q_2^P rather than Q_1^P planes), as shown in Panel (a), because the price has fallen. Total production of planes falls by *less* than the decrease in government purchases because the private sector buys more.

EXAMPLE

Originally, the price is P_1 and 3,000 planes are sold each year; the private sector buys 1,000 and the government buys 2,000. The government then reduces its demand by 1,000 planes, so the market demand for planes decreases by 1,000. (The market demand curve shifts to the left by 1,000 planes.) Production of planes falls by 400, from 3,000 to 2,600 planes per year. The government buys 1,000 fewer planes, but the private sector buys 600 more because the price is lower.

Resource Allocation

When one buyer buys less, does the economy cut production, or does the amount available for other buyers increase? As Figure 1 shows, both results occur. When the government buys less of a product, output of that good typically falls. But output does not decline by as much as the fall in government purchases, so more of the good is available for other buyers. Similarly, when the government raises its demand for a product, the economy typically raises production *and* other buyers reduce purchases.

The economy provides the additional goods purchased by the government in two ways: Production increases, and other people reduce their purchases. Elasticities of supply and demand determine the extent to which each method operates. With perfectly elastic supply, the increase in demand raises output of the product without reducing the amount purchased by other buyers. With perfectly inelastic supply, the increase in demand reduces the amount purchased by other buyers without changing output of the product. Generally, more elastic supply and more inelastic private demand mean that a rise in government demand for a product has a larger effect on its output and a smaller effect on the amount that the private sector buys.

Taxes

The government spends money that it gets from taxes, borrowing, or printing money. The next section discusses the first two possibilities. First, suppose that the government increases spending on roads and bridges, raising taxes to pay for the new spending.

The increase in government spending raises the demands for concrete, steel, and other materials. The increase in taxes, however, leaves people and businesses with less after-tax income or profits than they had before, so people and businesses reduce their spending. This decreases the demands for other goods.

If the tax increase causes people to reduce spending on new clothes and vacations, then the demands for clothes and vacations fall. Therefore, increased government spending financed by a tax increase raises the demands for some goods and lowers the demands for others.

> An increase in government spending financed by a tax increase raises demands for the goods that the government buys and lowers demands for the goods on which people reduce spending to pay the additional taxes.

Government Budget Deficits

The government can also borrow money to pay for new spending. The amount of money the government borrows is the government budget deficit.

> The **government budget deficit** is the amount of money that the government borrows each year when it spends more than it collects in taxes.

Changes in government borrowing affect the interest rate by changing the market demand for loans, similar to the way changes in government purchases of planes changes the market demand for planes.

Demand and Supply of Loans

Figure 2 shows the supply and demand for loans. Lenders (such as banks) supply loans by lending the money that people save. Borrowers demand loans. The interest rate is the

IN THE NEWS

Big deficit cut could sharply reduce rates

Credit markets

By Constance Mitchell
Staff Reporter of The Wall
Street Journal

"The deficit is costing us significantly in terms of long-term interest rates," says David Wyss, an economist at Data Resources Inc., a Boston economic consulting firm. Allen Sinai, chief economist at Boston Co., agrees.

Source: The Wall Street Journal

Data Resources, Boston Co., and WEFA Group in Bala Cynwyd, Pa.—three of the nation's leading economic consultants—each plugged hypothetical deficit cuts into the computer models they use to predict the behavior of the U.S. economy. All came to similar conclusions:

If the government cut the federal deficit by $100 billion, they say, the yield on the benchmark 30-year Treasury bond, now at 7.3 percent, would fall to between 6.4 percent and 6.6 percent.

As the U.S. government budget deficit fell in recent years, the government borrowed less, reducing the demand for loans and the interest rate.

price of a loan (per dollar loaned). The supply curve of loans slopes upward—an increase in the interest rate raises the incentive to lend money. The demand curve for loans slopes downward—a rise in the interest rate reduces the incentive to borrow.

Government Borrowing Raises the Demand for Loans

An increase in the government budget deficit raises the demand for loans, as Figure 3 shows. The demand curve D_1 shows the private demand for loans. If the government budget deficit is zero, then D_1 is also the market demand curve for loans. In this case, equilibrium occurs at Point A with an interest rate of i_1 and Q_1 dollars borrowed and lent each year.

Figure 2 | Demand and Supply for Loans

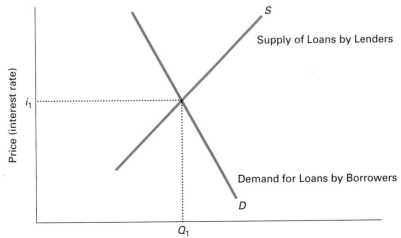

Some people save money and lend it to others (or put it in a bank account, in which case the bank lends it). These people supply loans. Other people, business firms, and governments borrow money. They demand loans. The supply and demand for loans determine the equilibrium interest rate i_1.

A $100 billion increase in government borrowing raises the demand for loans by $100 billion. This raises the interest rate from i_1 to i_2. It also raises total lending from Q_1 to Q_2 and lowers private-sector borrowing from Q_1 to Q_0.

Figure 3 | Increase in Government Borrowing Crowds Out Private Borrowing and Raises the Interest Rate

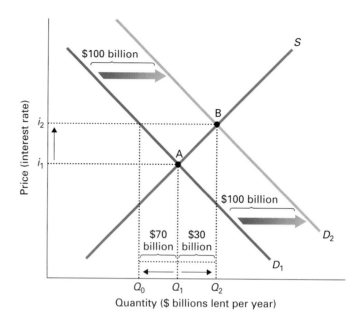

Now suppose the government budget deficit rises to $100 billion per year. This raises the market demand for loans, so the market demand curve shifts to the right by $100 billion. The new equilibrium occurs at Point B. The interest rate rises from i_1 to i_2 and total lending rises from Q_1 to Q_2. This rise in total lending is *less* than the $100 billion increase in government borrowing, because the private sector reduces borrowing from Q_1 to Q_0. For example, total lending might rise by $30 billion, and total private borrowing might fall by $70 billion. The original demand curve D_1 continues to show the private demand for loans, so the rise in the interest rate reduces the private sector's quantity demanded from Q_1 to Q_0. In this sense, government borrowing *crowds out* (reduces) private borrowing. Each dollar of government borrowing crowds out less than a dollar of private borrowing, however, because the rise in the interest rate increases total lending. In other words, the government can borrow more in one of two ways: Lenders can increase their lending, or the private sector can restrict its borrowing. In equilibrium, both occur in a combination determined by the elasticities of the supply of loans and private demand for loans.

Other Consequences

The government budget deficit has other consequences, as well. The decrease in private borrowing reduces the demands for houses, cars, vacations, and other goods that people would have bought with borrowed money. As a result, equilibrium outputs of those goods decline. The deficit also reduces the demands for new equipment that business firms would have bought with borrowed money, reducing equilibrium outputs of these goods as well.

Of course, a rise in the government budget deficit can result from either of two causes:

1. An increase in government spending (which raises demands for the goods the government buys)

2. A decrease in taxes (which leaves taxpayers with more money to spend than before and raises demands for the goods they buy)

An increase in the government budget deficit reduces demands for some goods and raises demands for others. Output falls in some parts of the economy and rises in other parts.

The deficit also reduces future *supplies* of many goods, because businesses that restrict equipment purchases today will have less equipment available for future production than they would have had without the deficit. As a result, the deficit reduces the economy's future output.

Review Question

1. Define (a) private demand; (b) government budget deficit.

Thinking Exercises

2. **(a)** Draw graphs similar to Figure 1 to show the effects of an increase in government spending on computers. How would this affect total production of computers and the number bought by the private sector? (Ignore the effects of rising taxes or government borrowing to pay for the increase in spending.)
   (b) How would your answer to Exercise 2a change if the supply of computers were perfectly elastic? Perfectly inelastic?
   (c) How is your answer to Exercise 2a affected by the elasticity of private demand for computers?

3. Draw graphs to show the effects of an increase in government spending financed by an increase in taxes, assuming that the government spends the money on schools and that the rise in taxes leads people to eat at restaurants less often.

4. Suppose that the government raises its budget deficit through a tax cut of $100 per person without a reduction in spending. Suppose that people use *all* their extra money from the tax cut to buy video games. What are the effects on:
   (a) The interest rate
   (b) Borrowing by the private sector
   (c) Prices and output of video games

Inquiries for Further Thought

5. (*More difficult*) Repeat Exercise 3, but assume that people pay the tax increase by reducing their *saving* rather than reducing their spending at restaurants. How does this affect the interest rate and the quantity of loans? (*Hint:* A fall in savings reduces the amount of money available for banks to lend, so it lowers the supply of loans.)

6. (*More difficult*) The government raises its budget deficit by cutting taxes by $100 per person without reducing its spending. (The government borrows the money to avoid changing its spending.)
   (a) How does this increase in the deficit affect the demand for loans? How far does the demand curve shift?
   (b) Assume that people save all the extra money that they get from the tax cut. (They put all this money into bank accounts.) Also assume that banks want to lend this money. Show how this increase in saving affects the supply of loans.
   (c) Combine Questions 6a and 6b. How does the tax cut affect the interest rate?

Governments all over the world run programs to change the prices of farm products. Governments of most developed countries try to keep prices of farm products high; governments of some less developed countries do the opposite.

GOVERNMENT FARM POLICIES

U.S. Government Policies That Affect Demand

The U.S. government buys many farm products to help keep their prices high. This program began to make large quantity purchases during the Great Depression of the 1930s. The Agricultural Adjustment Act of 1933 authorized the government to buy wheat, cotton, corn, dairy products, and other farm products to raise their prices. Sometimes the government stored the goods it bought, and sometimes it disposed of the goods in other ways. For example, the government bought and slaughtered pigs to reduce the total supply of pork.

The U.S. government keeps milk prices high by choosing a *support price* and then buying as much milk as dairy farmers want to sell at that price. The U.S. government typically buys a billion pounds of milk each year in an effort to keep milk prices high and help dairy farmers maintain their incomes, although they do so at the expense of consumers and taxpayers.

Figure 4 shows the private demand, government demand, and market demand for milk. The government's demand for milk is *perfectly elastic* at the support price, as in Panel (b). Therefore, the market demand curve in Panel (c) becomes perfectly elastic when it reaches the support price (in this example, $10.10 per hundred pounds of milk). The equilibrium occurs at Point A with an equilibrium price of $10.10 and an equilibrium quantity of Q_1^M. Panel (a) shows that the private sector buys Q_1^P milk at the support price, and the government buys the rest (Q_1^G). If the government did not buy milk, the price of milk would be lower and the private sector would buy more.

Occasionally the government buys so many farm products that it fills its storage facilities; then it either pays farmers to store more, or it destroys, sells, or gives away some of the goods. Selling those goods, of course, raises their supplies and lowers their prices.

U.S. Government Policies That Affect Supply

The U.S. government also started programs during the 1930s to limit supplies of farm products as a way to keep their prices high. The government paid farmers to destroy crops they had already planted and to slaughter young pigs and pregnant sows. These

IN THE NEWS

Continued fall in wheat prices is tied to U.S. program to reduce stockpiles

In November, the department launched a Friday wheat auction as part of its campaign to reduce a huge government-owned stockpile. While the long-term goal of the program is to boost prices by eliminating excess stockpiles, the infusions of government grain into the market depress prices.

Source: The Wall Street Journal

When the government sells a good that it has held in storage, the increased supply lowers the good's price.

Figure 4 | Government Price Supports

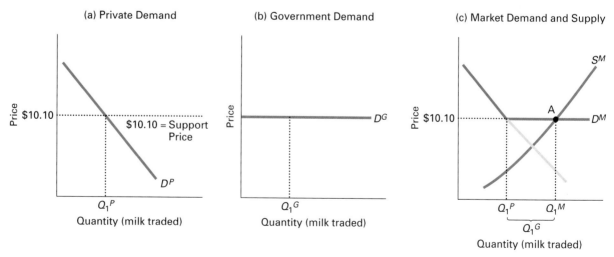

(a) At a price of $10.10 per hundredweight, the private sector buys Q_1^P milk. (b) The government's demand for milk is perfectly elastic at the support price of $10.10. (c) At the support price, dairy farmers supply Q_1^M milk. The private sector buys Q_1^P, and the government buys the rest (Q_1^G). Without the price support, the equilibrium price would be lower.

IN THE NEWS

U.S. program leads to rises in dairy prices

By Albert R. Karr
Staff Reporter of The Wall
Street Journal

To trim the oversupply of dairy products, the government pays farmers to sell milk-cow herds for slaughter.

Source: The Wall Street Journal

Also, throughout the U.S. dairy farmers now are assessed 52 cents a hundredweight for milk they sell—to help the government pay for the slaughter program.

While dairy products will cost more, the govern-

ment won't have to spend so much to buy surplus dairy products. "You will pay at your Safeway store instead of on your IRS form," says John Ford, a Washington, D.C., agricultural consultant.

Another program seeks to reduce the supply of milk and raise its price.

---

programs reduced supplies of farm products such as pork and raised their prices. The government also began paying farmers not to plant crops on part of their land.

Cotton output fell 20 percent when these programs began. The programs reduced supplies by less than they reduced total acreage planted, however, because farmers naturally chose to stop producing on their least productive land, while they kept farming their most productive land. Farmers also increased their yields per acre in other ways, such as increasing their use of fertilizer. When farmers began collecting money to reduce wheat production, they planted rice or soybeans instead (raising supplies of those products and reducing their prices). The government responded by changing the program to pay farmers to reduce the *total* acreage they planted for all crops. In recent decades, such programs have removed about 50 million acres of farmland from production—about one-sixth of all U.S. farmland. Other government programs also keep farm prices high—for example, government marketing orders sometimes prohibit California farmers from selling all their fresh oranges. If demand for oranges is inelastic, such an order raises the price of oranges enough that total spending on oranges increases, benefiting the farmers.

Advice
You can find more information on government farm programs, and most other topics in this book on the World Wide Web. (See www.dryden.com).

Thinking Exercises

7. Draw a graph to show the effects on the prices of farm products when government programs pay farmers to reduce output.

8. Draw a graph like Figure 4 to show why the price of milk would fall if the government were to eliminate its price-support program.

Inquiries for Further Thought

9. **(a)** The government says that one purpose of its farm policies is to help small, family farms. Argue for or against the government continuing these programs.
   (b) Do you think the government should offer similar programs to help other small, family run businesses? (It could pay motel owners not to rent all their rooms and pay grocers not to sell all their food.) What would be the effects?
   (c) Why do you think the government maintains farm-support programs but not similar programs for most other industries?

COSTS OF BUYING GOODS MAY DIFFER FROM PRICES

Sometimes the cost of buying a good includes more than its money price. When you must spend time to buy something, the total cost of the good equals its price plus the cost of your time. You may suffer social disapproval if you buy a certain good, so its total cost equals its price plus the cost of suffering social disapproval. In some countries and circumstances, people must pay bribes for opportunities to buy certain goods. Then the total costs of the goods equal their prices plus the bribery costs. The next sections of this chapter examine these issues. Earlier discussion showed why a 100-unit increase in government demand shifts the market demand curve *horizontally* to the right by 100 units. Now we will find that a $5 increase in time costs, costs of social pressures, and costs of bribes shifts the demand curve *vertically* downward by $5. First, we need to understand why the costs that buyers are *willing* to pay for a good determine the height of its demand curve.

Willingness to Pay

Would you be willing to pay 25 cents for your favorite beverage right now? What about 50 cents, $1, or $5? What is the highest price that you would be willing to pay, if you had to, to buy it? That highest price is your *reservation price:*

> The highest price that you would be willing to pay for a good, if necessary, rather than do without the good, is your **reservation price** for the good.

A buyer's reservation price measures his willingness to pay for a good. It does not say anything about the equilibrium price that buyers actually pay for it.

A person buys a good if her reservation price exceeds the cost of buying it, but not if her reservation price is less than the cost of the good. For example, you might be willing to pay $3, but not more than that, for something to drink. Beverages may sell for 75 cents each. Then your reservation price of $3 exceeds the 75-cent cost of buying the

**Figure 5
Height of Demand
Curve Shows
Reservation Prices**

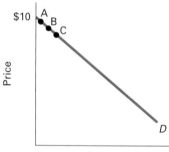

One buyer is willing to pay up to $10 for a unit of this good. A second buyer is willing to pay up to $9.98 for a unit of this good. A third buyer is willing to pay up to $9.95 for a unit of this good. Other buyers have lower reservation prices.

Buyers think about their reservation prices.

beverage, so you will buy it. If your reservation price were only 50 cents per beverage, less than its cost, you would not buy it.

Demand curves show reservation prices:

The height of a demand curve shows buyers' reservation prices.

The demand curve shows the highest prices that buyers would pay, *if they had to,* for each unit of the good. Figure 5 shows that one buyer has a reservation price of $10.00—he would be willing to pay up to $10.00, if necessary, to buy a unit of the good. Another buyer has a reservation price of $9.98; still others have lower reservation prices. The height of the demand curve shows these reservation prices, going from the highest reservation price to lower reservation prices as we move downward along the demand curve.

TIME COSTS AND MONEY PRICES

You spend both time and money to buy goods. You must travel to a store, find or choose what you want, pay for it, and go home. You also spend time using some of the goods you buy; you may have to assemble or prepare a good, read an instruction manual, or spend time in other ways learning how to use it. You spend time to watch a movie, get a haircut, or cook a meal and clean the kitchen.

You pay two kinds of prices for many goods: a money price that you pay at the store, and a time cost to buy, prepare, and enjoy the good.

The **time cost** of a good is the time required to buy, prepare, and use it.

Television shows, parties, and home-cooked meals have high time costs; fast food and home-delivered pizza have low time costs.

Time is valuable. Its opportunity cost is the extra income you could earn by working or by studying more (which could raise your future income), or the benefits you could enjoy from additional leisure time. The value of your time changes as your opportunities change; your time is probably more valuable during the week before final exams than during the week after exams end.

We can measure a time cost in units of time or its dollar value. Suppose that you attend a concert one evening when you could have worked for 3 hours instead, earning $5 per hour. Your time cost of the concert is $15 because you could earn $15 in the time you spend there; the value of your time is $5 per hour. Your money price of the concert is the price of your ticket, say $20, so the total cost you pay for the concert is $35. (If you have the evening off from work, the opportunity cost of your time might be less than $5 per hour; you could measure it by the value of what you would have done if you had not gone to the concert.)

Time Costs and Changes in Demand

A change in the value of time changes the demands for goods with high time costs, such as parties and movies. The demand for movies rises on weekends and during school vacations, when the value of time falls. The Chicago Cubs abandoned a long tradition and began playing baseball on weeknights because the demand for night games is higher than the demand for day games, when many people work.

When the cost of buying a good includes a money price *and* a time price, buyers usually care only about the total cost, not the separate money price and time cost. For example, four students rent an apartment near campus. They pay $300 per month in rent plus a monthly utilities fee of $50. They care only about their total cost of $350 per month, not its division into rent and the utilities fee. They would not care if the rent increased to $320 and the utilities fee decreased to $30, as long as the total remained at $350 per month. Similar logic applies to money and time prices.

Figure 6 shows the demand and supply for haircuts. Suppose that all buyers value their time at $8 per hour and that the time cost of a haircut is 30 minutes. Then the value of the time cost is $4 per haircut. When the demand curve is D_1, the equilibrium *money price* of a haircut is $10, so the *total* cost of a haircut (the money price *plus* the time cost) is $10 + $4 = $14. Buyers care about the $14 cost of a haircut, not the separate $10 and $4 costs.

Now suppose that technology improves, reducing the time cost by half. A haircut now takes only 15 minutes instead of 30 minutes. Buyers save 15 minutes in time, which they value at $2 (because each hour is worth $8). This $2 fall in the time cost shifts the demand curve upward (vertically) by $2. The new demand curve, D_2, is $2 above the old demand curve, D_1. Buyers are willing to pay $2 more for the good, because they pay $2 less in time cost. The equilibrium moves from Point A to Point B in Figure 6. The equilibrium money price rises by less than $2, from $10 to $11, so the total cost of haircuts falls by $1, from $14 ($10 money price plus $4 time cost) to $13 ($11 money price plus $2 time cost).

Equilibrium with Different Types of Buyers

Sometimes buyers can choose either high time costs with low money prices, or low time costs with high money prices. Convenience stores charge higher money prices than large grocery stores do, but many buyers still shop at convenience stores to reduce their time costs. Similarly, you can reduce your time cost of clothes by shopping at a store with a good selection of styles and sizes. The money price of clothes is often lower at a discount store than at a regular department store with a good selection, but the time cost is usually higher at a discount store. Buyers can choose whether to save time and pay higher money prices, or spend more time and pay lower money prices. The choice

Figure 6 | Effects of a Decrease in a Time Price

If the time cost of haircuts falls by $2, the demand curve shifts vertically by $2, and equilibrium moves from Point A to Point B. The money price of haircuts rises by an amount less than $2; it may rise by $1, from $10 to $11. The total price of haircuts, including the money and time costs, falls.

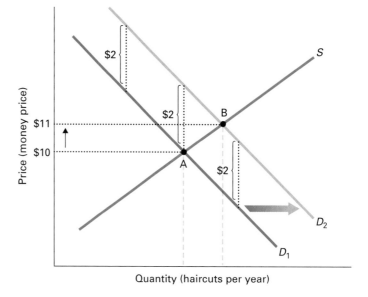

Quantity (haircuts per year)

depends on the value of a buyer's time at the moment. When a major university recently installed condom vending machines in dormitory bathrooms, some students complained that the machines charged a money price five times higher than the prices at pharmacies. Nevertheless, some students bought from the vending machines because the time cost was lower.

Figure 7 shows the demand and supply for a good at two types of stores: fast-service stores and slow-service stores. (It doesn't matter here why some stores provide faster service than others.) The demand curve at the fast-service stores is D^F; the demand curve at the slow-service stores is D^S. The equilibrium price is $25 at the fast-service stores and only $21 at the slow-service stores. If buyers must spend 20 minutes longer to buy the good at the slow stores, then those who value their time higher than $12 an hour go to the fast stores, and those who value their time lower than $12 an hour go to the slow stores. (The $12 an hour figure equals $4 for 20 minutes, the extra shopping time required at the slow stores.) People who value their time at exactly $12 an hour don't care where they shop; the money price is $4 lower at the slow stores, but the time cost is $4 higher there.

People with high time values are generally willing to pay high money prices to save time. High-wage people use money-saving coupons less frequently than do people with low wages. Apartments and houses at convenient locations cost more than comparable apartments and houses at less convenient locations; people with high values of time willingly pay higher rents to live at the convenient locations.

Buying Time

You can think of time as a good that people buy. People buy extra time when they spend money for time-saving goods or services. Microwave ovens, frozen dinners, and automatic dishwashers save time in meal preparation and cleanup. You can hire people to mow your lawn, clean your house, prepare your meals, and even help you find appropriate friends or romantic partners.

Figure 7 | Buyers' Different Time Prices

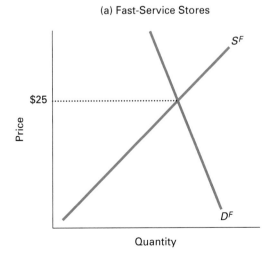
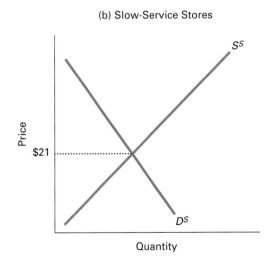

Goods might cost $4 more at fast stores, where shopping takes 20 minutes less than at slow stores. People with time values above $12 per hour shop at fast stores, and people with time values less than $12 per hour shop at slow stores.

SOCIAL AND ECONOMIC ISSUES

Demand for Sleep

Sleep has a high time cost. If you sleep 8 hours a night, you spend one-third of your lifetime asleep. Some evidence indicates that people reduce their sleep as the value of their time rises. Holding wealth fixed, a 20 percent increase in wages reduces sleep by about 1 percent. This relationship implies that a person who earns $40 an hour sleeps about half an hour less each night than a similar person who earns $10 an hour, but who has the same level of wealth, perhaps from an inheritance. (People employed full time work about 2,000 hours each year, so $10 an hour is about $20,000 per year.)

Evidence shows that employed people sleep about 1 hour less each night than unemployed people do. Increases in wealth also raise the demand for sleep, holding wages fixed. As a result, despite higher average wages, people in rich countries sleep more than people in poor countries.

Thinking Exercises

10. A local cafe adds a $1 "cleaning fee" to the $2 price of each beverage, so the total cost of a beverage is $3.
    (a) Draw a demand curve for beverages at the cafe, and show the quantity demanded at the $2 price.
    (b) Show how the demand curve changes if the cafe eliminates the cleaning fee.
    (c) Suppose the cafe eliminates the cleaning fee but raises the price of a beverage to $3. How many beverages will it sell? Will it sell more or fewer beverages than it sold when it charged a $2 price and a $1 cleaning fee?

11. Patrons can reach the Island Restaurant only by boat. The round trip used to take 1 hour, but now it takes only 40 minutes. Draw a graph to show how this change affects the demand for meals at the Island Restaurant if all potential diners value their time at $12 per hour.

12. Figure 7 assumes that buyers spend 20 minutes longer at slow-service stores than at fast-service stores. Suppose that slow stores improve their service so that now buyers must spend only 10 minutes longer there. Show on a graph how this change affects the equilibrium in Figure 7.

Inquiries for Further Thought

13. If you could save 15 minutes a day, every day, how much extra time would you gain each year? How much would you be willing to pay for this time? What good could you buy that would save you 15 minutes in an average day? How much would it cost?
    (a) What is the value of your time? Does its value differ in the morning, afternoon, and evening? Do you expect its value to rise after you finish college? How much? Why?
    (b) How long would you wait in line to save $10? How does your answer depend on what you can do while you wait in line?

14. Suppose that a business firm could save time for its customers by reorganizing the store, opening more checkout lines, or in some other way. Does the firm have an incentive to make the change? What factors affect the decision?

Bribery

A payola scandal rocked the popular-music industry in the 1950s, when record companies bribed disk jockeys to play their records. (The record companies hoped that the increased exposure would raise the demands for their records.) Bribes are a common part of business in some countries; sellers often obtain permits and licenses partly by bribing officials. Rumors circulate about bribery, particularly in certain occupations and cities where police and other local officials (such as health-and-safety inspectors) may ignore violations in exchange for bribes. In a burst of candor a few years ago, one politician complained that many friends who had contributed money to a successful presidential campaign "hadn't gotten anything" (such as government contracts and appointments) in return for their campaign contributions. Bribing ushers gets people better seats at theaters and ball games. Travel writers often accept free airfare, hotel stays, and meals in return for writing favorably about resorts, airlines, hotels, or restaurants. The so-called *casting couch* was once (and may still be) a feature of Hollywood movie-making.

Supply-and-demand analysis can reveal the effects of bribes on equilibrium prices and quantities. The opportunity to collect bribes is a partial substitute for formal wage payments. The total payment for a job includes bribes, so an increase in expected bribes within an occupation raises the supply of labor to that occupation. This increase in the supply of labor reduces the formal wage.

Bribes add to the total salaries in some occupations, just as paying time costs adds to the total costs of certain goods. Changes in bribery income affect supply curves just as changes in time prices affect demand curves. Figure 8 shows the supply and demand for disk-jockey services. The price axis measures the wage that radio stations pay disk jockeys. At equilibrium (Point A), disk jockeys earn a wage of W_1 per week.

When record companies begin paying bribes, disk jockeys get two kinds of income: wages and bribes. The supply of disk jockeys increases, and the supply curve moves downward (vertically) by the average weekly bribe. The equilibrium moves from Point A to Point B, and the formal wage for disk jockeys falls from W_1 to W_2. This fall in the wage is smaller than the average bribe, so disk jockeys earn higher total pay (including

IN THE NEWS

Clean, not laundered

BERLIN — Corruption is common because the rusty machinery of international business calls out for lubrication. Corruption's beneficiaries are rich-country companies and officials of third-world—and, increasingly, East European—governments. The International Chamber of Commerce has had rules against bribery and extortion since 1977, but most people ignore them. America's antibribery law is more effective, though it is hardly fool-proof.

Still, most of the anti-corruption drive has been directed at senior officials. Many say the biggest problem is at lower levels.

"They're probably too scared to attack it at the bottom because people don't make a living wage," said one shipping official. "So it's accepted that this subsidizes their income. But whenever it's accepted, it opens a Pandora's box, with the benefit to the smarter ones."

Source: The Economist and *Journal of Commerce*

Bribes are common in some places.

IN THE NEWS

Bye-bye to bribes

The industrial world takes aim at official corruption

By Thomas Omestad

A Kenyan newspaper cartoon depicts a man meeting St. Peter at heaven's gate and offering *kitu kidogo*—"something small" in Swahili—for a spot inside. In Kenya, the cartoon implies, bribing officials is so much a part of life that it may even transcend death. But bribes are just as common in dozens of other nations around the world. Chinese pay *huilu*, and Russians rely on *vzyaztka*. In the Middle East, palms are greased with *baksheesh*, while a bribe in Mexico is simply *una mordida*—"a bite."

As ancient as it is ubiquitous, official corruption has been casually accepted as an inescapable fact of life as far back as the time of the Pharoahs. But now passive acceptance of graft is finally giving way to hostility and action. This week in Paris, the industrialized nations are signing a treaty that criminalizes payoffs to foreign officials.

Source: U.S. News & World Report

When bribery becomes illegal, only criminals will pay bribes.

Bribery is common in many parts of the world, despite laws against it.

Figure 8 | Effects of Bribing Disk Jockeys

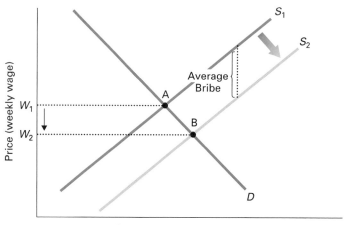

Quantity (disk-jockey services)

When bribery begins, the supply of disk-jockey services increases, shifting the supply curve downward (vertically), by the size of the bribes. The formal wage falls from W_1 to W_2, but this fall in the wage is smaller than the average bribe.

bribes) than they earned before. Honest disk jockeys who refuse to accept bribes earn lower incomes than before, however, so they may look for jobs in other professions.

Social Pressures

Some people feel social pressure not to buy certain products, such as the wrong kinds of sneakers or cars. Buying some goods (cigarettes, drugs, pornography, or the wrong clothes) can expose buyers to criticism and social ostracism. A buyer's total cost of those goods equals the sum of the money and nonmoney costs created by that social pressure. People who are more sensitive than others to these social pressures (criticism or ostracism) pay higher total costs than other people pay if they buy those goods.

Figure 9 | Increase in Social Pressure

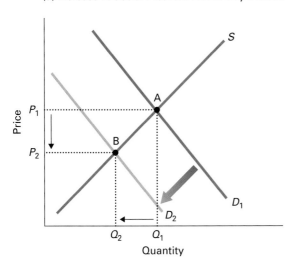

(a) Increase in Social Pressure Not to Buy a Good

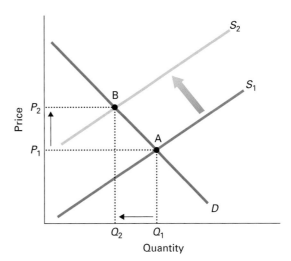

(b) Increase in Social Pressure Not to Sell a Good

An increase in social pressure not to buy a good raises the nonmoney price that buyers pay, decreasing their demand for the good. An increase in social pressure not to sell a good raises the nonmoney price that sellers pay when they sell the good, reducing their supply of it.

An increase in social pressure against buying a good raises its nonmoney cost and reduces demand for it. Figure 9a shows the effects of an increase in social pressure not to buy a good: Demand falls from D_1 to D_2, reducing the good's equilibrium price and quantity sold. Likewise, Figure 9b shows the effects of an increase in social pressure not to sell a good: Supply falls from S_1 to S_2, which raises the money price of the good and reduces the quantity sold. An increase in social pressure not to buy or sell a good reduces both supply and demand. The quantity sold falls and the money price rises or falls depending on whether social pressure has a larger effect on supply or demand.

Thinking Exercises

15. Draw graphs to show the effects on money prices and quantities sold when:
    (a) Social pressure to buy a good (such as a certain kind of sneakers) increases
    (b) Social pressure to sell a good (such as environmentally friendly soap) increases

16. Police officers in a major city obtain one-third of their income in the form of bribes until the government begins strict enforcement of anti-bribery laws. How does this new government policy affect the equilibrium salaries of police officers?

17. A dishonest university president plans to grant one pizza vendor the right to sell pizzas in the new student activities building. Many pizza vendors have offered bribes to the president in return for that right. What factors will determine the equilibrium size of the winning bribe?

18. Suppose that someone who works several years for a government regulatory agency can expect to land a lucrative consulting job in later years with the industry that the agency regulates. How does this opportunity affect the supply of people to government regulatory jobs?

19. Some sports stars earn extra income by making television commercials. Explain how this opportunity affects average salaries in sports.

IN THE NEWS

For better Mets seats, pay an usher

By H. Eric Semler

Paying ushers for better seats is a time-honored practice at many ball parks around the country. But at Shea, it has evolved into a tightly organized and accepted ritual in the last few years, say stadium guards, ushers, and dozens of spectators.

Aware that many season-ticket holders will not show up at games, at least a dozen ushers in the field-level and loge sections, the two lowest levels, openly and aggressively try to sell the empty seats to wandering spectators, sometimes called "floppers."

Working in teams, the ushers share their finder's fees. Many command payments as high as $50 a seat at the most popular games, said some ushers, who said they were not involved in such deals. To get into the stadium, the floppers have to pay at least $6 for a ticket.

When a reporter was asked to show his ticket stub to a field-level usher at a game between the Mets and Cubs June 15, he was told to "come back and see me if you want a better view."

"What will it cost?" the reporter asked.

"Ten or 15 bucks," the usher said.

The Mets organization, which employs about 140 ushers for each game, said such hustling is only a minor problem at Shea.

Ushers working on the upper deck at Shea said their colleagues on the field level sometimes earn more than $200.00 in extra payments during a game. The Mets pay each usher $37.50 a game.

It is Mets policy to suspend or dismiss any usher who accepts money to seat people where they do not belong, said Robert Mandt, the team's director of operations.

Source: New York Times

CHANCES

Life is filled with uncertainties. Fortunately, the economic analysis of supply and demand can apply to the *chances* of various events. Chance events include risks of accidents, chances of getting caught at illegal activities, and even the length of life.

Analysis of chance events requires an understanding of the concept of expected value. An *expected value* is a weighted average of various outcomes, in which the weights are the chances of those outcomes occurring. For example, if you have a one-half chance of getting an 80 on a test, and a one-half chance of getting a 90, then the expected value of your score—your *expected score*—is $(\frac{1}{2})(80) + (\frac{1}{2})(90) = 85$.

Illegal Activities

Economic analysis applies to illegal as well as legal activities. Buyers or sellers of an illegal good face a threat of formal punishment, with effects that resemble those of social pressure. The buyer's total cost includes a money price plus an expected-punishment cost that reflects the buyer's risk of being caught and punished.[2]

---

[2]The net price (price net of expected-punishment cost) that a seller receives, on the other hand, is the money price minus an expected-punishment cost based on the seller's risk of punishment; the possibility of punishment subtracts from the seller's money price.

I N   T H E   N E W S

Highway robbery! Aluminum thieves take metal and run

Current high price attracts pilferers to road signs, guardrails, and light poles

By James P. Miller
Staff Reporter of The Wall Street Journal

Don't look now, but robbers are dismantling America's highways.

Thieves are sweeping the USA, stealing traffic and road signs, guardrails, fire hydrant stems, even house siding, to cash in on scrap metal prices.

Increased prices for brass, copper, and aluminum—up between 40 and 90 percent—are fueling the recent crime wave.

Psst, Got Any Extra Coke Cans?

It isn't just big-time crooks who are playing the metals game. The city of Mountain View, Calif., recently cracked down on "or-

ganized rings" stealing bags of aluminum soda cans left outside homes for recycling. And even awnings have become the object of larcenous desire. "People go on vacation and when they come back their aluminum patio covers have been stolen," says Detective Readhimer.

Source: The Wall Street Journal and USA Today

Criminals respond to incentives.

Expected-Punishment cost

The expected-punishment cost of an illegal activity equals the chance of being caught times the money value of the punishment that would result. For example, suppose that a buyer takes a one-half chance of being caught buying an illegal good, and the punishment is a $100 fine. The expected-punishment cost is $50. If the chance of being caught rises to three-fourths, and the punishment stays at a $100 fine, the expected-punishment cost increases to $75. If the law breaker faces a jail sentence rather than a fine, the expected-punishment cost equals the chance of being caught times the money value of the jail sentence (the amount of money the criminal would be willing to pay to avoid jail).

The expected-punishment cost rises with any increase in either the punishment or the chance of being caught. A rise in buyers' expected-punishment cost reduces demand for the illegal good, which lowers its price and quantity sold. An increase in sellers' expected-punishment cost reduces supply of the illegal good, which raises its price and lowers the quantity sold. Whether an increase in the expected-punishment cost raises or lowers a good's price depends on whether it has a larger effect on the buyers' or sellers' expected-punishment costs.

EXAMPLE

Suppose that the punishment for someone caught buying illegal firearms rises from a $1,000 fine to a $1,500 fine, while the chance of being caught stays constant at one in ten. This change raises the expected-punishment cost by $50, from $100 to $150, shifting the demand curve for illegal firearms downward by $50, as in Figure 10. The equilibrium money price falls from P_1 to P_2. Notice that the money price falls by less than $50, so the total cost of the illegal firearms (money price plus expected-punishment cost) rises.

Figure 10 | Effect on Demand of a Rise in the Expected-Punishment Price

If the expected-punishment price of buying an illegal firearm rises by $50, the demand curve shifts downward (vertically) by $50. The equilibrium price falls less than $50.

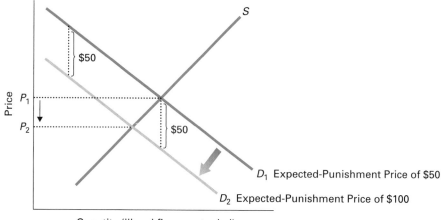

Risk and Safety

Safety is a good with a demand and a supply. Safety is not free—it also has a price. You buy safety when you drive carefully, fasten your seat belt, avoid smoking and ingesting dangerous substances, live in a safe neighborhood, eat healthy foods and exercise regularly, practice safe sex, and see your dentist twice a year.

We can measure safety as 1 minus the probability of death. A reduction in the chance of injury amounts to an increase in safety. (We could, instead, measure safety as 1 minus the probability of injury, leading to a similar discussion.) Figure 11 shows a person's demand for fire safety. The demand curve slopes downward as usual: When the cost of safety rises, people buy less safety.

Figure 11 | Supply and Demand for Fire Safety

The price of safety is the price of a 1 one-millionth reduction in the chance of death this year. The figure shows an equilibrium in which a person buys enough safety to reduce the chance of death by 3 one-millionths.

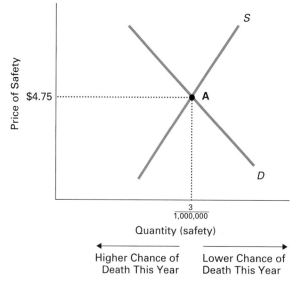

Safety can have a nonmoney cost as well as a money price, because risks sometimes lead people to avoid activities that they would enjoy. Higher costs of safety lead people to choose less safety, just as higher money prices do.

EXAMPLES

Suppose that you face a choice between two kinds of acne medication. One kind costs $3 per tube and causes brain damage in 2 out of 1 million (2/1,000,000) people. The other kind costs $10 per tube and causes brain damage in only 1 out of 1 million (1/1,000,000) people. The medications are identical in all other ways.

You can buy safety in your choice of medication. Reducing your chance of injury by 1 one-millionth (0.000001) costs $7. Many people would buy the additional safety at a cost of $7; fewer would buy the additional safety at a cost of $70. (The $7 price in this example reflects the amount that people pay, on average, to reduce the chance of death from accidents at work. Evidence shows that, on average, people are willing to take riskier jobs if they are paid about $7 more per year for each one-millionth increase in the chance of death in a year.)[3]

Figure 11 shows the supply and demand for fire safety in an apartment building. Producing safety costs money. Improving safety requires expenditures for smoke detectors and fire extinguishers, improvements in fire-escape systems, building with flame-retardant materials, and so on. Builders are willing to improve safety in apartment buildings if they can sell or rent them for higher prices to cover their higher costs. Therefore, the supply of safety slopes upward. The demand curve for safety slopes downward, because people want to buy less safety as its price rises. The equilibrium occurs at Point A in Figure 11. At this equilibrium amount of safety, people in the example choose a 3/1,000,000 chance of death by fire at an equilibrium price of $4.75; it costs $4.75 to reduce the chance of death from fire by one one-millionth.

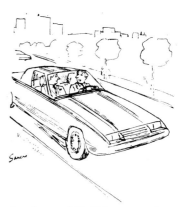

Buying a $40,000 car made me a safer driver.

People buy more safety when they have more to lose.
Source: The Wall Street Journal, October 18, 1987.

EXPLANATION

People sometimes say, "You can't place a value on a human life," but people place money values on chances of death every day. They drive inexpensive, small cars when evidence shows that larger cars (which cost more) are safer. They live in houses without smoke detectors. They drive cars on trips instead of spending more money to fly in airplanes, when passenger car travel exposes them to a death rate about 70 times larger than the death rate for airline travel.[4] The value of saving human lives enters many government decisions, from safety regulations to policies on drunken driving. Safety, like other goods, is amenable to economic analysis.[5]

Thinking Exercises

20. **(a)** Suppose that the government removes legal prohibitions against buying some good, so the expected-punishment cost falls from $100 to zero. Show (on a graph) how this change affects the money price of the good and its quantity sold.

[3]Some estimates of the price that people are willing to pay for safety are as low as $0.80 for a 1 one-millionth reduction in the chance of death; other estimates are as high as $11. Most estimates fall between $4 and $8.

[4]The death rate for car travel in a recent year was 22 deaths per 1 billion passenger miles, while the death rate for airline travel was about 0.3 deaths per 1 billion passenger miles.

[5]Some surprising implications grow out of the observations that people routinely sacrifice safety for other values, giving rise to an equilibrium quantity of safety. For example, laws that require use of seat belts in cars lead people to drive less carefully. (If you doubt the truth of this, ask yourself whether you would try to drive even more carefully if your seat belt were broken; most people answer "yes.") Lower speed limits, when enforced, have similar effects. As a result, seat belt laws and lower speed limits save fewer lives than they would save without these changes in behavior.

Gaining from the Misfortunes of Others

Emergencies are inevitable. A fire, hurricane, flood, or earthquake may destroy homes or a whole city; a traffic accident or an assault may cause injuries that require immediate care. Some people benefit from such disasters. Construction companies—and their workers—gain from the added demand to rebuild houses destroyed by natural disasters; health-care workers earn their pay by treating medical problems. Mental-health professionals gain customers whose lives fall apart because of unemployment or other misfortune; companies benefit if their competitors go out of business.

Is it fair that some people gain from the misfortunes of others? Although economics cannot answer that question, it can shed light on the consequences of laws or regulations that would prevent people from gaining from others' misfor-

tunes. This can help people to decide the merits of any such law or regulation.

Suppose that a natural disaster destroys homes and raises the demand for shelter, clothing, beds, medical supplies, and other goods. The increases in demand for these goods raise their prices in the stricken area. These high prices create incentives for sellers to raise the quantities of these goods that they supply to the area. (The high prices allow sellers to serve their own self-interests by providing the goods, so victims of the disaster need not only rely on the altruism of others.) Sellers respond to the price increases in two ways. They raise production of housing, beds, medical supplies, and other goods, and they divert supplies to the disaster area from outside that area. These decreases in supply in other areas raise prices there, inducing people who are not victims of the disaster to reduce their use of resources needed in the disaster area.

Decreased purchases by people outside the disaster area leave more resources available for disaster victims. For

(b) Suppose that that the government removes legal prohibitions against selling some good. Draw a graph to show the effects of legalizing the good on its money price and quantity sold.

21. Discussion on a television talk show makes people worry about getting mad-cow disease if they eat beef. Explain how this can affect the price of beef. Does the effect depend on whether the risk is real or imagined?

Inquiries for Further Thought

22. What choices have you made that involve a decision about your risk and safety? How much would you pay for a 1 one-millionth lower chance of death this year? (A 20-year-old in the United States has about a 1 in 1,000 chance of dying each year.) How much would you pay to reduce your chance to 1 in 2,000? Translate your answers into your demand curve for a smaller chance of death.

23. The National Research Council (a branch of the National Academy of Sciences) decided in 1989 that the government should not require seat belts in school buses. The council argued that the additional safety would not justify the cost, because seat belts on large school buses would save (on average) one child's life per year at a cost of $40 million. (The council suggested making other changes in buses that would cost less and save more lives per year.) How *should* people make decisions about how much money to spend to save a life?

24. Airline travel would be safer if pilots received more training and more rest between flights, if planes were inspected more often and more thoroughly, and if aging planes were scrapped. Each of these changes has a cost. How should people compare these costs with the additional safety that they would buy? How much

example, an increase in the cost of medical supplies leads hospitals in the rest of the country to use less where they can, freeing these supplies for sale to the disaster victims. Even buyers who are unaware of the disaster reduce their purchases of the goods that are in high demand in the disaster area. Similarly, sellers who are unaware of the disaster also raise their quantities supplied to the stricken area, because the high prices boost their profits. Sellers benefit from the high prices, but the victims of the disaster also benefit; they gain the opportunity to buy goods, albeit at high prices, rather than doing without them.

Some people find it unfair that sellers benefit from high prices when a disaster occurs. Critics suggest that the government should prevent sellers from raising prices above "normal" levels in a disaster area, or that it should tax away the "excess" profits made by sellers who gain from the misfortunes of others. What would be the results of government programs like these? Without opportunities to raise prices (or with increased taxes that prevent a rise in profits), sellers would lack the self-interest incentive to raise the quantity of beds, medical supplies, and other goods they would supply to the disaster area. Altruistic support for disaster victims would no longer be supplemented by assistance motivated by self-interest. Sellers would lack financial incentives to produce more of the goods that the victims need, and buyers in other areas would lack the financial incentive to buy fewer of these goods.

The mere prospect of profits from a disaster gives sellers an incentive to keep supplies readily available in case trouble strikes. For example, the mere prospect that someone might die keeps funeral businesses going even on days when no one dies, and the mere prospect that an ambulance might be needed keeps private ambulance companies in business on days without accidents. (The prospect of future demand induces these suppliers to buy ambulances and other equipment.) Similarly, the mere prospect of a disaster gives suppliers an incentive to make sure that they will be able to supply the goods that victims will need.

training and rest should pilots get? How often and how thoroughly should planes be inspected? Could any *general principles* guide these decisions?

IN THE NEWS

Genentech drug raises question on a life's value

By Marilyn Chase
Staff Reporter of The Wall Street Journal

Health economists and cardiologists now have a sticky issue to consider: Is a human life worth $200,000?

The question has been raised because of the slim but surprising survival edge shown by Genentech Inc.'s heart drug, TPA, over its less-expensive rival, streptokinase, in a huge international study.

"You have to treat 100 patients with TPA to save one additional life, and the cost differential [between the drugs] is about $2,000," Dr. Parmley said. "So for $200,000, you've saved one life."

"This makes it difficult for managed care to make decisions," said Mark A. Hlatky, a Stanford University health policy expert. "It's very expensive for the amount of time it adds to people's life expectancy."

Source: The Wall Street Journal

Doctors and other people must routinely decide whether additional safety is worth the price that someone would have to pay for it.

ECONOMICS OF
EVERYDAY LIFE

Lifestyles

You can buy a low-stress lifestyle by choosing a job that exposes you to little stress; the price you pay is a lower income. Figure 12 shows the supply and demand for labor services in stressful jobs and peaceful jobs. The equilibrium wage for the stressful job is W_1^S and the equilibrium wage for the peaceful job is W_1^P. The stressful job pays a higher wage, and the difference in the wages $(W_1^S - W_1^P)$ is the price of the peaceful lifestyle.

The same reasoning applies to other characteristics of jobs. People can buy increased job security, independence, schedule flexibility, or ability to take vacations or family leaves. Jobs with these desirable characteristics usually pay lower wages than other jobs that require the same education. The wage difference is the cost of the increased job security or other characteristic.

Honesty and Other Values

Honesty, fairness, compassion, patriotism, and other values also have prices, and their quantities demanded depend on those prices. People usually buy less honesty when its price rises; they tell more lies when they expect greater benefits from those lies. Athletes are more likely to cheat by using performance-enhancing drugs before important athletic events than unimportant events and before events where they are less likely to be caught. Politicians are more likely to vote based on their beliefs on the merits of an issue when they are not tempted or pressured by lobbyists. Married people are more likely to cheat on their spouses when an attractive opportunity arises or when their marriages have deteriorated so that the benefits of remaining married to the same person have declined. The temptation to deal illegal drugs is high when a dealer can earn thousands of dollars a week; more people choose illegal jobs when earnings from those jobs are high. People are more willing to help others when helping costs less time, effort, or money.

Figure 12 | The Economics of Stressful and Peaceful Lifestyles

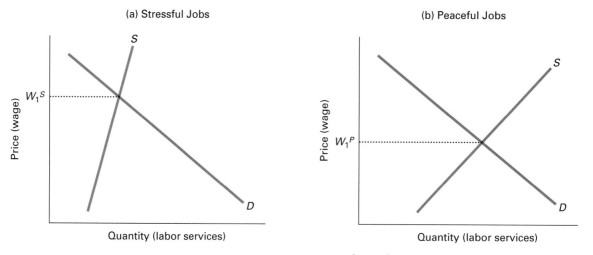

The price of a relatively peaceful job is $W_1^S - W_1^P$.

IN THE NEWS

Former executive happily traded rat race for slow pace of Montana

By Dave Zelio
The Associated Press

CASCADE, Mont.— Pasquale, 53, can't help but smile whenever he talks

about leaving the rat race in Washington, D.C., for a slower-paced life in rural Montana—something many executives only

dream of doing.

He says only that his "substantially lower" salary is offset by other, greater rewards.

Source: Rochester Democrat and Chronicle

The lifestyle you want is for sale.

People show more honesty as its price declines, and this tendency explains why vending machines for soft drinks and newspapers differ. Many newspaper dispensers expose their contents so that a buyer could take several newspapers after paying for only one. Soft-drink dispensers, on the other hand, prevent people from taking more than a single can at a time. The vending machines differ because people are unlikely to be dishonest when the benefits are small. (Few people want a second newspaper.) When the benefits of dishonesty are larger, as in the case of soft drinks, more people would choose dishonesty (if they could) by taking additional drinks without paying.

These examples make two points. First, living according to certain values has an opportunity cost; people sacrifice certain benefits to live honest, fair, or caring lives. Second, a change in the prices of these values can change behavior; people are less willing to live by these values when doing so entails larger sacrifices. When laws, customs, and social institutions increase the costs of certain values, fewer people adopt these values.

IN THE NEWS

Lobbyists who pay lawmakers $1,000 an hour have found an effective way to communicate

Source: The Wall Street Journal

Some politicians sell their integrity at a low price.

Dowries

In certain countries, such as India, a marriage often involves an exchange of a *dowry*. When a couple marries, the woman (or her family) pays a dowry to the man. Marriages in some other countries, such as Egypt, often involve payments of *bride prices* by men to women. The size of the dowry or bride price is influenced partly by culture and tradition, but also partly by economics. Think of a dowry as part of a price that a woman or her family pays to a man for his marriage services. Figure 13 shows the supply of males' marriage services, S, and the demand for males' marriage services by females, D. At the equilibrium (Point A), the dowry is P_1.

Dowries and bride prices also vary with the quality of the marriage partner. For example, Indian women can marry men from higher social classes by paying larger dowries. In other words, they can buy higher-quality husbands by paying higher prices.

Children

Although people do not (usually) buy children, raising children has a cost or price. Parents spend both money and time to raise children. The money price includes many

Figure 13 | Dowries

The equilibrium dowry is P_1.

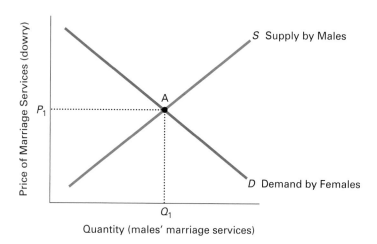

Quantity (males' marriage services)

expenses from prenatal medical expenses to food, clothing, a larger apartment or house, and the child's recreational expenses. The average money price of raising a child varies across families; estimates range from about $6,000 to $10,000 by the child's first birthday. The time cost of child-rearing is also large, but some parents reduce it by buying child-care services or simply spending less time with their children.

Throughout most of history, the demand for children by farm families has exceeded the demand by city families. Food and housing were cheaper on farms than in cities, and farm children helped with work. These factors made the price of chil-

IN THE NEWS

Tens of thousands of Indian women, poor and rich alike, have undergone amniocentesis for the sole purpose of learning whether their fetus is a boy or girl. If it is a girl, they have an abortion; if it is a boy, they don't.

The reason for this strong preference for male babies is both traditional and economic. In many

parts of India, boys are perceived as an economic benefit; girls are perceived as an economic burden. Although marriage dowries are technically illegal in India, they persist. And the price for marrying off a daughter can run as high as $10,000—the equivalent of a year's salary for a middle-class Indian. Several daughters and no sons can be a

prescription for bankruptcy.

The Indian state of Maharashtra has opted for a law that bans any prenatal test to determine a fetus' sex. This has driven the testing underground or to other states with no such laws. The economic pressures are simply too great on families with several daughters.

Source: Rochester Democrat and Chronicle

Economic forces affect decisions about children, sometimes with tragic results.

dren lower for farm families than for city families. This price difference diminished with the mechanization of farming, because children provided less help on farms than in the past. When the price difference fell, so did the difference in the average sizes of farm and city families.

Sometimes the costs of raising boys and girls differ, and this variation affects demand. Reports cite higher rates of female infanticide and abortion of female fetuses (after medical tests to determine fetal gender) in northern India than in southern India. Stronger boys can provide more help raising wheat in the north, while girls are as valuable as boys for raising rice in the south. Because the cost of raising a child declines when the child can help on a farm, the cost of girls is higher than the cost of boys in the north, while the costs are about the same in the south. This cost difference helps to explain why the preference for boys over girls is less strong in southern India than in the north.

The demand for children falls as a woman's wage rises, because women usually provide larger time inputs into children for both biological and cultural reasons. A rising wage raises the price of children by raising the opportunity cost of the parent's time. Economic forces also affect the timing of child-bearing; the demand for children is lower for women in their teens and twenties, who spend more time acquiring education, than for older women. For this reason, expanded education programs for women tend to reduce population growth.

Thinking Exercises

25. Suppose that people's tastes change, and they want to switch from stressful jobs to peaceful ones. Draw graphs to show how this increase in demand for a peaceful job affects wages in stressful jobs and peaceful jobs.

26. Alan Dershowitz, a Harvard law professor, has argued that parents in some countries choose abortions or even infanticide for female babies, because they prefer male babies due to tradition and to avoid the high cost of dowries. His argument goes on, "If this is allowed to continue and expand, it could affect the natural balance between males and females. Throughout history, of course, there have been other factors that have skewed the proportion of males and females: wars, certain sex-linked illnesses, even crime."[6] Use supply-and-demand analysis to discuss the effect on the size of dowries if the number of females per male in the society were to decrease.

Inquiries for Further Thought

27. Some people claim that you cannot buy friends. Can you? What kind of nonmoney costs would you pay? What factors affect your demand for friends?

28. Can people find higher-quality romantic partners by paying higher prices? (The prices may not involve money; they may involve more time to search for the right person, to improve oneself, or to devote to a relationship.) Does romance implicitly involve a money price? Could someone find a higher-quality partner if he or she were richer and shared this wealth with a partner?

---

[6]Alan Dershowitz, quoted in the *Rochester Democrat and Chronicle*, August 15, 1988

ADJUSTMENT TO EQUILIBRIUM

Market equilibrium is a situation in which quantity demanded equals quantity supplied. When a market is in equilibrium, the price and quantity traded tend to remain constant until supply or demand changes. When a market is in disequilibrium, the price tends to move toward the equilibrium price. The price tends to rise to eliminate any shortage or to fall to eliminate any surplus. In either case, the price and quantity traded tend to move toward equilibrium. This adjustment to equilibrium follows any change in demand or supply that changes the equilibrium price and quantity.

Price adjustments take only a few seconds or minutes in some markets, such as the stock market and other financial markets. Prices in other markets adjust over much longer periods. Retail stores, for example, often put price tags on goods and then wait for buyers to make their choices. A seller may recognize a surplus or shortage of a good only after a period of time. Even then, changing prices may require additional time. Some sellers publish catalogs with prices and wait for buyers to place orders. In these cases, price changes may take days, weeks, or even months.

IN THE NEWS

The plunge in world coffee prices that followed last week's collapse of coffee export quota talks in London will translate into big price cuts in supermarkets almost immediately—much more quickly than is normal in the industry.

The quick price cuts contrast with a normal lag of up to 12 weeks.

Source: The Wall Street Journal

Sometimes prices adjust rapidly, sometimes slowly.

EXAMPLES

A clothing store puts price tags on clothes and waits to see what customers buy. If the store develops a surplus of green shirts because fewer people buy them than the store manager expected, the store holds a sale and lowers the price. This adjustment may take weeks, however, because the store manager may initially believe that low sales of the shirt are temporary, and that sales will soon increase. Eventually, if sales remain low, the manager will conclude that the price is above the equilibrium and will reduce it.

When a busload of people unexpectedly arrive at a fast-food restaurant, lines form to order burgers and fries. Demand rises for the restaurant's food, but the price does not immediately increase. Over a period of time, though, increases in demand at these restaurants raise their food prices.

Inquiry for Further Thought

29. Why do prices of some goods adjust quickly to changes in supply or demand, while prices of other goods take longer to adjust?

Key Terms

private demand
market demand

government budget deficit

reservation price

time cost

Problems

30. Do goods that last twice as long, or are twice as big, cost twice as much? Explain why or why not.

31. You can buy fame! Many colleges will name a building, classroom, or professorship after you for a price. Hospitals will name an operating room or patient's room after you. Sports facilities, gardens, and even seats at performing-arts centers carry the names of donors. What determines their prices?

IN THE NEWS

What price fame?

For a donation, you can preserve your name on parking lots, elevators, and wig rooms

Now you can do more than cheer for your favorite college football player. You can "buy" him. At the University of Southern California, there's a Richard Alden center, a Chester H. Dolley quarterback, and 14 other named positions. Eight defensive positions remain, at $300,000 a pop.

If football's not your sport, how about fencing? At Brandeis University, a fencing room goes for $250,000. Locker rooms are just $50,000. Tennis courts anyone? Smith College will name indoor courts for $100,000. But if you're just a spectator, don't sweat: A block of 40 bleacher seats at Smith goes for $10,000.

Harvard will put your name on its new Medical Education Center for $12 million. Too pricey? Then how about a 10-person "study module" for $10,000.

Really good grass is awfully expensive these days.

Agnes Scott College, in Decatur, Ga., has several campus quadrangles available for $10,000 to $50,000.

Some of the best operators are in hospitals, and they're not all surgeons. At Children's Medical Center in Dallas, patient rooms cost $25,000 to name and operating rooms $250,000.

For $2,500, the Tampa Bay Performing Arts Center is putting plaques on individual seats.

Source: The Wall Street Journal

32. Extend your imagination and develop a supply-and-demand analysis to predict the economic effects—the effects on the prices and quantities of various goods—of the following changes:
    (a) The spread of AIDS
    (b) Sudden global warming
    (c) An increase in the average age of marriage
    (d) An increase in the fraction of the population over age 65
    (e) A new baby boom
    (f) A technological breakthrough that makes solar energy almost free
    (g) A worldwide ban on products that may contribute to global warming
    (h) A microelectronics revolution that makes supercomputers as cheap as shoes
    (i) A major, conventional war in some part of the world
    (j) A sudden and massive decrease in the demand for drugs

Inquiries for Further Thought

33. Single men in their twenties outnumber single women in their twenties in the United States by about a six-to-five ratio. (For every five women, there are six men.) A generation ago, the numbers were more equal. The ratio of men to women also varies across cities in the United States. What results would you anticipate from the increase in the supply of men relative to the supply of women? What effects would you expect for differences between cities? How might the economics of supply and demand apply to this situation?

34. Should the government limit the extent to which sellers profit from the misfortunes of others?
    (a) If you say "no," explain why not, then answer the following questions: Suppose that a

I N   T H E   N E W S

After first driving overland to Bulgaria, where the border guards refused him entry, he returned to Istanbul and eventually paid $300 to a man who promised to show him how to cross the frontier into Greece.

He cannot allow his real name to be used, so he asked to be called Ali. The lucky ones, he said, the ones who could pay $7,000 for a Canadian visa in Istanbul or buy a fake passport, or those with blood relatives in Frankfurt or London, have already gotten out.

Source: Washington Post

woman sees a man about to drown. She yells to the drowning man, "I will save you if you give me your life savings!" The man yells "Okay, I promise!" and she saves him. Should the courts enforce his promise, or should the government limit profits made in this way from the misfortunes of others? Under what conditions, if any, should the government limit profits made from the misfortunes of others?

(b) If you say "yes," how should this limit work? Does your argument suggest that the government should limit the incomes doctors earn by treating patients? Should it limit the gains of farmers from selling food to people who have the misfortune to be hungry? Doesn't a plumber gain from a person's misfortune by clearing clogged pipes? Doesn't every seller gain from the misfortune of buyers? How would you choose which gains to limit and which not to limit? What general principle would guide your decisions?

35. A person can buy the right to immigrate to some countries; sometimes, a person can buy citizenship in those countries. (Some of this trade involves illegal payments.) What factors determine the price of immigration rights? Do you think that the United States should sell rights to immigrate to the highest bidders?

36. Do you think that the demand for democracy and freedom rises when people become richer? Does freedom ever have a price? Does democracy? For example, do countries ever sacrifice national security for freedom or democracy? (Perhaps national security could be improved by increasing taxes to fund new spending on defense, or by instituting a military draft, or by permitting the police to search houses without search warrants.) Do countries ever sacrifice traditional cultures for freedom or democracy? What conditions affect the demand for freedom? The demand for democracy?

CHAPTER 7

INTERNATIONAL TRADE, ARBITRAGE, AND SPECULATION

Flug Flight		nach to	über via
LG	302	LUXEMBURG	
AZ	419	TURIN	
LH	1122	NEAPEL	
LH	1906	MADRID	
LH	1022	STUTTGART HBF.	
AF	1701	LYON	
AY	822	HELSINKI	
AA	071	SFRANCISCO-DALL	
AF	743	PARIS	
LH	1116	VENEDIG	
DL	023	DALLAS	

In this Chapter...

Main Points to Understand

▸ International trade creates economic links between countries.

▸ Arbitrage tends to equate prices in different locations.

▸ Through speculation, expectations about the future affect current economic conditions.

Thinking Skills to Develop

▸ Apply the supply-demand model to explain international trade.

▸ Understand the parallel logic of international trade, arbitrage, and speculation.

▸ Understand why arbitragers or speculators earn *no profits* in equilibrium.

You are part of a world economy. Events in distant countries touch your life, and your future will be affected by economic growth and government economic policies around the globe. The world economy is more integrated now than ever before. Each year, people in the United States export goods and services worth about $3,000 per person—about one-tenth of total U.S. output—and import even more. International trade has been growing: a quarter century ago, the United States exported only one-twentieth of its total output, half of the current proportion. More jobs involve producing goods for international trade today than ever before. Changes in supplies and demands around the world affect economic conditions—prices, wages, and employment—in every U.S. city and town.

Just as international trade links the economies of different nations, interregional trade between cities, towns, and states connects the economies of regions within a country. An earthquake in California affects prices, wages, and employment in Virginia. Economic changes in Michigan affect people in Texas.

Speculation links economic activities across time, between today and the future. People's expectations about the future affect today's economy. The prices people pay this week for food, houses, and other goods, and quantities of these goods supplied, depend on expectations about the future.

This chapter explains why the supply and demand for a good at any place or any time is related to its supplies and demands at other locations and other times. The chapter applies supply-and-demand analysis to three issues: international trade, interregional trade, and speculation. The same type of supply-demand diagram can illustrate all three issues.

INTERNATIONAL TRADE

The United States exports wheat, corn, cotton, chemicals, plastics, construction and industrial machinery, scientific equipment, computers, aircraft, and many other goods to foreign countries. It imports coffee, cocoa, crude oil, important raw materials (such as bauxite, cobalt, platinum, chromium, nickel, tin, and zinc), automobiles, clothing, toys, consumer electronics equipment such as televisions and audio equipment, and many other products. Why does the U.S. economy export computers and import televisions rather than exporting televisions and importing computers? What economic factors affect a country's exports or imports of a good? How do changes in demand or supply in one country affect prices and outputs in other countries? Supply-and-demand analysis can illuminate these questions.

Equilibrium with International Trade

Figure 1 shows how to graph international trade. Three side-by-side supply-and-demand diagrams illustrate markets in the United States, other countries, and the world as a whole. Without international trade, each country's curves would determine its own equilibrium price and quantity traded. With international trade, world supply and demand determine the equilibrium price. The quantity supplied in each country at the equilibrium price shows the amount that each country produces. The quantity demanded in each country at the world equilibrium price shows the amount that each country consumes.

> People consume a good when they use it to satisfy their wants; **consumption** is the total quantity consumed over some period of time.

People consume a good when they wear it, eat it, drive it, or watch it. The quantity demanded shows consumption; the quantity supplied shows production. A country's consumption and production differ when that country exports or imports a good:

> A country **exports** a good when it sells the good to buyers in other countries.
> A country **imports** a good when it buys the good from foreign producers.

When a country exports a good, it produces more of that good than it consumes. (It exports the rest.) When a country imports a good, it consumes more of that good than it produces.[1] One country's exports are another's imports.

EXPLANATION AND EXAMPLE

Figure 1a (labeled "United States") shows the U.S. supply and demand for film. The demand curve in Panel (a) shows the quantities demanded at various prices by U.S. buyers. Similarly, the supply curve in Panel (a) shows the quantities supplied at various prices by U.S. producers. Without international trade, equilibrium would occur at Point A at a U.S. price of $3 and a quantity of 5 million rolls of film per week.

Figure 1b (labeled "Other Countries") shows the demand and supply for film in all

---

[1]The discussion in this chapter applies to consumer goods (abstracting from investment and uses of goods as inputs to produce other goods). A more complete analysis would replace the term *consumes* with the phrase "consumes, invests, or uses as intermediate inputs."

Figure 1 | International Trade in Film

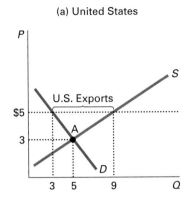

(a) United States

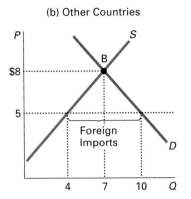

(b) Other Countries

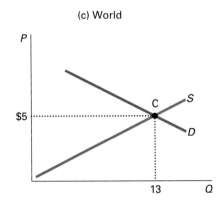

(c) World

		United States[a]		Other Countries[a]		World Market[a]	
	Price	Quantity Demanded	Quantity Supplied	Quantity Demanded	Quantity Supplied	Quantity Demanded	Quantity Supplied
	$9	0	17	6	8	6	25
	8	0	15	7	7	7	22
	7	1	13	8	6	9	19
	6	2	11	9	5	11	16
World Equilibrium	5	3	9	10	4	13	13
	4	4	7	11	3	15	10
	3	5	5	12	2	17	7
	2	6	3	13	1	19	4
	1	7	1	14	0	21	1

[a]Millions of rolls per week.

other countries of the world. The foreign supply and demand curves show demand by buyers in other countries and supply by foreign producers. Without international trade, the foreign equilibrium would occur at Point B at a foreign price of $8 and an equilibrium quantity of 7 million rolls per week.[2]

Without international trade, the foreign equilibrium price exceeds the U.S. price, giving U.S. sellers an incentive to sell film in foreign countries at the higher price. The price difference also gives buyers in other countries an incentive to buy film from the U.S. sellers at the lower price. For both reasons, the price difference creates incentives for international trade.

Figure 1c shows demand and supply by all buyers and sellers in the world.[3] World demand and supply determine the equilibrium price and quantity for an internationally traded good. At world equilibrium (Point C) the price is $5 and the quantity is 13 million rolls per week.

A horizontal line across the three panels in Figure 1 shows the world equilibrium price of $5. At that price, the supply curves in the three panels show the quantities supplied in the United States, other countries, and the world market. The demand curves in the three panels show the quantities bought by people in the United States, other

---

[2]Foreign prices are usually quoted as amounts of foreign currencies such as yen, francs, or pesos. The $8 price refers to the dollar value of the foreign price.

[3]Chapter 4 showed how to derive the market demand curve from the demand curves of individual buyers. Figure 1 derives the world market demand curve from the demand curves of individual countries. It then repeats this procedure for supply.

countries, and the world. At the equilibrium price of $5, the quantity of film demanded by U.S. buyers is 3 million rolls per week, as the U.S. demand curve shows. The quantity of film supplied by U.S. producers is 9 million rolls per week, as the U.S. supply curve shows. The United States produces and sells 9 million rolls per week, consuming 3 million and exporting 6 million.

Figure 1b shows that foreign countries import film from the United States. The supply curve shows that foreign countries produce 4 million rolls per week; the demand curve shows that they consume 10 million rolls. Foreign countries import 6 million rolls per week from the United States.

Notice that foreign imports equal U.S. exports. The horizontal distance between a country's demand and supply curves at the world equilibrium price shows that country's equilibrium exports or imports. If a country's quantity supplied exceeds its quantity demanded, it exports the good; if its quantity demanded exceeds its quantity supplied, it imports the good.

Another Way to Find the Equilibrium Price

You do not need the graph in Figure 1c to find the equilibrium price. Instead, you can use trial and error to find the price at which one country's exports equal the other's imports. If you guess a price that is too high (above the equilibrium price of $5), the graph in Figure 1a will show U.S. exports of more than 6 million rolls per week (the horizontal distance between the supply and demand curves will exceed 6 million), and Figure 1b will show that other countries import less than 6 million rolls per week. This situation is not an equilibrium, because U.S. exports do not equal foreign imports.

If, instead, you guess a price that is too low (below the equilibrium price of $5), Figure 1a will show U.S. exports of less than 6 million rolls per week, while Figure 1b will show other countries importing more than 6 million rolls. Again, this situation is not an equilibrium, because U.S. exports do not equal foreign imports. Only at the equilibrium price ($5) do U.S. exports of the good equal foreign imports. (The horizontal distance by which U.S. supply exceeds U.S. demand equals the horizontal distance by which demand in other countries exceeds supply there.)

Winners and Losers from International Trade

Some people gain from international trade, while others lose. Without international trade, the U.S. price of film would be $3 and the foreign price would be $8. International trade moves the price to $5 in all countries. U.S. film buyers lose from international trade in film, because it raises the price they pay. U.S. film manufacturers gain from international trade, because they can sell film at a higher price, and they choose to sell more film as a result (9 million rolls rather than 5 million rolls per week). Foreign buyers gain from international trade in film, because it reduces the price they pay from $8 to $5 per roll. Foreign sellers lose from international trade in film because it reduces the price at which they can sell their film.

Chapter 9 will show how to compare the sizes of these gains and losses, concluding that the winners from international trade gain more than the losers lose; U.S. sellers gain more from international trade than U.S. buyers lose, and foreign buyers gain more than foreign sellers lose. As a result, international trade is economically efficient.

Changes in Supply and Demand in International Trade

When a country engages in international trade, its economy reacts to changes in foreign economic conditions. Changes in foreign demand or supply affect prices, production, and consumption in the home country.

Some people gain from international trade, while others lose.

Rise in Foreign Demand

Figure 2 shows how a rise in foreign demand for film affects its price, output in each country, consumption in each country, and international trade. If foreign demand rises by 5 million rolls of film per week, the foreign demand curve shifts to the right by that amount. This raises world market demand and shifts the world market demand curve to the right by 5 million rolls. The equilibrium price rises from $5 to $6 and the equilibrium quantity rises from 13 million to 16 million rolls per week.

Output of film rises in each country, because the price increase raises the quantity supplied. U.S. film output rises from 9 million to 11 million rolls per week; output in

---

IN THE NEWS

U.S. drought a reprieve to South American farmers

Los Angeles Times

BUENOS AIRES, Argentina—This summer's drought may be devastating for North American farmers, but it has handed a multibillion dollar bonanza to grain growers in Argentina and Brazil, generating a glimmer of optimism in an otherwise desperate economic climate.

Argentina expects a windfall of up to $2 billion in extra revenue from agricultural exports because of higher prices this year, government officials said.

Nearly half the bonus is attributed directly to the drought in the United States and Canada.

In Brazil, too, agriculture ministry officials predicted an increase in farm exports of $1.2 billion this year, thanks to the extra price surge caused by the drought.

"I am sorry for the Americans, but I am happy for our own farmers, who have suffered for years," said Fernando Miguez, 37, a Buenos Aires agronomist who also is co-owner of a 340-acre farm in Rojas, near Buenos Aires.

Source: Rochester Democrat and Chronicle

A fall in U.S. supply raises both the world price and U.S. imports.

Figure 2 | Effects of a Rise in Foreign Demand

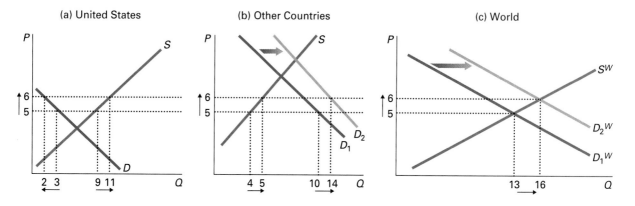

		United States		Other Countries		World Market	
				New		New	
	Price	Quantity Demanded	Quantity Supplied	Quantity Demanded	Quantity Supplied	Quantity Demanded	Quantity Supplied
	$11	0	21	9	12	9	33
	10	0	19	10	10	10	29
	9	0	17	11	8	11	25
	8	0	15	12	7	12	22
	7	1	13	13	6	14	19
New Equilibrium ⟶	6	2	11	14	5	16	16
Old Equilibrium ⟶	5	3	9	15	4	18	13
(Figure 1)	4	4	7	16	3	20	10
	3	5	5	17	2	22	7
	2	6	3	18	1	24	4

other countries rises from 4 million to 5 million. Altogether, total world output of film rises from 13 million to 16 million rolls per week. The price increase reduces U.S. consumption of film from 3 million to 2 million rolls per week. Film consumption in other countries rises from 10 million to 14 million rolls per week. (Notice that foreign consumption rises by 4 million rolls even though foreign demand increased—the demand curve shifted horizontally to the right—by 5 million rolls. Foreign consumption rises by less than the increase in demand, because the price increase moves foreign consumers upward along their demand curve from 15 million to 14 million rolls.) As in Figure 1, the horizontal distances between the supply and demand curves at the world equilibrium price show exports and imports. In Figure 2, U.S. film exports rise from 6 million to 9 million rolls per week (11 million produced minus 2 million consumed) as the United States produces more film and consumes less. Foreign film imports also rise from 6 million to 9 million (14 million consumed minus 5 million produced).

Rise in Foreign Supply

Figure 3 shows the effect of a rise in the foreign supply of film by 5 million rolls per week. This change reduces the world equilibrium price from $5 to $4 per roll and raises the world quantity traded from 13 million to 15 million rolls per week.

U.S. output of film falls from 9 million to 7 million rolls per week, and U.S. consumption rises from 3 million to 4 million rolls, so U.S. exports of film fall from 6 million to 3 million rolls per week. Foreign output of film rises from 4 million to 8 million rolls, and foreign consumption rises from 10 million to 11 million rolls, so foreign imports fall from 6 million to 3 million rolls per week.

Figure 3 | Effects of an Increase in Foreign Supply

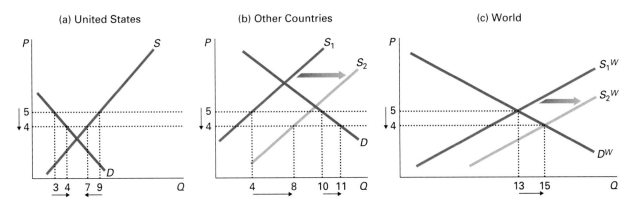

		United States		Other Countries		World Market	
	Price	Quantity Demanded	Quantity Supplied	Quantity Demanded	New Quantity Supplied	Quantity Demanded	New Quantity Supplied
	$9	0	17	6	13	6	30
	8	0	15	7	12	7	27
	7	1	13	8	11	9	24
Old Equilibrium	6	2	11	9	10	11	21
(Figure 1) ⟶	5	3	9	10	9	13	18
New Equilibrium ⟶	4	4	7	11	8	15	15
	3	5	5	12	7	17	12
	2	6	3	13	6	19	9
	1	7	1	14	5	21	6

Review Questions

1. How can a country's consumption of a good differ from its production of that good?

2. Draw three graphs side by side to show equilibrium in the world market for corn, U.S. exports of corn, and foreign imports of corn.

Thinking Exercises

3. Who would gain and who would lose if foreign governments were to prohibit imports of film from the United States?

4. Explain why an increase in the foreign supply of film reduces output of film in the United States.

The price of lobsters does not vary much between cities near ocean ports and cities far from the ocean. The price of corn does not vary much between America's heartland and distant cities like Boston or San Francisco. Prices of many goods tend to be about the same in different places. This results from arbitrage.

ARBITRAGE

> **Arbitrage** is the process of buying something at a place where its price is low, and selling it where its price is higher.

If a good sells at a much higher price in one place than another, people arbitrage—they buy it in the low-price place and resell it in the high-price place. This raises the price in the low-price location and lowers the price in the high-price location, which tends to equalize prices in the two places.

> A **price differential** is a difference between the prices of identical goods in two different locations.

Arbitrage tends to eliminate price differentials.

Anyone can arbitrage. Producers arbitrage when they decide to sell more goods where the price is high and fewer where the price is low. Other people arbitrage by buying and then reselling goods. Some people have full-time jobs arbitraging in financial markets, such as stock markets; they spend their days checking financial prices in different locations, looking for price differentials to eliminate.[4]

Arbitrage often has a cost, however. An arbitrager must identify a price differential, go to the low-price location, buy the goods, ship them to the higher-price location, and find buyers there. If the price differential across locations is small, people will not find it worthwhile (profitable) to arbitrage. When arbitrage is costly, it limits price differentials but does not eliminate them completely.

> You have an **arbitrage opportunity** if you know about a price differential that exceeds your costs of arbitrage.

Arbitrage opportunities are elusive in real life, because they disappear quickly as people take advantage of them. In equilibrium, they vanish:

> In equilibrium, there are no arbitrage opportunities.

When people find arbitrage opportunities and try to profit from them, their actions reduce the price differential until the arbitrage opportunity disappears.

Equilibrium with No Costs of Arbitrage

If the price of a good is lower in New York than in Los Angeles, people have an incentive to buy the good in New York and resell it at the higher price in Los Angeles. This arbitrage activity raises the price in New York and lowers the price in Los Angeles, reducing the price differential between the cities.

When arbitrage costs nothing, the equilibrium price differential is zero. Any price differential creates an arbitrage opportunity, so all price differentials must disappear in equilibrium. As a result, arbitragers do *not* earn profits in equilibrium, because the price differential is zero. The best way to understand this logical point is to think of a very small price differential that creates a profit just large enough to provide people with an incentive to buy and resell the goods.

Figure 4 shows an equilibrium with no costs of arbitrage.[5] Figure 4 resembles Figure 1, but it applies to different cities rather than different countries. Figure 4a, labeled *Here,*

---

[4]These people work for big banks and other financial institutions.

[5]In some real-life situations, such as financial markets, the costs of arbitrage are very small and the assumption no-cost arbitrage is a good approximation. A later section of this chapter discusses costs of arbitrage.

Figure 4 | Equilibrium with No-Cost Arbitrage

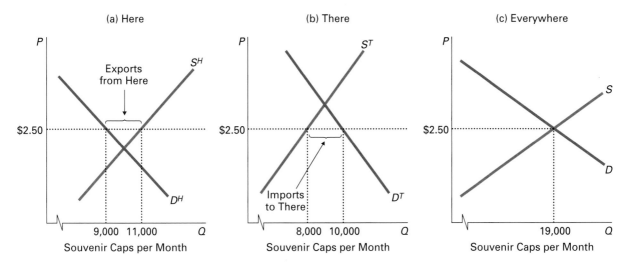

Arbitrage works like international trade. Arbitragers buy 2,000 caps per month *here*, and "export" them to *there*. Production *here* is 11,000 caps per month; consumption *here* is 9,000. Production *there* is 8,000, and consumption *there* is 10,000.

shows supply and demand in one place; Figure 4b, labeled *There,* shows supply and demand for the same good in another place. Figure 4c, labeled *Everywhere,* shows the total market supply and demand. Without arbitrage, the supply and demand in each place determine the equilibrium in that place. With costless arbitrage, however, the equilibrium is determined by the supply and demand everywhere; the equilibrium price is $2.50 in both places.

The demand curve D^H shows demand by consumers here. At the equilibrium price of $2.50, consumption here is 9,000 souvenir caps per month. The supply curve S^H shows supply by all producers *here,* so equilibrium production *here* is 11,000 caps per month. Arbitragers buy 2,000 per month *here* and resell them *there.* The supply curve S^T shows supply by producers *there.* At the equilibrium price of $2.50, production *there* is 8,000 caps per month. Arbitragers offer another 2,000 caps for sale, so equilibrium consumption *there* is 10,000.

Figure 4 shows an equilibrium, because the quantity supplied (*everywhere*) equals the quantity demanded (*everywhere*), and no one has an incentive to change the amount of arbitrage from its current level of 2,000 units per month. If arbitragers transferred less than 2,000 caps per month, the price *here* would be lower than the price *there,* creating an incentive for additional arbitrage. That would not be an equilibrium. Similarly, if arbitragers transferred more than 2,000 caps per month, the price here would be above the price *there,* creating an incentive to reduce arbitrage. That would not be an equilibrium, either. The only possible equilibrium occurs when arbitrage is 2,000 caps per month.

Hint on Thinking about Economics

Two of the most important questions economists ask themselves are:

▶ In this situation, what will people do to make themselves better off?

▶ When people do it, how will the situation change?

Asking these questions can help to clarify thinking about economics. For example, suppose that the price of bandages in New Orleans is below the price in Columbus. What will people do to make themselves better off? They will buy bandages at the low price in New Orleans and resell them in Columbus.[6] Alternatively, bandage-makers might arbitrage by reducing bandage shipments to New Orleans and increasing shipments to Columbus. Equilibrium occurs when people are *already* doing whatever is best for themselves; there is nothing else they can do (in this market) to make themselves better off.

Winners and Losers from Arbitrage

Arbitrage, like international trade, creates winners and losers. Arbitrage raises the price of a good in one location and reduces it somewhere else. Sellers gain and buyers lose in the location where the price rises. Sellers lose and buyers gain in the location where the price falls. Chapter 9 will show that, because the winners gain more than the buyers lose, arbitrage (like international trade) is economically efficient.

Review Questions

5. What is arbitrage? What is an arbitrage opportunity?

6. Explain why equilibrium allows no arbitrage opportunities.

Thinking Exercises

7. Explain why the equilibrium price differential is zero.

8. Who gains and who loses from arbitrage?

SPECULATION

Speculators have a bad reputation. Many people think of speculation as an ethically questionable activity pursued by people seeking quick profits for little effort. Most speculation, however, is rather mundane.

> **Speculation** is the process of buying something at a time when its price is low and storing it to sell later when its price might be higher (or storing it for later use).

The discussion in this section considers only storable goods such as lumber, rather than nonstorable goods such as fresh fish.

Speculation works like arbitrage or international trade across time rather than between locations or countries. Storing goods is like exporting them from the present to the future; using or selling stored goods is like importing them from the past.

Speculation differs from arbitrage or international trade because the future is uncertain. Speculators risk the chance that future prices might be lower rather than higher than current prices. Whenever people plan for the future, whether speculating or planning picnics, they base their plans on their beliefs or expectations about the future. Speculators expect to profit if they expect the prices of their goods to rise so that they can resell them at the higher, future prices. To avoid unnecessary complications, this discussion will consider only cases in which every speculator has the same expectations about the future.[7]

If people expect the price of a good to be much higher in the future than it is today, they speculate. They buy and store the good, planning to sell it at a profit in the future.

---

[6]They would continue to arbitrage as long as the price differential exceeded the cost of arbitrage, as discussed later in the chapter.

[7]If people's expectations differ, those who expect high future prices are likely to become speculators, just as people who expect good weather are more likely to plan picnics than people who expect bad weather.

Figure 5 | Equilibrium with Costless Speculation

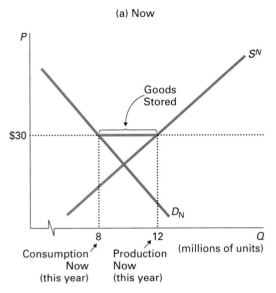

(a) Now

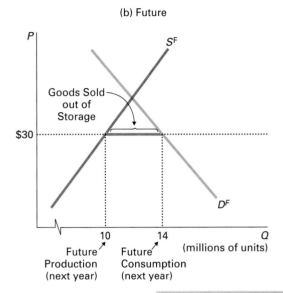

(b) Future

Speculation works like international trade, with speculators "exporting" goods into storage now and "importing" them out of storage in the future. In this equilibrium, current production is 12 million units per year, current consumption is 8 million units, and speculators buy 4 million units for storage. In the future, speculators take these goods out of storage, so future consumption exceeds future production by 4 million units.

This activity raises the price today and reduces the expected future price, so it tends to equalize the two prices.

Equilibrium with No-Cost Speculation

Figure 5 shows an equilibrium with speculation when there are no costs of speculating. Figure 5a shows supply and demand now. Figure 5b shows expected supply and demand next year. Figure 5 resembles Figures 1 and 4, except that it represents different times rather than different nations or regions. Without speculation, the expected future price exceeds today's price, creating an incentive for speculators to buy the good now, store it, and resell it in the future.[8]

With costless speculation, the equilibrium price now equals the expected future price, as in Figure 5. The reasoning is the same as in the discussion of arbitrage; if costs of arbitrage are zero, the equilibrium price is the same in both locations. Here the equilibrium price is the same in both time periods if speculation costs nothing.

The demand curve D^N shows current demand by consumers. Equilibrium consumption now is 8 units of the good. Equilibrium output now is 12 units of the good; people consume 8 units, and speculators buy 4 to store for the future. The expected future demand curve is D^F. The expected future supply curve by producers is S^F. At a future price of $30, the quantity supplied by producers is 10, and speculators sell the 4 units that they have stored. In equilibrium, the future price is $30, future consumption is 14 units, future production is 10 units, and speculators sell 4 units out of storage.

IN THE NEWS

Low natural-gas prices lure speculators

Natural-gas prices, ever the volatile kids on the energy block, are creeping down once again.

But despite the short-term pessimism in the trading pits—and a ballooning abundance of the fuel in underground storage tanks—the markets long view for prices is relatively bullish.

Natural-gas wholesalers, who control the storage tanks, are betting that they can buy cheap gas now on the spot market, hoard it, then retail it later this year at higher prices.

Source: The Wall Street Journal

As speculators buy natural gas for storage, their demand limits the fall in today's price, but also raises future supply, reducing future price increases.

---

[8]The opposite would happen if speculators expected a future price below the current price. Speculators would try to profit by selling more of the good now and storing less for the future. Their actions would reduce the current price and raise the expected future price. In equilibrium, the expected future price equals the current price. The situation becomes more complicated if the amount of the good that people store falls to zero because it becomes impossible to store less for the future. In that case, the current price can remain above the expected future price without speculators doing anything to profit from the situation.

Profiting from Differences in People's Expectations

When expectations about the future differ, people can gain from trade. Suppose that your friends expect your college football team to win its game against Rival State, and you know people at Rival State who expect *their* team to win. You can profit by arranging for these people to trade.

You issue an *asset* (or IOU) by writing on a piece of paper "I will pay the owner of this IOU $1 if our team wins." Call this note the *home-team asset*. You then issue another asset: a piece of paper that says "I will pay the owner of this IOU $1 if Rival State wins." Call this note the *Rival State asset*. You then *sell* these assets in equal numbers. (You must sell the same number of each kind of asset.)

People who expect your college's team to win will probably be willing to pay more than 50 cents for a home-team asset, which will pay $1 if your team wins. Someone who estimates your school's chances of winning at 3 out of 4 may be willing to pay up to 75 cents for this asset. This person will expect to *profit* by paying anything less than 75 cents. Suppose you sell a home-team asset to this person for 60 cents.

Similarly, people who expect Rival State to win will probably be willing to pay more than 50 cents for the Rival State asset, which pays them $1 if Rival State wins. Someone who estimates the chance that Rival State will win at 60 percent may be willing to pay up to 60 cents, and this person will expect to profit by paying anything less. Suppose you sell the Rival State asset to this person for 55 cents.

You collect more than a dollar ($1.15) by selling these two assets. After the game, you will have to pay $1 to one

Speculators, like arbitragers, earn zero expected profits in equilibrium. Positive expected profits would create incentives for people to increase speculation, while negative expected profits would create incentives to reduce speculation. Neither of those situations could be an equilibrium, because both create tendencies for change. As a result, equilibrium requires that speculators earn zero expected profits. As in the discussion of arbitrage, the best way to understand this logical point is to think of a very small expected price increase that would give speculators a profit just large enough to create an incentive to buy and store the goods for later resale.

Although expected profits are zero, future events may differ from people's expectations today. The figure shows the actual future price, production, and consumption if speculators' expectations accurately foretell the future. If speculators turn out to be wrong and the future price is below $30, speculators lose money. If the future brings a price above $30, speculators profit. No matter what happens, future consumption exceeds future output, because speculators will eventually sell the goods they have stored.

Who Are Speculators?

A speculator can be a producer who stores goods rather than selling them now, in expectation of selling for a higher price in the future. A buyer speculates when he avoids an expected price increase by buying extra goods now, while the price remains low, and storing them for future use. A speculator can also be a third party who believes that a good's price will rise and attempts to profit by buying now with plans to resell in the future. People speculate when they buy art or real estate that they plan to sell in the future.

Winners and Losers from Speculation

Speculation, like arbitrage and international trade, creates winners and losers. Speculation raises a good's price at times when it would otherwise be unusually low, so buyers lose and sellers gain at those times. Speculation also lowers the price (as speculators sell stored goods) at times when the price would otherwise be unusually high, so buyers gain and sellers lose at those times.

person or the other, depending on which team wins, and you will keep 15 cents in profit. Obviously, the size of your profit depends on how many pairs of assets you sell, as well as the prices that people are willing to pay for them. This idea generalizes to any difference in expectations about the future:

When people have different expectations about the future, they can gain from trade.

Each person with whom you trade gains from the trade, regardless of who wins the football game. These gains are similar to the benefits people get from purchasing fire insurance, even if they are lucky and a fire never erupts in their home. When they purchase insurance, people are uncertain about the future, so they gain by buying the insurance. Similarly, people gain from buying your assets because they are uncertain about the outcome of the football game.

Many sophisticated financial assets (such as options and futures contracts) function like these assets, and they are traded every day in major cities around the world. These real-life financial assets create trades between people with different expectations about the future. Financial institutions such as banks and the New York Stock Exchange play the role that you played in the football example; they profit by bringing together people with differing expectations who expect to gain by buying these assets.

Note: The general rule is this: A person who estimates the chance that your team will win at p percent (such as 55 percent) will expect to break even by paying p cents for the home-team asset. Someone who estimates the chance of winning at 75 out of 100 will expect to break even by paying 75 cents for the asset. By paying any price less than 75 cents, this person will expect to profit from the home-team asset.

I N   T H E   N E W S

The speculator as hero

By Victor Niederhoffer

I am a speculator. I own seats on the Chicago Board of Trade and Chicago Mercantile Exchange. . . .

Like hundreds of thousands of other traders, I try to predict the prices of common goods a day or two or a few months in the future. If I think the price of an item will go up, I buy today and sell later. If I think the price is going down, I'll sell at today's higher price. The miracle is that in taking care of ourselves, we speculators somehow ensure that producers all over the world will provide the right quantity and quality of goods at the proper time, without undue waste, and that this meshes with what people want and the money they have available.

When a harvest is too small to satisfy consumption at its normal rate, speculators come in, hoping to profit from the scarcity by buying. Their purchases raise the price, thereby checking consumption so that the smaller supply will last longer. Producers encouraged by the high price further lessen the shortage by growing or importing to reduce the shortage. On the other side, when the price is higher than the speculators think the facts warrant, they sell. This reduces prices, encouraging consumption and exports and helping to reduce the surplus. Of course, speculators aren't always correct. When they are wrong, their actions contribute to shortages or gluts. Manias such as the Tulipomania, the South Sea Bubble, the Mississippi Bubble, gold panics, stock market crashes, and violent swings in the value of the dollar are frequently cited as examples of occasions when speculators contributed to instability and imbalance. But who could do the job better?

Source: The Wall Street Journal

A speculator describes his job.

Figure 6 | Increase in Expected Future Demand

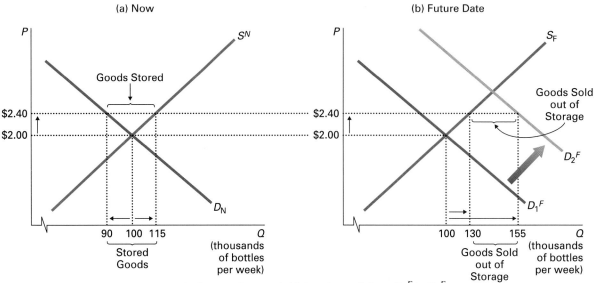

An increase in expected future demand, from D_1^F to D_2^F:

▶ Raises the price from $2.00 to $2.40
▶ Raises current production from 100,000 to 115,000
▶ Lowers current consumption from 100,000 to 90,000
▶ Raises future (expected) production from 100,000 to 130,000
▶ Raises future (expected) consumption from 100,000 to 155,000

Chapter 9 will show that, at each point in time, the gains from speculation exceed the losses if speculators act on reasonably accurate expectations about the future. In that case, speculation (like international trade and arbitrage) is economically efficient.

Effects of Changes in Expectations

Suppose that people's expectations about the future change, and they begin to expect an increase in future demand for mouthwash. Figure 6 shows that an increase in expected future demand from D_1^F to D_2^F raises the expected future price. This creates an incentive for speculators to buy and store mouthwash for future resale. The increase in expected future demand creates speculation and raises both today's price and the expected future price from $2.00 to $2.40. Current production rises from 100,000 to 115,000 bottles per week, current consumption falls from 100,000 to 90,000, and speculators store 25,000 bottles. Expected future production rises from 100,000 to 130,000 bottles. Because speculators will eventually sell 25,000, expected future consumption rises from 100,000 to 155,000 bottles. Notice that the change in beliefs about the future affects prices, production, and consumption now. This result illustrates an important point:

Economic conditions now depend partly on what people expect about the future.

Changes in expectations about the future affect the economy now.

Intertemporal Substitution

Suppose that you want to buy a computer, but you expect computer prices to fall next month. You might choose to wait until next month to make the purchase. Similarly, you

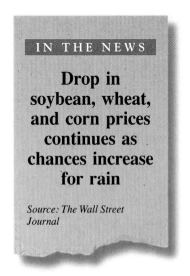

IN THE NEWS

Drop in soybean, wheat, and corn prices continues as chances increase for rain

Source: The Wall Street Journal

Current prices fall when an increased chance of rain raises expected future supplies.

might take a vacation during an off-season when prices are lower, or buy your textbooks early or late when the lines at the bookstore are shorter. How often have you waited for a product to go on sale at a lower price before buying it, or bought a good sooner than you planned because its price was low? You may have waited for a book to come out in paperback or a movie to come out on video. These examples illustrate intertemporal substitution, or substitution over time.

Intertemporal substitution refers to a change in current demand or supply of a good caused by a change in its expected future price. People often choose when to buy or sell goods to take advantage of expected price changes. You might wait to buy a good because you expect its price to fall, or you might buy now because you believe its price might soon rise. A change in the expected future price of a good causes a change in its current demand.

Intertemporal substitution resembles speculation, except it can affect even nonstorable goods. Although haircuts and beach vacations are not storable goods, you can get a haircut either today or next week; you can go to the beach either this year or next. If people expect the price of a good to rise, they have an incentive to buy it now. If it is storable, they can save it for later use. If it is not storable, they may be able to use it now instead of later. If people expect the price of a good to fall, they may wait until later to buy and use it.

Review Questions

9. What is speculation?

10. What are the effects of speculation?

Thinking Exercises

11. How is today's equilibrium price related to the expected future price? Explain why.

12. What happens to the current price of a storable good if its expected future demand rises?

COSTLY ARBITRAGE AND SPECULATION

The chapter noted earlier that arbitrage often has a cost that allows small price differentials, but limits their size. Figure 4 showed an equilibrium with costless arbitrage. This section discusses the logic of equilibrium with costly arbitrage or speculation.

Equilibrium with Costly Arbitrage

Costs of arbitrage can include money and time costs of purchasing goods in one place, transporting them to another place, and reselling them. Suppose that arbitrage costs total $2 per unit of the good. Then arbitrage is profitable only if the price differential exceeds $2. If the good costs $12 *Here* and $13 *There*, arbitrage is not profitable. If it costs $12 *Here* and $15 *There*, however, arbitragers earn profits. Any price differential that exceeds $2 creates an arbitrage opportunity. Since equilibrium allows no arbitrage opportunities, the equilibrium price differential cannot exceed $2.

Figure 7 shows an equilibrium with costly arbitrage. The per-unit cost of arbitrage, $2, means that arbitragers must pay $2 to buy, ship, and resell each unit of the good. The price in Boston, $14, exceeds the price in Minneapolis, $12, by the cost of arbitrage. Output in Minneapolis is 200 units, consumption there is only 160 units, and arbitragers buy 40 units of the good there for resale in Boston. Consumption in Boston is

Figure 7 | Equilibrium with Costly Arbitrage

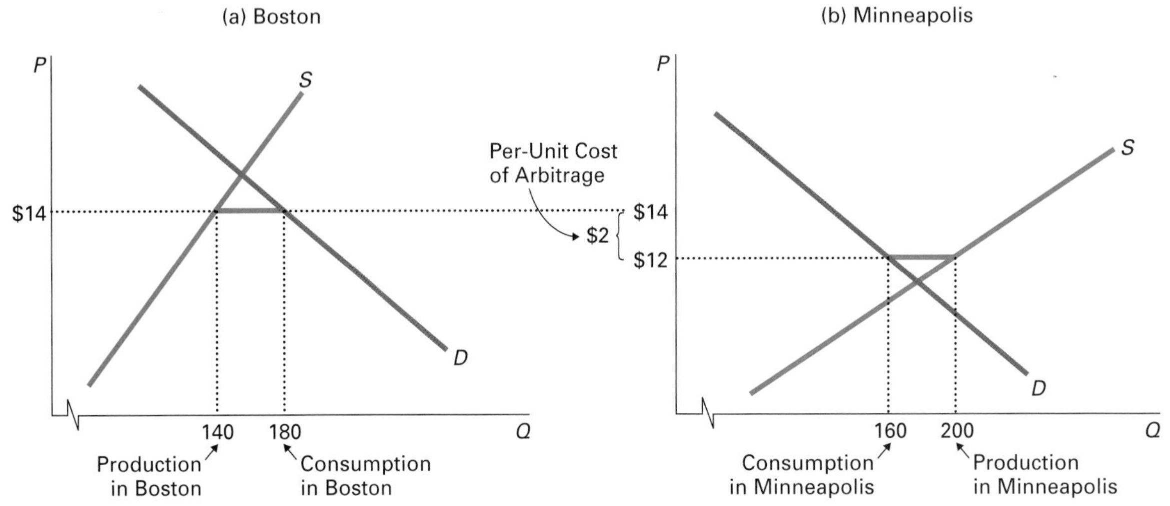

Boston imports 40 units of the good from Minneapolis. The price in Boston exceeds the price in Minneapolis by the per-unit arbitrage cost, $2.

180 units and production is 140 units. Consumption exceeds production in Boston, because arbitragers sell the goods they bought in Minneapolis; Boston effectively imports 40 units from Minneapolis. In this way, arbitrage creates interregional trade.

A price differential can occur in equilibrium when arbitrage is costly. You probably know many examples of goods that cost more in one place than in another. These differentials occur because arbitrage is costly. Otherwise, everyone would buy in the low-price place, or some would buy in the low-price place and profit by reselling in the high-price place. The per-unit costs of arbitrage limit the sizes of price differentials.

Some goods have low costs of arbitrage, so they sell for roughly the same prices in different cities. You can buy stock, bonds, or other financial assets for the same prices in any city. The costs of arbitrage are very low for these assets, because people can buy them over the phone, through the mail, or by computer. Low arbitrage costs keep the prices of soap, paper, pencils, books, baseballs, light bulbs, plastic cups, and comic books roughly the same everywhere. Other goods have high costs of arbitrage, and their prices can differ substantially across locations. Costly arbitrage allows the prices of land, houses, auto repairs, and haircuts to differ from city to city. Land and houses cannot be transported cheaply from one city to another, nor can services such as auto repairs and haircuts. The supply and demand in each city determine the equilibrium there, as long as the price differential remains smaller than the per-unit cost of arbitrage.

Equilibrium with Costly Speculation

Speculation, like arbitrage, may have a cost. If an expected future price increase is smaller than this cost, then speculation is not profitable. The cost of speculation limits the expected rise in the equilibrium price of a storable good. Costless speculation prevents a good's expected future price from exceeding its current price.

Speculation can be costly for several reasons. First, speculators must pay to buy a good now, but they do not collect anything from selling goods until later, so they tie up money in the speculation. Speculation has an opportunity cost equal to the interest income that the money could have earned in another investment or in a savings account. A speculator's opportunity cost (per dollar of speculation) is the interest rate.

A second cost of speculation is risk. A speculator profits by selling a good later at

Figure 8 | Equilibrium with Costly Speculation

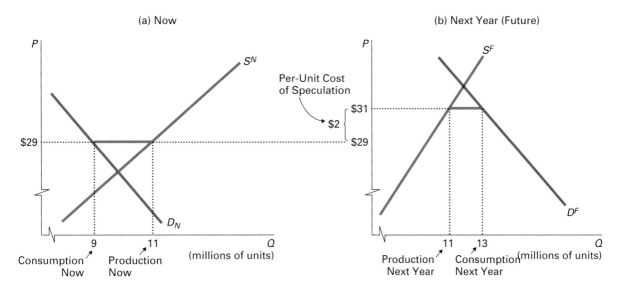

a higher price than the current price. A speculator loses money if the price later falls short of the price now. Most people do not like taking risks like this, so people are willing to speculate only if they expect, on average, to earn enough money to compensate them for taking risks. A payment for bearing risk is a second cost of speculation.

A third cost of speculation involves storage costs and depreciation of goods in storage. Speculators must pay to store goods in a warehouse or some similar place until a future time. Depreciation is the loss in value of goods because of spoilage or other wear and tear due to storage. Depreciation occurs each year as rats eat a certain fraction of the wheat stored in silos. Depreciation also occurs if only nine out of every ten goods a speculator puts into storage will remain in good condition for future sale. Storage costs and depreciation are additional costs of speculation.

Figure 8 shows an equilibrium with costly speculation. It resembles Figure 7, except that it applies to speculation over time rather than arbitrage across locations. The per-unit cost of speculation, $2 in Figure 8, includes foregone interest, risk, storage costs, and depreciation. People are willing to speculate only if the price of the good is expected to increase by at least $2. In Figure 8, the equilibrium current price is $29 and the equilibrium expected future price is $31. The expected future price exceeds the current price by the per-unit cost of speculation, $2. Equilibrium production today is 11 million units of the good. People consume 9 million units and speculators buy the other 2 million to store for the future. Expected future production is 11 million units. Expected future consumption is 13 million, which exceeds expected future production by the 2 million units that speculators will sell out of their inventories.

Review Question

13. What are the costs of arbitrage and speculation?

Thinking Exercise

14. Use a graph like Figure 7 to show how a fall in the cost of arbitrage affects (a) the price at each location, (b) production at each location, and (c) consumption at each location.

OTHER APPLICATIONS

International Borrowing and Lending

From the end of World War II until the 1980s, the United States was a lender in markets for international loans.[9] Since then, the United States has borrowed from the rest of the world.

> International borrowing or lending occurs whenever people in one country lend to or borrow from people in another country; it is international trade in loans.

International trade in loans resembles international trade in goods. People supply loans when they lend money, and they demand loans when they borrow money. The quantity of loans supplied is the amount of money that people are willing to lend, and the quantity demanded is the amount that others want to borrow. The interest rate is the price of a loan, per dollar loaned. Increases in the interest rate raise the incentive to lend money, so the supply curve for loans slopes upward as in Figure 9. Increases in the interest rate reduce the incentive to borrow money, so the demand curve for loans slopes downward.

Figure 9 shows equilibrium in international trade in loans. It resembles Figure 1, except it applies to loans. The equilibrium world interest rate is 6 percent per year in this example, and total world loans are $3,300 billion. The supply of loans in the United States, S^{US}, represents lending by people in the United States. The demand for loans in the United States, D^{US}, represents borrowing by people in the United States. At the equilibrium interest rate of 6 percent, U.S. lenders lend $800 billion, while U.S. borrowers borrow $900 billion. People in the United States borrow $100 billion from people in other countries. Figure 9b shows the foreign supply of loans, S^F, and foreign demand for loans, D^F, which represent lending and borrowing by people in foreign countries. At the equilibrium interest rate of 6 percent, foreign borrowers borrow $2,400 billion, while foreign lenders lend $2,500 billion, so foreign lenders lend $100 billion to borrowers in the United States.

What would happen if foreign countries could not lend to the United States? (Suppose, for example, that foreign governments prohibited lending to the United States.) Then the U.S. interest rate would be determined solely by U.S. supply and demand for loans (the curves in Figure 9a). The equilibrium U.S. interest rate would be 7 percent instead of 6 percent, and the foreign interest rate would be 5 percent. This shows how foreign lending to the United States keeps the U.S. interest rate lower than it would otherwise be.

Effects of Increased U.S. Government Borrowing

The government borrows money when it has a budget deficit—when it spends more money than it receives in tax revenues. Recall from Chapter 6:

> The **government budget deficit** is the amount of money that the government borrows each year when it spends more than it collects in taxes.

Although U.S. government budget deficits have fallen in recent years, they may increase again after a few years as the baby boom generation retires and begins collecting social security.

Changes in government borrowing affect the interest rate by changing the demand for loans. A $100 billion increase in the U.S. government budget deficit raises the U.S. demand for loans by $100 billion, from $D_1{}^{US}$ to $D_2{}^{US}$ in Figure 10. This raises the world

IN THE NEWS

Foreign buying of U.S. Treasurys helps keep interest rates down

*By Thomas T. Vogel Jr.
Staff Reporter of The Wall Street Journal*

NEW YORK—One reason U.S. interest rates are so low now is a surge of foreign buying of U.S. Treasurys during the fourth quarter of last year and the first quarter of this year.

Source: The Wall Street Journal

Foreign lending to the United States (by buying U.S. Treasury securities) lowers U.S. interest rates, as in Figure 9.

[9]This statement refers to total net lending by people, business firms, and governments. Some Americans borrowed from people in other countries, but as a whole the United States was a lender.

Figure 9 | International Borrowing and Lending

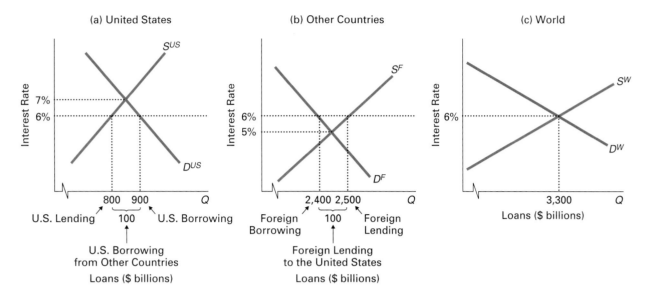

demand for loans, which raises the world interest rate from 6.0 percent to 6.5 percent. The interest-rate increase raises U.S. lending from $800 billion to $820 billion, while U.S. borrowing rises from $900 billion to $980 billion. The interest-rate increase also raises foreign lending from $2,500 billion to $2,530 billion, while foreign borrowing falls from $2,400 billion to $2,370 billion. Before the increase in the U.S. government budget deficit, the United States borrowed $100 billion from foreigners each year. After the increase, the United States borrows $160 billion from foreigners each year. Higher government budget deficits increase equilibrium borrowing from foreign countries.

Figure 10 | Effects of Higher U.S. Government Borrowing

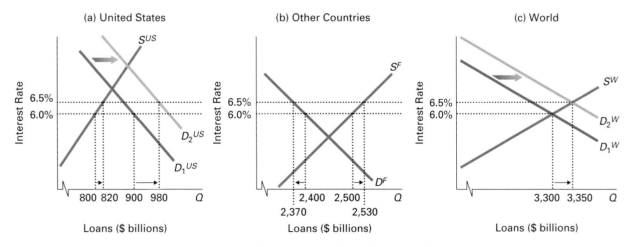

The interest rate starts out at 6.0 percent. An increase in U.S. government borrowing raises U.S. demand for loans from D_1^{US} to D_2^{US}, and the world market demand rises from D_1^{W} to D_2^{W}. This raises the world interest rate from 6.0 percent to 6.5 percent. U.S. lending rises to $820 billion and U.S. borrowing rises to $980 billion. Foreign lending rises to $2,530 billion and foreign borrowing falls to $2,370 billion. U.S. borrowing from other countries rises from $100 billion to $160 billion.

The interest-rate increase from 6.0 percent to 6.5 percent also reduces borrowing by the private sector in the United States (that is, by people and business firms). Total borrowing from foreign countries by people, business firms, and the government in the United States rises by $80 billion (from $900 billion to $980 billion), but total *government* borrowing rises by $100 billion. Thus, total borrowing by the private sector in the United States falls by $20 billion per year.

Futures Markets

When you buy a sweater at a store, you take it home with you. When you order a shirt from a catalog or a custom-made bike from a local shop, however, you receive your goods at a future time.

> **Futures markets** are markets in which people buy and sell goods for future delivery. **Future prices** are prices of goods for delivery at future dates.

Some futures markets, such as the Chicago Mercantile Exchange, are formal organizations. Financial pages of newspapers list futures prices of corn, wheat, barley, cattle, cocoa, cotton, orange juice, gold, silver, gasoline, lumber, and many other goods. Futures prices differ from spot prices.

> **Spot prices** are the prices of goods for current delivery.

Spot prices are prices as people normally think of them.

Speculation creates a link between today's futures price and the spot price that people expect in the future:

The equilibrium futures price equals the expected future spot price.[10]

EXPLANATION AND EXAMPLE

Suppose that you expect the spot price of wheat next April 1 to be $5.00 per bushel. If the futures price is $4.70, you would expect to profit from buying wheat futures. Suppose that you buy 5,000 bushels of wheat on the futures market at a cost of $4.70 per bushel; the wheat will be delivered to you on April 1, and you can sell it then. If your expectations turn out to be right and the future spot price is $5.00, you make a profit of 30 cents per bushel (or $1,500 on the 5,000 bushels). If the future spot price falls short of $4.70, you lose money because you sell the wheat for less than the $4.70 you paid for it. (Like other speculators, you would not wait until April 1 to sell the wheat. You would sell it before April 1 to avoid having the wheat actually delivered to you.)

If you expect the spot price of wheat next April 1 to be $5.00 and the futures price is $5.25, then you can profit by selling wheat futures. Suppose that you sell 5,000 bushels of wheat on the futures market at a cost of $5.25 per bushel. (If you don't have any wheat to sell, you can borrow wheat and sell it; you can buy wheat later to repay the loan.) The sale obligates you to deliver 5,000 bushels of wheat to someone on April 1. If your expectations turn out to be right and the spot price is $5.00 on April 1, you make a profit of 25 cents per bushel by purchasing wheat at $5.00 per bushel and delivering it to another buyer who pays you $5.25. If the spot price in April turns out to be more than $5.25, you lose money.

---

[10]Because people dislike risk, this conclusion is only an approximation that applies closely in most futures markets.

IN THE NEWS

Brazil's frost puts chill on coffee prices

Wholesalers have raised prices almost $1.00 a pound in the past month and the consumer, who had been paying about $3.69 a pound for preground coffee beans in markets, has seen the price go to $4.69.

Beans that were selling at about $1.30 a pound wholesale 3 months ago rose to more than $2.70 a pound this week.

The initial reason for the increases, according to Donald Schoenholt, founding chairman of the Specialty Coffee Association of America, a trade group of small specialty coffee shops and roasters, is "the nervous, frightening climate" in the coffee-growing world caused by news that frost in Brazil killed more than 40 percent of that country's coffee crop for sale in 1987. Brazil supplies one-third of all the coffee sold in the world.

Supplies of coffee are plentiful now, but the prospect of a shortage next year has caused wild speculation on contracts for future purchases in the New York Coffee, Sugar and Cocoa Exchange, the commodity market whose transactions ultimately determine prices. This speculation has driven up the prices for the coffee beans called Arabica.

Source: Rochester Democrat and Chronicle

Prices rise today when new information reduces expectations of future supplies.

If the futures price of wheat is below the expected future spot price of wheat, then people buy wheat futures. This raises the demand for wheat futures, which raises the futures price of wheat. This speculation continues until the futures price equals the expected future spot price. At that point, the market reaches equilibrium. If, instead, the futures price of wheat exceeds the expected future spot price, people sell wheat futures, raising the supply of wheat futures and lowering the futures price. This continues until the futures price equals the expected future spot price.

The futures price changes whenever expectations about the future spot price change. Rainfall in Brazil changes the futures price of coffee. Frost in Florida raises the futures price of orange juice.

Stock Prices

Every night, people watch television news reports on the stock market, yet few viewers know much about it.

> **Shares of stock** are legal rights of ownership in business firms. The stock market is an organized system for trading shares of stock. The prices of these shares are stock prices.

The costs of speculating on the stock market are small, so Figure 5 (which shows an equilibrium with no-cost speculation) approximates the stock market. This has an important implication:

> The equilibrium **stock price** today equals (approximately) the expected future stock price.

EXPLANATION

If the expected future price exceeded the price today, people could profit by buying stock now and selling it later. If the expected future price were lower than the current price, people could profit by selling the stock now and buying it back later at a lower price.[11] With costless speculation on the stock market, the equilibrium current price and expected future price are equal.

Stock Prices Take a Random Walk

In equilibrium, the expected future price of a stock approximately equals its current price. People know that the stock price might rise or fall, but, on average, they expect it to stay at about the same level.

> A price follows a **random walk** if it is equally likely to rise or fall by the same amount, so, on average, it will stay about where it is.

Stock prices approximate random walks.

Costs of Stock-Market Speculation

The costs of speculating on the stock market are not *exactly* zero. The opportunity cost of buying stock equals the interest you could have earned by depositing the same money in a bank or lending it. Another cost of buying stock is risk; the stock investment may lose money rather than make money. In real life, these costs are small enough that, from day to day, stock prices very closely approximate random walks.

Many investment advisors deny that stock prices approximate random walks. They claim to be able to tell you when to buy and sell certain stocks to make large profits. Maybe they can, but it is fair to ask them, "If you're so smart, why aren't you rich?" If these investment advisors knew which stock prices were likely to rise or fall, they would probably stop working and vacation for the rest of their lives! (They could also use their knowledge to earn large sums of money for charities.) Of course, a few investors earn high profits in the stock market by chance. These lucky investors are usually willing to tell you about their investment skills, but you are less likely to hear from the people who lose money by chance.

Some people have privileged information about certain companies and may be able to earn high profits in the stock market by trading based on that information. Most people lack access to this kind of special information, though. In equilibrium—and in real life—stock prices come close to random walks. To make large profits in the stock market, you must have better luck, better information, or better skills at using information than most other people have.

Review Questions

15. What is a futures price? A spot price?

16. How is the equilibrium futures price of lumber related to the spot price that people expect for a future date?

---

[11]Anyone who does not own stock can borrow it to sell through arrangements set up by organized financial markets to accommodate this kind of activity, called *short selling*. Later, you buy the stock and use it to repay the loan.

17. Explain why stock prices follow random walks.

18. Would the U.S. interest rate rise or fall if the government were to prohibit borrowing from people in foreign countries? Explain why.

19. Would the United States borrow more or less from people in other countries if people in the United States saved more? Explain why.

C o n c l u s i o n

International Trade

The world market determines prices of internationally traded goods. The quantity supplied in each country at the world equilibrium price shows that country's output of the good, while the quantity demanded at that price in each country shows its consumption. If a country's quantity supplied at the world equilibrium price exceeds its quantity demanded, the difference equals that country's exports. If a country's quantity demanded at the world equilibrium price exceeds its quantity supplied, the difference equals its imports.

An increase in demand in any country raises the world equilibrium price, which lowers consumption in other countries and raises output in all countries. An increase in supply of a good in any country lowers its world equilibrium price, which lowers output in other countries and raises consumption in all countries.

Arbitrage

Arbitrage means buying a good at a place where its price is low and selling it where its price is higher. Like international trade, arbitrage tends to reduce or eliminate price differentials. As arbitragers buy in low-price locations to resell in higher-price locations, the price rises in the low-price places and falls in the high-price places. An arbitrage opportunity arises when someone knows of a price differential that exceeds the costs of arbitrage. Equilibrium allows no arbitrage opportunities. If the cost of arbitrage is zero, the equilibrium price is the same in every location.

Speculation

Speculation means buying a storable good when its price is low and reselling it at a later time when its price may have risen. Speculation resembles arbitrage across time rather than across regions or between countries. If speculation costs nothing, the equilibrium price of a good today equals its expected future price. While international trade and arbitrage tend to equalize prices in different places, speculation tends to equalize expected prices in different

months or years. Because of speculation, a fall in the expected future supply of a product raises its price today. Intertemporal substitution resembles speculation: People time their buying or selling to take advantage of temporarily low or high prices.

Costly Arbitrage and Speculation

Arbitragers and speculators incur costs. Arbitrage costs include identifying a price differential, buying the goods at the low-price location, shipping them, and reselling them at the higher-price location. Costs of speculation include the interest rate (which is the opportunity cost of tying up money in speculation), the cost of bearing risk, storage costs, and depreciation.

When arbitrage is costly, the equilibrium price differential cannot exceed the per-unit cost of arbitrage. When speculation has a cost, the expected future price cannot exceed the equilibrium price today plus the per-unit cost of speculation.

Other Applications

International trade in loans resembles trade in goods. Some countries lend (or export loans), while other countries borrow (or import loans). The price of a loan is the interest rate, and the world equilibrium interest rate determines international trade in loans. Changes in the supply or demand for loans in any country affect the world interest rate. An increase in the government budget deficit in some country can raise that country's demand for loans, which raises the world interest rate and the amount that the country borrows on world markets.

People buy and sell goods for future delivery on futures markets. The equilibrium futures price of a good equals its expected future spot price. People buy and sell shares of stock on stock markets. The costs of speculating on the stock market are low, so the equilibrium price of a stock closely approximates its expected future price. Economists summarize this result by saying that stock prices follow a random walk.

Key Terms

consumption of a good	price differential	futures market	share of stock
export	arbitrage opportunity	futures price	stock price
import	speculation	spot price	random walk
arbitrage	government budget deficit		

Problems

20. Refer to the accompanying table to answer the following questions:
    (a) Fill in the rest of the table. What is the world market demand for radios? What is the world market supply?
    (b) Find the world equilibrium price and quantity.
    (c) Draw graphs of the U.S. demand and supply, the rest of the world's demand and supply, and the world market demand and supply.
    (d) Does the United States export or import radios in this example? How much does it export or import? What is the money value of these exports or imports? Does the rest of the world export or import radios? How much do other countries import?

How much does it export or import? How much does the rest of the world produce, consume, and export or import?
(b) Suppose that the foreign demand for radios increases by 4 units at every price. Find the new world equilibrium price and quantity. How much does the United States produce, consume, and export or import? How much does the rest of the world produce, consume, and export or import?
(c) Suppose that the U.S. supply of radios increases by 6 units at every price. Find the new world equilibrium price and quantity. How much does the United States produce, consume, and export or import? How much does the rest of the world produce, consume, and export or import?

	United States		Other Countries		World Market	
Price	Quantity Demanded	Quantity Supplied	Quantity Demanded	Quantity Supplied	Quantity Demanded	Quantity Supplied
$12	2	13	5	25		
11	4	12	6	22		
10	6	11	7	19		
9	10	10	8	17		
8	11	9	9	15		
7	12	8	10	14		
6	14	6	11	13		
5	16	0	12	12		
4	18	0	13	9		
3	20	0	14	0		
2	22	0	15	0		

21. Refer to the table from Problem 20 and give separate answers for each of the following questions:
    (a) Suppose that the U.S. demand for radios increases by 4 units at every price. (Add 4 to all numbers in the U.S. Quantity Demanded column, so the United States demands 6 if the price is $12, 8 if the price is $11, and so on.) Find the new world equilibrium price and quantity. How much does the United States produce now? How much does it consume?

(d) Suppose that the foreign supply of radios increases by 6 units at every price. Find the new world equilibrium price and quantity. How much does the United States produce, consume, and export or import? How much does the rest of the world produce, consume, and export or import?

22. Start with the equilibrium in Figure 1. Use graphs similar to Figures 2 and 3 to show what happens to

IN THE NEWS

Soybean prices surge as radio report on plant disease incites speculators

By Scott Kilman
Staff Reporter of The Wall
Street Journal

Soybean prices jumped yesterday after speculators heard Chicago radio commentator Paul Harvey re-

hash old news about a mysterious disease that suddenly kills soybean plants.

Grain brokers were stunned when Mr. Harvey's noon broadcast about "sudden death syndrome in the

soybean fields" helped fuel a buying binge in the last 10 minutes of trading, apparently on speculation that the disease could wipe out part of the crop.

Source: The Wall Street Journal

Futures prices respond quickly to any new information that people believe is important.

output, consumption, and exports or imports of film by the United States and other countries when:
(a) U.S. demand for film increases
(b) U.S. supply of film increases

23. Begin with the equilibrium in Figure 1. Show in a diagram what would happen to prices, production, and consumption of film in each country if the U.S. government were to *prohibit* international trade in film.

24. A drought in North America reduces output of oats in the United States. Use graphs to help explain why this increases U.S. imports of oats from Argentina.

25. Begin with the equilibrium in Figure 4 (which represents trade between *here* and *there*). Draw graphs to show what happens to the equilibrium price and equilibrium output and consumption in each place if:
(a) Demand for souvenir caps increases *there*
(b) Supply of souvenir caps increases *here*

26. Draw diagrams to show the effects of an increase in the expected future demand for a product next year on today's (a) price of the good, (b) quantity

produced, and (c) quantity consumed. Also show the amount of the good (d) produced next year and (e) consumed next year, along with (f) the price next year.

27. Snow in Florida reduces the number of oranges that will be available in the future. Comment on the following statement: "The price of orange juice may rise in the future, but the current price does not change because the weather in Florida does not change the amount of orange juice already in stores."

28. When the price of crude oil increases, gasoline prices rise immediately, even for gasoline that sellers already had in storage and that was produced from older, cheaper crude oil. Use graphs to explain why.

29. What can you do to try to profit if the futures price of eggs differs from the spot price of eggs that you expect next month?

30. Comment on this claim made by a well-known financial consulting firm: "Our stock analysts can help you pick the winners and avoid the losers, and our track record over the last year proves it."

Inquiries for Further Thought

31. Do you have any arbitrage opportunities? What price differentials do you know about? What would be your costs of arbitrage?

32. On what goods could you speculate? What would

be your costs of speculation? Under what conditions would you profit or lose money?

33. Do you think that profits from speculation result more from luck or from skill? How could you tell?

IN THE NEWS

Sudden impact: invasion of Kuwait sends U.S. gasoline prices soaring

Gasoline prices have shot up as much as 15 cents a gallon in the wake of Iraq's invasion of Kuwait and are likely to go higher despite outcries from motorists, politicians, and consumer groups.

Only hours after news of the hostilities broke, prices were being raised all along America's gasoline supply chain, from refineries to the corner service station. "I've never seen it happen so quickly," said Bill Dodd, a harried staff member at the Florida branch of the Automobile Association of America in Orlando. Pump prices in that state jumped two to 15 cents on Friday and "indications are they are going up higher," he said. "As we're speaking, the price is going up."

Increases across the Nation

Public irritation over the speedy price increases could cause unexpected results. Most troublesome is the possibility that the fear and furor—all by itself—could fuel further price increases.

Gasoline demand may jump sharply and stay unusually high in coming weeks simply because motorists, trying to beat the next price rise or worried about shortages, may insist on filling up their tanks and keeping them full. Normally, they might drive around on half a tank most of the time.

"If you put another quarter of a tank [of gasoline] in every car in the U.S., Western Europe, and Japan, it makes a huge difference," said Bryan Jacoboski, an oil analyst at PaineWebber Inc. in New York.

Source: The Wall Street Journal

Gasoline prices in the United States rose suddenly when Iraq invaded Kuwait in 1990. (See Problem 26.)

CHAPTER 8

PRICE CONTROLS AND TAXES

In this Chapter. . .

Main Points to Understand

▸ Maximum legal prices cause shortages and reduce output.

▸ Minimum legal prices cause surpluses and reduce output.

▸ A tax raises the price that buyers pay, lowers the price that sellers receive (net of tax), and reduces output.

Thinking Skills to Develop

▸ Recognize the effects of laws that keep prices higher or lower than equilibrium.

▸ Understand the effects of taxes on incentives.

▸ Predict the likely effects of a change in taxes.

General George Washington and his Continental Army troops spent the winter at Valley Forge, Pennsylvania, in 1777 and nearly starved to death. They could not buy enough food because government price controls on food left farmers unwilling to produce and sell food at those low prices. Governments throughout history have tried to keep prices low by making it illegal to charge prices above some level. But laws cannot repeal the forces of supply and demand, so price controls have unintended consequences.

Like price controls, taxes affect incentives to buy, sell, and produce. Taxes even affected the development of popular music. In the 1940s, a 20 percent tax on live vocal music in New York City nightclubs led those clubs to switch from vocal acts to bands playing instrumental music; this tax hindered the development of vocal jazz and encouraged instrumental jazz. Jazz musician Max Roach said, "That 20 percent tax was the most important thing," for American musical development in the mid-20th century.

PRICE CONTROLS: MAXIMUM LEGAL PRICES

Governments all over the world try to keep prices low by setting maximum legal prices. These price controls cause long lines and shortages and reduce production. Figure 1 shows what happens when the government places a maximum legal price on a good.

> A **maximum legal price** (price ceiling) is the highest price at which the government allows people to buy or sell a good.

The following discussion deals only with a maximum legal price *below* the equilibrium price.

In Figure 1, the maximum legal price, $\overline{P}$, is below the equilibrium price. A maximum legal price causes a shortage and reduces output.

> A **shortage** is a situation in which the quantity demanded exceeds the quantity supplied at the current price.

The maximum legal price reduces the quantity supplied from Q^E to Q^S and raises the quantity demanded from Q^E to Q^D. The shortage equals the quantity demanded minus the quantity supplied, $Q^D - Q^S$. Output falls (along with the quantity supplied) from Q^E to Q^S; although consumers would like to buy more, sellers are willing to sell only Q^S. Chapter 4 explained that a shortage usually causes the price to rise, but the price cannot rise if the government enforces the maximum legal price law.

Nonprice Rationing

A shortage prevents some buyers from buying as many goods as they want at the current price.

Figure 1 | Maximum Legal Price

A maximum legal price, $\overline{P}$ below the equilibrium price causes a shortage of $Q^D - Q^S$. Actual production and sales equal Q^S.

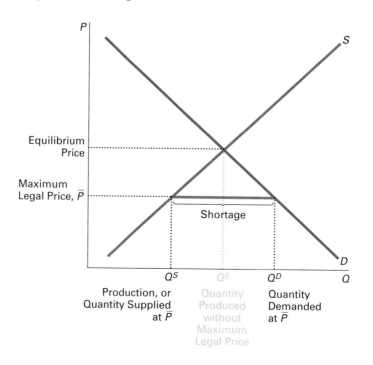

Price controls affected everyday life in the former Socialist countries of Eastern Europe. Shortages and long lines were commonplace. Still, some people were lucky. After hours in a queue caused by price controls, this jubilant woman celebrates the luck that allowed her to purchase a pair of Italian boots.

> **Nonprice rationing** is a system for choosing who gets how many goods during a shortage.

Rationing by waiting, rationing by coupons, and bribes are three common forms of non-price rationing. In each case, the people who actually get the goods may not be the people most willing to pay for them.[1]

Rationing by Waiting

Rationing by waiting occurs when people toward the front of a line can buy a good, but people further back in line cannot. Goods are allocated by a first-come, first-served method. Rationing by waiting is also called *queuing,* and the line is called a *queue.* The people who buy the good (those first in line) are the people who are willing to spend the most time to buy it. These people either value the good more than others or place a lower value on their time.

Rationing by waiting sometimes leads buyers to hire other people with lower time values to wait in line for them. This practice was common in the former socialist economies of eastern Europe and the former Soviet Union, where rationing by waiting was a daily experience. Retired people worked part-time waiting in long lines at stores to buy goods for other people. Buyers hired them on the streets in front of the stores.

When the U.S. government set a maximum legal price for gasoline in the 1970s, high-school students in the Los Angeles area earned money waiting in queues to fill up other people's tanks. They picked up cars in the morning, waited in line at gas stations, and returned the cars with the tanks filled to their owners.

Rationing by waiting forces buyers to pay more than the money price, $\overline{P}$; they also pay a time cost equal to the value of the time they spend waiting in line. The total cost of the good includes this time cost plus the money price.[2]

Sometimes buyers can choose either to wait in line for a low price or to pay a higher money price. If you pay someone to wait in line and buy a good for you, you increase your money price and reduce your time price. Some former socialist economies allowed

---

[1]Chapter 6 discussed buyers' willingness to pay for goods.

[2]Chapter 6 discussed time costs.

people to sell some of the goods they produced on their own. This option gave buyers a choice between government-owned stores with long queues for prices below equilibrium (along with the risk that the store would run out while the buyer waited in line) and private sellers charging higher prices but without queues.

Coupon Rationing

Soon after Japan bombed Pearl Harbor in 1941, the U.S. government set up the Office of Price Administration (OPA) with power to set maximum legal prices on 8 million types of goods and to oversee rationing. The OPA rationed goods by issuing books of colored stamps (coupons). Each stamp represented the right, valid until a certain date, to buy a certain good such as butter, beef, or sugar. At the store, a buyer exchanged the stamp and the money price for the good. People needed stickers on their cars to buy gasoline. (Many politicians got special *X* stickers that allowed them to buy unlimited amounts.) The U.S. government eliminated the OPA after the war.

Rationing by coupons occurs when the government distributes legal rights to buy a good among certain buyers. To do this, the government prints and distributes coupons that buyers must exchange along with money to buy the good. Each coupon lets a person buy one unit of the good at the maximum legal price of $\overline{P}$. Buyers exchange the coupon along with the $\overline{P}$ dollars when they buy the good. Coupon rationing may induce some people with coupons to buy more than they would have bought without the maximum legal price. Other people cannot buy as much because they lack enough coupons.

Rationing by Bribery

Bribery is another method for rationing with maximum legal prices. Sellers provide goods to their friends, to people who do favors for them, or to people who give them gifts or money. Buyers pay more than the explicit money price, $\overline{P}$; they also pay the cost of the bribe. Bribery is common in many parts of the world with maximum legal prices.[3]

Tie-in Sales

People sometimes avoid laws on maximum legal prices through tie-in sales.

> **Tie-in sales** occur when sellers sell only to buyers who also agree to buy other products from them.

When the government sets a maximum legal price on apartment rentals (rent controls), landlords sometimes require renters to rent furniture along with apartments. By charging a high rent for the furniture, a landlord evades the maximum legal price. For example, if the equilibrium rent is $300 per month and the maximum legal price is $200 per month, landlords might charge an extra $100 per month for required furniture rental or for cleaning fees.

Examples of Maximum Legal Prices

Price controls did not end with World War II. President Nixon imposed price controls in 1971. Several countries, including the United States, set maximum legal prices for gasoline in 1974 after the world price of oil quadrupled. These price controls caused long queues for gasoline. Again, in the late 1970s, the government printed coupons for rationing gasoline, though it never issued them.

Price controls have a long history, dating from about 2350 B.C. in ancient Sumeria. Later, Hammurabi's code of law for Babylon (around 1750 B.C.) set legal prices for medical services and other labor services. The Roman emperor Diocletian set maximum legal prices for many products in 301 A.D., with the death penalty for violators. The Roman price controls caused shortages and riots, and they were abandoned 4 years later when Diocletian abdicated.

Despite this ancient experience, price controls have remained common throughout history. During this century, governments of former socialist countries controlled prices on most goods and sold many goods only in government-owned stores. Even in nonsocialist countries, governments often control the prices of food, grain, houses, and many other goods and services. Price controls are major causes of low food production in many less-developed countries; governments there keep prices so low that farmers don't bother to produce much food beyond what their families eat. The governments of many

---

[3]Chapter 6 discussed bribery.

African countries have required farmers to sell their food output to the government, which pays them less than one-half, and sometimes less than one-fourth, of the world equilibrium price. African per-capita food production fell by about one-fourth from 1960 to 1985 as increasing numbers of governments imposed maximum legal prices and other regulations. Some countries have changed these policies since then, recognizing that price controls contribute to world poverty. Ghana once paid farmers about one-fifth of the world equilibrium value of their output; when the government there abolished maximum legal prices on food in 1987, corn production tripled.

Rent Controls

Rent controls—maximum legal prices on apartment rentals—are common in many cities around the world. Several U.S. cities, including New York, maintain rent controls in various forms. In many former socialist countries, people had to sign up years, even decades, in advance to get apartments. As a result, many young, married couples lived with parents for years as they waited for apartments of their own. Queuing is the usual method for rationing apartments with rent controls, although bribery also commonly occurs. Tie-in sales are less common, because governments often outlaw them.

The short-run and long-run effects of rent controls differ because the supply of apartments is very inelastic in the short run but not in the long run. Figure 2 shows an example with perfectly inelastic short-run supply. A maximum legal price reduces apartment rents without changing the quantity supplied in the short run. A shortage develops because people want more apartment space at the low, government-set monthly rent than they would want at a higher, equilibrium rent. In the long run, rent controls reduce incentives to build new apartments and to repair and maintain existing ones. As a result, these controls limit availability of new apartments and induce landlords to let old ones deteriorate. The results in many cities have included serious urban decay with poorly maintained and even abandoned buildings. In the long run, rent controls decrease the quality and number of available apartments.

Maximum Legal Prices of Zero

Sometimes a government effectively sets a maximum legal price for a good at zero by allowing people to give it away free of charge but prohibiting them from charging prices

Rent Controls in New York City—It's Who You Know

Many celebrities, including a former New York mayor, have lived in rent-controlled apartments in New York City. These renters pay only a fraction (often less than one-fourth) of the rents for similar apartments without rent controls. Since 1943, when rent controls in New York City began as a temporary program (and they are *still* legally temporary), they have covered nearly half of all apartments in the city. Some renters have gained these benefits simply through luck; many have inherited legal rights to stay in rent-controlled apartments. For many others, getting a rent-controlled apartment is a matter of "who you know."

Figure 2 | Rent Control: Short-Run and Long-Run Effects

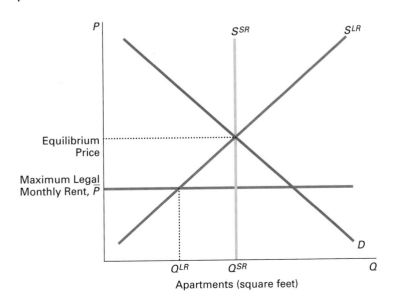

In the short run, rent control may not affect the number of available apartments, but in the long run, rent control reduces available apartment space to Q^{LR}.

IN THE NEWS

Another 'shadow economy'

Private medical practice has long flourished illegally in the Soviet Union, creating what has been called a "shadow medical economy." Influential people use connections and gifts to get appointments with hard-to-see specialists. State doctors are bribed with money and lavish presents to open their offices after hours. Nurses demand candy, flowers, or liquor to give basic hospital care to patients. These practices are so common that people consider them part of everyday life.

Source: New York Times

Maximum legal prices led to bribery in the former Soviet Union.

for it. One example of such a good is human organs. Medical advances have made organ transplants common. Doctors regularly transplant kidneys, for example, because a person can donate one of two kidneys and stay alive with the other one. Doctors also transplant hearts, livers, and other organs from people who have recently died. Most countries do not allow people to sell their organs, however, either while they are alive or at death; they allow people only to donate their organs without collecting payment. This restriction reduces the number of organs available for transplant.

Other examples of goods with maximum prices of zero include blood for transfusions (which people can donate, but not sell in most places), babies (adoption is legal, but baby-selling is not), and sexual services. The NCAA sets a maximum price of zero on the services of college athletes by prohibiting member colleges from making explicit payments to them. This causes a shortage and leads to subtle, indirect ways of paying college athletes.

Black Markets

When people buy or sell an illegal good, or sell a good at an illegal price, they trade on the black market.

> **Black markets** are markets for illegal transactions.

Some goods are illegal to trade at any price, such as certain drugs, alcohol during prohibition, abortions before 1973, and certain weapons. Other goods traded on black markets are legal, but subject to price controls. By preventing people from making voluntary, mutually beneficial trades, price controls give people incentives to find ways to avoid them and trade illegally. Black markets are common wherever governments impose price controls or prohibit trade. Of course, people who buy or sell goods on black markets risk being caught and punished, and this risk of punishment affects demands and supplies.

Maximum Legal Prices on Inputs

A government might try to reduce the cost of producing a good by setting maximum legal prices for its inputs. In fact, however, a maximum legal price on an input *raises* the price of the final good.

EXPLANATION

Figure 3 shows the supplies and demands for peanuts and peanut butter. Suppose that each jar of peanut butter requires 1 cup of peanuts. The equilibrium quantity of peanuts is 100 million cups per year, and 80 million jars of peanut butter sell each year for $3 per jar. In equilibrium, 80 million cups of peanuts become inputs for peanut butter each year, and the other 20 million cups sell as canned nuts.

A maximum legal price on peanuts reduces output of peanuts from 100 million to 50 million cups (the quantity supplied at the maximum legal price). The reduction in peanuts available to make peanut butter drives down the supply of peanut butter from S_1^{PB} to S_2^{PB}. Since each jar of peanut butter requires 1 cup of peanuts, producers cannot make more than 50 million jars each year.[4] The fall in supply raises the price of peanut butter from $3 to $4 per jar.

---

[4]The supply of peanut butter may be less than 50 million jars, because people may buy some of the 50 million cups of peanuts to eat. This possibility depends on how peanuts are rationed. Figure 3 assumes that peanut-butter producers get all the peanuts.

Figure 3 | Maximum Legal Price on an Input

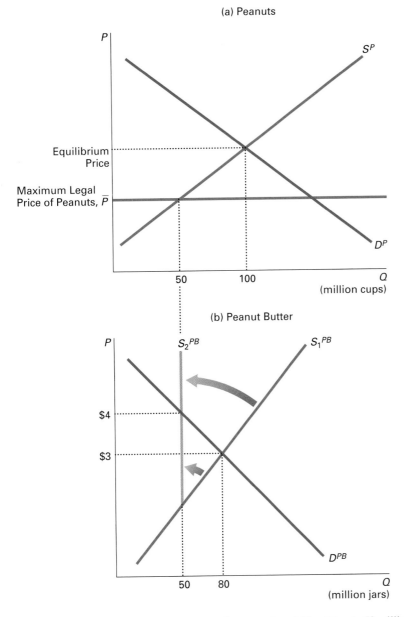

IN THE NEWS

Politics, as well as weather, also continues to play a significant role. The aftereffects of civil war in Sudan, Somalia, and Mozambique have left agriculture in disarray. In Angola, renewed civil war has affected food production and prevented relief distribution. New refugees in Rwanda, displaced by civil war, need food assistance. And in Kenya, politics has added a new twist to planting. With the government maintaining the price of cereal grains at an artificially low level while fertilizer prices have skyrocketed, many farmers are refusing to plant maize and wheat and are growing only enough food for themselves.

Source: New York Times International

Maximum legal prices keep food production low in many poor countries.

A maximum legal price on peanuts reduces output of peanuts from 100 million to 50 million cups, which reduces the supply of peanut butter, raising its price.

Governments sometimes impose price controls to keep prices *high*. For many years, the U.S. government kept airline and trucking prices high; airlines, for example, were not permitted to cut fares without government permission. Today, the best-known minimum legal price is the minimum wage.

> A **minimum legal price** (price floor) is the lowest price at which the government allows people to buy or sell a good.

PRICE CONTROLS: MINIMUM LEGAL PRICES

Figure 4 shows the effects of a minimum legal price, $\underline{P}$, above the equilibrium price. A minimum legal price causes a surplus and reduces output of the good.

> A **surplus** is a situation in which quantity demanded is less than quantity supplied at the current price.

A surplus results when sellers cannot sell all the goods they would like to sell at the minimum legal price. The minimum legal price reduces the quantity demanded from Q^E to Q^D and raises the quantity supplied from Q^E to Q^S in Figure 4. The surplus equals the quantity supplied minus the quantity demanded, $Q^S - Q^D$. Output falls, along with the quantity demanded, from Q^E to Q^D. Producers would like to produce and sell more, but buyers are not willing to buy more than Q^D, so producers reduce output rather than accumulate goods they cannot sell. Chapter 4 explained that a surplus usually causes the price to fall, but the minimum legal price prevents this adjustment.

Minimum Wage

The minimum wage is a minimum legal price of labor services. It currently mandates a wage of at least $5.15 an hour for most jobs in the United States. When the minimum wage exceeds the equilibrium wage, it causes a surplus of labor services—unemployment. Figure 5 shows the results. The minimum wage lowers the quantity of labor services demanded from Q^E to Q^D. Although more than Q^D people want jobs, employers are willing to hire only Q^D workers, so the minimum wage reduces employment.

The effect of a minimum wage is easy to understand if you think like an employer. Ask yourself, "Will I earn a profit by hiring a worker who will produce only $4.00 worth of output each hour if I have to pay $5.15 an hour (plus legally required fringe benefits such as worker's compensation insurance or retirement plans)?" A minimum wage reduces employment in two ways: by making fewer jobs available and by turning full-time jobs into part-time jobs (that is, it reduces the quantity of labor services demanded per week).

Figure 4 | Minimum Legal Price

A minimum legal price of $\underline{P}$, above the equilibrium price, creates a surplus of $Q^S - Q^D$. Sellers reduce production to Q^D rather than produce goods they cannot sell.

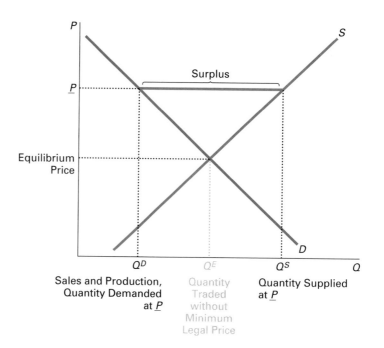

Figure 5 | Minimum Wage

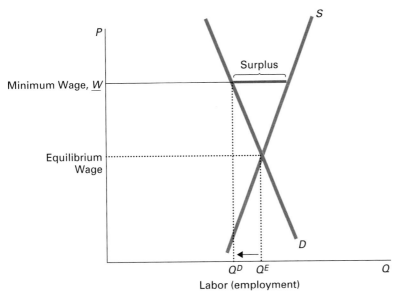

A minimum wage reduces employment from Q^E to Q^D.

Evidence

Statistical evidence shows that the minimum wage has a stronger effect on employment of teenagers than on employment of adults. A 10 percent rise in the minimum wage reduces employment of teenagers by about 1 to 3 percent (probably closer to 1 percent in the short run). This means that an increase in the U.S. minimum wage from $5.15 to $5.65 an hour would eliminate about 80,000 teenage jobs. The minimum wage has a much smaller effect on adult employment. Most evidence indicates that blacks and females lose more jobs as a result of a minimum wage than do whites and males.

The minimum wage helps some workers and hurts others. The winners include unskilled workers who keep their jobs and receive higher wages than they would earn without the minimum. The law also benefits skilled workers who (along with machinery) replace less-skilled workers. The losers from a minimum wage include the employers, who must pay the minimum rather than the equilibrium wage, and the unskilled workers who lose their jobs, never find jobs, or work fewer hours per week.

Review Questions

1. Draw a graph to show how a maximum legal price below the equilibrium price affects output. Why does it cause a shortage? Draw a graph to show how a minimum legal price above the equilibrium price affects output. Why does it cause a surplus?

2. Which buyers obtain goods under a system of rationing by waiting?

3. How does a maximum legal price on an input affect the price of the final good (the good that the input helps to produce)?

4. Discuss the effects of a minimum-wage law.

Thinking Exercises

5. State usury laws establish maximum legal interest rates (the prices of loans). Discuss the effects of a usury law that mandates a maximum legal interest rate below the equilibrium interest rate.

Minimum Wage— History and Impact

Minimum-wage laws began in New Zealand in 1894 and England in 1909. The U.S. government imposed a minimum wage in 1938, when the Fair Labor Standards Act set a lower limit of 25 cents per hour for some workers. This wage amounted to 40 percent of the average wage in manufacturing industries at the time. By 1998, the U.S. federal minimum wage was $5.15 per hour, about 40 percent of the average wage in manufacturing of about $13.00 per hour. A person who works 8 hours per day, 5 days a week, 50 weeks a year (with 2 weeks vacation) works 2,000 hours per year. (U.S. full-time workers average about 1,800 hours per year.) A worker earning the $5.15 per hour minimum wage for 2,000 hours per year earns $10,300 annually, an income close to the official government definition of poverty for a family of two.

About 5 million Americans earn the minimum wage, two-thirds of them part-time workers. Among people whose jobs pay hourly wages (1 out of 20 full-time workers and 1 out of 5 part-time workers), 5 percent of all men and 10 percent of all women earn the minimum wage. Of these workers, 2 million are older than 25, and 1 million live in families with incomes below the government's poverty line. Nearly 1 out of 3 working teenagers—but fewer than 1 out of 20 workers over age 25—earn the minimum wage. About half of minimum-wage earners work in retail trade, most as sales clerks.

6. Suppose that landlords avoid rent controls by making tie-in sales that require renters to rent furniture along with apartments. (Renters must pay separately for the furniture.) Draw a graph of supply and demand to show the equilibrium rental price of furniture. What would happen to the rental price for furniture if rent controls on apartments were eliminated?

TAXES

There is no known civilization that did not tax. The first civilization we know anything about began 6,000 years ago in Sumer, a fertile plain in modern Iraq. The dawn of history, and tax history, is recorded on clay cones excavated at Lagash, in Sumer. The people of Lagash instituted heavy taxation during a terrible war, but when the war ended, the tax men refused to give up their taxing powers. From one end of the land to the other, these clay cones say "there were the tax collectors." Everything was taxed. Even the dead could not be buried unless a tax was paid. The story ends when a good king, named Urukagina, "established the freedom" of the people, and once again, "There were no tax collectors." This may not have been a wise policy because shortly thereafter the city was destroyed by foreign invaders.[5]

Prices to Buyers versus Prices to Sellers

Most U.S. state governments charge sales taxes. When you buy a good with a price of $10, you pay $10 *plus* the sales tax. These taxes are often expressed as tax rates.

> The **tax rate** on a good is its per-unit tax, expressed as a percentage of its price.

A tax might be expressed as a fixed amount of money, such as 12 cents per gallon of gasoline, or as a percentage of the price, such as a 5 percent sales tax or a 28 percent income tax. When you buy a $5.00 good in a location that charges a 5 percent sales tax, you pay $5.25 to the store. The store keeps $5.00 and sends $0.25 to the government. The tax creates a gap between two prices: the *price buyers pay* ($5.25) and the *price sellers receive* after the government gets its money ($5.00). The difference between these prices is the per-unit tax ($0.25).

EXAMPLES

The federal government charges a tax of 14.1 cents per gallon of gasoline. This tax is included in the prices displayed on signs at gas stations. If you pay $1.259 per gallon for gasoline (the price to you, the buyer), the price the seller receives is $1.118, which is $1.259 minus $0.141.

Zach works for General Utilities, which pays him $14.00 per hour. He pays one-fourth of his income to the government as income taxes: His tax rate is 25 percent. Think of Zach as a seller of labor services, which his employer buys. The buyer pays a price of $14.00 per hour, but the seller (Zach) receives a price of $10.50 per hour. The per-unit tax is $3.50 per hour.

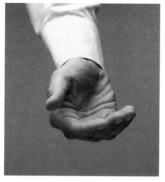

The hand of the tax collector drives a wedge between the price buyers pay and the price sellers receive.

[5]Charles Adams, *Fight, Flight, Fraud: The Story of Taxation* (Curacao: Euro-Dutch Publishers, 1982), pp. 9–10.

Equilibrium with a Tax

Figure 6 shows equilibrium with a tax on sales. The price buyers pay (including tax) is P_B. The price sellers receive (net of tax) is P_S. The difference, $P_B - P_S$, equals the per-unit tax. The equilibrium quantity bought and sold is Q_1. The equilibrium with a tax satisfies two conditions: The price buyers pay (including tax) exceeds the price sellers receive (net of tax) by the per-unit tax, and the quantity supplied equals the quantity demanded.

Without a tax, the equilibrium price would be P_0 and the equilibrium quantity traded would be Q_0. (See Figure 6.) A tax raises the price to buyers from P_0 to P_B, lowers the price to sellers from P_0 to P_S, and lowers the quantity bought and sold from Q_0 to Q_1.

EXPLANATION

The price buyers pay (including tax) is relevant for demand. The demand curve in Figure 6 shows a quantity demanded of Q_1 if buyers pay the price P_B. The price sellers receive (net of tax) is relevant for supply. The supply curve shows a quantity supplied of Q_1 units if sellers receive the price P_S. The price buyers pay, P_B, equals the price sellers receive, P_S, plus the per-unit tax, T. Since the quantity demanded equals the quantity supplied, Q_1 is the equilibrium quantity.

EXAMPLE

Figure 7 shows the supply and demand for tapes. The demand curve shows that buyers want to buy 7 million tapes if the price they pay (including tax) is $10.50. The supply curve shows that sellers want to sell 7 million tapes if the price they receive (net of tax) is $10.00. The two conditions for an equilibrium are met: The price buyers pay exceeds the price sellers receive by the 50-cent-per-tape tax, and the quantity demanded equals the quantity supplied. Figure 7 shows the equilibrium. The figure also shows that, without the tax, the equilibrium price would be $10.20 and 8 million tapes would be bought and sold.

Figure 6 | Supply and Demand with a Tax

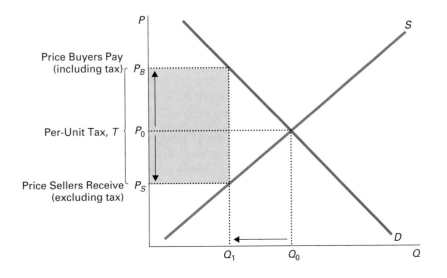

Buyers pay P_B dollars per unit of the good. Sellers keep P_S dollars after taxes, while T dollars per unit go to the government as taxes. The tax per unit, T, separates the price buyers pay and the price sellers receive net of taxes: $P_B = P_S + T$. The tax reduces the equilibrium quantity from Q_0 to Q_1. The area of the shaded rectangle shows total tax payments.

Figure 7 | Tax on Sales of Tapes

A 50-cent-per-unit tax on tapes raises the price that buyers pay, including tax, from $10.20 to $10.50, and it reduces the price sellers receive, excluding tax, from $10.20 to $10.00. The tax reduces the number of tapes sold from 8 million to 7 million. The area of the shaded rectangle shows total tax payments of $3.5 million (50 cents each on 7 million tapes).

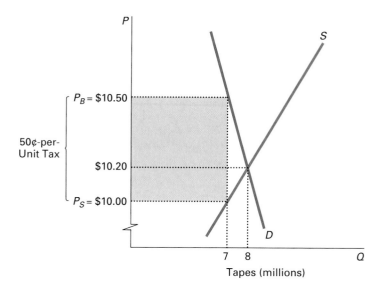

Drawing the Equilibrium

Figure 8 shows how to find the equilibrium with a tax in a graph. The tax creates a wedge between the the demand and supply curves. Draw a vertical line with a height equal to the per-unit tax, and move it horizontally in the supply-demand diagram until its top touches the demand curve and its bottom touches the supply curve. The top of the line shows the price that buyers pay, including tax; the bottom of the line shows the price that sellers receive, excluding the tax.

Total Tax Payments

The area of the shaded rectangle in Figure 6 shows total tax payments, that is, the total amount of money that buyers or sellers pay the government. Total tax payments equal the per-unit tax multiplied by the number of units of the good that people buy. The height of the shaded rectangle shows the per-unit tax (T) and its base shows the number of units

Figure 8 | How to Draw an Equilibrium with a Tax

1. Draw a vertical line with height equal to the tax per unit.
2. Fit the line into the supply-demand diagram.
3. Draw horizontal lines at the price buyers pay and the price sellers receive, excluding tax.

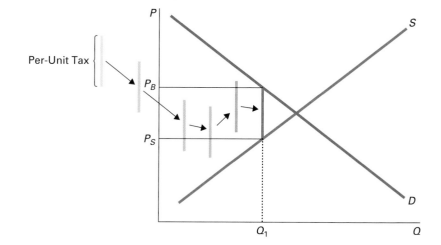

sold (Q_1), so total tax payments equal the area of the rectangle ($T \times Q_1$). Of course, total tax payments equal the government's tax revenue, its total receipt of money from the tax, so the shaded rectangle also shows the government's tax revenue. The area of the shaded rectangle in Figure 7 is $3.5 million, which equals the rectangle's height (50 cents per unit) times its base (7 million units).

How Buyers and Sellers Share the Tax Payment

Buyers and sellers each pay part of the tax on production or sales of a good. When the government imposes a tax, the price that buyers pay (including tax) rises by less than the amount of the tax, and the price that sellers receive (net of tax) falls by less than the amount of the tax. Sellers pass on part of a tax increase to consumers in the form of a price increase, but they pay the rest of the tax. As Figure 9 shows, the price to buyers rises a lot when demand is very inelastic or supply is very elastic. The price to buyers rises only a little when demand is very elastic or supply is very inelastic.

EXAMPLE

The 50-cent tax on tapes in Figure 7 raises the price that buyers pay (including tax) by 30 cents, from $10.20 to $10.50, so buyers pay 30 cents of the 50-cent tax. The tax reduces the price that sellers receive (excluding tax) by 20 cents, from $10.20 to $10.00, so sellers pay 20 cents of the tax. In a situation with more inelastic demand for tapes or more elastic supply, as in Figure 9a, the price to buyers rises more and buyers pay a larger fraction of the tax, as compared with Figure 7. (Figure 9a shows that buyers pay 45 cents of the 50-cent tax, and sellers pay only 5 cents.) In a situation with more elastic demand for tapes or more inelastic supply, as in Figure 9b, the price to buyers rises less than it does in Figure 7, and buyers pay a smaller fraction of the tax. (Figure 9b shows that buyers pay 10 cents of the 50-cent tax, and sellers pay 40 cents.)

Why Don't Buyers Pay the Whole Tax?
Sellers choose not to raise the price to buyers by the full amount of the 50-cent tax in Figure 7. If they raised the price by 50 cents per tape, the price to buyers would rise to

Figure 9 | How Buyers and Sellers Share a Tax Payment

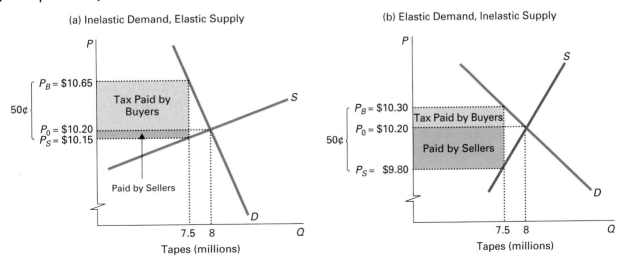

(a) Relatively inelastic demand and elastic supply shifts the tax toward buyers. (b) Relatively elastic demand and inelastic supply shifts the tax toward sellers.

$10.70 and buyers would want fewer than 7 million tapes. Since the price to sellers would remain at $10.20, sellers would want to sell 8 million tapes. This mismatch would create a surplus, and the price would fall toward the equilibrium ($10.50 to buyers and $10.00 to sellers). In equilibrium, sellers do not pass on the entire tax to consumers; buyers and sellers share the tax payments. Precisely how they share the payments depends on their elasticities of supply and demand.

Taxing Buyers versus Taxing Sellers

The price to buyers, including tax, does *not* depend on who is responsible (buyers or sellers) for sending the tax money to the government. Similarly, the price to sellers, net of tax, does not depend on who must send the tax money to the government. Buyers and sellers share the tax in the same way regardless of whether the government requires buyers or sellers to remit the tax payments.

EXPLANATION

Suppose that the government imposes a tax on sales of a good. Figure 6 shows that if the tax is T per unit, buyers pay the price P_B and sellers receive the price P_S. If the government requires sellers to send in the tax money (as is typical for sales tax payments in the United States), buyers pay P_B dollars at the store, and sellers send T dollars to the government and keep the remaining P_S dollars. If, instead, the government requires buyers to send in the tax money, buyers pay the price P_B in two parts. They pay P_S dollars to the store and T dollars to the government. Since $P_S + T = P_B$, buyers pay the same total price regardless of who must send the tax money to the government. Sellers keep P_S dollars (net of taxes) in either case. The responsibility for sending the tax money to the government does not matter, because buyers either pay the government directly, or they pay indirectly by giving sellers the money to send to the government.

EXAMPLES

If sellers are responsible for paying the tax money in Figure 7 to the government, buyers pay $10.50 to the store for a tape and the store sends 50 cents to the government and keeps $10.00. If, instead, buyers are responsible for paying the tax money to the government, buyers pay only $10.00 to the store for a tape, but they also pay 50 cents to the government. Either way, tapes cost buyers $10.50 each, and sellers get $10.00, net of the tax.

The U.S. social security tax includes two parts: an employer's part and an employee's part. If you earn $20,000 per year, your employer pays $1,530, 7.65 percent of your salary, in social security taxes. You pay an additional 7.65 percent for social security tax, which is deducted from your salary. You are the seller of labor services and your employer is the buyer in this analysis. The price that the buyer pays for your labor services is $21,530 per year; the price that you, the seller, receive, net of the tax, is $18,470 (your $20,000 salary minus the $1,530 you pay directly in social security taxes). So:

$$\text{Price to buyer} = \$21,530 \left.\vphantom{\begin{array}{c}a\\b\\c\end{array}}\right\} \$3,060 \; tax$$
$$\text{Price to seller} = \$18,470$$

If the law changes so that your employer must pay the entire $3,060 tax to the government, the equilibrium price of your labor services (your salary) falls from $20,000 to $18,470 per year. This makes no difference either to you or to your employer, who still pays $21,530 per year while you still get $18,470. If the law changes so that *you* must pay the entire $3,060 tax to the government, the equilibrium price of your labor services (your salary) rises to $21,530 per year. Again, neither you nor your employer care about the change: Your employer still pays $21,530 per year and you still get $18,470. Buyers and sellers share the tax the same way regardless of who pays the money to the government.

Review Questions

7. Explain the difference between the price that buyers pay, including tax, and the price that sellers receive, net of tax.

8. Draw a graph to show how a sales tax affects (a) output; (b) the price that buyers pay, including tax; (c) the price that sellers receive, net of tax; and (d) total tax payments.

9. In what sense do buyers and sellers share the payment of a sales tax?

Thinking Exercises

10. Suppose that the tax law changes so that buyers, rather than sellers, must remit sales tax payments to the government. Would sellers benefit from this change? Explain.

11. Draw a graph of the supply and demand for loans to show the effects of a tax on interest income earned by lenders.

Why Taxes Reduce the Quantity Traded

A tax reduces the quantity of a good bought and sold because the gains from some trades are smaller than the per-unit tax that the parties would have to pay.[6] People stop making those trades to avoid the tax. People make a trade only if it creates a total gain (to buyer and seller) that exceeds the tax.

EXAMPLE

Shelley wants to trade her car for Jake's stereo system. Jake agrees, because the car is worth $800 to him and the stereo is worth only $700 to him. The car is worth only $750 to Shelley, but the stereo is worth $800 to her. They both benefit if they trade: The value of Shelley's gain is $50, and the value of Jake's gain is $100. Their total gain from the trade is $150.

If the government puts a $200 tax on this trade, Shelley and Jake choose not to trade. By not trading, they avoid paying the tax. Shelley would trade only if the tax she would have to pay were less than her $50 gain from the trade; Jake would trade only if the tax he would have to pay were less than his $100 gain from the trade. If the tax on their trade totaled less than $150, they would trade because the total gains from the trade would exceed the tax, so they could share the remaining part of the gain. But the tax on their trade exceeds $150, so they choose not to trade.

IN THE NEWS

Sawmill closings were caused by tax on lumber: Lawmakers

OTTAWA (CP)—Five Northern Ontario sawmills have shut down and more closures are imminent because of Ottawa's 15 percent surtax on softwood lumber, says a task force of Liberal MPs from the region.

The MPs, who held hearings in six Northern Ontario communities in mid-February, said yesterday the region has lost 900 jobs so far due to a sharp decline in softwood exports to the United States.

"A lot of companies are losing money that never lost money before," said Maurice Foster, MP for Algoma and chairman of the group, at a news conference. "A lot of companies are operating one shift rather than three shifts."

Source: Montréal Gazette

---

[6]Chapter 3 discussed gains from trades.

In an economy with many traders like Shelley and Jake, a tax on trade usually prevents some trades but not all of them. A tax prevents trades with gains smaller than the tax, though trades that create larger gains occur despite the tax. For this reason, a tax reduces the equilibrium quantity traded.

Special Cases of Elasticities

Figure 10 shows four special cases of elasticities. These special cases are important to study, because some real-life situations closely approach these extreme cases. In studying them, compare the effects of taxes in these special cases with the general case in Figure 6.

Perfectly Inelastic Demand

Figure 10 shows how to draw supply-and-demand graphs with taxes in four special cases of elasticities of supply and demand. Panel (a) shows the effect of a tax with a perfectly inelastic demand curve. The tax raises the price that buyers pay, including tax, but it does not change the price that sellers receive, net of tax, nor does it change the quantity bought and sold. Because the price paid by buyers rises by the amount of the tax, buyers pay all the tax in this case. The shaded rectangle in the figure shows total tax payments.

Figure 10 | Taxes with Special Cases of Elasticities

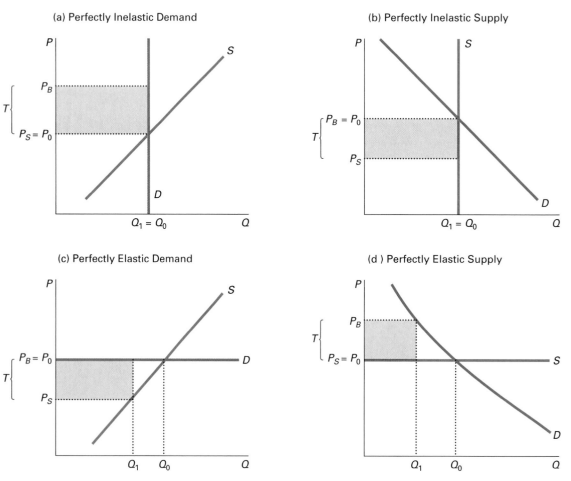

The per-unit tax is T. Shaded areas represent total tax payments.

EXPLANATION

Perfectly inelastic demand means that the quantity demanded is Q_0 regardless of the price. People want to buy as much when the price is P_B as when it is P_0. Sellers, however, are willing to sell the same amount only if the price they receive, net of tax, stays at P_0. Therefore, the price to sellers stays at P_0, and the price to buyers rises to P_B.

Perfectly Inelastic Supply

Panel (b) of Figure 10 shows the effects of a tax with perfectly inelastic supply. The tax lowers the price that sellers receive, net of tax, and leaves the price that buyers pay, including tax, unchanged. Sellers pay the full amount of the tax, and it does not change the equilibrium quantity bought and sold. The shaded rectangle shows total tax payments.

EXPLANATION

Perfectly inelastic supply means that the quantity supplied is Q_0 regardless of the price. Sellers offer a fixed amount of the good for sale. If the price that buyers pay were to rise above P_0, people would buy less, creating a surplus. Therefore, in equilibrium the price that buyers pay, including tax, remains at P_0. The price that sellers receive falls by the full amount of the tax, and the quantity traded remains at the fixed amount that sellers have available for sale.

Perfectly Elastic Demand or Supply

Panel (c) of Figure 10 shows the effects of a tax with perfectly elastic demand. The tax lowers the price that sellers receive, while leaving the price that buyers pay unchanged and reducing the equilibrium quantity. Panel (d) shows the effects of a tax with perfectly elastic supply. The tax raises the price that buyers pay, while leaving the price that sellers receive unchanged and reducing the equilibrium quantity.

EXPLANATION

Perfectly elastic demand prevents a tax from raising the price that buyers pay, because the quantity demanded would fall to zero, since no buyer is willing to pay a higher price. Therefore the price that buyers pay, including tax, remains the same and the price that sellers receive, net of tax, falls by the full amount of the tax. This fall in the price to sellers reduces both the quantity supplied and output.

The perfectly elastic supply curve means that sellers would not be willing to produce and sell the good at all at any price below P_0, so the price received by sellers does not fall. Instead, the price paid by buyers rises by the amount of the tax. Buyers do not want as much at the higher price, however, so a tax reduces the equilibrium quantity bought and sold.

Tax Rates and Total Tax Payments

You might expect total tax payments to rise after an increase in the per-unit tax on production, sales, or purchases of a good. An increase can actually *reduce* total tax payments, however, if it causes a sufficient reduction in the quantity traded.

Figure 11a shows the usual case, in which an increase in the tax rate raises total tax payments and government revenue from the tax. The area of each rectangle shows total tax payments at each tax rate; that area is larger with the higher tax rate, T_2, than with the lower tax rate, T_1.

Figure 11 | Per-Unit Taxes and Total Tax Payments

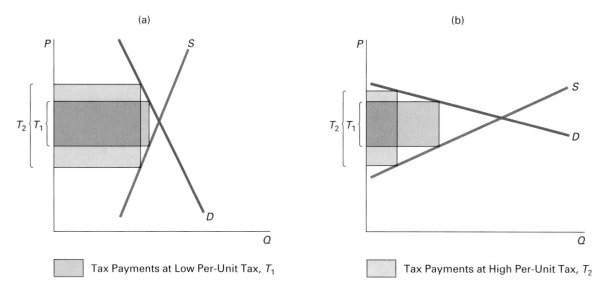

(a)

(b)

Tax Payments at Low Per-Unit Tax, T_1

Tax Payments at High Per-Unit Tax, T_2

An increase in the per-unit tax from T_1 to T_2 can (a) raise total tax payments or (b) reduce total tax payments.

**Figure 12
A Laffer Curve**

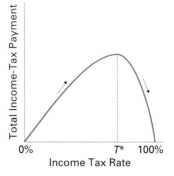

If the tax rate is below T^*, a tax rate increase raises total tax payments. If the tax rate is above T^*, a tax rate increase reduces total tax payments.

As Figure 11b shows, however, an increase in the tax rate can actually reduce total tax payments and government revenue. The area of the tall, narrow rectangle shows total tax payments with the higher of the two tax rates, T_2. That area shows a smaller total tax payment with the higher tax rate than with the lower tax rate, T_1. When the tax rate rises from T_1 to T_2, people pay more tax than before on each unit they buy and sell, but the amount that they buy and sell falls by enough that total tax payments fall.

The idea that higher tax rates can reduce government tax revenue is sometimes portrayed in a graph called a *Laffer curve,* like the one in Figure 12. At an income tax rate

IN THE NEWS

The taxes [in 19th–century England] were important not only because of the bite they put on people but because of their individual social consequences. Until repealed in 1861, for example, the tax on paper helped to keep books scarce and expensive. Soap was taxed until 1853 with the consequence of the poor personal hygiene which may have contributed to some of the epi-demics of typhus and other diseases that periodically devastated elements of the population. (In fact, a black market sprang up in soap, and it was smuggled in from Ireland, where there was no tax, to the western shore of England.) The tax on windows mentioned in [Jane Austen's] *Mansfield Park* was perhaps the most pernicious one, since even a hole cut in a wall for ventilation was counted as a window, making, among other things, for dark houses for the poor. The fact that a family was taxed £2.8s. for each male servant in 1812 (bachelors £4.8s.) helped to steer people toward women servants—both this and the tax on carriages were based on the government's (correct) assumption that these were two of the leading ways to get revenues from the wealthy.

Source: Daniel Poole, *What Jane Austen Ate and Charles Dickens Knew*

A tax on any good reduces its production and sales.

of zero, no one would pay income taxes; at an income tax rate of 100 percent, no one would bother working to earn taxable income, and total tax payments would again be zero. For this reason, both very low and very high tax rates create very low tax payments. Total tax payments are higher at intermediate tax rates, such as 40 percent. Figure 12 shows the general relationship between the tax rate and total tax payments. If the tax rate is less than T^* (a particular intermediate tax rate), then an increase in the tax rate raises total tax payments as in Figure 11a. If the tax rate exceeds T^*, a further increase reduces total tax payments, as in Figure 11b. In that case, the government could increase its tax revenue by lowering the tax rate.[7]

Statistical evidence shows that most real-life tax rates are below T^*. Some evidence does indicate, however, that U.S. tax payments increased as a result of cuts in the highest income tax rates from 70 percent to 50 percent and then to 33 percent in the 1980s.[8] Some evidence also suggests that government tax revenue falls as a result of increases in the tax rate on certain investment income.

SUBSIDIES

Government subsidies work like negative taxes. The price that buyers pay (net of the subsidy) is less than the price that sellers receive (including the subsidy). The difference is the per-unit subsidy.

The U.S. government subsidizes production of many goods with direct payments to producers, special tax breaks, loan guarantees, and other programs. Figure 13 shows the equilibrium for a good that the government subsidizes. The price that sellers receive including the subsidy, P_S, exceeds the price that buyers pay, P_B, by the per-unit subsidy, Y. The subsidy raises the price that sellers receive from P_0 to P_S, reduces the price buyers pay from P_0 to P_B, and raises the quantity traded from Q_0 to Q_1. The area of the shaded rectangle shows the total cost of the subsidy to the government. The height of the rectangle is the subsidy per unit, Y, and the base is the number of units subsidized, Q_1. The subsidy costs the government Y times Q_1.

Buyers and sellers share the benefits of the subsidy, because it raises the price that sellers receive and lowers the price that buyers pay. Neither the price to buyers, nor the

Figure 13 | Supply and Demand with a Subsidy

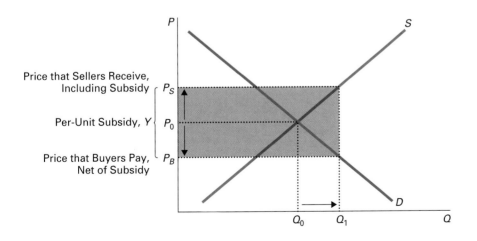

A subsidy creates a gap between the price that sellers receive and the price that buyers pay. The price that sellers receive, including the subsidy, P_S, exceeds the price that buyers pay, P_B, by the per-unit subsidy, Y. That is, $P_S = P_B + Y$. The subsidy raises the equilibrium quantity from Q_0 to Q_1. The area of the shaded rectangle shows the cost of the subsidy to the government.

---

[7]The tax rate T^* maximizes total tax payments, but this fact does not imply that T^* is in any sense a bad or good tax rate. It does imply, however, that tax rates higher than T^* cause economic inefficiency, because some lower tax rate would raise just as much tax revenue for the government at a lower cost to tax payers.

[8]See *The Growth Experiment* by Lawrence Lindsay, an economist who later became a governor of the Federal Reserve System (New York: Basic Books, 1988).

price to sellers, depends on which group (buyers or sellers) receives the subsidy payments from the government. Buyers and sellers share the subsidy in the same way, regardless of whether the government pays the subsidy to buyers or to sellers.

Review Questions

12. Draw graphs to show the effects of a tax on sales with (a) perfectly inelastic demand, (b) perfectly elastic demand, (c) perfectly inelastic supply, and (d) perfectly elastic supply.

13. Draw a graph to show why an increase in the tax rate can reduce government tax revenue. Explain in words why this can happen.

14. Draw a graph to show how a government subsidy for production of a good affects (a) its output, (b) the price that buyers pay, and (c) the price that sellers receive. (d) Use your graph to show the total cost of the subsidy to the government.

Thinking Exercises

15. Comment on this statement: "An increase in the tax rate on a good leads to a larger increase in tax revenue to the government when the demand and supply curves are more inelastic."

16. State governments subsidize education at many state colleges and universities. Draw a graph to help explain how these subsidies affect (a) college tuition, (b) the revenue colleges generate per student, and (c) the total number of students at these institutions. (d) How does subsidized education at state colleges and universities affect tuition and financial aid at private colleges?

TAXES AND OTHER RESTRICTIONS ON INTERNATIONAL TRADE

Tariffs

Almost all governments tax imports from other countries. They impose taxes called *tariffs*.

> A **tariff** is a tax on an imported good.

The U.S. government has imposed tariffs on many products, from televisions to pasta. The largest American tariffs affect imports of textiles and clothing, steel, automobiles, and sugar. The North American Free Trade Agreement (NAFTA) phases out all tariffs on trade between the United States, Canada, and Mexico. The World Trade Organization (WTO) is an international organization associated with several treaties that reduce trade restrictions.

Figure 14 shows the effects of a tariff that does not affect the world price of the good.[9] For example, the United States buys only a small fraction of the world's tea, so a fall in purchases of tea by people in the United States reduces the world demand for tea—and the world price—by such a small amount that economists can ignore it in practice.

Without a tariff, the world price is P^W, U.S. production is 10 units per month, and U.S. consumption is 34 units per month. The U.S. imports 24 units per month.

A tariff reduces international trade and raises domestic prices. The price buyers pay including the tax (the tariff) rises to P^{US}. As a result, U.S. consumption falls from 34 to

IN THE NEWS

USA hits Europe with tariffs

Source: USA Today

Most countries tax imports from other countries.

[9]When a country buys a large enough fraction of total world sales of a good, a tariff can reduce the world price of that good.

Figure 14 | Effects of a Tariff

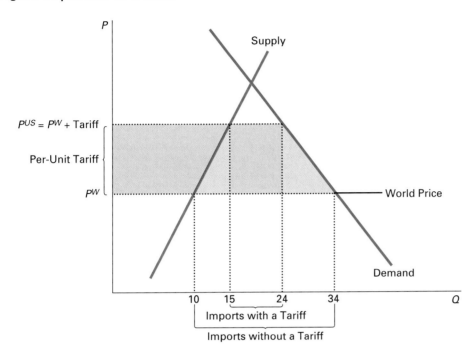

Without a tariff, the United States produces 10 units of the good, imports 24, and consumes 34. With a tariff, the U.S. price rises from P^W to P^{US}, U.S. production rises to 15 units, imports fall to 9, and consumption falls to 24.

24 units per month. The price that American sellers receive also rises to P^{US}, because the tariff does not apply to sales of American goods. As a result, American sellers raise production from 10 to 15 units per month. Foreign sellers receive the after-tax world price P^W. The difference, $P^{US} - P^W$, is the per-unit tariff that the government collects. Because American consumption falls to 24 units and American production rises to 15 units, American imports fall to 9 units per month.

Buyers and sellers share the tariff payment. The tariff hurts American buyers because it raises the price that they pay for the good and reduces the amount they buy.[10] The tariff helps American sellers because it raises the price they receive.[11]

Quotas on Imports

Most countries impose legal limits on imports of certain goods, or import quotas.

> An **import quota** is a limit on the quantity of a good that can enter a country from foreign sources.

Import quotas have the same effects as tariffs. An import quota of 9 units per month would have the same effects as the tariff in Figure 14. The quota would reduce imports from 24 to 9 units per month, raise the U.S. price from P^W to P^{US}, raise U.S. production from 10 to 15 units, and reduce U.S. consumption from 34 to 24 units per month.

A quota differs from a tariff in one way—the government collects tax revenue from a tariff, but not from a quota. A quota raises the price that U.S. buyers pay, but the extra money goes to foreign sellers who sell goods in the United States at higher prices than they would receive without the quota.

IN THE NEWS

Higher tax hits utility truck imports

By Jim Freschi and James R. Healey, USA Today

The U.S. government just added up to $3,000 to the price of some imported trucks.

The Treasury Department said Thursday that imported sport-utility vehicles with only two doors are meant for hauling cargo, not people, so must pay the truck tax—a tariff equal to 25 percent of what the truck costs its American importer.

Source: USA Today

A tariff on imports raises prices to consumers.

---

[10]Even though the tariff applies only to imports, the resulting price increase for imported goods reduces the foreign competition facing U.S. producers, so U.S. producers also raise their prices. As a result, buyers pay P^W for all units of the good, regardless of its source.

[11]Chapter 9 discusses the sizes of these gains and losses.

IN THE NEWS

Group seeks phase-out of steel-import quotas

The program is linked to high prices and shortages

By Jonathan P. Hicks

An association of steel importers pitted itself against the nation's major steelmakers yesterday, calling for the Government to modify the program that

Source: New York Times

limits steel imports.

"We are opposed to any effort to renew steel quotas or to broaden them," said William C. Lane, a trade specialist with Caterpillar Inc., the large machinery

manufacturer based in Peoria, Ill. "Quota-induced shortages of steel have hurt our efforts to meet export demand."

Import quotas, like tariffs, raise prices in the importing country.

Review Questions

17. Draw a graph to show the effects of a tariff on (a) production, (b) consumption, (c) the prices that buyers pay and sellers receive, and (d) total tariff (tax) payments.

18. Draw a graph to illustrate the effects of an import quota. How do the effects of a quota differ from the effects of a tariff?

Thinking Exercise

19. Who gains and who loses from elimination of a tariff or quota on imports? What groups might be expected to favor eliminating a tariff, and what groups might be expected to oppose the change?

Conclusion

Price Controls: Maximum Legal Prices

A maximum legal price below the equilibrium price causes a shortage by reducing the quantity supplied and raising the quantity demanded. It reduces production of the good and causes nonprice rationing based on some formal or informal system for choosing which buyers can buy goods and how much each can buy. This nonprice rationing may occur through queuing (rationing by waiting), coupons, or bribery.

Rent controls provide an example of a maximum legal price. They reduce the number of apartments available and create a shortage. Price controls often lead to formation of black markets where transactions take place at illegal prices. A maximum legal price on an input raises the price of the goods produced with it.

Price Controls: Minimum Legal Prices

A minimum legal price above the equilibrium price causes a surplus by reducing the quantity demanded and raising the quantity supplied. It lowers output of the good (along with the quantity demanded), because producers can sell only as many goods as people are willing to buy at the minimum legal price. One minimum legal price, the minimum wage, reduces employment (particularly among teenagers).

Taxes

A tax on sales or production of a good creates a gap between the price that buyers pay, including tax, and the price that sellers receive, net of tax; the difference is the per-unit tax. A tax raises the price to buyers, lowers the price to sellers, and lowers the quantity bought and sold. Buyers and sellers share the tax payment, since buyers pay more than they would pay without the tax and sellers receive less (net of tax). Neither the price buyers pay or the price sellers receive depends on who is legally responsible for paying the tax to the government, so neither buyers or sellers care who must remit the tax payments. A tax reduces output because the gains from some trades are smaller than the tax that people would have to pay if they were to complete those trades. An increase in the tax rate (the tax expressed as a fraction of the price) usually raises total tax payments and government tax revenue, but it can lower total tax payments and government revenue if it causes a sufficient reduction in the quantity traded.

With perfectly inelastic demand, a tax raises the price to buyers without changing the price to sellers or the quantity traded. With perfectly inelastic supply, a tax lowers the price to sellers without changing the price to buyers or the quantity traded. With perfectly elastic demand, a tax does not affect the price to buyers; with perfectly elastic supply, a tax does not affect the price to sellers.

Subsidies

Subsidies work like negative taxes. When the government subsidizes sales or production of a good, the subsidy lowers the price that buyers pay (net of the subsidy), raises the price that sellers receive (including the subsidy), and raises the quantity bought and sold. The government pays the cost of the subsidy, and buyers and sellers share its benefits. Neither the price buyers pay nor the price sellers receive depends on which group (buyers or sellers) receives subsidy payments, so the effects do not depend on whether the government subsidizes buyers or sellers.

Taxes and Restrictions on International Trade

A tariff (a tax on imports) raises the price of a good in the importing country by the per-unit tariff (per-unit tax). The tariff also raises output and reduces consumption in the importing country; it also reduces imports. A quota on imports has the same effects, except that the government collects revenue from a tariff but not from a quota.

Key Terms

maximum legal price	tie-in sale	surplus	tariff
shortage	black market	tax rate	import quota
nonprice rationing	minimum legal price		

Problems

20. Waiting in line (queuing) is part of the price that buyers pay when a maximum legal price leads to rationing by waiting. (a) What determines the equilibrium length of a line? (b) How would the lengths of lines at stores change today if people expected the government to raise maximum legal prices on food next week?

21. Comment on this statement: "An effective way to keep the price of clothing down would be to put price controls on fabric; this step would reduce the costs of making clothing and reduce clothing prices."

22. Suppose that the government prohibited selling shoes for more than a maximum legal price of $30 a pair, spurring development of a black market in shoes. Use supply-and-demand analysis to discuss the forces that would determine the equilibrium price of shoes on the black market. How would that price change if the government were to crack down harder on black-market sellers?

23. What would happen if the government were to raise the minimum wage to $50,000 per year for all workers? What if the government were to raise the minimum wage for college graduates to $100,000 per year?

24. **(a)** Use a graph to show how a 50-cent-per-gallon tax on gasoline would affect the quantity sold and the price. Also show on your graph the revenue that the government would collect from this tax.
    (b) Suppose that the supply of gasoline is perfectly inelastic and repeat your analysis.
    (c) Suppose that the supply of gasoline is perfectly elastic and repeat your analysis.

25. At a well-known prep school, freshmen who buy candy from machines in the dorms are "required" to give part of their candy bars to seniors. Why do seniors require freshmen to give only *part* of each candy bar instead of the whole thing? How should seniors decide how large a part to take if they want to maximize the amount of candy they collect?

Inquiries for Further Thought

26. Comment on this statement from the chair of a federal government commission: "A subminimum wage is inequitable. It would violate the requirements of social justice and ought to be rejected as a policy option even if we thought that it would substantially reduce youth unemployment."

27. Should the government set a minimum wage? How high should it be? Why? What are the costs and benefits of a minimum wage versus a welfare or "workfare" program as a means to raise the incomes of poor people?

28. Many colleges rent dormitory space at prices below the equilibrium prices. As a result, dorms often cannot accommodate all the students who want to live in them. Do you think that colleges should raise dormitory rental prices to the equilibrium levels? If not, how should they ration space? How would raising the prices of dorms affect off-campus rents?

29. Discuss the two news reports on markets for human organs reproduced nearby. If you favor allowing people to sell their organs, explain how you think that market would operate. If you oppose sales of organs, explain why you think a market for organs differs from a market for food or clothing, and how you think organs should be rationed. (How would you determine which patients get the organs and which do not?)

30. The maximum legal price on sales of children is zero. People can legally adopt children, but they cannot pay for them. What are the effects of this maximum legal price of zero? Does the limitation produce good or bad effects? Should married couples who are medically unable to have children be legally allowed to pay adoption agencies to speed up adoptions? Should they be allowed to pay adoption agencies to find children for them? Should they be allowed to pay biological parents to allow them to adopt children? Should they be allowed to pay women for surrogate mother services using sperm from either the father or a sperm bank? What would be the effects of eliminating the maximum legal price of zero?

IN THE NEWS

Trying to cure shortage of organ donors

By Glenn Ruffenach
Staff Reporter of The Wall
Street Journal

A rapidly growing gap between the number of people waiting for organ transplants and the supply of organs has educators and researchers searching for ways to increase organ donations.

Some studies suggest that the timing of a physician's or nurse's request to surviving family members can raise consent rates substantially. Other proposals call for some type of federal tax benefit to a donor's estate or assistance with funeral expenses. A physician writing in today's *Journal of the American Medical Association* broaches the once-heretical notion of paying families outright— say, $1,000—for an organ donation.

Though physicians, medical ethicists and patients differ, sometimes sharply, over the effectiveness of these strategies, there is little dispute about the need for added measures to procure organs.

Higher Success Rates

More people are being recommended for transplants, reflecting soaring success rates for these operations, but organ donations "haven't kept up with demand," says Wanda Bond, a spokeswoman for the United Network for Organ Sharing, a national clearinghouse that maintains the waiting list for organs and matches organs with recipients.

The supply of organs has not kept pace with the demand. The waiting list for kidney transplants has grown from 2,500 to 3,500 in the past five years; in the past two years the waiting lists for heart and liver transplants have increased by 60 percent. These shortages cost money—not to mention lives.

Source: The Wall Street Journal

IN THE NEWS

Ethical debate over selling body organs

By Jeff Kleinhuizen
USA Today

Paying for the kidneys, livers, hearts, and lungs of brain-dead patients might help those awaiting organ transplants, two surgeons say. But a medical ethicist says the proposal could create a black market for body organs.

Writing in today's *Journal of the American Medical Association,* Dr. Thomas Peters, Jacksonville, Fla., says that, despite public awareness programs, 1,878 people died awaiting organ transplants in 1989.

He suggests pilot programs offering $1,000 as a death benefit to the consenting next-of-kin. State and federal laws now prohibit buying and selling organs.

Ethicist Dr. Edmund Pellegrino, Georgetown University, Washington, D.C., writes that payments would subject the poor "to more duress and manipulation than the well-to-do, and this is discriminatory."

Transplant surgeon Dr. Jimmy Light, Washington Hospital Center, Washington, D.C., says blacks make up 35 percent of those on transplant waiting lists, but only 8 percent of donors. Nearly 2,400 people died last year awaiting transplants, he says.

"If education and altruism aren't working," asks Light, "is it more unethical to let people die waiting for transplants, or to offer some kind of incentive to stimulate donations?"

But Pellegrino says paying donors would replace altruism with selfishness.

"The body is not an object to be scavenged even for good purposes," he says.

Source: USA Today

---

31. A letter to a New York newspaper claimed that abolishing rent control would "turn New York City into a complete Yuppie City," with "no poor and no middle class." What really would happen? How could the poor afford to stay in New York without rent control? Discuss.

32. People who live in rent-controlled apartments benefit from low rents. Is it fair to require the owners of the rent-controlled buildings to pay for the renters' benefits (by collecting low rents), or should taxpayers pay for such benefits through taxes? Is rent control an unconstitutional taking of property without fair compensation (as the 5th amendment to the U.S. Constitution requires)? If not, how does it differ from a taking of property? By forcing landlords to give benefits to tenants, does rent control violate the equal protection clause of the 14th amendment?

33. Comment on this quote:

    Take filet mignon and chuck steak. Assume that consumers, holding all else constant, prefer filet mignon to chuck steak, a not too unrealistic assumption. The question is: Why is it, in spite of consumer preferences, chuck steak sells at all? The actual fact of business is that chuck steak outsells (is more employed than) filet mignon! How does something less liked compete with something more liked?

    It offers compensating differences. In other words, as you wheel your shopping cart down the aisle, chuck steak, in effect, says to you, "I don't look as nice as filet mignon; I'm not as tender and tasty; but I'm not as expensive either." . . .

    What would be the effect of a minimum steak [price] law . . . ? Again, put yourself in the position of the shopper wheeling the shopping cart down the aisle. Chuck steak says to you, "I don't look as nice as filet mignon, I'm not as tender and tasty, and I sell for the *same* price as filet mignon. Buy me." Such a message would fall on deaf ears. . . . The lower the price of discriminating, the more of it will be done.[12]

34. Discuss these statements.
    (a) "A large tax on printers and photocopying machines would violate the right of free speech."
    (b) "Applying the income tax to churches, or to businesses they own, would violate the separation of church and state."
    (c) "A large tax on guns would violate the second amendment to the Constitution."

---

[12]Walter Williams, *The State against Blacks* (New York: McGraw-Hill, 1982), pp. 40–41.

35. Do you think that the government should set taxes and subsidies to achieve some social goals, such as discouraging smoking or drinking, encouraging exercise or family farms, or promoting "family values"?

36. The government often assists people whose houses are destroyed by natural disasters. In what sense is this assistance a subsidy? What is the government subsidizing? What are the effects of this kind of program?

Appendix: Algebra of Equilibrium with Taxes

This appendix builds on the Chapter 4 appendix on the algebra of equilibrium. The demand and supply curves are straight lines represented by equations. The demand curve is:

$$Q^d = a - bP_B \qquad\qquad \text{Example: } Q^d = 10 - 2P_B$$

where Q^d is the quantity demanded (in millions of units per year) and P_B is the price that buyers pay.

The supply curve is:

$$Q^s = c + dP_S \qquad\qquad \text{Example: } Q^s = -5 + 3P_S$$

where Q^s is the quantity supplied (in millions of units per year).

The price to buyers exceeds the price to sellers by the per-unit tax, T:

$$P_B = P_S + T \qquad\qquad \text{Example: } P_B = P_S + 1$$

Substitute this last equation into the equation for the demand curve to eliminate the variable P_B. This manipulation gives a new equation for the demand curve:

$$Q^d = a - b(P_S + T) \qquad\qquad \text{Example: } Q^d = 10 - 2(P_S + 1)$$

To find the equilibrium, where the quantity demanded (Q^d) equals the quantity supplied (Q^s), set the equations for Q^d and Q^s equal:

$$a - b(P_S + T) = c + dP_S \qquad\qquad \text{Example: } 10 - 2(P_S + 1) = -5 + 3P_S$$

$$\text{or } 10 - 2P_S - 2 = -5 + 3P_S$$

Solve for the equilibrium price to sellers:

$$P_S = (a - bT - c)/(b + d) \qquad\qquad \text{Example: } P_S = 13/5 = \$2.60$$

The equilibrium price to buyers exceeds this price by the per-unit tax, so:

$$P_B = (a - bT - c)/(b + d) + T \qquad\qquad \text{Example: } P_B = \$3.60$$

Now substitute the solution for the price to sellers into the supply curve equation, or substitute the price to buyers into the demand curve equation, to solve for the equilibrium quantity:

$$Q = c + d(a - bT - c)/(b + d) \qquad\qquad \text{Example: } Q = 2.8 \text{ million units per year}$$

Total tax payments equal the per-unit tax times the quantity sold:

$$T[c + d(a - bT - c)/(b + d)] \qquad\qquad \text{Example: } \$2.8 \text{ million per year}$$

Problems

A1. Suppose that the demand curve for rental cars is:

$$Q^d = 500 - 2P_B$$

The supply curve is:

$$Q^s = 100 + 6P_S$$

Q^d is the quantity demanded (in cars per day), Q^s is the quantity supplied, P_B is the price per day paid by renters (including tax), and P_S is the price per day received by sellers (excluding tax). Suppose that the government taxes car rentals at $8 per day. Find the equilibrium prices to buyers (including tax) and to sellers (excluding tax), the equilibrium quantity, and total tax payments to the government.

A2. Suppose that the demand curve for a product is:

$$x^d = 1,000 - 120p$$

where x^d is the quantity demanded and p is the price (measured in dollars). Suppose that the supply curve for the product, with x^s as the quantity supplied, is:

$$x^s = 200 + 40p$$

(a) Find the equilibrium price and quantity.
(b) Suppose that the government imposes a per-unit tax of $4 on sales of the product. Find the new equilibrium quantity, price paid by buyers (including tax), price received by sellers (net of tax), and total tax payments to the government.

A3. Repeat Problem A2, but suppose that the government offers a subsidy of $4 per unit instead of imposing a tax. Find the equilibrium quantity, the price paid by buyers (net of the subsidy), the price received by sellers (including the subsidy), and the cost of the subsidy to the government.

CHAPTER 9

ECONOMIC EFFICIENCY AND THE GAINS FROM TRADE

In this Chapter. . .

Main Points to Understand

▶ Consumer surplus measures buyers' gains from trade.

▶ Producer surplus measures sellers' gains from trade.

▶ Economic efficiency combines the interests of consumers and producers.

▶ Deadweight social loss measures economic inefficiency

Thinking Skills to Develop

▶ Interpret measures of gains and losses.

▶ Diagnose economic inefficiencies.

▶ Recognize conflicts between economic efficiency and the interests of particular groups.

What *should* an economy do? How many houses, videocassette recorders, taxi rides, and French fries should it produce? How many people should be doctors, lawyers, plumbers, scientists, and accountants? What economic policies should the government adopt? Economics does not answer normative questions about actions that *should* occur, but it can help people to make informed and intelligent judgments about these issues. It cannot answer questions such as "Should we permit people to import foreign cars?" However, it can help to provide answers about who would gain and who would lose from changes in economic conditions or government policies.

When Supreme Court Justice Anthony Kennedy faced senators' questions during his confirmation hearings, one senator urged him "not simply to weigh economic efficiency" but also to consider how his decisions would affect consumers. What is economic efficiency? Why does anyone care about it? How does it affect consumers? How might it help to answer questions about which economic policies the government should follow? This chapter addresses these issues.

CONSUMER SURPLUS AND PRODUCER SURPLUS

You're thirsty and you would be willing to pay up to $3.00, if you had to, for a soft drink. Fortunately, a machine offers them for 75 cents each. When you buy the drink, you gain a *consumer surplus* of $2.25.

> **Consumer surplus** is the benefit to a consumer of buying a good at the equilibrium price.

Consumer surplus measures a buyer's gain from a trade. Economists calculate consumer surplus as a buyer's *willingness to pay* for a good minus the price the buyer actually pays. Consumer surplus measures the gain to buyers based on their own tastes and values, as revealed by their willingness to pay. If Valerie values a product more than Bruce does, indicated by her willingness to pay more for it, then Valerie gains higher consumer surplus from the good than Bruce gains.

Chapter 6 explained that the height of a demand curve shows buyers' willingness to pay for a good. The demand curve shows the highest prices that buyers would pay, *if they had to,* for each unit of the good. For example, the demand curve in Figure 1 shows that:

▶ Alice is willing to pay up to $10 to buy a pizza.

▶ Bill is willing to pay up to $9.

▶ Carol is willing to pay up to $8.

▶ Dave is willing to pay up to $7.

▶ Elaine is willing to pay up to $6.

▶ Fred is willing to pay up to $5.

Figure 2 shows each person's consumer surplus if the equilibrium price is $7. Alice, Bill, Carol, and Dave buy pizzas, while Elaine and Fred do not. Alice gains $3 in consumer surplus, because she would be willing to pay up to $10. Bill gains $2 in consumer surplus, and Carol gains $1. Dave gets zero consumer surplus, because he pays $7, the highest price he would be willing to pay. Total consumer surplus in this example equals

This man's consumer surplus equals his willingness to pay to attend the concert minus the ticket price.

Figure 1 | Height of a Demand Curve Shows Willingness to Pay

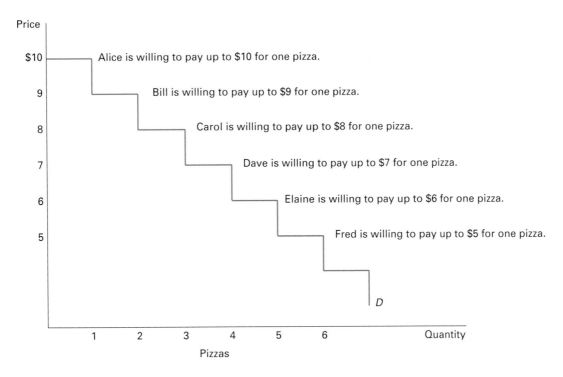

$6. Economists estimate consumer surplus by using statistical analysis to estimate the heights of demand curves.

Figure 3 shows consumer surplus in equilibrium. The total consumer surplus equals

Figure 2 | Consumer Surplus in the Example

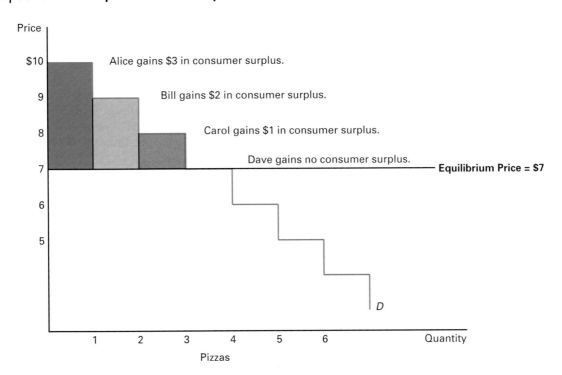

Figure 3 | Consumer Surplus

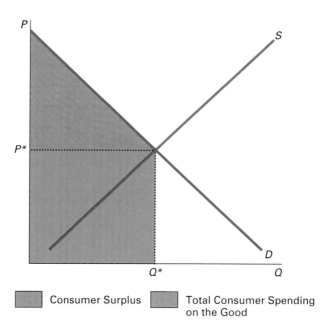

Consumer Surplus | Total Consumer Spending on the Good

the area under the demand curve, above the equilibrium price (P^*), and between the quantity zero and the equilibrium quantity (Q^*).

Discussion

Your willingness to pay for a good, minus the price you actually pay, measures your benefit from buying the good. If your willingness to pay increases, your consumer surplus increases. In this sense, your consumer surplus reflects your own tastes or values.

Your willingness to pay also depends on your ability to pay, that is, how rich you are. Adding together the consumer surpluses of different buyers gives total consumer surplus, as in the example above. This process amounts to adding your willingness to pay to someone else's willingness to pay. You might be willing to pay more than someone else would pay for a good because you are richer than that person, but you might not gain more happiness from the good than that poorer person would gain. Consumer surplus does *not* measure the happiness or enjoyment that consumers gain from goods. (It is probably impossible to measure this.) Instead, consumer surplus measures the total benefit to consumers based on their tastes or values and their abilities to pay (how rich or poor they are). This measurement reflects the current distribution of income and wealth across people, as well as their tastes and preferences.

Value and Price: Common Confusions

Many intelligent people have been confused by the fact that important goods like air and water are free or inexpensive, while less important goods like diamonds are expensive. They wonder why an important good like an ounce of water could cost less than an unimportant good like an ounce of diamonds. They are confused because they do not understand that the equilibrium price of a good does not measure its importance to people. Figure 4 shows the supplies and demands for clean water and diamonds. Clearly, the equilibrium price of diamonds (per ounce) exceeds the equilibrium price of clean water (per ounce). Consumer surplus for water, however, is much larger than consumer surplus for diamonds; in that sense, water is more valuable.

Producer Surplus

Just as consumer surplus measures buyers' gains from trade, producer surplus measures sellers' gains.

> **Producer surplus** is the benefit to a producer of selling a good at the equilibrium price.

Producer surplus measures a seller's gain from a trade. Economists calculate producer surplus as the price the seller actually receives for a good minus the lowest price that the seller would have been *willing* to accept.

The height of the supply curve shows the lowest prices that sellers would be willing to accept, *if they had to,* to produce and sell a good. For example, the supply curve for lawn-cutting services in Figure 5 shows that:

▶ George is willing to mow a lawn for $5.

▶ Elaine is willing to mow a lawn for $6.

▶ Jerry is willing to mow a lawn for $7.

▶ Kramer is willing to mow a lawn for $8.

▶ Newman is willing to mow a lawn for $9.

Figure 5 also shows the total producer surplus if the equilibrium price is $8 per lawn. George, Elaine, Jerry, and Kramer mow lawns, while Newman does not. George gains $3 in producer surplus because he would be willing to accept as little as $5. Elaine gains $2 in producer surplus, and Jerry gains $1. Kramer gets zero consumer surplus, because the price that he receives to mow a lawn, $8, is the lowest price that he would be willing to accept.

Producer surplus measures a seller's gain from a trade. Economists calculate producer surplus as the price a seller actually receives for a good minus the lowest price at which the seller would be *willing* to produce and sell the good.

Figure 4 | Water and Diamonds

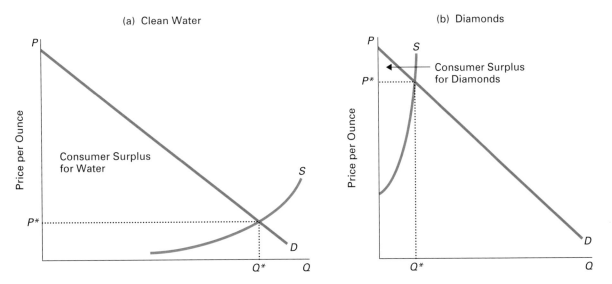

People gain greater consumer surplus from water than from diamonds; water is a human's best friend.

Figure 5 | Height of a Supply Curve Shows Willingness to Sell

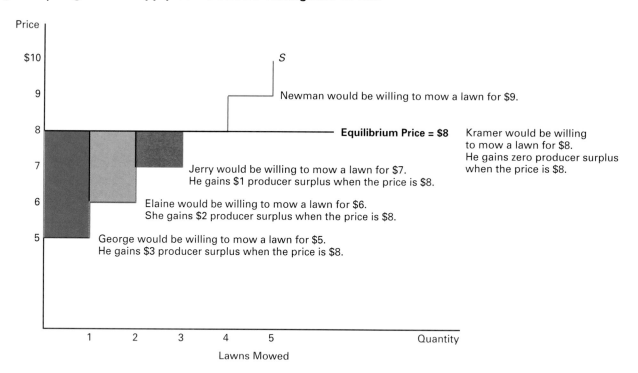

Cost and Willingness to Sell

A seller's willingness to sell reflects his opportunity costs. George's opportunity cost of mowing a lawn is $5 in the example above, so he would be willing to mow a lawn for any price above $5 but not for any price below $5. Elaine's higher opportunity cost means that her minimum price is also higher.

The lowest price at which any seller would be willing to sell a good equals that seller's cost of producing it (her opportunity cost). Therefore, the height of the supply curve shows sellers' costs.

> The height of a supply curve shows sellers' opportunity costs of producing various units of the good.

The height of the supply curve in Figure 5 is $5 at a quantity of 1 lawn, reflecting George's opportunity cost of $5. Its height at a quantity of 2 is $6, reflecting Elaine's opportunity cost. Its height at a quantity of 3 is $7, reflecting Jerry's opportunity cost, and so on.

The area *under* the supply curve, between the quantity zero and any given quantity, shows the total cost of producing that quantity.[1] In the lawn-mowing example, the total cost of producing four mowed lawns is $26. This amount equals George's opportunity cost of mowing one lawn ($5) plus Elaine's cost ($6) plus Jerry's cost ($7) plus Kramer's cost ($8).

The area under a supply curve shows the *total cost* of producing the good.

Consumer and Producer Surplus in Equilibrium

Figure 6 shows consumer and producer surplus in equilibrium. Producer surplus equals the area above the supply curve and below the equilibrium price (P_1), between the

---

[1]Chapter 11 gives a more precise statement when firms have fixed costs of production.

Figure 6 | Gains from Trade

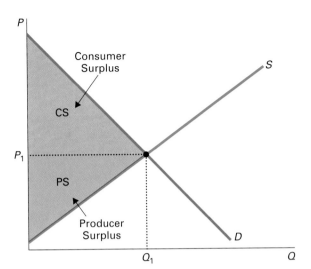

Buyers and sellers share the gains from trade; buyers gain the consumer surplus, and sellers gain the producer surplus.

quantity zero and the equilibrium quantity (Q_1). Consumer surplus (Area *CS*) shows the gains from trade to buyers. Producer surplus (Area *PS*) shows the gains from trade to sellers.

> The total gain from trade in some good equals the consumer and producer surplus that buyers and sellers receive from exchanges of that good.

The total gain from trade is the sum of Areas *CS* and *PS* in Figure 6.

Figure 7 shows another way to view the gains from trade. The shaded area under the demand curve in Figure 7a shows the benefit to consumers from drinking 3 million quarts of root beer each month. The shaded area under the supply curve in Figure 7b shows the total cost of producing that root beer. The difference—the shaded area in Figure 7c—

Figure 7 | Total Gain from Trade: Another View

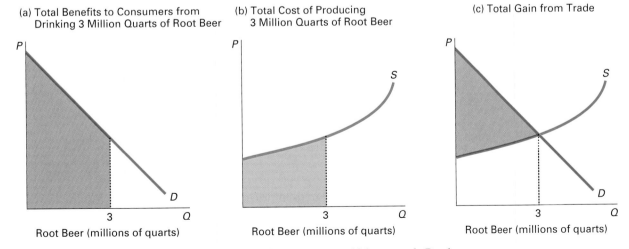

(a) Total Benefits to Consumers from Drinking 3 Million Quarts of Root Beer

(b) Total Cost of Producing 3 Million Quarts of Root Beer

(c) Total Gain from Trade

The total gain from trade equals the total benefit of the good to consumers, which appears in Panel (a), minus the total cost of producing the good, which appears in Panel (b). The benefit to consumers minus the cost to producers equals the gain from trade, which appears in Panel (c).

shows the total gain from trade in root beer. The total gain equals the benefit to consumers from drinking 3 million quarts of root beer each month minus the cost of producing that root beer. Consumers and producers then divide that total gain, as in Figure 6.

Review Questions

1. Define and show on a graph:
   (a) Consumer surplus
   (b) Producer surplus

2. Show on a graph:
   (a) A buyer's willingness to pay for a good
   (b) A seller's willingness to sell a good
   (c) The total cost of producing 10 units of a good
   (d) The total gain from trade (to consumers and producers) in equilibrium

3. Use a graph of supply and demand to show the effects on consumer and producer surplus of:
   (a) An increase in supply
   (b) An increase in demand

Thinking Exercises

4. Bill would be willing to pay up to $2.00 (but not more) for one roller-coaster ride. He would be willing to pay up to $1.50 for a second ride, $1.25 for a third ride, $1.00 for a fourth ride, and up to $0.75 for each additional ride. Elaine would be willing to pay up to $1.75 (but not more) for one ride, up to $1.75 for a second ride, up to $1.25 for a third ride, and up to $0.90 for each additional ride. Roller-coaster rides cost $1.00 each. How much consumer surplus do Bill and Elaine gain from roller-coaster rides?

5. Jennifer would be willing to baby-sit for up to 3 hours per day for $3 per hour (but not for less). She would be willing to baby-sit for a fourth hour for $4 per hour (but not less) and a fifth hour for $5 per hour. How much producer surplus does she receive if she baby-sits for 3 hours at $4 per hour? How much producer surplus does she receive if she baby-sits for 5 hours at $5 per hour?

6. How do the ideas of consumer and producer surplus relate to the shoe-store example at the beginning of Chapter 1 and the two-student examples in Chapter 3?

PARETO IMPROVEMENTS AND ECONOMIC EFFICIENCY

Jeff and Barb could eat at home or go out to eat. Barb doesn't care, but Jeff wants to eat out. Going out to eat makes Jeff happier and doesn't affect Barb's happiness. Eating out is *Pareto improving*.

> Any change is a **Pareto improvement** if at least one person gains and no one loses.

(*Pareto* is pronounced "par-ā-toh.")

Jeremy and Amy could go out to eat or eat at home. Jeremy wants to go out, and Amy wants to stay home. Even though Jeremy would be happier eating out, it would *not* be a Pareto improving choice, because Amy would lose. However, Jeremy might gain more than Amy loses. For example, Jeremy might be able to *compensate* Amy by doing something later that she wants. By compensating Amy later, the couple could turn their impasse into a win-win situation.

> A change is **economically efficient** if the winners *could* compensate the losers by enough to make the change a Pareto improvement.

In other words, a change is economically efficient if the winners from the change win more than the losers lose. In that case, the winners could compensate the losers by enough that they would no longer lose.

The word *could* is important in the definition. A change is economically efficient *even if no compensation actually occurs*. For example, suppose Betsy buys one T-shirt each month from Michael, who sells them for $12 each and earns $2 profit on each shirt. Now suppose she stops buying T-shirts from Michael and starts buying them from Pedro, who sells them for $7 each. Betsy saves $5 on each shirt she buys, while Michael loses only $2 in profit. It is economically efficient for Betsy to buy from Pedro instead of Michael. From her $5 gain each month, Betsy could compensate Michael for his $2 loss each month. If Betsy paid Michael $2 per month, then she would still gain $3 per month and Michael would not lose, so this compensation would create a Pareto improvement. Even if Betsy does not compensate Michael, it is economically efficient for Betsy to buy from Pedro instead of Michael, because Betsy wins more than Michael loses.[2] When winners win more than losers lose from a change, that change is economically efficient.

Note that every Pareto improvement increases economic efficiency because some people gain and no one loses. However, not all economically efficient changes are Pareto improvements. Betsy does not compensate Michael when she starts buying from Pedro, although she could do so. So this change is economically efficient, but not a Pareto improvement.

> ### Advice
> *An example may help you remember these ideas:* Your roommate throws a party in your room. If you are happy about the event, it is a *Pareto improvement.* If you want to go to sleep, your roommate may offer to pay you $5 to sleep down the hall. If this gesture is enough to compensate you for the inconvenience of the party, then the party is *economically efficient* even if your roommate never actually pays you.

EXAMPLE

Most people have gained from the technological developments in the computer industry. However, these changes have harmed some people. Losers include firms that produced mechanical adding machines and typewriters, as well as workers whose jobs have been replaced by computers. The development of computers was not a Pareto improvement, because some people lost. However, it was economically efficient, because the winners from these technological developments have gained more than the losers lost. Therefore, the winners *could* have compensated the losers enough to keep them from losing. Virtually every new development in technology is economically efficient, though not a Pareto improvement.

Economically Efficient Situation

A mountain climber reaches the top of a mountain when he has no further steps to take upward. The economy reaches a situation of economic efficiency when it has no further changes to make in the direction of efficiency.

> An **economically efficient situation** means there are no additional economically efficient changes to make.

---

[2]Pedro also gains from Betsy's business—otherwise he would not offer to sell the T-shirts for $7 each.

Tradeoff between Economic Efficiency and Equity?

Government policies on international trade often provoke loud public debate, and the debate on the North American Free Trade Agreement (NAFTA) was no exception. Some people claimed that NAFTA would raise economic effi- ciency, reduce prices to U.S. consumers, and help to im- prove the political climate in Mexico by boosting that coun- try's economy. Others claimed that NAFTA would cost jobs in the United States, as U.S. firms relocated to Mexico to gain access to cheaper labor, and that it would reduce wages in the United States. Virtually every economic study of NAFTA indicated that it would raise economic efficiency, but at the cost of economic harm to some people (such as un- skilled workers in many U.S. industries).

> An **economically inefficient situation** means some economically efficient changes have not yet been made.

An economically efficient situation is like being at the mountain top—there are no further steps to take toward improvement. An economically inefficient situation is like being on the side of the mountain—there are additional steps yet to be taken toward the top. After the economy has taken those steps—that is, after additional changes—the economy may reach an economically efficient situation.

Is Economic Efficiency Good?

It is easy to argue that Pareto improvements are good because no one loses and some people gain. People may disagree about whether a particular change is actually Pareto- improving in real life, but few argue that Pareto improvements are bad.[3]

In contrast, some economically efficient changes create losers as well as winners. Many innovations in technology throughout history have hurt some people while ben- efiting millions of others. A cure for cancer would obviously help millions of people, but some people would lose their jobs. The development of a cheap way to harness solar energy would help many people, but it would throw coal miners out of work. Radial tires last several times as long as old, bias-ply tires, so their development caused people to buy new tires less often. This fall in the demand for tires eliminated 40 per- cent of the jobs in the U.S. tire industry within a decade. The development of radial tires was not a Pareto improvement because it hurt some people (workers who lost their jobs). Like nearly every technical innovation, however, it was economically efficient.[4]

Are technical innovations good? The answer depends on how you weigh the gains to the winners and the (smaller) losses to the losers. Someone who does not care about the distribution of wealth among people would say that all economically efficient changes are good. Someone who cares about the distribution of wealth might say that some eco- nomically efficient changes are bad. That person might believe that certain economically

---

[3]There is usually room for disagreement about whether a change is actually a Pareto improvement. Suppose, for example, that Andy and Pat each have $100, then someone gives another $100 to Andy. Most people would say that this is a Pareto improve- ment because Andy gains and Pat does not lose. However, one could argue that Pat loses because he now feels envious of Andy. Similarly, suppose that the government were to repeal the laws that prevent under-age purchases of alcoholic bever- ages. Some people would say that they gain from being able to buy these drinks, while others would argue that the people who abuse alcohol as a result are actually worse off, though they may erroneously believe that they gain. Your judgment about whether the change is a Pareto improvement depends on whether you think people know and act in their own interests.

[4]Consumers could have compensated tire workers by paying them the same wages as before while they quit making tires and produced other goods instead. Then the workers would not have lost, and consumers would have gained (consumers would have enjoyed both their radial tires *and* these other goods). Therefore, the development of radial tires, like virtually all tech- nical innovations, increased economic efficiency.

The NAFTA debate centered on the question of whether an economically efficient change is good or bad. NAFTA would raise economic efficiency because the winners in each country would gain more than the losers would lose. Still, no provision in NAFTA would compensate the losers. Is a policy like this good or bad? Some people say that the losses to some people make the policy bad. Others say that the policy is good because the losses are outweighed by benefits to other people.

Nearly every change in government economic policy hurts some people. Should the government follow policies that promote economic inefficiency to prevent some people from losing from a policy change? Should the government adopt policies to promote economic efficiency even if some people lose from the policy changes? Economics alone cannot answer these questions; the answers require value judgments. Nevertheless, you implicitly answer these questions nearly every time you express an opinion about government policies.

efficient changes would be unfair to the losers, or that the losses they would suffer are more important than the larger gains to the winners. For example, some people would oppose a change that would help 100 rich people by $50 each if it would hurt 100 poor people by $10 each. Even though that change would increase economic efficiency (the rich people *could* compensate the poor people by paying them at least $10 each), some people would view it as bad because of its effects on the distribution of wealth.

Equilibrium of Supply and Demand Is Economically Efficient

The equilibrium quantity Q_1 in Figure 6 is economically efficient. Chapter 4 explained that the supply-demand model is based on competition between *price-takers*, which is also called *perfect competition*. The equilibrium of supply and demand is economically efficient because the equilibrium quantity Q_1 maximizes the total gain from trade.[5]

The height of the demand curve shows the benefit to buyers of each unit of a good, measured by their willingness to pay for the good. The height of the supply curve shows the cost of producing each unit of the good. If the benefit of the nth unit of the good exceeds its cost, then production of that nth unit is economically efficient. The equilibrium quantity Q_1 maximizes the total benefit of the good, minus its total cost.

EXAMPLE AND EXPLANATION

Suppose that firms were to produce *less* than the equilibrium quantity. If firms produced only 500 cans of soup per week in Figure 8, buyers and sellers would both gain from an increase in the quantity of soup. The height of the demand curve at the quantity 501 shows the benefit to buyers of the 501st can, indicating that some buyer is willing to pay 78 cents for that can of soup. The height of the supply curve shows the cost of producing the 501st can, indicating that a firm can produce it for only 61 cents. Because the demand curve lies above the supply curve at the quantity 501, buyers and sellers can share the gains from production of the 501st can of soup. Figure 8 shows a gain of 17 cents (78 cents minus 61 cents) from the 501st can. Any level of output less than the equilibrium quantity, Q_1, is economically inefficient, and buyers and sellers can share the gain from an increase in output.

Similar reasoning applies if output exceeds Q_1. The supply curve lies above the demand curve, so buyers and sellers can both gain by reducing output. If it costs 94 cents to produce the 1,321st can of soup, and buyers are willing to pay only 30 cents for it, then buyers and sellers jointly lose 64 cents on that can of soup. Buyers and sellers can share the 64-cent gain from not producing it.

---

[5]This conclusion that the equilibrium quantity is economically efficient assumes that no externalities complicate the analysis; a later chapter discusses externalities.

The equilibrium quantity, Q_1, is economically efficient. Higher or lower quantities would be economically inefficient.

Figure 8 | Equilibrium Quantity and Economic Efficiency

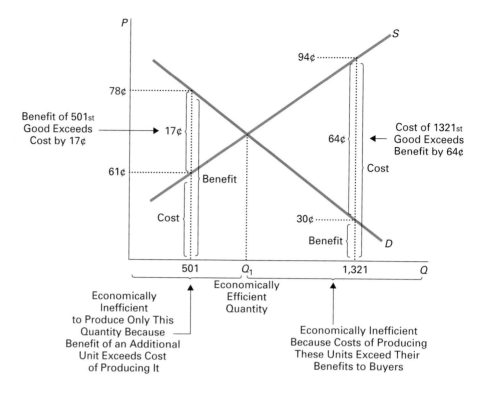

Deadweight Social Losses

This discussion suggests a way to measure the loss from an economically inefficient situation.

> The **deadweight social loss** from an economically inefficient situation is the consumer and producer surplus that people could gain by eliminating that inefficiency.

Roughly, a deadweight social loss is a loss to some people without corresponding gains to anyone else. The shaded area in Figure 9 shows the deadweight social loss from a restriction that keeps output at Q_0, below the equilibrium quantity.

EXPLANATION

Suppose that the government were to limit output of a good to 10 units when the equilibrium quantity was 15, as in Figure 10. The cost of producing an 11th unit would be $8, but the benefit to buyers would be $12. If the government were to allow production of an 11th unit, the buyer and seller could share the $4 gain from trade on that unit, so they would be willing to pay up to $4 to eliminate the prohibition on producing it. (For example, if they were to pay the government $3 to eliminate the prohibition, they could still share the remaining $1 gain from trade.) Therefore, the deadweight social loss from not trading the 11th unit traded would equal $4.

Similarly, the deadweight social loss from prohibiting the 12th unit would be $3, and the deadweight social losses from prohibiting the 13th and 14th units would be $2

Figure 9 | Deadweight Social Loss

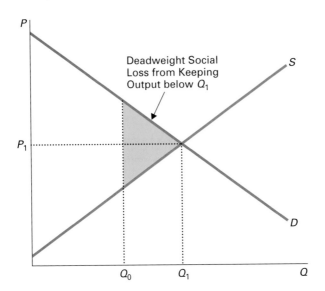

Deadweight social loss measures the size of the economic inefficiency from an output different than Q_1.

and $1. The prohibition of the 15th unit creates no deadweight social loss, so the total deadweight social loss from limiting output to 10 units would be $10, represented by the shaded area in the figure ($4 plus $3 plus $2 plus $1).

Earlier chapters introduced the idea of deadweight social loss without using that term. In the shoe-store example from Chapter 1, each person gains 1 hour of leisure time by trading. The deadweight social loss from prohibiting the trade would be the value of 2 hours of leisure time.

Figure 10 | Deadweight Social Loss Occurs when Benefit Does Not Equal Cost

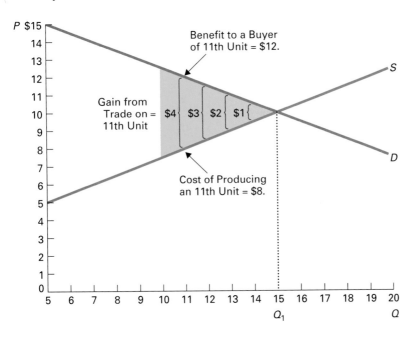

The deadweight social loss from limiting output to 10 units equals the gains from trade that people would have achieved if they had traded the 11th, 12th, 13th, 14th, and 15th units. The benefit of the 11th unit exceeds the opportunity cost of producing that unit; the difference is a deadweight social loss of $4. Similar deadweight social losses on the 12th, 13th, and 14th units create a total deadweight social loss of $10. The equilibrium quantity of 15 units is economically efficient because the benefit to buyers of the 15th unit, shown by the height of the demand curve, equals the opportunity cost of producing it, shown by the height of the supply curve.

> R e v i e w   Q u e s t i o n s

7. What is a Pareto improvement? Give an example.

8. When does a change increase economic efficiency? Give an example.

9. What is an economically efficient situation?

10. Why does the shaded area in Figure 9 show the deadweight social loss from limiting output to Q_0?

> T h i n k i n g   E x e r c i s e s

11. Why is it economically inefficient to produce more than the equilibrium quantity of a good?

12. In Thinking Exercise 4, what would be the deadweight social loss from a rule that prevented Bill from riding the roller coaster? What would be the deadweight social loss from a rule that limited him to one ride?

APPLICATIONS   Economists apply the concepts discussed in this chapter to measure the gains and losses from changes in underlying economic conditions. The following sections discuss some specific applications.

International Trade

Figure 11 shows the effects of international trade. (This figure resembles Figure 1 in Chapter 7.) Without international trade, the U.S. price is $3, and the foreign price is $8. The U.S. economy produces and consumes 5 million rolls of film and foreign countries produce and consume 7 million rolls.

Without international trade:

▶ U.S. consumer surplus is the sum of Areas A and B.

▶ U.S. producer surplus is Area D.

▶ Foreign consumer surplus is Area E.

▶ Foreign producer surplus is the sum of Areas F and H.

The equilibrium without international trade is not economically efficient. The benefit of an additional roll of film to foreign buyers is $8—the amount that some foreign buyer would be willing to pay for it. The cost of producing that roll of film in the United States is only $3, which is $5 less than its benefit. Buyers and sellers could share the $5 gain from producing one more roll of film in the United States and providing it to a foreign buyer. This change—allowing some international trade—would be economically efficient.

With international trade, the world price is $5. The United States produces and sells 9 million rolls per week, consuming 3 million rolls and exporting 6 million rolls. Foreign countries produce 4 million rolls per week, consuming 10 million rolls and importing 6 million rolls from the United States.

Figure 11 | Economic Efficiency of International Trade

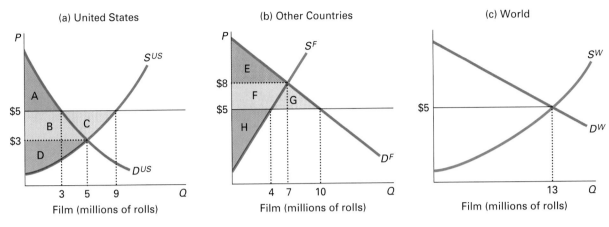

	Without International Trade		With International Trade	
	United States	**Other Countries**	**United States**	**Other Countries**
Consumer surplus	A + B	E	A	E + F + G
Producer surplus	D	F + H	B + C + D	H

The net gain from international trade is Area C + G.

With international trade:

▶ U.S. consumer surplus is Area A.

▶ U.S. producer surplus is the sum of Areas B, C, and D.

▶ Foreign consumer surplus is the sum of Areas E, F, and G.

▶ Foreign producer surplus is Area H.

The equilibrium with international trade is economically efficient. However, allow-ing international trade was not a Pareto improvement, because some people lose from international trade:

▶ U.S. consumers lose Area B.

▶ U.S. producers gain Areas B and C.

▶ Foreign consumers gain Areas F and G.

▶ Foreign producers lose Area F.

Notice that *U.S. producers gain more than U.S. consumers lose,* and *foreign con-sumers gain more than foreign producers lose.* Overall, then, each country gains from international trade in the sense that its winners win more than its losers lose. Area C represents the net gain to the United States, and foreign countries gain Area G. The deadweight social loss from prohibiting international trade would be the sum of Areas C and G.

This logical demonstration that international trade is economically efficient, and that prohibitions on international trade are economically inefficient, is one of the most famous results in economics. It is the basis for the near-universal support of free international trade among economists. Similar arguments apply to the effects of arbitrage and speculation.

Taxes

Figure 12 (like Figure 6 in Chapter 8) shows the effects of a tax. Without the tax, the equilibrium price and quantity are P_1 and Q_1, and consumer surplus is the sum of Areas A, B, and C. Producer surplus is the sum of Areas D, E, and F. The equilibrium without a tax is economically efficient.

A per-unit tax of T dollars raises the price that buyers pay to P_B (including tax), while sellers receive the price P_S (net of the tax), which is T dollars less than P_B. Output with the tax is Q_2, consumer surplus is Area A, and producer surplus is Area F. The sum of Areas B and D shows total tax payments, which the government collects as tax revenue. The sum of Areas C and E is a deadweight social loss.

▶ Consumers lose Areas B and C from the tax.

▶ Producers lose Areas D and E from the tax.

▶ The government gains Areas B and D from the tax.

▶ Areas C and E show the deadweight social loss from the tax.

EXPLANATION AND EXAMPLE

A tax causes a deadweight social loss, because it prevents some mutually advantageous trades. Chapter 3 first introduced this idea in the section, *How Taxes Create Economic Inefficiency: An Example.* (You may want to reread that section now.) Figure 13 shows that a $1 tax on haircuts causes a deadweight social loss. Without the tax, haircuts cost $10.00, and people in the United States buy 1 billion haircuts per year. With the tax, haircuts cost $10.50; the government gets $1.00 and barbers get $9.50. With the tax,

---

Figure 12 | Effect of a Tax

With no tax, the equilibrium price and quantity are P_1 and Q_1, consumer surplus is A + B + C, and producer surplus is D + E + F. With a per-unit tax, T, buyers pay P_B, sellers keep P_S, and Q_2 units are traded. Consumer surplus is A, producer surplus is F, government tax revenue is B + D, and the deadweight social loss is C + E.

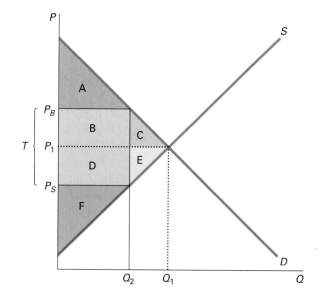

Figure 13 | Deadweight Social Loss from a Tax

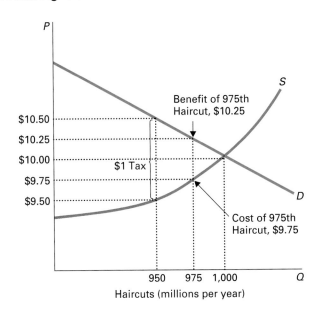

A tax of $1.00 reduces the number of haircuts traded per year to 950 million. Some buyer is willing to pay up to $10.25 for haircut number 975 million, and some seller is willing to provide that haircut for $9.75. The tax prevents this trade, however, causing a deadweight social loss.

people buy only 950 million haircuts per year. The figure shows that someone would be willing to pay $10.25 for haircut number 975 million, and a barber would be willing to provide that haircut for $9.75. They could share the $0.50 gain from trade by agreeing on any price between $9.75 and $10.25, but they choose not to trade because the gain from this trade, 50 cents, is smaller than the per-unit tax ($1.00) that they would have to pay. The tax causes a deadweight social loss because it prevents some mutually beneficial trades.

Special Cases of Elasticities

A tax on a good with perfectly inelastic supply does not cause a deadweight social loss. Figure 14 shows that without a tax, the price is $5 and the quantity sold is 120 units per week. Consumer surplus is Area A, and producer surplus is the sum of Areas B and C. A $1-per-unit tax leaves the price that buyers pay (including tax) at $5, but the price that

Figure 14 | Effects of a Tax with Perfectly Inelastic Supply

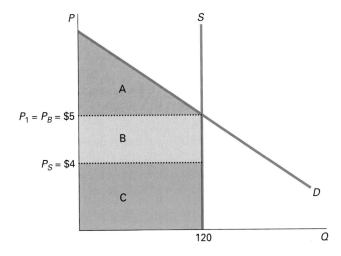

Without a tax, consumer surplus is Area A and producer surplus is Area B + C. With a tax, consumer surplus is Area A, producer surplus is Area C, and the government collects Area B. Because supply is perfectly inelastic, the tax does not cause a deadweight social loss.

sellers receive (net of tax) falls to $4. With the tax, consumer surplus remains Area A, producer surplus becomes Area C, and the government gains Area B in tax revenue. The total gain from trade to everyone, including the government, does not change. It remains the sum of Areas A, B, and C. A similar argument shows that no deadweight social loss results from a tax on a good with perfectly inelastic demand. (See Problem 19 at the end of this chapter.)

Comment

This discussion has ignored the costs of calculating and paying taxes. The time and expense that people and business firms spend to fill out forms, calculate, and pay their taxes is an additional source of deadweight social loss from the tax that does not appear in these diagrams. (This deadweight social loss occurs even with perfectly inelastic supply or demand.) This additional deadweight social loss can be large; the cost of filing personal and business income tax returns in the United States each year equals roughly 1 percent of the economy's total output.[6]

Subsidies

Taxes cause deadweight social losses, but do subsidies provide social gains? The answer is no; subsidies also cause deadweight social losses. Figure 15 shows the effects of a $20 per-unit subsidy for production of waterbeds. Without the subsidy, waterbeds cost $140 and 360,000 are sold each year. Consumer surplus is the sum of Areas A and B, and producer surplus is the sum of Areas F and G. The equilibrium without a subsidy is economically efficient.

With a per-unit subsidy of $20, buyers pay $125 (net of the subsidy), sellers receive $145 (including the subsidy), and 420,000 waterbeds are sold each year. Consumer surplus is the sum of Areas A, B, E, and F. Producer surplus is the sum of Areas B, C, F, and G. Consumers gain Area E + F from the subsidy and producers gain Area B + C. Who loses? The government loses because it provides the subsidy (that is, taxpayers lose). The subsidy costs the government $20 on each of the 420,000 waterbeds sold each year, so it loses the sum of Areas B, C, D, E, and F. The loss to the government is larger than the total gain to consumers and producers. The difference, Area D, is the deadweight social loss due to the subsidy. In summary:

▶ Consumers gain Areas E and F from the subsidy.

▶ Producers gain Areas B and C from the subsidy.

▶ The government loses Areas B, C, D, E, and F from the subsidy.

▶ Area D shows the deadweight social loss from the subsidy.

Price Controls

Figure 16 (like Figure 1 in Chapter 8) shows the effects of a maximum legal price. Without the maximum legal price, the equilibrium price and quantity are P_1 and Q_1. Consumer surplus is the sum of Areas A, B, and C; producer surplus is the sum of Areas D, E, and F. This equilibrium without price controls is economically efficient.

With a maximum legal price and a resulting shortage, the rationing system determines which consumers actually buy the goods. Therefore the effects of a maximum legal price on consumer and producer surplus depend on the form of rationing. If people with the

---

[6]Government programs provide benefits to people, of course, and the government probably cannot obtain enough revenue to finance its operations without taxes that cause deadweight social losses. The government can, however, choose its mix of taxes to try to minimize the resulting deadweight social losses.

Figure 15 | Effects of a Subsidy

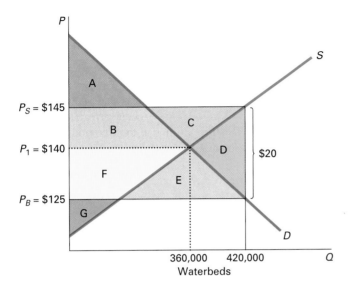

Without a subsidy, consumer surplus is Area A + B and producer surplus is Area F + G. With a subsidy, consumer surplus is Area A + B + E + F, producer surplus is Area B + C + F + G, the government pays Area B + C + D + E + F, and the deadweight social loss is Area D.

highest willingness to pay can buy the goods, then consumer surplus is the sum of Areas A, B, and D, and producer surplus is Area F. In this case, the maximum legal price causes a deadweight social loss equal to the sum of Areas C and E.

The deadweight social loss would be larger for a rationing system that did not provide the goods to buyers with the highest willingness to pay. For example, rationing by waiting provides units of a goods to people who are first in line. Some people with high willingness to pay for the good cannot buy it because they are near the end of the line; other people with lower willingness to pay for the good are able to buy it because they are near the front of the line. In addition, rationing by waiting adds to the deadweight social loss because people could use the time that they spend in line to do something else. Generally, gains from a rationing system accrue to people with a comparative advantage at obtaining goods within that system (such as people with a lot of free time

Figure 16 | Maximum Legal Price

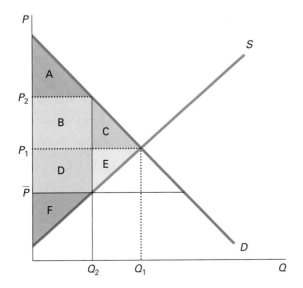

The effects of a maximum legal price of $\overline{P}$ depend on the rationing system. If buyers with the highest willingness to pay get the goods, then consumer surplus changes from A + B + C to A + B + D, and producer surplus falls from D + E + F to F. The deadweight social loss is Area C + E. The deadweight social loss would be greater than that amount with most forms of rationing.

to spend waiting in a line); other people lose. Experiments in economics have shown that the size of the deadweight social loss due to a price control often exceeds C plus E; the exact amount of the loss depends on the type of rationing system.

EXAMPLE: DEADWEIGHT SOCIAL LOSS FROM SELECTIVE PRICE CONTROLS ON GASOLINE

The California state government required Chevron gas stations in the state to reduce their prices, for about two months, to levels 16 to 21 cents per gallon below prices at other stations. This mandate created lines for gasoline at the Chevron stations, while other stations had no lines but higher prices. The wait to buy gas at a Chevron station averaged about 15 minutes.

If you wait 15 extra minutes to buy 10 gallons of gas and you save $0.20 per gallon, you effectively earn $2.00 in 15 minutes, which amounts to a wage of $8 per hour. Some California buyers, particularly people whose time was worth less than $8 an hour, waited in lines at Chevron stations. Other buyers, particularly those with a higher value of time, avoided the lines by buying gas elsewhere despite higher prices.

The size of the deadweight social loss from waiting in line depends partly on how much people dislike it. In California, lines were not important to some people, who enjoyed listening to music or talking to friends as they waited; these people tended to buy gas at Chevron stations. Others, who disliked the lines more, tended to buy their gasoline elsewhere.

The average customer bought about 10 gallons of gas. Chevron customers paid about $0.20 per gallon less by waiting in line, so they saved about $2.00 per 10-gallon fill-up. A study showed that the typical Chevron customer would have been willing to spend $1.00 to avoid waiting in the line, so an average Chevron customer had a net gain of $1.00 for each 10-gallon fill-up. Chevron stations, though, lost $2.00 on each 10-gallon fill-up. The difference between a *buyer's gain of $1.00* and a *Chevron station's loss of $2.00* was a deadweight social loss. This loss was $1.00 for each 10-gallon fill-up, so the deadweight social loss at each Chevron station that sold 20,000 gallons of gasoline per month was about $2,000 per month.

Review Questions

13. Draw a graph like Figure 11, and use it to show consumer and producer surplus (a) without international trade and (b) with international trade.

14. Draw a graph to show consumer and producer surplus:
    (a) Without a tax
    (b) With a tax on production of a good. (Also show the deadweight social loss.)

15. Draw a graph to show consumer and producer surplus:
    (a) Without a subsidy
    (b) With a subsidy for the production of a good. (Also show the deadweight social loss.)

16. Draw a graph to help explain why a tax does not cause a deadweight social loss if supply is perfectly inelastic.

Thinking Exercises

17. Use a graph to show how an increase in demand affects consumer and producer surplus.

18. Use a graph to show how an increase in supply affects consumer and producer surplus.

Conclusion

Consumer Surplus and Producer Surplus

Consumer surplus measures buyers' gains from trade. It equals their willingness to pay minus the price they actually pay. Consumer surplus appears on a graph as the area under the demand curve and above the price buyers pay, between the zero quantity and the equilibrium quantity.

Producer surplus measures sellers' gains from trade. It equals the price that sellers receive for their goods minus their opportunity costs of producing those goods. Producer surplus appears on a graph as the area above the supply curve and below the price sellers receive, between the zero quantity and the equilibrium quantity.

The total gain from trade equals the sum of consumer and producer surplus. This sum equals the total benefit to buyers of the good minus the total cost of producing the good.

Pareto Improvements and Economic Efficiency

Any change is a Pareto improvement if at least one person gains and no one loses. Any change is economically efficient if the winners *could* compensate the losers by enough to make it a Pareto improvement. The change is economically efficient whether or not that compensation actually occurs.

Every Pareto improvement increases economic efficiency. Not every increase in economic efficiency is a Pareto improvement.

An economically efficient situation exists if there are no additional economically efficient changes that could be made. An economically efficient situation is like being at a mountain top with no further steps to take toward the top. An economically inefficient situation is like being on the side of the mountain, with steps yet to take toward the top. Only by taking those steps can the economy achieve economic efficiency. A deadweight social loss measures the size of an economic inefficiency. It equals the consumer and producer surplus that people would gain from eliminating the inefficiency.

Applications

International trade is economically efficient. International trade helps people as consumers and hurts them as producers in the exporting country, though consumers gain more than producers lose. International trade hurts people as consumers and helps them as producers in the importing country, though producers gain more than consumers lose. The same argument applies to arbitrage and speculation.

Taxes cause economic inefficiencies (except with perfectly inelastic supply or demand). The government revenue from a tax is smaller than the losses in consumer and producer surplus caused by the tax. The difference is the deadweight social loss from the tax. Subsidies, like taxes, are economically inefficient. The cost of a subsidy to the government exceeds the gains to buyers and sellers, and the difference is a deadweight social loss. Price controls also cause deadweight social losses by reducing output below its economically efficient level.

Key Terms

consumer surplus	Pareto improvement	economically efficient situation	deadweight social loss
producer surplus	economically efficient change	economically inefficient situation	

Problems

19. Use diagrams to show the effects of a tax on consumer and producer surplus, and to show the deadweight social loss from the tax, when:
 (a) Demand is perfectly inelastic
 (b) Supply is perfectly inelastic
 (c) Demand is perfectly elastic
 (d) Supply is perfectly elastic
 Also explain your results in words.

20. Draw a diagram to illustrate the effects of a subsidy for the production of candy. Show the effects on (a) output of candy, (b) the prices paid by buyers and received by sellers, (c) consumer surplus, and (d) producer surplus. Also show (e) the cost of the subsidy to the government and (f) the social gain or loss from the subsidy.

21. Comment on these statements:
    (a) "Economists say that taxes cause a deadweight social loss, but this statement is misleading. Obviously, when one person *pays* money in taxes, another person *collects* money in taxes, so society as a whole suffers no loss."
    (b) "A tax causes a deadweight social loss to the extent that people change their behavior so that they don't have to pay it."

22. Draw a diagram like Figure 11 to show equilibrium with international trade. Suppose that foreign demand rises. How much do U.S. consumers gain or lose? What about U.S. producers, foreign consumers, and foreign producers?

23. Suppose that a foreign country puts a tariff on imports of U.S. beef. Use a diagram to discuss the effects of the tariff. Who gains and who loses? How much?

24. Explain why not every economically efficient change is a Pareto improvement.

25. Complete the following exercises to continue a problem from Chapter 7.
    (a) Use the table to find equilibrium prices, quantities produced, and quantities consumed with international trade.
    (b) Repeat Problem 25a *without* international trade.
    (c) Calculate the gains or losses to consumers and producers in each country and the deadweight social loss from a law prohibiting international trade. (*Hint:* Use the table to draw a graph of demand and supply in each country, and calculate consumer and producer surplus.)

	United States		Foreign Countries		World Market	
Price	Demand	Supply	Demand	Supply	Demand	Supply
$12	2	13	5	25	7	38
11	4	12	6	22	10	33
10	6	11	7	19	13	30
9	10	10	8	17	18	27
8	11	9	9	15	20	24
7	12	8	10	14	22	22
6	14	6	11	13	25	19
5	16	0	12	12	28	12
4	18	0	13	9	31	9
3	20	0	14	0	34	0
2	22	0	15	0	37	0

Inquiries for Further Thought

26. Think of a good you recently bought. How much did you pay for it? How much more would you have been willing to pay for it? What was your consumer surplus?

27. A magazine article says, "the pleasures of music are incalculable, either in wattage or in money." Do you agree? Can you think of a way to calculate a person's pleasure from music in terms of money?

28. Do you think the economy faces a tradeoff between equity and economic efficiency?
    (a) If so, give examples of increases in economic efficiency with unfair or inequitable consequences. Should government policies promote equity even at the cost of economic efficiency? What general principles should guide the government's decision about whether to promote equity or efficiency?
    (b) If not, explain the general principles behind your concept of equity. Can equity ever conflict with efficiency? Why or why not? If a conflict were to arise, how should the government decide whether to promote equity or efficiency?

29. When Supreme Court Justice Anthony Kennedy was questioned in the U.S. Senate during his confirmation hearing, one senator urged him "not simply to weigh economic efficiency" but also "to consider the impact on consumers" of his decisions. Did the senator's comment make sense? Discuss it.

30. People risk death to flee bad economic conditions or oppressive governments in many countries. U.S. immigration policy limits the number of foreigners who can come to live in the United States. Think of the right to come to the United States as a good that could be bought and sold. The U.S. government imposes a maximum legal price of zero on this good and then rations it. (The government chooses who gets to buy this good at the legal price of zero.)

(a) Discuss the effects of this maximum legal price on consumer and producer surplus.

(b) Suppose that the U.S. government were to decide to allow more immigration. Who would gain and who would lose? How much? What would be the effects on consumer surplus?

IN THE NEWS

Since most teenagers are sensitive to the disincentive effects of high tobacco taxes, a tax hike could be deemed "economically efficient" on the grounds that it might prevent many from starting to smoke in the first place—something they would not have done if they were fully aware of the risks.

Source: Business Week

Does the government promote economic efficiency when it sets taxes to prevent decisions that it believes better-informed people would not have made?

(c) What should U.S. immigration policy be? Why?

31. Discuss this statement: "People often make irrational choices, such as smoking despite the health risks. The government should tax goods such as cigarettes and alcohol to improve the economy's efficiency. A higher tax on cigarettes could reduce smoking by forcing people to make rational decisions."

32. Consider these issues that arise in relation to international trade.

(a) When the United States chooses its international trade policies, should it design policies to benefit only U.S. citizens or should it also take into account the effects on people in other countries?

(b) Suppose that U.S. residents would gain $100 and foreigners would lose $150 from some U.S. government policy, and that foreign residents would gain $100 and U.S. residents would lose $150 from a foreign government's policy. Should the government of each country take into account only the effects on its own residents? What else might the government do?

33. Farm wages rose when tighter immigration laws reduced the supply of labor. Who would gain and who would lose, and how much, if the U.S. government were to allow more immigrant workers into the United States?

Appendix A: Algebra of Consumer Surplus

Consider the straight-line demand and supply curves represented by these two equations:

$$Q^d = a - bP \qquad\qquad \text{Example: } Q^d = 10 - 2P$$

$$Q^s = c + dP \qquad\qquad \text{Example: } Q^s = -5 + 3P$$

where Q^d is the quantity demanded, Q^s is the quantity supplied, P is the price of the good, and a, b, c, and d are numbers.

The appendix to Chapter 4 showed that the equilibrium price is:

$$P_1 = (a - c)/(b + d) \qquad\qquad \text{Example: } P_1 = 3$$

The equilibrium quantity is:

$$Q_1 = a - b(a - c)/(b + d) \qquad\qquad \text{Example: } Q_1 = 4$$

Figure A1 illustrates these equations. Because the demand curve is a straight line, consumer surplus is the area of the shaded triangle. The height of the triangle is:

$$H = a/b - P_1 \qquad\qquad \text{Example: } 5 - 3$$

$$= a/b - (a - c)/(b + d) \qquad\qquad \text{Example: } 2$$

Figure A1 | Calculating Consumer Surplus

Consumer surplus is the area of the shaded triangle, which is $\frac{1}{2}(a/b - P_1)Q_1$.

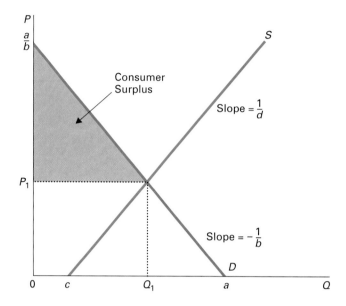

The base of the triangle is the equilibrium quantity, so the area of the triangle, consumer surplus, is half the area of the base times the height:

$$CS = (H)(Q_1)/2 \qquad\qquad \text{Example: } (2)(4)/2 = 4$$

Problems

A1. Suppose that the demand curve is:

$$Q^d = 30 - P$$

and the supply curve is:

$$Q^s = 2P$$

(a) Calculate the equilibrium quantity and price.
(b) Show the equilibrium on a graph.
(c) Calculate consumer surplus. Your answer should be a number. (*Hint:* Look at your graph and use the formula for the area of a triangle.)
(d) Calculate producer surplus. Your answer should be a number. (*Hint:* Use logic similar to that for finding consumer surplus.)

A2. Suppose that the demand curve is:

$$Q^d = 300 - 10P$$

and the supply curve is:

$$Q^s = 20P$$

(a) Calculate the equilibrium quantity and price.

(b) Show the equilibrium on a graph.

(c) Calculate consumer surplus. Your answer should be a number.

Appendix B: Calculating the Deadweight Social Loss from Taxes

This appendix builds on the appendixes to Chapter 4 and Chapter 8. Suppose that the demand curve is:

$$Q^d = 10 - 2P_B$$

where Q^d is the quantity demanded, in millions, and P_B is the price that buyers pay. The supply curve is:

$$Q^s = -5 + 3P_S$$

where Q^s is the quantity supplied, in millions, and P_S is the price that sellers receive. Without a tax, P_B and P_S are the same; the equilibrium price is $3 and the equilibrium quantity is 4 million units. (See the appendix to Chapter 4.)

The appendix to Chapter 8 showed that a tax of $1.00 per unit reduces the equilibrium price to sellers to $2.60, raises the equilibrium price to buyers to $3.60, and drops the equilibrium quantity to 2.8 million units. The deadweight social loss is represented by Area A in Figure B1. This region is a triangle, so its area is one-half of its base times its height. The base of the triangle is the change in quantity because of the tax. The quantity falls from 4.0 million to 2.8 million, so the base of the triangle is 1.2 million. The height of the triangle is the per-unit tax, which is $1. These numbers give an area for the triangle of the deadweight social loss of:

$$\tfrac{1}{2}(1.2 \text{ million})(\$1) = \$600{,}000$$

Figure B1 | Calculating Deadweight Social Loss

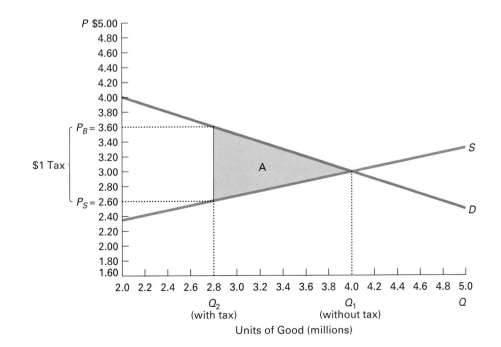

Area A is a triangle with a base of 1.2 million goods and a height of $1 per unit, so its area represents $600,000.

Problems

B1. (Follow-up to Problem A1 in the appendix to Chapter 8) Suppose that the demand curve for rental cars is:

$$Q^d = 500 - 2P_B$$

and the supply curve is:

$$Q^s = 100 + 6P_S$$

where Q^d is the quantity demanded (in cars per day), Q^s is the quantity supplied, P_B is the price per day paid by renters including taxes, and P_S is the price per day received by sellers excluding taxes. Suppose that the government taxes car rentals at $8 per day. Find the effects of this tax on consumer surplus and producer surplus, and find the deadweight social loss from this tax.

B2. (Follow-up to Problem A2 in the appendix to Chapter 8) Suppose that the demand curve for a product is:

$$x^d = 1,000 - 120p$$

where x^d is the quantity demanded and p is the price (measured in dollars). Suppose that the supply curve for the product, with x^s as the quantity supplied, is:

$$x^s = 200 + 40p$$

Suppose also that a per-unit tax of $4 is placed on the product. Find the effects of this tax on consumer surplus and producer surplus, and find the deadweight social loss from this tax.

B3. (Follow-up to Problem A3 in the appendix to Chapter 8) Reconsider Problem A2 for a subsidy of $4 per unit instead of a tax. Find the effects of this subsidy on consumer surplus and producer surplus, and find the deadweight social loss from this subsidy.

B4. Suppose that the demand curve for a good is:

$$x^d = 1,000 - 6p$$

and the supply curve is:

$$x^s = 4p$$

Suppose that the government places a tax of $30 per unit sold on this product. Find the equilibrium quantity, the price paid by buyers, the price paid by sellers, and the deadweight social loss from the tax.

PART 4

CHOICES
AND THEIR
IMPLICATIONS

CHAPTER 10

CHOICES AND DEMAND

In this Chapter . . .

Main Points to Understand

▶ Choices are determined by tastes and opportunities.

▶ The logic of rational choice implies decisions that equate marginal benefit with marginal cost.

▶ Sunk costs are irrelevant to rational choices.

Thinking Skills to Develop

▶ Recognize marginal costs and benefits.

▶ Distinguish *marginal* costs and benefits from *total* costs and benefits.

▶ Apply the logic of rational choice.

Success in most areas requires a variety of skills—imagination, drive, motivation, and smart decision making. Economics cannot help much with imagination, but it can help a lot with making decisions. The logic of rational choice is very general. It underlies computer algorithms as well as production decisions by business firms around the globe every day; money managers and global traders from New York to Tokyo to Shanghai to Bonn use the logic of rational choice 24 hours a day to guide their investment and financial decisions. The logic applies to personal decisions, as well—big decisions like career choices as well as everyday decisions like buying snacks. While people often make good decisions without comprehending the *logic* of choice, understanding and learning to apply that logic will help you to make even better decisions.

BUDGET LINES

Chapters 1 and 3 introduced the idea that everyone faces limits —limits on their time and their budgets. Figures 1 and 2 in Chapter 3 showed those limits on graphs. Graphs of limited budgets are called *budget lines*. As Chapter 3 explained, you can choose a

Figure 1 | Budget Line between Tape Rentals and Video Games

Tape rentals cost $1 each, while video games cost 25 cents each. A person with $10 can afford 40 games and no tapes, 10 tapes and no games, or other combinations along the budget line, such as 4 tapes and 24 games.

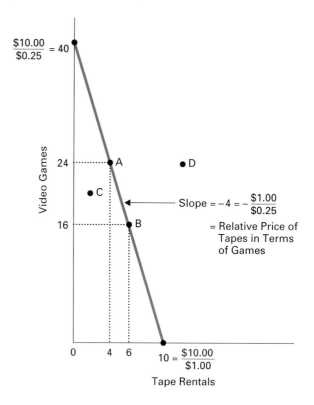

point on or below your budget line, but you cannot reach points above your budget line (given your limited budget).

> A **budget line** graphs a person's possible choices.

Figure 1 shows the budget line for a person with $10.00 to spend on renting video tapes for $1 each or playing video games for 25 cents each. If he spends all $10 on tapes, he can rent 10 tapes. If he spends all $10 on video games, he can play 40 games. The budget line shows the combinations of tape rentals and games that he can afford, such as points A, B, and C. The person does not have enough money to choose points above the budget line, such as Point D.

Slope of a Budget Line

The absolute value of a budget line's slope is the relative price of the good on the X-axis (tapes in this case) in terms of the good on the Y-axis (games in this case). Chapter 4 defined the relative price of one good in terms of another as the opportunity cost of the first good, measured in units of the second. If P_T is the nominal price of tapes, and P_G is the nominal price of games, then the relative price of tapes in terms of games is P_T/P_G.

Figure 2
An Increase in Income Shifts a Budget Line

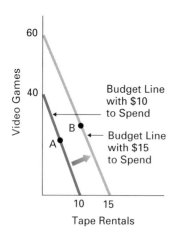

EXAMPLE

The nominal price of a tape rental is $1 and the nominal price of a video game is 25 cents, so the relative price of tapes in terms of games is 4 games per tape. Each time you rent a tape for $1, you sacrifice playing four video games for $0.25 each. In Figure 1, the absolute value of the budget line's slope equals 4.

Changes in Opportunities

A person's budget line shifts when her income changes. Figure 2 shows how an increase in income causes an upward shift in a budget line. The slope does not change. (The slope changes only if the relative price changes.) The shift in the budget line shows that you can afford to buy more goods when your income rises. A decrease in income would cause a downward shift in the budget line.

A person's budget line rotates when a price changes. Figure 3a shows how an increase in the price of tape rentals, from $1 to $2, makes the budget line steeper. (If the person spends all $10 to rent tapes, he can afford only 5 tapes after the price increase.) Figure 3b shows how an increase in the price of video games, from 25 cents to 50 cents, makes the budget line flatter. (If the person spends all $10 on games, he can afford only 20 games after the price increase.)

Tastes and Opportunities

Your budget line shows your opportunities. Your *tastes* determine which of those opportunities you actually choose. Appendix A in this chapter discusses indifference curves, which economists create to graph people's tastes. The main idea is that each person chooses the point on her budget line that she most prefers.

Changes in income and prices cause changes in opportunities, which often lead people to make new choices. For example, an increase in your income might lead you to change your choice from Point A to Point B in Figure 2. This change does not reflect a change in your tastes. It reflects a change in your opportunities.[1]

Review Question

1. Draw a budget line, and explain what it means and what its slope shows. Show how the budget line would change due to an increase in income or a price.

Thinking Exercises

2. Draw a graph to show how a fall in the price of a good affects your budget line.

3. Pedro has $100 to spend on caps and T-shirts. Caps cost $5 each and T-shirts cost $10 each.
   (a) Draw Pedro's budget line.
   (b) Show how his budget line changes if the price of caps rises to $10.

Figure 3
A Price Change Rotates a Budget Line

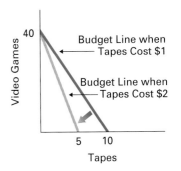

(a) Rise in the Price of Renting Tapes

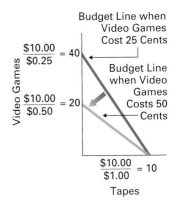

(b) Rise in the Price of Video Games

RATIONAL CHOICE

Economic models of consumer choice often assume that consumers choose rationally.

> A **rational choice** is the choice on your budget line that you most prefer.

Your choice is rational if you do not prefer any other choice on your budget line, given your own tastes and values. A rational choice is the best choice from your point of view. It does not imply any judgment about your tastes, values, or goals.

---

[1]A change in tastes would cause a change in your choice without any change in your opportunities, such as a change from Point A to Point B in Figure 1.

Sometimes people confuse the idea of rational choice with their judgments of good and bad choices. Someone might accuse you of having irrational tastes because you bought a good that person views as worthless. Instead, these critics should say that they disagree with your tastes. In economics, *rationality* does not refer to whether a person's choices show good or bad taste in some sense, but whether people do what is best based on their own tastes.

Rational choices are not necessarily selfish choices. People may be altruistic and make choices out of concern for other people or for animals or the environment. They may risk their lives to help other people or give anonymous gifts with no tangible returns to themselves. These actions may be rational based on their own values, tastes, and goals.

Choices and Behavior

Why do economists analyze the logic of rational choices? If people always behaved in simple ways—for example, if buyers always spent one-tenth of their incomes on restaurant meals and producers always invested half of their profits in new equipment—then economists might not need to analyze the logic of choice. However, people do not behave in such simple ways, particularly after changes in underlying economic conditions (such as technology, taxes, and foreign competition). Simple descriptions often give inaccurate views of behavior, particularly when totally new situations arise. For example, how would consumer spending change if the government were to replace the income tax with a consumption tax (so that people would pay taxes on money they spend but not on money that they save)? A simple rule such as "consumers always save 10 percent of their income" would probably give a wrong answer after the change, because consumers would probably spend less and save more than they did under the old tax law. To avoid these problems with simple rules, economists analyze the logic of choices to allow accurate descriptions and predictions about them.

Rule of Rational Choice
Rational choice follows a basic rule of logic:

> It is rational to do something until its marginal benefit equals its marginal cost.

(*Marginal benefit* and *marginal cost* are defined below.) This logical rule plays a central role in economic analysis, and it is one of the most important points for you to understand. The rule applies to any action, from how many socks you buy to how much food you eat; it applies to how long you study for an exam and how many friendships you cultivate. The next chapter will apply this rule to the decisions of business firms, and the rest of this book will make extensive use of the rule.

Marginal Benefit
You seek to obtain some benefit (money, happiness, fulfillment) from your actions. Your *total* benefit represents all the benefits you obtain from doing something. Your *marginal* benefit is the extra benefit you get from doing a little more of the same activity.

> The **marginal benefit** of doing something is the increase in total benefit from doing it a little more.[2]

Measuring Benefits: Utility and Revenue When economists discuss benefits to buyers, they often use the language of utility theory by measuring benefits in terms of utility. *Utility* is a catch-all term for measuring human goals (such as happiness, pleasure, fulfillment, accomplishment, understanding, love, approval, hope, sanctity, comfort, and so on).

---

[2]Readers who know calculus will recognize marginal benefit as the derivative of the total benefit from doing something with respect to the number of times you do it.

Utility is an abstract term for measuring human goals (such as happiness).

Economists often use the terms *marginal utility* and *total utility* to mean marginal benefit and total benefit measured in terms of utility.

When economists discuss benefits to sellers, they often use the terms *marginal revenue* and *total revenue* to mean marginal benefit and total benefit measured in terms of revenue (money income to sellers).

This chapter uses the general terms *marginal benefit* and *total benefit*. When applied to buyers, these terms may refer to marginal and total utility. When applied to sellers (as in the next several chapters), they refer to marginal and total revenue. More generally, the logic of rational choice applies to benefits measured in *any* kinds of units.

EXAMPLE OF MARGINAL AND TOTAL BENEFIT

Figure 4 shows a key example. If you do something once (see a movie, eat an apple, spend a day selling flowers on the street), your benefit may be 100 units measured in utility or dollars. Your *marginal* benefit of doing the action that one time equals 100. Your *total* benefit is also 100.

If you do the same activity twice, your benefit from the second time may be only 90 units (of dollars or utility). This is your *marginal* benefit. Your total benefit would be 190 units. Your marginal benefit from doing it the second time, 90 units, equals the increase in your total benefit (from 100 to 190 units).

If you do something a third time, your *marginal* benefit from that third time may be only 80 units. Your total benefit rises from 190 to 270 units. Again, your marginal benefit from doing it a third time equals the increase in your total benefit.

Panel (a) of Figure 4 shows how your *total* benefit depends on the number of times you do something: total benefit is 100 if you do it once, 190 if you do it twice, 270 if you do it three times, and so on. Figure 4b shows how your *marginal* benefit depends on the number of times you take the action. The marginal benefit of the first time equals 100; the marginal benefit of the second time equals 90; the marginal benefit of the third time equals 80, and so on.

Discussion Some actions, such as seeing movies, eating apples, or selling flowers, occur sequentially. In those cases it makes sense to discuss a first time or a fourth time, and the marginal benefit of the activity is the additional benefit from repeating it another time. However, the concept of marginal benefit also applies in nonsequential situations. For example, we can discuss the marginal benefit of larger beverages or television screens, faster computers, or more concentrated doses of medicine.

Why is the marginal benefit of doing something a second or third time smaller than the marginal benefit of the first time? The marginal benefit often declines for simple reasons—the movie isn't as entertaining the second time, because you already know the plot; the second apple is less satisfying, because you are less hungry after eating the first. The marginal benefit sometimes declines for more subtle reasons—the marginal benefit to a farmer of cultivating her most fertile fields exceeds the marginal benefit of additional cultivation on less fertile land. In still other cases, the marginal benefit does *not* decline—a child may enjoy the second ride on a roller coaster, after fear has subsided somewhat, more than the first ride. Still, even roller coaster rides may eventually become routine, with their marginal benefit declining as the number of rides increases sufficiently.

Marginal Cost

Every action has an opportunity cost, measured in money or utility. Total cost and marginal cost bear the same relationship as total benefit and marginal benefit: *Marginal cost* refers to the extra cost you pay to do something a little more.

Figure 4 | Total and Marginal Benefit and Cost

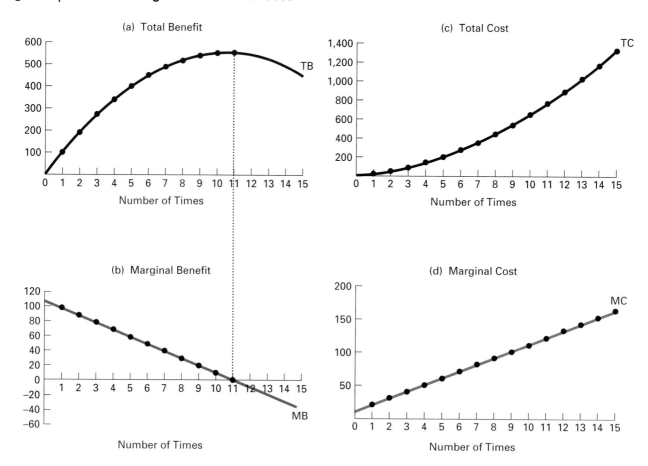

The **marginal cost** of doing something is the increase in total cost from doing it a little more.[3]

EXAMPLE

Suppose that the cost of doing something once is 20 (measured in utility or dollars), the cost of doing it a second time is 30, the cost of a third time is 40, and so on. Then the total cost of doing it once is 20, the total cost of doing it twice is 50, the total cost of doing it three times is 90, and so on. Figure 4c shows total cost; Figure 4d shows marginal cost.

Net Benefit

The net benefit of an action equals its total benefit minus its total cost:

Net benefit (or profit) equals total benefit minus total cost.

---

[3]Readers who know calculus will see that marginal cost is the derivative of total cost with respect to the number of times you do something.

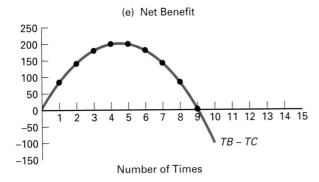

(e) Net Benefit

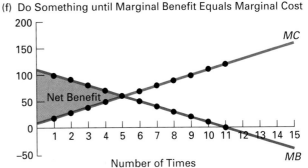

(f) Do Something until Marginal Benefit Equals Marginal Cost

Panel (e) shows the net benefit (profit) at various quantities. The net benefit of doing something once is 80, the net benefit of doing it twice is 140, and so on. The net benefit is maximized at a quantity of 5, and the highest possible net benefit is 200. The area under the marginal benefit curve and above the marginal cost curve, shown together in Panel (f), represents the net benefit or profit. To maximize net benefit, choose a quantity so that marginal benefit equals marginal cost; in this case choose to do the activity five times.

Panel (f) shows that the net benefit of doing it once is 100 minus 20, or 80. The net benefit of doing it twice is 140 because the marginal benefit of the second time (90) exceeds its marginal cost (30) by 60 units, raising the net benefit to 140. The net benefit of doing it three times is 180, because the marginal benefit of the third time (80) exceeds the marginal cost (40) by 40 units, raising the net benefit from 140 to 180. As long as marginal benefit exceeds marginal cost, net benefit rises as you do it more. You maximize net benefit at 200 when you do it 5 times. At that point marginal benefit equals marginal cost.

Number of Times	Total Benefit	Marginal Benefit	Total Cost	Marginal Cost	Net Benefit	MB − MC
1	100	100	20	20	80	80
2	190	90	50	30	140	60
3	270	80	90	40	180	40
4	340	70	140	50	200	20
5	400	60	200	60	200	0
6	450	50	270	70	180	−20
7	490	40	350	80	140	−40
8	520	30	440	90	80	−60
9	540	20	540	100	0	−80
10	550	10	650	110	−100	−100
11	550	0	770	120	−220	−120
12	540	−10	900	130	−360	−140
13	520	−20	1,040	140	−520	−160
14	490	−30	1,190	150	−700	−180
15	450	−40	1,350	160	−900	−200

EXAMPLE

In Figure 4, the net benefit of doing something once is 80 (dollars or utility) because the total benefit is 100 and the total cost is 20. The net benefit of doing it twice is 140. Figure 4e shows that net benefit rises to a maximum of 200 when you take the action four or five times. (The fifth time does not change the net benefit.) The net benefit falls below 200 if you do it more than five times, becoming negative for ten times or more. At that point, the total cost exceeds the total benefit.

This woman maximized her net benefit. She continued to shop until the marginal benefit equaled marginal cost.

Maximizing Net Benefit A rational choice maximizes the net benefit from an action. To maximize net benefit, you do something until its *marginal benefit equals its marginal cost*. This is the logical rule stated earlier in the chapter: It is rational to do something until its marginal benefit equals its marginal cost.[4]

EXAMPLE

Figure 4f shows marginal benefit and marginal cost on the same graph. Marginal cost equals marginal benefit when you do something five times. At that point, the marginal benefit and the marginal cost both equal 60, and the net benefit is 200. Doing it more or less cannot produce a higher net benefit.[5] The figure also shows that the net benefit equals the area above the marginal cost curve and below the marginal benefit curve.

Discussion Whenever the marginal benefit exceeds the marginal cost, the net benefit rises as you do something a little more. The extra benefit from the additional action exceeds the extra cost of that action. When the marginal benefit exceeds the marginal cost (at any number of times less than five in the last example), you raise your net benefit by expanding your action (doing a little more of it).

For example, Figure 4f shows that the net benefit of one action is 100 minus 20, or 80. The net benefit of two actions is 140, because the marginal benefit of the second time (90) exceeds the marginal cost (30) by 60 units, raising net benefit by 60 units from 80 to 140. The net benefit of three actions is 180, because the marginal benefit of the third time (80) exceeds the marginal cost (40) by 40 units, raising net benefit from 140 to 180. As long as marginal benefit exceeds marginal cost, net benefit rises as you do it more. You maximize net benefit at 200 when you do it 5 times. The fifth time does not affect your net benefit. At that point, marginal benefit equals marginal cost.

Similarly, if the marginal benefit is *smaller* than the marginal cost, then net benefit *falls* as you do something a little more. In that case, the extra benefit from the additional action is smaller than the extra cost. When the marginal benefit is *less* than marginal

---

[4]This basic logical rule (that rational people do something until its marginal benefit equals its marginal cost) applies to any action with decreasing or constant marginal benefits and increasing or constant marginal costs. With a decreasing (or constant) marginal benefit, the marginal benefit of an action gets smaller (or stays the same) as you do it more. With increasing (or constant) marginal costs, the marginal cost of an action grows (or stays the same) as you do it more. These conditions apply to almost all economic decisions.

[5]You could also get a net benefit of 200 by choosing a quantity of four, but you could not do better.

"Anything Worth Doing Is Worth Doing Well"—True or False?

You've heard the old saying, "Anything worth doing is worth doing well." Is it true? The logic of rational choice shows that sometimes it is worthwhile not to do something well. Rational choice suggests doing something until the marginal benefit of doing more equals the marginal cost. Sometimes that rule means doing a good job. Other times, it means doing only an adequate or passable job.

Examples are everywhere. Some people say that athletes should always give 100 percent of their energy to a game, but an athlete who works as hard as possible every minute of a game risks tiring earlier than an athlete who conserves energy for the most important times. Suppose that you are in a hurry to go somewhere important, but you are also hungry. Should you cook dinner only if you will do a good job of cooking? Not necessarily: perhaps you should spend only enough time to fix a quick, mediocre dinner. Should you take a course only if you intend to do well in it? Not necessarily, if the bulk of your time would be better spent on other courses or other activities. The old saying should be modified:

Anything worth doing is worth doing until the marginal benefit equals the marginal cost.

cost, you raise net benefit by doing something *fewer* times. In Figure 4, the marginal benefit of the sixth time is 50, but the marginal cost is 70. Therefore net benefit *falls* by 20, from 200 to 180, if you do it a sixth time. You could raise net benefit from 180 to 200 by doing it only five times instead of six times. If the marginal benefit of doing something is smaller than the marginal cost, you gain by doing it less.

Application to Demand

Your marginal benefit of candy bars probably decreases with the amount you eat; on any given day, a second candy bar probably gives you less utility than the first, and a fifth or sixth candy bar probably gives even less.[6] Suppose we measure the marginal benefit of candy bars in *dollars*. The marginal cost of buying a candy bar is its price, so you maximize net benefit if you buy a quantity that sets marginal benefit equal to the price. Whatever the price, the marginal benefit curve shows your quantity demanded. This implies that your marginal benefit curve is your demand curve.

A person's demand curve for a good is her marginal benefit curve.

Notice that the height of your demand curve for candy bars shows your marginal benefit of candy bars, measured in dollars. In other words, your marginal benefit curve shows your *willingness to pay*. That explains why the height of the demand curve shows willingness to pay (as discussed in Chapters 6 and 9).

EXAMPLE

Figure 5 shows Rebecca's marginal benefit and marginal cost of candy bars. Her marginal benefit of one candy bar per day is $1.50. Her marginal benefit of a second candy

Figure 5
A Demand Curve Is a Marginal Benefit Curve

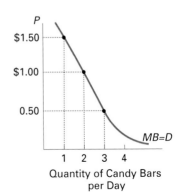

Rebecca's marginal benefit curve is her demand curve.

---

[6]Even if you enjoy your 100th candy bar in a day as much as your first, the dollar value of your enjoyment is likely to fall as you buy more candy bars. As you increase spending on candy bars, you must reduce spending on other goods, so the value of a dollar available to spend on them increases. This means that the dollar value of your enjoyment from candy falls. To see why, think about an extreme case. Suppose that you spent almost all your money on candy, so you had almost nothing else—no healthy food, few clothes, and so on. Then an extra dollar's worth of good food or other goods would probably be worth a lot to you. The value of a dollar to you rises as you have fewer available, so the dollar value of your enjoyment from a candy bar is smaller than if a dollar were not worth so much to you.

bar each day is $1.00. If the price of candy is $1.00, then she maximizes her net benefit by eating two candy bars per day. This quantity, two candy bars per day, equates her marginal benefit with the price (which is her marginal cost of candy). Rebecca's marginal benefit of a third candy bar each day is $0.50. If the price of candy fell to $0.50, she would maximize net benefit by eating three candy bars per day. This quantity, three candy bars per day, would equate her marginal benefit with the price. Whatever the price, Rebecca's marginal benefit curve shows her quantity demanded. Therefore, Rebecca's marginal benefit curve is her demand curve.

RATIONAL AND IRRATIONAL CHOICES

A large body of evidence on a wide range of economic issues supports the assumption underlying most economic models that people make most economic decisions rationally, or close to rationally. While people's responses to surveys and questionnaires sometimes appear irrational, evidence indicates that people's actions are more rational than their words.

Obviously, people do not consciously and formally calculate marginal benefits and marginal costs when they make decisions. That would be too difficult and time-consuming. Still, people's choices, at least in common situations, can match the choices they would make if they were to calculate marginal costs and benefits and choose quantities that would equate the two. In that sense, people act *as if* they were rational. (Many experiments show that even animals often behave as if they were making rational choices!) The rational choice model is a reasonably good predictor of actual economic decisions.

Some rational choices can appear to be irrational. For example, a rational choice made by someone with limited information may appear irrational to someone with more information. A person may buy a product for a high price at one store when another store nearby sells the same product for less. This may appear irrational, but the buyer may not know that the other store offers a lower price, or the trip to the other store may not seem worth the additional time it would require. Information is not free; buyers must spend time and sometimes money to obtain it. They must spend time to understand, digest, and remember information (such as the information in this book).

Some rational choices appear irrational for other reasons. You may say to yourself, "This term I'm going to study more," but as each day arrives, you find something else to do. You may decide to diet, but every day an ice cream sundae forces its way into your mouth. Are these actions rational? They might be. Someone may rationally plan to do something, decide later not to do it, and even to regret the decision after making it.[7]

Although evidence suggests that much economic behavior is rational, experiments reveal that people sometimes make irrational choices. Experiments have uncovered two main kinds of irrationalities. First, people sometimes ignore opportunity costs. For example, you might think that reading this book is free (since you already own it), because you are not paying money to anyone to read it. Of course, that ignores the opportunity cost of your time, so reading this book has a cost. A second form of irrationality also appears in experiments—people sometimes act irrationally by *not* ignoring sunk costs.

Sunk costs are costs that you have *already paid* and cannot recover.

Rational choices ignore sunk costs. Bygones are bygones; one cannot undo the past. Rational choices equate the marginal benefit and marginal cost of taking some action.

---

[7]If you behave this way, economists say that you have time-inconsistent tastes. You may rationally choose to commit (if you can) to your plan of action. You might commit not to do something (such as drinking) by avoiding certain situations (such as parties with alcohol). People usually cannot commit completely to specific actions, or they can do so only with great difficulty, but sometimes they can commit partially to a future action. For example, some people avoid carrying credit cards to make it more difficult for them to spend more than they had planned.

Economics of Personal Improvement

Many books and articles that give advice for personal improvement or self-help rely on basic economic principles. These books often warn about inefficient use of time, spending too much time doing unimportant activities and too little time doing important ones. The books do not use the language of economics, but they remind people of opportunity costs, since the time spent on one task could be spent doing something else. Although these books and articles use less precise language, they tell people to spend time on any project until its marginal benefit equals its marginal cost. They often suggest methods to calculate these costs and benefits. They tell you to list your goals, review the way you spend your time, and regularly examine whether your actions are helping you to achieve those goals. These techniques try to help people equate the marginal costs and marginal benefits of their actions.

Books and articles on personal improvement also emphasize that rational decisions ignore sunk costs. Without using the terms of economics, they tell people not to dwell on past misfortunes, mistakes, or failures, but instead to concentrate on the future. Ignoring sunk costs can be a difficult psychological challenge, so the articles often suggest techniques to help. These techniques include positive thinking, visualizing results, and concentrating on goals. They are designed to help you make choices that equate marginal benefits with marginal costs.

Source: [Cleveland] *Plain Dealer,* August 25, 1985.

The cost of that action is the best opportunity that you sacrifice when you take that action. The cost of the action does not include payments made in the past that you cannot now recover. For example, suppose that you paid $5 to see a movie. After 20 minutes, you realize that you made a mistake; the movie is really terrible. Should you leave now, or should you stay and watch the rest of the movie because you paid $5 to see it? A rational choice would ignore the $5 because it is a sunk cost. You have already paid the $5 and the theater will not return your money. Your decision to stay or leave should compare the benefit and time cost of staying. If you can find something better to do, you should leave. Experimental evidence suggests, however, that people do not always ignore sunk costs.

Although people sometimes behave irrationally, evidence also indicates that they learn. Their choices become more rational when they repeatedly face particular situations. People learn to ignore sunk costs and not to ignore opportunity costs; they learn to choose in an approximately rational way.[8]

Even when people behave irrationally, many conclusions of standard economic models remain the same as if they made rational choices. For example, demand curves likely show downward slopes. If you randomly choose how much to buy, a rise in the price of a good is likely to reduce your quantity demanded, because you cannot afford to buy as much as before at a higher price (unless your random spending on other goods falls by a sufficient amount). Demand curves are likely to slope downward whether people behave rationally or randomly.

Most economic theories assume that people make rational choices, though some consider the consequences of people making certain decisions irrationally.[9] Economists have even applied the logic of rational choice to behaviors that many people consider irrational, such as crime. Evidence shows that criminal behavior responds to incentives. Crime declines with increases in punishments and chances of being caught and punished. Two interesting cases of this effect appear in the history of basketball. The

---

[8]A summary of some of this evidence appears in an article by experimental economist: Vernon Smith, "Theory, Experiments, and Economics," *Journal of Economic Perspectives* 3 (Winter 1989), pp. 151–169.

[9]Certain models allow for irrational speculation on the stock market and other financial markets.

Atlantic Coast Conference raised the number of referees for its basketball tournament from two to three per game in 1979. This increased the chance that a player who committed a foul would be caught, and the number of fouls per game dropped by one-third. Similarly, a lower punishment for fouls raised the number of fouls. Before 1963, fouled defensive players took free throws; after 1963, an offensive foul cost a team only possession of the ball. This reduction in punishment—in the price of a foul—raised the number of fouls committed.

Review Questions

4. What is marginal benefit? What is marginal cost?

5. State and explain the basic rule of rational choice.

6. What is a sunk cost? Why do rational decisions ignore sunk costs?

Thinking Exercises

7. Suppose that the marginal cost in Figure 4 increases by 20 (changing from 20, 30, 40, . . . , 160 to 40, 50, 60, . . . , 180).
   (a) Show this increase in marginal cost on a graph.
   (b) How does this increase in marginal cost affect the rational choice of the number of times to take the action?

8. Suppose that the marginal benefit in Figure 4 increases by 20 (changing from 100, 90, 80, . . . , 40 to 120, 110, 100, . . . , 20).
   (a) Show this increase in marginal benefit on a graph.
   (b) How does this increase in marginal benefit affect the rational choice of the number of times to take the action?

Conclusion

Budget Lines

A budget line shows a person's opportunities. The absolute value of the budget line's slope equals the relative price of the good on the *X*-axis in terms of the good on the *Y*-axis. Changes in income shift the budget line without changing its slope. Changes in the relative prices of goods rotate the budget line. Each person chooses the point on his budget line that he likes best.

Rational Choice

Rational choice means choosing what you most prefer among your alternatives. Rational choices may seem either good or bad from another person's point of view. Rational choices are not necessarily selfish; they can be altruistic. The logic of rational choice leads to a simple rule: Do something until its marginal benefit equals its marginal cost. Marginal benefit is the increase in total benefit from doing something a little more. Marginal cost is the increase in total cost from doing it a little more. Net

benefit reaches its maximum when you do something until its marginal benefit equals its marginal cost. When marginal benefit is measured in dollars, a person's marginal benefit curve is her demand curve.

Rational and Irrational Choices

Considerable evidence indicates that people make rational choices, or almost rational ones, in most economic decisions. People are more rational in what they do than in what they say. Though people do not consciously calculate marginal benefits and marginal costs to make decisions, evidence suggests that they often act as if they did. One person's rational choice can appear (incorrectly) as irrational from the perspective of a person with more information.

   Although much economic behavior is rational, experimental evidence indicates that people sometimes make irrational decisions by ignoring opportunity costs or not ignoring sunk costs (previously paid costs that cannot be recovered). Rational decisions ignore sunk costs. The evidence also shows, however, that people learn. When they repeatedly face particular situations, they learn to ignore sunk costs and not to ignore opportunity costs, so their decisions become more rational.

K e y   T e r m s

budget line
rational choice

marginal benefit
utility

marginal cost
net benefit (or profit)

sunk cost

P r o b l e m s

9. Draw a budget line and show how it changes in response to:
   (a) A fall in income
   (b) A fall in the price of the good on the horizontal axis
   (c) A fall in the price of the good on the vertical axis

10. Suppose that the nominal prices of deodorant and soap both double. What happens to the relative price of deodorant in terms of soap? How does a budget line between them shift?
    (a) Suppose that your money income doubles along with the nominal prices of all the goods you buy. What happens to your budget line? Do you change what you buy? Explain.
    (b) If your tastes do not change in Problem 10a, what happens to your quantities demanded?

11. Judy must take midterm exams today in molecular biology and quantum physics. She can study for only one more hour, and she wants to maximize the total number of points she gets on the two exams added together. She expects the following scores depending on how much she studies each subject:

Minutes Studying Biology	Expected Score in Biology	Minutes Studying Physics	Expected Score in Physics
0	70	0	55
10	77	10	65
20	83	20	73
30	88	30	80
40	92	40	85
50	95	50	90
60	97	60	93

   (a) Create two new columns to show Judy's marginal benefit and marginal cost from studying biology for 10 more minutes.

   (b) How much time should she spend studying for each exam? Explain why.
   (c) Draw Judy's budget line between points on the biology exam and points on the physics exam. Show in your diagram which point on the budget line she should choose.
   (d) Suppose that Judy has 70 minutes rather than 60 minutes to study. How does this change affect her budget line? How long should she study biology? How long should she study physics? How many additional points could she expect to gain by studying the extra 10 minutes?

12. You organize a used-book exchange to buy used textbooks for half of their original prices and resell them for $1 more than you paid for them. This enterprise takes several hours, during which you could be working at a local store earning $5 per hour. You also have other costs (such as advertising). You calculate that your total benefits and total costs of working on the book exchange project are:

Hours Worked	Total Benefit	Total Cost
1	$ 20	$ 8
2	40	15
3	58	22
4	73	29
5	85	36
6	96	44
7	105	53
8	113	63
9	119	74

   Calculate the marginal benefit and the marginal cost of hours worked on the new project. How many hours should you work to maximize your net benefit?

13. Explain the economic principle behind the following comic strip.

Source: Plain Dealer, August 25, 1985.

Inquiries for Further Thought

14. You are a doctor in a city where an earthquake injured thousands of people yesterday. Your medical supplies are limited, though new supplies will arrive tomorrow. You must decide which victims get medical attention and supplies today (and how much) and who must wait. How would you make your decision? Express your answer in terms of marginal benefits and costs.

15. People leave tips at restaurants even if they never plan to return. Is this behavior rational? Is it rational to cooperate with other people? To be courteous, polite, and honest?

16. Are opportunities and choices the same as freedom? Nobel-laureate economist George Stigler once argued that wealth is the same as freedom. He argued that more wealth gives the ability to buy or do more things, just as freedom does. Do you agree? If not, how do wealth and freedom differ?

17. Discuss this statement: "People do not make rational choices. They buy some products they don't need and other products (like cigarettes) that harm them. They underestimate important risks, such as the risk of injury in automobile accidents while driving without a seat belt. People would benefit if the government would make more decisions for them."

Appendix A: Indifference Curves

Economists graph people's tastes with indifference curves.

> A person is indifferent between two combinations of goods if she does not prefer one to the other. An **indifference curve** shows combinations of goods between which a person is indifferent.

Each point on an indifference curve represents a combination of goods. A person is indifferent between the various points on her indifference curve: She does not care which combination of goods she consumes.

EXAMPLE

Figure A1 shows one of Lee's indifference curves. Lee does not care whether he consumes 5 hamburgers and 40 hot dogs per month, or 8 hamburgers and 25 hot dogs, or 10 hamburgers and 20 hot dogs, or 20 hamburgers and 10 hot dogs, or 40 hamburgers and 5 hot dogs. He does not prefer any of these combinations to any of the others.

Many Indifference Curves

Combinations of goods that do not lie on one indifference curve lie on other indifference curves, and a description of a person's tastes requires many indifference curves. Every possible combination of goods is a point on *some* indifference curve. As long as you want more of both of a pair of goods, you prefer combinations of goods on higher indifference curves.

Figure A2 shows several of Lee's indifference curves. He prefers points on higher indifference curves to points on lower indifference curves. For example, he is indifferent between Point A (16 hamburgers and 25 hot dogs) and Point B (20 of each), but he prefers both Point A and Point B to Point C (8 hamburgers and 25 hot dogs) and to other points on lower indifference curves.

The indifference curves of a rational person never cross. To see why, consider a person who likes to have as many concert tickets and movie posters as possible, and suppose that his indifference curves *do* cross, as in Figure A3. This person would be equally happy at Points A and B—he does not care whether he has eight posters and six tickets, or four posters and eight tickets. He would also be equally happy at Points B and C. However, that implies that he would be equally happy at Points A and C, even though he has

Figure A1 | One of Lee's Indifference Curves between Hamburgers and Hot Dogs

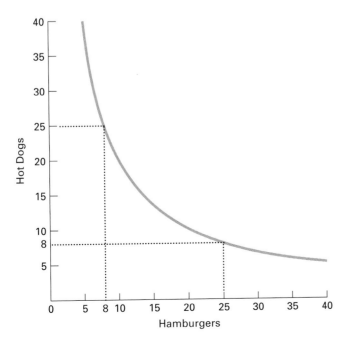

Figure A2 | More of Lee's Indifference Curves between Hamburgers and Hot Dogs

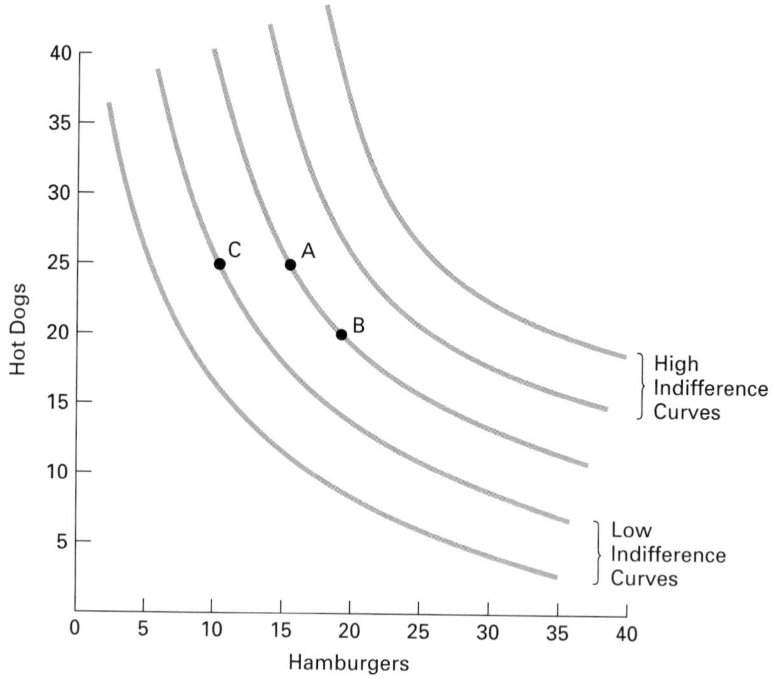

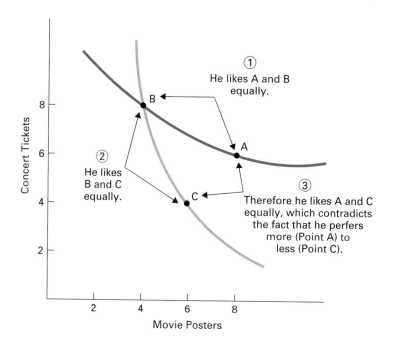

more posters *and* tickets at Point A than at Point C! This contradicts the assumption that he would always like more of both goods. To prevent that contradiction, we conclude that his indifference curves cannot cross.

Figure A3 | A Rational Person's Indifference Curves Cannot Cross

This person is indifferent between Point A (eight posters and six tickets) and Point B (four posters and eight tickets). He is also indifferent between Point B and Point C (six posters and four tickets), so he must be indifferent between Points A and C. This implication does not make sense, because he has more posters *and* tickets at Point A than at Point C. Therefore, economists conclude that indifference curves cannot cross.

A1. Choose two goods, such as pizza and ice cream, and graph one of your own indifference curves between them.

A2. Draw another of your indifference curves on the same graph.

Slopes of Indifference Curves

Indifference curves usually slope downward. If you get fewer hot dogs in one situation than in another, you need more hamburgers to compensate and make you indifferent between the two situations.[10] The number of hamburgers you need to compensate for the loss of one hot dog is your marginal rate of substitution between hot dogs and hamburgers.

> Your **marginal rate of substitution** between Goods X and Y is the largest amount of Y that you would be willing to trade away for an additional unit of X.

Your marginal rate of substitution between books and socks depends on your *willingness to pay* for an extra book, measured by the number of socks you would give up for it. Your marginal rate of substitution between vacation days and money shows the amount of money that you would be willing to pay for an extra vacation day.

Your marginal rate of substitution equals the absolute value of the slope of your indifference curve for two goods, such as Goods X and Y in Figure A4.

> The absolute value of the slope of your indifference curve shows your marginal rate of substitution between two goods.

The absolute value of your indifference curve's slope shows the amount of Y you would be willing to trade for one X. Indifference curves usually look something like the ones in Figure A2, but if two products are very good substitutes for each other, then you may not care whether you have five of one and ten of the other or vice versa. If you care only about the total amount of cola you drink, but you don't care whether you drink Coke or Pepsi, then those drinks are perfect substitutes to you. In this case, your marginal rate of substitution between the goods is constant and equal to 1, because you want one can of Pepsi as compensation for losing one can of Coke. Your indifference curves look like those in Figure A5.

By contrast, if two products are very strong complements for each other, like left shoes and right shoes, then you benefit from extra units of one only if you also have extra units of the other. Goods are perfect complements if one is useless to you without the other; your indifference curves for such goods would look like those in Figure A6.

Rational Choice with Indifference Curves

Rational choice means reaching the highest possible indifference curve by choosing the feasible consumption combination that a person most prefers. A budget line shows opportunities, so a rational decision would choose the highest indifference curve that a person's budget line could reach. The rational choice in Figure A7 is Point A, where the budget line just touches the highest indifference curve that it can reach. (The indifference curve is tangent to the budget line at Point A.) Any other point that you can afford

---

[10]Indifference curves slope upward if you like one of the goods but dislike the other.

Figure A4 | Marginal Rates of Substitution

Your marginal rate of substitution is the absolute value of the slope of your indifference curve. This value depends on how much you consume.

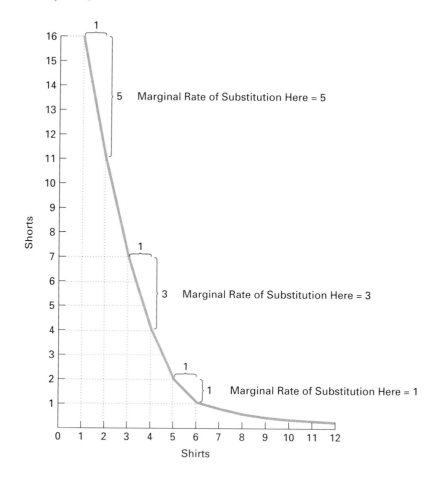

Figure A5 | Indifference Curves for Perfect Substitutes

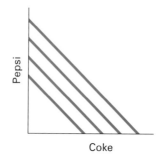

Figure A6 | Indifference Curves for Perfect Complements

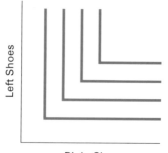

(such as Points B and C) lie on lower indifference curves than Point A. Point A shows the combination of goods that you prefer to all other combinations that you can afford.

The slope of the indifference curve at Point A equals the slope of the budget line. Recall that the absolute value of the indifference curve's slope is the marginal rate of substitution between X and Y; also, the absolute value of the budget line's slope is the relative price of X in terms of Y. Together, these relationships imply that:

> At Point A, the marginal rate of substitution equals the relative price.

This fact implies a rule to govern rational choice (the effort to reach the highest possible indifference curve): Buy quantities of products that set your marginal rate of substitution between a pair of products equal to their relative price.

Review Questions

A3. Explain why the absolute value of an indifference curve's slope shows a person's marginal rate of substitution between two goods.

A4. Draw a graph with a budget line and indifference curves.
   (a) Show the person's rational choice on your graph.
   (b) Explain your graph. Why is the point of tangency the rational choice?

Figure A7 | Rational Choice with Indifference Curves

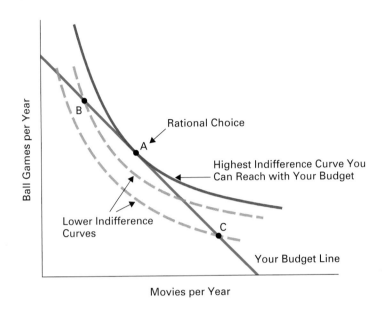

The rational choice is Point A, where your budget line reaches the highest possible indifference curve.

Demand Curves and Indifference Curves

When a budget line rotates in response to a price change, this movement changes the rational choice. Figure A8 shows an example. Elee has $200 per year to spend on movies and magazines. When movies cost $4 and magazines cost $2, she sees 30 movies and buys 40 magazines each year (Point A in the figure). When the price of seeing a movie

Figure A8 | Deriving a Demand Curve from Budget Lines and Indifference Curves

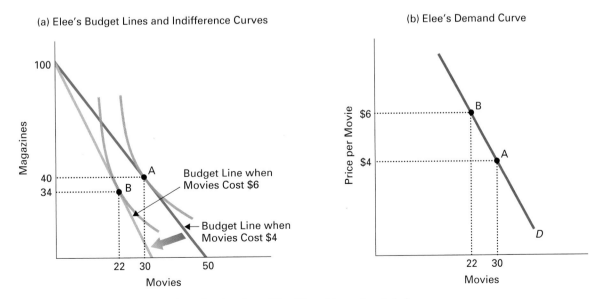

Elee's budget line rotates when the price of movies rises from $4 to $6, and her rational choice changes from Point A to Point B. Plotting the movie prices and her quantities demanded on a graph gives her demand curve for movies.

rises to $6, her budget line rotates, and she chooses Point B, where she sees 22 movies and buys 34 magazines, instead of Point A.[11]

These two choices are two points on Elee's demand curve for movies. When movies cost $4, she sees 30 movies, so Point A on her original budget line defines Point A on her demand curve. When movies cost $6, she sees 22 movies, and Point B on her new budget line defines Point B on her demand curve. As the price changes, the new budget line and the indifference curves identify new rational choices that define new points on the demand curve.[12]

Key Terms

indifference curve
marginal rate of substitution

Problem

A5. Use a graph with budget lines and indifference curves to show how to derive a demand curve. Find the rational choices at several prices and graph them as points on a demand curve.

Appendix B: Marginal Benefits and the Marginal Rate of Substitution

The rule for rational choice is to choose a number of times to do something to equate marginal benefit with marginal cost. For a price-taking buyer—one who cannot affect the prices of the goods she buys—marginal cost equals the price. In mathematical terms, a buyer chooses to buy pizzas and videos until the marginal benefit of pizzas equals the price of pizzas and the marginal benefit of videos equals the price of videos:

$$MB(\text{pizzas}) = P(\text{pizzas}), \text{ and}$$

$$MB(\text{videos}) = P(\text{videos})$$

where *MB* and *P* are the marginal benefit and price of each good.

Dividing the first equation by the second gives a new equation:

$$MB(\text{pizzas})/MB(\text{videos}) = P(\text{pizzas})/P(\text{videos})$$

The left-hand side of this equation, $MB(\text{pizzas})/MB(\text{videos})$, is called the *marginal rate of substitution* between pizzas and videos.

> The **marginal rate of substitution** between two goods equals the marginal benefit of one divided by the marginal benefit of the other.

---

[11]If her indifference curves were different (because her tastes were different), she would have made another choice. For example, she might have chosen 20 movies and 40 magazines.

[12]Notice that these changes in choice result from changes in opportunities (indicated by changes in the budget line), not from changes in tastes. A change in tastes would shift the indifference curves.

This marginal rate of substitution measures the number of videos *that you would be willing to trade away* for one pizza.

The rule of rational choice calls for a buyer to equate the marginal rate of substitution between two goods with their relative price. In the example, the relative price of pizzas and videos is *P*(pizzas)/*P*(videos). The general rule is:

A buyer maximizes net benefit by choosing quantities demanded so that the marginal rate of substitution between any pair of goods equals their relative price.

If you read Appendix 10A on indifference curves, you may notice that this general rule holds when the buyer chooses quantities demanded to make her *indifference curve tangent to her budget line*. In absolute values, the slope of her indifference curve is her marginal rate of substitution, and the slope of her budget line is the relative price. Tangency between an indifference curve and a budget line implies that their slopes are equal. Therefore that tangency implies the general rule equating the marginal rate of substitution with the relative price.

Key Term

marginal rate of substitution

Problems

B1. How is the marginal rate of substitution between magazines and paperback books related to their marginal benefits?

B2. Suppose magazines cost $2 each and paperback books cost $6 each. What marginal rate of substitution between books and magazines would a rational buyer choose? How does the buyer choose her marginal rate of substitution?

B3. Table B1 shows the combinations of goods that Jane can afford if she has $24, Good X costs $2, and Good Y costs $4.

Table B1 | Jane's Rational Choice

Amount of X	Total Benefit of X	Marginal Benefit of X	Amount of Y	Total Benefit of Y	Marginal Benefit of Y
0	0		6	180	20
2	44	20	5	160	24
4	74	14	4	136	28
6	96	10	3	108	32
8	110	6	2	76	36
10	119	4	1	40	40
12	124	2	0	0	

Advice to Students
Don't be confused by Table B1. Each row shows a quantity that Jane can afford. She can buy 0 units of X and 6 units of Y, or 2 units of X and 5 units of Y, and so on. Notice that the quantities of X in the first column rise by 2 units from one row to the next.

(a) Find the quantities demanded of X and Y that maximize Jane's net benefit.
(b) Explain how your answer satisfies the general rule for rational choice using the marginal rate of substitution.

Appendix C: Mathematics of Rational Choice[13]

Your total benefit from doing something depends on how much you do it. Your benefit is a function of the amount you do. Let B denote the total benefit from doing something Q times. B is a function of Q:

$$B = f(Q)$$

Your marginal benefit, MB, is the derivative of total benefit with respect to Q:

$$MB = f'(Q)$$

$$= dB/dQ$$

The total cost is also a function of Q. Let C be your total cost of doing something Q times. C is a function of Q:

$$C = g(Q)$$

Your marginal cost, MC, is the derivative of total cost with respect to Q:

$$MC = g'(Q)$$

$$= dC/dQ$$

Your net benefit is your total benefit minus your total cost, so your net benefit is also a function of Q:

$$\text{Net benefit} = f(Q) - g(Q)$$

To maximize your net benefit, take its derivative with respect to Q, and set the derivative equal to zero:

$$f'(Q) - g'(Q) = 0$$

$$f'(Q) = g'(Q)$$

$$MB = MC$$

To maximize net benefit, choose a quantity Q so that marginal benefit equals marginal cost.

Problems

C1. Suppose that the total benefit of doing something Q times is:

$$60\,Q - Q^2$$

and the total cost of doing something Q times is:

$$20 + Q^2$$

(a) Calculate the marginal benefit and marginal cost.
(b) Which choice of Q maximizes net benefit?
(c) When you choose Q to maximize net benefit, how large is your net benefit?

---

[13]*Note:* This appendix requires knowledge of calculus. It uses derivatives.

CHAPTER 11

BUSINESS DECISIONS AND SUPPLY IN THE LONG RUN

In this Chapter . . .

Main Points to Understand

▶ Business decisions follow the logic of rational choice.

▶ Supply curves are (portions of) marginal cost curves.

▶ Accounting measures of cost differ from economic (opportunity) cost.

Thinking Skills to Develop

▶ Apply the logic of rational choice to business decisions.

▶ Interpret connections between costs of production, supply decisions, and profit.

B usiness decisions mystify most people. Everyone knows that the cost of producing a good affects its price. However, few people understand how costs affect decisions such as quantities to produce, hiring or firing workers, using plastic or metal parts, choosing sucrose or fructose as a sweetener, launching new products, expanding into foreign markets, halting production of a product, or even going out of business. This chapter discusses the fundamental logic of business decisions, supply, and profits.

BUSINESS FIRMS

Nearly 20 million business firms operate in the United States, about one for every eight adults. In Japan, about 22 million firms operate, about one for every four adults. Most U.S. firms are small companies; about 60 percent of them generate annual revenues less than $25,000. A few large firms (about 4 percent of all firms) generate annual revenues of more than $1 million.

The three main types of firms are sole proprietorships, partnerships, and corporations. A sole proprietorship is a company owned by one person, such as a small store. Anyone can start a sole proprietorship and run it subject to relatively few government regulations.

Such a company pays no corporate income tax; instead, the owner pays personal income tax on the firm's revenue. The owner is personally responsible for all the debts of a sole proprietorship. Sole proprietorships rely mainly on the owner's personal funds and personal loans from banks or other financial institutions to finance their operations. Almost three-quarters of all U.S. firms are sole proprietorships, most of them small operations; together, they receive only about 6 percent of the total revenue (income) of all U.S. firms.

A partnership resembles a sole proprietorship, except two or more people share ownership according to terms stated in a written contract or informal agreement. The owners divide the firm's revenue and pay personal income taxes on it; they pay no corporate income tax. All partners bear responsibility for all the firm's debts, and the firm relies mainly on personal loans to finance its operations. Fewer than 10 percent of U.S. firms operate as partnerships, but they are larger, on average, than sole proprietorships. Partnerships receive about 4 percent of the total revenue of all U.S. firms.

A corporation is a business firm with special legal rights. The law treats it as an artificial person that lives on even if its owners change. Limitations on liability shield its owners, called *stockholders,* from personal responsibility for the firm's debts.[1] If the firm goes bankrupt and does not repay all its loans, the lenders cannot legally force the owners (stockholders) to pay them. Some corporations have only one or two owners. Others have many owners, because they issue shares of stock that trade publicly on stock markets such as the New York Stock Exchange or NASDAQ system. A firm's stockholders own the firm, collect its profits, and hire its managers, including the top manager, called the *CEO,* for *chief executive officer.*

Corporate income is taxed twice. First, the firm pays the corporate tax on its income. Second, the stockholders pay tax on distributions of the firm's income that they receive. The owners receive this income partly in the form of dividends, which are direct payments from the firm to its stockholders. They may also earn capital gains from increases in the price of the stock. Owners pay personal income tax on dividends, and they pay either personal income tax or a special capital gains tax on any gains they realize when they sell stock at a higher price than they paid for it.

Corporations often borrow money from banks and other financial institutions. They also borrow money directly from investors by selling IOUs called *corporate bonds* in financial markets. Bondholders loan money to a firm in exchange for IOUs on which they will collect in the future. About 20 percent of U.S. firms are corporations. Because many are large, they receive 90 percent of the total revenue of all U.S. firms.

Two Critical Business Decisions

Every producer must make two critical decisions: *how* to produce its good or service and *how much* to produce. These decisions may interact. A firm may use different kinds of equipment and production methods to produce 10,000 lampshades than it would use to produce a few hundred. Still, it is useful to separate these questions to analyze the logic of business decisions.

DECIDING HOW TO PRODUCE

A business firm's decision about how to produce a good includes three logical steps:

1. Choose a hypothetical quantity to produce, and list all the technically efficient methods of producing that quantity.

---

[1]This separation between the obligations of the corporation and those of its owners is sometimes called the *corporate veil.* Court decisions have sometimes *pierced the corporate veil* by ruling that owners must personally fulfill certain corporate obligations.

2. Choose the lowest-cost method from the list.

3. Repeat Steps 1 and 2 for all other possible quantities.

Step 1: List All Technically Efficient Methods

> A **technically efficient** method of production does not waste any inputs. (The firm could not produce the same amount using less of any one input without using more of some other input.)

A firm can identify many technically efficient methods to produce most goods. Some methods use many workers and little equipment; others use extensive equipment and few workers. A firm can use high-technology equipment or older equipment, relatively experienced or inexperienced workers, rubber or plastic, sugar or corn syrup, and so on.

Step 2: Choose the Lowest-Cost Method

While a firm can identify many technically efficient ways to produce, the firm maximizes its profits by using the method with the lowest cost. The lowest-cost method depends on prices of inputs.[2]

EXAMPLE

One technically efficient method may employ a worker to cut five cords of wood in 10 hours using an axe; another may complete the same work in 1 hour using a chain saw. Which method has a lower cost? The answer depends on the costs of workers, axes, and chain saws. Suppose that a worker costs $5 per hour, an axe costs $10, and a chain saw costs $50. Then the axe method costs $60 for 10 hours of work and one axe, while the chain saw method costs only $55 for 1 hour of work and a saw, so the chain saw method has the lowest cost. If chain saws cost $60, however, then the axe method has a lower cost, even though it takes 10 hours of work.

The lowest-cost method of production may depend on how much the firm produces. The lowest-cost way to cut one cord of wood uses an axe, because 2 hours of labor plus one axe costs $20, less than the cost of the chain-saw method. The lowest-cost way to cut 50 cords of wood, however, uses a chain saw.

Note on Quality

The discussion here applies to some *fixed* quality of the product. Think of high-quality goods and low-quality goods as different products. Producers decide which product (which quality level) to make, and then they determine the lowest-cost method of producing that quality.

Step 3: Repeat Steps 1 and 2 for All Other Possible Quantities

The first two steps give a firm the lowest-cost method of producing each possible quantity of the good. After the firm knows how to produce each possible quantity at the lowest possible cost, it can decide how *much* to produce.

[2]Chapter 12 applies the rules of rational choice to the selection of inputs that allow a firm to produce at the lowest cost.

IN THE NEWS

It's easy to find soybean substitutes or go without them when soybean prices rise too high.
• Food makers can switch to other oils, especially archrival palm oil.
• In industry, soybean oil can be replaced, too. For example, pesticides can be mixed with water instead of soybean oil.

Source: USA Today

There are many technically efficient ways to produce a product.

IN THE NEWS

A [representative] for PepsiCo Inc. said: "We have no immediate plans to go to sucrose. However, Pepsi is always exploring different, more economic ways to sweeten our drinks. If the price of sucrose becomes competitive with high fructose corn syrup, we'd consider our options." Sucrose is a sugar extracted from sugar cane or sugar beets.

Source: The Wall Street Journal

A beverage firm chooses the lowest-cost method of production by calculating whether it costs less to use sucrose or high-fructose corn syrup to sweeten its product.

DECIDING HOW MUCH TO PRODUCE

The general rule for rational choice discussed in Chapter 10 applies to the choice of how much to produce. If a firm decides to produce at all, it maximizes its net benefit by producing a quantity for which its marginal benefit equals its marginal cost.

Benefits and Revenues

A firm's net benefit from producing a good is its profit, equaling its total revenue minus its total cost.

> **Profit** is total revenue minus total cost.

If you sell 200 yearbooks at $10 each, your total revenue is $2,000. If your total cost of producing the yearbooks is $1,800, then your profit is $200.

The total benefit of producing a good is the total revenue it generates. The marginal benefit is marginal revenue, and the net benefit is the producer's profit.

▶ Total revenue is total benefit.

▶ Marginal revenue is marginal benefit.

▶ Profit is net benefit.

For example:

> **Marginal revenue** is the increase in total revenue from producing a little more of a good.[3]

A firm's net benefit may include nonmonetary benefits in addition to profit, such as a sense of accomplishment, a feeling of power, respect, fame, an air-conditioned office, or good feelings from contributing to the community. A producer faces tradeoffs between profits and nonmonetary benefits, because an improvement in working conditions may provide nonmonetary benefits, while adding to costs and reducing profits. Some producers may choose to sacrifice some profits to use relatively costly but environmentally friendly methods of production. Others might choose to earn those profits by generating more pollution than absolutely necessary but contribute money to an environmental cause. Many business decisions focus mainly on profit. Unless otherwise noted, this chapter will focus on cases in which the nonmonetary benefits are sufficiently small that the firm's profit approximates its net benefit of producing a good.

Table 1 shows an example of a firm's costs, revenues, and profit. If the firm charges $16, it sells 1 unit, generating total revenue of $16. If it charges $15, it sells 2 units for total revenue of $30. The *marginal revenue* (marginal benefit measured in dollars) of the second unit is the increase in total revenue from selling it, or $14. The table also shows the firm's total cost of producing goods and its marginal cost.

The basic logic of rational behavior from Chapter 10 applies directly to decisions like the quantity to produce. This chapter focuses on a firm's *long-run* decisions. Chapter 12 discusses more complex *short-run* decisions.

---

[3]Readers who know calculus will recognize marginal revenue as the derivative of total revenue with respect to the quantity produced. See the appendix following this chapter.

Table 1 | Choosing a Quantity to Produce

Quantity (Q)	Price (P)	Total Revenue (TR)	Marginal Revenue (MR)	Total Cost (TC)	Marginal Cost (MC)	Profit
1	16	16	16	28	28	−12
2	15	30	14	42	14	−12
3	14	42	12	44	2	−2
4	13	52	10	46	2	6
5	12	60	8	48	2	12
6	11	66	6	51	3	15
7	**10**	**70**	**4**	**55**	**4**	**15**
8	9	72	2	60	5	12
9	8	72	0	66	6	6
10	7	70	−2	73	7	−3
11	6	66	−4	81	8	−15
12	5	60	−6	90	9	−30

> The **long run** refers to a period of time over which people fully adjust their behavior to a change in conditions. Applied to a business firm, the long run is a period of time over which the firm can change the quantities of all its inputs.

A firm maximizes long-run profit by choosing its level of production in three steps. First, it chooses the level of output for which marginal revenue equals marginal cost, with rising or constant marginal cost. Second, it calculates total revenue and total cost at that level of output. Finally, it chooses whether to shut down or to produce the chosen level of output.

Step 1

Find the level of output at which *marginal revenue equals marginal cost,* at a point where the marginal cost curve either slopes upward or runs horizontally.[4] Figure 1a shows an example of this analysis, using the numbers from Table 1. Marginal cost equals marginal revenue at both Point A where output is 7 units and Point B where output is 2 units. The marginal cost curve slopes upward at Point A (economists say *MC* is rising at that point), but not at Point B. Step 1 says to choose Point A, with output equal to 7 units.

Step 1 shows the quantity that the firm will produce to maximize profit, if it chooses to produce rather than to shut down operations. The next two steps determine whether or not the firm should produce or shut down.

Step 2

Calculate total revenue *(TR)* and total cost *(TC)* at the level of output from Step 1. In Figure 1, the total revenue from selling 7 units is $70, and the total cost of producing that quantity is $55. Figure 1b graphs total revenue and total cost for various levels of

---

[4]Technically, a firm can also maximize its profit by producing a quantity at which marginal revenue equals marginal cost, with a falling marginal cost, if marginal cost falls more slowly than marginal revenue as output rises.

Figure 1 | Long-Run Profit Maximization with Rising Marginal Cost

Step 1 in the profit-maximization decision identifies the quantity at Point A: 7 units per year.

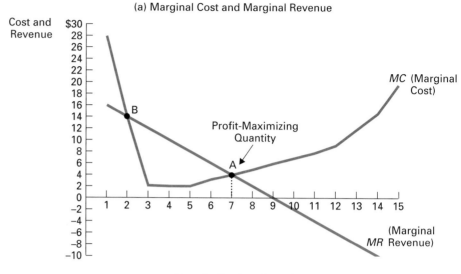

(a) Marginal Cost and Marginal Revenue

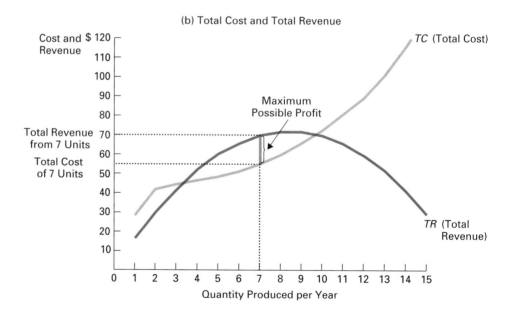

(b) Total Cost and Total Revenue

output. The firm earns the highest possible profit when it produces 7 units (the quantity from Step 1). Based on this information, the firm next decides whether to produce or shut down production.

Step 3

If total revenue is smaller than total cost at the level of output from Step 1, then producing that quantity would generate negative profit. (The firm would suffer a loss.) In this case, the firm should shut down (not produce anything). Shutting down would prevent the loss, because the firm would have zero revenue, zero cost, and zero profit. If total revenue equals or exceeds total cost, so that profit is positive, or at least zero, then the firm should produce the level of output from Step 1.

Step 3 says that a profit-maximizing firm should stay in business for the long run if its total revenue covers its total cost; otherwise, it should shut down to avoid losing money. To summarize Step 3 mathematically, *in the long run:*

1. If $TR < TC$, then shut down production.

2. If $TR \geq TC$, then produce the quantity from Step 1, and earn a profit equal to $TR - TC$.

In Figure 1 (and Table 1), total revenue ($70) exceeds total cost ($55), so the firm should produce the quantity from Step 1 (7 units) to earn a profit of $15. Figure 1b shows that the firm generates the highest possible profit, $15, when it produces 7 units. At this quantity, total revenue exceeds total cost by $15, so the firm produces.

Figure 2 shows an example in which the firm would shut down, because total revenue falls short of total cost. (If the firm were to produce, it would lose money; by shutting down, it avoids the loss.)

EXPLANATION

If marginal revenue exceeds marginal cost, the firm raises its profit by producing more. The extra revenue from an additional unit of output exceeds the cost of that additional unit, so profit rises. In Table 1, for example, the firm earns $6 profit if it produces 4 units of the good. The marginal revenue from a fifth unit ($8) exceeds the marginal cost of a fifth unit ($2) by $6, so producing a fifth unit raises the firm's profit by $6 (from $6 to $12).

Similarly, if marginal revenue is less than marginal cost, the firm raises its profit by producing less. If the firm produces 8 units, its profit is $12. Since the marginal revenue of the eighth unit is only $2 while its marginal cost is $5, producing the eighth unit reduces the firm's profits by $3 (from $15 to $12). In that case, the firm can raise its profit by reducing output from 8 units to 7. The firm earns the highest possible profit by producing the quantity for which marginal revenue equals marginal cost, when marginal cost is rising or constant. If this highest possible profit is *negative* so that the firm would suffer a loss by producing, then the firm shuts down to avoid that loss.

Figure 2 | A Firm That Shuts Down in the Long Run

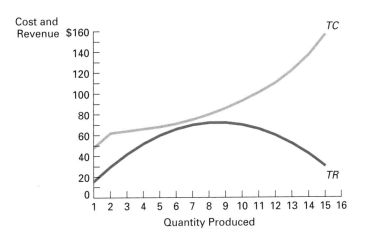

In a situation like this one, the firm should shut down rather than produce at a loss.

Review Questions

1. Discuss the differences between sole proprietorships, partnerships, and corporations.

2. What is a technically efficient method of production?

3. What do economists mean by the term *long run?*

4. Under what condition should a firm shut down in the long run?

Thinking Exercises

5. Explain why some technically efficient methods of production have lower costs than other technically efficient methods.

6. Change the numbers in Table 1 so that marginal cost equals 4 for every quantity (every number in the *MC* column is 4) and total cost equals 4 times the quantity. How does this revision affect the profit-maximizing quantity of output? How does it affect the firm's profit?

7. Repeat Thinking Exercise 6, but set marginal cost equal to 6 (instead of 4) at every quantity. How does this change affect the profit-maximizing quantity of output? How does it affect the firm's profit?

AVERAGE COST AND REVENUE

The steps for maximizing profit can be restated in terms of average costs and revenues.

> **Average revenue** *(AR)* is per-unit revenue (total revenue divided by the quantity produced).

> **Average cost** *(AC)* is per-unit cost (total cost divided by the quantity produced).

A firm stays in business in the long run if average revenue is greater than or equal to average cost, and it shuts down (to avoid a loss) if average revenue is less than average cost. For example, if a store sells 1,000 televisions at $300 each, it earns total revenue of $300,000, and its average revenue (revenue per unit sold) equals the price, $300 per television. If its total cost is $280,000, then its average cost is $280,000 divided by 1,000 televisions, or $280 per set. The firm does not suffer a loss, so it remains in business.

Marginal Cost Pulls Along Average Cost

Marginal cost and average cost are related in a simple way: Marginal cost pulls along average cost.

▶ When $MC > AC$, marginal cost pulls the average upward.

▶ When $MC < AC$, marginal cost pulls the average downward.

▶ When $MC = AC$, average cost does not change.

Figure 3 | Marginal Cost Pulls Along Average Cost

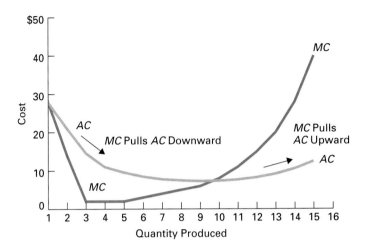

When *MC* is below *AC*, *AC* falls with an increase in output. When *MC* is above *AC*, *AC* rises with an increase in output.

An Analogy

Suppose your grades on the first two quizzes of a term are 80 and 90, giving you an average grade of 85. Your grade on a third quiz is 100, which raises your average for the three quizzes to 90. That *marginal* grade—the grade on the third quiz—was above your previous average, so it raised your average. If your grade on a fourth quiz is 86, below your average, then it pulls down your average for the four quizzes from 90 to 89. Whenever your grade on an additional quiz exceeds your previous average, it raises the average. Whenever it is below your previous average, it reduces the average. In a business, marginal cost pulls along average cost, just as your marginal grade on an additional quiz pulls along your average grade.

> **EXAMPLE**

When marginal cost is below average cost, at quantities up to 9 units in Figure 3, average cost falls as output rises. When marginal cost exceeds average cost, at quantities of 10 or more units in the figure, average cost rises as output rises. Notice that the marginal cost curve intersects the average cost curve at its lowest point (at the bottom of the *AC* curve). That occurs because the average is pulled down when marginal cost is below average cost, and it is pulled up when marginal cost exceeds average cost.

Figure 4 shows three common shapes for long-run average cost and marginal cost curves. Panel (a) shows *constant costs;* in which average cost equals marginal cost and both are independent of the quantity produced. In other words, all units of output cost the same regardless of how much the firm produces.

SHAPES OF COST CURVES

> A firm has **constant costs** if its long-run average cost is independent of the quantity it produces.[5]

---

[5]This is closely related to a concept called *constant returns to scale,* which means that the firm could double its output by doubling all its inputs (or raise output by 20 percent by raising all its inputs by 20 percent, etc.). If a firm has constant returns to scale and the prices of its inputs do not depend on how many units of input it buys, then the firm has constant costs. See Chapter 12.

Figure 4 | Three Common Shapes for Long-Run Average Cost Curves

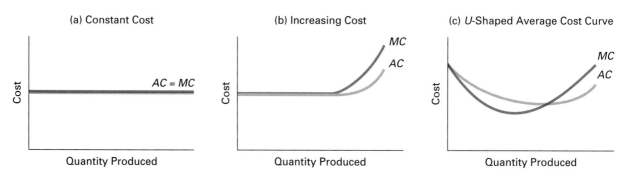

(a) Average cost is constant, and marginal cost equals average cost. (b) Costs increase for sufficiently high levels of output. (c) Costs decrease for a range of low quantities of output, and rise at higher quantities.

If a firm has constant costs, then its marginal cost must equal its average cost. If marginal cost were above or below average cost, then it would pull the average upward or downward, so average cost would depend on output.

Figure 4b shows a case of *increasing costs* at high levels of production: Average cost rises as output rises.

> A firm has **increasing costs** if its long-run average cost rises with increases in output.

Notice that average cost rises when marginal cost exceeds it, pulling it upward with increasing quantities. Increasing per-unit costs can result from problems of increasing firm size:

▶ As firms grow, they often face expanding problems of managing and coordinating workers.

▶ Larger firms have higher costs of monitoring workers (and managers) to ensure proper job performance.

These problems can cause average cost to increase along with output.

Figure 4c shows a *U*-shaped long-run average cost curve. At high levels of output, the firm's per-unit costs increase, as in Panel (b). However, at low levels of output, rising quantity brings *decreasing per-unit costs:* Average cost falls as the firm increases production.

> A firm has **decreasing costs** if its long-run average cost falls with increases in output.

Long-run average cost may decrease as output expands for several reasons:

▶ A firm producing a small quantity of output may not be able to use certain equipment to its full capacity. Raising production would reduce average cost as the equipment's use intensifies. For example, the oven in a pizza parlor may have the capacity to bake 10 pizzas per hour; as a result, the average cost of baking a pizza falls if the restaurant raises production from 5 to 10 pizzas per hour.

IN THE NEWS

Is your company too big?

Even as they argue that size is necessary to compete against global rivals, executives at many big companies are trying to mimic smaller firms. One corporate Goliath after another is trying to act like the Davids of the business world, creating smaller, highly decentralized business units and giving managers greater flexibility and freedom with less staff review.

To accomplish such aims, . . . corporate leaders are hacking away at bureaucracy by axing management layers, pushing down decision making, and shortcutting the approval process.

Source: Business Week

Costs of production may rise if a firm is either too large or too small for the most efficient operation.

▶ Employees of large firms can specialize in the activities at which they have comparative advantages. This specialization can reduce average cost. In the example from Chapter 3, a small firm may employ Lauren at $10 per hour to repair both windows and walls. In 12 hours, she could repair 3 windows and 3 walls. A larger firm could employ Lauren at $10 per hour to fix windows, and hire Steve at $10 per hour to fix walls. In 12 hours, they could fix 7 walls and 9 windows (or 6 walls and 12 windows)—*more* than twice as much output for only twice the cost. Therefore, the large firm has a smaller *average* cost of production than the small firm.

▶ Rising output can reduce average cost for technical reasons, as well. A firm may build a pipeline to transport water to a desert or heating oil to a city in a cold climate. Pipe with a 2-inch radius costs *twice* as much to make as pipe with a 1-inch radius, because the material required to make it increases in proportion to its radius. However, the larger pipe carries *4 times* as much water (or oil) as the smaller one, because a pipe's capacity rises with the *square* of its radius. Therefore, increasing the size of the pipe reduces average cost. The same logic applies to other inputs, such as trucks, boxes, and other products. Similarly, a large retail store can cost less per square foot to operate than a small retail store.

Review Questions

8. Explain the relationship between marginal cost and average cost.

9. Explain why a firm might have: (a) constant costs, (b) increasing costs, (c) decreasing costs.

Chapter 4 explained that the supply-demand model applies when buyers and sellers are price takers. We are now in a position to relate the supply curves of price-taking firms to their costs:

SUPPLY CURVES, COSTS, AND PROFIT

A firm's long-run supply curve is the portion of its marginal cost curve that lies on or above the average cost curve.

In other words, a firm's long-run supply curve is the same as its marginal cost curve as long as the price is high enough that it does not shut down operations.

When a firm is a price taker, its marginal revenue equals the price. For example, if a firm sells 101 Dalmatians instead of 100, its total revenue rises by the price at which it sells the 101st dog, so its marginal revenue equals the price. Because the firm chooses its output so that marginal cost equals marginal revenue, the marginal cost curve shows the firm's output at that price. In other words, the *marginal cost curve is the supply curve*. However, if average cost exceeds the price, then the firm shuts down in the long run rather than continuing to produce at a loss. Therefore, the marginal cost curve is the supply curve only if the price exceeds average cost. At lower prices, the quantity supplied is zero (the firm shuts its doors).

Profit and Producer Surplus

Chapter 9 defined *producer surplus* as benefit to a producer of selling a good at the equilibrium price. It explained that the height of the supply curve shows sellers' opportunity costs of producing various units of the good. We now see that the height of the long-run supply curve at each quantity shows the marginal cost of producing that quantity.

Chapter 9 also explained that the area under a supply curve measures the total cost of producing the good. We now see why: The area under a long-run supply curve equals the marginal cost of producing the first unit, plus the marginal cost of producing the second unit, and so on for additional units.

Chapter 9 explained that economists calculate producer surplus as the area above the supply curve and below the equilibrium price, between the quantity zero and the equilibrium quantity. That area equals total revenue from sales minus the total cost of producing the good. We now see that, in the long run, producer surplus equals profit.

The height of a supply curve at any given quantity shows the marginal cost of producing that quantity. The area under a long-run supply curve, between zero and a given quantity, equals the total cost of producing that quantity. The area above the supply curve and below the equilibrium price, rightward to a given quantity, shows profit (producer surplus).

EXAMPLE

Figure 5 shows the marginal cost curve by a price-taking firm that sells its product for $5 per unit. The firm maximizes profit by producing 7 units. Its marginal cost of producing the first unit is $2, so it earns a $3 profit on that unit. Its marginal cost of producing the second unit is also $2, so it earns another $3 profit on that unit. When the firm produces 7 units, its total profit is $15.

Measuring Cost and Profit

The cost of any action is the value of what you sacrifice or give up for it. It is the opportunity cost of that action, discussed in Chapter 1. Measures of cost on accounting statements usually differ from a firm's true (opportunity) costs. As a result, accounting measures of profit also differ from a firm's true profit (total revenue minus total cost).

Accounting measures omit certain costs and give inaccurate statements of others, because they value inputs at historical costs rather than current opportunity costs. (This does not imply a dispute between economists and accountants; firms calculate accounting measures of costs as they do for good reasons, such as the requirements of tax laws.)

Figure 5 | Producer Surplus and Profit

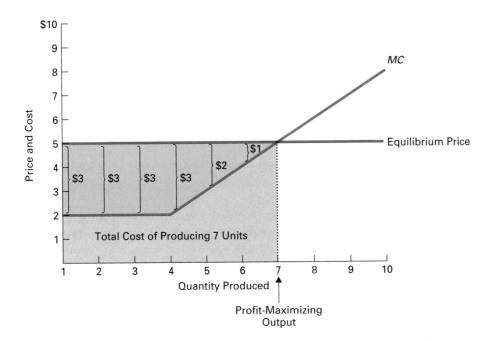

This firm earns $15 profit by producing 7 units.

Historical Costs of Inputs An input's historical cost is the price that a firm paid to buy the input in the past. An input's historical cost accurately reflects its current opportunity cost if the firm uses the input soon after buying it, before its price changes. For example, firms buy electricity to operate machinery as they use it; restaurants buy fresh foods soon before preparing and serving them. For inputs like these, historical costs closely measure opportunity costs of using the inputs. However, an input's historical cost differs from its current opportunity cost if its price has changed since the firm bought it. The historical costs of inputs that firms use over periods of many years, such as machinery, equipment, and buildings, seldom reflect current opportunity costs.

EXAMPLE

Suppose that a firm purchased 1,000 barrels of oil 6 months ago at $15 per barrel and 800 additional barrels last month at $18 per barrel. If the firm could now resell the oil for $20 per barrel, then the current opportunity cost of using any of this oil is $20 per barrel rather than *either* historical cost. One accounting measure, the FIFO (first-in, first-out) method, values inventory at historical costs and supposes that the firm uses its $15 oil first, then its $18 oil. Another accounting measure, the LIFO (last-in, first-out) method, values inventory at historical costs and supposes that the firm uses the oil that it purchased most recently first. Both measures misstate the current opportunity cost of the input.

A second reason that historical costs misstate current opportunity costs arises from depreciation.

Depreciation is the fall in the value of a resource over some period of time.

Accounting measures of depreciation usually do not accurately measure the fall in the resale value of a resource. When a firm increases the intensity of its use of a machine, the machine's resale value may fall faster than it would if the firm made less intensive use of the machine. (For example, the resale price of your car falls more during a year if you drive it 25,000 miles per year than if you drive it 5,000 miles per year.) When a firm uses a machine to produce a good, the fall in the price of the machine is a cost of production. Accounting measures of depreciation are not based on changes in the prices of inputs, so they misstate the opportunity costs of using those resources in production.

Omission of Certain Costs from Accounting Statements Accounting measures misstate a firm's opportunity costs for another reason: They omit some relevant costs. In fact, accounting statements omit many *implicit costs*.

> **Implicit costs** are costs that do not involve direct payments; they are solely opportunity costs.

The most important implicit cost that accounting statements omit is the opportunity cost of the financial capital that a firm's owners have provided to fund its assets and operations. If you save $10,000 and invest it in your own business, your opportunity cost is the income that you could have earned if you had invested that $10,000 in stocks or bonds. Similarly, a firm's owners provide entrepreneurial services; they generate and implement new ideas and take the risk that it will fail. If you start your own firm, you put in time, energy, and creativity that you could have spent on something else. You also take a risk that your business will fail and you will lose your investments of money, time, and effort; you could avoid that risk by investing your money, time, and effort in less risky endeavors. For these reasons, your firm has important implicit costs equal to the opportunity costs of your money, time, energy, creativity, and willingness to take risks. Similar logic applies to the stockholders of a large corporation; these owners invest their money and take the risk that they will lose that money. The firm's implicit cost of their money is the interest that the owners could have earned by investing elsewhere.

Another implicit cost is associated with intangible assets such as brand names and trademarks ("Coca-Cola," "Disney," "McDonald's," and so on). Firms incur opportunity costs if they do *not* use or license these intangible assets (just as the firm incurs an opportunity cost if it does not use some equipment that it owns, because it sacrifices revenue that it could have earned by using that equipment). A sports team sacrifices income if it does not sell or lease the right to use its name and logo (intangible assets) on clothing and other items; an entertainment firm like the Walt Disney Company can raise revenue by allowing its name on various products.

Overuse of a brand name or trademark also has a cost: depreciation. Depreciation of an intangible asset is an implicit cost. Many public figures, such as entertainment and sports stars, earn extra income by endorsing products or appearing in commercials. If a celebrity loses those opportunities because of a public scandal, that person pays an implicit cost in depreciation of his "brand name." Similarly, a firm's brand name can lose value due to overuse or if the firm puts its name on poor-quality products and loses a reputation for high quality.

Implicit costs are hard to estimate. How much must an entrepreneur be paid to start and invest in a risky firm? Still, these are real opportunity costs to a firm's owners.

Profit and Accounting Measures of Profit

Rational decisions must take into account *all* costs.

> **Economic cost** refers to all costs, explicit and implicit. Economic cost is the correct measure of cost for a firm's decisions.

Economic profit equals total revenue minus total economic cost.

Accounting profit equals total revenue minus total cost as measured on accounting statements.

Economic profit differs from accounting profit because accounting statements do not accurately measure economic costs. When accounting statements understate costs (e.g. by omitting implicit costs), they overstate profits—accounting profit exceeds economic profit.

Review Questions

10. What is the connection between a firm's long-run supply curve and its marginal cost curve? Explain why.

11. What does the area under the supply curve show?

12. How are profit and producer surplus related?

13. Explain two reasons why historical costs differ from opportunity costs.

14. Explain two reasons why accounting statements do not accurately measure economic costs.

Thinking Exercises

15. Suppose that the price in Figure 5 were $6 instead of $5 per unit. How much would the firm produce? How large would its profit be?

16. Draw a graph like Figure 6. Show how to represent profit on your graph (a) using the marginal cost curve, and (b) using the *average* cost curve. (*Hint* for 16b: Think about how profit and average cost are related.)

Figure 6 | Find Profit on This Graph (See Thinking Exercise 16)

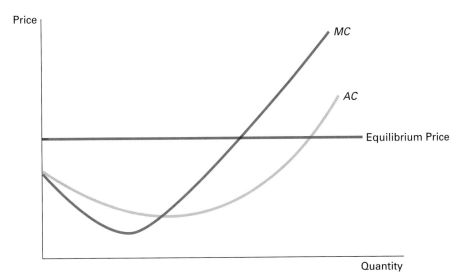

Conclusion

Business Firms

A firm is an organization that coordinates the activities of workers, managers, owners, lenders, and other participants to produce and sell a good or service. Most firms in the United States are sole proprietorships, which tend to be small, and some others are partnerships, which tend to be larger than sole proprietorships. About one-fifth of U.S. firms are corporations, which tend to be larger than both.

Deciding How to Produce

A business firm's decision about how to produce follows three logical steps. First, it chooses a hypothetical quantity and lists all the technically efficient methods to produce that quantity. Second, it chooses the lowest-cost method of production from that list. Third, it repeats the procedure for other possible quantities.

Deciding How Much to Produce

The term *long run* refers to a period of time over which people fully adjust their behavior to a change in conditions. For a firm, the long run is the time during which it can change the quantities of all its inputs.

A firm maximizes profit by choosing its level of production in three steps. First, it finds the level of output at which marginal revenue equals marginal cost, with an upward-sloping or horizontal marginal cost curve. The firm produces this quantity if it does not shut down to avoid losses. Second, the firm calculates total revenue and total cost at this level of output. Third, the firm shuts down in the long run if total cost exceeds total revenue.

Average Cost and Revenue

A firm's choice between producing and shutting down can be restated in terms of average (per-unit) costs and revenues. A firm shuts down in the long run if its average cost exceeds its average revenue.

Marginal and average cost are related: When marginal cost exceeds average cost, average cost rises as output increases. When marginal cost is less than average cost, average cost falls as output increases. When marginal cost equals average cost, average cost does not change as output increases.

Shapes of Cost Curves

A firm has constant costs if its long-run average cost is independent of its output quantity. In this case, marginal cost and average cost are equal, and the *MC* and *AC* curves are horizontal lines. A firm has increasing costs if its long-run average cost rises with increases in output; it has decreasing costs if its long-run average cost falls with increases in output.

Supply Curves, Costs, and Profit

A firm's long-run supply curve is the portion of its marginal cost curve on or above the average cost curve. That is, its long-run supply is given by marginal cost as long as the firm does not shut down to avoid losses.

The height of a supply curve, at any given quantity, shows the marginal cost of producing that quantity. The area under a long-run supply curve, between zero and a given quantity, equals the total cost of producing that quantity. The area above the supply curve and below the equilibrium price rightward to a given quantity shows profit (which equals producer surplus in the long run).

Accounting statements usually misstate a firm's true opportunity costs and profit. Accounting measures inaccurately state certain costs, because they value inputs at historical costs rather than current opportunity costs. Accounting measures also misstate total costs because they omit implicit costs, including the opportunity costs of the financial capital that owners have invested in the firm as well as their time, energy, creativity, and willingness to take risks. Implicit costs also include opportunity costs of the firm's trademark or brand name. When accounting statements understate costs, they overstate profits—accounting profit exceeds economic profit.

Key Terms

technically efficient method of production	long run	increasing costs	economic cost
	average revenue	decreasing costs	economic profit
profit	average cost	depreciation	accounting profit
marginal revenue	constant costs	implicit cost	

Problems

17. Discuss the differences between sole proprietorships, partnerships, and corporations.

18. Can the lowest-cost method of production be technically inefficient? Explain your answer.

19. Explain why a firm can raise its profits by reducing production if marginal cost exceeds marginal revenue.

20. (a) Explain why the firm in Table 1 (on page 261) is not a price taker.
    (b) Change the numbers in Table 1 to make the firm a price taker by assuming that the price is 8 for every quantity. (Every number in the Price column is 8.) Notice that marginal revenue also becomes 8 for every quantity. What is the profit-maximizing quantity of output? How large is the firm's profit in this case?

21. The equilibrium price of gourmet edible baseball caps is $20 each. Table 2 shows Josh's costs of production for the caps. Derive and fill in the missing numbers from the table, and indicate how many caps he should produce to maximize profit.

Table 2 | Data for Problem 21

Quantity (Q)	Price (P)	Total Revenue (TR)	Marginal Revenue (MR)	Total Cost (TC)	Marginal Cost (MC)	Profit
1	20			50		
2	20			80		
3	20			100		
4	20			110		
5	20			120		
6	20			130		
7	20			140		
8	20			150		
9	20			170		
10	20			200		
11	20			240		
12	20			290		

22. Your history professor gives five quizzes this term, each worth 10 points. You get 6 points on the first quiz, 7 on the second, 3 on the third, 5 on the fourth, and 8 on the fifth. Calculate your marginal and average scores. Explain why your marginal score pulls along your average score.

Inquiries for Further Thought

23. You own a fast-food restaurant, where you can package your food and drinks in biodegradable containers or in cheaper, nonbiodegradable containers. Your business could sacrifice profit to buy biodegradable containers that would benefit the environment. You want to make a profit for yourself, and you also want to help the environment. How would you decide between (a) reducing your profits by spending the extra money to use biodegradable containers, and (b) keeping your costs down and your profits high by using nonbiodegradable containers, but donating part of your profit to help a worthy cause? Under what conditions would you want your firm to maximize profit?

24. Do firms have a social responsibility to sacrifice profit to help the poor or pursue other worthy causes, or should they maximize profit and leave these other goals to individual people (including the firms' owners, private charities, and the government)? Who pays for a social program that a firm promotes at the expense of profit?

25. Do nonprofit firms (such as most colleges, hospitals, and charitable organizations) earn profits or losses? What do you think these firms maximize?

Appendix: Mathematics of Choosing How Much to Produce[6]

A firm wants to maximize its profit from selling swimming pools. First, summarize the demand for pools with a function $d(Q)$. To sell quantity Q, the highest price the firm can charge is P. This price is a function of the quantity the firm sells, Q, so:

$$P = d(Q)$$

The demand curve slopes downward, so the derivative of d with respect to Q is negative: $d'(Q) < 0$. This relationship means that the firm must reduce its price to increase sales of pools.

The firm's total revenue, *TR*, is the quantity that it sells multiplied by the price:

$$TR = QP$$

Rewrite this as:

$$TR = Qd(Q)$$

$$\equiv f(Q)$$

This expression defines the function $f(Q)$ and shows that the firm's total revenue is a function of the quantity that it sells.

Marginal revenue is the derivative of total revenue with respect to Q:

$$MR = f'(Q)$$

The firm's total cost of producing pools, *TC*, is also a function of the quantity:

$$TC = g(Q)$$

Marginal cost is the derivative of total cost with respect to quantity, so:

$$MC = g'(Q)$$

The firm's profit equals total revenue minus total cost:

$$\text{Profit} = TR - TC$$

$$= f(Q) - g(Q)$$

To maximize profit, set its derivative (with respect to Q) equal to zero. This step gives:

$$f'(Q) - g'(Q) = 0$$

$$f'(Q) = g'(Q)$$

This equation states that marginal revenue equals marginal cost. The firm maximizes its profit by choosing to produce a quantity at which marginal revenue equals marginal cost.

---

[6]*Note:* This appendix requires knowledge of calculus.

Price Takers

A special case occurs when firms are price takers. A price taker faces perfectly elastic demand. (A price-taking firm cannot raise its price without losing all its customers.) Therefore, the function $d(Q)$ is a constant; its value does not depend on Q. Therefore, $P = d$, where d is some number. (Price does not depend on Q.) Total revenue becomes:

$$f(Q) = Qd$$

Marginal revenue is:

$$f'(Q) = d$$
$$= P$$

This equation says that marginal revenue equals price for a price-taking firm. The firm maximizes profit by choosing a quantity so that:

$$P = g'(Q)$$

which says that marginal cost equals price.

CHAPTER 12

BUSINESS DECISIONS AND SUPPLY IN THE SHORT RUN

In this Chapter...

Main Points to Understand

▶ Variable costs influence a firm's decision of whether to shut down or stay in business, but fixed costs do not affect this decision.

▶ Diminishing returns cause a firm's short-run marginal cost and average variable cost to increase as its level of output increases.

▶ A firm's demand for an input depends on the value of its marginal product.

▶ A firm maximizes its value, which equals the discounted present value of its expected future profits.

Thinking Skills to Develop

▶ Recognize the implications of short-run limits on a firm's choices.

▶ Calculate and apply discounted present values.

The previous chapter discussed profit maximization in the long run, when people can fully adjust to any change in conditions. However, many adjustments take time. Months or even years pass as farmers grow crops and manufacturers build new equipment, factories, or offices. The short run is a period of time over which people cannot fully adjust to changes in underlying conditions.

> The **short run** refers to a period of time over which people cannot fully adjust to a change in conditions. Applied to business decisions, it refers to a period over which a firm cannot change the quantity of some input.[1]

Over the short run, a firm may have some inputs with fixed quantities—such as the number of machines installed in its factory or its available office space. While it can

PROFIT MAXIMIZATION IN THE SHORT RUN

---

[1]More precisely, the cost of adjusting quickly to a change in conditions is sometimes higher than the cost of adjusting slowly. The short run is the period of time before a complete adjustment occurs when people or firms choose their speed of adjustment. For example, suppose that a person wants to sell a house. She can sell it in *1 day* if she is willing to accept a low enough price. But if she is willing to wait, she is likely to find a buyer who is willing to pay more than she could get in such a short period of time. Her *cost* of a quick sale is higher (the house brings a lower price) than if she sells the house over a longer period of time. The short run, then, is the time before the owner chooses to accept an offer to sell the house; the long run encompasses later times.

This machine at a cookie factory is a fixed input; the dough that goes into the machine is made up of variable inputs.

change these inputs in the long run, the short run is the period of time over which it cannot change them.

> **Fixed inputs** are inputs whose quantities a firm *cannot change* in the short run. Other inputs, whose quantities a firm *can* change in the short run, are **variable inputs.**

Short-run costs differ from long-run costs because a firm faces an *extra limit on its choices* in the short run: It cannot change the quantities of fixed inputs.[2] Current decisions are limited by past choices on the number of machines in its factory or the office space it has previously rented. In the short run, a firm may be stuck paying some fixed costs.

> **Fixed costs** are costs of fixed inputs. **Variable costs** are costs of variable inputs.

A firm can reduce its variable costs by lowering production. However, it cannot change its fixed costs; these expenses remain fixed and unavoidable in the short run. A firm's total cost of production equals its total fixed cost plus its total variable cost.

In the long run, all inputs are variable because a firm can change the levels of all its inputs. Therefore, firms have no fixed costs in the long run. All long-run costs are variable costs.

EXAMPLES

If a firm has signed an unbreakable lease for office space, then its payment for office space is a fixed cost. If the firm has the right to terminate the lease without penalty, then its payment for office space is a variable cost. The cost of electricity to operate a firm's

---

[2]More precisely, it is more costly to vary these inputs quickly than to adjust them over a longer period. The distinction between the short run and the long run really involves the costs of changing inputs over various periods of time. The short-run constraint arises from the relatively high cost of quick variations in inputs. See the previous footnote.

Table 1 | Revenues and Costs With $10 Total Fixed Cost

Quantity (Q)	Price (P)	Total Revenue (TR)	Marginal Revenue (MR)	Total Cost (TC)	Total Variable Cost (TVC)	Marginal Cost (MC)	Profit	
1	16	16	16	38	28	28	−22	
2	15	30	14	52	42	14	−22	
3	14	42	12	54	44	2	−12	
4	13	52	10	56	46	2	−4	
5	12	60	8	58	48	2	2	
6	11	66	6	61	51	3	5	
7	10	70	4	65	55	4	5	MC = MR
8	9	72	2	70	60	5	2	
9	8	72	0	76	66	6	−4	
10	7	70	−2	83	73	7	−13	
11	6	66	−4	91	81	8	−25	
12	5	60	−6	100	90	9	−40	

machinery is a variable cost, because it can change over short periods. Table 1 is reproduced from Chapter 11 but now includes a $10 fixed cost. Total cost equals total variable cost plus the $10 total fixed cost.

How Short Is the Short Run?

The terms *short run* and *long run* do not refer to fixed amounts of calendar time. The short run may be measured in minutes in some situations and in years in other situations. Long-run decisions for a travel agency may span only a few days (the time required to buy and set up phones and desks); long-run decisions for another firm may involve commitments over decades (the time to grow trees for certain types of wood). Economists make these distinctions precise in the context of individual issues.

Why Marginal Cost Rises at High Levels of Output

Notice that marginal cost rises in Table 1 as output increases beyond 5 units. Marginal cost often rises with output in the short run, because the firm is limited by the quantities of fixed inputs that it has already chosen. To raise output in the short run, it must either use those fixed inputs more intensively than before (operate machinery at a higher speed, for example) or switch to other, more expensive methods of production. Marginal cost also rises because increases in production raise the costs of managing the firm. (See the discussion of *increasing costs* in Chapter 11.)

Step-by-Step Procedure for Choosing Short-Run Output

A firm chooses its short-run level of production in the same three-step process through which it chooses a long-run level. The decisions differ only in the condition under which a firm chooses to shut down production. It may choose to operate at a loss in the short run, though it would shut down if that loss were to continue in the long run.

Step 1
The first step is to find the level of output for which *marginal revenue equals marginal cost*, with an upward-sloping or horizontal marginal cost curve. (This is exactly the same

as the first step for choosing the long-run level of production. It shows the firm's level of production if the firm does not shut down.) The second and third steps differ slightly from the long-run case, because the conditions under which a firm shuts down differ in the short run and long run.

Step 2

Calculate total revenue *(TR)* and total *variable* cost *(TVC)* at the level of output from Step 1.

Step 3

Shut down the firm if total revenue is smaller than total *variable* cost.[3] If total revenue exceeds total variable cost, produce the quantity from Step 1. The firm earns a profit if total revenue *(TR)* exceeds total cost *(TC)*. It takes a loss if total revenue is less than total cost. A firm loses money but continues to produce in the short run if total revenue is less than *total* cost (variable *plus* fixed costs) but greater than total *variable* cost alone.

The key point to understand is this: Variable costs are *opportunity costs* of producing. However, fixed costs are *not* opportunity costs of producing, because a firm must pay fixed costs *even if does not produce*. (Fixed costs are unavoidable.) Therefore, *only* variable costs are relevant for the firm's decision of whether or not to produce. In the language of Chapter 10, fixed costs are *sunk costs*.

> Fixed costs are sunk costs, so rational choices ignore them. Fixed costs do *not* affect firms' decisions.

Fixed costs do, however, affect its profit.

The following table summarizes the three possible situations:

Situation	Firm's Best Action
(a) Total revenue > Total cost > Total variable cost	Produce, earn a profit
(b) Total cost > Total revenue > Total variable cost	Produce, suffer a loss
(c) Total cost > Total variable cost > Total revenue	Shut down, suffer a loss equal to fixed costs

Figure 1 graphs each situation. Panel (a) shows the conditions described in Table 1. Total fixed cost equals $10, and the firm produces and earns a $5 profit, because total revenue exceeds total cost with production of 7 units (the quantity of output from Step 1). Panel (b) shows the same situation as in Panel (a), except that total fixed cost is $20. The firm produces 7 units, but suffers a $5 loss. Its total revenue of $70 exceeds its total variable cost of $55 (so it continues producing), but it takes a loss because its $20 fixed cost pushes total cost to $75, which exceeds total revenue. The conditions in Panel (c) are the same as those in Table 1, except that total *variable* cost is $20 higher than the amount in that table. The firm shuts down production, because its total variable cost exceeds its total revenue at every level of output.

EXAMPLES

A firm maximizes its profit by producing 200 cans of beans per day. (At this quantity, marginal cost equals marginal revenue.) It has a fixed cost of $100 and a variable cost of $200, so its total cost is $300. The firm can face three possible situations. (a) If its

Advice to Students

Don't get confused by the suggestion that a firm might produce and take a loss instead of shutting down under certain conditions. To see how this decision might make sense, suppose you pay a $50 fee to set up a booth at a fair. You plan to sell 100 hamburgers for $2 each.

Unfortunately, no one at the fair is willing to pay $2 for a hamburger. You can sell them only if you reduce the price to 40 cents each, meaning that your total revenue will be only $40. Since you paid a $50 fee for the booth, you stand to lose $10.

But losing $10 is better than losing $50! If you were to shut down and not sell the hamburgers, you would take a $50 loss, because you paid a $50 fixed cost. It is better to sell the hamburgers and take a $10 loss than to shut down and take a $50 loss. Of course, if you had known that you would lose money, you never would have paid the $50 fee. But you learn the sad truth too late to avoid the loss; that $50 fixed cost is an unavoidable expense, because the fair operators will not refund your money.

---

[3]Note that a firm may temporarily shut down production without permanently going out of business.

Figure 1 | Short-Run Profit Maximization with Fixed Costs

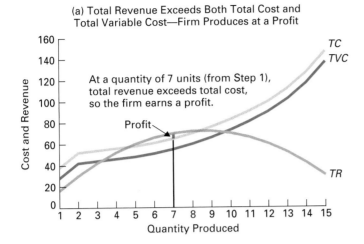

(a) Total Revenue Exceeds Both Total Cost and Total Variable Cost—Firm Produces at a Profit

At a quantity of 7 units (from Step 1), total revenue exceeds total cost, so the firm earns a profit.

Profit

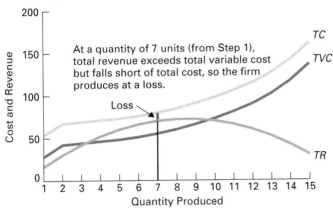

(b) Total Revenue Exceeds Total Variable Cost but Falls Short of Total Cost—Firm Produces at a Loss

At a quantity of 7 units (from Step 1), total revenue exceeds total variable cost but falls short of total cost, so the firm produces at a loss.

Loss

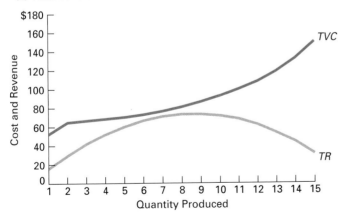

(c) Total Variable Cost Exceeds Total Revenue—Firm Shuts Down

Panel (a) shows the situation described in Table 1. Total fixed cost is $10, and the firm produces and earns a $5 profit, because total revenue exceeds total cost when it produces 7 units (the quantity of output from Step 1). Panel (b) shows the same conditions as in Panel (a) except total fixed cost is $20. The firm produces 7 units but suffers a $5 loss. Its total revenue of $70 exceeds its total variable cost of $55 (so it continues production), but it takes a loss, because its $20 fixed cost pushes total cost to $75, which exceeds total revenue. Panel (c) shows the same situation as in Table 1, except total variable cost is $20 higher than in that table. The firm shuts down production, because its total variable cost exceeds its total revenue at every level of output.

total revenue is $350, the firm earns a $50 profit and stays in business. (b) If its total revenue is $250, it takes a $50 loss, a smaller loss than the $100 it would lose by shutting down and sacrificing its entire fixed cost; the firm stays in business and produces at a loss. (c) If total revenue is only $150, the firm would suffer a $150 loss if it were to produce, so it shuts down to limit its loss to $100.

EXPLANATION

Economists distinguish between variable cost and total cost, because each serves a different purpose. Total cost helps analysts to evaluate the outcomes of decisions made in the past. To answer the question, "Has the firm been profitable?" we must subtract all costs—both fixed and variable costs—from total revenue. However, only variable cost is relevant to any current decision. The firm cannot avoid its fixed costs, which it has already either paid or agreed to pay. It cannot escape paying these fixed costs or get its money back. Fixed costs are sunk costs. As Chapter 10 explained, rational choices ignore sunk costs for current decisions, such as whether to stay in business or shut down production. Therefore, to answer the question, "Should the firm produce or shut down?" we compare total revenue with total *variable* cost.

Review Questions

1. What do economists mean by the term *short run?*

2. What are fixed inputs? Variable inputs? Give examples of each.

3. What are fixed costs? Variable costs?

Thinking Exercises

4. Under what conditions does a firm shut down in the short run? Under what conditions does it produce at a loss? Explain.

5. Change the numbers in Table 1 so that fixed cost is $15 instead of $10. Does this change affect other numbers in the table? Which ones? Explain how this change affects the firm's short-run decisions and profits.

AVERAGE COSTS

Chapter 11 discussed average cost and average revenue. For a price-taking firm, average revenue equals the product's price. Average (or per-unit) cost rises whenever marginal cost exceeds the average, and it falls when marginal cost is less than the average. (Recall the example about grades on quizzes.) Chapter 11 also explained that a firm shuts down in the long run if average cost exceeds average revenue. In the short run, however, a firm shuts down only if average *variable* cost exceeds average revenue.

> **Average variable cost (AVC)** is total variable cost divided by the quantity produced.

> A firm shuts down in the short run if average variable cost exceeds average revenue.

> **Average fixed cost (AFC)** is total fixed cost divided by the quantity produced.

Average total cost *(ATC)* is the overall per-unit cost (total cost divided by the quantity produced).

Average total cost equals average variable cost plus average fixed cost *(ATC = AVC + AFC)*. In the long run, all inputs become variable. That is, a firm can choose the levels of all inputs, even those that are fixed in the short run. As a result, all costs become variable costs in the long run, so average total cost and average variable cost become identical. (Chapter 11 called this amount simply *average cost.*)

Average fixed cost falls as output rises, because an increase in output spreads the fixed cost over more units. Table 2 shows average total cost, average variable cost, and average fixed cost for the firm in Table 1.

Capacity Output

The quantity at which average total cost reaches its lowest point is called *capacity output.*

Capacity output is the level of output that minimizes average total cost.

Capacity output is (loosely) the quantity that a factory was built to produce. A firm can produce more than its capacity output, but doing so raises its average total cost. (For example, a firm might operate its machinery more hours per day than the equipment was designed to withstand; this practice would produce more than capacity output, but it would wear out the machinery in a shorter time.) A firm can also produce at less than its capacity; such a practice would raise average total cost, because the firm would not fully utilize its fixed inputs. Figure 2 shows a firm's capacity output.

Short-Run and Long-Run Average Costs

At any quantity, a firm can produce that output at lower cost (or the same cost) in the long run than in the short run, when fixed inputs constrain its choices. For this reason, short-run average total cost curves are always above or the same as (but never below) long-run average total cost curves.

Table 2 | Average Costs With a $10 Fixed Cost

Quantity (Q)	Total Cost (TC)	Average Total Cost (ATC)	Variable Cost (TVC)	Average Variable Cost (AVC)	Total Fixed Cost (TFC)	Average Fixed Cost (AFC)
1	38	38	28	28	10	10
2	52	26	42	21	10	5
3	54	18	44	$14\frac{2}{3}$	10	$3\frac{1}{3}$
4	56	14	46	$11\frac{1}{2}$	10	$2\frac{1}{2}$
5	58	$11\frac{3}{5}$	48	$9\frac{3}{5}$	10	2
6	61	$10\frac{1}{6}$	51	$8\frac{1}{2}$	10	$1\frac{2}{3}$
7	65	$9\frac{2}{7}$	55	$7\frac{6}{7}$	10	$1\frac{3}{7}$
8	70	$8\frac{3}{4}$	60	$7\frac{1}{2}$	10	$1\frac{1}{4}$
9	76	$8\frac{4}{9}$	66	$7\frac{1}{3}$	10	$1\frac{1}{9}$
10	83	$8\frac{3}{10}$	73	$7\frac{3}{10}$	10	1
11	91	$8\frac{3}{11}$	81	$7\frac{4}{11}$	10	$\frac{10}{11}$
12	100	$8\frac{1}{3}$	90	$7\frac{1}{2}$	10	$\frac{5}{6}$

Figure 2 | Capacity Output

Capacity output is the quantity that minimizes average total cost *(ATC)*. The average total cost curve hits its lowest level at capacity output, the same point at which the marginal cost curve intersects the *ATC* curve.

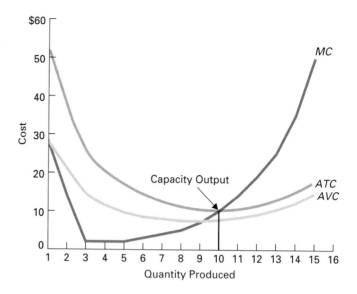

Figure 3 shows a firm's short-run and long-run average total cost curves. Each of the many short-run average total cost curves, such as $SRAC_1$, $SRAC_2$, and $SRAC_3$, shows the situation associated with a different quantity of fixed inputs (such as a different factory size). $SRAC_1$ shows a firm's short-run average total costs if it has a small quantity of fixed inputs (such as a small factory), giving it a capacity of 20,000 units per year. $SRAC_2$ shows the firm's short-run average total costs with a slightly larger quantity of fixed inputs (such as a larger factory) that boost capacity to 25,000 units per year. $SRAC_3$ shows the firm's short-run average total cost if still more fixed inputs (such as an even larger factory) give it a capacity of 50,000 units per year. The long-run average total cost curve just touches each of the short-run average total cost curves.

Figure 3 | Short-Run and Long-Run Average Total Cost Curves

A firm's short-run average total cost curve depends on its level of fixed inputs (its capacity). A firm has only one *LRAC* curve.

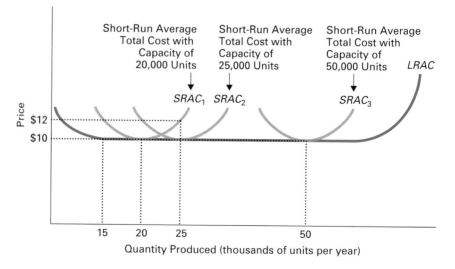

EXPLANATION

Short-run costs reflect limits or constraints on a firm's choices. Each firm must operate with quantities of fixed inputs that it has chosen in the past. These constraints prevent a firm from changing its fixed inputs to reduce its costs, but they disappear in the long run, when the firm can choose quantities of *all* its inputs. Therefore, all costs become variable in the long run. Long-run costs are free from the short-run constraints. The firm can only gain, not lose, by escaping those constraints. Therefore, long-run average total cost is always less than or equal to—never higher than—short-run average total cost. Figure 3 shows that *LRAC* always lies below, or on, the *SRAC* curves.

A firm with a small factory has the short-run average total cost curve $SRAC_1$ in Figure 3. The firm's capacity output is 20,000 units per year, and its average total cost of producing that quantity is $10 per unit. In the short run, its average total cost rises to $12 if it raises output to 25,000 units per year, because the factory was built to handle only 20,000 units. For example, the firm might operate its factory 24 hours per day and not allow equipment to cool down between shifts, raising output but reducing the useful life of the equipment and raising costs. In the long run, the firm can replace its factory with a larger one designed to handle the higher output, so in the long run, the firm's average total cost of producing 25,000 units per year is only $10 per unit. If the firm were to build a much larger factory with a capacity of 50,000 units per year, its short-run average total cost curve would be $SRAC_3$.

Similarly, if a firm with a capacity of 20,000 units per year reduces output to 15,000 units per year, its short-run average total cost rises to $12 per unit, because its costs include extra capacity (a larger factory than it needs to produce 15,000 units per year). In the long run, the firm could replace its factory with a smaller one designed to produce 15,000 units per year, so in the long run, its average total cost of producing 15,000 units per year is $10 per unit.

SHORT-RUN SUPPLY AND PROFIT

Chapter 11 explained that a firm's long-run supply curve is the portion of its marginal cost curve lying on or above the average cost curve. The results in the previous section modify this result for the short run:

> A firm's *short-run* supply curve is the portion of its marginal cost curve lying on or above the average *variable* cost curve.

In other words, a firm's short-run supply curve is identical to its marginal cost curve as long as the price is high enough that the firm does not shut down.

Profit and Producer Surplus in the Short Run

As Chapter 11 explained, the height of a supply curve, at any given quantity, shows the marginal cost of producing that quantity. Therefore the area under a short-run supply curve, between zero and a given quantity, equals the total *variable* cost of producing that quantity. However, a firm may also incur some fixed costs in the short run. Therefore, in the short run, profit equals producer surplus minus total fixed costs. Because a firm cannot avoid its fixed costs (they are unavoidable sunk costs), it maximizes profit by maximizing producer surplus. Since the firm has no fixed cost in the long run, producer surplus and profit are identical in the long run. However, they can differ in the short run, when:

> Profit equals producer surplus minus total fixed costs.

6. What are the definitions of average total cost, average fixed cost, and average variable cost?

7. What is capacity output?

8. Explain the connection between short-run and long-run average total cost curves.

9. How are short-run supply curves related to costs?

10. How are producer surplus and profit related in the short run?

T h i n k i n g   E x e r c i s e

11. What is the capacity output of the firm profiled in Table 2?

PRODUCTIVITY AND DIMINISHING RETURNS

What determines the shapes of short-run marginal and average cost curves? The answer to this question involves the concepts of productivity and diminishing returns. A firm's demand for inputs depends on their productivity:

> The **average product** of an input is a firm's total output divided by the quantity of that input.

For example, if 10 people work to produce 60 computers, their average product is 6 computers per worker.

> The **marginal product** of an input is the increase in a firm's total output when it adds a little more of the input while keeping quantities of other inputs fixed.

For example, if adding an 11th worker would increase output of computers from 60 to 65, then the *marginal product* of workers is 5 computers.

EXAMPLES

The average product of land where a farmer grows corn is the number of bushels of corn divided by the number of acres of land. The marginal product of this land is the increase in corn that the farmer could produce by using more land but *not* more seed, fertilizer, labor services, or other inputs. The average product of labor to repair transmissions is the number of repairs per worker-hour. The marginal product is the number of additional repairs per day the shop could complete by hiring another worker, but using the same tools and other equipment. A numerical example appears in Table 3.

Diminishing Returns

The *law of diminishing returns* summarizes the simple idea that a tenth person does not add much to a floor-cleaning crew equipped with only one mop.

Because of diminishing returns, doubling the number of workers on this assembly line will increase output by less than double.

Table 3 | An Example of Diminishing Returns to Labor

Input of Labor	Output (thousands of units)	Marginal Product of Labor (thousand units per worker)	Average Product of Labor (thousand units per worker)	Value of the Marginal Product of Labor[a] ($ thousands per year)
0	0	—	0.0	—
1	50	50	50.0	$25.0
2	120	70	60.0	35.0
3	180	60	60.0	30.0
4	230	50	57.5	25.0
5	270	40	54.0	20.0
6	300	30	50.0	15.0
7	320	20	47.1	10.0
8	330	10	41.2	5.0
9	332	2	36.9	1.0
10	333	1	33.3	0.5

[a]The numbers for the value of the marginal product assume a product price of $0.50 each.

> The **law of diminishing returns** is the principle that raising the quantity of an input eventually reduces its marginal product, if the quantity of some other input remains fixed.

Many firms use some inputs whose quantities are fixed in the short run. A firm's factory size and its quantity of specialized machines may be fixed. When it increases the quantities of its variable inputs, those inputs eventually generate diminishing returns. For example, an auto repair shop can double the number of cars it repairs each week if it doubles the number of mechanics it employs, the quantity of equipment, and the size of the repair shop. If it doubles the number of mechanics without changing the quantity of equipment or the size of the shop, however, the number of cars it can repair each week less than doubles. The shop experiences diminishing returns to additional mechanics while keeping fixed other inputs.

EXAMPLE

Table 3 shows the marginal and average products of labor for a firm with two machines. (Ignore the last column of the table for now.) If the firm employs one full-time worker, it produces 50,000 plastic containers per year. With two workers, it produces 120,000 containers per year; with three workers, it produces 180,000. The firm's output increases as it adds more workers, but if it still has only two machines, increases in its output slow as the number of workers rises. Increases in the quantity of labor, holding the number of machines fixed, eventually reduce the marginal product of labor. The marginal product of labor falls from 70,000 containers per year with two workers to 50,000 containers per year with four workers, to less than 10,000 containers per year with more than eight workers. The firm faces diminishing returns to adding labor, holding the number of machines fixed.

Figure 4 graphs the marginal product of labor, *MPL*, and the average product of labor, *APL*, from Table 3. Notice that the average product of labor rises when the marginal product exceeds the average product; it falls when the marginal product is smaller than the average product. The logic connecting average and marginal products is the same as the logic connecting average and marginal costs, as discussed in Chapter 11.

Figure 4 | Marginal and Average Product of Labor from Table 3

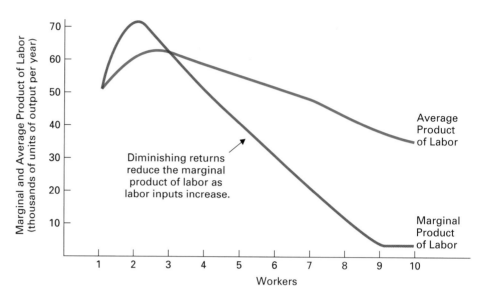

Advice to Students

Don't get confused by the intersection of the curves in Figure 4. The number of workers that a firm will actually hire depends on productivity *and* on wage rates.

Diminishing Returns and Costs

Short-run marginal cost and average variable cost rise with increasing output, at least after output reaches a certain level, because of the law of diminishing returns. Figure 5 shows the marginal and average variable cost curves for the firm in Table 3, assuming that workers earn $25,000 per year. The marginal cost curve slopes upward after output reaches 120,000 units per year; the average variable cost curve begins to slope upward when output exceeds 200,000 units per year. These cost curves begin sloping upward as quantities rise to these levels, because the firm has some fixed inputs (its two machines), so it encounters diminishing returns as it raises the quantity of its labor input.

Calculating marginal and average costs for Table 3 illustrates the reasons for the upward slopes of these curves. Assume that workers earn $25,000 per year. The firm in Table 3 has a total variable cost of $75,000 if it hires three workers and $100,000 per year if it hires four workers. It produces 180,000 containers with three workers and 230,000 containers with four workers. By spending the extra $25,000 for a fourth worker, the firm increases its production by 50,000 containers. The firm's marginal cost when it hires four workers and produces 230,000 containers becomes $25,000/50,000 containers, or $0.50 per container.

Now consider the firm's marginal cost when it hires eight workers. It produces an extra 10,000 containers by hiring the eighth worker, that is, by spending $200,000 rather than $175,000. Therefore the extra cost of those extra 10,000 containers is $25,000, and the firm's marginal cost when it hires eight workers and produces 330,000 containers is $25,000/10,000 containers, or $2.50 per container. These figures show how diminishing returns make the firm's marginal cost rise with increasing output after output reaches a certain level, as in Figure 5.

Now consider the *average variable cost* of the firm in Table 3. Workers earn $25,000 per year, so hiring four workers gives the firm a total variable cost of $100,000 per year. Because it produces 230,000 containers per year with four workers, its average variable cost is $0.435 per container ($100,000/230,000). If, however, it hires eight workers, its total variable cost rises to $200,000 and it produces 330,000 containers, so its average

Figure 5 | Marginal Cost and Average Variable Cost from Table 3 When Workers Cost $25,000 per Year

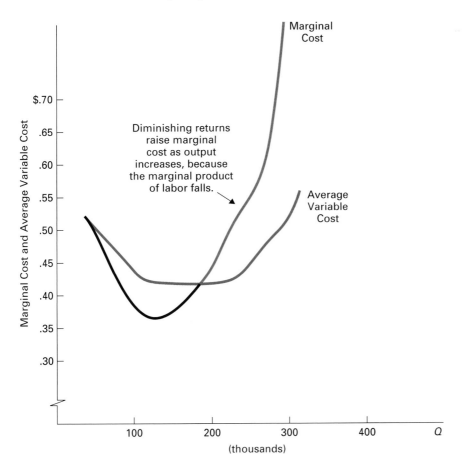

variable cost is $0.606 per container ($200,000/330,000). Clearly, diminishing returns make the firm's average variable cost rise with increasing output above a certain level, as in Figure 5.

Value of Marginal Product and Demand for Inputs

The marginal product of an input refers to the increase in the number of goods that a firm produces by adding a little more of that input while holding fixed other inputs. In contrast, the value of the marginal product of an input refers to the *value* of the additional goods produced.

> The **value of the marginal product** of an input is the increase in the money value of a firm's output when it adds a little more of the input, keeping fixed the quantities of other inputs.

If a firm is a price taker, then the value of the marginal product of an input equals its marginal product multiplied by the price of the final product. For example, suppose that adding one more full-time worker raises a firm's output by 20 shirts per week, and each shirt sells for $10. The marginal product of labor at the firm is 20 shirts per week, and the *value* of the marginal product of labor is $200. The last column in Table 3 shows the value of the marginal product in that example, assuming that the containers sell for $0.50 each.

The rule for rational decisions from Chapter 10 applies to decisions about how to produce a good. A rational firm chooses a quantity of each input that equates its marginal benefit and its marginal cost.

An input's marginal benefit is the value of its marginal product.

Most firms are price takers in input markets; they cannot affect the prices of the inputs they buy. A typical fast-food restaurant, for example, cannot reduce the costs of its inputs such as labor, ground beef, potatoes, and electricity by reducing its demands for those inputs, and it can buy more of those inputs without raising their prices; the restaurant is a price taker in input markets. For a price-taking firm, the marginal cost of an input is its price. Therefore the firm can equate marginal benefit with marginal cost by equating the value of an input's marginal product with the input's price.

A firm maximizes profit by choosing a quantity of each input so that the value of its marginal product equals its price. Therefore the demand curve for an input graphs the value of its marginal product.

The height of the demand curve for any input shows the value of the marginal product.

Review Questions

12. What is the marginal product of an input? What is the value of an input's marginal product?

13. Explain the law of diminishing returns.

14. Why does the short-run marginal cost curve slope upward? Why does a firm's short-run supply curve slope upward?

15. What determines a firm's demand for an input? How does your answer relate to the general rule for rational choice?

Thinking Exercises

16. How would the numbers in the last column of Table 3 (which show the value of the marginal product of labor) change if the product price were $2.00 each instead of $0.50 each?

17. Suppose that the firm in Table 3 hires six workers who earn $30,000 per year. What is its marginal cost of producing containers?

DISCOUNTED PRESENT VALUE AND THE VALUE OF A FIRM

Does short-run profit maximization imply *short-sighted* maximization? How do firms resolve the tradeoff between higher profits *this year* and higher *future* profits brought about by additional investment today in machinery, equipment, worker training, and research and development? (A firm could raise its current profit by spending less on new equipment, but this would reduce its future profits.) The answer requires an understanding of the concepts of *discounted present value* and the *value of a firm.*

Interest Rates and Discounted Present Value

Economists use the interest rate to calculate a discounted present value.

> An **interest rate** is the price of a loan, expressed as a percentage per year of the amount loaned.

EXAMPLES

If you borrow $100 for 1 year at an interest rate of 12 percent per year, you owe $112 at the end of the year. The price of the loan is the extra $12 that you must pay next year when you repay the loan. This amount is 12 percent of the $100 loan. Similarly, if you borrow $200 for 1 year at an interest rate of 12 percent, you owe $224 at the end of the year. The price of the loan is the $24 you must pay when you repay the loan. Expressed as a percentage, this $24 price is 12 percent of the $200 loan.

If you borrow $100 from a bank for 2 years at an interest rate of 10 percent per year, you owe the bank $121 at the end of 2 years. The bank charges you 10 percent per year *each* year. After one year, your debt to the bank is $110. This amount increases another 10 percent ($11) to $121 at the end of the second year. The price of the loan is $21 paid 2 years from now, when you repay the money you borrowed. This $21 is 10 percent of your loan amount per year.

More generally, if you borrow X dollars for 1 year, you must pay back $X(1 + i)$ dollars the next year, where the number i is the interest rate on the loan, stated as a decimal. (A 5 percent interest rate means that i equals 0.05; a 10 percent interest rate means that i equals 0.10.)

Discounted Present Value

One of the most useful formulas you will learn in economics is the formula to calculate the *discounted present value* of some future amount of money. Interest rates and discounted-present-value formulas are important for understanding any economic decisions that involve time.

> The **discounted present value** of a future amount of money is the money you would need to save and invest today to end up with a specific amount of money in the future.

In other words, it is the value, at the *present* time, of a certain amount of money to be received in the future. Discounted present value is based on a simple idea: It is better to receive $100 today than in the future because you can deposit the money in a savings account and earn interest on it. As a result, a dollar today is more valuable than a dollar in the future.

EXAMPLES

Suppose that you have $100 now, and the interest rate is 6 percent per year. If you invest your money for 1 year, you will have $106 next year, so the discounted present value of $106 next year is $100 now. This means $106 next year has the same value as $100 today, when the interest rate is 6 percent per year. Since the two amounts have the same value, you can trade one for the other. If you have $100 now, you can trade it for $106 next year by lending your money or depositing it in a bank account. If someone will pay you $106 next year, you can trade that money for $100 now by borrowing $100 and using the $106 you receive next year to repay the loan with interest.

If the interest rate is 10 percent per year, the discounted present value of $121 paid two years from now is $100. Again, $121 two years from now and $100 now have the same value when the interest rate is 10 percent per year. People can trade one for the other by borrowing or lending $100 for two years.

General Formula

Suppose that you put X dollars into a savings account today. Let the letter i represent the interest rate (expressed as a decimal, so that an interest rate of 12 percent per year is the number 0.12). Then a simple formula says that your X dollars this year will grow to be worth $X(1 + i)$ dollars next year. In other words, the *future value* of X dollars today is $X(1 + i)$ dollars next year. Simply turn this formula around to get the general formula for discounted present value:

$$\text{Discounted present value of } X \text{ dollars payable 1 year from now} = \frac{X}{1 + i}$$

EXPLANATION

If you had $X/(1 + i)$ dollars now, you could save it (put it in the bank or make another investment) and earn interest. Next year you would have X dollars. The value *now* (the *present value*) of the X dollars next year is $X/(1 + i)$ dollars. You can turn $X/(1 + i)$ dollars now into X dollars next year, and you can turn X dollars next year into $X/(1 + i)$ dollars now.[4] These statements mean that X dollars next year and $X/(1 + i)$ dollars now have the same value.[5]

Using the Formula

Suppose that you will receive $100.00 one year from now. If the interest rate is 10 percent per year, the discounted present value of the $100.00 next year is $100.00/(1.10), or about $91.91. If you had $91.91 now, and you saved it and earned a 10 percent interest rate for a year, you would have $100.00 next year.

To find the discounted present value of $1,000 two years from now, apply the general formula twice. Suppose that in 1999 the interest rate is 10 percent per year. Someone has promised to pay you $1,000.00 in the year 2001. You can find the discounted present value, in 1999, of that money in two steps. First, apply the formula to find out the value in 2000 of $1,000.00 payable in 2001. The formula gives a year-2000 value of $1,000.00/(1.10), or $909.09. You then apply the formula again to find the 1999 value of $909.09 gained in the year 2000. (This time, substitute $909.09 for X in the formula.) The formula shows a value of $909.09/(1.10), or $826.45. The discounted present value of $1,000.00 paid 2 years from now is $826.45 if the interest rate is 10 percent per year.

To find the discounted present value of $1,000.00 N years from now, apply the general formula N times. The formula for the discounted present value of X dollars paid N years from now is:

$$X \text{ dollars payable after } N \text{ years} = \frac{X}{(1 + i)^N} \text{ dollars now}$$

---

[4]You can do this by borrowing X dollars now and repaying $X/(1 + i)$ dollars next year.

[5]Notice that the term *discounted present value* refers to the fact that X dollars in the future have the same economic value as $X/(1 + i)$ dollars at the present time.

where i is the interest rate per year. That is, the discounted present value of X dollars paid N years from now is $X/(1 + i)^N$. For example, if the interest rate is 10 percent per year, the discounted present value of $2,000.00 paid 2 years from now is $2,000.00/(1.10)^2$, or $2,000.00/1.21, which is $1,652.89.

Using the Formula for Repeated Payments

To calculate the value of a firm, take the discounted present value of all its future profits, including its profits next year, the year after, the year after that, and so on. Repeated application of the general present value formula implies the following results:

> The discounted present value of X_1 dollars paid 1 year from now plus X_2 dollars paid 2 years from now plus X_3 dollars paid 3 years from now, and so on, is:

$$\frac{X_1}{(1 + i)} + \frac{X_2}{(1 + i)^2} + \frac{X_3}{(1 + i)^3} + \cdots$$

The sum goes on until some ending date, or it may go on forever.

> The discounted present value of X dollars paid every year forever is:

$$\frac{\$X}{i}$$

EXAMPLE

Suppose that the interest rate is 10 percent per year, and a firm earns $2,000 per year, every year, for 4 years. The discounted present value of these profits is:

$$\frac{\$2,000}{1.10} + \frac{\$2,000}{1.10^2} + \frac{\$2,000}{1.10^3} + \frac{\$2,000}{1.10^4} = \$6,340$$

If the firm earns $2,000 in profits every year forever, then the discounted present value of its profits is $2,000/0.10, or $20,000.

The formula for the discounted present value of X dollars paid every year forever, X/i, is a rough approximation to the discounted present value of X dollars paid every year for N years if N is 30 years or more. You can verify this statement by using a calculator or computer to solve for these discounted present values.

Value of a Firm

These formulas help to answer the questions introduced at the beginning of this section: How do firms handle the tradeoff between higher profits *this year* and higher *future* profits? Does short-run profit maximization imply *short-sighted* maximization? The answers come from the observation that a firm's owners do not maximize current profit alone; they usually seek to maximize the discounted present value of their expected future profits.

> The **value of a firm** is the discounted present value of its expected future profits.

Because *actual* future profits are uncertain today, a firm's value is the discounted present value of its *expected* future profits.

The formula for discounted present value determines how a firm trades off current profit against future profit. A firm's owners are willing to sacrifice current profit to boost future profit if the discounted present value of that extra future profit exceeds the value of the profit they lose today. For example, suppose a firm raises its spending on research and development by $1 million, reducing its current profit by $1 million. If the additional research and development raises the discounted present value of expected future profits by *more* than $1 million, then the firm's value rises. This would happen, for example, if the interest rate were 10 percent per year and the investment raised expected future profit by more than $100,000 per year in each future year.

Economists often use the phrase *maximizing profit* in place of the more precise phrase *maximizing value*. This book will follow that practice and adopt the usual term, *profit maximization*, except when the distinction is important for some issue.

Do Firms Make Rational Decisions?

Do business firms make rational decisions? More precisely, do the people associated with firms make rational decisions? Have they made rational choices in organizing their firms and setting the terms of the contracts that define their organizations?

Competition tends to eliminate firms that do not make rational choices. If the people in a firm repeatedly make irrational choices, competitors will likely drive that firm out of business. Firms that behave irrationally tend not to survive competition.

Of course, everyone associated with a firm—the owners, workers, managers, and creditors—pursues some personal interests. The personal interests of different parties often conflict with each other. The firm's owners usually want to maximize its value, while the managers and workers often prefer to sacrifice some profits and firm value to improve working conditions for themselves, their relations with co-workers, and so on. The personal interests of creditors such as bondholders (investors who have loaned money to the firm) also differ from the interests of the owners.

The owner of a small firm may make all its decisions. Owners of larger firms hire managers to make most decisions. Owners try to design managers' contracts to establish incentives for them to act *in the owner's interests*. In fact, owners design many details of business practices and organization to provide incentives for other people to act in the owners' interests (to make their goals correspond to the owners' goals). They cannot easily make these goals coincide, however, so owners design firms' business practices and organization to establish partial but not complete agreement in goals. Because a firm's owners cannot completely control its actions, those actions may not fully maximize its value.

Nevertheless, most decisions of most firms closely approximate an economic model in which firms maximize their values. If a firm's owners fail to create incentives that lead the firm to maximize its value (at least approximately), then someone can profit by *taking over* the firm—buying it, changing the way it operates (replacing the management or altering incentives for managers and workers), and then selling it at a higher value. This possibility of takeovers induces firms to maximize value, at least approximately.

Review Questions

18. What is a discounted present value?

19. What is the value of a firm?

20. Explain in words why $100 today is worth more than $100 to be received in the future, even if prices do not change.

21. What is the general formula for the discounted present value of X dollars paid every year forever?

22. What is the general formula for the discounted present value of X_1 dollars to be paid 1 year from now, *and* X_2 dollars to be paid 2 years from now, X_3 dollars to be paid 3 years from now, and so on?

Thinking Exercises

23. Perform the following calculations.
    (a) If the interest rate is 10 percent per year, what is the discounted present value of $200 to be paid 1 year from now? What if the interest rate is 5 percent?
    (b) Suppose that the interest rate is 10 percent per year. Find the discounted present value of $20,000 to be paid 2 years from now.
    (c) Suppose that the interest rate is 10 percent per year. What is the discounted present value of $10,000 to be paid 1 year from now plus $10,000 to be paid 2 years from now?

24. If people expect a firm to earn profits of $100,000 per year, every year, forever, and the interest rate is 5 percent per year, what is the value of the firm?

Conclusion

Profit Maximization in the Short Run

The term *short run* refers to a period of time over which people can make only incomplete adjustments. A firm cannot change the quantities of its fixed inputs in the short run, though it can change the quantities of its variable inputs. In the short run, therefore, a firm incurs fixed costs (sunk costs of its fixed inputs). A firm can alter its variable costs (the costs of its variable inputs) by changing its use of variable inputs and therefore its output. In the long run, all fixed costs become variable costs because a firm can vary the quantities of all its inputs.

In the short run, a firm either produces a quantity at which marginal revenue equals marginal cost, with a horizontal or upward-sloping marginal cost curve, or it shuts down production. It shuts down in the short run only if total variable cost exceeds total revenue at this level of output. A firm earns a profit if total revenue exceeds total cost, and it takes a loss if total revenue is less than total cost.

Average Costs

A firm's short-run decision to produce or shut down can be restated in terms of average costs and revenues. A firm shuts down in the short run if its average variable cost exceeds its average revenue. Capacity output is the level of output that minimizes average total cost.

Short-Run Supply and Profit

A firm's short-run supply curve is the portion of its marginal cost curve lying on or above the average variable cost curve. Its profit equals its producer surplus minus its total fixed costs.

Productivity and Diminishing Returns

The average product of an input is total output divided by the quantity of the input. The marginal product of an input is the increase in a firm's total output when it adds a little more of the input, keeping fixed the quantities of other inputs. The law of diminishing returns states that raising the quantity of an input eventually reduces its marginal product, if the quantity of some other input remains fixed. Diminishing returns imply that short-run marginal cost and average variable cost rise with increasing output. The value of the marginal product of an input is the increase in the value of a firm's output when it uses a little more of the input, keeping fixed the quantities of other inputs. With a price-taking firm, the value of the marginal product of an input equals its marginal product multiplied by the price of the good produced. A firm's demand curve for an input graphs the value of its marginal product.

Discounted Present Value and the Value of a Firm

The discounted present value of a future amount of money is the money that you would need to save and invest today to end up with a specific amount of money in the future. The discounted present value of X dollars to be paid 1 year from now is $X/(1+i)$ where i is the interest rate. The value of a firm is the discounted present value of its expected future profits. A firm's owners generally want to maximize its value, although conflicts between the interests of owners and managers may slightly alter this behavior.

Key Terms

short run
fixed input
variable input
fixed cost

variable cost
average variable cost
average fixed cost
average total cost

capacity output
law of diminishing returns
value of the marginal
  product

interest rate
discounted present
  value
value of a firm

Problems

25. Explain this statement: "Fixed costs are unavoidable in the short run."

26. Discuss this statement: "A rational firm might decide to produce in the short run but shut down in the long run, even if the demand for its product and its costs do not change."

27. Comment on this statement: "A good businessperson never sells a product for less than the cost of producing it."

28. Suppose that the firm in Table 1 has a fixed cost of $20 instead of $10. How does this change affect other numbers in the table? How does it affect the firm's short-run decisions and profit?

29. Change the numbers in Table 1 on page 279 to make the firm a price taker by assuming that the price is 8 for every quantity (so that every number in the Price column is 8). Notice that marginal revenue also becomes 8 for every quantity. How does this change affect the firm's short-run decisions and profit?

30. How does an increase in a firm's fixed cost affect:
    (a) Its profit-maximizing short-run level of output?
    (b) Its short-run profit?
    (c) Its decision to stay in business or shut down in the short run?

31. How is the short-run supply curve of a price-taking firm related to its costs of production? Explain the connection in as much detail as you can.

Inquiries for Further Thought

32. Why might the price of a share of stock be related to the discounted present value of the dividends that its owner will receive in the future?

33. What forces prevent a firm from operating in a short-sighted manner and raising its current profits at the expense of the firm's future?

Appendix: Isoquants

This appendix describes a graphical approach to choosing inputs to maximize the value of a firm. It introduces *isoquants,* which resemble indifference curves applied to production decisions. Recall that Appendix A in Chapter 10 discussed indifference curves, which show combinations of two goods that give a person equal utility; similarly, isoquants show combinations of two inputs that give a firm equal output.

> **Isoquants** graph technically efficient combinations of inputs that give the same amount of output.

Each isoquant applies to one level of output; successively higher isoquants indicate higher levels of output.

    Figure A1 shows examples of isoquants. Panel (a) shows an extreme example in which inputs are perfect complements; a firm must use exactly 1 unit of labor and 1 unit of capital to make 1 unit of output. (Think of cars, drivers, and taxi services.) With the isoquants in Panel (a), extra labor produces nothing unless the firm also provides extra capital, and extra capital produces nothing unless the firm hires extra labor. Panel (b) shows another extreme case in which labor and capital are perfect substitutes in producing an output; a firm produces the same amount with four workers and no machine as with no workers and two machines. Only the total amount of machines and pairs of workers affects total production. Panel (c) shows the usual shape of isoquants; the firm can produce the same amount of output with little capital and a lot of labor, or vice versa, but the inputs are *not* perfect complements or substitutes.

Isoquants differ from indifference curves in two ways:

▶ Each isoquant shows a certain quantity of output instead of a certain amount of utility.

▶ Isoquants show technical possibilities for production instead of people's tastes.

Whatever quantity of goods a firm chooses to produce, it wants to produce at the lowest possible cost to maximize its profit. Suppose that the firm wants to produce 75 units of a good per hour when labor costs $10 per hour and tools rent for $5 per hour. The isoquant for 75 units of output in Figure A2 shows the various combinations of workers and tools with which the firm can produce that quantity. To find the lowest-cost method of production, draw an *isocost* line (similar to a budget line from Chapter 10) with a slope equal to the negative of the relative price of labor in terms of tools. In the figure, the relative price of labor in terms of tools is two tools per worker, so the slope of the isocost line is −2. Now find the lowest isocost line (which represents the lowest possible level of spending on inputs) that touches the 75-good isoquant. In the figure, that line touches the isoquant at Point A, where the firm produces 75 units of output using six workers and eight tools for a cost of $100. This point identifies the lowest-cost way to produce 75 goods. Any other combination of workers and tools to produce 75 units would cost more than $100.

The slope of an isoquant equals the negative of the *marginal rate of substitution in production* between labor and tools, which is the ratio of their marginal products. (This explanation is similar to the definition in Appendix A in Chapter 10 of a buyer's *marginal rate of substitution* as the ratio of marginal benefits, or the absolute value of the slope of an indifference curve.) The firm minimizes its cost of production by choosing combinations of inputs so that the marginal rate of substitution in production equals the

Figure A1 | Isoquants

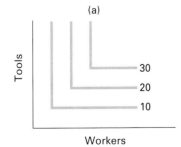
(a)

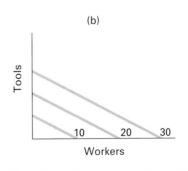
(b)

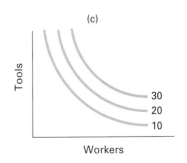
(c)

Each graph shows three isoquants; one for producing 10 goods per day, one for producing 20 goods per day, and one for producing 30 goods per day. In Panel (a), one worker and one tool are needed to produce 1 unit of output; tools and workers are perfect complements. In Panel (b), total output equals the number of tools plus twice the number of workers; tools and workers are perfect substitutes. In Panel (c), the normal case, tools and workers are neither perfect complements nor perfect substitutes.

Figure A2 | Economically Efficient Choices of Inputs

The straight line shows the combination of inputs that the firm can buy for $100. Its slope is the negative of the relative price of labor in terms of tools. Tangency at Point *A* between this isocost line and the 75-unit isoquant shows that the lowest-cost method of producing 75 units employs six workers and eight tools, and costs $100.

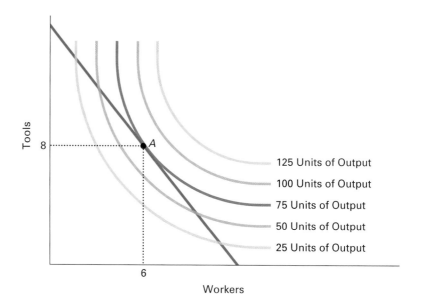

relative price of the inputs. This situation occurs at Point A in Figure A2, where the slope of the isocost line equals the slope of the isoquant. Changes in input prices cause changes in the slope of the straight line. For example, an increase in wages would make the line steeper, which would lead the firm to reduce labor and increase tools in production.

Problems

A1. Explain why isoquants cannot cross each other.

A2. How would isoquants between machines and workers change in response to these events:

   (a) Technical progress allows each machine to replace a larger number of workers.
   (b) The price of machines rises.
   (c) The average and marginal products of machines and workers all increase by 10 percent.

PART 5

COMPETITION AND STRATEGIC INTERACTIONS

CHAPTER 13

PERFECT COMPETITION

In this Chapter...

Main Points to Understand

- Certain economic conditions result when price-taking firms compete.

- Perfect competition leads to economic efficiency.

Thinking Skills to Develop

- Recognize the dynamic process of competition, and predict its consequences.

- Develop a deeper understanding of economic efficiency.

Everyone participates in some form of competition. Children compete for attention and toys; as people grow older, they compete for friends, for use of the family television and car, for victory in games and sports, for college admission, for good jobs, and for desirable spouses. Gas stations compete for customers, airlines compete for passengers, television networks compete for viewers, and colleges compete for students. Firms compete for customers by trying to offer lower prices, better quality, more selection or convenience, or other benefits that they think people want. The firms that most accurately anticipate and most fully satisfy the desires of customers at the lowest cost earn profits and survive the process of competition; other firms suffer losses and may go out of business.

Some people mistakenly believe that competition is the opposite of cooperation. Because cooperation is good, they reason, competition must be bad. The next few chapters will illustrate the confusion in that idea. Competition gives sellers an incentive to cooperate with buyers by providing the products that buyers want at the lowest possible prices. Competition does not replace cooperation; it channels and directs cooperation.

This chapter discusses the form of competition that characterizes (approximately) many farms and small businesses, including pizza parlors, gas stations, retail stores, computer and software vendors, interior decorating firms, investment firms, and so on. Competition promotes economic efficiency, often with dramatic results. Countries around the world where competition flourishes tend to enjoy high standards of living, while poverty tends to prevail in countries whose governments interfere with the process of competition, often to protect domestic firms from foreign rivals.

PRICE TAKERS

Chapter 4 defined *price takers* as buyers or sellers who can trade as much (or as little) of a good as they want at the equilibrium price, but whose transactions cannot affect that price. A price-taking firm faces a perfectly elastic demand curve for its product. It can sell as much as it wants at the equilibrium price, but it loses all its customers if it raises its price.

Elasticity of Demand for a Firm's Output

The elasticity of demand for the output of an individual firm is usually much higher than the elasticity of overall market demand for the product. Figure 1 shows the market demand curve for tomatoes in Panel (c) and the almost-perfectly-elastic demand curves facing two individual growers. Because each firm produces only a small fraction of total industry output, and because buyers do not care which firm's product they buy (since all tomatoes are perfect substitutes), each firm is approximately a price taker.

EXAMPLE

The elasticity of market demand for tomatoes is about ½, as Figure 1c shows. World output of tomatoes is about 20 million tons per year, grown on about 1 million acres of land. Sunny's 1,000-acre farm produces 20 tons of tomatoes per year (see Figure 1a), which is 1 one-millionth of world output. Suppose that Sunny's farm doubles its output of tomatoes. This 100-percent increase in Sunny's output raises world output by 0.0001 percent, from 20,000,000 tons to 20,000,020 tons. Since the elasticity of demand is ½, the equilibrium price falls by (0.0001/0.5) or 0.0002 percent, from $144.6000 per ton to $144.5997 per ton. Because the 100-percent increase in output on Sunny's farm reduces the price by only 0.0002 percent, the elasticity of demand for the tomatoes from that particular farm is 100/0.0002 = 500,000. Sunny's farm faces almost perfectly elastic demand.

Figure 1 | Approximate Price Taking

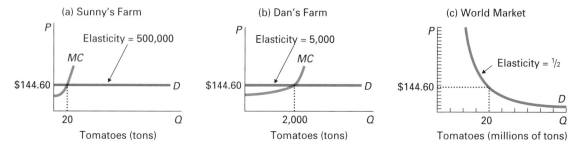

The elasticity of market demand is ½. Sunny's farm produces 1 one-millionth of world output, so it faces an elasticity of demand around 500,000. Dan's farm produces 1/10,000 of world output, so the elasticity of demand facing Dan's farm is about 5,000. Both Sunny and Dan are approximate price tak-

Dan's larger 100,000-acre farm produces 2,000 tons of tomatoes each year (see Figure 1b), or 1/10,000 of world output. If Dan's farm doubles its output, world output rises by 0.01 percent. Since the market elasticity of demand is ½, the equilibrium price falls by (0.01/0.5) or 0.02 percent, which is $0.0289 per ton. Dan's farm faces an elasticity of demand of 100/0.02 = 5,000. Dan's farm also faces almost perfectly elastic demand.

Competition is a process. It gives people incentives to innovate to achieve their goals. For example, two people competing for the same job promotion both have incentives to find new and improved ways to do their current jobs in the hope of getting promoted. Firms compete for customers by trying to provide the goods and services that people want at low prices and by looking for new ways to satisfy customers. This is the process of competition.

This chapter will focus on the results of this process. That is, it explores the equilibrium that results from the process of competition among price-taking sellers.

> **Perfect competition** means competition among price-taking sellers.

The model of perfect competition applies approximately when sellers are approximately price takers.

Short-Run Equilibrium with Perfect Competition

Figure 2 illustrates a short-run equilibrium with perfect competition. The graph shows the market demand and supply and the costs and outputs of two typical firms in the industry.

> In analyzing an equilibrium, the **short run** is a period over which the number of firms is fixed (though some firms may temporarily shut down production). The **long run** is a period over which the number of firms can change.

A firm may be a price taker in the long run, but not in the short run. In the early days of personal computers, for example, only a few firms manufactured and sold them. Each firm could raise its price without losing a large share of its customers; these firms were not price takers at the time. Since then, hundreds of firms have started manufacturing and selling personal computers, and most of them are now approximately price takers.

Figure 2c shows a market equilibrium price of $14.50 and a market equilibrium quantity of 240,000 units per week. Each firm takes the $14.50 price as given (a number that it cannot affect); it faces a perfectly elastic demand curve at that price. Each firm chooses output to maximize profit, so it produces the quantity at which its marginal cost equals its marginal revenue. Since marginal revenue equals the price, each firm chooses the quantity at which its marginal cost equals the price. For any price above the firm's average variable cost, its marginal cost curve is its supply curve.

The firm in Panel (a), Y.E.S., produces 600 units per week (1/400 of total industry output).[1] Its average cost of producing 600 units per week is $12.00, so it earns a $2.50 profit on each unit. Its markup or profit margin is $2.50.

> A firm's **markup** or **profit margin** is its price minus its average cost.

PERFECT COMPETITION

IN THE NEWS

Pizza makers slug it out for share of growing eat-at-home market

Source: The Wall Street Journal

Competition forces firms to try to provide the goods and services that customers want at the lowest price.

---

[1] If the elasticity of the market demand curve is 1, then Y.E.S. faces an elasticity of demand of about 400, so this firm is approximately a price taker.

Figure 2
Short-Run Equilibrium
with Perfect Competition

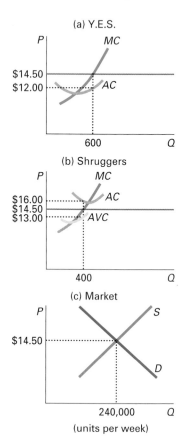

(a) Y.E.S.

P

MC

$14.50
$12.00

AC

600   Q

(b) Shruggers

P

MC

AC

$16.00
$14.50
$13.00

AVC

400   Q

(c) Market

P

S

$14.50

D

240,000   Q

(units per week)

(a) Y.E.S. earns a $2.50 profit margin, and it maximizes its total profit by producing 600 units. Its average cost of producing 600 units is $12.00, and it sells them for $14.50. (b) Shruggers takes a $1.50 loss on each unit it sells, because its average cost is $16.00, while the price is only $14.50. Shruggers stays in business because that price exceeds its average variable cost of $13.00. It minimizes its loss by producing 400 units.

Since Y.E.S. sells 600 units per week at a $2.50 markup per unit, its total profit is $1,500.00 per week.

The firm in Panel (b), Shruggers, has higher costs of production than Y.E.S. It minimizes its loss by producing 400 units per week (1/600 of industry output), but its average cost is $16.00, so it loses $1.50 on each unit it sells. Still, its average *variable* cost is only $13.00, because its total cost of production is $6,400.00, its total variable cost is $5,200.00, and its total fixed cost is $1,200.00. If Shruggers were to shut down production, it would lose $1,200.00 (its fixed cost); by producing 400 units per week, it cuts that loss to $600.00 per week ($1.50 per unit times 400 units). The price is higher than Shruggers' average variable cost, so it continues to produce.

Entrepreneurs

Why do some firms, like Y.E.S., earn profits while others, like Shruggers, lose money? Frequently, the difference is better entrepreneurial ability of some firms than others.

> An **entrepreneur** is a person who conceives and acts on a new business idea and takes the risk of its success or failure.

Profit is easier to study than to acquire. Costs of production and revenues from sales are not data that an owner or manager can find in a book. Firms must estimate costs and revenues under changing conditions and decide what, how, and how much to produce, taking the risk that their estimates will be wrong. Based on their guesses, an entrepreneur chooses how and when to start a firm, expand it, or shut its doors. Some people perform these tasks more effectively than others. Entrepreneurship involves not only discovering or inventing ideas, but also implementing them—not just dreaming, but also doing. In return for their work and the risks they take, entrepreneurs receive their firms' profits (or suffer the losses).

An entrepreneur is easy to identify in a small company. It is usually the person who

IN THE NEWS

Valentines came to this country as early as 1847, when a Worcester, Mass., woman, Esther Howland, became aware of her British cousin's use of Saint Valentine's Day as a commercial-printing bonanza.

In short order Howland set up an assembly line to produce Valentine cards. One of her staff glued paper flowers on the cards, another added lace. By 1850 Howland was doing a $100,000-a-year business.

The rest is history.

Not every invention is that successful, of course. Some are just plain wacky. Others are entirely practical but either aren't marketable or are ahead of their time.

Bathrooms seem to preoccupy many inventors. In Atlanta, Walter Hibbs's ex-wife used to complain that he didn't put down the seat after using the toilet. So he developed Seat Down, a hydraulic device that is attached to the seat of the toilet. Lifting the seat activates a timer that slowly closes the seat over two minutes, which Mr. Hibbs says is four times longer than the average man needs. The couple got a divorce anyway.

Sources: San Francisco Chronicle and The Wall Street Journal

Entrepreneurship is risky. Some projects succeed—and some fail.

IN THE NEWS

Day-care business lures entrepreneurs

Market growth, fragmentation spur ventures

By Lawrence Ingrassia
Staff Reporter of The Wall Street Journal

Day care is hot. Entrepreneurs, who once flocked into frozen yogurt or computer software, are now catering to kids. A half-dozen venture-capital firms have financed child-care start-ups recently.

And despite the presence of a few major child-care chains—led by Kinder-Care Inc. and La Petite Academy Inc.—no one dominates the business. There are an estimated 60,000 to 70,000 day-care centers nationwide. But only about a dozen companies operate more than 20 centers, and 90 percent of all for-profit companies in the field have fewer than five centers, according to Roger Neugebauer, publisher of Child Care Information Exchange, an industry magazine.

"It's very simple. You can make money where there's a market niche and growing demand," says an accountant who recently started a day-care center but doesn't want to be identified. Though the industry may be fragmented, competition is stiff because there are many nonprofit centers that charge lower fees. Start-up costs are steep—typically $150,000 to $300,000 per center. And salaries account for more than half of operating costs, but can't be cut much if things go wrong because of state rules setting maximum numbers of children per employee.

"Day care runs on a tight margin," says Cheri L. Sheridan, a day-care consultant in Silver Spring, Md.

Source: The Wall Street Journal

starts and runs the business. A larger company may include many entrepreneurs. The owners (stockholders) may act as entrepreneurs, since they receive the firm's profit or loss and choose the managers who run the company's daily activities. Managers and other workers may also be entrepreneurs, though. Their pay may depend on the firm's profit or loss, and its fortunes in the marketplace may depend on their ideas and implementation.

Review Questions

1. What is perfect competition?

2. What is an entrepreneur, and how does an entrepreneur collect payment?

Thinking Exercises

3. Explain why any one firm may face demand that is more elastic than the market demand for the product. How can a firm such as Y.E.S. in Figure 2 be approximately a price taker when the market demand curve slopes downward?

4. The elasticity of demand for breath mints is 2. If the industry is perfectly competitive and Mint-for-You produces $\frac{1}{25}$ of the industry's output, what is the elasticity of demand facing Mint-for-You?

LONG-RUN EQUILIBRIUM WITH PERFECT COMPETITION

In the long run, firms that continually suffer losses go out of business or drop their unprofitable products; they exit the industries that produce those losses. New firms enter an industry to capture potential profits, sometimes replacing other firms that generated profits in the short run but cannot avoid losses in the long run.

> **Entry** into an industry means that a firm begins producing and selling that industry's product; **exit** from an industry means that a firm stops selling that product.

Economic profits or losses, not the accounting measures of profit or loss, guide firms' decisions on entry and exit. The transition from short-run equilibrium to long-run equilibrium is a dynamic process, during which old firms may die and be replaced by new firms with lower costs. This process requires free entry and exit.

> **Free entry** means that no legal barriers prevent a firm from entering an industry. **Free exit** means that no legal barriers prevent a firm from exiting the industry.

Many industries in the United States and other developed countries allow free entry of new competitors. Laws or government regulations prevent free entry in some industries, however, such as first-class mail delivery, taxi-cab services, and cable television.

When new firms enter an industry, the goods they produce add to the total quantity supplied, shifting the short-run market supply curve to the right, as in Figure 3a. This change reduces the equilibrium price from P_1 to P_2, which reduces the profits that all producers earn. Positive economic profits in an industry give new firms an incentive to enter, tending to reduce profits. Similarly, when firms exit an industry, the total quantity supplied falls. The short-run market supply curve shifts to the left, as in Figure 3b, raising

---

IN THE NEWS

Dental hygienists seek to start practices on their own—raising the ire of dentists

By Rhonda L. Rundle
Staff Reporter of The Wall Street Journal

Judy Boothby, a dental hygienist in Sacramento, Calif., invested $10,000 in a van and portable equipment so she could make house calls as part of an experimental state project begun earlier this year.

Source: The Wall Street Journal

But the van is now parked and locked. By raising questions about the legality of the service, she says, some local dentists are scaring away her clients, many of which are nursing homes.

Mrs. Boothby's venture is mired in a struggle over the proper role of hygienists in dental care. Besides cleaning teeth, hygienists often take X-rays and give fluoride treatments. They usually work for dentists, but some of them—like Mrs. Boothby—want to go into business for themselves. The idea has dentists gnashing their teeth.

Restrictions sometimes hinder attempts to enter an industry.

Figure 3 | Effects of Entry and Exit

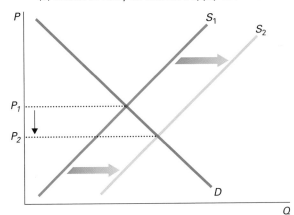

(a) Effects of Entry on Market Supply and Price

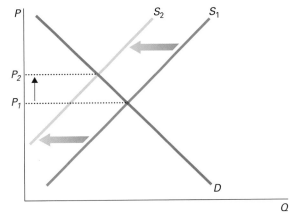

(b) Effects of Exit on Market Supply and Price

(a) As new firms enter an industry, short-run market supply increases and the price falls.
(b) As firms exit an industry, short-run market supply decreases and the price rises.

the equilibrium price from P_1 to P_2, which raises the profits of remaining firms. Negative economic profits give firms an incentive to exit the industry, tending to raise profits.

Entry and exit create a tendency for positive economic profits to fall and for negative economic profits to rise. In long-run equilibrium, entry and exit has already occurred until no further incentives induce firms to enter or exit.

> **Long-run equilibrium** occurs when no firm has an incentive to enter or exit an industry.

Case 1—All Firms Have the Same Costs

Suppose that all firms in an industry have the same costs of production. New firms have an incentive to enter this industry whenever they expect to earn positive economic profit. Similarly, current competitors have an incentive to exit the industry in the long run if their economic profit is negative. As a result, long-run equilibrium occurs when each firm earns zero economic profit.

> If all firms have the same costs of production, then each firm's economic profit is *zero* in long-run equilibrium.

Why do firms with zero economic profits stay in business? A firm that earns zero economic profit pays its owners enough income to cover their opportunity costs. The owners would not gain by shutting down the firm and doing something else; they cannot find a better opportunity than to keep the firm in business.

Figure 4 shows a long-run equilibrium with perfect competition. Panel (d) shows the market equilibrium price, $11, and the market equilibrium quantity, 360,000 units per week. Each individual firm faces a perfectly elastic demand curve at the $11 equilibrium price, so it chooses output to maximize its profit by producing the quantity at which its marginal cost *(MC)* equals the price. The figure also shows each firm's long-run average cost curve *(LRAC)*.

Figure 4 | Long-Run Equilibrium with Perfect Competition

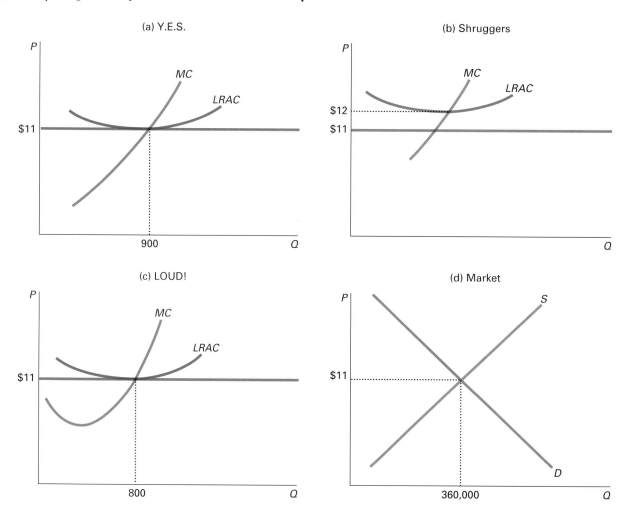

Y.E.S. produces 900 units of the good in long-run equilibrium. Its long-run average cost of $11 equals the price, so Y.E.S. earns zero economic profit. A new firm named LOUD! has entered the industry and produces 800 units in long-run equilibrium. Its long-run average cost is also $11, and its economic profit is zero. Shruggers has exited the industry because its lowest long-run average cost of $12 exceeds the $11 long-run equilibrium price.

Figure 4a shows that Y.E.S. has survived competition and produces 900 units of the good per week in long-run equilibrium. At its long-run average cost of $11, it earns zero economic profit. Its accounting statements might show a positive profit, though. For example, records might show a profit of $2,700 per week (a profit margin of $3 on each of the 900 units it sells), but that figure indicates accounting profit, not economic profit. As Chapter 11 explained, accounting profit includes payments to the firm's owners to cover the opportunity costs of their time, money, and willingness to bear risk. Since Y.E.S. has zero economic profit, it earns a normal (accounting) profit.

> A **normal (accounting) profit** is the level of accounting profit required for a zero economic profit.

A firm earns a normal accounting profit if its economic profit is zero.

Figure 4b shows that Shruggers has exited the industry. Shruggers operated unprofitably because its long-run average cost exceeded the $11 long-run equilibrium price, no matter how much it produced. Less efficient firms like Shruggers (firms with higher costs than their competitors) do not always survive competition in the long run.

Figure 4c shows a new firm named LOUD! has entered the industry and maximizes profit by producing 800 units per week. Its long-run average cost of $11 gives it an economic profit of zero. LOUD! may report a higher (or lower) accounting profit than Y.E.S. if its accounting statements show lower (or higher) costs, but this difference means only that its implicit costs are higher (or lower) than those at Y.E.S.

Figure 5 shows the short-run and long-run average cost curves for Y.E.S. In the short-run equilibrium (see Figure 2), Y.E.S. produced 600 units per week. Its average cost curve was $SRAC_1$, shown in Figure 5, and its average cost of production was $12. In the long run, Y.E.S. expanded its operation. It expanded its factory, purchased additional machinery and equipment, and hired and trained new workers. This shifted its short-run average cost curve to $SRAC_2$. Y.E.S. had to expand to survive competition, because new entry into the industry reduced the price from $14.50 to $11.00. In the long run, Y.E.S. produces 900 units per week, which minimizes its long-run average cost at $11.00.

Case 2—Firms Have Different Costs

Suppose some firms can produce more efficiently than other firms, giving them lower average costs. The relatively efficient firms earn positive economic profits in long-run equilibrium.

Not every firm that suffers a short-run loss (like Shruggers) must exit the industry in the long run. Some firms may experience short-run losses because they are too small (or too large) to keep their average costs of production low enough to earn short-run profits. In the long run, however, these firms can adjust. They can expand by acquiring new machinery and equipment and hiring and training new workers or shrink by selling machinery and equipment and making other changes to reduce costs. Figure 6 shows a new firm, Wetlands, that suffered a loss in the short run but managed to reduce its average cost in the long run by expanding, as Y.E.S. did. Unlike Shruggers, Wetlands reduced its cost low enough (to $11 or less) to stay in business in the long run.

IN THE NEWS

The Weyerhaeuser example

The Weyerhaeuser Company illustrates the point. This highly profitable wood and paper-products company reported a net income of $276.7 million last year.

That profit, however, represented only a 5.8 percent return on the billions of dollars the company had spent to build or purchase its network of paper mills and sawmills, its vast array of high-technology machinery, its forests, and its many other assets.

At this rate of return, Weyerhaeuser could have earned more money if it had sold off all those holdings and invested the proceeds in Treasury notes or bonds, which paid above 7 percent last year.

Source: New York Times

The opportunity cost of investing in new capital, such as paper mills, sawmills, machinery, and forests, is the interest that a firm could have earned on other investments. This is part of the firm's implicit costs. In this case, Weyerhaeuser had an accounting profit, but an economic loss, because it could have earned more money investing in Treasury notes.

Figure 5 | Y.E.S. Expands in the Long Run

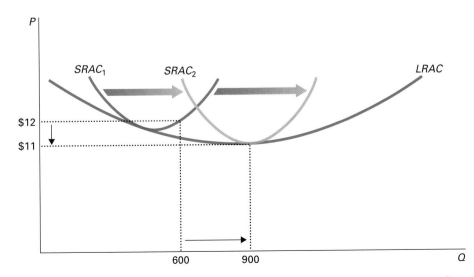

Y.E.S. builds a new factory with additional capacity, shifting its short-run average cost curve from $SRAC_1$ to $SRAC_2$ and reducing its average cost to $11.

In the original short-run equilibrium, Wetlands' short-run average cost curve is $SRAC_1$, and its marginal cost curve is MC_1. It produces 200 units in the short run at a price of $14.50. Its average cost is $16.00, so it takes a $1.50 loss on each good it produces. Wetlands expands in the long run, however, so its new short-run average cost curve is $SRAC_2$, and its new marginal cost curve is MC_2. In long-run equilibrium, it produces 1,000 units and earns a $1 profit (economic rent).

Figure 6 | Wetlands Expands and Eliminates Its Short-Run Loss

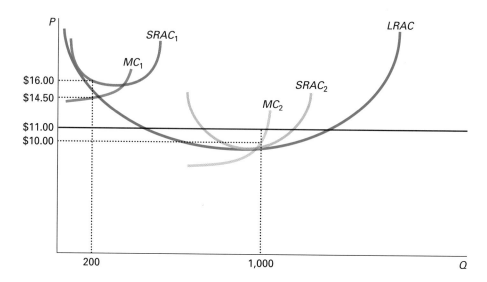

As Figure 6 shows, Wetlands reduced its long-run average cost of production below $11 by producing more efficiently than any other firm. In long-run equilibrium, Wetlands produces 1,000 units at an average cost of only $10 and earns a $1-per-unit economic profit in long-run equilibrium.

> If some firms have lower average costs of production than other firms, they earn positive economic profits in long-run equilibrium.

Economic Rents

How could a firm produce at a lower average cost than other firms? Perhaps its owner motivates workers more effectively than owners of other firms do. Perhaps the firm owns some unique resource that no other firm can acquire. For example, if it owns the only natural source of water in a desert, its cost of providing water to people there is lower than the costs of firms that transport water from other locations. Whatever the reason, its positive economic profit results from the special input—such as a superior owner-manager or other unique resource—that reduces the firm's costs below the costs of other firms. Economists often use the term *economic rent* for the economic profit created by such an input.

Review Questions

5. What happens to the price of a good when new firms enter an industry? Why?

6. What is a normal accounting profit?

Thinking Exercises

7. Explain why firms earn zero economic profit in long-run equilibrium with perfect competition, if all firms have the same costs. Why does a firm with zero economic profit stay in business?

8. Explain why a firm with a unique input could earn a positive economic profit (economic rent) in long-run equilibrium with perfect competition. Why don't other firms enter the industry in this case? What economic profits do *other* firms in the industry earn in long-run equilibrium?

LONG-RUN SUPPLY CURVES

Figures 7 and 8 show two possible shapes for long-run market supply curves: perfectly elastic curves and rising curves.

Perfectly Elastic Long-Run Supply

The long-run market supply curve is perfectly elastic, as in Figure 7, if many firms have the same long-run cost of producing the good and their costs do not depend on the total output of the industry. In this situation, an increase in demand raises the number of firms in the industry, but it does not change the price or the quantity that each firm produces.

> **EXAMPLE**

Suppose that many firms can produce flashlights at an average cost of $3 each if they produce 10,000 flashlights per month, so that many firms have the long-run average cost curve in Figure 7. Even though each firm has an upward-sloping supply (marginal cost) curve, as the figure shows, the long-run market supply of flashlights is perfectly elastic

Figure 7 | Perfectly Elastic Long-Run Market Supply: A Constant-Cost Industry

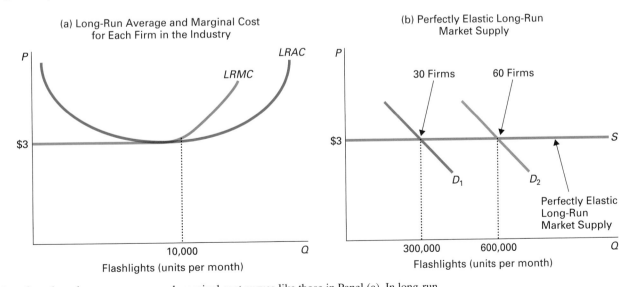

Many firms have long-run average and marginal cost curves like those in Panel (a). In long-run equilibrium, the price is $3 per flashlight and each firm earns zero economic profit by producing 10,000 flashlights per month. Even though each firm has an upward-sloping supply (marginal cost) curve, the long-run market supply of flashlights is perfectly elastic at the price $3. The number of firms in the industry depends on demand. If demand is D_1, the industry includes 30 firms in long-run equilibrium. If demand is D_2, the industry includes 60 firms.

Figure 8 | Upward-Sloping Long-Run Market Supply: An Increasing-Cost Industry

The long-run market supply curve slopes upward in an increasing-cost industry. In long-run equilibrium, the number of firms depends on demand. If the demand curve is D_1, the industry includes 20 firms. If the demand curve is D_2, it includes 35 firms.

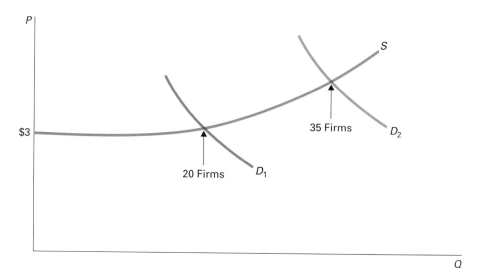

at the price $3. If the price is higher than $3, flashlight producers earn positive economic profits, and new firms enter the flashlight industry. These new entrants raise the quantity supplied and reduce the price back to $3 in long-run equilibrium. If the price is lower than $3, losses lead some firms to exit the industry, which reduces the quantity supplied and raises the price back to $3. In long-run equilibrium, each firm produces 10,000 flashlights per month, and the number of firms in the industry depends on demand. If the demand curve is D_1, with a quantity demanded of 300,000 flashlights per month at the $3 equilibrium price, then the industry includes 30 firms in long-run equilibrium. If the demand curve is D_2, with a quantity demanded of 600,000 units per month at the $3 price, then the industry includes 60 firms. Entry and exit maintain a perfectly elastic long-run supply curve. Industries like this are called *constant-cost industries*.

> A **constant-cost industry** is an industry with a perfectly elastic long-run market supply curve.

Rising Long-Run Supply

In an increasing-cost industry, the long-run market supply curve slopes upward, as in Figure 8. An industry may experience increasing costs for two reasons. First, each firm's average cost may depend on total output in the industry. Every ocean-front hotel requires ocean-front property as an input, but the fixed quantity of ocean-front property acts as a constraint. As more firms enter the ocean-front hotel industry, the demand for ocean-front land rises, driving up its price. This raises the cost of producing an ocean-front hotel. Since the average cost of producing an ocean-front hotel rises with total industry output, the long-run market supply curve slopes upward. The equilibrium number of firms in an increasing-cost industry depends on demand. If the demand curve is D_1 in Figure 8, the industry includes 20 firms in long-run equilibrium. If the demand curve is D_2, the industry includes 35 firms.

> An **increasing-cost industry** is an industry with an upward-sloping long-run market supply curve.

Figure 9 | Upward-Sloping Long-Run Supply Curve When Some Firms Have Lower Average Costs than Others

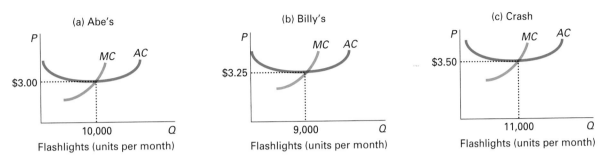

If the equilibrium price is $3.00, only firms like Abe's compete. If the price is $3.25, firms like Billy's enter the industry, and some inputs at firms like Abe's earn economic rents. If the equilibrium price is $3.50, firms like Crash also enter the industry, and certain inputs at firms like Abe's and Billy's earn economic rents.

A second reason for increasing costs concerns industries in which some firms have lower costs than others. In Figure 9, Abe's can produce flashlights at an average cost of $3.00 each. However, Abe's might be one of only a few firms with such low costs. Other firms might have higher costs; for example, Billy's can produce at a minimum average cost of $3.25, and Crash can produce at a minimum average cost of $3.50. If equilibrium industry output is sufficiently low, then only firms like Abe's produce in this industry. At higher equilibrium levels of output, higher-cost firms like Billy's and Crash enter the industry. Because they have higher average costs, the long-run supply curve slopes upward as they enter. With firms like Billy's and Crash in the industry, Abe's earns a positive economic profit (economic rent) in long-run equilibrium.

An industry's costs determine the short-run and long-run effects of a change in demand on the equilibrium number of firms and output of each firm. Suppose an industry has constant costs, giving it a perfectly elastic long-run supply curve. Then a fall in demand reduces the equilibrium quantity, but not the price. If each firm has a U-shaped average cost curve, as in Figure 7, the long-run fall in quantity results entirely from a fall in the number of firms in the industry, without any change in output per firm. Each firm continues to produce the quantity at the lowest point on its long-run average cost curve.

In an industry with increasing costs, a fall in demand reduces both the quantity and the price. In the long run, the fall in quantity results from both a fall in the number of firms in the industry and a fall in output per firm. Figure 10 shows the effect of a fall in demand in an increasing-cost industry. In the short run, the price falls from $10 (at Point A) to $6, and all firms reduce output (Point B). Some firms, those whose average variable costs exceed $6, immediately exit the industry. Other firms may continue to produce, but suffer losses. The most efficient firms earned economic profits before the fall in demand (due to economic rents to their unique inputs); after the change, they earn lower profits. In the long run, more firms go out of business, and equilibrium moves to Point C. The quantity supplied falls, and the price rises from $6 to $8. This price increase helps some of the firms that suffered losses in the short run (at the $6 price) to stay in the industry in the long run and earn zero economic profits at the $8 price. Firms that exit the industry are those that would suffer losses even at a price of $8, that is, the firms

FROM THE SHORT RUN TO THE LONG RUN

Figure 10 | Effects of a Fall in Demand

The fall in demand moves the equilibrium from Point A to Point B in the short run and to Point C in the long run.

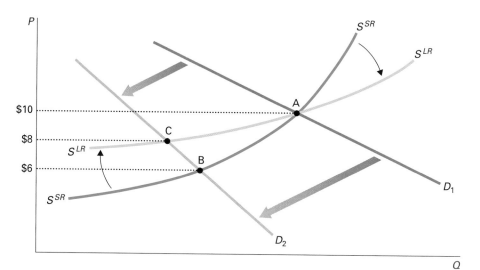

whose lowest average costs exceed $8 in the long run. Firms that stay in business are the relatively efficient ones that can earn at least zero economic profits at a price of $8, that is, firms whose lowest average costs are less than or equal to $8 in the long run.

Review Questions

9. What is a constant-cost industry? What is an increasing-cost industry?

10. Explain how a fall in demand affects the price, total output, and number of firms in an increasing-cost industry.

Thinking Exercise

11. Explain how an *increase* in demand affects the price, total output, and number of firms in (a) a constant-cost industry and (b) an increasing-cost industry.

WHAT IS PERFECT ABOUT PERFECT COMPETITION?

Under certain conditions, the equilibrium quantity with perfect competition is economically efficient.[2] It may seem obvious that equilibrium is economically efficient whenever people trade voluntarily. After all, if a situation is not economically efficient, people can share the gains from changing that situation. They could get together and find a Pareto-improving change. Because people would do this voluntarily, you might think that voluntary trading always creates economic efficiency.

---

[2]One important condition for this result is that no externalities affect the situation. Essentially, this requirement means that the producer of a good must pay *all* the costs of producing it, and the people who buy the good must receive *all* of its benefits. This condition is often violated in cases where firms pollute the air or water when they produce. See Chapter 20. The efficiency result also requires a few technical conditions that fall outside the scope of this book.

In fact, things are not quite this simple. For example, many small retail stores have gone out of business in recent years because they could not compete with Wal-Mart and various wholesale clubs. The voluntary trades between Wal-Mart and its customers suggest that each side expects to gain. How do we know that the gains to Wal-Mart and its customers exceed the losses to the small stores that went out of business and their customers? Remarkably, logic can provide an answer to this question under conditions of perfect competition. Perfect competition leads to an economically efficient equilibrium. Perfect competition creates losers, but their losses are always smaller than the gains to successful sellers and to buyers.[3]

Equilibrium with perfect competition achieves economic efficiency because it equates the marginal benefit of a good to the economy with its marginal cost. Each equals the good's price. The economy faces tradeoffs between producing food and cars, health-care services and video games, education and houses. People also face tradeoffs between buying these goods; they can spend more money on food and less on cars, or vice versa.

> In equilibrium with perfect competition, the economy makes the tradeoffs that consumers desire, as revealed by their willingness to pay for various goods.

Figure 11 shows the economy's production possibilities frontier (PPF) for producing T-shirts and hamburgers, as discussed in Chapter 3. The absolute value of the slope of the PPF shows the economy's tradeoff between producing T-shirts and hamburgers. It shows the economy's opportunity cost of producing T-shirts, measured in terms of hamburgers. If the economy produces the combination of goods at Point A, the production tradeoff is 4 hamburgers per T-shirt. That is, the economy can produce 1 additional T-shirt per month by producing 4 fewer hamburgers. On the other hand, if the economy produces the combination of goods at Point B, the production tradeoff is 6 hamburgers per T-shirt. That is, the economy can produce 1 more T-shirt if it produces 6 fewer hamburgers.

This production tradeoff between T-shirts and hamburgers equals the economy's marginal cost of producing T-shirts, measured in terms of hamburgers. With perfect competition, firms produce quantities at which marginal cost equals price. In other words, they choose Point A if the relative price of T-shirts is 4 hamburgers per T-shirt, and they choose Point B if the relative price is 6 hamburgers per T-shirt.

Suppose that consumers prefer the combination of hamburgers and T-shirts shown by Point A to all other possible combinations. Then Point A is the economically efficient point for the economy, *and* it is the long-run equilibrium with perfect competition. At Point A, the tradeoff between production of T-shirts and hamburgers is exactly the tradeoff that consumers want to make. In contrast, at Point B (or any other point on the curve) consumers' and producers' tradeoffs differ. At Point B, the producers' tradeoff (6 hamburgers for 1 T-shirt) is higher than the tradeoff that consumers want to make. Buyers may be willing to sacrifice up to 4 hamburgers for one T-shirt, but at Point B the economy sacrifices 6 hamburgers for each T-shirt it produces. At Point B, the economy would produce too many T-shirts and too few hamburgers. Similarly, at a point on the curve above Point A, the economy would produce too few T-shirts and too many hamburgers.

The prices that consumers are willing to pay inform producers about the tradeoffs that consumers want to make. At Point A in Figure 11, the relative price of T-shirts equals the rate at which buyers are willing to trade hamburgers for T-shirts. Firms choose levels of output at which the relative price of T-shirts equals the marginal cost of producing them. Relative prices adjust to guarantee that the economy makes the production tradeoffs that consumers want.

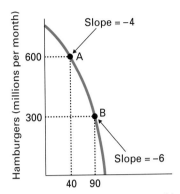

Figure 11
Perfect Competition Is Economically Efficient

The economy's production possibilities frontier shows possible combinations of output. In equilibrium with perfect competition, the economy produces the combination that consumers most prefer.

IN THE NEWS

Expect competition and be prepared for it

If you are the first to come up with a great idea for a product or service, you might have the market to yourself for a couple of years. After that, though, you must assume that your success will attract others to the field.

Source: The Wall Street Journal

The first firms in an industry may earn profits, which attract new firms to enter and the resulting increase in supply eventually reduces the price and each firm's profits.

---

[3]The proof of this fact is actually a deep mathematical theorem that far exceeds the scope of this book. The following chapters will discuss conditions of competition in which outcomes are *not* economically efficient.

In equilibrium with perfect competition:

▶ The relative price of each good equals the tradeoff that consumers are willing to make to buy that good.

▶ The relative price of each good also equals the tradeoff in production, that is, the marginal cost of producing the good, measured in terms of other goods.

▶ The tradeoff that consumers want to make equals the tradeoff that the economy can make to produce the goods.

EXPLANATION

Why is the tradeoff that consumers are *willing* to make equal to the tradeoff that the economy *can* make? To answer this question, suppose that these tradeoffs are *not equal*. Then the situation is not economically efficient. The situation could be *changed* in an economically efficient way. For example, suppose that people are willing to trade one T-shirt for 4 hamburgers, but the economy's actual tradeoff in production is one T-shirt for 6 hamburgers, as at Point B in Figure 11. What economically efficient change could the economy make? Economic efficiency would improve if the economy were to produce six more hamburgers and one less T-shirt. Consumers would give up that T-shirt in return for four hamburgers, so they would be no better off or worse off with one less T-shirt and four more hamburgers. However, this change leaves 2 *extra* hamburgers, so someone can gain from this change in production without anyone else losing. That is, the change would be Pareto efficient (see Chapter 9). Whenever the tradeoff that the economy *can* make differs from the tradeoff that consumers *want* to make, there are economically efficient *changes* that could be made. Equilibrium with perfect competition is economically efficient because it equates these tradeoffs.

The economic efficiency of equilibrium under perfect competition is a formal statement of the proposition advanced by Adam Smith in his 1776 book *The Wealth of Nations*. Smith argued that competition and voluntary exchange in free markets automatically coordinate people's activities to promote general welfare:

> Every individual . . . neither intends to promote the general interest, nor knows how much he is promoting it. He intends only his own security, his own gain. And he is in this led by an invisible hand to promote an end which was no part of his intention. By pursuing his own interest he frequently promotes that of society more effectually than when he really intends to promote it.[4]

Economists in the 20th century have proved a very strong version of Smith's *invisible hand* proposition: Not only do people "frequently promote" the interests of society when they pursue their own gains through trade in free markets, but (under certain conditions) perfect competition leads to an economically efficient equilibrium.

Review Questions

12. How does Figure 11 show the economy's opportunity cost of producing T-shirts?

13. What was the name of Adam Smith's famous book? What did Smith say relating to the economic efficiency of equilibrium?

---

[4]Adam Smith, *The Wealth of Nations* (Chicago: University of Chicago Press, 1976), pp. 477–478.

14. Explain why equilibrium with perfect competition equates the tradeoff that consumers want to make between any two goods and the tradeoff that the economy can make in producing those goods.

15. Explain why equilibrium with perfect competition is economically efficient.

C o n c l u s i o n

Price Takers

A price-taking firm faces a perfectly elastic demand curve for its output. Its marginal revenue equals its price. Its short-run supply curve is the portion of its marginal cost curve above its average variable cost curve. Its long-run supply curve is the portion of its marginal cost curve above its average total cost curve. When consumers don't care which firm produces a good, a firm that produces only a small fraction of total industry output is approximately a price taker.

Perfect Competition

Perfect competition is competition between price-taking firms. Short-run equilibrium with perfect competition refers to equilibrium with a fixed number of firms in the industry. Long-run equilibrium with perfect competition refers to equilibrium when the number of firms can change. In short-run equilibrium, some firms may have lower costs and higher profits than other firms. Costs differ across firms for many reasons. Some firms benefit from better entrepreneurial abilities than others. Entrepreneurs are people who conceive and act on new business ideas, taking the risk that their efforts will succeed or fail.

Long-Run Equilibrium with Perfect Competition

Firms with negative economic profits (losses) eventually exit an industry. Long-run equilibrium occurs when no firms have further incentives to enter or exit the industry. Entry and exit create a tendency for positive economic profits to fall or for negative economic profits to rise. If all firms have the same costs, economic profits are zero in long-run equilibrium. Firms earn a normal accounting profit, that is, the accounting profit that reflects a zero economic profit. If some firm has lower costs than others because it has a unique input, then it earns a positive economic profit (economic rent to the unique input) in long-run equilibrium.

Long-Run Supply Curves

A constant-cost industry is an industry with a perfectly elastic long-run supply curve. Each firm in an industry may have an upward-sloping supply curve, but the industry supply curve is perfectly elastic if all firms have the same average cost curve and each firm's average cost does not depend on total industry output. Total output in a constant-cost industry rises or falls with changes in the number of firms, each of which produces the quantity that minimizes its average cost. If firms do not have the same average cost curve or each firm's average cost depends on total industry output, then the long-run supply curve may slope upward and the industry has increasing costs.

From the Short Run to the Long Run

A fall in demand in a constant-cost industry reduces output and the number of firms in the industry in the long run without changing the price or output at each firm. In the short run, the price may fall and firms may incur losses, leading some to exit the industry. A fall in demand in an increasing-cost industry reduces the price, which reduces economic profits (economic rents) at some firms, creates losses at other firms, and leads some firms to exit the industry. In the long run, output falls through a combination of a reduction in the number of firms in the industry and a fall in output per firm. Firms with low costs survive, while higher-cost firms exit.

What Is Perfect about Perfect Competition?

Under certain conditions, the equilibrium quantity with perfect competition (and *only* that quantity) is economically efficient. Equilibrium is economically efficient because it equates the marginal benefit of a good to the economy with its marginal cost. Each equals the price. This equality means that the economy makes the production tradeoffs that consumers want to make, as revealed by their willingness to pay. In equilibrium with perfect competition, the relative price of each good equals both the tradeoff that consumers are willing to make when they buy the good and the marginal cost of producing the good. Whenever the tradeoff the economy can make differs from the tradeoff that consumers want to make, the situation is economically inefficient. Equilibrium with perfect competition is economically efficient because it equates these two tradeoffs.

Key Terms

perfect competition

short-run equilibrium

long-run equilibrium

markup (or profit margin)

entrepreneur

entry and exit

free entry and exit

long-run equilibrium

normal (accounting) profit

constant-cost industry

increasing-cost industry

Problems

16. Suppose that the elasticity of market demand for computers equals 1, and Cool Technologies produces 1 of every 1,000 computers. Suppose Cool Technologies then doubles its output of computers. If all computers are alike, regardless of who produces them,
    (a) By what percentage will the price of computers fall?
    (b) What is the elasticity of demand for computers produced by Cool Technologies?

17. Suppose that new firms enter a perfectly competitive industry. Draw a graph to show the effects on the market supply curve, the price, the demand curve facing each firm, and the output of a typical firm. Repeat the same analysis for a situation in which firms exit an industry.

18. Discuss two reasons for increasing costs in an industry.

19. Draw a graph to help discuss the short-run and long-run effects on the price, total industry output, and the number of firms in the industry of:
    (a) An increase in demand in a constant-cost industry
    (b) An increase in demand in an increasing-cost industry

20. Suppose that the government forces all firms competing in an industry at the beginning of the current year to pay a one-time, $10,000 fine. How does this fine affect industry output, the price, and the number of firms? Explain.

Inquiries for Further Thought

21. In which of the following industries do you think sellers are approximately price takers? Why?
    (a) Aspirin and other pain relievers
    (b) Ice
    (c) Valentine cards
    (d) Gasoline
    (e) Donuts
    (f) Movies
    (g) Jeans
    (h) Antiques
    (i) Videotape rentals
    (j) Houses
    (k) Auto repair
    (l) Candy
    (m) Breakfast cereals

22. The government restricts entry into some industries, sometimes by laws and regulations that directly prevent entry and other times by requiring sellers to pay certain costs (such as license fees) to enter.
    (a) How do restrictions on entry into an industry affect the price, total output of the good, and output per firm?
    (b) What would be the effects of restricting entry into the fast-food industry?
    (c) What would be the effects of removing restrictions on entry into the prescription-drug dispensing industry?

IN THE NEWS

Doctors stir controversy by selling drugs directly to their patients . . .

By Rhonda L. Rundle
Staff Reporter of The Wall
Street Journal

The $20-billion market in prescription-drug sales has some new players, a group of competitors that pharmacists are finding impossible to ignore.

Although the practice is still unusual, increasing numbers of doctors are selling drugs directly to patients. The trend alarms many pharmacists.

Benefits for Patients

For patients, the change appears to offer several immediate benefits. Buying drugs from a doctor might mean fewer trips to the pharmacy and less standing in line for prescriptions. Patients might also save money.

Arguments about doctors dispensing drugs are usually couched in terms of patient care, but there is no doubt that the economic stakes are high. At some walk-in care centers with large staffs of doctors, annual profits from drug sales can run into six figures.

Source: The Wall Street Journal

See Question 22.

CHAPTER 14

MONOPOLY

In this Chapter . . .

Main Points to Understand

▶ A monopoly produces a quantity at which marginal cost equals marginal revenue, and charges the highest price at which it can sell that quantity.

▶ Monopolies create economic inefficiency.

▶ Sellers sometimes collude to raise prices, though collusion usually fails in the long run.

▶ Monopoly sellers can sometimes profit by charging different prices to different customers.

Thinking Skills to Develop

▶ Recognize the causes of monopoly, their incentives, and the long-run limits they face.

▶ Formulate and criticize arguments about government policy on monopoly.

Monopoly—the word connotes power and its abuse, a failure of competition, rich corporations exploiting workers and buyers. Many years ago, the U.S. government passed laws to tame monopolies, limit their powers, or break them up into smaller firms. What are monopolies and what do they do? What logic drives their behavior?

Loosely, a monopoly is the only seller of some product. More precisely:

> A firm is a **monopoly** if it (a) faces a downward-sloping demand curve for its product and (b) makes decisions without considering the reactions of other firms.

The first condition means that a monopoly is *not* a price taker; it can raise its price without losing all its customers, and it must reduce its price to increase sales. The second condition means that the monopoly can ignore the possibility that its decisions will cause some competing firm to change its price in a way that shifts the monopoly's demand curve. (See Chapters 16 and 17 for further discussion of this point.)

INTRODUCTION TO MONOPOLIES

The U.S. Postal Service has a monopoly on first-class mail delivery.

IN THE NEWS

In free rein of cable TV, fees are up

Moreover, most areas that have cable television are served by only one company, so there is no direct competition to restrain prices.

Pricing Like Monopolies

"In a monopoly situation, they are pricing like monopolies," said Nicholas Miller, a partner in the law firm of Miller, Young & Holbrook, which represents many municipalities on cable issues.

Source: New York Times

Most local cable television companies are monopolies.

EXAMPLES

The post office and most local telephone, cable television, gas, electric, and water companies are approximately monopolies. Microsoft has a near monopoly on operating systems for personal computers. Other firms have had monopolies on products they invented such as aluminum foil, photocopying machines, and various medications.

KEY EXAMPLE

Loretta catches fish and sells them on a street corner in town. Today she has eight fish to sell, and she is the only person in town who sells fish. Figure 1 shows the demand curve for her fish. She can sell all eight fish if she charges $1 per fish, seven fish if she charges $2 per fish, and so on. If she charges $8, she sells only one fish.

Does Loretta maximize her profit by selling all eight fish? Figure 1 shows that selling all eight fish at a price of $1 gives her total revenue of only $8. In contrast, she earns total revenue of $20 by charging $4 or $5 per fish, in which case people buy only five or four of her eight fish. She is actually better off throwing away the other fish than selling them.

Since she has *already* caught the fish, Loretta's marginal cost is *zero* (ignoring the time she spends on the street corner). The time she spent at the lake catching the fish is now a *sunk cost* that does not affect her rational choice about how many fish to sell today, though it will affect her choice of how many fish to catch tomorrow, as a later discussion will explain. Figure 1 also shows Loretta's marginal revenue. She maximizes profit by choosing the quantity (five fish) at which her marginal revenue equals her marginal cost (zero).

Loretta sells one fish if she charges $8 each and two fish if she charges $7 each. Why is her marginal revenue of selling the second fish only $6? The answer is important: *To sell to another customer, a seller usually must lower the price to* ALL *customers*. If Loretta charges $8, one customer buys a fish. To sell two fish, she must reduce the price to $7. She then gains $7 by selling the second fish, but loses $1 that she could have earned on the first fish (because she charges only $7 instead of $8). Therefore, her marginal revenue from selling the second fish, only $6, is less than the $7 price.

The same argument applies to larger quantities. To sell three fish, Loretta must charge only $6, so she gains $6 from the sale of the third fish but loses $2 because she

Figure 1 | Loretta's Demand and Marginal Revenue

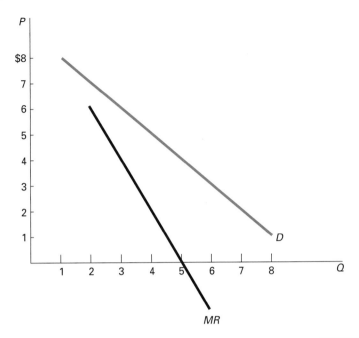

Loretta maximizes revenue by selling five fish at $4 each. Since her marginal cost is zero, this is the quantity at which marginal revenue equals marginal cost.

Price	Quantity of Fish Sold	Total Revenue	Marginal Revenue
$8	1	$ 8	$ 8
7	2	14	6
6	3	18	4
5	4	20	2
4	5	20	0
3	6	18	−2
2	7	14	−4
1	8	8	−6

sells the first two fish for only $6 each rather than $7 each. Therefore, her marginal revenue is only $4, less than the $6 price. Figure 2 shows how selling another unit causes both an increase in revenue equal to the price and a loss in revenue from lowering the price to buyers who would otherwise have paid a higher price. Loretta earns a higher profit by charging $4, selling five fish, and throwing out three fish, than by selling all her fish—because if she sold more than five, she would have to reduce the price and earn a lower profit on the first five fish.

What if Loretta could charge different prices to different customers? She might charge $4 and sell five fish to the customers who would pay that much, and *then* reduce the price so that *other* customers would buy her other fish. Instead of throwing out the last three fish, she could sell them for $1 each and raise her profit by $3. If she were to try this, however, her customers might wait until she reduced the price before buying their fish, so she might not sell any fish at the $4 price. *Most of this chapter will assume that she must charge the same price to all of her customers.*[1] In this case, she maximizes profit by selling five fish and throwing away the other three.

Throwing away fish is wasteful. It creates a deadweight social loss (a loss to the economy) of three fish. Some buyer would be willing to pay $3 for one of those fish. (Loretta could sell an additional fish by reducing the price to $3.) Another buyer would be willing

---

[1] A later section on price discrimination returns to this issue.

Figure 2 | Why Marginal Revenue Is Less than Price

Loretta loses Area A ($2) if she reduces the price from $7 to $6 to sell a third fish, but her revenue rises by Area B ($6). The $2 loss and $6 gain mean that the marginal revenue of selling three fish is $4 (Point C).

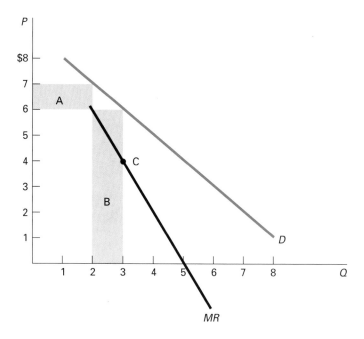

to pay $2 for one of those wasted fish, and a third buyer would pay $1 for the last fish. The prices that people are willing to pay measure the values that they place on the fish. Since the three fish that Loretta throws out are worth $3, $2, and $1 to buyers, the value of the deadweight social loss is $6. Figure 3 shows the deadweight social loss.

Price takers would never throw away fish. They would sell all their fish because they would not have to reduce the price to sell additional units. Sellers who face downward-sloping demand curves for their goods can sell more, however, only by reducing the price. If reducing the price would reduce their profits, they don't reduce the price. Instead, they choose to sell fewer units.

If Loretta catches fish regularly, she will choose to catch fewer than eight fish rather

Figure 3 | Deadweight Social Loss Because Loretta Sells Only Five Fish

The deadweight social loss is $6 ($3 + $2 + $1).

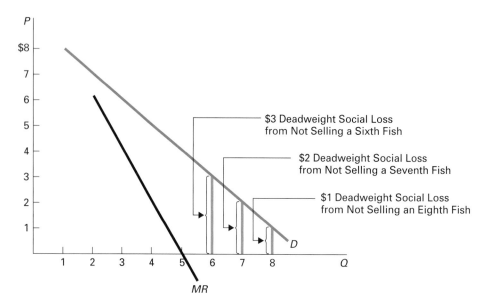

than catching them and throwing them out; she will reduce her output. Even if fishing is a costless activity, she maximizes her profit by catching and selling only five fish per day. Her choice causes a $6 deadweight social loss, because people would like to have three more fish. They would be willing to pay $6 in total for those fish ($3 for the first one, $2 for another, and $1 for the last), but Loretta doesn't provide them.

This situation seems peculiar. Catching fish is costless, and some people would like to buy more fish, but the only seller in town chooses *not* to provide them. Why doesn't someone else compete with Loretta by catching fish and selling them to these potential buyers? Another seller could sell two fish for $2 each and earn $4. If other sellers enter the business, then Loretta would lose her monopoly on selling fish in the town. She can maintain her monopoly only if some barriers to entry stop potential competitors. Such barriers might take several forms:

▶ Perhaps no one else can legally sell fish in the town.

▶ Perhaps Loretta owns the only nearby stream with fish, and the town has no other source of fresh fish.

▶ Perhaps Loretta's costs of catching fish are lower than anyone else's costs. If no one else can profit by selling fish for $5 or less, no other sellers will enter the business.

You should look for features from this example in the general discussion that follows.

SHORT-RUN EQUILIBRIUM WITH A MONOPOLY

A monopoly faces a downward-sloping demand curve, as in Figure 4. If it charges the price P_1, it can sell the quantity Q_1; if it charges P_2, it can sell Q_2, and so on. A monopoly chooses which price to charge, recognizing that its choice affects the quantity that it sells. A monopoly has no supply curve.[2] It chooses the price-quantity combination along its demand curve (such as Point A, B, or C in Figure 4) that maximizes its profit.

A monopoly maximizes its profit by producing the quantity at which its *marginal cost* equals its *marginal revenue,* and selling that quantity for the highest price that buyers will pay (the price on the demand curve at that quantity). Figure 5 shows the logic of profit maximization for a monopoly. The marginal revenue curve, *MR,* differs from the demand curve, *D.* The monopoly chooses the quantity, Q_M, at which marginal cost *(MC)* equals marginal revenue (where the curves intersect). It then charges the highest price at which it can sell this quantity, P_M.

EXPLANATION AND EXAMPLE

The marginal revenue curve *(MR)* differs from the demand curve *(D)* because the firm must reduce its price to all customers to raise the quantity that it sells. The first two columns of the table in Figure 6 show a demand schedule; the third and fourth columns show total and marginal revenue; the remaining columns show total, marginal, and average cost, and the firm's profit. Figure 6 graphs the demand curve, the marginal revenue curve, and the marginal and average cost curves. If the firm charges a $12 price, it can sell 5 units of the good per week for a total revenue of $60 per week. The firm could sell 6 units per week only by reducing the price to $11. This would raise its total revenue to $66 per week, so the marginal revenue of a sixth unit

---

[2]The supply curve of a perfectly competitive firm (as in Chapter 13) is the portion of its marginal cost curve above its average variable cost curve. That supply curve is independent of the demand curve; changes in demand do not change supply. In contrast, no supply curve accurately portrays the choices for a monopoly because the quantity supplied at any one price depends on demand.

**Figure 4
Demand Curve for a
Monopoly's Product**

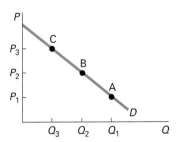

A monopoly faces a downward-sloping demand curve. If it charges the price P_1, it can sell the quantity Q_1 (Point A). If it charges P_2, it can sell Q_2 (Point B). If it charges P_3, it can sell Q_3 (Point C). A monopoly chooses the point on its demand curve (such as A, B, or C) that maximizes its profit.

**Figure 5
Monopoly Price
and Output**

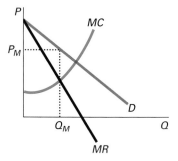

A monopoly maximizes its profit by choosing the quantity, Q_M, at which its marginal cost *(MC)* equals its marginal revenue *(MR)*. It charges the price P_M and sells the quantity Q_M.

per week is $6. The difference between the demand and marginal revenue curves is the difference between the second and fourth columns of the table.

In words, marginal revenue is less than price for a monopoly because to sell an additional unit of the good, the monopoly must reduce its price to all customers. Its marginal revenue from selling a tenth unit equals the gain in revenue from selling that unit, which is the price, minus the loss in revenue from selling the other 9 units at a lower price. (See also Figure 2.)

A firm maximizes its profit by choosing a quantity that sets marginal revenue equal to marginal cost. (See Chapter 10.) The monopoly illustrated in Figure 6 maximizes profit by producing 7 units per week and charging $10 per unit (the price at which the quantity demanded equals 7). It earns a $48 profit, and cannot raise its profit by charging more and selling less or charging less and selling more.

Figure 6 | Monopoly Decision Making

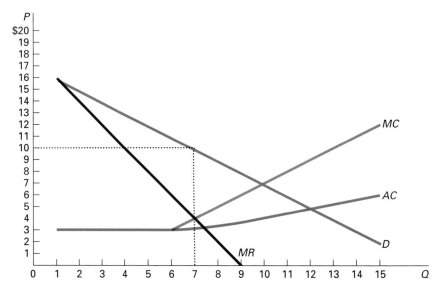

	Quantity per Week (Q)	Price (P)	Total Revenue (TR)	Marginal Revenue (MR)	Total Cost (TC)	Marginal Cost (MC)	Average Cost (AC)	Profit
	1	$16	$16	$ 16	$ 3	$ 3	$3.000	$ 13
	2	15	30	14	6	3	3.000	24
	3	14	42	12	9	3	3.000	33
	4	13	52	10	12	3	3.000	40
	5	12	60	8	15	3	3.000	45
	6	11	66	6	18	3	3.000	48
MR = MC	7	10	70	4	22	4	3.143	48
	8	9	72	2	27	5	3.375	45
	9	8	72	0	33	6	3.667	39
	10	7	70	−2	40	7	4.000	30
	11	6	66	−4	48	8	4.364	18
	12	5	60	−6	57	9	4.750	3
	13	4	52	−8	67	10	5.154	−15
	14	3	42	−10	78	11	5.571	−36
	15	2	30	−12	90	12	6.000	−60
	16	1	16	−14	103	13	6.437	−87

In this example, the monopoly maximizes its profit by producing 7 units per week and charging $10 per unit. Its profit is $48.

Monopoly Profit

Figure 7 shows the profit for a monopoly without fixed costs.[3] People buy Q_M units of the good and pay P_M for each unit, so the area of the rectangle with height P_M and base Q_M shows the monopoly's total revenue from its sales. The area under the marginal cost curve shows the variable cost of producing the good, so the remainder of the rectangle shows the monopoly's profit.

Figure 8 graphs monopoly profit in a second way. The monopoly's profit equals its markup (price minus average cost) times the number of goods that it sells. This is the area of rectangle A in Figure 8. These two graphs illustrate two equivalent ways to show monopoly profit.

Deadweight Social Loss from a Monopoly

Monopolies cause economic inefficiency. Figures 7 and 8 both show the deadweight social loss from a monopoly. As in the fish example (Figure 3), the deadweight social loss occurs because the monopoly sells less than the economically efficient quantity.

The economically efficient quantity, Q_1 in Figure 9b, is the quantity at which the marginal cost of producing the good equals the marginal benefit of the good to buyers (the height of the demand curve). The marginal cost curve and demand curve intersect at this quantity. Panel (b) shows the gain from trade—consumer and producer surplus—when the economically efficient quantity, Q_1, is traded. Panel (a) shows the gain from trade—consumer and producer surplus—with a monopoly. The gain from trade in Panel (a) is smaller than that in Panel (b). The difference, Area A in Panel (a), is the deadweight social loss due to the monopoly.

The deadweight social loss occurs because the monopoly charges a price above its marginal cost. At this higher price, people buy only Q_M rather than Q_1 units. The deadweight social loss represents the potential gains from the trades that do not occur because of the monopoly. It results from a monopoly's choice not to sell additional units of the good even though some people are willing to pay more than the cost of

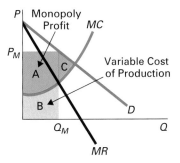

**Figure 7
Monopoly Profit and
Deadweight Social Loss**

Areas A and B together give total spending on the monopoly's product (the firm's total revenue). Area A shows the monopoly's profit, and Area C gives the deadweight social loss.

Figure 8 | Monopoly Profit: Another Way to Graph It

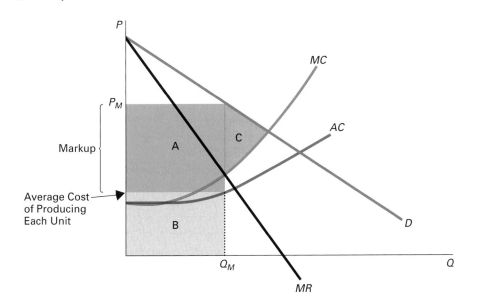

Area A shows monopoly profit (markup times Q_M). Area B shows the total variable cost of producing Q_M units. Area C shows the deadweight social loss.

---

[3]If the monopoly has a fixed cost, its profit is smaller than this area by that amount. The area under the marginal cost curve equals the variable cost of producing the good.

Figure 9 | Monopoly versus Perfect Competition

Total consumer and producer surplus is smaller with the monopoly quantity, Q_M, than with the economically efficient quantity, Q_1. The difference, Area A, is the deadweight social loss from the monopoly.

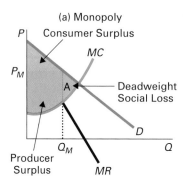

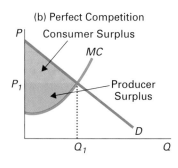

producing them. The firm chooses not to sell to these potential customers because if it did, it would have to lower the price to all customers, even those who would willingly pay more.

EXAMPLE

Ralph has two candy bars to sell. (He does not want to eat them.) Luke is willing to pay up to 50 cents for one; Violet is willing to pay up to 20 cents. Neither Luke nor Violet wants two candy bars. Suppose that Ralph must charge the same price to both Luke and Violet. He maximizes his profit by selling only to Luke, for 50 cents, and throwing away the other candy bar. (If he were to sell both candy bars, he could charge only 20 cents each, so he would earn only 40 cents for both.) This is economically inefficient because Ralph throws away something that Violet is willing to buy. An economically efficient trade with Violet does not occur because it would reduce Ralph's total profit. The deadweight social loss from Ralph's monopoly in this example is 20 cents (the value of the candy to Violet).

Comparing Monopolies and Perfect Competition

An industry with perfect competition produces the economically efficient quantity and charges a price equal to marginal cost. A monopoly produces less than that quantity and charges a price above marginal cost. Figure 9 contrasts a monopoly with perfect competition, assuming the same marginal cost.

Suppose that the market supply curve with perfect competition is the *MC* curve in Figure 9.[4] Industry output with perfect competition is then Q_1, the economically efficient quantity, while monopoly output, Q_M, is smaller. The monopoly charges a higher price (P_M instead of P_1) and earns a higher profit than the perfectly competitive firm. (Producer surplus is larger with the monopoly.) Consumer surplus with a monopoly is smaller for two reasons: Buyers pay more for each good, and they buy less.

These conclusions apply only if a monopoly has the same costs of production as a perfectly competitive industry. In some cases, however, a monopoly may have lower costs of production. In fact, a firm might become a monopoly *because* its costs are much lower than those of any potential competitors.[5] A later section titled "Natural Monopoly" discusses a related situation.

---

[4]The supply curve of each firm under perfect competition is the portion of its marginal cost curve above its average variable cost, so the market supply curve is the industry marginal cost curve, *MC* in the figure.

[5]In this case, economic efficiency would result if the monopoly were to produce the good (gaining the advantage of its low costs) but at the economically efficient quantity, Q_1 in Figure 9, which is higher than Q_M. The monopoly would not voluntarily produce this higher quantity, of course.

Review Questions

1. Draw a graph to show:
   (a) Monopoly output
   (b) Monopoly price
   (c) Monopoly profit (with no fixed costs)
   (d) Deadweight social loss from a monopoly

2. Contrast the prices and quantities produced by a monopoly and a perfectly competitive industry.

Thinking Exercises

3. Why is a monopoly's marginal revenue less than its price?

4. Why does a monopoly produce less than the economically efficient quantity?

LONG-RUN EQUILIBRIUM AND BARRIERS TO ENTRY

Monopoly profits tempt other firms to enter the industry. If enough new firms enter, the industry may reach perfect competition (and zero economic profits) in the long run. If only a few firms enter, the industry may become an oligopoly, which is the subject of Chapter 16. A firm can remain a monopoly in the long run only if some barrier to entry keep other firms out.

> **Barriers to entry** are costs high enough to prevent potential competitors from entering an industry.

Barriers to entry may be *natural,* resulting from lower costs of production at the monopoly firm, or *artificial,* resulting from laws or government regulations.

EXAMPLES

Laws and regulations sometimes prohibit new firms from entering an industry. No firm other than the U.S. Postal Service can legally deliver first-class mail in the United States. Legal barriers to entry do not fully protect monopolies from competition, however, because potential competitors can often produce substitute products. The Postal Service, for example, competes with private overnight-delivery companies, parcel carriers, fax machines, and electronic mail. Advertising inserts in newspapers were invented in the 1960s as a way to compete with the Postal Service by substituting newspaper delivery for mail delivery.[6]

Most countries prohibit new firms from competing with their government-owned airlines. The U.S. government prohibited new firms from entering the trucking industry for several decades. Many state governments operate lotteries but prohibit private firms from operating competing lotteries. State governments often limit the number of restaurants and gas stations along toll roads. In the former Soviet Union (and many other socialist

---

[6]Although the post office is a government agency, it hires private firms to transport and deliver some of its mail, particularly in rural areas. This practice has a long tradition; King William III of Britain contracted the first colonial postal service to Thomas Neale in 1692; in 1785, the U.S. Congress authorized the postmaster general to hire private stagecoaches to carry mail.

Should the Post Office Have a Monopoly?

The U.S. Postal Service has a legal monopoly on delivery of first-class mail in the United States; the government prohibits entry by other firms. Other companies can compete in delivery of packages, overnight mail, magazines, and so on, but not first-class mail.

Critics argue that competition would lower prices and raise the quality of service. Supporters of the restriction say that other firms would deliver mail only on the most profitable routes and leave the government Postal Service with the unprofitable routes. They say that competition would raise prices for people who live in out-of-the-way places. Currently, the Postal Service charges everyone the same price, so it makes profits on low-cost routes and suffers losses on high-cost routes. Those who favor allowing competition reply that mail delivery costs more in out-of-the-way places than in easily accessible areas, so the government unfairly forces everyone else to subsidize mail delivery to those places. People in those places, they say, should have to pay the high costs of living there. (To limit their costs, they might choose to pick up their mail at the post office instead of buying home delivery, or they might take only weekly delivery.)

Opponents of postal competition also argue that mail delivery is a natural monopoly; if many firms were to deliver mail, they may all have higher average costs than the government agency incurs, potentially raising the overall cost of mail delivery. Supporters of postal competition argue that mail delivery is not a natural monopoly, but that even if it were, competition would keep prices down and raise incentives for efficient service.

countries), the government had a monopoly on production and sales of most goods, and it prohibited competition. Until recently, a national law in Japan prevented large retail stores from competing with smaller, "mama-papa" stores. It was illegal for a store of more than about 5,000 square feet in size to open in any town without permission from the community's store owners with whom it would compete.

License requirements also set up artificial barriers to entry. The U.S. government requires licenses to run radio and television stations, and historically, it has used this requirement to limit the number of stations. Governments require people to obtain licenses to become doctors, pharmacists, lawyers, barbers, and hairdressers; to operate stores and restaurants; and to stage rock concerts.

Patents and copyrights (which protect rights to intellectual property) are also artificial barriers to entry. A patent is the legal right to produce and sell a product that you have designed. Polaroid's patent on the instant-picture cameras invented by its founder prevented other companies from producing and selling such cameras without Polaroid's permission. A copyright resembles a patent, but it protects rights to works of art, books, music, movies, television programs, and paintings. This book is copyrighted, as are most songs. (Even the song "Happy Birthday" is copyrighted; you are legally required to pay the copyright owner if you perform it for pay, though the law allows you to sing it at a party if no one pays you!) Patents and copyrights raise the incentive to invent new products and create new intellectual property and works of art, but they also create barriers to entry.

Some barriers to entry result from natural cost advantages. A firm that owns the only spring in a desert may have a monopoly in the long run because no other firm can provide water there at a sufficiently low cost. More than 90 percent of the world's output of boron, an ingredient in bleach, glass, ceramics, electronics, and other products, comes from just two mines, one in California and another in Turkey, both owned by the same company, RTZ Borax. A Canadian company once owned almost all the world's nickel reserves. The Louvre is the only museum in the world with the Mona Lisa; it has a monopoly on showing that painting because it owns the only original.

Figure 10 | Natural Monopoly

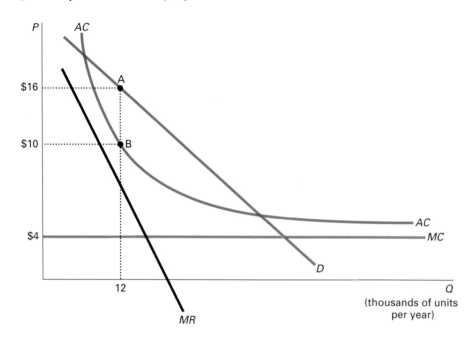

A natural monopoly has a downward-sloping average cost curve. This single firm can produce any given quantity at lower cost than any combination of more than one firm. This natural monopoly has a fixed cost of $72 thousand and marginal cost of $4 per unit of output. It maximizes profit by producing 12,000 units (the quantity at which $MC = MR$) and charging $16 (Point A). The average fixed cost of producing 12,000 units is $6 per unit, so the average total cost of producing that quantity is $10 per unit (Point B).

Natural Monopoly

One type of natural barrier to entry occurs when the average cost of producing a good falls as quantity increases. In that case, it is cheaper for one firm to produce all of the industry output than for many small firms to produce portions of that output. This situation creates a natural monopoly.

> A firm has **increasing returns to scale** if its average cost of production decreases as output rises.

Figure 10 shows increasing returns to scale as the downward slope of the average cost curve, *AC*.

> An industry with increasing returns to scale over sufficiently large quantities is a **natural monopoly.**

The phrase "sufficiently large quantities" refers to all quantities demanded at prices high enough to cover the firm's average cost.[7]

A natural monopoly may occur if production requires high fixed costs. The monopoly is natural because it is cheaper for one firm, rather than several firms, to produce all units of the good. (This avoids several firms paying the fixed cost.) Figure 10 shows an example. Any firm that produces this good must pay total fixed costs of $72 thousand and a marginal cost of $4 per unit of output. If two firms were to produce 12 thousand units each, their average costs would be $10 per unit. If one firm produces 24 thousand units per year, its average cost is lower than $10 per unit. So average cost is lower if only one firm produces all units of the good.

---

[7]A firm with a *U*-shaped average cost curve has increasing returns to scale at low levels of output but not at higher levels. Such a firm is not a natural monopoly unless low market demand for its product makes the demand curve intersect the average cost curve at a point where that curve slopes downward.

IN THE NEWS

Another monopoly bites the dust

By Seth Lubove

Anthony Tortoriello, a blunt-talking Chicago car dealer and industrial oil seller, has a hot deal for you: 1,400 megawatts of electricity, enough to power 40 small towns. Asking price: at least 15 percent to 20 percent lower than you're likely to get from your local electric monopoly.

Source: Forbes

Interested? For now, you can buy Tortoriello's electricity only if you're another utility. But Tortoriello anticipates the end of the local electric companies' monopoly privileges—a day, not far off, when electric consumers can buy power from whomever they want, much as they now choose their long distance carriers.

Local electric monopo-

lies in the high-tax states fear that they'll be stuck with billions of dollars' worth of excess capacity, or "stranded investment," if their big customers are allowed to shop around for cheaper power. Says Goodman of Howell, "If you don't hear the fear in the utility executives voices, you're not listening carefully."

Public utilities, traditionally protected by government on the grounds that they are natural monopolies, will face increasing competition in the years ahead.

Public utilities such as local telephone companies; cable television companies; and electric, gas, and water companies are often cited as natural monopolies. These industries require heavy fixed costs of setting up telephone wires and switching systems, cable and electrical wires, and gas and water pipes. It would be economically inefficient for several competing firms to duplicate these costs, with multiple wires or pipes to the same neighborhood. While a few cities have permitted competition between more than one cable television firm, few neighborhoods have more than one set of cable lines; each cable company avoided installing lines where the other company had already installed them. If CableRight has already wired a neighborhood, it is not likely to be profitable for CableFamily to install its own, separate wires in the same neighborhood.

Some people argue that these duplication problems imply that natural monopoly creates a barrier to entry, making natural monopolies more immune than other monopolies to long-run competition. New firms would lose money if they were to compete with an entrenched firm, because they would have to pay high fixed costs that the entrenched firm has already paid. However, this argument ignores the potential *benefit* to a new firm from entering a natural monopoly industry. While a new entrant faces high fixed costs, if the new firm succeeds it is likely to capture the *entire* market (at least until some other new firm mounts another new challenge). The costs of entry are big, but so are the potential gains. Operating systems for computers, for example, involve high fixed costs (of development) and low marginal costs (of making new copies of the software). While Microsoft currently sells operating systems for almost all personal computers, it faces continual threats of entry from potential alternatives (such as OS-2 and Java-based alternatives). Similarly, Netscape once sold nearly all Web browser software, but that has not prevented new entrants (including Microsoft) from paying the fixed costs and mounting competitive challenges. With few exceptions, only government regulations prohibiting entry are likely to shield any monopoly firm from competition in the long run.

Other goods with high fixed costs include satellite television broadcasts (where the fixed cost involves the satellite itself, with a low marginal cost of broadcasting a show). Movies and videos have high fixed costs of initial production but low marginal costs of showing at theaters or copying onto videotape. Computer software, books, and the Internet also involve high fixed costs and low marginal costs. In each case, the high fixed costs create increasing returns to scale. Nevertheless, competition in many of these areas has begun to flourish in recent years as government regulation has declined.

Although natural monopoly makes it efficient to have a single producer, the monopoly level of output is not economically efficient. A natural monopoly, like any other monopoly, chooses its quantity to equate marginal cost and marginal revenue. In the short run, the natural monopoly in Figure 10 maximizes profit by producing 12,000 units per year and charging a price of $16. Its average cost is $10 at that level of output, so its markup is $6. In the long run, continual challenges by new firms seeking to become the natural monopoly may lead the firm to reduce its price to maintain its monopoly position. For example, Netscape stopped charging for its Web-browser software after a competitor, Microsoft, began giving away its own similar software.

How Do Monopolies Start?

How does a firm become a monopoly? Some monopolies begin under the protection of government regulations or laws that create artificial barriers to entry. A firm may also become a monopoly by acquiring most or all of a unique input needed to produce a good (such as the boron mines mentioned earlier). Other firms become monopolies by inventing new products and obtaining patents on their designs. Some firms become monopolies by reducing their costs of production enough that other firms cannot profitably compete with them.

Without other barriers to entry, monopolies based on patents end when legal protections expire, and monopolies based on low costs of production end after other firms copy the inexpensive production methods. Consequently, only temporary monopolies result from new or improved products or from new technology that reduces costs. The monopoly power that results temporarily from an entrepreneur's success can provide an incentive (much like the incentive from a patent or copyright) for people to try to create new and better products that customers will want to buy. Monopolies may also begin with mergers or with implicit agreements among firms to stop competing and cooperate in acting like a monopoly. These cartels are the subject of the next section.

Review Questions

5. What happens to a monopoly in the long run if no barriers to entry deter potential competitors? State three examples of barriers to entry.

6. What is a natural monopoly?

Thinking Exercise

7. Discuss this statement: "If an industry is a natural monopoly, it is economically efficient to have a monopoly in that industry."

People of the same trade seldom meet together, even for merriment and diversion, but the conversation ends in a conspiracy against the public, or in some contrivance to raise prices.—Adam Smith, *The Wealth of Nations,* 1776.

CARTELS

If a monopoly does not already exist, competitors can profit by forming one. They could form a monopoly through a merger (in which two firms legally become one) or an acquisition (in which one firm buys another). Sometimes firms collude (make joint decisions) without legally merging. Laws in many countries, including the United States, prohibit mergers to form monopolies as well as certain kinds of collusion.

When firms collude and agree to act jointly as a monopoly, they form a cartel.

> A **cartel** is a group of firms (members of the cartel) that try to collude to act like a monopoly and share the monopoly profit.

Perhaps the most famous cartel is OPEC—the Organization of Petroleum Exporting Countries. A successful cartel works like any other monopoly, producing the monopoly level of output and charging the monopoly price. Cartels are illegal in most countries.

Problems Facing Cartels

A cartel faces special problems that a single-firm monopoly does not. The cartel must convince its members to reduce output to the monopoly level, it must decide how to divide the monopoly profit among its members, and it must prevent members from cheating on the cartel agreement by reducing their prices to boost their own sales.

Suppose that ten firms in a perfectly competitive industry each produce 20 units of a good per month, so that industry output is 200 units per month. These firms' cost curves appear in Figure 11. At the $12 equilibrium price, each firm earns zero economic profit.

IN THE NEWS

OPEC set to discuss output cut

*By Youssef M. Ibrahim
Special to The New York Times*

PARIS, Feb. 9—The president of the Organization of Petroleum Exporting Countries said today that he would press for a significant cut in oil production to prop up sagging prices, which have dropped by 20 percent since November.

Source: New York Times

OPEC, the oil cartel, tries to reduce output to raise the price of oil and its profit.

IN THE NEWS

Cola sellers may have bottled up their competition

Agreements on pricing and marketing of Coke and Pepsi are alleged

*By Andy Pasztor
and Larry Reibstein
Staff Reporters of The Wall
Street Journal*

When four executives of local Coca-Cola and Pepsi Cola bottling companies gathered at a popular, late-night restaurant in Norfolk, Va., four years ago, they did more than share a meal.

By the end of the meeting, the executives allegedly established a single wholesale price—$5.50 a

case—for cans of Coke and Pepsi sold in much of Virginia, according to sworn testimony, government filings, and other federal court documents in Norfolk. The participants also agreed on the sizes and timing of future price increases for both cans and bottles, Justice Department prosecutors and government witnesses allege.

Over the next year and a half, executives of the two

area bottlers conspired to share confidential price and marketing information at meetings in such places as hotel bathrooms and lounges, parking lots, fast-food outlets, and an airport coffee shop, according to prosecutors and the testimony, filings, and other court documents.

The result, prosecutors charge, was to inflate soft-drink prices paid by consumers.

Source: The Wall Street Journal

Adam Smith's observation is as true today as it was two centuries ago.

Figure 11 | Forming a Cartel

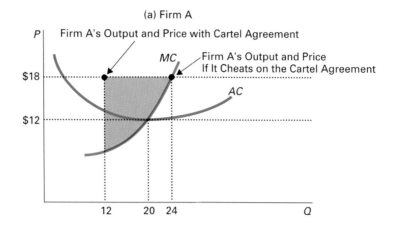

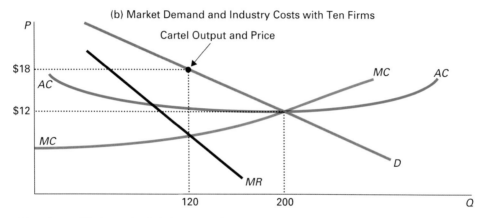

Under perfect competition, the equilibrium price is $12, and ten firms produce 20 units each per month; industry equilibrium output is 200 units per month. If the firms form a cartel, they act like a monopoly. They maximize the cartel's profit by reducing industry output to 120 units per month (so that each firm produces 12 units per month) and raising the price to $18. If Firm A cheats on the cartel agreement, however, it can earn extra profits, represented by the shaded area in Panel (a).

If the firms form a cartel, they can maximize the cartel's profit by reducing industry output to 120 units per month and raising the price to $18.

The cartel's first problem is how to divide production and profit among firms. The amount of output that each firm is supposed to produce is called its output *quota*. In this example, each firm's quota might be 12 units. Cartel members often find it difficult to agree on the quotas.

Another problem for a cartel is how to prevent member firms from cheating on the agreement by producing more than their quotas. Cartel members rarely rely on legally enforceable contracts, because laws prohibit most cartel agreements. In Figure 11, each firm can raise its profit by producing more than 12 units. As long as the other firms restrict output to keep the price at $18, Firm A can maximize its profit by producing the quantity at which marginal cost equals $18, that is, 24 units.[8] Figure 11a shows the extra profit that this firm would earn by cheating on the agreement, assuming that other firms honor it.

Every individual member of a cartel has an incentive to cheat by producing more

IN THE NEWS

OPEC members agree to reduce output but must decide who cuts by how much

Source: The Wall Street Journal

[8]If Firm A cheats by producing more than 12 units and other members of the cartel produce their quotas, total industry output rises, so the price falls slightly below $18; the example ignores this effect for simplicity. It does not change the conclusion that each firm has an incentive to cheat.

All cartels face the problem of agreeing how to divide output and profits.

Collusion in the Classroom

A classic classroom experiment shows why it is hard for a cartel to prevent cheating. Each of 15 students in a class secretly writes the number 1 or 2 on a sheet of paper and gives it to the professor. The professor pays students depending on what they write, as in the following table:

If This Many Students Write 1	Then Each Student Who Wrote 1 Gets	And Each Student Who Wrote 2 Gets
0	—	$0.45
1	$0.05	0.50
2	0.10	0.55
3	0.15	0.60
4	0.20	0.65
5	0.25	0.70
6	0.30	0.75
7	0.35	0.80
8	0.40	0.85
9	0.45	0.90
10	0.50	0.95
11	0.55	1.00
12	0.60	1.05
13	0.65	1.10
14	0.70	1.15
15	0.75	—

If everyone writes 1, then everyone gets $0.75. If everyone writes 2 (and no one writes 1), then everyone gets only $0.45. You might think that everyone would write 1, but if everyone else writes 1 and you write 2, you get $1.15 and everyone else gets $0.70. If students in the class can successfully collude, they will all write 1. However, every student has an incentive to cheat by writing 2.

Experiments show that if students are not allowed to talk to each other before choosing a number, then most write 2. If students are allowed to talk to each other first, they usually try to form a cartel by agreeing that they will all write 1. If you think that most people would honor this kind of agreement, you will be disappointed in the result. Time after time, when this experiment is performed in classrooms, many students write 2 after agreeing to write 1. Cheating is a persistent problem for cartels.

than its quota. However, if many firms begin cheating, the increase in output reduces the price below $18, destroying the cartel. Except where cartels are legal (so that quota agreements can be enforced in courts), the incentive to cheat tends to destabilize cartels.

To understand the incentive to cheat in a cartel, imagine that your professor grades on a curve. Each student can get the same grade with less studying if *everyone* agrees to limit studying. Suppose that students form a cartel and all agree to study only 15 minutes for an exam. Each student has an incentive to cheat on this agreement by studying for a longer period. If other students study only 15 minutes, a cheater can raise his grade substantially by studying for a few hours. Of course, if everyone cheats on the agreement, the cartel breaks down. The incentive to cheat grows even stronger if cartel members think that others might cheat; if other people study for a few hours and one person studies for only 15 minutes, that person is likely to fail the exam. Without some outside enforcement mechanism, members cannot prevent cheating, and the cartel becomes unstable.

Cartels can operate for long periods of time when the government helps to prevent cheating. In 1931, Texas and other oil-producing states made it illegal for any firm to produce more than a certain amount of oil. The state governments intended these laws to reduce oil production, and therefore to raise the price of oil and the profits of oil producers, that is, to establish a cartel. The U.S. government helped by raising the tax on imported oil, protecting the domestic cartel from foreign competition.

International oil companies had never formed a successful cartel on their own, but in 1970 the government of Libya began to suggest that countries restrict their oil output. By 1973, the OPEC members—national governments—had formed a cartel agreement and

The ostrich cartel could be staring at disaster

By Bill Keller
Special to The New York Times

OUDTSHOORN, South Africa—Smirk, if you like, at the ostrich-egg lamps and ostrich jerky on sale in the curio shops, the ostrich jockeys at the Safari tourist farm, the South African flag composed of ostrich feathers, the ubiquitous, low-cholesterol ostrich steak platter, the ostrich crossing sign posted on Langenhoven Street.

Go ahead, roll your eyes at the Feather Inn, the Early Bird television repair shop, and Chez L'Austriche. But be advised that in Oudtshoorn, which bills itself without exaggeration as the world's ostrich capital, they take their ostriches seriously.

Almost somberly, in fact, these days. For after nearly 50 years of controlling the world's supply of this comical but lucrative commodity, the Oudtshoorn ostrich cartel faces an alarming threat: competition.

With two new rival ostrich associations beginning to challenge from inside South Africa, and smugglers spiriting breeding stock away to ranchers overseas, farmers here fear that the days of the $500 ostrich-hide handbag may be numbered.

Source: New York Times International

The government of South Africa successfully protected the ostrich cartel from competition from 1945 until recent times. Every cartel faces potential competition unless governments limit rivalry by restricting entry.

Fighting quotas: Independent farmers oppose rules letting cartels decide output

Fruit, nut growers challenge depression-era legacy; Will almond butter sell?
Repealing curb on grapefruit

By Marj Charlier
Staff Reporter of The Wall Street Journal

SANGER, Calif.—Inside a big metal building on the Riverbend International Corp. farm here, shiny oranges bounce jauntily along conveyor belts and down chutes, automatically joining like-sized fruit in boxes bound for Pacific Rim markets.

But outside, in orchards that stretch across the San Joaquin Valley, oranges just as fine plop off trees and rot in the scorching heat. Perry Walker, Riverbend's vice president, says that the fruit wouldn't be going to waste if it weren't for restrictions imposed by a government-backed cartel.

Rotting fruit and lost profits have become a cause.

Fifty-year-old federal regulations allow farmers to form cartels to control supplies, share marketing efforts, and allocate production rights through "marketing orders" approved and enforced by the U.S. Agriculture Department.

Source: The Wall Street Journal

The government enforces some cartel agreements.

quadrupled the price of oil. Even before the OPEC cartel, firms in other industries had tried—and often failed—to form successful cartels. Cartels have been attempted in the tin, nickel, cocoa, coffee, potash, bauxite, natural rubber, nutmeg, and banana industries (though the Organization of Banana-Exporting Countries never achieved OPEC's fame or success). The International Tin Council (ITC) cartel collapsed in 1985. Many member countries of the International Coffee Organization (ICO) cheated on the cartel agreement by producing more coffee than their quotas and selling it for less than the ICO price; the cartel collapsed in 1989 and the wholesale price of coffee fell from $1.25 to about $0.50 a pound. Seven Latin American countries later formed a new group, the Association of Coffee Producing Countries, as the basis for a new cartel. A bauxite cartel lasted for only a few years. Governments of the United States, Canada, Australia, Russia, and the 12-nation European Union set up an informal aluminum cartel in 1994, agreeing to reduce output of aluminum by about 10 percent to raise its price.

ANTITRUST POLICY

When governments are not busy forming or assisting monopolies and cartels, they often fight these organizations with antitrust laws.

> **Antitrust laws** prohibit monopolies and cartels or monopoly-like behaviors.

In the United States, the main antitrust laws are the Sherman Act (1890) and the Clayton Act (1914). These laws outlaw monopoly behavior and attempts to form monopolies, as well as certain other actions *if* those actions help to create monopolies. The prohibited actions include predatory pricing (charging less than average cost to try to drive a competitor out of business); tie-in sales (offers to sell products only to people who also buy other products); mergers (two firms joining together to form one firm); and price discrimination (discussed in the next section).

In a famous early application of antitrust law, the U.S. government broke up the Standard Oil Company into various smaller companies. The Supreme Court ruled in 1975 that Xerox had a monopoly of photocopying equipment because it sold 65 percent of industry output. The court required Xerox to increase competition by allowing some of its competitors to produce its patented products. The government applied antitrust law to the telephone industry in the 1980s, dividing AT&T into smaller companies.

More recently, Wal-Mart has been accused of violating antitrust laws through predatory pricing. Whatever the truth in that case, predatory pricing is rare because the predator loses money. You might expect that a large predator firm with extensive resources could outlast a small victim firm with less money in a price war. That assumption would be true if each firm were to lose the same amount of money each week from predatory pricing, but a predator with twice the sales of a victim (and with the same costs and price) loses twice as much money as the victim firm.[9] (If each firm loses $1 on each sale, a firm with 1,000 sales per week loses $1,000 per week, while a firm with 100 sales per week loses only $100 per week.)

The U.S. government has investigated the Microsoft Corporation for possible violations of antitrust laws. One accusation involves tie-in sales in which Microsoft agreed to sell rights to its Windows operating system only to computer makers that also bought its Web-browser software. Microsoft claimed in its defense that its operating system and browser software were sufficiently integrated that they formed one product, not two products in a tie-in sale. Microsoft has also argued that even though it sells nearly all personal computer operating systems, it does not have a monopoly, because continual competition from other firms forces it to maintain low prices. Moreover, says Microsoft,

IN THE NEWS

OPEC is reining in runaway output despite some cheating by its members

By James Tanner
Staff Reporter of The Wall Street Journal

The Organization of Petroleum Exporting Countries has reined in runaway oil production despite cheating by some members on their March quotas.

Source: The Wall Street Journal

The OPEC oil cartel, like all cartels, faces the problem of members cheating on the agreement.

---

[9]A victim of predatory pricing may be able to reduce its short-run loss through a temporary shutdown, during which it remains ready to produce again when the predatory pricing stops. A monopoly that understands this possibility may have little incentive to try predatory pricing.

IN THE NEWS

Wal-Mart on trial on 'predatory pricing' charges

By Kathryn Jones

Wal-Mart Stores Inc. and its pricing practices went on trial yesterday in an Arkansas courtroom, where three independent pharmacies are trying to prove that the nation's largest retailer sold merchandise below its costs in an effort to drive competitors out of business.

The retail druggists in Conway, Ark., north of Little Rock, contend that their business suffered from Wal-Mart's "predatory prices" on a range of items, from toothpaste to mouthwash to over-the-counter drugs, sold at its Conway supercenter store. The drugstores charge that Wal-Mart violated the Arkansas Unfair Practices Act, which forbids selling merchandise below cost "for the purpose of injuring competitors and destroying competition." They are seeking $1.1 million in damages.

In court filings, Wal-Mart has acknowledged selling some products for less than they cost, but insists that the policy has not damaged competition in the Conway area.

"It would be better if you could make a profit on everything you sell, but in the real world, that isn't possible," David Glass, Wal-Mart's president and chief executive officer, testified yesterday in Faulkner County Chancery Court in Conway. "That's the principal reason why we do it."

The sheer size of Wal-Mart, with $55.5 billion in revenues last year and more than 2,300 discount stores and warehouse-club outlets, allows it to buy in volume and offer "everyday low prices." But smaller merchants, especially those in small towns, have complained that they cannot match Wal-Mart's prices and are often forced out of business when one of the mega-stores moves into their markets.

The Supreme Court in June rejected predatory pricing charges by the Brooke Group Ltd. and its Liggett unit against a rival cigarette manufacturer, the Brown & Williamson Tobacco Corporation. The court upheld lower-court decisions against Liggett, saying it believed predatory pricing was generally impractical, since a company would have to endure long-term losses to drive competitors out of business.

Source: New York Times

Is Wal-Mart guilty of predatory pricing, or does it charge lower prices than rivals simply because it beats their costs?

IN THE NEWS

Intel is hit with FTC antitrust charges

The federal trade commission filed antitrust charges against Intel Corp., alleging that the giant chip maker stifled innovation and competition by retaliating against companies that challenged Intel over their rights to key technology.

The move against Intel brings both pillars of the personal computer industry under attack on antitrust charges. Last month, the Justice Department filed a broad lawsuit against Microsoft Corp., alleging that it abused monopoly power in basic PC software.

Intel "used its monopoly power to impede innovation and stifle competition," said William Baer, chief of the FTC's competition bureau.

Intel said that the FTC's complaint relies on "a new legal theory under antitrust law. Although the key legal requirement of an antitrust claim is harm to competition, the FTC is unable to show harm to competition in any market," the company said.

Source: The Wall Street Journal

competition drives rapid innovation in the industry. Microsoft's competitors and potential competitors counter that this competition could be temporary, and that it could disappear if recent competitive challenges to Microsoft fail.

Countries throughout the world differ in their antitrust laws and policies. Cartels operate legally in some countries such as Switzerland and, in some cases, Japan. Antitrust law in Japan and many European countries is considerably less restrictive (prohibiting fewer actions) than U.S. law.

Review Question

8. Why can firms benefit by forming a cartel?

Thinking Exercise

9. Why do members of a cartel have an incentive to cheat?

PRICE DISCRIMINATION

An earlier section raised the possibility that a monopoly could charge different prices to different buyers. It could charge a high price to buyers who would willingly pay a lot and lower prices to others who would not buy the product at the high price. A monopoly can raise its profit through price discrimination.

> **Price discrimination** means charging different prices to different buyers for the same good.

Two goods are not the same if their costs of production differ, so selling them for different prices would not constitute price discrimination. For example, a music store incurs higher costs to deliver a piano to a fourth-floor, walk-up apartment than to a ground-level apartment, so the store does not practice price discrimination if it charges more for delivery to the fourth floor; piano delivery to a fourth-floor apartment is a different good than piano delivery to a ground-level apartment.

"$200 for a loaf of bread! I told you never to go shopping in uniform!"
Source: The Wall Street Journal, May 20, 1988.

EXAMPLES

Pharmacies sometimes charge lower prices to senior citizens than to younger people for the same prescription medicines. Theaters and airlines sometimes charge less for children than for adults. Some stores and theaters give student discounts. Antique stores quote higher prices to expensively dressed customers or those who show particular interest in specific objects than to less prosperous-looking customers or those who show only mild interest. These may all be cases of price discrimination.

Perfect Price Discrimination

> Perfect price discrimination occurs when a seller charges each customer the highest price that she is willing to pay.

Figure 12 illustrates perfect price discrimination. The monopoly seller produces the economically efficient quantity, Q_1 (the same quantity it would produce under perfect competition). A monopoly that practices perfect price discrimination creates no deadweight social loss. It captures all the gains from trade; consumer surplus is zero and producer surplus is the shaded area in Figure 12.

EXPLANATION

The height of the demand curve shows the highest prices that buyers are willing to pay. As long as the demand curve lies above the marginal cost curve, some buyer is willing to pay more for another unit of the product than its cost of production, so the seller profits by producing and selling that extra unit. The seller maximizes profit by selling to every buyer who is willing to pay more for a good than it costs to produce, so the seller in Figure 12 maximizes profit by producing and selling Q_1 units, the same quantity that would result from perfect competition. Since this is the economically efficient quantity, there is no deadweight social loss. The seller charges $20 to a buyer who is willing to pay up to $20, $19 to a buyer who is willing to pay up to $19, and so on. Because the seller charges the highest price that each buyer is willing to pay,

Figure 12 | Perfect Price Discrimination

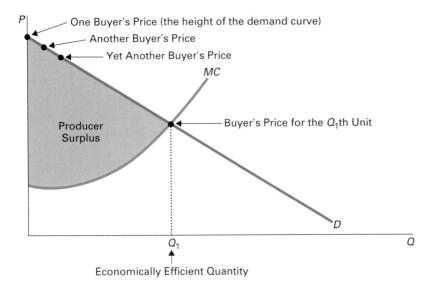

no buyer gets any consumer surplus. The perfectly price-discriminating monopoly captures all the gains from trade.

EXAMPLES

Recall the example in which Ralph has two candy bars to sell. (He does not want to eat them.) Luke is willing to pay up to 50 cents for one; Violet is willing to pay up to 20 cents. Neither Luke or Violet wants two candy bars. An earlier example in this chapter showed that if Ralph must charge the same price to both Luke and Violet, he maximizes his profit by selling only to Luke, for 50 cents, and throwing away the other candy bar. This economically inefficient result gives Ralph a profit of 50 cents.

If Ralph can perfectly price-discriminate, however, he charges Luke 50 cents for one candy bar and charges Violet 20 cents for the other. Notice that neither Luke nor Violet gets any consumer surplus in this case, but Ralph's profit is 70 cents and this situation is economically efficient. Perfect price discrimination eliminates the deadweight social loss from a monopoly and raises the monopoly's profit.

Figure 1 showed the demand for Loretta's eight fish. Recall that if she must charge the same price to all buyers, she maximizes profit at $20 by charging $4, selling five fish, and throwing away the other three fish. If Loretta can perfectly price-discriminate, however, she sells one fish for $8 to the buyer willing to pay that much, another fish for $7 to the buyer willing to pay $7, another for $6, a fourth for $5, a fifth for $4, and the sixth, seventh, and eighth for $3, $2, and $1. She earns more profit—$36—and she doesn't throw away any fish. This situation is economically efficient.

Difficulties with Perfect Price Discrimination

Perfect price discrimination creates two problems. First, the seller must know the highest price that each buyer is willing to pay—something sellers seldom know and buyers have no incentive to tell them. Second, the seller must prevent buyers from reselling their goods. Otherwise Violet may buy a candy bar for 20 cents and resell it to Luke for 50 cents. A theater that gives student discounts must prevent students

IN THE NEWS

Prices tumble on Big Macs, but fries rise

By Richard Gibson
Staff Reporter of The Wall Street Journal

The most dramatic price cut in the history of the fast-food industry may not be quite as dramatic as it seems.

Today, the price of the Big Mac falls to 55 cents from about $1.99—a discount of about 75% for McDonald's Corp.'s flagship hamburger.

But before the promotion kicked in, a number of McDonald's restaurants have quietly raised their prices on french fries and soft drinks—which it so happens customers have to purchase in order to get the hamburger discount.

Source: The Wall Street Journal

Not all tie-in sales are illegal. McDonald's customers could buy Big Macs for 55 cents only if they also purchased french fries and drinks.

from buying discounted tickets and reselling them to nonstudents. When a seller has trouble preventing resale, it has trouble price-discriminating.

Imperfect Price Discrimination

Often, sellers can price-discriminate only imperfectly, charging higher prices to some groups of buyers than to others. A firm can increase its profit if it can charge a higher price to people in a group that, on average, is willing to pay more, and a lower price to people in a group that, on average, is not willing to pay as much. The seller still must determine which people are willing to pay which prices, and it must prevent resales.

EXAMPLES

On average, students will not pay as much for theater tickets as people with full-time jobs will pay. By giving student discounts, a seller can charge a higher price to people who, on average, are willing to pay more, and a lower price to people who are, on average, unwilling to pay as much. By requiring students to present IDs to receive the discount, the seller can discriminate between the two groups.

Airlines charge lower round-trip air fares to people who stay over Saturday night. This practice reflects imperfect price discrimination between business travelers, who are usually willing to pay more but not to stay over Saturday night, and personal travelers, who are usually not willing to pay as much and who are more likely to stay over Saturday night. Airlines also prohibit their customers from reselling their tickets to other people.

Discount coupons permit sellers to charge lower prices to people who spend the time to clip, sort, and use the coupons than to people who don't. On average, people who don't use discount coupons are willing to pay higher prices than people who do. (A person who does not bother to use discount coupons is not likely to bother with comparison shopping and searching for the lowest price.) In this way, discount coupons allow sellers to price-discriminate by charging more to people who, on average, are willing to pay more, and less to people who, on average, are not willing to pay as much.

Some stores promise to sell products for the lowest prices and to give rebates to customers who later see lower advertised prices at other stores. This is a method of imperfect price discrimination, because some customers search through advertisements

Discount coupons are a tool of price discrimination.

after buying a product to try to find lower prices and collect the rebates, while other customers don't bother. This allows the seller to charge higher prices to customers who are less concerned with price than others.

Monopolies' Incentives for Cost Reduction and Innovation

A monopoly, like a perfectly competitive firm, has an incentive to produce at the lowest possible cost to earn the highest possible profit. Some people argue that a monopoly may feel a weaker incentive than a perfectly competitive firm, because its owners might become complacent and fail to control costs or maintain efficient production. On the other hand, monopolies sometimes achieve lower costs than perfectly competitive firms could manage. After all, monopolies can result from successful innovations that allow particular firms to produce at lower cost than others.

Some economists have argued that the same weakness in incentives for monopolies to limit costs can also reduce their success in research and innovation. Others have argued the opposite, reasoning that a monopoly or cartel is more likely than a competitive firm to succeed at research and development, partly because it can use its monopoly profit to finance large-scale research projects. Perfectly competitive firms may struggle to convince lenders to fund a risky research project; a monopoly's internal funds may allow it to avoid this difficulty. Research has uncovered mixed evidence on this issue.

Product Durability

Does a monopoly benefit by making its products fall apart quickly or become obsolete?[10] A company once advertised that its roach-killer product would permanently rid a home of roaches The ads claimed that the product was available only by mail because stores refused to sell it, fearing that its effectiveness would eliminate customers who would never have to buy roach killers again! This argument makes no sense. Although planned obsolescence may seem likely to raise profits by making sure that people buy the product more often, this argument ignores the effect of obsolescence on price. People are willing to pay more for products that last longer or work more effectively.

Most people are willing to pay about twice as much for a gallon of milk as for a half-gallon or for a box of cereal that is twice as large as another. They are willing to pay about twice as much for a 1-year health-club membership as for a 6-month membership. Similarly, people are willing to pay about twice as much for an alarm clock that will last 2 years as for one that will last only 1 year. Since clothing styles change over time, people are not willing to pay twice as much for clothes that will last twice as long. Every good has some optimal durability that takes into account style changes, costs of producing long-lasting goods, and other relevant factors. A seller, even a monopoly, has no incentive to make products wear out more quickly than is optimal.

Competition to Become a Monopoly

Honeoye Falls is a rural community without cable television. Several cable television firms want to serve the town, and each has asked the town government to designate it

[10]This idea was immortalized in an old movie, *The Man in the White Suit* (1952, starring Alec Guiness). A man invents a fabric that never gets dirty or wears out. Garment producers set out to suppress the invention, because they believe that their profits will fall since people will never have to replace their clothing. You should be able to see what is wrong with the economic premise of this movie plot.

as the only legal cable-service supplier. The firms point out that most U.S. cities have given monopoly rights to single cable companies. The town government has decided to grant monopoly cable rights to whichever company pays the town the most money. This policy forces the companies to compete for the right to be the monopoly seller.

How much would a firm be willing to pay to become a monopoly? The highest price it would pay is the discounted present value (see Chapter 12) of all future monopoly profits it would gain. If the town government sells the right to become the monopoly and many firms bid for that right, they are likely to outbid each other until the winner pays that discounted present value. This competition reduces the winner's economic profit to zero, and the government collects a fee equal to the discounted present value of the monopoly profit that the winning firm would have earned.

Competition to become a monopoly also occurs when television networks bid for the monopoly right to broadcast a special event such as the Super Bowl or the Olympic Games. The highest price that a television network is willing to pay the National Football League or the Olympic Committee for broadcast rights is the discounted present value of its expected monopoly profit from broadcasting the event. When the networks bid against each other for the monopoly broadcasting rights, the equilibrium price is usually close to that discounted present value. The National Football League and the Olympic Committee capture most of the monopoly profits from these broadcasts.

Rent Seeking

When firms compete for rights to a legal monopoly or to obtain other special favors from the government, their actions can create a deadweight social loss because they spend time and other resources arguing about the division of the economy's wealth rather than creating new wealth. This activity, which economists call *rent seeking,* can create economic inefficiency.

> **Rent seeking** is competition for favors from the government.

The term comes from *economic rent,* as discussed in Chapter 13 in connection with economic profit from unique resources. In this case, the unique resource creating economic profit would involve a favor from the government.

People or firms engage in rent-seeking behavior when they try to obtain or keep special favors or status from the government. Many firms and special-interest groups lobby the government; they hire lobbyists to wine, dine, and entertain government officials in an effort to convince them to act in ways that benefit those firms or special-interest groups. Lobbying wastes resources, because the lobbyists could be producing goods rather than spending resources haggling over how to divide existing resources (trying to get the government to do favors for *them* rather than others).

If monopolies had to spend all of their profits on rent seeking to keep their monopolies, then Figures 7 through 9 would change. The deadweight social losses would grow, because all the areas marked "Monopoly Profit" or "Producer Surplus" would become part of the deadweight social losses.[11] Estimates of the total deadweight social loss from monopoly in the United States range from 0.1 percent of the country's annual output to more than 5.0 percent when rent seeking is included.

---

[11]You might think that no deadweight social loss would result if a monopoly simply bribed government officials, (creating only a redistribution of resources). After all, when a firm pays a $1 million bribe, a government official collects that $1 million bribe. But the economy suffers a deadweight social loss from the competition among people to be the government officials who can collect such bribes! A well-known New York madame of the 1920s, Polly Adler, wrote in her book, *A House Is Not a Home,* that her "house" (and others like it) were much less profitable than they seemed to outsiders, because madames had to make large payoffs to the police and politicians. Competition among corrupt police officers and politicians takes wasteful forms well-known to viewers of gangster movies.

Monopoly Buyers

Previous sections of this chapter have discussed monopoly sellers. However, similar logic applies to monopoly buyers (often called *monopsonies*). A monopoly buyer can reduce the price it pays for a product by reducing its purchases. A monopoly buyer buys a quantity that sets its marginal benefit equal to its marginal cost, paying the lowest price at which sellers will sell that quantity. Because the monopsony buys less than the economically efficient quantity, it causes a deadweight social loss.

EXAMPLES

Blackair Gulch is a one-company mining town, and Old Dig is the only employer in town. It keeps its wages lower and its profit higher than those of a perfectly competitive industry by hiring fewer workers.

The De Beers diamond cartel (a South African company that buys diamonds from mines in most parts of the world) has been the only major buyer of diamonds in the world market for most of the 20th century. It uses its monopoly-buyer status to reduce the price that it pays for diamonds.[12]

The NCAA, in combination with professional sports leagues, exercises its monopoly-buyer power to limit payments to college and high-school athletes. Top college players probably would command high salaries if the NCAA and professional leagues would permit the payments.[13] Payments-in-kind to top college athletes, such as loans that can be repaid after signing professional contracts or gifts of various kinds, are attempts to avoid the NCAA rules.

Before U.S. professional baseball and football adopted free-agency systems, each team was a monopoly buyer of the services of its players. The players could not offer their services to other teams in the leagues. This restriction kept players' salaries low, until changes in rules led to free agency, reducing teams' monopoly power and vastly increasing players' salaries.

Review Questions

10. What is price discrimination? Cite an example.

11. Discuss this statement: "If a monopoly's marginal cost of production rises by $5, the monopoly raises the price by $5."

12. What happens when many firms compete for the legal right to operate as a monopoly?

Thinking Exercises

13. How large is the deadweight social loss if a monopoly perfectly price-discriminates? Explain your answer.

14. Explain why rent seeking can cause a deadweight social loss.

15. Explain how a monopoly buyer reduces the price it pays, and why this causes a deadweight social loss.

---

[12]De Beers also approximates a monopoly; it sells more than 80 percent of all diamonds sold in the world. It produces about one-third of the world's diamonds and buys the others to resell. As a buyer and reseller, it coordinates a cartel.

[13]Colleges have an incentive to keep payments to athletes low. They gain from low-cost sports on campus that help attract students, raise money from alumni, and publicize their institutions. Also, professional sports players may benefit from the reduction in competition from college athletes.

C o n c l u s i o n

Introduction to Monopolies

A monopoly faces a downward-sloping demand curve for its product and makes its decisions independently of the reactions of other firms.

Short-Run Equilibrium with a Monopoly

A monopoly chooses a price-quantity combination that lies along its demand curve. To maximize profit, it chooses the quantity at which marginal cost equals marginal revenue, and it charges the highest price at which it can sell that quantity. A monopoly earns a higher profit than a firm in a perfectly competitive industry would earn with the same costs of production. Consumer surplus is lower with a monopoly than with a perfectly competitive industry. A monopoly causes economic inefficiency, because it produces less than the economically efficient quantity. The deadweight social loss represents the potential gains from the trades that do not occur because the monopoly charges a price higher than its marginal cost.

Long-Run Equilibrium and Barriers to Entry

Monopoly profit tempts other firms to enter an industry. A monopoly can persist in the long run only if barriers to entry keep out other firms. These barriers to entry may be natural (resulting from lower costs of production at the monopoly firm) or artificial (resulting from laws or government regulations).

One type of natural barrier to entry results from increasing returns to scale (average cost that falls with output). A natural monopoly is a firm with increasing returns to scale over sufficiently large quantities.

Cartels

A cartel is a group of firms that try to collude to act like a monopoly and share the profits. A cartel faces special problems. Its members must decide which firms produce what goods and how the firms share the monopoly profits. It must also prevent member firms from cheating on the cartel agreement by reducing their prices and increasing sales, which is individually profitable for each firm but not jointly for all firms.

Antitrust Policy

Antitrust laws prohibit monopolies, cartels, and monopoly-like behaviors.

Price Discrimination

Price discrimination occurs when a seller charges different prices to different buyers for the same good. A seller can raise its profit by price-discriminating. The extreme case is perfect price discrimination, in which a seller charges each customer the highest price that the customer is willing to pay. In that case, the seller maximizes profit by producing the economically efficient quantity. The seller gets all the gains from trade, so consumer surplus is zero. In the less extreme case of imperfect price discrimination, a seller charges higher prices to some groups of buyers than to other groups.

Applications of Monopoly

Although monopolies create economic inefficiency, they generally have no incentive to produce products with inferior quality or that become obsolete quickly. Firms sometimes compete against each other for the right to operate as a monopoly. The process of competition can reduce the winner's monopoly profit to zero. This is a special case of rent seeking (competition for favors from the government), which can create a deadweight social loss because firms spend time and other resources fighting about how to divide the economy's wealth rather than creating new wealth. A monopoly buyer can reduce the price it pays for a product by reducing its purchases, causing a deadweight social loss.

K e y   T e r m s

monopoly	increasing returns to scale	cartel	price discrimination
barrier to entry	natural monopoly	antitrust law	rent seeking

P r o b l e m s

16. Rebecca can produce lemonade for $1 per gallon. (Her marginal cost and average cost both equal $1 per gallon.) She faces the demand schedule in Table 1.
    (a) How much should she produce and what price should she charge to maximize her profit?
    (b) How big is her profit?
    (c) How much consumer surplus do her customers get?
    (d) How big is the deadweight social loss from Rebecca's monopoly?

Table 1

Price	Quantity Demanded
$7.00	1
6.00	2
5.00	3
4.00	4
3.00	5
2.00	6
1.00	7
0.50	8

(e) Repeat Questions 16a through 16d assuming that Rebecca can perfectly price-discriminate.

17. Explain why colleges often charge higher tuition (perhaps full tuition, without rebates or any other form of financial aid) to students with government scholarships.

18. Discuss this statement: "A natural monopoly would lose money if it were to charge a price equal to its marginal cost."

19. Comment on this statement: "Producers could raise their profits by making their products fall apart or go rapidly out of style."

20. The city of Santa Barbara, California, passed a law to prevent any new hookups to the city's water supply. Discuss the effects of this law on the value of houses in Santa Barbara.

21. Hot-Time Amusement Park does not allow people to bring their own food into the park. The park sells food at concession stands, which charge prices twice as high as those at restaurants outside the park. The park charges an admission fee for entrance.
   (a) Suppose that everyone who comes to the park buys exactly one hamburger and one soft drink. How would the profit-maximizing price of an admission ticket change if the park were to lower the price of food? Would the amusement park gain by charging a high price for food in this case?
   (b) Suppose that people have different demands for food at the amusement park. Some people are willing to pay much more than others. Some people would pay very high prices for food at the park, while others prefer to eat before going there and not buy any food inside its gates. Explain why the park could maximize its profits by charging a high price for food.

22. Many towns have laws and regulations to limit growth by prohibiting or raising the costs of building new houses and apartment buildings. Who gains from these restrictions?

23. Who benefits and who loses if a monopoly practices predatory pricing to try to drive a competitor out of business? Does predatory pricing increase or decrease the deadweight social loss from a monopoly?

Inquiries for Further Thought

24. **(a)** Suppose you were the lawyer for the U.S. government trying to charge Microsoft with monopoly behavior. Present your case in as much detail as you can, using economic analysis in your arguments. What would you propose that the government do about the situation?
   (b) Suppose you were the lawyer for Microsoft defending your company against the government. Present your case in as much detail as you can, using economic analysis in your arguments.

25. Should major-league baseball be exempt from antitrust laws, as it was when this book went to press? What would happen to player salaries and to other features of the business if antitrust laws applied to baseball?

26. Should the NCAA eliminate its rule that prevents colleges from paying student athletes? What would be the effects?

27. Do you think that cable television is a natural monopoly? Should local governments allow more than one cable television company to serve a single area? What would be the results of cable competition? Should governments regulate or control cable television companies? If so, how?

28. U.S. colleges and universities share information about tuition increases. In 1989, the U.S. government charged some private colleges with forming a cartel to maintain high tuitions. Do you think that colleges have a cartel? What evidence would you want if you were to argue this case before the Supreme Court?

29. U.S. drug manufacturers have asked the government for an exemption from antitrust laws on the grounds that collaboration may reduce their costs of developing new treatments for AIDS and other diseases. Opponents of this idea believe that the

exemption would simply allow the companies to form a cartel and raise prices. What should the government do? Why?

30. A news clipping in this chapter reported charges that Wal-Mart has engaged in predatory pricing. If you were a judge, how would you decide Wal-Mart's guilt or innocence? What should the law say about the prices that business firms charge? Should it prohibit certain kinds of pricing decisions? If so, which ones and why? If not, why not?

31. Discuss this statement: "U.S. immigration laws create a cartel of U.S. workers and keep U.S. wages high by limiting the number of foreigners that can enter the U.S. labor market."

32. Name three firms that you think are monopolies. How did they get to be monopolies? Why don't other firms enter their industries and compete with them?

33. After Adam Smith's famous quote on collusion cited in this chapter, Smith went on to write, "It is impossible, indeed, to prevent such meetings, by any law which either could be executed, or would be consistent with liberty and justice." Do you agree or disagree? Why? What (if anything) should the government do about monopolies?

34. Discuss this statement: "Monopolies are good because the potential to earn a monopoly profit provides a strong incentive for people to create new products and patent them."

35. In 1998, the U.S. government charged Intel Corp. with violating antitrust laws. Intel had stopped sharing information about its computer chips with certain companies that had disputes with Intel. The government argued Intel was illegally using its monopoly power (as the dominant maker of microprocessors with market share over 80 percent) to "impede inovation and stifle competition." Intel responded that information about its chips is its own intellectual property, and that is has the right to share, or not to share, that information with anyone.

(a) The government has hired you to present its case in court. What would you argue?

(b) Intel has hired you to defend it in court. What would you argue?

36. How much protection should a patent provide to an inventor? How long should a patent last? Should Nintendo have been able to prevent Atari from making games for Nintendo systems?[14] Should the author of an encyclopedia of trivia have been able to prevent the inventors of Trivial Pursuit from selling that game, as one author tried to do? Should researchers in genetic engineering be permitted to patent new forms of life, such as bacteria that would aid farmers or new kinds of farm animals (such as geeps, combinations of goats and sheep)? What about Dolly, the cloned sheep?

If patents and copyrights create valuable incentives for new products and ideas, but also result in economically inefficient monopolies, what should the government do? How would you make decisions on these matters? Can you formulate some *general principles* to use as a guide?

37. Should the U.S. government allow firms to collude so that they could better cope with foreign competition?

---

[14]This case arose in the early 1990s. Another issue involves why Nintendo would care. You might think that Nintendo would want to keep Atari from making the games so that Nintendo could sell more games instead, but if Atari makes any games that people want—because they are either better or cheaper than alternatives—then more people will buy the Nintendo system to play those games and the ability to play those other games raises the price that Nintendo can charge for its machines. Nintendo would benefit by allowing other firms to make games for its machines. The reasons why Nintendo did not want Atari to make games for its machines are more complicated and beyond the scope of this book.

CHAPTER 15

MONOPOLISTIC COMPETITION

In this Chapter...

Main Points to Understand

- Monopolistic competition combines elements of monopoly and perfect competition.

- Firms compete in product features as well as price.

- Free entry drives economic profit to zero in the long-run, even when firms are *not* price takers.

Thinking Skills to Develop

- Apply the logic of free entry leading to zero economic profit.

- Recognize the tradeoff between variety of goods and efficient production of each good.

- Explain why firms advertise, and formulate arguments about the economic roles of advertising.

M any real-life industries match neither the monopoly nor perfectly competitive models. Burger King can raise the price of a Whopper without losing all its customers to Wendy's, Hardee's, or Benny's Burger Palace, so Burger King is not a price taker. A perfectly competitive firm would not advertise to try to attract customers, because it could sell as much as it wanted to sell at the equilibrium price; fast-food restaurants advertise aggressively to convince people that they offer the best food and unique features (such as salad bars and prizes in children's meals). Yet no one in the fast-food industry has a monopoly. As in a perfectly competitive industry, new competitors can freely enter: virtually anyone can start a fast-food restaurant. Similar remarks also apply to many other industries, such as music recordings (CDs), movies, novels, clothing and other retail stores, and computer software. This chapter discusses a form of competition that lies between perfect competition and monopoly.

Restaurants are not all alike. They produce differentiated products.

> Firms produce **differentiated products** if buyers regard the products as good, but not perfect, substitutes.

MARKET CHARACTERISTICS

IN THE NEWS

Beefpackers are trying to win back consumers by selling leaner cuts, brand names, and convenience

The packers are hoping that the brand-name approach could do for beef sales what designer labels did for blue jeans and Frank Perdue did for chicken: create distinctions where none existed—and do so at higher prices and, presumably, higher profits. If the industry's innovators have their way, a steak will no longer be a steak; it will be a steak by Excel or IBP.

Source: New York Times

Differentiating a product

If buyers view each seller's product as slightly different from the products of other sellers, these firms produce differentiated products. The products may differ in appearance, design, quality, location, image, or other features. The difference can be real or merely perceived by customers. Advertising may differentiate products by creating unique images for them. Other differentiated products include hair salons, cars, and college educations.

When many firms in an industry produce differentiated products, the result is monopolistic competition.

> **Monopolistic competition** means that (1) each firm sells a differentiated product; (2) enough firms compete in the industry that when one cuts its price, every other firm loses only a small quantity of its sales; and (3) the industry has free entry.

Monopolistic competition requires all three conditions. The first condition implies that firms are *not* price takers. Each faces a downward-sloping demand curve like that of a monopolist. If a firm raises its price, it loses some but not all of its customers; some customers continue to buy from the firm because they would rather pay the higher price than switch to other firms' slightly different products.

The second condition for monopolistic competition means that the actions of any one firm have only small effects on sales by any other firm. Unlike a cartel, each firm acts independently, making decisions without considering the reactions of other firms. To understand this condition, think about a situation in which firms do *not* act independently. Suppose that three gas stations compete near an exit along a divided highway, each serving 100 customers per hour. If one station cuts its price by 2 cents per gallon it gains 20 customers per hour, 10 from each of the other stations. The other stations, seeing 10 percent reductions in business, cut their prices by 2 cents per gallon to regain their customers. Each station then has a lower price, but the same number of customers as before. If the first gas station knows that other stations will react to its actions, it may choose not to lower its price. Such a firm does not act independently, because it takes account of the reactions of its competitors when it chooses its price.

If 21 gas stations compete near the same exit, however, and one gains 20 customers by cutting its price by 2 cents, each other station loses only about *one* customer. Because they experience such small losses, the other firms may not react to the price cut; they may keep their prices unchanged. In this case, the firm acts independently because it need not take into account the reactions of its competitors. (Chapter 16 on oligopoly returns to this issue.)

The third condition for monopolistic competition guarantees that new firms enter the industry in the long run if it offers positive economic profits, and some firms exit the industry if they suffer losses. These possibilities imply that monopolistic competition generates zero economic profits in the long-run equilibrium, just as perfect competition does.

EXAMPLES

The credit-card market is an example of monopolistic competition. Many banks issue credit cards such as Visa and MasterCard. Each bank tries to differentiate its product by giving its credit card a better picture, a higher credit line, a lower interest rate or annual fee, or by providing prizes or other services.

The restaurant industry is also monopolistically competitive, with many different types of restaurants offering different atmospheres and types of food. Some people prefer some types of restaurants; other people prefer other types. As a result, most restaurants are not price takers—they face downward-sloping demand curves. Nevertheless, enough restaurants compete to ensure that changes in price at any one restaurant have only a small effect on business at any other particular restaurant. Each restaurant acts independently without having to consider the reactions of other restaurants to its decisions. Finally, potential competitors can

Product differentiation creates a variety of different styles.

enter freely into the restaurant business. Other examples of monopolistic competition include clothing, soaps and detergents, movies, pain relievers, sneakers, and music.

Product differentiation does not guarantee success, though. Duncan Hines once tried to sell cookies that it advertised as crispy on the outside and soft on the inside. This differentiated product failed; customers did not buy the cookies because, according to an industry consultant, "the package tasted better than the product."[1]

Short-Run Equilibrium with Monopolistic Competition

EQUILIBRIUM

Each firm in a monopolistically competitive industry faces a downward-sloping demand curve, so its marginal revenue curve lies below its demand curve, as in Figure 1. Like a monopoly, it chooses a combination of price and output along its demand curve. It

Figure 1 | One Firm under Monopolistic Competition

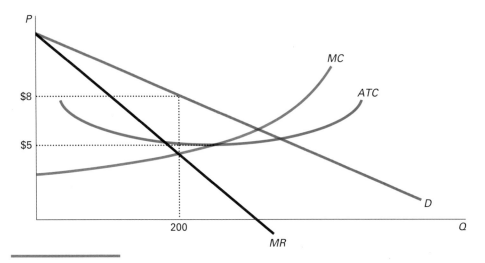

A monopolistically competitive firm chooses a quantity that equates marginal revenue and marginal cost. It then charges the highest price at which it can sell that quantity. In the short run, the firm can earn a positive economic profit. In this example, the firm's average cost is $5 and the price is $8, so it earns a $600 profit ($3 on each of 200 units sold).

[1]*New York Times*, August 15, 1987.

Free Entry and Zero-Profit Equilibrium

As Chapter 13 explained, free entry and exit drive economic profit to zero in long-run equilibrium with perfect competition. We now see that free entry and exit drive economic profit to zero in long-run equilibrium even when firms face downward-sloping demand curves.

When all firms in a perfectly competitive industry have the same costs of production, long-run equilibrium occurs when each firm earns zero economic profit. (Whenever economic profit is positive, new firms have an incentive to enter the industry; whenever economic profit is negative, firms have an incentive to exit the industry. Entry and exit stop, in long-run equilibrium, only when economic profit is zero.) That chapter explained that firms with zero economic profits stay in business because zero economic profit covers all a firm's opportunity costs. If a firm earns zero economic profit,

its owners could not gain by shutting down the firm and doing something else; they cannot do better than to keep the firm in business. Because accounting measures of profit differ from economic measures (see Chapter 11), a positive accounting profit is consistent with a zero economic profit.

EXPLANATION: As Chapter 11 explained, accounting measures omit certain implicit costs of producing goods. One important implicit cost is the opportunity cost of the financial capital that a firm's owners invest in the firm. Suppose that you save $10,000 and invest it in your own pizza business—you use the $10,000 to buy a pizza oven. The opportunity cost of this investment is the interest that you could have earned if you had put your $10,000 in stocks or bonds. Perhaps your opportunity cost is $1,000 per year, because the best alternative investment would have paid 10% per year interest ($1,000 per year on a $10,000 investment).

If investors believe that they can earn more on their investments in pizza ovens than in other investments, then they will start more pizza businesses (and invest in ovens for

maximizes profit by choosing a quantity that gives a marginal cost equal to its marginal revenue and charging the highest price at which it can sell that quantity. Figure 1 shows the profit-maximizing output and price for a monopolistically competitive firm: 200 units at a price of $8 per unit.

Figure 1 also shows the firm's average cost curve, which indicates that the average cost of producing 200 units equals $5. The firm charges $8, so it earns a $3 profit on each unit it sells. (It has a $3 markup.) In the short run, with a fixed number of firms in the industry, monopolistic competition resembles monopoly, and Figure 1 looks like the basic graph for a monopoly.

Long-Run Equilibrium with Monopolistic Competition

In the long run, positive economic profits induce new firms to enter the industry and produce good substitutes for the products of the older firms. As more firms share the industry's customers, the demand for each firm's output falls. Figure 2 on page 354 shows that entry of new firms reduces demand for the product of a firm that already competes in the industry. This new entry shifts the demand curve for the existing firm's product to the left. As demand shifts from D_1 (a short-run equilibrium) to D_2 (the long-run equilibrium), the marginal revenue curve shifts from MR_1 to MR_2.

Long-run equilibrium occurs when new firms see no further incentives to enter the industry and old firms see no reason to exit, that is, when economic profits are zero. Figure 2b shows long-run equilibrium with monopolistic competition. Each firm maximizes profit by producing 120 units of the good (the quantity at which marginal revenue equals marginal cost) and charging a price of $6 per unit. This price equals average cost, so each firm earns zero economic profit. Long-run equilibrium occurs when entry of new firms has reduced demand sufficiently to position the demand curve tangent to (just touching) the firm's average cost curve.

these businesses). As new pizza firms enter the industry, the increase in supply of pizzas reduces the equilibrium price of pizzas, reducing profits in the pizza business.

If investors believe that they can earn less on their investments in pizza ovens than in other investments, then they stop buying pizza ovens to replace those that wear out. Pizza businesses exit the industry, and the decrease in supply of pizzas raises their equilibrium price, raising profits in the pizza business.

In long-run equilibrium, investors who put their money in pizza ovens expect to earn the same return on their investment that they could get on alternative investments (in stocks and bonds, or investments in other industries such as buying computers for accounting firms). This payment to investors for the use of their money is an implicit cost of running a pizza business, or any other business.

Similar logic applies to other implicit costs. For example, a firm's owners provide entrepreneurial services to the firm—they generate and implement new ideas, and take the risks of failure. If you start your own firm, you put in time, energy, and creativity that you could have spent on something else. You also take a risk that your business will fail and you would lose your investments of money, time, and effort; you could have avoided that risk by investing your money, time, and effort in less-risky endeavors. So your firm has implicit costs equal to the opportunity costs of your time, creativity, and willingness to take risks.

Your pizza firm may earn zero economic profits, but it compensates you for your investments of your money and your time. You could not do any better by shutting down your firm and doing something else with your time and money. So your firm stays in business. You would like a higher profit, but whenever economic profit in the pizza business begins to rise above zero, these profits attract new firms to the industry, reducing the price of pizzas and reducing economic profit back to zero. Free entry and exit drive economic profit to zero in long-run equilibrium.

If firms lose money in short-run equilibrium, then some exit the industry in the long run. Their exit raises demand for the products of the remaining firms, shifting demand curves rightward until the industry reaches a long-run equilibrium with zero economic profit, as in Figure 2b.

Economic profit is zero when price equals average total cost. Therefore, in long-run equilibrium, price equals average total cost. With perfect competition, the price also equals marginal cost; with monopolistic competition, the price exceeds marginal cost. In both cases:

Free entry and exit drive economic profit toward zero.

EXPLANATION

Why does demand for each firm's output fall, as in Figure 2a, when new firms enter the industry? Consider competition among ice-cream stands along a beach. Figure 3a on page 355 shows a short-run equilibrium with three ice-cream stands. They all sell the same kinds of ice cream, but their products are differentiated by their locations. The sellers are not perfectly competitive because they face downward-sloping demand curves. If they all charge the same price, a person closest to Joanne's stand goes there. Joanne could raise her price somewhat without losing all her customers because people close enough to her stand would still buy from her rather than walk farther to other stands. For this reason, Joanne faces a downward-sloping demand curve. Donna and Linda face downward-sloping demand curves for the same reason. These ice-cream stands are monopolistic competitors.

If enough people on the beach buy ice cream, then each stand earns positive economic profits and in the long run new firms enter the industry. Figure 3b shows the long-run equilibrium. Two new firms, Kerk's Ice Cream and Shinji's Ice Cream, have entered the industry and now compete with Donna, Joanne, and Linda. The new firms have

(a) Economic profits earned in the short run by current competitors attract new firms to enter the industry, reducing demand for the products of old firms. Each firm's marginal revenue curve shifts downward along with the demand curve for each differentiated product. (b) Long-run equilibrium occurs when the demand curve shifts far enough that each firm earns zero economic profit when it produces the quantity at which marginal revenue equals marginal cost. A firm earns zero economic profit when the demand curve is tangent to the average cost curve (so average cost equals price).

Figure 2 | Effects of Entry in a Monopolistically Competitive Industry

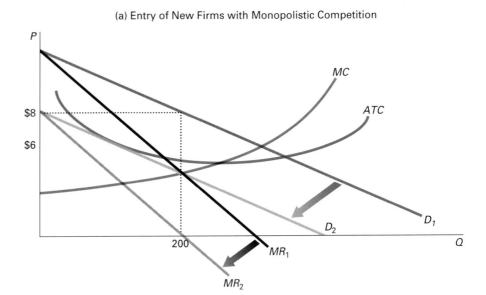

(a) Entry of New Firms with Monopolistic Competition

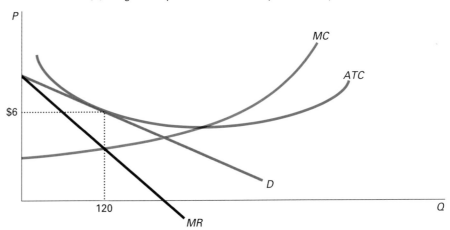

(b) Long-Run Equilibrium with Monopolistic Competition

located their stands to attract the largest number of customers, and some people who would previously have bought from Donna, Joanne, or Linda now buy from Kerk or Shinji. Donna, Joanne, and Linda have experienced falling demands for their ice cream; the demand curves for their ice cream have shifted leftward, as in Figure 2a. New entry occurs until firms earn zero economic profits, as in Figure 2b.

Review Questions

1. What three conditions characterize a monopolistically competitive industry?

2. How does entry by new firms shift the demand curve for the product sold by a firm already in the industry?

3. **(a)** Why don't monopolistically competitive firms earn economic profits in long-run equilibrium?
   (b) Why do firms stay in business if they earn only zero economic profit?

Figure 3 | Short-Run and Long-Run Equilibrium with Monopolistic Competition

(a) Short-Run Equilibrium with 3 Ice-Cream Stands

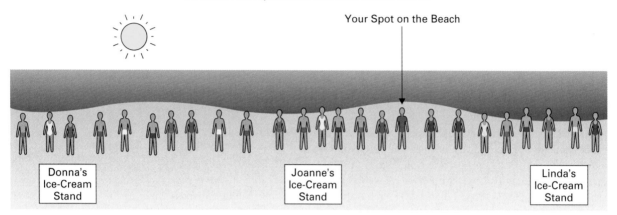

(b) Long-Run Equilibrium with 5 Ice-Cream Stands

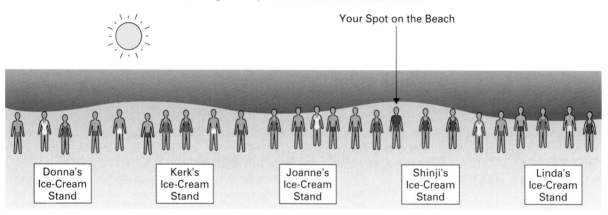

(a) In the short run, Donna, Joanne, and Linda earn positive economic profits. (b) Seeing their success, Kerk and Shinji enter the industry by setting up their own ice-cream stands. They locate their stands where they can attract the most customers: halfway between the other stands. Their entry reduces demand for ice cream at the three original stands, and in the long-run equilibrium, each seller earns zero economic profit.

Thinking Exercises

4. Consider the beach example in Figure 3a, in which each of three sellers earns a profit in the short run. (a) Draw a graph showing the demand for Joanne's ice cream, Joanne's marginal and average costs, the quantity of ice cream that Joanne sells, and the price of ice cream. (b) Draw similar graphs for the long run, after two new firms have entered the industry and reduced long-run economic profits to zero.

5. Draw a graph of short-run equilibrium like Figure 1, but raise the *ATC* curve so that average total cost exceeds the price, and the firm takes a loss in the short run. (Assume that average *variable* cost is less than the price, so the firm stays in business in the short run.) What happens as the economy moves to the long run? Draw a new graph to show the long-run equilibrium.

A Firm in Monopolistic Competition: McDonald's

The fast-food industry is a good example of monopolistic competition. Burger King, Hardee's, Wendy's, McDonald's, and many other fast-food restaurants differentiate their products and face downward-sloping demand curves. They tend to act independently of other firms, because they are numerous enough that, when one cuts its price, each other restaurant suffers only a small loss in customers. New competitors can freely enter into the fast-food business. The table shows estimated sales and costs at a typical McDonald's franchise.

Over 2,000 people apply each year to start McDonald's franchises. The firm accepts only about 1 applicant out of 20. Each accepted franchisee (franchise owner) spends about $310,000 to open a McDonald's outlet and about $500,000 more a few years after opening. Most of these payments cover equipment; they also include a franchise fee and a se-

Estimated Annual Sales, Costs, and Profit of a Typical McDonald's Restaurant

Sales	$1,865,600
Costs	1,674,160
Costs of food and paper	684,796
Food costs	603,973
Paper costs	80,823
Crew labor costs	301,899
Management labor costs	113,069
Advertising and promotion	117,648
Utilities	65,522
Royalties/rent (set by McDonald's at 11.5 percent of sales)	214,544
Other expenses	169,682
Operating profit (accounting profit)	191,440
Cost of capital (interest and depreciation)	88,531
Pretax net revenue to franchisee	$ 102,909

curity deposit. The franchisee must also spend about 2,000 hours in training (working and attending the company's

---

FEATURES OF EQUILIBRIUM WITH MONOPOLISTIC COMPETITION

Excess Capacity and Product Variety

Monopolistically competitive firms maintain excess capacity in long-run equilibrium.

> A firm has **excess capacity** if it could reduce its average cost by raising its output.

Recall from Chapter 12 that a firm's capacity output is the quantity that minimizes its average total cost. A firm has excess capacity if it produces less than its capacity output. A monopolistically competitive firm could reduce its average costs if it were to produce more, but it chooses not to do so because the increase in production would reduce its profit.

EXPLANATION AND EXAMPLE

The connection between average cost and excess capacity is easy to understand. Suppose that a person moves from one apartment to another and rents a larger truck than she needs because a smaller truck is not available. The extra space in the truck is excess capacity. Suppose that the truck costs $40 for the day and it can hold 200 boxes. If the person moves 100 boxes, the average cost of moving a box is 40 cents per box. If she had moved 200 boxes, the average cost would have been 20 cents per box. Excess capacity implies that average cost declines as quantity rises.

Figure 2b shows a firm producing 120 units in long-run equilibrium with monopolistic competition. Its capacity output exceeds 120 units, so it could reduce its average

Hamburger University without pay) before being allowed to open the franchise.

The $102,909 net revenue to the franchise owner equals the sum of:

▶ The opportunity cost of the owner's time and effort running the franchise

▶ A partial payment toward the owner's opportunity cost of the 2,000 hours of training

▶ A payment to the owner for bearing risk

▶ Economic profit (or economic rent to the owner for entrepreneurial services)

Source: Patrick Kaufmann and Francine Lafontaine, "Costs of Control: The Source of Economic Rents for McDonald's Franchisees," *Journal of Law and Economics,* October 1994, 417–453; transformed to 1998 dollars by the author.

cost by increasing production. However, the firm would have to lower its price to sell the additional units, and the price cut would reduce profit, despite the reduction in average cost. For example, the firm in Figure 2b might reduce its average cost from $6 to $5 by raising output to 150 units per month. However, to sell 150 units, the firm would have to reduce the price from $6 to $4. In that case, the firm would lose $150 (a $1 loss per unit, on 150 units) each month. Instead, the firm chooses to produce 120 units and earn an economic profit of zero.

Is Monopolistic Competition Inefficient?

Excess capacity may *appear* to imply that monopolistic competition leads to economic inefficiency. In long-run equilibrium, the price is higher than marginal cost (as in Figure 2b), and firms could reduce their average costs by raising production. When price exceeds marginal cost, some buyer is willing to pay more for an additional unit of the good than the supplier would spend to produce that unit. As Chapter 14 explained, this is what makes monopoly output economically inefficient. Before you draw similar conclusions about the efficiency of monopolistic competition, however, notice two points:

▶ In some industries, average total cost exceeds marginal cost, and firms would lose money if they charged a price equal to marginal cost.

▶ Monopolistic competition creates product variety. Buyers may like variety, and monopolistic competition may be the best way to provide it.

A film studio pays high fixed costs to produce a movie. However, the marginal cost of showing the film in a theater, or producing a videotape, is very low. Because average total cost exceeds marginal cost, a film studio would never charge a price equal to marginal cost—it would lose money. An industry like this—with average total cost above marginal cost—requires a more sophisticated application of the concept of economic efficiency. It would not be correct to conclude that the film industry, or any other monopolistically competitive industry, is economically inefficient simply because its price exceeds marginal cost or because its average total cost declines with increasing output.

Similarly, monopolistically competitive industries provide consumers with the benefits of product variety. These firms face tradeoffs between average cost and product variety. Average total cost would fall if fewer firms operated in the industry, because each firm would produce more units, but product variety would also fall. The lower average cost would be good, but the smaller variety of products might be bad. Buyers usually like a large variety of products because each buyer can choose the type of product he likes best. In that sense, excess capacity under monopolistic competition is the price that the economy pays for more product variety and choice. In conclusion, monopolistic competition might *appear* to create economic inefficiency simply because marginal cost exceeds price and average total cost would fall with an increase in output, but this conclusion is misleading. Whether any particular monopolistically competitive industry is economically efficient requires more sophisticated analysis.

Monopolistic Competition versus Perfect Competition and Monopoly

Monopolistic competition resembles perfect competition in two important ways:

▶ Each firm acts independently, without regard to the responses of its competitors.

▶ Free entry guarantees that firms earn zero economic profits in long-run equilibrium.

Monopolistic competition also differs from perfect competition in two ways:

▶ Each firm faces a downward-sloping demand curve because each produces a differentiated product; monopolistic competitors are not price takers.

▶ Each firm's equilibrium price exceeds its marginal cost (see Figure 2b), and its average total cost would be lower if its output were higher.

The difference between monopolistic competition and perfect competition vanishes as demand becomes large enough to accommodate many firms in an industry in long-run equilibrium. As the number of firms increases, the similarity rises between one firm's product and those of its closest competitors, so products become less differentiated from one another. For example, as more ice-cream stands open on the beach, the distance between the *closest* and *second-closest* stands declines and the demand curve facing each firm becomes more elastic. If the number of firms in the industry grows very large, each firm becomes a price taker and monopolistic competition turns into perfect competition.

Monopolistic competition differs from monopoly mainly in its application to situations with free entry in the long run. Free entry guarantees zero economic profit in long-run equilibrium.

Nonprice Competition

Firms in a monopolistically competitive industry engage in nonprice competition to raise demands for their products. Nonprice competition occurs when firms compete by providing better-quality products or product characteristics designed to match the preferences of specific groups of consumers. Better-quality products might provide faster or friendlier service, longer warranties, quicker delivery, and so on. Firms match product

Figure 4 | A Business Location Decision

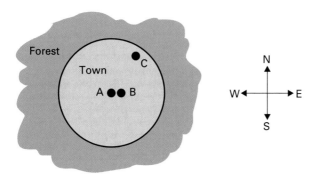

Billy's gas station is at Point A. Joe-Bob can attract more customers by locating his new gas station next to Billy's, at Point B, than by opening at a more remote location like Point C.

characteristics with the preferences of certain groups of consumers when they produce products tailored to the demands of those consumers, such as baby strollers for twins and triplets, mango soda, and designer hearing aids.

Sometimes nonprice competition involves location, as in Figure 4. Suppose that Billy opens the first gas station at Point A in the middle of town. When Joe-Bob establishes a competing gas station, he will attract more customers if he chooses Point B, right next to Billy, than at another location like Point C, where he would be farther away from most people in town. If Joe-Bob were to locate at Point C, Billy would be closer to most of the town's population, and Joe-Bob could attract those customers from Billy only by charging a lower price. By locating at Point B, Joe-Bob guarantees that he is about the same distance as Billy from customers. Joe-Bob is slightly closer to customers on the east side of town, while Billy is slightly closer to customers on the west side. You have probably seen the real-life results of this logic, with several gas stations located close to each other, often at the same intersection.

This same logic applies in many industries.[2] Similar reasoning also applies to *characteristics* of goods other than the location of the seller. Suppose that an organization on your campus earns a large profit by selling brownies, and your club decides to go into the brownie business, too. Brownies range from very soft to very chewy, as Figure 5 illustrates, with many in-between varieties. Suppose that equal numbers of people like each possible type of brownie, and the other organization sells an in-between type (not too soft and not too chewy). Your club is likely to maximize its profit by selling brownies

Figure 5 | Profit-Maximizing Product Differentiation: Don't Be Too Different

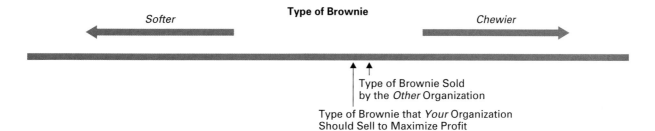

People who like *softer* brownies buy from you.

People who like *chewier* brownies buy from the other organization.

---

[2]A more complicated model is necessary to explain some business location decisions. When many businesses want to locate at the center of town, the high demand for land there raises land prices. A business may choose to locate at a remote location like Point C if the lower land price more than offsets the disadvantages of that remote location.

Is Advertising Good or Bad?

Advertising bombards people daily in newspapers and magazines, on television and radio, by direct mail, and even by telephone, fax, and electronic mail. Advertising is a major industry that accounts for more than 2 percent of U.S. gross domestic product (the total value of all goods and services produced in the United States). Firms advertise to gain customers; some of these new customers may come at the expense of other firms in the same industries, and some may come as a result of product demand generated by advertising.

Some People Say . . .

Some people say that advertising is a socially wasteful extravagance. It tries to convince people to buy products they don't want or need. It tries to mold people's tastes and values, and it diverts their attention from the important things in life toward whatever raises advertisers' profits. Because of advertising, firms do not provide the goods that people really want; instead, it induces people to want whatever firms supply.

Critics see advertising as mostly image-making. According to them, most advertising provides little information about products; instead, it creates images without any basis in reality. They criticize advertising as socially wasteful because it encourages the wrong kind of competition. Customers lose when sellers compete with images rather than price, the quality of goods and services, or socially responsible business practices.

Advertising raises prices, say its critics. Advertisements by any *one* car dealer may add to that dealer's sales, but mainly at the expense of other car dealers. When *all* car dealers in a city advertise, the advertisements tend to neutralize each other, so advertising wastes money. Each seller gets about as many customers as it would get without advertising, but consumers pay the costs of advertising. By raising the cost of selling products, advertising raises prices.

Advertising discourages competition by raising the cost of a new entry into an industry. To compete successfully with entrenched firms, a new firm needs enough money to launch a major advertising campaign.

Advertising creates wasteful product differentiation. People don't really need 100 kinds of laundry detergent, each of which is really about the same as the others, or 20 brands of toilet paper. Advertising all these brands is economically inefficient.

Other People Say . . .

Advertising is socially useful, according to its defenders. It provides valuable information about a product's

that are only *slightly* softer or *slightly* chewier than those sold by your competitor. (If your brownies were *very* soft or *very* chewy, fewer people would buy them.) By making your product only slightly different from the product of your competitor, you maximize the number of your customers.

Competition among Cities and States

Cities compete against each other to attract new businesses, sports franchises, and tourists. Monopolistic competition represents this competition well. Many cities freely enter this competition, and variations in their characteristics create product differentiation. Cities compete vigorously by offering tax breaks, new stadiums, and other desirable benefits to induce major-league football and baseball teams to move from elsewhere or to obtain new teams when leagues expand. Similarly, cities compete to attract other types of businesses by offering low tax rates or special tax exemptions along with other benefits. States and countries compete in this way for tourists and residents, as well as businesses. Warm-weather states compete for retirees by offering free fishing licenses, free college tuition, retail discounts, and other benefits. France and Spain competed for Disney's European theme park; France won partly because it offered more tax breaks and other assistance. All these examples share an important feature: New players can freely enter the competitions. As a result, cities, states, and countries earn zero economic profits in the long run from these activities.

availability, what it does, how much it costs, and who sells it. It reminds people of their opportunities.

Advertising cannot influence people to continue to buy things they don't really want. Of course, advertising creates images. People *like* images, and advertising must entertain to catch and hold people's attention. Entertainment is the best way to provide (or to get people to seek) information about a product; few people would watch a commercial that sounded like a dry, college lecture. Celebrities, jingles, and entertainment help people to remember the commercials and therefore the products. Sellers of arcane goods such as aluminum ingots and special industrial parts advertise in trade journals read mainly by hard-headed businesspeople, and even these advertisements try to be entertaining and eye-catching to get their information across to readers.

Advertising does not discourage competition, say its defenders; it encourages competition, because it provides information about the availability of alternative products. Without advertising, some buyers might not realize that they could find good alternatives to the products they usually buy. Advertising helps new firms to enter an industry and compete by providing them with a forum in which to tell potential customers about their products. Evidence shows that advertising makes demand curves more elastic by increasing the willingness of customers to switch to the products of new firms.

Other evidence shows that advertising increases competition. A famous study compared the prices of eyeglasses in states that allowed advertising of eyeglasses against prices where such ads were prohibited. It found that eyeglasses cost 28 percent more in states that prohibited advertising. Advertising reduced the price by helping sellers to compete with each other and attract customers through low prices. Evidence also indicates that other goods, such as toys and prescription drugs, are cheaper when advertising is allowed than when it is prohibited.

Even if advertising sometimes raises prices, consumers must want the advertising. If people preferred lower-priced, unadvertised products (or goods with less advertising), firms would have an incentive to sell them. A firm could reduce its price and raise its profit by reducing advertising costs. (If a firm could save $1 per unit by reducing its advertising, it could reduce its price by 90 cents and still increase its profit by 10 cents per unit.) If customers preferred less advertising and lower prices, firms would not advertise. They advertise because people want (and are willing to pay for) that advertising.

Advertising gives firms an incentive to improve service to their customers. Its messages create consumer recognition of brand names that helps to make these brand names valuable to firms. This raises the incentives of firms to protect their brand names by providing quality goods and services.

Advertising

Under perfect competition, each firm's marginal cost equals the price. As a result, no firm seeks additional customers. (Because the cost of producing another unit equals the price, the firm would gain nothing from another sale.) Moreover, under perfect competition, all firms sell essentially identical products, so no firm has any incentive to tell customers how its product differs from those of other firms—the products don't differ.

Under monopolistic competition, in contrast, marginal cost is less than price. As a result, each firm stands to profit by attracting additional customers, so it will spend money to attract those customers. In other words, monopolistically competitive firms have an incentive to advertise.

The marginal benefit from advertising to a monopolistically competitive firm is the increase in sales that it will gain, multiplied by the difference between price and marginal cost. Firms choose quantities of advertising that equate the expected marginal benefits from advertising with its marginal costs.

A firm's incentive to advertise depends on the extent of its product differentiation. The more differentiated a firm's product, the greater its incentive to advertise. If a firm produces a product *very* similar to other, competing products, a large fraction of the extra sales from its advertising may go to the similar products of competing firms. On the other hand, a firm that produces a well-differentiated product is likely to capture a large fraction of the extra sales that its advertising creates, so it has a strong incentive to advertise.

R e v i e w   Q u e s t i o n s

6. What is excess capacity, and why do monopolistically competitive firms have excess capacity?

7. What is nonprice competition?

8. How does monopolistic competition resemble perfect competition, and how does it differ? How does it resemble monopoly, and how does it differ?

T h i n k i n g   E x e r c i s e s

9. Why do competing firms often locate near each other? Why do they often sell products that differ only slightly from those of their competitors?

10. What issues are involved in evaluating the economic efficiency of a monopolistically competitive industry?

C o n c l u s i o n

Market Characteristics

In monopolistic competition, many firms in an industry produce differentiated products. Each firm faces a downward-sloping demand curve and produces a quantity at which its marginal revenue equals its marginal cost. Enough firms compete in the industry that the actions of any one of them have only small effects on sales by each of the others. As a result, each firm acts independently, making decisions without considering the reactions of other firms. The industry has free entry.

Equilibrium

Short-run equilibrium with monopolistic competition resembles short-run equilibrium with many monopoly firms. However, free entry drives economic profits to zero in long-run equilibrium.

Features of Equilibrium with Monopolistic Competition

Firms maintain excess capacity in equilibrium: each firm could reduce its average cost by raising output, but doing so would cause it to lose money. Excess capacity may *appear* to imply economic inefficiency in monopolistic competition. However, that conclusion would ignore important facts: (1) Average total cost exceeds marginal cost in some industries, and firms in such industries would lose money if they charged prices equal to marginal cost. (2) Monopolistic competition provides customers with desirable product variety. Nonprice competition is common in monopolistically competitive industries. To maximize their profits, firms often follow

incentives to produce products that are different, but not *too* different, from those of competitors. Also, monopolistically competitive firms have incentives to advertise their products. Table 1 sums up price and profit characteristics in several types of industries.

Table 1
Long-Run Prices and Profits with Different Kinds of Markets

Structure of Competition	Markup of Price over Marginal Cost	Economic Profit

Perfect competition
    Many sellers, no entry
    barriers, identical
    products
	0	0

Monopoly
    One seller, entry
    barriers, one
    product
	+	+ or 0

Cartel
    Few sellers, entry
    barriers, identical
    or differentiated
    products
	+	+ or 0

Monopolistic competition
    Many sellers, no
    entry barriers,
    differentiated
    products
	+	0

Key Terms

differentiated product   monopolistic competition   excess capacity

Problems

11. (a) Why do monopolistically competitive firms advertise? Why don't perfectly competitive firms advertise?

(b) Present a case in favor of advertising.

(c) Present a case against advertising.

12. What arguments can you advance for the economic inefficiency of monopolistic competition? What arguments can you advance for benefits to society from monopolistic competition?

13. Draw a graph of a short-run equilibrium with monopolistic competition in which firms suffer losses. Explain what happens in the long run, and draw a graph of the long-run equilibrium.

14. Over 100,000 fast-food restaurants operate in the United States. Some people say that these restaurants have been overbuilt, that the industry has excess capacity. Can this situation be a long-run equilibrium? Explain.

15. Apply the economic analysis in this chapter to explain why politicians often take middle-of-the-road positions on issues in public, even if they privately hold more liberal or conservative views than their public positions indicate.

16. Three hot-dog stands plan to operate around Circle Lake (which, surprisingly enough, has the shape of a circle). People live in apartments evenly spaced around the lake. Draw a picture of Circle Lake and show locations for the three hot-dog stands that are consistent with equilibrium, so that no stand wants to move to a different location.

IN THE NEWS

If the battle continues much longer, many fast-food businesses will close or merge, predicts Vincent Morrissey, who owns a string of Kentucky Fried Chicken stores in the Midwest. "The industry is overbuilt," he says. "Fast-food franchisers have managed to squeeze in stores into every corner available."

Source: The Wall Street Journal

Is there excess capacity in the fast-food industry?

Inquiries for Further Thought

17. Do people like variety? Is it good or bad to have many choices of products? Does variety cause wasteful duplication?

18. What markets do you think are monopolistically competitive? Why? Do you see too much or too little variety in these markets? Why?

19. Suppose that advertising misleads some people to view Brand X as the best cleanser, when scientific evidence proves that other brands provide more effective cleaning. Is the advertising harmful if people believe that they have the best product? Do people benefit if advertising convinces them that a product makes them sexier? Would they be better off if the government were to ban such advertising? What should the government do if it could identify a case like this? Do you think it could identify such a case?

20. Consumers usually benefit from standardization of certain products rather than using products in different, incompatible formats—think of computer operating systems and software, videotape systems, television systems, and so on. Can the economy standardize products if the government does not let companies collude (which would risk letting them develop a cartel)? Do free markets choose the best standards? Discuss.

CHAPTER 16

OLIGOPOLY

In this Chapter...

Main Points to Understand

▶ Oligopoly is competition among a few firms interacting strategically with each other.

▶ Firms formulate business strategies by anticipating how competitors will react to price changes, and these anticipations affect their own output and pricing decisions.

Thinking Skills to Develop

▶ Recognize competitive situations that give rise to strategic interactions.

▶ Recognize how strategic interactions affect incentives.

▶ Analyze results of strategic interactions.

No major airline is a price taker. No airline is a monopoly, either, since several major companies compete with each other. None of them is a monopolistic competitor, because when American Airlines cuts ticket prices, United Airlines may respond by cutting its prices, too.

When an airline decides whether to cut prices, it must take into account how its competitors will respond. They do *not* act independently of one another (as monopolistic competitors would). Instead, each anticipates the reactions of others to its own actions and chooses its own actions based on these expectations. Their business strategies can involve complex matrices of "If I do this; they'll do that, so I'll do X, and they'll do Y."

Oligopoly roughly means competition among a small number of sellers. More precisely:

INDUSTRY CHARACTERIS-TICS

Oligopoly occurs when (1) firms are not price takers (each faces a downward-sloping demand curve), and (2) each firm acts strategically, taking into account its competitors' likely reactions to its decisions and how it will be affected by their reactions.

365

IN THE NEWS

Cigarettes are sold in this country by a six-company oligopoly that has demonstrated the market power to raise prices at will. . . . The top two sellers—now Philip Morris and R. J. Reynolds—together hold about two-thirds of the market.

Source: New York Times

The tobacco industry is an oligopoly.

An oligopolist reasons as follows: "What *I* do affects what *they* will do, and what *they* do affects *me*." Each firm anticipates its competitors' reactions to its own actions when it decides what to do; firms interact strategically. The airline industry, like the automobile industry and the tobacco industry, is an oligopoly. Other oligopolies include television broadcasting (despite increased competition from cable networks), breakfast cereals (in which Kellogg and General Mills share about two-thirds of total industry sales), the soft-drink industry (which Coca-Cola and PepsiCo dominate), the video-game industry, and the sports-shoe industry.

Strategic Interaction

Strategic interactions take many forms. When a company builds a new hotel in a resort area, it must consider how its rivals will respond. Will they react by building even more hotels or by canceling their own expansion plans? Industries with perfect competition or monopolistic competition have sufficiently many firms that when one boosts sales, the loss in sales at *each* other firm is small enough to ignore. For this reason, those industries do not exhibit strategic interaction.

If only five firms compete in an industry, however, and one firm doubles output from 100 to 200 units per month, each of the other four firms may lose 25 sales per month (25 percent of its business). These competitors are likely to react to such an action. Knowing that its competitors will react, each firm anticipates these likely reactions in its decision making. This process leads oligopolistic firms to act strategically. Table 1 contrasts oligopoly with monopolistic competition and perfect competition.

Examples of Strategic Interaction

Governments evaluate the likely reactions of allies and adversaries in their foreign-policy decisions. Personal decisions (particularly romantic ones) often take into account the reactions of other people and the likely effects of those reactions. Candidates for public office consider their opponents' reactions to public statements, positions, and political advertisements. Each of these cases illustrates a strategic interaction—each decision maker considers the reactions of others in choosing her own actions.

Barriers to Entry

Oligopolistic firms, like monopolies, can earn positive economic profits in the long run only if barriers to entry protect them from new competition. Otherwise, additional firms enter, creating a perfectly competitive or monopolistically competitive industry. Barriers to entry (costs high enough to prevent new firms from entering) can take many forms. Artificial barriers to entry include laws against new firms joining an industry, license requirements or other government regulations that hinder entry, and patents or copyrights. Natural barriers to entry include the fixed costs of starting a firm and increasing returns to scale (average costs that fall with a rising scale of production). Also, established firms may have prohibitive cost advantages if they own unique inputs that new firms cannot obtain or operate more efficiently than new firms can, perhaps due to their experience in the industry.

Product Differentiation by Oligopolies

The logic of oligopoly sometimes applies to industries with *many* firms and differentiated products. For example, many firms sell ice cream, but perhaps only a few offer close substitutes for Jim's Gourmet Ice Cream. Jim may take into account the reactions of those close competitors when he makes decisions about output and prices. Although

Like chess players, business firms must anticipate the reactions of their rivals.

Table 1 | Differences between Monopolistic Competition, Oligopoly, and Perfect Competition

Monopolistic Competition	Oligopoly	Perfect Competition
Many firms produce closely related products When one firm lowers its price, it gains sales. *Each* other firm loses only a few sales, because so many other firms compete. When one firm changes its output or price, other firms *do not react.*	Few firms produce closely related products When one firm lowers its price, it gains sales. *Each* other firm loses a significant amount of sales, because only a few other firms compete. Those firms react, perhaps by lowering their prices. Each firm knows that other firms will react to its decisions, and it anticipates these reactions when making its decisions.	Many firms produce the same product Any firm can sell more without reducing its price. With many firms, each one loses only a very small amount of sales. When one firm changes its output, other firms *do not react.*

many firms compete in the real-life ice-cream industry, Ben and Jerry's may be a closer substitute for Baskin-Robbins than for generic ice cream. Kellogg's Raisin Bran and Post Raisin Bran are closer substitutes for each other than either is for Batman or Lucky Charms cereal. Even in an industry with many firms, if only a few sell close substitutes, those firms may strategically interact with each other.

Prices and Profits in the U.S. Economy

Industries with only a few firms that together sell a large fraction of total industry output are often called *highly concentrated* industries. Highly concentrated industries tend to have certain characteristics. While price equals marginal cost in perfectly competitive industries, price exceeds marginal cost in industries with oligopoly, monopoly, or monopolistic competition. Evidence suggests that price exceeds marginal cost in many U.S. industries, and the ratio of price to marginal cost is higher on average in more concentrated industries. Evidence also suggests that prices in more concentrated industries change less often and by smaller amounts than other prices; these industries show more *price rigidity.*

> **Price rigidity** refers to slow adjustments of prices to changes in costs or demand.

Magazines at newsstands, like tickets to rock concerts and major sporting events, tend to show some price rigidity. Economists do not yet fully understand the reasons for price rigidity and its variation across industries. Nevertheless, evidence indicates that prices change more often in some industries than in others, and they tend to change less often in more concentrated industries. Wholesale prices remain fixed for 6 to 18 months on average, depending on the industry. For example, the average length of time between price changes is about 6 months for household appliances and plywood, 1 year for glass and paper, and 18 months for cement, steel, and chemicals.

Firms tend to earn higher profits (on average) in more concentrated industries. There are two possible interpretations of this fact. An increase in concentration might reduce competition, leading to higher prices and profits. In such a case, profits are high because industry sales are concentrated among a few firms. Alternatively, firms that succeed in earning high profits (perhaps because they successfully reduce their costs) tend to expand, raising concentration in their industries. In such a case, the industry becomes concentrated because some firms have been more successful than others at reducing their costs, so those firms earn higher profits.

I N T H E N E W S

Dominant firms attract antitrust probes and investors

By Greg Ip
Staff Reporter of The Wall Street Journal

Microsoft Corp., Intel Corp. and Coca-Cola Co. have been among the biggest creators of shareholder wealth during the 1990s bull market. They have also all come in for antitrust scrutiny.

It may not be a coincidence.

These blue-chip growth companies boast enormous market shares, strong fran-

chises and brand names and often the ability to expand profit margins in a highly competitive economy. These qualities are key to delivering consistent, above-average earnings, which is why investors attach such high values to them. But they are also the characteristics often associated with near-monopolies. As such, they are likely to attract antitrust scrutiny from regulators or competitors.

There is nothing illegal

about a dominant market share per se. Indeed, whether these companies have actually done anything wrong is the subject of debate in Washington and in the courts. Coke, for example, owes its 50% share of the world soft drink market not to government-granted monopoly or a costly fixed infrastructure, but to its painstakingly developed brand and distribution network.

Source: The Wall Street Journal

Review Questions

1. What is oligopoly? How does it differ from monopolistic competition and perfect competition?

2. Why do oligopolistic firms interact strategically with one another?

3. What are two characteristics of highly concentrated industries?

EQUILIBRIUM

Each firm in an oligopoly must anticipate other firms' likely reactions to its actions. The equilibrium in an oligopoly depends on *what firms believe* about the likely reactions of their competitors. Each type of belief leads to a different model of oligopoly. This section discusses one famous oligopoly model called the *Cournot* model.

The logic of strategic interactions is based on the concept of a Nash equilibrium, which occurs when each firm's action is optimal *given* the actions of the other firms.[1] More precisely:

> A firm's **best response** to a situation is the action that maximizes its profit, *given* the actions of its rivals.

> A **Nash equilibrium** is a situation in which each firm makes its best response.

---

[1]Chapter 17 discusses the general theory of strategic interactions—game theory—and its application.

In other words, a Nash equilibrium is a situation in which each firm's action maximizes its profit, *given* the actions of rival firms. In a Nash equilibrium, each firm's action is its best response to its competitors' actions, and no firm has an incentive to change its actions.

Cournot Model

> In the **Cournot model,** each firm believes that other firms will react to its decisions by changing their prices to maintain fixed levels of output.[2]

In the Cournot model, each firm looks at other firms and says, "I'll take the demand that is *leftover* after their sales, and act like a monopoly." In Nash equilibrium with the Cournot model, price exceeds marginal cost, but is below the monopoly price.

Explanation of the Cournot Model

Suppose that the sports-shoe industry has two firms, Kiwi Sports Shoes and Mango Super-Sport Footwear. Kiwi believes that, whatever it does, Mango will *react* by changing its price to keep its output constant.

> If we cut our price to sell more shoes, Mango will also cut its price to compete with us and keep its sales from falling below 3 million shoes per month. If we raise our price, Mango will also raise its price enough to increase its own profits while still selling 3 million pairs of shoes per month. Mango will always sell 3 million pairs of shoes, no matter what we do.

The owner of Kiwi Sports Shoes would continue her reasoning:

> We'll have to take whatever demand for shoes is left over after Mango sells 3 million pairs per month. We can maximize our profit by acting like a monopoly facing this leftover demand. We will choose the quantity at which marginal cost equals marginal revenue, based on this leftover demand.

Figure 1 shows what Kiwi will do. The figure shows the market demand for shoes,

---

Figure 1 | Nash Equilibrium with Cournot Competition

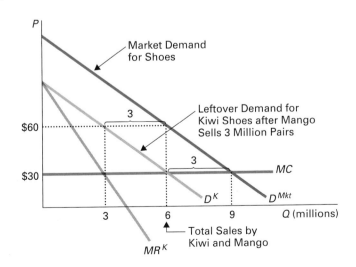

Total market demand for shoes is D^{Mkt}. Kiwi believes that Mango will always change its price to sell 3 million pairs of shoes, so the demand for Kiwi shoes is market demand minus 3 million, giving the demand curve D^K. The curve MR^K shows Kiwi's marginal revenue. Kiwi maximizes profit by producing a quantity at which its marginal revenue equals its marginal cost, so it produces 3 million pairs of shoes and sells them for $60 per pair.

---

[2]Other oligopoly models apply when firms have other beliefs about the likely reactions of their competitors. For example, a firm might believe that if it reduces its own price to increase its sales, its competitors will reduce their production levels and keep their prices fixed.

Business Strategies in Oligopoly

Business strategies in an oligopolistic market take many forms and involve complex issues, including commitment to flexible or inflexible technologies, inventory decisions, industrial secrecy, product differentiation, and investments in experience.

Flexible and Inflexible Technologies

Some firms can choose between relatively flexible or inflexible technologies for producing their goods. Suppose that a firm could use either of two technologies with average costs as in Figure 2. Curve AC_1 shows the average cost curve with one technology, and Curve AC_2 shows the average cost curve with a second technology. Technology 1 is the lowest-cost method of producing 100 units per month, but the increased

flexibility of Technology 2 makes it the lowest-cost way to produce most other levels of output. The average cost of production using Technology 2 does not change much if the firm changes its output, allowing flexibility in output level. Technology 1, in contrast, gives the firm little flexibility, since it would experience a big jump in average cost at any output that differs much from 100 units per month.

Flexibility benefits a firm that is uncertain about the demand for its product. It can also help a firm to raise or lower output in response to the actions of another firm. Inflexibility can also provide benefits, though. If potential competitors are aware of a firm's commitment to inflexible technology, they may be less likely to begin competing with that firm than if they believe that flexible technology would allow it to reduce its output easily. Because choosing an inflexible technology can help to deter entry, it can be an advantageous business strategy in an oligopolistic market.

An inflexible technology can also help a cartel to prevent cheating by its members. If member firms rely on inflexible technologies designed to produce the quantities that the cartel has set, each firm has little incentive to cheat by raising output, because its average cost would also rise.

Inventories

Firms in an oligopolistic industry can sometimes deter new firms from entering by holding large stocks of inventories. A firm can threaten to sell these inventories all at once to reduce the price if a new competitor enters. If potential competitors are aware of these inventories, they may choose not to enter the industry. Holding inventories has the same effect as using a flexible technology: It allows a firm to increase supply quickly without a large increase in costs of production. Of

Figure 2 | Flexible and Inflexible Technologies

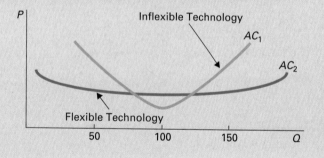

D^{Mkt}, and D^K, the leftover demand for Kiwi shoes after Mango sells 3 million pairs per month. Kiwi maximizes its profit by choosing a quantity at which its marginal cost ($30 per pair) equals its marginal revenue, MR^K. The figure shows that it chooses to produce 3 million pairs of shoes per month and sell them for $60 per pair.

Mango faces the same situation as Kiwi. Mango believes that Kiwi will adjust its price to keep selling 3 million pairs of shoes, no matter what Mango does. Mango takes the demand *left over* after Kiwi sells 3 million pairs per month; it calculates its marginal revenue curve and chooses a quantity at which its marginal cost equals marginal revenue, based on this leftover demand. A figure just like Figure 1 could show Mango's profit-maximizing decision to produce 3 million pairs of shoes per month and sell them for $60 per pair.

Notice that based on Kiwi's belief that Mango will sell 3 million pairs of shoes, Kiwi chooses to sell 3 million pairs itself. Also, based on Mango's belief that Kiwi will sell 3 million pairs of shoes, *Mango* chooses to sell 3 million pairs itself, which is just what Kiwi expects it to do. This situation is a Nash equilibrium. Kiwi is maximizing its course, a firm can deter entry by threatening price reductions only if it produces at lower costs than potential competitors do. Otherwise, the firm would take a loss itself if it were to reduce the price enough to force a loss on the new competitor; knowing this, new firms enter the industry.

Information

A firm can deter entry into its industry if it can make other firms *believe* that its costs are lower than theirs would be, so that new firms would expect to lose money if they enter the industry. This possibility gives firms an incentive to keep their costs secret and make potential competitors believe that they produce at particularly low costs. Of course, potential competitors know that an entrenched firm has an incentive to deceive them about costs. They may try to obtain information on the firm's true costs in various ways, providing one motive for industrial espionage.

Product Differentiation

Studies show that a new firm cannot successfully enter an industry dominated by a single firm unless it has lower costs than the dominant firm or a differentiated product that consumers want. [See, for example, Michael Porter, *Competitive Strategies* (New York: Free Press, 1985). Porter studied hundreds of industries and summarized his results in this book.] The new entrant must also overcome other advantages of the dominant firm and prevent a strong reaction from that firm. A new entrant has the best chance of succeeding if it produces a differentiated product that the dominant firm could produce only at a higher cost.
Japanese car makers, for example, successfully challenged the three big American car makers in the 1970s by producing small, fuel-efficient cars at a time when most American cars were big gas guzzlers. The Japanese firms saw an opportune moment to enter the American market, because the price of gasoline had risen dramatically at about the same time, giving consumers an incentive to buy small cars with good fuel efficiency. American car makers could not quickly switch to making good, small cars because of the time required to design, test, and produce the new models. After succeeding in that portion of the car market, Japanese firms later expanded to larger and more expensive cars.

Federal Express provides another example of successful entry because of a cost advantage. FedEx successfully entered the parcel-delivery business, competing with United Parcel Service (UPS) and other such firms, by inventing a new kind of delivery system with a single hub (in Memphis, Tennessee) that allowed it to provide reliable overnight delivery at a lower cost than its rivals. The hub technology was later copied by other firms in the industry.

Experience

Experience can affect the cost of producing a good. A more experienced firm with better-trained workers often has lower costs of production. If learning by doing can reduce costs sufficiently, then the first firm in an industry has an incentive to charge a low price rather than the monopoly price, even if it loses money in the short run! By keeping the price low, it sells more and gains more experience, reducing future costs. These lower future costs can help deter future entry by potential rivals who lack this experience. The firm trades off a lower price and losses in the short run for lower costs, less competition, and higher profits in the long run.

profit, based on its correct beliefs about Mango's reactions, and Mango is maximizing its profit, based on its correct beliefs about Kiwi's reactions.

Notice that each firm's price exceeds its marginal cost of production. More sophisticated analysis would show that the equilibrium price approaches marginal cost as additional firms compete in the industry. This happens because the additional competition decreases the leftover demand for any one firm, reducing the price that each firm charges.

Comments on the Cournot Model

The Cournot model applies to situations in which each firm expects other firms to react to its actions by keeping their levels of output constant, and varying their prices. In some real-life situations, this is not a reasonable assumption because other firms have no incentive to react in this way. The Cournot model applies in *some* real-life situations, though. For example, firms sometimes choose their production levels or capacities before they know what prices will be. The Cournot model applies in many such cases, particularly if production or capacity is fixed for a long period of time. (For example, a firm may take a long time to build a new factory with added capacity.) Evidence from economic experiments also shows that the Cournot model accurately describes most situations of duopoly (oligopoly with two firms). The Cournot model is also consistent with the observation that industries with fewer firms generate higher profits.

Dominant-Firm Model

The *dominant-firm* model applies to an industry with one large, dominant firm and several (perhaps many) small firms. The dominant firm acts like a Cournot competitor; it takes the demand curve leftover after the smaller firms have sold their outputs and acts like a monopoly facing this leftover demand.

A firm may become dominant if it enters the industry before other firms and learns about cost-reducing techniques or grows to a size that gives it the lowest average cost. Alternatively, a firm can become dominant if it begins operating under the protection of a patent and remains larger than new competitors who enter the industry after expiration of the patent. Even with free entry, single firms dominate some industries. The Cheerleader Supply Company, for example, sells more than half of all cheerleaders' products sold in the United States, even though free entry has allowed many other firms to enter the industry.

Unless a dominant firm can keep its costs lower than those of its competitors, it cannot retain its position in the long run. Often, a dominant firm can earn economic profits only temporarily, before other firms enter the industry. Apple and IBM, for example, were the first major producers of personal computers, earning high profits for a time, until many new firms entered that industry. U.S. Steel had a 66 percent market share when it was formed by a merger in 1901, but its market share and profits fell over time as new steel producers appeared. Harley-Davidson had the entire U.S. motorcycle market in 1962, but only 36 percent of the market 20 years later; Xerox saw its market share of photocopying machines fall from 100 percent to 42 percent over the same period.

Review Questions

4. What is a Nash equilibrium?

5. In the Cournot model, how do firms expect rivals to react?

6. Why is the dominant firm model a special case of Cournot competition?

Thinking Exercise

7. Suppose that a dominant firm operates in an industry. Draw a graph to show the connection between market demand and demand for the product of the dominant firm. Also show the dominant firm's marginal cost and profit-maximizing level of output.

SUMMARY OF MARKET BEHAVIOR

Experimental evidence on prices and quantities generally supports these conclusions:

1. The monopoly model applies when only one firm operates in an industry.

2. The Cournot model applies when two firms compete.

3. If the same people make price and output decisions repeatedly in an oligopoly, the monopoly (cartel) model eventually applies best.

4. Otherwise, perfect competition begins when three or more firms compete.

Table 1 in Chapter 15 summarized the difference between price and marginal cost as well as economic profit in long-run equilibrium with perfect competition, monopolistic competition, cartels, and monopoly. With perfect competition, price equals marginal cost and firms earn zero economic profits in the long run. With monopolistic competition, price exceeds marginal cost in the long run and firms earn zero economic profits. With oligopoly or monopoly, price exceeds marginal cost and firms often earn positive economic profit. The difference between oligopoly and monopoly is mainly in the size of the profit and the markup of price above marginal cost. Monopolies usually charge higher prices than oligopolies with the same marginal costs. Short-run profits can be positive or negative in any of these cases. Positive economic profits create incentives for entry, and negative profits lead firms to exit the industry. Whether an industry resembles a monopoly, a cartel, or an oligopoly in the short run, perfect competition or monopolistic competition can prevail in the long run if no barriers to entry deter potential competitors.

IN THE NEWS

"It only takes two competitors to keep prices down," says Robert Joedicke, a securities analyst with Shearson Lehman Brothers. "When you had Macy's and Gimbel's on the same block in New York, you didn't need 12 other department stores to have low prices."

Source: The Wall Street Journal

Oligopolies, even with only two firms, typically charge prices lower than the monopoly price.

Conclusion

Industry Characteristics

An industry is an oligopoly if a small number of firms interact strategically with one another. In strategic interaction, each firm's decisions take into account the likely reactions of other firms and the effects on themselves of those reactions. In the short run, oligopolies may earn economic profits, but new firms enter in the long run and reduce economic profits to zero unless barriers to entry prevent this.

In a *highly concentrated* industry, only a few firms sell a large fraction of total industry output. Such an industry tends to show a high ratio of price to marginal cost and relatively high price rigidity. High concentration sometimes causes high profits through oligopoly behavior; in other cases, both high concentration and high profits result from the success of certain firms in reducing their costs.

Equilibrium

A firm's best response to a situation is the action that maximizes its profit, given the actions of its rivals. In a Nash equilibrium, each firm follows its best response, that is, the action that maximizes its profit, given the actions of rival firms. The equilibrium in an oligopoly depends on what firms believe about the likely reactions of their rivals; different sets of beliefs lead to different models of oligopoly.

In the Cournot model of oligopoly, each firm believes that others will react to its decisions by changing their prices to maintain fixed output levels. As a result, each firm acts like a monopoly using the demand *left over* after other firms have sold their outputs. In equilibrium, price exceeds marginal cost. A related model applies to any industry with a dominant firm that acts like a monopoly facing the demand left over after other, smaller firms have sold their outputs.

Summary of Market Behavior

Experimental evidence suggests that the monopoly model applies when only one firm operates in an industry, the Cournot model applies when two firms compete, and perfect competition is a good approximation when three or more firms compete. However, when the same people or firms act repeatedly in an industry with only a few firms, the monopoly (cartel) model best captures their behavior.

Key Terms

oligopoly
price rigidity

best response
Nash equilibrium

Cournot model

Problems

8. Why does the Nash equilibrium price exceed marginal cost in the Cournot model? (*Hint:* Assume that price equals marginal cost in the Kiwi/Mango example, and ask what Kiwi would do to increase its profit.)

9. Reproduce Table 1 from Chapter 15 and fill in a new row for Oligopoly.

10. Consider the Cournot example in the text. What would Kiwi Sports Shoes do differently if it expected Mango Super-Sport Footwear to respond to its actions by changing output and keeping price constant? (*Hint:* Start from Figure 1 and think about what Kiwi could do to raise its profits in this case.)

11. Summarize the experimental evidence on market behavior.

12. **(a)** How can oligopoly firms use inventories to help prevent entry?
    (b) What advantage can an oligopoly firm gain by maintaining secrecy about its plans?
    (c) Why might a new firm in an emerging industry have an incentive to charge such a low price that it loses money, even if other firms have not entered the industry to compete with it?

Inquiries for Further Thought

13. What industries do you think are oligopolies? Why?

14. A high concentration ratio does not insulate a firm from competition. Nike had a large share of the sports shoe market until Reebok expanded rapidly in the 1980s and surpassed Nike's sales in 1987. Can you think of other examples of firms that had large shares of their industries' sales until new firms entered and eventually surpassed the old leaders?

15. What, if anything, should government do about oligopolies?

CHAPTER 17

GAME THEORY

In this Chapter...

Main Points to Understand

▶ Game theory involves the logic of strategic behavior.

▶ Certain games, such as the prisoner's dilemma, have many real-life applications.

▶ A player's best strategy usually depends on the strategies of other players.

▶ Tit-for-tat is a good strategy in repeated games.

Thinking Skills to Develop

▶ Recognize game situations in real life.

▶ Analyze how one person's strategy affects another person's strategy.

▶ Predict the Nash equilibrium of a game.

▶ Understand multiple equilibria and subgame perfection.

▶ Recognize the value of commitments.

In a simple child's game, two players place five sticks on the ground. The players take turns picking up either one or two sticks, and the player who picks up the last stick loses. If you can leave your opponent with only one stick to pick up, you win. You can leave only one stick if two or three remain on the ground when you start your last turn. You can guarantee this position if you take the first turn and pick up one stick. With four sticks remaining, your opponent must leave you with either two or three at the end of his turn. When both players understand this game, the first player wins. If the game starts with seven sticks, on the other hand, the second player wins.

The logic of games like this extends beyond entertainment; it applies when two stores compete for customers, when three employees compete for a promotion, when governments conduct foreign policy, and when U.S. senators trade votes on bills in Congress. It applies to economic situations like the oligopolies discussed in Chapter 16 and to personal interactions in many areas of life. Firms employ highly paid executives largely to carry out strategic planning: making decisions for the firms after considering the likely reactions of competitors, consumers, and suppliers. Most people recognize how other people will react to their decisions, and they take these reactions into account in their decisions. You can apply game theory to any situation in which your actions affect other people, and their actions affect you.

BASIC IDEAS OF GAME THEORY

The general logic of strategic behavior is known as *game theory*.

> **Game theory** is the general theory of strategic behavior.

Game theory was developed by the mathematician John von Neumann around 1928 and extended by von Neumann and an economist, Oskar Morgenstern, in their 1944 book, *The Theory of Games and Economic Behavior*.[1] The theory, usually written in mathematical form, plays an important role in modern economics; it also has applications in biology, political science, psychology, military planning, and other disciplines.

Most games involve strategic interactions among the players. As each player decides what to do, she must consider how her actions will affect the actions of other players. What she does affects what others do, and what they do affects her. Each player takes into account the actions and reactions of other players. Chapter 16 presented some examples of strategic behavior in the context of an oligopoly.

Rules, Strategies, Payoffs, and Equilibrium

When economists apply game theory, they think of economic situations as games. To successfully analyze such a situation, you must think carefully about the rules of the game, the possible strategies for each player, and the players' payoffs. Then you can choose the players' *best* strategies and find an *equilibrium* of the game, that is, a prediction of the likely outcome.

The rules of the game describe its economic, legal, and social environment.

> The **rules** of a game say who can do what and at what times.

Suppose that two aircraft manufacturers bid for a government contract. The rules might require that each firm submit a price at the same time, without seeing the price that the other firm submits. The government then chooses the lowest price, and the winning firm must sell ten planes to the government at that price.

> A player's **strategy** is a plan for actions in each possible situation in the game.

You might ask a friend to go to a movie, planning to go if the answer is "yes" and stay home if the answer is "no." That is a strategy of a simple game; other possible strategies might include going to the movie alone or asking someone else if the first person says "no." The strategies available to bidders on a government contract involve the prices they could charge.

The next step in analyzing a game is to list the payoffs to the players: what they would win or lose in various situations.

> A player's **payoff** is the amount that the player wins or loses in a particular game situation.

The payoffs in a game might state the profits or losses of the bidders on a government contract or the utility (happiness) of family members deciding how to spend their joint holiday.

A game with strategic interaction: The pitcher wants to fool the batter with his pitch. The batter knows that the pitcher wants to fool him, and the pitcher knows that the batter knows that he knows.

---

[1]John von Neumann and Oskar Morgenstern, *The Theory of Games and Economic Behavior* (Princeton, N.J.: Princeton University Press, 1944).

Once you know the rules, possible strategies, and payoffs, you can find the players' *best strategies* or *best responses*. A player's best strategy often depends on what other players do. Your best strategy in the 50-yard dash may be simply to run as fast as you can, but your best strategies in chess and football depend on how your opponents play. If a player's best strategy does not depend on what other players do, it is called a *dominant strategy*.

A player has a **dominant strategy** if that player's best strategy does not depend on what other players do.

Nash Equilibrium

A Nash equilibrium occurs when each player's strategy is optimal, given the strategies of the other players. Recall the more precise definitions from Chapter 16:

A player's **best response** (or best strategy) is the strategy that maximizes that player's payoff, given the strategies of other players.

A **Nash equilibrium** is a situation in which each player makes her best response.

In a Nash equilibrium, each player's strategy is a best response to other players' strategies, so no player has an incentive to change strategies. Examples of rules, strategies, payoffs, and Nash equilibria will appear throughout this chapter.

Prisoner's Dilemma

A famous example in game theory called the *prisoner's dilemma* has many applications. The police catch two people, Bonnie and Clyde, and charge them with a crime. The police take them into separate rooms, where each prisoner must decide either to confess or not to confess without knowing what the other prisoner will do. The police tell each prisoner that they have collected enough evidence to send both to prison for 3 years. If only one prisoner confesses and testifies against the other, that prisoner will get only 1 year and the other will get 8 years. If both confess, each will get 4 years.

Table 1 summarizes these payoffs to Bonnie and Clyde for each possible choice. Bonnie chooses a row of the table (top or bottom). In the top row, she confesses; in the bottom row, she does not confess. Clyde chooses a column of the table (left or right). In the left column, he confesses; in the right column, he does not confess.

Table 1 | Prisoner's Dilemma

		Clyde	
		CONFESS	NOT CONFESS
Bonnie	CONFESS	4 years each	1 year for Bonnie and 8 years for Clyde
	NOT CONFESS	8 years for Bonnie and 1 year for Clyde	3 years each

Figure 1 | Bonnie's Decision Tree

What is each prisoner's best strategy when neither knows what the other will do? Figure 1 graphs Bonnie's choices in a *decision tree* with two parts. If Clyde confesses, Bonnie can:

▶ Confess and serve 4 years in prison.

▶ Not confess and serve 8 years.

Her best strategy in this situation is to confess. If Clyde does not confess, Bonnie can:

▶ Confess and serve 1 year in prison.

▶ Not confess and serve 3 years.

Again, her best strategy is to confess. No matter what Clyde does, Bonnie gains by confessing. Confessing is Bonnie's dominant strategy. By the same reasoning, Clyde concludes that he should confess regardless of what Bonnie does, so confessing is also a dominant strategy for Clyde.[2]

Since each player's best response is to confess, the Nash equilibrium of the prisoner's dilemma game is for both players to confess, and each gets a 4-year prison term. The dilemma is that both would fare better if neither were to confess, but they lack the proper incentives to achieve this better outcome.

Review Questions

1. What is a strategy in a game?

2. What is a Nash equilibrium?

Thinking Exercises

3. Draw a decision tree for Clyde in the example from Table 1 and indicate his best strategy.

4. The police charge Rat and Skunk with shoplifting. If both plead not guilty, each will get a $300 fine. If both plead guilty, each will get a $500 fine. If Rat pleads

---

[2]This ignores issues of retaliation by either one after both leave prison; that question would complicate the game, but it would not change the main ideas.

guilty and implicates Skunk (who pleads not guilty), Rat will go free and Skunk will get a $1,000 fine. Skunk faces the same choice if Rat pleads not guilty. Draw a table to summarize the *payoffs* in this game and find each player's best response. What is the Nash equilibrium of this game?

This section considers three applications of the prisoner's dilemma game to economics— cheating on a cartel, an international trade war, and advertising—in which the players have dominant strategies. The section also discusses a fourth example of a game in which the players have no dominant strategies.

ECONOMIC APPLICATIONS OF GAME THEORY

Cheating on a Cartel

Suppose that the Coca-Cola Company and PepsiCo form a cartel, agreeing to charge the monopoly price for soft drinks and split profits equally. Chapter 14 explained that firms have incentives to cheat on cartel agreements because each firm could raise its own profit by charging a slightly lower price and taking customers away from the other cartel members. Each firm must choose its own price without knowing which price others will choose. Each firm in a two-firm soft-drink cartel has two possible strategies: it can either charge the monopoly price or charge a low price.[3]

Table 2 shows the payoffs. Coca-Cola chooses a row of the table, and PepsiCo chooses a column. If Coke and Pepsi both charge the monopoly price (Coke chooses the bottom row and Pepsi chooses the right column), each earns a $6 million profit. If Coke cheats on the cartel by charging a low price (the top row) while Pepsi charges the monopoly price (the right column), Coca-Cola earns $8 million and Pepsi earns only $2 million. The reverse is true if Pepsi charges a low price and Coca-Cola does not. If both charge a low price (Coke chooses the top row and Pepsi chooses the left column), each earns only $3 million.

Figure 2 graphs Coke's decision tree. If Pepsi charges the monopoly price, Coke can either charge the low price and earn $3 million or charge the monopoly price and earn $2 million. Coke's best strategy in this situation is obviously to charge the low price. If Pepsi charges the monopoly price, Coke can choose the low price and earn $8 million or the monopoly price and earn $6 million; again, Coke's best strategy is to charge the low price. No matter what PepsiCo does, Coca-Cola gains by charging the low price,

Table 2 | Cheating on a Cartel

		PepsiCo	
		CHEAT ON CARTEL (CHARGE LOW PRICE)	DON'T CHEAT (CHARGE MONOPOLY PRICE)
Coca-Cola	CHEAT ON CARTEL (CHARGE LOW PRICE)	$3 million each	Coke earns $8 million, Pepsi earns $2 million
	DON'T CHEAT (CHARGE MONOPOLY PRICE)	Coke earns $2 million, Pepsi earns $8 million	$6 million each

[3] The assumption that each could charge only one possible low price simplifies the analysis. The analysis is more complicated, but the main point remains the same, when the firms could choose from *many* low prices.

A Hint on Studying Games

Games often become clear if you write out a table with payoffs (as in Table 1) and draw arrows to show the best responses of each player. The vertical arrows show Bonnie's best strategy in the prisoner's dilemma game. They point from the worse outcome to the better outcome for Bonnie for each possible situation. The horizontal arrows show Clyde's best strategy; they point toward his preferred outcome in each situation.

When two arrows point to the same place (such as the upper, left-hand corner, where each player confesses to the crime), they point out a Nash equilibrium.

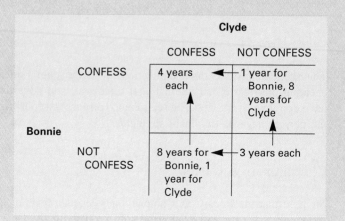

and no matter what Coke does, Pepsi gains by charging the low price. Each company has a dominant strategy: Charge the low price. As a result, in the Nash equilibrium of this game, both companies charge the low price and earn only $3 million profit each.

Trade Wars between Countries

Suppose that two countries, the United States and Japan, carry on international trade. The United States produces only food, and Japan produces only televisions. The United States exports food and imports televisions; Japan exports televisions and imports food. Assume also that food and television production are perfectly competitive industries.[4]

The United States can gain by imposing a *tariff* on Japanese televisions, that is, by taxing television imports. Figure 3 shows the effects of this tax. The U.S. government collects revenue represented by Areas A and B. The tax raises the price to U.S. buyers from $300 to $350, so U.S. consumer surplus falls by Areas A and C. Therefore, the United States gains Area B minus Area C from the tariff. (The government could give

Figure 2 | Decision Tree for the Coca-Cola Company

---

[4]Similar but somewhat more complicated reasoning applies for monopoly, monopolistic competition, or oligopoly.

Figure 3 | Effects of a Tariff on Japanese Televisions

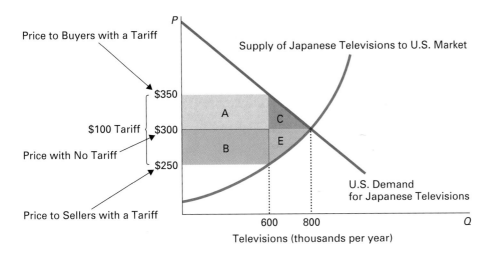

In this example, the United States imports all of its televisions from Japan. Without a tariff, the equilibrium price is $300 per television. A $100 tariff raises the price to buyers to $350 and reduces the price to sellers to $250. U.S. consumer surplus falls by the sum of Areas A and C, but the U.S. government gains the sum of Areas A and B. (The government could give this money back to U.S. consumers.) Net U.S. gains are Area B minus Area C. As long as Area B is larger than Area C, the United States as a whole gains from the tariff. (Japan loses the sum of Areas B and E in producer surplus. The world as a whole loses Areas C and E from the tariff.)

the money in Area A + B to consumers, which would more than offset their loss.) Of course, the tariff hurts Japanese producers, who lose Areas B and E in producer surplus. The United States gains B − C, but Japan loses B + E, so the tariff causes a deadweight social loss of Areas C and E.

The same logic applies to Japanese imports of American food. Japan can gain by imposing a tariff on imports of American food, but its gain would be smaller than the loss of producer surplus to the United States.

Table 3 shows the payoffs in this application of the prisoner's dilemma game. If *neither* country adopts a tariff (both maintain *free trade)*, then each country gains $8 million in consumer and producer surplus. If either country imposes a tariff on imports while the other does not, it gains $9 million and the other country gains only $4 million.[5] If both countries put tariffs on imports, each country gains only $5 million from trade.

The decision tree in Figure 4 shows that, regardless of what Japan does, the United States has an incentive to put a tariff on television imports. The same argument applies to Japan; it gains from a tariff on food, regardless of U.S. policy. Imposing a tariff on imports is a dominant strategy for each country, so each country imposes a tariff in the Nash equilibrium of this game, and each country gains only $5 million from trade. The Nash equilibrium is economically inefficient because both countries would gain from free trade.

Table 3 | Trade War Payoffs ($ millions)

		Japan	
		TARIFF	NO TARIFF
United States	TARIFF	$5 each	$9 for United States, $4 for Japan
	NO TARIFF	$4 for United States, $9 for Japan	$8 each

[5]Total producer and consumer surplus in the world without tariffs is $16 million ($8 million in each country). If the United States puts a tariff on televisions, total world producer and consumer surplus falls to $13 million ($9 million for the United States and $4 million for Japan). The difference—the $3 million fall in total world consumer and producer surplus—is the sum of Areas C and E in Figure 3.

Figure 4 | Decision Tree for the United States

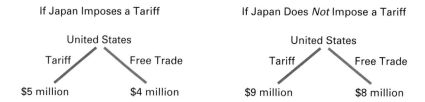

Advertising

The prisoner's dilemma game also applies to advertising. Folger's advertisements take away business from Maxwell House, and Maxwell House advertisements take away business from Folger's. Suppose that advertising does not change the total amount of coffee that people buy; it affects only which brand they choose. If neither seller advertises, each firm earns $1 million profit. If either firm spends $1 million on advertising while the other does not advertise, the advertiser gains $5 million in revenue, or a $4 million profit, and the other firm loses $5 million. If *each* firm spends $1 million on advertising, their advertisements cancel out one another, and neither firm gains revenues; each firm earns zero economic profit. (The $1 million in advertising costs eliminate each firm's profit.) Table 4 shows the payoffs. If each firm must decide at the same time whether to advertise, then in the Nash equilibrium, *both* firms advertise, even though each would gain if neither were to advertise.

Games without Dominant Strategies

In the previous examples, each player had a dominant strategy. In many games, however, players have no dominant strategies; a player's best strategy often depends on the strategies of other players. Table 5 shows an example for the noted gangsters, Ma and Pa. The police have caught them and, like Bonnie and Clyde, isolated them in separate rooms, where each prisoner must decide either to confess or not to confess without knowing the other prisoner's choice. If both confess, Ma (the mastermind of their crimes) gets 6 years in prison and Pa gets 1 year. If neither confesses, Ma gets 4 years in prison and Pa gets 2 years. If only Ma confesses, she gets 5 years in prison and Pa gets 3 years. If only Pa confesses, Ma gets 8 years in prison and he goes free. Table 5 shows the results in each case; Ma chooses a row of the table (showing whether she confesses or not) and Pa chooses a column.

What is each prisoner's best strategy when neither knows what the other will do? Figure 5 shows Ma's decision tree. If Pa confesses, Ma gains by confessing, but if Pa

Table 4 | Advertising Payoffs ($ millions)

		Maxwell House	
		ADVERTISE	**DON'T ADVERTISE**
Folger's	ADVERTISE	$0 each	$4 for Folger's, −$5 for Maxwell House
	DON'T ADVERTISE	−$5 for Folger's, $4 for Maxwell House	$1 each

Figure 5 | Ma's Decision Tree

If Pa Confesses

Ma

Confess / \ Not Confess

6 Years in Prison   8 Years in Prison

↑
Best
Strategy

If Pa Does *Not* Confess

Ma

Confess / \ Not Confess

5 Years in Prison   4 Years in Prison

↑
Best
Strategy

Ma has no dominant strategy. She wants to confess if Pa confesses, but she prefers not to confess if he does not confess.

Table 5 | A Game with No Dominant Strategy

		Pa	
		CONFESS	NOT CONFESS
	CONFESS	6 years for Ma, 1 year for Pa	5 years for Ma, 3 years for Pa
Ma	NOT CONFESS	8 years for Ma, 0 years for Pa	4 years for Ma, 2 years for Pa

does not confess, she gains by not confessing. Ma's best strategy depends on what Pa does, so she has no dominant strategy. Pa, on the other hand, has a dominant strategy: confess. As a result, Pa confesses, so Ma also confesses. Both players confess in the Nash equilibrium of this game.

Multiple Equilibria

Every game discussed so far has a single Nash equilibrium. Some games, however, have more than one Nash equilibrium: They have multiple (Nash) equilibria.[6] When a game has multiple equilibria, the game theorist requires some extra information (information from outside the game itself) to predict what will happen when people actually play the game.[7]

EXAMPLE

A famous example of a game with multiple equilibria involves two friends, Carolyn and Mark, who plan to go out tonight. They have two choices: a party or a movie. Carolyn wants to go to the party; Mark wants to see a movie. Most important to both of them, however, is that they do something together. Table 6 shows the happiness that each person would gain from each activity.

If they go to a party, Carolyn gets 2 units of enjoyment and Mark gets 1 unit. The reverse occurs if they go to a movie. If they choose different activities, each loses 2 units of enjoyment. This game has two Nash equilibria, one in which both go to a movie, and one in which both go to a party.

---

[6]Some economists believe that multiple equilibria occur in the stock market and the foreign-exchange market. Multiple equilibria may also play important roles in business cycles and unemployment.

[7]This information might include culture, history, or other influences on behavior.

Table 6 | Payoffs in a Game with Multiple Equilibria (units of utility)

		Mark	
		PARTY	MOVIE
Carolyn	PARTY	Carolyn gets 2 units, Mark gets 1 unit	Each loses 2 units
	MOVIE	Each loses 2 units	Carolyn gets 1 unit, Mark gets 2 units

Review Questions

5. What does it mean for a player to have no dominant strategy?

6. Explain why Carolyn and Mark reach a Nash equilibrium in Table 6 when they go to (a) a party, and (b) a movie.

Thinking Exercises

7. Draw decision trees for Folger's and Maxwell House in the example from Table 4.

8. Draw a decision tree for Pa in the example from Table 5.

SEQUENTIAL GAMES AND CREDIBILITY

Some games require *sequential* actions, that is, players take turns making moves.

A **sequential game** is a game in which players make at least some of their decisions at different times.

A diagram like Figure 6 gives useful insight into a sequential game. The figure combines the decision trees of two players, a monopoly and a new firm.[8] Each small circle shows a point at which someone makes a decision; arrows indicate possible decisions and payoffs.

Beginning at the top of the diagram (at the point labeled "New Firm Chooses"), the new firm decides whether or not to enter the industry and compete with the monopoly. If the firm enters, move down the arrow on the left side of the decision tree to the circle labeled "Monopoly Chooses." If the new firm does not enter, move down the arrow on the right side of the decision tree. Next, the monopoly chooses whether to charge a high price or a low price. If it chooses a high price, move down the corresponding arrow to the left; if it chooses a low price, move down the arrow to the right. At the bottom of the decision tree are the payoffs, which also appear in Table 7.

The bottom half of Figure 6 (below the "Monopoly Chooses" circles) describes the second half of the game. This part resembles some decision trees discussed earlier in the chapter. In the second half of the game, the monopoly has a dominant strategy: Charge a high price. Knowing that the monopoly will choose a high price, the new firm would reasonably choose to enter the industry. (The new firm earns $2 million if it enters and the monopoly

---

[8]The diagram is called the *extensive form* of the game.

Figure 6 | A Sequential Game

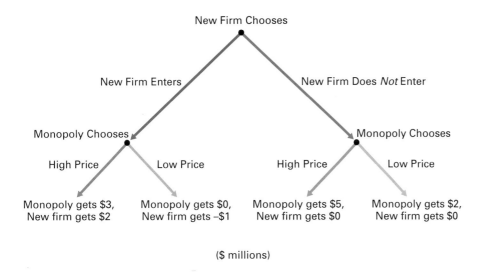

New Firm Chooses

New Firm Enters   New Firm Does *Not* Enter

Monopoly Chooses   Monopoly Chooses

High Price   Low Price   High Price   Low Price

Monopoly gets $3,
New firm gets $2

Monopoly gets $0,
New firm gets –$1

Monopoly gets $5,
New firm gets $0

Monopoly gets $2,
New firm gets $0

($ millions)

This sequential game has two steps. First, a new firm decides either to enter or not enter the industry and compete with the monopoly. Second, the monopoly chooses whether to charge a high price or a low price. The monopoly's *four possible strategies* are: high price if new firm enters, low price otherwise; low price if new firm enters, high price otherwise; high price in either case; and low price in either case. In one Nash equilibrium of this game, the monopoly charges a high price in either case and the new firm enters. Footnote 10 discusses two other Nash equilibria of this game.

Table 7 | Payoffs in a Sequential Game of Entry ($ millions)

		New Firm	
		ENTER	DO NOT ENTER
Monopoly	HIGH PRICE	Monopoly gets $3, New firm gets $2	Monopoly gets $5, New firm gets $0
	LOW PRICE	Monopoly gets $0, New firm gets –$1	Monopoly gets $2, New firm gets $0

charges a high price, and it earns nothing if it does not enter.) In fact, this situation is a Nash equilibrium of the game: The new firm enters, and the monopoly charges a high price.

This equilibrium, in which the monopoly chooses a high price regardless of what the new firm does and the new firm chooses to enter, is called the *subgame perfect Nash equilibrium* of this game.

> A **subgame perfect Nash equilibrium** is a Nash equilibrium in which every player's strategy is credible (no player makes incredible threats).[9]

A strategy is credible if a player would have an incentive to carry out that strategy.

This new idea of a subgame perfect equilibrium is important because the monopoly would like to tell the new firm, "If you enter, we'll cut our price and you'll lose $1 million, so don't enter!" This threat is not credible, however, because once the new firm enters, the monopoly has no incentive to carry out the threat. For this reason, the only

IN THE NEWS

Still, some analysts doubt that soft-drink makers are seriously considering a switch to refined sugar from high-fructose corn syrup, and suggested the reports could be a ploy to frighten corn processors into keeping a lid on syrup prices.

Source: The Wall Street Journal

Business firms routinely strategically interact, but their threats are not always credible. Do these firms really have an incentive to switch sweeteners, or is the threat just a ploy?

[9]More precisely, a subgame perfect Nash equilibrium is a Nash equilibrium in which each player's strategy is consistent with what that player would do in a Nash equilibrium in every part of the game (every subgame). Think about the second part of the game in Figure 6 after the new firm has already decided to enter the industry. The monopoly's best response is to charge a high price, so the only Nash equilibrium of this subgame is for the monopoly to charge a high price. For this reason, a subgame perfect Nash equilibrium of the original game in Figure 6 requires that the monopoly choose a high price if the new firm enters. The same logic applies if the new firm chooses not to enter, so a subgame perfect Nash equilibrium of the original game requires that the monopoly follow its dominant strategy: Choose a high price no matter what the new firm does. Therefore the only subgame perfect Nash equilibrium of the game in Figure 6 is for the monopoly to charge a high price in either case and for the new firm to enter.

A threat gains credibility if the player has the teeth to act on it.

subgame perfect Nash equilibrium of the game in Figure 6 is for the monopoly to charge a high price in either case and for the new firm to enter. The monopoly then earns $3 million and the new firm earns $2 million.[10]

In some real-life games, one player may *not know* whether another player's strategy is credible. The player with incomplete information must make decisions based on beliefs about the credibility of the other player's threats. This gives players an incentive to seek information about the strategies and incentives of other players.

Review Questions

9. What is a sequential game?

10. What is a subgame perfect Nash equilibrium?

Thinking Exercises

11. Give examples of a credible threat and an incredible threat.

12. Consider the example of Carolyn and Mark in Table 6, but suppose that they play a *sequential game*. First, Carolyn chooses whether she will go to the party or the movie, then Mark chooses where he will go.
    (a) Draw a diagram like Figure 6 to describe this game.
    (b) Find the subgame perfect Nash equilibrium of the game.

COMMITMENTS

Commitments are valuable. Although it may seem paradoxical, people can benefit by committing even though it limits their future choices.

> People can benefit from being able to limit their future actions so that they cannot do what they would otherwise want to do in the future.

Commitments allow people to limit their future actions in beneficial ways.

> A person **commits to a future action** if she does something now to limit her future options or change her future incentives so that she will have an incentive to take that action in the future.

A person commits not to take a future action by doing something to make that action either impossible or contrary to her own future interest. Commitments can provide valuable benefits by restricting future choices in a way that changes other people's actions to one's own benefit.

---

[10]The game in Figure 6 has two other Nash equilibria, but these others are not subgame perfect. In the first, the monopoly can threaten to charge a low price if the new firm enters and charge a high price if it doesn't, so the new firm chooses not to enter. This is a Nash equilibrium because (a) the monopoly earns $5 million and cannot do any better by changing its strategy, given that the new firm does not enter, and (b) the new firm cannot do any better by changing its strategy (to enter the industry) given that the monopoly would then charge a low price. Of course, the monopoly does not actually have an incentive to charge a low price if the new firm enters (it would lose $3 million by charging a low price instead of a high price). That is why this Nash equilibrium is not subgame perfect.

In the other Nash equilibrium that is not subgame perfect, the monopoly can charge a high price if the new firm enters and threaten a low price if the new firm does not enter, so the new firm enters. This possibility may seem like a silly strategy for the monopoly, because it would have no incentive to charge a low price if the new firm failed to enter. That fact explains why this situation is not a subgame perfect Nash equilibrium, but it is a Nash equilibrium.

EXAMPLES

Many governments try to commit *not* to bargain with kidnappers or terrorists. If potential terrorists know that governments cannot bargain, they are less likely to conduct terrorist attacks. People try to commit to romantic relationships by getting married; this limits the options of each partner, but each may gain from the commitment of the other. People try to commit to diets by avoiding places with candy machines or eating before shopping for groceries. The phrase "burning your bridges behind you" comes from an important military application of commitment—an advancing army may literally burn bridges behind it to prevent a future retreat and commit the soldiers, seeing no escape, to fight hard instead.

Commitment Mechanisms

It is often difficult or impossible to commit to a future action. Governments may proclaim that they will not deal with terrorists, but they may back down when terrorists hold hostages. Marriage does not perfectly commit people to relationships. Sometimes, however, people can commit by using the legal system to enforce explicit contracts. Other times people commit by relying on social pressure and etiquette to enforce promises; in many cultures honor plays this role. The next example illustrates one of many other ways to commit.

Commitments are valuable because they change people's incentives and actions.

Excess Capacity as Commitment

Consider a game like the one in Figure 6, but suppose that a monopoly can choose whether to invest in extra capacity by adding new machines and equipment before playing the game. Extra capacity reduces the monopoly's marginal cost of increasing its output, so it raises the profit that the monopoly would earn by reducing its price and increasing sales.

If the monopoly does *not* invest in extra capacity, then it and the new entrant play the game in Figure 6. If the monopoly invests, they play the game in Figure 7. These games differ only in the payoff when the monopoly charges a low price. The games in Figures 6 and 7 are parts (or subgames) of the complete game that includes the monopoly's decision of whether or not to invest in extra capacity.

The game in Figure 7 has only one subgame perfect Nash equilibrium: The monopoly charges a low price if the new firm enters the industry and a high price otherwise, while the new firm chooses not to enter.[11] The monopoly's threat to charge a low price if the new firm enters is credible because the monopoly would have an incentive to take this action if the new firm were to enter. The monopoly's investment in extra capacity gives credibility to the threat because it allows the monopoly to commit to a future action. Because of this commitment, the new firm chooses not to enter, and the monopoly never has to carry out its threat to cut the price.

Now consider the complete game, which begins with the monopoly's decision to invest. If the monopoly invests in added capacity, it will play the game in Figure 7 and end up earning a $5 million profit. If it does not invest, it will play the game in Figure 6 and earn only a $3 million profit. Therefore, in the subgame perfect Nash equilibrium of the expanded game, the monopoly invests in new capacity, the new firm chooses not to enter, and the monopoly charges a high price.

---

[11]To see why this situation is the only subgame perfect Nash equilibrium in Figure 7, begin at the bottom of the figure and suppose that the new firm enters the industry. The monopoly then earns $3 million if it charges the high price and $4 million if it charges the low price, creating an incentive to charge the low price. Now suppose that the new firm does not enter the industry. The monopoly then earns a higher profit if it charges a high price than if it charges a low price, so the monopoly would charge a low price if the new firm were to enter and a high price otherwise. The new firm, recognizing these incentives, realizes that it will lose $3 million if it enters the industry, and it will earn zero otherwise, so the new firm chooses not to enter. The monopoly then charges the high price and earns a $5 million profit.

Figure 7 | Game with Monopoly Investing in Additional Capacity

The monopoly and the new firm play this game if the monopoly decides to invest in additional capacity (raising production capability). If not, they play the game in Figure 6, which differs from this game only in the payoffs when the monopoly charges a low price.

This game (a subgame of the complete game) has only one subgame perfect Nash equilibrium: The monopoly charges a low price if the new firm enters and a high price otherwise, while the new firm chooses not to enter. The monopoly then earns $5 million, and the new firm earns nothing.

The monopoly earns a higher payoff than in the subgame perfect Nash equilibrium of the game in Figure 6, leading it to choose to invest in new capacity. This decision commits the monopoly to charge the low price if the new firm enters. Recognizing this commitment, the new firm does not enter, and the monopoly charges the high price. Investing in additional capacity allows the monopoly to raise its profit by committing to a future action.

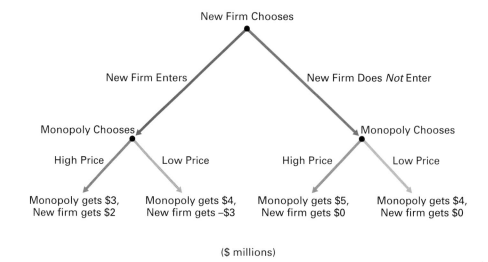

($ millions)

Notice that *the monopoly never uses its extra capacity* in equilibrium, because it charges the high price and keeps output low. The monopoly benefits from investing in new equipment *that it knows it will never use.* The sole benefit of the equipment is to make its threat credible. This situation resembles deterrence in national defense: If one country stockpiles enough weapons and it convinces potential enemies that it will use them if attacked, then the other side has an incentive not to attack, and the weapons go unused.[12]

Commitment in Other Games

The ability to commit would help the criminals in the prisoner's dilemma game. If *both* prisoners could commit not to confess, both would gain. (However, if only one prisoner could commit not to confess, the other still would have an incentive to confess.)

By limiting their own capacity to produce, firms may commit not to cheat on a cartel. If a firm sells all that it can produce when it charges a high price, it has no incentive to cut its price. Firms sometimes commit to future actions by convincing the government to regulate them; the government can then require them to take the actions to which they want to commit. For example, the government may prevent firms from reducing prices, as it did in the trucking and airline industries for many years.

REPEATED GAMES

People and firms face some real-life situations repeatedly. Understanding the logic of these situations requires an analysis of repeated games.

A **repeated game** is a game that the same players play more than once.

[12]Commitment to massive retaliation to any attack was an important part of nuclear deterrence during the Cold War. Similarly, incumbent politicians sometimes prevent serious opposition in elections by amassing large "warchests" of money before their campaigns begin. This potential campaign weapon deters opponents from challenging incumbents because they anticipate high costs of matching the incumbents' spending. Opponents decide not to run, and without serious opponents, incumbents win reelection without spending all the money in their warchests, saving it to deter entry in future campaigns.

Repeated games differ from one-shot (nonrepeated) games because people's current actions can depend on the past behavior of other players. In the prisoner's dilemma, neither prisoner can punish the other for confessing, but in a repeated game, players can punish other players for bad behavior in previous rounds of the game. One-shot games differ from repeated games particularly when players have limited information about other players' incentives. In a repeated game, each player can learn from experience what other players are likely to do in various situations.

Repeated games encourage cooperative behavior more than one-shot games do. Experimental evidence shows, for example, that the equilibrium in an oligopoly tends to be closer to the monopoly (cartel) solution if the same firms compete repeatedly than if they compete only once.

Think about repeating the game in Table 2 (the Pepsi-Coke example) many times. For a single round of this game, the only Nash equilibrium is for both players to charge the low price. If this game is repeated indefinitely, however, other subgame perfect Nash equilibria emerge.[13] In equilibrium, each firm says, "We will start by charging a high price, but if the other firm ever charges a low price, we will punish that firm by charging a low price the next day. Each day we'll look at what they do, and copy it the following day." This strategy is called *tit-for-tat,* that is, doing to others what they just did to you.

> You follow a **tit-for-tat** strategy, if you (1) cooperate on your first move and (2) for each later move, copy the other player's action in his previous move.

In one Nash equilibrium of the repeated prisoner's dilemma, players adopt this strategy. Unless players care very little about the future, no prisoner ever confesses. Similarly, firms in the indefinitely repeated Pepsi-Coke game always charge the high price. Each firm believes that if it were to charge a low current price, the other firm would reduce its price in the future. The first firm would gain $2 million currently (its profit would rise from $6 million to $8 million), but it would lose $3 million in the next round of the game (its profit would fall from $6 million to $3 million), when the other firm would reduce its price. If the discounted present value of this $3 million loss exceeds the $2 million gain from reducing the price, then the firm will not reduce its price. In this case no punishment ever occurs, because every firm charges a high price every round of the game. The threat of punishment prevents the need to carry it out. Experimental evidence confirms that repeated games tend to produce cooperative behavior.

Experimental Evidence on Tit-for-Tat

Political scientist Robert Axelrod reports on his studies of a repeated prisoner's dilemma in his book, *The Evolution of Cooperation.*[14] Axelrod invited economists, political scientists, and others to submit strategies for playing a prisoner's dilemma game. Some players chose very complicated strategies. After repeating the game many times, Axelrod found that the winning strategy was tit-for-tat. He announced this result and held another game to allow players to devise strategies to beat tit-for-tat. Again, the best strategy turned out to be tit-for-tat.

This result surprised most game theorists, because tit-for-tat is not an aggressive strategy. It says to cooperate, never be the first one to cheat, always punish with "an-eye-for-an-eye," then forgive and cooperate again. Axelrod speculates that the success of the tit-for-tat strategy lies behind social customs and etiquette. In fact, animals sometimes seem to play strategies like tit-for-tat in natural game situations.

IN THE NEWS

Oil ultimatum

Saudis plan to pump all the crude they can sell if OPEC can't agree on new quotas

Outside the kingdom, it is assumed that the Saudis' recent opening of the oil spigot is aimed at lowering prices to punish other exporters for their excesses. One widely held theory says that the kingdom wants to teach them a lesson so they will return to the OPEC bargaining table chastened.

Source: The Wall Street Journal

In repeated games, players can threaten each other with future punishment for bad current behavior.

---

[13]The new equilibria emerge if the game never stops, or if some *chance* always remains that the game will continue.

[14]Robert Axelrod, *The Evolution of Cooperation* (New York: Basic Books, 1985).

I N   T H E   N E W S

Nice guys finish first

When dealing with your neighbor, a business rival, or the
Soviet Union, the way to get ahead is to get along.

By William F. Allman

Captain J. R. Wilton, an officer in the British Army, was having tea with his fellow soldiers in the mud near Armenières, France. It was August 1915, and World War I had become a trench-lined struggle for barren stretches of countryside. Wilton's teatime was suddenly disrupted when an artillery shell arced into the camp and exploded. The British soldiers quickly got into their trenches, readying their weapons and swearing at the Germans.

Then from across no-man's-land, writes Wilton in his diary, a German soldier appeared above his trenches. "We are very sorry about that," the soldier shouted. "We hope no one was hurt. It is not our fault, it is that damned Prussian artillery."

Enemy soldiers might seem like the last people on Earth who would cooperate with each other, but they did. Despite exhortations to fight and threats of reprisals from their commanders if they didn't, peace often broke out among the German and English infantry. Sometimes there were truces arranged through formal agreements, but many times the soldiers simply stopped shooting at each other, or at least shot where it would do no harm. According to an account by one German soldier, for example, the English battalion across the way would fire a round of artillery at the same spot every evening at seven, "so regularly you could set your watch by it. There were even some inquisitive fellows who crawled out a little before seven to watch it burst."

The World War I trench soldiers' tacit cooperation arose because, unlike most wars, the troops were stationed so that the enemies faced each other day after day; they knew that the same people they shot at one day would be shooting at them the next. According to one soldier, "It would be child's play to shell the road behind the enemy's trenches . . . but on the whole there is silence. After all, if you prevent your enemy from drawing his rations, his remedy is simple: He will prevent you from drawing yours."

Source: Science '84

*Even soldiers in wartime have discovered the
benefits of cooperating through the
tit-for-tat strategy.*

R e v i e w   Q u e s t i o n s

13. Explain, with an example, why people can benefit from commitments.

14. Explain how a firm can deter entry by investing in excess capacity.

15. Explain why repeated games can have different Nash equilibria than one-shot games.

16. Explain the tit-for-tat strategy. What evidence suggests that it is a good strategy in some games?

C o n c l u s i o n

Basic Ideas of Game Theory

Game theory is the general theory of strategic behavior. A game is described by its rules, strategies, and payoffs.

A Nash equilibrium of a game is a situation in which each player's strategy is a best response to other players' strategies.

The prisoner's dilemma is a famous example of a two-person game. Each player gains by deviating from the cooperative solution regardless of what the other player does, so both players deviate and end up receiving lower payoffs than the cooperative solution would have given them.

Economic Applications of Game Theory

The prisoner's dilemma applies to many situations such as cheating on a cartel, trade wars between countries, and advertising wars. A player has a dominant strategy when that player's best strategy does not depend on other players' actions. In some games, players have dominant strategies; in other games, they do not. Some games have multiple Nash equilibria.

Sequential Games and Credibility

Players make decisions at different times in a sequential game. A subgame perfect Nash equilibrium is a Nash equilibrium in which every player's strategy is credible, that is, when players have incentives to carry out their strategies.

Commitments

A person commits to a future action by taking some current action that limits her future options or raises her future incentives to take that future action. People can gain from commitments, even though they limit future choices, because they affect the actions of other people.

Repeated Games

A repeated game is a game that the same players play more than once. Players' actions can depend on the past behavior of other players, so their current actions can punish others for bad behavior in the past. Players can also learn from experience about the strategies and incentives of other players. A game that is repeated indefinitely can have more Nash equilibria than a one-shot game. These other equilibria may involve more cooperation between players than in a one-shot game (as in the repeated prisoner's dilemma). One strategy that has achieved widespread success in repeated games is tit-for-tat, in which a player cooperates on the first move, and thereafter copies the other player's action in the previous move.

Key Terms

game theory	payoff	Nash equilibrium	commitment to a future action
rules of a game	dominant strategy	sequential game	repeated game
strategy	best response (best strategy)	subgame perfect Nash equilibrium	tit-for-tat

Problems

17. What is the Nash equilibrium of the following game?

		Player 2	
		HEADS	**TAILS**
Player 1	HEADS	$5 each	$0 for Player 1, $9 for Player 2
	TAILS	$10 for Player 1, $1 for Player 2	$2 each

18. Explain how the prisoner's dilemma may apply to:
   (a) Picnickers in a park with competing boom boxes
   (b) The nuclear arms race
   (c) Children sharing a birthday cake or friends sharing a pizza

19. Make up an example of a game with multiple equilibria.

20. Think of a real-life example of a repeated game.

21. Find all the multiple equilibria in the following game. Two cars drive toward each other on a road.

If both drive on the left-hand side (as in England) or on the right-hand side (as in most other countries), they pass each other safely. If one drives on the left and the other on the right, however, they crash.

		Boris	
		DRIVE ON LEFT	DRIVE ON RIGHT
Natasha	DRIVE ON LEFT	Each gains 1	Each loses 2
	DRIVE ON RIGHT	Each loses 2	Each gains 1

22. Explain how a monopoly might deter entry of new competitors by accumulating large inventories of goods. (*Hint:* Review the example in which a monopoly invests in extra capacity to deter entry and follow a similar logic.)

23. Comment on this statement: "Committing is never a good idea, because it takes away your flexibility to respond to a situation in whatever way is best at the time."

24. Comment on this statement: "Nuclear deterrence is most effective if the government is willing to respond to a nuclear attack by completely destroying the other country, even if such destruction would be pointless because it would be too late to prevent damage from the initial attack."

25. What are the subgame perfect Nash equilibria of the game in Figure 8?

Figure 8 | A Game of Compromise

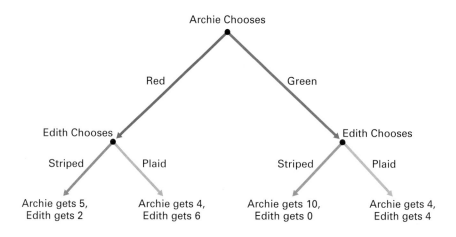

Inquiries for Further Thought

26. A Stanford professor of education and psychology, Robert Calfee, recommends teaching tit-for-tat in grade school. "It's a technology . . . [for] how to deal with others in society. What do you do when you're mad at someone you love? Nothing in our schools teaches that."[15]

    How can you apply the tit-for-tat strategy in everyday situations? Discuss examples and likely results. Is tit-for-tat an effective way to behave in these situations? Is it a fair or moral way to behave? Would other behaviors be better in some way (more likely to produce good results or satisfy higher ethical standards)? Be as specific as you can. Is tit-for-tat a *bad* strategy in any situation?

27. In what recent real-life situation has your strategy for behavior depended on the strategies or behaviors of other people? Can you analyze the situation using game theory?

[15]Quoted in William F. Allman, "Nice Guys Finish First," *Science '84*, October 1984.

WORK AND WEALTH

CHAPTER 18

LABOR MARKETS

In this Chapter. . .

Main Points to Understand

▶ Equilibrium wages reflect labor productivity.

▶ Jobs that require greater human capital tend to pay higher wages.

▶ Jobs with high risks or low amenities tend to pay higher wages than similar jobs with low risks or better amenities.

▶ Job tournaments can create superstars, who earn much higher wages than similar people for only slightly higher productivity.

▶ Unemployment results from normal labor turnover, and from wages that exceed the equilibrium level.

Thinking Skills to Develop

▶ Analyze reasons for differences in wages across people and jobs.

▶ Recognize incentives affecting labor supply by workers and labor demand by employers

▶ Recognize market forces that affect equilibrium hours of work, types of wage payments, and investments in human capital.

▶ Understand features of labor markets such as unemployment and superstars.

In 1931, Babe Ruth earned more than the president of the United States. When asked about this fact, Ruth, perhaps the most talented baseball player of all time, is said to have responded, "Why not? I had a better year than he did." (Ruth hit .373 with 46 home runs; President Herbert Hoover contended unsuccessfully with the Great Depression.) Why have Michael Jordan and the Spice Girls earned more than scientists researching cancer or AIDS? Why do some people work overtime while others struggle with unemployment? The discipline of labor economics addresses these issues.

LABOR SUPPLY AND DEMAND

Labor markets differ from markets for shoes or lumber. People in most countries, including the United States, earn about 70 percent of their income from selling their labor services. (The other 30 percent comes from returns on investments, that is, from owning capital.) In 1997, for example, the total personal income of everyone in the United States amounted to $6.9 trillion; $4.8 trillion of this income came from selling labor.

Labor markets also require special consideration because labor services are physically connected to people. Machines don't care where they work, but people do. People care about their work environments, their fellow workers, flexibility of hours, and risks of injury on the job.

One person's labor is not necessarily equivalent to another's. People differ in their abilities, education, and experience. Therefore economists often analyze separate markets for specific types of labor, such as the markets for unskilled labor in Philadelphia, dental hygienists in Dallas, or airline pilots in the entire country.

Labor Supply

A person's labor supply decisions include whether to work at all, what occupation to choose, which job offer to take (or whether to operate an independent business), and how many hours to work each year. Economists say that a person *works in the market* if she works for monetary pay. A person *works in the home* if his work brings no explicit pay (such as caring for children or volunteering at a charity). Although most of this chapter concerns work in the market, economists estimate that the value of work in the home averages about $30,000 per year, and nearly $40,000 if the person cares for children under age 6.

> A person is in the **labor force** if she works in the market or is looking for a job in the market.

In 1900, almost nine out of ten men, but only two out of ten women, were in the labor force. Today, about 75 percent of men and 60 percent of women over age 16 are in the labor force. People tend to be in the labor force when they face low opportunity costs of working (for example, they have no children at home or they find child care at low cost) or they see high benefits from working (for example, the family has no other source of income).

Occupation choice also depends on a person's job preferences and opportunities, including wages, possibilities for advancement, flexibility, job security, and location. Job opportunities depend partly on worker abilities, training, and experience. In 1900, more than one-third of U.S. workers worked on farms. Today, farm jobs amount to only 3 percent of total jobs. In 1900, service industries provided only about 20 percent of U.S. jobs; today, that figure is about 60 percent. Only 20 percent of U.S. workers held white-collar jobs in 1900; today, more than half do.

Most workers have some choice about the number of hours they work each week. While most self-employed workers can easily make this choice, others can also choose their weekly hours by their choices of jobs, options to work overtime, or decisions to take second jobs. At the beginning of the 20th century, U.S. manufacturing workers averaged about 55 hours per week; today they average about 35 hours per week.

Labor supply curves may take two possible shapes, shown in Figure 1. They may slope upward, as in Panel (a), or bend backward, as in Panel (b).

> A **backward-bending labor supply curve** is a labor supply curve with a negatively sloped portion.

Labor supply curves can display either shape, because a wage increase can lead a person to work either more *or* less.

Substitution and Income Effects of a Wage Increase

The *substitution effect* of a wage increase makes people want to work *more* hours than before. As the wage rises, the opportunity cost of leisure time also increases, leading people to choose less leisure time and more time at work. The *income effect* of a wage increase makes people want to work *fewer* hours than before, because it makes them richer and raises their demand for leisure time.

EXAMPLE

If you work 40 hours per week and earn $10.00 per hour, you earn $400.00 per week. If your wage were to rise to $12.50 per hour, you might:

Figure 1
Labor Supply Curves

(a) Upward-Sloping Labor Supply

Hours
of Work
per Week

(b) Backward-Bending Labor Supply

Hours
of Work
per Week

▶ Work 8 hours less each week (only 32 hours per week) and *still* earn $400 per week. In this case, your labor supply curve bends backward as in Figure 1b.

▶ Continue to work 40 hours and earn $500 per week, giving you a perfectly inelastic labor supply curve.

▶ Work 4 hours more each week (44 hours per week) and earn $550, giving you an upward-sloping labor supply curve, as in Figure 1a.

The income effect is stronger for a *permanent* wage increase than for a temporary increase. For example, you would not become much richer if your wage were to double for one day, so the income effect would probably be smaller than the substitution effect, leading you to work more hours that day. However, you would become much richer if your wage were to double *permanently*, and the large income effect may lead you to work less than before. For this reason, labor supply curves are more likely to bend backward when a wage increase is permanent than when it is temporary.

Evidence on Labor Supply

Labor supply curves for most adult males are very inelastic, with slight backward bends. The same shape describes labor supply curves for unmarried females who work full time. Evidence suggests that a permanent 10 percent wage increase reduces the quantity of labor supplied by about 1 or 2 percent. On the other hand, labor supply curves slope upward when wage changes last only a few days or a few months. Evidence indicates that labor supply curves of married females, teenagers, and older workers slope upward even for permanent wage changes.[1]

Labor supply increases when nonpay features of a job (its work environment) improve or when family income from other sources falls. Labor supply decreases when nonpay features of a job lose attractiveness, family income from other sources rises (a spouse gets a big raise), or the opportunity cost of working rises (as with the birth of a child).

Market Supply of Labor

The market supply of labor, for a given occupation and skill level, can slope upward even if the supply by each worker is backward-bending or perfectly inelastic. The market supply curve may slope upward because an increase in wage attracts people to choose the occupation. A wage increase in any one occupation or industry leads workers to switch from other occupations and industries. Similarly, an increase in the demand for labor in Texas raises wages there and leads workers to move from other states, raising the quantity of labor supplied in Texas.

Labor Demand

Chapter 12 explained that the marginal product of any input, including labor, is the increase in a firm's total output when it adds a little more of the input, while keeping fixed quantities of other inputs. That chapter also defined the *value* of the marginal product of an input as the increase in the *value* of those goods. This concept applies to labor:

> The **value of the marginal product of labor** is the increase in the money value of a firm's output when it employs a little more labor, keeping fixed quantities of other inputs.

---

[1]Historically, the income effects of wage changes have been smaller for married females than for unmarried females, because married females have obtained income from their spouses; the difference between married females and married males apparently reflects the facts that females have earned (and still earn) less on average than males and that fewer males have worked in the home. Whether these differences will continue in the future remains to be seen.

If a firm is a price taker in the labor market (rather than a monopoly buyer of labor), then the value of the marginal product of labor equals its marginal product multiplied by the price of the final product. For example, adding one full-time worker may raise a firm's output by 20 shirts per week, with each shirt selling for $10. Then the marginal product of labor is 20 shirts per week, and the *value* of the marginal product of labor is $200 per week. Chapter 12 also explained:

The demand curve for labor graphs the value of its marginal product.

EXAMPLE

The demand for labor by a grocery store slopes downward due to the law of diminishing returns. A grocery store can increase its sales by hiring additional cashiers to keep lines short and additional workers to stock shelves, assist customers, unload new shipments of food, and so on. Some inputs (such as the size of the store) are fixed in the short run, however, so the marginal product of labor falls as the store hires more workers. The height of the demand curve for labor shows the value of the marginal product of labor at the grocery store.

Evidence on Labor Demand

Several factors affect the demand for labor. A firm's demand for labor rises when:

▶ An advance in technology raises the marginal product of labor

▶ An increase in worker skills raises the marginal product of labor

▶ A firm acquires new machinery or equipment that raises the marginal product of labor

▶ The price of the firm's final product rises, raising the *value* of the marginal product of labor

Some changes in technology reduce the demand for particular types of labor. For example, advances in computer technology in the last decade have reduced firms' needs for middle-management, white-collar workers to handle information. The invention of the plow reduced the demand for farm workers—not because workers became less productive (in fact, the plow raised their productivity), but because the plow raised farm output, reducing food prices and decreasing the value of the marginal product of farm workers' labor. If robot technology continues to improve, prices of industrial robots may fall, decreasing the demands for manual labor.

Evidence suggests that the long-run elasticity of demand for labor for the entire U.S. economy is between 0.15 and 0.50. Therefore, a 10 percent wage increase would reduce the quantity of labor demanded by between 1.5 percent and 5.0 percent. Evidence suggests an even more inelastic short-run demand for labor. On the other hand, the long-run demand for unskilled teenage labor is very elastic, with an elasticity of about 8.

LABOR MARKET EQUILIBRIUM

Figure 2 shows equilibrium in the labor market. The United States has about 132 million workers and over 5 million employers. In equilibrium, people work about 260 billion hours per year and receive an average hourly wage of about $19 per hour.[2]

---

[2]The average wage for nonsupervisory workers is about $13 per hour.

Employment and Hours in Equilibrium

Equilibrium of supply and demand for labor determines total labor hours, but how does a firm using 1,400 hours of labor per week decide whether to employ 35 people each working 40 hours per week, or 40 people each working 35 hours per week? Will the firm offer 40 jobs or only 35 jobs? The answer depends on the costs and benefits of adding employees versus increasing hours per employee.

A firm hires relatively *few employees,* each working relatively *longer hours* if:

▶ High hiring and training costs allow a firm to reduce total training costs by hiring few workers with each working many hours.

▶ Working requires setup time, so fewer employees working longer hours raises productivity. For example, it may be more efficient for one person to spend long hours writing a computer program than for several people to write the program jointly, with each person working fewer hours per day. (Each worker would face a high setup cost of becoming familiar with the entire structure of the program.)

▶ Laws and regulations make it cheaper to have fewer employees. For example, some government regulations apply only to firms with 5 or more workers.

▶ Employees want to work long hours. They may prefer the pay they earn during long hours, or they may face fixed costs of commuting to work or arranging child care.

Figure 2
Equilibrium in the Labor Market

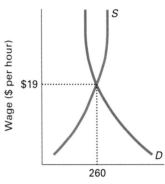

Wage	Labor Supply	Labor Demand
$ 6	120	420
12	200	320
19	260	260
24	280	210
30	300	200

IN THE NEWS

Fewer jobs filled as factories rely on overtime pay

Hiring is 'a last choice'

By Louis Uchitelle

For decades, overtime encouraged hiring. Companies found it cheaper to hire a new worker rather than assign more hours to existing employees, who have to be paid a 50 percent premium for the extra work.

But particularly in the last two years, the cost of a new employee—recruiting, training, and ever-more-costly health insurance—has made overtime the less expensive choice.

Source: New York Times

Heavy Demand for Product

"You almost always hire people now only as a last choice," said Robert Cizik, chairman of Cooper Industries and also of the National Association of Manufacturers.

When Cooper had a surge in orders for the computer cables it makes, more than 2,000 workers were asked to work an additional two hours a day, on overtime pay. Only as a last resort has Cooper recently begun to hire. "People got

tired of working 10-hour days," Mr. Cizik said.

The Costs of Hiring

The overtime phenomenon is most evident in manufacturing. Factory workers, who represent 17 percent of the nation's employees, are generally skilled and well paid, and they usually work full time because factory shifts require full timers. Each new worker, as a result, means a considerable investment not only in benefits but also in recruiting and training.

The number of new jobs in equilibrium depends partly on the costs of adding employees versus the costs of increasing hours per employee.

The average nominal wage in the United States rose from $4.53 per hour in 1975 to $12.26 in 1980, an increase of 171 percent. The average real wage fell over that time period. Real wages of unskilled workers fell by about 6 percent in the past two decades while real wages of college graduates increased by about 12 percent.

Wages in Equilibrium

The equilibrium price of labor is the wage or salary. The *real* wage refers to the inflation-adjusted wage.

> The **nominal wage** is the wage rate measured in money (such as dollars, yen, or pesos). The **real wage** is the wage rate adjusted for inflation, that is, the wage measured in purchasing power units.

The real wage, rather than the nominal wage, guides decisions by workers and firms, because it measures wages in purchasing power units.

The average hourly real wage in the United States has risen about 2 percent per year since early in the 20th century, as Figure 3 shows. The graph demonstrates the striking fact that the average real wage has fallen in the last quarter of the century. The figure overstates the fall in the average real wage somewhat because of increases in fringe benefits paid to workers and because of changes in the composition of the labor force. For example, an increase in the number of women in the labor force has led *average* wages to fall because women earn, on average, less than men do. Holding fixed a person's education, experience, and gender, the average hourly real wage has changed little since 1973. Average wages of women have increased over the last quarter-century, while average wages of men have remained about the same.

Review Questions

1. What affects a person's decision to be in the labor force?

2. What affects a firm's decision to hire 200 full-time workers or 300 part-time workers?

3. Explain the difference between real and nominal wages.

Figure 3 | Real Hourly U.S. Wages in the 20th Century

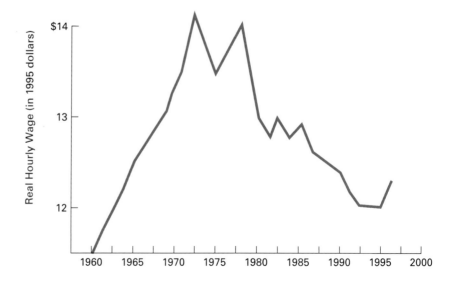

4. Why might a labor supply curve bend backward? What would make it slope upward?

5. Explain how a permanent improvement in technology is likely to affect real wages and employment. How would the effects differ if the improvement in technology were to raise productivity for only a few months?

Human Capital

FEATURES OF EQUILIBRIUM IN LABOR MARKETS

Wages differ across occupations mainly because some occupations require higher levels of skill and training than others.

> **Human capital** means the skills, knowledge, and abilities of people.

The value of a person's human capital is the discounted present value of the higher future wages that it creates.

EXAMPLE

Consider a 22-year-old worker who earns an annual salary that starts at $30,000 per year, rises 8 percent per year until age 50, and then stays the same until retirement at age 65. If the interest rate is 5 percent per year, the value of this person's human capital is:

$$\$30,000 + \$\frac{(30,000)(1.08)}{1.05} + \$\frac{(30,000)(1.08)^2}{1.05^2} + \ldots + \$\frac{(30,000)(1.08)^{28}}{1.05^{28}}$$

$$+ \$\frac{(30,000)(1.08)^{28}}{1.05^{29}} + \ldots + \$\frac{(30,000)(1.08)^{28}}{1.05^{43}}$$

$$= \$2,333,676$$

Wages and Human Capital

Graphs in the Appendix to Chapter 2 showed that people with more education earn higher wages throughout their lives. Because education raises their productivity, it raises the demand for their labor and their equilibrium wages.

Firms must pay higher wages for jobs requiring more education; otherwise, people would not acquire that additional education. Whenever jobs pay *more* than enough to compensate people for costs of additional education, more people seek these jobs. The increase in labor supply reduces the wage until it *just* compensates for the costs of additional education required in that job. In equilibrium, the difference in the discounted present values of wages in any two jobs (that are otherwise similar) equals the discounted present value of the difference in the required education costs.

The cost of investing in human capital is high. Direct expenditures such as tuition and supplies, along with the opportunity cost of time spent in school, sum to about 10 percent of U.S. GDP (the nation's total output of goods and services). However, the benefits are also high. The rate of return on investment in human capital—essentially, the

IN THE NEWS

Jersey cows face uncertain future

JOHN, JERSEY—The realities of modern farming are intruding upon the cozy world of the Channel Islands where men and women lovingly raise real Jersey and Guernsey cows.

Every evening at about 7, Philip Romeril goes out to the field behind his 18th-century farmhouse to check on his 60 Jerseys.

Their golden brown hides glow in the soft, re- ceding summer light. Their tails swish and their round, brown eyes blink. They have names like Carol and Marie, and they ooze contentment.

Romeril scratches the tops of a few heads, tugs at a floppy ear here and there, runs his hand over a pregnant cow's bulge.

And then he has a chat with them.

"People think I'm crazy because I talk to my cows," Romeril said. "But it's important. A cow that runs away from you is not a happy cow."

Explained Anne Perchard, another Jersey dairy farmer, who serves as chairman of the World Jersey Cattle Bureau, "There has to be a tremendous feeling towards the cow itself, otherwise there are easier ways of making a living."

Source: Rochester Democrat and Chronicle

Compensating differentials: The nonpay benefits of certain jobs lead people to take them despite low pay.

interest rate that a worker receives on that investment—is about 10 to 15 percent per year, adjusted for inflation, and this figure has risen over the last quarter-century.[3]

On average, wages rise with a worker's age, partly due to gains in experience which increase human capital and productivity. Wages in most occupations rise until around age 40-55, then remain about constant (or fall slightly) as a worker gets older.[4] Young workers gain more benefits than older workers from investments in human capital, because younger workers have more years to *use* that human capital.

Some jobs offer workers opportunities to gain experience while working through *on-the-job training.* If workers believe that this experience or training will be valuable in the future, they raise the supply of labor to jobs offering those opportunities. As a result, jobs offering relatively attractive opportunities for experience or training tend to pay lower wages than other, similar jobs. In that sense, workers pay for their on-the-job investments in human capital by accepting lower wages during the training periods. Of course, workers would not invest in this additional human capital if they did not expect to earn even higher wages later in their careers.

Signaling

Some firms hire only workers who meet certain standards for education, even for jobs that appear unrelated to that education. These firms may use education as a *signal* that the person will be a good employee. A person with the motivation and ability to do well in school, they reason, will probably be a good employee. Other signals, such as how a person dresses and speaks, the appearance of a resume, conduct during an interview, and so on, provide similar information to firms. Education is an expensive signal, however;

---

[3] The estimated rate of return is imprecise because people differ. People who are particularly good at academic work tend to stay in school longer than other people. Their rate of return from education may be higher than the rate of return that others get. The rate of return on human capital is higher than the figures quoted here before the adjustment for inflation.

[4] Wages stop rising between age 40 and 55, partly because of diminishing returns to additional experience, and partly because workers start losing human capital through depreciation as their skills start becoming old and obsolete.

Figure 4 | Compensating Differentials

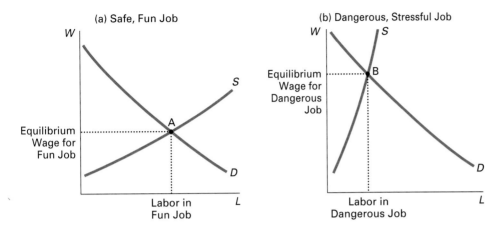

(a) Safe, Fun Job

(b) Dangerous, Stressful Job

a trial period on the job could indicate ability at much lower cost. Still, firms may use education as a signal partly because it *also* provides human capital likely to contribute to job performance.

Compensating Differentials

Differences in job environments, such as safety or ambience, create differences in equilibrium wages. Contrast a dangerous, stressful job with a relatively safe, fun job that requires the same skills and experience. Since workers prefer the safe, fun job, the supply of labor for that job exceeds the supply for the dangerous job. If the demand for labor is the same for each job, as in Figure 4, then the dangerous job pays a higher equilibrium wage to attract workers. Firms must pay higher wages to compensate workers and persuade them to take unattractive jobs. In equilibrium, no worker in either job is tempted to quit and try to obtain the other type of job. The wage in the dangerous job is just high enough to compensate for the danger or stress.

> A **compensating differential** is a difference in wages that offsets differences in the nonpay features of two jobs.

Review Questions

6. How and why does human capital affect wages?

7. How does a typical worker's wage vary over that worker's lifetime? Why?

Thinking Exercises

8. Make some guesses about your future wages and use a calculator or computer to calculate the value of your human capital. (Choose an interest rate for your calculation from a newspaper or the television news. How does your choice of an interest rate affect your answer?)

9. What factors are likely to affect the investments in human capital that people choose?

Paying for Risk of Death on the Job
Riskier jobs pay compensating differentials to the extent that workers are aware of the risks. Compensating differentials range from about $30 to $500 per year when the chance of being killed on the job in any given year rises by 1 in 10,000. This means that a firm with 1,000 workers could save between $3,000 and $50,000 in wage costs every year by investing in safety equipment that would, on average, prevent one death every ten years. Of course, when workers are unaware of a job's risks, those risks do not create a compensating differential.

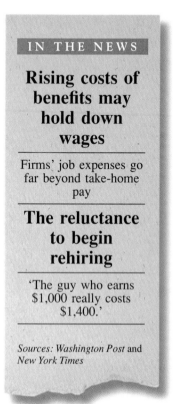

IN THE NEWS

Rising costs of benefits may hold down wages

Firms' job expenses go far beyond take-home pay

The reluctance to begin rehiring

'The guy who earns $1,000 really costs $1,400.'

Sources: Washington Post and New York Times

Changes in nonwage labor costs affect equilibrium wages.

Nonwage Labor Costs

Firms pay more than wages for workers. Total worker compensation averaged about $17.49 per hour in U.S. industry in 1996, but wages accounted for only $12.58 of this amount. The remaining $4.91 was nonwage compensation, including $1.14 per hour for insurance, $0.55 for paid vacations, $0.38 for paid holidays, $0.19 for paid sick days and other paid leave, $0.52 for extra pay and benefits, $0.55 for pensions and other savings plans for employees, $1.05 for Social Security payments, $0.40 for workers' compensation insurance to cover job-related injuries, and $0.15 for unemployment benefits.[5]

Firms' nonwage labor costs also include the costs of hiring and training workers. Hiring costs include advertising job openings, testing and evaluating applicants, and filling out government-required forms to comply with tax laws and other regulations. Hiring and training costs in the U.S. economy typically total more than $1,000 (and sometimes several thousand dollars) per employee. Because hiring and training costs depend on the number of workers a firm employs rather than the number of hours worked, ten part-time workers may cost a firm more than five full-time workers.

Types of Pay

Most workers collect hourly wages or weekly or monthly salaries; their pay depends on the time they spend at work. About 15 percent of U.S. workers collect piece-rate pay based on how much they produce. Some workers receive commissions (shares of total sales) or shares of their employers' accounting profits in profit-sharing programs. Firms have an incentive to provide pay in forms that workers like, because if they provided pay in some way that workers find unattractive, they would have to pay higher average wages to attract good workers.

Piece Rates

Piece-rate pay gives workers an incentive to work quickly and not to shirk, but it can also give them an incentive to sacrifice quality for high quantities. As a result, piece-rate pay is common mainly in industries in which quality is unimportant or easy to judge (so the firm can easily enforce a minimum quality standard).

Time Rates

Hourly wages give workers less incentive than piece-rate pay to work hard, but they avoid creating an incentive to sacrifice quality for quantity. Time-rate pay is common in industries in which it is easy to judge quantity, but hard to determine quality. A second reason for time-rate pay is that piece-rate pay creates risk in workers' weekly paychecks. A worker's productivity may depend partly on circumstances beyond individual control, such as changes in weather or equipment problems. These random factors do not affect the incomes of workers who receive time-rate pay, but they create risks for workers who receive piece-rate pay. Most workers prefer the more predictable incomes that time-rate pay provides.

When the quality of work is observable and luck plays only a small role, time-rate pay (such as annual salaries) can create nearly the same incentives as piece-rate pay. For example, a study found that the annual salaries of professional baseball players closely approximate piece-rate pay, with a one-year delay. Position players earn $9,000 in the following year for each additional home run and $6,000 for each run scored or run batted in they compile; pitchers earn $3,000 per inning pitched, $38,000 per victory, and $16,000 per save.

Profit Sharing

Some workers, particularly top executives, receive part of their pay through profit-sharing plans. They collect part of their firm's accounting profit, so their pay changes

---

[5]Firms sometimes reduce nonwage labor costs by outsourcing work to temporary workers, that is, by hiring people who are not permanent employees. This practice can reduce labor costs, because government regulations that create some of these costs do not apply to "temp" workers.

along with demand for its product. Profit sharing gives workers an incentive to watch each other and ensure that everyone contributes to that profit. Also, because worker pay falls in times of low profits, profit sharing reduces a firm's incentive to lay off these workers in lean times. For this reason, some analysts believe that firms should move toward profit sharing and away from time-rate pay.[6] Although profit sharing reduces the risk of layoff, it can be risky for workers because their pay becomes unpredictable, possibly varying substantially from one year to the next.

Profit sharing is not common in the United States, although it may be growing. Profit-sharing arrangements are more common for top executives than for other employees. In contrast, most workers in Japan receive bonuses based on their firms' profits; in fact, these bonuses comprise about one-fourth of a typical Japanese worker's total pay.

Superstars and Tournaments

The best barber cannot cut everyone's hair, the best cook cannot make everyone's meal, and the best mechanic cannot fix everyone's car. It *is* possible, however, for everyone to watch the best athlete or actor on television or in movies. Everyone can listen to the best musical performers (on CDs) and read novels by the best authors. The quantity supplied can rise without any increase in the number of performers, because more people can watch the *same* performance or read copies of the *same* novel.

When many people want to watch or read only the best (and they agree on who that is), there may be little demand for the services of people who are almost as good as the best. As a result, the best become *superstars,* and the rest, the *almost-contenders,* may be relegated to low pay and obscurity.

As a result, superstars like Madonna and Leonardo DiCaprio earn tens of millions of dollars per year, while most musicians and actors earn very low salaries. Superstar athletes receive millions of dollars per year while many others who are almost as good never succeed in professional sports. Stephen King and John Grisham earn millions, while most authors earn little or nothing from their novels. Small differences in ability may separate superstars and almost-contenders, but they may create huge differences in equilibrium pay, because a superstar's large audience translates into a very high marginal product of labor.

These cases illustrate *job tournaments,* in which one person lands a job earning a much higher wage than other people for only slightly higher productivity. Job tournaments create superstars. A job tournament requires technology that allows a single supplier to provide services to a large number of buyers at little extra cost, and some occupations do not meet this criterion. As a result, there are no superstar barbers, cooks, or mechanics.

Job tournaments occur in some occupations when only one person *can* fill a certain job. For example, only *one* person plays starting quarterback or runs a big corporation. As a result, the person who wins a top executive job may receive triple the salary of people who did not get the job, despite a much smaller difference in productivity. Firms also use tournaments to motivate workers; the *chance* of winning the good job motivates workers to perform well at their current jobs. Of course, a worker who misses out on the good job may feel overlooked or unappreciated, leading to poor performance. Firms often pay early retirement bonuses to get rid of these "deadwood" workers. In the past, many firms also imposed mandatory retirement rules that required people to retire at specified ages. The U.S. government now prohibits those rules.

Executive Compensation

Executives of large corporations receive high levels of pay. The average (median) compensation of chief executive officers (CEOs) of the 100 largest U.S. corporations exceeds $1 million per year. This amount is about three times higher than the average salary of top executives in Japan, although perks—nonmoney wage payments

Some labor markets operate like tournaments, in which the winners become superstars with high pay, and the losers—who may be *almost as good as the winners*—receive much lower pay.

"He may be a highly paid anchorman but I have the power to zap him away."

Source: The Wall Street Journal, August 12, 1993.

---

[6]See Martin Weitzman, *The Share Economy* (Cambridge, Mass.: Harvard University Press, 1984).

SOCIAL AND ECONOMIC ISSUES

Perks

Perks often include health insurance and health-care services, paid vacations, paid sick leave, discounts on product purchases, and child care. Top executives sometimes get perks such as chauffeur service; access to company cars or airplanes; free memberships in country clubs, health clubs, and other clubs; and home security systems. A small scandal developed in 1993 when a U.S. automobile manufacturer hired a new chief executive officer who had relied on the perk of a free car for so long that he couldn't remember the last time he had bought or even owned a car.

such as access to company yachts, country estates, home entertainment, and long vacations—are much more generous in Japan. The average pay for all U.S. CEOs is about $200,000 to $250,000. Average CEO salaries in Germany, France, and the United Kingdom are smaller (about $100,000 to $150,000), but firms in those countries also provide more perks. Economists disagree about whether executive pay results from tournaments and allocates resources efficiently or whether corporate laws and regulations create an economically inefficient situation that supports artificially high executive pay.[7]

Labor Turnover

Even in equilibrium, the labor market constantly changes. Every year some people finish school and look for jobs, while other people retire. Still others enter or leave the labor force, quit their jobs to take or look for other jobs, or get fired or laid off.

> **Labor turnover** refers to the continuing flows of people into and out of the labor force, employment and unemployment, and various jobs.

In the United States, the quit rate in manufacturing is 1 to 2 percent per month. Each month, about 3 percent of workers in manufacturing industries were hired over the previous month. About half of all workers have spent less than 4 years in their current jobs, though about half of all adult workers eventually find jobs that they keep for over 20 years.

The equilibrium amount of labor turnover depends on:

▶ Labor mobility—how easily people can move—and how willingly they will move to a new city, to take new jobs

▶ Information available to workers about new job opportunities

▶ Information available to workers and firms about each other, which affects how well they will match and fit together

▶ Underlying economic change (in technology, demographics, tastes, and government policies) that affect demands and supplies, causing some firms to shut down and others to expand, destroying some jobs and creating others

IN THE NEWS

Milken's pay boggles the mind

By Steve Swartz
The Wall Street Journal

NEW YORK—The U.S. government said it, so it may be true; Michael R. Milken, the Drexel Burnham Lambert Inc. junk bond king, was paid $550 million in salary and bonuses in 1987.

I can't imagine paying anyone $550 million. What do you say to him in his performance review? "Now Mike, if you don't work even harder next year, we won't be able to give you a raise?"
—Nelson Peltz,
wealthy former client

Source: Rochester Democrat and Chronicle

Michael Milken's pay was second only to that of gangster Al Capone, who pocketed $105 million in 1927, comparable to about $600 million after adjusting for inflation between 1927 and 1987.

[7]A related disagreement among economists concerns the extent to which executives' pay provides them with the proper incentives. Executives often receive various types of pay based on their firms' performance levels (profits, stock-market values, sales, and so on) that are designed partly to affect their performance incentives.

> A person is **unemployed** if that person does not have a job, but wants one.

> A person is **underemployed** if that person does not have a job that makes use of his or her training and skills, but wants one.

These definitions are somewhat vague because they include the phrase *wants one*. The federal government measures unemployment in the United States through a monthly survey called the *Current Population Survey* conducted by the Bureau of Labor Statistics (BLS), an agency in the U.S. Department of Labor.[8] The BLS randomly chooses about 58,000 households to survey; it counts people as unemployed if they are:

1. Not working, but have actively looked for work in the last month

2. Waiting to be recalled by firms after being laid off

3. Waiting to start new jobs within the next month

The measurement of unemployment is imperfect for at least three reasons. First, it does not count people as unemployed if they have become so discouraged that they have stopped looking for jobs. The survey classifies them as not in the labor force rather than as unemployed. Second, it counts underemployed workers (mathematicians driving cabs, and so on) as employed. Also, it counts people who work part-time as employed, although they may want full-time jobs. Third, it counts people as unemployed if they say they looked for work within the previous month, even if they did not look seriously or were unwilling to accept job offers with realistic wages. The first two problems lead the BLS survey to underreport unemployment; the third problem has the opposite effect. Figure 5 shows the rate of unemployment in the United States since 1948. Table 1 shows the composition of unemployment in a typical month.

Most newly unemployed people find jobs within 1 or 2 months. While most spells of unemployment end within 1 month, some drag on for much longer periods. As a person remains unemployed longer, the likelihood that he will find a job declines, as does the wage he will eventually earn upon finding a job. People lose their skills when unemployed, so they become less productive. Also, firms regard unemployment as a signal that a person may not be a good worker.

IN THE NEWS

U.S. jobless rate drops to 28-year low

Source: The Wall Street Journal

Table 1 | Unemployment in the United States: April 1998

Civilian labor force	137.3 million people	Unemployment rate	4.3 %
Employed	131.4 million	Men age 20 and over	3.4 %
Unemployed	5.9 million	Women age 20 and over	4.1 %
Unemployed less than 5 weeks	2.6 million	Teenagers (both sexes age 16 to 19)	13.1 %
Unemployed more than 15 weeks	1.4 million	Whites	3.6 %
		Blacks	8.9 %
Not in labor force	67.5 million	Hispanics	6.5 %

Source: Survey of Current Business

---

[8]Nations measure unemployment by different methods; Japan and Canada also use surveys, while most European countries count the numbers of people collecting unemployment compensation payments.

SOCIAL AND ECONOMIC ISSUES

Mommy Track

An article in the *Harvard Business Review* argued that firms should offer two types of career opportunities: one for "career-primary" women and men who would plan to devote most of their time to their careers, and another for "career/family" women and men who wanted to balance career goals with their roles in raising their children and who would be willing to sacrifice some career growth and salary for the freedom and flexibility to do so. Pundits soon dubbed the career/family track the *mommy track,* although *daddy track* would do as well in principle.

The proposal advocated allowing workers to choose career options. Workers themselves, not their employers, would make these decisions. Workers in the so-called *mommy track* would (on average) earn lower pay and fewer promotions than career-primary workers, and they would accumulate less human capital, but they would also work fewer hours and gain flexibility in hours and employment choices, perhaps choosing to stop working or work part-time for several years to raise children.

Proponents have argued that this proposal would enhance workers' control over their own lifestyles. Opponents have argued that firms would use the idea as an excuse to discriminate against women and not permit true choice. Some also have argued that the mommy track would reinforce undesirable social customs that concentrate responsibility for raising children on women. (Recall from the chapter on game theory that people can sometimes gain from committing themselves and limiting their own options. If no

Why Unemployment?

Unemployment can occur if the wage exceeds the equilibrium wage, as in Figure 6. Ordinarily, the wage falls toward its equilibrium level in this situation. However, wage changes may take months or even years, so the wage may temporarily exceed its equilibrium level after a fall in demand, creating a temporary surplus of labor services and temporary unemployment. Unemployment can also be created by government regulations, minimum wage laws, or union actions that prevent the wage from falling to its

Figure 5 | Unemployment Rate in the United States Since 1948

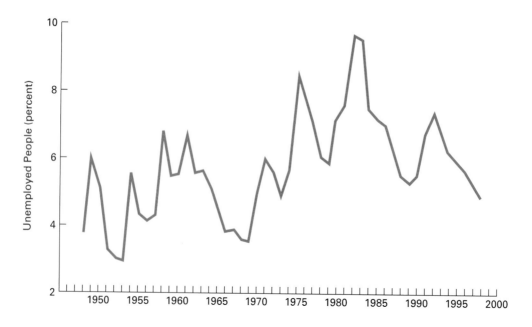

mommy track is available, women can commit to choose either the regular career track or no career at all. Faced with this choice for their wives, men might choose to expand their roles in raising children.) Other people have argued that the mommy-track idea does not go far enough; firms should permit greater flexibility in career paths for *all* workers, with each worker choosing his or her own commitment to career versus other aspects of life.

Questions

1. How much sacrifice must people make in their personal or family lives to advance to the top of the business world? Do you think the reward is worth the sacrifice?

2. Would women work more or less if firms were to offer a mommy track? How would the mommy track affect the wages of men and women in the career-primary track?

3. What kinds of jobs are best-suited for a mommy or daddy track? What kinds are least well-suited?

4. Should firms offer a mommy track? Defend your position, then argue against it.

5. Why don't firms permit more choice and flexibility in careers now? Does flexibility have a cost?

Source: See Felice Schwartz, "Management Women and the New Facts of Life," *Harvard Business Review,* January-February 1989. Schwartz is president of Catalyst, an advisory group on women's leadership.

---

equilibrium level. Union workers, who already have jobs at the prevailing wage and do not want it to fall, may have greater influence on union decisions than workers who would gain jobs if the wage were to fall.

Some unemployment results from normal labor turnover. New people enter the labor force, some firms expand, and others go out of business. This continual reshuffling of workers and jobs creates some unemployment. Workers who quit their jobs or get laid off often experience periods of unemployment before finding new jobs, although *most* job changes do not involve unemployment. Some people experience unemployment after leaving school before finding jobs. Workers and firms take time to find the right matches. As a result, job vacancies persist alongside unemployment.

Review Questions

10. Name some advantages and disadvantages of (a) piece-rate pay; (b) time-rate (e.g. hourly or weekly) pay; (c) profit sharing.

11. Why do superstars earn such high salaries? What is a labor tournament?

12. What conditions affect the degree of labor turnover?

13. How does the U.S. government measure the unemployment rate?

Thinking Exercises

14. How is an increase in hiring costs likely to affect wages, employment, and hours worked per week for an average worker?

15. Suppose that an increase in government regulations creates obstacles to firing workers. How is this likely to affect wages, employment, and hours worked per week for an average worker?

**Figure 6
Unemployment with the Wage above Equilibrium**

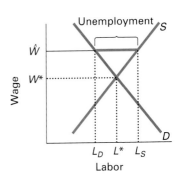

The equilibrium wage is W^* and the equilibrium quantity of labor is L^*. If the wage is $\hat{W}$, which is above the equilibrium wage, the quantity of labor demanded is only L_D, which is smaller than the equilibrium quantity. Therefore, only L_D hours of labor are actually employed (only that many people actually get jobs at the wage $\hat{W}$), while the quantity of labor supplied is L_S. Unemployment is L_S minus L_D.

ADDITIONAL ISSUES

Population Changes

The supply of labor expands with increases in population due to rising birth rates, falling death rates, and immigration. Unless corresponding increases in technology or other inputs such as land and capital raise the marginal product of labor by a sufficient amount, population increases create diminishing returns to labor and reduce the equilibrium wage. The same effect works in reverse: When the black plague killed between 17 percent and 40 percent of the population of England and about one-third of the entire European population from 1347 to 1351, the resulting fall in labor supply raised wages by 30 to 100 percent.

Baby Boom

People born in the 1950s and early 1960s, when U.S. couples had many more babies than usual, are part of the so-called *baby-boom* generation. By 1980, for example, the labor force included 44 percent more 22-year-olds than two decades earlier. The increase in labor supply by young, inexperienced workers reduced their wages by nearly 15 percent.

The effects of the baby boom on wages continue to this day. By 2000, the baby-boom generation will have accumulated about 20 to 25 years of work experience, which will raise the supply of workers with that level of experience and reduce their wages. Members of the baby-boom generation are likely to receive lower wages throughout their lives than they would have received as part of a less populous generation.

Advances in Technology

Improvements in technology raise the marginal products of labor in industries that use the new technologies. As a result, the demand for labor rises in those industries, raising equilibrium wages and employment. The wage increase attracts workers from other industries, thereby reducing labor supply in other industries and spreading wage increases throughout the economy.

Changes in Tastes

Changes in consumer demands affect jobs and wages. When the demand for one good falls and demand for another rises, the resulting price changes reduce the value of the marginal product of labor in the first industry and raise it in the second. This decreases demand for labor in the first industry, lowering wages and employment by its firms. It also increases the demand for labor in the second industry, raising wages and employment there. Temporary unemployment results as workers shift from the first industry to the second.

Labor Unions

Labor unions are organizations of workers intended to represent their interests in negotiations with firms over wages and working conditions and to provide other services.

> **Labor unions** are organizations of workers designed to improve the working conditions and pay of their members and to provide other services.

Labor unions are also social and political institutions that help to represent their members in the political arena and to provide social support of many kinds, from parties to college scholarship funds.

Industrial unions like the United Auto Workers usually cover workers in different occupations within the same firm or industry. Craft unions (such as an electrician's union) typically cover workers in some occupation regardless of the industry in which they work. Most U.S. unions are members of the AFL–CIO, the American Federation of Labor–Congress of Industrial Organizations, which is roughly a union of unions. Some occupational organizations, such as the American Medical Association and the American Bar Association, share many features of unions but are not legally considered labor unions in the United States.

Unions play roles in several scenarios. Nonunion members can work at a firm with an open shop. A closed shop, prohibited in the United States in 1947 by the Taft-Hartley Act, required every worker to be a union member. In a union shop, a firm can hire nonunion workers, but those workers must join the union after a short period of time. About 20 U.S. states have enacted right-to-work laws that prohibit union shops or mandate open shops. *Collective bargaining* refers to negotiations between firms and unions about labor contracts. A strike occurs when a group of workers (usually members of a union) refuses to work until the firm meets certain conditions in collective bargaining. A lockout occurs when a firm refuses to allow employees to work until their union meets certain conditions in collective bargaining.

Unions as Monopoly Sellers of Labor

Unions can raise the wages of their members by acting as monopoly sellers of labor. Workers sell labor services, and a union is essentially a legal cartel of workers that restrict the number of workers in an industry to raise wages. Figure 7 shows a labor market equilibrium when a union is a monopoly seller of labor to an industry. Without the union, the marginal cost of working would define the supply curve for labor. The equilibrium wage with no union would be W^N and equilibrium employment would be L^N. Members of a union can gain by restricting the quantity of labor supplied, just as any monopoly restricts its quantity. Figure 7 shows the marginal revenue curve, *MR*, associated with the industry

Figure 7 | Unions as Monopoly Sellers of Labor

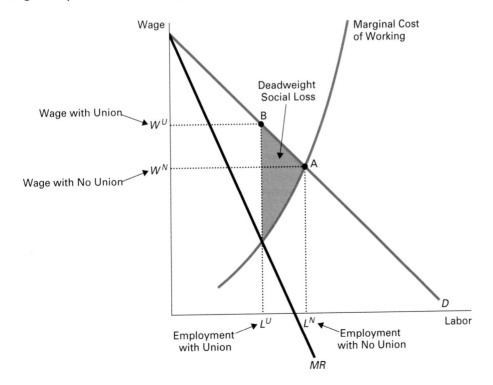

The marginal cost of working curve would be the labor supply curve with no union, and Point A would be the equilibrium point. The union's influence moves the equilibrium to Point B.

demand for labor, D. The union maximizes its profit (total wage payments minus the opportunity cost of working) by raising the wage to W^U, which it can do by restricting employment or hours per worker to L^U.

The reasoning is the same as that for any monopoly or cartel. The union can divide the gains it achieves among its member workers. As in any monopoly situation, the gain to the union is smaller than the loss to employers, so the union's actions cause a deadweight social loss, indicated by the shaded area in Figure 7.

Economists estimate that unions raise wages about 10 percent to 20 percent, on average. They estimate the deadweight social loss from union monopoly power and strikes to be about 0.8 percent to 1.0 percent of the economy's total output (GDP) each year.[9]

About one-fifth of all nonfarm workers are union members in the United States today. This rate is lower than the rate earlier in the 20th century and the rates in most European countries.[10]

Explicit and Implicit Contracts

Firms and workers in a unionized industry usually agree to detailed, formal labor contracts. The contracts usually set wages, articulate procedures for resolving issues such as layoffs and job vacancies, and address other issues. Many employees without these formal, explicit contracts have implicit labor contracts with their firms.

An **implicit labor contract** is an informal agreement or understanding about the terms of employment.

Courts cannot enforce implicit labor contracts, because the terms are not stated in writing in signed, binding agreements. Still, competition among firms to maintain good reputations helps to enforce the informal agreements. A firm would risk losing its good reputation if it were to renege on the terms of an implicit contract. Firms value good reputations because they help to attract good workers without paying higher wages than other firms; workers prefer to work for firms that typically treat employees fairly and live up to their implicit agreements.

Efficiency Wages

Sometimes a firm has an incentive to pay workers more than the value of their marginal product to keep them from quitting. A firm can increase employees' incentives to do high-quality work by paying a higher wage than the employees could get at similar jobs elsewhere. This gives employees more to lose if they lose their jobs. A worker with a particularly good job has a stronger incentive to keep it than a worker who could easily find a similar job at another firm. A worker with a strong incentive to keep a job is likely to do high-quality work and maintain high productivity. By paying unusually high wages, firms can give employees incentives for good performance. In this way, high wages can substitute to some extent for active supervision of workers, reducing a firm's management costs.

When Henry Ford started the Ford Motor Company, he encountered a very high quit rate among his employees. (Also, he frequently fired workers.) The company's employee

---

[9]Some evidence indicates that unions also raise productivity by improving worker-firm relations and reducing quit rates..

[10]Union membership in the United States may have declined because fewer people now work in industries with traditionally strong unions, such as manufacturing, construction, and transportation. Employment in those industries has fallen from one-half of the labor force in the mid-20th century to one-third of the labor force today. More people now work in service industries, which tend not to be unionized because high elasticity of demand for their products prevents unions from raising wages much without large decreases in employment. Foreseeing smaller gains from unionization, workers in these industries have not tended to form unions. However, union membership increased in Canada as it declined in the U.S., despite close similarities in other changes affecting the U.S. and Canadian economies. Some economists conclude from this difference that much of the decline in U.S. union membership reflects U.S. government policies or greater employer opposition to unions in the United States.

turnover rate was 370 percent in 1913; Ford had to hire 370 people each year just to keep 100 jobs filled. On an average day, more than 10 percent of workers failed to show up for their shifts. Despite worker unhappiness, Ford could choose among long lines of people who wanted to work there, so it could easily hire new workers. Nevertheless, the company decided in January 1914 to double its wage from $2.50 to $5.00 per hour (in today's dollars). The $2.50 wage was an equilibrium wage. (If it had been below equilibrium, Ford would not have easily found new employees to hire.) Setting the wage above the equilibrium level, however, reduced the quit rate by 87 percent, and absenteeism fell 75 percent. Workers improved their performance, and firings fell 90 percent.

> When firms pay wages above equilibrium to try to raise worker productivity, economists say they pay **efficiency wages.**

Efficiency wages can cause unemployment. To see why, ask yourself what happens if all firms try to pay unusually high wages, competing to beat the pay that other firms offer. Of course, they cannot succeed. As all firms try to pay more than other firms, however, wages rise above the equilibrium level, which causes unemployment, as in Figure 6. The incentive effects of the high wages still operate, but in a different way; now a worker who shirks responsibility and loses a job risks unemployment rather than a drop in income.

Review Questions

16. How can unions affect wages?

17. Why might firms pay efficiency wages? What are the likely results of doing so?

Thinking Exercises

18. Explain how an improvement in technology might hurt unskilled workers.

19. If workers in half of the industries in the economy formed new unions to increase their wages, how would this affect wages and employment in other, nonunionized industries?

Conclusion

Labor Supply and Demand

People make labor supply decisions, including whether to be in the labor force at all, what occupations to choose, which job offers to accept, and how many hours to work. Labor supply curves slope upward if the substitution effect of a wage increase outweighs the income effect; those curves bend backward if the income effect outweighs the substitution effect. The demand for labor reflects the value of its marginal product. Technology, worker skills, the amount of capital machinery and equipment, and the price of a firm's final product affect a firm's demand for labor.

Labor Market Equilibrium

Labor market equilibrium combines an equilibrium real wage and an equilibrium number of hours worked for each type of labor. Hiring and training costs, government regulations, and other factors determine how a firm chooses between hiring new employees and increasing hours per week for each employee. The real wage is the wage measured in purchasing power. (It adjusts the nominal wage for inflation.)

Features of Equilibrium in Labor Markets

Improvements in skills (human capital) and equipment (physical capital) raise a worker's equilibrium wage by increasing her productivity.

Wages differ across jobs mainly because some require more human capital (education, skills, knowledge, experience, and ability) than others. People invest to develop their own human capital through education, on-the-job training, and experience. Jobs that require comparatively high human capital must pay high wages to compensate workers for the cost of acquiring that human capital. Jobs that offer on-the-job training pay lower wages than other, similar jobs.

Wages also differ across jobs because of differences in work environments. To attract workers, dangerous jobs must pay higher wages than similar, less dangerous jobs. Generally, compensating differentials in wages offset differences in nonpay aspects of jobs.

Firms may pay workers based on the time they work (a time rate), the quantity they produce (a piece rate), or the firm's profits (profit sharing). Each type of pay creates different incentives. A job tournament occurs when a single supplier can provide services to a large number of buyers at little extra cost. Job tournaments create superstars, who earn much higher wages than other people with almost equal job performance. Tournaments also help to explain high levels of executive compensation.

Constant labor turnover generates continuing unemployment. The amount of labor turnover depends on factors such as labor mobility, information available to workers and firms about their opportunities, and the extent of underlying changes in the economy.

Unemployment

The U.S. government measures unemployment through a monthly survey. Its measurement is imperfect because of discouraged and underemployed workers, and because some people do not search seriously for work. Most newly unemployed people find jobs within 1 or 2 months, though some spells of unemployment drag on for long periods. Some unemployment results from normal labor turnover. Unemployment also results when the wage exceeds its equilibrium level.

Additional Issues

Labor unions can raise the wages of their members by acting as monopoly sellers of labor that restrict the number of workers in their industries. Implicit labor contracts are informal agreements between firms and employees about the terms of employment. While courts cannot enforce implicit labor contracts, firms have some incentive to honor them to maintain valuable reputations. Firms may pay wages above equilibrium—efficiency wages—to provide workers with incentives for hard work.

Key Terms

labor force
backward-bending
   labor supply
   curve

value of the marginal
   product of labor
nominal (money) wage
real wage

human capital
compensating differential
labor turnover
unemployed person

underemployed person
labor union
implicit labor contract
efficiency wage

Problems

20. If wages differ because of compensating differentials, why do business executives earn more money and enjoy nicer working conditions than garbage collectors?

21. Explain why a worker may be willing to sacrifice a higher wage this year in return for an increase in the discounted present value of future wages.

22. What are some deficiencies of the U.S. government's measure of unemployment?

23. Comment on this statement: "Workers with more seniority than others receive higher wages because they are more likely to have families and need higher incomes." Why do firms pay more to workers with more seniority than others?

24. A college dean said in a speech that colleges will see fewer students in the coming decade because the population will include fewer people of college age. He said that colleges will reduce tuitions to compete with each other for students, and that this will create a problem because professors' salaries have been rising. How would you expect a fall in the demand for college admission to affect professors' salaries?

25. How would wages, employment, and average weekly hours per worker be affected by:

(a) A change in tastes so that people want to work more than they did before

(b) An earthquake that destroys much of a city

(c) A law that requires firms to buy health insurance for workers

(d) Worsening traffic problems that increase commuting times for workers

26. Suppose that people irrationally believe that a job is safer or more dangerous than it really is. Does this irrational belief affect wages? Explain.

Inquiries for Further Thought

27. Why do people buy and sell labor services? Why don't all workers work for themselves, as many doctors, lawyers, accountants, plumbers, artisans, and farmers do, rather than working as employees of business firms?

28. Why are people unemployed? If someone wants a job and cannot find one, why doesn't this person say to a firm, "Look, calculate the value of what I can produce for your firm, and then pay me less than that. Then you will profit from hiring me and we'll both benefit"? Alternatively, why doesn't this person start an independent business?

29. Is unemployment involuntary or voluntary?

30. What should the government do about unemployment, if anything?

(a) Do you think that the government should be involved in job training? What incentives induce workers and firms to provide this training themselves?

(b) Should the government subsidize moves by people in areas with high unemployment to areas with more job opportunities? What would be the results of such a subsidy?

(c) Should the government require job sharing to try to reduce unemployment?

(d) Should the government subsidize companies to increase employment? Would this policy reduce unemployment?

31. How would increased immigration affect U.S. employment and wages?

(a) Should the United States permit increased immigration or unlimited immigration, allowing anyone who wants to enter the country to do so?

(b) Should immigrants be eligible for welfare? Should they be eligible to vote?

(c) Should the United States sell immigration rights to the highest bidders?

(d) Should a country give priority in immigration to political refugees (those who are subject to punishment in their home countries for their political views)? What about people who want to immigrate to the United States to avoid poverty in their home countries?

32. In *The Wealth of Nations,* Adam Smith wrote, "We trust our health to the physician; our fortune and sometimes our life and reputation to the lawyer and attorney. Such confidence could not safely be reposed in people of a very mean or low condition. Their reward must be such, therefore, as may give them that rank in society which so important a trust requires."[11] Do you agree? What does this argument have to do with efficiency wages?

33. Do top executives deserve the pay they get? How about sports figures, musicians, and actors?

34. How are technical progress and economic growth (an increase in per-person income and output of goods and services in the economy) likely to affect people's willingness to work hard in their jobs?

35. The number of hours that an average person spends working each year is higher in Japan than in the United States, and higher in the United States than in most European countries.

(a) Why might countries differ in this way?

(b) Comment on the following claim: "Profit-driven employers will always seek to encourage long working hours."

---

[11]Adam Smith, *The Wealth of Nations* (1776; reprint, New York: Knopf, 1991).

CHAPTER 19

RICH AND POOR: INCOME DISTRIBUTION, POVERTY, AND DISCRIMINATION

In this Chapter. . .

Main Points to Understand

- On average, people have become wealthier over time, although inequality has increased in the last quarter century.
- The distribution of wealth is less equal than the distribution of income.
- Although poverty is temporary for most people in developed countries, persistent and severe poverty remains a serious problem for at least one-fifth of the world's population.
- Alternative views of justice and fairness are associated with egalitarianism, utilitarianism, the implicit contract view, and natural rights views.

Thinking Skills to Develop

- Evaluate evidence about poverty and the distribution of income.
- Evaluate alternative normative statements about justice and fairness.
- Formulate arguments for and against various ideas of justice and fairness.
- Apply economic analysis to social issues such as discrimination.

The distribution of income is one of the most volatile subjects of public discussion, and it runs like an undercurrent through many political debates. Are the poor getting poorer while the rich get richer? How poor are the poor? How rich are the rich? Are economic conditions improving or deteriorating for the average family? How does poverty in the United States compare to poverty in the rest of the world? How large are the income differences between men and women, different racial groups, and people in different countries? What are the effects of discrimination or remedies for it?

Preliminary Definitions

> **Income** is the value of money and goods that a person receives during some time period.

People earn income from working, as returns on investments, and as gifts or inheritances.

DISTRIBUTION OF INCOME AND WEALTH IN THE UNITED STATES

> **Wealth** is the total value of a person's accumulated savings plus the discounted present value of expected future labor income.

Income refers to a *flow* of dollars per year, and wealth refers to a *stock* of dollars at some specific time. The accumulated-savings portion of wealth is called *nonhuman wealth;* the discounted present value of expected future income is called *human wealth* (the value of human capital). Economists measure wealth in dollars; they measure income in dollars per year.

The *distribution of income* or *wealth* refers to comparisons of income or wealth across people or families.

> **Median income** is the income level at which half of the population receive more income and half receive less.

> **Mean income** is total income divided by the number of people.

If one person earns $10, another person earns $20, and a third earns $60, their median income is $20. This is the income level of the person in the middle; one person earns more and one person earns less. Their mean income is $30 = (10 + 20 + 60)/3.

Unless the text states otherwise, all statistics quoted for the United States refer to 1995 dollars and use the government definition of *money income*, which refers to income *before* paying taxes and:

▶ Includes transfer payments of money from the government (sometimes called *entitlements),* such as social security and unemployment compensation.

▶ Excludes noncash transfers from the government, such as food stamps, health benefits like Medicare and Medicaid, and subsidized housing.

▶ Excludes noncash benefits paid by employers such as free housing for farm workers, employee medical care, and health insurance.

The definition of *money income* overstates U.S. poverty somewhat because it does not include *noncash* income such as food stamps.

The U.S. government reports separate income data for families and for households. The category *families* includes people living with others to whom they are related by biological or marriage ties; *households* includes families plus individuals living alone. About 102 million households live in the United States, of which about two-thirds (71 million) are families by this definition.

Main Facts of Income Distribution

Figure 1 shows the percentages of U.S. households with incomes in various ranges in 1996 and 1970. Because the distribution is skewed (not symmetric like a bell curve), median household income, about $35,500, is less than mean household income, about $47,000. The figure shows that the percentage of U.S. households with incomes over $75,000 (in 1995 dollars) has doubled in the last quarter-century, while the percentage with incomes below $10,000 has decreased. (Recall that all incomes have been adjusted for inflation to avoid misleading comparisons, as discussed in Chapter 2, so differences between years do not reflect inflation.)[1]

---

[1]Actual money incomes from earlier years (such as 1970) were smaller than shown in the figure. The actual median income in 1970 was $8,734, but prices were (on average) 4.04 times higher in 1996 than in 1970, so an $8,734 income in 1970 was equivalent to an income of $35,319 in 1996.

Figure 1 | Percentages of Households in Various Income Ranges

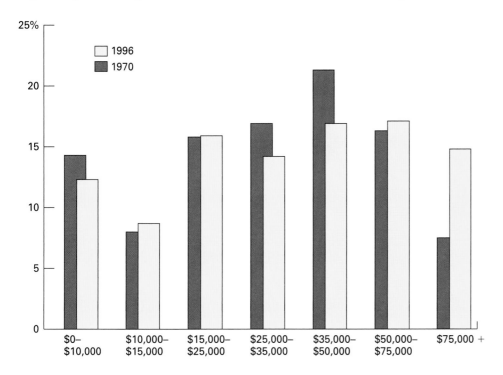

Figure 2 shows the fraction of total income earned by U.S. households in various ranges of the income distribution. The *highest fifth* of the income distribution refers to the 20 percent of households with the highest incomes; the *lowest fifth* refers to the 20

Figure 2 | Percentages of Total Income Earned by Households in Five Income Ranges, 1996

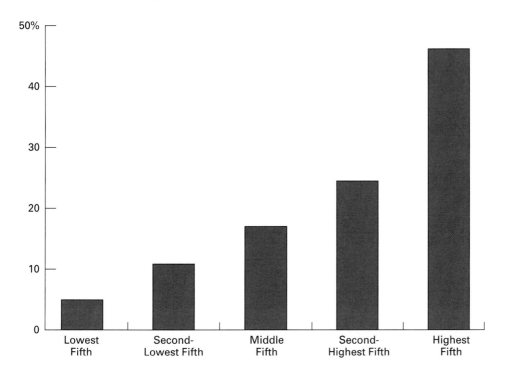

Figure 3 | Median Family Income in 1996 Dollars

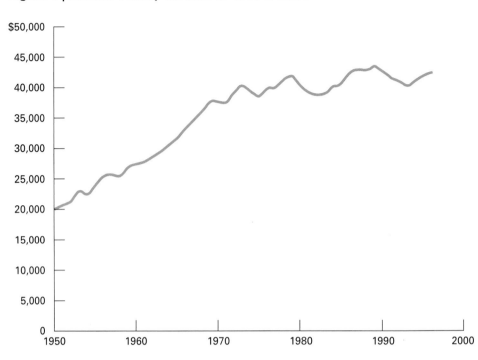

percent with the lowest incomes. People in the highest fifth of the income distribution earn about 45 percent of all income, while people in the lowest fifth earn less than 5 percent.

The main facts of the distribution of income in the United States include:

1. Median household and family income have doubled since the middle of the 20th century. Figure 3 shows median family income over time in 1996 dollars. However, income increased much more slowly in the last quarter of the century than in the third quarter.

2. Each year, households in the top fifth of the U.S. income distribution collect just under one-half of all the country's income, and households in the bottom fifth get only about 4.4 percent, down from close to 5 percent two decades ago.

3. Family income inequality in the United States has not changed much since 1950. Inequality fell in the third quarter of the 20th century but increased in the last quarter. More households now have incomes from *two* wage-earners, and more receive *no* earned income at all. Government programs have helped to mitigate increases in income inequality resulting from these changes. However, the average income of people in the bottom fifth of the income distribution still has fallen in the last quarter-century.

4. People in the United States are economically mobile; a low income in one year does not rule out a higher income in future years, and a high income in one year does not guarantee high incomes in future years. About half of all people with incomes in the bottom fifth of the income distribution move to higher fifths of the distribution within seven years.

5. About 10 to 15 percent of U.S. citizens live in households with incomes below the government-defined poverty level. About 2 percent remain below the poverty level for many years; the others move out of poverty after a few years. Poverty is higher

Figure 4 | Poverty in the United States

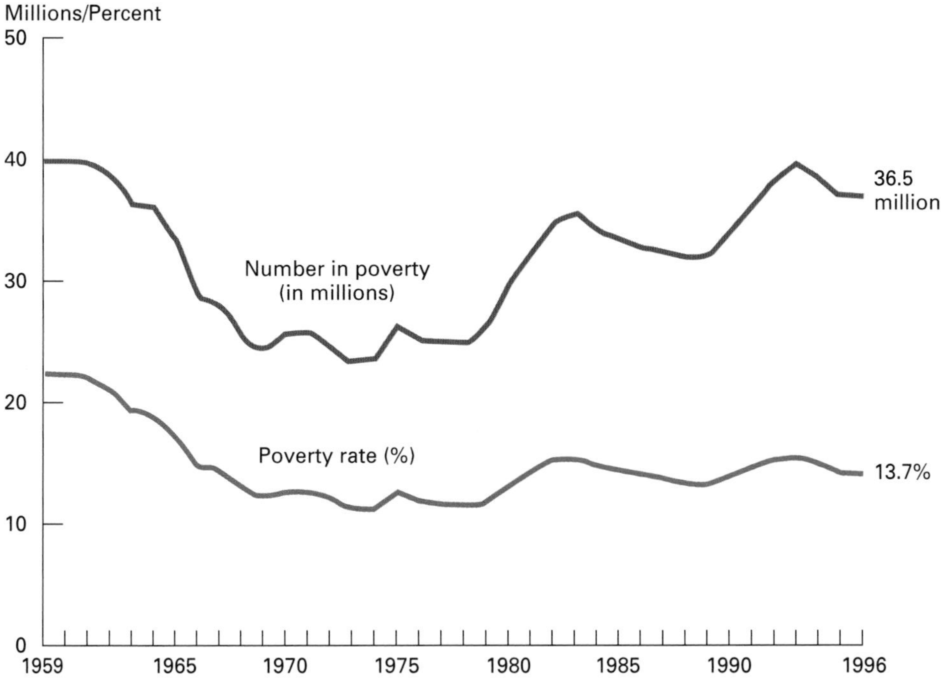

Millions/Percent

among women, children, blacks, and Hispanics than among other groups. Figure 4 shows the number of people living below the government-defined poverty level, $16,036 for a family of four in 1996.[2]

Discussion

Median household income rose only 7 percent between 1970 and 1996. However, total U.S. output of goods and services increased from $18,095 per person in 1970 to $28,082 per person in 1996 (both in 1995 dollars).[3] Why has median household income risen so slowly despite such a rapid increase in output of goods and services per person? The explanation has several parts. First, *mean* income has risen faster than *median* income since 1970 as the distribution of income has become more unequal over that period. Second, household size has declined, so income *per person* has increased faster than income per *household*. Third, the median household income figures do *not* include noncash income, which has risen over time.

The doubling of median income since 1950 understates the increase in material living standards since that time. Many goods that people now take for granted had not even been invented in 1950, and the quality of many goods has increased since then.[4] Further, white males accounted for two-thirds of the labor force in 1950; opportunities for blacks and women were much more restricted at that time than they are today.

Incomes differ substantially across different types of households. Figure 5 shows the median incomes of several household types in 1996. Households with only female

---

[2]The poverty level was originally calculated to equal three times estimated basic minimum food costs, based on a survey of food consumption.

[3]These figures are adjusted for inflation to avoid a misleading comparison, as discussed in Chapter 2.

[4]Even pollution was worse then in many respects; the air and various products contained significant amounts of toxic lead, for example.

Figure 5 | Median Income by Household Type, 1996

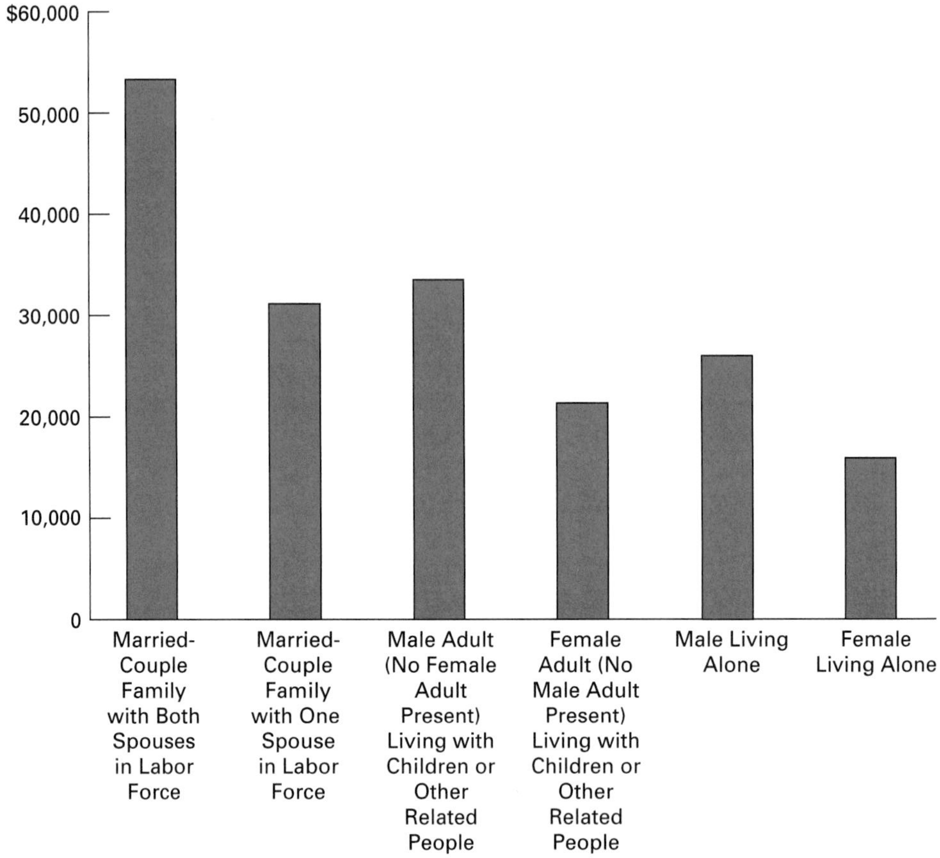

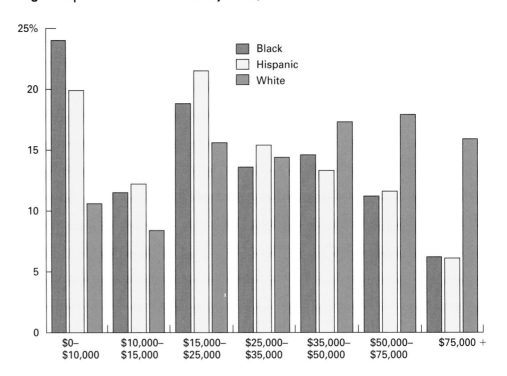

Figure 6 | Household Incomes by Race, 1996

adults clearly have lower incomes than those with only males or with both. Figure 6 shows the percentages of whites, blacks, and Hispanics with 1996 incomes in various ranges.

Poverty

Poverty has struck children particularly hard, as Figure 7 shows. The percentage of U.S. children living below the poverty level has increased in recent decades. More than 14 million children, and nearly one-fourth of all children under age 6, lived in households with incomes below the poverty line in 1996. Studies show that children who grow up in poverty generally get less education and face higher chances of living in poverty as adults. Much of the increase in the fraction of children living in poverty in recent decades has been associated with increases in the number of teenage mothers living in households without fathers and in the number of young, two-parent households with low incomes.

To view U.S. poverty in perspective, compare it with average world output of goods and services per person. The U.S. government-defined poverty level for a person living alone in 1996, $7,995 per year, was about 33 percent *above* average world output per person (about $6,000). The poverty level for an average family of four, $16,036, was about two-thirds of average world output per four-person family.

About half of all people below the poverty level in any year remain there for a full year, while the rest rise out of poverty in that time. About one-fourth of the U.S. population receive help from government welfare programs at some time over the course of a decade, though only a small percentage depend on welfare over long periods. As a result, households in the lowest fifth of the income distribution spend almost twice as much as their incomes. They spend more than they take in because they expect, usually correctly, that their low incomes will be only temporary. By borrowing or digging into their savings, they can spend more than they earn for short periods. The typical person in the lowest fifth of the U.S. income distribution in 1996 spent more than the income per-person of the *median* U.S. household in 1950.

These facts show that, for most people in the United States, poverty is a temporary problem. However, some people remain in poverty for many years and experience more

Figure 7 | Percentages of Children Below Poverty Level

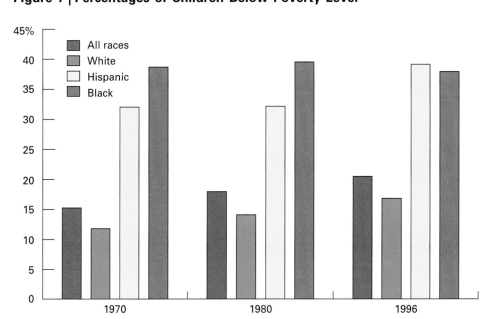

serious difficulties. This information also indicates that temporary receipt of government welfare payments does not, for most people, automatically create a dependence on welfare. However, evidence shows a strong connection between incomes of parents and incomes of their children when they grow into adults. One study found that for every 10 percent increase in parent income, their children's adult income rises by 8 percent. While economic mobility is common in the United States, the children of the poor are more likely than others to become poor adults, and the children of the rich are more likely to become rich adults.

Wages

Average wages have fallen over the last quarter century. Hourly wages (in 1997 dollars) averaged $8.57 in 1950, rose steadily to $14.24 in 1973, and then began falling to $12.97 by 1980, before falling further to $12.03 in 1993 and then rising slightly to $12.26 in 1997.[5] Average weekly earnings rose 48 percent from 1950 to 1973, then fell 21 percent from 1973 to 1997. Wages for college graduates rose, but wages for workers with less education fell. These changes mainly reflect advances in technology that have reduced demand for low-skilled workers and raised demand for skilled workers. Because equipment that exploits technological advances can replace people in many low-skill jobs, wages of low-skilled workers have fallen. Meanwhile, these advances in technology have raised wages of highly skilled "knowledge workers." Some economists believe that increased world economic integration and the waning power of unions in the United States may also have contributed to the decline in wages for low-skilled workers in the United States.

Although wages have fallen, total labor income has not. Instead, more people have worked and total payments to workers have increased along with the economy's total output. While hourly wages among males became more unequal in the last two decades, hourly wages among females did not.

Distribution of Wealth

Wealth is distributed less equally than income. In the United States, the richest 2 percent of the population own about one-fourth of all household assets (nonhuman wealth). The richest 25 percent own about three-fourths of all household assets.

The distribution of wealth has gradually become more equal throughout most of the 20th century in the only three countries for which long-term data are available: the United States, the United Kingdom, and Sweden. In 1922, the richest 0.5 percent of the U.S. population owned 30 percent of all household wealth. This figure fell to 21 percent by mid-century and to less than 15 percent by 1975. It has increased in the last quarter century, though.

Blacks and whites in the United States differ much more in their average wealth than in their incomes. The median nonhuman wealth of white households is about $75,000, but this figure is only about $5,000 for black and Hispanic households.[6] Married couples hold much more nonhuman wealth than individuals living alone. Figure 8 shows estimates of nonhuman wealth for various groups, illustrating the greater racial disparity in wealth than in income. Even blacks with the same incomes as whites have less wealth, on average; the average wealth of black families with incomes above $30,000 per year (roughly the richest third) is only one-third of the average wealth of white families with the same incomes. The figures for Hispanics are about the same as those for blacks.

---

[5]This statement refers to production workers, excluding supervisors and agricultural workers, and includes overtime.

[6]This statement measures nonhuman wealth as financial assets minus debts, plus the value of real estate and motor vehicles.

Figure 8 | Median Nonhuman Wealth

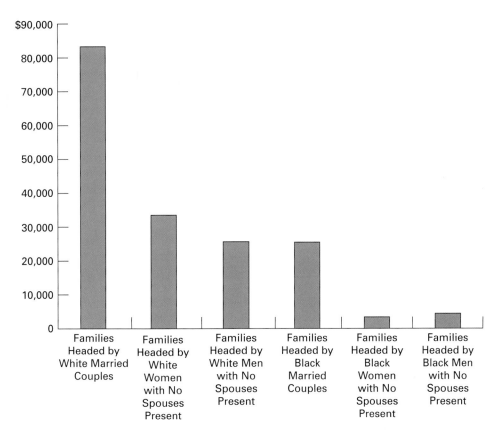

How did the very wealthy get that way? Of the 400 people on the *Forbes* magazine list of the richest people in America (with an average wealth of about $500 million each), about one-fourth got rich through inheritance. The other three-fourths, such as Bill Gates of Microsoft, got rich through working, starting their own businesses, inventing new products, and so on.

Review Questions

1. List the main facts about the distribution of income in the United States.

2. Why has median U.S. household income increased less than total U.S. output of goods and services per person in the last quarter century?

3. Compare average world output per person with the U.S. government-defined poverty level.

Thinking Exercises

4. What is the connection between an economy's production of goods and services and its income?

5. What hypotheses can you construct to explain the fact that children from poor families are more likely than others to become poor adults, and children from rich families are more likely to become rich adults?

IN THE NEWS

The rich really aren't different

America has lots of millionaires. They aren't who you think they are

By James K. Glassman

Mention the word millionaire, and Americans tend to think of *Fortune 500* honchos (Lawrence Coss, the CEO of Green Tree Financial Corp., just received a bonus of $102 million). Or perhaps they think of sports stars (Michael Jordan earned $53 million in 1996, according to *Forbes*) or Hollywood actors (Jim Carrey received $20 million for a single movie in 1996).

But the typical millionaire in America isn't a corporate executive, a sports hero, a film star, or even a coupon-bond-clipping retiree. Instead, two thirds of millionaires are self-employed, mostly as entrepreneurs in small, boring busi-

nesses. They are welding contractors, pest controllers, rice farmers, owners of mobile-home parks. They live well below their means and save a large chunk of what they make. Their actual incomes are surprisingly low—a median of $131,000 a year.

These are a few of the remarkably mundane facts that emerge from an extensive survey by two marketing experts, Thomas Stanley and William Danko, who published their findings in a book called *The Millionaire Next Door* (Longstreet Press, 1996). Other studies, including one last year by the Rand Corp., confirm many of the findings.

"Very few rich people," writes John Weicher of the Hudson Institute, "have received much in the way of inheritance." The Stanley-Danko survey found that fewer than one fifth of millionaires inherited 10 percent or more of their wealth, and most did not get a single dollar. Even billionaires, these days, are self-made. "Great fortunes are being created almost monthly in the United States today by young entrepreneurs who hadn't a dime when we created this list 14 years ago," write the authors of the *Forbes 400*. The six richest Americans all built businesses from scratch.

Source: U.S. News & World Report

WORLD DISTRIBUTION OF INCOME

Income comparisons across countries encounter a problem because prices of similar goods and services differ across countries. Adjusting for these price differences, the distribution of income across countries is much less equal than the distribution within the United States. As Figure 9 shows, the poorest 60 percent of countries receive less than 20 percent of world income. The richest 20 percent of countries receive 58 percent, and the richest 5 percent of countries receive 18 percent of world income.

Table 1 compares countries according to their distributions of income across people. The table shows the fractions of national income received by the highest and lowest fifths of the populations in ten countries. Some countries, like Japan, have more equal distributions of income than the United States. Others, like Mexico, have less equal distributions.

Many people in the world live in conditions of poverty that probably defy the imaginations of readers of this textbook. The United Nations defines *absolute poverty* as the income level below which a person cannot afford a nutritionally adequate diet and nonfood requirements. The United Nations estimates this income to be $525 per year in

Figure 9 | Distribution of Income across Countries

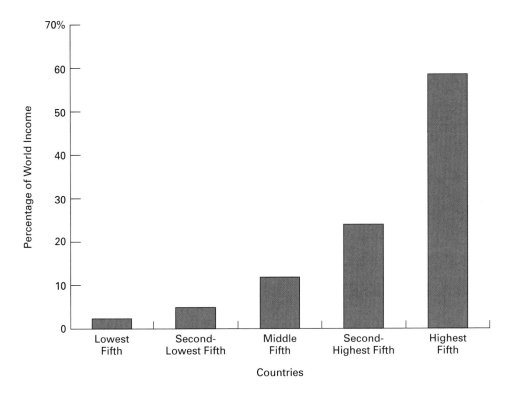

IN THE NEWS

The poverty of economic policy that is driving black Africa deeper into poverty

It will take 40 years for the region to reach the level of wealth of 20 years ago, says the World Bank

By Michael Holman, Africa Editor

Unless sub-Saharan Africa's "poor" economic policies improve, it will be 40 years before the region returns to its per-capita income of the mid-1970s, warns a World Bank report on the region published tomorrow.

Even Ghana, rated the best of Africa's reforming countries which has achieved real growth of about 5 percent a year, is still among the world's poorest countries: "At this growth rate, the average Ghanaian will not cross the poverty line for another 50 years," says the report.

Source: Financial Times

1995 U.S. dollars (adjusted for price differences across countries). Using this definition, about 1 billion people—nearly one-fifth of the world's population—live in absolute poverty. Two-thirds of these people live on less than $400 per year. About half of them live in southern Asia and many others in sub-Saharan Africa. While these numbers overstate world poverty because measured incomes do not include home-produced food and some other sources of income, the extent of world poverty is clearly enormous. For perspective, the U.S. poverty level for a family of four is $16,404, or about $4,100 per person, which is over 7 *times* the absolute poverty income and two-thirds of average

Table 1 | Income Distributions in Ten Countries

COUNTRY	Percentage of National Income Received by	
	LOWEST FIFTH OF POPULATION	HIGHEST FIFTH OF POPULATION
Mexico	2.9%	57.7%
Singapore	5.1	48.9
Hong Kong	5.4	47.0
United States	4.7	41.9
India	8.1	41.4
United Kingdom	5.8	39.5
Bangladesh	10.0	37.2
Germany	6.8	38.7
Japan	8.7	37.5
Sweden	8.0	36.9

Source: World Development Report, World Bank (various issues).

The economic policies of governments in sub-Saharan Africa have contributed to a fall in per-capita output in the last two decades.

Although extreme poverty remains a horrifying problem for one-fifth of the world's population, long-run trends show improvements in nutrition.

IN THE NEWS

African thugs keep their continent poor

By George B.N. Ayittey

The key to Africa's prosperity is investment. But even domestic investors have not found Africa an attractive place to put their money. Africa is the least economically free continent, according to the Index of Economic Freedom, published jointly by the Heritage Foundation and The Wall Street Journal. Onerous state controls, unstable currencies, runaway government expenditures, confiscatory taxes, political instability and crumbling infrastructure have conspired to create an environment inimical to development.

Source: The Wall Street Journal

Government policies keep many African countries in poverty.

world output per person. If total world income were distributed equally (assuming that this redistribution would not affect the total), each person in the world would receive an income about 10 times the absolute poverty level.[7]

Poverty in America is bad enough, but no words written here can impart to most readers the full impact of poverty among one-fifth of the world's population. One should remember that *people* live behind these statistics. Even when these people can get enough calories for physical survival under normal conditions, most of them lack even the most basic medications for sickness. In poor countries, infant mortality rates, mortality rates of children under age 5, and death rates of mothers during childbirth are orders of magnitude higher than in richer countries.

Trends in World Poverty

In the long run, there are reasons for optimism on alleviation of world poverty. When countries become richer, poverty tends to decline. In addition, income tends to be more equally distributed within richer countries. As a result, economic growth may significantly reduce problems of world poverty.

Overall, world poverty declined through most of the 19th and 20th centuries, and the poorest fifth of the world's population is less poor now than it was a century ago or even two decades ago. World food production per person has risen despite worldwide government policies that reduce food production. Governments in most developed countries pay farmers not to grow certain crops, and government policies in many developing countries discourage food production by placing maximum legal prices on agricultural output. The price limits reduce the quantities supplied, create shortages, and create dependence on higher-priced food imported from developed countries. Consumption of food, however, has risen more slowly in poorer countries than in advanced countries.

Occasional setbacks have disrupted the general trend toward less world poverty. Income per person in sub-Saharan Africa has remained stagnant or even fallen in the last quarter-century. Progress has not stopped in many other parts of the world, though. Income per person in southern Asia (which has the largest concentration of the world's

---

[7]Any attempt to redistribute income on this scale would cause a massive fall in the total.

absolute poverty) rose more than 7 percent in the last quarter of the century, after stagnating in the previous quarter century. Most studies predict that economic growth and development will continue to reduce world poverty in the coming years.

What Affects Inequality and Poverty?

Seventy percent of personal income in the United States comes from working (selling labor services). The other thirty percent comes from returns on investments (stocks, bonds, real estate, and so on). People's incomes differ because they differ in:

▶ Education

▶ Experience

▶ Ability (intelligence, creativity, talents, and so on)

▶ Effort (Some people work harder than others.)

▶ Luck (fortunate investments; being born at a certain time, in a certain country, into a certain type of family environment, or with certain abilities)

▶ Inheritance

▶ Discrimination encountered (in education, employment, and other opportunities)

▶ Willingness to take risks (which raises average earnings)

▶ Past savings (People earn income on money they have saved in the past.)

What affects inequality in a society? What affects poverty? A poor society could have little inequality, but much poverty. A rich enough society could virtually eliminate poverty while maintaining considerable inequality. On average, however, relatively rich countries have more equal distributions of income, and less poverty.

Cultural attitudes and government policies that inhibit economic mobility can affect inequality. They may raise inequality by preserving traditional differences among people or limiting opportunities for the poor to advance. At the same time, they may prevent new inequalities from emerging as some people become wealthy through business successes or by exploiting their unique talents in entertainment or sports.

The United States has seen increasing inequality in recent decades mainly because technical change has increased the wages of skilled, educated workers, but has also limited wage gains for low-skilled, less-educated workers. In addition, expanded international trade with increased competition from producers in lower-wage countries may have increased inequality in the United States by reducing the demand for low-skilled American workers.

What Is Just?

Opinions differ about criteria for a fair, equitable, or just distribution of income or wealth. Questions of fairness or justice arise whenever people make judgments about these distributions or the desirability of government economic policies that affect them.

Egalitarianism

Egalitarianism is the view that fairness requires equal results.

EVALUATING POVERTY AND WEALTH

A simple version of egalitarianism holds that fairness requires the same income for every person. Another version holds that fairness requires more income for some people than for others to compensate them for certain differences. Perhaps a handicapped person or a person with unusual medical needs should receive more income than other people. Perhaps a person who is physically unattractive should get more income than a good-looking person. Perhaps a person who works in an unpleasant job should get more income than a person with a personally satisfying job (such as an artist). Karl Marx advocated another version of egalitarianism in the principle, "From each according to his abilities, to each according to his needs." Egalitarianism in some form has obvious appeal to many people. It is, after all, one reason for giving every person one vote in an election.

Problems arise, however, in the choice of the best version of egalitarianism and in designing policies that would create an egalitarian society. The main problem is that egalitarian policies reduce incentives to work. If egalitarianism is desirable for its own sake, people may choose to sacrifice some economic efficiency to achieve a more equal distribution. These issues raise many questions: What is the best tradeoff between equality and efficiency? Which is better, a society in which half of the people have $1,000 and half have $2,000, or an egalitarian society in which everyone has $1,001? What if everyone could have $1,250 or $1,500 instead? Is it just to punish a poor person who robs from a rich person, or does the robbery contribute to justice? Should socially valuable behavior, such as curing a disease or producing a good that people want, be rewarded with extra income? Should esteem (bestowed by other people) be distributed equally like income? Can it be? Should people with high esteem receive low incomes, and people with low esteem receive additional income as compensation? Can people give material or physical tokens of esteem (or gifts) in an egalitarian world, or do these tokens count as income?

Another set of issues arises when people become unequal through their actions. Suppose that two people have the same wealth at age 20, but one saves more than the other. In later years, the saver will have investment income that the other person will lack. Is this just? Is it consistent with egalitarianism?

One need not be an egalitarian to favor a relatively equal distribution of wealth. One may oppose egalitarianism and yet believe that government policies should try to reduce poverty. These views can be deduced from other views of justice considered in the following sections.

Utilitarianism

Utilitarianism is the view that justice results from maximizing the total amount of human happiness.[8]

Only total happiness matters to a utilitarian, not its distribution (that is, not who is happy and who is not). In this sense, utilitarianism differs strongly from egalitarianism, which argues for an equal distribution. Despite this concentration on total happiness rather than its distribution, utilitarianism can support an argument for redistributing income from the rich to the poor. Some utilitarians argue that taking a dollar from a rich person and giving it to a poor person produces a loss in happiness to the rich person smaller than the gain in happiness to the poor person. The poor person, according to this argument, values money more than the rich person does, because he has less of it. The marginal utility (benefit) of the money is larger for the poor person than for the rich person, so redistributing income from the rich to the poor raises total utility (happiness).[9]

---

[8]Some versions of utilitarianism may also include the welfare of animals in evaluating justice. Utilitarianism was developed largely by the English philosophers Jeremy Bentham and John Stuart Mill.

[9]See Abba Lerner, *The Economics of Control: Principles of Welfare Economics* (1944; reprint, New York: Augustus M. Kelley, 1970).

Critics of this argument say that it requires an impossible *interpersonal comparison of utility*. They assert that no one can compare one person's happiness with another person's. Perhaps redistributing income from the rich to the poor would actually reduce total happiness. A utilitarian might reply that while one can never be sure of these comparisons, it seems reasonable that poor people gain more happiness from an extra $10 than rich people lose when they give up $10. Indeed, a utilitarian might say, people make interpersonal comparisons of utility regularly when they decide to give money to charities.

Critics of utilitarianism have advanced numerous arguments against it. Many people object to utilitarianism because it ignores the *distribution* of happiness. A utilitarian would prefer a situation in which Jeremy has 10 units of happiness and John has 1 unit to a situation in which Jeremy and John each have 5 units of happiness; an egalitarian would prefer the latter situation.

A second criticism claims that utilitarianism ignores people's fundamental rights. If someone needs an emergency kidney transplant to stay alive and no one offers to donate a kidney, a utilitarian might say that the government should force someone to donate, because the gain in happiness to the recipient would exceed the loss in happiness to the donor, who can live with one remaining kidney. Some critics of utilitarianism say that, while the situation is unfortunate, forcing someone to donate a body part would violate that person's rights. Many philosophers believe that utilitarianism has "morally monstrous" implications.[10]

Justice as an Implicit Contract

Before you play a game with a friend, you agree on rules. Football teams agree on the rules that will govern their play before they know the outcome of the coin toss that determines which team will receive the first kickoff.

Suppose that people could meet with each other and agree on the *rules of life* before the toss of a coin (that is, luck) turns them into unique individuals living in diverse circumstances around the world. Imagine people meeting together before they are born, before they find out if they will be smart or dumb, beautiful or ugly, lucky or unlucky, whether they will have rich or poor parents, tastes for material goods or for spiritual fulfillment, and so on.[11] This imagined conference is called meeting in the *original position* or *behind the veil of ignorance*.[12]

According to the view of justice as an implicit contract, the government should act like a referee, enforcing rules that people would have chosen behind the veil of ignorance.

At this meeting, people would choose the legal rules and government policies that would affect their lives. They would decide whether the government should redistribute income from rich people to poor people and how much it should transfer. They would decide what rights and obligations everyone would have. Because people would not yet know their own individual circumstances when they made these decisions, they could not make rules to give themselves special benefits. Instead, they would presumably choose rules that would benefit the whole society in some sense; in that sense, the rules that they chose would define fairness and would give meaning to the concept of justice.

According to one view of justice, judgments of fairness or justice can apply only to rules, not to outcomes like who wins a game or how equally income is distributed. Further, rules are fair or just if everyone would agree to them at this magical meeting behind the veil of ignorance. Because this meeting is impossible to arrange, however, no one knows for sure what rules would command agreement. In his book *A Theory of Justice*,

[10]As one critic has explained, "It might well be the case that more good and less evil would result from your painlessly and undetectedly murdering your malicious, old, and unhappy grandfather than from your forebearing to do so: he would be freed from his wretched existence; his children would be rejoiced by their inheritances and would no longer suffer from his mischief. . . . Nobody seriously doubts that a position with such a consequence is monstrous."—Alan Donagan, "Is There a Credible Form of Utilitarianism?" in Michael D. Bayles, ed., *Contemporary Utilitarianism* (Magnolia, Mass.: Peter Smith, 1968), pp. 187–188.

[11]All generations—and everyone in each generation—would have to attend this meeting.

[12]This idea was developed by economist John C. Harsanyi and later expanded by philosopher John Rawls. See John C. Harsanyi, "Cardinal Utility in Welfare Economics and the Theory of Risk-Taking," *Journal of Political Economy* 61 (1953); and John Rawls, *A Theory of Justice* (Cambridge, Mass.: Harvard University Press, 1971).

John Rawls has guessed that people would favor considerable redistribution from the lucky to the unlucky—from the rich to the poor—to make certain that no one would fall below a certain level of income. Justice would then amount to enforcement of this agreement. Other proponents of justice as an implicit contract have made other guesses about what rules people would choose.

Natural Rights

Some philosophers have formulated arguments implied by the statement in the U.S. Declaration of Independence that people "are endowed by their Creator with certain inalienable rights . . . ." Justice, in the natural-rights view, consists of enforcing these rights. Some people believe that these rights come from God; others agree with English philosopher John Locke that certain rights can be deduced from human nature. Perhaps in the original position behind the veil of ignorance, people would choose a society that would guarantee a set of fundamental rights, and perhaps this choice is the source of human rights.[13] The main shortcoming of the natural-rights argument comes from the potential for disagreement about precisely what those rights *are*. Some people may claim that everyone has a right to a minimum amount of food, health care, and so on. Others may claim that one has rights to one's own body and property, and that any government-enforced redistribution, however needy the recipient, violates those rights. Some alleged rights obligate other people to perform specific tasks. For example, a right to health care would require someone to provide that care, yet the person forced to do so might complain that such compulsion violates her rights.

Review Questions

6. How does the United Nations define absolute poverty? Compare the absolute poverty level, the official U.S. government poverty level, and average per-person income in the world.

7. List at least six reasons for differences in people's incomes.

Thinking Exercises

8. What evidence would you gather to decide why one person earns a higher income than another?

9. If you were appointed to chair a United Nations commission on reducing world poverty, what evidence would you try to gather to determine successful and unsuccessful approaches to this problem?

GOVERNMENT PROGRAMS AND POVERTY

Governments of many developed countries pursue antipoverty programs. Some countries, such as Sweden, have established welfare systems much more comprehensive than that in the United States. Judgments of the effects of such welfare programs generate heated controversies. Many people believe that welfare programs reduce poverty and human misery for recipients who temporarily accept such benefits when bad luck strikes their

---

[13]This position is sometimes called *rule-utilitarianism*, because it involves a choice of rules (laws and government policies) made in the original position, behind the veil of ignorance, that people in that original position think will maximize their happiness.

lives, although some people may depend on support over long periods of time and a few may abuse the system. Critics of the welfare system argue that it discourages people from seeking productive work and fosters a culture of welfare dependency, sometimes creating socially disruptive incentives to break up families or avoid employment. Some critics argue that U.S. welfare programs have failed to reduce poverty and have actually caused some poverty.[14] Other scholars dispute this claim, but economists generally agree that government welfare programs have had some perverse effects on incentives that have contributed to the problems of the poor.[15] Economists disagree mainly on the sizes of these effects and on their importance compared to the benefits of welfare programs.

Severe poverty in less-developed countries often results from government policies and wars.[16] Maximum legal prices for food reduce food production by eliminating the potential to profit from it. High taxes, regulations, and threats of confiscation weaken incentives to produce food and other products. They also reduce incentives for foreign investment that would provide capital equipment to raise the productivity of local labor and improve living standards. Like a tax, business firms in many countries labor under the need to bribe local officials in conducting normal business operations; this graft sometimes prevents businesses from operating in certain countries or investing there. Civil wars, attempts by dictators to expand or maintain their power, and corruption in the military and civil branches of government all help to create poverty. Famines and other natural disasters do not cause long-term world poverty. People would not stay in an area of persistent poverty if they could leave. Without government policies that keep people from leaving some countries and entering others, most people would not continue to live in places where they could not hope to grow food or earn incomes in some other way.

Technology is now sufficiently advanced, and the world's capital stock is large enough, that everyone in the world (even people without skills) could produce enough goods and earn enough income to stay well above the absolute poverty level. To achieve this goal, however, people need access to that technology and capital equipment or natural resources. Owners of capital equipment would profit by providing that equipment to poor people if government policies did not prevent it. The additional equipment would raise productivity of poor workers, allowing both higher wages for workers *and* profits to investors. In this sense, government policies are largely responsible for absolute poverty in the modern world. Policies prevent people from making use of current world technology and capital and receiving the higher incomes they could then earn.[17]

DISCRIMINATION

Income inequality has also resulted from discrimination against minorities and women. Discrimination may reduce a person's job opportunities or introduce obstacles to buying a house in a certain neighborhood or joining some organization. Discrimination raises the costs of certain actions to its victims, because they suffer negative reactions from other people. Discrimination can also have indirect effects. For example, a business may refuse to hire minorities, not because its owner is prejudiced but because the business fears losing sales to prejudiced customers.[18] Discrimination in employment can result from the prejudices of employers, other workers, or customers.

[14]Charles Murray, *Losing Ground* (New York: Basic Books, 1984).

[15]Frank Levy, *Dollars and Dreams: The Changing American Income Distribution* (Ithaca, N.Y.: Russell Sage Foundation, 1987).

[16]The developing countries of the world spend about five times as much on armed forces as they receive in foreign aid.

[17]For an interesting case study (of Biafra), see Dan Jacobs, *The Brutality of Nations* (New York: Alfred A. Knopf, 1990). Ethiopia in the 1970s and 1980s is another clear example. A good summary of other cases is contained in Karl Zinsmeister, "All the Hungry People," *Reason,* June 1988, pp. 22–30.

[18]Of course, a prejudiced employer could falsely claim that the business would lose customers.

Discrimination in Labor Markets

Two decades ago, the average black man's weekly earnings were only 66 percent of the average white man's. At the same time, the average woman's weekly earnings were only 62 percent of the average man's, and the average black woman earned only 88 percent as much as the average white woman. The average hourly wage for women was 65 percent of that for men, though the fraction varied by age. Women ages 20 to 24 earned hourly wages that were 86 percent of men's; women over 35 had hourly wages that were only 56 percent of men's. These numbers have changed only slightly in recent years. Economists generally agree that the wage differences between these groups result partly from factors other than discrimination; they disagree on the extent to which discrimination explains the remaining differences.

Wage Differences between Women and Men

The hourly wage of women averaged about 60 percent of that of men over most of the twentieth century (and, scarce data suggest, long before that).[19] Recently, however, women's average hourly wages have risen to about 80 percent of men's. Relatively young women have made the largest wage gains.

Women and members of minority groups earn less than white men for at least three reasons: They face discrimination in labor markets, they have less human capital on average (possibly due to discrimination earlier in life and low-quality educational opportunities), and they take lower-paying jobs on average (partly due to discrimination and below-average human capital).

Wages of women have actually risen more quickly than the 80 percent figure indicates, due to changes in education and experience.[20] Today, the average woman in the labor force has less education and experience, compared to the average man, than in the past. While women have gained education and experience, relatively large numbers of less-educated and low-skilled women have entered the labor force in recent years. As a result, one study concludes that "Women's wages are rising more rapidly than commonly believed, but they are also lower relative to men's than is commonly believed."[21] At least half of the male/female wage difference is due to measurable differences in education and experience.

Some part of the male/female wage difference may reflect the typical division of child-rearing responsibilities in U.S. society.[22] A person's sex or race may help to *predict* other (relevant) characteristics of the person. As a result, it may affect firms' hiring decisions even when sex and race are otherwise irrelevant to job performance.

> **Statistical discrimination** involves making predictions about a person based on membership in a certain group.

Insurance companies practice statistical discrimination when they charge higher prices for life insurance to older people than to younger people; on average, younger people are less likely to die soon. Statistical discrimination also occurs when insurers charge lower prices for women than for men, because women tend to live longer than men.

---

[19] This 60 percent figure may date to biblical times. Leviticus 27:1–4 indicates that women may have earned only 60 percent of the wages of men.

[20] The average woman's weekly earnings are only about 75 percent of the average man's, reflecting the fact that women work in the market (for pay) fewer hours per week.

[21] Claudia Goldin, "Development of the American Economy," *NBER Reporter*, Winter 1989/1990. Economists can measure some differences in education, such as the number of years of school, but other differences, such as quality of education, may defy measurement.

[22] This fact itself may reflect discrimination in a larger sense, as traditional social roles may persist partly because of discrimination in the form of social pressures, differences in education and socialization of boys and girls, and so on. Of course, it could also result from differences in the typical priorities and choices of males and females.

IN THE NEWS

Studies link subtle sex bias in schools with women's behavior in the workplace

By Sharon E. Epperson
Staff Reporter of The Wall Street Journal

What's holding women back as they climb the success ladder?

Classrooms may be partly to blame.

Overt discrimination it isn't, for schools are increasingly offering equal opportunities to girls and boys in both formal courses and extracurricular activities, including sports. But several studies suggest that, from first grade through college, female students are the victims of subtle biases. As a result, they are often given less nurturing attention than males.

Researchers maintain that a chilly climate for women in the classroom undermines self-esteem and damages morale. They believe, too, that some of these patterns of student-teacher interaction may help set the stage for expectations and interactions later in the workplace.

Source: The Wall Street Journal

Past discrimination can affect a woman's wage (even without current discrimination) by affecting her human capital.

Traditional differences in gender roles imply that women, on average, have less time available than men to work at formal jobs, or work overtime. These differences imply that women accumulate less experience than men, on average, if they leave their jobs for a few years to raise children. Finally, because women are more likely than men to leave jobs to raise children, employers are less willing to hire women and invest in training them. These forces reduce the average wage of women relative to that of men. This may explain why childless women earn higher wages than similarly-educated women with children.[23]

Job segregation also results from discrimination. Employers may place minorities or women in lower-level jobs or jobs in different locations than white, male workers. Some studies indicate that about half of the education-adjusted wage difference between men and women results from placement of women in lower-level jobs than men with equivalent qualifications.

Wage Differences between Blacks and Whites

The median weekly wage of black men is less than three-fourths that of white men. Wages of black women are about 87 percent of those of white women. These ratios have not changed in the last two decades. Over longer periods, however, blacks have made large gains relative to whites. For example, in the middle of the 20th century, black men earned only half of what white men earned.

About half of the difference in the black/white wage differential is due to measurable differences in average education. Adjusted for measured differences in education, black men earn 85 percent of the average wage of white men. The remaining 15 percent wage differential may reflect discrimination or other factors such as unmeasured differences in education. Studies evaluate the effect of education differences on the wage gap

---

[23]Because most of these women would not expect to remain childless, they would make the same education choices as other women. They would also be subject, on average, to the same discrimination in education as other women. Earlier in this century, when unmarried women were less likely to bear children than they are today, many firms maintained so-called *marriage bars;* they refused to hire married women, and they fired single women who married.

by measuring the number of years of schooling, but they omit the quality of education, which might be expected to be lower among blacks partly because, on average, they grow up in lower-income areas that spend less on schooling than whites.

Discrimination may also play a more subtle role in wage differences. The lower average education of blacks relative to whites may reflect past discrimination in educational opportunities. Job discrimination against blacks in the past may produce continuing effects if that discrimination adversely affected the family lives of black children. Children acquire human capital through interactions with their parents. Parents with low levels of human capital are likely to supply their children with below-average levels of human capital. As a result, the effects of past racial discrimination may last for generations.

Equilibrium with Discrimination

A person who discriminates pays a price; as a result, prejudiced people do not always discriminate. Consider a business owner who is prejudiced against blacks and women. This person wants both high profits and a workforce made up only of white males. If only a few business firms were to discriminate against blacks and women, then in equilibrium blacks and women would work at nondiscriminating firms. Discrimination would affect where they work, but not not their wages. However, when many firms discriminate against blacks and women, discrimination reduces the demand for their labor, lowering their equilibrium wages. As a result, white men earn higher wages than equally skilled women and blacks.

Each firm that discriminated by hiring only white males would pay for this discrimination, however, by sacrificing a potential increase in profits that it could earn by hiring lower-wage women and blacks with equally good skills. (Unless its customers were prejudiced, the firm could not raise its price to cover its high labor costs. Even prejudiced customers might not willingly pay higher prices to buy from a firm that employed only white males.) In this situation, the least prejudiced firms might choose not to discriminate in hiring decisions, because they would not be willing to pay the price.[24]

Now suppose that prejudiced customers want to buy from a firm that does not employ blacks. Customers seldom know whether blacks or whites, or men or women, produce the goods they buy. However, for some goods and most services (such as haircuts), buyers have direct contact with workers. Because blacks earn lower average wages than whites, firms raise their marginal costs if they employ only whites, so buyers must pay higher prices to buy from these firms. The higher product prices represent a cost of discrimination to buyers. An interesting application of this logic appears in the market for baseball cards. Cards of nonwhite players sell in used-card markets for about 10 percent less than cards of white players with comparable accomplishments, suggesting customer discrimination.[25]

---

[24]You can easily estimate the cost of discrimination to a business firm. Suppose you own and manage a firm with ten workers who are identical in every way except their race and salary: Nine workers are white and one is black. The equilibrium wage of white workers is $50,000, but, because of widespread discrimination, the equilibrium wage of black workers is only $30,000. If you pay those equilibrium wages to each of your workers, and your own wage is $120,000, then your total wage bill is $600,000 per year (nine white workers at $50,000 each, plus one black worker at $30,000, plus $120,000). In real life, a typical firm's accounting profit equals about one-third of its total wage bill. Assuming your firm is typical, it generates a $200,000 accounting profit, which you earn as its owner. (Chapter 11 explained that this normal accounting profit reflects implicit costs.)

If you were to replace your expensive white workers with equally productive black workers, your labor costs would fall from $50,000 to $30,000 per worker. If you are prejudiced against blacks, you might choose to pay the higher cost to work only with white workers. However, your profit would rise if you could overcome your prejudice and hire blacks. Instead of paying nine white workers $50,000 each (for a total payment of $450,000), you could pay nine black workers $30,000 each (for a total payment of $270,000), and save a total of $180,000. This would almost double your firm's accounting profit. This enormous increase in potential profit reflects an opportunity cost to your firm of continuing its discrimination. As this exercise illustrates, a firm's cost of discriminating can be very large. See a similar calculation by Steve Landsburg in "Pay Scales in Black and White: Does discrimination explain the differences in salaries?" *Slate Magazine*, http://www.slate.com/default.asp, May 29, 1997.

[25]In his 1987 *Bill James Baseball Abstract* (New York: Villard, 1987), pp. 68–71, Bill James also finds evidence of discrimination against blacks.

The price of discrimination explains why laws have often *forced* people to discriminate. In the 19th century, public transportation was not racially segregated in southern U.S. cities (including Montgomery, Alabama, the site of Rev. Martin Luther King's famous boycott). Laws requiring segregation in these cities were passed around 1900.[26] Many streetcar companies had voluntarily segregated smokers and nonsmokers into different parts of their streetcars, but they opposed laws requiring segregation by race, because discrimination had a price and racial segregation would reduce their profits.

Many countries have mandated discrimination. South African mining companies opposed laws requiring them to hire white workers rather than black workers, because they had to pay higher wages to white workers.[27] Businesses in South Africa often tried to evade the laws that limited hiring of blacks, not necessarily because the business owners valued fairness, but because discrimination raised their labor costs.[28] Similarly, immigration laws in many countries arose from attempts to prevent foreigners from competing for jobs by offering to work at low wages; immigration laws force employers to discriminate against foreigners by not allowing them to work in the country. Even a firm that is prejudiced against foreigners has an incentive to hire them if they will work for lower wages than domestic workers will accept. White neighborhoods that want to exclude blacks can often do so only with regulations, because even a prejudiced home-owner is unlikely to refuse a good offer from a black buyer.[29]

Remedies for Discrimination in the United States

Before 1963, many U.S. states enforced laws limiting the job opportunities of women, their hours of work, and work during pregnancy. The federal Equal Pay Act overturned these laws. The following year, Congress passed the Civil Rights Act of 1964, which outlawed many forms of discrimination (such as discrimination in hiring and promotions) based on "race, color, religion, sex, or national origin." The law also established the Equal Employment Opportunities Commission. When firms claim to be "equal-opportunity employers" they are complying with this law.

In 1965, the U.S. government began requiring firms with large government contracts to take "affirmative action" to increase employment of women and minorities or risk losing their government contracts.[30] The government expanded the requirements for affirmative action (actions to redress imbalances in employment, whether due to discrimination or other causes) in the 1970s. Affirmative action plans usually required firms to prove that they were taking actions to hire and retain women and minorities, particularly in cases where they employed fewer such workers than seemed appropriate to the government or to the courts.

Opponents of affirmative action claim that it creates reverse discrimination against white males or other people not in the favored groups. They also claim that affirmative action rules presume guilt until firms prove their innocence, and that chance employment of fewer or more women or minorities does not imply discrimination. Finally, opponents argue that affirmative action weakens incentives, because people in the favored groups lose some incentive to acquire skills if the affirmative-action policy can guarantee a job,

---

[26]See Thomas Sowell, *Preferential Policies* (New York: William Morrow, 1991).

[27]After the Rand Rebellion, the new government subsidized the mining companies by enacting tariffs to protect them from foreign competition. This helped to offset the higher cost of white labor.

[28]Some of the strongest proponents of these laws were white workers with few skills who relied mainly on their white skin to find employment.

[29]Blacks were able to buy land after the Civil War, despite organized attempts of whites to prevent the sales. The price of discrimination was too high to allow racial identity to stop the land sales.

[30]The term comes from an executive order by President Kennedy requiring equal treatment of all job applicants, "without regard to race, creed, color, or national origin." The meaning of the term has changed to state a requirement that employers pay specific attention to those characteristics and try to hire and promote people from underrepresented groups.

while people in the disfavored group lose some incentive to acquire skills if they believe that affirmative action reduces the value of those skills. Affirmative action, according to its critics, is unfair and economically inefficient.[31]

Proponents of affirmative action argue that discrimination is usually (even if not always) the cause of large differences in employment, promotions, and wages of different groups. They also argue that all firms, even those not guilty of discrimination themselves, should be required to try to remedy the past discrimination of others by making efforts to hire women and minorities. They argue that affirmative action promotes diversity, mixing people from different groups, and that this diversity and mixing has (in the language of Chapter 20) a positive externality; it creates benefits for society as a whole by raising tolerance of differences, creating the habit of associating with members of other groups, and reducing social and economic barriers. Affirmative action and other proposed remedies for discrimination remain nearly as controversial in public discussions as discrimination itself.

Review Questions

8. How large are black/white and male/female wage differentials? What reasons other than current employer discrimination may create these wage differentials?

9. Describe a typical study of discrimination and discuss its limitations.

10. What is statistical discrimination? Why might it reduce the wages of women relative to wages of men?

Thinking Exercises

11. How would a decrease in discrimination affect the equilibrium price of discrimination?

12. Suppose that many firms discriminate against hiring blacks. What happens if one firm in a perfectly competitive industry decides not to discriminate?

Conclusion

Distribution of Income and Wealth in the United States

The term *distribution of income* refers to comparisons of incomes across people or families. The U.S. median income has doubled since the middle of the 20th century, though its growth slowed in the last quarter-century. Households in the top fifth of the income distribution receive almost one-half of all of the nation's income, and households in the bottom fifth get about 4 percent. Family income inequality has stayed about the same in the last half-century, partly because of government programs.

Poverty in the United States occurs mainly among blacks, Hispanics, women, and children. However, few people stay in poverty for long periods. While 10 percent

to 15 percent of the population live in households with incomes below the poverty line, about 2 percent remain below the poverty line for many years. About half of all people with incomes in the bottom fifth of the income distribution move to higher fifths within 7 years.

Average wages have fallen in the last two decades, mainly due to advances in technology that have raised demand for highly-skilled workers but reduced demand for low-skill workers.

Wealth is distributed much less equally than income. In the United States, the richest 2 percent of the population own about one-fourth of all household assets, and the richest 25 percent own about three-fourths. Black families have, on average, about one-tenth the household

---

[31]In Malaysia, the government has required universities to adjust grades to achieve "ethnic balance." See Gordon P. Means, "Ethnic Preference Policies in Malaysia," in Neil Nevitte and Charles H. Kennedy, eds., *Ethnic Preference and Public Policy in Developing States* (Boulder, Colo.: Lynne Reinner, 1986), p. 108.

assets of white families. Despite these inequalities, the distribution of wealth has gradually become more equal throughout the 20th century.

World Distribution of Income

The world distribution of income is more unequal than that in the United States. About one-fifth of the world's people—1 billion people—live in absolute poverty, with incomes of less than $525 per person per year. The official U.S. poverty level is about 7 times higher than this absolute poverty income. If all the income in the world were distributed equally with no effect on the total, each person would have an income about twice the U.S. poverty level and about 10 times the absolute poverty level. World poverty declined through most of the 19th and 20th centuries, and it has declined further in the last several decades. Wars and government policies are major reasons for persistent poverty in the modern world.

Evaluating Poverty and Wealth

Luck, effort, and other factors are among the many reasons why some people are poor while others are rich. Opinions differ on what is fair, just, or equitable. However, questions of fairness and justice arise whenever people make judgments about government economic policies. Egalitarianism is the view that every person deserves an equal share of wealth (or some measure of happiness). Utilitarianism is the view that government policies should maximize total happiness, regardless of its distribution. Another view holds that justice applies only to rules, and rules are just if people would choose them in a fictional original position, behind a veil of ignorance. Still another view holds that people have natural rights that government policies should not violate. Good arguments can be made for and against each of these views.

Government Programs and Poverty

Governments have developed many programs designed to reduce poverty; policy analysts disagree about their effects and desirable changes in policies. Some disagreements result from differences in opinions about justice and fairness; other disagreements continue in the absence of conclusive evidence about the effects of various government policies. Economists agree that some government policies have disastrous effects and contribute to the plight of the 1 billion people who live in absolute poverty.

Discrimination

One reason for income inequality has been discrimination against minorities and women. Discrimination in the labor market affects wages, creating an equilibrium price of discrimination. This price takes the form of a loss of potential profits by any firm that discriminates. About half of male/female and black/white wage differences can be explained by measured differences in education and experience (although differences in education and experience may themselves reflect past discrimination). The remainder of the wage differences may result from current discrimination in labor markets, from other unmeasured factors such as quality of education, or from statistical discrimination.

Key Terms

income	median income	egalitarianism	statistical discrimination
wealth	mean income	utilitarianism	

Problems

13. How has average household income changed in the last quarter-century?
    (a) About how large is the difference in average nonhuman wealth (measured by household assets) between white families and black or Hispanic families?
    (b) Roughly how many people in the world live below the United Nations' absolute poverty line?
    (c) On average, does more or less poverty occur in richer countries than in poorer ones? More or less income inequality?

14. Define *egalitarianism,* then argue (a) for it, and (b) against it.

15. Define *utilitarianism,* then argue (a) for it, and (b) against it.

16. Explain the view that justice is an implicit contract, then argue (a) for it, and (b) against it.

17. Would a fall in employment discrimination against women raise the wages that women earn or reduce the wages that men earn, or both? Explain, using supply and demand analysis.

18. Who gains from laws that require firms to discriminate in their hiring? Explain why.

Inquiries for Further Thought

19. A song from the 1960s said, "What the world needs now is love, sweet love. It's the only thing that there's just too little of." A commentator recently said, "That song is wrong. Many people lack food to eat, basic health care, and any opportunity or hope for the future." Discuss these two claims.

20. Are some people richer than others mainly because of luck or because they work harder than others? How would you find data to support your claim?

21. Comment on this statement: "Income differences are all due to luck; even differences in effort are due to luck, because some people are lucky enough to have the motivation to educate themselves and work hard at their jobs."

22. Does the market system produce an equitable or inequitable, moral or immoral distribution of income? What could be done about it? What should be done? What would be the costs?

23. Should ugly people get to pay lower taxes that others as compensation for their appearance? Should handicapped people get similar benefits? People with less physical ability than others? People with less mental ability?

24. Would people rather live (a) in a society that offers many opportunities, but also much risk (so that one could end up rich, but at the risk of ending up poor) or (b) in a society with the same average income, but no chance of wealth or poverty?

25. Write a critical essay arguing for and against alternative concepts of justice. What criteria, in your opinion, determine justice?

26. Comment on the implications for justice of the following statements. In each case, what would be the effects of a government policy to implement this view of justice?
    (a) The government should ensure an equal distribution of income.
    (b) People who work harder than others should earn higher incomes.
    (c) People who face unusual medical expenses should earn higher incomes than others without such costs.
    (d) People who have large families to support should earn high incomes.
    (e) Everyone should be made as happy as everyone else.
    (f) From each according to her abilities, to each according to her needs.

    (g) Especially virtuous people should get unusually high incomes.

27. What government policies and laws would you choose behind the veil of ignorance?

28. (a) Does a rich person have a moral obligation to give money to poor people? How much money? (b) Does a rich country have a moral obligation to give money to poor countries? How much money?

29. Discuss these statements and questions:
    (a) It is unjust not to help a poor person, even if you did not cause his poverty.
    (b) It is unjust not to help a person who is injured, even if you did not cause the injury.
    (c) If justice requires people to help in either (a) or (b), how much help does it require? Should the law mandate helping in either case? (Many Good Samaritan laws do mandate assistance; this was not simply invented for the final episode of the television show, Seinfeld!)
    (d) Is it important to distinguish between harming a person and failing to help her?

30. A utilitarian argues that people get less happiness from watching sports events than poor people could get if the money were used instead to buy food, housing, and medical care for them. The utilitarian convinces the government to outlaw sports events. Discuss whether this action is just or unjust, and why.

31. Should the government redistribute income to increase equality? To what extent should it redistribute income? How much should it take from whom, and how much should it give to whom?

32. Is it just for the U.S. government to redistribute wealth from rich Americans to poor Americans if most of the poor Americans are already richer than 1 billion other people in the world? Should redistribution include only people who live in the United States or everyone in the world? Why?

33. Is it fair to take wealth away from people who gained it by working harder than others? Would (or does) this affect how hard people work?

34. Should sports and entertainment figures be permitted to make as much money as they do? What would happen if the government were to limit their incomes?

35. Should people with high incomes pay higher percentages of their incomes in taxes than people with low incomes pay?

36. Should the government replace an income tax with a tax on wealth? What would be the effects?

37. Should the government tax inheritances? How much? What would be the effects of a 100 percent tax on inheritances? Would a smaller tax be better for any reason? What criteria should determine the size of this tax?

38. Should wealthy countries forgive the foreign debts of poor countries? If private lenders have loaned the money, should governments compensate those lenders? What would be the effects on poverty? Why don't the poor countries just refuse to pay?

39. Suppose a firm hires mostly black workers because they command lower wages than equally productive white workers. Can the firm morally continue to pay low wages to black workers simply because poor alternatives make them *willing* to *accept* lower wages? If government were to prohibit paying lower wages to blacks than to equally productive whites, would a firm respond by raising its wages for blacks or replacing black workers with white workers? Why?

40. Women live about seven years longer than men, on average. Suppose that a firm has a pension program for its workers. It pays the same amount of money into the pension program for every worker, male or female. If a man and a woman both work at the firm for the same number of years, the firm has saved the same amount of money in the pension program for each of them.

(a) Suppose that the firm gives each worker all of the pension money that it saves for the worker over the years on the day the worker retires. Since women live longer on average, the same amount of money at retirement means that women have less money to spend per year (on average) after retirement. Is this fair? Is this discrimination?

(b) Suppose that the firm does not give the worker all of the pension money on the day of retirement. Instead, the firm pays the worker a certain amount of money each month. Since women live longer than men on average, the firm pays women retirees less per month than men. Is this fair? Is it discrimination?[32]

(c) Suppose the firm gives workers monthly payments, but it gives male and female retirees the same monthly pensions. To do this, the firm must save more money in the pension fund for each female employee than for each male employee, so it finds that it can save money by hiring male employees for equal wages. As a result, it wants either to hire men instead of women or to pay women less than men. Would this policy be fair? Would it be discrimination?

IN THE NEWS

Proposals for equal insurance fees for men and women spark battle

Insurance companies, almost unanimously, say that the two sexes should pay different rates because their claims patterns are different. "It's a basic issue of fairness," says Sean Mooney, a senior vice president and economist with the Insurance Information Institute, a trade group. "The price should reflect the risks involved. If I'm a maker of fireworks I should pay more for insurance than a garment maker does."

Charges of Discrimination

Logical as all that seems to insurers, the current system is blatant sex discrimination in the eyes of many people. Says a spokeswoman for the National Organization for Women: "There's no compelling reason to divide the human race in that fashion."

Unisex insurance pricing is controversial wherever the issue is raised. Indeed, beset by complaints—many from parents whose daughters' auto-insurance rates had soared—Montana lawmakers voted this year to repeal the law. But Democratic Gov. Ted Schwinden vetoed their action, and an override attempt failed by a few votes.

Source: The Wall Street Journal

---

[32] The U.S. Supreme Court ruled that this practice is illegal discrimination under U.S. law.

41. Should the law prohibit discrimination on the basis of race or sex? What would be the effects of changing the law?

42. Discuss this statement: "[E]conomic studies have consistently shown that rising female wages encourage work and inhibit fertility, and that, more directly, marriages where women earn more are likely to dissolve. . . . As a result, one price of the very labor market success women have enjoyed may well be a less stable American family."[33]

43. A disproportionately large number of National Merit Scholarship finalists and people listed in *Who's Who* are firstborn children.
    (a) Does this fact suggest discrimination against non-firstborn children? Discuss alternative explanations. (Note: This result is not likely to be due to chance.)
    (b) Should the government adopt policies to help non-firstborn children, perhaps taxing them at a lower rate than firstborns later in life?

44. Argue both sides of the following proposal: The government should compensate people who are members of groups that were victims of discrimination or slavery in the past, such as African Americans, Native Americans, and Japanese Americans (for internment during World War II). Even though many of the actual victims are dead, their children, grandchildren, and great-grandchildren suffer because of that past discrimination; they live in poorer families, get poorer educations, have fewer opportunities and less stable families, and face poorer prospects for their children than they would in the absence of the past discrimination. The effects of discrimination do not die with the victims. While compensation cannot undo the effects of past discrimination, it can and should help to remedy the lingering effects.

45. A firm must pay more to provide life insurance to men than to women (because men will die sooner, on average). Men must pay more for auto insurance than women (because men—particularly young men—drive more recklessly, on average). Is it discrimination for an insurer to charge different prices to men and women for insurance?[34] Is it fair?

46. Discuss the issue of discrimination raised in the news item about the auto dealer's "Christian Plan." Should the law allow this kind of selective discounting? What would be the economic effects of either decision?

IN THE NEWS

Auto dealer's 'Christian plan' is called bias

Special to
The New York Times

FAIRFAX, Va., May 26—One night last August the letters *C, M, B* and *P* popped into Freddy (Action) Jackson's head. Business at his car dealership has never been the same since.

The next morning, he said, he had it: "Christian Members Buying Plan." Christians would buy cars at bargain prices and a percentage of his profit would go to their church.

The American Civil Liberties Union and the Anti-Defamation League of B'nai B'rith say Brown Lincoln-Mercury discriminates against non-Christians.

A lawyer for the A.C.L.U., Victor Glasberg, told the Federal Trade Commission this month that the policy violated equal-opportunity credit laws.

Three years ago, the Anti-Defamation League was involved in a similar dispute in Pensacola, Fla., where Jerry Harrison, an Exxon station owner, had put up a sign reading, "For Christians Only: 10 percent discount on labor."

"We are sick and tired of Christians and Christian values being expunged from every area of public life," he said. "This isn't separation of church and state; this is a private merchant."

Source: New York Times

---

[33] Smith and Ward, "Women in the Labor Market," p. 22.

[34] At most ages, a woman has a 40 percent lower chance of dying within the following year than a man does.

ADVANCED
TOPICS IN
MICROECONOMICS

CHAPTER 20

ECONOMICS OF INFORMATION

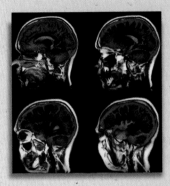

In this Chapter. . .

Main Points to Understand

- ▶ Imperfect information can create differences in prices across stores.
- ▶ Diversification reduces risk.
- ▶ Limited information about other people's actions can create moral hazard problems, with important applications to labor markets, insurance, and financial markets.
- ▶ Limited information about the quality of a product or service can create adverse selection problems, with many important applications, particularly to insurance markets.

Thinking Skills to Develop

- ▶ Recognize the problems that limited information can create.
- ▶ Predict how economies resolve problems caused by limited information.

O ur time has been called the information age. Technical advances have made information easier to obtain, transfer, manipulate, and utilize than ever before. Firms spend billions of dollars gathering and processing information. Consumers are increasingly bombarded with information from the media, the government, and the labels on products they buy. Yet *useful* information often remains costly to obtain, difficult to understand, and hard to remember. The accuracy of information received can be difficult or costly to verify. People make decisions based on limited and imperfect information, and some have better information than others, creating opportunities to exploit information advantages. How do you know if a taxi driver overcharges you in a strange city? How do you know if a service agent overcharges you for repairing a car or a television? How do you know whether the information you receive in a college course is accurate? If the college track team is particularly anxious for you to join, doesn't that indicate something about the speeds of their current runners? When a person suddenly takes out a particularly large insurance policy, shouldn't the company suspect something? The economic consequences of imperfect information can be large and pervasive, and they help to explain many subtle characteristics of markets, contractual arrangements, and the organization of the business world.

EXPECTATIONS ABOUT THE FUTURE

Expected Values

People often guess at numbers they don't know, such as the score of tomorrow's ball game or their incomes ten years from now. Under certain conditions, a rational guess is the expected value.[1]

> An **expected value** is an average of the sum of every possible number, weighted by the probabilities (chances) that they will occur.

We calculate an expected value in three steps:

1. List the number (e.g., the score or the income) in each possible situation.

2. Multiply each number by its probability or chance of occurring.

3. Add the results from Step 2.

EXAMPLES

1. Consider the expected value for the points that a team will score in the last 20 seconds of a game. If the team has a one-third chance of scoring 0, a one-third chance of scoring 1 point, and a one-third chance of scoring 2 points, the expected value of the score (or expected score) is:

$$(1/3)(0) + (1/3)(1) + (1/3)(2) = 1 \text{ point}$$

2. Suppose you have a nine-tenths chance of earning $50,000 per year ten years from now and a one-tenth chance of earning $300,000. Then your expected salary is:

$$(9/10)(\$50,000) + (1/10)(\$300,000) = \$75,000$$

LIMITED INFORMATION ABOUT PRICES

Why do some stores charge higher prices than others charge? With perfect competition, a seller that raises a price above the equilibrium loses all his customers. In many markets, however, limited information prevents all buyers from immediately switching to other sellers. When a store raises its price, many buyers may not realize that they can buy the product at a lower price elsewhere, so the store may lose only some of its customers. When a store reduces its price, many people may continue to buy from higher-priced competitors, because they have not learned about the price cut. When buyers have limited information about prices, firms face downward-sloping demand curves.

Search Costs

Buyers with limited information often check several stores to try to find the best price or product quality. This search activity has costs.

> **Search costs** are the time and money costs of obtaining information about prices and products.

---

[1]The expected value is also called the *mean* of a distribution of numbers.

The optimal amount of search occurs when the expected marginal benefit of searching (the expected benefit from trying one more store) equals its expected marginal cost.[2]

EXAMPLE

Suppose that four stores sell a product that a buyer wants. The average price is $40, but some stores charge more and others charge less. Table 1 shows that two stores charge $40, one store charges $35, and one store charges $45.

Table 1 A Search Example	
Number of Stores	**Price**
1	$35
2	40
1	45

The buyer is willing to pay up to $50 for the product, and knows that one store charges $35, two stores charge $40, and one store charges $45, but does not know which store charges which price. Choosing a store at random, the buyer has a one-fourth chance of choosing the low-price store and buying the product for $35. The buyer also has a one-fourth chance of choosing the high-price ($45) store and a one-half chance of choosing a store that charges $40. If the first store charges $40 or $45, the buyer must decide whether to go to another store to look for a lower price.

Suppose that the first store charges $40, and the buyer decides to go to one, and only one, other store. This person has a one-third chance of visiting a store that charges $35 and a one-third chance of visiting a store that charges $40; in either case, the buyer would buy the product. The buyer also faces a one-third chance that the second store will charge $45, in which case the buyer would return to the original store and pay $40.[3] In summary, if the first store charges $40, a buyer who tries one more store has a one-third chance of saving $5 and a two-thirds chance of not saving any money. The expected marginal benefit of search at the second store is:

$$(1/3)(\$5) + (2/3)(\$0) = \text{about } \$1.67$$

If this expected marginal benefit exceeds the expected marginal cost of visiting the second store, then the buyer expects to gain from searching. If not, then a rational buyer would stop searching.

Similarly, if the first store charges $45, the buyer must compare the expected marginal benefit of searching with its expected marginal cost. By visiting one more store, the buyer faces a two-thirds chance that it will charge $40 and a one-third chance that it will charge $35. The expected marginal benefit from search is:

$$(2/3)(\$5) + (1/3)(\$10) = \text{about } \$6.67$$

If this amount exceeds the expected marginal cost of the search, the buyer gains by trying another store; if not, a rational buyer stops searching.

In most situations, people do not know how many stores charge which prices. They must learn from experience and from other sources, such as advertising and talking with friends, about the expected benefits of searching.

Price Differences between Stores

Some buyers know more about prices than others. Tourists, for example, usually have less information than local residents have about which stores charge high prices. For that reason, tourists are more likely than locals to buy products at high-priced stores.

When some customers have better information than others, a distribution of prices can persist in equilibrium.

---

[2] This statement abstracts from risk; it applies strictly to risk-neutral consumers. A later section of the chapter discusses the effects of risk.

[3] In this example, the buyer could also try a third store at random. That third store would charge either $35 or $40, so the buyer could do at least as well as going back to the original store. To avoid additional complexity, the discussion ignores this possibility (which seldom arises in real life, because buyers usually choose among more than four stores).

> A **distribution of prices** means that some sellers charge higher prices than others.

Informed consumers buy from low-price stores. Some uninformed consumers go to the low-price stores by chance, but others buy from high-price stores, because they don't know that other stores offer lower prices.

In a market with generally well-informed consumers, all stores charge low prices (equal to marginal cost, as in perfect competition). Any store that tried to charge a higher price would lose enough customers to reduce its profits. For this reason, a market with well-informed consumers may fit the perfect competition model well. However, when many consumers are poorly informed and face high search costs, a distribution of prices can persist in equilibrium. Some stores charge high prices, while others charge low prices. The high-price stores sell less than the others, but earn higher profits on each item sold; the low-price stores earn less per item, but sell larger quantities.

A firm may sell a single good under different brand names at different prices. Some firms operate more than one store (perhaps one at each of several shopping malls), charging more for a single good at some stores than at others. Informed consumers buy the cheaper brands or shop at the low-price stores. Many uninformed consumers buy the high-price brands or shop at the high-price stores, so the sellers earn high profits on sales to them. These methods allow firms to price-discriminate by charging higher prices to some relatively uninformed buyers.

Searching for a Good Match

Products as well as prices differ between stores. Buyers search not only for the best prices, but also for the types of products they want. Some people prefer a music store with a good selection of rock music; others look for a good selection of vintage jazz. This kind of search is often more costly than searching for the lowest price, which may take only a phone call.

EXAMPLES

"I know it's true love, because my marginal cost of searching for someone better equals my marginal benefit."

Search is important in labor markets. People want jobs that pay good wages, but they also search for jobs that suit them well—they search for the best match between jobs and workers. Firms also search for workers who match their needs well. Similarly, people search for good matches when they look for husbands or wives. Romantic notions aside, some couples marry, not because they have found the perfect match, but because they have found a satisfactory match and the costs (especially the time costs) of continuing the search are not worth the expected benefits. Even though they might find someone who matches them better if they were to search more, the chance is small so the expected marginal benefit from search is less than its cost, and they stop searching. (In these cases, divorce may result from the additional information that comes free with everyday life.)

Applications of Search Theory

Many aspects of life involve imperfect information and search. A fair number of students enter college not knowing whether they want to major in economics, physics, history, engineering, or some other field of study. Most students take classes in various disciplines, partly to learn which ones they find most interesting. The cost of search involves time (the opportunity cost of taking other classes or working) and direct payments of money (tuition). The benefit comes from an improved match between individual interests and an ultimate field of concentration and career.

Adults have often complained that younger generations "revolt" against their elders' lifestyles, experimenting with new or different lifestyles. Perhaps this tendency to revolt (which has been noted throughout history) involves rational searching for the lifestyle that best matches each person's interests. Young people may sample alternative lifestyles, not because they dislike their parents' lifestyles, but because they are searching to see if any alternatives better match their own values and interests. Many people already have some information about how well their parents' lifestyles might satisfy their desires for fulfillment in life. By experimenting with alternative lifestyles, they learn how well those alternatives satisfy them. People search and experiment more when they are young than when they are older because the benefits of the information are larger for younger people (who have more years left to live their lives and make use of that information).

Firms Have Limited Information about Demand

Firms have limited information about the prices that buyers are willing to pay, so they must learn in some way about the demand curves they face. They may learn by trial and error, charging different prices at different times. Putting a product on sale can help a firm to learn about the demand curve, because it can observe the quantities that consumers buy at the regular and sale prices. A firm with limited information about demand often profits by charging a high price at first, then reducing the price over time and putting the good on sale if it does not sell well enough. (Some retail stores carry nothing but goods that have previously been offered at higher prices elsewhere.) The firm benefits from this pricing strategy because it charges high prices to buyers who are willing to pay them. The strategy has two costs. First, some consumers would pay the high price if necessary, but they expect the price to fall, so they postpone buying until the firm reduces the price. Also, the firm sells goods more slowly this way than it would with a low initial price, raising inventory costs.

EXPLANATION

Suppose that all buyers are the same; each is willing to pay (at most) P dollars for one unit of the good, and no buyer wants more than one unit. Sellers, though, do not know the exact value of P; they know only that P is between $10 and $20. Suppose that a seller's best guess of P (its expected value) is $15; if the seller charges $15, there is a one-half chance that people will buy the good.

The seller could charge less than $15 to raise the chance of selling the good, but it would then sacrifice profit if people were actually willing to pay a higher price. To avoid this loss of profit, a seller might initially charge $19 or $20, then reduce the price slowly over time if people did not buy the good. This method may allow the seller to charge people the highest price they are willing to pay. Of course, if buyers believe that the seller will reduce the price further, they may wait for lower prices before buying. In that case, the seller cannot obtain the highest price buyers are willing to pay. However, if buyers differ in the prices they are willing to pay, some might pay a high price to buy the good now rather than waiting for a lower price.

Review Questions

1. What would be the expected value of your starting salary in your first job if you had a one-tenth chance of earning $60,000; a one-tenth chance of earning $50,000; a three-tenths chance of earning $40,000; and a five-tenths chance of earning $20,000?

2. What is a distribution of prices? Why can a distribution of prices persist in equilibrium?

PERSONAL DECISION MAKING

Some Information That Sellers Try to Hide

Sometimes stores don't sell designer clothes after a normal period of time. If they were simply to cut the prices, consumers would realize that they could eventually buy the clothes at still lower prices. To prevent consumers from learning this possibility, and to keep uninformed consumers willing to pay the high initial prices, stores cut off designers' labels. Informed consumers may know this, and some can even determine who made a product because federal law requires labels to carry RN or WPL numbers that identify manufacturers. (You can find out which companies have which numbers by consulting a directory in your local library.) Uninformed consumers pay high prices.

3. Why do firms charge high prices for new products, then later put them on sale at reduced prices?

4. Why do tourists often pay more than local residents for the same goods?

Thinking Exercises

5. Calculate expected values in two situations:
   (a) You bought a raffle ticket. The chance is $\frac{999}{1,000}$ that your ticket will not win anything, and $\frac{1}{1,000}$ that it will win a stereo system valued at $500. What is the expected benefit from your raffle ticket?
   (b) You face a one-half chance that you will lose $100 on an investment, a one-quarter chance that you will break even (zero profit), and a one-quarter chance that your profit will be $400. What is your expected profit on the investment?

6. You are shopping for a television set, and you learn the price at a local store. You could visit other stores, with a one-tenth chance that the next store you visit will charge $25 less for the same television set, and a nine-tenths chance it will charge the same price as the current store. What is your expected benefit from visiting the other store to check the price there?

RISK

Some activities are riskier than others. You take a greater risk going hang gliding than watching soap operas. You assume a bigger risk to your ego by talking to an attractive stranger than by sitting alone in the corner. You take a bigger risk with your money by investing it to start your own business, which might fail, than by depositing it in a savings account and taking a job at a stable corporation.

Diversification

An old adage, "Don't put all your eggs in one basket," is usually the best investment advice you can get. People can reduce the risks of their investments by diversifying.

> **Diversification** refers to spreading risks across many different, unrelated investments.

IN THE NEWS

Portfolios tango the best when they're out of step

Your money matters

By Barbara Donnelly
Staff Reporter of
The Wall Street Journal

When it comes to building an investment portfolio, there's a crucial distinction between true diversification and simply holding a hodgepodge of securities.

An investor could hold dozens of small-company stocks, for instance, and still be ravaged by the special perils that affect this volatile sector. Even if the holdings comprised many small-company mutual funds, which themselves are diversified, the investor's portfolio would still be vulnerable.

The real secret of portfolio diversification, investment professionals say, is to mix investments that don't move in tandem— then regularly readjust the mix to maintain its original proportions.

The basic objective is always to have at least some investments that do well, to offset others that are lagging.

Right Place at Right Time

In effect, diversification insures that at least part of the portfolio will always be in the right place at the right time. Consequently, it makes money for investors through a series of base hits, rather than home runs—a feature that could seem disappointing to some individuals who crave more action.

Source: The Wall Street Journal

The basics of diversification.

The following example shows the benefits of diversification.

EXAMPLE

Beth has $100 to invest, and she can buy stock in either of two companies: the Romer Corporation or the Solow Corporation. Romer is on the verge of inventing a new medical-research technology that may replace one sold by Solow. The new technology has a flaw, however, and Romer has a one-half chance of correcting the flaw. A share of stock in either company sells for $50, so Beth can buy 2 shares. She must decide whether to buy 2 shares of Romer and no Solow, 2 shares of Solow and no Romer, or 1 share of each.

If Romer corrects the technical flaw, the price of Romer stock will rise to $80 and the price of Solow stock will fall to $30. In this case, Beth will gain $30 on each share of Romer stock and lose $20 on each share of Solow stock. If the flaw remains uncorrected, the price of Romer stock will fall to $30 and the price of Solow stock will rise to $80. In that case, Beth will lose $20 on each share of Romer stock and gain $30 on each share of Solow stock.

If she buys either 2 shares of Romer stock or 2 shares of Solow stock, Beth has a one-half chance of gaining $60 and a one-half chance of losing $40. Her expected profit is $10:

$$(1/2)(\$60) + (1/2)(-\$40) = \$30 - \$20 = \$10$$

If she diversifies by buying 1 share of stock in each firm, Beth gains $30 on one of the stocks and loses $20 on the other, so her profit is $10 with no risk. Whether or not

Diversifying Risks

The key to diversifying risks is to choose investments whose returns move in opposite directions. An investor is better diversified if some of that person's investments provide high returns in those situations where her other investments provide low returns, and vice-versa. This mixture of investments protects the investor, rather like insurance, because at least some investments are likely to do well in any set of conditions. With some doing well, poor performance by others creates less damage to the overall portfolio.

The example in the preceding section is a special case. The two investments (Romer and Solow stock) move in opposite directions with perfect consistency. Few real-life investments move so perfectly in opposite directions, but optimal diversification requires choosing investments that approximate this kind of relationship. In the stock market, an investor gains by choosing stocks that perform out of step. Some should provide their highest returns at times when others provide low returns, and vice versa.

A homeowner with a variable-rate mortgage makes increasing payments when interest rates rise and lower payments when interest rates fall. That homeowner can diversify by choosing investments that pay high returns in times that high interest rates rise and low returns when interest rates fall. If interest rates rise, the increasing returns on the investments help to offset the increasing mortgage payments; if interest rates fall, the investments pay less, but lower mortgage payments reduce overall costs. Similarly, a person with a risky job can partly diversify the income risk from that job by choosing investments likely to generate their highest returns under conditions that cause low employment income.

she diversifies, Beth's expected profit is $10. However, diversifying reduces her risk—she earns $10 with certainty rather than taking a one-half chance of earning $60 and a one-half chance of losing $40.

Risk Aversion

Diversification provides valuable benefits to anyone who dislikes risk.

> A person is **risk averse** if he prefers a less risky income, holding fixed its expected value.[4]

Risk-averse people prefer to avoid risks unless the risks carry with them sufficiently large expected gains; risk averse people would diversify in the example above. In fact, risk-averse people would choose the less risky investment even if it had a slightly smaller expected profit; they are willing to sacrifice some expected profit in order to eliminate some risk. However, risk-averse people *will* take risks if the expected profits are high enough to make risk taking worthwhile.

> A **risk-neutral** person does not care about risk.

Risk-neutral people would not care whether they invest in Solow stock or Romer stock, or both, in the example; diversifying provides no gain to them. A person who likes risk would not buy insurance or diversify investments. Such a person would actually pay to take chances. While many people pay to take certain risks—they buy lottery tickets and vacation at gambling resorts—these activities involve entertainment. Most of the

---

[4]More precisely, a person is risk averse if she would dislike an increase in the standard deviation of her future wealth, holding fixed its expected value.

people who gamble also buy insurance against big risks such as fire, theft, and accidents; their behavior shows that (at least for large gambles) they are risk averse. Evidence from financial markets, indicating that risky investments must pay higher expected returns to induce people to buy them, implies that most people are risk averse.

People often lack important information about others' actions. Firms may not know how hard their employees work; a person with a house for sale may not know how hard a real-estate agent tries to sell it. These examples illustrate hidden action or moral hazard. We begin with definitions of important terms:

> A **principal** is a person who hires someone else, an **agent,** to do something.

A home seller is a principal; a real-estate broker is an agent. The owner of a firm is a principal; an employee is an agent. A principal sets goals for the agent to achieve. Those goals, such as high profits or a well-built house, would benefit the principal. The agent's success may depend on luck as well as the amount of effort he exerts. Interesting economic issues arise when the principal can observe the outcome, but not the agent's actions or his luck. The principal does not know the extent to which the outcome resulted from the agent's effort and the extent to which it resulted from luck. As a result, the agent can try to take credit for a good outcome that results from luck. If the agent's shirking leads to a bad outcome, the agent can blame bad luck.

> **Moral hazard** occurs when an agent lacks an incentive to promote the best interests of the principal, and the principal cannot observe the actions of the agent.

MORAL HAZARD

"Naughty or nice? You mean you'll just take my word for it?"

Incomplete information about an agent's actions creates moral hazard.
Source: The Wall Street Journal, December 22, 1989.

Optimal Contracts

In any moral hazard situation, the principal is likely to recognize an incentive for the agent not to act in the principal's interests. The principal can respond by creating an incentive for the agent to try hard by paying more for good results than for bad results. If the principal were to pay the agent a large enough bonus for good results, the agent would have a reason to act in the principal's interest. A contract between a principal and an agent is an agreement that states how the agent's pay depends on the results.

> An **optimal contract** between a principal and an agent is an agreement that maximizes the principal's profit while providing an incentive for the agent to participate in the agreement.

In a moral hazard problem, the optimal contract is a compromise between the benefit to the agent of a flat salary (low risk), and the incentive to act in the principal's interest that comes from a salary increase for an improved outcome. The optimal contract determines the sensitivity of the agent's pay to the results by setting the marginal benefit of additional sensitivity equal to the marginal cost. The marginal benefit of additional sensitivity is the incentive it provides for the agent to increase his effort. The marginal cost of additional sensitivity is the additional effect of luck on the agent's pay, which makes the agent bear additional risk and thereby raises the expected salary that the principal must pay to attract an agent to the job. The optimal contract equates the marginal benefit of better incentives with their marginal cost.

Table 2
Chance of a High Profit Depends on the Agent's Action

	Agent's Action	
	TRY HARD	SHIRK
$300,000 profit	2/3	1/3
No profit	1/3	2/3

EXAMPLE

A business owner (the principal) hires a salesperson (the agent) to sell new, biodegradable food containers. The amount the agent sells depends on both the agent's effort and luck. Suppose that the firm's profit will be either $300,000 or zero. The chance of earning $300,000 depends on the agent's effort, as in Table 2.

If the agent tries hard, the firm has a two-thirds chance of earning $300,000 and a one-third chance of earning nothing. Therefore the firm's expected profit is $200,000 if the agent tries hard. If the agent shirks, the chance of a $300,000 profit is only one-third, and the expected profit is only $100,000. The principal will never find out how hard the agent tries. The principal will see only the final result—the firm's profit.

A $30,000 salary would give the agent an incentive to shirk. The agent would earn the money without the effort of trying hard, and the principal would never know. If the firm were to earn a zero profit, the agent could falsely claim that, despite vigorous effort, the poor profit resulted from bad luck.

Now consider some alternative payment schemes to the $30,000 salary.

Case 1 Suppose that the agent receives nothing if the firm earns zero profit, and $45,000 if it earns $300,000. If the agent shirks, this payment plan gives him an expected salary of:

$$(1/3)(\$45,000) + (2/3)(\$0) = \$15,000$$

If the agent tries hard, this payment plan gives him an expected salary of:

$$(2/3)(\$45,000) + (1/3)(\$0) = \$30,000$$

The agent has an incentive to try hard because effort can raise his expected salary from $15,000 to $30,000.

However, the agent may not like bearing the risk of earning a zero salary. A risk averse agent, like most people, would prefer to take another job that would guarantee a $30,000 salary in return for working hard. To attract a worker to this job, the firm must raise the expected salary to compensate the worker for the risk of earning nothing.

Case 2 Suppose that the agent receives $32,000 if the firm earns a profit of $300,000 and $29,000 if it earns zero. An agent who shirks can expect a salary of:

$$(1/3)(\$32,000) + (2/3)(\$29,000) = \$30,000$$

An agent who tries hard can expect a salary of:

$$(2/3)(\$32,000) + (1/3)(\$29,000) = \$31,000$$

The agent bears much less risk than in Case 1, so even a risk averse worker might prefer this risky job to one that would guarantee $30,000. The expected salary rises by $1,000 if the agent tries hard instead of shirking. Whether this difference gives the agent an incentive to try hard depends on how much expected salary the agent is willing to sacrifice in order to shirk. If the agent enjoys shirking sufficiently, this $1,000 difference in expected salary will not be enough to induce hard work. Now consider a payment scheme that compromises between the high-incentive scheme, Case 1, and the low-risk scheme, Case 2.

Case 3 Suppose that the agent will try hard if effort would increase the expected salary by $3,000. The firm can pay the agent $37,000 if it earns a profit of $300,000 and

IN THE NEWS

Even so, the economics of a losing network [are] different from the economics of a winning one. CBS is being asked to pay producers more for its series because, as the losingest network, CBS cancels more of them.

Source: The Wall Street Journal

Firms must pay risk averse employees higher expected incomes when they require employees to take higher risks; similarly, television networks must pay higher prices to producers on whom the networks impose higher risks.

Table 3 | Chance of a High Profit and Three Possible Agent Actions

	Agent's Action		
	TRY HARD	TRY A LITTLE	SHIRK
$300,000 profit	2/3	1/2	1/3
No profit	1/3	1/2	2/3

$28,000 if it earns zero. An agent who shirks can expect a salary of:

$$(1/3)(\$37,000) + (2/3)(\$28,000) = \$31,000$$

An agent who tries hard can expect a salary of:

$$(2/3)(\$37,000) + (1/3)(\$28,000) = \$34,000$$

Now the agent is willing to try hard. The agent bears less risk than in Case 1, but more than in Case 2. The agent may be willing to take this risk, however, for the expected salary of $34,000, which is $4,000 more than other jobs would pay. (If the firm paid only $36,000 for a high profit and $27,000 for a zero profit, the agent's expected salary from working hard, $33,000, may not be enough to ensure an attractive job.)

Case 4 Suppose that the agent is not willing to take the job (because of the risk) even for expected pay of $34,000, as in Case 3. Perhaps the agent could try a little, however, as a compromise between shirking and hard work. (See Table 3.)

If the agent tries a little, the firm has a one-half chance of a $300,000 profit and a one-half chance of nothing for an expected profit of $150,000. (Expected profit is $100,000 if the agent shirks, and $200,000 if the agent really makes an effort.) This possibility suggests another payment scheme.

Suppose that the agent receives $35,000 for a $300,000 profit and $29,000 if the profit is zero. The agent expects a salary of $31,000 for shirking, $32,000 for trying a little, and $33,000 for hard work. In this case, the agent may be willing to try a little to earn an expected salary of $32,000 rather than $31,000 but unwilling to try hard just to raise the expected salary by another $1,000.

An optimal contract may give the agent an incentive to try a little, but not to try hard. The agent may try hard only if the principal offers much higher pay for a $300,000 profit than for a zero profit. That may raise the expected salary more than it would raise the principal's expected profit, though, so the principal would be unwilling to pay enough to induce hard work.

Monitoring

In many moral hazard situations, the principals can obtain some information about the agents' actions by monitoring them.

> **Monitoring** an agent means obtaining information about that person's actions (perhaps by watching).

Perfect monitoring—learning exactly what an agent does—is usually too costly to be practical for a principal. (Sometimes it is impossible.) Imperfect monitoring—developing some indication of the agent's action—can be less costly, though. A company's owner

"It's called moral hazard— Mom thinks that I worked hard to clean my room and that dog messed it up again."

may not know exactly how hard an engineer is working to prepare a new design for a complex product, but some indication of the engineer's effort comes from the volume and nature of research reports, performance at staff meetings, hours of work, and so on. James Ritty, a bar owner in the 1870s, invented the cash register to help prevent bartenders from dipping their fingers in the till—stealing money. The cash register recorded every sale, so at the end of a day, Ritty could see how much money it should contain. He later sold his bar to a person who added a bell to the cash register. With the bell, a store owner could hear when a sale occurred (even from the back of the store), preventing a cashier from selling a good and pocketing the money without using the cash register.

Monitoring has costs because the principal must either spend time watching the agent or hire someone else to do so.[5] Owners of firms employ accountants and auditors to monitor company managers and make sure they try hard to maximize profits.

Principals can choose how closely they monitor agents. Principals monitor until the expected marginal cost equals the expected marginal benefit. Sometimes firms ask employees to monitor each other. Employees who work together in small groups may easily observe how hard other employees work. By paying each worker a wage that depends on the group's output, each member of the group loses if any worker shirks. Employees who fail to work hard feel pressure from the rest of the group to improve their performance.

Firms have tried innovative methods of monitoring. One firm had to deal with employees prone to go fishing rather than show up at work. It awarded points for showing up at work that employees could redeem for prizes. The firm gave the points to the workers' spouses rather than directly to the workers, which gave their spouses an extra incentive to monitor them.

On the other hand, some firms benefit by creating new ways for agents to cheat principals. The frequent-flyer plans of airlines encourage employees to take actions that oppose the interests of their employers. Many firms allow their employees to use frequent-flyer miles they collect during business travel for personal travel. This policy gives employees an incentive to take more business trips than necessary to acquire frequent-flyer miles for personal use.

Applications of Moral Hazard

Insurance

Insurance is a classic example of moral hazard. Insurance protection reduces a person's incentive to prevent a loss. The insurance company (the principal) does not know if the policy holder (the agent) is doing everything possible to prevent a loss. The optimal insurance contract sets up a compromise between incentives and risk, so insurance companies sell only incomplete insurance. For example, insurance policies may pay only 80 percent of a loss or only the part of a loss above a certain amount called a *deductible*. Incomplete insurance provides the policy holder with an incentive to prevent a loss while still reducing her risk.

Product Guarantees

Like insurance, a product guarantee reduces an owner's incentive to take proper care of a product. If an electronics store were to guarantee that your personal stereo would operate perfectly for the first two years, that guarantee would reduce your incentive to care for it properly. A guarantee does not create a moral hazard problem if the manufacturer can distinguish problems due to defects from problems due to careless use. However, manufacturers often lack the ability to distinguish between these types of defects, resulting in moral hazard problems.

---

[5]In addition, workers may dislike being watched, so another cost of monitoring may be the extra wages required to attract workers willing to work while monitored.

THE LOCKHORNS HOEST

"Since we took out that million-dollar insurance policy, I notice you don't remind me to use my seat belt anymore."

Insurance creates problems of moral hazard.
Source: Washington Post, November 22, 1988.

The optimal contract again involves a compromise between a complete guarantee (which would eliminate a consumer's risk) and no guarantee (which would give consumers strong incentives for proper use and care of the product). In the compromise, a guarantee reduces risk while leaving some incentive for proper use and care. For example, guarantees that pay for new parts but not for labor reduce the risks of owning a product while maintaining an incentive to take care of it to avoid the labor costs of repairs.

Some sellers offer service contracts under which they agree to repair products without charge if they ever break. Service contracts are subject to moral hazard because they reduce people's incentives to properly care for and use products, so products break more often when people buy service contracts. One study found that a 10 percent increase in the number of service contracts leads to a 5 percent increase in product repairs.

Executive Compensation

The interests of top corporate executives can differ from those of a firm's owners. Owners want to maximize the value of the firm. However, owners cannot closely monitor an executive's activities without high cost, so executive employment involves moral hazard. This problem is sometimes called the *separation of ownership and control* of a firm: A firm's owners—its stockholders—are the principals, and the managers or executives are the agents.

The optimal contract between a firm's owners and managers ties managers' pay to the value of the firm to equate the expected marginal benefit and the marginal cost of creating incentives for managers to act in the owners' interests by maximizing the firm's value. The contract provides these incentives only partially, to avoid exposing managers' pay to too much risk. Evidence suggests that the chief executive officer (CEO) of a typical American corporation gains only $325 in additional salary and other forms of compensation when the value of the firm rises $100,000. Many economists believe that $325 per $100,000 in firm value does not provide a sufficiently strong incentive for a typical CEO to maximize a firm's value. Suppose, for example, that a CEO can undertake a pet project worth $1,000 to him or her personally (perhaps in extra prestige) that costs the firm $100,000. The CEO would expect to lose $325 in compensation from the project, leaving a net gain of $675 ($1,000 minus $325). The CEO would choose to undertake the project, though it would be contrary to the interests of stockholders, because it would reduce the value of the firm.

Economists disagree about the reasons for the apparent shortfall in incentives for CEOs to maximize profits. Perhaps stockholders can monitor CEOs well enough that the moral hazard problem is not important for executive compensation; perhaps executives have little control over profits (which would also make the moral hazard problem unimportant for executive compensation). Other economists believe that social pressures prevent firms from increasing CEO pay much when profits rise. Evidence suggests that profits rise with progressively closer links between CEO compensation and firm performance, a finding that suggests the importance of the moral hazard problem for executive compensation. In fact, some economists argue that CEO pay is already optimal, creating a situation analogous to Case 4 in the earlier example of contracts, in which an optimal contract paid an agent for moderate rather than hard effort.

Interest Rates on Personal Loans

Most borrowers repay their loans, but some default and declare bankruptcy. (In this legal procedure, a debtor gives up all but a small amount of personal property and the court liquidates the rest of the person's property to eliminate debts.)[6] Firms can also declare bankruptcy. The possibility of declaring bankruptcy creates a moral hazard problem by reducing borrowers' incentives to try hard to earn enough money to repay their debts. This option of bankruptcy also gives borrowers incentives to choose risky actions that raise their expected profits but also raise their chances of bankruptcy.

EXAMPLE

Derek is $5,000 in debt. He has assets worth $6,000 and no other source of income. He meets someone who offers him a double-or-nothing bet on a football game; the chance of winning the bet is one-half. If Derek refuses the bet, he has $1,000 in assets after paying his debt. If Derek bets and wins, he has $12,000, or $7,000 after paying his debts. If he bets and loses, he has no assets and declares bankruptcy, which wipes out his debt. The bet gives Derek a one-half chance of winning $6,000 and a one-half chance of losing only $1,000; his expected profit from the bet is:

$$(1/2)(\$6,000) + (1/2)(-\$1,000) = \$2,500$$

Derek dislikes risk, but the expected profit on the bet is high enough that he takes the risk.

The lender would want Derek to refuse to bet. If he bets and loses, he will not repay the loan. The bet exposes the lender to risk, with no chance of gain. This moral hazard problem reduces the willingness of lenders to lend money, raising the interest rates they charge on loans. To prevent borrowers from taking actions that jeopardize loan repayment, lenders often require them to pledge property (such as cars or houses) as collateral, which the lenders can take if the borrowers default.

Bondholders and Stockholders

Stockholders own firms. Bondholders are firms' creditors—people who have loaned money to the companies. When someone lends money to a firm by purchasing its bonds, that investor takes a chance that the firm will go bankrupt and not repay the loan. After the firm has already borrowed the money, stockholders would like the firm to choose

---

IN THE NEWS

Marriott to revise terms of split

By Paul Farhi
Washington Post Staff Writer

Marriott Corp. agreed yesterday to change some of the terms of its plan to split into two companies, backing down in the face of a challenge from bondholders angered by the restructuring.

"We were surprised by how hurt and angry [the bondholders] were when we first announced the restructuring," said Stephen F. Bollenbach, Marriott's chief financial officer. "So what we did was change it."

Source: Washington Post

The interests of stockholders and bondholders can conflict. When the Marriott Corporation split into two companies in 1993, stockholders tried to say that one of the companies, Host Marriott, would owe most of Marriott's debts, while the other, Marriott International, would be relatively free of debts. This structure would raise the chance that Host Marriott would go bankrupt and bondholders would lose. Meanwhile, stockholders would gain, because the other company could operate relatively free of debt. Bondholders filed lawsuits to prevent the original plan from going into effect.

---

[6]The precise amount of personal property that escapes liquidation varies across states in the United States. The bankruptcy court uses the property it takes from the person to repay creditors in part for the outstanding balances of the debts.

risky investments, because they keep the gains if a risky investment pays off and they can force some of the loss onto bondholders (by declaring bankruptcy) if not. The logic is precisely the same as in the personal loan example; the agent (the firm and its owners, the stockholders) has an incentive to engage in risky actions that raise the chance of bankruptcy, and the principal (the bondholder) cannot perfectly observe the firm's actions. The principal sees only the results (repayment of the loan or bankruptcy). For this reason, stockholders and bondholders frequently disagree about a firm's optimal business strategies. Stockholders prefer riskier business activities (such as investments in new product lines) than bondholders.

Review Questions

7. Explain how diversification can reduce risk.

8. Explain moral hazard and present an example, identifying the principal and the agent.

Thinking Exercises

9. Explain why a person's incentive to shirk depends on the compensation method.

10. With an optimal contract in a moral hazard situation, do agents have an incentive to try as hard as the principal would like? Why or why not?

Moral hazard occurs when a principal has imperfect information about an agent's actions. Sometimes people lack relevant information about the reasons for the actions of others with whom they interact. A potential buyer knows that you are selling your car, but not whether you are selling it because it is a bad car or simply because you want a newer model. This example illustrates hidden information or adverse selection.

ADVERSE SELECTION

> **Adverse selection** refers to a situation in which sellers have relevant information that buyers lack (or vice versa) about some aspect of product quality.

The market for used cars is the classic example of adverse selection. Someone who sells a car knows something about its quality that a buyer does not know: how well the car has worked in the past. The car might be reliable or it might be faulty. Because most buyers cannot readily identify a faulty car, good used cars and faulty ones sell for the same prices. In a sense, buyers overpay for faulty cars and underpay for good ones. If they had better information, buyers would not be willing to pay as much for the faulty cars as for the good cars.

Because good cars are underpriced, people who own them are relatively unlikely to sell them. Because faulty cars are overpriced, people who own them are relatively likely to sell them. For this reason, good cars are under-represented in the used-car market, and faulty cars are over-represented. The term *adverse selection* refers to this result. The cars that people offer in the used-car market tend to be those of lower-than-average quality. The low-quality cars offered for sale tend to drive the higher-quality cars out of the used-car market.

Moral hazard differs from adverse selection. Moral hazard occurs when one person does not know what another person is doing; a principal cannot see whether an agent is acting in the principal's best interest. Adverse selection occurs when people know what an agent is doing, but not why.

EXAMPLE

Suppose that good cars are worth $1,000, faulty cars are worth $500, and each car has a one-half chance of being good or faulty. Also suppose that people are risk neutral. Buyers would be willing to pay $1,000 for a car if they could be certain that it was good and only $500 for a clearly faulty car. Buyers do not know if a car is faulty, however, so the expected value of a particular car is:

$$(1/2)(\$1,000) + (1/2)(\$500) = \$750$$

Buyers are willing to pay $750 for a car that might turn out to be either good or faulty. Buyers pay a price equal to the expected value of the car and take their chances. They end up overpaying for faulty cars by $250 and underpaying for good cars by $250.

Most people with good cars (worth $1,000) will not choose to sell them for $750, however. Also, some people who would not sell their faulty cars if they could fetch only $500 will choose to sell them for $750. In the extreme case, if every owner of a good used car were to value it at $1,000 and every owner of a faulty car were to value it at $500, then no one would ever want to sell a good used car for $750 and every owner of a faulty car would want to sell it at that price. All used cars offered for sale would be faulty! Knowing this, buyers would be unwilling to pay $750 for used cars. Because all used cars would be faulty, they would be willing to pay only $500. This would push the equilibrium price down to $500. Low-quality cars would drive all high-quality cars out of the used-car market.

In a more realistic case, owners differ in valuations of their cars. If some owners of good cars were willing to sell them for less than $1,000, then some good cars might be sold in equilibrium, allowing an equilibrium price above $500. Perhaps some owners of good cars would be willing to sell them for $600, though all buyers value good cars at $1,000 and faulty cars at $500. This could create an equilibrium in which the price of a used car would be $600, one-fifth of all used cars for sale would be good, and four-fifths would be faulty, giving an expected value of a car to a buyer of:

$$(4/5)(\$500) + (1/5)(\$1,000) = \$600$$

which is the equilibrium price. In this case, low-quality products would tend to drive out high-quality products, but not completely.

Examples of Adverse Selection

Medical Insurance

Adverse selection applies to many kinds of insurance, and insurance professionals fully understand the economic issues. Someone with a high risk of medical problems is more likely to buy medical insurance, and to buy a more comprehensive policy, than someone with a lower risk of medical problems. The same argument applies to life insurance.

People may know about their risks from family histories, health habits, and their own health histories. Insurance companies try to obtain this information, but their information remains imperfect, so they end up selling more insurance to high-risk people than to low-risk people. The price of insurance reflects an average of the costs of insuring people with different levels of risk. As a result, low-risk people overpay for insurance and high-risk people underpay. Low-risk people pay more for insurance than they would pay if insurance companies had more information.

Labor Markets

Adverse selection is also important in labor markets. A job applicant usually knows more about the quality of her labor than prospective employers know. Whatever wage a firm offers to pay, it will get many applicants with worse job alternatives, but few job applicants with better alternatives. Firms try to obtain information on the quality of job applicants, but they never gather perfect information. To protect themselves, they often hire people for low-level jobs and then, after learning about the quality of their labor, promote the high-quality people and not the low-quality people. Firms may also offer high wages to attract high-quality applicants.

Credit Cards

Because some people do not pay their bills, banks take risks when they issue credit cards. Even after spending money on lawyers and collection agencies, banks still never collect payments from some people. Banks also incur interest costs and collection costs on the many late payments that they receive. Banks must judge each applicant's credit risk based on limited information. If they could separate high-risk people from low-risk people, they would charge a higher interest rate to the high-risk people. Limited information prevents this distinction, so banks charge an interest rate that reflects the average credit risks of their customers. This practice creates adverse selection, because low-risk (creditworthy) people overpay interest and high-risk people underpay. This encourages a relatively large number of high-risk people to apply for credit cards, further raising the interest rates that banks must charge to earn zero profits in equilibrium.

Limits on Adverse Selection Problems

Guarantees

Firms that sell high-quality goods can try to limit the adverse selection problem by offering guarantees to buyers. For example, a firm might give a money-back guarantee to buyers or offer free repairs or replacement for products with defects. Guarantees can communicate information about quality to buyers, because a firm selling high-quality products will not hesitate to offer a guarantee, expecting few of its products to be returned or need repair. Firms selling low-quality products must pay high costs to honor guarantees, however, so they hesitate to provide them. Therefore, buyers properly view a good guarantee as a signal of a high-quality product. Guarantees reduce the problem of adverse selection by allowing producers of high-quality products to command higher prices than other firms charge for low-quality products.

Guarantees cannot completely eliminate adverse selection problems, because a guarantee must provide a way to enforce the promise in order to convey reliable information to buyers. Firms that make low-quality products may issue guarantees and then go out of business; a buyer may not trust a guarantee offered by a stranger selling a used car. A firm that sells a low-quality product may try later to escape responsibility for its guarantee.

Moral hazard problems also limit the use of guarantees. A buyer may not take proper care of a product with a guarantee, but a seller may have to pay for repairs or replacement if it cannot show that a problem arose from misuse or poor care. This moral hazard problem leads sellers to give the strongest guarantees only for products that buyers cannot ruin through negligence or for which sellers can monitor buyers' care. For this reason, automobile guarantees require regular servicing of cars.

Adverse selection is a less serious problem when the buyers and sellers deal with each other repeatedly, because sellers can develop reputations for high-quality goods. Good reputations for quality allow sellers to raise prices, so firms have incentives to develop good reputations by maintaining high quality.

When buyers do not deal repeatedly with the same sellers, franchising can help to reduce the adverse selection problem by providing a signal of quality. Franchising gives sellers a way to buy reputations. Consumers tend to trust stores with franchise names

IN THE NEWS

Credit-card issuers ease their standards to get new accounts

Lured by hefty profits, they sign up many customers who may prove risky

Typically, card losses run 3 percent to 4 percent of outstanding debt. Thanks to interest-rate deregulation, issuers make up those losses with the high rates—usually from 18 percent to 24 percent—charged on credit-card debt; borrowers who repay their debts thus pick up the tab for those who don't.

Source: The Wall Street Journal

Adverse selection problems raise interest rates on credit cards.

Limited Consumer Information and the Role of Government

Liability laws and government regulations can limit adverse selection problems. The government can reduce sales of low-quality goods by requiring firms to sell only products that meet minimum quality levels.

Some people argue that guarantees issued by sellers provide better results than government regulations. Some consumers may prefer to pay low prices for low-quality products, rather than buying high-quality products at high prices. Firms selling high-quality products can issue guarantees to help consumers to identify those products, leaving buyers free to choose which levels of quality they want to purchase. Those who favor government regulations and liability laws respond that private guarantees give insufficient protection, because some people mistakenly buy lower-quality products than they want, and some people have limited information about quality differences. Government regulations, they argue, help to protect people from making bad choices.

Some people believe that the government should license

that they view positively from past experience, such as McDonald's, The Limited, or The Gap. Franchises charge fees to allow stores to use their names, and they monitor stores' quality levels to prevent damage to their valuable reputations.[7]

Product Reviews

Consumers can sometimes buy information from product reviewers such as movie and book reviewers, auto magazines, stereo magazines, and publications like *Consumer Reports*. The information provided in these reviews can help to limit adverse selection problems. However, consumers can buy only limited amounts of information in this way, because information is a public good, and people who sell it cannot easily limit information to buyers who pay for it. If someone spends time and money to investigate a product's quality and then sells that information to one group of people, these recipients may provide it to others who have not paid. This possibility limits the incentive to provide information and reduces the amount of product information provided in equilibrium.

Separating Equilibrium

Sometimes innovative price and product schemes can reduce adverse selection problems. Suppose that an insurance company sees two types of customers: high-risk people and low-risk people. The company incurs higher costs to insure high-risk people because they have more accidents as a group. If the company offers only one type of insurance policy, some customers will be high-risk people and others will be low-risk people. If the insurance company cannot identify high-risk customers, it must charge the same price to every customer. Low-risk people then overpay for insurance and high-risk people underpay compared to the prices that each would pay if firms could charge more to high-risk people. As a result, some low-risk people would choose not to buy insurance, raising the average risk of the insurance company's customers.

Suppose, however, that the insurance company offers people a choice of two kinds of policies. One policy provides basic insurance with limited coverage and limits on payments. The other provides more comprehensive coverage that pays a larger amount in case of an accident. If the insurance company were to allow people to buy only one of these policies, low-risk people might be satisfied with the basic policy. High-risk people, however, would prefer the more comprehensive insurance. The insurance company could then identify or separate the high-risk and low-risk people by the choices they

[7]About one-half million franchised stores operate in the United States, generating more than one-third of all U.S. retail sales.

only high-quality sellers when consumers have limited information about product quality. Of course, the government may face the same problems as consumers in obtaining information about product quality. If the government can obtain better information than consumers, perhaps it should simply provide that information to consumers rather than licensing sellers or regulating product quality. The government could either provide information about product quality directly or require sellers to provide the information on product labels.

Licensing brings another disadvantage by restricting the number of sellers and reducing competition. Although consumers may benefit from improvements in quality, they may lose from reduced competition among sellers. Like government regulations on product quality, licensing also prevents consumers who want lower-quality products at lower prices from exercising their choices.

Some argue for licensing or regulation instead of government-provided information or labeling laws, claiming that consumers may not always obtain the information or read the labels, and they may not understand the information they receive. In that case, people might make choices they would later regret, errors that government regulations or licensing might be able to prevent.

made. The firm could set the price for each type of policy based on the knowledge that only low-risk people would buy the limited, basic policy, while everyone who bought the more comprehensive policy would be a high-risk person.

Review Questions

11. Explain adverse selection and present an example of it. Explain how adverse selection differs from moral hazard.

12. Why can't guarantees completely solve adverse selection problems? Explain how moral hazard limits the use of guarantees.

IN THE NEWS

How much should patients be told?

As with most medical procedures, a person considering genetic testing must give "informed consent"—not just agreeing to take the test but understanding just what the test shows and how reliably, the stresses of coping with a positive result, possible treatments, and the stresses that might result from not taking the test.

Explaining all this is demanding. The Johns Hopkins Huntington's program, for example, gives people extensive counseling before even asking for a decision on whether they want to take the test.

"Informed consent is an enormous problem," says Joan Marks, who oversees a Sarah Lawrence College program training graduate students to be genetic counselors. "If a patient doesn't understand what he is being told, how can he give informed consent? And many physicians are just not that great at communicating."

What about Doctors Who Are Ill-Informed?

Some see a strong role for government in this area, to make sure that biotechnology firms don't oversell their tests' abilities and to ensure a high standard of laboratory work.

Source: The Wall Street Journal

Do these information problems create a role for government policy? What role?

Thinking Exercises

13. Discuss this statement: "Adverse selection means that all products will be of the lowest possible quality."

14. Firms that sell medical insurance try to judge the risks of applicants by investigating their current health indicators (such as their blood pressure readings), family medical histories (to look for diseases that might run in a family), and personal habits (such as smoking). The firms charge high prices to insure high-risk applicants. Suppose that the government requires firms to offer everyone who lives in a community the same price, based on the average risks of people in that community. How would this mandate affect the decisions of people to buy medical insurance?

Conclusion

Expectations about the Future

An expected value is an average of numbers weighted by the probabilities (chances) that they will occur. Under certain conditions, the expected value of a number is a rational guess of that number.

Limited Information about Prices

When consumers have limited information about prices and they incur costs of searching for the lowest price, sellers face downward-sloping demand curves. The optimal amount of search occurs when the expected marginal benefit of search (the expected benefit from trying one more store) equals its expected marginal cost.

When some customers have better information than others, a distribution of prices can persist in equilibrium. Some sellers charge higher prices than others and well-informed consumers buy from low-price sellers. High-price stores sell lower quantities than low-price stores, but they earn higher profits on each item they sell; low-price stores earn less profit per item, but they sell larger quantities. A firm can price-discriminate between well-informed buyers and poorly informed buyers by operating several stores that charge different prices or by selling essentially the same product under different brand names at different prices. Poorly informed consumers are more likely than well-informed ones to buy at the high-price stores or to buy the high-price brands.

Firms with limited information about demand can learn about the demand curves they face by trial and error. They may put products on sale at reduced prices to evaluate demand. They may also put goods on sale to price-discriminate by charging high prices to buyers who are willing to pay more to buy goods without waiting for sales.

Risk

Diversification—spreading risks across many different, unrelated investments—can reduce overall risk. Most people are risk averse, so diversification is a valuable investment strategy for most people.

Moral Hazard

When a principal has imperfect information about the actions of an agent, that agent may not have an incentive to act in the best interests of the principal. This creates a problem of moral hazard. To give the agent an incentive to take actions consistent with the principal's interests, a compensation scheme can pay the agent for good results, even those due to good luck. As the agent's pay becomes more sensitive to outcomes prone to the influence of luck, the agent faces an increasingly risky income. Agents who are risk averse (as most people are) dislike this risk, so the principal must pay a higher expected income to attract agents than other, similar positions that pay reliable compensation. An optimal contract between a principal and an agent compromises between the benefit to the agent of a flat salary (low risk) and the incentive to act in the principal's interest that results from higher pay for better outcomes. Such a contract sets the marginal benefit of improved incentives equal to their marginal costs. Principals can often obtain some information about an agent's actions by monitoring, although perfect information is often too costly, or even impossible, to obtain. Moral hazard problems arise in insurance, product guarantees, executive compensation, interest rates on personal loans, and conflicts between bondholders and stockholders.

Adverse Selection

Adverse selection occurs when two people might trade with each other, and one person has important information about product quality that the other person lacks. It results from a lack of relevant information about the motivations of other people. A classic example involves used cars. Buyers do not know whether someone wants to sell a car because it is faulty (a bad car) or for other reasons. When buyers lack information about quality, high-quality products and low-quality products sell for the same price. In this case, sellers offer mainly low-quality products, because those who own high-quality products cannot charge high prices for them. Low-quality products tend to drive high-quality products out of the market under adverse selection. Adverse selection applies to insurance, labor markets, interest rates on credit cards, and other situations. Firms can reduce the problem of adverse selection by offering guarantees. The problem also becomes less severe when buyers and sellers deal repeatedly with each other or when people can buy information about quality.

Key Terms

expected value	diversification	principal	optimal contract
search cost	risk averse	agent	monitoring
distribution of prices	risk neutral	moral hazard	adverse selection

Problems

15. A new business has a one-tenth chance of succeeding and earning a profit with a discounted present value of $500,000. It has a nine-tenths chance of failing and incurring a loss with a discounted present value of $40,000. What is the discounted present value of the expected profit from starting this business? How would this figure change if the $40,000 loss were to change to $60,000?

16. Explain two ways that firms price-discriminate in selling to uninformed consumers. Why does increasing availability of consumer information reduce prices?

17. Why do very low monitoring costs prevent moral hazard problems?

18. Explain how adverse selection applies to:
   (a) Medical and life insurance
   (b) Firms hiring workers
   (c) Credit cards

19. Real-estate agents earn sales commissions when they sell houses. Does this compensation system give a real-estate agent the same incentives as the owners of the house? Explain how agents' incentives might differ, and discuss obstacles to improving their incentives.

20. Describe the incentives of an investment advisor who earns a fraction of the profits of recommended investments. How does your answer depend on whether the advisor has to pay for part of any losses from those investments?

21. Suppose people were to pay doctors every week that they remain well and stop the payments whenever their health deteriorates. How would this compensation scheme affect doctors' incentives? Why aren't doctors paid this way?

22. Explain why the average used car offered for sale provides lower quality than the average used car not offered for sale.

23. Discuss the following quotations and situations.
   (a) "Do you really want to pay $100 for that 'oil well'? If it's such a great deal, why isn't everyone trying to buy it? Why are they so anxious to sell it to you? Maybe you have overestimated its value."
   (b) "Whoever bids the most either knows more than everyone else or has bid too much!"
   (c) "I wouldn't join any club that would have me as a member."
   (d) Mary has applied for jobs at five firms. Each firm has limited information about the quality of her labor, and each makes a different guess. Discuss the following argument:

   The firm with the highest guess of Mary's labor quality probably overestimates it, just as the firm with the lowest guess underestimates it. The firm with the highest guess will offer the highest wage, and she will take that job. That firm will end up overpaying her, because it will have overestimated the quality of her labor. The same argument applies to sports teams that hire players; the team that outbids others for a player is the one that most overestimates the player's ability and then overpays the most. In situations like this, every employee is paid more than he or she is worth.

24. Monte Carlo, where Cooley sells ice cream on the beach, has hot days and normal days. On a hot day, Cooley earns a $1,000 profit. On a normal day, he earns a $200 profit. He always faces a one-half chance that tomorrow will be a hot day.
    (a) What is Cooley's expected profit from selling ice cream tomorrow?
    (b) Suppose that the casino at Monte Carlo starts a new weather gambling game. Every day, the casino sells weather tickets for $100 each. If the next day is normal, the weather ticket pays $200. If the next day is hot, the weather ticket pays zero. What is the expected profit from buying a weather ticket?
    (c) Suppose that Cooley buys one weather ticket every day. What is his net profit on a normal day after selling ice cream and buying a weather ticket? What is his net profit on a hot day?
    (d) Could Cooley eliminate all risk by buying weather tickets? How many tickets would he have to buy each day to eliminate all of his risk? What income would he receive?

Inquiries for Further Thought

25. To what extent can the government increase consumer information about quality or prices? How? Should it do so? What other policies should the government follow to deal with problems of limited consumer information?

26. If information is costly to produce, disseminate, and remember, how much information is it economically efficient to produce? Can an economy produce this information without government regulations? What might the government do?

27. Why can't or don't people buy insurance, from private insurance companies, against becoming unemployed? (The insurance might pay people when they are unemployed, just as fire insurance pays them if their houses burn down.) Should the government provide this kind of insurance? How should the program be run? Should the government require unemployment insurance or make it voluntary? If the government requires participation, should it provide the insurance itself or require that people buy unemployment insurance from private insurance companies? What problems of moral hazard or adverse selection might emerge?

28. Discuss these statements:
    (a) "Economists see an adverse selection problem with health insurance that would be solved if insurance companies could gather more information about people. If insurance companies had more information, however, that might create a new problem. Some people are born with medical problems. If an insurance company knows about the problem, it will charge that person a high price for insurance. If the company does not know about the problem, then people with and without such problems will pay the same price for insurance. Insurance companies should not have this information, so people can insure against such pre-existing conditions."
    (b) "The government should require insurance companies to issue health insurance without a test for HIV (the AIDS virus)."
    (c) "New medical tests can determine whether a person's genes make her likely to contract a disease later in life. The government should outlaw use of these tests, because insurance companies will use them to deny insurance to certain people, creating economic inefficiency as these people become unable to buy insurance."

29. Is more information always better than less information? Would you want information about how long you will live or that you have some disease that might be treatable if you could take prompt action? Information about your birthday gifts next month or about what someone else thinks of you? What factors affect the demand for information? What factors affect its supply?

30. Does competition in the creation and dissemination of information provide the economically efficient amount of information? If not, does competition produce too little or too much information? Explain your answer.

CHAPTER 21

ENVIRONMENTAL ECONOMICS AND PUBLIC GOODS

In this Chapter. . .

Main Points to Understand

- ▶ Negative externalities (and economic inefficiency) occur when people do not bear responsibility for all the costs of their own actions.
- ▶ Side payments can internalize externalities when transactions are sufficiently low. Otherwise economic efficiency depends on the legal assignments of property rights.
- ▶ Unowned resources are overused. Private property rights eliminate overuse and provide incentives to conserve resources for the future.
- ▶ Strong positive externalities from public goods lead to inefficiently low equilibrium production of those goods.

Thinking Skills to Develop

- ▶ Recognize differences between private and social costs.
- ▶ Diagnose fundamental economic causes of environmental (and related) problems.
- ▶ Debate alternative solutions to environmental (and related) problems.

P ollution, destruction of rain forests and the ozone layer, extinction and annihilation of biodiversity—all these problems involve economics. Economics addresses incentives to pollute the air and water, incentives to conserve or destroy natural resources, and incentives to conduct activities that affect ecological systems and could eradicate entire species. What are the appropriate economic solutions? A complete answer cannot be found in this chapter, or anywhere else, but this chapter discusses the fundamental economic analysis of these problems, on which people must someday build an answer.

EXTERNALITIES

Pollution and similar problems occur when people do not bear all the costs of their actions. They force polluted air or water on the rest of society; they overuse or destroy natural resources. Analysis of these problems must begin with a careful distinction between the private costs and social costs of human actions.

Definitions and Examples

Economists distinguish between private and social costs.

> The **private cost** of producing a good is the cost paid by the firm that produces and sells it.

Private costs include all the costs discussed in earlier chapters, including costs of all inputs and implicit costs.

When a factory causes air pollution as it produces a good, the people harmed by that pollution pay a cost—the harm they suffer from the pollution. Elements of that cost might include increased medical bills, shortened life spans, health problems, or simply less pleasant lives than they would enjoy without the pollution. The social cost of producing the good includes *all* costs—private costs paid by the producer *plus* costs forced on other people by pollution.

> The **social cost** of a good is its cost to everyone in the society, including people who do not produce or consume it. The social cost of producing a good equals the private cost of producing it plus the cost to other people.

Private and social costs differ whenever production or use of a good directly affects people who do not buy or sell it. When a factory pollutes the air as it produces goods, the social cost of those goods includes the harm to other people from that pollution. Similarly, the social cost of driving a car includes the cost of gasoline and use of the car *plus* the harm to other people from the pollution created by driving.

> A **negative externality** occurs when the social cost of a good exceeds its private cost.

Economists also distinguish between private and social benefits.

> The **private benefit** of consuming a good is its benefit to the people who buy and consume it. Its **social benefit** equals its total benefit to everyone in the society.

> A **positive externality** occurs when the social benefit of an activity exceeds its private benefit.[1]

When economic activity produces externalities, economists sometimes call this a *market failure*.

Negative externalities harm other people; positive externalities help them. Most of this chapter concentrates on negative externalities. Pollution is not the only example; negative externalities result from poor health practices that increase other people's chances of contracting contagious diseases. Negative externalities arise from someone's installation of a security system on a house or car, because it redirects burglars to other,

Each driver creates negative externalities by polluting the air and by contributing to highway congestion (imposing costs on other drivers).

Activities That Create Externalities
- Driving a car
- Dumping waste into a river, killing fish
- Spreading flu germs by sneezing
- Planting a beautiful garden
- Using dangerous chemicals that might spread through the ecosystem
- Using a product that may damage the ozone layer
- Advancing scientific knowledge

---

[1]An activity can produce both positive and negative externalities if it helps some people and hurts others. For example, some people may like to hear the music from a loud rock concert near their neighborhood, while other people may dislike it. The Eiffel Tower produced both positive and negative externalities in Paris when it was first built—some people liked it and others hated it. Strictly, a negative externality occurs when the social cost minus the social benefit is larger than the private cost minus the private benefit. A positive externality occurs when the social benefit minus the social cost is larger than the private benefit minus the private cost.

Figure 1 | Equilibrium with a Negative Externality

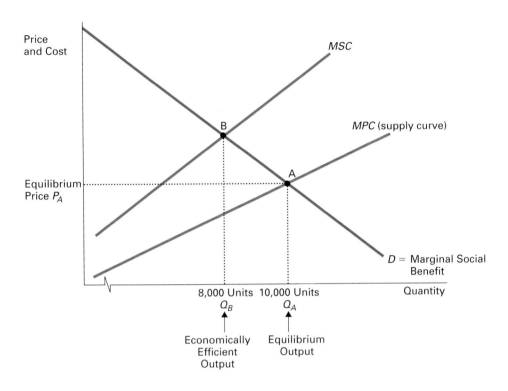

The *MPC* curve shows the marginal private cost of producing the good. The *MSC* curve shows its marginal social cost. The vertical distance between the two curves shows the marginal cost to other people. The demand curve shows the marginal social benefit of the good. Equilibrium occurs at Point A, where the supply and demand curves intersect. The economically efficient quantity of this good equates its marginal social cost and marginal social benefit.

nearby houses or cars. Similarly, increased law enforcement in one area of a city may move crime to other areas. Activities that contribute to global warming, the noise level in a city, or overcrowded beaches, the disappearance of wilderness, and extinction of species create negative externalities.

Equilibrium and Economic Efficiency

Figure 1 shows the basic demand and supply graph with a negative externality. The marginal private cost of producing a good, *MPC*, is the increase in total private cost from producing an additional unit. The marginal social cost of producing a good, *MSC*, is the increase in the total social cost from producing an additional unit. The demand curve shows the marginal social benefit of the good (the benefit to buyers).[2]

The marginal social cost curve lies above the marginal private cost curve. The vertical distance between the *MSC* and *MPC* curves represents the *marginal cost to other people* (such as the harm from pollution) from producing or using this good.

With perfect competition, the marginal private cost curve is the industry supply curve. Therefore, equilibrium with perfect competition occurs at Point A with equilibrium quantity Q_A and equilibrium price P_A. The economically efficient quantity, however, is Q_B. The quantity Q_B is economically efficient because the marginal social cost equals the marginal social benefit at that quantity.[3]

---

[2]Figure 1 applies to *negative* externalities. If this good had a *positive* externality, then the marginal social benefit would exceed the marginal private benefit to buyers.

[3]The situation becomes somewhat more complicated when a producer can alleviate the cost to other people without reducing production, by installing pollution-abatement devices. Still, the main lessons of the analysis continue to apply. The situation also becomes more complicated if the marginal social benefit and the marginal private benefit differ. A later section discusses differences in social and private benefits.

A negative externality creates economic inefficiency, because the equilibrium quantity exceeds the economically efficient quantity.

EXPLANATION

Output of a good is economically efficient if its marginal social benefit equals its marginal social cost, as at Point B in Figure 1. Equilibrium with perfect competition, Point A, is economically inefficient because the marginal social cost of the good exceeds its marginal social benefit. The height of the demand curve shows the good's marginal benefit to society, that is, society's gain from an additional unit of the product. The height of the marginal social cost curve shows what society sacrifices to produce that unit. That sacrifice includes both the private cost of producing the good and the cost to other people, such as the harm they suffer due to pollution from producing or using the good.

Chapter 9 explained that an economically efficient quantity of a product is the one at which its marginal social benefit equals its marginal social cost, as at Point B in Figure 1. At the equilibrium level of output (10,000 units in Figure 1), the marginal social benefit of the good (the height of the demand curve) is less than the marginal social cost of the good, so society could gain by *reducing* production of the good. The logical argument is identical to the logic from Chapter 9 to show that government subsidies cause economic inefficiency.

Deadweight Social Losses from Externalities

Figure 2 shows the deadweight social loss from a negative externality. At the equilibrium, Point A, the quantity is 10,000 units and the price is $100. In equilibrium, the

Figure 2 | Equilibrium and Economic Inefficiency with a Negative Externality

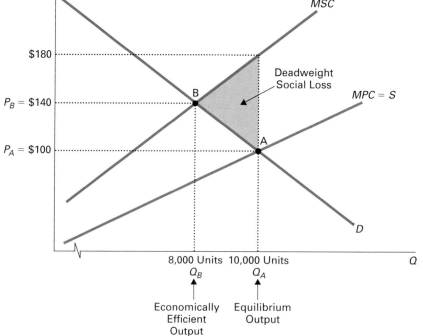

marginal private cost of the good equals this price. The marginal social cost of the good is $180, however, because *other people* pay a marginal cost of $80. The shaded area of the graph shows the deadweight social loss from the externality. The deadweight social loss from a negative externality resembles that from a subsidy.

People would buy the economically efficient quantity of the product if its price were $140, but the equilibrium price is less than that, so people buy too much of the product in equilibrium; they buy more than the economically efficient quantity (Q_B). Notice that this quantity is a positive value, not zero. Applying this analysis to pollution suggests that completely eliminating pollution would *not* achieve economic efficiency because it would require doing without the product entirely.

> The economically efficient level of pollution is not zero.

Instead, the economically efficient level of pollution occurs when the marginal benefit of reducing it equals the marginal cost of reducing it.[4]

For example, people pollute the air when they drive cars. Without any taxes, fees, or restrictions on driving, the equilibrium use of cars would exceed its economically efficient level. On the other hand, if the law completely prohibited polluting the air, no one could drive cars at all. Requiring cars to use emission-reducing equipment and unleaded gasoline raises the private cost of driving, bringing it closer to the social cost. Economic efficiency requires that the marginal *private* cost curve coincide with the marginal *social* cost curve to eliminate any discrepancy between private and social costs. Economic efficiency also requires that reduction of pollution be accomplished in the least-cost manner.[5]

Review Questions

1. Explain the distinction between private costs and social costs.

2. Explain in words why an equilibrium with a negative externality is not economically efficient.

3. Draw the basic demand and supply diagram with a negative externality. Show (a) the marginal private cost of the good, (b) the marginal social cost of the good, (c) the marginal cost to other people from the good, (d) the marginal private benefit and marginal social benefit of the good, (e) the economically efficient quantity of the good, (f) the equilibrium quantity, (g) the equilibrium price, and (h) the deadweight social loss from the externality.

Thinking Exercises

4. Explain how an analyst might determine the economically efficient level of pollution.

5. Why do factories dump chemicals into the air and water and not on people's lawns or in their houses or cars? What does your answer suggest about ways to tackle problems of pollution?

---

[4]Reducing pollution has a cost because people must sacrifice other things they want to achieve this goal. People could reduce air pollution by limiting their driving or doing without CFC-based air conditioners. Air pollution from burning oil and other fossil fuels would also be lower if people used more efficient cars, trucks, light bulbs, and electric generators that recover more useable energy than current models from the same amount of fuel. Increasing energy efficiency in these products would create costs, however, and the people who pay these costs would sacrifice other things of value.

[5]Economic efficiency requires the lowest-cost method to reduce total pollution from *all* sources. This may imply reducing pollution in *some* industries (where firms can cheaply do so) but not others (where reducing pollution would require very expensive methods).

IN THE NEWS

Wide overuse of antibiotic cited in study

By Carol Gentry
Staff Reporter of The Wall Street Journal

BOSTON—Doctors are consistently overprescribing the last-line-of-defense drug against a common, lethal hospital infection, a new study finds.

The study comes amid alarming reports of bacteria resistant to the antibiotic, vancomycin, which are raising concerns that the drug could be losing its effectiveness.

A vancomycin-resistant organism "is the one we're afraid of—the one that's going to take us to a public health disaster," says Dr. Stuart Levy of Tufts University Medical School; founder of the international Alliance for Prudent Use of Antibiotics.

The problem is that the more vancomycin is prescribed, the greater the chance that the deadly microbes will find a way to defeat it. The same fate befell penicillin, once the standard treatment for staph infections.

Source: The Wall Street Journal

Prolonged use of an antibiotic creates a negative externality by increasing the risk that bacteria will develop resistance to it.

INTERNALIZING EXTERNALITIES

A negative externality occurs when people do not pay all the costs of their own actions, that is, when other people bear some of the costs. An externality is *internalized* when people must assume responsibility for all costs of their own actions.

> **Internalizing an externality** means changing private costs (or benefits) so that they equal social costs (or benefits).

Internalizing an externality eliminates the deadweight social loss that it would otherwise cause. For this reason, internalizing an externality achieves economic efficiency. One way to internalize externalities is with *side payments.*

Side Payments

People can make side payments to other people or firms who perform specified actions. (You can think of a side payment as a kind of bribe.) In some cases, side payments can internalize externalities. People who suffer harm from a factory's pollution may offer to pay the polluter to stop. This payment may seem unfair, but it could effectively achieve their goal. This offer of a side payment creates an opportunity cost for the factory, because it sacrifices the side payment if it keeps polluting. The offer of a side payment raises the factory's private opportunity cost of producing. A side payment of the right size would equalize the factory's private costs with its social costs, internalizing the externality.

EXAMPLES

For many years, a small factory has dumped wastes into a lake a few miles away, through a pipe running from the factory to the lake. Twelve families who build cottages around the lake ask the factory to stop dumping wastes there. The factory refuses, so the families offer to pay the factory $600 per year ($50 per family) to stop. The factory stops polluting and uses its $600 annual side payment to pay for waste treatment.

Similar payments occur in many situations. A store in a gang-infested area or in a city with corrupt police may pay protection money to prevent destruction of property. People say to their roommates, "Look, the noise you're making is bothering me while I'm trying to study (or sleep); please quiet down, and I'll return the favor some time."

In 1990, the Unocal Corporation paid people in Los Angeles to turn in old cars that caused pollution. (The company presumably did this as a public-service gesture that would also generate good publicity.) Unocal paid $700 each for the first 7,000 old cars. In the same year, the city of St. Paul, Minnesota, paid a sex-oriented business $1.8 million to leave town and not return.

Willingness to Make and Accept Side Payments

The highest price that a person would be willing to pay to reduce pollution is the value of the harm that the pollution causes that person. If pollution causes someone $500 worth of harm (including health costs, cleaning costs, unpleasantness, and all other types of harm), he would be willing to pay up to $500 to eliminate the pollution. If a person were to place a value of $120 per year on a 10 percent reduction in pollution from a factory, he would be willing to pay up to $120 per year to reduce pollution by 10 percent. The harm that people suffer from additional pollution when the production of a good rises by one unit—the marginal cost to other people—equals the highest side payment that people would be willing to make to prevent that increase in pollution.

Consider a firm that usually produces 1,000 tons of steel per month and that can reduce pollution only by reducing output. Suppose that people offer to pay the firm $10 for each ton it does not produce up to 1,000 tons per month. In this case, the firm could

IN THE NEWS

Vehicle-recycling plan put in first gear

Cash for clunkers?

By G. Chambers Williams III

Metroplex transportation planners want to retire those old cars that belch smoke and fumes as they chug down the highway. And if the planners have their way, the government soon might cough up as much as $1,000 per vehicle to get 1979 and older vehicles off the road. . . .

Source: Fort Worth Star-Telegram

A similar cash-for-clunkers program in Southern California has taken more than 21,000 vehicles off the road since 1994, Claudia Keith, spokeswoman for the South Coast Air Quality Management District in Los Angeles, said yesterday.

That program, however, is funded by companies

that are allowed to buy clunkers and take them off the road in return for being permitted to continue certain levels of pollution from their manufacturing operations—a system that environmental regulators refer to as "credits."

Side payments take old cars off the road, reducing pollution.

collect $2,000 per month in side payments by reducing output to 800 tons per month. The offer of a side payment would raise the marginal private cost by $10 per ton. The firm's marginal private cost *(MPC)* curve would shift upward and coincide with the marginal social cost *(MSC)* curve, as in Figure 3. The firm would then choose its level of output to maximize its profit, taking into account *all* its costs, including the opportunity cost of losing side payments if it were to increase production. The resulting equilibrium level of output would be economically efficient.

Figure 3 | Side Payments to Internalize an Externality

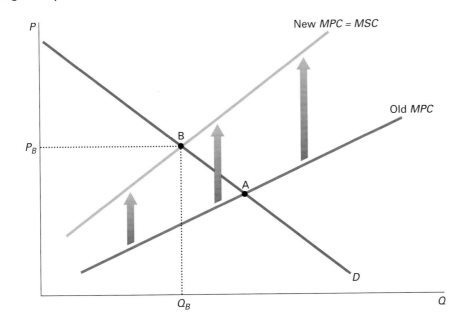

The offer of side payments equal to the marginal cost to other people raises the marginal private cost to equal the marginal social cost. The resulting equilibrium quantity, Q_B, is economically efficient.

Side Payments in Reverse

Side payments can also work in reverse. For example, if laws prohibit pollution, a firm might pay people to allow the pollution, that is, pay them not to bring lawsuits to enforce the law. The largest side payment that the firm would be willing to make would equal the extra profit that it would earn if it could pollute. The smallest side payment that people would accept to allow the pollution would equal the harm that they would suffer from that pollution. These side payments could lead to economic efficiency; instead of producing zero output to create zero pollution, the firm would produce the economically efficient quantity, Q_B.

EXAMPLE

Quantum Corporation builds a new research facility, but its electronic equipment interferes with television reception at a nearby hotel. Without good television reception, the discounted present value of the hotel's profit falls by $20,000. Quantum could eliminate the interference by modifying its equipment at a cost of $50,000. The hotel could eliminate the interference by replacing its televisions at a cost of $12,000.

Economic efficiency requires eliminating the interference at the lowest possible cost, that is, by spending $12,000 to replace the televisions rather than $50,000 to modify Quantum's equipment. This conclusion does not settle the matter of who should pay this $12,000 cost, though. Perhaps the hotel should pay; perhaps Quantum should pay. Replacing the televisions is economically efficient regardless of who pays.

If Quantum Corporation has a legal right to use its equipment despite the problems at the hotel, then the hotel will pay $12,000 to replace the televisions. It has an incentive to spend the money to replace them because its profits will then rise by $20,000, which exceeds the cost of the replacements. If Quantum has no legal right to cause this problem for the hotel, then Quantum maximizes its profit by paying the hotel to replace its televisions rather than spending $50,000 to modify its equipment. Quantum gains as long as it pays the hotel less than $50,000; the hotel gains (and is willing to replace its televisions) as long as it receives at least the cost of the replacements, $12,000. We can expect Quantum Corporation and the hotel to reach a voluntary agreement that helps them both. Quantum pays the hotel some amount of money between $12,000 and $50,000, the hotel replaces its televisions, and Quantum continues to use its research equipment.

This example shows that the same outcome (replacement of the televisions) occurs regardless of whether the law permits Quantum to create the interference. The economically efficient outcome can result from side payments in either direction. The law determines the direction of the side payments, so it affects the *distribution of income* (who pays whom) but not the *allocation of resources* (actual production and modification or replacement of equipment).

Review Questions

6. What does the phrase *internalize an externality* mean?

7. Explain how side payments can internalize an externality.

8. What determines who makes side payments to whom (i.e., the direction of side payments)?

Thinking Exercises

9. Alter the Quantum Corporation example so that Quantum could eliminate the television interference at the hotel by spending only $4,000.

a. What happens if Quantum Corporation has a legal right to use its equipment despite the reception problems it causes at the hotel?

b. What happens if Quantum has no legal right to cause this problem for the hotel?

Problems with Side Payments

In reality, side payments do not internalize all externalities. People harmed by pollution find it impractical to get together, identify polluters, agree on the side payments and on how to share their costs, make the offers, and verify that polluters honor the agreements. Economists say that transactions costs are sometimes too high to allow side payments to solve the problem.

Transactions Costs

> **Transactions costs** are the costs of trading (buying and selling).

Transactions costs include the time and money that a person spends to go to a store or arrange an appointment, obtain information, bargain with people, wait in a line, transport products, and so on.

Side payments can internalize externalities in situations with sufficiently low transactions costs. Low transactions costs give people incentives to arrange side payments that eliminate economic inefficiencies and share the gains from creating economic efficiency. Laws and property rights determine who makes side payments to whom.

High transactions costs make side payments impractical when it is too difficult or costly to bring people together, bargain and agree on side payments, and enforce an agreement. In that case, an equilibrium may be economically inefficient as in Figure 2; high transactions costs prevent side payments that could create efficiency. Laws and property rights (for example, laws limiting the amount of pollution a firm can generate) affect marginal private costs, so they affect equilibrium prices and quantities.

The Coase theorem summarizes these results:[6]

> Coase theorem: With sufficiently low transactions costs, the equilibrium is economically efficient regardless of whether firms have the right to pollute, though the law affects who makes side payments to whom. With high transactions costs, however, laws and property rights affect the equilibrium quantity, perhaps producing an economically inefficient equilibrium.

EXAMPLE: LOW TRANSACTIONS COSTS

Railroad tracks run by a farm, and sparks from passing trains damage crops near the tracks. A farmer loses $50 from the sparks, and the railroad could prevent sparks by spending $100. Economic efficiency calls for the railroad to emit sparks because the social cost of preventing them ($100) exceeds the social benefit from preventing them ($50). The transactions costs are low because the farmer and the railroad can fairly easily discuss the situation; for simplicity, suppose that the costs are zero.

If the farmer has the legal right not to suffer crop damage, the railroad will offer a side payment to the farmer to buy the right to emit sparks. The railroad is willing to pay up to $100 for this right; the farmer is willing to sell the right for any price above $50.

---

[6]This theorem is named for Ronald Coase, a recipient of the Nobel Memorial Prize in Economic Science.

The railroad and farmer will agree on a voluntary trade in which the railroad will pay the farmer some amount between $50 and $100, and its trains will continue to emit sparks.

Suppose, instead, that the railroad has the legal right to emit sparks. The highest price that the farmer will offer the railroad to prevent the damage is $50, but the railroad will not accept this payment because it would have to spend $100 to prevent sparks. The railroad and farmer will not agree on any side payments, and the trains will continue to emit sparks.

This example shows that the result is economically efficient (the railroad emits sparks) regardless of how the law assigns property rights. The law does affect the distribution of income, though. The railroad benefits if it has the legal right to emit sparks, because it does not have to make side payments to the farmer; the farmer benefits if the law does not give the railroad the right to emit sparks, because the railroad will then pay for that right.

EXAMPLE: HIGH TRANSACTIONS COSTS

Suppose that Quantum Corporation's research equipment interferes with television reception in 1,000 nearby houses, each with one television. (The hotel from the earlier example has gone out of business.) Modifying the televisions to prevent the interference would cost $60 per house for a total cost of $60,000. Quantum, however, could modify its equipment for $50,000 to prevent interference. The transactions costs are higher in this example than in the hotel example, because Quantum might incur large costs to negotiate separately with each of 1,000 households. For simplicity, assume that such negotiation would be prohibitively expensive.

Assume also that good television reception is worth more than $60 to each homeowner. Each homeowner would prefer to pay $60, if necessary, to modify her television to avoid suffering from the interference. The economically efficient outcome requires modifications to Quantum's equipment, because this is the cheapest way to stop the interference. This solution is economically efficient because the benefit of good reception exceeds its cost ($50,000).

Suppose that Quantum Corporation has the legal right to use its equipment, even if it causes interference. With sufficiently low transactions costs, people would get together and pay Quantum to modify its equipment. High transactions costs prevent this possibility, though. Instead, Quantum will go on using its equipment, and each homeowner will prefer to spend $60 rather than suffer the interference, so 1,000 homeowners will spend $60 each. This result is economically inefficient because modifying Quantum's equipment would cost less.

If, on the other hand, Quantum has no legal right to interfere with television reception, then it will spend $50,000 to modify its equipment and stop the interference, the economically efficient outcome. This example shows that with high transactions costs, the law affects the economic efficiency of the outcome.

Government Policies

In principle, government policies could improve a situation that is economically inefficienct due to high transactions costs. Government could increase efficiency by imposing taxes or regulations, or by issuing a limited set of sellable rights to pollute. In reality, whether government policies will promote economic efficiency depends on the political forces that determine those policies. (Chapters 22 and 23 discuss influences on government policies.)

Taxes and Regulations

The government can internalize an externality by taxing or fining firms that pollute. The tax or fine raises the private cost of production. If the tax for each additional amount of pollution equals the *marginal cost to other people* of that pollution, then the tax equalizes the private and social costs and internalizes the externality.

Figure 4 | Tax on Pollution

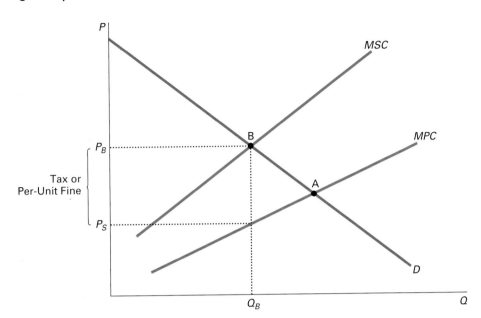

A per-unit tax on production of a good, equal to its marginal cost to other people, $P_B - P_S$, causes the equilibrium quantity to fall to Q_B, the economically efficient level.

Economists distinguish between the *total tax*—the total amount of money that a firm must pay to the government if it pollutes—and the *marginal tax*—the extra amount that the firm must pay if it *increases* its output of pollution. If the marginal tax equals the marginal cost to other people from the pollution, then the tax internalizes the externality. Figure 4 shows the equilibrium at Point B, where buyers pay the price P_B (including tax), sellers receive the price P_S (net of tax), and equilibrium output is Q_B, the economically efficient quantity.

The government can impose the tax in Figure 4 only if it has sufficient information to calculate the marginal cost to other people. This calculation allows it to set the appropriate level of the tax and to change the tax when the marginal cost to other people changes. An alternative to such a tax or fine is a government regulation. The government may require the industry to produce output at the economically efficient level, Q_B. Regulations can achieve this goal, however, only if the government has reliable, up-to-date information about the economically efficient quantity and if it can impose that quantity on firms in an efficient manner.

Taxes can provide better incentives than regulations. For example, suppose that the government wants to limit the total amount of pollution from an industry. If it does so through regulation, a firm that learns of a new method to reduce pollution may have no incentive to adopt that method. However, if the government limits pollution by taxing it, the firm may be able to raise its profits by adopting the new method. Taxes can provide firms with more effective incentives to use new, lower-cost methods of reducing pollution than regulations can provide.[7]

Taxes offer a second advantage over regulations to internalize externalities. They generate revenue for the government, allowing reductions in other taxes. If the government were to receive $100 billion from taxes on pollution, for example, it could reduce income taxes by that amount, lowering the deadweight social losses from both income taxes and pollution.

---

[7] If the government could always learn about a new method at the same time that firms learn about it, the government could change its regulations. If firms sometimes obtain technical information that the government lacks, however, then taxes create stronger incentives to adopt new methods.

IN THE NEWS

Taxes fail to cover drinking's costs, study finds

By Gina Kolata

Taxes on cigarettes cover the costs imposed on society by smoking, but taxes on alcohol do not pay for the costs of drinking, a new study reports.

The findings published in today's issue of the *Journal of the American Medical Association,* reflected the fact that smokers tend to die sooner than nonsmokers, saving society the cost of their pensions and other benefits. This saving would offset the extra costs of smoking, like the cost of days lost from work and extra medical care.

Taxes on alcohol, in contrast, did not reimburse society for the cost of

drinking because the costs of drunken driving were so high, the researchers found.

Although there have been numerous discussions in Congress about raising the taxes on cigarettes and alcohol, legislators have considered raising these taxes to alleviate the budget deficit, not to repay society for the costs of smoking and drinking.

Looking for Cost of Bad Habits

"What we were looking at was economic reasons for not wanting to subsidize bad health habits," said Willard G. Manning of the University of Michigan in Ann Arbor, an author of the study.

The state and federal

taxes on a pack of cigarettes averaged 37 cents. The researchers calculated that the cost to society of smoking was about 15 cents per pack of cigarettes, but if they also included the cost of fires and the health effects of passive smoking on other family members, the cost to society of smoking was 38 cents a pack.

The average taxes on an ounce of alcohol were about 23 cents per ounce. But the researchers found that the cost to society of drinking was about 48 cents per ounce of alcohol consumed.

The researchers calculated that from the age of 20 a smoker lost 137 minutes of life expectancy for

(continued)

Sellable Rights to Pollute

The government can limit the total amount of pollution at the lowest possible cost by issuing sellable rights to pollute, as the U.S. government began doing in 1991. For example, the government may limit total pollution of a certain type to 3 million units per year (measured in tons of particulates, gases, etc.). It issues 300,000 pollution certificates, each of which gives the owner the legal right to emit 10 units of that type of pollution each year. The law prohibits polluting without a certificate. The government sells these pollution certificates to the highest bidders, and allows owners to buy and sell their certificates. Firms with the highest costs of reducing pollution have incentives to pay the highest prices for the certificates; firms with lower costs of reducing pollution have incentives to reduce pollution rather than buy the certificates.

This system has an important economic advantage: It promotes adoption of the lowest-cost method of reducing pollution to the specified level. Suppose that the steel and rubber industries cause the same kind of pollution. If the government taxes both industries, both will respond by reducing pollution. The rubber industry may be able to reduce pollution more cheaply than the steel industry, however. In that case, an economically efficient solution would allow the steel industry to pollute and concentrate pollution-reduction efforts on the rubber industry, where it is cheaper. It is difficult for taxes and regulations to create the efficient outcome in a changing world. However, pollution certificates easily accomplish this goal. Firms in the steel industry outbid firms in the rubber industry for the every pack of cigarettes smoked. They said a heavy drinker lost 20 minutes of life expectancy for every ounce of pure alcohol consumed in excess of 2.3 ounces a day, or approximately five drinks.

The study distinguished between the external costs tobacco and alcohol abusers inflict on others and the internal costs they and their families pay. The researchers said the study, which considered only the external costs, was the first to compare those costs to tax revenues from tobacco and alcohol sales.

Results Were Not Expected

The research was financed by the National Center for Health Services Research and was conducted by Dr. Manning and Ennett B. Keeler of the Rand Corporation, a private research organization in Santa Monica, Calif.

Source: New York Times

Dr. Manning said that the group decided to look at the costs of smoking and drinking because "there's a sense that smokers don't pay their own way." He and his colleagues strongly suspected that when they added up the costs of medical care, time lost from work, and other expenses, they would find that society was subsidizing smokers.

"It is true that smokers use more resources, but they also die early," he said. "They don't get to collect on the Social Security and Medicare services that they have paid for. The net result is that the differences between smokers and non-smokers are not as great as we thought."

With drinking, Dr. Manning said, "drunk driving is the principal cost." Drunken driving each year kills 7,400 people who were not drinking, Dr. Manning said. The researchers calculated a

value to society of $1.6 million for each life lost. "That's the dominant figure in the calculation," he said.

Dr. Manning added that there are other reasons besides economic costs to think of increasing taxes on cigarettes and alcohol. Some studies have found that when cigarettes cost more, teenagers are less likely to start smoking. Other studies have found that when beer costs more, young adults drink less.

The researchers said that there were strong reasons to increase federal taxes on beer and wine, which are taxed at a much lower rate than distilled spirits.

"Higher beer taxes would make particular sense," Dr. Manning said in a statement, "because it's the drug of choice for teens and young adults who drive when they're drunk."

Taxes and the Externalities of Alcohol: What policies would you recommend to the government on the basis of this study?

certificates, giving firms with the lowest-cost methods of reducing pollution the incentives to do so, while allowing pollution by firms that face high costs of reducing it.

Review Questions

10. Explain the Coase theorem.

11. Explain why an equilibrium with externalities and high transactions costs can be economically inefficient.

12. Draw a graph to show how taxes can internalize externalities with high transactions costs.

Thinking Exercise

13. What would be the effect on the amount of chocolate sold and the price of chocolate if manufacturers were made legally liable for increases in dental bills as a

result of chocolate consumption? (Assume that a dentist could easily figure out how much of each patient's bill is due to eating chocolate, and assume that the law does not affect the frequency of tooth brushing or flossing.)

EXTERNALITIES AND PROPERTY RIGHTS

Many externalities occur because no one in particular owns some resources. When no one owns a resource, no one is likely to protect it from misuse. Throughout history, people have destroyed forests without specific owners, used farming methods that destroyed soil on unowned land and then moved on to other land, and polluted unowned lakes and streams. No one owns the ozone layer; no one owns the earth's upper atmosphere.

Some externalities would not occur if all resources were owned and property rights were clearly defined and well-enforced. No one, for example, would permit pollution of a lake on her land without adequate compensation. The requirement that a polluter must compensate the owner raises the polluter's costs so that the private costs of his actions equal the social costs; it eliminates the externality. While property rights in some resources are easy to define and enforce, this process is much harder for other resources, such as the air outside a person's house or the ozone layer.

With low transactions costs, well-enforced property rights in all relevant resources eliminate externalities, because side payments can equate private and social costs. The assignment of property rights (the decision about who owns what resources) affects only the distribution of income. With high transactions costs, however, the assignment of property rights can determine whether the resulting equilibrium is economically efficient or inefficient. The earlier Quantum Corporation example contrasted two assignments of property rights; either Quantum owns the right to create electromagnetic interference, or people own the right to freedom from that interference. The legal assignment of property rights determines whether Quantum will modify its equipment to prevent the radiation (the economically efficient equilibrium in the example) or whether each family will modify its television (the economically inefficient equilibrium).

Private Ownership and Common Resources

> A **property right** is a legal right to determine the use of a scarce resource or to sell the resource to someone else.

> **Private ownership** means that one person (or a small group of people) has a property right to use or sell a resource.

Most people privately own their clothes, cars, stereo equipment, and other personal goods. People also privately own businesses or shares of stock in corporations.

If a resource is not privately owned, it may be unowned or it may legally belong to society as a whole.

> A **common resource** is something that belongs to no one or to society as a whole.

Legally, property rights are matters of degree rather than being all-or-nothing. An owner has the legal right to determine certain uses of his property, but not others. Zoning laws, for example, can prevent a homeowner from establishing a business in his home or painting his house fluorescent orange. Restrictive covenants control uses of some land.

These legal restrictions prevent owners from carrying on certain activities on their property, such as cutting down trees or constructing buildings.[8]

Owners of private property have incentives to protect their properties' values. Logging reduces the value of land by removing valuable trees, so an owner of private land allows logging only if loggers pay the owner an amount that exceeds the fall in the value of the land. Loggers will pay this amount only if someone values the wood highly enough to pay a price that will cover this cost. However, no similar mechanism prevents destruction of unowned rain forests or other valuable common resources. Property rights tend to place decisions in the hands of accountable people who have incentives to protect their property values.

Because everyone has the right to use common resources, they frequently suffer from overuse. No one has a strong incentive to conserve a common resource; each person wants to be a *free rider* (a person who takes advantage of other people's contributions but does not himself contribute) and let other people work to protect the resource. This results in the *tragedy of the commons*.[9]

> The **tragedy of the commons** is the overuse of a common resource (relative to its economically efficient use).

EXAMPLES

The tragedy of the commons is, unfortunately, a common tragedy. Many species of life are endangered because, as common resources, they are overhunted. Rain forests and other valuable lands are overused and destroyed. Crowds often clog roads and highways, public parks, and beaches. Lakes and oceans are overfished. For example, cod, once plentiful off the New England coast, is now scarce; deep-sea fish may be the next victims.

The problem is not new. Throughout history, wilderness has been an overused common resource. Wood was the major source of energy and an important construction material for houses, ships, furniture, tools, and carriages in 15th-century to 18th-century Europe. The forests destroyed in the process of cutting wood were common resources, so no one limited harvesting or replaced trees. As historian Fernad Braudel puts it, "Common land was the enemy of the forest." By the beginning of the 18th century, a much reduced supply of wood was available because of deforestation in the earlier centuries, causing a dramatic increase in the price of wood. In response, people substituted coal as a major source of fuel.[10] The tragedy of the commons also led to overgrazing of medieval pastures, air pollution associated with the industrial revolution, and destruction of prairies through overgrazing in the early United States. In the Middle East, people cut trees for firewood, destroying forests and expanding the desert.

The tragedy of the commons afflicts many common resources, including public parks and beaches, highways, air and water, the Internet, and endangered species. Traffic jams in Los Angeles alone have been estimated to cost $10 billion per year in lost output. If drivers had to pay the social cost of their road use, they would drive at different times to reduce traffic jams at peak hours, switch to less congested roads, car pool more, and

Throughout history, common resources have been overused. One result has been deforestation.

---

[8]Some environmental groups, such as the Nature Conservancy, protect wildlife by buying restrictive covenants on land. For example, a firm may own land with a forest that is home to a rare species of bird. The group may pay the firm for a restrictive covenant that would prevent activities on the land that might harm the birds. Even if the company were to sell the land, the restrictive covenant would remain and prevent the new owner from carrying on the destructive activities.

[9]The term comes from the classic paper by biologist Garrett Hardin, "The Tragedy of the Commons," *Science* 162 (December 13, 1968), p. 1244.

[10]Fernad Braudel, *The Structures of Everyday Life*, vol. 1 of *Civilization and Capitalism, 15th–18th Century* (New York: Harper & Row, 1986), pp. 363–367.

limit driving. For several years, Singapore has charged drivers to use certain roads at peak hours by requiring badges on cars. New technologies will allow electronic monitoring and billing for road use, reducing the costs of collecting tolls.

NUMERICAL EXAMPLE: LAKE NESS

Lake Ness is a common resource with many fish that can be sold for $2 each. One person fishing on Lake Ness can catch 400 fish on an average day. Two people fishing on the lake can expect to catch 350 fish each on an average day. Table 1 shows how the number of fish caught per person depends on the number of people fishing. The opportunity cost of each person's time working at another job is $200 per day, and the other job is exactly as much fun as fishing. The marginal private cost and marginal social cost of fishing both equal $200 per day.

Because Lake Ness is a common resource, it is overused. To see why, think about the private incentives to fish. A person has an incentive to fish if he can expect to catch at least 100 fish per day, earning at least $200. Otherwise, he will take the other job for $200 per day. If fewer than seven people were to fish on the lake, then someone else would have an incentive to join them, until seven people were fishing on the lake. No one would choose to be the eighth person fishing on the lake, however, because that person would earn only $100 from fishing, less than the $200 that the other job would pay. Equilibrium occurs when the marginal private benefit from fishing equals the marginal private cost ($200), so the equilibrium number of people fishing is seven.

It is economically inefficient, however, for seven people to fish on the lake. Each of them would catch 100 fish, so their total catch is 700 fish worth $1,400. If only six people were to fish the lake, each person would catch 150 fish for a total catch of 900

IN THE NEWS

U.N. talks combat threat to fishery

Seek to control overfishing that is said to be wiping out several species

By David E. Pitt
Special to The New York Times

UNITED NATIONS, July 23—In a basement conference room a world away from the klieg-lighted talks upstairs on Bosnia, Iraq, and Haiti, more than 150 diplomats here have been grappling with what most agree is a grave but less photogenic crisis: the threat to the earth's fisheries.

Alarmed by evidence that cod, tuna, mackerel, pollack, and scores of other valuable species are being wiped out by overfishing, the United Nations opened a three-week conference on July 12 to try to lay the groundwork for a global system to manage and re-propagate the fish that are still left.

"Fish are a common property resource," Ross

Reid, Canada's newly installed Minister of Fishing and Oceans, said at the conference last week. "There is a natural tendency for each fishing vessel, and each fishing country, to try to take as much as it can from the common resource. The result is as predictable as it is disastrous."

Source: New York Times

The tragedy of the commons.

Table 1 | Fishing on Lake Ness

Number of People Fishing	Number of Fish Caught per Person	Total	Marginal Private Benefit	Total Value of Fish Caught	Marginal Social Benefit
1	400	(400)	$800	$ 800	$ 800
2	350	(700)	700	1,400	600
3	300	(900)	600	1,800	400
4	250	(1,000)	500	2,000	200
5	200	(1,000)	400	2,000	0
6	150	(900)	300	1,800	–200
7	100	(700)	200	1,400	–400
8	50	(400)	100	800	–600

fish; six people catch more fish overall than seven people. That fact is not the only reason to limit fishing to six rather than seven people, though. If a seventh person fishes, the economy loses the productivity of that person at the other job (paying $200 per day). The economy's loss from the seventh person fishing equals 200 fish worth $400 plus $200 worth of work that the seventh person could have done at the other job. A similar argument shows that the economy suffers a loss if six or five people fish on the lake.

Economic efficiency calls for four people to fish. To see why, think about the marginal social benefit from fishing (the last column in the table). The marginal social benefit is the value of the extra fish that society obtains if one more person fishes. The marginal social benefit of a fourth person fishing, $200, equals the marginal social cost (the value of the person's work at the other job). Adding a fifth person would reduce economic efficiency, because it would not add to the total value of fish caught in the lake and it would reduce the value of output at the other job by $200. Economic efficiency requires that only four people fish on the lake.[11]

When the lake is a common resource, people overfish: The equilibrium amount of fishing exceeds the economically efficient amount. Figure 5 graphs the tragedy of the commons on Lake Ness. The marginal private benefit of fishing is the value of the fish that one additional person would catch. The marginal social benefit of fishing is the value of the increase in the total number of fish that would be caught if one additional person fishes. An externality results, because the marginal social benefit is smaller than the marginal private benefit. For example, suppose four people fish on Lake Ness. Table 1 shows that if a fifth person fishes, she catches 200 fish worth $2 each, so the marginal private benefit of fishing is $400. But the marginal social benefit of fishing (the last column) is *zero*. Figure 5 shows that the equilibrium quantity is seven people, while the economically efficient quantity is four, so there is overfishing.

In this example, each person creates an externality by reducing the number of fish that other people catch. This negative externality reflects the loss due to overfishing, just as negative externalities from pollution reflect the losses from overproduction of products that cause pollution.[12] In many real-life cases, overfishing a lake also causes a fall in the fish population that reduces the number of fish that people will catch in the future. The logical analysis of the tragedy of the commons is similar regardless of whether the externality falls mainly on other people fishing today or people who want to fish in the future. In both cases, the Lake Ness example illustrates that analysis.

Advice to Students
Notice that although the Lake Ness example shows how a common resource can be overused, the example does not show how this overuse affects the *future*. In some real-life cases, the biggest problems created by common resources involved effects on the future. For example, the biggest problem with overfishing is not that it reduces the *current* overall catch of fish, but reduces the future fish population and affects fishing in the future. However, the basic logic of the Lake Ness example also applies when the main harm is in the future.

---

[11]Another economically efficient solution would allow three people to fish in this example. If a fourth person fishes, the value of fish output rises by $200 (from $1,800 to $2,000), but the value of other output in the economy (the goods that the fourth person could have produced at the other job) falls by $200.

[12]Negative externalities cause equilibrium quantities of those goods to exceed the economically efficient levels.

Q_A shows the equilibrium quantity with a common resource. Q_B shows the economically efficient quantity. $Q_A - Q_B$ gives the amount of overuse of the common resource (overfishing in the example).

Figure 5 | Tragedy of the Commons: Overuse of a Common Resource

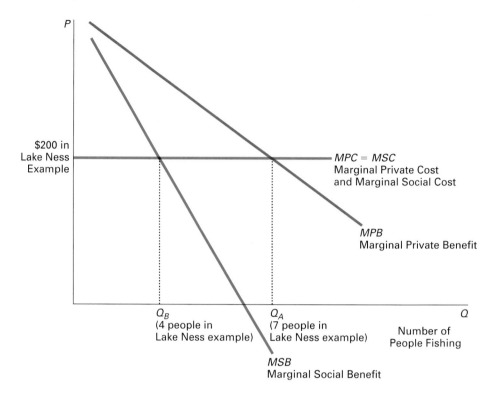

Discussion

The problem of overfishing led the United States to extend its claim on off-shore ocean waters from the traditional 3 miles to 200 miles. Though this action reduced fishing by foreigners, it did not reduce overfishing by Americans. Despite government attempts to limit overfishing through restrictions on nets, catches, and the length of the fishing season, overfishing continues. Private ownership of harvesting rights would provide a solution, as success in Canada, Alaska, and Delaware shows. Some policy analysts have suggested that the government auction off these rights, as it does mineral rights.

Excessive logging in forests, a similar problem, generally occurs on government lands. Sweden has considerable forest land, most of it privately owned, yet Sweden imports wood, because land owners do not want to cut down their trees fast enough to satisfy demand. The situation in Finland was similar until the Finnish government tried to encourage more cutting by taxing land owners on the value of the timber they could have cut (even if they didn't). Governments of third-world countries frequently subsidize harvesting of forests. In the decade of the 1980s alone, for example, the government of Brazil subsidized deforestation of an area in the Amazon basin larger than France. In the decade of the 1990s, deforestation continued on common-resource land around the world in an area twice this size, mostly in poor countries where people burn wood as a main source of energy and property rights do not protect woodlands.

Private Ownership to Internalize Externalities

Private ownership of a resource can internalize externalities and eliminate the tragedy of the commons. Property rights create incentives for owners to care for property by preventing overuse. Private ownership shifts the marginal private benefit curve in Figure 5 downward so that it coincides with the marginal social benefit curve, creating an economically efficient equilibrium.

IN THE NEWS

The new range war has the desert as foe

Hundreds of millions of acres are being lost

By Myra Klockenbrink

Before the era of great cattle drives, bison, bear, and other wildlife were abundant. Giant trees paved the mountain sides and commanded flood plains and grasses grew as high as a horse's belly.

"Now it's hard to find anything growing that would scratch a horse's ankles," said Norbert Riedy

of the Wilderness Society. "The natural grasslands are all but gone."

Chief among the expensive habits that have depleted the land in the West is overgrazing. The cattle industry began with millions of acres of free and unrestricted pasturage. Though much of the damage was done in the great cattle drives of the late

1800s, the number of cattle on the land has reached an all-time high of more than 19 million head in the 11 western states today.

The number of cattle and the long periods they are kept in one area are what lead to overgrazing, and repeated overgrazing undermines tissue reserves until the plant grows weak and dies.

Source: New York Times

Overuse of a common resource.

IN THE NEWS

World's whales worth more alive than dead

International Whaling Commission meeting

By Bronwen Maddox
Environment Correspondent

Whales are worth more alive than dead, UK and US officials will argue when they meet in Mexico tomorrow ahead of the annual meeting of the International Whaling Commission.

Potential revenues from whale watching—an increasingly popular form of tourism—could soon reach several hundred million pounds worldwide.

Source: Financial Times

Can whales be saved from extinction by private property rights?

EXAMPLE: LAKE NESS CONTINUED

Now suppose that someone owns Lake Ness so it is no longer a common resource and the owner can charge people to fish on her lake. She maximizes her profit by allowing only four people (the economically efficient number) to fish on the lake. To see why, think about the fees that she can charge. If she charges a fishing fee of $300 per day, four people will fish, each catching 250 fish and selling them for $500. After paying the $300 fee, each person retains $200. These people earn as much fishing as at the other job ($200 per day), so they are willing to pay the fee and fish. The owner of the lake earns a profit of $1,200 ($300 from each of the four fishermen).

The $1,200 profit is the highest amount that the lake's owner can obtain. If she were to charge a higher fishing fee, fewer people would be willing to fish, reducing her profit. For example, if she were to charge $350, only three people would fish.[13] If she were to reduce her fishing fee, more people may fish, but again her profit would fall. For example, a $200 fee would generate a profit of only $1,000, because five people would pay the fee and fish, each catching 200 fish, selling them for $400, paying the $200 fee, and retaining $200. Private property rights create an incentive for the owner to set fees that induce economically efficient use of that property. In this way, private ownership of a common resource eliminates the tragedy of the commons.

OTHER EXAMPLES

Many private game farms charge fees for hunting. Like the owner of Lake Ness, they have incentives to avoid overhunting. The National Wildlife Sanctuary manages thousands

Advice
To help understand the example, think of the fishing fee as $299 rather than $300, giving four people an incentive to choose fishing over the alternative job.

---

[13]She can also earn a $1,200 profit by charging a $400 fishing fee. In that case, three people pay the fee and fish, another economically efficient solution, as Footnote 11 explained.

SOCIAL AND ECONOMIC ISSUES

Externalities, Actions That Hurt Other People and the Role of Government

Consider the following ("libertarian") idea:

People have the right to do whatever they want with themselves and their own property as long as they do not hurt other people.

Some opponents of this view believe it creates problems, including how to decide what actions hurt other people. Suppose, for example, that some people feel seriously offended because other people use drugs, alcohol, or pornography; listen to songs with lyrics that offend others; act in rude and ill-mannered ways; dress in fashions that offend others; or advocate government policies that other people find abhorrent. Knowledge of these actions may cause people moral anguish, and such psychological feelings may even contribute to physical health problems. If a person is clearly affected badly by these actions, do other people have a right (or should they have a right) to continue these actions, or does the harm to other people limit that right? Should the government limit these behaviors?

How does harm caused by pollution differ from harm caused by knowledge or a belief about what another person is doing? Some people see no difference, and they assert that the government is as justified in using taxes and regulations to reduce use of pornography or songs with offensive lyrics as to reduce air pollution. In this view, both pollution and these other behaviors have negative externalities that justify government actions.

Other people see a difference between the physical harm caused by polluted air and the moral or psychological harm, and even the physical harm, that results from knowing that others engage in offensive behaviors. Supporters of such a distinction cite at least two arguments. First, some distinguish between a physical invasion of property, such as polluting someone's water or air, and other harms (such as moral or psychological distress from private behaviors of other people) that do not result from physical invasions. Pollution is a physical invasion of property, because the polluter causes actual physical particles to go into someone's water or air. (Presumably sound waves count as a physical invasion for this purpose, also.)

At least two problems complicate this view. First, it does not clearly show why anyone should care about this distinction between physical invasion and other harm. Psychological

of acres of wildlife preserves for the benefit of birds. It charges fees for people to watch the birds and for cattle to graze on the land. Private ownership prevented extinction of abalone; when the price of abalone rose far enough, preservation became profitable. Similarly, private turtle farms have helped to prevent extinction of sea turtles. In Scotland, water pollution of streams has not been a serious problem because people there have private property rights to streams.

Indigenous peoples living in the Labrador Peninsula developed private property rights to reduce externalities in the fur trade. In the mid-1600s, before fur trade was an important business, people hunted mainly for food and clothing. Although animals were a common resource, they were plentiful and hunting created only small externalities. In the 1700s, however, increasing demand for fur by European settlers raised its price and increased hunting, raising the externalities from common ownership. The indigenous groups solved this problem by establishing private property rights that gave families ownership of hunting land to the exclusion of other families. Poaching (illegal hunting) of animals continues to be a problem throughout the world.

Saving Resources for Future Generations

Overuse of a common resource frequently leads to its depletion, leaving fewer resources for future generations than would be economically efficient.[14] Private ownership can eliminate this problem and provide owners with incentives to conserve resources for

---

[14] How many resources is it economically efficient to save for future generations? That is a subject of controversy; a brief discussion of this topic appears in Chapter 22 in the section on cost-benefit analysis.

and moral distress can result in as much harm, or more, to a person's well-being as many physical invasions. (One response is that the harm from a physical invasion of property is clearly caused by the invader, while psychological harm may result as much from the beliefs and psychological makeup of the person who claims harm as the person he blames for offensive behavior.) Second, it may be hard to distinguish between a physical invasion and a psychological invasion. If Bob paints his house bright orange, and his neighbor Ray finds the color offensive, is Ray's distress merely a psychological harm rather than a physical invasion? After all, photons of light travel from Bob's house into Ray's eyes; these photons may constitute a physical invasion. The same is true of sound waves from Bob's stereo, or from his mouth when he advocates some action that is morally offensive to Ray.

A second argument for distinguishing physical invasion of property from other cases is that people may have natural rights to their property that are violated by physical invasions such as pollution, but not by their own mental or psychological responses to other people's actions. This argument is subject to many of the same problems as the first argument. In addition, this view must explain the source of these natural rights, and why those rights are violated in one case but not the other.

Even if people were to agree that only a physical invasion of someone's property constitutes an externality, additional problems arise. Anyone who breathes exhales carbon dioxide particles that spread to other people's property. (What if someone has bad breath?) Is this discharge a physical invasion of property? Obviously, the government cannot stop people from exhaling. Should government policy distinguish between a situation in which a person lights a candle or flashlight at night and slightly illuminates her neighbor's property and a situation in which she shines a very bright light on her neighbor's property at night? Perhaps you can just hear your neighbor's television through an open window; is this sound an externality that calls for the same government policy response as if your neighbor were to play loud music at full volume all night, every night, or open an explosives-testing business in his backyard?

In one sense, the idea of externalities is straightforward and this chapter discusses the main issues associated with them. On a deeper level, however, the idea of externalities involves rather complex issues on which people have fundamental disagreements, despite the immediate importance for real-life government policies.

future generations. A person who owns a resource has an incentive to conserve it for the future because conservation raises its value, that is, it raises the price at which the owner can sell the resource to someone who plans to use it in the future. For this reason, people take care of their own property; firms invest in new machinery, equipment, and research and development; and mining companies limit the rates at which they extract minerals from the earth.

Drawbacks of Private Property Rights

Although private property rights can provide a powerful way to internalize externalities, three main drawbacks complicate this kind of solution. First, high costs may prevent a society from defining or enforcing property rights in some resources. For example, it is hard to define and enforce property rights in the air because the wind blows and air moves. How could anyone know whose air is whose? This drawback makes private property rights in some resources nearly impossible. New technologies provide solutions in other cases, however. For example, when grazing lands in the American West became crowded in the mid-19th century, people found it difficult to keep their cattle separate, and enforcement of property rights in cattle became a problem. Fences might have helped, but few people could afford enough wood to build extensive fences. A solution emerged from two new ideas: branding cattle and barbed-wire fencing, which was much cheaper than wood. More recently, innovations allow for "branding" of whales by recording genetic prints and tracking the animals by satellite, creating a possibility for defining and enforcing private property rights in whales. Soon, profitable opportunities may emerge to establish property rights in many endangered species; if those species generate profitable sales for their owners, the establishment of property rights could prevent their extinction.

A second drawback of private property rights reflects the difficulty of charging people to use certain types of property. For example, streets are common resources and become overcrowded, particularly at certain times of day. Each person who drives on a street adds to its congestion, creating a negative externality for other drivers and passengers. If streets were privately owned, owners could charge tolls for their use (as in the Lake Ness example). Streets would become less crowded, reducing driving times and accident rates. However, toll booths are costly to set up and operate.[15] These problems are not easily solvable by government policies. Sometimes the only relevant choice for society may be overuse of a resource or no use at all.

When transactions costs are high, correct assignment of property rights is important for the reasons discussed earlier in the chapter. Recall that Quantum Corporation had property rights to use its equipment despite creating electromagnetic radiation that interfered with reception for nearby televisions. High transactions costs led homeowners to modify their televisions, which was economically inefficient.

Review Questions

14. Explain the tragedy of the commons and why private property rights prevent this problem.

15. What difficulties arise in attempts to prevent the tragedy of the commons with private property rights?

Thinking Exercises

16. (a) Consider the Lake Ness example in the text. Recall that a private owner of the lake earned a $1,200 profit by choosing a $300 fee, which induced economically efficient use of the lake (four people fished). Show that the owner's profits would fall if she changed the fee to $200, or $500, or $600. (In each case, use Table 1 to find the number of people who would pay the fee and fish, and then calculate the owner's profit.)
    (b) Rework the Lake Ness example assuming fish sell for $1 each.

17. Many of the world's rain forests are common resources. If governments were to make the rain forests private property and give property rights to specific people, who would gain and who would lose? Could compensations to the losers allow everyone to gain from creating private property rights in the rain forests?

POSITIVE EXTERNALITIES AND PUBLIC GOODS

Positive externalities generate less attention in political discussions than negative externalities, but they can be quite important. If a scientist discovers an improved medicine to treat a disease, her gains (and her firm's profits) from selling this medicine are private benefits. The gains to people who use the medicine are also private benefits. The social benefits of the new medicine include these private benefits plus gains to other people, perhaps because the scientist's discovery provides new ideas that help other scientists work-

---

[15] New electronic devices to monitor road use can automatically recognize a sticker on a car and mail a bill to its owner, but these devices are also costly.

ing on other problems. Similarly, the private benefit from planting a tree may be its beauty or shade; the social benefit includes the enrichment of the atmosphere from the oxygen that the tree produces. Many economists believe that positive externalities from scientific research and production of knowledge play major roles in long-term economic growth. The development of cities as dynamic centers of business and culture may reflect the effects of positive externalities, and it may also have promoted economic growth. Culture itself is a product of positive externalities from the creation of music, art, and literature. Education and manners create positive externalities that enhance social interactions.

Equilibrium and Economic Efficiency with Positive Externalities

Figure 6 shows the basic graph of equilibrium with a positive externality. The marginal private cost equals the marginal social cost; there is no marginal cost to other people. However, the activity creates a marginal benefit for other people, so its marginal social benefit *(MSB)* exceeds its marginal private benefit *(MPB)*. The marginal private benefit curve is the demand curve; the marginal private cost curve is the supply curve.

If high transactions costs prevent people from making side payments, the equilibrium with perfect competition occurs at Point A, where the demand and supply curves cross, giving the equilibrium quantity Q_A. The economically efficient quantity, however, is Q_B, where the marginal social cost equals the marginal social benefit. The positive externality creates underproduction with an equilibrium quantity less than the economically efficient quantity. Underproduction occurs because people who buy and sell the good ignore its benefits to other people. The area of the shaded triangle shows the deadweight social loss from the underproduction. The figure also shows the producer surplus, consumer surplus, and total gain to other people in equilibrium.

With high transactions costs, the government could raise equilibrium output to the economically efficient level by doing the opposite of what it would do for a negative externality. For example, it could raise economic efficiency by subsidizing production of an activity with positive externalities. Just as a tax can create economic efficiency with

Figure 6 | Positive Externality

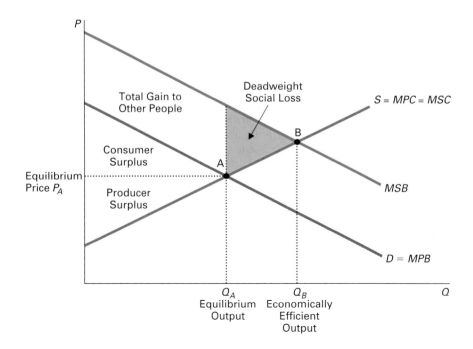

negative externalities, a subsidy can create economic efficiency with positive externalities.[16] With sufficiently low transactions costs, side payments can internalize positive externalities just as they internalize negative externalities, giving an economically efficient equilibrium without subsidies (Point B).

EXAMPLE: SIDE PAYMENTS

Apple growers and beekeepers provide one example of side payments to internalize positive externalities. Apple trees have a positive externality for nearby beekeepers because apple blossoms provide nectar from which bees make honey. Beekeepers sometimes make side payments to apple growers to increase the number of apple trees to the economically efficient level (from Q_A to Q_B in Figure 6). Interestingly, beekeeping also has a positive externality for apple production, because bees pollinate apple blossoms. For this reason, apple growers sometimes make side payments to beekeepers rather than the reverse.

Public Goods

Positive externalities are particularly important for certain types of goods, such as information, television broadcasting, and national defense.

Nonrival Goods

If you eat an apple, one less apple remains for other people. If you watch a television show, however, you do not reduce the number of other people who can watch that show on their own televisions. When a farmer plants wheat on 100 acres of land, that land becomes unavailable for other people's use. But when a scientist or engineer uses technical knowledge to create new insights into biology or new types of computer chips, other people can use that same technical knowledge at the same time.

> A good is **nonrival** if the quantity available for other people does not fall when someone consumes it.

Your use of a nonrival good does not reduce the quantity that other people can consume, either now or later.

EXAMPLES

Knowledge is an important nonrival good. One person's knowledge of science, technical formulas, computer algorithms, product designs, or methods for operating business firms does not reduce the amount of knowledge available to other people. Similarly, songs and music, stories, national defense, television and radio broadcasts, and (to some extent) police protection are nonrival goods.

Nonexcludable Goods

> A good is **nonexcludable** if it is prohibitively costly to provide the good only to people who pay for it (and prevent or exclude other people from obtaining it).

Positive externalities flow in both directions between beekeepers and apple growers. Apple blossoms provide nectar for bees to make honey, and bees pollinate apple blossoms.

---

[16]Governments of many countries subsidize the arts—painting, music, theater, literature, and so on. One rationale for these subsidies asserts that the arts generate positive externalities for society, and the subsidies prevent underproduction of paintings, music, theater, and literature. The subsidies could raise output from Q_A to Q_B in Figure 6. A more likely reason for these subsidies, however, is that they benefit consumers (patrons) of the arts, who comprise the main political constituency for the subsidies.

EXAMPLES

It may be prohibitively costly for a television station, such as a Public Broadcasting Service affiliate, to restrict access to its shows to people who pay or donate money to the station. Unless it scrambles its broadcast signals and sells descrambling services, anyone with a television can watch its show. Its broadcasts are nonexcludable if descrambling is prohibitively costly. National defense is also a nonexcludable good; it is hard to exclude a few houses or isolated individuals from protection against a foreign aggressor.

Problems of Public Goods

> A **public good** is a nonrival and nonexcludable good.

Public goods present a unique economic problem because firms have little incentive to produce them. Few buyers willingly pay for nonexcludable goods, because they can get them free, as long as someone produces them. (Some people do pay for nonexcludable goods, as when people voluntarily contribute to PBS fund-raising drives, but these payments usually fall short of the stations' costs.) A consumer might be willing to pay $100 for a public good if he could get it in no other way, but he might prefer to be a *free rider* and let other people pay for the good. However, if everyone tries to be a free rider (intending to enjoy the benefits of other people's contributions, but not to contribute anything himself), then no one pays for the good, and no firm is willing to produce it. Even if a few people choose to pay, their total payments may not be enough to make it profitable for firms to produce the good, or may make the good available only on a limited scale. For example, a television station may limit its broadcast hours or broadcast only inexpensive shows.

> The **free-rider problem**, the challenge of getting anyone to help pay for a public good when each individual can enjoy it freely if other people buy it, keeps the equilibrium quantity of a public good below its economically efficient level.

In the extreme case, the equilibrium quantity of a public good is zero. No firm is willing to produce the good because no one pays for it; although people may value the good at more than its cost, they all try to be free riders. This equilibrium is economically inefficient. Suppose, for example, that 5,000 people would be willing to pay up to $1 each for a public good that costs $2,000 to produce. Economic efficiency calls for production of the good, because its value to buyers exceeds its cost of production. However, if fewer than 2,000 people resist the chance to be free riders and pay $1 each, no firm will produce the good.

Potential buyers of a public good might try to join together and share the payment for a public good. Even if low transactions costs would allow them to join together, however, many potential buyers would try to be free riders. They would falsely deny that they really wanted the public good or understate their willingness to pay for it, secretly hoping that other people would pay more and give them a free ride. As the number of people in the group increases, so does the free-rider problem.[17]

Private Supply of Public Goods

Firms have devised methods to reduce the free-rider problem enough to allow profitable production of certain public goods. For example, television broadcasts are public goods, but private firms in the United States produce them by combining them with advertising,

---

[17]Economists have devised complex methods to give people incentives to tell the truth about their willingness to pay for goods, but these methods have not yet found widespread use (and for some problems, they are not practical solutions).

so that advertisers, rather than viewers, pay for the broadcasts. This method loses effectiveness as more people videotape shows and fast-forward through commercials. Some advertisers try to avoid this problem by placing commercials within shows or movies and by having characters conspicuously use products. Some cable and satellite broadcasters exclude free riders by scrambling their broadcasts. Computer software firms achieve partial exclusion by providing technical support only to registered users. Some Internet sites use passwords to restrict access to paid subscribers. Increases in the cost of excluding free riders reduces the incentive for firms to develop and produce new products.

Role for Government

The free-rider problem provides a fundamental rationale for government to provide certain public goods. The government may produce a public good, such as national defense, and require people to pay for it through taxes. In a previous example, the government might tax 5,000 people 40 cents each to obtain $2,000 in tax revenue that it could spend to pay for the public good. Government coercion can solve the free-rider problem without the government actually producing the public good itself; the key role of the government is to eliminate free riders. The government could raise the funds for the public good through taxes and then buy it from the private firm that would produce it at the lowest cost.

Government provision of public goods has two main drawbacks. First, the government lacks information about the amount of money that various people are willing to pay for any particular public good. This creates two more problems: The government cannot calculate the economically efficient level of the public good, and it may tax some people more and others less than they are willing to pay for the public good. The counter-argument to this objection states that the government may at least provide a solution closer to the economically efficient level of the public good than the free market would provide. Government provision of a public good has a second main drawback, though, because actual government programs may reflect political pressures to benefit special-interest groups rather than considerations of economic efficiency. As a result, government provision of public goods may solve the *free-rider* problem but create *forced-rider* problems.

Governments help to exclude free riders through patents and copyrights that provide limited-time property rights in ideas, product designs, and artistic creations. Patents increase scientists' incentives to produce new knowledge by giving them temporary property rights that (if enforced) help them to exclude others from using the new ideas. Similarly, copyrights help artists to exclude free riders from their artistic creations such as stories and songs.

Social Responsibility

If one could change human behavior, the problems of externalities could be solved. Education and propaganda may be part of a socializing process influencing people to adopt certain values or behave in certain ways. Clearly, people sometimes behave in ways that reduce externalities; people recycle, practice good manners, and contribute to charities. Experimental evidence suggests that people do not always free ride when given the opportunity; they often cooperate with other people, particularly when they interact with others repeatedly in the same kind of situation. (Interestingly, experimental studies with college students show that economics majors are more likely to try to be free riders than students with other majors. Most economists are not very comfortable with the implications of this result!) Evidence also suggests that persuasion can affect the level of charitable contributions. Whatever the chances for changes in human behavior in the future, however, externalities remain a problem in today's world.

IN THE NEWS

Copied software now common

Although the industry remains hugely profitable and competitive, some experts say the amount of theft reduces the incentives that developers have to create programs. But software creators are trying to fight back.

Last year, the Software Publishers Association, a trade group, conducted 75 raids, sent 561 warning letters, and filed 33 lawsuits against organizations and individuals it suspected of software piracy.

The problem will only get worse, industry executives say, as each new technology makes it easier to copy digital information.

Many in the industry feel that finding a way to protect copyrights is essential for the industry to avoid a crisis.

Source: New York Times

Private firms produce software, despite its public-good features, though the inability to exclude nonpayers may reduce incentives for innovation.

Review Questions

18. Draw a graph of an equilibrium with a positive externality. Show the equilibrium quantity, the economically efficient quantity, and the deadweight social loss.

19. What is a public good, and what special problem does it present?

IN THE NEWS

Equations patented; Some see a danger

By Edmund L. Andrews
Special to The New York
Times

WASHINGTON, Feb. 14—Encouraged by a new attitude in the courts and at the Patent and Trademark Office, universities and corporations are rushing to stake patent claims in a whole new arena of intellectual property: mathematical equations.

The equations, known more technically as *algorithms,* use mathematics to solve such problems as how an airline can most efficiently schedule its planes or how a computer should handle data to operate as fast as possible.

But the growing number of the patents is causing concern among some math-

ematicians that basic research and the free exchange of information could be inhibited.

"We face the real prospect that mathematics will become poorer as mathematicians become richer," said John Barwise, a mathematician and philosopher at Stanford University's Center for the Study of Language and Information. "If you suddenly create barriers so that people are not able to freely use the results of others, you're changing the rules that mathematicians have used for centuries."

Other scientists, university officials, and patent attorneys, however, say the patents are necessary to provide incentives for future research.

Ronald Bracewell, a professor of electrical engineering at Stanford who developed a new way to calculate what is known among mathematicians as a Fast Fourier Transform, said that without patent protection future research would be inhibited.

"By the time you've spent six months writing 10,000 lines of computer code, you know darn well it isn't something nature put there," he said. "The world of industry is demanding protection for what they very well know is proprietary information. Without the protection of patents, the incentive to get into the hard work of development would be lost."

Source: New York Times

To what degree should the government use patents
to encourage the production of knowledge?

Thinking Exercises

20. Well-attended parties are more fun than poorly attended parties. Explain the application of this observation to this chapter.

21. A movie company sued people who made and sold pirated (unauthorized) copies of a movie on videotape. The movie originally cost $100 million to make and appeared at theaters last year. Draw a graph to show the marginal cost and average cost of providing the movie to a person on videotape. Would the courts promote economic efficiency by allowing people to make copies of videotapes (a) for their own use, (b) to lend to their friends, (c) to sell? How is this problem related to natural monopoly?

Conclusion

Externalities

A negative externality occurs when the social costs of an action exceed its private costs. A negative externality raises the equilibrium quantity above the economically

efficient quantity. The economically efficient quantity of pollution is not zero; it occurs when the marginal social benefit of reducing pollution equals the marginal social cost of reducing it.

Internalizing Externalities

Negative externalities occur when people do not pay all of the costs of their own actions so that other people bear some of those costs. Internalizing an externality makes people responsible for all of the costs of their own actions to equate private and social costs. Internalizing an externality moves the economy to an economically efficient equilibrium.

Low transactions costs allow side payments to internalize externalities and achieve an economically efficient equilibrium, regardless of whether the law gives firms the right to pollute. The law determines only who makes side payments to whom.

High transactions costs prevent side payments. In this case, laws and property rights affect the equilibrium quantity, perhaps leading to economic inefficiency. The government may improve economic efficiency with taxes or regulations or by issuing sellable rights to pollute.

Externalities and Property Rights

A property right is a legal right to decide the use of a scarce resource or to sell the resource to someone else. Private ownership of a resource gives one person or a small group of people a property right to use or sell that resource. A common resource is something that belongs to no one or to society as a whole.

Owners of private property have incentives to protect its value. But common resources are overused, because no one has an incentive and legal right to prevent their overuse. Private ownership of a resource can eliminate this *tragedy of the commons* by giving the owner an incentive to care for the resource and prevent its overuse. The main drawbacks to this solution are the costs of establishing and enforcing property rights and the problems of economic inefficiency that high transactions costs may create.

Positive Externalities and Public Goods

A positive externality occurs when the social benefits of an action exceed its private benefits. With a positive externality, the equilibrium quantity is lower than the economically efficient quantity. Underproduction occurs because people who buy and sell a good ignore its benefits to other people. Low transactions costs allow side payments to internalize positive externalities. In situations with high transactions costs, the government may raise equilibrium output to the economically efficient level through subsidies or regulation.

The quantity of a nonrival good available for other people does not fall when someone consumes it. It is prohibitively costly to restrict access to a nonexcludable good to people who pay for it, and exclude other people from obtaining it. A public good is a nonrival and nonexcludable good.

Public goods present problems because firms have little incentive to produce them. Most buyers are unwilling to pay for nonexcludable goods because they can get them free if anyone produces them; most consumers want to be free riders, enjoying the benefits of the goods without contributing to their cost. However, if everyone tries to free ride, no one pays for the good, so no firm produces it. The free-rider problem reduces the equilibrium quantity of a public good below the economically efficient quantity. Firms have devised methods to reduce the free-rider problem enough to make it profitable to produce certain public goods, but a higher cost of excludability creates a smaller incentive for firms to develop and produce new products. The free-rider problem provides a fundamental rationale for government financing of public goods.

Key Terms

private cost	negative externality	property right	nonrival good
social cost	positive externality	private ownership	nonexcludable good
private benefit	internalizing an	common resource	public good
social benefit	externality	tragedy of the commons	free-rider problem
externality	transactions cost		

Problems

22. Governments usually limit the hunting seasons for most animals. What does this policy have to do with common resources?

23. Explain, with a graph, why subsidizing the production of goods that generate positive externalities can eliminate a deadweight social loss and create economic efficiency in situations with high transactions costs.

24. Suppose that the owners of a company have no legal liability to pay hospital bills, sick leave, and similar costs for their employees who are injured on the job. Do the owners have an incentive to invest in equipment and programs that reduce the probability and severity of job-related accidents?

25. A dentist and a writer live next door to each other, and each has her office at home. Screams of pain

from the patients in the dentist's office interfere with the writer's creativity, causing her to write inferior novels and lose $800 per year in income. The dentist would have to spend $600 to install sound-absorbing material on her office walls, and this material would have to be replaced each year. (It is a rowdy dentist's office.) The writer sues the dentist. The court can rule in favor of the author and require the dentist to soundproof her walls, or it can rule in favor of the dentist and dismiss the case. Explain what would happen under each ruling if:

(a) The dentist and the writer are on speaking terms (small transactions costs, ignoring court fees).

(b) They are not speaking to each other under any circumstances (large transactions costs).

26. Turkeys run wild on Turkey Island. The island is not the property of anyone in particular, and people are free to hunt turkeys there and sell them to food wholesalers. Turkey Island is fairly small, though, and several hunters at once tend to scare away the turkeys, reducing the number remaining available to shoot. One hunter alone can shoot 20 turkeys on an average day, and two hunters hunting at once can each get 15 turkeys, on average. If three hunters are on the island at once, each will get 12 turkeys, on average. Each of four hunters will get 9 turkeys on an average day. With more than four hunters, no one gets any turkeys. All of the people who live in the vicinity of Turkey Island (those who might come to the island to hunt) could earn $80 in a day if they were not turkey hunting. (Of course, this $80 reflects the social value of the goods they would produce if they were not hunting turkeys.) If they go turkey hunting, they can sell the turkeys they shoot for $10 each. Assume that turkeys reproduce adequately to eliminate any danger of extinction, and that all of the numbers stay the same over time.

(a) In long-run equilibrium, how many people would hunt turkeys on Turkey Island when anyone could freely do so? Why?

(b) What is the economically efficient number of hunters on the island? Why? Does the island experience overhunting, underhunting, or the economically efficient amount of hunting?

(c) Suppose that the island were owned by someone interested in earning the largest possible profit. What is the maximum price that someone would be willing to pay to hunt turkeys on the island for a day if he were the only hunter allowed? What is the maximum price per day that someone would pay to hunt on the island if one other person were also allowed to hunt? What is the maximum price per day a person would pay if two other hunters were allowed on the island? Three others?

(d) How many hunters would an owner allow to maximize his own profit from owning the island? How much profit would he make? If the island were owned, would overhunting, underhunting, or the economically efficient amount of hunting occur?

27. A geneticist who specializes in recombinant DNA research invents a new bacteria that is harmless and unnoticeable to humans, but obnoxious to insects that feed on farm crops. The bacteria can be easily spread on farmland along with seed. The scientist obtains a patent on this new bacteria and sets up a company to sell it to farmers. The research that led to the discovery cost thousands of dollars, but enough bacteria to protect 1 acre of farmland costs only 3¢ now that the scientist has perfected the technique. The patent prevents anyone but the scientist's company from selling the product.

(a) Draw a graph to illustrate the forces that determine the equilibrium price and quantity sold of the bacteria.

(b) Illustrate on your graph the economically efficient amount of bacteria to be produced and sold, now that it has been developed.

(c) If the government were to force the scientist's company to produce and sell the economically efficient amount of the product (assuming that the government could determine this number exactly), would the company make a profit or suffer a loss?

(d) Does a conflict emerge between the economically efficient use of a product that has already been invented and the economically efficient amount of research on new inventions and discoveries?

28. Suppose that someone builds a house near an airport and later complains about noise from the planes. Does an externality arise in this case? Does the answer depend on whether or not the homeowner was aware of the airport before building the house?

29. Many scientists believe that carbon dioxide emissions will lead to global warming, with average temperatures rising 2 to 9 degrees Farenheit within the next century. Assume that this possibility could be prevented by reducing carbon dioxide emissions. How would an economist determine the economically efficient choice between reducing the emissions (at a cost that the U.S. government calculates to be in excess of $100 billion per year) or spending the resources on irrigation, dikes, and air conditioning to help reduce negative effects on people of global warming?

Inquiries for Further Thought

30. Do you think that social costs or benefits differ from private costs or benefits for the goods or activities on the following list? Explain why in each case. For each externality that you identify, explain what, if anything, you think the government (or someone else) should do about the externality.
    (a) Drug use
    (b) Pornography
    (c) Violence on television or in the movies
    (d) Rock lyrics advocating violence, drugs, sex, or suicide
    (e) Fast driving on a freeway
    (f) Abortions
    (g) Births and world population growth
    (h) Social customs
    (i) Celebrations of holidays
    (j) Good manners and etiquette
    (k) Physically fit, well-dressed, and attractive people
    (l) Well-educated people
    (m) Nearby hazardous waste sites or nuclear reactors
    (n) Someone lights a candle, and the photons of light shine on the house next door.
    (o) Someone turns on a 1,000-watt searchlight, which shines on the house next door.
    (p) Jane plans to marry Peter until Dick comes along, then Jane dumps Peter for Dick.

31. How much economic growth should a country sacrifice to improve the environment? On what basis should this decision be made? Who should make the decision?

32. Does culture have a positive externality? Art? Music? Plays? Sports? Is this a good reason for the government to subsidize any of these activities (such as paying grants to support the arts or constructing new sports facilities)?

33. Do cultural diversity and racial diversity have positive externalities? Discuss them. Does an externality result from the spread of English-language music, television, and movies and American culture in general around the world? (Some countries refer to this as U.S. *cultural imperialism.*)

34. Does trash disposal involve externalities? How would you estimate the benefits of recycling? How would you estimate the costs? Should governments require people to recycle? What alternative policies might governments adopt?

35. When a pregnant woman drinks a significant amount of alcohol or uses a drug that is dangerous to her fetus, does she create an externality? What if the mother's use of some product creates only a chance of a long-term problem to a baby? How big does that chance have to be before an externality arises?

36. Most people would feel guilty after stealing a videotape or almost anything else. Many fewer people seem to feel guilty when they take public goods without paying by copying computer software, music tapes, and movies on video, or by receiving cable television without paying for it. Is this activity stealing? Is it as bad as stealing an ordinary, nonpublic good? Explain why or why not. Why do people feel less guilty about these

crimes than about others? What, if anything, should the government do to enforce property rights in computer software, audio and video materials, and similar products?

37. **(a)** Discuss this statement: "An externality arises every time a child is born. The world must share its limited resources with one more person. It will feed her, clothe her, and educate her at public expense. It will provide her with highways, police protection, and other public services. Each new person imposes a burden on limited resources such as water, clean air, fossil fuels, and even space on the ground. Each person has a negative externality."

 (b) Which would be better, a world with 5 billion people and a $6,000 per-person average annual income, or a world with 3 billion people and a $10,000 per-person average annual income?

 (c) Which would be better, a world with 5 billion people and a $6,000 per-person average annual income, or a world with 3 billion people earning $9,000 per person and 2 billion people earning $1,500 per person? Compare your answer to this question with your answer to Question 37b.

38. The U.S. government bans smoking on all domestic, commercial airline flights; some cities have banned smoking in all restaurants. Are bans of this sort necessary to internalize externalities from second-hand smoke? Are they economically efficient? Are they good public policy?

39. How should the government choose its policies when genuine scientific uncertainty surrounds some possible environmental disaster?

40. In 1965, the Supreme Court decided the case of *Griswold* v. *Connecticut,* striking down a law that made use of contraceptive devices a crime, even for married couples. In a 1971 article in the *Indiana Law Journal* criticizing the court's reasoning, Judge Robert Bork wrote,

> In Griswold a husband and wife assert that they wish to have sexual relations without fear of unwanted children. The law impairs their sexual gratification. . . . The majority finds use of contraceptives immoral. *Knowledge that it takes place* and that the State makes no effort to inhibit it *causes the majority anguish,* impairs their gratifications. Neither case is covered . . . in the Constitution. . . . Why is sexual gratification more worthy than moral gratification? . . . Courts must accept any value the legislature makes unless it clearly runs contrary to a choice made in the framing of the Constitution. (Emphasis added.)

Does the knowledge or belief that other people engage in certain sexual acts of which some people disapprove constitute an externality? If government policies should deal with externalities, is this a rationale to overturn the *Griswold* decision, as Judge Bork favored?

41. In what ways would global warming (a possible effect of carbon dioxide emissions) benefit or harm people? How would you estimate the effects on human health and productivity? Compare your answers with the 1991 study by the U.S. National Academy of Sciences, available through your library.

CHAPTER 22

GOVERNMENT REGULATIONS AND TAXES

In this Chapter. . .

Main Points to Understand

▶ Government regulations are pervasive and controversial, with a wide range of rationale, criticisms, and economic effects.

▶ Political forces affect the regulations that a government actually adopts and the effects of those regulations.

▶ Economists often use cost–benefit analysis to evaluate regulations.

▶ Optimal taxation minimizes the deadweight social loss from collecting a certain amount of revenue for the government.

Thinking Skills to Develop

▶ Debate the appropriateness of government regulations.

▶ Apply cost–benefit analysis.

▶ Recognize political forces determining government regulations.

People face government regulations and taxes every day. You wake up on a mattress with a tag printed with, "Do not remove this tag under penalty of law," and shower in water sold by the local government in a bathtub made to satisfy government-approved specifications.[1] You dress in clothes with labels required by the government, eat breakfast foods made from government-subsidized grains by firms subject to long lists of government regulations. You may take a prescription medicine that has been approved for sale by the government and which you can buy only if a doctor with a government license writes a prescription to be filled by a government-licensed pharmacist. When you leave your house, built to conform to government regulations and purchased from a government-licensed real-estate broker, you drive a government-licensed car with government-required safety and emissions features on a government-owned road. Your driver's license shows your permission from the government to do so. Your workplace must meet government health and safety regulations; your employer spends money to fill out reports required by government regulatory agencies, perhaps after consulting lawyers for advice about these regulations. If you are a manager, you may meet with the personnel department to discuss compliance with government hiring regulations. Your business travel will probably involve taking a government-licensed taxi to a government-owned or government-regulated airport.

---

[1]You can legally remove the tag after you buy the mattress.

Your paycheck shows deductions for income taxes and social security taxes. You may stop on the way home at the government-regulated store, where you pay sales taxes on most of your purchases and buy gasoline for your car at a price that is about one-third taxes. When you return home, you check the mail that the government has delivered, mow your lawn with a government-approved lawn mower, or watch a television program from a network with a government-issued broadcast license or from a government-regulated cable company.

Governments are heavily involved in our lives. They raise money through taxes, buy goods, make direct payments of money (transfer payments such as social security payments and unemployment compensation), produce goods and sell them or provide them free (such as roads, education, and national defense), and regulate many aspects of the economy and the society.[2] Government regulations serve varied purposes: to protect the environment, limit the power of monopolies, guarantee minimum standards of workplace safety, and many others. Critics also cite varied arguments against regulation; often concluding that regulations create economic inefficiencies, reduce competition, and stifle innovation and economic growth.

Taxes and regulations are alike in many ways. Both represent government-imposed limits on private property rights, restricting either the uses of property or the proceeds from some use. Both serve similar goals. Taxes raise revenue for the government, encourage or discourage production or purchases of certain products, and affect the distribution of income. If the government wants to transfer income from one group to another, it may tax one group and give the money to another group, or it may impose minimum-wage laws, rent controls, requirements that firms provide certain benefits for their employees, and so on. If the government wants to discourage consumption of certain goods (such as alcoholic beverages or cigarettes), it may raise taxes on these goods or impose regulations. Government mandates require most firms to provide employees with a type of insurance called *workers' compensation;* evidence shows that this expense operates like a tax on employment, with 85 percent of its costs paid by employees in the form of lower wages than they would earn without the requirement.

Different combinations of taxes can create the same total revenue for the government while producing different effects on economic efficiency. This chapter discusses how a government can choose a combination of taxes to raise revenue or achieve its other goals with the lowest possible deadweight social loss from economic inefficiency.

REGULATION

Proposed new government regulations of the tobacco industry, intended to reduce under-age smoking, were defeated in Congress in 1998 after strong lobbying by the industry.

Some government regulations, like prohibitions on underage drinking and smoking and limits on industrial pollution, limit actions of people or business firms. Others, like mandatory labels on food packages, require certain actions. Although legislation creates some regulations, many result from rulings of regulatory agencies such as the Food and Drug Administration and Environmental Protection Agency.

Purposes of Government Regulations

Because government regulations result from a political process, they tend to serve the interests of groups with political power. Sometimes those interests coincide with broad social interests (such as consumer interests); other times they do not. However, most regulations are at least *ostensibly* intended to serve one of the following purposes:

---

[2]Governments also perform other tasks such as setting rules for publicly owned resources (speed limits and fees at government parks) and dealing with foreign governments.

	Examples
1. Protect the environment by internalizing externalities (in the language of Chapter 21) when high transactions costs prevent other methods	Government regulations limit industrial emissions that would pollute the air, require preparation of environmental impact statements for certain activities, and restrict disposal methods for hazardous waste materials.
2. Reduce economic inefficiencies that may result from monopolies, oligopolies, or imperfect information of consumers	Government regulations control prices charged by cable-television companies, insurance companies, and utilities (electricity, gas, and water suppliers). Regulations also require sellers to provide certain types of information about their products.
3. Increase fairness (by some view of fairness) or redistribute income	Government regulations require firms to provide working conditions that meet certain health and safety standards and to provide certain benefits for their employees. Regulations also help to prevent discrimination against minorities, women, and people with disabilities.
4. Protect people from making bad decisions (by some view of those decisions)	Government regulations require people to use seat belts and to buy cars with air bags. They prevent people from buying certain drugs without prescriptions from licensed physicians or from using unproven or experimental drugs. They also prevent people from buying or selling certain products deemed harmful or immoral by regulators, and from trading with hairdressers, insurance agents, or real-estate brokers who have not obtained licenses.
5. Improve products	U.S. government regulations prevent the use of certain chemicals in food, require cars to meet minimum levels of fuel efficiency, ban all food additives that induce cancer in humans or animals (no matter how large the doses required to do so), require minimum standards for doctors, and require building materials and other products to meet certain standards.
6. Set rules for the use of common resources	Government agencies control use of public parks and speed limits on roads.

Scope of Regulation in the United States

Government regulations have a long history in the United States. The first big, independent U.S. regulatory agency, the Interstate Commerce Commission, was created in 1887. Regulation in the United States grew rapidly after that, increasing dramatically during World War I (when the U.S. government nationalized the railroads and telephone lines, regulated prices, and controlled production and distribution of many goods) and again during the Great Depression of the 1930s and World War II.[3] Over the last several decades, U.S. government regulation has increased in some areas (such as environmental protection) but decreased in others, with active deregulation in the airline, trucking, petroleum and natural gas, and financial services industries. The same mix of increased regulation in certain areas and *deregulation* (a decrease in government regulations) in others has also characterized recent decades in many other countries.

Estimates of the total costs of complying with U.S. federal government regulations vary widely, from about $200 billion to $700 billion per year, or about $800 to $2,700 annually for every person in the country each year, and state and local government regulations add considerably to this total.[4] Table 1 lists some of the (more than 50) U.S. regulatory agencies, and Table 2 gives a few examples of regulations. All regulations generate both costs and benefits. Most economists regard some regulations as reasonable and justified measures for one or more of the reasons listed earlier, while they criticize other regulations for creating economic inefficiencies primarily to benefit certain special-interest groups at the expense of others.

Some government regulations require certain actions, like labels. Others prohibit certain actions, like using unapproved medications.

---

[3]World War I served as a period of training in regulation for many officials in the U.S. government. They put their training to use later in the Great Depression of the 1930s and World War II, when regulation showed another dramatic increase. See Robert Higgs, *Crisis and Leviathan* (Oxford: Oxford University Press, 1987); and Paul Johnson, *Modern Times* (New York: Harper & Row, 1983).

[4]See Thomas D. Hopkins, "Regulatory Costs in Profile," Center for the Study of American Business, Washington University, 1996.

Table 1 | Some U.S. Regulatory Agencies

Interstate Commerce Commission (ICC)	Regulates the operations of railroads, trucks, buses, and water carriers
Consumer Product Safety Commission (CPSC)	Regulates the design, use, and labeling of products to reduce injuries
Food and Drug Administration (FDA)	Regulates manufacturing, sale, and labeling of foods and drugs
Environmental Protection Agency (EPA)	Deals with regulations on pollution and other environmental issues
Occupational Safety and Health Administration (OSHA)	Regulates the health and safety conditions at firms
National Highway Traffic Safety Administration (NHTSA)	Regulates vehicles to reduce traffic accidents
Nuclear Regulatory Commission (NRC)	Regulates nuclear power facilities
Federal Aviation Administration (FAA)	Regulates the airline industry
Federal Communications Commission (FCC)	Controls licenses for television and radio and regulates telephone service
Federal Energy Regulatory Commission	Regulates energy industries
Federal Maritime Commission	Regulates ocean freight traffic
Federal Trade Commission (FTC)	Regulates advertising to prevent deception
Securities and Exchange Commission (SEC)	Regulates stock exchanges and other financial markets
Commodity Futures Trading Commission (CFTC)	Regulates futures markets
National Labor Relations Board (NLRB)	Regulates labor issues and collective bargaining
Equal Employment Opportunity Commission (EEOC)	Investigates and enforces laws against discrimination in employment
Antitrust Division of the Justice Department	Enforces antitrust laws
Federal Reserve System, or Fed	Regulates banks and conducts monetary policy
Federal Deposit Insurance Corporation (FDIC)	Regulates banks and insures bank deposits

Table 2 | Examples of Regulations in the United States

Limits on the number of people who can immigrate from other countries

Ban on all food additives that have been found to induce cancer in humans or animals, no matter how large the doses required to do so (See the 1958 Delaney Amendment to the Food, Drug, and Cosmetics Act.)

Occupational licensure (requirements for people to have government-issued licenses before practicing some professions, such as doctors, real-estate agents, barbers, and so on)

Regulations on toxic waste disposal

Emission standards for automobiles

Fuel-economy requirements for automobiles

Rent controls

Minimum-wage rates

Regulations of public utilities such as electricity, gas, and water suppliers

Regulations of cable-TV providers and prohibitions on new competitors in the industry

Regulation of broadcast television and radio, licensing of stations, and restrictions on commercials

Affirmative action rules on hiring and other antidiscrimination rules

Dumping regulations that penalize foreign companies for selling in the United States at low prices

Health regulations

Safety regulations for homes and public facilities like schools, stores, cars (seat belts, airbags), hotels, and firms; regulations affecting the construction of many consumer products

Zoning regulations that state what kinds of houses or businesses can locate on certain property

Compulsory schooling requirements

Child labor laws that limit the number of hours worked by young people

Building codes that require certain kinds and qualities of materials, certain types of construction, and work by government-licensed workers

Regulations on investments by banks and other financial institutions, on interest rates they can charge, and interest rates they can pay; also, regulations requiring them to hold certain assets

Regulations preventing people from buying drugs without doctors' prescriptions and preventing sales of prescription drugs without clear evidence of their safety and effectiveness

Food regulations outlawing certain additives, restricting the uses of others, and requiring labels with specified information

Required health warnings on products such as cigarettes and alcohol

Mandatory bottle deposits

Regulations on insurance company charges and the types of policies they can offer to customers

Medical regulations

Regulation of day-care centers and old-age homes

State laws complicating or preventing takeovers of firms

Laws against smoking on airlines or requiring restaurants to set aside nonsmoking areas

Laws prohibiting sales of certain products such as drugs, prostitution services, etc.

Laws prohibiting sales of certain goods that are legal to possess such as babies, surrogacy services, human organs, etc.

Laws on possession or registration of guns

Laws requiring people to participate in the social security system

EXAMPLES

Regulations that restrict pollution may be justified as attempts to reduce the economic inefficiencies created by externalities, as discussed in Chapter 21. Speed limits on public roads govern use of common resources in a way that may raise their value. Prohibiting discrimination on the basis of race or sex responds to widely shared notions of fairness. Government-required health warnings and label requirements may be justified as providing a public good—information—that might raise economic efficiency. The actual effect of any specific regulation on economic efficiency, however, depends on its costs as well as its benefits. Some government regulations mainly benefit certain groups at the expense of everyone else. The list includes restrictions on buying goods from foreign sellers, restrictions on the hours that stores are allowed to be open, farm programs that raise consumer prices, and restrictions on entry into various professions or industries (such as regulations requiring licenses for barbers and hair stylists).[5]

Economists use cost–benefit analysis to compare benefits and opportunity costs of a regulation or tax.

> **Cost–benefit analysis** is the process of identifying and comparing the costs and benefits of a regulation, tax, or other policy.

Economists measure the costs and benefits of a regulation or tax by the changes it causes in consumer surplus and producer surplus and the effects on people of related externalities such as pollution.

As Chapter 9 explained, a change in the economy is a Pareto improvement if at least one person gains while no one loses. A change is economically efficient if it would be *possible* for the winners to compensate the losers by enough to make the change a Pareto improvement. Cost–benefit analysis implements these ideas. If a regulation's benefits exceed its costs, then the regulation is economically efficient. Although some people may lose from the regulation, the people who would gain could (in principle) compensate the losers by enough to prevent their losses. Cost–benefit analysis can help to settle the question of which regulations and taxes enhance economic efficiency and which do not.

A regulation or tax may generate intangible costs or benefits, such as a reduction in the chance of accidental death or freedom from airplane noise. In these cases, economists measure the benefits by the amounts of money that people are willing to pay to reduce their chances of death or eliminate noise in their neighborhood.

Uncertain Costs and Benefits

The costs and benefits of a government policy are usually uncertain when the government adopts the policy. Because of this uncertainty, economists compare the expected values of benefits and costs. The expected value of a benefit or cost is an average of

EVALUATING REGULATIONS: COST–BENEFIT ANALYSIS

---

[5]While U.S. stores now face few restrictions on hours of operation, these regulations remain common in other countries. Japan began in the first half of the 1990s to ease regulations that prevented large stores from opening and competing with existing, small stores. In many countries, including Japan and Germany, regulations prevent stores from remaining open after a certain time (such as 5 or 8 P.M.) or from opening on certain days. These regulations help the retailing industry by reducing competition while allowing each firm to reduce costs by limiting its operating hours. The losers are customers, who face limited choices of hours in which to shop.

How should the government evaluate the costs and benefits of regulations on alcohol?

each possible benefit or cost, weighted by the chance that it will occur.[6] For example, if there is a one-half chance that the benefit of a regulation will be $1 million and a one-half chance it will be $2 million, the expected benefit is:

$$(1/2)(\$1 \text{ million}) + (1/2)(\$2 \text{ million}) = \$1.5 \text{ million}$$

Expected costs can be calculated in the same way.

Using Cost-Benefit Analysis: An Example

Raising the tax on alcoholic beverages, or tightening regulations on their use, would reduce consumption of alcohol and reduce deaths from traffic accidents caused by drunk drivers.[7] This reduction is the benefit of the potential tax or regulation. It would have two costs. First, the tax or regulation would hurt responsible drinkers; a tax would raise the price and reduce their consumer surplus, and a regulation might raise the price or limit access. The second cost of a tax or regulation is the loss in producer surplus.

Consider a 30 percent tax on beer. We can measure its costs by estimating the elasticities of demand and supply. The elasticity of demand for beer is about $1/3$.[8] Suppose that supply is perfectly elastic (which is a good approximation to the actual elasticity).[9] Figure 1a shows the cost of the tax, equal to the deadweight social loss it causes, ignoring the externality from alcohol consumption (traffic accidents). The tax would reduce consumer surplus, with consumers losing Areas A and C. The government would gain Area A, so the cost of the tax would be Area C.

How large is this cost? With perfectly elastic supply, the price would rise by the full amount of the 30 percent tax, so the price of 12 ounces of beer would rise from about 70 cents to about 91 cents, as the figure indicates. With an elasticity of demand of $1/3$, the quantity demanded falls by one-third of 30 percent, or 10 percent, roughly

---

[6]See Chapter 20.

[7]A tax would also raise revenue for the government, but this would not benefit society as a whole because consumers would lose the tax money that the government would gain.

[8]Stanley I. Ornstein, "Control of Alcohol through Price Increases," *Journal of Studies on Alcohol* 41 (1980), pp. 807–818.

[9]This discussion follows the analysis in a study by Charles E. Phelps, "Death and Taxes: An Opportunity for Substitution," unpublished paper, University of Rochester, 1987.

Figure 1 | Cost–Benefit Analysis of a 30 Percent Tax on Beer

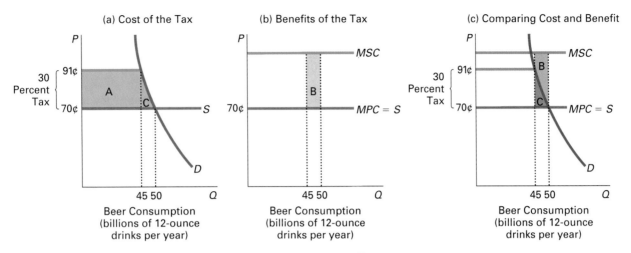

Panel a: Consumers would lose Areas A and C from a 30 percent tax on beer. The government would gain revenue equal to Area A, leaving a cost equal to Area C. This is approximately the area of a triangle: (5 billion)(21¢)/2, or $525 million. *Panel b:* The marginal private cost of beer, *MPC,* is its price, 70¢ before the tax. The marginal social cost of beer, *MSC,* is higher than that amount because of externalities from drunk drivers. Area B shows the value of the benefit of a reduction in highway deaths from drunk drivers due to a fall in the equilibrium quantity of beer from 50 billion to 45 billion drinks per year. Estimates show that Area B is at least $1,752 million per year, and probably closer to $14,600 million per year. *Panel c:* Area C shows the cost of the tax, and the portion of Area B that does not overlap Area C shows its net benefit. In this case, cost–benefit analysis shows that the benefits of the tax would exceed its costs.

from 50 billion to 45 billion 12-ounce drinks per year. The base of Area C in Figure 1a (the cost of the tax) is 5 billion beers per year, and the height of the triangle is 21 cents. The area of the triangle is one-half of the base times the height:

$$(0.5)(5 \text{ billion})(\$0.21) = \$525 \text{ million per year}$$

This equation gives the cost of the tax.[10]

Would the benefit of fewer deaths from traffic accidents outweigh this cost? Figure 1b shows the marginal social cost of alcohol consumption. It lies above the supply curve (the marginal private cost curve) by a distance equal to the marginal cost to other people of the externality (traffic accidents), as discussed in Chapter 21. The benefit of the tax, Area B in the figure, would equal the fall in costs to other people as the equilibrium quantity of beer falls from 50 billion drinks per year to 45 billion. One study has estimated that this change would save 2,920 lives per year by reducing traffic accidents from drunk drivers.[11] About 1,650 of these lives would be the drunk drivers, and about 1,270 would be lives of other people. This analysis does not identify individuals whose lives would be saved, it says only that the chance of death would fall for many people.

To measure the dollar value of this reduction in the chance of death, economists ask, "How much are people willing to pay to reduce the chance of death in some situation by 1 percent?" To answer this question, they look at how much money people are willing to pay for safety equipment at home or in their cars, how much of a wage increase

---

[10]A similar procedure would give an estimate of the cost of a regulation. A more thorough analysis would also include the costs of paying the tax (including recordkeeping by sellers) and collecting the tax (an increase in government bureaucracy), or the costs of operating the government regulatory agency.

[11]Phelps, "Death and Taxes." For several reasons, this estimate probably understates the benefit.

people demand to accept work at risky jobs, and so on. Estimates of this price vary from around $0.60 to $8.00 for a one-millionth reduction in the chance of death. This evaluation implies that people are willing to pay somewhere between $600,000 and $8 million to save one life, probably around $5 million. Even with the lowest figure, $600,000, a savings of 2,920 lives per year would be worth:

$$(2,920)(\$600,000) = \$1,752 \text{ million per year}$$

This benefit is more than three times the estimated cost of the tax.[12] The $5 million per-life estimate would give a benefit from the tax of $14,600 million per year, 28 times its estimated cost. The benefit of the tax would actually exceed this estimate, because the tax would also reduce injuries and property damage from accidents. Clearly, cost–benefit analysis indicates that the benefits to society of this tax would outweigh its costs.

Figure 1c graphs these costs and benefits of the tax together. Area C shows the cost of the tax, while the portion of Area B that does not overlap Area C shows its net benefit. As Chapter 21 explained, the economically efficient quantity of beer is the quantity at which the marginal social benefit (the height of the demand curve) equals the marginal social cost (the height of the *MSC* curve). At the quantity of 45 billion drinks per year, Figure 1c shows that the marginal social benefit is slightly below the marginal social cost. Therefore, economic efficiency would require a slightly higher tax than in the example.

Criticisms of Cost–Benefit Analysis

Some critics of cost–benefit analysis claim that costs are less important than benefits, that money expenditures are less important than human values. The beer-tax example shows the error in this criticism. That example measures costs, including human lives, and benefits, including human enjoyment. More generally, this criticism shows a misunderstanding of costs. Costs are foregone values. If a regulation costs $100 million, people lose $100 million that they might have spent for food, housing, health care, or computer games.

Similarly, some people criticize cost–benefit analysis because, they say, human lives and certain other values cannot be measured in money terms. This criticism ignores the fact that people do sometimes choose to accept increased chances of death or injury in return for money. For example, they buy relatively small, cheap cars that are, on average, less safe in accidents than large, expensive cars. They spend money on curtains rather than smoke detectors; they take riskier jobs for higher pay. These choices allow economists to measure the amount of money that people are willing to accept in return for an increased chance of death. In this sense, reducing the chance of death does have a money value.

A third, more substantial criticism charges that cost–benefit analysis ignores people's rights and the distribution of costs and benefits. Cost–benefit analysis finds the total benefits and costs of a regulation, but the people who pay the costs and those who gain the benefits may differ.[13] If the benefits of a regulation exceed its costs, then the regulation raises economic efficiency but is not necessarily a Pareto improvement (see Chapter 9). The winners could compensate the losers, but in reality no compensation usually

---

[12] The benefit calculation assumes that the analysis should value the lives of the drinkers. One might argue that drinkers know they increase their chances of death and choose to drink anyway, so they must think the benefits they get from drinking outweigh the rise in their chances of death. In that case, perhaps the analysis should count only the deaths of the 1,270 non-drinking people whose lives would be saved each year by the tax. This change would give a benefit between (1,270)($600,000), or $762 million and (1,270)($5 million), or $6,350 million per year; even the lowest figure exceeds the cost of the tax.

[13] In the beer-tax example, responsible drinkers might lose more than they gain, while people who do not drink beer (and do not pay the beer tax) gain from the fall in traffic accidents without paying any of the cost.

occurs. For this reason, cost–benefit analysis cannot determine whether a tax or regulation would be a good policy choice. An action that increases economic efficiency may subject some people to unfair treatment or violate their rights.

Proper application of cost–benefit analysis requires consideration of the costs and benefits of various alternative solutions to a problem, leading to a choice of the solution with the greatest net benefit. For example, one alternative to an increase in the tax on beer would be an increase in the penalty for drunk driving. This solution would refrain from penalizing people who consume beer but do not drive drunk. A cost–benefit analysis of this solution would have to consider the costs of catching drunk drivers, prosecuting them, and punishing them (including the costs of enforcing punishments such as suspended licenses, so that such people would not drive without valid licenses). The analysis would also have to estimate the size of the incentive effects of punishment. (How much less drunk driving would an increase in the penalty induce?) If the incentive effects are large, then the costs of prosecuting and punishing drunk drivers are small because few people would commit the offense; if the incentive effects are small, the cost may become an important consideration.

Future Costs and Benefits

A regulation or tax may generate benefits now and costs in the future, or vice versa. In such a situation, economists compare the discounted present values of the costs and benefits.

EXAMPLE

Suppose that consumers are willing to pay $20 billion this year to build a giant, virtual-reality amusement park. The park would permanently destroy a beautiful forest that people value at $2 billion per year, every year. The discounted present value of the benefit from the project is $20 billion; the discounted present value of the project cost is the discounted present value of $2 billion per year, every year, forever:

$$\frac{2}{1+i} + \frac{2}{(1+i)^2} + \frac{2}{(1+i)^3} + \frac{2}{(1+i)^4} + \frac{2}{(1+i)^5} + \ldots$$

This cost is measured in billions of dollars, where i is the interest rate (measured so that 0.05 means a 5 percent per year interest rate). Because the sum goes on forever, this formula can be simplified to:

$$\frac{2}{i}$$

If the interest rate is 10 percent per year, the discounted present value of the cost equals ($2 billion)/(0.10), or $20 billion. If the interest rate is 5 percent per year, the discounted present value of the cost equals $40 billion, while if the interest rate is 12½ percent per year, the discounted present value of the costs is $16 billion. The benefits of the virtual-reality park exceed its costs if the interest rate is higher than 10 percent per year and fall short of its costs at a lower interest rate.

Another Criticism of Cost–Benefit Analysis

Another criticism of cost–benefit analysis involves the use of discounted present values when some people affected by a policy are not yet born. According to this criticism, discounted present values improperly give less weight to costs and benefits to future generations than to people currently alive. This happens because discounted present values divide future benefits or costs by an interest rate. For example, with an interest rate of 10 percent per year, cost–benefit analysis using discounted present values would suggest adopting a regulation that would prevent the death of one infant today even if that regulation would cause the deaths of 100 infants 50 years from now. Some critics advocate calculating discounted present values differently so that effects on future generations carry greater weight; they propose reducing the interest rate for intergenerational calculations.

Choosing among Alternative Policies with Cost–Benefit Analysis

Studies of U.S. government regulations intended to reduce chances of accidental death show that the cost of regulation, per life saved, ranges from $150,000 to $110 billion per life. Overall, the government tends to adopt the most cost-effective regulations, with the lowest cost per life saved resulting from regulations on motor vehicles—the collapsible steering column requirement, the passive restraint (seat belt or airbag) rule, the fuel system rule, and a regulation on side-door strength. Overall, evidence suggests that health regulations cost much more per life saved than safety regulations. For example, regulations intended to prevent cancer cost much more per life saved than safety regulations, on average. Many proposed regulations cost more than $5 million per life saved, so with an estimated value of saving a life of about $5 million (based on the average prices people are actually willing to pay to avoid risks), the benefits of those regulations would not be worth their costs.

A Harvard School of Public Health study explored 587 government regulations and health-care practices intended to save lives. The researchers concluded that medical care tends to save lives at a much lower cost than regulations on workplace safety or environmental conditions. In particular, the study found some enormous costs of alleviating very minor cancer risks. For example, each year of life saved by a heart transplant costs, on average, $104,000, but each year of life saved by preventing factories from releasing carcinogens costs over $2.5 million. The study also concluded that the U.S. government could prevent 60,000 deaths per year by reallocating the roughly $20 billion per year it spends on about 200 major life-saving programs according to the results of cost–benefit analysis. Similarly, cost–benefit analysis of health-care spending could save about $31 billion per year without increasing the death rate. Childhood immunizations, drug and alcohol treatment programs, and prenatal health care are among the lowest-cost methods of saving lives, while the most expensive are government regulations on chloroform (a carcinogen) at pulp mills, which cost nearly $100 billion for each year of life saved.

EXAMPLES

The government proposed a regulation to require infants traveling in airplanes to sit in approved infant safety seats. Previously, parents had been allowed to carry small infants on their laps on airplanes. Everyone agrees that infant seats would help to save lives of infants in airline accidents. The cost may appear to be limited to the extra money that parents would pay for additional airline seats for infants. However, because the regulation would raise the cost of airline travel for families with infants, it would make them more likely to drive rather than fly on vacations. But the death rate in passenger cars is about 22 deaths per billion passenger miles, about 70 times larger than the death rate for airline travel (about 0.3 deaths per billion passenger miles). If enough people were to switch from flying to driving because of the regulation, the death rate could rise rather than fall.[14] Perhaps because of this calculation, the regulation has not been adopted.

[14]Estimates of the substitution between flying and driving show that enough people would probably switch to cars to cause a rise in the death rate. Because the death rate is about 70 times larger in cars, even a small substitution to driving could raise the overall death rate.

Government regulations called CAFE standards (for *corporate average fuel economy*) are intended to help the environment by reducing gasoline use. CAFE standards require every auto manufacturer to achieve a certain minimum level of fuel efficiency measured in miles per gallon averaged over all of the cars it produces. The company can produce some cars with low fuel efficiency ratings as long as it produces others with high ratings. Critics of CAFE standards argue that these regulations cause thousands of deaths in auto accidents, because they force manufacturers to produce more small, fuel-efficient cars that expose passengers to more danger than larger models do. Studies indicate that CAFE standards have reduced the average weight of an automobile by about 500 pounds, which translates into about 3,000 deaths and 15,000 injuries every year. Supporters of CAFE standards argue that auto manufacturers should be forced to meet the fuel-efficiency requirements with alternative technologies rather than lower average car sizes and that, when firms reduce car sizes, they should be required to add other safety features. Critics respond that these additional regulations would raise car prices and that, even after adding other safety features to cars, the safety costs of CAFE standards exceed the benefits of increased fuel efficiency.

Review Questions

1. List six government regulatory agencies and the activities they oversee. List ten government regulations, and state their intended purposes.

2. Explain cost–benefit analysis and the main criticisms of it.

3. Explain how economists measure the value of saving lives as amounts of money.

Thinking Exercises

4. Suppose that the government were to require all colleges to find or provide jobs for their graduates and that the jobs must pay at least three-quarters of the average wages for new graduates in those occupations. What costs and benefits would this regulation generate?

5. How would you calculate the costs and benefits of reducing the maximum speed on highways to 40 miles per hour? Raising it to 80 miles per hour?

PROBLEMS WITH REGULATION

While some regulations are intended to save lives, protect the environment, reduce inefficiencies, and so on, other government regulations seem mainly to benefit special-interest groups. For many years, U.S. government regulations prevented both fare reductions by existing airlines and entry into the industry by new airlines. Regulations also kept prices of interstate trucking services high by preventing any existing firm from reducing its price or any new firm from entering the industry. Government regulations have also prevented firms from reducing the prices of many other goods, such as natural gas.

Following deregulation of the airline industry nearly two decades ago, the average price per mile flown (adjusted for inflation) has fallen, the number of flights has increased, the number of passengers flying has increased, and the number of towns served by more than one airline has increased. Deregulation has saved consumers several billion dollars per year; the average fare per passenger mile (adjusted for inflation) fell roughly by half, despite increased monopoly power of certain airlines at hub cities such as Chicago, Pittsburgh, and Atlanta. Despite increased air traffic, the death rate did not increase. Deregulation in the trucking industry also reduced prices and has saved consumers about $50 billion per year.

Critics of government regulations contend that their actual effects frequently differ from their intended effects. There are three main views of regulation.

> The **public-interest view of regulation** asserts that regulations serve the public interest.

According to the public-interest view, politicians do what most voters want in order to win reelection; these officials establish and operate regulations to serve the majority of voters.

> The **special-interest view of regulation** asserts that government regulations respond to the demands of certain interest groups.

According to this view, special-interest groups have enough political power to convince the government to create and operate regulations for their benefit, even if the regulations reduce economic efficiency and harm most people.

> The **capture view of regulation** asserts that regulatory agencies originally established to serve the general public interest end up serving the special interests of the industries they were intended to regulate.

According to this view, regulations help industries to maximize their producer surplus at the expense of other groups. Members of an industry or occupation with enough political power to influence the government will try to control entry into that industry or occupation. Under this influence, many government regulations benefit the special interests of firms in the regulated industries at the expense of consumers.

Diffuse and Concentrated Interests

Proponents of the special-interest and capture views of regulation argue that concentrated interests exert more political power than equal-sized diffuse interests.

> A **concentrated interest** is a benefit limited to a small group of people or firms; a **diffuse interest** is a benefit spread across many people.

For example, 200 million people might gain 10¢ each if the government were to abolish some regulation. While the gain might total $20 million, each individual would receive only a small benefit. As a result, the potential beneficiaries have little incentive to learn about or study the regulation, or to pressure the government to abolish it. The $20 million cost of the regulation is too diffuse, spread among too many people, to motivate them to exert strong political pressure to abolish it. On the other hand, the regulation may provide benefits concentrated among a few recipients. If five firms gain $1 million each from the regulation, then each one has an incentive to spend time and money to support it politically. As a result, the government may adopt the regulation even though its total costs ($20 million) exceed its total benefits ($5 million).

Similarly, the government may *not* regulate or tax an industry if the regulation or tax imposes concentrated costs and provides more diffuse benefits. For example, the cost–benefit analysis earlier in this chapter suggested that the benefits of an increase in the tax on beer would exceed the costs. The costs tend to be more concentrated than the potential benefits, however, because the regulation would harm a relatively small number

IN THE NEWS

Higher-cost gasoline

Clean air is not cheap, as many motorists will soon discover. On Jan. 1, gas stations serving 30 percent of the national market will start selling a cleaner burning fuel that costs 3 cents to 8 cents more per gallon than conventional gasoline.

Motorists in the affected area—the Northeast and mid-Atlantic states, and parts of the Midwest, Texas, and California—will have no choice but to buy it. But as they learn more about the new, reformulated gasoline, they may well wonder why drivers, as opposed to other polluters, must pay so much of the bill for cleaning up urban smog.

Motorists, however, are responsible for less than one-third of overall emissions in major cities; factories, refineries, and power plants, along with other mobile sources such as trucks and buses, are bigger polluters. So why were drivers stuck with most of the bill for keeping the air clean? The American Automobile Association, the drivers' lobby, says the reasons have more to do with politics than with science or economics. AAA suggests, plausibly enough, that local and state officials decided to spread the costs widely among the driving public rather than concentrate them in specific, politically influential industries.

Source: Journal of Commerce

Concentrated interests usually have more political power than diffuse interests have.

of firms that produce and sell the product. These firms can organize opposition on behalf of themselves and their customers. Even if a regulation is originally designed to help consumers, the concentrated interests of producers may soon capture the regulatory agency, changing regulations and their enforcement for the benefit of producers. The airline and trucking industry regulations mentioned earlier are examples.

Why would regulators allow their agencies to be captured by these interest groups? Critics believe that many people who work in regulatory agencies intend to promote the public interest, but they also care about their own careers and families. A person who works as a regulator learns about the regulated industry, acquiring knowledge and skills with particular value to its employers. A regulator who leaves government service can often become a valuable employee or consultant within the same industry. Bureaucrats have incentives not to jeopardize these opportunities by alienating the firms in the industries they regulate; instead, their incentives may lead them to formulate and enforce regulations in ways that benefit the industries.

More generally, any understanding of government regulations requires an understanding of regulators' incentives. The important question then focuses on where those interests lie, and what political and institutional forces affect regulators' incentives. Evidence suggests, for example, that regulators lose more from clearly visible mistakes, such as allowing sales of harmful products, than from less visible mistakes, such as keeping potentially valuable products off the market. The incentives to avoid clearly visible mistakes may lead regulators to restrict innovation and risk-taking below economically efficient levels. Critics of regulation suggest that this better-safe-than-sorry incentive is particularly important in food and drug regulations, resulting in overregulation that keeps useful medicines off the market because of excessive concern with safety.[15]

---

[15] In his book *Breaking the Vicious Circle* (Cambridge, Mass.: Harvard University Press, 1994), Stephen Breyer, now a justice on the U.S. Supreme Court, argues that government regulators do not face the proper incentives to implement reasonable procedures for calculating the costs and benefits of government regulations.

Slippery-Slope Hypothesis

Does one regulation lead to another? Does any amount or type of censorship threaten freedom of speech for everyone? Do a few steps in the wrong direction lead people down a slippery slope to a place they do not intend to go? This slippery-slope argument has many applications. Political conservatives often make the slippery-slope argument when they discuss government regulation of the economy; they argue against a regulation partly because it creates a slippery slope leading to other bad policies. Political liberals often make the slippery-slope argument when they discuss freedom of speech; they argue against any restriction on freedom of speech because it creates a slippery slope leading to

threats against all speech. Libertarians often make slippery-slope arguments in both cases.

In *The Road to Serfdom* (Chicago: University of Chicago Press, 1944), economist Friedrich Hayek, who later won a Nobel Memorial Prize in Economic Science, argued that increased regulation of the economy eventually leads to complete government control. Hayek argued that increased government involvement sets into motion a process that, through political pressures, tends to create other government regulations. For example, the U.S. government sets a minimum price for milk above the equilibrium price and buys all the milk required to keep the price at this level. This commitment has created political pressures to reduce government spending on the program by paying farmers not to produce milk, to slaughter cows, and to get out of the dairy business. It also has led the government to limit the amount of milk that

Rent Seeking

The mere possibility that the government will help producers through its regulations gives those producers an incentive to spend resources trying to obtain beneficial regulations. Rent seeking, or competition for favors from the government, occurs when these producers spend time, money, and other resources seeking regulations that benefit themselves. Rent seeking is economically inefficient because it consumes resources to fight over how to divide the economy's wealth rather than to create new wealth.

Thinking Exercises

6. Discuss this statement:

> Opium and morphine are certainly dangerous, habit-forming drugs. But once the principle is admitted that it is the duty of the government to protect the individual against his own foolishness, no serious objections can be made against further encroachments. A good case can be made out in favor of prohibition of alcohol and nicotine. And why limit the government's benevolent providence to the protection of the individual's body only? Is not the harm a man can inflict on his mind and soul even more dangerous than bodily evils? Why not prevent him from reading bad books and seeing bad plays, from looking at bad paintings and statues, and from hearing bad music? The mischief done by bad ideologies, surely, is much more pernicious, both for the individual and for the whole society, than that done by narcotic drugs. If one abolishes man's freedom to determine his own consumption, one takes away all freedoms.[16]

7. Does one regulation lead to another? Does one restriction on free speech lead to another?

---

[16]Ludwig von Mises, *Human Action* (New Haven, Conn.: Yale University Press, 1949).

Americans can import from countries with lower milk prices. Programs like this raise the prices of milk and milk products, in turn creating political pressures to help poor people buy milk products. Governments then create programs to redistribute income through the tax system, and so on.

One argument against the slippery-slope hypothesis notes that the United States and many other countries have practiced some degree of government regulation for a long time and it has not yet led to complete government control. Similarly, government agencies in the United States have long exerted some control over free speech and engaged in various kinds of censorship, but these restrictions have not yet led to complete control over speech. Of course, *yet* may be a key word here, though complete government control does not appear to be a near-term threat in the United States. Nevertheless, the size of government in the United States has expanded over time more rapidly than the U.S. economy, so this argument against the slippery-slope hypothesis may be inconclusive.

Another argument against the slippery-slope hypothesis postulates an equilibrium amount of regulation, so that some regulations do not necessarily lead to others. While some special-interest groups have enough power to create government regulations that help them, they cannot get everything they want from those regulations, nor can all special-interest groups obtain the regulations they desire. (Just because some people can get away with robbing you doesn't mean that everyone can.) An equilibrium amount of regulation may emerge from the balance of political powers. Changes in political forces may raise the equilibrium amount of regulation, but that increase in regulation does not automatically lead to further increases. The same argument may apply to restrictions on free speech.

Regulations and Their Alternatives

The effects of regulations, and alternatives suggested by policy analysts, differ from case to case depending on the details of the regulations and the situations. This section considers a few examples.

Occupational Licensure

Governments license people to work as doctors, lawyers, real-estate agents, hair stylists, and so on. Occupational licensure reduces competition by creating a barrier to entry. The main argument for occupational licensure is that it guarantees a minimum level of quality in the licensed occupation. The main economic arguments against occupational licensure state that it raises prices to consumers by restricting competition; also, it creates economic inefficiencies by preventing people from choosing low-quality goods or services at low prices, if they so desire.

Proponents of licensure argue that licenses provide people with information about quality; opponents argue that the government could provide that information directly to consumers.[17] As an alternative, it could license high-quality suppliers, but allow other people to enter professions without licenses, as governments do in some occupations such as plumbing.[18] Proponents of licensure argue that the license requirements prevent people from making mistakes; a person might not realize she is seeing a low-quality doctor, for example. Opponents of occupational licensure argue that this limitation prevents people who want to buy lower-quality services and pay lower prices from doing so. They also argue that licensure does not protect people from mistakes about quality, it only shifts the possibility of mistakes to the licensure process. Further, they claim, the cost of licensure in reduced competition and increased prices is not worth the benefits from preventing mistakes.

---

[17]Do consumers need government licenses to convey this information to them? *Consumers Reports* magazine regularly rates products; Underwriter's Laboratory (UL) sets standards for electrical equipment; *Motor Trend, Audio,* and other magazines regularly rate specialty products such as automobiles and hi-fi equipment; newspapers, magazines, and television carry reviews of books and movies. Could similar arrangements work for doctors, lawyers, barbers, and so on?

[18]The government would still enforce laws on fraud, so an unlicensed person could not legally claim to hold a license.

IN THE NEWS

How children's safety can be put in jeopardy by day-care personnel

Human tragedy
Ashley Snead, 10 months old, died in the home
of sitter with child-abuse record
The crusade for regulations

By Cathy Trost
Staff Reporter of The Wall
Street Journal

The quality of care ranges from "absolutely excellent

to absolutely awful," says Yale University child-care expert Edward Zigler. "You knock on one door and it may be wonderful.

You knock on another door and your kid may be dead that night."

Should a 'mother down the block' be regulated as day-care provider?

By Cathy Trost
Staff Reporter of The Wall
Street Journal

Many providers of child care go unregulated under a hodgepodge of state laws, while a controversial proposal to impose federal child-care standards recently met defeat.

Children's advocacy groups intend to press their case in the next Congress. Marian Wright Edelman, president of the Children's Defense Fund, says she questions the judgment of a nation that has "no qualms" about licensing hairdressers,

restaurants, and plumbers but not the people who care for children.

Standards are no guarantee of safety, says DeAnn Lineberry, an official of Virginia's Department of Social Services. But she says regulated care is still "much less risky" because it gives child-care providers rules to follow and gives parents more resources to deal with problems.

Others, however, argue that burdensome regulation would force many day-care providers out of business, while the survivors would

have to increase their prices beyond the reach of many parents. Moreover, says Robert Rector, policy analyst for the conservative Heritage Foundation, unlicensed child-care "is far from being the onerous type of dangerous cesspool facility." He adds, "It's one mother down the block who has a preschooler of her own, and is taking care of one other preschooler. . . . All the scientific evidence we have," shows that informal, unlicensed day-care is as safe as regulated care.

Source: The Wall Street Journal

Should the government license child-care services? Try to argue both sides.

Television and Radio Broadcasting

The government licenses television and radio broadcasters and assigns them frequencies at which they can legally broadcast. This policy gives the government greater control over the broadcast media than over printed media, such as newspapers and magazines. Occasionally, the government has exercised this control in controversial ways. Some argue in favor of regulation of broadcasting, because only a limited number of broadcast frequencies can carry radio and television signals. However, scarcity of a resource does not imply that unregulated market forces create economic inefficiencies; land, food, and original Picasso paintings are also scarce resources. If people had private property rights in broadcast frequencies, so that someone owned the right to a particular frequency

I N   T H E   N E W S

Anti-acne drug faulted in birth defects

By Gina Kolata

Government officials estimate that the popular anti-acne drug Accutane has caused hundreds, perhaps more than 1,000, babies to be born with severe birth defects in the past six years.

Officials say they are seriously considering removing the drug from the market or asking the maker to severely limit its distribution.

Despite clear warnings that the drug can cause devastating and sometimes fatal deformities if taken by pregnant women, experts estimate that thousands of women have taken Accutane in their pregnancies.

Although Dr. Oakley suggests that it might be best to remove the drug from the market, some dermatologists disagree.

'Extremely Important Drug'

Dr. Robert Stern, a dermatologist at the Harvard Medical School, agreed that the situation "is a serious problem," but he said Accutane is the only treatment available for many patients with disfiguring acne.

"Accutane is an extremely important drug," he said. "There are thousands—perhaps tens of thousands of patients a year—for whom this drug really changes their lives. There is no alternative that is anywhere near as effective." He stressed that severe acne, left uncontrolled, "scars patients both physically and psychologically."

Source: New York Times

Safety regulations cannot always prevent damage from dangerous products.

band in a particular region, then free markets could operate for broadcasts just as they operate for land and other goods.[19] In fact, the government has created private property rights in certain other frequency bands (those associated with cellular phone and paging technologies).

Food and Drug Regulations

Current U.S. regulations require sellers to prove that foods are safe for human consumption and that drugs are both safe and effective. Critics of drug regulations complain that clinical trials to prove effectiveness cause long delays in bringing valuable new drugs to the market.

One alternative calls for abolishing all regulations intended to ensure health by preventing sales of certain foods and drugs; instead, say critics, let people buy and sell what they want. The government would still enforce laws against fraud; if a producer were to make false claims that a drug was safe, consumers or their heirs could sue the producer for damages and compensation. Limitations on liability of producers create one problem with this method of guaranteeing safety, since a court can force a producer to pay only limited amounts or it may declare bankruptcy. One possible solution to this problem would be to change the laws on limited liability and make producers fully liable (completely responsible for the results of their own actions) in certain cases.

Another alternative to current regulations would be for the government to provide information about food and drug products but not prohibit their sale or purchase. The government might require producers to distribute information (on labels or in pamphlets packaged with products). Still another alternative would require proof of safety, but not

---

[19] The government could sell property rights in broadcast frequencies through an auction, as it has done with other parts of the electromagnetic spectrum. One argument against this move is that rich people might buy up all of the broadcast frequencies. However, rich people do not buy all units of other goods in the economy. (Of course, rich people own most of the luxury yachts and private mansions; do you think that ownership of television and radio broadcasting frequencies would be different?)

proof of effectiveness. This change would reduce the length of time before a producer could sell a drug, and people would be free to buy any safe medicine. People would benefit from this reform if a drug turned out to be effective. If a drug turned out to be ineffective, some people would have wasted their money. Critics of this idea argue that ineffective drugs may encourage false hopes in people with serious diseases. They also argue that people might take ineffective medications rather than seeking more promising professional help.

Private Supply or Government Supply?

An extreme case of regulation and taxation occurs when the government makes *all* the decisions of a firm and takes all its profits—that is, when it *owns* the firm. Governments provide many goods and services that private firms could (and sometimes do) provide, such as collecting garbage, operating airports, delivering mail, running schools, and selling unemployment insurance. Private garbage-collection firms, airports, and schools also perform these services. Private postal companies operated until the government shut them

IN THE NEWS

Public Services

Like never before, the U.S. is unleashing the turbulent forces of the market: competition and choice, prices and profits.

Profit-making companies are invading areas once thought the exclusive preserve of government. Roughly one in 20 federal inmates is now in a for-profit prison, and more than one in eight community hospital beds is in an investor-owned hospital. Deregulation is shaking up once drowsy industries like electric utilities, prompting a frantic scramble for dominance. Skilled people in endeavors from singing to software find that, like baseball's free agents, they can command once-unimaginable salaries if they exploit the market.

The changes are found in unlikely places. In the land of the freeway, a privately owned stretch of Route 91 in Southern Cali-

fornia charges a 60-cent toll at night and $3.20 at rush hour to discourage peak-hour travel. In Kansas, the state hires private contractors to find homes for foster children, paying a fixed per-child fee to provide an incentive for prompt placement. Even the government is learning to play the game: The Federal Aviation Administration took bids to operate its payroll computers. Interestingly, the Department of Agriculture beat IBM and two other companies.

At the other end of the spectrum, some government functions still are widely seen as unsuitable for privatization. No one is proposing to privatize the criminal courts (though a significant number of business disputes are handled outside the public court system) or to hire private companies to sail aircraft carriers.

But in between using private janitorial services and hiring Wackenhut to run the Marines Corps are a host of activities where relying more on market forces raises vexing questions and emotional debate. Should the government continue to ban the sale of human organs for transplant? (Nobel laureate Gary Becker and a few other economists say no.) Should the government proceed with a plan to sell its uranium-enrichment operations, even though the organization has been assigned the delicate task of buying uranium from Russia? (President Clinton says yes, though his former economic adviser Joseph Stiglitz says "absolutely not!")

And, most controversial, is making a profit by serving the poor a terrible notion that smacks of a Dickens novel, or is it a welcome move towards efficiency?

Source: The Wall Street Journal

What are the proper roles of government and free markets?

down, and several private firms deliver overnight letters and packages. Private firms sell many kinds of insurance; presumably, they could also sell unemployment insurance. (As New York governor, Franklin Roosevelt signed a state law prohibiting private insurance companies from selling unemployment insurance.)

When a government provides goods and services, the political process determines quantities supplied, quality levels, prices, and methods of production. Sometimes a low quantity supplied or low quality level induces private firms to enter the industry and provide supplementary goods and services. For example, some people and businesses hire private police and security guards to protect themselves or their property; these services substitute for government-provided, public police services. Some firms resolve legal disputes through private courts and arbitrators; they sign contracts that specify arbitrators to handle any disputes that later arise.[20] Even private prisons and jails operate in the United States.

As an alternative to supplying a good itself or allowing private firms to supply it, government can finance private production. For example, governments of some communities pay for garbage collection out of tax revenues without actually operating those services; instead, they hire private companies to collect garbage. This system gives firms incentives to provide goods at low prices (assuming that governments want to buy from the lowest-cost suppliers), but it requires everyone to pay for the service through taxes. Some analysts have suggested similar schemes for other goods and services. For example, the government could use tax revenues to pay for education without actually operating schools by hiring private firms to operate schools. It could also provide people with education vouchers that the recipients could exchange for education services at the schools of their choice or any government-approved schools.

Controversies surround many proposals for privately supplying products currently supplied mainly by governments, including schools, prisons, fire fighting, and health-care services. The main argument for private supply is that private firms can provide higher-quality products or services at lower prices than the government. The main argument against private supply is that government supply can ensure uniform quality standards. Other arguments on both sides vary case by case.

Review Questions

8. Explain the public-interest view, special-interest view, and capture view of regulation.

9. Explain diffuse and concentrated interests and how the difference between them may affect government regulations.

10. Discuss arguments for and against occupational licensure (licensing requirements to work in certain occupations).

11. Discuss arguments for and against current U.S. food and drug regulations.

Thinking Exercises

12. What are the effects of regulations that require restaurants to provide no-smoking sections? How do these regulations affect prices at the restaurants, profits in the restaurant industry, lines at restaurants, and so on? Without these regulations, would a restaurant have an incentive to offer a no-smoking section to customers who wanted it? Why or why not? (Note that no-smoking sections became common at about the same time that laws began to require them.) Who gains and who loses from these regulations?

---

[20] You may be familiar with examples of arbitration from professional sports.

13. Some people who make textile products work in factories, and others work in their homes. The union in the textile industry wants the government to prohibit work at home, as it did for about four decades in the middle of the century. They argue that work at home can violate workplace fire and safety regulations, maximum-hours laws, child labor laws, and other regulations. The industry says that allowing work at home gives workers flexibility, and that the union wants to restrict competition from people who work at home in order to raise wages. Who would gain and who would lose from a regulation banning textile work in the home?

TAXES

Taxes, like regulations, serve several purposes. Governments impose taxes to fund their programs, redistribute wealth, and achieve other social goals like discouraging or encouraging activities such as smoking, driving, polluting the air, buying imported goods, saving money, or spending money. Most taxes create economic inefficiencies. As a result, different combinations of taxes can provide the same revenue to the government while creating different amounts of economic inefficiency and exerting different effects on the government's goals.

How can the government choose a combination of taxes that best meets its objectives? This section begins with a discussion of how a government can choose a combination of taxes to raise a certain amount of revenue with the lowest possible cost in economic inefficiency.

Reducing Deadweight Social Losses from Taxes

Chapter 9 explained that taxes create economic inefficiency; the deadweight social loss from a tax consists of the gains from trades that it prevents. A tax on a good reduces the quantity traded, because some people choose not to trade because of the tax; the economy loses the consumer and producer surplus that these foregone trades would have created. The size of the deadweight social loss depends on the elasticities of supply and demand. Chapter 9 showed that a tax causes *no* deadweight social loss with perfectly inelastic demand or perfectly inelastic supply. As elasticity of supply and demand increases, the deadweight social loss from a tax also increases. By placing high tax rates on goods with low elasticities of demand and supply, and low tax rates on goods with high elasticities, the government can reduce the deadweight social loss from taxes and achieve optimal taxation.

> **Optimal taxation** minimizes the total deadweight social loss from taxes while raising a certain amount of revenue for the government.

The example in Table 3 shows the main idea. Suppose that the government wants to raise $4,000 in tax revenue. It could generate this income in many ways. It could tax labor income at 20 percent and collect $4,000 with a deadweight social loss of $800, or it could tax investment income at 40 percent and raise $4,000 with a deadweight social loss of $1,600. However, the government can do even better by combining the taxes. If it taxes labor income at 10 percent and investment income at 20 percent, it raises $2,000 from each tax, for a total of $4,000, with a total deadweight social loss of only $600 ($200 from the tax on labor income and $400 from the tax on investment income). Even better, it could tax labor income at 15 percent and investment income at 10 percent to raise $4,000 with a total deadweight social loss of only $550 ($450 from the tax on labor income and $100 from the tax on investment income). These proportions indicate the optimal tax rates when the government wants to raise $4,000 in revenue. Other optimal tax rates would raise other levels of revenue.

Table 3 | Example of Optimal Taxation

Tax on Labor Income			Tax on Investment Income		
TAX RATE	TAX REVENUE	DEADWEIGHT SOCIAL LOSS	TAX RATE	TAX REVENUE	DEADWEIGHT SOCIAL LOSS
5%	$1,000	$ 50	5%	$ 500	$ 25
10	2,000	200	10	1,000	100
15	3,000	450	15	1,500	225
20	4,000	800	20	2,000	400
25	5,000	1,250	25	2,500	625
30	6,000	1,800	30	3,000	900
35	7,000	2,450	35	3,500	1,225
40	8,000	3,200	40	4,000	1,600

This logic implies that the government can minimize the economic inefficiency from its taxes by taxing only goods with perfectly inelastic demands or supplies, if it can identify any such goods and if taxes on these goods alone would raise sufficient revenue. Some people have argued that the perfectly inelastic supply of land ensures that taxes on it would not create economic inefficiency. However, real-life taxes on land are partly taxes on improvements to the land (such as buildings, care for soil or plant life, cultivation, and so on), and improvements do not show perfectly inelastic supply. Another suggestion is a head tax in which everyone pays a fixed amount of money. This tax on live people targets a quantity with close to perfectly inelastic supply (although a head tax would affect the number of births).

Criticisms

While taxes on goods with perfectly inelastic demands or supplies would be the most economically efficient way for the government to collect a certain amount of revenue, many people criticize their fairness. Most people believe that the government should choose tax rates partly on the basis of fairness or equity. Therefore, the government may choose to sacrifice economic efficiency to increase fairness or equity. Great Britain replaced property taxes with a head tax (called a *poll tax*) in 1988; despite some rebates for poor people, the public viewed the head tax as unfair and it was soon repealed.

To see the tradeoff between economic efficiency and fairness, suppose again that the government wants to raise $4,000 in revenue from the taxes in Table 3. It could minimize economic inefficiency by choosing a 15 percent tax on labor income and a 10 percent tax on investment income for a deadweight social loss of $550. Some people may regard these taxes as unfair, however; they may want higher taxes on investment income and lower taxes on labor income. This view of fairness may lead the government to tax labor income at 10 percent and investment income at 20 percent, despite the higher deadweight social loss, $600. Obviously, the conclusions about whom to tax depend on one's ideas of equity and fairness. People may disagree on principles of equity; economic analysis alone cannot settle these issues.

Of course, actual government tax policies may be guided more by the political power of various groups than by actual considerations of either economic efficiency or fairness. If investors' political power were strong enough, for example, the government might choose to tax labor income at a 20 percent rate and not tax investment income at all, raising the total deadweight social loss to $800.

Economists distinguish between two dimensions of fairness in taxes: horizontal equity and vertical equity. Horizontal equity is the principle that calls for equal treatment of people with the same characteristics. Applied to taxes, it says that people in equal conditions should pay equal taxes. According to this principle, for example, men and women should not pay different taxes solely due to their gender difference. Vertical equity is the principle that calls for unequal treatment of people in unequal conditions, suggesting, for example, that taxes should be based partly on ability to pay.

Taxes in the United States

Table 4 shows total U.S. federal income taxes and self-employment taxes (which are the social security taxes paid by a self-employed person) for various income levels in 1997.

> A person's **average tax rate** equals her tax obligation divided by her income.

> A person's **marginal tax rate** equals the increase in taxes she would pay if her income were to increase, expressed as a percentage of that increase in income.

The relationship between marginal and average tax rates resembles that between marginal and average costs. Your average tax rate rises when your marginal tax rate exceeds your average, and it falls when your marginal tax rate is less than your average.

Taxes often apply only to part of a person's income. For example, people can deduct certain charitable contributions and other expenses from their incomes. *Taxable income* refers to the part of income that the government considers when it sets tax payments (income minus allowed deductions).

Table 4 shows that a single, self-employed person paid $7,483 in federal and self-employment taxes in 1997 if she earned $30,000 and took the standard deduction on her tax return. Her average tax rate, therefore, was 25 percent, and her marginal tax rate was 28 percent—if she had earned another $100, she would have paid an extra $28 in federal taxes.

The U.S. government began collecting federal income tax in 1913 with a maximum tax rate on personal income of 7 percent that applied only to the richest 2 percent of

Table 4 | U.S. Federal Income Taxes and Self-Employment Taxes for a Single, Self-Employed Person, 1997

Gross Income	Total Tax[a]
$ 10,000	$ 1,867 (28%, 19%)
20,000	4,675 (28, 23)
30,000	7,483 (28, 25)
40,000	11,354 (41, 28)
50,000	15,371 (39, 31)
60,000	19,388 (39, 32)
80,000	26,413 (34, 33)
100,000	33,071 (32, 33)
150,000	51,074 (40, 34)
250,000	89,923 (38, 36)
500,000	193,900 (42, 39)
1,000,000	402,640 (42, 40)

Note: Figures in parentheses are marginal and average tax rates (marginal rate, average rate).
[a]The tax figures assume that the taxpayer takes one exemption and the standard deduction.

people in the country.[21] The top rate was raised to 15 percent in 1916 and to 77 percent during World War I, after which it fell to 25 percent. This rate increased again to 55 percent in 1931 (during the Great Depression) and to 77 percent during World War II. By the early 1960s, the highest federal income tax rate was 91 percent. The government again reduced it, this time to 70 percent, then to 50 percent in 1982, and to 33 percent in 1987, before raising it again.

Graduated Tax Rates

If everyone were to pay the same percentage of taxable income in taxes, people with high incomes would pay more than people with low incomes. A flat-rate tax system requires the same percentage for everyone. However, most countries, including the United States, set graduated income tax rates that rise with income, so people with higher incomes than others pay higher percentages of their incomes as taxes.

Some people have proposed replacing the graduated tax rates with a modified flat-rate system. One such proposal would place a 20 percent tax on all income above a certain level, such as $20,000 earned per person, with no deductions allowed. Under this proposal, people earning less than $20,000 per year would pay no income tax, and people earning more than $20,000 would pay 20 percent of their income in excess of that amount. For example, a person earning $30,000 would pay 20 percent of $10,000, or $2,000 in federal income tax. This proposal would probably raise about the same amount of government revenue as the current tax system does while providing two main advantages—simplicity (since it would reduce the time that people must spend to calculate their taxes) and a reduction in marginal tax rates (which would raise people's incentives to work).

The main argument against a flat-rate tax centers on fairness. Its critics believe that people with higher incomes than others should pay higher percentages of their incomes in taxes. The modified flat-rate proposal attempts to remedy this problem by taxing only incomes above a certain level, such as $20,000 per year. With a 20 percent flat-rate tax on income above $20,000 per year, people who earn $30,000 annually would pay income taxes of $2,000, or 6.7 percent of their income, while people who earned $100,000 annually would pay 16 percent of their income. In this way, the average tax rate would rise with income.

Taxes on Corporations

The corporate income tax provides the U.S. government with slightly more than 10 percent of its total tax revenue. Where do corporations obtain the money to pay corporate income taxes? Do the owners of corporations—the stockholders—pay the tax by receiving lower profits than they would receive without it? Do customers pay the tax in the form of higher prices for the products they buy than they would pay without it? Do workers bear the burden of the corporate income tax in the form of lower wages than they would otherwise earn?

Owners, customers, and workers share payment of corporate income taxes in a way that reflects the alternative opportunities available to each group. The better the alternative opportunities of workers, that is, the better their job opportunities outside of corporations, the less corporate income tax the workers pay and the more owners and customers pay.[22] The better the alternative opportunities of customers, that is, the better their opportunities to buy products from firms not subject to corporate taxes (such as partnerships or sole proprietorships, which do not pay the corporate income tax), the less

---

[21]An income tax was proposed in the United States, but never passed, during the War of 1812. The U.S. government began collecting income taxes, with tax rates rising to 10 percent of income, during the Civil War, but the tax lasted only until 1872.

[22]This is easy to understand if you think about elasticities of demand and supply. Suppose that workers have very good job opportunities at firms not subject to the corporate income tax, creating a very elastic supply of labor to corporations. In such a case, corporations could not reduce wages without losing large numbers of workers to noncorporate jobs, so they could not shift the burden of a corporate income tax increase to their workers by cutting or limiting wages.

corporate income tax that customers pay and the more owners and workers pay. Finally, the better the alternative investment opportunities of the firm's owners, the less they pay and the more workers and customers pay. It is very difficult to calculate precisely who actually pays corporate income taxes. Current evidence, although weak, indicates that owners of corporations (stockholders) pay most of the corporate income tax.

Many economists favor abolition of the corporate income tax on grounds of efficiency and equity. The efficiency argument cites double taxation of some corporate income. First, corporations pay taxes on their profits; second, people who receive those profits in the form of stock dividends or capital gains pay personal income taxes on it. This duplication raises the overall tax rate on savings and investment, which may reduce the economy's overall output and decrease its rate of growth.

Taxes on business firms, like taxes on individuals, can require extensive record-keeping and other costs. The costs of obeying corporate income tax laws is particularly high. For example, nine out of ten U.S. corporations have assets of less than $1 million; for each dollar of corporate income tax that such a firm pays, it spends more than $3 on recordkeeping, filling out and submitting required forms, and other related costs.

The equity argument for abolishing the corporate income tax notes that corporate profits are taxed at the same rate regardless of their distribution to high-income owners or low-income owners. The argument says that low-income people who own stock in a corporation should pay lower tax rates on their shares of the corporation's profits than high-income people should pay; this would occur if the corporate tax were abolished and everyone were to pay only individual income taxes on the income they received from corporate profits.

Review Questions

14. What is optimal taxation?

15. What is the average tax rate? The marginal tax rate?

16. Roughly how large is the combined federal income tax rate and social security tax rate on most people in the United States?

Thinking Exercises

17. Explain why the burden of the corporate income tax may fall on customers, workers or owners. What conditions determine how they share the burden of the tax?

18. Who would gain and who would lose if the corporate income tax were eliminated? How would elimination of this tax affect economic efficiency?

Conclusion

Regulation

Government regulations restrict the actions of people and firms, and they require people and firms to take certain actions. Government regulations are intended to protect the environment, reduce economic inefficiency, increase fairness, protect people from their own bad decisions, improve products, or set rules for using common resources. Some regulations are intended mainly to benefit certain special-interest groups at the expense of other people.

Evaluating Regulations: Cost–Benefit Analysis

Economists use cost–benefit analysis to compare the benefits and costs of regulations, taxes, and other government policies. The cost of a regulation results from a reduction in economic efficiency (lost consumer and producer surplus and costs to other people from externalities such as pollution). Economists measure intangible benefits (such as safety) by the amount of money that people are willing to pay for them in other situations.

When a regulation or tax has future costs or benefits, economists compare discounted present values. To cope with uncertainties about costs or benefits, economists compare the discounted present values of expected values. One criticism of cost–benefit analysis cites separation of the winners and losers from a regulation or tax; cost–benefit analysis shows only whether a policy would increase economic efficiency, but not whether it would be a Pareto improvement. A second criticism notes that use of discounted present values causes cost–benefit analysis to place lower weights on the effects on future generations than seems appropriate to some critics.

Problems with Regulation

Critics of government regulations contend that the actual effects of regulations frequently differ from their intended effects. The three main economic views of regulation are the public-interest view (that regulations serve the public interest), the special-interest view (that regulations serve special-interest groups), and the capture view (that regulatory agencies originally established to serve the general public interest end up serving the special interests of the industries they were intended to regulate). The special-interest and capture views are based on the argument that the political power of concentrated interests exceeds that of equal-sized diffuse interests, so regulations tend to benefit groups with concentrated interests such as firms in the regulated industries. The possibility that government will help producers through regulation gives them an incentive to spend resources to obtain beneficial regulations; this rent seeking is economically inefficient.

Taxes

Taxes, like regulations, serve several purposes: They fund government programs, redistribute income, and achieve other social goals. Different combinations of taxes that give the government the same amount of revenue can create different amounts of economic inefficiency. Optimal taxation sets tax rates that minimize the total deadweight social loss from taxes while raising a certain amount of revenue for the government. Optimal tax rates are higher on goods with more inelastic supplies and demands and lower on goods with more elastic supplies and demands. If the government could identify goods with perfectly inelastic supplies or demands, optimal policy would tax only those goods. Other considerations, such as fairness, may suggest that the government should not choose tax rates solely to minimize economic inefficiency. Economists distinguish between horizontal equity (equal treatment for people with the same characteristics) and vertical equity (different treatment for people in unequal conditions). Actual taxes, like regulations, result from political forces.

A person's average tax rate equals his tax payment divided by his income. His marginal tax rate is the increase in taxes he would pay if his income were to rise, expressed as a percentage of the increase in income . The average tax rate rises when the marginal tax rate exceeds the average, and it falls when the marginal rate is below the average. Most countries set graduated income tax rates rather than flat rates. Corporate taxes are paid partly by employees (in the form of lower wages than they would receive without the tax), customers (in the form of higher prices), and owners (in the form of lower after-tax returns on their investments). Evidence suggests that owners probably pay the largest share of corporate taxes.

Key Terms

cost–benefit analysis	special-interest view of regulation	concentrated interest	average tax rate
public-interest view of regulation	capture view of regulation	diffuse interest optimal taxation	marginal tax rate

Problems

19. Suppose that a proposed regulation will generate benefits of $250,000 every year forever, with a one-half chance of costs of $2 million and a one-half chance of costs of $6 million. In either case, all costs are paid this year, and no future costs will arise. Use cost–benefit analysis to evaluate this regulation, assuming an interest rate of 5 percent per year.

20. A proposed regulation would raise prices, boosting consumers' costs for a product by $10 million, and raising sellers' profits by $10 million. Is the $10 million a cost or a benefit of the regulation? Explain.

21. Why do regulated firms have incentives to raise their costs?

22. Explain why a military draft resembles a tax. Who pays the tax?

Inquiries for Further Thought

23. Should the government try to protect adults from their own, possibly bad decisions, or should people be free to make their own mistakes?

24. The government restricts smoking and taxes cigarettes partly to protect the health of smokers. The government requires seat belts and airbags to raise safety in cars. Should the government also regulate weight, exercise, sleep, and consumption of high-cholesterol foods? Should it tax people based on their health? What would be the effects on quantities and prices of such taxes or regulations? How far should the government go to protect people from their own bad choices? Should the government require people to buy health insurance? To save for retirement? To do other good things? (Which things and why?)

25. Discuss this statement: "If people want more energy-efficient refrigerators and other appliances, better gas mileage in their cars, and so on, they can freely buy products that provide these benefits without any need for government regulation. If people were willing to pay enough to cover the cost of enhanced energy efficiency, producers would make these products, because they could raise their profits by doing so. No argument justifies government regulation of energy standards."

26. Suppose that a government regulation saves one life in this country, but kills two people in a distant country. Suppose that another government regulation saves one life today, but destroys two lives in the distant future. Are the costs and benefits the same or different in these two cases? Should cost–benefit analysis take discounted present values of the losses in the future, but not current losses in other countries?

27. Several government regulations create obstacles to firms that want to fire employees. Should regulations ever prevent a firm from firing an employee? Under what circumstances?

28. Some people claim that U.S. government regulations hurt the country's businesses that compete with foreign sellers. Should the government take this effect into account in forming its regulations? If so, how? How could foreign competition affect the cost–benefit analysis of government regulations?

29. Should the government regulate product quality or safety? Is an improvement in quality or safety always better, even if it raises costs? How should the government decide on quality and safety regulations? Who gains and who loses from government regulations on minimum quality or safety? Apply this analysis to the quality of (a) medical care, (b) schools, and (c) food and drugs.

30. U.S. government regulations require drug makers to prove the safety and effectiveness of their products. What are the likely effects of these regulations?

31. Suppose that two people are identical in every way, except that one person has saved more and spent less in the past than the other. Should the government tax them at the same rate or different rates? Should it tax the interest income received by the person who saved money? What incentives are created by taxing (or not taxing) interest income?

32. Being as specific as possible, argue for and against:
    (a) Graduated income tax rates
    (b) A flat-rate income tax
    (c) A head tax

33. Discuss this statement: "Horizontal equity does not suggest that men and women should be taxed at the same rate, because women live longer than men, so they are likely to collect social security income over longer periods. Therefore, women should pay higher social security taxes than men pay."

34. The U.S. government has occasionally bailed out a large company that was about to go bankrupt by giving the company enough money to stay in business. Should the government do this? Why or why not? If so, which companies should it bail out, and which should it allow to fail?

CHAPTER 23

ECONOMICS OF PUBLIC CHOICE AND LAW

In this Chapter. . .

Main Points to Understand

▶ The political process often creates results favored by the median voter.

▶ Voting can create paradoxical (inconsistent) results.

▶ People who feel very strongly about an issue can increase their political strength through logrolling.

▶ Economically efficient laws create incentives for economically efficient behavior.

Thinking Skills to Develop

▶ Apply economic logic to voting and the equilibrium of a political process.

▶ Apply economic logic to the design of laws and institutions.

Every person makes her own decisions on most issues affecting her life. However, many decisions result from a political process—voting outcomes and government decisions. The political process determines the taxes you pay and the levels of government services you receive from local police and public schools to highway repair, welfare programs, and national defense. The political process determines laws and regulations that affect jobs available to you, environmental quality, and your choices in medical care. It determines the systems that administer justice and set rules for settling disputes.

What determines the results of the political process? Does the political process, like a market for goods and services, have an *equilibrium* that we can analyze with logical thought and evidence? If so, what affects the equilibrium results of the political process? How does that political process, and the laws and rules that it creates, affect the economy?

People have faced these issues directly in recent years as the political landscape in eastern Europe has undergone dramatic change. Formerly communist countries have adopted new, democratic political procedures and new legal systems for their emerging free-market economies. In the process, these nations have created entirely new systems of business law and entirely new institutions for their new political and economic systems. Similar issues have faced other nations around the world, and they may soon face many developing nations in Africa and Asia. How would you design new laws and institutions? Intelligent decisions on these issues require analyzing the effects of laws and political institutions on incentives.

PUBLIC CHOICE

Most readers of this book will be working and paying taxes in 2020, when mass retirement by baby boomers threatens a large increase in social security taxes. The U.S. social security system essentially taxes young and middle-aged working people and provides money to older, retired people. Because the large baby-boom generation will retire starting about 20 years from now, each worker paying into social security will have to support increasing numbers of retired people. As a result, either social security taxes will increase or social security benefits will fall. Every recent proposal for social security system reform requires some combination of tax increases and benefit cuts.

Decisions about social security reform, like those about many other social and economic issues, will result from a political process. That process will depend on the political strength of winners and losers from any potential reform. Retired people typically oppose reductions in social security benefits, while young workers typically oppose increases in taxes. Middle-aged workers fall in between; a worker nearing retirement may prefer increases in taxes, which he would pay for only a few more working years, to cuts in benefits, which would affect his income over many years of retirement. The older the worker, the larger the gains from increasing taxes instead of cutting social security benefits.

When retired people and young workers vote in roughly equal numbers, the middle-aged workers hold the swing votes that can affect the result of an election. This observation is formalized in the median voter theorem.

Median-Voter Theorem

The median-voter theorem states a logical result about equilibrium in political markets (under certain conditions). To define the term *median voter,* recall that the median of any distribution is the number with half of the distribution below it and half of the distribution above it. For example, in the list of numbers {1, 4, 10}, the median is 4, although the average, or mean, is 15/3, or 5. In a class of four students, if three students get *A*s while one fails, the median grade is an *A,* but the mean is lower than an *A.*

> The **median voter** is the voter whose views on a policy issue are in the middle of the spectrum; half of the other voters fall on one side of this voter's views, and half fall on the other side.

Suppose that five voters disagree about the level of government spending on roads. Voter A wants the government to spend $10, Voter B wants it to spend $20, Voter C wants it to spend $30, Voter D wants it to spend $40, and Voter E wants it to spend $100. The median voter is C, because 2 people want the government to spend more and the same number of people, 2, want it to spend less.

> The **median-voter theorem** states that, under certain conditions, the equilibrium government policy chosen by the political process is the policy favored by the median voter.

EXPLANATION AND EXAMPLE

The median voter can alter the result of an election. Suppose that Smith and Jones are running for Congress. If Smith promises to support $20 in road spending, Jones can win the election by promising to spend $30 because Voters C, D, and E will prefer that position to Smith's. The winner will be the candidate who supports the policy favored by Voter C, the median voter.

Will this man's vote swing the election?

Smith, knowing that a promise to spend $20 would give the election to Jones, may instead promise to spend $30 (as Voter C favors). In that case, Jones faces losing the election by choosing any other position, so both candidates will choose the policy favored by the median voter. (In fact, politicians do commonly try to appeal to middle-of-the-road voters.) In that case, both candidates support the same views, and the election's outcome depends on some other issue, on the candidates' personal characteristics, or on chance.

More generally, if only one issue (such as social security reform) determines the outcome and an analyst can list all voters in order of their preference on this issue, the median voter is in the middle of the list.[1] If one of two candidates for office advocates the policy favored by the median voter, that person will receive more votes than an opponent who advocates a different policy. The median-voter theorem states that in such a situation, both politicians are likely to choose the same political position—a middle-of-the-road position favored by the median voter. In real life, of course, politicians must guess at the positions held by the median voter, and their guesses may differ. Still, the median-voter theorem explains the tendency for politicians to take similar, middle-of-the-road positions on public issues.

Limitations of the Median-Voter Theorem

In reality, government policies often appear to differ (sometimes substantially) from the policies favored by the median voter. In fact, the median-voter theorem has several limitations. It does not apply to certain situations with more than two candidates or more than one issue, nor does it apply to certain situations in which voters prefer either high spending or low spending to a moderate level of spending. (Some voters, for example, might want either high levels of spending on a public park or no spending at all, rather than some moderate amount of spending.)

Finally, the median-voter theorem does not apply to situations that present voters with limited choices because someone has previously established an agenda for the votes. For example, suppose that a local school board wants the highest possible spending on schools, while all voters want spending as close to $10 million as possible. If current spending on schools is $8 million, the school board may propose a $3.9 million increase in spending, so voters must decide between spending $11.9 million or the status quo spending level of $8 million. Because the school board's proposal is closer to the $10 million level that voters prefer, they vote for the spending increase. In this case, spending is higher than the level preferred by the median voter (who, like all voters, prefers to spend $10 million). Of course, in the long run, voters might choose a school board that would better represent their preferences. In the short run, however, evidence suggests that this model explains spending on local schools better than the median-voter model does. School boards generally propose higher spending than the median voter wants and require voters to choose between that high level and a lower level of spending that most voters like even less. This indicates that spending on local public schools exceeds the level desired by the median voter.

Paradox of Voting

The simple logic of the median-voter model applies well to some political situations. However, many others give rise to strange and surprising equilibrium results. Suppose that three voters will evaluate three possible government actions, as in Table 1. Alan favors Policy A, considers Policy B second best, and thinks Policy C is the worst policy. Bill favors Policy B, thinks Policy C is second best, and thinks Policy A is the worst choice. Cindy thinks that Policy C is best, Policy A is second best, and Policy B is the worst option. If they vote on Policy A versus Policy B, Policy A wins because Alan and Cindy vote for A over

---

[1]The results may differ, and the logic becomes much more complicated, for situations with more than two candidates. It also becomes more complicated when many issues are at stake in the same election.

Table 1 | Paradox of Voting

Person	First-Choice Policy	Second-Choice Policy	Last-Choice Policy
Alan	A	B	C
Bill	B	C	A
Cindy	C	A	B

B, and only Bill votes for B over A. Policy A beats Policy B in an election. If, instead, they vote on Policy B versus Policy C, Policy B wins because Alan and Bill vote for B and only Cindy votes for Policy C. Policy B beats Policy C in an election.

You might think that Policy A would beat Policy C in an election because A beats B, and B beats C. However, if the three people vote between Policies A and C, Policy C wins! Bill and Cindy vote for C and only Alan votes for A. Such an election produces strange results: A beats B, B beats C, and C beats A! Even if every voter makes a rational choice in the sense that each has a clearly defined first, second, and third choice, voting by society as a whole produces no clearly defined first, second, or third choice. This example illustrates the Arrow impossibility theorem.

> The **Arrow impossibility theorem** states that, under very general conditions, voting can produce inconsistent results (in the sense that A can beat B in an election while B beats C, but A does not beat C) even if all voters make consistent choices.

The Arrow impossibility theorem actually states a stronger result. Arrow's theorem shows the *logical impossibility* of defining the "public good" or "social good" in a way that it has certain reasonable properties, such as transitivity, which means that if A is better than B, and B is better than C, then A is better than C.

If a majority of voters prefer Policy A to either Policy B or Policy C (or any other policy), then Policy A may seem, in one sense, to coincide with the public interest. The Arrow impossibility theorem shows that it is usually impossible to define the public interest in this way. One generally cannot combine the preferences of individual people, expressed by voting, into a consistent set of preferences for society as a whole.

This result also shows the importance of setting an agenda for voting. The outcome of voting between several alternatives can depend on the order in which people consider those alternatives. If people must choose *first* between A and B, and *then* between C and the winner in the first election, Policy C wins. If people first choose between B and C, then choose between A and the winner in that election, Policy A wins. If people first choose between A and C, then between B and the winner in that election, Policy B wins. This example illustrates that a political equilibrium can depend crucially on factors other than the views or preferences of voters.

Intensity of Preferences and Logrolling

Simple majority voting on an issue usually allows people only to vote yes or no. As a result, voters cannot directly express varying intensities of their views. Nevertheless, this variation can affect the equilibrium of a political system indirectly. For example, intensities of views affect the willingness of legislators to trade votes. Legislator A might promise to vote for a bill that Legislator B favors, if B will vote for a bill that A favors. This informal vote trading, or *logrolling,* provides a way for a minority that feels strongly about some issue to obtain majority support. In return, the minority changes its votes on other issues less important to its members.

Table 2 shows a simple example of logrolling in a town with three people. The government could spend $9 to build a new park and pay this cost by increasing taxes by $3 for each person. Pat would gain $11 from the new park, for a net after-tax gain of $8, so she wants the local government to build the park. Liz and Jean would gain only $1

Table 2 | Opportunity for Logrolling

| | Net Gain (or loss) from Each Policy | |
PERSON	NEW PARK	NEW LIBRARY
Pat	$ 8	$–4
Liz	–2	9
Jean	–2	–4
Society as a whole	4	1

each from the park, for a net after-tax loss of $2 each, so they oppose the park. Society as a whole—the three people—would gain from the park because Pat's net gain of $8 would exceed the net loss of $4 to Liz and Jean. Society's net gain from the park would equal the difference, $4, making the park an economically efficient project. In a majority-rule vote, however, the proposal would lose by a vote of two to one. Majority rule does not take into account the intensity of preferences.

The outcome changes when people can trade votes, however, because vote trading allows the intensities of preferences to affect the result. Suppose that the government of the same town could also spend $15 to build a new library, paying the cost with a $5 tax increase on each person. Suppose that Liz values the library at $14, giving her a net after-tax gain of $9 if it is built. Suppose Pat and Jean each value the library at $1, for net after-tax losses of $4 each. Society as a whole would gain $1 from the library, because the $9 gain to Liz would exceed the $8 loss to Pat and Jean. Again, however, the majority would vote, two to one, *not* to build it.

Now introduce vote trading. Pat offers to support a new library if Liz will support a new park. On net, Pat would gain $8 from the park and lose only $4 from the library, so she is willing to make this trade. Liz would gain $9 from the library and lose only $2 from the park, so she is also willing to make this trade. As a result, Pat and Liz out-vote Jean on each issue by two to one, and the local government builds *both* a new park and a new library.

While vote trading seldom occurs among ordinary voters, it is common among legislators. Bills in Congress often include multiple, unrelated provisions that result from such trades. Two proposed policies that might each lose on their own may win when combined into one piece of legislation. Skilled lawmakers use these strategies everyday to advance their own agendas. Congressional committees often decide whether to approve proposed bills for votes by the whole legislature based on committee members' beliefs about how the bills will affect vote trading in the larger body. Controversies about the line-item veto also relate to this issue because this power would allow the president to eliminate one part of a bill without vetoing the entire bill, thereby reversing the results of vote trading.

Sometimes a minority can register a strong preference on an issue in a different way. In the park example, Pat could choose to spend her *own* money to build the park. She would spend $9 and personally gain $11, for a net gain of $2. However, she gains *more* than $2 if she can get the government to build the park and force taxpayers to pay the cost. (In the vote-trading example, Pat gains $4 from trading votes with Liz so that the government builds both the park and the library.)

This option is not always open for individuals, though. Liz would be unwilling to build the library on her own. She gains from the library on net only if other people share the cost. The government might provide the library in a case like this based on the rationale that Liz would incur prohibitive costs negotiating with Pat and Jean to get them to contribute. While negotiations between three people, as in this example, are seldom very costly, real-life applications of this logic often involve thousands or millions of people. Logrolling provides flexibility for the political system and alters its results. Decisions on

Lights shine from Capitol building offices as lawmakers arrange to trade votes.

Table 3 | Inefficient Results from Logrolling

PERSON	Net Gain (or loss) from Each Policy	
	NEW BALLPARK	NEW PLAYGROUND
Homer	$ 5	$–3
Lisa	–3	5
Marge	–3	–3
Society as a whole	–1	–1

public goods such as national defense emerge from similar processes. A minority with a strong view on the best level of national defense spending may be unwilling to pay for it themselves, but they may be willing to trade votes on other issues to achieve their goal on that issue.

While logrolling raises economic efficiency in the park/library example, it often reduces economic efficiency in the real world. Table 3 shows an example. Homer would gain $5 if the town built a new ballpark. Lisa and Marge would each lose $3, because the taxes they would pay exceed their benefits from the ballpark. As a result, society as a whole would lose $1 from the project. Similarly, building a new playground would provide a $5 net gain to Lisa but net losses to Marge and Homer of $3 each. As a result, society as a whole would lose $1 from a new playground.

If people voted separately on the ballpark and playground, each project would lose by a 2-to-1 vote. However, logrolling can change the result. Homer may agree to vote for a new playground if Lisa votes for a new ballpark. Because Homer gains $5 from the new ballpark and loses $3 from the new playground, he receives a net gain of $2 from the combination. The same calculation applies to Lisa. Therefore Homer and Lisa are willing to trade votes in this way. This vote trading allows both the new ballpark and new playground to pass by 2-to-1 margins, with a net loss to society of $1 from each project. In this case, logrolling creates economic inefficiency—a deadweight social loss of $2.

Information Costs and Organizing Costs

The political power levels of groups with *concentrated* interests usually exceed those of groups with *diffuse* interests. Recall that a group has a concentrated interest if a small number of people would enjoy most of the benefits from a policy or suffer most of its costs. A group has a diffuse interest if costs or benefits are spread over a large number of people, with very small costs or benefits to each *individual*.

For example, ten people may *each* gain $1 million from some government policy that wastes $26 million. However, the total $26 million cost of the policy may spread across 260 million other people, at a cost to each one of only 10 cents. Proponents of the policy have a concentrated interest; opponents have a diffuse interest. Despite the economic inefficiency of the policy (since it would create a deadweight social loss of $16 million), none of the 260 million losers have much incentive to spend time or money to fight it. It may prevail because of the costs of organizing, bargaining, and trading. Because information has a cost, the losers even lack much incentive to *find out* about the policy or evaluate its benefits and costs. Many government policies have big effects on small groups and small individual effects on everyone else. For example, the U.S. government sugar program raises prices to consumers, but few individual consumers lose enough money to motivate them to learn about that program. As a whole, consumers suffer a large loss, but the cost is diffused over many people. As a result, this program and many similar policies persist in equilibrium.

IN THE NEWS

Constituent service is pivotal to way Congress works, and ethical line is fuzzy

WASHINGTON—Nobody is groaning louder about the federal farm-spending cuts than wheat growers. But once they look a little deeper into the 1990 farm bill, they're apt to change their tune.

Hidden in the legislation is a perk tailor-made for them, a provision that pays them for idling their wheat fields while allowing them to profit from the sale of another crop grown on the same acreage.

It's all part of the congressional rite for making winners out of losers when agriculture spending is on the line. Take a few bursts of legislative creativity, add raw political power, and act quickly—preferably late at night. Tag teams of lobbyists, working almost round-the-clock in the waning days of budget reconciliation, succeeded in taking much of the sting from the $13.6 billion in five-year subsidy cuts for their commodity-group clients.

Source: The Wall Street Journal

Lobbyists for groups with concentrated interests frequently influence legislation.

Why Vote?

Why does anyone vote? The cost of voting is small—only a few minutes of time. However, the combined actions of millions of voters ensure an even smaller chance that *your* vote will affect the outcome of an election. Even in a local election with only a few thousand voters, any individual's vote is extremely unlikely to affect the outcome. Of course, if this logic led most people *not* to vote, and only a few people voted, then any individual vote would have a larger chance to affect the outcome. However, when many other people vote, the benefits to any one voter appear much smaller than the costs.

Many people *do* vote, however. Presumably, they vote for reasons other than the chance of affecting the outcome of the election. Perhaps they enjoy voting for or against certain candidates or issues; perhaps they view voting as a responsibility of a good citizen. Whatever their reasons, studies have shown that people are more likely to vote when they expect close elections than when they confidently expect certain outcomes.

Some Consequences

If your vote could swing an election, you would have a strong incentive to become informed about candidates or issues that affect you. However, that incentive is absent when there is almost no chance that any one person's vote will affect the results of an election. As incentives, voters fall for people with diffuse interests to become informed, political power rises for groups with concentrated interests. Low incentives for people with diffuse interests also make it more difficult for politicians to create winning coalitions by informing voters about policies. These increased difficulties raise politicians' susceptibility to the influence of special-interest groups. In addition, as average voters become less informed, politicians suffer weakening backlash if they support policies favored by special-interest groups.

As the typical voter's information diminishes, the incentive grows for politicians to favor policies with short-run benefits and long-run costs. A politician may expect to be out of office long before the costs of his policies grow large. One force operating in the opposite direction is the endorsement of a political party. Even though an individual politician may have a limited term in office, a political party has an incentive to maintain its reputation. Because a party's reputation may suffer in the long run if its elected officials ignore the longer-run costs of policies, political parties may provide some incentives for politicians to consider long-run costs and benefits. This incentive operates, however, only if voters are sufficiently well informed to change their views of a political party based on these considerations.

Bureaucrats

Many government decisions are made, not by elected officials, but by bureaucrats: unelected government workers, such as the heads of government regulatory agencies. Bureaucrats, like elected politicians, pursue varied interests. They care about their own careers, salaries, prestige, families, and friends. Despite deep concern about promoting justice, helping the needy, defending the country, and pursuing the perceived national interest, even dedicated public servants are subject to personal pressures that may influence their perceptions of the national interest. Most people are motivated by wide-ranging desires that sometimes conflict, and people in government service are no exceptions.

Because their productivity is hard to measure, bureaucrats' salaries seldom reflect their efficiency. A bureaucrat may gain personal influence, power, and prestige by increasing his agency's budget and number of employees. Of course, a bureaucrat whose only concern is doing a good job might also favor a larger budget and more employees. Bureaucrats typically try to increase the sizes and budgets of their agencies by influencing elected politicians. These incentives lead bureaucrats to exaggerate the importance of their own agencies. For example, the Defense Department is likely to exaggerate the need for increased defense spending.

Review Questions

1. Explain the median-voter theorem. What are its limitations?

2. Explain why the costs of gathering information and organizing for action increase the political power of groups with concentrated interests relative to groups with diffuse interests.

Thinking Exercises

3. Consider the example in Table 1, but suppose that the three people decide to vote on the order of voting. What will happen? Suppose that they vote on a way to decide how to decide the order of voting. Explain what will happen.

4. You and *two* other people vote yes or no on a proposed project. If the other people each have a 1/2 chance of voting yes and a 1/2 chance of voting no, what is the chance that *your* vote will affect the outcome? What happens to that chance as the number of other voters increases?

ECONOMIC ANALYSIS OF LAW

The 11 nations of the European Union designed the new European Central Bank to conduct their joint monetary policy starting in 1999, knowing that the rules governing the bank's operation would affect its results. When the formerly socialist countries of eastern Europe designed contract laws and business laws for their emerging free-market economies, they knew that their work would affect standards of living in their countries for decades to come. Every nation designs laws and regulations dealing with medical care and health insurance, environmental issues, the responsibility of producers for accidents involving their products, copyright laws on the Internet, and crime. These laws affect incentives. A society's overall economic performance depends heavily on its laws and the procedures to enforce them. Economies without clear, enforceable laws on property rights and contracts experience difficulties attracting investment; they have low levels of output and high levels of economic inefficiency.

Laws promote economic efficiency when they create incentives to solve problems in the most economically efficient ways and to minimize transactions costs through quick, inexpensive settlement of disputes (without overusing the court system). For example, laws on product liability determine a firm's responsibility when someone is injured while using its product; liability laws affect incentives for producers to make safe products, for consumers to use products carefully, and for both sides to settle disputes efficiently. Liability laws affect costs of production, so they affect equilibrium prices and quantities.

Precedents, Incentives, and Justice

Suppose that Carston takes Jones Corporation to court after suffering an injury while using a defective product made by the company. The court must decide how much money Jones should pay Carston as compensation for the injury. One important question for the court to answer is, "What is fair or just?" Another important question concerns how the outcome of the case will affect future incentives. The outcome may establish a legal precedent that will affect decisions in similar cases in the future; such a precedent affects incentives.

Carston's accident has already happened, so the harm that Carston has suffered is a sunk cost; the court cannot eliminate that harm, it can only transfer resources from Jones to try to compensate Carston. This action does not reverse the harm, it merely redistributes wealth. It shifts some of the harm to Jones. The incentives created by the court decision can affect future behavior, however, along with the total amount of future harm in similar cases, by influencing the number of similar accidents in the future, the severity of those accidents, and the methods by which people try to avoid future accidents. The court's decision has costs and benefits associated with the incentives that it creates.

Suppose that the court requires Jones to pay Carston enough money to compensate for all of Carston's costs from the accident, including the court's estimate of psychological costs. With complete compensation, Jones would pay Carston enough money that Carston would no longer care that the accident happened. What incentives would this decision create? Jones Corporation, and other, similar firms, would have an incentive to avoid future cases like this, either by making very safe products or discontinuing those products entirely. On the other hand, buyers would have little incentive to use the products carefully if they could rely on complete compensation in any future accident. Because Jones knows that buyers have little incentive to use the product carefully, Jones must make an essentially foolproof product.

Would this court decision promote economic efficiency? The answer depends on the relative costs to producers and consumers of safety. If Jones can make very safe products more cheaply than customers can avoid accidents through careful use, then this court decision may be economically efficient. It would lead to production of safety by the person who could produce it at the lowest cost. On the other hand, Jones may lack the ability to make the product completely safe, while users can take precautions relatively easily. The court decision would then create economic inefficiency by eliminating users' incentives to take those precautions. The economically efficient court decision may require users to be careful and relieve Jones of any responsibility to compensate Carston.

More generally, the economically efficient court decision would provide incentives to everyone who might help prevent a future accident. It would give users incentives to take precautions up to the point at which the marginal social cost of additional precautions equals their marginal social benefit by reducing accidents. This decision might require a firm like the Jones Corporation to pay part, but not all, of the cost of an accident, or to pay only if its negligence contributed to the injury (that is, if it had failed to take reasonable measures to produce a safe product). Perhaps a decision might allow Jones to avoid paying if Carston was negligent (careless) in using the good. Sometimes the economically efficient court decision may correspond to a person's sense of justice; other times the two may conflict.

Torts

Torts are acts that injure other people, either intentionally or by accident. Common tort cases focus on auto or airline accidents, libel and defamation of character, product liability, and medical malpractice. A *liability rule* is a legal statement of who is responsible under what conditions for injuries or other harms in a tort.

In most accidents involving two (or more) people, anyone involved could have taken some actions to reduce the risk or severity of the accidents. One person might bear most or all of the blame or moral responsibility, but even an innocent victim can take precautions to reduce the chance or severity of a potential accident. An economically efficient liability rule gives *each* person the incentive to exercise the economically efficient amount of precaution to avoid accidents. The economically efficient level of precaution for each person usually depends on the precautions taken by other people. For example, a potential sex partner's careful precautions in the past to avoid contracting a sexually transmitted disease reduce the precautions you need to take now. The general rule for the economically efficient level of caution is to set the expected marginal cost of taking precautions equal to the expected marginal benefit.

Suppose you buy a cup of coffee at a drive-through window of a restaurant, and burn yourself badly by spilling the coffeee as you drive away. The risk of this kind of accident could be reduced by actions of the restaurant, such as serving lukewarm coffee, using

IN THE NEWS

Failure to wear seat belts can cut crash-suit awards

By Paul M. Barrett
Staff Reporter of
The Wall Street Journal

A drunk driver slams into a car idling at a stop light. The victimized driver isn't wearing a seat belt. Should a jury in a subsequent lawsuit reduce the victim's award if failure to buckle up contributed to the victim's injuries?

An increasing number of state appellate courts are saying yes, and that has plaintiffs' lawyers worried. These attorneys fear that the seat-belt defense will distract juries from the cause of an accident—whether it is driver negligence or a defective car part—and shift the blame to the injured person.

Supporters of the trend applaud the courts' creation of incentives for drivers to use seat belts. The legal decisions "do have a deterrent effect, especially when the cases get a lot of publicity," says David A. Westenberg, a Boston, Mass., lawyer who has written academic articles on the issue.

Source: The Wall Street Journal

Tort law often tries to give everyone an incentive to take economically efficient precautions.

SOCIAL AND ECONOMIC ISSUES

Economics of Broken Promises

Jill signs a contract to produce a new machine for Jack's factory, for which Jack agrees to pay $10. Before the machine arrives, Jack spends $2 to train his assistant to operate it. Jack expects the machine to increase his firm's revenue by $15. After paying $10 for the machine and $2 to train his assistant, he expects a $3 profit.

Jill builds the machine but breaks her contract with Jack and sells the machine to Peter for $13. Jack sues Jill for breaking the contract. How much money should the court force Jill to pay to Jack?

One rule that courts have used is based on Jack's expectations. The rule says Jill should pay $5, so that Jack would get the same $3 profit that he expected to earn if Jill had kept her promise. (The other $2 covers the cost that Jack paid to train his assistant.) Courts have sometimes applied a second, different rule stating that Jill should pay

only $2 to reimburse Jack for the money he spent in expectation that Jill would honor the contract.

In this simple case, the first rule is economically efficient, and the second rule is not. Economic efficiency requires that the machine go to its highest-valued use. Jack values the machine at $15. (That is the highest price he would be willing to pay for the machine. If Jack paid $15, his economic profit would be zero, although his accounting profit would show a $2 *loss* due to the sunk cost of training his assistant.) The law enhances economic efficiency by providing an incentive for Jill to break the contract *if and only if* Peter values the machine at more than $15. Therefore, an economically efficient law would require Jill to pay $5 to Jack if she breaks the contract. This law would raise Jill's opportunity cost of selling to Peter from $10 to $15 (the $10 Jack would have paid her plus the $5). With this law, she would sell to Peter if and only if Peter offers to pay more than $15. If the law required Jill to pay more than $5, or less than $5, to Jack, then it would create economically inefficient incentives for breaking contracts in similar, future cases.

spill-proof cups, or refusing to sell coffee at the drive-through window. The risk could also be reduced by your actions, such as carefully securing the cup of coffee before you begin driving. Economic efficiency may call for the restaurant *not* to spend the money for spill-proof cups; the economically efficient solution is likely to involve mainly reasonable precautions by drivers who buy hot coffee. The same principle applies to other, more complex cases. The general rule for economic efficiency says that the marginal cost of precautions by each person must equal the marginal benefit of those precautions.

What Should Laws Try to Accomplish?

Some economists believe that laws, and the way courts interpret and enforce them, should maximize economic efficiency. When an accident occurs, a court could compare people's *actual* levels of precaution with their economically efficient levels to determine whether one person must pay compensation to the other. While courts cannot usually measure precautions as accurately as in the example, courts can estimate the efficient levels of precaution.

Careful with that coffee!

Other people criticize the idea that laws and their enforcement should maximize economic efficiency. They argue that laws should *also* be designed for fairness and justice, and consider issues such as the distribution of wealth. For example, some people would find it unfair for the law to require a poor consumer to take precautions when using a product sold by a large company owned by wealthy investors. Nevertheless, economic efficiency might require that buyers take precautions if the cost of producing a safe product exceeds the cost of the precautions required for safe use.

Economic efficiency also requires that laws encourage quick, inexpensive resolution of disputes without expensive court battles. For example, sexual harassment cases often involve conflicting accounts of events that occurred behind closed doors, creating "he said/she said" disputes that courts have no clear way to settle. Economically

IN THE NEWS

Liability insurance needs rise with jury awards

Can you afford a dog that bites or icy walks?

When it comes to snow, however, New Yorkers face a dilemma. If they fail to shovel, they face a $25 fine. If they clear a path, they become liable to any passerby who slips on a stray icy patch and decides to sue. Many lawyers advise that if you don't want to be sued, don't shovel. "It may be ridiculous, but it's the law," Sullivan said.

Source: Rochester Democrat and Chronicle

Tort law and jury awards of damages affect a wide variety of everyday activities.

Advice

Note the similiarity between the idea from Chapter 19 of justice as an implicit contract and the idea that tort law can try to duplicate the contract that people would have chosen prior to the accident. This similiarty illustrates how to apply ideas from one economic topic to another. Practice finding other similiarities among various ideas and logical arguments in this book.

efficient laws discourage use of the legal system to settle such disputes, giving people and companies incentives to avoid potentially problematic situations. Similarly, no-fault automobile insurance laws (in which insurance companies share costs and do not even try to assign blame for auto accidents) can promote economic efficiency. Although these laws reduce incentives for careful driving, they also reduce costs of fact-finding and settling disputes.

When someone dies or suffers an injury in an accident, courts must decide how to measure those damages in terms of money. It cannot restore a healthy arm, let alone a life. Earlier chapters have already introduced the idea of the price of safety—people often choose other values at the expense of safety. Courts use evidence of the tradeoffs that people actually make—and the implicit prices that they are willing to pay to avoid risks of injuries or death—to determine the values of health, lost limbs, and lost lives. Courts use these estimates to set damage payments in personal injury or death cases. In addition, courts usually use other criteria such as the discounted present value of lost wages, the amount of pain and suffering, and reduced ability to enjoy life.

Tort Law and Contracts

Suppose that people could meet before any accident occurs and agree on rules governing the precautions that people should take in various situations. They could also set penalties for people who fail to take those precautions in the event of an accident. They would have incentives to sign a contract establishing the economically efficient levels of precautions. Such a contract would eliminate the need for tort law; the contract's provisions would determine who owes how much to whom in the event of an accident. Courts would simply have to enforce the contract terms.

Of course, in real life, people cannot meet and sign such a contract prior to accidents. However, tort law can try to *duplicate* the contract that people *would have* chosen if they had met in advance. This, some people argue, should be the goal of tort law. In fact, some analysts suggest replacing tort law with contract law in certain cases, such as product liability, where people can easily and inexpensively negotiate contracts before any accident occurs. In the case of product liability, for example, a buyer and seller would enter into an implicit contract whenever they exchange a good. (Whenever you buy a good, you implicitly contract with the seller. Your implicit contract says that the cereal box contains the amount and kind of cereal specified on the label, with the ingredients listed on that label. These terms of the contract are enforceable in a court of law.) That contract, and not tort law, would determine liability and compensation payments in the event the buyer has a problem with the product.

Product Liability

Product-liability law relates to accidents in which people who suffer injuries while using products seek damages from the firms that sold or made the products. Suppose that courts hold firms responsible for injuries that people suffer while using their products, even if the firms take reasonable (economically efficient) precautions. This *strict liability rule* essentially requires a firm to provide an implicit *insurance* policy to people who use its product; if an accident happens, and the user was not negligent or reckless with the product, then the firm pays for resulting injuries.

This implicit insurance policy is not free. It raises prices, because it raises firms' marginal costs. The price increase reflects the cost to the firm of providing the implicit insurance. The cost of this implicit insurance accounts for 30 percent of the price of a stepladder, 95 percent of the price of childhood vaccines, and one-third of the price of a small airplane. It adds more to the price of a football helmet than the cost of making

IN THE NEWS

Business struggles to adapt as insurance crisis spreads

Price increases and profit cuts are common; some drop products, exercise greater caution

*A Wall Street Journal
News Roundup*

The soaring cost and worsening shortage of liability insurance are taking their toll on businesses, professionals, and local governments across the country. The crisis is forcing companies to raise prices or accept smaller profits, change their operations, and eliminate products and services.

Day-care centers, hotels, restaurants, bars, ski resorts, ice-skating rinks, and other service businesses face sharply higher premiums or a lack of liability coverage. While some smaller operations are closing up, others are trying to make themselves less vulnerable to lawsuits or are passing higher costs to their customers.

The insurance crisis is also making life difficult for many professionals. While the rising cost of medical malpractice insurance has dominated the headlines, malpractice premiums for architects, engineers, and accountants are rising even more sharply.

For big companies, which can more easily absorb higher insurance costs, the most serious problem is the lack of coverage at any price in such areas as directors' and officers' liability, pollution liability, and product liability.

Source: The Wall Street Journal

Product-liability laws affect prices and production levels of various products as well as research on new products.

the helmet itself. It adds about $300 to the price of delivering a baby and prevents U.S. production of certain drugs, even some certified as safe and effective by the Food and Drug Administration.[2]

Product-liability claims fall under tort law, although some people argue that it should be part of contract law. This distinction relates to an important difference between an accident involving use of a product and an auto accident (a classic example of a tort). In the product-liability case, the buyer and seller already had a contract to pay for and deliver a product. That contract could state how the buyer and seller will divide the costs of any accident and what precautions each side must take. A firm might offer to sell a product on the condition that it accepts no liability whatsoever for injuries that people might receive while using it, or it might offer to sell a product on the condition that it is liable only if the product is defective or does not meet certain standards, but not otherwise. A firm might offer full insurance to buyers as in the strict liability case.

Some economists argue that courts should enforce whichever contract to which buyers and sellers voluntarily agree. Until recently, U.S. law enforced most contracts that buyers and sellers agreed on. In situations with no contractual agreement on liability, the law served as a standard contract, and standard tort law applied. Laws in many countries still enforce such contracts, but modern U.S. tort law does *not* enforce these

---

[2]See Peter W. Huber, *Liability: The Legal Revolution and Its Consequences* (New York: Basic Books, 1988). This discussion presumes throughout that the government enforces property rights and ignores issues associated with private police, courts, and so on. For a discussion of these issues, see David Friedman, *The Machinery of Freedom*, 2d ed. (La Salle, Ill.: Open Court, 1989). Also see Gary S. Becker and George J. Stigler, "Law Enforcement, Malfeasance, and Compensation of Enforcers," *Journal of Legal Studies* 3 (January 1974), and David D. Friedman, "Efficient Institutions for the Private Enforcement of Law, *Journal of Legal Studies* 13 (June 1984).

Product-Liability Crisis

Should firms and customers be permitted to sign contracts that determine liability in the case of accidents? Should courts overrule such contracts and impose another liability rule?

Arguments for Enforcing Contracts That Determine Liability

- It is economically efficient to enforce mutually voluntary contracts in the absence of externalities. People can then share risks as they choose. Enforcing contracts allows freedom of choice. Buyers and sellers can freely agree on liability rules for products.
- Buyers and sellers can determine the economically efficient distribution of liabilities better than courts can. For example, an insurance company might sell accident insurance to people more cheaply than a product manufacturer

could, because the insurance company may pool the risks more effectively than the manufacturer would. (Critics reply that, in such cases, manufacturers can always buy liability insurance.)
- Competition among sellers helps to achieve economically efficient contracts. Economic efficiency would suffer if courts were to overrule the contracts that emerge from this competition and apply some other liability rule.
- The court system works poorly for product-liability cases, because juries award such high damage payments to victims that they distort incentives. Manufacturers spend too much on safety and decline to produce some products at all, even though many people want them. These problems would be reduced if courts were to enforce contracts that determine liability.
- The court system works poorly for another reason, as well. With many different lawsuits, the same manufacturer may repeatedly pay punitive damages. The punitive damages can sum to economically inefficient levels, resulting in overly safe products, in the sense that the extra

contracts; instead, it often imposes a strict liability rule (or some variant of this rule) for nearly all product-liability cases. The chance that the *plaintiff* (the person who brings the lawsuit against the firm) will win a product-liability suit has increased substantially in recent decades, as have the sizes of damage payments to the winners. This development has led some people to speak of a *liability crisis* in the United States. The Social and Economic Issues box discusses whether courts should enforce contracts between firms and customers that determine liability in case of accidents.

Property and Theft

Economically efficient tort law weighs the costs and benefits of precautions that could be taken by either party to a dispute and tries to provide incentives for people to take economically efficient actions in the future. Economically efficient laws on property rights similarly weigh costs and benefits to create efficient incentives. For example, theft almost always impairs economic efficiency. The inefficiency does *not* result because someone suffers a loss; if Bill steals $100 from you, you lose $100, but Bill gains $100. That fact does not create inefficiency, merely a redistribution of income. (Of course, you may not like this redistribution, but Bill probably does.) Instead, theft reduces economic efficiency because its mere *possibility* leads people to spend money, time, and energy to protect their property. This activity creates economic inefficiency, because those people could have spent their time and energy to produce more goods rather than fighting with thieves over the distribution of existing goods. The thieves could better use their time and skills to produce goods that people would be willing to buy, and the victims could avoid spending money on locks, security systems, and police resources. Economic inefficiency increases when a thief takes an item with sentimental value to its owner. If Bill were to steal such an item from you, your loss would exceed his gain, adding to the inefficiency.

safety is not worth its cost. Excessive punitive damages also induce firms to withdraw some good products from the market, as has happened, for example, with some children's vaccines.

Arguments for Imposing Strict Liability and Not Enforcing Contracts

- People do not always act in their own best interests. The law must protect people from their own bad decisions.
- People underestimate the risks they take with some products, so contracts will not result in economic efficiency, because people will take more risks than they should.
- People do not buy enough insurance on their own. They are better off if the law forces them to buy it through product-liability laws.
- Society will not let the people who fail to buy insurance suffer big losses; society will pay for them through the welfare system. To reduce welfare costs, people should be required to buy insurance through the product-liability laws, even if they don't want it.

- Even if people were to act in their own best interests, they would incur costs to gather information. The law should protect people who don't read the small print or don't understand the complexities of a contract that includes liability clauses.
- People benefit if they don't have to bother reading all the fine print and worrying about different liability rules in different contracts, and they don't have to bother if the law sets a product-liability rule that applies to all products.
- Sellers can insure risk more cheaply than buyers can, so imposing strict liability divides risk in an efficient way. (The other side replies, if this were true, then people would choose contracts in which the seller provides insurance for accidents; the law would not have to impose it. The usual responses repeat the previous arguments—that people do not act in their own best interests and would not buy this insurance, and that they are better off if the government forces them to buy it.)

Suppose a poor woman steals $100 from a rich man. Some people may think that her gain exceeds his loss, because she may value that money more than he does. Economics alone cannot resolve issues like this, because they require comparing one person's happiness with another's. Even if her gain did exceed his loss, it may be economically inefficient for the law to permit theft, because that would create incentives for rich people to spend more time and money to protect their property and for poor people to steal rather than work.

IN THE NEWS

Victims of violent crimes increasingly sue for damages—and many win big awards

Not only are the perpetrators of violent crimes being hit for damages, increasingly, the owners and managers of properties where the crimes occur are also targets of civil actions for restitution.

This increased emphasis on victims' rights, many law-enforcement officials and criminal-justice experts agree, is likely to prompt far-reaching changes in how courts operate and how they punish criminals.

Third-Party Targets

Civil suits are frequently aimed at third parties because the average criminal doesn't have the resources to pay damages; courts have been known to make multi-million-dollar awards.

Some lawmakers and critics denounce the practice of victims suing third parties with deep pockets.

Source: The Wall Street Journal

Would it be economically efficient to replace criminal law with tort law?

Theft *can* be economically efficient in unusual situations with high transactions costs. Even in those situations, however, economic efficiency requires eventual compensation to the victim. Suppose, for example, that you are lost in the woods and starving when you notice a cabin. No one is home, but the owner has left food inside. You break in and eat the food. Because you placed an extremely high value on that food at that moment, your theft may be economically efficient. If the cabin's owner had been present, you could have bought the food from her. In her absence, however, the transactions costs were too high to arrange a voluntary trade. Economically efficient laws would allow theft in a case like this, while requiring that you later pay the cabin owner for the food (plus any damage to the cabin caused by your break-in). That payment may serve *justice,* but it also serves two important economic functions. First, if the law did not require such payments, then it would encourage people to steal goods instead of buying them. Second, if it did not require such payments the law would encourage cabin owners to take additional, costly precautions against theft (such as more locks and sophisticated alarms, or removing valuables from their cabins when they leave). The law, in this case, tries to recreate the contract that you and the cabin owner would have made if the cabin owner had been home. Of course, courts may find it hard to determine whether a thief would actually have been willing to pay for a stolen item. With low transactions costs, therefore, the law requires that people *demonstrate* their willingness to pay for a good by *actually* paying for it rather than stealing it.

Review Questions

5. In what ways can a law promote economic efficiency?

6. What is a legal precedent? Explain how a precedent can affect economic efficiency.

7. How does a product-liability case differ from an automobile accident case? Why do some people suggest that contract law should apply to product-liability cases?

8. Explain why theft is usually economically inefficient, but can sometimes be economically efficient.

Thinking Exercises

9. Would a government promote economic efficiency by imposing a severe punishment (the death penalty, life imprisonment, or a giant fine) for every crime? How would this policy affect crime?

10. When a court finds someone liable for an injury, the court may require payment of punitive damages as extra punishment in addition to compensation for the person who was injured. Is this requirement economically efficient? Explain.

Conclusion

Public Choice

The median-voter theorem states that, under certain conditions, the equilibrium government policy chosen in political markets is the policy favored by the median voter. Although the median-voter model explains the tendency of politicians to establish middle-of-the-road positions, several limitations complicate its application. For

example, it does not apply to certain situations in which voters' choices are limited by previously established voting agendas.

The Arrow impossibility theorem shows that, under very general conditions, voting can produce inconsistent results. When voters choose among three alternatives, they may vote for Policy A over Policy B, and B over C, but not for A over C, even if each voter follows consistent first, second, and third choices. This result shows a fundamental problem in defining an unambiguous public interest, and it shows the importance of setting agendas prior to voting, because the order of voting can determine the outcome.

Logrolling allows voters with very strong preferences on one issue to obtain support on that issue by trading their support on other issues. Logrolling can increase the economic efficiency of the political equilibrium.

Groups of people with concentrated interests may wield more political power than groups with diffuse interests. Information costs reduce the incentives for groups with diffuse interests to learn about government policies that hurt them. Organization costs may prevent them from eliminating such government policies, even if they learn about the policies.

The likelihood is very small that any one person's vote will directly affect the outcome of an election; the observation that people vote suggests that they see other benefits of voting, such as fulfilling civic responsibilities or pure pleasure of voting for or against certain people or issues.

Economic Analysis of Law

Laws can promote or hinder economic efficiency because they affect incentives and behavior. Economic efficiency is one important criterion (in addition to justice) for designing laws and government institutions.

Tort law deals with accidents. Liability rules state conditions under which someone bears responsibility for injuries suffered by others. An economically efficient liability rule would give everyone the incentive to exercise the economically efficient degree of caution so that the marginal cost of precautions would equal their marginal benefits.

Some economists believe that the government and courts should choose and interpret laws to maximize economic efficiency. Other people criticize the idea that liability rules should maximize economic efficiency on the grounds that this policy would ignore fairness or justice. If people involved in an accident could have gathered before the accident, they could have chosen the precautions that each would take, the penalties for failing to take those precautions, and who must pay how much money to whom if an accident were to occur anyway. Although people usually cannot sign contracts to resolve these issues before accidents occur, economically efficient tort law can try to duplicate the contracts that people would have chosen if they had met in advance. Some analysts believe that contracts should replace tort law in cases where people can easily and inexpensively negotiate contracts, such as product-liability cases.

Enforcement of property rights nearly always promotes economic efficiency. Theft increases inefficiency, because it creates incentives for people to fight over the distribution of resources rather than to create resources. However, theft can improve economic efficiency in unusual cases with extremely high transactions costs.

Key Terms

median voter	median-voter theorem	Arrow impossibility theorem

Problems

11. Suppose that Anna, Bob, and Clara would vote on complete versus partial national health insurance (NHI) as in the table:

Person	First Choice	Second Choice	Last Choice
Anna	Complete NHI	Partial NHI	No NHI at all
Bob	Partial NHI	No NHI at all	Complete NHI
Clara	No NHI at all	Complete NHI	Partial NHI

   (a) Suppose that people must first vote on the type of national health insurance to consider—complete coverage versus partial coverage. People would then vote on whether to adopt national health insurance at all. Which policy would win?

   (b) Suppose that people must first vote for or against national health insurance with partial coverage. If they chose to have some national health insurance, they then vote on expanding the program to provide full coverage. Which policy would win?

12. Aaron wants to raise taxes by $100 billion to eliminate the government budget deficit. Butch wants to raise taxes by $60 billion. Cory wants to raise taxes by $20 billion. Danny wants to cut taxes by $40 billion. Emmy wants to cut taxes by $60 billion. Assume that two candidates are running for office, tax policy is the only issue, and the candidates care only about winning the election. Use the logic of the median-voter theorem to explain what positions the candidates will support.

13. Suppose that candidates for public office care about supporting the policies that seem best to them. How would this affect the median-voter theorem?

14. Suppose that everyone could legally buy and sell their votes. What would determine the equilibrium price of votes? Discuss the likely effects.

15. An intrauterine birth control device made in the 1970s, the Dalkon Shield, severely damaged the reproductive systems of many women, causing pain and infections and leaving them unable to bear children. The device also apparently caused several deaths. About 200,000 women later filed suits against the manufacturer with claims totaling $4 billion. Eventually the manufacturer filed for bankruptcy with the intent of preventing any new lawsuits by other women; the court handling the bankruptcy ordered the firm to set up a trust fund of $2.4 billion to pay compensation. Most of the money for this trust comes from the company that bought the bankrupt manufacturer.
    (a) What is the best procedure for determining the sizes of damages, obtaining payments for the injured women, and setting incentives to reduce the chance of a similar disaster in the future?
    (b) Suppose that a corporation loses a product-liability suit and goes bankrupt so that it cannot pay all legitimate claims. What should the law do about these situations? What incentives for firms are created by the ability to avoid payments by declaring bankruptcy?

16. Suppose that an accident occurs at a nuclear power facility, causing injuries such as increased risks of cancer or other diseases to its workers and nearby residents. How would you decide (a) who should pay the costs of this accident, and (b) how much the payment should be?

Inquiries for Further Thought

17. What is the economically efficient punishment for a college student who cheats on an exam or plagiarizes a paper? What is the correct marginal punishment for cheating or plagiarism?

18. Does the law promote economic efficiency or inefficiency by allowing criminals to profit from books, magazine articles, and television interviews related to the crimes they commit? Discuss this question again with reference to your ideas of justice or fairness; do the answers differ?

19. Marriage is a contract; divorce means breaking the contract.
    (a) What legal rules would promote economically efficient divorce? Discuss economically efficient compensation of a spouse, division of property, and responsibilities for children.
    (b) Courts have enforced so-called *palimony* suits, ruling that implicit promises resemble marriage contracts, and palimony payments take the place of alimony when the couple separates. Does the government promote economic efficiency by enforcing these contracts? How might a court determine the terms of any such implicit contract?

20. What are the effects of laws making bars legally responsible for accidents committed by patrons who drive drunk after leaving? Under what conditions, if any, should a smoker (or family after a smoker's death) be able to sue a cigarette manufacturer and collect damages for health problems? What economic efficiency issues are involved?

21. Under what conditions, if any, should courts decline to enforce private, voluntary contracts?

22. Would economic efficiency increase from a policy to require victim compensation in criminal cases? How would the requirement of victim compensation affect the economically efficient level of other punishments such as fines or prison terms? How should the sizes of victim compensation payments be determined for various crimes? Should they depend on criminals' ability to pay? What if a criminal cannot afford to pay victim compensation?

23. A very rich man marries a very poor woman, who quits her job to travel full-time with her husband. After a few years, the man breaks the marriage contract and leaves his wife. She takes him to court and asks for damages (alimony) for breaking the contract. Her lawyer argues that her former husband should pay her enough money to make her as wealthy as she would have been without the divorce, which would make her a rich woman. Her former husband's lawyer argues that she should receive only enough money to make her as wealthy as she would have been if she had never quit her job and married, which would leave her living in poverty. What should the court do?

24. Should the government set liability limits in lawsuits related to medical malpractice, accidents, or product-liability cases? How should courts decide the maximum liability levels in these cases?

25. Suppose scientists agree that a certain product will cause cancer in 10 percent of all people who have used it. Should the law allow a person to collect damages based on the *fear* and *possibility* that he will be among the unlucky 10 percent? Should only those people who actually develop cancer collect? Explain the economic efficiency issues involved.

26. The U.S. Supreme Court ruled in a 1992 case, *Lucas* v. *South Carolina Coast Commission,* that the government must compensate people who effectively lose the entire value of private property due to a government regulation. The ruling was based on the eminent domain clause in the fifth amendment to the U.S. Constitution, which says "Nor shall private property be taken for public use without just compensation." In the *Lucas* case, David Lucas bought two beach-front lots, on which he planned to build two houses. Two years later, before construction began, the state government instituted an environmental regulation that banned construction on the lots, severely reducing their value. The Supreme Court said that the U.S. Constitution requires the state government to compensate Lucas for the loss of "all economically viable use" of his land.

    Should the government compensate people for all losses in property values due to any changes in regulations, or only large losses, or only in certain cases? Why? What about losses due to changes in taxes?

27. Should losers in lawsuits have to compensate winners for their legal costs (lawyer fees, time spent on the cases, and other expenses) as is required in many countries outside North America? Should losers also pay court costs (the judge's salary and so on)?

PART 8

MACROECONOMICS: MYSTERIES, MEASUREMENT, AND MODELS

CHAPTER 24

MACROECONOMIC ISSUES AND MEASUREMENT

In this Chapter . . .

Main Points to Understand

- Macroeconomics is the study of the economy as a whole—total production of goods and services, total employment and unemployment, the average level of prices, foreign exchange rates, interest rates and financial market activity, and the overall effects of government policies.
- GDP measures the economy's total production of final market goods and services
- The GDP deflator, consumer price index, and producer price index are three measures of the average level of prices.

Thinking Skills to Develop

- Recognize the connection between the economy's total production of final goods and services, its total income, and its total spending.
- Distinguish between nominal and real GDP.
- Recognize key issues in measurement and interpretation of economic statistics.

When you finish college and look for a job, your employment opportunities will probably depend on the nation's overall economic situation. If the economy is growing rapidly with low unemployment rates, your chances of finding a good job will be higher than if the economy is in a recession with low growth and high unemployment. In the first half of 1998, the unemployment rate in the United States was 4.5 percent, down from 7.5 percent only six years earlier. What will happen when you look for a job?

If your job has an international flavor—as many do through world trade, international business connections, or foreign competition—then international factors such as financial crises and recessions in Asia, inflation in Latin America, and high unemployment in Europe may directly impact your career. Even middle-class Americans will see their lives dramatically altered in the coming decades by economic growth in China, Africa, Mexico and Latin America, Russia, and eastern Europe. Distant as these places may seem, events there will affect your job opportunities, your salary, the prices you pay, and the products available to you. They will affect the interest rates at which you can borrow money for cars and vacations, the taxes you will pay, and the new technologies that drive the goods and services you consume in the coming decades.

Momentous economic events have transformed people's lives over the last 100 years. The 20th century saw the highest inflation rates in history; the Great Depression of the 1930s, with the highest unemployment rates ever recorded; and interactions of economics and politics that led to war—as economic penalties imposed on Germany after World War I helped bring hyperinflation and the rise of Adolf Hitler. The 20th century saw dramatic increases in government spending and taxes. In the United States, federal government spending rose from under 3 percent of the total U.S. income in 1900 to almost 20 percent in 1998. Economic catastrophes in the former Soviet Union and eastern Europe helped to bring down communism, ending the cold war and spreading freedom and democracy. The century also saw the development of new financial markets around the globe, along with the fastest growth in living standards in all of history, the biggest drops in national death rates and infant mortality rates, and the biggest increases in life expectancy. No one was isolated from these events—economic issues affected not only people's jobs and incomes but the challenges and opportunities that shaped their lives. Economics shaped the 20th century, and it will probably help shape your life in the 21st.

Macroeconomics is the study of the economy as a whole—*total* production of goods and services, rather than production of individual goods such as pizzas and painting services; *total* employment and unemployment rather than employment in the computer industry or unemployment in the auto industry; the *average* level of prices rather than the prices of haircuts and hats. You will see that macroeconomics also involves interest rates, foreign exchange rates, stock markets and other financial markets, and the overall effects of government policies. You need to understand macroeconomics before you can understand many of the major social and political issues that affect our lives. You must understand macroeconomics if you want to contribute to the design of thoughtful government policies, and to the solutions to economic problems impacting people around the globe.

This book explores the key issues of macroeconomics, including:

▶ What affects a country's living standards?

▶ Why do standards of living differ across countries?

▶ Why are average standards of living higher now than in the past? What affects the speed at which living standards *grow*?

▶ What affects available job opportunities, total employment, unemployment, and wages?

▶ What causes *business cycles* in which periods of rising incomes and low unemployment are followed by *recessions* in which incomes fall and unemployment rises?

▶ What affects the average level of prices and the increases in this average that we call *inflation?*

▶ How does international trade affect our economy? What affects exchange rates between moneys in different countries, and how do changes in foreign exchange rates affect the economy?

▶ What creates changes in interest rates and stock prices, and how do these changes affect our lives?

▶ How do government policies affect the economy? What policies are best?

TOTAL PRODUCTION OF GOODS AND SERVICES

In 1997, the U.S. economy produced final goods and services that sold for $8,080 billion (or about $8 trillion). This is the economy's *GDP*, or *gross domestic product*. With a population of 268 million, U.S. GDP per capita (per person) was $30,149.

Gross domestic product (GDP) is the value of a country's production of final market goods and services during some time period (usually a year).

World GDP is currently about $36 trillion per year. With a world population of about 6 billion people, this amounts to about $6,000 per person each year.[1]

Nominal GDP refers to GDP measured in money (dollars, yen, pesos, Euros, etc.).

Real GDP, to be defined formally below, refers to *inflation-adjusted* GDP.

Notice the phrase "final market goods and services." Final goods are products or services intended for sale to consumers, such as hamburgers or tattoo services. Products such as steering wheels, that become inputs into the production of other goods such as cars, are *not* final goods. In other words, GDP includes the economy's production of french fries, but it does not separately include the production of potatoes that were inputs into those french fries. The term *market goods* refers to products that people sell to others; GDP does not include the food you eat from your own garden or services that people perform without explicit pay, such as housework, child care by parents, and volunteer work.

Four decades ago, in 1960, U.S. nominal GDP was only $527 billion, or about $2,915 per person, as Figure 1 indicates. What explains the change since then? Two factors are at work: (1) increases in production, and (2) increases in prices.

Increases in Production

If prices had been the same in 1997 as in 1960, then the final goods and services produced in the United States in 1997 would have sold for $1,728 billion. In other words, U.S. GDP in 1997, *measured in 1960 prices,* was $1,728 billion.

Real GDP refers to GDP measured in the prices of a certain *base year*.

Figure 2 shows U.S. real GDP measured in *base year 1960 prices.* In 1960, U.S. real GDP in 1960 prices was $527 billion; by 1997, it was $1,674 billion. The scale on the right-hand side of Figure 2 shows U.S. real GDP measured in *1997 prices.* Measured in *1997 prices,* U.S. real GDP was $2,544 billion in 1960 and $8,080 billion in 1997. As Table 1 shows, the choice of a base year affects only the scale of measurement; it does not affect the picture of how real GDP changes over time. Figure 2 shows that U.S. real GDP more than tripled between 1960 and 1997.

The U.S. population increased from 181 million in 1960 to 268 million in 1997, so real GDP per person in 1997 dollars rose from:

$$\frac{\$2,544 \text{ billion}}{181 \text{ million people}} = \$14,055 \text{ per person in 1960}$$

to

$$\frac{\$8,080 \text{ billion}}{268 \text{ million people}} = \$30,149 \text{ per person in 1997}$$

In other words, U.S. real GDP per person more than doubled during that time.

GDP Update
In the first half of 1998, U.S. GDP reached $8,435 billion at an annual rate, meaning that GDP for the year would equal $8,435 billion, or $31,177 per person, if production in the second half of the year continued at the same pace as in the first half. See the Web pages for this book (www.dryden.com) for the latest economic statistics.

Only Final Goods Appear in GDP
To see why GDP includes only *final* market goods and services, consider an example. Suppose that National Sugar sells sugar to Nabisco for $1,000, and Hershey sells chocolate to Nabisco for $500. Nabisco uses sugar and chocolate to produce final goods: 100,000 Oreo cookies. If cookies sell for 3 cents each, people spend $3,000 to buy 100,000 cookies. If these cookies were the *only* final market good in the economy, nominal GDP would be $3,000. It would not make sense to include the $1,000 of sugar and the $500 of chocolate in GDP *in addition* to the cookies, because they are *part* of the cookies. (Should we also add the value of the cocoa beans that were used to produce the chocolate?) Only the value of *final* market goods appears in GDP.

---

[1]Estimates of world GDP differ, ranging from about 10 percent below this estimate to about 20 percent above it.

Figure 1 | Nominal GDP in the United States, 1929–1998

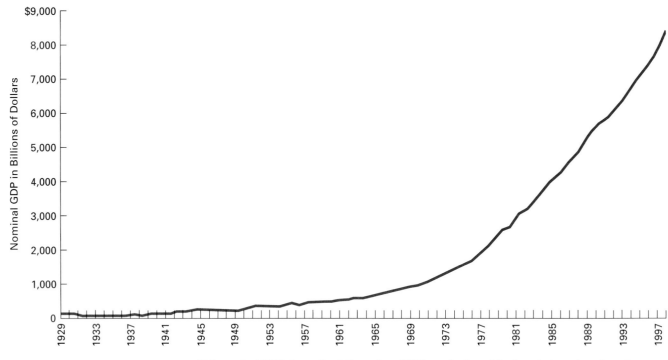

U.S. nominal GDP shows the dollar value of U.S. production of final market goods and services during each year.

Figure 2 | U.S. Real GDP, 1929–1998

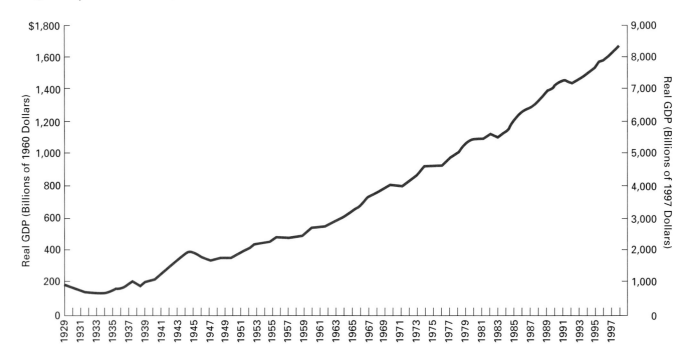

U.S. real GDP has generally increased over time. The scale on the left-hand side shows real GDP measured in base year 1960 prices; the scale on the right-hand side shows real GDP measured in base-year 1997 prices.

Table 1 | Measuring U.S. GDP in Base-Year Prices

U.S. GDP	Nominal GDP	Real GDP, Measured in 1960 Prices	Real GDP, Measured in 1997 Prices
In 1960	$527 billion	$527 billion	$2,544 billion
In 1997	$8,080 billion	$1,674 billion	$8,080 billion
Percentage increase	1,433 percent	218 percent	218 percent

Increases in Prices

Most nominal (money) prices increased between 1960 and 1997. (Chapter 4 explained the difference between nominal prices and relative prices.) One way to measure the average increase in prices over that period is to compare two figures:

▶ The money value of the economy's production in 1997 (nominal GDP in 1997)

▶ The money value of the economy's production in 1997 *if prices had been at their 1960 levels* (real 1997 GDP measured in 1960 prices)

The ratio of these two numbers shows the average increase in prices between 1960 and 1997. If prices had remained constant over that period, then these two numbers would be the same, and their ratio would equal 1. If every price had doubled between 1960 and 1997, then the first number would be twice as high as the second number, and their ratio would equal 2, indicating that prices had doubled. The *GDP deflator* measures the average change in prices between two years:

The **GDP deflator** equals nominal GDP divided by real GDP:

$$\text{GDP deflator} = 100 \times \frac{\text{Nominal GDP}}{\text{Real GDP}}$$

Figure 3 shows the U.S. GDP deflator, sometimes called the *implicit price deflator,* from 1960 to 1998. The scale on the left side shows the GDP deflator with base year

Advice: Understanding Base-Year Prices

Don't be confused by the idea of base-year prices—the idea is really very simple. Imagine comparing GDP per person in the United States and Mexico. In 1997, Mexican GDP was 3,248 billion pesos. To compare this amount to U.S. GDP of $8,080 billion, you need to know that about 8 pesos had the same value as $1. Then you can calculate that Mexican GDP, *measured in dollars,* was about $406 billion.

The same reasoning applies when you compare *1960 dollars* with *1997 dollars.* U.S. GDP in 1960 was $527 billion, and U.S. GDP in 1997 was $8,080 billion. To compare them, you need to know that $1.00 in 1960 was about the same as $4.83 in 1997. Then you can calculate that 1960 GDP, *measured in 1997 dollars,* was $2,544 billion.

IN THE NEWS

Big Upward Revision in 1st-Qtr Growth

A 5.4% GDP surge shows the economy was even hotter than thought

The nation's economy roared in the first quarter, with the fastest growth in nearly 2 years.

Gross domestic product grew at a 5.4% annual rate in the first quarter, revised up from the previous estimate of 4.8%, the Commerce Department reported. That's the fastest growth since the second quarter of 1996, when the economy rose at a 6% pace.

Source: Investor's Business Daily

News reports, like this one, usually mean "real GDP" when they refer to GDP.

Figure 3 | U.S. GDP Deflator, 1929–1998

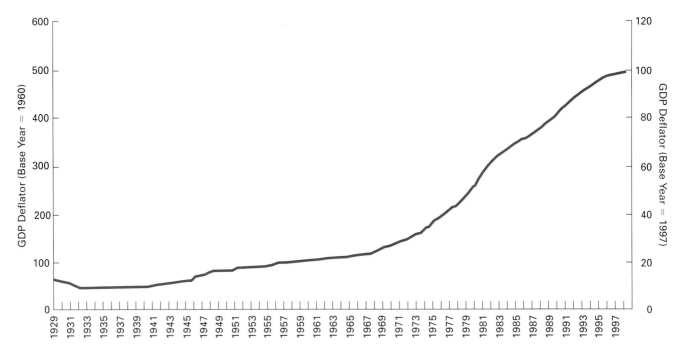

The GDP deflator, or implicit price deflator, equals nominal GDP divided by real GDP.

1960. In other words, it shows the GDP deflator when the denominator of the formula is real GDP measured in 1960 prices. The GDP deflator equaled 100 in 1960 by definition; it rose to 483 by 1997. In other words, the average level of nominal prices in the United States in 1997 was about 5 times as high as the level in 1960.

The scale on the right-hand side of Figure 3 shows the GDP deflator for base year 1997. In other words, it shows the GDP deflator when the denominator of the formula is real GDP measured in 1997 prices. With this scale, the GDP deflator equals 100.0 in

IN THE NEWS

GDP up, inflation at bay

NEW YORK (CNNfn) - The American economy grew by a stronger-than-expected 1.4 percent in the second quarter, the Commerce Department said Friday. Real gross-domestic product, or the total value of goods and services produced by the U.S. economy, expanded at a 1.4 percent annual rate from April through June, down sharply from a revised 5.5 percent growth spurt in the first quarter.

Inflation, meanwhile, appeared to be held in check. The implicit price deflator, a key inflation measure, rose only 0.9 percent in the second quarter.

Source: http://cnnfn.com/hotstories/economy/9807/31/gdp/

GDP and the GDP deflator, often called the implicit price deflator, frequently appear in the news.

1997 by definition, and it rose from 20.7 in 1960. Conclusions about changes in the average level of nominal prices do not depend on which scale we choose.

EXAMPLE: MEASURING REAL GDP IN BASE-YEAR PRICES

Suppose that the economy produces six videos and eight pillows in 2002, as Table 2 shows, and that videos cost $20 each and pillows cost $10 each in that year.

Nominal GDP in 2002 = (Output of videos in 2002)(Price of videos in 2002)
+ (Output of pillows in 2002)(Price of pillows in 2002)
= (6 videos)($20 per video) + (8 pillows)($10 per pillow)
= $120 + $80 = $200

Now choose a base year, such as 1990, and calculate real GDP.

Real GDP in 2002 measured in 1990 dollars
= (Output of videos in 2002) (Price of videos in 1990)
+ (Output of pillows in 2002)(Price of pillows in 1990)

Suppose that, as Table 2 shows, videos cost only $10 each in 1990, and pillows cost only $5 each. Then real GDP in 2002 measured in 1990 dollars equals:

(6 videos in 2002)($10 per video in 1990)
+ (8 pillows in 2002)($5 per pillow in 1990)
= $60 + $40 in 1990 dollars
= $100 in 1990 dollars

Real GDP in 2002 is $100 measured in 1990 dollars. Table 2 shows similar calculations for other years.

This measurement of real GDP allows sensible comparisons of the economy's output of goods and services in different years. To see why, suppose that the economy produces the same number of videos and pillows in 2002 as it did in 1998, but that prices are higher in 2002 than in 1998. Then nominal GDP rises between 1998 and 2002, while real GDP remains unchanged at $100, measured in 1990 dollars. This is a sensible conclusion: real GDP remains constant because production of goods does not change.

Now suppose that the economy produces 9 videos and 12 pillows in 2005, 50 percent more of each good than in 2002. In this case:

Real GDP in 2005 measured in 1990 dollars
= (9 videos in 2005)($10 per video in 1990)
+ (12 pillows in 2005)($5 per pillow in 1990)
= $90 + $60 in 1990 dollars
= $150 in 1990 dollars

Table 2 | Measuring GDP in an Economy with Videos and Pillows

	Videos	Price of Videos	Pillows	Price of Pillows	Nominal GDP	Real GDP in 1990 Dollars
1990	4	$10	4	$ 5	$ 60	$ 60
1998	6	18	8	8	172	100
2002	6	20	8	10	200	100
2005	9	21	12	10	309	150
2010	9	21	16	10	349	170

Real GDP in 2005 is $150 measured in 1990 dollars. Real GDP rises by 50 percent from 2002 to 2005, because production of each good rises by 50 percent. Finally, suppose that the economy produces 9 videos and 16 pillows in 2010. Real GDP in 2010 rises to $170 in 1990 dollars.

The change in real GDP between any two years is an average of the changes in output of the goods that the economy produces, weighted by their base-year prices. The price deflator in 2002 becomes:

$$\text{GDP price deflator in 2002 (base year 1990)}$$

$$= \frac{\text{Nominal GDP in 2002}}{\text{Real GDP in 2002 in 1990 dollars}}$$

$$= \frac{\$200}{\$100 \text{ in 1990 dollars}}$$

$$= 2 \text{ (relative to base year 1990)}$$

In this case, the price level doubles from 1990 to 2002. Notice that the equation for real GDP applies to this example: Nominal GDP in 2002 is $200, the price deflator is 2, and real income in 1990 dollars is $100.

Review Questions

1. What is the difference between real GDP and nominal GDP?

2. Roughly how large is the U.S. GDP? Roughly how large is world GDP? How big is GDP per person in the United States? GDP per person in the world?

Thinking Exercises

3. Use the numbers in Table 2 to calculate real GDP in 2010 measured in 1998 dollars.

4. A nation of elves produces only one good: cookies. In 1990, cookies sold for 2 cents each; in 1998, they cost 3 cents each; in 2000, they cost 4 cents each. How is this nation's real GDP related to the number of cookies it produces? How does your answer depend on your choice of the base year for measuring real GDP?

THE ECONOMY'S TOTAL SPENDING AND INCOME

What happens to all the goods and services the economy produces? People *consume* some of them—they wear clothes, eat pizzas, and watch movies. *Consumption* refers to the goods and services that people buy and use. Business firms *invest* some of them—they build new machinery, equipment, and office buildings. *Investment* refers to the creation of new *capital*—machinery, equipment, tools, buildings, and new knowledge (such as the technical knowledge of how to build a computer chip). The *government purchases* some of the goods and services. Finally, we may *export* some goods to people in foreign countries, perhaps more than we *import* from them. As a result, GDP equals the sum of consumption, investment, government purchases, and net exports (exports minus imports):

$$GDP = C + I + G + NEX$$

where C is consumption, I is investment, G is government purchases, and NEX is net exports (exports minus imports). Table 3 and Figure 4 show that consumption accounts for

Table 3 | GDP in the United States, 1997

	Total ($ billions)	Dollars Per Person	Percent of GDP
Nominal gross domestic product (GDP)	$8,080	$30,149	
Consumption	5,486	20,469	68%
Investment	1,243	4,636	15
Government purchases	1,453	5,421	18
Net exports	−101	−377	−1

about two-thirds of GDP in the United States, investment accounts for about 15 percent, government purchases account for 18 percent, and net exports account for −1 percent (because the United States imports more than it exports). The percentages are very similar for most other countries.

Definitions and Discussion

People consume goods when they use them—when they eat, wear, or drive them:

> **Consumption** is spending by people on final goods and services for current use.

People often buy goods, such as cars and houses, partly for future use. Official government statistics measure consumption as total household spending on goods and services except for purchases of new housing, which the official statistics count as investment.

Advice to Students
Don't be confused by the *NEX* part of this equation. *Net* exports (exports *minus* imports) appears in the GDP equation, because consumption and investment already include imports from other countries. For example, suppose GDP is $10, consumption is $8, investment is $1, government spending is $2, and exports are zero. How can consumption, investment, and government purchases sum to $11 when the nation produces only $10 in goods? Easy—the country imports $1 worth of goods, making *net* exports equal to *minus* $1. Then $C + I + G + NEX = $ $10, which equals GDP.

Figure 4 | Categories of Spending in GDP

Net Exports − $101 | NEX | − 1%
Government Purchases $1,453 | G | 18%
Investment $1,243 | I | 15%
Consumption $5,486 | C | 68%

GDP = $8,080

Consumption accounts for about two-thirds of U.S. GDP; investment accounts for about 15 percent; government purchases account for 18 percent.

Consumption.

Advice: Understanding Investment

In everyday life, people say they *invest* if they buy stocks or bonds. However, when you buy stocks or bonds, someone else sells them. In that case, the economy as a whole does not invest. The economy as a whole invests when it increases its capital stock (machinery, tools, knowledge, etc.). Economists use the term *investment* to refer to such increases in the economy's capital stock.

In principle, whenever you buy a durable good, such as a stereo or a car, part of that spending is investment, because you will continue to use the good in the future. However, official statistics count spending on durable goods, except new houses, as consumption.

Business firms *invest* when they buy new machines, computers, office buildings, and lab equipment. They also invest when they build new factories, train their workers, and add to knowledge through research and development.

> **Capital** is the stock of equipment, structures, inventories, human skills, and knowledge available to help produce goods and services. **Investment** is spending to create new capital.

Capital also includes inventories—stocks of spare parts and unsold final goods. For example, an auto dealer may invest in cars for its showroom or oil filters for its repair shop. In principle, you invest when you acquire skills by attending school or when you buy a durable good; however, these kinds of investments appear in official consumption statistics rather than investment statistics. The government also invests when it spends money on roads and buildings, but all government spending falls in a separate category. The term *investment* means *private* (nongovernment) investment spending.

The government purchases goods and services when it buys military equipment, builds roads, and pays school teachers and police.

> **Government purchases** include total spending on goods and services by federal, state, and local governments.

Not all government *spending* consists of government *purchases*. Government spending also includes *transfer payments* of money to people—payments that simply transfer money without any exchange of goods and services. The social security program is the largest transfer payment program in the United States. This spending is *not* included in the GDP category of government purchases of goods and services.

> **Exports** are goods and services sold to people and firms in other countries.

Investment creates new capital.

> **Imports** are purchases of goods and services from people and firms in other countries.

> **Net exports,** or the **balance of international trade,** equals exports minus imports.

A country with positive net exports (its exports exceed its imports) has an international trade surplus; one with negative net exports (its exports fall short of imports) has an international trade deficit.

Every good produced in the economy is consumed, invested, purchased by the government, or exported.[2] If a firm produces a good that no one buys, it becomes an investment in the firm's inventory of goods not yet sold.

Figure 5 and Table 4 show flows of money and goods in the United States in a year. All numbers in the figure show *average* amounts *per person*.[3] The figure shows four types of actors in the economy: people, firms, the government, and foreign countries. The arrows show flows of money between these actors; the green arrows show flows of money to buy *final goods*. In 1997, nominal GDP was about $30,000 per person. People spent about $20,500 per person for consumption; an arrow from people to firms shows

Figure 5 | GDP per Person in the United States

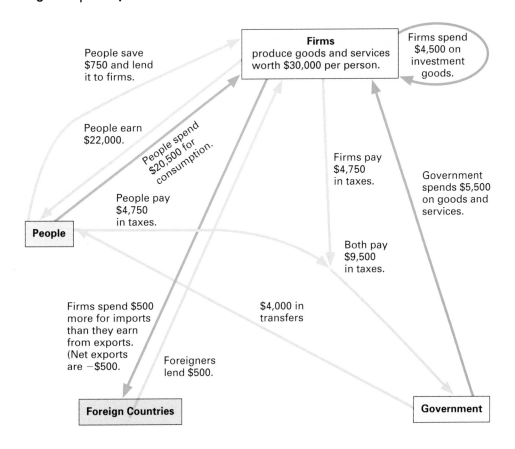

The numbers show *dollars per person* for flows in the U.S. economy. For example, wages and other income from firms averages about $22,000 per person, and consumption spending averages $20,500 per person.

---

[2] If you buy an ice cream cone and it melts before you eat it, you might not want to say that you consumed it. Still, this spending counts as consumption in economic data.

[3] All per-person amounts refer to the entire U.S. population—about 268 million people in 1997.

Table 4 | Flows of Money in Figure 5[a]

People		Firms		Government	
MONEY IN	MONEY OUT	MONEY IN	MONEY OUT	MONEY IN	MONEY OUT
$22,000 wages and profits	$20,500 consumption	$20,500 consumption $4,500 investment $5,500 government purchases	$22,000 wages and profits $4,500 investment		$5,500 government purchases
$4,000 transfer payments	$4,750 taxes		$4,750 taxes	$9,500 taxes	$4,000 transfer payments
	$750 loaned to firms	$750 borrowed from people $500 borrowed from foreign countries	$500 for imports in excess of exports		
TOTAL = $26,000	TOTAL = $26,000	TOTAL = $31,750	TOTAL = $31,750	TOTAL = $9,500	TOTAL = $9,500

[a]All Figures in dollars *per person* in the United States, 1997.

payments of $20,500 for this purpose. Firms spent about $4,500 per person on investment. The curved arrow leading from firms back to firms shows $4,500 per person in payments for that investment. Government purchases were $5,500 per person in 1997, and the arrow from government to firms shows the payment for those goods. Notice that the sum of consumption, investment, and government purchases, $30,500 per person, is $500 *more* than GDP. Where did the other $500 in spending go? The answer is that net exports totaled *minus* $500 per person; imports exceeded exports by that amount. In sum, the U.S. economy produced $30,000 in goods per person and imported $500 more, so total spending on consumption, investment, and government purchases was $30,500 per person.

The Economy's Total Income

Where did people get the $20,500 that they spent on consumption? Gold arrows show other flows of money in the economy. On average, each person earned $22,000 by working at firms and by sharing in firms' profits. In addition, the government provided money to people through *transfer payments* that averaged $4,000 per person. In total, then, an average person acquired $26,000 from these sources. After subtracting $20,500 in consumption spending and $4,750 per person in taxes, people had $750 per person left (on average) in savings. They loaned this money to firms (usually with banks acting as intermediaries).

Where did firms get the $4,500 that they spent on investment? They obtained $20,500 per person by selling goods to people for consumption. They also earned $4,500 per person by selling goods to other firms for investment. Finally, they earned $5,500 per person by selling goods to the government. In total, then, firms obtained $30,500 per person from these sources. In addition, they borrowed $1,250 per person, partly from foreign countries. Firms spent $22,000 to pay people wages and profits, $4,500 for investment, $4,750 in taxes, and $500 for imports in excess of exports.

The economy's total income—*national income*—is less than its total production, because some of that production replaces capital that wears out over the year. In 1997, two-thirds of the money that firms spent on investment, or $3,000 per person, paid for replacing capital that *depreciated* (wore out) during the year. As a result, gross investment of $4,500 per person increased the capital stock by about $1,500 per person. Figure 6 illustrates this point. If you build 4½ new machines, and 3 old machines explode or wear out (depreciate), then you have increased the number of machines by 1½.

Figure 6 | Gross and Net Investment

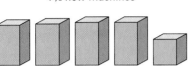

Gross investment =
4¹/₂ new machines

Minus *depreciation*
(3 old machines explode)

Leaves *net investment*
(increase in the capital stock) =
1¹/₂ additional machines

Income and GDP

Figure 5 and Table 4 suggest another way to calculate GDP—by adding incomes instead of expenditures. Income and spending are closely related: When you spend $5 for a movie, your spending creates $5 of income for the theater. Because every trade involves a buyer and seller, the buyer's spending equals the seller's income. Each person's income is connected with someone's spending:

> GDP = total value of production of final market goods and services
> = total spending on those goods and services
> = total income from selling those goods and services

U.S. firms produced $30,000 in final market goods and services per person in 1997. After replacing capital that depreciated ($3,000 per person), the economy was left with $27,000 per person in final market goods and services. Firms sold those goods, and the revenues from those sales created income for people and the government, as shown in Figure 5 and Table 4.[4]

Measuring Employment and Unemployment

GDP,
EMPLOYMENT,
AND
UNEMPLOYMENT

Over six million adult Americans were *unemployed* in 1998, while 131.2 million had jobs, and 68 million adults were *not in the labor force*. These terms represent some simple basic concepts: People with jobs are *employed;* people are *unemployed* if they are jobless and looking for jobs; other people are *not in the labor force*. Official statistics on total employment, unemployment, and the labor force in the United States come from the government's Current Population Survey. Each month, the Census Bureau interviews about 60,000 households and classifies the members as employed, unemployed, or not in the labor force. The *unemployment rate* is the percentage of unemployed people in the labor force.

> The **unemployment rate** is the percentage of unemployed people in the labor force.

$$\text{Unemployment rate} = 100 \times \frac{\text{Number of unemployed people}}{\text{Number of employed people} + \text{Number of unemployed people}}$$

---

[4]Details of the tax system complicate the precise calculations. The appendix to this chapter shows more details on the connections between production and income in the National Income Accounts. Also see the Web page (www.dryden.com) for this book.

IN THE NEWS

World recession possible, '30s rerun not?

TOKYO—World financial market turmoil, the collapse of growth in Asia, and fears of a global credit crunch are forcing economists to rachet down forecasts for global growth and admit that recession cannot be ruled out.

Comparisons to the debacle of 70 years ago are nonetheless falling more frequently from commentators' lips these days. Mutterings of a potential global depression are also being heard more often in the financial community.

But despite a case of crisis jitters, many economic experts say that unless world policymakers suffer collective amnesia, a rerun of the 1930s Great Depression is unlikely. Many economists believe that lessons from policy mistakes that tilted the world into depression in the 1930s have been learned well enough to avoid a rerun now.

Source: Reuters News

The last recession in the United States occurred in 1990 and 1991. When do you expect the next one?

IN THE NEWS

Unemployment jumps to record in South Korea

Rate hits 7% as government increases pressure on insolvent companies to end operations

SEOUL—With nearly 2,000 people losing jobs every day, South Korea's unemployment rate has soared to a record 7 percent of the work force, or 1.49 million people, the government reported Tuesday.

More than 2 million people are likely to be out of work by the end of the summer, according to projections by the National Statistical Office, as some of the country's largest companies make good on promises to cut losses by laying off workers.

Source: International Herald Tribune

With 6.2 million people unemployed and 131 million employed, the unemployment rate is $100 \times 6.2/(137.2) = 4.5$ percent.

Key Economic Issues about GDP, Unemployment, and Prices

Figure 7 shows the unemployment rate in the United States; Figure 8 shows total employment. Key economic issues call for explanations:

▶ Why did the U.S. unemployment rate average 5.7 percent in the last half of the 20th century, rather than 2.0 percent or 10.0 percent?

▶ Why is the unemployment rate in Europe about twice as high as in the United States? Why is the unemployment rate in Japan only about half as high as the U.S. rate?

▶ Why does the unemployment rate change over time? Why did it reach nearly 10 percent in 1982 and fall almost to 4 percent in 1998? Why did it reach almost 25 percent during the Great Depression of the 1930s?

▶ Why does unemployment increase as the growth of real GDP slows its growth or declines, as in the *recessions* of 1975, 1982, and 1991 (see Figures 2 and 7) and the Great Depression?

A **recession** occurs when real GDP is unusually low relative to its trend value. Some economists define a recession as a period when real GDP falls for two consecutive quarters (3-month periods), although official recession dates set by the National Bureau of Economic Research are based on more sophisticated criteria.

▶ Why do total employment and real GDP grow over long periods of time (see Figures 2 and 8)? What economic forces create additional jobs and additional production?

▶ How can government policies contribute to long-run growth of real GDP and employment? What can policies help to prevent recessions and maintain low unemployment?

▶ What causes prices to rise over time (as in Figure 3)? What causes foreign exchange rates to change? How can government policies contribute to low inflation?

These and other related issues will be the subjects of later chapters. Before beginning those discussions, this chapter discusses some reasons for cautious interpretations of the data and alternative measures of the average level of prices.

Problems with Measurement and Interpretation

Economists lack ideal measurements for most economic data. Three big problems complicate measurement and interpretation of gross domestic product.

First, GDP figures omit production of goods and services that are not sold on markets, such as housework, meals cooked at home, and child care provided by parents, as well as services volunteered for charities and other groups. When you repair your own apartment, your repair services do not appear in GDP. However, if two people repair each other's apartments, and each pays the other $100, the exchange adds $200 to GDP. When parents care for their own children, the value of their care does not appear in GDP. However, when parents pay for child care, those services appear in GDP. When volunteers take a group of scouts to camp, their services do not appear in GDP; however, when a camp hires paid leaders, their services appear in GDP.

Second, GDP includes only a very imperfect estimate of production of goods and services sold on the underground economy (or black market). This activity includes production of illegal goods and services (such as drugs and prostitution). It also includes production of legal goods that goes unreported to avoid taxes. Many estimates suggest that the underground economy in the United States amounts to between 5 and 10 percent of GDP; this figure is even larger in many other countries. In some episodes (such as experiences in Peru and Russia), underground economies may have been as large as above-ground (official) economies, creating huge errors in GDP measurement.

Third, special measurement problems result when GDP includes certain goods that are

IN THE NEWS

U.S. Jobless Rate Drops to 28-Year Low

American businesses created 262,000 new jobs last month, and unemployment fell to an astoundingly low 4.3%, a level not seen since February 1970.

Source: The Wall Street Journal

Each month the government reports the unemployment rate calculated from its survey. As Figure 7 shows, the U.S. unemployment rate fell from 1992 through 1998.

IN THE NEWS

The ruble: an hour-by-hour disaster

MOSCOW, Sept. 3— Moscow's Central Interbank Exchange re-opened Thursday for the first time since trading was halted on Aug. 26. The ruble has lost more than half its value since late August, and the long downward plunge continues unabated. Meanwhile, worried Moscovites crammed banks in a frantic and mostly fruitless attempt to withdraw savings being eroded by the hour as the ruble continued its free-fall.

Source: CNBC

Exchange-rate crises have hit many countries in recent years, including Russia, Mexico, Indonesia, and South Korea. One key issue of macroeconomics involves the causes and prevention of crises like these. When do you expect the next one?

Figure 7 | Unemployment Rate in the United States

A monthly government survey measures the unemployment rate as the percentage of unemployed people in the labor force. People are unemployed if they are jobless but looking for jobs. People are in the labor force if they are either employed or unemployed (people are not in the labor force if they are jobless but not looking for jobs).

not sold on markets. When you rent a house or apartment, your expenses appear in GDP as payments for housing services. However, if you *own* your house or apartment, GDP includes the government's estimate of the rent that you *would* pay if you were renting.

Figure 8 | Total Employment in the United States

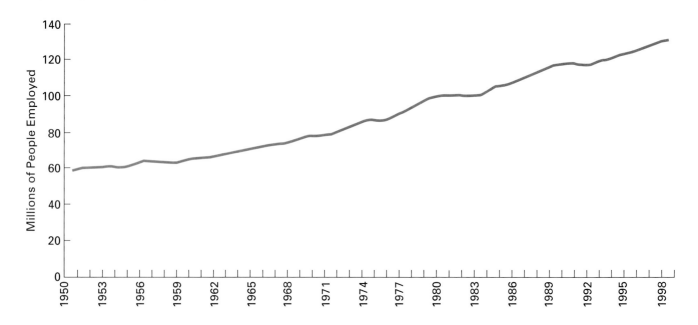

Similarly, the costs of environmental cleanups present special problems. Ideally, GDP would include the value of the improvement to the environment—the amount of money that people would be willing to pay for the cleaner environment (as measured by the equilibrium prices at which these benefits would be sold on markets). Instead, GDP includes the *costs* of environmental cleanups, which may differ significantly from their benefits. Similarly, GDP includes the *costs* of government services, such as police and public-school services, rather than their market values.

Measurement of unemployment also suffers from imperfections, and its interpretation requires caution. First, unemployment tends to be understated by official numbers, which ignore *discouraged workers,* who do not have jobs but have given up hope of finding them and stopped looking. The government classifies these people as not in the labor force. Second, unemployment tends to be understated, because it counts *underemployed* workers (mathematicians driving cabs, and so on) as fully employed. Similarly, official statistics count people who work part-time as employed, although they may want full-time jobs. Third, official statistics overstate unemployment to the extent that people are not truthful or not serious about looking for work.

Despite imperfections with measurement of GDP and unemployment, statistics on these and other economic concepts provide important evidence about the economy. It is important to remember that GDP is intended to measure production, not human happiness. GDP does not measure pollution, crime, leisure time, health, beauty, values, the qualities of goods, the qualities of relationships, or the quality of life. GDP is merely a convenient, if incomplete, summary measure of the total production of final goods sold on markets. Nevertheless, increases in GDP have been associated with increases in life expectancy, improvements in health, and increases in leisure time, as well as with increases in material comforts such as food, shelter, and entertainment. While interpreting changes in GDP and other economic statistics requires care, we can learn much about the economy from these statistics. Before turning to *how* we can use these concepts to learn about the operation of the economy, we turn to the concepts of the price level and inflation.

Review Questions

5. Consumption is (roughly) what fraction of GDP?

6. How is the unemployment rate measured in the United States?

7. What is a recession? What happens to unemployment during a recession?

8. List three main problems in measurement (or interpretation) of GDP.

9. List three main problems in measurement (or interpretation) of unemployment.

Thinking Exercise

10. Explain how you could try to estimate a broader concept of GDP that would *include* final goods and services that are currently omitted or measured poorly.

The economy's *price level* is an average of the prices of its goods and services. We have already encountered one measure of the price level: the GDP deflator. Other common measures are the *consumer price index (CPI)* and the *producer price index (PPI)*.

MEASURING THE PRICE LEVEL

IN THE NEWS

CPI increase on target

NEW YORK (CNNfn) - U.S. consumer prices rose slightly in July, the Labor Department reported Tuesday. The Consumer Price Index, the government's main inflation gauge, rose 0.2 percent, following a 0.1 percent increase in June.

Source: http://cnnfn.com/hotstories/ economy/9808/18/cpi/

Due to compounding, a monthly rise of 0.2 percent equals an annual increase of about 2.7 percent per year. A monthly rise of 0.1 percent equals an annual increase of about 1.3 percent per year.

The consumer price index measures the average nominal prices of goods and services that a typical family living in an urban area buys. The CPI is a weighted average; goods such as salt and shoelaces (on which people spend small fractions of their incomes) receive less weight in the average than goods like cars and televisions, on which people spend more money. The PPI is a weighted average of the prices of inputs—crude goods and intermediate goods (sometimes called *wholesale prices*)—that producers buy to make final goods. On average, the CPI has doubled every 25 years in the 20th century, meaning that consumer prices now are 16 times higher than they were 100 years ago. The PPI and GDP deflator, on the other hand, are about 10 times higher than a century ago.

Figure 9a shows the price level in the United States as measured by the CPI, PPI, and GDP deflator; Figure 9b shows *inflation rates*—annual percentage changes in the price level—using the same three measures. The GDP deflator includes all final market goods and services produced in the country, while the CPI includes only the goods and services that an average household buys, and the PPI includes only those that an average producer buys. The CPI and PPI include the goods we import, but not those we export. The GDP deflator, in contrast, measures prices of goods we produce rather than goods we buy, so it includes the goods we export, but not those we import.

The CPI and PPI result from government survey data. Every several years, the U.S. Census Bureau conducts a Consumer Expenditure Survey to see what goods and services the typical family buys. Each month the Bureau of Labor Statistics (BLS) sends researchers to stores to find out the prices of about 400 goods and services, recording a total of about 90,000 prices. The BLS computes the total cost of buying the quantities of these goods that the typical family buys. The BLS also computes the total cost of buying these goods at base-year prices. It then calculates the consumer price index from the formula:

$$\text{CPI} = 100 \times \frac{\text{Total cost of the goods now}}{\text{Total cost of the goods in the base year}}$$

EXAMPLES

Suppose that the typical family buys ten pizzas, eight half-gallons of ice cream, and two bottles of antacid tablets every month, and that pizzas cost $10, ice cream costs $4 per half-gallon, and antacids cost $3 per bottle. (See Table 5.) The family's total spending is:

$$(10)(\$10) + (8)(\$4) + (2)(\$3) = \$138$$

Suppose that *in 1990* pizzas cost $8, ice cream cost $3, and antacids cost $3. At these 1990 base-year prices, ten pizzas, eight half-gallons of ice cream, and two bottles of antacids would have cost:

$$(10)(\$8) + (8)(\$3) + (2)(\$3) = \$110$$

The CPI, measured in 1990 dollars, is then:

$$\text{CPI} = 100 \times \frac{\$138}{\$110} = 125$$

A typical family spends $138 today to buy goods that cost only $110 in 1990. In other words, it must spend about $125 today to buy the same goods that it could have bought for only $100 in 1990. In other words, the average level of prices has increased by about 25 percent.

Figure 9 | Three Measures of the Price Level and Inflation

(a) CPI and PPI, 1913 – 1998; GDP Deflator, 1921 – 1998

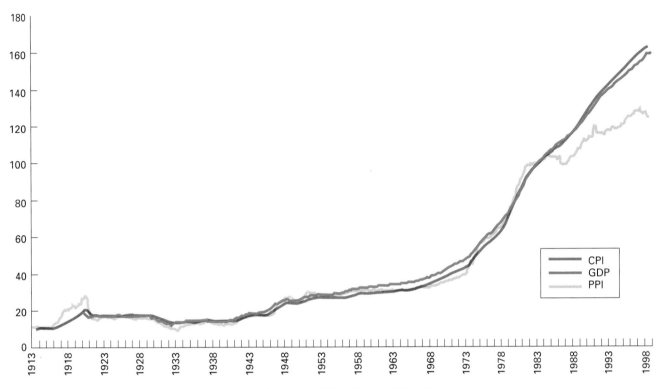

(b) Inflation: (CPI, PPI, and GDP Deflator)

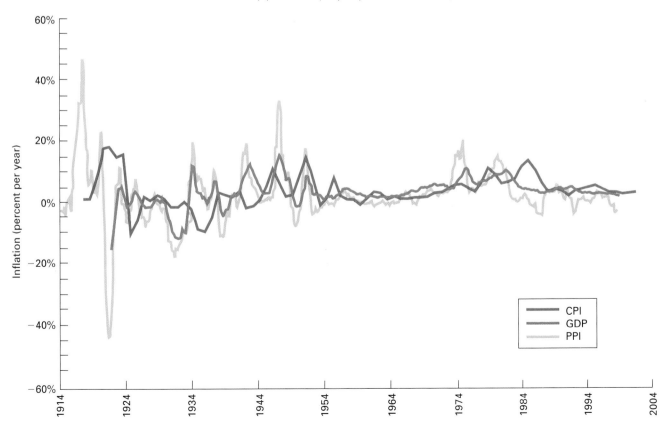

Table 5 | Measuring the CPI in an Economy with Pizzas, Ice Cream, and Antacids

Good	Price in 1990	Current Price	Quantity Purchased
Pizza	$ 8	$ 10	10
Ice cream	3	4	8
Antacids	3	3	2
Total cost of goods	110	138	

Limitations of Price Indexes

The right measure of the price level for *you* is a weighted average of the goods that *you* buy. For example, the cost of tuition, room, board, and fees for an undergraduate at Harvard increased by 343 percent over the last two decades, while the CPI increased by 171 percent over the same period.

The GDP deflator, the CPI, and the PPI all measure average prices only imperfectly, and each has limitations. Together, these sources of bias may lead the CPI to overstate inflation by about 1 percent per year. The three main problems are substitution bias, new-good bias, and quality-change bias. These measurement issues are important because they affect people's incomes. For example, changes in the CPI affect the amount of income elderly people receive in social security.

Substitution Bias

The first problem with price-level measurement is *substitution bias*. When a decrease in the supply of coffee raises its price, people buy less coffee and buy more tea. However, the CPI measures the increase in the cost of buying the *same amounts* of coffee (and other goods) as before. Obviously, when an increase in the price of coffee leads people to substitute cheaper goods (such as tea) for the more expensive good (coffee), they spend less than if they had continued to buy the same amounts of the goods. As a result, the change in the CPI *overstates* the increase in the cost of living.

IN THE NEWS

Wholesale-Price Fall Sets 11-Year Record

Washington—Inflation has rarely been so scarce.

In 1997, prices paid by wholesalers fell by 1.2%, the sharpest drop since they were pushed down 2.3% by collapsing oil prices in 1986, the Labor Department said.

Source: The Wall Street Journal

The report showed no evidence of inflationary pressures in the pipeline. Consider the cost of a dress, which is influenced by the price of the cloth used to make it, called an intermediate good, and of the yarn used to make the cloth, called a crude good. In December, the prices of intermediate goods dropped 0.2%, after climbing 0.2% in November, while prices of crude goods plunged 5.6%, after rising 1.6% the month before.

The PPI, CPI, and GDP deflator give slightly different results for inflation, because they measure different prices and because substitution bias, new-good bias, and quality-change bias affect each price index differently.

EXAMPLE

Suppose people buy a lot of orange juice and very little apple juice when orange juice costs $2.00 and apple juice costs $1.00. Now suppose that the price of orange juice doubles, while the price of apple juice falls 20 percent, leading people to buy mainly apple juice and very little orange juice. Did the price level double, or did it fall by 20 percent? A reasonable answer is something between the two. However, the CPI would show that the price level almost doubled, overstating the increase in the cost of living by ignoring consumer substitution to apple juice.

New-Good Bias

What do Viagra, CDs, Internet service, personal computers, cellular phones, Prozac, snowboards, personal satellite dishes, in-line skates, and DVDs have in common? They all emerged as new consumer products within the last decade or two, and they all create problems for the consumer price index. How can anyone compare the average level of prices today with the average level before introduction of these new goods? After all, the prices of these goods were *infinite* before they were invented—no one could buy them at *any* price. In fact, the government actually puts new goods into the CPI with a delay (typically several years). If a new good appears in the CPI for the first time in 1999, the government calculates inflation from 1998 to 1999 without including the new good, overstating the rate of inflation for that period.

Quality-Change Bias

George de Mestral and his dog returned from a country walk one beautiful day, both covered with burrs. Before removing them, the Swiss engineer looked through his microscope to see why the burrs stuck so stubbornly to his clothes and his dog's fur. Thus was born the hook and loop fastener that he called Velour Crochet (since the burrs stuck to his velour pants) and that we know as velcro, which he patented in 1955. Consumers certainly noticed quality improvements when velcro fasteners began appearing on a wide variety of consumer products. But how much better is a product that uses velcro rather than some other fastening method (zippers, etc.)? How much better is a "new, improved" laundry detergent, breakfast cereal, or computer program? If the prices of products rise by 10 percent but their qualities also improve, by how much have prices really increased? The government tries in a variety of ways to adjust the CPI for changes in quality. Sometimes the government can use statistical methods to estimate the effect of a change in quality; other times, the people collecting the data must use their subjective judgments.

The invention of a new service or good, such as in-line skates, creates a bias in the consumer price index.

Review Questions

11. Explain three problems with measurements of the average price level.

12. How is the consumer price index calculated?

Conclusion

Macroeconomics is the study of the economy as a whole—total production of goods and services, total employment and unemployment, the average level of prices, foreign exchange rates, interest rates and financial market activity, and the overall effects of government policies.

Total Production of Goods and Services

Gross domestic product (GDP) is the value of a country's production of final market goods and services during some time period (usually a year). Nominal GDP refers to GDP measured in money (dollars, yen, pesos, Euros, etc.). Real GDP refers to GDP measured in the prices of a certain base year. The GDP deflator, a measure of the average level of prices in the economy, equals nominal GDP divided by real GDP.

The Economy's Total Spending and Income

GDP equals the sum of consumption, investment, government purchases, and net exports (exports minus imports). Consumption is spending by people on final goods and services for current use. Investment is spending to create new capital, which is the stock of equipment, structures, inventories, human skills, and knowledge available to help produce goods and services. Government purchases refers to total spending on goods and services by federal, state, and local governments. Total government *spending* includes government purchases plus transfer payments (payments that simply transfer money without any exchange of goods and services). Exports are goods and services sold to people and firms in other countries; imports are purchases of goods and services from people and firms in other countries. Net exports, or the balance of international trade, equals exports minus imports.

Income and spending are closely related: Every trade involves a buyer and seller, so the buyer's spending equals the seller's income. GDP equals the total value of production of final market goods and services, which equals total spending on those goods and services, and also equals the total income created by that spending.

GDP, Employment, and Unemployment

People with jobs are employed. People are unemployed if they are jobless but looking for jobs. Other people are not in the labor force. The unemployment rate is the fraction of unemployed people in the labor force. The unemployment rate in the United States is measured with a monthly survey.

Key issues involving GDP, employment, and unemployment include the causes of recessions (periods in which real GDP falls for two consecutive quarters) and associated increases in unemployment, long-run growth of real GDP and employment, and the effects of government policies on recessions and long-run growth.

Measuring the Price Level

Like the GDP deflator, the consumer price index (CPI) and producer price index (PPI) measure the economy's price level. The CPI measures the average price of goods and services that a typical consumer buys, while the PPI measures the average price of goods that a typical producer buys. No price indexes measure price levels perfectly; all have limitations. Three main problems include substitution bias, new-good bias, and quality-change bias.

Key Terms

gross domestic product (GDP)	consumption	government purchases	net exports (balance of international trade)
nominal GDP	capital	exports	unemployment rate
real GDP	investment	imports	recession
GDP deflator			

Questions and Problems

13. Which issues of macroeconomics listed in the introduction to this chapter involve *normative* judgments?

14. Roughly what fractions of U.S. GDP are spent on consumption, investment, and government purchases of goods and services?

15. Why doesn't GDP include *all* government spending, including transfer payments (such as social security)?

16. How is GDP affected when (a) you buy a used textbook? (b) You buy a video? (c) You rent a video? (d) A town cleans up after a tornado? (e) Microsoft introduces a new computer operating system? (f) Someone buys cocaine from Colombia? (g) The government raises taxes? (h) A town builds a new school?

17. Purchases of cars and stereo systems are part of consumption spending. Why might someone sensibly decide to count them as investment instead of consumption?

18. Do the three main problems in measuring price indexes also create problems in measuring real GDP? Explain whether and how each problem applies to real GDP.

19. Why should we adjust a price index, like the CPI, for changes in the *quality* of goods? What is wrong with simply measuring price changes and ignoring changes in quality?

20. Why does substitution bias always lead the CPI to *overstate* inflation? Why doesn't it lead the CPI to understate inflation?

Inquiries for Further Thought

21. What factors do you think might cause changes in consumption? Investment? Government purchases? Net exports?

22. How will the main issues of macroeconomics affect your life in the next year? In the next 10 years?

Appendix: Measuring Production and Income: National Income Accounting

Table A.1 shows a more detailed accounting table for U.S. GDP in 1997 than the data that appears in the chapter text. This table reports data in the form adopted by the government and with the government's terminology. The table shows GDP as total spending, $C + I + G + NEX$, and the main categories of consumption and the other components. The table then adds "Receipts of factor income from the rest of the world," which mean payments of money to Americans who worked or invested in other countries. The table also subtracts "payments of factor income to the rest of the world." The result is *gross national product,* or GNP. While GDP measures the total output of final market goods and services by people and property within the country, GNP measures the country's total income.

Subtracting depreciation (called *consumption of fixed capital* in the table) from GNP gives *net national product.* Subtracting indirect business taxes (mainly sales taxes) and some other small items from net national product gives *national income.* The table makes some adjustments to national income to obtain *personal income* (which is mainly wages and salaries). Subtracting personal taxes (and nontax payments such as fees for auto licenses) gives *disposable personal income,* which is essentially the after-tax income of ordinary people. The table shows that people spend most of their after-tax income for consumption, and they save most of the rest.

IN THE NEWS

Consumer Spending Rose Faster in April Than Income, and the Savings Rate Fell

By John Simons
Staff Reporter of
The Wall Street Journal

Washington—Undaunted by foreign financial crises—or even by their own poor savings habits—Americans continue to spend, spend, spend.

While personal income rose 0.4% in April to a seasonally adjusted annual rate of $7.18 trillion, following March's 0.3% increase, consumer spending jumped 0.5% to $5.72 trillion, the Commerce Department said. Disposable after-tax incomes were up 0.4% in April, but adjusted for inflation, they posted a mere 0.2% increase, the smallest in nine months.

The earn-it-and-spend-it cycle lowered personal savings as a portion of disposable income to 3.5% in April.

Source: The Wall Street Journal

Many of the concepts in Table A.1 appear regularly in news articles.

Table A.1 | U.S. NATIONAL INCOME AND PRODUCT, 1997

United States GDP, 1997	Total ($ billions)	Per Person ($)
Nominal gross domestic product (GDP)	$8,080	$30,149
Personal consumption expenditures	5,486	20,469
Durable goods	659	2,460
Nondurable goods	1,592	5,940
Services	3,235	12,069
Gross private domestic investment	1,243	4,636
Fixed investment	1,174	4,381
Change in business inventories	68	255
Government consumption expenditures and gross investment	1,453	5,421
Federal	524	1,954
State and local	929	3,466
Net exports of goods and services (exports minus imports)	−101	−377
Exports	957	3,571
Imports	1,058	3,948
GDP	$8,080	$30,149
Plus: Receipts of factor income from the rest of the world	262	978
Less: Payments of factor income to the rest of the world	282	1,052
Equals: Gross national product	$8,060	$30,075
Less: Consumption of fixed capital (i.e., depreciation)	868	3,238
Equals: Net national product	7,192	26,837
Less: Indirect business taxes, business transfer payments, and statistical discrepancy; Plus: Subsidies minus surpluses of government enterprises	543	2,024
Equals: National income	$6,650	$24,812
Less: Corporate profits	805	3,004
Less: Net interest	449	1,674
Less: Taxes for social insurance	733	2,736
Plus: Personal interest and dividend income	1,090	4,068
Plus: Government Transfer Payments to Persons	1,094	4,082
Plus: Business Transfer Payments to Persons	27	101
Equals: Personal Income	$6,874	$25,649
Wages, salaries, and other labor income	4,294	16,022
Proprietors' income	545	2,032
Rental income	148	552
Personal interest and dividend income	1,090	4,068
Transfer payments to persons minus taxes for social insurance	797	2,975
Personal income	$6,874	$25,649
Less: Personal tax and nontax payments	989	3,689
Equals: Disposable personal income	$5,885	$21,960
Less: Personal outlays	5,659	21,114
Personal consumption	5,486	20,469
Interest payments	155	578
Transfer payments to foreigners	18	67
Equals: Personal saving	$ 227	$ 846

Notes: The national income and product accounts of the United States are prepared by the Bureau of Economic Analysis, a division of the U.S. Department of Commerce. The data come from tax returns and surveys of people and business firms. For further information, see the Web pages (www.dryden.com) for this textbook.

CHAPTER 25

SIMPLE ECONOMIC MODELS OF GDP, PRICES, AND EMPLOYMENT

In this Chapter . . .

Main Points to Understand

▶ Economic models—logical stories about the economy—are necessary for serious thinking about our real-life economy.

▶ Technology and inputs of labor, capital, and natural resources determine the economy's total production of goods and services.

▶ The equation of exchange defines the velocity of money.

▶ Equilibrium wages equate the quantity of labor demanded with the quantity supplied.

Thinking Skills to Develop

▶ Create simple economic models to think about economic issues.

▶ Develop the implications of simple economic models.

▶ Reason by analogy from economic models to real-life issues.

Picture yourself: ten years from now. You're vice-president of a business, listening to e-mail from the company president. She wants you to report on how the latest recession in Europe will affect your company's profits and whether the situation will improve if the European Central Bank loosens its monetary policy. First, though, you have to decide whether to invest in a new facility near Beijing. Will the Chinese economy continue to grow as rapidly as it has over the past two decades, making the new facility a profitable investment?

Fortunately, you are prepared to formulate answers to questions like these, because you have learned how to think logically about economic issues. (Your coworkers vaguely remember studying current economic conditions in their economics courses, but the boss seldom asks about conditions way back in 1999 or 2001.) This chapter introduces simple models of GDP and the price level; later chapters will use these basic models as building blocks for more sophisticated analysis.

A good way to begin learning a craft is to watch an expert. Similarly, a good way to begin learning economic analysis is to listen to an expert. The following section reprints the text of a commencement speech delivered at the University of Chicago by Professor Robert E. Lucas, Jr., who won the 1995 Nobel Prize in Economic Sciences for his work on macroeconomics. His talk on "What Economists Do" introduces some new terms, which are highlighted in bold type and explained briefly nearby in the margin.

IN THE NEWS

Chicago professor wins Nobel

For the fifth time in six years, a University of Chicago professor has won the Nobel Memorial Prize in economics. This year's winner, announced Tuesday, is Robert Lucas, 58. Lucas won for his research 25 years ago that showed the ineffectiveness of government attempts to use monetary and fiscal policies as cures for economic ailments such as poverty or rising inflation.

He "has had the greatest influence on macroeconomic research since 1970," the Royal Swedish Academy of Sciences said Tuesday in announcing the $1 million award.

He says he doesn't know yet what he'll do with the money. "I'm already doing what I really want to do: teaching and research."

Source: USA Today

Robert E. Lucas, Jr.

You can find out more about Professor Lucas and other famous economists on the Web site (www.dryden.com) for this book.

Before reading Lucas's essay, recall from Chapter 2 that economic models are like artificial, robot economies. You can think of Professor Lucas's story of the Kennywood amusement park in this way.[1]

WHAT ECONOMISTS DO

Essay by Robert E. Lucas, Jr.

Economists have an image of practicality and worldliness not shared by physicists and poets. Some economists have earned this image. Others—I and many of my colleagues here at Chicago—have not. I'm not sure whether you will take this as a confession or a boast, but we economists are basically story-tellers, creators of make-believe economic systems. Rather than try to explain what this story-telling activity is about and why I think it is a useful, even essential, activity, I thought I would just tell you a story and let you make of it what you like.

My story has a point: I want to understand the connection between changes in the **money supply** and economic **depressions.** One way to demonstrate that I understand this connection—I think the only really convincing way—would be for me to engineer a depression in the United States by manipulating the U.S. money supply. I think I know how to do this, though I'm not absolutely sure, but a real virtue of the democratic system is that we do not look kindly on people who want to use our lives as a laboratory. So I will try to make my depression somewhere else. The location I have in mind is an old-fashioned amusement park—roller coasters, fun house, hot dogs, the works. I am thinking of Kennywood Park in Pittsburgh, where I lived when my children were at the optimal age as amusement park companions—a beautiful, turn-of-the-century place on a bluff overlooking the Monongahela River. If you have not seen this particular park, substitute one with which you are familiar, as I want you to try to visualize how the experiment I am going to describe would actually work in practice.

Kennywood Park is a useful location for my purposes because it has an entirely independent monetary system. One *cannot* spend U.S. dollars inside the park. At the

The term *money supply* refers to the amount of money available for the economy to use; this term will appear later in this chapter, and a more detailed discussion will follow in Chapter 29.

Economists usually use the term *depression* for a particularly severe recession (such as the Great Depression of the 1930s); here, Professor Lucas uses it in the sense of any typical *recession*.

---

[1]Often economists tell their stories in the language of mathematics instead of the languages of English or Spanish. That choice doesn't change the fact that the models are stories like this one. (As Chapter 2 explained, that is what economic models *are*.)

gate, visitors use U.S. dollars to purchase tickets, then they enter the park and spend those tickets. Rides inside are priced at a certain number of many tickets per ride. Ride operators collect these tickets, and at the end of each day tickets are cashed in for dollars, like chips in a casino.

For obvious reasons, business in the park fluctuates: Sundays are big days; July 4 is even bigger. At most attractions—I imagine each ride in the park to be independently operated—there is some flexibility: An extra person can be called in to help take tickets or to speed people getting on and off the ride, on short notice if the day is unexpectedly big or with advanced notice if it is predictable. If business is disappointingly slow, an operator will let some of his help leave early. So "GDP" in the park (total tickets spent) and employment (the number of man hours worked) will fluctuate from one day to the next due to fluctuations in demand. Do we want to call a slow day—a Monday or a Tuesday, say—a depression? Surely not. By an economic depression we mean something that ought not to happen, something pathological, not normal seasonal or daily ups and downs. This, I imagine, is how the park works. (I say "imagine" because I am just making most of this up as I go along.) Technically, Kennywood Park is a **fixed exchange rate system,** since its **central bank**—the cashier's office at the gate—stands ready to exchange **local currency**—tickets—for **foreign currency**—U.S. dollars—at a fixed rate. In this economy, there is an obvious sense in which the number of tickets in circulation is economically irrelevant. No one—customer or concessioner—really cares about the number of tickets per ride except insofar as these prices reflect U.S. dollars per ride. If the number of tickets per U.S. dollar were doubled from 10 to 20, and if the prices of all rides were doubled in terms of tickets—6 tickets per roller coaster ride instead of 3—and if everyone understood that these changes had occurred, it just would not make any important difference. Such a **doubling of the money supply** and of prices would amount to a 100 percent inflation in terms of local currency, but so what?

Yet I want to show you that changes in the quantity of money—in the number of tickets in circulation—have the capacity to induce depressions or booms in this economy (just as I think they do in reality). To do so, I want to imagine subjecting Kennywood Park to an entirely operational experiment. Think of renting the park from its owners for one Sunday, for suitable compensation, and taking over the functions of the cashier's office. Neither the operators of concessions nor the customers are to be informed of this. Then, with no advance warning to anyone inside the park, and no communication to them as to what is going on, the cashiers are instructed for this one day to give 8 tickets per dollar instead of 10. What will happen?

We can imagine a variety of reactions. Some customers, discouraged or angry, will turn around and go home. Others, coming to the park with a dollar budget fixed by mom, will just buy 80 percent of the tickets they would have bought otherwise. Still others will shell out 20 percent more dollars and behave as they would have in the absence of this change in "exchange rates." I would have to know much more than I do about Kennywood Park patrons to judge how many would fall into each of these categories, but it is pretty clear that no one will be induced to buy more tickets than if the experiment had not taken place. Many people will buy fewer, so the total number of tickets in circulation—the **"money supply"** of this amusement park economy—will take a drop below what it otherwise would have been on this Sunday.

Now how does all this look from the point of view of the operator of a ride or the guy selling hot dogs? Again, there will be a variety of reactions. In general, most operators will notice that the park seems kind of empty for a Sunday and that customers don't seem to be spending like they usually do. More time is being spent on "freebies," the river view or a walk through the gardens. Many operators take this personally. Those who were worried that their ride was becoming passé get additional confirmation. Those who thought they were just starting to become popular, and had had thoughts of adding some capacity, begin to wonder if they had perhaps become overoptimistic. On many concessions, the extra employees hired to deal with the expected Sunday crowd are sent home early. A gloomy, "depressed" mood settles in.

An economy has a *fixed exchange rate system* when its government fixes the price at which its money *(local currency)* trades for foreign money *(foreign currency).* The government agency that fixes the exchange rate is the *central bank.* For example, the Central Bank of Argentina fixes the exchange rate between the Argentine peso and the U.S. dollar at one peso per dollar; the Hong Kong Monetary Authority fixes its exchange rate at about 7.75 Hong Kong dollars per U.S. dollar. Similarly, the management of Kennywood Park fixes the price of tickets in terms of dollars at 10 tickets per dollar.

The change in *exchange rates* means the change in the price of tickets in terms of dollars—from ten tickets per dollar to eight tickets per dollar for this particular day.

Real output *means real GDP*.

The *money supply* in Kennywood Park is the number of tickets that customers have available to spend on rides. Doubling the money supply in the park means doubling the number of tickets. Notice Professor Lucas's point here: No one cares whether tickets cost 10 cents each and the roller coaster costs 3 tickets or tickets cost 5 cents each and the roller coaster costs 6 tickets. (In either case, you pay 30 cents for a ride.) Doubling the prices of rides in terms of tickets (which amounts to 100 percent inflation in the park), while simultaneously doubling the number of tickets that a person can buy for $1, makes no difference to customers or to the park. This concept is the principle of *neutrality of money* defined later in this chapter.

What I have done, in short, is to engineer a depression in the park. The reduction in the quantity of money has led to a reduction in **real output** and employment. And this depression is indeed a kind of pathology. Customers are arriving at the park, eager to spend and enjoy themselves. Concessioners are ready and waiting to serve them. By introducing a glitch into the park's monetary system, we have prevented (not physically, but just as effectively) buyers and sellers from getting together to consummate mutually advantageous trades.

That is the end of my story. Rather than offer you some of my opinions about the nature and causes of depressions in the United States, I simply made a depression and let you watch it unfold. I hope you found it convincing on its own terms—that what I said would happen in the park as the result of my manipulations would in fact happen. If so, then you will agree that by increasing the number of tickets per dollar we could as easily have engineered a boom in the park. But we could not, clearly, engineer a boom Sunday after Sunday by this method. Our experiment worked only because our manipulations caught everyone by surprise. We could have avoided the depression by leaving things alone, but we could not use monetary manipulation to engineer a *permanently* higher level of prosperity in the park. The clarity with which these effects can be seen is the key advantage of operating in simplified, fictional worlds.

The disadvantage, it must be conceded, is that we are not really interested in understanding and preventing depressions in hypothetical amusement parks. We are interested in our own, vastly more complicated society. To apply the knowledge we have gained about depressions in Kennywood Park, we must be willing to argue by analogy from what we know about one situation to what we would like to know about another, quite different situation. And, as we all know, the analogy that one person finds persuasive, his neighbor may well find ridiculous.

Well, that is why honest people can disagree. I don't know what one can do about it, except keep trying to tell better and better stories, to provide the raw material for better and more instructive analogies. How else can we free ourselves from the limits of historical experience so as to discover ways in which our society can operate better than it has in the past?

In any case, that is what economists do. We are story-tellers, operating much of the time in worlds of make believe. We do not find that the realm of imagination and ideas is an alternative to, or a retreat from, practical reality. On the contrary, it is the only way we have found to think seriously about reality.

Economists tell stories, like Professor Lucas's story about the amusement park. Then they reason by analogy from the stories to real-life economies.

IN THE NEWS

Japanese Slip into Recession; Outlook is Dim

TOKYO—Japan's once-mighty economic engine has ground into reverse for the second time this decade, and there are few signs that the world's second-largest economy will pick up soon. Economic output fell for the second quarter in a row, throwing Japan into recession by the common yardstick of two consecutive quarterly contractions. Preliminary economic data for April also suggests that consumer demand and business investment may be continuing to worsen.

Source: The Wall Street Journal

Japan is one of several Asian countries that slipped into recessions in 1997 and 1998. To understand real-life recessions, economists build models that mathematically describe stories similar to the Kennywood Park story.

In a way, there is nothing more to this method than maintaining the conviction that imagination and ideas matter. I hope you can do this in the years that follow. It is fun and interesting and, really, there is no practical alternative.

Review Questions

1. Professor Robert Lucas said in his essay that we can reason by analogy from Kennywood Park to our own, vastly more complicated society. In his analogy (his story), what plays the role of U.S. GDP?

2. In his thought experiment, Professor Robert Lucas considered a change in underlying conditions at Kennywood Park. What was that change in underlying conditions? What were its *effects?*

Thinking Exercises

3. Why do you think Professor Lucas decided to "make" a depression and "let you watch it unfold" rather than stating his "opinions about the nature and causes of depressions in the United States"? Why would he think this method is more valuable to you?

4. Professor Lucas says that "by increasing the number of tickets per dollar we could as easily have engineered a boom in the park." Explain how that could happen by retelling his story with an *increase* in the number of tickets that customers can purchase for each dollar.

What determines the economy's GDP? Rather than simply stating an answer—which would give you little help in learning to *use* economic analysis to solve real-world problems that you will confront in your life—this chapter follows Professor Lucas and constructs a *model*. We examine a model precisely because we are interested in understanding *real-world* GDP in the United States and other countries. If we simply listed data about the U.S. economy in a spreadsheet, without a model, we would not be able to answer *"what if" questions* that interest us: What if technology changes? What if people decide to consume more and save less? What if the government cuts taxes? A model suggests how the various bits of data are interrelated—it tells us how changing *some* numbers in a spreadsheet are likely to change *other* numbers. As Professor Lucas asks, how else can we free ourselves from the limits of historical experience (the U.S. economic numbers in the spreadsheet) and discover ways to do better than in the past, by seeing how the numbers would *change* in various *"what if"* scenarios?

It is usually easier to begin with very simple models, and then to add more realistic features, than to dive in to a complicated model that may be difficult to understand. Therefore, we begin with a very simple model of an economy in which no one trades— a Robinson Crusoe economy.

A VERY SIMPLE MODEL OF GDP

Spreadsheet with data for the U.S. economy:

LABOR	GDP	MONEY	CPI
136,206	8,013.6	1,080.8	121.5
137,169	8,103.5	1,065.4	121.9
137,447	8,204.2	1,073.7	122.6
137,962	8,340.7	1,075.0	123.1

We need a *model* to help us interpret economic data and tell us how changing *some* numbers in the spreadsheet are likely to change *other* numbers. We need to answer such *what-if* questions in order to formulate good economic policies and make good business decisions.

A Robinson Crusoe Economy

Robinson Crusoe lives in his own economy. He produces goods for his own consumption by picking berries from trees. Crusoe's *real GDP* each day equals the number of berries he picks that day, and depends on the number of hours he works that day.

Table 1 shows Crusoe's *production function*—the first two columns show how his real GDP (berries picked per day) depends on the number of hours he works at picking berries.

> A **production function** is a mathematical description of an economy's technology, showing the total production that an economy can obtain from its inputs of labor, capital, and natural resources.

Crusoe's input of labor is his work effort; his capital is a basket he has woven to carry berries back to his camp, his skills at picking, and his knowledge of which berries are safe to eat; the natural resources are the bushes and trees on which berries grow. Figure 1 graphs Crusoe's production function, with hours worked on the X-axis and total production on the Y-axis.

The third column of Table 1 shows Crusoe's *average product of labor:*

> The **average product** of a person's labor equals total production divided by the number of hours worked.

For example, the table shows that Crusoe picks 3,000 berries if he works 3 hours, making his average product of labor equal to 1,000 berries per hour.

The fourth column of Table 1 shows Crusoe's *marginal product of labor:*

> The **marginal product** of labor is the *additional* production obtained from *increasing* labor a little, without changing the amounts of capital or natural resources.

For example, the table shows that Crusoe can pick a total of 1,200 berries if he works 1 hour or a total of 2,200 berries if he works 2 hours. If he *increases* his work time from 1 hour to 2 hours, he picks 1,000 *additional* berries (2,200 − 1,200), meaning that his marginal product of labor is 1,000 berries per hour.

Similarly, the table shows that Crusoe can pick a total of 3,000 berries if he works 3 hours or a total of 3,500 berries if he works 4 hours. If he *increases* his work time from 3 hours to 4 hours, he picks 500 *additional* berries (3,500 − 3,000), meaning that his marginal product of labor is 500 berries per hour.

Table 1 | Crusoe's Production Function

Hours Worked Picking Berries (per day)	Real GDP per Day (total berries picked per day)	Average Product of Labor (berries per hour, on average)	Marginal Product of Labor (*additional* berries from one *additional* hour of work)
0	0		
1	1,200	1,200	1,200
2	2,200	1,100	1,000
3	3,000	1,000	800
4	3,500	875	500
5	3,800	760	300
6	4,000	667	200
7	4,100	586	100
8	4,150	519	50
9	4,160	462	10
10	4,165	416	5

Figure 1 | Robinson Crusoe's Production Function

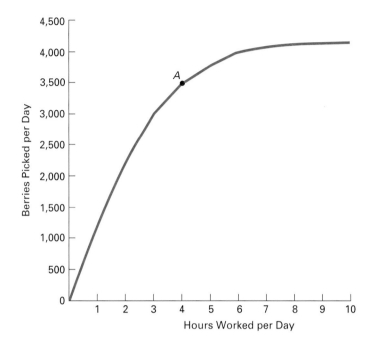

Diminishing Returns

Notice that Crusoe's marginal product of labor is higher if he only works a few hours than if he works many hours. This illustrates the important concept of diminishing returns.

> The **law of diminishing returns** is the principle that raising the quantity of an input eventually reduces its marginal product, if the quantity of some other input remains fixed.

Holding fixed the number of trees and bushes, as well as the size of Crusoe's basket and his knowledge and skills, Crusoe faces diminishing returns as he works additional hours. As Table 1 shows, his marginal product of labor falls as his hours of work rise. Several factors contribute to diminishing returns. Crusoe may get tired as he works, working more slowly in each additional hour. If he works only a few hours, he picks the berries that are easiest to reach; however, if he works many hours, he must pick hard-to-reach berries, reducing his marginal product of labor. The curved shape of Crusoe's production function in Figure 1 illustrates diminishing returns.

Production Possibilities Frontier

Crusoe must choose: He can work a lot and eat a lot of berries, or he can increase his leisure time and eat less. His *production possibilities frontier (PPF)* in Figure 2 illustrates that choice. He can take 24 hours of leisure time each day and have nothing to eat, or he can work 24 hours and have 4,175 berries to eat each day. He can also choose positions such as Point A, in which he takes 20 hours of leisure time each day, working 4 hours and eating 3,500 berries each day. In this way, Crusoe chooses his real GDP.

Notice that Crusoe's PPF and his production function (in Figure 1) show the *same* information, but in different ways.

Investment

Now add some additional realism to the model. Crusoe is not likely to spend all his time picking berries with the tools provided by nature; instead, he is likely to realize that he can build some tools. In other words, he can *invest*. Crusoe can build an automatic

Figure 2 | Robinson Crusoe's Production Possibilities Frontier

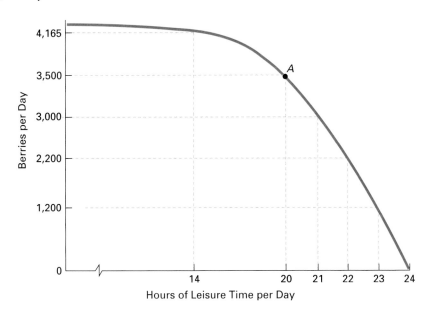

berry-picker by spending less time picking berries or relaxing by the shore. When he completes his new machine, he will be able to pick more berries in less time than before. By investing, Crusoe sacrifices consumption and leisure time *today* to obtain more consumption and leisure time *in the future*. Whether he is willing to build the machine depends on the terms of that tradeoff—how much can he gain in the future by sacrificing consumption and leisure today? How much is he *willing* to sacrifice?

If automatic berry pickers are highly productive, and if Crusoe is sufficiently willing to sacrifice consumption today for future consumption, then he might even build several berry-picking machines. The amount of investment Crusoe undertakes, and the *capital stock* that he ends up with, depend on his choices.

Suppose that Crusoe must sacrifice 3,000 berries for each automatic berry-picking machine he builds. In other words, the time he requires to build each machine is the same as the time he requires to pick 3,000 berries. Then Crusoe can, in essence, "buy" a machine for 3,000 berries—the relative price of a machine is 3,000 berries per machine. (Recall the discussion of relative prices in Chapter 4.)

Real GDP

Crusoe's production function depends not only on his labor input (hours worked) and the natural resources available to him but also on his *capital* stock. The production function can take the form of an equation:

$$\text{Real GDP} = F(l, k)$$

where l represents the number of hours that Crusoe works, k represents his capital stock (the number of machines he uses), and real GDP is *total* production of berries and machines, counting each machine as equivalent to 3,000 berries.

For example, Crusoe may work 8 hours, building one machine and picking 1,150 berries. If he had not built the machine, he would have picked 4,150 berries in 8 hours of work. Building the machine took time—the same amount of time in which he *could have* picked 3,000 of those 4,150 berries. Because he built the machine, he could pick only 1,150 berries in his 8-hour work day.

Crusoe's production function describes how his real GDP depends on his inputs of labor and capital.

Crusoe's real GDP is also the sum of his consumption and investment:

$$\text{Real GDP} = c + i$$

where c is Crusoe's consumption and i is his investment (measured in the number of berries he gave up for his machines). In the example, Crusoe's consumption is 1,150 berries and his investment (building one machine) is 3,000 berries, for a total real GDP of 4,150 berries.

The numbers in Table 1, graphed in Figures 1 and 2, showed Crusoe's production of berries when he had no automatic berry-picking machines. Once he has those machines, however, they can help him boost berry production, changing the numbers in Table 1 and shifting the curves, as in Figure 3.

Changes in GDP

Each evening, Crusoe spends time thinking about how to improve his economic situation. Eventually, he figures out how to build a better automatic berry-picker. Over the next weeks or months, he spends time building that new, better machine. To make time for this investment, he works more hours and spends a little less time picking berries. As a result, his GDP rises, although his consumption of berries falls. Finally, he completes his new machine. Now he can stop working so many extra hours per day. Although this decrease in work hours for investment tends to reduce his real GDP, the new machine helps him pick more berries per hour than before. As a result, his real GDP rises to a new, higher level. Technical change, which resulted from Crusoe's investment of time in thinking about new ideas for a better machine, raises investment and real GDP in the short run, and raises consumption and real GDP in the long run.

Crusoe's production changes over time for other reasons, as well. The weather varies, and he picks fewer berries per hour on a stormy day than on a pleasant one. Seasons change, and in the winter he finds fewer berries to pick than in the summer. Some days he doesn't feel energetic, and his production is lower than usual. Other days, he wants to avoid working at all, taking time to sleep, write in his journal, or explore the island. As a result, Crusoe's real GDP fluctuates over time, and an observer might interpret these fluctuations as booms and recessions.

Figure 3 | Effects of an Increase in Capital

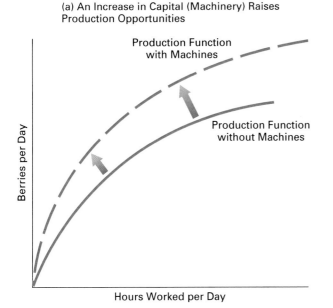

(a) An Increase in Capital (Machinery) Raises Production Opportunities

Production Function with Machines

Production Function without Machines

Berries per Day

Hours Worked per Day

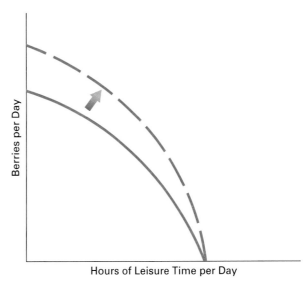

(b) An Increase in Capital Shifts Crusoe's PPF

Berries per Day

Hours of Leisure Time per Day

In fact, some economists *do* interpret real-life booms and recessions in this way. They note that Crusoe is "unemployed" on days that he doesn't work, making his "unemployment rate" high when his real GDP is low, as in recessions. Most economists, however, believe that a simple model like this cannot explain key features of real-life recessions. (For example, people who are unemployed in a real-world recession may struggle to find jobs. In contrast, Crusoe is self-employed and he can stop being "unemployed" simply by deciding to pick berries.)

So far, it is impossible to examine *nominal* GDP and nominal prices in this model, because Crusoe doesn't use money. In fact, he doesn't even *trade* with anyone. The next sections extend the model to include trade and nominal prices.

Review Questions

5. How does Table 1 show diminishing returns to Crusoe's labor?

6. In what way does Crusoe choose his real GDP?

Thinking Exercises

7. How would the shape of the production function in Figure 1 change if there were *not* diminishing returns, so that Crusoe would pick 1,200 berries per hour *regardless* of how many hours he worked? Draw the production function for that case.

8. The text claimed that Crusoe's production function (in Figure 1) and his PPF (in Figure 2) show the same information in different ways. Explain why.

A Model with Trade

Imagine an economy with a large number of people just like Crusoe, except that they produce and sell different goods. Everyone wants to consume a little bit of each good. Some people have comparative advantages in producing food, and other people have comparative advantages creating housing, entertainment, and other goods and services. As a result, people specialize in production and then trade with one another. They receive gains from trade as discussed in Chapters 1 and 3. Trade will create two other changes in the model: labor markets, and the use of money.

Labor Markets

Trade among people will create a labor market in our model, in which people buy and sell labor services. Some people will form business firms and hire workers, and other people will decide to work for those firms. Unlike Crusoe, who was self-employed, many people in the model will participate in labor markets. The desire by firms to hire workers creates a demand for labor, and the desire by some people to work for firms instead of becoming self-employed creates a supply of labor.

Figure 4a shows the supply of labor by people who want to work, as well as the demand for labor by firms that want to hire workers. The price of labor services is the *wage* rate. Equilibrium occurs at Point A, with an equilibrium wage of w_0 and equilibrium employment of l_0.

At the equilibrium wage, everyone who wants to work has a job. In equilibrium, there is no surplus or shortage of labor. When labor demand or supply change, the wage adjusts to restore equilibrium.

IN THE NEWS

Ruble Withering? So What? Russians Survive on Barter

Novgorod, Russia—Russia's currency may be tumbling. Its stock market may lie in ruins. But Yevgeny Shulman is used to operating without money.

Mr. Shulman's factory sure churns out valves for nuclear power plants and heavy industry. What his company receives in return

is clear from a stroll around headquarters: Newly minted cars and trucks are lined up near small mountains of railroad car break pads and raw metal.

Mr. Shulman even set up a small chain of drugstores to sell the medicines he receives in his transactions with drug companies.

"This is the way everybody in Russia does business these days," Mr. Shulman said. "Of course, we'd prefer to receive cash. But it is barter that has saved us."

Now, with economic shock waves rippling across Russia, companies are counting more than ever on barter to survive.

Source: New York Times

Although barter sometimes occurs, as in Russia in recent years, most trades in most economies involve exchanges of goods and money.

Labor Markets and Real GDP

Our model determines real GDP in two steps. First, equilibrium in the labor market determines equilibrium employment, l_0 in Figure 4a. Second, the economy's *aggregate* production function, which relates *total* real GDP in the economy to *total* labor hours worked, determines equilibrium real GDP as in Figure 4b.

Money

People in our model economy will want to use *money* for their trades, rather than bartering like the two students in Chapter 3. We will assume that they form a government,

---

Figure 4 | Equilibrium Employment and Real GDP

(a) Supply and demand for labor determine employment...

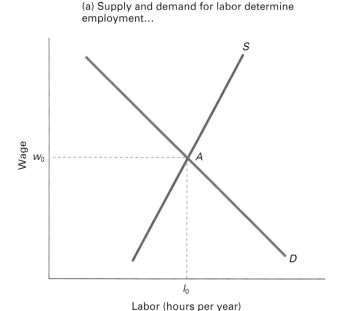

(b) ...And the economy's production function then determines real GDP, y_0

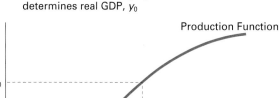
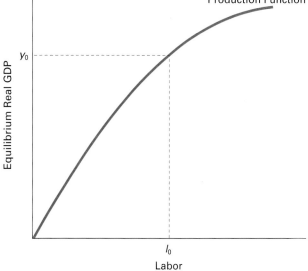

whose sole task is to print some dollar bills and distribute them equally to every person in the economy. Sellers are willing to accept these dollar bills as payments for goods and services, because they know that they can later exchange those dollars for goods and services from *other* sellers. The *nominal money supply* in this model is the total amount of money that the government has printed and distributed.

> The **nominal money supply** is the total amount of money in the economy, measured in monetary units such as dollars or yen.

The term *nominal* refers to measurement in money units such as *dollars*. For example, the government may print 1,000 $1 bills for people to use, making the nominal money supply equal to $1,000.

Circular Flow

Figure 5 shows the *circular flow* of economic activity in the model; it resembles a simple version of Figure 5 from the preceding chapter (which showed a circular flow for the U.S. economy).

The outside circle shows the flow of money in the economy. People pay money to firms in exchange for goods and services. Firms pay people to work for them, and they pay profits to their owners for providing capital (tools and machines). Money travels clockwise around the circle.

The flow of money from firms to people shows this economy's nominal GDP, which equals total spending on goods and services (for consumption or investment), that is, the total monetary value of the economy's production of goods and services. The inside circle in Figure 5 shows flows of physical goods and services. The arrow from people to firms represents flows of labor and capital services from people to firms. The arrow from firms to people represents the final goods that people buy from firms. While the outside circle shows aggregate nominal income and spending, measured in money terms, the inside circle shows the economy's *real GDP* measured in terms of actual goods and services. It represents a weighted average of berries, automatic berry-picking machines, and other goods and services, using relative prices of the goods as weights in the average (as explained earlier with berries and berry-picking machines in the Crusoe model).

Equation of Exchange

Suppose that the circular flow in Figure 5 occurs *once per year*. The money in the economy flows once each year from people to firms and back to people. Each dollar in the

Figure 5 | Circular Flow of Economic Activity

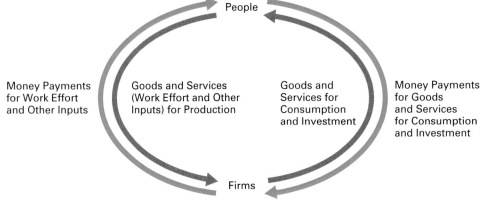

| Money Payments for Work Effort and Other Inputs | Goods and Services (Work Effort and Other Inputs) for Production | Goods and Services for Consumption and Investment | Money Payments for Goods and Services for Consumption and Investment |

economy is used once each year by people to buy goods, and once each year by firms to pay people. In this case, the flows of money in Figure 5 show the economy's nominal GDP for one year, and the flows of goods show its real GDP for that year. (If the circular flows in the figure occurred *twice* each year, then the money in the economy would flow from people to firms and back twice each year. In that case, annual GDP would be *twice* the amount shown by the arrows in the figure.)

With the circular flow in Figure 5 occurring once annually, each dollar in the economy is spent once per year. As a result, this economy's nominal GDP equals its nominal money supply. Both the nominal GDP and the money supply equal the flow of money shown by the outer arrows in Figure 5. If, instead, the circular flow occurred *twice* each year, then each dollar would be spent *twice* per year on goods, so the economy's nominal GDP would be *twice* its nominal money supply. The number of times that each dollar bill gets spent each year is the *velocity* of money.

> The **velocity of money** is the average number of times per year that money is spent in the circular flow; velocity equals nominal GDP divided by the nominal money supply.

If the circular flow occurs once annually, then the velocity of money equals 1 per year. If the circular flow occurs twice per year, then velocity equals 2 per year. In that case, nominal GDP equals twice the money supply. More generally:

Nominal GDP equals the nominal money supply multiplied by the velocity of money.

Using the letter M for the nominal money supply and the letter V for velocity, this relationship gives the equation:

$$\text{Nominal GDP} = MV$$

Recall that nominal GDP equals real GDP multiplied by the GDP price deflator. Using the letters P for the GDP deflator and y for real GDP:

$$MV = Py$$

This equation is called the *equation of exchange*.

> The **equation of exchange** says that $MV = Py$.

In words, the equation of exchange says that the nominal money supply multiplied by the velocity of money equals the GDP price deflator multiplied by real GDP.

Now rewrite the equation of exchange to express the GDP deflator in terms of the money supply, velocity, and real GDP:

$$P = MV/y$$

This equation shows that the economy's price level equals the nominal money supply times its velocity, divided by real GDP. Note that the nominal money supply is determined by the number of dollar bills that the government has printed, and real GDP is determined as in Figure 4, by the economy's equilibrium level of employment and production function. After determining the velocity of money—the number of times per year each dollar is spent in the economy—the equation of exchange gives the economy's price level.

Your true height does not change if we switch our units of measurement from feet to inches; only the units of measurement change. Similarly, the economy's real GDP and employment do not change if we switch our units of measurement by raising the nominal money supply and all nominal prices and wages in the same proportion. Nominal GDP may rise from $1,000 to $2,000, but every dollar is worth only one-half of its previous value.

Real wages adjust nominal wages for inflation. Real wages are measured in *base-year* dollars, like real GDP. To compute the real wage in 1999, measured in 1992 base-year dollars, we divide the 1999 *nominal* wage, W, by the consumer price index measured in 1992 base-year dollars:

$$\text{real wage (in 1992 base-year dollars)}$$
$$= \frac{\text{nominal wage}}{\text{CPI (in 1992 base-year dollars)}}$$

Neutrality of Money

We can use the equation of exchange to find the effects of an increase in the money supply. Suppose the money supply rises permanently from $1,000 to $2,000, because the government prints up additional dollar bills and distributes them equally to every person in the economy. This 100 percent increase in the money supply raises all *nominal* prices (prices measured in monetary units) by 100 percent. Because all prices rise in the same proportion, *relative* prices remain unchanged. Similarly, the 100 percent rise in the money supply raises *nominal* wages (wages measured in monetary units) by 100 percent. However, *real wages*—wages measured in *base-year* dollars to adjust for inflation—remain unchanged, because nominal wages and prices rise proportionally.

> **Nominal wages** are payments for labor services, measured in monetary units like dollars or yen.

> **Real wages** are wages measured in *base-year* dollars.

Because the increase in the money supply does not affect real wages, it does not affect the quantities of goods and services that people can afford to buy. After the 100 percent increase in nominal prices and nominal wages, goods and services cost twice as many dollars as before, but people earn twice as many dollars per hour as before. Only our *unit of measurement* has changed (the value of a dollar has fallen in half), but nothing real—nothing of importance to people—has changed. The 100 percent increase in the money supply leaves consumption, employment, and real GDP unchanged. This result is called the *neutrality of money:*

> **Neutrality of money:** The implication of an economic model that an increase in the nominal money supply raises all *nominal* prices and wages but leaves real GDP, employment, and *relative* prices unaffected.

Doubling the money supply from $1,000 to $2,000 doubles the price level; people spend twice as many dollars to buy the same goods and services, at twice the prices.[2] The economy's technology is unaffected by printing pieces of paper for use as money, so the aggregate production function in Figure 4b is unaffected by a change in the money supply. Similarly, printing money does not affect the supply of labor or the demand for labor in Figure 4a, so it does not affect equilibrium employment or the equilibrium real wage. What happens in Figure 4a when an increase in the money supply raises nominal wages? The answer is *nothing*. Chapter 4 explained that the price on the Y-axis of a supply-demand diagram is the *relative price* of the product, *not* the *nominal* price. The relative price of labor services is the *real wage*, so the *real wage* appears on the Y-axis in Figure 4a. Because an increase in the money supply raises the nominal wage and the CPI in the same proportion, it leaves the real wage unchanged. Because the increase in the money supply does not affect equilibrium employment or technology, it does not affect real GDP.

Because equilibrium employment remains at l_0 and the production function does not change, real GDP remains at y_0 in Figure 4. In Professor Lucas's words, raising the money supply from $1,000 to $2,000 would not make any important difference. "Such a doubling of the money supply and of prices would amount to a 100 percent

---

[2] For now, we *assume* that the velocity of money does not change. A later chapter will discuss velocity in more detail, reaching the conclusion that a permanent change in the level of the money supply does not affect the long-run level of velocity. However, even if velocity were to change, this change would *not* affect the neutrality-of-money conclusion that real GDP is unaffected by doubling the money supply.

inflation in terms of local currency, but so what?" No one in the economy would really care, because they would work the same number of hours as before, and they would consume the same goods and services as before.

In summary, this model says that real GDP and employment are determined by the labor market and the economy's production function, as in Figure 4. Knowing real GDP, the equation of exchange allows you to solve for the equilibrium price level in terms of the nominal money supply and its velocity.

Recessions: Return to Kennywood Park

The story that Professor Lucas told early in the chapter about Kennywood Park leads to the conclusion that a decrease in the money supply causes a recession. In other words, that model does *not* predict the neutrality of money. Why not? What is different about the Kennywood Park story and the model developed in this chapter? There is one key difference: In the Kennywood Park story, prices do not fall along with the money supply.

Recall the reactions of customers in Kennywood Park when they learn that they can get only eight tickets per dollar instead of ten. They were disappointed, and the total number of tickets sold at the park decreased that day. In Professor Lucas's story, the number of tickets people need for each ride remains unchanged. Imagine how different the story would be if the number of tickets needed for each ride were to fall by 20 percent along with the exchange rate of tickets for dollars, publicly announced to customers at the park entrance. Although people could get only eight tickets per dollar instead of ten, rides that previously required ten tickets would now require only eight tickets; rides that required five tickets before now would require only four. In that case, customers would not care about the changes. They would say, in Lucas's words, "So what?" The change would not affect the number of people in the park or how many rides they choose to buy. This change in the money supply would be *neutral*, with no effect on real GDP.

A fall in the money supply creates a recession in Professor Lucas's Kennywood Park model because prices inside the park (the number of tickets per ride) do *not* adjust to the change in the money supply. In Professor Lucas's story, prices fail to adjust because no one inside the park becomes informed about the change in the money supply. Later chapters will discuss other reasons for prices not to change, and for violations of the *neutrality of money*.

IN THE NEWS

Inflation-Adjusted Wages Are on the Rise for Typical U.S. Worker, Shifting Trends

Something good must be happening in the U.S. economy: the latest government data showed the inflation-adjusted wages of the typical American worker are rising, and the gap between the best-paid and worst-paid workers is beginning to narrow. Inflation-adjusted wages for the median male worker climbed at an annual rate of 2.6 percent between 1996 and the middle of 1998. Between 1989 (the last business cycle peak) and 1996, medium wages fell 0.8 percent.

Source: The Wall Street Journal

Real wages (inflation-adjusted wages) have grown more rapidly in the past several years than in previous years.

Review Questions

9. What determines real GDP in the model with many people specializing and trading? Use graphs to help explain your answer.

10. Explain the equation of exchange and how it relates to the circular flow of economic activity.

11. What is the *neutrality of money*?

Thinking Exercises

12. Suppose the nominal money supply is $4,000, velocity equals 2 per year, and real GDP is 1,000 goods per year. What is the equilibrium price level?

13. Suppose your nominal wage rises by 10 percent and the consumer price index rises by 5 percent. What happens to your real wage?

14. Explain why doubling the nominal money supply and all nominal prices is similar to changing units of measurement from gallons to half-gallons, or miles to half-miles.

EQUILIBRIUM EMPLOYMENT AND UNEMPLOYMENT

Although the macroeconomic model developed in this chapter is very simple, many of its conclusions carry over to the more complicated models that economists analyze using computers. This chapter's model assumes equilibrium in the labor market (Figure 4a); as a result, *unemployment* occurs in the model only when people choose not to work, as when Crusoe decides to take a day off from picking berries. However, real-life unemployment often occurs when people have lost their old jobs and have not yet found suitable new jobs. Fortunately, the logic in this chapter also applies when the economy experiences unemployment. To see why, think about the causes of unemployment.

Some unemployment results from continuing economic changes. Changes in demand and supply cause some industries to expand and others to contract, raising the demand for labor in some parts of the economy and reducing labor demand in other parts. For example, steel manufacturers lay off workers when the demand for steel falls; computer firms hire workers when the demand for computers rises. Some people suffer unemployment as they take time to search for suitable jobs. Although someone who is willing to take a low-paying job can usually find one quickly, it takes longer for people to find good jobs that suit their interests and skills. Unemployment occurs partly because continuing changes always force some people to look for new jobs.

Some jobs go unfilled while people are unemployed and looking for work. Job vacancies occur because firms, like people, need time to find suitable employees who match their needs for skills, experience, and other characteristics. This *matching* process takes time. While firms are looking for suitable workers, and workers are looking for suitable jobs, unemployment and job vacancies occur together. Meanwhile, continuing changes in technology, consumer tastes, population, weather, government policies, international competition, and other factors, create new unemployment.

> **Equilibrium unemployment** refers to unemployment that results from continuing changes in supplies and demands and the costs of searching for and matching jobs in labor markets.

IN THE NEWS

Labor Day Reflects a Changing World for Job Seekers and Employers

With the passage of Labor Day, the hiring outlook for employers is daunting as they face the tightest employment market in three decades. Since unemployment is hovering at historically low levels, employers are devising new and creative methods, including technology-based solutions, to help them find, attract and hire new candidates. And employees on the hunt for a new job are quickly adapting to a new set of rules to succeed in today's job market. Now and in the future, employers and employees alike can expect a remarkably different playing field in their hiring and job-hunting quest.

Source: PRNewswire

Changes in technology have made it easier than in the past for people to obtain information about jobs, and for firms to obtain information about prospective workers. Will these new technologies help reduce the equilibrium level of unemployment?

The equilibrium rate of unemployment is often called the *natural* rate of unemployment (though there is little *natural* about it). When economists refer to *full employment,* they do not mean an economy with *zero* unemployment; they mean an economy with unemployment equal to its equilibrium (or natural) rate.

Full employment refers to a situation with equilibrium unemployment.

Determinants of Equilibrium Unemployment

Equilibrium unemployment occurs when the rate of job creation equals the rate of job destruction.[3]

> The **rate of job creation** is the number of new workers hired each month.

> The **rate of job destruction** is the number of people who quit or lose their jobs each month.

The rate of job destruction depends on the size and speed of changes in technology, government policies, and other factors that reduce the demand for labor in certain industries. The rate of job creation depends partly on the speed with which workers can learn about job opportunities and the speed with which firms can learn about candidates for hiring. The rate of job creation also depends on the number of people unemployed at the time; when the number of people looking for jobs and the number of firms looking for workers increase, so does the rate of new job matches each month. For example, if 20 percent of unemployed workers find jobs each month, then the rate of job creation is 1 million jobs per month if 5 million people are unemployed, or 2 million jobs per month if 10 million people are unemployed.

Equilibrium unemployment occurs when job destruction equals job creation, that is, when the number of people who lose their jobs each month equals the number of unemployed people who find jobs, leaving total unemployment unchanged. If unemployment exceeds its equilibrium level, then the rate of job creation exceeds the rate of job destruction, and unemployment falls. If unemployment falls below its equilibrium level, then the rate of job creation falls below the rate of job destruction and unemployment rises. In this way, the rate of unemployment tends to move toward its equilibrium level.

EXAMPLES

Suppose that continuing changes in demand and supply cause 1 million job losses each month, and each month one-third of all unemployed people find jobs. In this case, equilibrium unemployment is 3 million people. Each month one-third of these 3 million people find jobs, so the rate of job creation is 1 million jobs per month. Because 1 million jobs are destroyed each month, unemployment stays at 3 million people, composed of 2 million people who were already unemployed and did not find jobs plus 1 million newly unemployed people.

To see why unemployment tends toward its equilibrium level, suppose that 6 million people are unemployed at the beginning of January. Because one-third of them find jobs in January, only 4 million remain unemployed by February. Because 1 million other

IN THE NEWS

Jobless Rate Held Steady in August

The U.S. unemployment rate held steady at 4.5% in August as job losses in other industries outweighed the return to work of laborers affected by strikes at General Motors earlier this summer. Net job growth across all employment sectors in August was 365,000.

Source: USA Today

The unemployment rate remains the same when the rate of job creation equals the rate of job destruction.

[3]When the labor force—the number of people who have or want jobs—grows over time, perhaps due to population growth, equilibrium unemployment occurs when the rate of job creation equals the rate of job destruction *plus* the increase in the labor force. Employment then rises along with the size of the labor force and unemployment is constant.

people lose their jobs, however, total unemployment in February falls to 5 million, 1 million less than in January. One-third of these 5 million people (about 1,667,000 people) find jobs in February, and 1 million new people lose their jobs, so unemployment falls by 667,000 people, to 4.33 million, by March. Each month, unemployment falls toward its equilibrium level of 3 million people, although the process takes time.

What If the Economy Lacks Enough Jobs?

What if the economy does not create enough jobs to employ everyone who wants to work? What if the number of workers looking for jobs exceeds the number of firms looking for workers? People and firms then create new jobs. Jobs are not products like houses and food; the number of jobs available in the economy is not limited by available resources. Jobs are *trades*—voluntary agreements in which people exchange labor services and money. The only limit to the number of jobs the economy can create comes from the number of voluntary trades that people are willing to make. As long as a person can produce goods or services that are valuable to other people, that person can create a job by offering to work for a wage below the value that the other people place on those goods or services. The economy can always create enough jobs for everyone who can produce something valuable and who is willing to accept a wage equal to or below the value of his production.

> Jobs are trades; the number of jobs the economy can create is limited only
> by the number of trades that people are willing and able to make.

Unemployment results as people take time to find the trading opportunities that provide them with the greatest benefits. You may decide *not* to hire Mark to paint your house, even if you would gain from that trade, if you expect to find *someone else* who offers to paint it for a lower price that Mark charges. By waiting, you may find a *better* trade. Meanwhile, your house goes unpainted. Similarly, an unemployed person may not accept a job offer if he expects that an even *better* offer may soon arise; meanwhile, he remains unemployed.

Think about a person who drops out of college to look for a job. This person's work effort may be worth $8 per hour to many businesses, and yet the person may have difficulty finding a job. What creates this difficulty? Why don't business firms offer him a job at $6 per hour—leaving the firm with a $2 per hour profit from hiring the worker? Two reasons may prevent firms from hiring this person. First, firms may believe that the worker will soon quit to go back to school or look for a different job. Firms do not want to spend money to hire and train workers whom they will soon lose. Second, firms may expect to find other job applicants with better or more appropriate skills or experience. Even if the job applicant meets the basic qualifications for the job, these firms may prefer to wait for an even more suitable job applicant. Factors like these increase the time required to match people to jobs. These factors reduce the rate of job creation and create equilibrium unemployment.

Why don't unemployed people create jobs by becoming self-employed, like Crusoe? They might offer services as barbers, carpenters, caterers, designers, painters, plumbers, maintenance workers, baby-sitters, consultants, or taxi drivers. They might sell handicrafts or provide lawn and landscape care, music lessons, tutoring services, or laundry services; they could open restaurants or video-rental stores. (Centuries ago, when most people were self-employed, unemployment was virtually unknown.) Self-employment has several drawbacks. Although it eliminates the need for a person to find a job at a firm, self-employment requires people to find other things, such as suppliers (of inputs) and customers. A self-employed person may need to find and arrange a business location (for a barber shop or restaurant); tools (to work as a carpenter or computer repairer), and money for machinery, office space, and advertising. A self-employed person may need organizational skills, marketing skills, and other inputs that an employer would have provided. Self-employment requires potentially difficult and costly efforts to buy all these inputs, organize them, and make key business decisions. As a result, many people prefer to remain unemployed while they search for suitable jobs at established firms.

Automation

Throughout history, many people have worried about automation causing unemployment, as new machines gain capabilities to replace workers at lower cost. How does the economy create new jobs to replace those that automation destroys? The answer does not come from jobs producing the new machines, because one worker may produce a machine that replaces ten workers. Instead, the economy solves this problem by creating new jobs through new trades; firms are willing to hire the people who lose their jobs to automation, because those people offer valuable labor services. Because firms and workers need time to create suitable matches, automation temporarily drives unemployment above its equilibrium level. In time, however, it falls back toward its equilibrium level. People who lose their jobs may suffer greatly from unemployment, and the new jobs they find may not be as good as the jobs they lost, but the new machines raise the economy's aggregate GDP. The economy produces more goods and services for people than before technology improved. Although automation creates losses for some people (particularly those who lose their jobs), the average person gains from automation and other technical progress.

Unemployment in Kennywood Park

In the Kennywood Park story, ride operators become partially "unemployed" as fewer customers buy their rides after the money supply falls. As explained earlier, the fall in the money supply creates a recession in Kennywood Park because prices (tickets per ride) do *not* fall along with the money supply. As a result, customers make fewer trades with ride operators. This decrease in trading creates unemployment.

Unemployment in the Kennywood Park story illustrates another type of unemployment that economists often call *cyclical unemployment*. Cyclical unemployment refers to unemployment created by the economic forces that cause recessions, in contrast to the unemployment resulting from job destruction and creation in normal times. Because the distinction between cyclical unemployment and other unemployment is based on its *cause*, economists need *models* to distinguish cyclical unemployment from other unemployment in real-life data.

Chapter 2 explained that models have three purposes: understanding, prediction, and interpretation. This chapter has explained how a simple economic model helps with *understanding*, and why it helps with *prediction* by helping economists answer "what-if" questions; we now see that economists also need a model to *interpret* real-life unemployment data. The next chapter develops the model further by introducing financial markets and then using the model to answer some basic "what-if" questions.

Review Questions

15. List some reasons for unemployment.

16. Explain why the rate of unemployment tends to move toward its equilibrium level.

Thinking Exercises

17. Discuss this statement: "Advances in technology that replace workers with machines are likely to raise the rate of unemployment over the next several decades by reducing the number of jobs available in the economy."

18. Consider the Kennywood Park story. (a) Explain how changes in consumer tastes might create unemployment among ride operators in the park. (b) How would you identify job destruction and job creation in the park? (c) Explain how the fall in the money supply described by Professor Lucas creates unemployment among ride operators. (d) What could ride operators do to become re-employed in the park, after a fall in the money supply? (e) How would you estimate equilibrium unemployment in the park? How would you estimate cyclical unemployment?

C o n c l u s i o n

What Economists Do

Economists construct models, which are like logical stories, and then reason by analogy from those models to real-life economies. They construct models *because* they want to understand *real-world* economies. Models allow economists to answer *"what if"* questions about the economy, understand the economy, make real-life decisions, and give advice about government policies.

In the Kennywood Park story told by Professor Lucas, a decrease in the money supply and a proportional decrease in prices inside the park (the number of tickets per ride) would not make any difference to customers. Professor Lucas considers an experiment in which the money supply in the park decreases and prices do *not* decrease because the fall in the money supply was a surprise. He explains why this combination creates a recession. This "story" is an example of an economic model.

A Very Simple Model of GDP

In the Robinson Crusoe economy, Crusoe's real GDP is determined by his production function and the number of hours he chooses to work. Crusoe also decides how much to invest in building new capital. His investment decisions depend on his willingness to sacrifice consumption or leisure time today to increase his consumption in the future, and his opportunities for doing so. Crusoe's real GDP fluctuates over time. These fluctuations may resemble recessions and booms, but they may also differ from them in important ways.

In a model with many people who specialize and trade, equilibrium in labor markets determines employment and the real wage. Given equilibrium employment, the aggregate production function determines real GDP.

The circular flow diagram illustrates the equation of exchange, which says that the nominal money supply, multiplied by its velocity, equals the price level multiplied by real GDP. This equation *defines* velocity. The equation of exchange shows how the price level depends on the nominal money supply, velocity, and real GDP.

In this chapter's basic model (which *assumes* a constant velocity of money), doubling the nominal money supply causes nominal prices to double without changing

real GDP and employment. The prediction that real GDP does not depend on the money supply is called the *neutrality of money.* Economic controversies about business cycles and recessions surround discussions of the neutrality of money. The Kennywood Park story is one example of a model without the neutrality of money.

Equilibrium Employment and Unemployment

Unemployment results from continuing changes in underlying conditions such as technology, consumer tastes, population, weather, government policies, international competition, and other economic factors. Some industries contract while others expand. Unemployed people require time to find jobs that suit their interests and skills. Firms also require time to find workers who match their needs. Unemployment occurs because this matching process takes time.

Economists use the term *full employment* to refer to an economy with the equilibrium level (or natural rate) of unemployment, resulting from continuing changes in labor markets. Unemployment reaches it equilibrium level when the rate of job creation equals the rate of job destruction. At this level, the number of people who lose their jobs each month equals the number of unemployed people who find jobs, so total unemployment does not change. If unemployment exceeds its equilibrium level, then the rate of job creation exceeds the rate of job destruction and unemployment falls. If unemployment falls below its equilibrium level, then the rate of job creation falls below the rate of job destruction and unemployment rises. This activity moves the rate of unemployment toward its equilibrium level.

Jobs are trades, not products with limited supplies. The only limit to the number of jobs the economy can create is the number of profitable, voluntary trades to which people can and will agree. Anyone who can produce something of value to other people can obtain a job at some wage. Unemployment occurs because searching and matching take time; some people choose unemployment while they search for better opportunities. Cyclical unemployment results from additional factors that cause recessions, as in the Kennywood Park story.

Key Terms

production function
average product
marginal product
law of diminishing returns

nominal money supply
velocity of money
equation of exchange

nominal wages
real wages
neutrality of money

equilibrium unemployment
rate of job creation
rate of job destruction

Questions and Problems

19. Explain the Kennywood Park story of Professor Robert Lucas.

20. Why do you think Professor Lucas says that "we could *not* use monetary manipulation to engineer a *permanently* higher level of prosperity in the park"? What might happen if the park tried to do that?

21. In what ways are fluctuations in Robinson Crusoe's real GDP like recessions and booms in the U.S. economy? In what ways do they differ?

22. Suppose the nominal money supply is $2,000, velocity equals 1 per year, and real GDP is 1,000 goods per year. What happens to the equilibrium price level if real GDP rises to 2,000 goods per year?

23. How large is equilibrium unemployment if the rate of job destruction is 300,000 workers per month, and one-tenth of unemployed workers find jobs each month? Suppose that 10 million people are currently unemployed, and explain why unemployment falls over time toward its equilibrium level.

24. A professor at Stanford University, Alvin Rabushka, suggested that the government of Japan should try to end its 1998 recession by organizing a "national fire sale" in which all businesses, large and small, would be subsidized to reduce the nominal prices of their products.[4] Use the economic analysis of this chapter to explain why and how this policy might end a recession.

Inquiries for Further Thought

25. Professor Lucas says, "In any case, that is what economists do. We are storytellers, operating much of the time in worlds of make believe. We do not find that the realm of imagination and ideas is an alternative to, or a retreat from, practical reality. On the contrary, it is the only way we have found to think seriously about reality." Do you agree, or not? Defend your answer.

26. Why are people unemployed? Why don't unemployed people create their own jobs by going into

business for themselves? What could governments do to reduce unemployment? What government policies add to unemployment?

27. Why don't people buy unemployment insurance like they buy fire insurance?

---

[4] "On Sale Now," Alvin Rabushka, *The Wall Street Journal*, August 19, 1998.

SAVINGS, INVESTMENT, AND GROWTH

CHAPTER 26

INTEREST RATES, SAVINGS, AND INVESTMENT

In this Chapter...

Main Points to Understand

▶ The supply of loans by savers and demand for loans (mainly for investment) jointly determine the equilibrium interest rate and equilibriums levels of savings and investment.

▶ Equilibrium in the loan market is equivalent to equilibrium in the market for goods and services.

▶ The real (inflation-adjusted) interest rate affects saving and investment decisions.

▶ The economy's responses to changes in underlying conditions (such as technology or taxes) depend on the willingness of consumers to sacrifice current consumption for additional future consumption.

Thinking Skills to Develop

▶ Develop skills in working with economic models.

▶ Add new features to a simple model to address new issues.

▶ Use an economic model to examine changes in underlying conditions.

▶ Recognize the role of Adam Smith's "invisible hand" in macroeconomic issues.

As a college student, you are making a sacrifice. By attending school rather than working full time, you sacrifice income and consumption. You have probably made this choice on purpose, because you expect (quite correctly, on average) that a college education will raise your *future* income and consumption. In this and many other decisions in life, you make "now or later" choices that require current sacrifices for future gains or provide current gains at the expense of the future. Everyone regularly makes this kind of decision: A child decides whether to eat all her candy now or save some for next week; a worker decides whether to take time away from work and family to upgrade his skills; a business firm decides whether to pursue short-term profits or sacrifice them by investing in research and development in pursuit of increased long-term gains; every society somehow makes decisions about using natural resources or conserving them for future generations.

These "now or later" decisions affect the economy as a whole: They affect the amounts that people work, consume, and save. They affect the economy's current GDP and the opportunities that it will offer to future generations of workers and consumers. This chapter explains how a basic financial market and an important price—the market for loans and the interest rate—coordinate these decisions.

Think about the basic model of real GDP, employment, and the price level discussed in the previous chapter. In that basic model, each person produces and sells a good or service, and each buys goods and services from other people. (Some people work for

As a student, you sacrifice income now to improve your future. Similarly, the economy as a whole can sacrifice consumption now to invest in its future.

firms rather than producing goods as individuals, but that distinction does not affect our story.) People in the basic model have opportunities to invest in new tools, equipment, buildings and factories, skills, and technical knowledge, just as Robinson Crusoe had the opportunity to invest in automatic berry-picking machines. Robinson Crusoe's situation differs in two important ways from the situation of people in the basic model.

1. When Robinson Crusoe invests, he must either spend more time working or spend less time picking berries for consumption. As a result, Crusoe can invest only by reducing consumption or leisure time. In contrast, a person in the basic model can *borrow* to invest without reducing consumption or sacrificing leisure time.

2. Sometimes Robinson Crusoe enjoys a large berry harvest, because random changes in the weather or seasons allow him to pick a lot of berries in a short time. On those days, Crusoe has a high income (a high real GDP), and he can either eat a lot of berries, or work fewer hours and take more leisure time. On bad-harvest days, Crusoe has a low income; even by working extra hours, he picks fewer berries than normal to eat. If he could, Crusoe would like to store berries on days when he earns a high income for use on days when he has a low income. However, he cannot store berries (because they spoil quickly in the island heat). As a result, each day, Crusoe eats whatever he picks that day. In contrast, a person in the basic model can *save* on days when she has a high income. She saves by spending less than her income and lending the difference.

In the basic model, some people want to borrow money to spend on investments. Other people want to save money. As a result, people can gain from trades, and their trades create a *loan market* in which people borrow and lend.

INTEREST RATES AND LOAN-MARKET EQUILIBRIUM

Figure 1 shows equilibrium in the loan market. The price of a loan is the *interest rate*. The *demand for loans* shows the behavior of borrowers: *Borrowers demand loans.* The demand curve slopes downward because a rise in the interest rate raises the cost of borrowing. The *supply of loans* shows the behavior of lenders: *Lenders supply loans.* The supply curve slopes upward because a rise in the interest rate raises the interest income that lenders receive when loans are repaid.

Borrowers demand loans. Lenders supply loans.

Equilibrium in the loan market occurs at Point A in the figure, where the quantity of loans supplied equals the quantity demanded. The equilibrium interest rate is R_0 and the equilibrium quantity of loans is L_0. At interest rates above R_0, the quantity of loans supplied exceeds the quantity demanded, leading interest rates to fall toward the equilibrium. At interest rates below R_0, the quantity of loans demanded exceeds the quantity supplied, leading interest rates to rise toward the equilibrium.

Interest Rates

> An **interest rate** is the price of a loan, expressed as a *percentage per year* of the amount loaned.

EXAMPLES

If you borrow $100 for one year at an interest rate of 12 percent per year, you owe the lender $112 at the end of the year. The interest on the loan is the extra $12 you must pay; the interest rate expresses this amount as a percentage of the $100 loan; paying $12 on a loan of $100 gives an interest rate of 12 percent per year. If you borrow $200 for one year at an interest rate of 8 percent, you owe the bank $216 at the end of the year. You pay $16 in interest, which is 8 percent of the $200 loan.

If you borrow $100 for *two* years at an interest rate of 10 percent per year, you will owe $121 at the end of two years. The interest rate is 10 percent per year, *each year.* Your debt is $110 after one year ($100 plus $10 interest), so the interest on the second year of the loan is $11 (10 percent of $110), and you owe $121 at the end of two years. The $21 interest that you pay reflects an interest rate of 10 percent per year for two years.

Interest Rate Formula

If you borrow X dollars for one year, you must pay back:

$$X(1 + R)$$

dollars the next year, where R is the interest rate on the loan, measured as a decimal. In other words, an 8 percent interest rate means R is 0.08, and a 10 percent interest rate means R is 0.10.

Discounted Present Value

One of the most useful formulas in economics is the formula for a discounted present value. The discounted present value of some amount of money in the future is its value today.

> The **discounted present value** of a future payment of money is its market value *today.*

In other words, the discounted present value of $100 paid next year is *today's* equilibrium price of the right to receive $100 next year.

The general formula for a discounted present value is:

X dollars payable 1 year from now is worth $\dfrac{X}{1 + R}$ dollars now

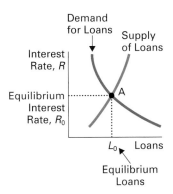

Figure 1
Equilibrium in the Market for Loans

Equilibrium occurs at Point A, with an equilibrium price of R_0 per year and an equilibrium quantity of L_0 per year.

where R is the interest rate, measured as a decimal. For example, 12 percent per year is the number 0.12.

EXPLANATION AND EXAMPLES

The idea of discounted present value is very simple: A dollar today is worth more than a dollar in the future, because if you have the dollar today you can save it and earn interest. For example, suppose the interest rate is 10 percent per year. If you have $91 today and you save it and earn interest on it, then you will have $91 + $9.10 = about $100 next year. Therefore, $91 *today* is worth about $100 paid next year. In other words, if the interest rate is 10 percent per year, then the *discounted present value* of $100 paid next year is about $91 today.

Notice that, with an interest rate of 10 percent per year, you can *trade* $91 today for about $100 next year by saving and earning interest. Similarly, you can trade $100 payable next year for about $91 *today* by *borrowing*. Suppose you will earn $100 next year. You can trade that money for $91 *today* by borrowing $91 now, for 1 year. You will owe the lender about $100 next year, and you can pay off the loan, with interest, by using the $100 that you will earn next year. In this way, you can trade $100 next year for $91 today. In summary, when the interest rate is 10 percent per year, people can trade $91 today for $100 next year, or they can trade $100 next year for $91 today. As a result, these amounts have the same value. We say that (when the interest rate is 10 percent per year) the discounted present value of $100 payable next year is about $91.

Consider some more examples: If the interest rate is 12 percent per year, then the discounted present value of $112 payable next year is $100 now. A person with $100 now can trade it for $112 next year, and a person who will have $112 next year can trade it for $100 today. If the interest rate is 8 percent per year, then the discounted present value of $20,000 payable next year is $20,000/1.08 = $18,518.52.

Investment and the Demand for Loans

The demand curve for loans in Figure 1 slopes downward because a rise in the interest rate raises the cost of borrowing. Think about a firm that wants to borrow to invest $1,000 in a new machine. Suppose that the new machine would add $1,200 to the firm's production next year, and would fall apart immediately after that. Borrowing $1,000 to invest in this machine is profitable if the interest rate is less than 20 percent per year, but not profitable if the interest rate is above 20 percent. For example, if the interest rate is 10 percent per year, then the firm will owe $1,100 to repay its loan. Because the firm gains $1,200 from the machine, the firm can repay the loan and keep $100 in profit. If the interest rate were 25 percent, however, the firm would owe $1,250 to repay its loan, and the revenue from the machine would not be enough to repay the loan. Loosely speaking, borrowing to invest is profitable only if the *rate of return* on the investment—20 percent per year in this example—exceeds the interest rate. More precisely:

> An investment is profitable if the discounted present value of the benefits from the investment exceeds the expenditure on the investment.

Suppose, in the example, that the interest rate is 10 percent per year ($R = 0.10$). Then the discounted present value of the benefit from the investment is $1,200/1.10 = $1,091. This amount exceeds the expenditure on the investment ($1,000), so the investment is profitable. However, if the interest rate were 25 percent per year ($R = 0.25$), then the discounted present value of the benefit would be only $1,200/1.25 = $960. This amount is less than $1,000, so the investment is *not* profitable.

Applying the Discounted Present Value Formula

Suppose an investment will pay $1,000 two years from now (but nothing before or after that time). Find the discounted present value of $1,000 paid two years from now by applying the formula *twice*. Suppose that in 2000 the interest rate is 10 percent per year. Your investment will pay you $1,000 in 2002, and you want to find the discounted present value, in 2000, of that money. First, apply the formula to find out how much $1,000 payable in 2002 is worth in 2001; the formula shows that this amount is worth $1,000/(1.10), or $909.09 in 2001. Then apply the formula again to find out how much $909.09 in 2001 is worth in 2000. (This time, substitute $909.09 for X in the formula.) The formula shows that it is worth $909.09/(1.10), or $826.45. The discounted present value of $1,000 paid two years from now is $826.45 if the interest rate is 10 percent per year.

Using this logic, you can apply the formula N times to find the discounted present value of $1,000 in N years from now. The formula for the discounted present value of X dollars paid N years from now is:

X dollars payable N years from now is worth

$$\frac{X}{(1 + R)^N} \text{ dollars now}$$

A nearby box shows how to calculate discounted present values of more complicated investments. Notice that a rise in the interest rate reduces the discounted present value of the benefit from the investment. In this example, the firm will borrow and invest if the interest rate is less than 20 percent, but not if the interest rate exceeds 20 percent. Other firms have their own investment ideas. Some of those ideas would be profitable even with a 30 percent interest rate; many more would be profitable if the interest rate were only 5 percent per year. The result is a downward-sloping demand curve for loans, as in Figure 1.

For example, suppose a firm has an idea for building new equipment that would cost $100,000 but would add $130,000 to the firm's revenue next year (and nothing in years after that). Then the investment is profitable—the discounted present value of the benefit exceeds the initial expenditure on the investment—if the interest rate is less than 30 percent per year, but not if the interest rate is higher than 30 percent. Suppose another firm has an idea for an investment that would cost $100,000 and would add $110,000 in revenue next year (and nothing in years after that). This investment is profitable only if the interest rate is less than 10 percent per year. Both firms would want to borrow if the interest rate is below 10 percent per year; only the first firm would want to borrow at an interest rate between 10 percent and 30 percent; neither

IN THE NEWS

The Powerball Payout Dilemma

Every player has to choose whether he would prefer to take any winnings up front or over a number of years. Making the right choice is tougher than it seems.

When a machinist from Westerville, Ohio, drove 100 miles recently to buy Powerball tickets for himself and a dozen buddies, he—like every other player in the huge lottery—faced a decision about how to get paid if he happened to win. He could either take the prize as a single lump sum—or as a stream of payments stretched out over 25 years.

As it happened, he chose the lump sum. And that's why, when the "Lucky 13," as they call themselves, claim their winnings, they will collect only $161.5 million, rather

than a total of $295.7 million over the next 25 years.

Did they make the right choice? Answering that question turns out to be more difficult than it might appear, financial planners told *Money Daily* on Thursday. But the answer has implications for how people facing more commonplace financial dilemmas—such as whether to take an annuity or a lump sum upon retirement—ought to analyze their situation.

In the case of Powerball, the choice works like this. You must decide when you buy your ticket whether to take the full prize—in this case, a total of $295.7 million over 25 years—or a much smaller sum ($161 million) up front. Yet the two are really equivalent. That's because

the way the lottery pays the $295 million is to buy a series of government bonds timed to mature in one year, two years, three years and so forth up to the full 25-year period. Buying those bonds costs about $161 million. So in either case, the lottery will pay out only $161 million.

Which type of payment is better for you depends critically on what you do with the money. "The difference between the lump sum and the annualized payout is equivalent to the government paying you 5.35% yearly interest on your money," says tax attorney Walker Arenson of Austin, TX. "So if you can beat that rate by investing the money, then you come out ahead."

Source: Money Daily

where R is the interest rate *per year*. The previous example shows how this formula applies when $N = 2$.

You can easily extend this logic to find the discounted present value of more complicated future payments. For example, suppose that someone will pay you $1,000 one year from now and another $1,000 two years from now. What is the discounted present value of these two payments? The discounted present value of $1,000 paid one year from now is $1,000/(1 + R)$. The discounted present value of $1,000 paid two years from now is $1,000/(1 + R)^2$. So the discounted present value of both payments is:

$$\frac{\$1,000}{(1 + R)} + \frac{\$1,000}{(1 + R)^2}$$

If the interest rate is 10 percent per year, the result is $909.09 plus $826.45, or $1,735.54.

Finally, you can apply this logic to payments that occur every year without stopping. The discounted present value of $1,000 per year paid *every year, forever* turns out to be:

$$\frac{\$1,000}{R}$$

If the interest rate is 10 percent per year, this amount equals $10,000. This result is also a rough approximation to the discounted present value of $1,000 paid every year for more than about 30 years ($9,370 if the interest rate is 10 percent per year).

The article goes on to explain how tax laws complicate the calculation. Additional information can be found on the Web pages for this book.

Opportunity Cost and Investment

Firms in the U.S. economy sometimes pay for investments with money they already have (from sales of their products) rather than by borrowing. Firms face an opportunity cost of using their money in this way, because they *could have* loaned the money to someone, earning interest on it. As a result, the interest rate affects investment decisions in the same way regardless of whether firms borrow money to fund investments or whether they use money they already have. Consequently, you can think of firms that use their own money for investments as *borrowing the money from themselves*. This borrowing appears as part of the demand for loans in Figure 1, and this saving and lending by firms appears as part of the supply of loans in Figure 1.

firm would want to borrow at an interest rate above 30 percent. This creates the demand curve for loans in Figure 2. With additional firms and additional investment ideas, the demand for loans appears as in Figure 1.

Adjustments to the Logic of Investment

These criteria for profitability of investments require three adjustments for many real-life applications. First, the future benefits of investments in real life are uncertain, so the logic above applies to *expected* benefits rather than actual benefits (which are unknown at the time a firm invests).

Second, firms must often pay taxes on returns from their investments, so they must adjust the logical reasoning for the effects of taxes. Essentially, the logic above applies to *after-tax* costs and benefits.

Third, people tend to dislike risk. A firm may have a 6/10 chance of gaining $1,000 on an investment and a 4/10 chance of losing $1,000. Although the chance of winning is better than the chance of losing, a firm may not want to accept the risk of this investment. In real-life investment decisions, firms adjust the logic of the decision to account for risk. Essentially, the discounted present value of the expected future benefits from the investment must exceed the required expenditure by an amount sufficient to repay people for taking risks. The fundamental logic of investments is not affected by these adjustments.

Government Budgets and the Demand for Loans

The demand for loans shows the amount of money that *everyone* in the economy—people, firms, and the government—would want to borrow at various possible interest rates. In the U.S. economy, the demand for loans is *mostly* demand by firms to pay for investments. Until recent years, however, the second-largest part of the demand for loans came from the *government budget deficit*.

Figure 2 | Example of Demand for Loans

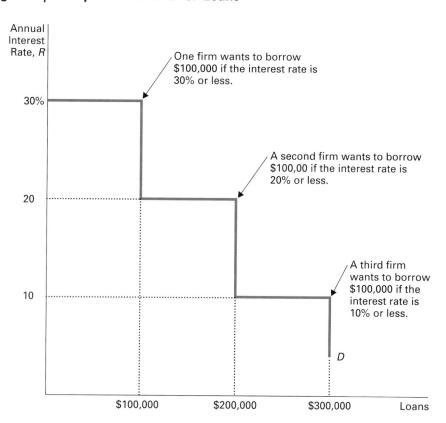

IN THE NEWS

American dream is back

Low interest rates light up home sales

Falling mortgage rates are adding fuel to an unseasonably hot market for home sales. Not since the 1960s has the housing market been so uniformly strong across the USA.

From Boston to San Francisco, Charleston, S.C., to Des Moines, people are buying homes at a record rate. Behind the boom: a strong economy, low interest rates and easy credit as more banks offer low- or no-down-payment loans.

"I never thought I could have a home of my own," says Mary Kutsch, who moved from El Segundo, Calif., to Las Vegas last year. Lured by low interest rates, the family first looked to buy a new home. And mortgage applications are at near-record levels, lifted by lower interest rates.

Source: USA Today

Decreasing interest rates raise investments in housing as well as investments in factories, equipment, and research.

The **government budget deficit** equals government spending in excess of tax receipts during some period of time.

A government budget deficit creates a demand for loans. When the government spends more than it collects in taxes, it borrows money to *finance* its deficit. If the government spends $2,500 billion, and collects $2,400 billion in taxes, it borrows the other $100 billion. As recently as 1996, the U.S. government's annual budget deficit exceeded $100 billion. However, state and local governments had budget surpluses that year (revenues that exceeded their spending), so the combined budget deficit of U.S. federal, state, and local governments was only $5 billion in 1996, meaning that units of government in the United States borrowed $5 billion. Back in 1992, the combined government budget deficit was almost $200 billion; by 1998, even the federal government had a *surplus* rather than a deficit. While U.S. government budget deficits may appear to be a topic of history, economists expect them to reemerge in future years as the baby-boom generation retires and begins collecting social security. Figure 3 shows the connection between investment demand, the government budget deficit, and the demand for loans.

The total demand for loans equals demand by firms for investment plus the government budget deficit.

Review Questions

1. Who supplies loans? Why does the supply curve for loans slope upward?

2. What is a discounted present value? Explain this concept in words. What is the formula for it?

Figure 3 | Equilibrium in the Market for Loans

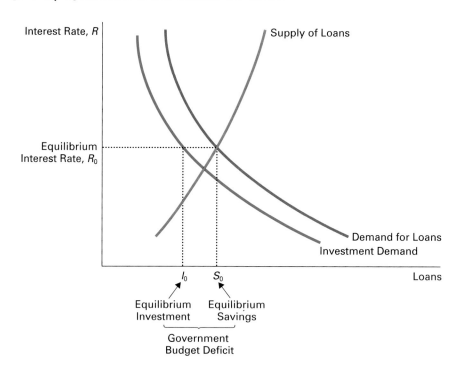

Thinking Exercises

3. If the interest rate is 10 percent per year, what is the discounted present value of $200 paid one year from now? What if the interest is 5 percent?

4. How does an increase in the interest rate affect the discounted present value of a certain future payment?

5. If the interest rate is 10 percent per year, what is the discounted present value of $20,000 paid two years from now?

SAVINGS AND THE SUPPLY OF LOANS

People supply loans when they lend money that they have *saved* by spending less than their incomes:

$$\text{Savings} = \text{Income (after taxes)} - \text{Consumption}$$

After-tax income is often called *disposable income*.

When people save, they usually put their money in bank accounts (or some similar accounts) or they buy financial assets such as stocks and bonds. When you put your money in a bank account, the bank lends your money to someone else. The bank is essentially a middleman or intermediary between savers (lenders) and borrowers. (Further analysis of the role of banks in this process appears in Chapter 27.)

You also lend money when you buy bonds; you lend to the business firms that sell those bonds. Each bond is an I.O.U.—a piece of paper printed with a promise to pay a specified amount of money at a future date. If a bond promises to pay $1,000 one year from now, and you buy that bond for $909.09, then you are actually lending $909.09 for a year at a 10 percent interest rate. The business firm that issues the bond gets the $909.09 now, and it repays you $1,000 next year. (As this example shows, the price of a bond is the discounted present value of its future payments.) A later chapter will discuss stocks, bonds, and other financial assets in greater depth. The current discussion can ignore the details of banks, stock markets, and similar complications: In the basic economic model, savers lend money directly to borrowers to fund investments.

Supply of Loans

The supply of loans slopes upward as in Figure 1 because a rise in the interest rate raises the return from lending. People gain more from lending money at a 10 percent interest rate than at a 5 percent interest rate. As a result, the quantity of loans supplied rises as the interest rate rises, creating the upward-sloping supply curve.

> The supply of loans shows the amounts of money that people would want to save and lend at various possible interest rates.

Total saving by people and businesses in the United States equals about $1.4 trillion per year. Almost all of this money is loaned to business firms for investment; a small fraction funds loans to households for cars, houses, vacations, and other purchases. (A few years ago, when the U.S. government was running a large budget deficit, the government also borrowed a portion of this money.)

Equilibrium in the Loan Market and Goods Market

Equilibrium in the loan market occurs when the quantity of loans demanded equals the quantity supplied, as at Point A in Figure 1. The equilibrium interest rate is R_0 and the equilibrium quantity of loans is L_0. The supply of loans reflects saving and lending, so *equilibrium saving equals L_0*. Similarly, the demand for loans reflects investment and the government budget deficit, so *equilibrium investment equals L_0 minus the government budget deficit*.

When business firms take out loans from banks, they borrow money that other people have saved and spend it on investments.

Equilibrium in the loans market is closely connected with equilibrium in the economy's overall market for goods and services reflected in the circular flow diagram (Figure 5 in the previous chapter). For the moment, ignore all international trade. Equilibrium in the loan market implies that the quantity of loans supplied—savings—equals the quantity of loans demanded—investment plus the government budget deficit:

$$S = I + DEF$$

where S is total savings, I is investment, and DEF is the government budget deficit. Recall that savings equals income minus taxes and minus consumption spending:

$$S = Y - T - C$$

Therefore, equilibrium in the loan market implies:

$$Y - T - C = I + DEF$$

However, the government budget deficit equals government spending minus taxes, so

$$DEF = G - T$$

Therefore, loan-market equilibrium implies:

$$Y = C + I + G$$

In the absence of international trade, this expression is the equation for equilibrium in the market for goods and services—GDP equals consumption plus investment plus government purchases.[1] In other words, equilibrium in the loan market and equilibrium in the goods market are *the same*.

What about International Trade?

International trade fits easily into the previous analysis. The key point to notice is the connection between net exports and international trade in loans: When we export to other countries more goods than we import from them (when we have an international trade surplus), other countries *borrow* from us to pay for the difference. For example, suppose we export $500 in goods to another country, and we import $300 in goods from them; our net exports equal $200. People in the other country need to obtain $500 to pay us for their purchases; they earn $300 of that money by selling goods to us, and they borrow the other $200. Similarly, when we import more goods than we export (when we have an international trade deficit), other countries *lend* the difference to us. For example, suppose we export $500 in goods to another country, and we import $600 in goods from them; our net exports equal *minus* $100. In that case, we *borrow* $100 from people in foreign countries. Figure 5 in Chapter 24 showed that the United States currently has an international trade deficit of about $500 per person, meaning that net exports, NEX, is *negative* and foreigners lend about $500 per person to Americans.

International trade enters the loan-market analysis because lending by foreigners adds to the total supply of loans. Therefore equilibrium in the loan market implies that

---

The idea that loan-market equilibrium and goods-market equilibrium are the same is easiest to understand with no government spending, no taxes, and no international trade.

In this case, loan-market equilibrium implies that savings equals investment, or

$$S = I$$

However, savings is simply income minus consumption, so:

$$S = Y - C$$

Substituting for S and rearranging:

$$Y = C + I$$

which is the same as goods-market equilibrium.

---

[1] An alert reader might recall the difference between government *spending* and government *purchases. Spending* includes transfer payments (such as social security payments). This difference does not affect these conclusions, however. To see why, let G represent government purchases. Then the government budget deficit is $DEF = G +$ transfer payments $-$ taxes. Now define T as taxes minus transfer payments. (In other words, we count transfer payments as *negative* taxes, which makes sense because transfer payments add to people's incomes in the same way that taxes reduce the incomes of others.) Then $DEF = G - T$, as in the text.

the quantity of loans supplied, or savings *minus net exports (NEX)*, equals the quantity of loans demanded, or investment plus the government budget deficit:

$$S - NEX = I + DEF$$

Therefore, equilibrium in the loan market implies $Y - T - C - NEX = I + DEF$, or

$$Y = C + I + G + NEX$$

This expression is the equation for equilibrium in the market for goods and services. GDP equals the sum of consumption, investment, government purchases, and net exports. As before, equilibrium in the loan market and equilibrium in the goods market are the same thing.

Intertemporal Allocation of Resources

Why is equilibrium in the loan market the same as equilibrium in the goods market? The answer is connected with the "now or later" choices mentioned in the introduction to this chapter—choices that people make every day, such as your decision to sacrifice current consumption to invest in a college education and raise your future consumption. Economists refer to these "now or later" choices as *intertemporal* choices. These choices affect the the economy's overall use of labor, capital, and other resources to create consumption *now* versus consumption in the *future*.

Goods-market equilibrium occurs when the *current* supply of goods and services equals the *current* demand (for consumption, investment, government purchases, and net exports). Loan-market equilibrium occurs when the amount of *current* goods that some people want to trade away in return for *future* goods (by lending) equals the amount that other people want to acquire (by borrowing).

Suppose people suddenly want more consumption now—and they are willing to pay for it by having less in the future. This decision creates *excess demand* in the goods market *now*, as well as excess supply in the future goods market. It also creates excess demand for loans, as people save less than before and spend more on consumption. As a result, the interest rate rises, bringing the loan market *and* the goods market into equilibrium.

As the interest rate increases, investment falls, reducing excess demand for loans. This fall in investment also reduces excess demand in the goods market. As the interest rate adjusts to create equilibrium in the loans market, it also automatically creates equilibrium in the market for current goods and services. That reasoning expresses in *words* the logic behind the *algebra* showing the equivalence of loan-market equilibrium and goods-market equilibrium.

The logic connecting loan-market equilibrium and goods-market equilibrium points out the important role of the interest rate. It also shows that the interest rate is connected to the *relative price* of consumption now versus consumption in the future. The next section explores this important issue.

Review Questions

6. Who demands loans? Why does the demand curve for loans slope downward?

7. In what way is the demand for loans related to the government budget deficit?

8. Use equations to show why equilibrium in the loan market is the same as equilibrium in the goods market.

T h i n k i n g   E x e r c i s e s

9. Discuss this statement: "Investors gain from a higher interest rate. By making investments more attractive, an increase in the interest rate raises investment."

10. Suppose an increase in the supply of loans leads to a new equilibrium in the loan market, with a $100 billion increase in equilibrium savings and investment. If government purchases, net exports, and GDP do not change, what happens to keep the goods market in equilibrium—that is, what happens to guarantee that $Y = C + I + G + NEX$?

REAL AND NOMINAL INTEREST RATES

In 1990, interest rates reached more than 1,000 percent per year in Argentina and Brazil, but they were only about 35 percent per year in Mexico and 8 percent per year in the United States and Japan. Why do interest rates differ so much between countries? Are they connected with inflation, which was above 1,000 percent per year in Argentina and Brazil, much lower in Mexico, and even lower in the United States and Japan?

The interest rates that people usually talk about or read about are *nominal* interest rates.

> The **nominal interest rate** on a loan is the annual dollar interest payment expressed as a percentage of the dollar amount borrowed.

The formula for the discounted present value of a certain amount of money to be delivered in the future involves the nominal interest rate. The nominal interest rate is actually a relative price.

> The nominal interest rate (expressed as a decimal), plus one, equals the *relative price* of $1 this year in terms of dollars next year.

In other words, when a person borrows $500 for a year, he buys $500 *this year* at a price of $500(1 + R) *next year*. For example, if the nominal interest rate is 6 percent per year, then 1 plus the nominal interest rate expressed as a decimal is 1.06, so the relative price of $500 this year is 1.06 times $500, or $530 next year. This price is the amount of money that a borrower must repay on the loan.

The *real* interest rate corrects the nominal interest rate for inflation:

> The **real interest rate** is the interest rate *adjusted for inflation*.

The real interest rate plays an important economic role, because it is the *relative price* of a good at two points in time.

> The real interest rate (expressed as a decimal), plus one, is the relative price of goods *this year* in terms of the same goods *next year*.

To see how the real interest rates corrects the nominal interest rate for inflation, suppose that you lend someone $100 for one year at 10 percent interest; you get back $110 at the end of the year, which is 10 percent more money than you originally loaned. If inflation has occurred, however, the borrower repays you in dollars that have lower purchasing power than the dollars you lent. Each dollar buys less at the end of the year than

Example

If the nominal interest rate is 10 percent per year, then the relative price of $1 this year is 1.10 dollars next year: If you borrow $1 now, you will owe $1.10 next year.

it bought at the beginning of the year. The nominal interest rate shows how much you gain in dollar terms from the loan; the real interest rate adjusts for inflation to measure your gain in purchasing power.

Fisher Equation

Real and nominal interest rates are connected by a formula called the *Fisher equation,* named after the famous American economist, Irving Fisher. The Fisher equation says:[2]

$$R = r + \pi$$

where R is the nominal interest rate, r is the real interest rate, and π is the rate of inflation.

   The Fisher equation shows why countries with high rates of inflation have high nominal interest rates. Whatever the level of the real interest rate, a high rate of inflation, π, causes a high nominal interest rate, R. Figure 4 shows the nominal interest rate, inflation rate, and real interest rate in the United States since 1955. Notice that decreases in the nominal interest rate in the 1980s and 1990s accompanied decreases in the rate of inflation. Rearranging the Fisher equation gives the real interest rate in terms of the nominal interest rate and inflation:

$$r = R - \pi$$

Figure 4 | Interest Rates in the United States, 1955–1998

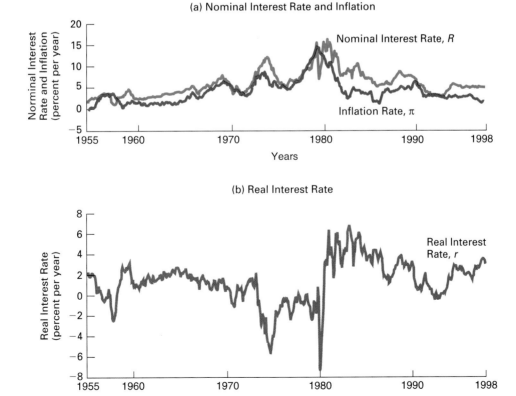

(a) Nominal Interest Rate and Inflation

(b) Real Interest Rate

[2] This version of the Fisher equation is an approximation for interest that is not continuously compounded; the actual equation in that case is $(1 + r)\, e^{\pi} - 1$ where e is the natural exponent. The formula in the text is exact for continuously compounded interest.

IN THE NEWS

Inflation is driving global rates higher

Inflation and fears of inflation are driving interest rates higher around the globe.

Source: The Wall Street Journal

Higher inflation inevitably leads to higher nominal interest rates, as the Fisher equation indicates. Similarly, lower inflation rates in recent years have reduced nominal interest rates, as Figure 4 illustrates.

EXAMPLES

Suppose that the nominal interest rate is 10 percent per year. If you lend someone $100, that borrower pays you $110 next year. Without inflation, π equals 0, and the Fisher equation gives a real interest rate of 10 percent ($r = 0.10 - 0 = 0.10$). When the borrower repays the loan, you gain 10 percent more dollars and 10 percent more purchasing power than you had before you made the loan. (You can buy 10 percent more goods next year with $110 than you could buy this year with $100.) Your 10 percent gain in purchasing power means that you can buy 11 goods worth $10 each next year instead of 10 goods this year, so the relative price of each good this year is 1.10 goods next year. In other words, 1 plus the real interest rate (expressed as a decimal) is 1.10, so the real interest rate is 0.10, or 10 percent per year.

Now suppose that inflation is 10 percent per year, while the nominal interest rate remains at 10 percent per year. In this case, the Fisher equation gives a real interest rate of zero (because $r = 0.10 - 0.10 = 0$). Prices next year will be 10 percent higher than prices this year, so you will need $110 next year just to buy the *same* amount of goods you could buy for $100 this year. Lending money gives you a 10 percent gain in dollars, but no increase in purchasing power. (This shows the meaning of a zero real interest rate.) The relative price of goods now in terms of goods in the future is 1.

Finally, suppose that the nominal interest rate is 10 percent per year and inflation is 4 percent per year. In this case, the Fisher equation gives a real interest rate of 6 percent per year, because 0.10 minus 0.04 equals 0.06. If you lend $100 for one year at 10 percent interest, you collect $110 at the end of the year. The $110 gives you 6 percent more purchasing power next year than you would have with $100 this year. In other words, the relative price of goods this year in terms of goods next year is 1.06. Since this relative price is 1 plus the real interest rate, the real interest rate is 6 percent per year.

These three examples illustrate an important point: The real interest rate states the interest rate in terms of the purchasing power that a borrower pays and a lender receives on a loan.

Relative Prices over Time

Higher real interest rates mean that goods now (this year) are relatively more expensive in terms of future goods because people sacrifice more future goods for each good they buy now. This sacrifice occurs because higher real interest rates give people higher returns, measured in purchasing power, on their savings. A person who spends today, rather than saving for the future, sacrifices more future consumption when the real interest rate is high than when it is low. Lower real interest rates make goods today relatively cheaper in terms of future goods; people sacrifice fewer future goods for each good they buy now. This is the same as saying that future goods are relatively more expensive measured in terms of current goods. The real interest rate is the *relative price* that plays the key role in the economy's "now or later" decisions, and connects loan-market equilibrium with equilibrium in the market for goods and services.

EXAMPLE

Suppose that a can of soda pop costs $0.50 this year and everyone expects it to cost $0.55 next year (a 10 percent increase). Bob loans Tom $10.00 for one year at a 15 percent nominal interest rate; Tom will repay $11.50 next year. If Bob had spent $10.00 on soda pop, he could have bought 20 cans, so his opportunity cost of $10.00 is 20 cans of soda pop this year. His benefit from lending $10.00 equals the amount of soda pop that he can buy with the $11.50 that he collects from Tom next year. If soda pop really does cost $0.55 next year, he will be able to buy 21 cans, this amount is 5 percent more than the 20 cans he sacrificed this year.[3] The real rate of interest on the loan, measured in soda pop, is 5 percent per year. The relative price of soda pop this year in terms of soda pop next year is 1.05.

If the nominal interest rate were 20 percent per year instead of 15 percent, then Tom would repay Bob $12.00 next year. In this case, Bob would have enough money to buy 22 cans of soda pop next year, so the relative price of soda pop this year in terms of soda pop next year would be 1.10. A rise in the nominal interest rate, combined with the same rate of inflation of soda-pop prices, raises the real interest rate and the relative price of soda pop this year in terms of soda pop next year.

Uncertainty and Expected Inflation

In real life, future inflation is uncertain. No one knows what the rate of inflation will be over the next year. The Fisher equation applies with the term π representing the *expected* rate of inflation—the rate of inflation that people, on average, believe will occur.

Uncertainty about inflation also creates uncertainty about the real interest rate. For example, if the nominal interest rate is 10 percent and people don't know whether inflation will be 3 percent, 4 percent, or 5 percent over the next year, then they don't know whether the real interest rate will turn out to be 7 percent, 6 percent, or 5 percent. Economists distinguish the *expected* real interest rate from the *actual* real interest rate. If the nominal interest rate is 10 percent per year and people *expect* inflation of 4 percent, then the *expected* real interest rate is 6 percent per year. If inflation *turns out* to be 3 percent over the year of the loan, then the *actual* real interest rate is 7 percent.

> The *expected* real interest rate equals the nominal interest rate minus the *expected* rate of inflation. The *actual* real interest rate equals the nominal interest rate minus the *actual* rate of inflation during the period of the loan.

When this chapter refers to the *real interest rate,* it means the expected real interest rate.

Why the *Real* Interest Rate Matters

It is important to understand why the real interest rate, not the nominal interest rate, affects investment. Suppose that the nominal interest rate and expected inflation rise equally. The Fisher equation, $R = r + \pi$, indicates that these increases do not affect the real interest rate. These equal changes in the nominal interest rate and inflation do not affect a firm's investment decisions because two terms in the discounted present value formula cancel each other. First, the increase in expected inflation raises the firm's expected future income from investments. Second, the increase in the nominal interest rate reduces the discounted present value of each future dollar that the firm earns. When the nominal interest and expected inflation change equally, leaving the real interest rate constant, these two terms exactly offset each other in the discounted present value formula. As a result, only changes in the *real* interest rate affect investment.

---

[3]He is $0.05 short of the price of 21 cans. This reflects the fact that the Fisher equation is an approximation when interest is not continuously compounded. See footnote 2.

> ### EXAMPLE
>
> Sammy's Sports Store could spend $15,000 for a new machine that would produce 6,000 baseball caps each year for the next 3 years. More precisely, the machine would produce 6,000 caps 1 year from now, another 6,000 caps 2 years from now, and another 6,000 caps 3 years from now. After that, the machine would be worthless. The store can sell the caps for $1.00 each. Suppose there is *no* expected inflation, so the nominal and real interest rates are equal. Then the machine would provide expected income of $6,000 after 1 year, another $6,000 two years from now, and another $6,000 three years from now.
>
> Is it profitable to invest in the machine? You can verify that investing in the machine is profitable if the interest rate (real and nominal, since they are equal) is less than 9.7 percent per year. The discounted present value of the three future receipts of $6,000,
>
> $$\frac{\$6{,}000}{1+R} + \frac{\$6{,}000}{(1+R)^2} + \frac{\$6{,}000}{(1+R)^3}$$
>
> exceeds the $15,000 cost of the machine if R is less than 0.097.[4] For example, if the (real and nominal) interest rate is 3 percent per year, then the discounted present value of these three receipts is $16,972.
>
> Now suppose that expected inflation rises from zero to 5 percent per year, while the real interest rate remains at 3 percent per year. The Fisher equation shows that the nominal interest rate rises to about 8 percent per year. In fact, the Fisher equation is an approximation (as footnote 2 explained), and the nominal interest rate actually rises to 8.15 percent per year. With expected inflation of 5 percent per year, the expected price of baseball caps rises at 5 percent per year from its current level of $1.00 to $1.05 next year, $1.103 two years from now (another 5 percent increase), and $1.158 three years from now. Therefore, the discounted present value of the store's extra revenue from buying the machine is:
>
> $$\frac{(6{,}000)(\$1.\,05)}{1.0815} + \frac{(6{,}000)(\$1.103)}{1.0815^2} + \frac{(6{,}000)(\$1.158)}{1.0815^3} = \$16{,}972$$
>
> Notice that the discounted present value of the benefits from the investment does not change if inflation and the nominal interest rate rise together, with the real interest rate unchanged. Only changes in the *real* interest rate affect the profitability of investment.

> ## Review Questions
>
> 11. What is the real interest rate? Explain it in words. What relative price equals 1 plus the real interest rate?
>
> 12. What is the relationship between the real interest rate, the nominal interest rate, and the expected rate of inflation?
>
> 13. What is the difference between the expected real interest rate and the actual real interest rate?

---

[4]On the other hand, if the interest rate exceeds 9.7 percent per year, then the discounted present value of the three future receipts from the investment is smaller than the cost of investment, and it is not profitable.

Thinking Exercises

14. Concert tickets cost $20 now, but the price will rise to $24 next year. The nominal interest rate is 10 percent per year. What is the relative price of concert tickets this year in terms of concert tickets next year?

15. When the real interest rate rises, do current goods become cheaper or more expensive compared to goods in the future? Explain.

SUMMARY OF THE BASIC MODEL

We now have a basic model with several parts, summarized in Figure 5. The economy has a money supply, chosen by the government, and a capital stock that has resulted from *past* investments. It also has some technology, described by its production function, which shows how its real GDP depends on its inputs of labor and capital. It has firms that demand labor. Finally, it has people who supply labor services.

The demand for and supply of labor determine equilibrium employment, as in Figure 5a. With this level of employment and with the capital that the economy has created in the past, the production function determines real GDP, as in Figure 5b. The equation

---

Figure 5 | The Basic Model of the Economy

(a) Labor Market Equilibrium Determines Employment

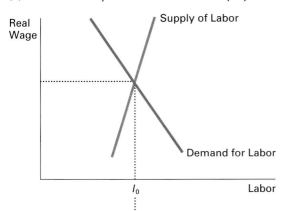

(c) The Price Level
- Government chooses money supply, M_0
- Velocity is assumed fixed at V_0
- Price Level $= P_0 = \dfrac{M_0 V_0}{y_0}$

(d) Savings and Investment
- People decide how much of real GDP, y_0, to consume, and how much to save. The interest rate affects their decisions, resulting in the supply of loans.
- Firms decide how much to invest. The interest rate affects their decisions, resulting in the demand for loans.

(b) Production Function Determines Real GDP

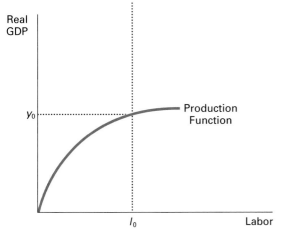

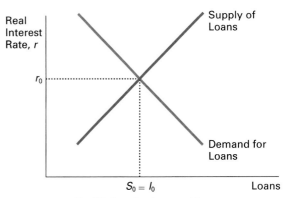

Equilibrium Savings and Investment

Equilibrium Consumption $= y_0 - S_0$
Nominal Interest Rate, $R_0 = r_0 +$ Expected Inflation

of exchange determines the price level: $P = MV/y$, where y represents real GDP, M represents the money supply (the number of dollars printed by the government), and V represents the velocity of money (which we treat as a constant for now). Changes over time in M, V, and y lead to changes in the price level, creating inflation. The supply of loans and demand for loans determine the equilibrium real interest rate, savings, and investment, as in Figure 5d. Consumption equals after-tax income minus saving. The nominal interest rate equals the real interest rate plus expected inflation. Finally, next year's capital stock rises as a result of this year's investment.

APPLYING THE MODEL

We now apply this basic macroeconomic model to answer "what-if" questions about the effects of changes in underlying economic conditions, such as the economy's technology and its government's policies. We use the model to examine the effect of these changes on variables such as consumption, savings, investment, and the real interest rate.

The following results will emerge from our analysis:

▶ An increase in consumer patience, that is, an increase in people's desire to save for the future, reduces the equilibrium real interest rate and raises equilibrium savings and investment. The additional investment raises the economy's future capital stock, raising future GDP and consumption.

▶ Technical progress raises the production that the economy can obtain from its labor and capital inputs. It thereby raises investment and the real interest rate. In the long run, it raises consumption and real GDP.

▶ The effects of a tax cut on the economy depend on two main factors:

1. How the tax cut affects incentives to work, incentives to save money rather than spend it, and incentives for firms to invest

2. Whether people choose to spend or save the money from the tax cut

The next sections explain these results. We analyze the effects of each change in conditions separately, one at a time. For example, the discussion of the effects of a change in consumer tastes assumes that technology and taxes remain unchanged. In real life, of course, many changes occur at the same time. However, logical thinking benefits by studying the effects of each change separately.

Effects of an Increase in Consumer Patience

Suppose that people become more concerned about the future and decide to reduce spending on current consumption and save more for the future. This kind of change is sometimes called an *increase in consumer patience*, or a *fall in consumer confidence*. This change raises the supply of loans, as in Figure 6, lowering the real interest rate and raising the equilibrium quantity of loans. It increases equilibrium savings from S_1 to S_2, along with the equilibrium quantity of loans. For now, we ignore the government budget deficit since deficits are currently close to zero in the U.S. economy. Equilibrium investment rises from I_1 to I_2. Equilibrium investment and savings rise by the same amount because savings *equals* investment plus the (zero) government budget deficit. Firms invest more than before because the real interest rate falls, making more investment projects profitable. Equilibrium consumption falls because consumption equals GDP minus investment minus government purchases, and investment rises while GDP

Figure 6 | Increase in Consumer Patience

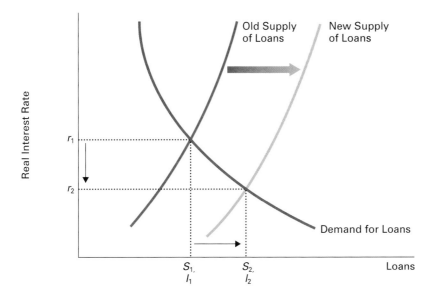

An increase in consumer patience, or desire to save, raises the supply of loans. This reduces the equilibrium real interest rate from r_1 to r_2, raises equilibrium savings from S_1 to S_2, and raises equilibrium investment from I_1 to I_2.

and government purchases remain unchanged. As a result, equilibrium consumption falls by the same amount that equilibrium investment rises.

The increase in investment eventually raises the economy's capital stock, so it eventually raises real GDP. No one has to work harder or more hours for this increase in real GDP; the economy produces more than before because each person works with more capital (such as machinery or equipment). This future increase in real GDP raises future consumption. In this way, the economy responds to the desires of consumers. When people want to reduce current consumption and raise *future* consumption, the economy increases investment, making fewer goods available for current consumption and more goods available for future consumption. When people want more *current* consumption and less future consumption, the economy provides this result through a decrease in investment. Adam Smith's metaphor of the "invisible hand" (see Chapter 1) applies here: As business firms make investment decisions to maximize their own profits, they are led "as if by an invisible hand" to provide consumers with the "now or later" choices that they *want*.

IN THE NEWS

Worries about future spur rise in savings

By Jim Henderson
USA TODAY

The USA's personal saving rate has jumped sharply in the past 2 years, and a survey on personal finances released Wednesday sheds light on why.

We're getting nervous.

Source: USA Today

People spend less and save more if they expect lower incomes in the future. Although this news item refers to the U.S. economic situation a decade ago, the situation is likely to repeat itself when signs of the next recession occur.

IN THE NEWS

Consumer confidence hits 29-year high

A strong job market helped propel Americans' confidence in the economy to a 29-year high in June, despite worries about financial woes in Asia.

Consumer confidence is important because consumer spending accounts for two-thirds of economic activity.

Source: USA Today

Increases in confidence about the future lead consumers to raise their spending, and reduce their saving.

Effects of Technical Progress

Suppose now that technical progress permanently increases productivity, shifting the production function, as in Figure 7. This raises the quantity of output that the economy can produce with each possible level of labor and capital inputs. To simplify this analysis (without affecting its main results), we consider the case in which the quantity of labor supplied is *perfectly inelastic* (indicated by a vertical supply curve), as in Figure 8.

The increase in productivity has two main effects. First, it raises total production of goods and services, real GDP, as in Figure 9. Second, it raises the demand for loans,

Figure 7 | Technical Progress

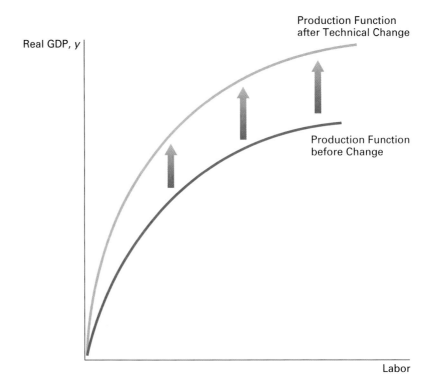

Figure 8 | Perfectly Inelastic Labor Supply

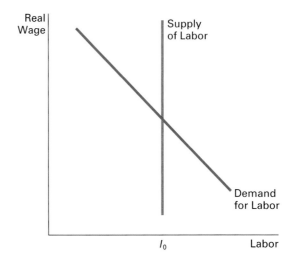

Figure 9 | Technical Progress Raises Real GDP

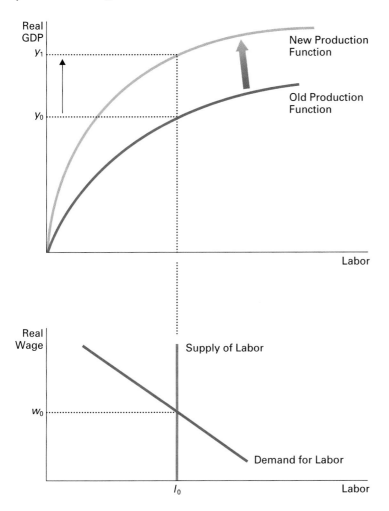

because it raises the benefits of new investments by boosting the productivity of new capital goods. For example, technical progress might allow companies to produce a new generation of computers that are faster than older computers or new farm equipment that increases output per acre. The increase in demand for loans raises the equilibrium real interest rate, and it raises equilibrium saving and investment, as in Figure 10.

The increase in equilibrium investment begins to raise the economy's capital stock. As the capital stock rises, the economy's real GDP increases, as in Figure 11. This increase in GDP allows consumption to increase along with production.

Notice that the economy's precise response to technical progress depends on the desires of consumers. The economy faces a trade-off: When its real GDP rises by $10 billion per year, consumption could rise by $10 billion per year *or* investment could rise by $10 billion per year, raising the future capital stock and creating an even larger increase in future real GDP than would otherwise occur. The economy's response to this trade-off depends on its available *opportunities* for investment and the *preferences* of consumers. These forces operate through the supply and demand for loans. Would people rather consume $10 billion more each year, starting *now,* or would they rather postpone the increase in consumption in return for a larger future increase (perhaps $12 billion more each year, starting two years from now)? The economy's investment opportunities determine the combinations of current and future consumption from which consumers can choose. Consumers decide which of these combinations of current and future consumption they like best. Consumer choices affect their savings, so they affect the supply of loans and the economy's equilibrium level of investment.

Figure 10 | Technical Progress Raises Demand for Loans

Technical progress makes investments more profitable than before, raising the demand for loans and raising equilibrium savings, investment, and the real interest rate.

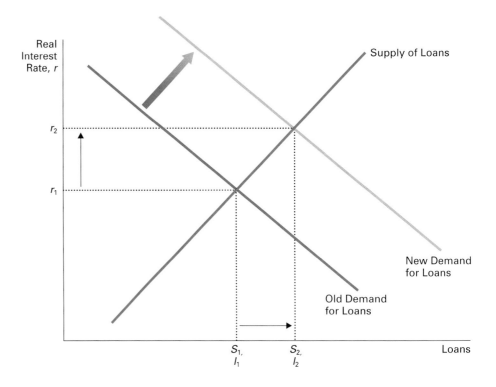

Figure 11 | Investment Raises the Capital Stock, which Raises Production

Technical progress raises investment. The increase in investment raises the economy's capital stock. The increase in capital raises production, increasing real GDP from y_1 to y_2.

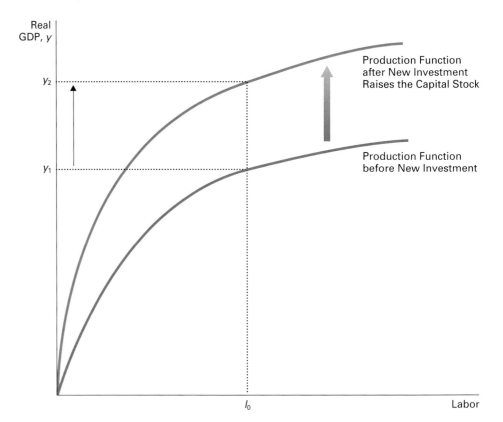

Effects of a Tax Cut

Suppose that the government cuts taxes without changing its spending. The effects of a tax cut depend on two main factors: (1) how the tax cut affects incentives to work, incentives to save money rather than spend it, and incentives for firms to invest; and (2) whether people choose to spend or save the money from the tax cut.

Before-Tax Wages and After-Tax Wages

A person who earns $20,000 per year before taxes might pay $6,000 in income taxes (to federal, state, and local governments) and social security taxes. This person has a 30 percent *tax rate*.

> The **tax rate** on income is the tax per dollar, as a percentage.

The tax drives a wedge between the *before-tax* wage of $20,000 and the *after-tax* wage of $14,000. Because employers pay the before-tax wage, that is the price they care about:

The demand for labor depends on the before-tax wage.

Workers, however, care about the after-tax wage they receive:

The supply of labor depends on the after-tax wage.

Figure 12 shows equilibrium in the labor market with a tax on wages. Employers pay the equilibrium wage *before* taxes of $15 per hour. Workers collect the equilibrium wage *after* taxes of $10 per hour. The government collects $5 in taxes per worker-hour, or a 33 percent tax rate (based on before-tax income). The equilibrium level of employment is 400 billion worker-hours, so the government collects $2,000 billion in revenue.

Figure 12 | The Labor Market With an Income Tax

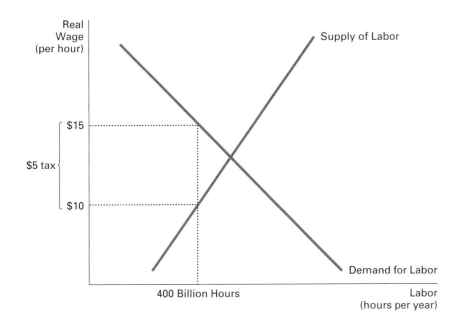

With an income tax, firms pay workers $15 per hour, and the quantity of labor demanded is 400 billion hours. Workers collect an after-tax wage of $10 per hour, and the quantity of labor supplied is 400 billion hours. The graph shows an equilibrium, because the quantity of hours demanded equals the quantity supplied.

Marginal and Average Tax Rates

Suppose you must pay taxes at a 20 percent rate on the first $20,000 that you earn each year, and a 30 percent tax rate applies to each dollar you earn above that amount. If you earn $20,000, you pay 20 percent, or $4,000, in taxes. If you earn $30,000, you pay $4,000 plus 30 percent of the *extra* $10,000, or $3,000, for a total tax payment of $7,000. Your *average* tax rate equals your taxes divided by your income: If you earn $30,000, your average tax rate is $7,000/$30,000 or about 23 percent. Your *marginal* tax rate equals the *extra* taxes you must pay if your earnings rise a little. If you earned $30,100 instead of $30,000, your taxes would rise from $7,000 to $7,030, so your marginal tax rate is 30 percent. In this example, the marginal tax rate exceeds the average tax rate, as it usually does in real life.

This distinction is important because some changes in taxes affect mainly average tax rates, and others affect mainly marginal tax rates. For example, an increase in the personal deduction on U.S. income taxes reduces the average tax rate without affecting the marginal tax rate (for most people). A drop in the average tax rate leaves people with more after-tax income than before, and they may choose to work less, reducing the supply of labor and lowering equilibrium employment and GDP. In contrast, a cut in the *marginal* tax rate, with little change in the average tax rate, means that people keep more of the

Incentive Effects of a Cut in Tax Rates

Figure 13 shows the effects of a tax cut. With a tax rate of 25 percent instead of 33 percent, the before-tax wage becomes $14 per hour, the after-tax wage becomes $10.50 per hour, and equilibrium employment rises from 400 billion to 440 billion hours. The government collects $3.50 per worker-hour (25 percent of the new $14 before-tax wage). Although the government collects less than before in taxes per worker-hour, it collects the tax on more worker-hours (440 billion instead of 400 billion). In this example, the tax cut reduces government revenue from $2,000 billion to $1,540 billion (equal to $3.50 per worker-hour times 440 billion worker hours).

The tax cut raises the equilibrium level of employment because the lower tax rate raises the gains from potential trades between employers and employees. Recall the discussion in Chapter 3 about why a tax reduces incentives to trade. A tax reduces the quantity bought and sold, because the gains from some trades are smaller than the per-unit tax that the parties would have to pay. People stop making those trades to avoid the tax. People make a trade only if it creates a total gain (to buyer and seller) that exceeds the tax. A cut in the tax rate reduces the *disincentive* to trade, raising the equilibrium quantity, as in Figure 13.

By raising equilibrium employment, as in Figure 13, a cut in the income tax rate raises employment and real GDP. Similar logic applies to other taxes. For example, a cut in the tax rate on income from savings raises the equilibrium quantities of saving an investment. Similarly, a cut in taxes that business firms must pay on income earned from their investments in new machinery raises the equilibrium saving and investment.

Figure 13 | Effects of an Income Tax Cut

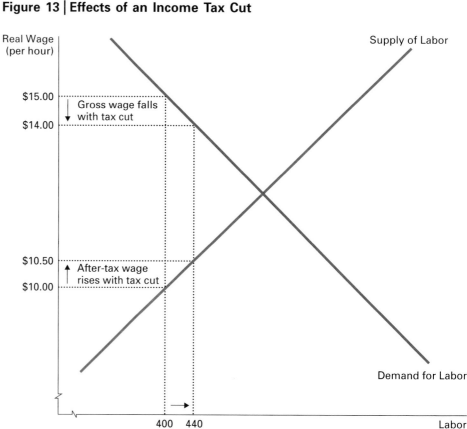

The gross wage falls from $15.00 to $14.00 with a tax cut; the after-tax wage rises from $10.00 to $10.50.

You might expect total tax payments to fall after a tax cut, as in Figure 13. In fact, a cut in a tax rate *can* (logically) raise tax revenue, although evidence indicates that *most* real-life tax cuts reduce tax revenue. Logically, a cut in a tax rate can increase total tax revenue collected by the government if demand and supply curves are sufficiently elastic. Figure 14 shows an example. The following discussion applies to the *usual* case in which a cut in the tax rate lowers government revenue from taxes, as in Figure 13.

Tax Revenue and Government Borrowing

A tax cut with no cut in government spending raises the government budget deficit if it reduces government revenue. As a result, the government must borrow more to finance the increased deficit. This increase in government borrowing raises the demand for loans, as in Figure 15. The demand for loans shifts *to the right* by the amount of the cut in tax revenue, as in the figure. If a cut in the tax rate reduces government tax revenue by $100 billion, then the government creates a $100 billion budget deficit, and the demand for loans shifts rightward by $100 billion.

Next, we must ask, "What do people do with the money they gain from the tax cut?" There are two extreme cases (as well as many in-between possibilities). First, suppose that people *spend* all the money from the tax cut on consumption. Then the supply of loans does not change. Figure 15 shows the results. Ignoring the incentive effects on savings already discussed the equilibrium moves from Point A to Point B, with the real interest rate rising from 10 percent to 12 percent. Before the tax cut, the government budget deficit was zero, so equilibrium savings and investment were equal at $1,000 billion. After the tax cut, the increased interest rate raises equilibrium savings to $1,060 billion. As a result, total loans rise to $1,060 billion. However, $100 billion of these loans go to the government, leaving only $960 billion for business

extra income they earn if they work more than before. As a result, a cut in the marginal tax rate tends to *raise* equilibrium employment as in Figure 13 and raise equilibrium real GDP. Clearly, the distinction between average and marginal tax rates is important.

Figure 14 | A Cut in the Tax Rate Can Raise Tax Revenue

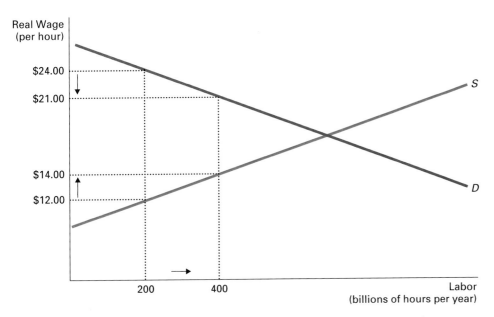

With a 50 percent income tax rate, the before-tax wage is $24 and the after-tax wage is $12. The equilibrium quantity of labor is 200 billion hours per year. The government collects a tax of $12 per hour, so it collects $2,400 billion in tax revenue. With a smaller 33 percent tax rate, the before-tax wage is $21, the after-tax wage is $14, and the equilibrium quantity of labor is 400 billion hours per year. The government collects $7 per hour in taxes, so it collects $2,800 in tax revenue. In this special case, the government's tax revenue rises when it cuts the tax rate.

Why Rational People Might Save all the Tax-Cut Money

Some (though not most) economists believe that evidence suggests people tend to *save* money from tax cuts, as in Figure 16, rather than *spend* it, as in Figure 15. A logical argument explains why people might choose to save the money from a tax cut. When the government reduces taxes without reducing spending, it collects the same amount of money from taxpayers as before! However, it *calls* some of this money it collects *loans* rather than *taxes*. People give the government less money than before in the form of taxes, but more money in the form of loans. Either way, the government collects the money required to pay for its (unchanged) spending.

The main difference between paying taxes and lending money to the government, is that the government promises to repay loans. However, where will the government get the money to repay these loans? Unless the government cuts spending some time in the future, it is likely to get that money by *raising taxes* in the future. Perhaps you loan the government some money, and it promises to repay you $100 in the future. However, you will not gain from the loan repayment if the government repays that $100 by raising your taxes by $100! In that case, lending money to the government is the same as paying taxes, because the government collects the same discounted present value of

Figure 15 | Effects of a Tax Cut and Rising Budget Deficit when People Spend the Money They Gain from the Cut

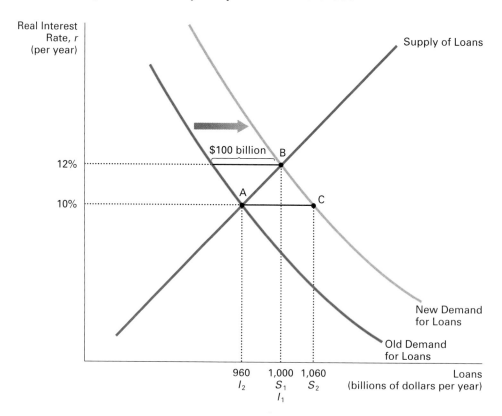

firms to borrow for investment. As a result, equilibrium investment falls by $40 billion to $960 billion.

This fall in investment caused by an increase in government borrowing is called *crowding out* investment. Government borrowing crowds out borrowing for private investment by business firms. Although the tax cut raises savings, savers lend more to the government to finance the budget deficit, leaving less for business firms to borrow to finance private investments.

> **Crowding out** of private investment means that government borrowing raises the real interest rate, reducing the equilibrium amount of investment.

The increase in government borrowing in Figure 15 is the distance from Point A to Point C, that is, the $100 billion amount by which the demand curve shifts to the right. This amount exceeds the amount of the increase in the equilibrium quantity of loans, which rises by $60 billion, so part of the increase in government borrowing comes from an increase in savings, and part comes from a decrease in investment. Because government borrowing rises by $100 billion but total savings rises by only $60 billion, the government borrows $40 billion that firms would otherwise have borrowed to finance investment. In this way, government borrowing crowds out $40 billion in investment. Figure 16 shows the opposite extreme case, in which people *save* all the money they gain from the $100 billion tax cut. In this case, the supply of loans increases by $100 billion, shifting the curve rightward by exactly the same amount as demand. As a result, the equilibrium real interest rate remains unchanged. Because equilibrium savings rise by the same amount as the increase in government borrowing, investment remains unchanged.

Figure 16 | Effects of a Tax Cut and Rising Budget Deficit when People Save the Money They Gain from the Cut

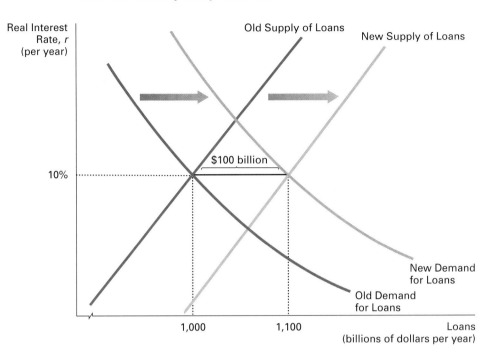

Other Changes in Underlying Conditions

Now that we have used the basic model to examine the effects of changes in the people's desires to save versus spend, advances in technology, and changes in tax rates, you can try to apply the model to other changes in underlying conditions. The next chapter will apply the basic model to help understand real-life experiences of economic growth.

IN THE NEWS

Retailers see public using fall tax cut mostly for Christmas buying, not saving

What's in store?

Administration officials who expect much of the tax reduction to be saved point to the aftermath of the Kennedy-era tax cut. In 1964, 1965, and 1966, personal savings rose by an amount equaling about 75 percent of the tax cut, and

in 1967 the rise in savings equaled 121 percent of the tax cut. This time around, the Treasury Department estimates that at least 50 percent and perhaps 60 percent of the tax cut will be saved. Stephen Entin, a deputy assistant Treasury

secretary, describes this projection as "deliberately conservative."

JCPenney Co. believes it isn't nearly conservative enough. Penney expects taxpayers to save only one-third of the initial tax cut.

Source: The Wall Street Journal

If people spend part of the money from a tax cut, then the tax cut raises the equilibrium real interest rate.

---

your money in either case. Knowing this, you may save the money from a tax cut because you will need those savings to pay the increased future taxes.

For example, suppose that the government cuts taxes by $100 per person, and the interest rate is 10 percent per year. Then the government owes $110 more next year and raises taxes next year by $110 to pay its debt. If people save all the money from the tax cut and earn 10 percent interest on their savings, they will have $110 next year; that is exactly the amount that they need to pay their taxes next year. Alternatively, suppose that the government cuts taxes by $100 per person and the interest rate is 10 percent per year, but that the government *never* repays its debt—instead, it pays $10 per year interest on that debt every year, forever. The government permanently raises taxes by $10 per year to make these interest payments. If people save all the money from the tax cut and put it in bank accounts earning 10 percent interest, they earn enough interest each year to pay the permanently increased taxes. After 1 year, people have $110 each in their bank accounts; they can withdraw $10 each to pay the increased taxes and leave the $100 in the account. Next year, they will have $110 again, and they can again withdraw $10 to pay the taxes and leave $100 in the account. They can repeat this process every year for as long as the government pays interest on this debt. By saving all of the money from the tax cut, people can afford to pay their raised future taxes without reducing their future consumption spending.

While this logical reasoning shows that people may have reasons to save the money from a tax cut, other factors may lead them to spend it. For example, some people may not care about the future tax increase if those bills will be paid by *future generations*. In that case, they may spend the tax cut and let future generations worry about paying the future taxes on the government's debt.

Review Questions

16. Explain how the basic model determines equilibrium employment, real GDP, the real interest rate, consumption, and investment. Also explain how it determines the price level and the nominal interest rate.

17. Suppose that people decide that they are willing to reduce consumption now if they can increase consumption in the future. In what way does the economy respond to their wishes?

18. Explain why government borrowing may *crowd out* investment.

Thinking Exercises

19. Suppose that the government runs a budget deficit and raises taxes to eliminate that deficit. Discuss the likely effects on the real interest rate, savings, investment, consumption, employment, real GDP, and the price level.

20. What are the effects of a tax increase that creates a budget surplus? In what way does your answer depend on how people obtain the money to pay the increased taxes?

Conclusion

Interest Rates and Loan-Market Equilibrium

Savers lend money—they supply loans. Firms borrow money to pay for investments in new capital equipment, tools, buildings, skills, and knowledge—they demand loans. The government also borrows when it runs a budget deficit (when it spends more than its tax revenue), adding to the demand for loans. Equilibrium in the loan market determines the interest rate and equilibrium quantity of loans. The equilibrium quantity of loans equals savings, which equals investment plus the government budget deficit.

An interest rate is the price of a loan, expressed as an annual percentage of the amount borrowed. The discounted present value of a future payment of money is its market value today, which equals the amount of money that you would need to save and lend today to end up with that amount of future money. The discounted present value of X dollars next year is $X/(1 + R)$ dollars now, where R represents the annual interest rate (measured as a decimal, so that an 8 percent interest rate means R equals 0.08).

An investment is profitable if the discounted present value of the benefits from the investment exceeds the expenditure on the investment. A rise in the interest rate reduces the discounted present value of the benefit from an investment. As a result, the demand curve for loans slopes downward to the right: A fall in the interest rate raises the quantity of loans demanded.

Savings and the Supply of Loans

Equilibrium in the loan market is identical to equilibrium in the market for goods and services. Loan-market equilibrium occurs when saving plus lending by foreigners equals investment plus the government budget deficit. This relationship implies that GDP equals the sum of consumption, investment, government purchases, and net exports.

Real and Nominal Interest Rates

The nominal interest rate on a loan is the dollar interest payment expressed as a percentage of the dollar amount borrowed. The nominal interest rate, expressed as a decimal, plus one, is the cost a borrower must pay next year if she borrows $1 to spend this year. Therefore, the nominal interest rate plus 1 is the relative price of $1 this year in terms of dollars next year.

The real interest rate corrects the nominal interest rate for inflation. It measures the interest rate in terms of purchasing power. The real interest rate, expressed as a decimal, plus one, is the relative price of *goods* this year in terms of the same *goods* next year. Higher real interest rates mean that goods this year are relatively more expensive in terms of future goods; lower real interest rates mean the opposite.

The Fisher equation shows the connection between real and nominal interest rates: The nominal interest rate is the real interest rate plus the expected rate of inflation.

Because future inflation is uncertain in real life, economists distinguish between the expected and actual real interest rates. The expected real interest rate is the nominal interest rate minus the expected rate of inflation; the actual real interest rate is the nominal interest rate minus the actual rate of inflation during the period of the loan.

Summary of the Basic Model

The labor market determines equilibrium employment. The economy's production function shows the real GDP that the economy produces with this level of employment and the available capital stock. The equilibrium price level equals the economy's money supply multiplied by the velocity of money and divided by real GDP. The loan market determines equilibrium savings and investment and the equilibrium real interest rate. Consumption equals after-tax income minus saving. The nominal interest rate equals the real interest rate plus expected inflation.

Applying the Model

An increase in consumer patience—an increase in people's desire to save for the future—reduces the equilibrium real interest rate and raises equilibrium savings and investment. The additional investment raises the economy's future capital stock, raising future GDP and consumption. Technical progress raises the production the economy can obtain from labor and capital inputs, so it raises investment and the real interest rate. In the long run, technical progress raises consumption and real GDP. The effects of a tax cut on the economy depend on (a) how the tax cut affects incentives to work, to save money, and to invest; and (b) whether people choose to spend or save the money they gain from the tax cut. An increase in the government budget deficit raises the real interest rate and crowds out private investment, except in the extreme case in which people save all the money from the tax cut.

Key Terms

interest rate
discounted present value
government budget deficit

nominal interest rate
real interest rate

tax rate
crowding out

Questions and Problems

21. Find the discounted present value in the following cases:
    (a) You will receive $540 one year from now and the nominal interest rate is 8 percent per year.
    (b) Your employer promises to pay you a $1,000 bonus 10 years from now, and the the nominal interest rate is 10 percent per year. Approximately what is the discounted present value of your bonus? (You may want to use a calculator.)
    (c) A state lottery promises to pay the winner $1 million, in the form of a $50,000 payment each year for 20 years. Use a calculator or computer to find the discounted present value of the prize if the nominal interest rate is 8 percent per year.
    (d) A perpetuity is a financial asset that pays interest every year, forever. If the nominal interest rate is 10 percent per year, what is the discounted present value of a perpetuity that pays $1,000 every year?

22. If the nominal interest rate is 8 percent per year and the expected rate of inflation is 5 percent per year, what is the real interest rate? If the real interest rate is 2 percent per year and expected inflation is 2 percent per year, what is the nominal interest rate?

23. Suppose that the nominal interest rate rises by 4 percent per year, because the expected rate of inflation rises by 4 percent per year. Explain why this change does not affect investment.

24. Discuss this statement: "The interest rate plays no role in the investment decisions of firms that use their own profits to pay for investments in new equipment."

25. Explain the flaw in the following argument: "A fall in the real interest rate reduces savings. But savings equals investment plus the government budget deficit, so a fall in the real interest rate must also reduce investment." (*Hint:* Recall the difference between changes in demand and changes in the quantity demanded.)

26. Show in a diagram how a tax on interest income affects the economy's savings and investment.

27. Suppose the government runs a budget surplus (it spends less than it collects in tax revenue), and it cuts taxes. Discuss the likely effect of the tax cut on the real interest rate, savings, investment, consumption, employment, real GDP, and the price level.

28. (a) Suppose the government cuts taxes by $100 million without changing its spending, and borrows $100 million to finance its deficit. Also suppose the interest rate is 10 percent per year. How much additional money will the government owe in the future? (b) If the government pays its future debts by raising taxes in the future, how much will future taxes rise? (c) What is the discounted present value of the tax increase that you calculated in part (b)? (d) Explain why this calculation may lead rational people to save all the money that they receive from a tax cut.

29. Comment on this statement: "A tax increase to reduce a government budget deficit is more likely to reduce the real interest rate if people pay the increased taxes by saving less instead of spending less."

30. A *fall in business confidence* occurs when firms reduce investments in new equipment because of increased uncertainty about future demand for their products. Discuss the effects of a fall in business confidence on the real interest rate, savings, investment, and consumption.

31. The baby-boom generation (people born in the 1950s) will retire after two or three more decades. Most retired people spend more than their incomes. The U.S. population now has about 3.4 workers for each retired person; by 2030, it may have only about 2 workers for each retired person.
    (a) Explain how this change will affect total savings in the United States.
    (b) Explain how this change will affect the real interest rate, savings, consumption, and investment.

Inquiries for Further Thought

32. Some economists believe that people in the United States do not save enough for the future.
    (a) What affects the amount of money that people choose to save? How much *should* people save? Who should decide?
    (b) Do people voluntarily save the amount that they should save, or should government policies provide incentives for people to increase saving? What government policies might lead people to increase saving? Do any current government policies encourage or discourage saving?

    (c) Discuss this statement: "Free-market economies do not provide enough savings, investment, and other resources for future generations. The government should adopt policies to raise savings and investment for future generations."

33. The social security system taxes workers' incomes and gives money to retired people.
    (a) How do you think the social security system affects the amount of money that people choose to save? Why?
    (b) How do you think the social security system affects equilibrium investment? Explain.

CHAPTER 27

ECONOMIC GROWTH

In this Chapter...

Main Points to Understand

▶ Long-run economic growth is perhaps the most important topic in economics, with the greatest effects on people's lives.

▶ Economic growth requires savings and investment.

▶ Economic growth has increased rapidly over the last two centuries. Some people speculate that diminishing returns will soon cause growth to slow down or even stop; others speculate that economies can avoid diminishing returns for many more centuries.

▶ Current evidence provides only limited knowledge about which government policies best promote long-run economic growth.

Thinking Skills to Develop

▶ Evaluate a model with evidence, and change the model with evidence as a guide.

▶ Develop speculative questions that raise new issues, and use them to guide logical thought in new directions.

Real GDP per person in the United States has doubled since 1964. Many of the products that you take for granted, such as CD players and VCRs, were not even available then. What does the future hold? Will real GDP double again in the next 30 or 40 years and give you the opportunity to use products unimaginable today?

Long-run economic growth—a continuing rise in real GDP per person over several decades—is one of the most important topics in economics. For most of history, people have lived in conditions of extreme poverty without even the basic goods that we now regard as necessities. Life was brutal, filled with hard work, little food or health care, short life spans, and high infant mortality rates.

Economic growth has lifted billions of people out of these conditions, although many people continue to live in poverty. World real GDP is about $6,000 per person today, roughly 12 times higher than the level in 1800, and 5 times higher than the level in 1900. Real GDP per person in the United States is almost $32,000 today, about 20 times higher than the level during the American Revolution, 12 times higher than the level during the Civil War, 6 times higher than the level in 1900, and twice as high as 34 years ago. The economies of some countries, such as Hong Kong (now a special zone of China), Japan, Singapore, South Korea, and Taiwan, have grown much faster than that of the United States in recent years, while others have grown much more slowly. Not only has the level of per-capita real GDP risen over time, but the rate of economic growth has also increased over most of the last 200 years. Economic growth has been much higher in the last 200 years than over all previous history.

Will the economy continue to grow rapidly in your lifetime and raise your material standard of living, or will economic growth slow down or stop? These issues have profound effects on people's lives. As one economist puts it, "The consequences for human welfare involved in questions [of economic growth] like these are simply staggering: Once one starts to think about them, it is hard to think about anything else."[1]

BASICS OF GROWTH

An economy's real GDP depends on its technology and its available inputs of labor and capital. Real GDP also depends on laws, regulations, taxes, and other factors that affect people's incentives for efficient use of technology and inputs, so that the economy produces at a point *on* its production possibility frontier rather than below it.[2]

Throughout most of history, real GDP and population grew at the same rates, leaving GDP *per person* roughly constant over time. Then, about 200 to 300 years ago, total real GDP began growing much faster than population (despite continuing increases in population), so real GDP per person began growing rapidly.

Figure 1 shows estimates of average real GDP per person in the world over the past million years. Despite some small changes, until 300 years ago, real GDP per person stayed about the same as it had been throughout all of human history—just high enough to keep people alive and reproducing. Then, things changed. Real GDP per person began to rise enormously—for example, about *1 percent per year* in the 19th century. While 1 percent per year may seem small, its cumulative effects are awesome—people's lives began to change dramatically—health improved, death rates declined, common people gained leisure time, and vast arrays of new products and services became available. Figure 2 shows the growth of world real GDP per person by century over the last millennium.

Figure 1 | World Average GDP per Capita

Source: Bradford De Long, "Estimating World GDP, One Million B.C.–Present."

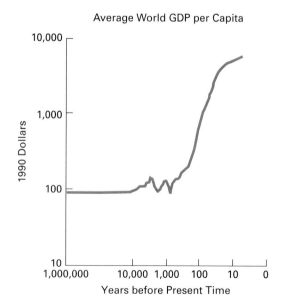

---

[1] Robert E. Lucas, "On the Mechanism of Economic Development," *Journal of Monetary Economics* 22, no. 1 (July 1988), pp. 3–42.

[2] Chapter 3 introduced production possibility frontiers.

Figure 2 | Growth of World Real GDP per Person

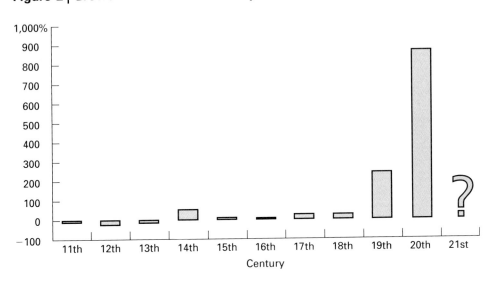

Source: Bradford De Long, "Estimating World GDP, One Million B.C.–Present."

We will define economic growth as an increase in a country's real GDP per person:

> **Economic growth** is a rise in real GDP per person.

We will measure economic growth by the *average annual growth rate* (percentage change) in real GDP per person. For example, the rate of economic growth in the 100-year period from 1900 to 2000 is:

$$\text{Rate of economic growth, 1900 to 2000} = \frac{1}{100} \times \frac{(\text{Real GDP per person in 2000} - \text{Real GDP per person in 1900})}{\text{Real GDP per person in 1900}}$$

Rule of 72

How is the actual change in real GDP per person connected to the rate of economic growth? What does growth of *2 percent per year* mean for your actual standard of living? A simple method called the *rule of 72* helps to answer these questions.

> The **rule of 72** says that if the growth rate of a variable is X percent per year, then the variable doubles after about $72/X$ years.

For example, if GDP grows at 2 percent per year, then it doubles after about 36 years. If it grows at 3 percent per year, then it doubles after about 24 years. World economic growth of 1 percent per year in the 19th century meant that real GDP per person doubled after about 72 years. Never before in history had living standards changed by so much.[3]

Using the rule of 72, you can estimate the effect on your future standard of living of various growth rates. If economic growth in the future is only 1 percent per year, you can expect average income to have doubled 72 years from now—a long time to wait.

---

[3]You can also use the rule of 72 backwards—if some quantity doubles in X years, then its average growth rate is about $72/X$ percent per year. For example, the U.S. consumer price index roughly quadrupled from 1970 to 1994. Because it doubled about twice in that 24-year period, on average it doubled every 12 years, so the price level grew at a rate of about 72/12, or 6 percent per year over that period.

However, if economic growth is 3 percent per year, average income will double in 24 years and quadruple in 48 years. So the difference between 1 percent and 3 percent economic growth—which may seem small—could have a major impact on your future standard of living, and the living standards of your children and grandchildren.

MAIN FACTS ABOUT ECONOMIC GROWTH

World Economic Growth

World per-capita real GDP is about $6,000 today. In 1900, it was only $1,200 to $1,300, and in 1800, it was only about $500 (all in today's dollars). The rate of world economic growth has generally increased over time for the last 300 years, meaning that the average person has been getting richer at a faster rate than in the past. World real GDP per capita grew at about 1 percent per year in the 19th century and 1.7 percent per year in the 20th century. World economic growth averaged 1.1 percent per year from 1900 to 1950, and it has averaged 2.1 percent per year since then. Per-capita world real GDP is now almost 5 times as high as in 1900.

One major exception to this experience involves a slowdown in world economic growth starting in 1973. World economic growth averaged about 1.4 percent per year from 1973 to 1998, higher than in the 19th century, but below that earlier in the 20th century.[4]

Economic Growth in the United States and the United Kingdom

Table 1 shows economic growth in the United States for the last two centuries. The rate of U.S. economic growth has generally increased over time, although it has fallen to an average of 1.6 percent per year for the period from 1973 to 1998.

Gross domestic product per capita in the United States is approaching $32,000 today. At the time of the American Revolution, U.S. real GDP per capita was about $1,450 (in 1998 dollars). Output per person was just slightly higher in the United States than in England and France. By 1860, on the eve of the Civil War, per-capita real U.S. GDP was $2,550 (in 1998 dollars). Table 2 shows levels of real GDP per person in selected years in the United States and the United Kingdom. U.S. output of goods and services per person is now more than 20 times its level at the time of the American Revolution, about 12 times its level at the time of the Civil War, and 2½ times its level in 1950.

Table 1 | Rising Economic Growth in the United States

Time Period	Growth Rate of Per-Capita U.S. Real GDP (percent per year)
1800–1855	1.1%
1855–1900	1.6
1900–1950	1.7
1950–1998	1.9

---

[4]Although economists lack good statistics on economic growth in earlier centuries, we know that the rate of economic growth must have been much lower in those centuries. Here is the basic logic: In 1800, per-capita world real GDP was about $500 (in today's dollars). If economic growth had averaged 1 percent per year in earlier centuries (its rate in the 19th century), then world real GDP per person would have been only $25 in the year 1500, and about $0.16 in 1000 (measured in today's dollars). This is impossible because people need more food than this to survive. Moreover, historical records prove that incomes were higher than this at those times. Therefore, the rate of world economic growth must have been much lower before the 19th century.

Table 2 | Per-Capita Real GDP in 1998 Dollars

	United States	United Kingdom
1776	$ 1,450	$ 1,350
1860	2,550	3,000
1900	5,450	5,300
1950	12,500	8,150
1998	31,500	22,000

You can use the rule of 72 to estimate the annual growth rate of per-capita real GDP in the United States. U.S. real GDP per capita doubled in the 34-year period from 1964 to 1998. Since 72 divided by 35 is about 2, you can estimate that U.S. real GDP per capita grew at about 2 percent per year over that period. If growth continues at that rate, real GDP per capita will be twice as high as in 1998 by the year 2033.

Economic Growth in Japan

In 1860, at the time of the U.S. Civil War, per-capita real GDP in Japan was about $850—about one-third that of the United States. The Japanese economy then grew at about the same rate as the U.S. economy, so Japanese real GDP per capita stayed at about one-third the U.S. level, until World War II. That war cut Japanese per-capita real GDP in half; when the war ended, it was about one-sixth of U.S. per-capita real GDP. After the war, Japan began a period of rapid growth. By 1960, Japanese real GDP per capita was again one-third of the U.S. level. This rapid growth continued, and by 1998, per-capita real GDPs in Japan and the United States were about equal, depending on the method of comparison.[5]

Economic Growth in Other Countries

Economic growth rates differ substantially across countries. Japan's economy has grown much faster than that of the United States in recent years. Table 3 shows the rates of economic growth in several countries. (For comparison, recall that U.S. economic growth in the 20th century has averaged 1.8 percent per year.)

Per-capita real GDP has grown despite the fact that people work *less* than they did in earlier times! The number of worker-hours per person in developed countries has fallen by about one-fourth since the mid-19th century.[6] Real GDP is much higher today, despite the decrease in work per person, because people are more productive today, due to better technology and greater quantities of capital (tools, equipment, and worker skills).

Economic growth is not inevitable, however. Chapter 24 noted that India, China, Bangladesh, Indonesia, and Pakistan experienced negative economic growth from 1900 to 1950; their per-capita GDPs fell. Similarly, Afghanistan, Angola, Chad, Madagascar, Mozambique, and Zambia have experienced negative economic growth since 1960. Many other countries have experienced negative economic growth over 5-year or 10-year periods.

[5]One way to compare amounts in Japanese yen with those in U.S. dollars is to use the foreign exchange rate between yen and dollars. Another way adjusts for differences in the prices of goods in Japan and the United States.

[6]An average worker in the United States, England, France, Germany, and Japan worked about 2,600 hours per year in 1913, but only 1,700 hours by the 1980s. A higher fraction of the population worked, however, so the average number of hours worked per person (not per worker) stayed about the same from 1913 to 1950, rose from 1950 to 1973, and has fallen since 1973, except in the United States and Japan.

Table 3 | Annual Rates of Economic Growth in Various Countries

Country	Growth Rate, 1900–1998	Country	Growth Rate, 1950–1998
Japan	3.2%	Taiwan	6.1%
Finland, Norway	2.6	Japan	6.0
Canada	2.3	South Korea	5.7
Switzerland	2.0	Thailand	3.7
Belgium, Mexico	1.6	Germany	3.6
Australia	1.5	Mexico	2.3
United Kingdom	1.4	India	1.7
Argentina	1.1	Chile	1.0
Bangladesh	0.1	Bangladesh	0.3

Source: Maddison, *The World Economy in the 20th Century* (Paris: OECD, 1989). Figures updated by author.

In contrast, the so-called *four tigers of Asia* (Hong Kong, Singapore, South Korea, and Taiwan) have posted rapid economic growth. Between 1965 and 1998, annual economic growth averaged 7.8 percent in Hong Kong, 7.5 percent in Singapore, and 9.5 percent in South Korea. (Despite the economic recessions that began in many Asian countries in 1998, average real GDP per person in these countries remains far higher than in previous decades.)

Countries with low per-capita incomes are sometimes called *third-world countries* or *LDCs* (for less developed countries). Many high-income countries are members of the OECD, or Organization for Economic Cooperation and Development. The richest of these nations account for 20 percent of world population and about 60 percent of world GDP. The second-richest 20 percent of the world population produce about 20 percent of world GDP. LDCs account for 60 percent of world population and only 20 percent of world GDP. An average person in an OECD country has an income about nine times higher than an average person in an LDC. The low-income countries had faster economic growth (about 3.1 percent per year) from 1965 to 1998 than the OECD countries, which grew at about 2.4 percent per year in that period.

LOGIC OF ECONOMIC GROWTH: A BASIC MODEL

Discussions of international differences in growth rates raise questions that require a *model* of economic growth. Why do some countries grow faster than others? This section begins with a simple model of growth. It then discusses the problems with that model and adds some realistic features.

Economist Robert E. Lucas explains why economists need models of economic growth:

> At the close of World War II, South Korea was less than twice as well off as India. . . . By 1980 Korea's income was four times higher than India's. If present trends continue, by the year 2000 Korea's per-capita income will be over 10 times India's . . . comparable to those in the U.S. and Western Europe today.
>
> With such a range of experience, why do we need theoretical models? Why not simply use success stories—like Korea—as models? Why can't India send a fact-finding delegation to Korea, find out how they do it, and then go home and get Indians to do the same?

This sounds easy enough, but it is not really operational. . . . An economy is just too complex an entity—there are just too many things going on at once—for getting all the facts to be either possible or useful.

Faced with so much data, an observer who is unequipped with a theory sees what he wants to see, or what his hosts want to show him. One needs some principles for deciding which facts are central and which are peripheral. This is exactly the purpose of an economic theory: to isolate some very limited aspects of a situation and focus on them to the exclusion of all others. . . . We need to make some hard choices about what to emphasize and what to leave out before we can think in an organized way at all.[7]

Per-Person Production Function

The basic model from the previous chapter implies that the *level* of real GDP depends on technology and available inputs of labor and capital. The economy's input of labor results from equilibrium in the labor market. Its input of capital results from its previous investments—the amount of equipment and tools it has created in the past.

We can write the economy's production mathematically:

$$\text{Real GDP} = A\ \mathrm{F}(l, k)$$

where l is the economy's labor input (measured as the total number of workers, or total worker hours per year) and k is its capital input. The function F shows how the economy combines inputs of labor and capital to produce real GDP. The variable A measures the economy's technology. Increases in A reflect improvements in technology. An increase in A raises real GDP, even if the amounts of labor and capital do not change.

Now add an assumption to the basic model: The economy's production function has *constant returns to scale*. This statement means that doubling all inputs doubles real GDP. Similarly, increasing all inputs by 20 percent boosts real GDP by 20 percent. (Evidence about real-life production functions indicates that this is a realistic assumption.) This assumption implies that we can write the economy's production function in *per-person* terms:

$$\text{Real GDP per person} = \frac{y}{l} = A\ \mathrm{f}\!\left(\frac{k}{l}\right)$$

In other words, real GDP *per person* depends on technology and capital per person, $\frac{k}{l}$.

Figure 3 shows this production function—it shows how real GDP per person depends on capital per person. When capital per person is low, at $\frac{k_1}{l}$, real GDP per person is low, at $\frac{y_1}{l}$. When capital per person is higher, at $\frac{k_2}{l}$, real GDP per person is higher at $\frac{y_2}{l}$.

Figure 4 shows how an increase in technology—an increase in A—changes real GDP per person. Even with the same amount of capital per person, an increase in A raises real GDP per person. In fact, they increase in proportion: If capital per person remains constant, a 10 percent rise in A raises real GDP per person by 10 percent.

An increase in technology shifts the production function. In contrast, an increase in capital per person moves the economy *along* the production function as in Figure 5. That figure shows that an increase in capital per person, $\frac{k}{l}$, raises real GDP per person. However, diminishing returns imply that increases in capital per person create proportionally smaller increases in real GDP per person, as the economy moves from Point A to Point

Advice

Here is one way to understand constant returns to scale and the per-person production function. Remember the Robinson Crusoe economy from an earlier chapter? Crusoe's production function was obviously a *per-person* production function, because he was the only person in the economy. Think about an economy with lots of people like Crusoe, each with the same *per-person* production function. That economy's production function has constant returns to scale—if you double the number of people like Crusoe, total production doubles.

---

[7]Robert E. Lucas, 1991 Fischer-Schultz lecture, European meetings of the Econometrics Society, September 1991.

Figure 3 | GDP per Person Depends on Capital per Person

When each person has k_1 capital to work with—so that capital per person is $\frac{k_1}{l}$, real GDP per person is $\frac{y_1}{l}$. At a higher capital per person, $\frac{k_2}{l}$, real GDP per person is higher, at $\frac{y_2}{l}$. The production function is steep at Point A, so small increases in capital per person have big effects on real GDP per person. The production function is relatively flat at Point B.

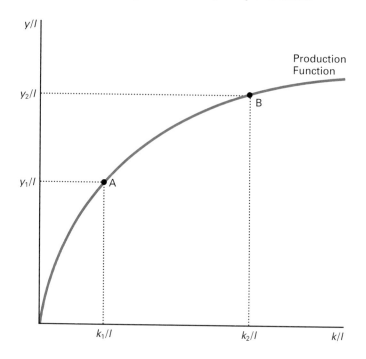

Figure 4 | Increase in Technology Raises Real GDP per Person

An increase in technology shifts the production function. It raises real GDP per person from $\frac{y_2}{l}$ to $\frac{y_3}{l}$, even if capital per person remains at $\frac{k_2}{l}$.

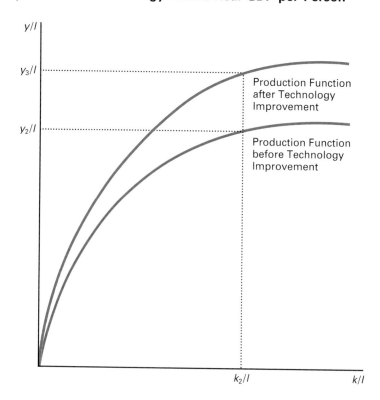

Figure 5 | Increase in Capital per Person Raises Real GDP per Person

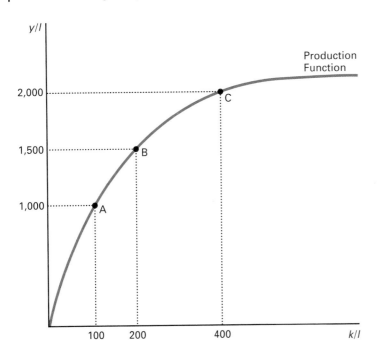

When capital per person is 100, real GDP per person is 1,000. When capital per person rises, real GDP per person rises. Because of diminishing returns, increases in capital per person raise real GDP per person in smaller proportions. In this example, when capital per person doubles from 100 to 200, real GDP per person rises by 50 percent, from 1,000 to 1,500. When capital per person expands to 400, real GDP per person rises to 2,000.

B to Point C. Doubling capital per person from 100 to 200 raises real GDP per person by only 50 percent. Doubling capital per person again, from 200 to 400, boosts real GDP by an even smaller proportion.

Economic Growth without Technical Change

Think about the logical question: Can an economy grow without technical progress? The answer is *yes,* because capital per person can grow, raising real GDP per person as in Figure 5. The economy can increase its capital by investing. The loan-market equilibrium discussed in the previous chapter shows the equilibrium amount of savings and investment. Each year, investment adds to the economy's capital, raising real GDP, as in Figure 5. With sufficiently high equilibrium investment, capital per person and real GDP per person rise over time. The economy grows.

The rate of economic growth depends on the equilibrium amount of investment. Raising investment accelerates growth in capital per person and real GDP per person. Increases in capital per person, however, are not sufficient to create *permanent* economic growth. As capital per person rises, the benefit of additional investment falls due to *diminishing returns*, discussed in Chapter 25. Because of diminishing returns, the benefit of additional investment falls over time as the capital–labor ratio rises. As capital per person rises, the demand for loans falls, as in Figure 6, from D_1 to D_2 to D_3, reducing equilibrium investment from I_1 to I_2 to I_3. Over time, investment falls and *economic growth slows*.

Eventually, capital per person stops increasing, so real GDP per person also stops increasing. Economic growth *stops*. At this point, economists say the economy reaches a *steady state*.

> A **steady state** is a long-run equilibrium in which capital per person remains constant.

Figure 6 | Economic Growth toward a Steady State

When the economy has low capital per person, investment demand is D_1, so equilibrium investment is I_1 and the equilibrium real interest rate is r_1. Investment adds to the economy's capital stock, but, because capital provides diminishing returns, investment demand falls as the economy's capital stock rises. As the economy grows and adds to its capital per person, equilibrium investment and the real interest rate fall. Eventually, the economy reaches a steady state. Steady state investment, I_{SS}, is just enough to replace capital that wears out, so the economy's capital stock stops rising. The steady state real interest rate is r_{SS}. (Note: This figure assumes that all loans fund investments, so the demand for loans is investment demand.)

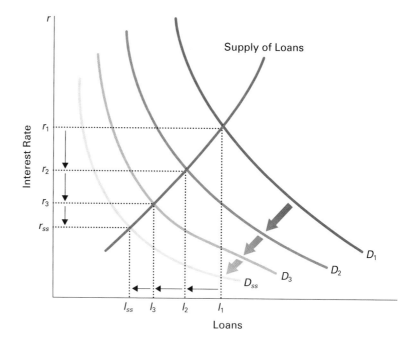

In the steady state, investment of I_{SS} in Figure 6 is just high enough to replace the capital that depreciates (wears out) each year and to keep up with rising population, so that capital per person remains constant.

Will you live in a steady state world in which economic growth has slowed and finally *stopped?* Or can we extrapolate the growth of the last half-century and expect that living standards will *double* in the next 36 years? Obviously, these two scenarios lead to entirely different lives for you and your children. To examine the issues underlying these questions, this chapter first analyzes this model of growth more carefully by using a numerical example, then it discusses evidence related to the model.

Numerical Example of Growth that Stops at a Steady State

Suppose that real GDP per person, $\frac{y}{l}$, depends on capital per person, $\frac{k}{l}$, in the following way:

$$\text{IF } \tfrac{k}{l} \text{ is } \leq 20 \text{ THEN } \tfrac{y}{l} = 2 \left(\tfrac{k}{l}\right)$$

$$\text{IF } \tfrac{k}{l} > 20 \text{ THEN } \tfrac{y}{l} = 30 + \left(\tfrac{k}{l}\right)/2.$$

Advice

Don't get confused by the strange formula for the production function in this example. If you have trouble understanding the formula, then ignore it and concentrate on the *numbers* from that formula in Table 4 and its *graph* in Figure 7.

Figure 7 graphs this production function, and the first two columns of Table 4 show various levels of capital per person and the resulting real GDPs per person. If capital per person is 20, real GDP person is 40; if capital per worker is 40, real GDP per person is 50, and so on.

Now assume that people save exactly one-tenth of GDP per person. The third column of the table shows total savings. Finally, assume that exactly one-tenth of capital depreciates (wears out) each year. The fourth column of the table shows total depreciation—if capital per person is 20, then depreciation equals 2 per year.

Suppose the economy's capital per person equals 20. Then real GDP per person is 40, and people save 4. Equilibrium in the loans market implies that savings equals investment, so the economy invests 4. Since only 2 units of capital wear out, the economy replaces those 2 units and adds 2 more to its capital stock. Therefore, next year

Figure 7 | Production Function in the Numerical Example

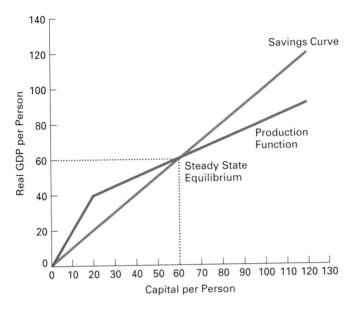

the economy's capital per person will be 22 instead of 20, and its GDP per person will rise. *The economy grows.*

The economy continues to grow as long as it saves more than enough to replace the capital that wears out each year. That is, it grows as long as the number in the savings column exceeds the number in the depreciation column. Eventually, the economy's capital per person reaches 60. When that happens, the table shows that real GDP per person also equals 60.[8] At that point, savings equals depreciation per person—each equals 6. The economy saves and invests just enough to replace the capital that depreciates each year. Therefore, capital per person stops growing, and real GDP per person stops increasing. The economy reaches a steady state, and economic growth stops.

Figure 7 shows a straight-line *savings curve* that intersects the production function at the steady state capital per person. The height of the savings curve shows the real GDP per person required to create enough savings to replace the capital that depreciates each year. When the production function lies above the savings curve (as in the left portion of the graph), real GDP per person is high enough that savings can replace all the capital that depreciates and still *add* to the capital stock. In this case, the capital stock rises over time—the economy grows.

Table 4 | Numerical Example of Growth that Stops at Steady State (billions of base-year dollars)

Capital per person	Real GDP per person	Savings per person	Depreciation per person
0	0	0	0
20	40	4	2
40	50	5	4
60	60	6	6
80	70	7	8
100	80	8	10

[8]The numbers for steady-state capital and steady-state GDP are equal in this example purely by coincidence.

When capital per person reaches 60, GDP per person is high enough to create *just enough* savings to replace the capital that depreciates. In this case, the capital stock does not increase further, and growth stops. This is the steady state equilibrium.[9]

Figure 8 shows a more general case of a production function and a savings curve in which people save 5 percent of GDP. At the steady state equilibrium, capital per person is 1,000 and real GDP per person is 2,000. One-tenth of capital depreciates each year, so the economy needs investment of 100 per year to replace it. With GDP per person of 2,000, people save 100—just enough to replace the depreciating capital. As a result, the capital stock remains constant, and the economy remains at its steady state equilibrium.

Evidence on the Model

How well does this model of economic growth correspond to real-life experiences? It applies well to certain situations. For example, World War II destroyed a large amount of capital in Germany and Japan (buildings, machinery, and so on). At the end of the war, these countries' economies had lower levels of capital per person and real GDP per person than they had before. For several decades after the war, investment levels in Germany and Japan far exceeded those in other countries, such as the United States, where little capital had been destroyed. Germany and Japan had high rates of economic growth as they rebuilt their capital stocks. Similar increases in investment and rapid growth typically occur after cities are struck by natural disasters such as earthquakes, floods, or hurricanes.

Figure 8 | Steady State Capital per Person and GDP per Person

At Point *SS* (for *steady state* equilibrium), capital per person is 1,000. One-tenth of this capital wears out each year, so firms must invest 100 just to replace depreciated capital, and capital per person remains at 1,000. At Point *SS*, real GDP per person is high enough (2,000) that people save 100, lending this amount to firms for investment and keeping capital per person at 1,000.

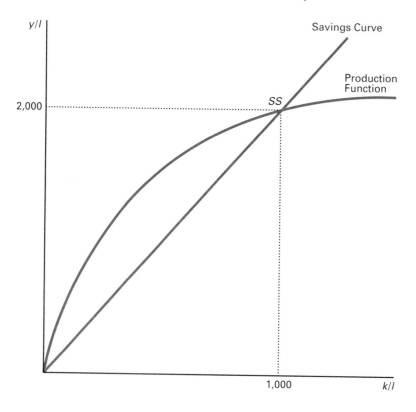

---

[9]When the production function lies below the savings curve (as in the right portion of the graph), real GDP per person is not high enough to create sufficient savings to replace the capital that depreciates. As a result, the capital stock falls over time, so real GDP also falls. Capital and real GDP rise when capital per person is less than 60, and they fall if capital per person exceeds 60. These forces create a tendency for the economy to move toward its steady state equilibrium.

The model does not apply so well, however, to most real-life economic growth. Two main observations about real-life growth are inconsistent with the model. First, the model implies that economic growth slows down and eventually stops. However, as Figures 1 and 2 and Table 1 indicate, the rate of economic growth has *increased* over time, except in the last quarter of the 20th century. Do people today live in an era of slowing economic growth as the economy approaches a steady state? No one knows for sure, but the overall experience of increasing rates of growth over the past two centuries does not support the predictions of the model. Second, the model predicts a falling real interest rate over time, as in Figure 6. However, evidence indicates that the real interest rate has *not* fallen over time; the real interest rate is about the same now as a century ago. Clearly, the basic model is missing certain important features of economic growth, such as technical progress.

Review Questions

1. Roughly how long does it take real GDP per person to double if it grows at 2 percent per year? What if it grew at 3 percent per year?

2. What does it mean to say that the economy's production function has constant returns to scale?

3. Draw graphs of a production function to show how real GDP per person changes when (a) capital per person rises; (b) technology advances.

4. What is a steady-state equilibrium?

5. What main observations about data contradict the basic model of economic growth without technical change?

Thinking Exercises

6. Comment on this claim: "People produce more today than in the past because they work more than in the past."

7. Explain why (a) increases in capital per person can create economic growth without technical change, and (b) without technical change, economic growth would slow down over time.

8. Change the numerical example in Table 4 to make people save ⅙ of GDP per person. How does this increase in savings affect the numbers in the table? How does it affect steady state capital per person and real GDP per person?

LOGIC OF GROWTH: EXTENSIONS

The model of growth discussed so far says that an economy grows by saving and investing. However, when its capital per worker reaches the steady state, the economy stops growing. That model is not consistent with the observations that economic growth has increased over time (except in the last quarter-century) and that the real interest rate has remained about constant over time. However, the model ignores an important fact: As time passes, our economy can produce more output than it did in the past *without* using additional inputs. In other words, the economy experiences *technical change*.

A classic study of American economic growth since 1929 found that about one-third of increases in U.S. real GDP per person resulted from increases in capital per person.

SOCIAL AND ECONOMIC ISSUES

Technical Change *Rearranges* Natural Resources

Technical progress does not mean that the economy produces *more* output with the same inputs. That would violate a basic law of physics—the law of conservation of mass and energy. Instead, technical progress refers to *rearrangements* of resources that increase their *value* to people. When metals such as gold, silver, copper, and (later) iron were discovered thousands of years ago, people developed technologies to heat them and transform them into products such as ornaments, utensils, tools, and weapons. Today, advances in technology have shown people how to use silver in photographic film, and iron oxide to carry information magnetically on videotapes.

Thousands of years ago, people learned to produce glass by heating quartz or sand (often mixed with ground seashells and other materials), and then quickly cooling it. They used glass for beads and other decorations. Today, advances in technology have shown people how to use different types of glass (with various characteristics) and to use glass for fiber optics that carry messages over telephone lines and the Internet.

By rearranging natural resources in new ways, technical change can increase the *value* of those resources to people. Economic growth results not from increases in the *quantity* of resources, but from increases in the *value* of resources.

About two-thirds of increases in U.S. real GDP per person resulted from increases in technology, knowledge, education, and increases in economic efficiency (meaning that the economy improved its use of its resources). A classic study comparing economic growth in Singapore and Hong Kong also illustrates the important role of technological change. Since 1965, economic growth has averaged over 7 percent per year in both countries. However, very different factors accounted for this growth. Singapore grew almost entirely through increases in capital per person (resulting from very high rates of saving and investment). In contrast, a large fraction of economic growth in Hong Kong resulted from technical progress.

Technical changes appear as increases in the variable A in the per-person production function,

$$\text{Real GDP per person} = A\ f\left(\tfrac{k}{l}\right)$$

Technical Change and Economic Growth

Think about the logical question: What does technical change add to the previous model? Technical change raises production per person without any increase in capital per person, as in Figure 4. An economy can grow indefinitely as long as technical progress continues, even if capital per person remains constant as in Figure 4. But can technical progress continue indefinitely? What creates technical change, and what policies can a country follow to promote technical change?

Investment in Technical Change

Technical change results from progress in science, engineering, and application of scientific knowledge to improve capital equipment and production methods. Some technical change occurs by accident, but most results from *investments* in research and development and in education and skills.[10]

Does technical change have diminishing returns? Do the benefits of additional knowledge fall as the economy adds to its stock of knowledge? If so, the logic from

---

[10]Practice and experience also raise productivity; economists call this learning by doing.

the last section would apply: Equilibrium investment in scientific research and its applications would fall over time. Technical change would slow down and eventually stop. As a result, economic growth would slow down and eventually stop at a steady state equilibrium. On the other hand, if knowledge does *not* have diminishing returns, then continuing technical change may cause economic growth to continue indefinitely without slowing. Economists can only speculate about the answers to these questions, although those answers will profoundly affect the lives of our children and grand-children.

Investment in Human Capital

Future economic growth *might* not slow down, even if technical change were to slow. Economic growth could continue indefinitely if the economy could continually add to its *effective* labor input by investing in human capital through education and training. To see why, suppose that technical change stops. When the variable *A* in the production function stops growing, economic growth can continue only if inputs of capital and labor continue to grow. *Both* inputs must grow; if the economy adds to only *one* input without adding to the other input, diminishing returns to the growing input cause economic growth to slow down and eventually stop.

The economy can add to its capital stock by producing additional machinery and equipment, but how can it add to its labor input? People could try to work harder, or to work more hours per year, but there are clear limits to human effort and work hours per week. However, improvements in skills and knowledge can make people more *effective* as workers. Investments in human capital—education and training—can raise *effective* labor per person.

> An economy's **effective labor input** is its labor input adjusted for knowledge and skills.

Because one skilled, educated person may do the work of two or three less knowledgeable people, increases in human capital resemble increases in the quantity of labor. They add to the economy's effective labor input.

If the economy can increase its effective labor input per person along with its capital stock, real GDP per person can grow even without technical change. With constant returns to scale, doubling the capital stock and the *effective* input of labor per person doubles real GDP per person. By increasing *both* inputs proportionally, the economy may avoid diminishing returns. If so, economic growth could continue indefinitely without slowing. Will this happen? Like questions about diminishing returns to technical progress, the answer is a matter for speculation.

Fixed and Exhaustible Natural Resources

Diminishing returns may cause economic growth to slow and perhaps eventually stop for another reason: The economy has fixed physical quantities of natural resources. We can distinguish three types of natural resources:

> **Renewable resources** are natural resources that can be replenished, such as trees.

> **Fixed resources** are natural resources that cannot be replenished, but are not depleted in production, such as land.[11]

---

[11]Of course, *fertile* land can be replenished as well as depleted.

> **Exhaustible resources** are resources that cannot be physically replenished and that are depleted in production, such as coal.[12]

Renewable resources play the same role that capital played in the earlier discussions. They create no complications for economic growth. In contrast, fixed resources may prevent economic growth from continuing indefinitely without slowing. By the law of diminishing returns, as the economy adds capital and labor to a fixed quantity of land and other fixed resources, the benefits of further increases in capital and labor fall. At some point, the economy reaches a steady state at which economic growth stops. In this way, fixed resources could limit per-capita real GDP. Exhaustible resources may create even more severe problems. As people use oil and other fossil fuels, the earth's remaining quantities of these resources fall over time. Some people worry that depletion of exhaustible resources will cause world real GDP to *fall* in the future.

Malthus on Population

The idea that fixed resources restrain economic growth goes back to Thomas Malthus and his famous "Essay on the Principle of Population," published in 1798. Malthus argued that as the population rises and increasing numbers of people work with a fixed amount of land, diminishing returns to land would reduce output of food per person. As a result, Malthus predicted that wages would fall over time as the population rose. When the wage fell far enough, he theorized, malnourishment and death would stop the population

Is world population at a good or bad level?

IN THE NEWS

Losing faith: Many Americans fear U.S. living standards have stopped rising

They believe their children face a tougher future; but Boomers have hope

Alan Murray
Staff Reporter of The Wall Street Journal

For nearly three decades after World War II, the rise in American living standards was as reliable as a Maytag washer.

The march of material prosperity created the easy assurance that each gener-

ation would live better than the last.

Today, that has changed.

The economic confidence of the postwar years has faded. In a painful awareness striking at the heart of American life, many no longer assume that their children will be better off than they are.

Expectations about the future may vary—but what is that future really likely to hold? Has the American dream of ever-rising living standards vanished, dwindled to a faint hope or merely gone into hibernation?

Source: The Wall Street Journal

This news article, appeared a decade ago, when most American had more pessimistic expectations about the U.S. economy than they have today. Economists draw lessons about long-run economic growth from long-run data, rather than economic experiences of a few years.

---

[12]Economists say that people *deplete* a resource if they transform it into a *less valuable* resource.

increase, and the population would stabilize at a subsistence wage just large enough for people to live and reproduce with zero population growth. This Malthusian view of growth became very popular and led people to call economics "the dismal science."

Was Malthus right? The world population numbered about 275 million people in the year 1000. It reached 750 million by 1750, 3.0 billion by 1960, and 6 billion by 1998. Obviously, the growth rate of the world population has increased rapidly. From 1000 to 1750, the human population grew at about 0.13 percent per year; from 1750 to 1960 it grew at about 0.66 percent per year, and from 1960 to 1998 it grew at almost 1.8 percent per year. Most experts predict that world population will reach 9.3 billion by the middle of the 21st century.

Malthus assumed that the population would rise as long as people earned incomes high enough to survive. Modern studies of fertility and population growth show clearly that people *choose* family sizes in relation to their incomes, the usefulness of children (to help raise food or support parents in old age), and other factors. People do not choose to have enough children to drive their wages down to subsistence levels. Instead, wages have increased over time as the world population has grown; these wage increases have resulted from technical advances and increases in physical and human capital that have raised the demand for labor faster than population growth has raised the supply. A century after Malthus published his book in Britain, that country's population had quadrupled and people's incomes had increased greatly.[13]

Scarcity of Natural Resources

Despite the evidence against the Malthusian model of population and wages, his argument about diminishing returns to a fixed quantity of land and natural resources raises serious issues. Even with moderate population growth diminishing returns could cause economic growth to slow down and eventually stop. Many social commentators have argued that this may happen, and some have argued for government policies intended to reduce the use and depletion of resources, and to reduce the rate of world population growth. According to their arguments, population growth reduces economic growth and could even reduce the level of real GDP per person. Population increases with fixed quantities of land may also reduce quality of life through crowding, pollution, and other factors that GDP calculations ignore.

Other analysts have argued that people respond to scarcity of a resource by innovating and creating new ways to replace scarce resources with more plentiful resources. History is filled with examples, as the Social and Economics Issues box on the next page illustrates. The evidence suggests that scarcity of natural resources has not limited economic growth in the past. As people deplete the remaining quantity of an exhaustible resource, its supply falls and its price rises. If economic growth were limited by depletion of exhaustible resources, the prices of those natural resources would rise. However, the evidence suggests the opposite: Historically, relative prices of most exhaustible resources have *fallen* over time.

Prices of exhaustible resources have fallen for two reasons. First, technical progress has increased their supply (for example, by locating new mines, reducing the cost of mining, and decreasing waste). Second, technical progress has reduced the demand for these resources by creating substitutes. (For example, satellite links and fiber-optic lines have replaced copper wires for telephone calls.) If technical change provides methods to increase output with reduced inputs of fixed and exhaustible resources, then economic growth may continue indefinitely without slowing or stopping.[14]

This debate on the future of economic growth continues today. One side says that economic growth will slow down and eventually stop because of diminishing returns to

---

[13]Even in the years from 1500 to 1700, when technical progress was slow, the situation differed from Malthus's scenario. The population grew at a rate well below the biological maximum. Europeans lived in conjugal rather than extended families, and married in their mid-20s rather than at puberty to keep fertility low; priests enforced prohibitions on premarital sex with reasonable success. Average living standards remained well above the subsistence level.

[14]Though the quantity of land is physically finite, it has not inhibited economic growth in the past. The development of better techniques for land use (for irrigation, fertilization, cropping, and breeding) have reduced the importance of land for agriculture. Similarly, the developments of elevators and high-rise buildings have helped to reduce the importance of land in cities.

SOCIAL AND ECONOMIC ISSUES

Will the Finite Quantity of Natural Resources Cause Economic Growth to Slow Down or Stop?

Yes

The earth provides a finite amount of many important natural resources. Some of these, like total land area, don't change over time, but population growth reduces the amount available per person. People are using up many others, such as fossil fuels (oil and natural gas) and metals. Future generations will have diminishing quantities of these resources available, even if the population stops growing.

World population growth shows no indication of slowing any time soon. Most experts expect massive increases in world population over the next century. Population growth is already outstripping the world's supplies of fresh water, food, and minerals.

The inaccuracy of earlier warning of doom is irrelevant to today's situation. The forecasters were wrong at the time, but the real crisis will come soon.

Finite natural resources will soon get more expensive, because they are being consumed. The fact that they became cheaper in the past proves nothing, because people were not near the point of running out; the world is near that point now.

No

Scarce resources haven't run out yet, and for a good reason. When resources become scarce, people respond with innovations and substitutes. This process has continued throughout history. The Greeks moved from the Bronze Age to the Iron Age 3,000 years ago because wars in the eastern Mediterranean disrupted trade and reduced the supply of tin for bronze production. The Greeks responded to the bronze crisis by starting to use iron instead. Timber shortages in 16th-century Britain led to the use of coal as a substitute fuel. As a resource becomes scarce, people find new ways to produce its services with resources that are more abundant, and the alternatives usually turn out to be better than the old ways. The most important natural resource for production of new ideas is human ingenuity, and its supply is unlimited.

As a result, neither the finite physical quantities of natural resources nor population growth will limit economic growth. An increase in population growth causes short-term problems, because children do not produce goods, but it does not create long-term problems because adults produce both goods and new ideas.

Serious people have claimed many times in the past—wrongly—that the world was about to run out of some natural resource. The current claims are wrong for the same reason that similar warnings were wrong in the past.

Many physically finite natural resources have become cheaper rather than more expensive over time because of new discoveries that have raised their supplies or the development of substitutes that have reduced their demand. Similar changes will likely occur in the future.

Investment in new ideas is a key source of economic growth.

finite resources, and perhaps because real GDP per capita will fall as the economy depletes exhaustible resources. The other side says that economic growth can continue indefinitely, driven by technical change and accumulating knowledge and human capital. Many past predictions have incorrectly warned that the world would soon run out of some finite resource.[15] This record of inaccuracy does not necessarily imply that similar claims will be wrong in the future.

Externalities and Growth

People and firms have incentives to invest in research and development to create technical change, because the results of the research can add to their profits. These additional profits are the private benefits of investing in research and development. Other people

---

[15] In his famous book The Coal Question: An Enquiry Concerning the Progress of the Nation (London, U.K.: Macmillan, 1865), economist Stanley Jevons warned that the world would soon run out of coal. The U.S. Federal Oil Conservation Board said in 1926 that the United States had only a 7-year supply of oil left. In The Population Bomb (New York: Ballantine Books, 1968), Paul Ehrlich warned that "The battle to feed humanity is over. In the 1970s the world will undergo famines—hundreds of millions of people are going to starve to death." Ehrlich warned that "nothing can prevent a substantial increase in the world death rate." He predicted that "America's vast agricultural surpluses are gone." In Ehrlich's book with Anne Ehrlich, The End of Affluence, the authors warned of a "nutritional disaster that seems likely to overtake humanity in the 1970s (or, at the latest, in the 1980s)," and said that "before 1985 mankind will enter a genuine age of scarcity" in which "the accessible supplies of many key minerals will be nearing depletion." These predictions were all wrong.

SOCIAL AND ECONOMIC ISSUES

A Famous Bet

In 1980, economist Julian Simon offered a bet to environmentalist Paul Ehrlich. For years, Ehrlich had been forecasting doom as the world runs out of resources. Simon had been arguing that continual innovations would prevent resource depletion, and that the prices of natural resources would continue to fall as in the past.

Simon offered to bet on the *relative prices* of natural resources. Ehrlich could choose any five metals for the bet, with quantities chosen so that they cost a total of $1,000 in 1980. If the relative prices of the metals increased by 1990, so the total value of the metals (adjusted for inflation) exceeded $1,000 in 1990, then Ehrlich would win the bet. If the

relative prices of the metals fell by 1990, so their total value (adjusted for inflation) was less than $1,000 in 1990, then Simon would win. The loser would pay the winner the difference in the total value of the metals, above or below $1,000. Ehrlich accepted the bet and chose copper, chrome, nickel, tin, and tungsten.

By 1990, the relative prices of all five metals had fallen below their levels in 1980. Ehrlich lost the bet, and sent Simon a check for $567.07. (In fact, the relative prices fell enough that Simon would have won the bet even if prices had not been adjusted for inflation.) Simon (who died in 1997) offered to renew the bets and increase the ante to $20,000, but Ehrlich was not interested.

More information on this bet, and other related bets offered by Simon and by Ehrlich, can be found on the Web site for this book.

---

may gain directly from these investments as well, so the social benefits of investments in research may exceed the private benefits.

> The **private benefit** of producing a good or investing in research is the benefit to the people who produce it or invest. The **social benefit** is the benefit to everyone in society of the production or investment.

Firms often copy technical changes they see in other firms or industries. Countries copy technical changes they see in other countries. New ideas often lead to even more ideas. Technical knowledge and ideas tend to spread throughout the economy, sometimes through written media in books and technical reports and sometimes through products that can be studied by reverse engineering (in which people take apart products to see how they work). You may know of many examples such as clones of brand-name computers, designer clothes, and other consumer products. Knowledge can be such a valuable asset that some firms undertake industrial espionage (spying) to gain information about technical developments at other firms.

> A **positive externality** occurs when the social benefit of producing a good or investing in research exceeds the private benefit.

Some economists believe that positive externalities play important roles in economic growth. Countries that invest more than others may grow faster partly because the new ideas generated by these investments create positive externalities that spread throughout the investors' economies.

If investments in knowledge or human capital generate positive externalities, then the economically efficient quantity of these investments exceeds the equilibrium quantity. This fact has led some economists to suggest that government policies should encourage savings and investment, perhaps through subsidies or lower taxes.

Similarly, positive externalities from investments in knowledge or human capital mean that doubling the amounts of physical and human capital may *more* than double real GDP. While doubling inputs of physical and human capital at any one firm may double *that* firm's output, the increase may also create positive externalities that raise output at other firms. Some economists cite this possibility as one reason for the increase

SOCIAL AND ECONOMIC ISSUES

Externalities and Government Policies

Evidence indicates that when a typical business firm invests in research and development, it gains only about one-half of the benefits from its investments. One study found that the *private benefit* to investment in research and development has been about 25 percent per year (before taxes), while the *social benefit*, has been about 50 percent per year. When business firms decide on a level of investment in research and development, they weigh the *private* benefits of investment against the costs. As a result, businesses invest less in research and development than they would if they had an incentive to take into consideration *all* the benefits of those investments. This discrepancy has led the U.S. government to reduce taxes for businesses that invest in research and development (by about 20 cents per dollar of investment). One study found that for every $1 billion in tax revenue the government sacrifices for these tax incentives, businesses raise investment in research and development by about $2 billion. These tax policies provide one important channel through which government policies can promote economic growth.

in the rate of economic growth over time. Of course, no one knows whether the rate of growth will continue to increase in the future, but the suggestion that growth results partly from positive externalities emphasizes this possibility.

Review Questions

9. What do economists mean by an economy's *effective* labor input? What increases the effective labor input? How do these increases contribute to economic growth?

10. (a) Explain why fixed and exhaustible natural resources might cause economic growth to decrease in the future. (b) Explain how the economy might avoid decreasing growth, despite the limited physical quantities of natural resources.

11. Explain and criticize Malthus's views of population and wages.

IN THE NEWS

The pump on the well

Unforeseen consequences of technology

When a solar-powered water pump was provided for a well in India, the village headman took it over and sold the water, until stopped. The new liquid abundance attracted hordes of unwanted nomads. Village boys who had drawn water in buckets had nothing to do, and some became criminals. The gap between rich and poor widened, since the poor had no land to benefit from irrigation. Finally, village women broke the pump, so they could gather again around the well that had been the center of their social lives.

Moral: Technological advances have social, cultural, and economic consequences, often unanticipated.

Source: New York Times

With enough economic growth, they could socialize at the local gourmet coffee shop.

12. What is a positive externality and how might externalities contribute to growth?

13. Suppose economic growth were limited by the earth's finite quantities of exhaustible resources. Why would economists expect the relative prices of these resources to rise over time? Why have their relative prices not risen over time?

14. Why would economic growth eventually slow and stop if investments in knowledge and technical change had diminishing returns?

The term *economic development* refers to economic growth in low-income countries. Economic development is generally accompanied by increases in life expectancy, health, and literacy, and by decreases in infant mortality. In 1900, average life expectancy at birth was only 49 years in the OECD countries and 35 years in LDCs (less developed countries). Economic growth in the 20th century has raised life expectancy to 77 years in OECD countries and 64 years in LDCs. Countries with highly developed economies tend to have more political freedom; more stable governments; fewer civil wars, coups and revolutions; and fewer government restrictions on people's activities than LDCs have. Developed countries tend to have more equal distributions of income than LDCs. Although development often raises inequality in the short run, it reduces inequality in the long run.

Why are some countries poorer than others are? What can a poor country do to increase its economic growth? Why have *some* countries risen from poverty by growing rapidly and joining the developed countries of the world? What have *those* countries done that other poor countries have not? Will poor countries ever catch up with rich countries? These are some of the key questions of economic development.

ECONOMIC DEVELOPMENT: GROWTH IN LESS DEVELOPED COUNTRIES

Differences among Countries

Two centuries ago, no country was as rich as developed countries are today, but no one was much poorer than the poorest country today. In 1900, real GDP per person in the world's richest country was about 8 times higher than real GDP per person in the world's poorest country. By 1998, real GDP per person in the world's richest country (the United States) was about 60 times higher than real GDP per person in the world's poorest country (Ethiopia). Clearly, inequality among countries of the world has increased as some countries have grown rapidly and others have remained far behind. Inequality among *developed* economies has fallen, however. Real GDP per person in OECD countries (with the exception of Asian countries) has become more equal in the 20th century, especially since 1950. Figure 9 shows growth in various regions around the world over the past 250 years.

Conditions that Promote Growth

Evidence suggests that several factors contribute to a country's economic growth. Poor countries tend to grow faster than richer countries (they tend to "catch up" with richer countries) *given* other conditions that affect growth. One advantage that less developed countries have in economic growth involves imitation. Poorer countries can copy techniques and

Does Economic Growth Create Problems?

Economic growth has improved people's lives enormously over time. Nevertheless, some people argue that growth has negative effects. These people often favor government policies designed to prevent or solve the problems, even if the policies reduce the rate of economic growth. Other people disagree, seeing negative aspects of growth as illusory or small issues. They favor government policies to promote fast growth. Here are some arguments on the positive and negative aspects of growth.

Positive Results of Growth

Economic growth brings people out of poverty. It raises health and expected life span, increases literacy, and opens new opportunities for people to have fulfilling lives. It gives people both the material goods they want and more leisure time. People can use this leisure time as they choose, for recreation or to pursue other goals and promote nonmaterial values.

Growth provides resources that can help the environment. A good summary measure of environmental quality as it affects people is expected life span, which has increased with economic growth, largely due to improvements in health and medicine that accompany growth. Economic growth also provides the resources that offer people some insurance against many risks, such as famine and disease. While economic growth requires change, and any change has risks, changes can produce good as well as bad effects.

Economic growth creates new opportunities for people to pursue fulfillment through work. People who want to be artists or self-dependent producers of their own food can still do so. In fact, with the increased technical knowledge made possible by economic growth, a self-dependent person can have a higher standard of living now than people could in the past. The romantic image of life and jobs before economic growth is completely different from the reality that life and work for most people are better—not worse—

Figure 9 | Real GDP per Capita around the World, 1750–1998

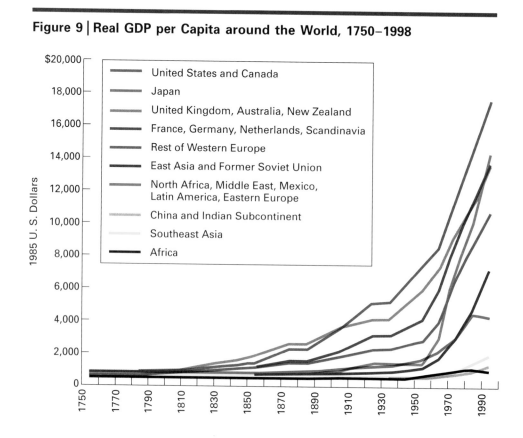

after economic growth. Future economic growth can continue to improve the quality of life.

Economic growth generates riches for some people. Although it may initially raise income inequality, it eventually reduces inequality. (For example, compare the amount of income inequality in developed countries and LDCs.) Any government policies to reduce economic growth would not reduce inequalities; they would entrench existing ones and reduce opportunities for people to advance themselves through innovation, hard work, or luck.

Problems that Some People See in Economic Growth

Some people claim that economic growth reduces the quality of life by leading people to focus on material goods that do not provide real satisfaction and to ignore the nonmaterial values that are important to satisfying lives. Others claim that economic growth increases income inequality and allows some people to get rich but not others.

Some people say that growth ruins the beauty of nature,

harms the environment, and threatens a fragile ecosystem. They say it threatens the welfare of future generations of people as well as nonhuman life.

Some people assert that growth alienates people from the most important values in life. It moves them from basic, fulfilling work such as farming, craft work, and building to unfulfilling jobs in factories and offices. Economic growth reduces a worker's understanding of how his efforts fit into a larger scheme and help other people. Some jobs, like investment banking, encourage gross materialism and discourage important values like honesty and charity. The increased specialization that goes with economic growth, in this view, alienates people from each other; it reduces shared experiences, makes it harder for people to understand each other, and breaks down the social bonds that support a civilized community.

What do you think? What evidence could you obtain to support your position?

technologies that were invented in richer countries. Copying does not always create success, however, because the technologies that are most appropriate in a country with highly-paid, skilled workers may differ from the best technology in a country with lower-paid, less-skilled workers.

While evidence suggests that poor countries tend to grow faster *given* other conditions, many countries are poor precisely because these other conditions differ. Differences in these other conditions can prevent poor countries from catching up with rich countries. Several other conditions affect economic growth. First, a country tends to grow faster than others if it has a skilled, educated population. Education and skills allow people to take greater advantage of advanced technologies. Often however, people in poor countries spend more time working and less time investing in education and skills than people in richer countries.

Countries tend to grow faster if their governments place few restrictions on international trade. International trade creates incentives for the nation's producers to specialize in the goods and services in which they have a comparative advantage. International trade also provides competition for domestic producers, creating stronger incentives for efficient uses of resources. A later chapter discusses other benefits from international trade.

Countries tend to grow faster if they attract high levels of investment from foreign countries. While the savings of people living in a country can provide resources for investment, poor countries generate low levels of saving. As a result, a poor country can raise its level of investment and economic growth by attracting foreign investment.

Countries tend to grow faster if they have stable economic and political conditions. High rates of inflation (discussed in the next chapter) inhibit economic growth. Countries with more coups, civil wars, and revolutions show lower economic growth than countries with more political stability.

Finally, countries tend to grow faster if they have well-developed and well-enforced systems of property rights, commercial and contract law, and legal methods for resolving

ON ECONOMICS—

Rich in Cash, But Not in Happiness

You say money can't buy happiness? It must be you just don't know where to shop. Most economists accept, nearly as an article of faith, that individual satisfaction tracks closely with income. Their faith isn't blind, either: Most of us seek raises, wish we could afford a bigger house and dream about winning the lottery.

But a small band of economists are breaking ranks. They cite numerous studies showing paradoxically that as society grows richer over time, the average level of happiness—as measured by the percentage of people who rate themselves "happy" or "very happy" in national surveys—doesn't grow in tandem. If true, the implications are potentially enormous. These findings should challenge economists—and everyone else for that matter—to re-examine the merits and consequences of economic growth.

Richard Easterlin, now an economist at the University of Southern California,

published a seminal study reporting no clear trend in surveys of Americans' reported happiness. Average happiness rose from the 1940s to the late 1950s, then gradually sank again to the early 1970s, even as personal income grew sharply. Returning to the subject three years ago, Easterlin cited an annual U.S. survey that showed a slight downward trend in the percentage of Americans saying they were "very happy" from 1972 to 1991—even though per capita income, adjusted for inflation and taxes, rose by a third.

Even more striking evidence came from Japan, where a Dutch scholar, Ruut Veenhoven, tracked self-reported levels of satisfaction from 1958 to 1987. During that period, Japan's economy defined the "Asian miracle." Real per capita income soared nearly fivefold, taking Japan from a developing country to an industrial superpower in a generation. Yet average levels of

reported satisfaction didn't budge at all.

Psychologists find that few things permanently budge individuals from their normal level of happiness, which is determined above all by inherited temperament. But income does matter. At any given time, the higher your income, the more likely you are to report being happy, so there's still reason to envy the rich.

How can these findings be reconciled? Easterlin believes people feel more satisfied if their consumption exceeds the social norms. But as an economy grows, so do material aspirations. That moving target keeps the average person from ever feeling better.

An economy with no growth, on the other hand, can turn ugly as people continue striving to climb the social ladder. The only way for people to get more out of a fixed pie is to grab someone else's slice. A static economy promotes nasty fights over distribution; growth promotes civility and altruism.

Source: San Francisco Chronicle

What do you believe? Does economic growth contribute to human happiness? Would you be as happy if you lived in the conditions of 1000 years ago? 100 years ago? How would human happiness be affected if economic growth were to end this year, or sometime in the near future? Should governments pursue policies to promote economic growth?

legal disputes. Economic growth in Russia in the 1990s, for example, has been hindered by absence of well-developed and well-enforced property rights. Property rights, along with economic and political stability, helps ensure businesses that they can reap the returns

---

IN THE NEWS

The development gap

Most developing countries will gain little from new technologies

Developing countries face a series of obstacles in their efforts to participate in the Third Industrial Revolution. First, a pool of highly trained scientific and technical personnel is essential for the successful diffusion of the new technologies. But only 13 percent of the world's scientists and engineers are in the third world, and they are concentrated in only a few countries in East Asia and in Brazil, India, and Mexico.

Second, new technologies require large amounts of capital. But many developing countries lack access to capital markets and already are heavily burdened by debt.

Third, shifts in world consumption and technical innovation have cut demand for traditional raw materials—bad news for the nearly 40 developing countries that depend on raw materials for at least 15 percent of their total export earnings.

Source: New York Times

---

of their investments. When business firms are reluctant to invest in a country, perhaps because they fear future government confiscation of the returns from their investment, that reluctance reduces economic growth.

Investment and Government Policies

Very poor countries tend to save smaller fractions of their incomes than rich countries save. Consequently, they have very low levels of investment in equilibrium unless they borrow from rich countries. Foreign investment in poor countries can increase their incomes, partly by bringing equipment to boost their workers' productivity and partly by bringing technical knowledge, organizational skills, and information about how to export their products. Foreigners have an incentive to invest in a poor country if it offers sufficiently low wages compared to worker productivity.

In practice, poor countries attract little foreign investment and wages remain much lower in poor countries than in rich ones. This difference may reflect low skill levels of workers in poor countries, which offsets the benefits of their low wages, or it may reflect risks of investing in those countries because of uncertainty about property rights. Potential investors evaluate the risk that the government of a less developed country may confiscate their property in the future, impose new taxes or regulations that reduce the returns on their investments, or limit their ability to take their profits out of the country.

Other factors further limit foreign investment in LDCs. Many LDCs have poor infrastructures with unreliable or nonexistent transportation and communication systems (roads, telephone systems, and so on). Governments of LDCs often limit foreign investment to avoid the perception that foreigners are taking over their countries or in response to political pressures from people who would lose from foreign investments. Government bureaucrats, for example, often benefit from maintaining the status quo.

Many governments of LDCs adopt economically inefficient policies such as limiting international trade and controlling domestic trade. Economists may see these inefficient policies as mistakes, but the policies may also benefit powerful special-interest groups within these countries, at the expense of reduced economic growth. Government policies also affect the extent to which people divert resources from production to economically inefficient activities such as seeking political influence through lobbying, bribes, legal battles, and other activities to increase their shares of the country's output. Countries that spend comparatively high levels of resources fighting over the distribution of output have comparatively low levels of real GDP and low rates of economic growth.

Success Stories

Among the most famous successes of economic development are the so-called *four tigers of Asia* mentioned earlier: Hong Kong, Singapore, South Korea, and Taiwan. These countries have averaged more than 7 percent annual growth of per-capita real GDP—more than four times the world average—since 1965. (The rule of 72 estimates that 7 percent annual growth would double these countries' incomes every decade.)

Why did these countries succeed so well at development? Economists do not yet have a complete answer, but the reason seems partly related to free markets and international trade. Evidence shows that economic growth is connected with increased international trade, particularly for small countries. All four Asian tigers imposed less government regulation and control than most LDCs, and all experienced large increases in international trade along with their rapid growth. Their governments left more economic decisions to free markets than did officials in low-growth countries; this policy promoted economic efficiency and probably raised economic growth. International trade promotes efficiency by allowing countries to specialize in the products at which they have comparative advantages, which raises their income, as Chapter 3 explained. In addition, increased specialization can raise a country's rate of economic growth under certain conditions. Increased international trade also raises competitive pressures on firms, which may reduce inefficiencies and raise output. Finally, increased international trade can help pressure governments to follow economically efficient policies.

Some economists look at the evidence on development and conclude that countries can develop and grow most rapidly if their governments eliminate restrictions on international trade, promote private property rights and free markets, reduce regulations and controls on the economy, and encourage foreign investment. Others believe that economic development can speed up if the government actively promotes international trade by subsidizing exports. While most agree that governments of less developed countries follow many policies that cause inefficient uses of resources, some question the extent to which changes in government policies alone can raise economic growth rates.

Review Questions

15. List some factors that promote fast economic growth.

16. How can foreign investment raise the rate of growth in a less developed country?

Conclusion

Basics of Growth

Economic growth is a rise in real GDP per person, measured by the annual percentage increase in per-capita real GDP. Throughout most of history, real GDP per person remained roughly constant until about 200 to 300 years ago, when it began a rapid increase. The rule of 72 says that if the growth rate of a variable is X percent per year, then the variable doubles after about $72/X$ years.

Main Facts about Economic Growth

World real GDP per person is about $6,000 today, 12 times higher than in 1800 and more than 4 times higher than in 1900. U.S. real GDP per person is about $32,000 today, almost 6 times as high as in 1900. It has doubled since 1964. Economic growth rates differ substantially across countries. Some countries have had annual growth rates over 7 percent in recent decades, with real GDP per person doubling every 10 years; others have roughly the same living standards as a century ago.

Logic of Economic Growth: A Basic Model

An economy can grow by saving and investing in new capital. However, without technical change, diminishing returns cause growth to slow down and eventually stop as the economy reaches a steady state equilibrium. Evidence indicates, however, that economic growth has increased over time (with the possible exception of the last quarter-century), which conflicts with the implication of this model. In addition, this basic model implies that the real interest rate falls over time, but evidence indicates a constant real interest rate.

Logic of Growth: Extensions

Technical change results from investments in research and development and in education. An economy can continue to grow indefinitely if technical change continues. If technical change were to have diminishing returns (a highly speculative question), then technical change and economic growth would slow down and eventually stop. Similarly, economic growth could continue indefinitely if the economy could indefinitely add to its *effective* labor input per person—through education—along with its capital per person.

Fixed and exhaustible natural resources cause diminishing returns for investments in physical and human capital, so they may lead growth to slow down and eventually stop. However, growth may continue indefinitely without slowing down if technical progress allows the economy to reduce its use of fixed and exhaustible resources or to substitute replenishable resources such as trees and sunlight for those resources. Some technical change may occur by accident, but the economy may be able to increase technical progress and long-run growth by increasing investments in education, research, and development.

Economic Development: Growth in Less Developed Countries

Countries tend to grow relatively rapidly if they are poor, have educated or skilled populations, limit government restrictions on international trade, and stimulate high levels of investment. Countries in Africa and Latin America have grown more slowly than similar countries elsewhere, perhaps because they have tended to suffer more political instability and less certain property rights. The fact that poor countries tend to grow faster than others does not mean that they are catching up with rich countries. Many countries remain poor because of frequent wars and inefficient government policies.

Key Terms

economic growth
rule of 72
steady state

effective labor input
renewable resource
fixed resource

exhaustible resource
private benefit

social benefit
positive externality

Questions and Problems

17. Explain why a country cannot keep growing at the same rate indefinitely simply by adding indefinitely to its physical capital.

18. Use a graph of the supply and demand for loans to help explain why an increase in savings raises the speed at which the economy grows toward its steady state.

19. How might increases in savings and investment raise the rate of economic growth as well as the level of per-capita real GDP?

20. Discuss this statement: "Poor countries are likely to catch up, eventually, with rich countries."

21. Why do some countries grow faster than others?

22. (*More difficult problem.*) Suppose the economy's per-person production function is

$$\text{Real GDP per person} = k^{\frac{1}{5}}$$

where k represents the capital stock per person. Also suppose that people save 2/10 of real GDP each year, and that 1/10 of the economy's capital depreciates (wears out) each year. Find the steady state capital stock and steady state real GDP.

23. Suppose that people in France begin saving more than before and people in England begin saving less. Is this change likely to raise the rate of economic growth in France and reduce the growth rate in England? (*Hint:* What happens to international borrowing and lending and to the world equilibrium real interest rate?)

Inquiries for Further Thought

24. Are we at a turning point in history beyond which economic growth is likely to decline?

25. Does economic growth create winners and losers? Who are they?

26. **(a)** Would further economic growth in the United States be good or bad? Why? If you are opposed to more economic growth, would you have opposed more growth in 1800? In 1900? In 1950?
    (b) How fast should countries' economies grow? What general principles should guide the answer to this kind of question?

27. What government policies would you recommend for an LDC that wants fast economic growth?

28. Discuss this statement: "To feed starving populations is desirable, but if new crops help add a billion new people to a crowded globe, is that necessarily a good thing?"

29. Discuss these statements.
    (a) "Population growth may raise economic growth, because it adds more brains as well as more mouths and hands."
    (b) "Population growth that increases the volume of trash may increase our problems in the short run, but it bestows benefits on future generations. The pressure of new problems leads to the search for new solutions. The solutions constitute the knowledge that fuels the progress of civilization, and leaves us better off than if the original problem had never arisen. That is the history of the human race."

30. Suppose that a higher population would reduce per-capita real GDP but raise aggregate real GDP. Would this increase in population be good or bad?

31. Discuss this statement: "Allowing foreigners to immigrate to our country can raise our rate of economic growth, particularly if the immigrants are well educated."

Appendix: Mathematics of Production Functions

A realistic production function for an economy is

$$\text{Real GDP} = A l^{2/3} k^{1/3}$$

This equation provides a good approximation to real-life production functions in the United States and many other countries. The variable A represents the level of technology, with increases in A representing technical progress. Real GDP rises with increases in A, k, or l.

This production function implies constant returns to scale: Doubling all inputs, doubles real GDP. To see why, multiply labor and capital by 2 in the equation:

$$\begin{aligned}
\text{Real GDP with twice the inputs} &= A(2l)^{2/3}(2k)^{1/3} \\
&= A 2^{2/3} l^{2/3} 2^{1/3} k^{1/3} \\
&= 2Al^{2/3} k^{1/3} \\
&= \text{twice the original GDP}
\end{aligned}$$

This result shows that doubling all inputs doubles real GDP. Similarly, multiplying all inputs by *any* number, such as X, multiplies GDP by that same number. This fact means the production function has constant returns to scale.

Now we let X be $1/l$. In other words, we multiply both inputs by $1/l$, which also multiplies real GDP by $1/l$. This gives an expression for real GDP per person:

$$\begin{aligned}
\frac{\text{Real GDP}}{l} &= \frac{Al^{2/3} k^{1/3}}{l} \\
&= A\left(\tfrac{k}{l}\right)^{1/3}
\end{aligned}$$

This expression shows that real GDP per person depends on capital per person, as in the chapter.

PART 10

INFLATION, MONEY, AND BANKS

CHAPTER 28

INFLATION

In this Chapter. . .

Main Points to Understand

▶ *Inflation* refers to continuing increases in the average level of *nominal* prices.
▶ Nothing affects inflation without affecting the growth rate of the money supply, the growth rate of velocity, or the growth rate of real GDP.
▶ Equilibrium between the supply of money and the demand for money determines the price level, as in the equation of exchange.
▶ No one would care about inflation if it reflected a change in units of measurement, like a reverse currency reform. Economic and social problems from inflation result from the *differences* between inflation and reverse currency reforms.

Thinking Skills to Develop

▶ Distinguish between factors that affect *relative* prices of various goods and services and factors that affect the *nominal* price level.
▶ Apply the economics of supply and demand to money.
▶ Reason by analogy (between inflation and currency reforms), and evaluate the limits of an analogy.

A t the beginning of the 20th century, basketballs cost about $2 each; at the end of the century they cost about $30. Prices of most goods and services are higher now than a century ago, or even a decade ago. On average, prices in the United States in 1998 were more than 18 times higher than prices in 1900, and twice as high as in 1980.

In 1998, after years of rapidly rising prices, Russia removed three zeros from the ends of all its money, prices, wages, bank accounts, and debts. The price of cheese, for example, fell from about 30,000 rubles per kilogram to about 30 rubles. People exchanged their old 100,000 ruble bills for newly designed 100 ruble bills and other new money printed by the government.

This Russian experience was not unique. In Germany from August 1922 to November 1923, inflation averaged 322 percent per month. Prices at the end of that German hyperinflation—a term for particularly high inflation—were 10 billion times the original level. Someone who lived through hyperinflation once defined it as a situation in which it's cheaper to pay for your lunch before you start eating it than after you finish. Indeed, people have sometimes resorted to eating money itself, or burning it for heat or cooking fuel as in the picture that opens this chapter.

Less than 20 years ago, inflation reached almost 5,000 percent per year in Argentina, 2,000 percent per year in Brazil, and several hundred percent in Israel. Bolivia's inflation rate reached 60,000 percent per year in the summer of 1985. Other countries, including

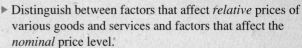

IN THE NEWS

BUENOS AIRES, May 31—Rioting over runaway inflation increased in the Argentine capital today.

Source: New York Times

Inflation causes social upheavals.

IN THE NEWS

A weary Buenos Aires family wonders how to keep afloat

By James Brooke
Special to
The New York Times

BUENOS AIRES, June 15—With his 2-year-old son squirming on his lap, Guillermo Dietrich pondered how to keep his family afloat in Argentina's rising sea of inflation.

"My wife, my mother, and my aunt are the antibodies of hyperinflation," the drawn father of two said, cracking a rare smile. "Every morning, they pool price information and try to save before prices are marked up again."

Last month, food prices jumped 78 percent, a record here. Argentina's working class neighborhoods erupted in the worst riots in a decade.

'We Live Day to Day'

This month, prices are expected to jump 100 per-cent. With businessmen projecting this year's inflation to be 12,000 percent, Argentina's middle class feel pushed to the edge.

"We live day to day," Mr. Dietrich said. "We only pay bills when the money comes in."

The descendants of immigrants from Europe, the Dietrichs grew up to think of themselves as middle class. Guillermo was a construction foreman. Elida, his wife, is a lawyer.

"We grew up with inflation of 7 to 15 percent a month," Mr. Dietrich, 31 years old, said of the annual inflation rate common to Argentina in the 1970s and 1980s. "But now, prices don't mean anything any more."

"I bought this last week at 37 australes," he said, toying with a half-smoked pack of L&M Light cigarettes. "Now it is selling for 55 australes. Next week, it will be 78 australes. What is the price?"

Elida Dietrich juggled her 4-year-old daughter, Valeria, and said: "It makes you feel very insecure."

"This morning, I went into one store, looking for detergent," she continued. "In one place, it was 140. The next place, 100. Finally, I bought it at a third store at 80. But tomorrow all the prices will change."

In late May, sudden rises of food prices triggered the sacking of hundreds of food shops across Argentina. In a shock to the nation, 15 people were killed, dozens were injured, and hundreds were arrested.

Source: New York Times

Living with inflation.

Austria, Greece, Hungary, and Peru, have had similar experiences in the last century. Around the world, the 20th century saw the biggest price increases in all of history.

Inflation—defined as a continuing increase in the price level—has a long history. Emperor Diocletian tried to stop inflation in the Roman Empire by imposing wage and price controls in A.D. 301. Despite the death penalty for violaters, inflation continued and many people were executed until Diocletian abdicated the throne in A.D. 305.

Personal hardships and social upheavals have accompanied periods of high inflation in the last century. Riots in the streets and changes in government make the news, but just as devastating are the difficulties that many families face when prices rise hourly, when their money loses value faster than they can spend it, and when increases in prices wipe out the values of their life savings.

Inflation in the United States today—about 2½ percent per year since 1991—is low by 20th-century standards, but high by standards of earlier centuries. Prices in the United States today are about one-fourth higher than in 1990. In contrast, the U.S. price level in 1940, at the beginning of World War II, was only about one-third higher than it was a century and a half earlier, when George Washington became the nation's first president. Clearly, the continuing inflation that people in the United States take for granted today is a relatively recent phenomenon.

IN THE NEWS

Hunger spreading in Peru inflation

Food is plentiful in markets but soaring prices put it out of reach for many

By Alan Riding
Special to
The New York Times

LIMA, Peru—Wandering around a street market near her home with the equivalent of just 60 cents in her pocket, Sara Chaverry seemed almost in a daze as she tried to imagine how she would provide the next three meals for the 10 members of her household.

"There's plenty of food in the stalls," the 28-year-old mother said, waving at unsold chickens and cuts of meat, "but things I could afford a couple of months ago are now out of reach. Sometimes I just buy the tail, skin, and head of a fish and boil it up with rice."

Since this country's deepening economic crisis brought a surge of inflation of 114 percent in September alone, food—or the lack of it—has become the central concern of millions of Peruvians who were already living below the poverty line.

Source: New York Times

Inflation creates winners and losers.

Who gains from inflation? Who loses? Why do some countries have higher rates of inflation than others? Why are policy makers around the world concerned about inflation? What causes inflation and what can prevent it? These are the subjects of this chapter.

DEFINITIONS AND BASIC MODEL

One of the most basic concepts in economics involves the distinction between nominal and real variables:

Nominal variables are quantities measured in units of money (U.S. dollars, Mexican pesos, etc.).

Real variables are quantities measured in units of goods and services or in units of *base-year* money.

A previous chapter explained one example—the distinction between nominal GDP and real GDP. Economists measure nominal GDP in units of money; they measure real GDP in units of *base-year* money. In an economic model with only one good (such as berries in the Robinson Crusoe model), real GDP represents the number of goods that the economy produces in a year.

A related distinction concerns nominal and relative prices (first discussed in Chapter 4):

Nominal prices are money prices of goods and services.

Relative prices are the opportunity costs of goods, measured in terms of other goods.

If a sandwich costs $3, and a drink costs $1, then the nominal prices of sandwiches and drinks are $3 and $1, and the relative price of a sandwich, measured in terms of drinks, is 3 drinks per sandwich. If we measure an average nominal price by giving equal weight in the average to sandwiches and drinks, we find that the average nominal price level in this example is $2.

These distinctions are extremely important because inflation involves nominal prices and other nominal variables, while the supply–demand model discussed in Chapter 4 involves relative prices and real variables. Many economic fallacies (some discussed later in this chapter) result from confusing relative prices and nominal prices. You should notice, for example, that the price level can change without any changes in relative prices. For example, all nominal prices may double, doubling the price level, but leaving all relative prices unaffected. Similarly, relative prices can change without any change in the price level—for example, the relative price of sandwiches can rise from 3 to 4 drinks per sandwich, with the nominal price of sandwiches rising to $3.20 and the nominal price of drinks falling to 80 cents. This change raises the relative price to 4 drinks per sandwich but leaves the average nominal price of the goods at $2.

The term *price level* refers to the average level of *nominal* prices of goods and services. An earlier chapter discussed three measures of the price level—the GDP deflator, the consumer price index (CPI), and the producer price index (PPI). Inflation refers to continuing increases in the average level of nominal prices:

> **Inflation** is a continuing increase in the (nominal) price level.

Economists measure inflation by the *percentage increase* in the CPI (or GDP deflator or PPI) over some period of time, such as a year.

The basic model discussed in previous chapters used the *equation of exchange*, represented by the circular flow diagram, to determine the equilibrium price level. We begin analyzing inflation—the *growth rate* of the price level—by examining this model in greater detail.

Equation of Exchange

Figure 1 shows the basic version of the circular flow of economic activity that Chapter 25 introduced to discuss the price level. The outer circle shows money flowing from people to firms as people buy goods and services (aggregate nominal spending). That flow of money shows the economy's total spending, or nominal GDP. Money also flows back to people as firms pay wages and distribute profits (another way to measure nominal GDP). The inner circle shows the flow of final goods from firms to people (real GDP) and the flow of work effort and other inputs from people to firms (another way to measure real GDP).

Chapter 25 defined the *nominal money supply* as the total quantity of money in the economy, measured in monetary units such as dollars or yen. That definition will continue to apply in this chapter: the nominal money supply is the total amount of dollar bills that the government has printed, minus those lost or destroyed. (The following chapter will add additional new real-life features of money and banking to the model and discuss several alternative measures of the money supply.)

> The **nominal money supply**, *M*, is the total dollar value of all paper money and coins in the economy.[1]

Example of Calculating Inflation

The U.S. CPI (measured using a base period of 1982 to 1984 = 100) was 160.3 in June 1997, and 163.0 in June 1998. Therefore the rate of inflation over this period was $100 \times (163.0 - 160.3)/160.3$, or 1.7 percent per year.

---

[1]This is the *currency* definition of money, to be discussed in the next chapter.

Figure 1 | Circular Flow

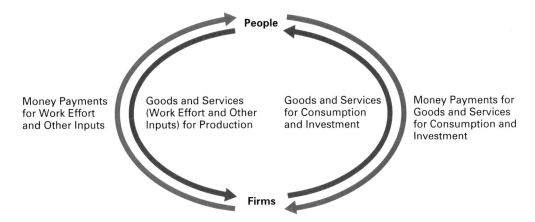

The velocity of money, *V,* equals the number of times someone spends each dollar (or yen) each year, on average. The price level, *P,* is the average nominal price of goods and services in the economy, measured by a price index such as the GDP deflator or the consumer price index.

The equation of exchange says that the nominal quantity of money (*M*) multiplied by the velocity of money (*V*) equals nominal GDP, or the price level (*P*) multiplied by real GDP (*y*):

$$MV = Py$$

This relationship implies that the price level equals the nominal money supply times velocity, divided by real GDP:

$$P = MV/y$$

The second equation shows that the price level depends on the nominal money supply, real GDP, and the velocity of money. Increases in the nominal money supply or velocity raise the price level, while increases in real GDP reduce the price level.

EXAMPLES

Think about an economy that produces 10 final goods each month, for a real GDP of 120 goods per year. Suppose also that its nominal money supply is $60. Each time the circular flow occurs, people spend $60 on goods. If people spend the money once per month, so velocity equals 1 per month (or 12 per year), then they buy 10 goods per month with $60, implying that each good costs $6. In this case, the equation of exchange becomes:

$$(\$60)(1 \text{ per month}) = (\$6 \text{ per good})(10 \text{ goods per month})$$

On an annual basis:

$$(\$60)(12 \text{ per year}) = (\$6 \text{ per good})(120 \text{ goods per year})$$

These equations can be rewritten in terms of the price level,:

$$\$6 \text{ per good} = \frac{(\$60)(1 \text{ per month})}{10 \text{ goods per month}} = \frac{(\$60)(12 \text{ per year})}{120 \text{ goods per year}}$$

Similarly, if people spend the nominal money supply *once* (rather than 12 times) per year, so that annual velocity equals 1, then they spend $60 each year to buy 120 goods, so each good must cost $0.50. In this case, the equation of exchange becomes:

$$(\$60)(1 \text{ per year}) = (\$0.50 \text{ per good})(120 \text{ goods per year})$$

SUPPLY AND DEMAND FOR MONEY

While the equation of exchange shows the relationship of the price level to the nominal money supply, real GDP, and velocity, it does not indicate the forces that affect those variables. Who controls the economy's nominal money supply? What determines the velocity of money, and what factors affect it? These questions lead to a discussion of supply and demand for money.

Money Supply

The government controls the economy's nominal supply of money, as defined earlier, printing paper money and minting coins.[2] U.S. nominal money supply, by this chapter's definition, was about $400 billion in 1998 (though people outside the United States hold much of it). This figure is about 8 times higher than a quarter century ago, and 350 times higher than a century ago. Governments of other countries have also increased their nominal money supplies. For example, the nominal money supply in Japan, by the same definition, is now about ¥50 trillion, 6 times its 1970 level.

Money Demand

Most people own some money, and carry it in their wallets. But money is just one of many assets that you can own. Other assets include stocks, bonds, bank accounts, land, art, jewelry, and Beanie Babies. When you save, you must decide what assets to own, and how much of each. You probably make your choice by comparing the benefits of each type of asset. For example, stocks, land, and Beanie Babies might increase in value; bonds and bank accounts pay interest; money is useful if you want to buy something at a store.

Costs and Benefits of Holding Money

Stocks, bonds, and bank accounts pay interest or dividends, but paper money and coins pay no direct returns. In fact, money *loses* value in times of inflation, because each dollar can buy fewer goods and services after prices increase. The *opportunity cost of owning money* is the nominal interest rate that you *could have* earned by putting that money in a bank account (or lending it by buying a bond).

Of course, holding money has benefits as well as costs. You cannot exchange a stock certificate, corporate bond, or piece of land for food at the grocery store. The special benefit of money is that you can spend it to buy goods and services.[3] The size of this benefit depends on many factors, such as the extent to which sellers accept credit cards or debit cards, and the time required for buyers to use such cards.

---

[2] The next chapter discusses other measures of the money supply and shows that the government does not have complete control over them. This result does not affect the main conclusions or logic in the current chapter.

[3] This fact ought to strike you as rather peculiar—why should other people give you goods and services you want in exchange for certain pieces of paper? Why will they accept some kinds of paper and not others? The answer to these questions are not obvious; these questions raise deep issues. Learning to raise questions, even if you cannot answer them, is an important skill that will make you a better economist.

Relative Price of Money in Terms of Goods

The relative price of sandwiches in terms of drinks is the opportunity cost of sandwiches; it equals the number of drinks you sacrifice for each sandwich. Similarly, the *relative price of money* in terms of goods is the opportunity cost of money—the number of goods you sacrifice for each unit of money. If goods cost $1 each, then you sacrifice one good for each dollar that you keep (rather than spending). If goods cost $2 each, then you sacrifice *half* of a good for each dollar that you keep (rather than spending). Clearly, the *relative price of money* in terms of goods equals the inverse of the price level (*P*):

$$\text{Relative price of money in terms of goods} = \text{Inverse of price level} = 1/P$$

Quantity of Money Demanded

As Chapter 4 explained, your quantity of CDs demanded, at some relative price of CDs, is the amount that you would choose to buy at that price, *given* your income, wealth, tastes, the prices of related goods, and so on. Similarly, your *quantity of money demanded,* at some relative price of money, is the amount of money that you would choose to own, *given* your income, wealth, tastes, and other conditions.

> The **quantity of money demanded** at some relative price of money, is the amount of money that people would choose to own, given current conditions such as their income and wealth, the usefulness of money, and the costs and benefits of owning other assets.

Figure 2 graphs the demand for money. As usual, the demand curve slopes downward: As the relative price of money (1/*P*) falls, the quantity of money demanded rises. Because the relative price of money is the inverse of the price level, you can see that increases in the price level raise the quantity of money demanded.

Studies of money demand have drawn several conclusions:

1. The quantity of money demanded is proportional to the price level, *P*. Doubling the price level (cutting the relative price of money in terms of goods by half) doubles the quantity of money demanded. It is easy to understand why. When nominal prices double, people need twice as much money to buy the same goods and services as before, so they carry twice as much money in their wallets.

2. The quantity of money demanded rises as real GDP rises. On average, each 1 percent increase in real GDP raises the quantity of money demanded by about 1 percent. Again, it is easy to understand why. When people become 1 percent richer, they buy about 1 percent more goods and services, so they carry about 1 percent more money in their wallets.

3. The quantity of money demanded falls when the nominal interest rate rises. A rise in the nominal interest rate raises the opportunity cost of holding money, so it decreases the amount of money that people want to hold. Estimates of the magnitude of this effect vary, but an increase in the nominal interest rate from 5 percent to 6 percent per year may reduce the quantity of money demanded by about 5 percent.

4. The demand for money has changed in recent decades in the United States and many other countries. Economists do not yet fully understand the reasons for those changes.

In summary, a mathematical expression gives the demand for money:

$$M^d = Py/V$$

Advice

Don't get confused about money demand. A common confusion is to think, "My demand for money is 1 billion dollars—or maybe an infinite amount, because I would always want more." Of course you want more! So does everyone! They also want more vacations and movie tickets and CDs, but they do not have infinite quantities demanded for these things. The quantity demanded of any good refers to the amount that people would choose to buy, given their incomes and other conditions. (See Chapter 4.) Similarly, the quantity of money demanded refers to the amount that people would choose to own, given their incomes and other conditions.

Example: You have saved a total of $1,000. If you decide to put $900 into the stock market and keep $100 in money to carry in your wallet, then your quantity of money demanded is $100. If conditions change, and you decide to put only $800 in the stock market and keep $200 cash in your wallet, then your demand for money *increases.* If conditions change, and you decide to put only $950 in the stock market and keep only $50 in your wallet, then your demand for money *decreases.*

Increasing the relative price of money in terms of goods and services, 1/P, reduces the quantity of money demanded.

Figure 2 | Demand for Money

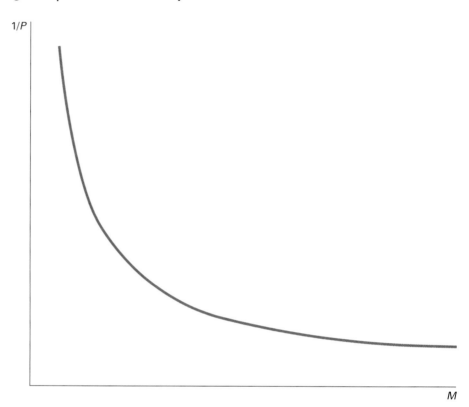

where M^d is the quantity of money demanded, P is the price level, y is real GDP (so Py is nominal GDP), and V is the velocity of money. Because the nominal interest rate is the opportunity cost of holding money, velocity is not a constant. It rises and falls with the nominal interest rate.

> Increases in the nominal interest rate raise the velocity of money; decreases in the nominal interest rate reduce velocity.

When the nominal interest rate rises, people spend their money faster than before. To see why, think about a country with a *very* high rate of inflation. That country has a very high nominal interest rate (recall the Fisher equation, discussed in Chapter 26). People in that high-inflation country spend their money very quickly after they receive it, before price increases reduce its value. As they quickly spend money, they create a very high velocity. In other words, an increase in the nominal interest rate raises the velocity of money.

An increase in the nominal interest rate raises the opportunity cost of holding money. As a result, people want to hold less money (and hold other assets, such as stocks and bonds, instead). Therefore, the quantity of money demanded falls. In the previous equation, an increase in the interest rate raises V, reducing M^d.

Equilibrium Price Level

Economists use the model of the supply and demand for money to analyze the equilibrium price level. Figure 3 shows equilibrium between the demand for money and the supply of money. The perfectly inelastic (vertical) supply of money curve shows the amount of money that the government has printed. The equilibrium relative price of money in terms of goods, $1/P_0$, gives the equilibrium price level, P_0.

> The **equilibrium price level** is the price level that equates the quantity of money demanded with the quantity supplied.

Essentially, the supply of money shows the amount of money *available* for people to hold, while the demand for money shows the amount that they *want* to hold (given their incomes, the relative price of money in terms of goods, and the benefits of holding other assets instead). Equilibrium occurs when people *want* to hold exactly the *available* amount. Mathematically, the quantity of money demanded equals the quantity supplied, M, so $M^d = M$, therefore:

$$MV = Py$$

where M is the quantity of money supplied, V is velocity, P is the price level, and y is real GDP. In other words, the equation of exchange, discussed earlier along with the circular flow, shows equilibrium between the demand and supply of money. Our analysis of the demand for money, however, shows that velocity is *not* a constant number; it rises and falls along with the nominal interest rate.

We can use the equation of exchange to examine factors that affect the equilibrium price level. We conclude that the equilibrium price level (P) rises when:

▶ The nominal money supply, M, rises

▶ The nominal interest rate rises, raising V

▶ Real GDP, y, falls

We also conclude that changes in underlying economic conditions do *not* affect the equilibrium price level *unless* they affect the nominal money supply, real GDP, or velocity.

Figure 3 | Equilibrium of Money Demand and Money Supply

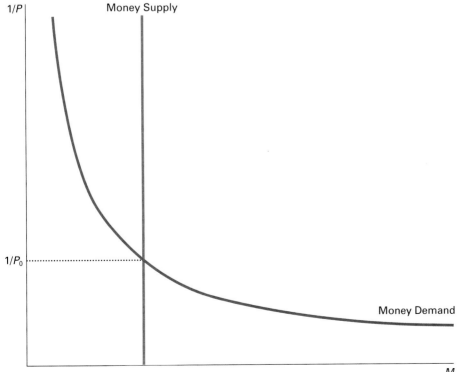

Equilibrium between money demand and money supply determines the equilibrium relative price of money in terms of goods (the inverse of the price level). Therefore, it determines the equilibrium price level.

If the price level is below its equilibrium level (P_0 is less than P_1), then the relative price of money in terms of goods exceeds its equilibrium level, creating a surplus in which the quantity of money supplied exceeds the quantity demanded. As a result, people spend the excess money, driving up prices until the price level rises to P_1, that is, until the relative price of money falls to its equilibrium.

Figure 4 | Adjustment to Equilibrium

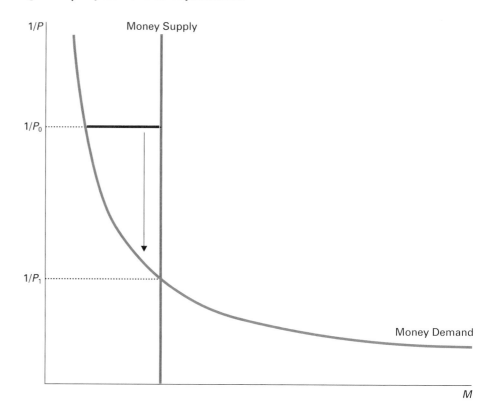

Adjustment to Equilibrium

If the price level is below its equilibrium level—so the relative price of money is *above* its equilibrium level—then the quantity of money supplied exceeds the quantity demanded, as in Figure 4. In this situation, people have more money (and fewer other assets such as stocks and bonds) than they want to hold, so they begin spending more money.

Any *one person* can trade money for stocks, bonds, and other assets, but *society as a whole* cannot trade away money.[4] Whenever one person spends the money, someone else receives it. Society as a whole is stuck with the amount of money that the government has printed—*someone* must hold it. However, as people spend more money, nominal prices rise moving the economy toward equilibrium. The relative price of money, $1/P$, falls as in Figure 4, raising the quantity of money demanded. In other words, the increase in the price level, P, raises Py/V. The price level rises until the quantity of money demanded equals the quantity supplied. At that point, the economy reaches its equilibrium.

Changes in Money Supply or Money Demand

Figure 5a shows the effect of an increase in the supply of money—the equilibrium relative price of money falls from $1/P_0$ to $1/P_1$, so the equilibrium price level rises from P_0 to P_1. Figure 5b shows the effect of an increase in the demand for money, perhaps due to an increase in real GDP, y, or a fall in velocity, V. A rise in the demand for money raises the equilibrium relative price of money from $1/P_0$ to $1/P_2$, reducing the equilibrium price level from P_0 to P_2.

---

[4]Thinking otherwise is an example of the *fallacy of composition*, discussed in Chapter 2.

Figure 5 | Effects of Changes in the Money Supply or Money Demand

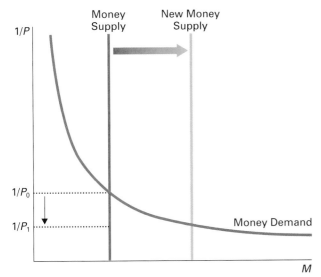

(a) Increase in the Money Supply

An increase in the money supply lowers the equilibrium relative price of money in terms of goods, raising the equilibrium price level.

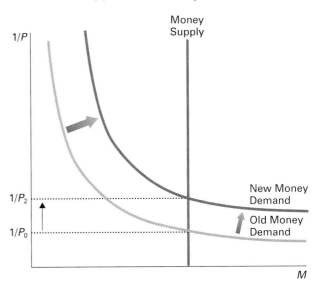

(b) Increase in Money Demand

An increase in money demand raises the equilibrium relative price of money in terms of goods, lowering the equilibrium price level.

Review Questions

1. State and explain the equation of exchange.

2. Explain why an increase in the nominal interest rate reduces the quantity of money demanded.

3. Explain why an increase in the price level raises the quantity of money demanded.

4. Explain the relationship between the velocity of money and the quantity of money demanded. How is velocity affected by the nominal interest rate?

5. What happens if the price level is below its equilibrium? Explain why.

Thinking Exercises

6. Discuss this claim: "The quantity of money demanded is infinite because people always want more money."

7. How would the equilibrium price level react to: (a) an increase in the money supply? (b) an increase in the nominal interest rate caused by an increase in expected inflation? (c) an increase in real GDP?

An important real-life example of a change in the money supply occurs during a currency reform.

CURRENCY REFORMS

IN THE NEWS

Argentina slims peso by stripping off 0,000

By a Wall Street Journal Staff Reporter

With the Argentine peso wracked by a 210 percent inflation rate last year, the military government has decided to lop four zeros off each peso note.

When the measure takes effect in about a month's time, a current 10,000-peso note will be called 1 peso. By the end of the year, the government hopes to phase out all the old notes and replace them with new units.

In 1967, the authorities resorted to a similar measure during a bout of inflation by converting 100 pesos into 1 peso. The new Argentine peso will be the equivalent of 1 million pesos of 1966.

Source: The Wall Street Journal

A currency reform that reduced money and prices to 1/10,000 of their previous levels.

A **currency reform** occurs when the government of a country (a) replaces one kind of money with another, new kind of money, and (b) automatically adjusts all nominal values in existing contracts (such as nominal wages in employment contracts and nominal debts in loan contracts) for the change in money to keep *real* values the same.

The new money introduced in a currency reform often has a different name than the old money. Usually each unit of new money is worth many units of the old money. For example, each new dollar may be worth 1,000 old dollars. In that case, nominal values specified in existing contracts would automatically fall to one one-thousandth of their previously stated levels. If a firm owes a bank 2 million old dollars, and each *new* dollar is worth 1,000 in old dollars, then the firm owes 2,000 new dollars after the currency reform.

A currency reform does not affect real GDP. It does not affect the amount of goods and services a country produces, consumes, or invests; it leaves all *real* variables unchanged. Also, it leaves *relative* prices unchanged. It affects nominal values, however, because the nominal values are measured in the new, different money. When the new money is worth 1,000 units of the old money, all nominal prices measured in the new money equal one one-thousandth of the prices measured in the old money; nominal GDP and other nominal variables fall to one one-thousandth of their values before the currency reform. (Note one exception: The nominal interest rate does *not* change in this way.)

EXPLANATION AND EXAMPLE

The following fictional news report gives an example of exactly what happens every several years in some country, somewhere in the world: "President Announces New Money: One 'New Dollar' Worth Ten Old Dollars; Crossing off Zeros; Prices Fall," *America Today,* February 1, 2002:

The president announced today that the United States would immediately issue "New Dollars" in place of old ones. Effective immediately, every $10 bill is now called one "New Dollar," every old $1 bill is now called one "New Dime." Every old $5 bill is now called 50 "New Cents," and so on. People must cross a zero off each $10 and $20 bill they own (making the bills $1 and $2 bills). The same requirement applies to larger bills (a $100 becomes a $10 bill, for example). Also, people must relabel $1 bills as 10 cents, and so on. Pennies become 0.1 cent coins, and nickels become 0.5 cent coins. The government has announced that it will soon issue "New Dollars," which will look different than the familiar green paper money.

As part of the change, all wages, salaries, debts, and payments stated in all contracts will automatically fall to one-tenth of their previous levels. For example, anyone who has earned $10 per hour will now earn one New Dollar per hour. Anyone who owed a debt of $2,000 in old money automatically owes 200 New Dollars.

In a related development, major retailers announced reductions in prices to one-tenth of their previous levels. For example, a television that previously sold for $300 will now sell for 30 New Dollars. The president described the measure as a "victory for consumers." He called the policy a "currency reform" and said similar policies have been very successful in other countries.

The speaker of the House, a long-time political foe of the president, opposed the measure. "This is just a political ploy by the president," he said. "Sure, a bag of groceries that used to cost $40 will now cost $4, but so what? It still takes the same four $10 bills as before to pay for those groceries—all we've done is to cross a zero off of each bill and rename it. Now we'll call each of those $10 bills 'one dollar' and say that we pay only $4 for those groceries. Any fool can see this does not change anything except the name of the dollar bills. It doesn't change anything of real importance to American consumers."

A currency reform changes the units of measure for nominal prices and other nominal variables without affecting real prices and real variables.

If the United States were really to make this change, the move would have almost *no* effect on real GDP, real consumption and savings, real investment, and employment.[5] Everything real in the economy would continue as before, except the names of the pieces of paper money that people exchange to buy and sell. Where once people paid $10 they would pay one (new) dollar; where they once paid $4.50 they would pay 45 (new) cents.[6] The currency reform would affect only nominal values. Each person would have one-tenth as many dollars and collect one-tenth of her previous nominal wage, and all nominal prices would fall to one-tenth of their previous levels. This is what has happened in real-life currency reforms throughout the world.[7] It is also the main idea behind the *neutrality of money* discussed in Chapter 25.

Real-Life Currency Reforms

History records many cases of currency reforms. In every case, nominal prices changed by the same percentage as the nominal money supply, and the change had no perceptible effect on real variables such as real GDP or on relative prices. The most recent example of a currency reform occurred in 1998 when Russia dropped three zeros from its money, the ruble. As a result, the money supply fell to one one-thousandth of its

[5] The word *almost* appears in this sentence because a currency reform could make the economy somewhat more efficient by reducing the time required to count money and make change when people buy and sell goods. Clerks would spend less time counting the zeros on paper money after the currency reform.

[6] Where people once paid 25 cents for something, they would pay 2.5 new cents. If the government had issued no half-cent coin, then payments involving half cents would have to be rounded up or down to the nearest whole cent. The effects of this rounding on real variables, such as real GDP, would be very small.

[7] Economists' use of the term *nominal* reflects the fact that only the name of the money changes in a currency reform.

IN THE NEWS

And in Bolivia: Weary from inflation that has hiked the price of a hamburger to 3 million pesos ($1.56), Bolivia will create a new currency by lopping six zeros from the peso's value and renaming it boliviano. One U.S. dollar now buys 1.9 million pesos; after Jan. 1, it will be worth 1.9 bolivianos. Argentina, Brazil, and Israel have taken similar steps.

Source: USA Today

A currency reform in Bolivia.

previous level, and nominal prices (in rubles per good) fell to one one-thousandth of their previous levels. This typical currency reform occurred, as most do, after a period of extremely high inflation.[8]

Similarly, Brazil introduced a new money in 1989, eliminating three zeros from its money and all nominal prices. As in Russia, the money supply and nominal prices fell to one one-thousandth of their previous levels, and the money's name changed. Brazil had another currency reform in 1994, introducing another new money. Bolivia had currency reforms in 1963 and 1987 (losing three zeros from its money and nominal prices in 1963 and six more zeros in 1987). Argentina had currency reforms in 1970 (losing two zeros from money and nominal prices), 1983 (losing five more zeros), 1985 (losing three more zeros), and 1992 (losing four more zeros). After several decades of extreme inflation, Argentina has had low inflation since the last currency reform. Other countries that have had currency reforms include France, in 1960, and Israel in 1980 and 1985.

Currency Reform in Reverse

Inflation resembles a *reverse* currency reform, introducing a new money worth *less* than the old money it replaces. For example, suppose that the government were to tell people to *add* a zero to every piece of money, so that $1 becomes $10, $5 becomes $50, and so

IN THE NEWS

Argentina returns to peso, saving numerous zeros

By Nathaniel C. Nash
Special to
The New York Times

BUENOS AIRES, Feb. 8— For the fifth time in 21 years, Argentina has switched currencies. The country has officially stopped using the austral and returned to the peso, the name of the currency in many Spanish-speaking countries.

In leaving the austral behind last month, the administration of Carlos Saúl Menem is hoping to send a signal that stable times are here.

Introduced in June 1985, the austral, whose name refers to the southern-

most extremes of Argentina, was at first worth $1.40. Then hyperinflation took over. By the end of last year, the austral was worth one-hundredth of 1 cent. That implies that the dollar's appreciation against the austral was 1.39 million percent.

When the switch was made on Jan. 1, $1 was equal to almost 10,000 australs. With 10,000 australs converted to one peso, the dollar and the peso are equal in value.

"When we came to the point of considering the need to print a bill of a million australs, that touched

off an alarm that said we had to change," said Alvaro Otero, a spokesman for the country's central bank. "The calculator and computers we import do not have the capacity to do such large sums."

But lopping off zeros— this time four—is not new for Argentina. In the last 21 years, the national currency has lost 13 zeros. If no such changes had occurred, the price tag for a $1,400 stereo system in an electronic shop on Avenida Florida in downtown Buenos Aires would have to read 14,000,000,000,000,000.

Source: New York Times

A currency reform in Argentina.

---

[8]Some countries impose government controls on nominal prices that prevent prices from changing in proportion to the money supply. Uncontrolled prices and black-market prices, however, change in rough proportion to the money supply.

on. The nominal money supply would be ten times higher after the change, and all nominal prices would rise to ten times their previous levels. Real variables and relative prices would not change, though.

Inflation works like a reverse currency reform. The main difference is that a currency reform does not redistribute income, so it does not create winners and losers. In real-life episodes of inflation, however, some people may gain and others may lose as inflation redistributes income. A later section discusses these redistributions.

EQUILIBRIUM INFLATION

The rate of inflation is the growth rate of the price level.

> The **equilibrium rate of inflation** is the growth rate of the equilibrium price level.

Economists take growth rates of the variables in the equation $P = MV/y$ to solve for the equilibrium rate of inflation:

$$\%\Delta P = \%\Delta M + \%\Delta V - \%\Delta y$$

In this equation, $\%\Delta$ indicates the percentage change in the variable, which is its growth rate. For example, the $\%\Delta M$ from 1998 to 1999 equals the change in the money supply from 1998 to 1999, divided by its 1998 level.

This equation says that the rate of inflation equals the growth rate of the nominal money supply plus the growth rate of velocity minus the growth rate of real GDP. For example, if the growth rate of the money supply is 8 percent per year, the growth rate of V is zero (which means that velocity remains constant over time), and the growth rate of real GDP is 3 percent per year, then inflation is 5 percent per year.[9] Nothing affects the equilibrium rate of inflation unless it affects either growth rate of the money supply, the growth rate of velocity, or the growth rate of real GDP.

The equation indicates the sense in which inflation is caused by "too much money chasing too few goods," as a famous quote explains. If velocity is constant (its growth rate is zero), then inflation occurs if the growth rate of the nominal money supply exceeds the growth rate of real GDP. An increase in the growth rate of real GDP reduces the rate of inflation.

Short-Run and Long-Run Inflation and Money Supply Growth

Over short periods of time, the growth rate of the money supply often increases without raising inflation, and decreases without reducing inflation. Figure 6 shows the annual inflation rate and growth rate of money in recent years in the United States.[10] As the figure indicates, money growth and inflation are not closely related in the short run. Although large increases in the money growth rate preceded large increases in inflation in 1973 through 1975 and 1978 through 1980, short-run changes in inflation and money growth have not usually been closely connected.

Over longer periods of time, however, money growth and inflation move more closely together. Figure 7 shows the relationship between the average inflation rate and the average growth rate of the nominal money supply in the United States in various decades from 1870 to 1998. With only three exceptions (the decades of the 1880s, the

[9]If something remains constant, its growth rate is zero.
[10]The next chapter will discuss the definition of the nominal money supply, called *M2*, that appears in these Figures.

Figure 6 | Inflation and Money Growth in the United States (1960–1998)

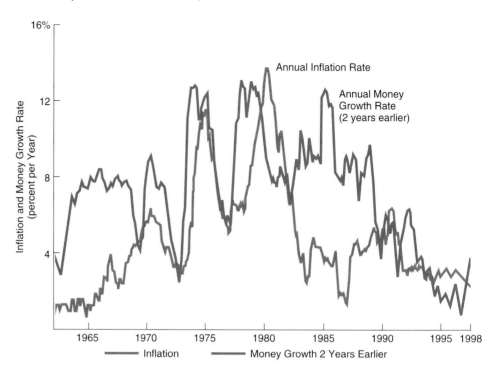

1930s, and the 1950s) the rate of inflation and the rate of money growth lie close together along the same line. This figure shows that nominal money growth and inflation are closely connected in the long run.

Similarly, differences in average inflation rates between countries over periods of several years or more are also related to differences in money growth rates. Countries whose nominal money supplies grow at high rates have high rates of inflation, and countries with low rates of nominal money growth have low rates of inflation.

Famous Episodes of Inflation

During the American Revolution, the colonies printed Continental Currency to pay for the war. The increase in the money supply caused inflation of 8.5 percent per month. Similarly, an increase in the growth rate of the money supply during the French Revolution caused inflation to average 10 percent per month.

During the U.S. Civil War, the money supply doubled in the North as the government printed paper money called *greenbacks* to pay for the war; the inflation rate was high enough that the wholesale price level doubled between 1861 and 1864.

The Confederacy (the South) also printed money to pay its cost of the U.S. Civil War. Inflation averaged 10 percent per month from October 1861 to March 1864. In May 1864, the Confederacy stopped increasing the money supply and actually reduced it with dramatic results. As one study put it, "Dramatically, the general price index dropped . . . in spite of invading Union armies, the impending military defeat, the reduction in foreign trade, the disorganized government, and the low morale of the Confederate army. Reducing the stock of money had a more significant effect on prices than these powerful forces."[11]

---

[11]Eugene Lerner, "Inflation in the Confederacy," in *Studies in the Quantity Theory of Money,* ed. by Milton Friedman (Chicago: University of Chicago Press, 1956).

Figure 7 | U.S. Inflation and Money Growth Rate by Decades, 1870s–1990s

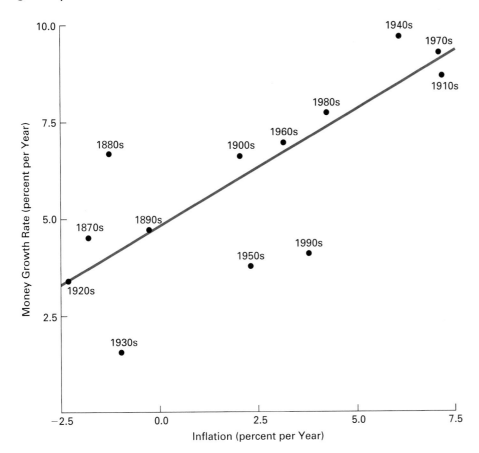

A famous case of hyperinflation occurred in Germany after World War I. The Treaty of Versailles that ended the war forced Germany to make large reparation payments to the Allied countries. The German government printed money rapidly to meet this obligation, and between August 1922 and November 1923, its money supply grew at an average rate of 314 percent per month. Inflation averaged 322 percent per month. The money supply and price level both increased by a factor of 10 million. In October 1923 alone, prices increased 32,000 percent.

In this case, as in many other times of hyperinflation, money lost value so fast that people could not wait to spend it. People would go to work, receive their pay (daily), and quickly spend the money before it lost value. Eventually, many German workers were paid two or three times a day; they would go to work in the morning, receive their pay, go out and spend the money before it lost value, then go back to work in the afternoon, receive partial pay again, and then quickly spend that money before it lost value. People took wheelbarrows full of money to stores to buy goods. Often the money weighed more than the groceries people could buy with it. Money became so worthless that people gave it to children as toys. It was cheaper to tie bundles of money together to make blocks than to buy blocks for children.

Other episodes of hyperinflation followed World War I in Austria, Hungary, Poland, and Russia. Greece experienced hyperinflation during World War II. But the biggest hyperinflation in recorded history occurred in Hungary after World War II. From August 1945 to July 1946, the money supply grew at 12,200 percent per month, and inflation averaged 19,800 percent per month. This rate amounts to 19.3 percent per day, or 0.74 percent per hour. In a year—the length of this

IN THE NEWS

When inflation rate is 116,000%, prices change by the hour

In Bolivia, the pesos paid out can outweigh purchases; No. 3 import: More pesos

LA PAZ, Bolivia—A courier stumbles into Banco Boliviano Americano, struggling under the weight of a huge bag of money he is carrying on his back. He announces that the sack contains 32 million pesos, and a teller slaps on a notation to that effect. The courier pitches the bag into a corner.

"We don't bother counting the money anymore," explains Max Loew Stahl, a loan officer standing nearby.

"We take the client's word for what's in the bag."

A 116,000% Rate?

Bolivia's inflation rate is the highest in the world. Prices go up by the day, the hour, or the customer. Julia Blanco Sirba, a vendor on this capital city's main street, sells a bar of chocolate for 35,000 pesos. Five minutes later, the next bar goes for 50,000 pesos. The two-inch stack of money needed to buy it far outweighs the chocolate.

The 1,000-peso bill, the most commonly used, costs more to print than it purchases. It buys one bag of tea. To purchase an average-size television set with 1,000-peso bills, customers have to haul money weighing more than 68 pounds into the showroom. (The inflation makes use of credit cards impossible here, and merchants generally don't take checks, either.)

Source: The Wall Street Journal

Living with hyperinflation.

period of hyperinflation—Hungary experienced an inflation rate of 3.81×10^{27} (3,810,000,000,000,000,000,000,000,000) percent. (Note that inflation compounds; a 10 percent per month inflation rate amounts to 214 percent per year, not 120 percent per year.)

Inflation and the Nominal Interest Rate

Inflation causes high nominal interest rates. The Fisher equation says that the nominal interest rate, R, equals the real interest rate, r, plus the expected rate of inflation, π^e:

$$R = r + \pi^e$$

Suppose that the real interest rate does not change when expected inflation changes. In this case, the equation shows that each 1 percentage point increase in expected inflation raises the nominal interest rate by 1 percentage point. Studies show that the real interest rate does not change, at least not very much, when inflation changes. Some studies show that the real interest rate falls slightly with higher inflation, but the fall in r is smaller than the rise in π^e, so an increase in expected inflation raises the nominal interest rate. Figure 8 shows the nominal interest rate and actual inflation in the United States from 1962 to 1998. When inflation rises, the nominal interest rate tends to rise also, because expected inflation tends to rise. For this reason, countries with high inflation also experience high nominal interest rates.

Following World War I, Germany's currency became virtually worthless. Its value declined so much that parents could allow children to play with actual bundles of money more cheaply than they could buy building blocks.

Daily inflation struggle obsesses Brazil

Nation looks to president-elect for relief from price shock

By Thomas Kamm
Staff Reporter of
The Wall Street Journal

RIO DE JANEIRO—It was a balmy evening in Rio, the sort of weather that invites one to relax at an outdoor cafe in Copacabana or Ipanema and take in the beachfront action.

But on this particular recent evening the hottest spot in town wasn't one of the cafes, bars, or restaurants that line the city's coast. The place to be was the gas station.

"The price of gas is going up 60% at midnight, so I want to fill up my tank before that happens," explained a taxi driver as he pulled into the line at the Petrobras gas station on Copacabana's Avenida Atlantica. It was close to 11:30 p.m. and there were a good 30 cars ahead of him.

"I hope I reach the pump before midnight," he said. "Otherwise, my money will buy only 20 liters instead of 34."

In the 12 months ended in February, consumer prices here increased 2,751 percent. Restaurant patrons complain that the cost of their meals goes up as they eat. Shoppers complain that prices are marked up while they wait in checkout lines.

Sources: New York Times,
The Wall Street Journal

High inflation diverts people's time and resources from producing goods and enjoying life.

Inflation and Foreign Exchange Rates

From 1990 to 1997, Brazil had one of the highest rates of inflation in the world. The price level in 1997 was about *50,000 times* higher than it was in 1990. Over the same period, the price level in the United States rose only about 23 percent. As a result, the *foreign exchange rate* between Brazilian money and U.S. dollars increased by a factor of about 50,000.[12]

> An **exchange rate** is a price of one money in terms of another.

Most countries have their own forms of money. People buy and sell moneys on the foreign exchange market.

Table 1 shows foreign exchange rates between the U.S. dollar and the moneys of some other countries. The first column shows the country and the name of its money. (For example, Argentina uses pesos.) The next two columns show the price of the foreign money in terms of U.S. dollars, and the price of one U.S. dollar in terms of the foreign money. For example, one Japanese yen cost $0.0075, or about three-fourths of one cent. Stated the opposite way, one U.S. dollar cost ¥133. Similarly, one French franc costs about 17.5 cents, and $1 cost about 5.7 French francs.

For clarity, this chapter will refer to the exchange rate as the *price of foreign money*—the amount of domestic currency (such as U.S. dollars) needed to buy one unit of foreign money. This corresponds to the first column of the table. We will use the letter *e* to represent the exchange rate.

---

[12]Brazil had two currency reforms during this period, removing zeros from its money. Brazil's money is now called the *real*.

Figure 8 | Inflation and the Nominal Interest Rate in the United States, 1962–1998

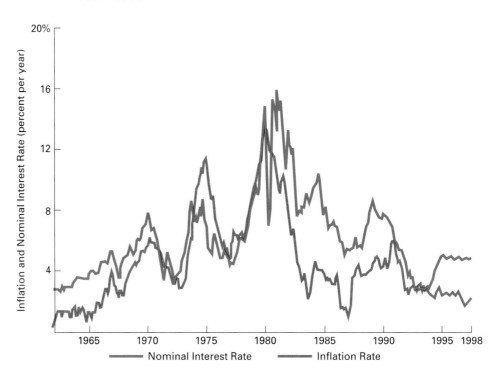

The exchange rate *e* is the price of foreign money—the amount of home money required to buy one unit of foreign money.

(You will sometimes see exchange rates quoted the other way around, as in the second column in Table 1.)

When the exchange rate changes, *appreciation* means that the money becomes more valuable in terms of the other money (*e* falls); *depreciation* means that the money becomes less valuable (*e* rises).

> A currency **appreciates** when less of that currency is needed to buy one unit of foreign money (*e* falls).

> A currency **depreciates** when more of that currency is needed to buy one unit of foreign money (*e* rises).

For example, in January, 1996, about 100 Japanese yen were required to buy 1 U.S. dollar. By September, 1998, about 133 Japanese yen were needed to buy 1 U.S. dollar. Over that period, the yen depreciated, and the U.S. dollar appreciated.

How Exchange Rates Have Changed

Figure 9 shows the change in the exchange rate between the U.S. dollar and the Japanese yen since 1980. This graph shows the exchange rate from Japan's point of view: the Y-axis of the graph shows the *price of dollars* measured in terms of yen. An increase in the exchange rate in the figure means depreciation of the yen and appreciation of the U.S. dollar. The figure also shows the ratio of the price level in Japan to the price level

Table 1 | Exchange Rates, September, 1998

Country and Currency	US$ per Unit of Foreign Money	Units of Foreign Money per US$
	An increase in the number in this column represents *depreciation* of the U.S. dollar and *appreciation* of the foreign money.	An increase in the number in this column represents *depreciation* of the foreign money and *appreciation* of the U.S. dollar.
Argentine Pesos	1.0002	0.9998
Brazilian Real	0.8476	1.1798
British Pounds	1.6771	0.5962
Canadian Dollars	0.6596	1.5161
Chilean Pesos	0.0021219	471.20
Chinese Renmimbi	0.1208	8.2794
French Francs	0.1751	5.7126
German Marks	0.5872	1.7026
Indian Rupees	0.02355	42.451
Italian Lira	0.0005943	1682.9
Japanese Yen	0.007506	133.22
Mexican New Pesos	0.09511	10.514
Russian Rubles	0.1176	8.5000
South Korean Won	0.00072027	1388.4

Updated data are available on the Web page for this book at www.dryden.com

in the United States. Inflation was lower in Japan than in the United States over this period, so that ratio fell over time.

Exchange Rates and Prices

The exchange rate allows people to compare prices in different countries. Suppose that a compact disk costs £8.00 (8 British pounds) in England. If the exchange rate between the British pound and the dollar is $2.50 per pound, then the CD costs

Figure 9 | Exchange Rate: Japan-USA, 1980–1998

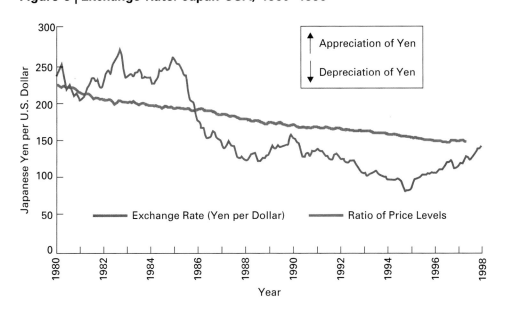

$20.00. To restate a foreign-money price in domestic money, multiply the foreign price by the exchange rate, where the exchange rate is defined as the price of foreign money.

> If P^f is an amount of foreign money and e is the exchange rate (the price of one unit of foreign money), then the equivalent amount of domestic money is eP^f.

In our example, the foreign price Pf is £8.00 and the exchange rate e is $2.50 per pound, so the equivalent dollar price is (£8.00)($2.50/£) = $20.00.

Suppose you see the same CD for sale on two Internet sites. One site, in London, quotes a price of £8.00, and the other site, in the United States, quotes a price of $20.00. Clearly, these two prices are equal if the exchange rate is $2.50 per pound. More generally, let P represent the price of a good in dollars and P^f denote the price in foreign money. The prices are the same if

$$P = eP^f.$$

If P exceeds eP^f then the good is cheaper in the foreign country; if P is less than eP^f then the good is cheaper in the United States.

The equation makes it easy to see how exchange rates are connected to inflation. Because the United States had higher inflation than Japan between 1980 and 1998, prices of goods in the United States increased faster than prices in Japan. If the exchange rate had not changed, U.S. goods would have become more expensive than Japanese goods, leading Americans to buy more from Japan at the lower prices there. Because Americans need yen to buy goods in Japan, this increase in imports raises the demand for yen, raising its price, the exchange rate. As a result, the U.S. dollar depreciated in terms of the yen between 1980 and 1998, as in Figure 9. Notice that while the exchange rate tracks the ratio of price levels on average over the period, it does not track the ratio of price levels every year.

> A country's money tends to *depreciate* on the foreign exchange market if that country has higher inflation than other countries.

Review Questions

8. Describe how a currency reform works. Explain why it changes nominal prices but not relative prices, without affecting real variables.

9. Cite examples of (a) currency reforms and (b) periods of high inflation or hyper-inflation. What caused such high inflation?

10. How does a reverse currency reform resemble inflation?

11. What does it mean to say that a currency depreciates on foreign exchange markets?

Thinking Exercises

12. (a) If the growth rate of the money supply is 1 percent per year, the growth rate of velocity is 2 percent per year, and the growth rate of real GDP is 3 percent per year, what is the equilibrium rate of inflation? (b) If the growth rate of the money supply rises from 1 percent per year to 5 percent per year, what happens to the rate of inflation?

13. If the growth rate of the money supply is 5 percent per year, the growth rate of velocity is 1 percent per year, the growth rate of real GDP is 2 percent per year, and the real interest rate is 3 percent per year, what is the nominal interest rate?

14. You want to buy a T-shirt in Mexico that costs 50 pesos. If the exchange rate is $0.10 per peso, how many dollars does the T-shirt cost? A hotel in Italy charges 64,000 lira for a room for the night. If the exchange rate is 1,600 lira per dollar, what is the price of the room in dollars?

WHAT AFFECTS— AND DOESN'T AFFECT— INFLATION?

The equation of exchange, in its percentage-change form, is the key equation for inflation. Anything that raises inflation must either raise the growth rate of the money supply, raise the growth rate of velocity, or reduce the growth rate of real GDP. This section discusses commonly cited forces that do—and do not—cause inflation.

News reporters and commentators often blame inflation on some special forces that affect relative prices. However, these special forces may not affect the overall price level, which is an average of the nominal prices of the economy's goods and services. While relative prices depend on the supplies and demands for particular goods and services, the economy's price level is determined by the supply and demand for money.

A second common fallacy confuses a high price level with a rising price level. Some factor, such as a low level of real GDP, may cause the price level to be high without causing it to continue to rise. The words *high* and *rising* do not mean the same thing! For example, the equation $P = MV/y$ implies a high price level associated with low real GDP. It also implies that the price level rises when real GDP falls. It does not say, however, that the price level *rises* due to a low *level* of real GDP, so it does not say that a low level of real GDP causes inflation. An analogy may help to explain the distinction. If you maintain a high effort level in a class, you will likely receive high grades on exams. However, a high level of effort does not imply that your exam grades will *increase* as the class continues. Improving grades would require *increases* in effort as the class continues. *High* levels of effort and *increasing* levels of effort are not the same thing.

Any change in conditions can raise inflation if that change causes the government to raise the growth rate of the money supply. Similarly, any change in conditions can raise the price level, raising inflation temporarily, if it causes people to reduce the quantity of money they demand, raising velocity. Except as indicated, the following paragraphs assume that the government does not change the money supply.

Suggested Causes of Inflation

1. Greed

Business firms want high profits, but greed for high profits does not cause inflation. Two fallacies mar the reasoning that greed causes inflation. First, sellers almost always want more profits. If sellers could increase their profits by raising their prices, they would already have done so![13] While greed might make prices high, it does not cause prices to continually *increase* over time. (The assertion to the contrary is an example of the fallacy of equating high prices with rising prices.) The episodes of hyperinflation discussed earlier did not occur because sellers suddenly became greedy—they were *always* greedy, looking for the highest profits they could capture. Nor did the episodes end because sellers suddenly became

---

[13] Why doesn't a seller increase its profits by raising its prices? Because the seller would lose enough sales to competitors, including sellers of other, substitute products, that raising prices would not increase its profits. That is, sellers charge the prices that give them the highest profits they can get, so any further price increases would reduce profits by changing prices from their profit-maximizing levels.

less greedy. Similarly, the fall in U.S. inflation from over 5 percent in 1991 to 2 percent in 1998 did not occur because sellers' greed decreased; greed has nothing to do with inflation.

The second fallacy in the claim that greed causes inflation results from ignoring equilibrium between the quantity of money demanded and quantity supplied. If the nominal money supply, velocity, and real GDP do not change, then the equilibrium price level does not change. Only factors that affect the growth rates of money, velocity, or real GDP can affect inflation.

2. Monopoly Sellers

Monopoly sellers charge higher prices than sellers that face more competition, but monopolies do not cause inflation. The idea that they do suffers from the same two fallacies as the idea that greed causes inflation. First, it confuses high levels of prices with increasing prices, as discussed above. A monopoly does not continually raise prices; it charges the price that gives it the highest profit and keeps its price at that level.

Second, the idea that monopolies cause inflation ignores equilibrium between the demand and supply of money, confusing relative prices with the price level. A monopoly charges a high *relative* price, but the equilibrium price level averages *nominal* prices of goods and services. It reflects equilibrium between the quantities of money demanded and supplied, as in the equation of exchange.

3. Low Productivity

Low productivity means that real GDP is lower than it would otherwise be (with higher productivity). Low productivity, therefore, means that the price level is higher than it would otherwise be, but not that the price level is *increasing*. Low productivity does not cause inflation.

A low *growth rate* of productivity, however, may cause a low growth rate of real GDP and therefore a high rate of inflation. The percentage change equation shows that high inflation occurs with a low growth rate of real GDP. However, a change in productivity growth has only a small effect on inflation. For example, a 1 percentage point fall in the growth rate of real GDP, from 3 percent per year to 2 percent per year (a large fall in the growth rate of real GDP), raises inflation by only 1 percentage point, such as from 3 percent per year to 4 percent per year. As a result, changes in the growth rate of real GDP explain only a small fraction of changes in real-life inflation. Similarly, differences among countries' growth rates of real GDP explain only small fractions of differences in inflation rates between countries.

4. Government Regulations

Government regulations, like low productivity, may cause low real GDP and a high price level. Regulations cause a *rising* price level, however, only if they reduce the growth rate (not just the level) of real GDP. As in the case of low productivity growth, regulations have a very small effect on inflation.

5. Increase in the Price of an Important Good

News reporters and commentators often say that inflation results from an increase in the price of some particular good or set of goods. Such a statement is usually a mistake. An increase in the price of any particular good or service can cause inflation only if it raises the growth rate of money or the growth rate of velocity, or if it reduces the growth rate of real GDP.

It is easy to see why someone might make this mistake. Whenever inflation occurs, most prices rise, so someone might easily think, incorrectly, that the price increases cause inflation when, in fact, the price increases *are* inflation. Saying that a price increase causes inflation is like saying that falling raindrops cause rain.[14]

IN THE NEWS

Auto insurance, clothing push consumer prices up

Inflation advances

Sharp increases in the cost of clothing and auto insurance helped send inflation back into the 5 percent annual range last month.

Food price rises push up inflation

Sharper price increases for food were the main influence behind the rise in inflation last month, official figures showed yesterday.

Sources: Washington Post, Financial Times

Fallacies about inflation in the news media.

---

[14]A similar fallacy states that unemployment is caused by people losing their jobs, a famous observation of President Calvin Coolidge.

Think about a change in demand. If people decide to eat more vegetables and less meat than before, then the demand for vegetables rises and the demand for meat falls. This raises the *relative* price of vegetables and reduces the *relative* price of meat, but it does not change the overall price level, because the money supply, velocity, and real GDP do not change. The nominal price of vegetables rises, but the nominal price of meat *falls,* leaving the overall price level roughly unaffected.

6. High Wages

High wages, perhaps due to strong unions, do not cause inflation. The idea that they do confuses levels with changes, as discussed earlier. High wages might cause high prices, or vice versa, but high wages do not cause *rising* prices.

Increases in wages can raise the price of a good by reducing its supply. An *increase* in union power could raise wages throughout the economy and reduce employment. Figure 10 shows the demand for labor by firms, which depends on the *real wage* (the purchasing power of the nominal wage). Figure 10 represents the real wage by the nominal (money) wage, W, divided by the price level, P. If the money wage, W, and the price level, P, rise by the same percentage (for example, if they both double), then the purchasing power of the wage, the real wage, remains unchanged.

If unions raise the nominal wage from W_1 to W_2 when the price level does not change, the real wage rises from W_1/P to W_2/P, and the quantity of labor demanded falls from L_1 to L_2. This reduces employment from L_1 to L_2 and increases unemployment. This fall in employment reduces the economy's total output of goods and services, real GDP, which raises the equilibrium price level. As a result, the economy experiences *cost-push inflation* (inflation due to an increase in wages or other costs of production) as the price level rises to reach its new, higher equilibrium level. However, this inflation is only temporary; it stops when the price level reaches a new, higher level associated with the lower level of real GDP. In addition, this effect is small in real life. Even a permanent 2 percent fall in real GDP, which would be fairly large compared to most real-life changes in real GDP, would raise the price level permanently by only 2 percent, temporarily adding 2 percentage points to inflation. This increase in inflation is small compared to most real-life inflation experiences.

Cost-push inflation may also occur for a second reason. The increase in unemployment resulting from an increase in wages above the equilibrium level might lead the government to increase the money supply.[15] Such an increase in the money supply, sometimes said to "validate the wage increase," would raise the price level. The rise in the price level in turn would reduce the real wage (the increase in P would reduce W/P), raising the quantity of labor demanded, and employment, back to L_1, and reducing unemployment. Although firms would pay higher nominal wages than before, they could also charge higher prices for their products, allowing them to hire L_1 workers.

If unions and the government act this way, a wage–price spiral can result. Unions see that the increase in the price level reduces the real wage, so they raise nominal wages again. Similarly, the government may again increase the money supply, further raising the price level. Inflation continues, and the rate may even increase, until either the unions or the government change their behavior. While the wage–price spiral may be important in some episodes of inflation, especially in countries with strong unions that operate in many industries, it is not the main explanation for most episodes of inflation. Evidence shows no strong connection between a country's rate of inflation and the strength of its unions.[16]

7. Rising Interest Rates

Sometimes people claim that inflation results from rising interest rates. They see interest

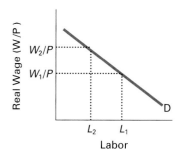

**Figure 10
Demand for Labor**

IN THE NEWS

Higher pay may be pushing up prices

Our wages and benefits are rising at a faster pace and may soon land in shopping bags as slightly higher prices.

Robert Dederick, chief economist at Northern Trust Co. in Chicago, says you can bet businesses "will certainly make every effort to pass those costs on to consumers."

Source: USA Today

Another fallacy about inflation in the news media—the article never mentions the fact that the price level will increase only if the government raises the money supply.

---

[15]Later chapters will discuss possible reasons for this reaction.

[16]Of course, wages do usually rise with prices during inflation, but this effect is part of the process of inflation (as rain drops are part of the process of rain), not a cause of inflation.

IN THE NEWS

Inflation Stays Under Control

Washington—Inflation stayed under control in July, helped in part by falling prices for energy, produce and telephone service.

Despite labor shortages that have begun to drive up wages—which can prompt price increases from companies seeking to maintain their profits—inflation has remained contained. It's running at a 1.6 percent annual rate this year, compared to 1.7 percent for all of last year. That's partly because hard times in other countries have dampened world demand for many products, lowering prices on commodities from gasoline to coffee.

Source: Associated Press

Find the economic errors in this news article.

rates as a cost of doing business, so rising interest rates seem to them to raise business costs and create higher prices. This argument confuses relative prices with the nominal price level by forgetting that the equilibrium nominal price level is determined by the equation between the supply and demand for money. A rise in the nominal interest rate is more likely to *result* from an increase in inflation (as discussed earlier) than to cause that increase.

8. Government Budget Deficits

Government budget deficits can cause inflation in two ways. When the government spends more than it collects in taxes, it must choose from two options:

1. Print money to spend in excess of its tax revenue.

2. Borrow money to spend in excess of its tax revenue.

If the government prints money, the money supply and the price level increase. In this way, a deficit causes temporary inflation, and deficits that continue year after year can create continuing inflation, if the government finances them by printing money.

If the government borrows money to finance its deficit, the increased demand for loans can raise the interest rate, which, in turn, raises the velocity of money and therefore the price level. An earlier chapter discussed the effects of a government budget deficit, which raises the real interest rate unless people save all the money that they get from the tax cut.

Government budget deficits and inflation show no close relationship in the United States, however. For example, inflation in the United States decreased during the 1980s as government budget deficits rose. In some countries, though, particularly less developed countries, governments often finance budget deficits by printing money, and deficits and inflation tend to occur together.

9. International Competition

Sometimes people claim that increases in international competition hold down inflation, because sellers cannot then raise prices without losing business to those foreign sellers. This incorrect claim confuses relative prices with nominal prices. An increase in international competition in the automobile industry reduces the relative price of automobiles, but has no direct effect on the nominal price level, unless it affects the money supply, velocity, or real GDP.

IN THE NEWS

Keener competition among producers keeps price increases, inflation at bay

By Erle Norton and
David Wessel
Staff Reporters of
The Wall Street Journal

In most recoveries, companies use increased demand as an excuse to raise prices—and with them, the inflation rate. But not this time.

The difference is intense competition. In this recov-ery, producers have been plagued by a fear that cutthroat rivals will rob them of market share if they raise prices. That market-share mentality, particularly in industries without dominant producers, has fostered intense competition that outweighs the normal tendency toward higher prices and profit margins.

Producers in many industries—diaper makers, tire manufacturers, food companies, clothing peddlers and electronics concerns, among others—are complaining that competition has kept price increases off the books. That keeps inflation at bay.

Source: The Wall Street Journal

Find the economic errors in this news article.

Review Questions

15. Explain the effects on inflation of:
    (a) Greed
    (b) Low productivity
    (c) An increase in international competition
    (d) High wages
    (e) A fall in the government budget deficit

Thinking Exercises

16. What would happen if unions were to raise wages, sellers were to raise nominal prices to "pass along the higher wage costs to consumers," and the money supply were to remain unchanged?

17. Identify at least one error in economics in the news article, "Keener Competition among Producers Keeps Price Increases, Inflation at Bay." Explain why it is an error.

Winners and Losers

EFFECTS OF INFLATION

Some people lose from inflation, but others gain. Everyone who holds money loses, because the real value of the money (its purchasing power) falls.

> The loss that people suffer when inflation reduces the purchasing power of their assets is called the **inflation tax.**

Inflation acts like a tax on holding money. Your money loses 10 percent of its value if prices rise 10 percent. You suffer the same loss as if you were required to give 10 percent of your money to the government as a tax payment.

The government gains when it prints money, because it can spend the money. Saying that "the government gains" really means that certain people gain—those people who benefit from whatever the government buys with the money. Suppose that the government raises the money supply by 10 percent, raising prices 10 percent. The government's gain from printing money equals 10 percent of the money supply. Because prices rise 10 percent, the money that people already have in their wallets loses 10 percent of its value. In this way, the people who hold money pay an inflation tax equal to 10 percent of the money supply. The gain to the government from the inflation tax equals the losses to holders of money.

Unexpected Inflation

If inflation is unexpected—if prices rise more rapidly than people thought they would—then it creates winners and losers:

▸ Debtors (people who have borrowed money) gain.

▸ Creditors (people who have loaned money) lose.

Debtors gain because they repay loans in dollars with lower purchasing power than the dollars they borrowed. They repay the same number of dollars, but each dollar buys fewer goods, so inflation reduces the purchasing power of the debt repayment. Unexpected inflation reduces the opportunity cost of paying off the loan. Creditors lose what debtors gain, because they collect dollars with lower purchasing power than those they lent.

Similarly, if inflation is lower than people had expected, debtors lose and creditors gain. The nominal interest rate reflects the inflation rate that people had expected, so unexpectedly low inflation means that the nominal interest rate overcompensates lenders for their loss in purchasing power.

Expected Inflation

When inflation is fully expected—when people correctly anticipate the actual rate of inflation—the nominal interest rate exceeds the real interest rate by the rate of inflation. In this way, the interest rate on the loan rises enough to offset the reduction in purchasing power of the dollars with which the borrower repays the loan. Even though each dollar that a borrower repays to a lender buys fewer goods due to inflation, the rise in the nominal interest rate requires borrowers to pay enough to counteract that loss in purchasing power. Neither debtors nor creditors gain or lose from fully expected inflation.

Indexing Contracts

Unexpected increases in inflation help debtors at the expense of creditors only if loans are not *indexed* to inflation. A wage is indexed to inflation if the nominal wage automatically changes with the price level (that is, if the wage contract specifies a cost-of-living adjustment, or COLA). With complete indexing, the nominal wage rises by the same percentage as the price level, keeping the real wage constant. Most wages in the United States and (most) other countries are *not* indexed to inflation. However, social security payments in the United States are indexed to inflation: Increases in the price level automatically raise nominal social security payments.

When a wage is *not* indexed to inflation, an unexpected increase in inflation reduces the real wage, so firms gain and workers lose. Similarly, an unexpected fall in inflation raises the real wage, so workers gain and firms lose.

Is Inflation Bad?

If inflation worked exactly like a reverse currency reform, no one would care much about it. After all, nominal prices are not very important. In a currency reform, all nominal prices change, but nothing real changes: relative prices, real GDP, and people's real incomes remain unaffected.

Most people think that inflation is bad because rising prices reduce the amount of goods that people can afford. This statement is true for an individual with a fixed income, but it is false for society as a whole. Inflation does not necessarily make society, as a whole, poorer. A country's real income is its real GDP, which is determined primarily by technology, available inputs, and other factors that do not respond to changes in nominal prices. In the long run, at least, the government cannot affect real GDP simply by printing *pieces of paper* called money.

Some economists, in fact, believe that inflation is *not* very important as long as it remains steady so that everyone can learn to expect it and adjust to it. In that case, inflation does not redistribute income from creditors to debtors. Although people lose from inflation as the purchasing power of their money falls (the inflation tax), the government gains by printing the extra money that causes prices to rise. In this case, the inflation tax is like any other tax, and the government must collect *some* taxes, after all, to finance its spending. According to this view, steady inflation has little or no effect on the economy's real income, so steady inflation is not a serious problem as long as the rate does not become too high (not above about 2 or 3 percent per year, for example).

Other economists believe that inflation is a serious problem that creates economic inefficiencies and harms people. Inflation differs from a reverse currency reform, because it redistributes income and continually changes the basic unit of measurement for prices, the dollar (or yen, franc, or peso). A currency reform changes the

IN THE NEWS

Inflation: Some like it

Just when you thought inflation was history, here it comes again. But while most of us nervously await its arrival, some are secretly rolling out the red carpet.

They're the USA's closet inflation-lovers, the ones for whom the gains of rising prices outweigh the losses.

To the rest of us, though, inflation is still a bogeyman. "Inflation is bad and has a very insidious effect in that it erodes value while people aren't looking," says Wayne Gantt, an economist at SunTrust Banks Inc. in Atlanta. "For every winner in inflation, there's a loser."

Source: USA Today

Some people gain from inflation.

IN THE NEWS

Argentina in chaos as prices rise hourly

By James Brooke
Special to
The New York Times

BUENOS AIRES— "Weimar Germany never had an I.B.M. computer," Adrián Rodríguez Boero said today, explaining with a wry smile how he manages to keep his supermarket ahead of Argentina's annual inflation rate of 12,000 percent.

"Every four hours, these prices lose 1 percent of their value," he said, surveying the well-stocked aisles of the Disco supermarket. With all produce tagged with bar codes, the prices are adjusted daily on a central computer.

The rub for Argentines is that their salaries do not increase by 1 percent every four hours.

In the last week, food prices jumped 27 percent. With food climbing out of reach, poor people responded by sacking hundreds of food stores across the nation.

The riots have left 15 people dead and about 80 wounded. In addition, about 1,700 people have been arrested around the country.

Here, at the Disco in downtown Buenos Aires, shoppers pushed loaded carts through the aisles in panic shopping.

"People want their money in something solid," Mr. Rodríguez Boero said, grasping a box of oatmeal for emphasis.

Source: New York Times

Redistributions of income caused by inflation create social problems.

IN THE NEWS

When inflation runs out of control, when no one really knows if next month's inflation will be 50 or 500 percent, only the most rudimentary transactions can take place in the currency.

Turning to Dollars

Generally, of course, wages go up almost as fast as prices or people wouldn't be able to survive. But the uncertainty wreaks havoc on the daily lives of ordinary people.

That explains why Latin American economies in the midst of hyperinflation typically end up using United States dollars as the medium of exchange, whether or not government authorities make such transactions legal. It also explains why the remedy for hyperinflation usually combines a change in the name and look of the local currency with more tangible measures to rebuild confidence in the economy.

Source: New York Times

Inflation creates uncertainty and erodes confidence.

amount of money that everyone has in the same proportion, but inflation redistributes income. When the government prints additional money, most people don't get any! Furthermore, critics of inflation point out, low and predictable inflation might not be a serious problem; however, few if any real-life episodes of inflation have stayed low and predictable over any sustained period of time. While a relatively harmless low and predictable inflation is a theoretical possibility, it may be difficult to maintain in real life.

We can summarize the main points on both sides. Inflation may be *bad* for several reasons:

▶ Inflation wastes valuable time and resources as people adjust to rising prices. For example, inflation raises the nominal interest rate and reduces the quantity of money demanded, raising velocity and reducing the benefits of money as a convenient method of payment. During hyperinflation, people try to spend the money they receive very quickly before it loses value. Sometimes they resort to barter and other inefficient methods of trade.

▶ Inflation wastes resources in financial markets by creating costly new methods for people to avoid personal losses due to inflation.

▶ Inflation is like changing the length of an inch every year or continually changing the definition of a pound or a quart. Inflation distorts nominal prices and prevents people from easily comparing prices of different goods at different times. This leads people and business firms to make mistakes in their economic decisions, creating inefficiencies.

▶ Inflation creates uncertainty that causes economic inefficiency. For reasons that economists do not yet fully understand, high rates of inflation are more variable and unpredictable than low rates. People generally dislike the increased uncertainty associated with inflation.

▶ Inflation raises certain taxes in a subtle way without an open and honest government policy of raising taxes.

▶ Unexpected inflation harms people by redistributing income. It penalizes people who work and save, because savers usually become creditors who lose from unexpected inflation. Similarly, the redistributions caused by inflation take from some people and give to others with no regard for either property rights or any notions of fairness.

On the other hand, inflation may have *good* effects. People may feel happier, perhaps irrationally, when their nominal wages rise, even if their real wages remain constant (because their nominal wage increases merely compensate them for price-level increases).

Suppressed Inflation

Many governments have imposed price and wage controls to try to reduce inflation, often while they were printing money at rapid rates.

> **Suppressed inflation** refers to inflation that would occur without government controls on wages and prices, but that does not fully occur due to those controls.

Government efforts to suppress inflation have a long history. The money supply in the Roman Empire rose rapidly starting in A.D. 296 under Emperor Diocletian, causing the Roman inflation mentioned in the introduction to this chapter. In response, Diocletian issued a famous Edict on Maximum Prices that set maximum legal prices on 900 goods and maximum legal wages for 130 types of work, imposing the death penalty for violations on both buyers and sellers. These wage and price controls failed to stop inflation, although numerous people were executed before Diocletian abdicated the throne. Almost 1,700 years later, President Nixon imposed price controls in the United States in 1971 when the country's inflation rate reached 4.5 percent per year. Between the Roman and U.S. episodes, many other tries at price controls (often during wartime bouts of inflation) nearly always created shortages and economic inefficiencies, led to black markets (illegal transactions to avoid the controls), and ultimately failed to stop inflation.[17] A recent attempt to control inflation with price controls began in Russia in 1998, when the government imposed price controls on food and other items in an attempt to prevent inflation while it began increasing the money supply more rapidly.

Review Questions

18. Who gains from inflation? Who loses? Does the answer depend on whether inflation is expected or unexpected? Why?

19. Is inflation bad? Defend both *yes* and *no* answers to this question.

IN THE NEWS

Moscow puts price controls on food

Now merchants struggle along with their customers

MOSCOW—In this time of crisis, store manager Farik Dabibov is having trouble remaining diplomatic about a decision by Moscow's mayor to control the price of baby food. "It's going to be a serious problem, and our salaries are going to get cut," said Dabibov, a store manager with a baby goods chain in Moscow. "Now we're just waiting to see what the government is going to do with us next."

Mayor Yuri Luzhkov decreed Tuesday that city retailers may not mark up basic food products by more than 20 percent, at least until Nov. 1. The list includes 27 categories such as sausage, cooking oil, sugar, matches—and baby food. Many small stores already pummeled by the crisis said the decree would push them closer to bankruptcy. "It's turning my work into a total mess," said Mikhail Kochetkov, who runs a small market. "I think about 20 percent of businesses will survive the decree. We're certainly not going to survive."

Source: Associated Press

Price controls will create shortages without stopping the underlying causes of inflation.

IN THE NEWS

Russia's New Government to Print Rubles to Pay Debts

MOSCOW—Russia's new Communist-influenced government indicated Thursday that it plans to satisfy old debts and bail out old friends by printing billions of new rubles, a decision that drew a swift and strong reaction from President Boris Yeltsin's capitalist allies.

Hours later in Washington, Deputy Treasury Secretary Lawrence Summers told a House subcommittee that Russia was heading toward a return of the four-digit inflation rates that savaged consumers and almost toppled Yeltsin's government in 1993. Russia's new leaders cannot repeal "basic economic laws," he said. "They must resist pressures to spend and lend which will doom the economy to another bout of high, perhaps hyperinflation."

Source: New York Times

As this textbook went to press, Russia had just announced that it would start increasing the supply of money. Has Russia followed through with this plan? Has inflation in Russia increased?

---

[17]Some people argue for wage and price controls in periods of high inflation on the grounds that by enacting them, a government shows people it is serious about reducing inflation. This action could help reduce expected inflation, reducing the nominal interest rate and the velocity of money and helping to hold down price increases until the government can attack inflation in other ways. However, wage and price controls can create serious distortions in the economy, and they cannot ultimately reduce inflation unless the government also reduces the rate of growth of the money supply. Moreover, if people view wage and price controls as a desperate measure or an indication that the government lacks the political will to fight inflation by reducing the rate of money growth, then wage and price controls may actually raise inflationary expectations and compound the difficulty of stopping it.

A fascinating history of wage and price controls appears in Robert Schuettinger and Eamonn Butler, *Forty Centuries of Wage and Price Controls: How Not to Fight Inflation* (Thornwood, N.Y.: Caroline House, 1979).

Thinking Exercises

20. How does inflation impose a tax? What does it tax? Who collects the tax revenue?

21. Explain why fully expected inflation does not redistribute income from creditors to debtors.

Conclusion

Definitions and Basic Model

Nominal variables are quantities measured in units of money (U.S. dollars, Mexican pesos, etc.). In contrast, *real* variables are quantities measured in units of goods and services or in units of base-year money. *Nominal* prices are money prices of goods and services. *Relative* prices are the opportunity costs of goods, measured in terms of other goods. Inflation, a continuing increase in the (nominal) price level, refers to changes in *nominal* variables, not (necessarily) *real* variables such as relative prices.

The circular flow diagram of economic activity illustrates the equation of exchange, $MV = Py$, where M is the nominal money supply, V is velocity, P is the price level, and y is real GDP. The equation of exchange implies that the price level can be expressed as $P = MV/y$.

Supply and Demand for Money

The government controls the nominal money supply, defined as the total dollar value of all paper money and coins in the economy. Money is just one among many assets that people can own. Each asset has costs and benefits. A benefit of owning money is that you can spend it at a store. However, money does not pay interest. The nominal interest rate measures the opportunity cost of holding money (rather than putting the money in a bank account or lending it).

The *relative price of money* in terms of goods is the opportunity cost of money—the number of goods you sacrifice for each unit of money you keep (rather than spending). The relative price of money in terms of goods equals $1/P$, the inverse of the price level. The *quantity of money demanded* at some relative price of money, is the amount of money that people would choose to own, given current conditions such as their income and wealth, the usefulness of money, and the costs and benefits of owning other assets. Evidence shows that the nominal quantity of money demanded is proportional to the price level. It rises as real GDP rises, and falls as the nominal interest rate rises.

Economists summarize the demand for money with a formula that defines the quantity of money demanded as proportional to GDP, $M^d = Py/V$. Increases in the nominal interest rate raise the velocity of money, so they reduce the demand for money. The equilibrium price level, the price level for which the quantity of money demanded equals the quantity supplied, can be expressed as $P = MV/y$. The equilibrium price level rises with increases in the money supply and velocity, and falls with increases in real GDP.

Currency Reforms

A currency reform occurs when the government of a country replaces an old unit of money with a new unit of money and automatically adjusts all nominal values in existing contracts (such as nominal wages and debts) for the change in money to keep real values the same. Each unit of new money is usually worth more than a unit of old money. (The new money often crosses off several zeros from the old money.) A reverse currency reform would add zeros to money, effectively raising the nominal money supply and nominal prices. Inflation resembles a reverse currency reform, except that inflation may create winners and losers by redistributing income in ways that a currency reform does not.

Equilibrium Inflation

The equilibrium rate of inflation is the growth rate of the equilibrium price level. It equals the growth rate of the nominal money supply, plus the growth rate of velocity, minus the growth rate of real GDP. Over long periods of time, inflation and the growth rate of the money supply are closely related. Over short periods of time, however, they are not closely related. High rates of inflation raise the nominal interest rate.

An exchange rate is a price of one money in terms of another. A currency appreciates when its value rises in terms of foreign money, so that fewer units of the currency are required to buy one unit of foreign money. A currency depreciates when its value falls in terms of foreign money. A country's money tends to depreciate on the foreign exchange market if that country runs higher inflation than other countries.

What Affects—and Doesn't Affect—Inflation?

Anything that raises inflation must either raise the growth rate of the money supply, raise the growth rate of velocity, or reduce the growth rate of real GDP. News commentators commonly blame inflation on special forces that do not affect those variables; their assertions involve a fallacy of confusing changes in relative prices with changes in the price level, which is an average of nominal prices. In another common source of error, people often confuse a high price level with a rising price level, although the words *high* and *rising* have different meanings.

These fallacies explain why the greed of business firms, the actions of monopoly sellers, low levels of productivity, and high levels of government regulation do not cause inflation. Similarly, they explain why an increase in the price of a particular good, however important that good, need not cause inflation unless it accompanies a fall in the economy's overall real GDP. For the same reasons, high wages do not cause inflation. *Increases* in wages, however, may lead the government to raise the nominal money supply, and in this way, create inflation. Increased foreign competition reduces the relative prices of products experiencing that competition, but increased foreign competition does not directly affect the (nominal) price level or inflation.

Effects of Inflation

Some people lose and others gain from inflation. Everyone who holds money loses, because inflation reduces the purchasing power of money. This loss is the inflation tax. The government collects revenue from the inflation tax, because it prints and spends the money that causes the inflation. The government also gains from inflation, because some taxes (those not indexed to the price level) automatically rise with inflation.

Unexpected inflation redistributes income from creditors to debtors. Debtors gain from unexpectedly high inflation, because they repay loans in dollars with lower purchasing power; creditors lose what debtors gain. When people fully expect inflation, in contrast, the nominal interest rate exceeds the real interest rate by the rate of inflation, and the higher nominal interest rate offsets the reduction in purchasing power. Although each dollar that a borrower repays buys fewer goods because of inflation, borrowers pay sufficiently more dollars that they do not gain, and creditors do not lose, from fully expected inflation.

Unexpected inflation can redistribute income from workers to firms if previously-set nominal wages do not automatically rise with prices. Similarly, unexpected inflation can redistribute income away from certain people such as retirees who live on pensions fixed in nominal terms.

If inflation worked exactly like a reverse currency reform, no one would care much about it. However, high, unexpected inflation can disrupt the economy by creating massive redistributions of income. Suppressed inflation can create serious economic inefficiencies. Economists disagree, however, over the question of whether low, steady inflation poses a serious problem.

Key Terms

nominal variable	inflation	currency reform	depreciation
real variable	nominal money supply	equilibrium rate of inflation	inflation tax
nominal price	quantity of money demanded	exchange rate	suppressed inflation
relative price	equilibrium price level	appreciation	

Questions and Problems

22. How is an increase in the growth rate of the nominal money supply likely to affect the nominal interest rate?

23. Comment on this statement: "If the demand for money rises over time, then eventually the government will be forced to increase the supply."

24. Suppose that velocity rises at 1 percent per year and real GDP grows at a rate of 2 percent per year. If the money supply rises at 6 percent per year, what is the equilibrium rate of inflation?

25. Suppose that velocity is constant and real GDP grows at a rate of 2 percent per year.
    (a) Explain why the government can increase the money supply at a rate of 2 percent per year without causing inflation.
    (b) Note that the government can spend the new money it prints. Who loses the purchasing power that the government gets from printing money? What would happen—and who would gain—if the government did not raise the money supply at a rate of 2 percent per year?

26. A counterfeiter prints money and spends it. Does this activity hurt anyone? Explain.

27. Comment on this situation: In an old movie, Doris Day plays a teenager whose father is a banker. Her boyfriend, trying to impress her father, asks him for

a $10 bill and then tears it up, saying, "See? Money is really worthless! Even though I have destroyed this money, there is no less food, clothing, cars, houses, or love in the world than there was before!" Doris's father is not impressed. Is the boyfriend correct? Who (if anyone) gained or lost when he tore up the money?

28. Discuss the following quotation from Milton and Rose Friedman:

    Money is a veil. The "real" forces that determine the wealth of a nation are the capacities of its citizens, their industry and ingenuity, the resources at their command, their mode of economic and political organization, and the like.[18]

29. An airline ticket from London to New York costs $400 in the United States or £300 in England. Where is it cheaper to buy the ticket? (Use Table 1.)

30. Discuss the likely effects of suppressed inflation.

31. *Disinflation* means a fall in the (positive) rate of inflation. Who gains and who loses from disinflation? *Deflation* refers to negative inflation (a falling price level). What could cause deflation? Who would win and who would lose from deflation?

Inquiries for Further Thought

32. Is inflation good or bad? Is deflation (negative inflation) good or bad? If both are bad, why are both increases *and* decreases in the price level problems? What is so good about the current price level that makes you want to keep it?

33. Why isn't every nominal wage indexed for inflation? Why don't people have cost-of-living adjustments for everything?

34. Discuss this statement:

    Inflation is a disease, a dangerous and sometimes fatal disease, a disease that if not checked in time can destroy a society. Examples abound.

    Hyperinflations in Russia and Germany after World War I . . . prepared the ground for communism in one country and nazism in the other. The hyperinflation in China after World War II eased Chairman Mao's defeat of Chiang Kai-shek.[19]

35. Why do people in the United States use dollars and not Swiss francs? Why don't Canadians and Mexicans use U.S. dollars in their every day trades? Why will many Europeans soon use Euros, rather than dollars, Swiss francs, or Russian rubles?

---

[18] Milton Friedman and Rose Friedman, *Free to Choose* (New York: Harcourt Brace, 1979), p. 238.
[19] Ibid., p. 242.

CHAPTER 29

MONEY AND FINANCIAL INTERMEDIARIES

In this Chapter...
Main Points to Understand

▶ Money is a medium of exchange, a store of value, and a unit of account. Important measures of the money supply include M1, M2, and the monetary base.

▶ The Federal Reserve—the U.S. central bank—controls the money supply, mainly through open-market operations.

▶ Actions of banks and depositors affect M1 and M2, creating a money multiplier.

▶ Financial intermediaries play important roles in the market for loans, creating connections between the monetary system and the loan market.

▶ Actions of the Fed to change the money supply can have short-run effects on the *real* interest rate.

Thinking Skills to Develop

▶ Understand connections between different markets, such as the money market and the loans market.

▶ Understand how actions of various groups, such as the Fed, banks, and depositors, can interact to determine the sizes of M1 and M2.

▶ Recognize the roles of financial intermediaries and the economic problems associated with them.

▶ Understand the incentives created by deposit insurance and the resulting economic problems.

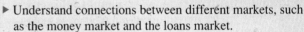

How would you like to grow your own money? In some southern colonies before the American Revolution, people did. Tobacco functioned as money, and people could literally grow their own money with which to buy other goods.

Today, people think of money mainly as paper notes printed by the government. Throughout much of the 19th century in the United States, however, people used paper money created by regular private banks. Each bank's money was a little different from others. (Imagine owning your own bank, printing your own money with your picture on it, and watching people spend your money to buy groceries!) Today, people use paper money issued by the government, as well as checks and electronic money on the Internet, but banks still affect the money supply. Banks, in fact, play important roles not only in the monetary system but also in the market for loans. When these roles are disrupted, the economic effects can devastate people's lives, as in the 1997–1998 financial crises in Japan, Russia, Indonesia, South Korea, Malaysia, the Philippines, and Thailand. Although the government's monetary policies may profoundly affect your life, few people know much about the Federal Reserve System, the independent U.S. government agency that controls that policy. This chapter will introduce the Federal Reserve, its operations, and its monetary policy tools.

HISTORY AND ROLES OF MONEY

While the economic model developed in previous chapters treats money as paper notes printed by the government, real-life "money" includes checks and other means of payment. Systems of money and payments have changed frequently throughout history, and our current system is likely to continue to change in the future.

Money and Barter

Not all civilizations have used money, and certainly not all used money as people know it today. Some primitive societies relied mainly on barter. In ancient Egypt, people paid taxes by giving goods, not money, to the government. The same was true in medieval Europe under the feudal system; serfs paid goods rather than money to lords. Barter was common during the Middle Ages, except for international trade. In America, money transactions began to replace barter during the 16th century.

Advantages of Money over Barter

People use money because it is more convenient than barter. It avoids the problem of creating a *double coincidence of wants* in which you find a trading partner who wants to sell goods that you want to buy *and* wants to buy goods that you want to sell. A modern economy cannot function well if every trade requires a double coincidence of wants. Can you imagine professors trying to barter lectures on chemistry or economics for food and rent, or computer programmers trading their services for movie tickets and gasoline? Money simplifies trading. People can sell goods for money and then spend that money to buy the goods they want from other sellers. A monetary transaction does not require a double coincidence of wants. This function is the main role of money: as a medium of exchange.

> A **medium of exchange** is an asset that sellers generally accept as payment for goods, services, and other assets.

Money also acts as a store of value and a unit of account.

> A **store of value** is any good or asset that people can store while it maintains some or all of its value.

Many goods can serve as stores of value, although goods such as gold and land function better than others, such as perishable food, by maintaining their values better over time. Any good that people use as a medium of exchange must be an effective store of value; otherwise it could lose its value between the time you earn it and the time you spend it.

Money also serves as a unit of account:

> A **unit of account** is a measure for stating prices.

The unit of account in the United States is the dollar: People quote prices in dollars. When buyers and sellers negotiate prices, they discuss dollar amounts. A unit of account requires a homogeneous good—all units of it must be roughly equivalent, like ounces of gold or paper money. In contrast, shoes would be a poor unit of account because they are not all alike. Throughout history, the kinds of goods that have served as money have been reliable stores of value and effective units of account.

Types of Money

Although people exchange paper money and coins today, cigarettes served as money in World War II prisoner-of-war camps and in Germany immediately after the war ended. People have traded shells, salt, silk, cattle, furs, dried fish, beads, and even stones as money in various societies. Gold, silver, copper, tin, iron, and other metals have been used as money. Some Native Americans used seashells (called *wampum*) as money. Tobacco served as money in the colonies of Virginia, Maryland, and North Carolina in the 1600s and 1700s. Of course, since farmers could grow tobacco, they could literally grow money, and they did, boosting the supply of money 40-fold over half a century, which caused a giant surge of inflation.

Gold and Silver Coins

Coins first circulated in China in 1091 B.C. and in Greece in about 750 B.C. Nearly 2,000 years later, the Chinese first invented and traded paper money around A.D. 900.

In economies that designated gold or silver coins as money, the money supply could increase in three ways: debasement of coins, new discoveries of gold or silver deposits, or imports of gold or silver. First, governments could *debase* coins by making more of them from the same amount of gold or silver, either by reducing the size of each coin slightly (shaving the edges and using the shavings to make new coins) or by mixing other, cheaper, metals with the gold or silver. By increasing the number of coins, debasement created inflation. Governments gained by creating more coins to spend, and people paid an inflation tax, as described in the previous chapter.

Inflation in ancient Rome resulted from frequent debasement of money. Rome first used copper coins, then switched to silver coins, and then switched again to gold coins. The government debased them all. The money supply in the Roman empire rose rapidly starting in A.D. 296 under Emperor Diocletian, who tried and failed to stop inflation with wage and price controls. In contrast, governments in ancient Athens and other Greek city-states did not debase their coins even in times of war. As a result, ancient Greece did not experience inflation. However, Greece was an exception: Debasement of coins has been common throughout history.

New discoveries of gold or silver raise the money supply in economies that use gold or silver coins as money. For example, inflation resulted from gold discoveries in the United States and Australia from 1848 to 1851 that increased world gold output by 8 percent per year for 15 years.

Finally, a country's money supply increases if it imports gold or silver from other countries to make coins. Suppose that an increase in the supply of gold money in Spain raised the Spanish price level. Goods and services would cost more gold coins than before. People in Spain would have an incentive to buy goods in other countries where prices had not changed, such as England, and bring those goods to Spain. To buy English goods, they would pay gold coins to English sellers, raising the supply of gold in England. As England exported goods and imported gold, the gold imports would raise the English money supply and price level. Meanwhile, the Spanish money supply would fall as Spaniards spent their gold coins in England. The fall in the Spanish money supply would reduce the Spanish price level. At the same time, the price level in England would rise until prices were again equal in the two countries. At that point, Spanish people would stop exporting gold to England.

During the Middle Ages, when barter was common, people often exchanged gold coins in international trade—coins minted by the Byzantine Empire before the 8th century and Moslem Arabic coins after that. Later, in medieval Europe, various feudal lords, kings, and ecclesiastics minted, and frequently debased, silver coins for local use. International trade expanded in the 13th century, and gold coins issued in Florence became the medium of exchange for international trade. By the 14th century, England, France, Germany, and other European countries had begun issuing gold coins.

PRINT YOUR OWN MONEY! It's Fun. It's Legal. But you need your own design . . .
Two kinds of paper money circulate in Ithaca, New York. One kind, printed by the U.S. government, is familiar throughout the United States. The other money, printed right in Ithaca, uses an entirely different unit of account: the "Ithaca hour." Since 1991, people in Ithaca have been using Ithaca hour notes to pay for home repairs, groceries, childcare, movies, restaurant meals, and other goods and services. The multi-colored notes are a form of *private money*, issued in five denominations: 2 Hours, 1 Hour, ½ Hour, ¼ Hour, and ⅛ Hour. Private moneys like this are completely legal, as long as they are distinct from Federal Reserve notes. The idea may spread: in recent years, several other communities have issued their own local currencies.

In modern times, European countries have begun replacing their national currencies with a new continentwide standard called the *Euro*.

Europe experienced a long period of inflation in the 16th and early 17th centuries due to gold and silver discoveries in the New World, which nearly doubled the European gold stock and more than tripled the silver stock. Although inflation rates in this period appear low by today's standards—inflation was about 2 percent per year—this *Price Revolution,* as it is commonly known, was the longest period of inflation in history up to that time, with a higher inflation rate than in any preceding century.

In the 18th century, the Bank of England began issuing paper money, which began to replace silver and gold coins. The Bank of Amsterdam did the same in Holland, and paper money began to replace coins in Spain, as well.

Gold Standard

Gold is the most historically important commodity that has served as money. Countries have adopted the gold standard in two different forms.

> In a **pure gold standard**, people use gold coins as money.

> In a **gold exchange standard**, people use paper money that is backed by gold stored in warehouses.

The gold standard is one type of *commodity standard* of money, in which money consists of some commodity, or is backed by that commodity. The silver standard, which resembles a gold standard except that it is based on silver instead of gold, is another historically important commodity standard.

A pure gold standard functioned for many centuries, before most countries replaced it with a gold exchange standard. In the gold exchange standard, paper money initially served as a sort of warehouse certificate for gold. People found paper certificates more convenient than gold coins to carry and store. Although anyone could exchange paper money for the gold that backed it, few people did so.

Imagine that the U.S. government were to adopt a gold exchange standard at a $300-per-ounce gold price. Anyone could bring $300 to a government office to buy or sell an ounce of gold for $300. The government would sell as much gold as anyone wants to buy for $300 an ounce, and buy as much as anyone wants to sell for that price. This policy would fix the price of gold at $300 per ounce, for two reasons. First, no buyer would be willing to pay more to another (non-government) seller, so the price would not rise above $300 per ounce. Second, no seller would be willing to sell for less than $300 per ounce to another (non-government) buyer, so the price would not fall below $300 per ounce. Gold would back paper money in the sense that anyone could exchange one for the other at the $300 price.

To fix the price of gold at $300, the government must have enough gold to sell to people who want to buy it at that price. If the government does not have enough gold, it cannot fix the price at $300. Under any commodity standard, paper money works like a warehouse certificate for the commodity. However, when people are willing to hold and accept paper money without exchanging it for the commodity in the warehouse, then the commodity may seem to lose its importance. Why let the commodity sit unused in a warehouse when it could be used for other purposes? When the government does *not* back its paper money with any commodity (such as gold or silver)—when people cannot trade the paper money for a commodity at a fixed price—that money becomes *fiat money.*

A government that fixes the nominal price of gold (in terms of its money) requires a sufficient quantity of gold to sell. In the same way, a modern government that tries to fix the price of its currency in terms of foreign money (the *exchange rate*) needs sufficient reserves of foreign money to sell. When a country lacks sufficient reserves, it cannot continue to fix its exchange rate. This situation has arisen in recent years in Mexico, Russia, and a number of Asian countries such as Indonesia.

> **Fiat money** is paper money that is not backed by a commodity in the sense that people cannot trade it for a particular commodity at a fixed nominal price.

Money in American History

Before the American Revolution, the 13 colonies relied on paper money denominated in British pounds. During the revolution, the colonies printed paper money known as *continental currency* to pay war expenses, causing inflation of 8.5 percent per month during that time. The continental currency was denominated in dollars, a word for Spanish pesos (pieces of eight). From 1775 to 1779, the colonial money supply rose to ten times its previous level, causing massive inflation. Prices climbed to as much as 100 times their previous levels. In a famous phrase, something utterly worthless was said to be "not worth a continental."

After 1783, the continental currency lost all its value. The United States adopted a type of silver standard until 1834, followed by the gold standard after that year. U.S. inflation remained virtually zero for the first 70 years of U.S. independence. From the time that George Washington became the first president in 1789 until the Civil War, the U.S. price level stayed about the same.

Money took several forms in the United States besides silver or gold coins, such as paper money issued by the Bank of the United States early in the 19th century and paper money issued by private banks. The federal government first printed fiat money (money not convertible to gold) in 1862 to help pay for the Civil War. These so-called *greenbacks* were measured in dollars and were designated as *legal tender,* meaning that the government required sellers to accept greenbacks in payment for goods and services (even if the sellers would rather be paid in gold or some other kind of money). The U.S. money supply doubled during this time, creating inflation that roughly doubled prices.

After the Civil War, the government began reducing the supply of greenbacks, creating *deflation* (negative inflation). By 1879, the wholesale price level had fallen all the way back to its pre–Civil War level. Once again, people could exchange paper money for gold. The United States remained on the gold exchange standard until World War I began in 1914. Countries often suspended the gold standard temporarily during wars, and World War I was no exception. Germany returned to the gold standard in 1924, after its hyperinflation discussed in the previous chapter. Britain and France returned to the gold standard in 1925 and 1928, respectively. As the United States returned to the gold standard after World War I, the new *Federal Reserve System* (discussed later in this chapter) began operation.

Review Questions

1. Why is trade based on money often more efficient than barter?

2. Name some commodities that have served as money.

3. What are three important properties of money?

Thinking Exercise

4. What is a gold standard? Use a supply–demand diagram to explain how that monetary system worked.

The basic model developed in previous chapters, defined the nominal money supply as the total nominal value of the paper money and coins created by the government. Because people in modern economies often pay for goods and services without using paper money or coins, economists have developed several alternative measures of the money supply.

MEASURING THE MONEY SUPPLY

IN THE NEWS

Overseas travels by U.S. dollar follow in tracks of world economy

In the ad, a little boy in Arab dress leads a confused American couple down side streets and through a crowded market, finally depositing them triumphantly in front of an automated teller machine.

The Americans, who'd just gotten cleaned out buying a driverless camel, gasp with amazement to discover that, no matter where they go, there's easy access to American money.

Obviously it was their first trip abroad or they wouldn't be the least bit surprised to find greenbacks in even the remotest corners of the world. In fact, to currency experts, the definition of overseas is that vast place where most American money is kept.

According to the Federal Reserve, 60 percent of all American currency in circulation—$500 billion at last count—is held somewhere outside the United States. Other experts think the number could be as high as 80 percent. What's more, the dollar outflow may be matched by a similar movement of other hard currencies.

Some of the money is in drugs and the underground economy, but most is used as legal tender.

Source: Journal of Commerce

Mystery of the Missing Money

Who has all the paper money? By 1998, U.S. currency (paper money and coins) in circulation totaled almost $500 billion. That amounts to an average of about $1,800 per person for everyone (including children) in the United States. You probably don't have that much cash. (I don't.) Where is the missing money?

Most of it is held by people in other countries. People in less developed countries, particularly countries with high inflation rates, often hold U.S. dollars. People also use dollars to buy goods on black markets in many countries. U.S. currency is also used for illegal transactions such as those in the drug trade. Some of it, obviously, has been lost at the bottom of the ocean and burned in fires. No accurate sources of data show precisely where all the currency is.

By extending the model to include new features associated with these measures of the money supply, we can use it to address important economic issues such as the causes of the 1997–98 economic crises in Korea, Japan, and other Asian countries.

The most important measures of the U.S. money supply are M1, M2, and the monetary base. These measures reflect the facts that you can pay for some goods by writing checks, and money in the bank is almost like money in your wallet. These measures distinguish between currency, demand deposits, and bank reserves:

Currency is the paper money and coins owned by people and business firms.

The basic model of previous chapters has treated currency as the money supply. We now consider other measures of the money supply. The first measure adds balances in checking accounts, because people can buy goods and services with these balances by writing checks.

Demand deposits are balances in bank accounts that you can withdraw on demand by writing a check.

In addition to demand deposits, *other checkable deposits* include balances in other, similar accounts on which people can write checks.

M1 equals the sum of currency, demand deposits, other checkable deposits, and traveler's checks.

The M1 measure of the money supply recognizes that money in a checking account is almost like cash in your wallet—you can spend it by writing checks. Traveler's checks appear in M1 because you can use them like currency to buy goods and services.

You might wonder why a definition of money should include balances in checking accounts but not balances in savings accounts. After all, you can easily transfer deposits from your savings account to your checking account or withdraw cash from your savings account. Perhaps a definition of money should include balances in money market mutual funds, because people who own them can often write checks on their account balances. A second measure of the money supply, *M2*, includes balances in these accounts:

> **M2** equals M1 plus the sum of balances in savings accounts, money market mutual funds, and similar accounts.

Figure 1 plots M1 and M2, and their growth rates, for the United States since 1960.

Choosing a measure of the money supply is somewhat like choosing a measure of intelligence. Scientists could measure a person's ability to learn mathematics, memorize poetry, recognize and deal with complex issues in human relationships, succeed in creating a happy life, and so on, but the many different ways to measure intelligence have different purposes, and not all people are intelligent in the same ways. To predict how well a person will succeed in an engineering course, one would choose some definition or measurement of intelligence that could predict that kind of success. Similarly, to predict inflation, economists want to use a measure of the money supply suited to that purpose. No one can supply a unique answer to the question of which is the best definition of money.

Basics of Bank Accounts and Money

Suppose that you have money in a checking account at a bank. When you write a check for $20 to pay for food at a grocery store, the store deposits the check at its bank. That bank gets $20 from your bank and adds it to the balance in the store's bank account. In that way, the store gets your $20.

When you deposit $100 in paper money in a bank account, the bank does not keep all of this $100 in its vault. Instead, it lends most of that money to someone who wants to borrow. The money the bank keeps (the part of the $100 that it does not lend) becomes part of its reserves.

> **Bank reserves** are the deposits that banks have *not* loaned.

Figure 1 | Measures of the U.S. Money Supply, 1960–1998

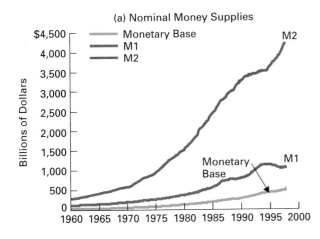

(a) Nominal Money Supplies

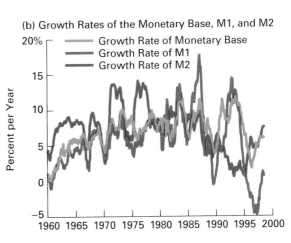

(b) Growth Rates of the Monetary Base, M1, and M2

Choosing between alternative measures of the money supply is like choosing between alternative measures of *performance* in sports. You might measure a player's performance as total points that the player scores, but team cooperation and other complexities of the game may suggest other, perhaps better, measures of performance. Similarly, economists might measure money as the number of dollars the government has printed, but complexities of real-life economies suggest other, perhaps better, measures.

A simple model of a team sport—like Figure 1 in Chapter 2, showing a model of a play in American football—neglects some of a game's subtle features, such as how players respond when the other team changes its tactics. Discussing those features of the game requires adding new complexities to the model beyond the features in that figure. Similarly, our basic economic model has omitted certain aspects of real-life monetary and payments systems. By extending the model to include new features, the model can be applied to new issues such as the details of U.S. monetary policy and the causes of the recent Asian economic crises.

Bank reserves in the United States include the currency that banks keep in their offices and vaults (called *vault cash)*, plus the balances they keep at the Federal Reserve (an independent agency of the federal government, discussed later in this chapter).

Banks hold reserves for two reasons. First, they need cash to give to people who withdraw from their accounts. The practice of keeping only a fraction of deposits as reserves and lending the rest is called *fractional reserve banking.* Fractional reserve banking provides banks with funds to lend, turning them into intermediaries between borrowers and lenders rather than simply safe places to store money or bookkeeping firms that record who owes how much to whom. However, fractional reserve banking also creates the possibility that people may try to withdraw more cash than a bank has available to give them. Because only a small fraction of depositors typically withdraw funds each day, banks generally have enough reserves to satisfy those depositors. Banks also hold reserves because the government *requires* them to hold a small fraction of deposits (in 1998, 3 percent of total checking-account deposits below $49 million and 10 percent of checking-account deposits above that amount). Every day, some banks find that they have more reserves than they want while other banks have less, so some banks borrow reserves from others.

Banks earn profits by lending the money that people deposit and charging higher interest rates to borrowers than the interest rates that they pay to depositors. For example, you may earn 4 percent annual interest on the money in your bank account, but the bank lends most of the money you deposited, perhaps charging 10 percent interest. The difference covers the bank's costs and provides a profit for its owners. A bank incurs an opportunity cost by holding reserves, because it could lend that money and earn interest on the loans. Banks balance the costs and benefits of reserves when they choose the amounts of reserves they choose to hold.

The Monetary Base

Because of fractional reserve banking, the government cannot directly control M1 or M2, although it can control a narrower measure of the money supply, the *monetary base.*

> The **monetary base** equals currency plus bank reserves.

Figure 2 compares the monetary base, M1, and M2.

The U.S. government—specifically, the Federal Reserve—has nearly complete control over the country's monetary base, which changes only when the Federal Reserve changes it or when money is lost (as in a shipwreck). However, the Federal Reserve cannot control the amount of the monetary base that flows outside the United States. People in other countries, particularly countries with high inflation rates, hold U.S. dollars because they provide a better store of value than local money. Dollars also serve as the main means of payment for illegal international drug trades and similar activities around the world. Only rough estimates, not precise data, are available on foreign holdings of dollars, so the Federal Reserve can only estimate the size of the monetary base held inside the United States. Nevertheless, these estimates give the Federal Reserve reasonably strong control over changes in the monetary base held within the country.

The Federal Reserve has incomplete control over M1 and M2 because these measures of money respond to actions of people and banks. To see why, you need to understand how banks help to create money.

How Banks Help to Create Money

Suppose you take $100 from your wallet and deposit it in your bank account. The bank might keep $10 of this money as reserves and lend the other $90 to your economics professor. Your professor then has $90 in cash and you have $100 in your bank account. Even though your professor has $90 of the paper money you deposited,

Figure 2 | Measures of the Money Supply

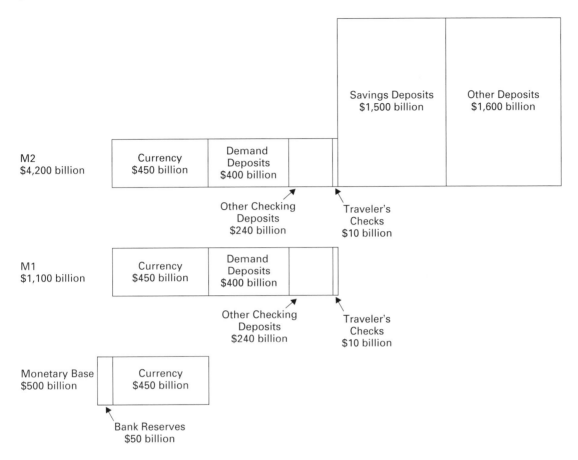

you still feel as if you have the entire $100. In a sense, you do; you have a $100 balance in your bank account. Your actions, along with those of your bank and your professor, have increased the M1 measure of the money supply by $90. M2 also increases by $90.

The story does not end there. M1 and M2 rise by more than $90 when your professor uses the borrowed money. When your professor deposits the $90 into a bank account, that bank lends most of the money to someone else. This process continues through many rounds, and eventually M1 rises by a larger amount. That amount depends on how much reserves banks hold and how people choose to divide their money between cash in their wallets and money in the bank.

EXAMPLE

Suppose that banks always hold reserves equal to 10 percent of the balances in checking accounts. Table 1 shows the results. Initially, you take $100 in cash from your wallet and deposit it in your checking account. The monetary base does not change, even though currency falls by $100, because bank reserves rise by $100 (since the bank has your money). M1 and M2 also remain unchanged, because currency falls by $100, while the balance in your checking account rises by that same amount.

The bank, however, keeps only $10 of the money you deposited and lends the other $90 to Andrea. At this point, M1 rises by $90 because you still have $100 in your bank account, but Andrea has $90 that she did not have before. Andrea spends the $90 to buy

Table 1 | How the Banking System Creates Money: An Example

Actions	Effects on Money Supply
You take $100 cash from your wallet and put it in your checking account.	No change in monetary base or M1.
The bank keeps $10 (10 percent of your $100 deposit) as reserves and lends $90 to Andrea.	No change in monetary base; M1 rises by $90.
Andrea spends the $90 to buy something from Bob, who deposits the $90 in his checking account.	No change in monetary base; M1 rises another $81, bringing its total increase to $171.
Bob's bank keeps $9 (10 percent of $90) as reserves, and lends the other $81 to Celine.	
Celine spends the $81 to buy something from Dave, who deposits the $81 in his checking account.	No change in monetary base; M1 rises another $72.90, bringing its total increase to $243.90.
Dave's bank keeps $8.10 (10 percent of $81) and lends the other $72.90 to Elaine.	
Elaine uses the money to buy something from Fran, who deposits the money in her checking account, and the process continues. . . .	Eventually, M1 rises by $900.[a]

[a]The $900 figure comes from adding:

$$\$90 + \frac{(.9)(\$90)}{\$81.00} + \frac{(.9)^2(\$90)}{\$72.90} + \frac{(.9)^3(\$90)}{\$65.61} + \frac{(.9)^4(\$90)}{\$59.05} + \ldots$$
$$= \$90(1 + 0.9 + 0.9^2 + 0.9^3 + 0.9^4 + 0.9^5 + \ldots)$$
$$= \$90/(1 - 0.9)$$
$$= \$90/0.1$$
$$= \$900$$

boots from Bob, who deposits it in his bank account. His bank keeps $9 (10 percent of the $90) as reserves and lends the other $81 to Celine. At this point, M1 rises by another $81, for a total increase of $171, because Celine now has $81 that she did not have before, while you still have your $100 in the bank and Bob still has his $90 in the bank. Celine spends the $81 to buy daggers from Dave, who deposits the money in his bank account. His bank keeps $8.10 (10 percent of the $81.00 deposit) and lends the other $72.90 to Elaine, raising M1 by another $72.90. By this time, M1 has increased by $243.90. Next, Elaine spends the money to buy flowers from Fran, and this process continues. After three more rounds, M1 rises by a total of $421.70; eventually, M1 rises by a total of $900 as a result of your initial $100 deposit.

Money Multiplier

The example showed how M1 eventually rises by $900 when a person deposits $100 in the bank, and banks hold reserves equal to 10 percent of their deposits. Because a $100 rise in deposits raises M1 by $900, economists say that the money multiplier is 9 in this case.

> The **M1 money multiplier** is the ratio of M1 to the monetary base.

For example, the money multiplier for M1 is defined as:

$$\text{M1 money multiplier} = \frac{\text{M1}}{\text{Monetary base}}$$

A similar definition applies to the M2 money multiplier.

In the example, the M1 money multiplier was 9 because the ratio of bank deposits to reserves equaled 9, that is, banks lent $9 for every $1 they held in reserves. For each dollar of deposits, banks lent $0.90 and kept $0.10 as reserves. In that example, the M1 money multiplier equaled:

$$\text{M1 money multiplier} = \frac{\text{Deposits}}{\text{Reserves}}$$

In that example, however, each seller deposited all newly received money into a bank account. More generally, a seller may keep some of that money as cash in a wallet, giving a more general formula for the M1 money multiplier:

$$\text{M1 money multiplier} = \frac{1 + \dfrac{\text{Currency}}{\text{deposits}}}{\dfrac{\text{Reserve}}{\text{deposits}} + \dfrac{\text{currency}}{\text{deposits}}}$$

(See the Appendix that follows this chapter for a derivation of this formula.) The ratio of currency to deposits shows how much currency (paper money and coins) people hold as a fraction of their total checking-account balances; the ratio of reserves to deposits shows how much reserves banks hold as a fraction of their total checking-account balances.

Using the Money Multiplier

The money multiplier measures the effect of a change in the monetary base on M1. Suppose that the government raises the monetary base by printing $1,000 in new money and spending it to buy something. The seller now has the $1,000, so the monetary base has risen by $1,000. The typical M1 money multiplier of 2.2 suggests that M1 will eventually rise by $2,200 (2.2 times $1,000). The general rule is:

Change in M1 = M1 money multiplier × Change in monetary base

Money Multipliers in the United States

The M1 money multiplier in the United States is about 2.2. The ratio of currency to deposits in the United States is about 0.70 (70 percent), and the ratio of reserves to deposits is about 0.075 (7.5 percent). Plugging in these values, the formula gives an M1 money multiplier of about 2.2. Figure 3 shows the changes in the U.S. M1 money multiplier in recent years.

Figure 3 | M1 Money Multiplier in the United States

Table 2 | How a Change in the Monetary Base Raises M1

	Starting Amount	Kept as Currency	Deposit in Bank	Bank Reserves	Bank Loans	Cumulative M1 Increase
Megan	$1,000.00	$412.00	$588.00	$44.10	$543.90	$1,543.90
Ned	$543.90	$224.09	$319.81	$23.99	$295.83	$1,839.73
Oprah	$295.83	$121.88	$173.95	$13.05	$160.90	$2,000.63
Pete	$160.90	$66.29	$94.61	$7.10	$87.51	$2,088.14
Quentin	$87.51	$36.06	$51.46	$3.86	$47.60	$2,135.74
Robert	$47.60	$19.61	$27.99	$2.10	$25.89	$2,161.63
Sandra	$25.89	$10.67	$15.22	$1.14	$14.08	$2,175.71
Tom	$14.08	$5.80	$8.28	$0.62	$7.66	$2,183.37

EXPLANATION AND EXAMPLE

Suppose that the government prints $1,000 in new currency and buys something from Megan, a typical person whose currency–deposit ratio of 0.7 indicates that she holds $0.70 in currency for each $1.00 in her bank account. Therefore, as a typical person, Megan puts $588 of her newly earned $1,000 into her checking account and keeps $412 as currency (since $412 is 70 percent of $588). These actions appear in the first row of Table 2. Megan's bank has a reserve–deposit ratio of 7.5 percent, so it keeps $44.10 of Megan's deposit as reserves and lends the other $543.90 to Ned.

Ned, another typical person with a currency–deposit ratio of 0.7, keeps $224.09 in cash and deposits $319.81 in his checking account. His bank keeps $23.99 as reserves on this deposit, and lends the other $295.83 to Oprah, another typical person. The money supply grows as the process continues down the rows of Table 2. Eventually, by the eighth round of this process (when Tom's bank has loaned $7.66 to someone), M1 has increased by $2,183.37, as shown in the last row of the table. If the table were to continue even further, it would show that M1 eventually rises by $2,200. The money multiplier simply gives a quick way to calculate the final change in M1.

Review Questions

5. If you pay for a new shirt with a check, how does the store get your money?

6. How can you (with the help of a bank) increase the money supply? Explain.

7. Define and explain who controls (a) the monetary base, (b) M1, and (c) M2.

8. Explain how the banking system creates money.

Thinking Exercises

9. Suppose that banks hold $0.10 of reserves for every $1.00 of deposits and that the currency–deposit ratio is 0.5. How large is the M1 money multiplier?

10. Suppose that people choose to increase the fraction of their money that they hold in the form of currency and reduce the fraction that they hold in the form of bank deposits. How would this change affect M1 and M2?

We now have three measures of the money supply (the monetary base, M1, and M2), with varying degrees of control by the government. We have a model to describe how the actions of banks and depositors affect the sizes of M1 and M2. We now turn to the actions of *government* that affect the money supply.

Many countries, including the United States, operate central banks that serve as banks for other banks. The U.S. central bank is the Federal Reserve System, often simply called the *Fed*.

> A **central bank** is a bank for banks. The **Federal Reserve System** is the central bank in the United States.

The Federal Reserve conducts monetary policy (controlling the money supply) and regulates banks in the United States. Similar agencies in other countries include the Bank of Canada, Bank of England, Bank of Japan, Bank of Mexico, the Bundesbank in Germany, and the new European Central Bank. These central banks conduct monetary policies and regulate banks in their countries.

The Fed was created by the Federal Reserve Act in 1913. Before that time, the United States had no central bank. Although the Fed affects the life of every citizen through its policies, most people know little about how it operates. The Federal Reserve System consists of three main parts:

1. The Board of Governors, a seven-member panel in Washington, D.C., employs a large supporting staff of statisticians and researchers. Members of the board are appointed by the U.S. president and confirmed by Congress to serve 14-year terms. The long terms are intended to help shield board members from political pressure, much as judges' life terms shield them. Board members' terms are staggered so that one becomes vacant every 2 years. The president appoints one governor to chair the board for a 4-year term. The chairman, currently Alan Greenspan, wields more influence and power than the other governors, partly through control of meeting agendas.

2. Regional Federal Reserve Banks are centered in 12 cities around the country, shown in Figure 4. Nine directors oversee each Federal Reserve Bank, three appointed by the Fed's Board of Governors and six elected by private banks in the Federal Reserve Bank's district. These nine directors choose the president of the Federal Reserve Bank. The New York Federal Reserve Bank carries out most of the Fed's monetary policy actions.

3. The Federal Reserve's Federal Open Market Committee, or FOMC, meets about every four to six weeks in Washington to discuss the economy, set the nation's monetary policy, and choose Fed policy actions. The FOMC's 12 members include the 7 governors in Washington D.C., the president of the Federal Reserve Bank of New York, and the presidents of 4 of the 11 other Federal Reserve Banks, who take turns serving on the committee. The bank presidents who do not serve on the FOMC can participate in its meetings, but they cannot vote on policy. The Federal Reserve Bank of New York is responsible for carrying out the policies chosen by the FOMC.

The Fed, unlike most government agencies, operates somewhat independently of the rest of the government. This independence is intended to isolate Fed decision making from political forces that might compromise its choices of the best policies for the economy. The Fed does not receive money directly from Congress. Instead, the Fed pays its expenses (staff salaries and so on) out of the interest it earns on its financial assets, mostly

One of the most powerful people in the world: Federal Reserve Chairman Alan Greenspan.

Figure 4 | Regional Federal Reserve Banks

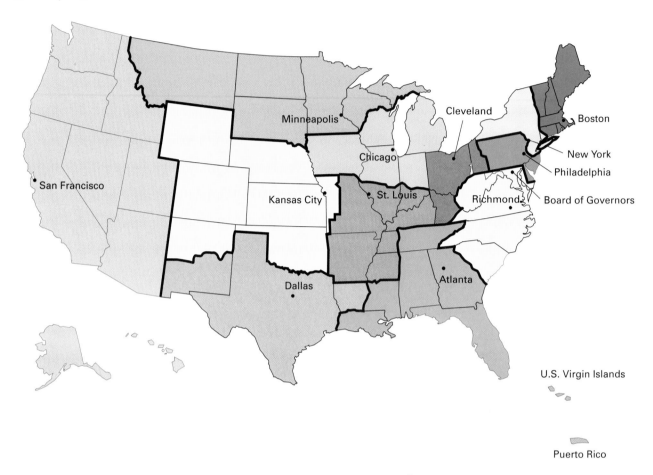

U.S. Treasury bills and government bonds.[1] After paying its expenses, the Fed returns any leftover money to Congress. In addition, the Fed does not undergo audits by the General Accounting Office, the federal accounting agency that audits the books of most other government agencies. This separation helps to reduce political pressures on the Fed.

Federal Reserve Policy Tools: How the Money Supply Changes

The Fed relies on three main tools to conduct monetary policy:

▶ Open market operations

▶ Discount window lending

▶ Reserve requirements and other bank regulations

Open Market Operations

The Fed's primary policy tool is the open market operation: Think of the Fed increasing the money supply by using newly printed money to buy government bonds.

> An **open market operation** is a Federal Reserve sale or purchase of U.S. government bonds. In an open market *purchase*, the Fed buys bonds, expanding the monetary base. In an open market *sale*, the Fed sells bonds, contracting the monetary base.

---

[1]Chapter 34 discusses government bonds and other financial assets.

The FOMC makes decisions about open market operations, and the Federal Reserve Bank of New York does the actual buying and selling. An open market purchase increases the monetary base, because the Fed creates money to buy financial assets. When the Fed buys bonds from a bank, the bank receives an increase in its reserves at the Fed. When the bank wants currency and coins to lend, it withdraws reserves from its account at the Fed. The Treasury Department prints currency and mints coins, and the Fed provides them to banks for lending. This increase in the monetary base sets into motion the money-multiplier process described earlier, raising M1 and M2.

An open market sale reduces the monetary base, because the Fed collects payments for the bonds it sells by taking reserves out of the accounts of the banks that buy those bonds. (Think of the Fed destroying the money that it receives for selling the bonds.) This fall in reserves sets into motion the money-multiplier process described earlier, only in reverse, so the open market sale reduces M1 and M2.

Discount Window Lending
The Fed sometimes lends reserves to banks. The bank is said to borrow at the Fed's discount window, and the interest rate the bank pays is called the *discount rate*.

> The **Federal Reserve discount rate** is the interest rate the Fed charges banks for short-term loans.

When the Fed lends reserves to a bank, the monetary base rises. Broader measures of the money supply, such as M1 and M2, then increase through the money-multiplier process. By raising and lowering the discount rate, the Fed can affect the amount of bank borrowing at the discount window.

As noted earlier, banks borrow and lend reserves among themselves every day. Banks with more reserves than they want lend to other banks with fewer reserves than they want. The interest rate that banks charge each other for short-term loans of reserves is called the *federal funds rate*.

> The **federal funds rate** is the interest rate that banks charge each other when they borrow and lend reserves for short periods.

The federal funds rate has nothing to do with the federal government, although it is often a target of Federal Reserve monetary policy.

Figure 5 shows changes in the Federal Reserve discount rate and the federal funds rate in recent years. When the federal funds rate is less than the discount rate, banks can borrow from other banks more cheaply than from the Fed. When the discount rate is less than the federal funds rate, banks would prefer to borrow from the Fed. The Fed discourages banks from borrowing too much or too often at the discount window, however, and it does not always lend to banks that want to borrow. (Banks that try to borrow from the Federal Reserve too often or too much attract increased scrutiny by its bank regulators, creating inconvenience and costs for those banks.)

The Fed lends reserves to banks at the discount window for two purposes: acting as a lender of last resort in an emergency situation and conducting monetary policy. The discount window was originally intended to make the Fed a lender of last resort—a source of loans to banks that could not easily borrow funds elsewhere and that needed reserves so depositors could withdraw their money (or for other purposes such as meeting legal reserve requirements). Banks that borrow at the discount window frequently could choose instead to borrow in the federal funds market, but only at a higher interest rate.

If only one bank needs to borrow reserves for depositors to meet withdrawal demands, it can borrow from other banks. However, if *all* (or many) banks simultaneously experience large withdrawals, they may be unable to borrow enough, because the

IN THE NEWS

Federal bank regulators move forward with plans to increase lending scrutiny

WASHINGTON—Federal bank examiners, worried about the slippage in lending standards, have begun stepping up their supervision of bank lending practices and, for the first time, going directly to bank directors to identify specific risky loans and lending practices.

Source: The Wall Street Journal

Figure 5 | Two Key Interest Rates for Monetary Policy

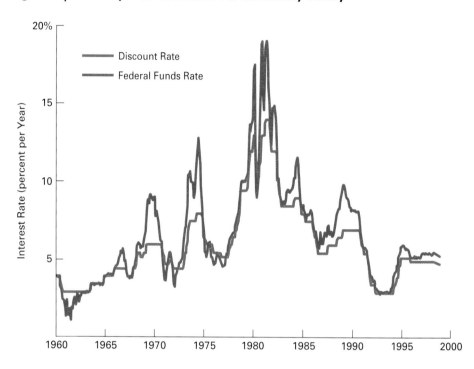

entire economy may not contain enough currency to pay all depositors who want to withdraw at once. As a lender of last resort, the Fed provides additional currency in such a situation; by assuring people that they can always withdraw their money whenever they want, it can help to prevent such a situation from developing out of panic. This function was originally intended as the main role of the Federal Reserve, and discount window lending was the main tool of Fed policy in its early years.[2]

The second purpose of discount window lending is to help conduct monetary policy, that is, to control the money supply. By lending reserves to banks, the Fed can raise the monetary base and broader measures of the money supply (such as M1 and M2).

Reserve Requirements and Other Bank Regulations

As an earlier section noted, the Fed requires banks to hold minimum proportions of reserves per dollar of deposits.

> **Required reserves** are reserves that the Fed requires banks to hold.

The Fed can increase the M1 money multiplier by reducing required reserves. A fall in required reserves increases the fraction of deposits that banks can lend, raising the M1 money multiplier. Similarly, the Fed can reduce the M1 money multiplier by raising required reserves, reducing the fraction of deposits that banks can lend. Although changes in reserve requirements can affect M1 and M2, the Fed seldom changes money supplies in this way.

The Fed also supervises and regulates banks. Its officials make sure that banks actually hold the reserves they are required to hold. It monitors their investments to make sure that they meet certain legal requirements, such as those intended to prevent banks

---

[2]As an option, banks could give people only $0.90 for each $1.00 in their accounts. This has actually happened in many banking panics.

from choosing particularly risky investments. The Fed also enforces a variety of other bank regulations. Other functions of the Federal Reserve include acting as a clearing-house to clear checks and distributing new currency.

Review Questions

11. Describe the Federal Reserve System and its three main policy tools.

12. Explain open market operations and how they affect the money supply.

13. What is the Federal Reserve discount rate? The federal funds rate?

Thinking Exercise

14. Why might the Federal Reserve be more effective than a private bank as a lender of last resort?

FINANCIAL INTERMEDIARIES

Earlier chapters discussed the supply and demand for loans and used these concepts as thinking tools to examine the effects of changes in consumer spending, government budget deficits, and other macroeconomic issues. The supply of loans mainly reflects lending by people who save, while the demand for loans mainly reflects borrowing by firms for investments (and by governments to finance budget deficits). In a modern economy, financial intermediaries participate in a large fraction of borrowing and lending transactions.

> A **financial intermediary** gathers money from savers and lends it to borrowers.

Banks are financial intermediaries; other financial intermediaries include savings and loan associations and credit unions.

Financial intermediaries provide three main benefits to the economy. First, they essentially bring borrowers and lenders together, so that savers can find people who want to borrow money, and borrowers can find people who want to lend money. Second, financial intermediaries combine small amounts of savings by many people into large sums of money to lend. A business firm that wants to borrow $1 million can borrow directly from a bank, rather than borrowing $1,000 each from 1,000 different savers.

The third important role of financial intermediaries involves information and monitoring. Before banks lend money to a firm, they study the firm's financial position and plans, carefully estimating the likelihood that the firm will repay the loan in full and on time. After lending money, banks often monitor its use by making sure that the firm follows through with its investment plans. By obtaining information about borrowers and monitoring their activities, financial intermediaries reduce the risks involved in lending money.

While financial intermediaries were not part of the basic economic model discussed in earlier chapters, they play a key role in the real-life loan market. They *also* play a key role in the real-life money market, by affecting M1 and M2. The combination of these roles is natural. Any firm that *safeguards* a person's money, like a bank, might as well lend it and earn interest. Consequently, monetary functions of banks affects their intermediary functions. Similarly, when banks lend, they create money through the money-multiplier process, so the intermediary functions of banks affects their monetary functions. Unfortunately, this natural connection between the money system and the loan market creates some important economic problems, to which we now turn.

IN THE NEWS

Russia's turmoil hammers young commercial banks

Crisis may force many to shut down

MOSCOW—Russia's financial crisis is tearing away the glittery facade of the country's young commercial banks. As the ruble falls, many have failed to meet obligations to either depositors or Western creditors, and government and central-bank officials warn that the crisis is likely to force many of the country's 1,500 banks eventually to close their doors.

The immediate reason: The collapse of financial markets has shrunk the assets of banks an average of 90% since their peak last fall, forcing some banks to default on loans to Western creditors.

Source: The Wall Street Journal

Banking Crises

If banks kept *all* their deposits as reserves—if they did *not* lend the money they receive in deposits—then the money market and loan market would not be closely connected, and banks would play no role in either creating money or lending it. Banks would simply safeguard money and transfer it to sellers' accounts when people paid for purchases by writing checks. Banks would always have enough money to give to people who came to withdraw their money. However, under the *fractional reserve* system (in which banks lend most of the money deposited with them), banks sometimes do *not* have enough currency to satisfy people who want to withdraw their deposits.

Two types of problems can arise. First, a bank may lose so much money on its loans that it becomes *insolvent*—even if all its current loans are repaid with interest, it would lack enough money to give to its depositors if they wanted to withdraw their money. This problem can occur if a bank makes a large number of bad loans—loans that borrowers simply cannot or do not repay. Some banks in Japan, Korea, and other countries faced insolvency during the Asian financial crisis of 1997–98. Most Russian banks also faced insolvency in 1998.

In the second, less severe type of problem, a bank may lack enough money to cover withdrawal demands *unless* it calls in its current loans—that is, asks borrowers to repay their loans ahead of schedule. This second type of problem is often called a *liquidity* problem—banks can obtain enough money to cover withdrawals with sufficient time, but they cannot quickly get that money. Many Asian banks did not become insolvent during the 1997–98 financial crises, but faced severe liquidity problems.

When *many* banks in the economy face either problem, the economy may experience disastrous consequences. Either type of problem reduces the supply of new loans, raising the interest rate and the cost for business firms to borrow money to finance investments. Some business firms may seek loans to continue operations despite short-run losses, and bank insolvency or bank liquidity problems may prevent them from obtaining these loans. Essentially, the *monetary* problems that can occur with fractional reserve banking can disrupt the operation of the economy's loan market. As a result, these troubles can reduce investment and disrupt normal operations of business firms. Recessions in Korea, Japan, and other Asian countries in 1998 resulted partly from the problems created by economy-wide banking crises.

Sometimes these problems lead to *bank runs*.

> A **bank run** occurs when many people try at the same time to withdraw their money from a bank that lacks enough reserves to accommodate all of them. In a **banking panic**, many banks face runs at the same time.

Banking panics frequently resulted from suspensions of convertibility in the United States prior to the beginning of the Federal Reserve System. Banking panics occurred in 1814, 1819, 1837, 1839, 1857, 1873, 1893, and 1907–08. When a bank lacked sufficient reserves to let people withdraw money from their accounts, it often suspended convertibility, that is, it stopped letting people withdraw their money. *Convertibility* means that depositors can convert bank balances into currency; in suspending convertibility, banks refused to let people make this conversion. Banking panics swept Russia in the summer of 1998, as the central bank became unable to keep the foreign exchange rate of the ruble pegged (see the nearby box) and most Russian banks became insolvent.

Banks that closed during historical U.S. banking panics were not usually insolvent; they simply faced liquidity problems. A bank closed when it lacked enough currency at the time to provide to depositors who wanted to withdraw funds. In most cases, though, banks could and did eventually allow depositors to withdraw all of their money once people had repaid their loans. Some banks went out of business permanently during banking panics, usually because people who borrowed money from them failed to repay their

A bank run in Russia in 1998 has depositors pushing and shoving to get into a bank to try to withdraw rubles and exchange them for dollars.

loans. (Loans to farmers, which were common, exposed banks to great risk, because bad weather could prevent farmers from repaying.) In these cases, depositors divided up whatever money the banks held, but they did not get their full balances.

The vast majority of banks, however, reopened after runs without any ultimate losses to depositors. Even in the worst banking panic, in 1893, 98.7 percent of banks later reopened. On average, depositors lost about $0.02 out of every dollar of their deposits in banks.[3] Of course, averages do not always accurately portray effects on people; this average loss of $0.02 per dollar reflects little or no loss for many people but major losses of lifetime savings did occur for a few people.

Banking panics often occurred with recessions. Real GDP fell 8.5 percent during the banking panic of 1907–08, convincing many people that the United States needed a cen-

IN THE NEWS

During the bank run, $250 million an hour left First Republic

By Michael J. Lyon

The silent run was accelerating at the First Republic Bank Corporation's offices in Texas—silent because retail customers

were not lining up on the streets. This run was being fueled by large institutions, including other banks, racing to electronically withdraw uninsured

deposits. Alarm bells went off around Washington, as the nation's top bank regulators met in an emergency session.

Source: New York Times

Today, bank runs can occur over electronic links.

Fixed Exchange Rates

Many countries today operate systems of *fixed exchange rates*. A central bank keeps the price of foreign money fixed by following procedures like those described earlier in the discussion of the gold standard. For example, the central bank of Argentina pegs the exchange rate between the Argentine peso and the U.S. dollar at $1 per peso. It does this by selling as many dollars (for pesos) as anyone wants to buy at that price, and buying as many dollars (with pesos) as anyone wants to sell for that price. This is the same procedure that central banks followed to fix the price of gold under the gold exchange standard. Under the gold exchange standard, a central bank could fix the price of gold only if it had enough gold to sell to people who wanted to buy it at the fixed price. Similarly, a central bank can operate a pegged exchange rate only if it has enough *reserves* of foreign money to sell to people who want to buy it at the fixed exchange rate. When a central bank lacks sufficient reserves, it can no longer keep its exchange rate fixed. That happened in Indonesia, South Korea, Malaysia, the Philippines, and Thailand in 1997, and central banks of those countries had to stop fixing their exchange rates. The central bank of Russia lacked sufficient reserves and was forced in 1998 to stop fixing the foreign exchange rate of the ruble. Mexico went through a similar experience several years earlier.

---

[3]The banking panic during the Great Depression of the 1930s was worse than this one, however.

IN THE NEWS

Japan to draft laws to clean up banking mess

Agency would be set up to take over operations of failed institutions

TOKYO—Japan is fleshing out a few of the details of its sweeping promises to mop up its banking crisis with a new plan to take over, shut down or merge weak banks.

Japanese leaders told visiting U.S. officials of their plans to set up a "bridge bank" that would take over the operations of failed lenders—Japan's latest of several largely unsuccessful attempts to mimic the U.S. Resolution Trust Corp.

Source: The Wall Street Journal

tral bank to prevent recurrences. (To put this drop in GDP in perspective, note that no recession in the United States since the Great Depression of the 1930s has seen such a large decline.) The Federal Reserve System was intended to prevent banking panics by acting as a lender of last resort and supervising banks.

Deposit Insurance

Despite the actions of the Federal Reserve System, the United States (and many other countries) experienced banking panics in the Great Depression from 1929 through much of the 1930s. In 1934, following the banking panic associated with the Great Depression, the federal government started the Federal Deposit Insurance Corporation (FDIC) to insure bank deposits. Deposit insurance was intended to protect people from losing their deposits if a bank lacked sufficient funds to meet withdrawal demands or went out of business. If a bank lacks sufficient funds for people to withdraw their deposits, the FDIC provides those funds. Banks pay the FDIC to provide this deposit insurance.

Without deposit insurance, a bank run may occur simply because people *believe* that it will occur. Suppose you believe that a bank run will occur at your bank tomorrow, and the bank has no deposit insurance. What would you do? Most people would quickly go to the bank and withdraw all of their money while the bank still has it—before other people withdraw all their money, and the bank runs out of funds. In other words, everyone wants to be near the beginning of the line at the bank to withdraw their money, because the people at the end of the line may find the vault empty. As many people rush to the bank to withdraw simply because they expect a bank run, they cause that bank run. The bank run becomes a self-fulfilling belief—when the bank run occurs, people see their beliefs confirmed.

Deposit insurance can prevent bank runs. Even if people expect a bank run, deposit

"Yeah, but who guarantees the federal government?"
Source: *The Wall Street Journal*, August 15, 1986, p. 15.

insurance takes away their incentive to rush to the bank to be near the front of the line by guaranteeing that all of them can withdraw their money. Because people have no incentive to rush to the bank to withdraw, a bank run becomes less likely.[4]

Private Deposit Insurance

Many banks in the United States arranged private deposit insurance in the 19th century. Banks often joined together and agreed that if any one of them failed, the others would pay depositors their money. In this way, the banks jointly acted as an insurance company for one another.

These insurance arrangements differed across states because of differences in state laws. Some states prohibited branch banking and required each bank to have only one office (one bank building). These laws were intended to protect small banks by preventing large banks from opening many conveniently located branch offices that would draw customers away from small competitors. However, large banks usually took the leadership roles in creating private deposit insurance, so states that prohibited branch banking often lacked effective deposit insurance.

Bank clearinghouses began to provide deposit insurance in the mid-19th century. A clearinghouse moves money between banks to clear checks. If you wrote a $50 check to pay for a new horse, the seller would deposit the check in a local bank. The seller's bank would then collect money from your bank. If the seller's bank already owed your bank $30, then your bank would owe a net amount of $20 to the seller's bank. The clearinghouse figures out all of this detail and moves the money. Privately operated clearinghouses flourished in the 19th century, as they also acted as lenders of last resort. Unfortunately, state laws against branch banking limited the benefits of clearinghouses, including deposit insurance and lender-of-last-resort services. The creation of the Federal Reserve essentially put an end to private deposit insurance and many private clearinghouse activities. Today, the Federal Reserve and several private firms function as bank clearinghouses in the United States.

Problems with Deposit Insurance

Until the last two decades, government-provided deposit insurance seemed to most analysts like a safe way to prevent bank runs. Then the government agency that provided deposit insurance for savings and loan associations went bankrupt. (Savings and loan associations, or S&Ls, resemble banks, but are a legally distinct type of financial intermediary.) The FSLIC (Federal Savings and Loan Insurance Corporation) lacked enough money to reimburse depositors of failed institutions, and the country plunged into a savings and loan crisis that ultimately cost the government over $100 billion.[5]

This episode highlighted the fact that deposit insurance changes the incentives of banks. With deposit insurance, banks want to make riskier investments than they would choose otherwise. With good luck, these risky investments pay off well, and the banks or savings and loan associations earn high profits. With bad luck, they go out of business, and deposit insurance covers depositors' balances.

Suppose that a bank without deposit insurance can choose between investing depositors' money in a safe way or a risky way. If the risky investment pays off, the bank's owners make a big profit. If not, they suffer a big loss. If the bank goes out of business, the bank's owners lose, but so do the depositors, who lose part or all of the money in their accounts. This threat gives depositors, particularly people with large balances, an incentive to monitor the bank and prevent it from making risky investments. Any bank that began to make risky investments would lose deposits as people moved their money to other banks with safer investments.

IN THE NEWS

Bonfire of the S&Ls

It's the biggest financial mess in U.S. history, and the bills will be coming due for the next 40 years. And that isn't all: the nation's banks may be next.

Source: Newsweek

Deposit insurance offered by the U.S. government affected the incentives of savings and loans, leading to bankruptcies by many.

---

[4]Some economists believe that by preventing a banking panic, deposit insurance can prevent a repeat of the Great Depression, when a large number of bank failures caused a large fall in the M1 and M2 measures of the money supply. Chapter 34 will discuss the connection between money-supply changes and the Great Depression.

[5]For various reasons, the costs are difficult to estimate and are not summarized in any convenient form in U.S. government financial accounts.

Asian Economic Crisis—1997–1998

The economic crisis in Japan, South Korea, Indonesia, Thailand, the Philippines, and Malaysia in 1997 to 1998 grew out of banking crises created by fractional reserve banking and (implicit) deposit insurance. Banks in these countries made a number of bad loans, often due to political pressures on banks. A second factor operated in Japan, where some major borrowers became unable to repay their loans to banks, after suffering losses when real estate prices fell from all-time highs. Because depositors expected governments to guarantee that they could withdraw their money, bank runs did not occur. However, insolvency at some banks and illiquidity at others contributed to recessions and created costs of bailing out depositors. The supply of loans decreased substantially in these countries, disrupting investment and the daily operations of many business firms. Similar problems have plagued many other countries in recent years.

Deposit insurance takes away the incentives of depositors to monitor their banks. Knowing that they can get their money out of the bank no matter what happens, depositors do not care whether banks make risky investments. The insurer, such as the FDIC, has an incentive to establish rules that limit the riskiness of banks' investments and to monitor banks to make sure that they follow these rules. If a bank suffers losses from risky investments, after all, the insurer must pay.

In the 19th century, private deposit insurers regulated and monitored bank investments. Similarly, when the government provides deposit insurance, it could either establish regulations that prevent banks from making risky investments or charge insurance premiums in proportion to the riskiness of investments, just as private health and life insurance companies raise insurance premiums for people who smoke.

Review Questions

15. What is a bank run and why might one occur?

16. How is deposit insurance intended to prevent bank runs?

17. What problem does deposit insurance create? How was this problem connected with the U.S. savings and loan crisis of the 1980s and the Asian financial crises of 1997–98?

Thinking Exercise

18. Suppose that a banking panic occurs and banks close, reducing the amount of bank deposits enough to raise the currency–deposit ratio from 1 to 2. If the reserve–deposit ratio is 10 percent, how does the money multiplier change? How would M1 change if the monetary base were to remain constant at its previous level?

IN THE NEWS

Perils of insuring bank deposits

By Lindley H. Clark, Jr.

Any insurance plan has to deal with a basic problem: something insurance men call "moral hazard." The idea is simple. If you have no fire insurance on your home, you are extra careful. If, on the other hand, you are insured, you relax. You may not let the kids play with matches, but you don't stay awake nights trying to smell smoke.

Similarly, when a bank deposit is insured, the depositor doesn't worry about the safety of his funds. He has little incentive to check up on the bank to try to learn if its operations are safe and sound. The bank, for its part, pays a fixed rate for deposit insurance regardless of the riskiness of its assets. If the bank's loans go bad, it knows the government will be standing by to pick up the pieces. There's a substantial incentive to make riskier loans to improve bank profits.

Source: The Wall Street Journal

Deposit insurance, like all insurance, creates a problem of moral hazard.

Connections between the monetary system and the loan market discussed in the previous sections imply connections between changes in the money supply and changes in the supply of loans. This section explains an additional *short-run* connection between the money market and the loan market.

When the Federal Reserve expands the money supply through an open market purchase, the long-run effects fall entirely on *nominal* variables, and money is neutral. In the long run, an increase in the money supply raises all nominal prices in the same proportion. For example, a 10 percent rise in the money supply eventually raises all nominal prices by 10 percent, so that relative prices do not change. Like a currency reform in reverse, an increase in the money supply has no long-run effects on real GDP, employment, or other real economic conditions.[6] Similarly, in the long run, a fall in the money supply reduces all nominal prices in the same proportion, without altering relative prices or real economic conditions.

In the short run, however, a Federal Reserve open market purchase may affect *real* variables rather than only *nominal* variables. The essay "What Economists Do," by Professor Robert Lucas (in Chapter 25) showed how a change in the money supply in Kennywood Park can affect real GDP and employment in the park. The real effects of changes in the money supply have inspired much economic research and controversy, as the next two chapters will explain. Most economists agree that one key element involves the connection between the *money market* and the *loan market*. This section discusses a simple model of this connection that explains why Fed actions affect the real interest rate in the short run.

Think about the supply and demand for short-term loans among banks. The equilibrium interest rate on these loans is the equilibrium federal funds rate. When the Fed adds reserves to the banking system through an open market purchase, the supply of loans increases, as in Figure 6a, reducing the equilibrium federal funds rate. Similarly, the supply of loans decreases when the Fed withdraws reserves from the banking system through an open market sale.

SHORT-RUN EFFECTS OF FEDERAL RESERVE POLICIES

Figure 6 | Effects of an Open Market Purchase

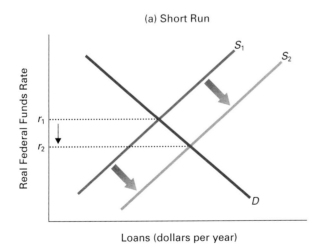

(a) Short Run

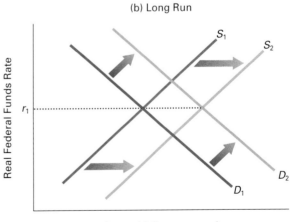

(b) Long Run

In the short run, an open-market purchase raises the money supply and the supply of loans. If the price level does not rise in the short run, as in the Kennywood Park story, then the real interest rate falls.

In the long run, the increase in the money supply raises the price level proportionately, raising the demand for loans and raising the equilibrium real interest rate back to its original level.

[6]Unlike a currency reform in reverse, however, the change in the money supply may redistribute income, creating winners and losers. In a reverse currency reform, everyone would share the increase in the money supply (essentially by adding zeros to their money). However, not everyone receives additional money when the money supply rises through an open market purchase, so the open market operation can redistribute wealth from some people to others.

IN THE NEWS

Fed cuts discount rate to 6.5%; move signals concern on economy

Lower funds rate is also seen backed at earlier meeting

By David Wessel
Staff Reporter of
The Wall Street Journal

WASHINGTON—The Federal Reserve Board, signaling its concern about the weakening U.S. economy, cut the highly visible discount rate one-half percentage point to 6.5 percent.

The unanimous decision by the six Fed governors came hours after a meeting of the Fed's larger policy-making committee. The committee is believed to have authorized an immediate reduction of one-quarter percentage point in the key federal funds rate, which banks charge on loans to one another.

Market reaction to the cut in the discount rate— which the Fed charges on loans to banks—was swift and enthusiastic. Stock and bond prices rose, driving interest rates down.

The discount-rate move, and the expected reduction in the federal funds rate to 7 percent as early as today, are likely to force banks to finally cut their lending rates.

Just two weeks ago, the Fed cut the federal funds rate one-quarter percentage point and made the unusual move of reducing the fraction of deposits that banks must hold as reserves— two moves aimed at stimulating the economy.

Symbolic Move

Moves in the discount rate have little direct effect on the economy, but are used by the Fed to send loud and clear signals. "Symbolism is important," said Mr. Moran.

"This will be on the front pages rather than the credit market columns. It will be on the evening news. It will be seen by individuals and small-business people who might not otherwise know [what the Fed is doing]. It will be a boost to confidence."

The Fed governors directly set the discount rate in response to requests from district Fed banks. But the Fed's Open Market Committee—for which the voting members consist of the six current governors plus five of the 12 district bank presidents—controls the federal funds rate by buying and selling Treasury securities. The fed funds rate is more significant in determining the level of interest rates in the economy.

Source: The Wall Street Journal

Federal Reserve policy actions affect interest rates.

Suppose the Fed raises the money supply by 10 percent, by increasing reserves that banks lend to people. If the *demand* for loans also were to increase by 10 percent, then the equilibrium real federal funds rate would not change. In the long run, a 10 percent increase in the money supply raises all nominal prices by 10 percent. As a result, the nominal quantity of loans demanded also rises by 10 percent in the long run, so equilibrium federal funds rate does not change. Figure 6b shows the long-run effect of the open market purchase on the federal funds market. An open market operation has no long-run effects on the real federal funds interest rate.

In the short run, however, an open market purchase tends to reduce the real federal funds rate. Suppose that the price level does *not change* in the short run, despite the 10 percent increase in the money supply. (Recall that a surprise decrease in the money supply in Kennywood Park left the price level in the park unaffected in the short run.) In this case, the increase in the money supply raises the *supply* of loans but leaves the *demand* for loans unchanged in the short run. As a result, the equilibrium real federal funds rate *falls* in the short run.

In this way, Federal Reserve actions affect the real interest rate in the short run. Specifically, the Fed's actions affect the real federal funds interest rate. The Fed can reduce the real interest rate through open-market purchases (which raise the money supply), or raise the real interest rate through open-market sales. These changes in the real federal funds rate also tend to be reflected in the nominal federal funds rate, unless the Fed's action has a large effect on expected inflation. As a result, the Fed lowers or raises the nominal federal funds rate through open-market purchases or sales.

The change in the federal funds rate affects other interest rates. A fall in the federal funds rate reduces the cost to banks of borrowing reserves, and competition then leads banks to reduce the interest rates that they charge to borrowers. Similarly, a rise in the federal funds rate raises the cost to banks of borrowing reserves, leading them to raise the interest rates they charge. An open market operation has no long-run effects on real interest rates. After changing in the short run, real interest rates return to their original levels.

Because open market purchases temporarily reduce the real federal funds rate, and open market sales temporarily raise it, commentators often describe Federal Reserve policies in terms of their effects on interest rates. The Fed itself usually describes its policies in this way—as raising or lowering interest rates.

> A **looser monetary policy** refers to Fed actions that increase the growth rate of the money supply or decrease the federal funds rate.

The Fed loosens monetary policy by expanding open market purchases or increasing its lending to banks at the discount window.

> A **tighter monetary policy** refers to Fed actions that reduce the growth rate of the money supply or increase the federal funds rate.

The Fed tightens monetary policy by reducing open market purchases (or expanding open market sales) or by reducing its lending to banks at the discount window.

The next two chapters discuss the short-run effects of monetary policy as they explore business cycles and recessions. A later chapter discusses alternative views of the role of monetary policy.

Review Questions

19. How does a Federal Reserve open market purchase affect the federal funds rate? Why does this effect occur? How do the short-run effects of such a policy differ from the long-run effects?

IN THE NEWS

Fed votes against cutting short-term rates for now

Open Market panel opposes immediate move, signals inaction in weeks ahead

By David Wessel
Staff Reporter of
The Wall Street Journal

WASHINGTON—Federal Reserve policy makers decided this week against any immediate cut in short-term interest rates, people familiar with the Fed's deliberations said.

The Fed influences the federal funds rate, which banks charge each other for overnight loans, by buying and selling government securities.

Source: The Wall Street Journal

IN THE NEWS

Federal Reserve's chief suggests a new rate rise may be needed

By Keith Bradsher
Special to
The New York Times

WASHINGTON, July 20— The chairman of the Federal Reserve said today that the four increases in interest rates this year might not have been enough to keep inflation under control.

Marc W. Wanshel, an economist at J. P. Morgan in New York, said that the comment made likely an additional tightening of monetary policy and higher interest rates.

Source: New York Times

The Fed tightens monetary policy to fight inflation.

20. What does the Fed do when it loosens or tightens monetary policy?

Thinking Exercise

21. If an open market sale raises the real interest rate by 1 percentage point and reduces expected inflation by 2 percentage points, how does it affect the nominal interest rate?

Conclusion

History and Roles of Money

Many commodities have served as money, and some civilizations have not used money at all. Money offers advantages, however, because it avoids the problem with barter of creating a double coincidence of wants. In its main role as a medium of exchange, money acts as an asset that sellers generally accept as payment for goods, services, and other assets. Money also serves as a store of value and a unit of account.

The most common form of commodity standard for money has been a gold standard. In a pure gold standard, people use gold coins as money, and the economy includes no paper money. In a gold exchange standard, people trade paper money that is backed by gold stored in warehouses. A silver standard resembles a gold standard, but silver instead of gold backs paper money. Fiat money is paper money that is not backed by a commodity in the sense that people cannot trade it for a particular commodity at a fixed nominal price.

Measuring the Money Supply

Banks help to create money. An increase in bank reserves leads to an increase in bank lending, which raises broad measures of the money supply. Definitions of the money supply include the monetary base and broader measures such as M1 and M2. M1 includes currency plus traveler's checks and bank balances against which people or firms can write checks; M2 combines M1 with balances in most savings accounts and similar accounts. The money multiplier is the ratio of a broad measure of the money supply, such as M1 or M2, to the monetary base.

Federal Reserve System

A central bank is a bank for banks. The Federal Reserve is the central bank of the United States. The Federal Reserve System consists of the Board of Governors, 12 regional Federal Reserve Banks, and the Federal Open Market Committee (FOMC).

The Fed's three main tools of monetary policy are open market operations, discount window lending, and changes in reserve requirements. The primary tool of monetary policy is the open market operation, in which the Fed buys or sells financial assets, usually U.S. government Treasury bills and Treasury bonds. In an open market purchase, the Fed buys financial assets; in an open market sale, it sells them.

Financial Intermediaries

Financial intermediaries, such as banks and similar kinds of firms, gather funds from many savers to lend to borrowers. They also monitor borrowers' activities to try to ensure timely repayment of loans.

A banking panic refers to many bank runs at the same time. Deposit insurance can help to prevent bank runs, but it changes the incentives of financial intermediaries, increasing their willingness to choose risky investments and reducing the incentive of depositors to monitor banks' investments and choose low-risk banks. The U.S. savings and loan crisis resulted from these incentives, coupled with a failure of the insurer (the government, in that case) to prevent risky investments or raise insurance premiums to risky institutions. Banking crises are usually associated with recessions, as in many Asian countries in recent years.

Short-Run Effects of Federal Reserve Policies

In the long run, an increase in the money supply raises all nominal prices proportionally and does not affect relative prices or the real interest rate. In the short run, however, an open market purchase reduces the real federal funds interest rate, leading other real interest rates to fall. Nominal interest rates also fall unless expected inflation rises sufficiently.

Economists commonly describe Fed policies in terms of raising or lowering interest rates. A looser monetary policy increases the growth rate of the money supply or decreases the federal funds rate, usually by increasing open market purchases. A tighter monetary policy reduces the growth rate of the money supply or increases the federal funds rate, usually by reducing open market purchases or increasing open market sales.

Key Terms

medium of exchange
store of value
unit of account
pure gold standard
gold exchange standard
fiat money

currency
demand deposit
M1
M2
bank reserves
monetary base

M1 money multiplier
central bank
Federal Reserve System
open market operation
Federal Reserve discount rate
federal funds rate

required reserves
financial intermediary
bank run
banking panic
looser monetary policy
tighter monetary policy

Questions and Problems

22. What is a double coincidence of wants?

23. When and why was the Fed created?

24. Why do banks hold reserves?

25. Suppose that banks hold reserves equal to 20 percent of deposits in checking accounts and that people always keep equal amounts of currency and checking-account balances (making the currency–deposit ratio equal to 1). If the Fed raises the monetary base by $1 million with an open market purchase, how much will M1 increase? Explain why.

26. What does a government do when it debases coins?

27. Suppose that the United States and Russia were on a gold standard and that large quantities of gold were discovered in Russia. Explain the process by which this discovery would affect prices in the United States.

28. Suppose that prices take 6 months to increase after the Fed increases the money supply. Suppose that the Fed raises the money supply by 10 percent through open market purchases.
    (a) Explain why this action could reduce the real interest rate for 6 months.
    (b) Explain why this action would not reduce the long-run real interest rate (after nominal prices have increased by 10 percent).

Inquiries for Further Thought

29. (a) Why are sellers willing to trade goods for the pieces of paper that people call dollar bills? What makes those pieces of paper different from other pieces of paper that sellers would refuse to accept as payment?
    (b) Why do sellers in the United States usually insist on payment in U.S. dollars rather than Canadian dollars, while Canadian sellers display the opposite preference?
    (c) Why do people use the money issued by their own governments? Why not other moneys? What advantages and disadvantages might accompany attempts by people in another country to use U.S. dollars rather than their own country's money?

30. What would happen if banks were allowed to issue their own money, as they were in 19th-century America?

31. What would happen to the U.S. economy if many

communities began using their own local currencies, such as the Ithaca Hours in Ithaca, N.Y.?

32. What would happen if the government were to stop providing deposit insurance to banks? What would happen if the government were to privatize deposit insurance?

33. Do you think that people will use money 50 years from now? Some people have predicted that cash will disappear as computers keep track of who owes what to whom. How might that work? Could inflation exist with that system?

34. Some people have proposed that the United States eliminate pennies. (The federal government mints about 12 billion pennies each year, about 50 for every person in the country. Sales clerks at stores take a few extra seconds to deal with pennies, and this time adds up to a large expense, in the millions of dollars, for stores. Banning the penny

would eliminate these expenses.) If the penny were abolished and all prices were rounded to the nearest $0.05, would stores always round the price upward, or would they maintain the psychological advantages of a $12.98 price by rounding down to $12.95? What would happen? Who would gain and who would lose from eliminating the penny? Would it be a good or bad idea?

Appendix: The Formula for the Money Multiplier

One can derive the M1 money multiplier from the definitions of M1 and the monetary base. If C stands for currency (cash), D stands for deposits, and R stands for bank reserves, then M1 equals:

$$M1 = D + C$$

and the monetary base, B, equals

$$B = R + C$$

The M1 money multiplier equals the ratio of M1 to B:

$$M1 \text{ money multiplier} = \frac{M1}{B}$$

Substituting the definitions for M1 and B:

$$= \frac{D + C}{R + C}$$

Dividing both the numerator and denominator by D:

$$= \frac{(1 + C/D)}{(R/D + C/D)}$$

This is the expression in the text. Money multipliers for broader measures of money can be derived in a similar way, with more complicated results.

BUSINESS CYCLES

CHAPTER 30

BUSINESS CYCLES 1: AGGREGATE DEMAND AND SUPPLY

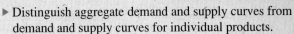

In this Chapter...

Main Points to Understand

▶ The aggregate demand curve graphs the equation of exchange for given levels of the money supply and velocity. It shows the total amount of goods and services that people, firms, and the government would buy at each possible price level, given the money supply and velocity.

▶ The aggregate supply curve graphs the total amount of goods and services that firms would produce and try to sell at each possible price level.

▶ The long-run aggregate supply curve is a vertical line.

▶ The short-run aggregate supply curve slopes upward because of sticky prices.

▶ Decreases in aggregate demand can cause recessions.

Thinking Skills to Develop

▶ Distinguish aggregate demand and supply curves from demand and supply curves for individual products.

▶ Use a special case of a model to help understand a more general case.

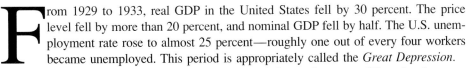

From 1929 to 1933, real GDP in the United States fell by 30 percent. The price level fell by more than 20 percent, and nominal GDP fell by half. The U.S. unemployment rate rose to almost 25 percent—roughly one out of every four workers became unemployed. This period is appropriately called the *Great Depression*.

The Great Depression may seem long ago and distant from your life today, but people in Mexico, Russia, Japan, and other countries have experienced major recessions within the last few years. In 1998 alone, real GDP fell about 15 percent in Indonesia, 8 percent in South Korea, 7 percent in Thailand, 6 percent in Russia, and 2.5 percent in Venezuela. Unemployment in Japan reached a new record high in late 1998, and leaders around the world began to talk openly of policies to avoid a repeat of the 1930s. Even smaller recessions, like the United States recession of 1991 when unemployment reached 7.5 percent, brought hardships for many families.

The basic model developed in earlier chapters is not capable of explaining these recessions. This chapter will extend the model in the direction suggested by the Kennywood Park story from Chapter 25. The extended model will help explain recessions and predict complex connections between real and nominal variables. For example, economists have noted that the money supply, measured by M2, fell by one-third during the Great Depression.[1]

---

[1]The government did not purposely reduce the money supply. The Federal Reserve kept the monetary base roughly constant, but the money multiplier (discussed in the previous chapter) fell as banks failed and the currency-deposit ratio increased.

IN THE NEWS

Japan's unemployment at record high

TOKYO, Oct. 1—Japan's unemployment rate bounced back to a record high 4.3 percent in August, boosted by an increase in corporate restructurings and bankruptcies, the government said Friday. The labor figures were the latest in the series of data that showed further deterioration of the Japanese economy.

Source: Associated Press

Many economists believe that if the Federal Reserve had prevented the fall in the money supply, it would have averted the Great Depression or dramatically reduced its severity. The extended model will explain why. It will also explain the logic that the Federal Reserve uses when it decides to loosen monetary policy to help fight a potential recession, as it did in September 1998.

Connections between real and nominal variables are controversial subjects in economics. Economists do not yet fully understand these connections; evidence is less complete than economists would like; and disagreements abound on details of these issues. However, governments cannot wait for additional evidence to formulate their policies, nor can business firms postpone their decisions on operations and investments. They must act on the best available information, even if that information is incomplete. This chapter studies the logic that underlies economists' current understanding of these key issues that have such profound impacts on our lives.

BOOMS AND RECESSIONS

Economic growth does not proceed smoothly—it fluctuates in patterns called *business cycles*.[2] A typical business cycle has two parts: a recession and a recovery or expansion. During a recession, which typically lasts between two quarters and two years, real GDP falls, employment falls, and unemployment rises. Some commentators define a recession as two consecutive quarters of falling real GDP. However, the National Bureau of Economic Research, a private organization generally regarded as the authority on dates of business cycles, uses a more complex definition involving an extended period of decline in real GDP and other related variables. Figure 1 shows recessions in the United States in the last quarter-century. Note that decreases in real GDP occur along with rising unemployment.

A recession begins at the *peak* of a business cycle and continues until its *trough* (low point), when a *recovery* or expansion begins, continuing until the next peak. The last U.S. recession occurred from July 1990 (the peak of the last business cycle) until March 1991 (the trough). Since that time (at least until late 1998) the U.S. economy continued in a long expansion.

Why do business cycles occur? Economists disagree on the details of the answer to this fundamental question, because available evidence is not yet strong enough to create full agreement. The basic model of previous chapters suggests one possible reason for business cycles: Perhaps business cycles result from changes in technology or

---

[2] The economy also experiences seasonal cycles throughout each year. These seasonal variations, which are much easier to predict than business cycles, share other features of business cycles. For example, unemployment rises as real GDP falls.

Figure 1 | U.S. Business Cycles, 1950–1998

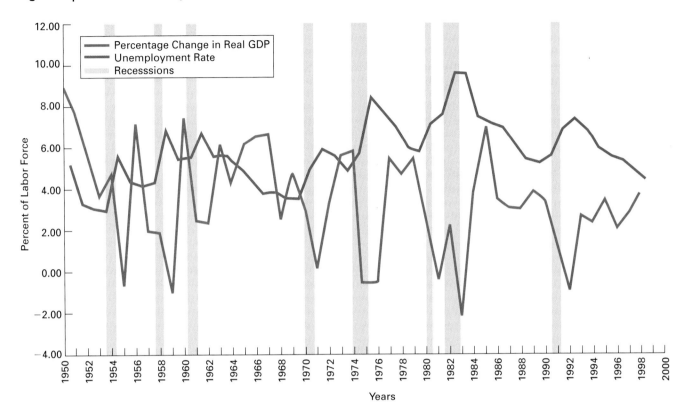

equilibrium quantities of inputs. (Chapter 27 showed how changes in technology and available capital affect real GDP.) However, available evidence leads most economists to doubt this explanation. Changes in overall technology occur too smoothly over time to cause the yearly fluctuations in GDP shown in Figure 1, or the Great Depression and the recent recessions throughout the world. Evidence indicates connections between recessions and *monetary policy,* a connection that the basic model of previous chapters cannot explain. This chapter modifies the basic model by adding *short-run* features that most economists believe are important in understanding business cycles.

We can use the circular flow diagram of Chapter 28 to create a simple model of a recession based on the equation of exchange, $MV = Py$. In Figure 2, firms produce 100 goods per year, so real GDP is 100 goods per year. The nominal money supply is $1,000, and the velocity of money is 1 per year, so people spend $1,000 per year to buy 100 goods, and the price level is $10 per good.

Suppose the money supply falls from $1,000 to $900 with no change in velocity. People spend only $900 per year, so the equilibrium price level falls from $10 to $9 per good. The 10 percent fall in the money supply reduces *nominal* variables by 10 percent, so nominal GDP falls from $1,000 to $900 per year. However, the fall in the money supply does not affect *real* variables, such as production and employment. Real GDP remains at 100 goods per year. In the language of previous chapters, *money is neutral.* Now consider a new complication to the circular-flow model. *Suppose that the price level cannot change.* Again, the money supply falls from $1,000 to $900 with constant velocity, so people spend only $900 per year. However, the price level remains at $10 per good,

A SIMPLE MODEL OF A RECESSION

Figure 2 | Key Example

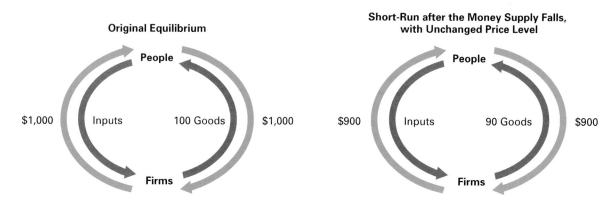

At first, people spend $1,000 to buy 100 goods each year. Velocity is 1 per year, and the price is $10 per good. The money supply then falls from $1,000 to $900. The completely sticky price level keeps the cost of goods at $10 each. Unless velocity rises, people spend only $900 each year, so they can afford to buy only 90 goods each year. Firms reduce output from 100 goods per person to 90 goods per person, and a recession occurs.

so *people can afford to buy only 90 goods.* Figure 2 shows the results. Firms have enough technology and inputs to produce 100 goods, but they can sell only 90. As a result, firms reduce production from 100 to 90, laying off workers and raising unemployment. The economy enters a *recession.*

In mathematical terms, these results appear in the equation of exchange:

$$MV = Py$$

The money supply, *M,* falls and velocity, *V,* remains constant, so the left-hand side of the equation falls. In the basic model of previous chapters, a fall in the price level, *P,* reduces the right-hand side of the equation, restoring equality. The price level falls by the same percentage as the money supply. Real GDP, *y,* remains unaffected. However, if the price level *cannot* fall, then real GDP must fall to balance the equation. Even though firms *could* continue to produce 100 goods per year, they would not be able to sell all those goods. As a result, they reduce production, decreasing real GDP and raising unemployment. If the price level cannot fall, money is *not* neutral, and the economy enters a recession.

Return to Kennywood Park

The recession in Professor Lucas's Kennywood Park story, discussed in Chapter 25, occurs for a similar reason. The money supply in Kennywood Park—the total number of tickets sold at the park—decreases one Sunday. However, nominal prices—the numbers of tickets required for the rides—remain unchanged. As a result, the park's real GDP falls; people buy fewer rides, and the park enters a recession.

Short Run and Long Run

Suppose that the price level remains fixed for 6 months following a fall in the money supply, then changes to its new equilibrium level. During the first 6 months, the economy will experience a recession. After the price level falls to its new equilibrium level, the recession ends. Economists distinguish the *short run* from the *long run*: The short run is the time period *before* the price level adjusts fully to its new equilibrium level after a change in conditions (like a fall in the money supply). The long run refers to the time period *after* prices have fully adjusted to a change in conditions.[3] If the price level cannot fall in the short run, then a decrease in the money supply causes a recession in the short run, but the recession ends in the long run. Money is *neutral* in the long run, though not in the short run.

Sticky Prices

The simple model of a recession says that the price level does not change in the short run, even after a change in underlying conditions: The price level is *sticky* in the short run.

> Nominal prices are **sticky** if they take time to adjust to their new equilibrium levels following changes in supply or demand.

Some prices adjust very quickly to changes in demand or supply. Prices of homogeneous commodities (such as gold, silver, tin, wheat, and soybeans) traded on organized markets such as the Chicago Mercantile Exchange change every few seconds. Prices of some consumer goods, such as computers, change very frequently. These prices are not sticky. Other prices adjust more slowly: prices of magazines at newsstands, prices of clothing in mail-order catalogs, apartment rental prices, and prices of steel, cement, chemicals, and glass bought by manufacturing firms. Prices in some industries remain unchanged for periods of several years.

Overall, evidence suggests that the *price level* is sticky in the short run—it adjusts only slowly after changes in underlying conditions, such as the money supply. Although economists disagree about interpretations of available evidence, most believe that the price level may take one or two years to adjust to its new equilibrium after a change in the money supply. Economists also disagree about the *causes* of short-run price-stickiness. Do firms remain unaware of changes in conditions that would otherwise prompt them to adjust prices? Or do firms postpone price adjustments because they involve costly reprinting of catalogs, menus, and price tags? Fortunately, logical analysis of the *consequences* of price stickiness can proceed without full answers to those questions. That logic begins with the model of *aggregate demand and supply.*

The price level is sticky in the short run—it moves only slowly to its new equilibrium after a change in underlying conditions.

AGGREGATE DEMAND

Loosely, a country's aggregate demand is the total demand for all the goods and services produced in that country in a given year. More precisely,

> The **aggregate demand curve** shows the total amount of goods and services that people, firms, and the government would choose to buy at each possible price level, given the nominal money supply and velocity.[4]

The aggregate demand curve graphs the equation of exchange, solved for the price level:

$$P = MV/y$$

for given values of M and V. The aggregate demand curve shifts when M and V change, rising when MV rises.

---

[3] This *macroeconomic* distinction between *short run* and *long run* differs from the distinction between those terms common in microeconomics.

[4] If you take additional courses in economics, you may encounter a different, more complex definition of aggregate demand.

Figure 3
Aggregate Demand Curve

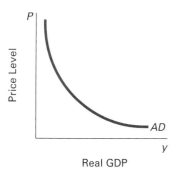

Figure 3 shows an aggregate demand curve. Given total nominal spending, *MV,* the graph shows that the price level (*P*) and real GDP (*y*) vary inversely with one another: Increases in *y* accompany decreases in *P.* For example, suppose that the money supply is $100 and velocity is 2 per year. Then *MV* is $200 per year, so *Py* must be $200 per year. At a price of $10 per good, *y* equals 20 goods per year (Point A in Figure 4). At a price of $20 per good, however, *y* equals only 10 goods per year (Point B in Figure 4).

The total amount of money you spend at a grocery store equals the sum of your spending on each type of good you buy (spending on marshmallows, plus spending on graham crackers, plus spending on chocolate). The term *MV* equals the economy's total spending in a year—the number of dollars in the economy (*M*) multiplied by the number of each times each dollar is spent in that year. This total equals the sum of spending on each type of good: consumption, plus investment, plus government purchases, plus net exports. Therefore, consumption (*C*), plus investment (*I*), plus government purchases (*G*), plus net exports (*NEX*) equals total spending.

$$MV = C + I + G + NEX$$

Both sides of this equation show total spending: both sides show the level of aggregate demand.

For example, suppose that the money supply equals $1 trillion and the velocity of money equals *7 times per year.* Then total spending on final market goods and services, *MV,* is $7 trillion per year. Perhaps people spend $5 trillion on consumption, firms spend $1 trillion on investment, the government spends $1 trillion, and exports equal imports (so net exports equal zero). Then total spending—aggregate demand—equals:

$$C + I + G + NEX = \$5 + \$1 + \$1 + 0 = \$7 \text{ trillion}$$

Figure 4
Example of an Aggregate Demand Curve

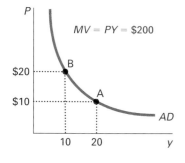

Changes in Aggregate Demand

The aggregate demand curve *shifts* when the money supply changes or velocity changes. Chapter 29 showed that Federal Reserve open market operations (and other Fed policy actions) can change the money supply, as can actions of banks and depositors. When the money supply increases, aggregate demand increases, as in Figure 5.

Our basic economic model shows how various factors can change the velocity of money. Chapter 28 explained that the velocity of money rises when the nominal interest rate rises. Many factors can affect the equilibrium nominal interest rate by affecting the demand or supply of loans. Three important sources of changes in velocity include consumption, investment, and government purchases:

IN THE NEWS

Consumption, the engine of the economy

A decline in consumer confidence often points toward recession because lower confidence is generally translated into lower sales of such things as cars and refrigerators. The effect of canceled or postponed purchases ripples through the economy as, say, the auto-mobile salesman decides he'll wait another year to add a patio to his house and the mason's helper begins to worry about being laid off.

Source: New York Times

A change in spending has indirect effects that ripple through the economy.

IN THE NEWS

Market turmoil makes some spenders pause a bit

Some big-spending consumers, feeling queasy from the stock market's recent gyrations, are deep-sixing some of their purchase plans.

For much of this decade, consumers have been powering the economy. They've been inspired by plentiful jobs, healthy income growth, low inflation—and heady stock-market gains.

But this time, people say there's enough uncertainty about global political and financial unrest that they're feeling uneasy. And at least for now, some are thinking twice about buying that summer home or third car.

Source: The Wall Street Journal

A rise in uncertainty about the future can lead people to raise savings and reduce consumption, decreasing aggregate demand.

1. **An increase in consumption, *C*:** When people decide to consume more and save less, the decrease in savings reduces the supply of loans, increasing the equilibrium real interest rate, as in Figure 6. Given the expected rate of inflation, this increase in the real interest rate raises the nominal interest rate, raising velocity. The increase in velocity raises aggregate demand as in Figure 5.

2. **An increase in investment, *I*:** When firms decide to increase investment, the demand for loans rises, increasing the equilibrium real interest rate. Given the expected rate of inflation, this increase in the real interest rate raises the nominal interest rate, raising velocity. The increase in velocity raises aggregate demand as in Figure 5.

3. **An increase in government purchases, *G*:** If the government borrows money to pay for its additional spending, then the demand for loans rises, increasing the equilibrium real interest rate. Alternatively, the government may raise taxes to pay for its additional spending, reducing people's after-tax income. The fall in after-tax income may lead people to reduce savings, decreasing the supply of loans and raising the equilibrium real interest rate. The demand for loans rises, increasing the equilibrium interest rate. Given the expected rate of inflation, this increase raises the nominal interest rate, raising velocity. The increase in velocity raises aggregate demand as in Figure 5.

Summarizing these results:

Increases in consumption (*C*), investment (*I*), or government purchases (*G*) raise aggregate demand, as in Figure 5.

You can personally raise aggregate demand in the U.S. economy by increasing your spending and reducing your saving. A business firm can raise aggregate demand by borrowing for new investment. The government can raise aggregate demand by boosting spending.

Review Questions

1. What do economists mean when they say that the price level is sticky in the short run?

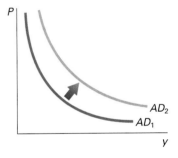

Figure 5
Increase in Aggregate Demand

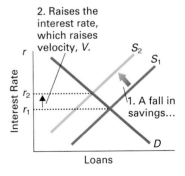

Figure 6
A Fall in Savings Raises Velocity

An increase in consumption spending reduces saving, which reduces the supply of loans from S_1 to S_2. This raises the real interest rate from r_1 to r_2, which raises the nominal interest rate and velocity. Therefore, aggregate demand (MV) rises.

An Important Reminder
The aggregate demand curve differs from the demand curves for individual products introduced in Chapter 4. Those demand curves involve *relative prices* of goods. When the relative price of a good rises, its opportunity cost increases, so the quantity demanded falls as people substitute other goods in its place. In contrast, the aggregate demand curve involves the economy's overall *nominal price level*. A rise in the nominal price level does not affect the opportunity costs of the economy's goods and services. However, it reduces the overall purchasing power of the money that people have available to spend. Understanding the distinction between relative prices and the nominal price level, and the related distinction between demand curves for individual products and the aggregate demand curve, will help you avoid logical fallacies.

"Whether the marriage lasts or not, we've certainly given the economy a boost."

A small increase in aggregate demand.
Source: The Wall Street Journal, October 25, 1988, p. A27.

2. Draw a circular-flow diagram and explain why a decrease in the money supply leads to a fall in real GDP if prices are completely sticky and velocity remains constant.

3. What does the aggregate demand curve show? Why does it slope downward? What makes it shift?

4. Why is the money supply multiplied by velocity equal to the sum of consumption, investment, government purchases, and net exports?

Thinking Exercise

5. Recall that the aggregate demand curve graphs the equation of exchange for given money supply and velocity. Explain how and why the following changes shift the aggregate demand curve: (a) a decision by people to reduce consumption and increase savings; (b) a decrease in investment demand; (c) a decrease in government purchases.

AGGREGATE SUPPLY

Loosely, a country's aggregate supply is the total supply of all the goods and services produced in that country in a given year. More precisely,

> The **aggregate supply curve** shows the total amount of goods and services that firms would produce and try to sell at each possible price level.[5]

---

[5]If you go on in economics, you may encounter a different, more complex definition of aggregate supply that distinguishes the amount that firms want to sell from the amount they want to produce.

The most important facts about the aggregate supply curve are:

The aggregate supply curve is vertical in the long run.

The aggregate supply curve slopes upward in the short run.

Long-run aggregate supply measures the total supply of goods and services after the economy has had time to adjust fully to a change in underlying conditions. *Short-run aggregate supply* refers to the total supply before that adjustment is complete.

Long-Run Aggregate Supply

The long-run aggregate supply curve is a vertical line, as in Figure 7. In the long run, a country's production of goods and services does *not* depend on *nominal* variables, such as the price level. Long-run production depends *solely* on *real* variables, such as available technology and inputs such as capital, labor, natural resources, as well as the laws, property rights, regulations, and taxes that affect people's incentives to use technology and inputs efficiently. This is an application of the idea from Chapters 25 and 27 that *money is neutral* in the long run. Changing the units by which we measure money and nominal prices, as in a currency reform, does not affect real variables such as production and relative prices.

The long-run level of real GDP in Figure 7, often called the *full-employment level of output*, y^{FE}, is the equilibrium level from the basic model of previous chapters. The supply and demand for labor determine equilibrium employment, and the production function then determines equilibrium real GDP, as in Figure 5 of Chapter 26.[6]

Changes in Long-Run Aggregate Supply

Increases in technology raise long-run aggregate supply, as in Figure 8. Long-run aggregate supply also rises with increases in the economy's equilibrium inputs of labor or capital, workers' skills, or the quality of capital equipment. Finally, long-run aggregate supply increases when changes in taxes, government regulations, or the legal system lead to more efficient use of the economy's resources. Long-run aggregate supply *decreases* when equilibrium inputs fall, workers' skills erode, or the quality of capital equipment falls, and when changes in taxes, government regulations, or the legal system lead to less efficient use of the economy's resources. Changes in the prices of imported inputs, such as oil from foreign countries, also shift the long-run aggregate supply curve. For example, a quadrupling of the price of oil a quarter-century ago contributed to the recession of 1973 to 1975 by reducing aggregate supply.

Long-Run Equilibrium of Aggregate Supply and Demand

The intersection of the long-run aggregate supply curve with the aggregate demand curve, as in Figure 9, shows the long-run equilibrium real GDP and price level. This graph summarizes the *same* equilibrium as in Figure 5 of Chapter 26. The supply and demand for labor determine equilibrium employment, and the production function then determines equilibrium real GDP; given this level of real GDP, together with the money supply and velocity, the equation of exchange determines the price level.

Changes in Aggregate Demand

Figure 10 on page 729 shows the long-run effects of a rise in aggregate demand from AD_1 to AD_2 (perhaps due to an increase in government purchases or the money supply). The price level rises from P_1 to P_2 and real GDP remains unchanged at y^{FE}, the full-employment rate of output.

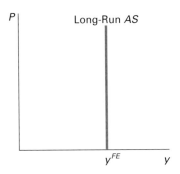

Figure 7
Long-Run Aggregate Supply Curve

The long-run aggregate supply curve is a vertical line at the full-employment level of output, y^{FE}.

An Important Reminder, Part 2

The aggregate supply curve differs from the supply curves of individual products introduced in Chapter 4. Those supply curves involve *relative prices* of goods. In contrast, the aggregate supply curve involves the *nominal price level*.

Understanding this distinction will help you avoid logical fallacies. For example, someone might say that the aggregate supply curve must slope upward, reflecting the upward slopes of the supply curves of individual goods, like pizzas and parkas. This claim is incorrect because it ignores the distinction between the price level and relative prices of individual goods. When the relative price of pizzas

(continued)

---

[6]The economy's capital stock and its technology result from its past investments, as Chapters 26-27 explained.

rises, production of pizzas rises as existing pizza restaurants boost production and new firms (such as hamburger restaurants) start selling pizzas. With a rise in the *relative* price of pizzas, sellers trade each pizza for *more* units of other goods, such as T-shirts and vacations. However, when the price *level* rises, with no change in relative prices, the incentive to sell pizzas remains unchanged, because each pizza trades for the same number of other goods as before the general price increase. You must understand these distinctions to understand why the slope of the aggregate supply curve is *vertical* in the long run, *regardless* of the shapes of supply curves of individual products. Similarly, the slope of the short-run aggregate supply curve depends on factors such as the degree of price stickiness; the slope is *unrelated* to the slopes of supply curves of individual products.

Figure 8 | An Increase in Long-Run Aggregate Supply

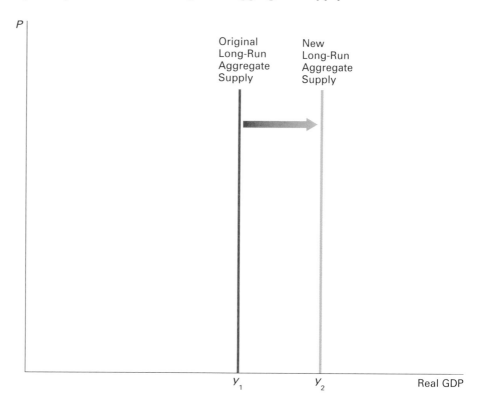

Figure 9 | Long-Run Equilibrium

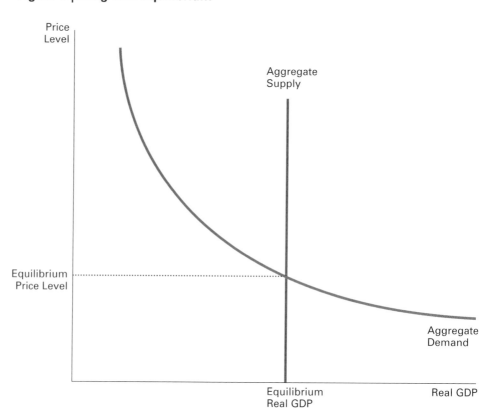

EXPLANATIONS

Suppose aggregate demand rises, because the government increases the money supply by 10 percent. The price level rises by 10 percent in the long run, and real GDP does not change. You may wonder how one can know that the price level will rise by 10 percent rather than 5 percent or 15 percent. To get this answer, use the equation of exchange, $MV = Py$. An increase in the money supply does not change real GDP, y, or velocity, V, in the long run, so these variables do not change; therefore, P must rise to balance the equation (raising the right-hand side by the same amount as the left-hand side). A 10 percent rise in M requires a 10 percent rise in P to balance the equation. As a result, the aggregate demand curve shifts *upward* by 10 percent, raising the equilibrium price level by 10 percent.

Now suppose an increase in government purchases raises aggregate demand. You may wonder why this increase in spending does not raise real GDP in the long run. The answer is that long-run real GDP depends on technology and available inputs, which are not affected by the increase in government purchases. When the government buys more goods and services than before, fewer remain available for people's consumption and business firms' investments. The increase in government purchases reduces the amount of goods that go to consumption and investment, and raises the price level.

The logic behind this result depends on how the government pays for its spending. If the government borrows money to pay for its additional spending, then the demand for loans rises, increasing the equilibrium real interest rate and reducing investment. Alternatively, suppose the government raises taxes to pay for its additional spending. This tax increase reduces people's after-tax income. With less after-tax income, people reduce their consumption. They also may save less, which decreases the supply of loans, raises the equilibrium real interest rate, and reduces investment. Either way, the increase in government purchases reduces consumption and investment in the new long-run equilibrium, and leaves real GDP unchanged.

Changes in Aggregate Supply

Figure 11 shows the long-run effects of a rise in aggregate supply from AS_1 to AS_2. The price level falls from P_1 to P_2, and the full-employment level of real GDP rises from y_1 to y_2.

Short-Run Aggregate Supply: Special Case

Suppose that *the price level cannot change* in the short run, as in the simple model of a recession earlier in this chapter—the price level is *completely sticky* in the short run. We can show this on a graph by drawing a horizontal line, as in Figure 12. This line shows that the price level P is completely sticky and that real GDP, y, adjusts to keep $MV = Py$ when MV changes. In this special case of a completely sticky price level, this horizontal line is the *short-run aggregate supply curve.*

Earlier, we defined the aggregate supply curve as a curve showing the total amount of goods and services that firms choose to produce and sell at each possible price level. The short-run aggregate supply curve in Figure 12 shows the total amount of goods and services that firms choose to produce and sell when the price is stuck at P_1. This is often called the simple Keynesian (pronounced *kane'-zee-en*) case of a horizontal short-run aggregate supply, after British economist and statesman John Maynard Keynes (pronounced like *canes),* the most famous economist of the 20th century. Keynes's 1936 book, *The General Theory of Employment, Interest, and Money,* revolutionized economics and led to economic models like the model of aggregate demand and supply.[7]

---

[7]If you go on in economics, you may encounter the *IS–LM* model, which resulted from the work of Keynes and his followers. The *IS* part of that model refers to *investment equals savings,* which corresponds to loan-market equilibrium in this book's model. The *LM* part of that model refers to the equation of exchange, which appears in this book's graphs as the aggregate demand curve. Therefore, if you study the *IS–LM* model in a future course, you may recognize it as the model from this chapter expressed in a different graphical language.

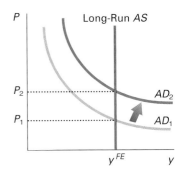

Figure 10
Long-Run Effects of an Increase in Aggregate Demand

An increase in aggregate demand raises the price level in the long run and leaves real GDP unchanged at the full-employment level of output, y^{FE}.

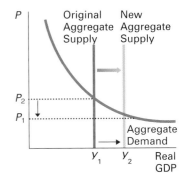

Figure 11
Long-Run Effects of an Increase in Aggregate Supply

Figure 12
Short-Run Aggregate Supply Curve—A Special Case

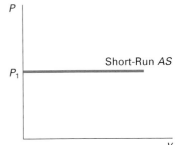

**Figure 13
Short-Run Effects of a
Decrease in Aggregate
Demand**

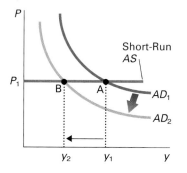

**Figure 14 | Short-Run and Long-Run Effects of a Decrease
in Aggregate Demand**

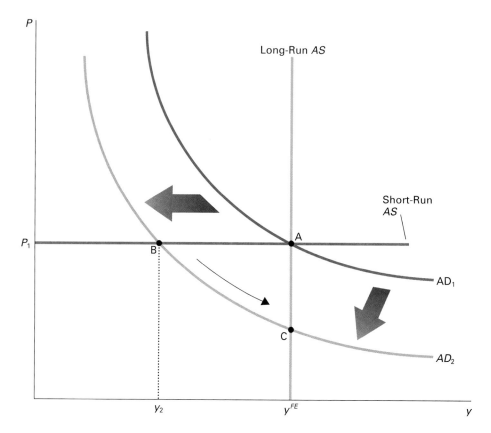

Short-Run Equilibrium of Aggregate Supply and Demand

The Kennywood Park recession in Professor Lucas's story, like the recession in the simple model discussed at the beginning of this chapter, resulted from a decrease in aggregate demand as in Figure 13. In the short run, the decrease in aggregate demand decreases real GDP from y_1 to y_2, moving the economy from Point A to Point B, creating a recession. In the long run, the price level falls and the recession ends, as real GDP returns to its full-employment level (Point C), as in Figure 14.

IN THE NEWS

Italy's GDP shrinks as Asia woes bite

ROME—Italy's economy unexpectedly shrank in the first quarter as Asia's economic slump knocked back Italian exports to the region.

Tumbling currencies and economies in Asia have eroded shoppers' appetite for Italian-made goods, notably clothing.

Source: International Herald Tribune

*A fall in aggregate demand spreads
throughout the world.*

IN THE NEWS

Recession hits Hong Kong

Economy shrinks five percent, biggest quarterly decline on record

HONG KONG—Hong Kong slipped officially into recession Friday as the government announced that the economy had shrunk by about five per-

cent in the second quarter, the biggest quarterly decline on record.

The decline reflected the further slackening in both local and consumer

demand as well as the territory's export performance in the second quarter, the government said.

Source: CNNfn

A fall in aggregate demand can cause a recession.

Short-Run Aggregate Supply—General Case

The horizontal short-run aggregate supply curve illustrates a special case in which the price level is completely sticky in the short run. More generally, the price level can change *partly* but not fully in the short run toward its long-run equilibrium level after a change in aggregate demand. As a result, the short-run aggregate supply curve slopes upward as in Figure 15.

The short-run aggregate supply curve in Figure 15 generalizes the special case in Figure 12. The price level is sticky, but not completely so, in the short run. As indicated earlier, some prices are not sticky even in the short run; prices of gold and wheat change continuously in organized markets; prices of computers change almost every day. However, other prices, such as prices of hamburgers at fast-food restaurants, prices of new books, and prices of clothes from catalogs, tend to be sticky in the short run. The aggregate supply curve in Figure 15 combines the results from these different markets. An upward movement along the short-run aggregate supply curve shows a rise in the nominal price level, resulting from increases in prices for some goods, and an increase in real GDP, resulting from sticky prices and increases in production of other goods.

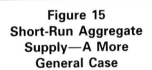

**Figure 15
Short-Run Aggregate
Supply—A More
General Case**

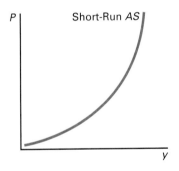

In the general case with upward sloping aggregate supply, a rise in aggregate demand raises the price level and real GDP in the short run, as in Figure 16a. A fall in aggregate demand lowers the price level and real GDP in the short run, as in Figure 16b.

If a change in aggregate demand is *temporary*, then its effects on the price level and real GDP are temporary. After moving from Point A to Point B in Figure 16 in the short run, the economy returns to Point A in the long run.

Figure 17 shows the effects of a *permanent* change in aggregate demand. Panel (a) shows the effects of a permanent rise in aggregate demand. In the short run, real GDP and the price level both rise, as the economy moves from Point A to Point B. In the long run, the economy moves to Point C, with unchanged real GDP, but a higher price level. Panel (b) shows the effects of a permanent fall in aggregate demand. In the short run, real GDP and the price level both fall (from Point A to Point B). In the long run, the forces that created sticky prices disappear. As a result, the price level falls further to its new long-run equilibrium level, and real GDP returns to its full-employment level (Point C).

**SUMMARY OF
CHANGES IN
AGGREGATE
SUPPLY AND
DEMAND**

SOCIAL AND ECONOMIC ISSUES

Does the United States Spend Too Much? Should the United States Save More?

Throughout the second half of the 20th century, Japan has saved a much larger fraction of its GDP than the United States has saved. As Chapter 27 indicated, the Japanese economy has also grown much faster over that period than the U.S. economy. Japan's GDP per person grew from about one-sixth of the U.S. level in 1950 to one-third of the U.S. level in 1960 (its pre–World War II ratio), to near equality with the United States today. For the past decade, Japan has saved about one-third of its GDP, more than twice as much as the United States.

Many economists argue that the United States should increase its saving. Because an economy needs savings to provide investment, which is necessary for long-run economic growth, they argue that the United States sacrifices the incomes of future generations by saving only a small fraction of GDP.

One natural response to this argument notes that people must not *want* to save more. If they would benefit by saving more and spending less, they would do so. Don't people know their own interests better than economists or government officials?

Many economists respond that government policies are partly to blame for low savings in the United States. Government policies have reduced savings in three main ways. First, government budget deficits in the last half of the 20th century contributed to low savings in the United States. Chapter 26 explained that an increase in the budget deficit raises the demand for loans as the government expands borrowing to finance its spending. Most economists believe that U.S. government budget deficits over that period raised the real interest rate and crowded out private investment. While the equilibrium quantity of loans increased, the savings available to the private sector for investment decreased.

Second, government policies reduce savings through the social security system. That system reduces private savings by providing income for elderly people, reducing the amount that people need to save for themselves. The more a person pays in social security taxes, and expects to receive in social security benefits, the smaller the incentive for that individual to save. If savings by the government replaced savings by individuals, then total savings would remain unaffected by the social security system. However, the U.S. government does not actually *save* the money that people pay in social security taxes. Until the late 1990s, the government simply collected these taxes from workers and immediately paid that money to social security recipients. Currently, the government saves the excess of social security tax revenue over payments (although this "saving" is only an accounting entry, since the government actually spends that money in other ways, as Chapter 33 will discuss). *Most* of the money that people pay in social security taxes continues to finance current social security expenditures. As a result, the social security system reduces U.S. national savings.

Third, the government's tax policies reduce savings. People pay income taxes on the money they earn regardless of whether they spend it or save it. However, if they save, and invest, they pay additional taxes on the interest (and capital gains) that their savings generate.

Figure 16 | Short-Run Effects of Changes in Aggregate Demand

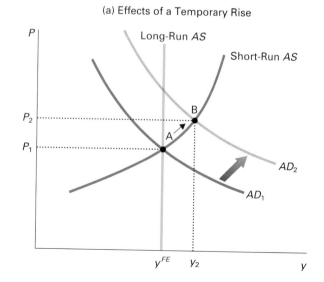

(a) Effects of a Temporary Rise

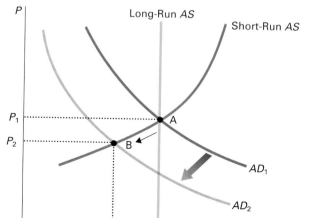

(b) Effects of a Temporary Fall

The income from investment is also taxed twice: corporations pay the corporate income tax on the income from investments, and then people pay personal income taxes (or capital gains taxes) when they receive this income. For example, suppose a person saves and buys stock in a corporation. That firm uses the money to invest in new equipment, and it earns $100, paying a corporate income tax of $40. The corporation pays the remaining $60 to the investor as stock dividends. The investor pays one-third of this income, $20, in personal income taxes. This leaves the investor with only $40 after taxes, on an investment that earned $100. Many economists have proposed changes in the tax system to reduce the features that discourage savings and investment.

Together, the government budget deficit, the social security system, and the negative effects of taxes on savings probably reduce U.S. savings below the level that people would choose without these policies. In that sense, one could say that the United States saves too little.

Suppose that the U.S. government were to adopt policies to raise savings by changing the tax system, altering the social security system, or encouraging people in other ways to increase savings. The resulting increase in savings would raise investment, which in turn would raise the economy's future productive capacity and its future real GDP. Therefore, the increase in savings would raise people's incomes in the long run.

The short-run effects of increased saving, however, could differ from the long-run effects. The model of aggregate demand and supply, with sticky prices, implies that an increase in savings would *reduce* real GDP in the short run by reducing consumption and aggregate demand, as in Figure 16b. This short-run analysis was first developed by John Maynard Keynes in his famous book, *The General Theory of Employment, Income, and Prices*. Many Keynesian economists (those who adopted Keynes's arguments) influenced governments in subsequent years. After World War II, the United States adopted policies to provide people with incentives to spend more and save less. These policies included taxes, legal limits on interest rates available to most savers, and expansion of a social security program that, by helping to provide income to retirees, reduced the incentive to save.

Increased savings clearly produce long-run benefits by raising long-run economic growth. With short-run price stickiness, however, increased savings during a recession could deepen the downturn. Choosing tax policies that encourage enough savings for rapid long-run growth while avoiding the short-run problems raised in this chapter is a difficult job, and it can raise questions of tradeoffs between short-run and long-run benefits.

Figure 17 | Effects of a Permanent Rise and Fall in Aggregate Demand

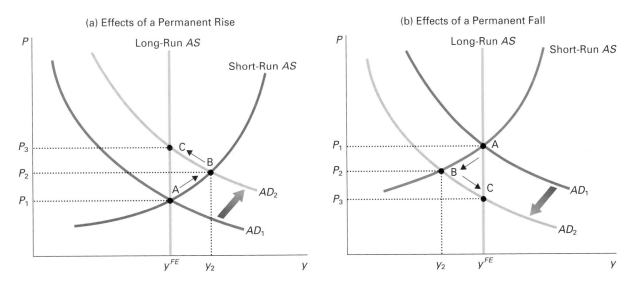

In Panel (a), aggregate demand rises from AD_1 to AD_2. In the short run, the economy moves from Point A to Point B as the price level rises from P_1 to P_2 and real GDP rises from y^{FE} to y_2. In the long run, the economy moves to Point C, where the new aggregate demand curve intersects the long-run aggregate supply curve. The price level rises all the way to P_3, and real GDP falls back to its full employment level, y^{FE}. In Panel (b), aggregate demand falls from AD_1 to AD_2. In the short run, the economy moves from Point A to Point B as the price level falls from P_1 to P_2 and real GDP falls from y^{FE} to y_2. In the long run, the economy moves to Point C, where the new aggregate demand curve intersects the long-run aggregate supply curve. The price level falls all the way to P_3, and real GDP rises back to its full employment level, y^{FE}.

IN THE NEWS

Experts say a lack of hiring stems from weak spending

By Louis Uchitelle

Americans are being bombarded with explanations of why the nation cannot generate enough jobs: a shortage of skilled workers, they are told, holds down hiring, along with higher taxes, global competition, expensive government regulations, technology that automates work, and cutbacks in military spending.

American consumers—and for that matter European consumers who buy American goods—have simply not purchased with their usual gusto. As a result, fewer workers are needed to make goods or provide services to the nation. The problem, in short, is weak demand, not a new world that has found a way to prosper without workers.

Source: New York Times

This news story from 1993, as the U.S. economy began recovering from a recession, illustrates the role of aggregate demand in recessions.

This model of aggregate demand and supply forms the basis for most economic analyses of the short-run effects of changes in underlying conditions on real GDP and other variables. However, economists disagree about certain issues such as whether the short-run aggregate supply curve is very flat or very steep, the period of time over which the price level remains sticky, and the sizes of real-life shifts in aggregate demand and aggregate supply. Economists may differ about the extent to which a particular recession results from a fall in aggregate demand and the extent to which it results from a fall in aggregate supply. For example, economists disagree about the relative importance of increases in aggregate *supply*, and increases in aggregate *demand*, in creating the long

Source: *Richmond Times-Dispatch*, December 16, 1987, p. 12.

A fall in spending can contribute to a recession by reducing aggregate demand, but a rise in savings raises long-run economic growth.

expansion of the 1990s (and before that the long expansion of the 1980s). Current evidence is not sufficient to resolve these disagreements.

The next chapter explores some additional aspects of the model developed in this chapter. It also uses the model to discuss interest rates, unemployment, and recessions in the United States and other countries.

Review Questions

6. What does the long-run aggregate supply curve show? Why is it a vertical line? What makes it shift?

7. What does the short-run aggregate supply curve show? Why does it slope upward? What makes it shift?

8. Draw a graph of aggregate demand and supply to show how a fall in the money supply causes a recession in the short run, and why the recession ends in the long run.

Thinking Exercises

9. Discuss this claim: "The long-run supply curves for housing, food, and every other good in the economy are upward sloping. Therefore the long-run aggregate supply curve, which shows total supply for *all* goods in the economy, is also upward sloping."

10. Draw a graph to show the short-run and long-run effects on real GDP and the price level of an increase in aggregate demand.

11. The text said that changes in the prices of imported inputs shift the aggregate supply curve. Draw a graph to show the long-run effects on real GDP and the price level of an increase in the price of imported oil.

IN THE NEWS

Typically, a slowdown in money-supply growth leads to slower overall economic growth. And indeed, Japan's economy has slowed somewhat, owing to the tight monetary policy the central bank has pursued since May 1989, when it began a series of interest-rate increases.

Source: The Asian Wall Street Journal

Japan's economic slowdown of the 1990s began with tighter monetary policy starting at the beginning of the decade.

Conclusion

Booms and Recessions

Some people define a recession as two consecutive quarters of falling real GDP, although the National Bureau of Economic Research uses a more complex definition. A recession begins at the peak of a business cycle and continues until its trough, followed by a recovery or boom until the next peak. Economists are divided on the causes of business cycles.

A Simple Model of a Recession

A fall in the money supply, with a given velocity of money, reduces the left-hand side of the equation of exchange, $MV = Py$, so the right-hand side also must fall. If the price level is sticky in the short run, P cannot fall, so real GDP, y, falls instead. Real GDP falls because the fall in the money supply reduces total spending, so people cannot afford to buy all the goods that the economy can produce.

Nominal prices are sticky if they take time to adjust to their new equilibrium levels following a change in supply or demand. The short run is the time period over which the price level has not fully adjusted to its new equilibrium level (because it is sticky) after a change in conditions. The long-run is the period after prices have fully adjusted to a change.

Aggregate Demand

The aggregate demand curve shows the total amount of goods and services that people, firms, and the government choose to buy at each possible price level, given the nominal money supply and velocity. The curve graphs the equation of exchange, $MV = Py$, for given values of M and V.

The economy's total spending each year, MV, equals the sum of spending by people on consumption, by firms on investment, by the government for purchases of goods and services, and net exports. As a result, $MV = C + I + G + NEX$. Both sides of this equation show aggregate demand.

The aggregate demand curve shifts in response to changes in the money supply or velocity, rising with an increase in *MV.* Increases in consumption, investment, and government purchases raise aggregate demand by increasing velocity.

The aggregate demand curve differs from the demand curves for individual products. Unlike those demand curves, which involve *relative prices,* the aggregate demand curve involves the economy's (nominal) *price level.*

Aggregate Supply

The aggregate supply curve shows the total amount of goods and services that firms choose to produce and sell at each possible price level. The aggregate supply curve differs from the supply curves of individual products, which involve relative prices of those individual products. In contrast, the aggregate supply curve involves the nominal price level.

The aggregate supply curve is a vertical line in the long run, because money is neutral in the long run: A country's long-run real GDP does not depend on *nominal* variables such as the price level. Instead, it depends solely on *real* variables—available technology and inputs, and the laws, property rights, regulations, and taxes that affect people's incentives to make efficient use of inputs. Because long-run aggregate supply is vertical, changes in aggregate demand affect the price level, but not real GDP, in the long run.

The aggregate supply curve slopes upward in the short run. (In a special case with *completely* sticky prices in the short run, it is a horizontal line.) The price level is sticky in the short run; it can change *partly* but not fully to its new long-run equilibrium level following a change in conditions.

Summary of Changes in Aggregate Supply and Demand

A rise in aggregate demand raises the price level and real GDP in the short run; a fall in aggregate demand lowers them in the short run. If a change in aggregate demand is permanent, then the price level continues to rise (or fall) farther in the long run, while real GDP returns to its long-run equilibrium level. This model of aggregate demand and supply forms the basis for most economic analyses of business cycles.

Key Terms

sticky price   aggregate demand curve   aggregate supply curve

Questions and Problems

12. Explain why aggregate demand rises if:
    (a) The money supply increases
    (b) The velocity of money increases
    (c) Investment demand increases
    (c) Government spending increases

13. Suppose that people decide to save less money and increase spending on entertainment. Explain how this change affects:
    (a) The real interest rate and the nominal interest rate
    (b) The velocity of money
    (c) Aggregate demand
    (d) Real GDP and the price level in the short run and long run
    If people spend $10 million more than before on entertainment, does real GDP change by more or less than $10 million? Explain.

14. Suppose that the government raises spending by $20 billion and raises taxes by $20 billion to pay for the higher spending.

    (a) Explain how this action affects consumption and saving, the interest rate, investment, velocity, and real GDP in the short run.
    (b) How would your answer change if the government did not raise taxes to pay for increased spending, but borrowed the money instead?
    (c) How would your answer change if the government did not raise taxes to pay for increased spending, but printed money to pay for the higher spending?

15. Suppose the economy is currently in a recession. Use the model of aggregate demand and supply to explain how a tax cut could raise real GDP and reduce unemployment.

16. Suppose the money supply is $500 and velocity is 5 per year. Also suppose the long-run aggregate supply curve is represented by the equation,

$$y = 500$$

and the short-run aggregate supply curve is represented by the equation,

$$P = (1/100)\,y$$

(a) Find the long-run equilibrium price level and real GDP.

(b) Suppose the money supply increases from $500 to $720. Find the new *long-run* equilibrium price level and real GDP. Then find the new *short-run* equilibrium price level and real GDP. (*Hint:* Find the *two* equations that hold in the short-run equilibrium, then solve them for the two unknown variables.)

17. Suppose the money supply is $1,000 and velocity is 3.6 per year. Also suppose the long-run aggregate supply curve is represented by the equation,

$$y = 360$$

and the short-run aggregate supply curve is represented by the equation,

$$P = (1/36)y$$

(a) Find the long-run equilibrium price level and real GDP.

(b) Suppose velocity rises from 3.6 per year to 4.9 per year. Find the new *long-run* equilibrium price level and real GDP. Then find the new *short-run* equilibrium price level and real GDP. Your answer for the price level may be rounded to the nearest dollar.

18. How is aggregate demand likely to react to an increase in consumer confidence about the future of the economy?

Inquiries for Further Thought

19. Should the United States adopt policies to reduce consumption spending and increase savings? What are the benefits and costs of a policy like this? Why did earlier chapters imply that an increase in savings raises productivity and future output, while according to this chapter, an increase in savings reduces aggregate demand and real GDP?

20. Why are prices sticky in the short run? Does price stickiness imply inefficiency in the economy?

CHAPTER 31

BUSINESS CYCLES 2: APPLICATIONS OF AGGREGATE DEMAND AND SUPPLY

In this Chapter...
Main Points to Understand

▶ Because the price level is sticky in the short run, changes in the money supply affect the real interest rate in the short run.

▶ The short-run Phillips Curve shows an inverse relationship between inflation and unemployment, although the curve shifts frequently over time. The long-run Phillips Curve shows *no* relationship between inflation and unemployment.

▶ Three models of short-run aggregate supply have different implications for unemployment and for government economic policies.

▶ Effects of a change in aggregate demand ripple throughout the economy, leading to further changes in aggregate demand.

Thinking Skills to Develop

▶ Interpret specific economic episodes in light of a model.

▶ Develop new implications of a model by extending its logic.

▶ Use a model to answer "what if?" questions.

▶ Learn to look at the *indirect* effects of a change as well as its direct effects.

A round the world, the 1990s witnessed major economic events: the collapse of the Soviet Union and the end of socialism in eastern Europe; rapid economic growth in China; a recession in the United States in 1990 to 1991, followed by a long period of rapid growth; an economic crisis in Mexico in 1995; economic crises in Korea, Indonesia, Thailand, the Philippines, and Malaysia in 1997 to 1998; a long recession in Japan; and the beginnings of new economic crises in other countries, such as Brazil and Russia. While entire courses could focus on each of these events, this chapter examines some of these events by applying the economic model developed in previous chapters, extending the model in a few places and delving deeper into it in other places. To understand macroeconomics, you must learn more than the model of aggregate supply and demand: You must learn how to *apply* that model to real events. You must learn to analyze news reports with economic reasoning, and adopt economic reasoning as a practical tool for thinking about new issues.

It was November 1991, and the United States was in a recession. Unemployment climbed above 7 percent; real GDP remained below its level from the previous year. The Federal Reserve decided to conduct open market purchases (buying assets) to reduce the federal funds rate (the interest rate on short-term loans between banks) from 5 percent to 4.75

MONEY AND INTEREST RATES IN THE SHORT RUN

percent per year. The action was very unusual, because it was the second cut in the federal funds rate within a single week and the 13th cut within two years. It would not be the last: The Fed cut the federal funds rate twice more before the end of the year, bringing it down from 8 percent in mid-1990 to 4 percent at the end of 1991. (Figure 5 in Chapter 29 showed the federal funds rate over a longer period of time.)

These actions of the Federal Reserve in 1990 and 1991 were intended to raise aggregate demand and help pull the U.S. economy out of its recession. The model of aggregate demand and supply shows why an increase in the money supply can raise real GDP and help end a recession. We begin this chapter by examining the connection between changes in the money supply and changes in the interest rate. These connections help to explain why increases in the money supply generally reduce the real interest rate in the short run. Understanding these connections will help you to understand news reports about Federal Reserve policies, such as its more recent actions to reduce interest rates starting in 1998.

Most news reports about monetary policy focus on interest rates: Will the Fed reduce interest rates? Will it raise them? Will the Bank of Japan change Japanese interest rates? Chapters 26 and 27 explained that changes in the money supply affect inflation, which affects *nominal* interest rates. However, as Chapter 29 explained, changes in the money supply also affect *real* interest rates in the short run. The model of aggregate demand and supply can help to clarify the effects of monetary policy on the real interest rate.

Long-Run Effects of a Federal Reserve Open Market Purchase
The easiest way to understand the effects of Fed policy (or the policy of a foreign central bank) on interest rates is to think about the special case of aggregate supply in the previous chapter, in which prices are *completely* sticky in the short run. In that case, the short-run aggregate supply curve is a horizontal line. Suppose the Fed permanently raises the money supply through an open market purchase, raising aggregate demand and temporarily raising real GDP as in Figure 17a of Chapter 30. What happens to the real interest rate? To answer that question, think about the demand and supply of loans. As in Chapter 29, focus on the supply and demand for short-term loans between banks and the federal funds rate.

The Fed's open market purchases raises the supply of loans. Figure 1 shows the results. Look first at Figure 1b, which shows the *long-run* results. In the long run, the increase in the money supply will raise all nominal prices in the same proportion. The long-run results will resemble a currency reform in reverse, with real variables remaining unchanged. For example, a 5 percent increase in the money supply will raise all nominal prices by 5 percent. With 5 percent higher prices of capital goods (such as new equipment), business firms will borrow 5 percent more money for the same real investments in capital equipment. Therefore the demand for loans (measured in dollars) rises *in the long run* by 5 percent, along with the supply of loans. Because the supply *and* demand for loans (measured in nominal terms) *both* rise by 5 percent in the long run, the real interest rate does not change. Therefore the Fed's open market purchase leaves the real interest rate unchanged in the long run.

Because the Fed's action raises the money supply, it raises the price level in the long run. As Chapter 26 explained, that rise in the price level (a temporary jump in the rate of inflation) raises the *nominal* interest rate while the price level falls toward its new long-run level.

Short-Run Effects of an Open Market Purchase
In the short run, however, the price level is sticky. Figure 1a shows the short-run results of the open market purchase. The prices of new equipment and other capital goods remain unaffected in the short run, so the demand for loans remains unchanged. However, the Fed's open market purchase increases the supply of loans, *reducing the real interest rate* in the short run.

What happens to the nominal interest rate in the short run? Two opposing forces affect the nominal interest rate. First, the decline in the real interest rate tends to

Figure 1 | How Open Market Operations and Interest Rates

(a) Short-Run Effects

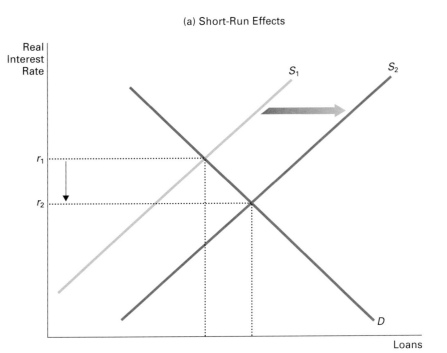

In Panel (a), an open market purchase raises the supply of money. By raising the supply of loans, it lowers the real interest rate in the short run (while the price level remains sticky). In Panel (b), a fall in the supply of money leaves the real interest rate unchanged in the long run. A 5 percent rise in the money supply raises the price level by 5 percent. As a result, the demand and supply of loans each rises by 5 percent, leaving the equilibrium real interest rate at r_1.

(b) Long-Run Effects

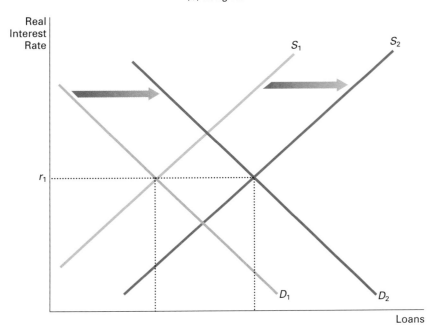

Money and the Nominal Interest Rate: a Complex Connection

The connection between the nominal interest rate and the money supply is complex. If the price level is sufficiently sticky in the short run, a Federal Reserve open market purchase reduces the nominal interest rate in the short run. However, that open-market purchase raises the price level in the long run, boosting inflation and *increasing* the nominal interest rate. So the same change in the money supply that *lowers* the nominal interest rate in the short run *raises* it afterwards.

reduce the nominal interest rate. Second, the jump in inflation, as the economy moves upward along its short-run aggregate supply curve (as in Figure 17a of Chapter 30), tends to raise the nominal interest rate. If the price level is sufficiently sticky, the short-run jump in inflation is small, so the nominal interest rate falls. (The first effect dominates the second effect: the nominal interest rate falls because the real interest rate falls.)

The discussion so far involves the federal funds interest rate, but the Fed's policy

IN THE NEWS

U.K. cuts key interest rate

THE BANK OF ENG-LAND cut the repo rate, the lowest rate at which the central bank loans money to commercial banks, by a quarter percentage point to 7.25 percent. The rate had been at 7.50 percent since June 4 when it was raised by 0.25 percentage points. That was the sixth rise in interest rates since Labor won power.

Labor removed authority over interest rates from politicians and gave it to the Bank of England within days of taking office. The bank then tightened monetary policy in line with a government target of low 2.5 percent inflation. But as world economic turbulence worsened, Britain's treasury chief, Gordon Brown, indicated this week that recession is now a greater risk than inflation, encouraging speculation that Britain would follow the U.S. Federal Reserve and cut rates.

Source: MSNBC News

England's central bank loosened monetary policy in late 1998 to help prevent a recession. A sticky price level allows the Bank of England to reduce the real interest rate in the short run.

also affects other interest rates. When the federal funds rate rises, banks must pay more to borrow from other banks, so they raise the rates they charge on their own loans. The rise in the federal funds rate ripples through the economy, raising other interest rates in the short run. Similarly, when the Fed reduces the federal funds rate through an open market purchase that raises the money supply, interest rates throughout the economy fall in the short run.

This model of the connections between Federal Reserve policies and interest rates can help you interpret news articles on those policies and their effects. To raise the interest rate, the Fed conducts open market sales, reducing the money supply. To reduce the interest rate, the Fed conducts open market purchases, raising the money supply.

These short-run effects of Fed policies result from short-run price stickiness. In the long run, the price level adjusts to its new equilibrium level, and the real interest rate returns to its original equilibrium level as the economy moves from the short-run aggregate supply curve to the long-run aggregate supply curve.

Figure 2 shows that the federal funds rate and the interest rate on U.S. government treasury bills tend to move together. Some analysts interpret their common movements as the effects of Fed policies: changes in the federal funds rate affect the treasury bill rate. However, other analysts note that the common movements in these interest rates are more complex: changes in the federal funds rate often occur *after* changes in the treasury bill rate. Some economists say that this occurs because loan-market participants *expect* changes in the federal funds rate, changing demand and supply so that the equilibrium treasury bill rate responds to these expectations. Others say the treasury bill rate often changes before the federal funds rate because the Federal Reserve *responds* to economic events. According to this view, changes in treasury bill rates cause the Fed to change the federal funds rate, and evidence on their common movement does not reflect the ability of the Fed to control the treasury bill rate or other interest rates.

EXAMPLE

The Federal Reserve conducted open market purchases in September 1998 to reduce the federal funds rate from 5.50 percent to 5.25 percent. The 3-month U.S. treasury bill interest rate dropped from 4.9 percent to 4.4 percent during that month, but the drop occurred throughout the month, *before* the September 29 date when the Federal Reserve reduced the federal funds rate. To some extent, the drop in the treasury bill rate probably reflected expectations that the Fed would reduce the federal funds rate; to some extent, the drop in the treasury bill rate probably occurred for other reasons, with the Fed merely responding. Until economists can find evidence to distinguish these two possibilities, the *magnitude* of the Fed's influence on the treasury bill interest rate (and other interest rates) remains uncertain.

The Federal Reserve, like other central banks, decides on its monetary policy by analyzing data on recent changes in the price level, real GDP, unemployment, and other variables. When the Fed believes the economy is "slowing down," because aggregate demand is falling (or growing less rapidly than aggregate supply), it tends to follow an *expansionary* monetary policy to raise aggregate demand. It conducts open market purchases that raise the money supply and reduce interest rates. When the Fed believes the economy is "speeding up" or "overheating," meaning that aggregate demand is rising more rapidly than the Fed would like (creating a threat of inflation), the Fed tends to follow a *tight* monetary policy to reduce aggregate demand. It conducts open market sales that reduce the money supply and raise interest rates.

The Fed monitors many economic variables for signals of changes in aggregate demand. Two important areas of focus are unemployment rates and inflation; its attention to unemployment results from a set of observations about the economy and its controversial interpretation as a *Phillips Curve*, to which the next section turns.

Figure 2 | Federal Funds Rate and Treasury Bill Interest Rates, 1991–1998

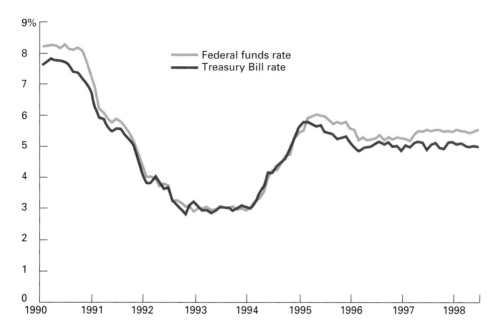

1. What actions does the Fed take to reduce the real interest rate? Why do these actions work in the short run but not in the long run?

2. Draw a graph to help show the short-run effects of a Federal Reserve open market *sale* on (a) the real interest rate, (b) the nominal interest rate, and (c) investment.

3. What factors complicate evidence on the extent to which the Fed's influence on the federal funds rate extends to the treasury bill rate and other interest rates?

Suppose an economy experiences temporary changes in aggregate demand. When aggregate demand temporarily rises, output and the price level both increase along the short-run aggregate supply curve, AS^{SR}; when aggregate demand falls again, output and the price level both decrease. Large increases in aggregate demand create a high growth rate of real GDP and high inflation, as in Figure 3; smaller increases in aggregate demand create smaller growth rates of real GDP and lower inflation, as in Figure 4. These temporary changes in aggregate demand cause inflation and the growth rate of real GDP to move together, as in Figure 5.[1]

A statistical generalization called *Okun's Law* indicates that each one percentage-point increase in the growth rate of U.S. real GDP typically accompanies a 0.5 percentage-point

PHILLIPS CURVES

---

[1]Permanent changes in aggregate demand also cause inflation and the growth of real GDP to move together in the short run.

Figure 3
Large Rise in Aggregate Demand

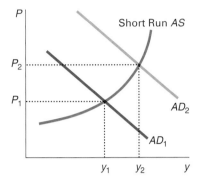

Figure 4
Small Rise in Aggregate Demand

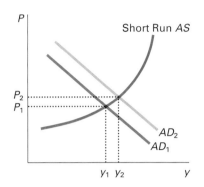

Figure 5
Short-Run Results of Changes in Aggregate Demand

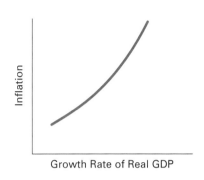

Figure 6
Short-Run Phillips Curve

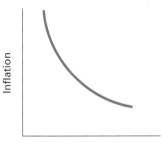

fall in the unemployment rate.[2] Because higher growth in real GDP accompanies lower unemployment, we can redraw Figure 5 as Figure 6.

Figure 6 shows the short-run relationship between inflation and unemployment predicted by the model with an upward-sloping short-run aggregate supply curve and temporary changes in aggregate demand, or the short-run effects of permanent changes in aggregate demand. In the short run, high inflation accompanies low unemployment, and low inflation accompanies high unemployment.

IN THE NEWS

Brazil's harsh attack on inflation is risking deep economic slump

Shrinkage of its money supply hobbles many companies, forces people to cut back. A housemaid loses her job.

SAO PAULO, Brazil—When Fernando Collor de Mello took office in March, he said he had "only one shot" to halt Brazil's hyperinflation. But instead of firing a bullet, the new president dropped a bomb.

"The monetary contraction we imposed on society is fantastic," acknowledges

Ibrahim Eris, one of the architects of the harsh anti-inflation plan and now the president of the central bank. "It's probably the first time in the world that a country in time of peace has practically destroyed its monetary standard and replaced it."

But in stopping inflation, the government has

also stopped the economy. "To kill the cockroach, they set the apartment on fire," complains former Economic Planning Minister Antonio Delfim Netto.

Deprived of cash, consumers stopped buying, companies stopped producing, and exporters stopped exporting.

Source: The Wall Street Journal

In any country, policies intended to reduce inflation risk causing a recession, as the economy moves along a short-run Phillips Curve.

---

[2]For example, a rise in the growth rate of real GDP from 2 percent to 3 percent per year typically occurs with a fall in the unemployment rate from 6 percent to 5.5 percent.

Most economists interpret available evidence as supporting the short-run relationship in Figure 6. They refer to it as the *short-run Phillips Curve*—a statistical relationship between inflation and unemployment.

> The **short-run Phillips Curve** is a statistical relationship between inflation and unemployment: In the short run, unemployment is low when inflation is high, and unemployment is high when inflation is low.

Figure 7 shows unemployment rates and inflation rates for the United States since 1986. While the points from 1986 through 1993 are consistent with a downward-sloping short-run Phillips Curve similar to the curve in Figure 6, the points from 1992 through 1998 would indicate an *upward*-sloping relationship. Clearly, the short-run Phillips Curve is not as simple a relationship as Figure 6 would indicate.

Two issues complicate the analysis:

▶ *Short-run* relationships between inflation and unemployment differ from *long-run* relationships.

▶ The short-run Phillips Curve *shifts* as people's *expectations* change.

The Short Run versus the Long Run

In the long run, when the price level adjusts to its new equilibrium, the economy returns to the equilibrium, full-employment level of output, y^{FE}, and the associated equilibrium level of unemployment, called the *natural rate of unemployment*.[3]

> The **natural rate of unemployment** is the unemployment rate that occurs when the economy produces the full-employment level of output.

Figure 7 | Phillips Curve for the United States, 1986–1998

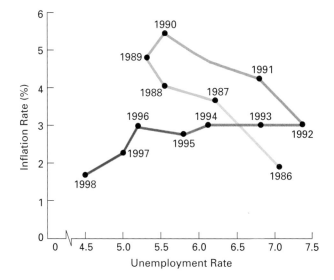

---

[3]Chapter 25 discussed the equilibrium level (natural rate) of unemployment, and the factors that affect it.

The natural rate of unemployment corresponds to equilibrium unemployment discussed in Chapter 25. Unemployment results from inevitable changes in any real economy, including changes in population, technology, consumer preferences, government policies, and world economic conditions. The natural rate of unemployment is not a constant; it changes over time. Its size depends on many factors, such as:

▶ Larger and more frequent changes in supply and demand raise equilibrium unemployment by raising the number of people who lose jobs each year.

▶ A decrease in the costs of searching for jobs and finding good matches between employers and employees reduces equilibrium unemployment.

▶ An increase in availability of good information about job opportunities reduces equilibrium unemployment by reducing the time people require to find new jobs.

▶ An increase in labor mobility reduces equilibrium unemployment by increasing the extent to which people will accept jobs in other cities.

▶ Increases in incomes of unemployed people, due to an increase in unemployment compensation or increases in incomes of other family members, raises equilibrium unemployment by reducing the willingness of people to accept new job offers.

▶ Union policies that raise wages, and increases in legal minimum wages can raise equilibrium unemployment by reducing the quantity of labor demanded.

▶ Government regulations and taxes can raise equilibrium unemployment. For example, regulations in European countries make it costly for firms to fire employees, which reduces their willingness to hire new workers.

No one knows exactly the size of the natural rate of unemployment in the United States. A decade ago, many economists estimated it to be about 5.5 percent; more recent estimates put it at about 4.5 percent.

Because unemployment returns to its natural rate in the long run, the long-run Phillips Curve is a vertical line as in Figure 8.

> The **long-run Phillips Curve** is a vertical line at the natural rate of unemployment.

Figure 7 showed unemployment and inflation rates in the United States since 1986; Figure 9 shows them in earlier periods during the second half of the 20th century. Some periods show downward sloping short-run Phillips Curves. However, notice that scales differ among the plots in Figure 9. Consequently, a plot that combines all the data, as in Panel (f), does *not* show a short-run Phillips Curve. Apparently, the short-run Phillips Curve shifts over time.

Shifts in the Short-Run Phillips Curve

Evidence indicates that the short-run Phillips Curve shifts when expected inflation changes. An increase in expected inflation shifts the short-run Phillips Curve upward and to the right. Figure 10 shows a short-run Phillips Curve shifting upward from PC_1 to PC_2 as expected inflation rises. A fall in expected inflation shifts the short-run Phillips Curve downward and to the left. Figure 10 shows a short-run Phillips Curve shifting downward from PC_1 to PC_3 as expected inflation falls. In contrast, the long-run Phillips Curve remains unaffected by changes in expected inflation.

Figure 8
Phillips Curves

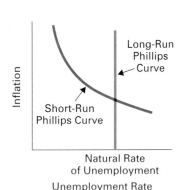

Suppose that the economy begins at Point A in Figure 10, in a long-run equilibrium. One day, the Federal Reserve, in a surprise policy change, permanently raises the growth rate of the money supply. As a result, inflation rises above the level that people had expected. In the short run, unemployment falls as the economy moves from Point A to Point B in Figure 10. After a while, however, people learn to expect this new, higher rate of inflation, so expected inflation rises. The rise in expected inflation shifts the short-run Phillips Curve upward and to the right, from PC_1 to PC_2, until the economy reaches Point C in the long run. Unemployment returns to its natural rate. A permanent increase

Figure 9 | Inflation and Unemployment in the United States

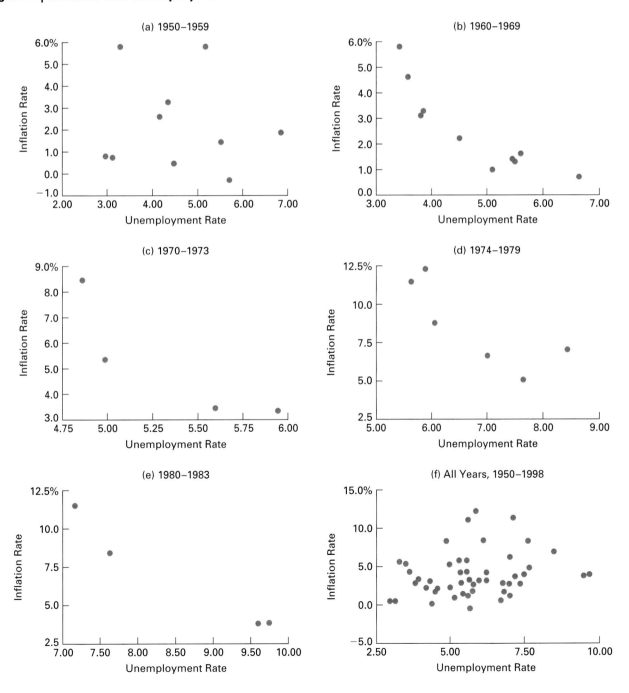

Figure 10 | Shifting Short-Run Phillips Curves

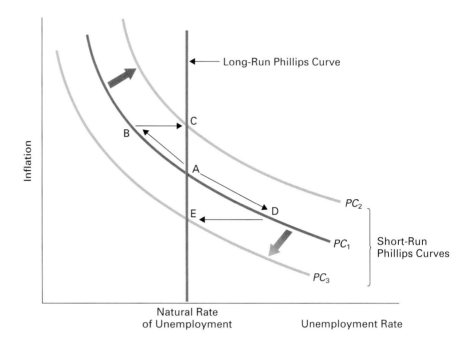

in the growth rate of the money supply raises inflation, but reduces unemployment only temporarily. It has no long-run effect on unemployment.[4]

Figure 10 also shows the effects of a permanent decrease in the growth rate of the money supply. Starting from Point A, inflation falls and unemployment rises in the short run, as the economy moves from Point A to Point D. As expected inflation falls, the short-run Phillips Curve shifts from PC_1 to PC_3. In the long run, unemployment falls back to its natural rate as the economy moves from Point D to Point E. A permanent fall in the growth rate of the money supply permanently lowers inflation, and temporarily raises unemployment. It has no long-run effect on unemployment.

Figure 11 shows the way most economists view the U.S. data on Phillips Curves. According to the standard interpretation, the figure shows a short-run Phillips Curve for the 1960s, which shifted upward when expected inflation increased in the early 1970s, and then shifted upward again in 1974 (as the world economy experienced a fall in aggregate supply due to a major increase in the price of imported oil). As inflation continued to increase in the late 1970s, expected inflation rose again, shifting the short-run Phillips Curve to an even higher level. As inflation decreased from 1980 to 1983, the U.S. economy moved downward to the right along that short-run Phillips Curve. Then, as expected inflation fell, the short-run Phillips Curve shifted downward to its 1986–94 level. Finally, as inflation remained lower in the 1990s than previous years, expected inflation declined throughout the decade as unemployment fell toward its natural rate. Some economists, questioning the standard interpretation, view Figure 11 as misleading. They argue that the figure groups years together in a way that artificially creates the *appearance* of short-run Phillips Curves. These economists argue that there is no reliable statistical relationship between inflation and unemployment that can guide policymakers in predicting the effects of alternative policies.

---

[4]If you exercise your thinking skills in economics, you may wonder *why* changes in expectations shift the short-run Phillips Curve. What economic *model* logically predicts these shifts? The answer requires a more complex analysis than the models in this book. Roughly, the short-run Phillips Curve shifts (as in Figure 10) when the short-run aggregate supply curve shifts, moving the economy from a short-run equilibrium to a long-run equilibrium (as in Figure 17 of the previous chapter). These changes are not quite the same, because the short-run Phillips Curve shifts due to changes in expected inflation, while the short-run aggregate supply curve shifts when the price level completes its adjustment to its new equilibrium. The precise logical connections between the model of aggregate demand and supply and the short-run Phillips Curve lie beyond the scope of this book.

Figure 11 | Shifting Short-Run Phillips Curves for the United States, 1960–1998

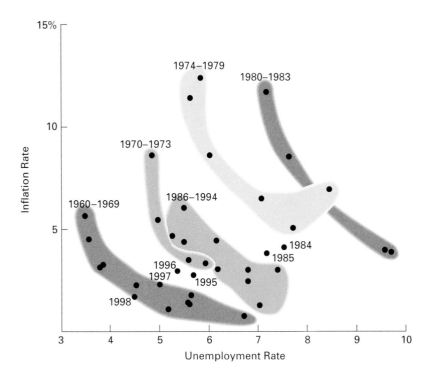

The difference between these two views of the evidence represents conflicting predictions about the answer to a "what-if" question: What would happen *if* the Federal Reserve changed its policies to raise or reduce inflation? Would a policy to raise inflation also reduce unemployment in the short run? Would a policy to reduce inflation create a recession and raise unemployment temporarily? Some economists argue that these policies would affect unemployment and real GDP; others disagree. For example, in the Kennywood Park story of Chapter 25, Professor Robert Lucas argued that changes in monetary policy could not repeatedly create recessions or expansions ("Sunday after Sunday"). He argued that monetary policy affects real GDP "only because our manipulations caught everyone by surprise." Economists will probably continue to disagree on the answers to these questions until stronger evidence on these issues becomes available.

Review Questions

4. Draw a short-run Phillips Curve and a long-run Phillips Curve.

5. What factors affect the natural rate of unemployment?

6. Summarize the evidence presented in this chapter about the short-run Phillips Curve, including criticisms of the usual interpretation of the evidence.

Thinking Exercises

7. A politician recently argued that the Federal Reserve should reduce interest rates to prevent an increase in unemployment. However, a Fed official warned that looser

monetary policy may ignite inflation. What do economic models and evidence say about the short-run and long-run effects of looser monetary policy on unemployment and inflation?

8. Economists disagree about the interpretation of the short-run Phillips Curve and its implications for policy. Explain that disagreement. What evidence would help resolve the disagreement?

THREE THEORIES OF AGGREGATE SUPPLY

The previous chapter explained that the short-run aggregate supply curve slopes upward because the price level is sticky in the short run—it does not immediately and fully adjust to its new long-run equilibrium level after a change in conditions. That chapter explained one of three alternative models of the short-run aggregate supply curve. The sticky-price model of aggregate supply is often called the *New Keynesian theory*. The other two models, the *sticky-wage model* and the *imperfect-information model*, explain the upward slope of the short-run aggregate supply curve in alternative ways. Each model differs in its explanation of unemployment and the short-run Phillips Curve. The three models also differ in their predictions about other macroeconomic variables and their implications for government policies.

Sticky Product Prices

The first model of short-run aggregate supply, the *sticky-price* or *New Keynesian* theory, states that the nominal price level is sticky in the short run. This stickiness makes the short-run aggregate supply curve slope upward, as discussed in the previous chapter.

Although evidence suggests that the price level is sticky, economists do not fully understand the causes of price stickiness. The most prominent explanation involves *menu costs*—a term for the actual costs of changing prices. Menu costs include the costs of printing new menus at restaurants, new catalogs for mail-order firms, and the costs of attaching new price tags to products at retail stores. More generally, menu costs include the costs of gathering information to decide which prices to change, and how much to change them.

When firms pay menu costs to change their prices, they must think carefully about the future when choosing their prices. For example, suppose a firm experiences an increase in demand for its product, but believes that this high demand is only temporary, and that demand will return to normal next month. The firm may leave its price unchanged, rather than paying the menu costs of raising the price today and reducing it again next month. As this example illustrates, a firm that faces menu costs must anticipate changes in future conditions when it sets prices.

Firms facing menu costs are less likely to change their prices in the short run, but they change them in the long run. If a firm's price is close to its equilibrium level, a firm may leave its price unchanged rather than pay the menu costs to change it. However, when the difference between the firm's price and the equilibrium price becomes large, the firm will change its price despite the menu costs.

Firms facing menu costs may not all change their prices at the same time, because they face different supply and demand conditions. For example, changes in the supply or demand for coffee or airline tickets may lead coffee sellers and airlines to change their prices more often, and at different times, than firms selling books. When aggregate demand falls, *some* firms will be ready to adjust their prices almost immediately, while others will leave their prices unchanged for some time. Consequently, in the short run the overall price level will fall only *part* of the way to its new long-run equilibrium level. Firms that have not changed their prices will see sales drop, and they will reduce production. As a result, the fall in aggregate demand reduces real GDP in the short run. Eventually, all firms reduce their prices to the new long-run equilibrium level, and real GDP returns to its full-employment level.

Sticky Wages

A second model, the *sticky-wage theory,* states that the short-run aggregate supply curve slopes upward because *nominal wages* are sticky in the short run. Nominal wages may be sticky because workers sign long-term employment contracts that set the levels of wages for an extended period of time (such as a year, or even longer).

Suppose the equilibrium nominal wage is $20 per hour, and a firm and its workers sign a contract fixing the nominal wage at that rate for the coming year. After the contract is signed, suppose the money supply and the price level fall by 5 percent. The new *equilibrium* wage is now $19 per hour. If all *nominal* prices and *nominal* wages fell by 5 percent, no *real* variables (such as real GDP or real wages) would change; money would be neutral. However, the employment contract creates stickiness in *nominal* wages. Because the nominal wage is sticky, the falling price level raises the *real* wage above its equilibrium level. This increase in the real wage reduces the quantity of labor demanded as in Figure 12. In that figure, the nominal wage is sticky at $20, so a fall in the price level from P_1 tp P_2 raises the real wage from $20/$P_1$ to $20/$P_2$. The firm sells its product for 5 percent less than before, in nominal terms, but it must pay workers the same nominal wage as before. As a result, the firm wants fewer workers—its quantity of labor demanded falls from L_1 to L_2. This decrease in employment reduces real GDP. In summary, when nominal wages are sticky, a fall in aggregate demand raises the real wage but reduces employment, raising unemployment and reducing real GDP. With short-run stickiness in nominal wages, a fall in aggregate demand creates a recession.

Nominal wages are not permanently sticky, though. Eventually, firms and workers sign new employment contracts, and nominal wages adjust to their new equilibrium levels. When the new contracts become effective, the real wage returns to its equilibrium, bringing employment and production back to their equilibrium levels. The recession ends and the economy returns to its full-employment level of real GDP.

Figure 12 | Effects of a Fall in the Money Supply
With a Sticky Nominal Wage

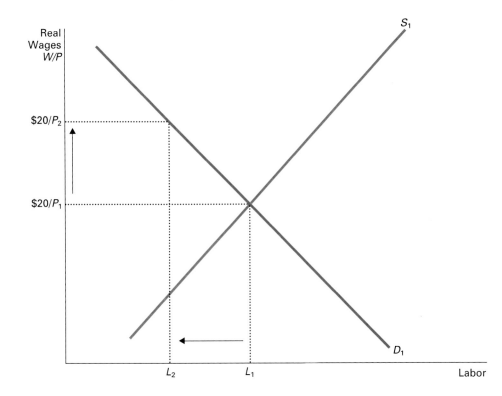

After workers sign labor contracts fixing the nominal wage at $20 per hour, the money supply falls by 5 percent. This reduces the price level by 5 percent, from P_1 to P_2. Because the price level falls by 5 percent, and the nominal wage, W, remains at $20, the real wage, W/P, *rises* by 5 percent. Employment falls from L_1 to L_2.

Comparing the Sticky-Wage and Sticky-Price Models

The sticky-price model and sticky-wage model differ in explaining when recessions end. Both models say that a recession ends when the short-run aggregate supply curve shifts and the economy returns to a long-run equilibrium. The sticky-price model says that this happens when the nominal price level completes its adjustment (after a change in aggregate demand). The sticky-wage model, in contrast, says that this happens when people sign new employment contracts and the nominal wage adjusts to its new long-run equilibrium.

The sticky-wage model predicts that a change in the money supply affects employment and real GDP only if it was *unexpected* at the time the nominal wage was set. Any changes in the money supply and price level that workers and firms expect when they sign the contract will affect the nominal wage. For example, suppose that workers and firms know that all nominal prices will rise 10 percent in the second year of the labor contract discussed in the last section. They could keep the real wage at its equilibrium level by writing a contract that would set the nominal wage at $20.00 per hour in the first year of the contract, and $22.00 per hour (10 percent higher) in the second year.

The prediction that only unexpected changes in the price level affect employment and real GDP receives support from evidence that surprise (unexpected) changes in the money supply have larger effects on real output than do predictable changes. This relationship remains controversial, however, because some evidence suggests that even predictable changes in the money supply or inflation temporarily affect real GDP. Still, surprise changes in the money supply and inflation seem to have larger effects on real GDP than do predicted changes. This evidence supports the sticky-wage model.

Imperfect Information

A third model of the short-run aggregate supply curve, the *imperfect-information* model, does *not* assume that menu costs make prices sticky, or that nominal wages are sticky. Instead, it states that the short-run aggregate supply curve slopes upward because sellers sometimes make mistakes: They sometimes *confuse* nominal price changes with relative price changes.

Suppose that a surprise fall in the money supply creates a surprise fall in the price level. When a firm sees an unexpected fall in the nominal price of the good it sells, it may mistakenly believe that the *relative* price of that good has fallen. Of course, in reality, the relative price may not have changed; instead, *all* nominal prices may have fallen by the same percentage. But the firm may not know that. It may incorrectly believe that the relative price has fallen, so it may reduce production. As other sellers make similar mistakes, the unexpected fall in the price level reduces real GDP.

The Kennywood Park story in Chapter 25 illustrates the imperfect-information model. Neither prices nor wages are sticky in that story. Instead, a fall in aggregate demand reduces *real* GDP and employment in the short run because each ride operator mistakenly believes that his ride is becoming passé—that the *relative* demand for his ride has decreased. If ride operators were aware that the park's money supply has decreased, they would all reduce their nominal prices and the recession would not occur.

Unemployment in the Three Models

The three models of aggregate supply differ in their interpretations of unemployment. According to the sticky-price model, people who become unemployed may not be able to find jobs even by offering to work for a reduced wage. When aggregate demand falls, firms become unable to sell all of the products that they produce. As a result, they reduce production and employment. Firms would be unable to sell the additional goods that they could produce by employing additional workers, so they are unwilling to hire additional workers regardless of the wage. In the long run, the fall in aggregate demand reduces the price level, and unemployment returns to its natural rate. With the price level sticky in the short run, government policies to raise aggregate demand would allow firms to sell additional products, thereby raising production and employment.

According to the sticky-wage theory, unemployment occurs when the real wage exceeds its equilibrium level. Unemployed people could find jobs if firms could reduce wages, but the sticky-wage model postulates that labor contracts or other forces prevent nominal wages from decreasing in the short run. In the long run, unemployment falls as the nominal wage falls to its equilibrium level. In the short run, the only way to reduce unemployment is to reduce the real wage, and the only way to reduce the real wage is to raise the price level by increasing aggregate demand.

The sticky-price and sticky-wage models both imply that increases in aggregate demand can reduce unemployment in the short run. Consequently, many economists propose government policies to raise aggregate demand in response to rising unemployment or the threat of a recession. The incomplete information model sees unemployment as a voluntary response to a situation of bad opportunities. According to that model, any unemployed worker could find a job by offering to work at a sufficiently low wage. Wages are not sticky in that model, so firms can reduce wages. Nominal prices are not sticky, so firms can sell the additional output that new workers would produce. According to the incomplete information model, people are unemployed when they prefer unemployment to their current job opportunities, which may fall short of the opportunities they expect to encounter if they continue searching for better options.

Review Questions

9. Why does unemployment develop in a recession according to the (a) sticky-price model? (b) sticky-wage model? (c) incomplete information model?

10. A recession ends when the economy moves from its short-run equilibrium (on a short-run aggregate supply curve) to its new long-run equilibrium. What change creates this movement according to the (a) sticky-price model? (b) sticky-wage model? (c) incomplete-information model?

Thinking Exercises

11. Suppose the Fed suddenly raises the money supply by 10 percent. Explain the effects on real GDP, unemployment, and the price level, according to (a) the sticky-price model; (b) the sticky-wage model, and (c) the incomplete information model. In each case, explain the *reasoning* involved, as well as the results.

12. Explain why only *unexpected* (surprise) changes in the money supply affect real GDP and unemployment in the incomplete-information model. Draw aggregate demand and supply curves to distinguish the effects of expected and unexpected changes in the money supply, according to that model.

13. How do the effects of expected and unexpected changes in the money supply differ, according to the sticky wage model? Draw aggregate demand and supply curves to distinguish the effects of expected and unexpected changes in the money supply, according to that model.

Example: Unemployment in the Sticky Price Model
Recall the simple example at the beginning of Chapter 30, illustrated in Figure 2 of that chapter. The economy begins in long-run equilibrium: firms produce 100 goods per year, the money supply equals $1,000, velocity equals one per year, and the price level is $10 per good. When the money supply falls from $1,000 to $900 with no change in velocity, people spend only $900 per year, so the equilibrium price level falls from $10 to $9 per good. However, if the price level is completely sticky and remains at $10 per good, people can afford to buy only 90 goods per year (spending $900). While firms could produce more than 90 per year, they cannot sell more than that as long as the price level exceeds its long-run equilibrium. Consequently, firms would be unwilling to hire additional workers, even if their wages were low.

You might think that if you spend $100 more and save $100 less than before, you will raise aggregate demand by $100. Actually, your spending will create *ripple effects* in the economy—in the end, aggregate demand may increase by *more* than $100, or it may increase by less. The size of the total change in aggregate demand depends on the *aggregate-demand multiplier*.

THE AGGREGATE DEMAND MULTIPLIER

A change in spending creates ripple effects in the economy, which are summarized by the aggregate-demand multiplier. When you understand the logic of these ripple effects, you will learn an important lesson of economic reasoning.

The **aggregate-demand multiplier** shows the ultimate increase in aggregate demand that results from an exogenous $1 rise in spending.

An *exogenous* change refers to a change in underlying conditions that affects other variables in a model. A model predicts *results* of exogenous changes. For example, a change in consumer tastes for pizza is an exogenous change in the model of supply and demand, which predicts the reactions of prices to that change. Similarly, a change in tastes can create an exogenous $1 rise in total spending. That exogenous increase in spending may have economic effects that lead to *further* changes in spending, which the aggregate-demand multiplier measures. For example, if spending rises exogenously by $100 and the multiplier is 2, then aggregate demand rises by $200. If the multiplier is 1, aggregate demand rises by $100. If the multiplier is ½, aggregate demand rises by $50; see Figure 13.

Direct and Indirect Effects—A Lesson in Logical Reasoning

A common explanation of the aggregate-demand multiplier involves a logical fallacy, and you can learn an important lesson in logical reasoning by studying the fallacy in the argument. That logical lesson can help you avoid making similar mistakes when you apply the logic of economics to real-life problems that you will face in the future.

The common, but incorrect, explanation of the multiplier goes like this: Suppose that Al decides to reduce his savings by $100 and increase spending by $100 to buy bread from Bill the baker. This purchase raises Bill's income by $100. Bill decides to save $50 of this extra income and spend the other $50 to buy candy from Cindy, so Cindy's income rises by $50. She decides to save $25 of this extra income and spend the other $25 to buy dishes from Dave. Dave's income rises by $25, and so on. If each person spends half of any increase in income and saves the other half, total spending eventually rises by $200. (That is, $100 + $50 + $25 + $12.50 + $6.25 + ⋯ = $200.) Therefore, the common argument goes, Al's $100 increase in spending has a *ripple effect* on the economy that raises total spending by $200.

The analysis in the preceding paragraph is incorrect, because it looks only at the *direct* effects of Al's spending and ignores the *indirect* effects. The *indirect* effects occur because when Al raises his spending by $100, he *reduces his saving* by $100. He puts $100 less in his bank account for the bank to lend, so someone else—say, Marcia—borrows $100 less than she would otherwise have borrowed. Marcia spends $100 less

Figure 13 | The Aggregate Demand Multiplier

Suppose that autonomous spending rises by $100. If the multiplier is 2, aggregate demand rises by $200, from AD_1 to AD_4. (The AD curve shifts to the right by $200.) If the multiplier is 1, aggregate demand rises by $100 and the AD curve shifts from AD_1 to AD_3. If the multiplier is ½, aggregate demand rises by only $50 and the aggregate demand curve shifts from AD_1 to AD_2.

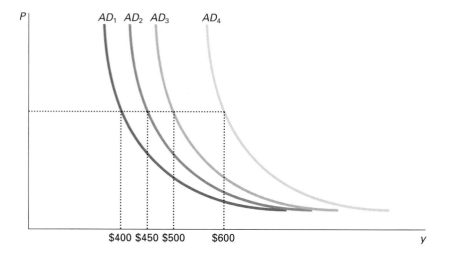

on nachos from Ned. Ned's income falls by $100, so Ned spends $50 less on oranges from Ollie. Ollie's income then falls, and so on.

Now compare the direct effects of Al's increased spending with the indirect effects. Al spends $100 more, but Marcia spends $100 less, so those changes in spending cancel each other. Bill spends $50 more, but Ned spends $50 less, so their changes in spending also cancel each other. Similarly, Cindy's increase in spending cancels Ollie's decrease, and so on. Clearly, the common argument incorrectly ignores these offsetting decreases in spending.

It is easy to notice the direct effects of Al's spending. For example, a reporter might interview Bill or Cindy, whose incomes have increased because of Al's spending. It is harder to notice the indirect effects. After all, Marcia might not know that she *could have* borrowed Al's money, if only he had saved it and deposited it in a bank account, so that the bank could have loaned it to her. These indirect effects indicate events that *would have* happened if Al had *not* increased his spending. Looking at direct effects but ignoring indirect effects is a common source of fallacies in economics. You will encounter this fallacy again in a later chapter on international trade. One of the important lessons you can learn from studying economics is not to ignore indirect effects.

> In logical thinking about economics, remember the *indirect* effects as well as the *direct* effects.

The Logic of the Multiplier

Despite the logical error in the common explanation of the multiplier, the assertion that a change in spending has ripple effects on the economy is correct. A $100 increase in spending may raise aggregate demand by more (or less) than $100. The economic model developed in earlier chapters provides a logical explanation of the multiplier. Consider the supply and demand for loans in Figure 14. When Al boosts spending by $100 and reduces savings by $100, the supply of loans falls. This fall in supply raises the equilibrium real interest rate from r_1 to r_2. This increase in the real interest rate raises the nominal interest rate, which raises velocity. The increase in velocity, in turn, raises

Figure 14 | Why the Multiplier Exceeds Zero

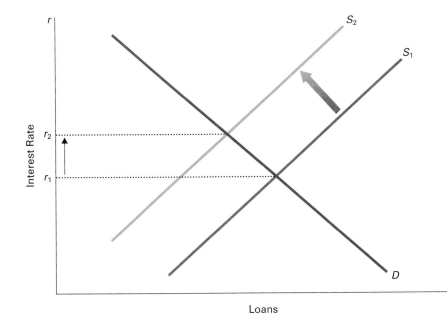

An increase in consumption spending reduces saving, which reduces the supply of loans from S_1 to S_2. This raises the real interest rate from r_1 to r_2, which raises the nominal interest rate and velocity. Therefore, aggregate demand (MV) rises.

IN THE NEWS

From Alaska fisheries to Australian outback, Asian crisis hits home

'Like ripples in the water.'

Asia's financial crisis has taught a lesson in the world's new geography to the residents of Monroe County, the taproot of southern Alabama's pulp country.

In January, Monroe's Alabama River Pulp Mill and Alabama Pine Pulp Mill shut down temporarily, idling 700 of 900 workers. The reason: shrinking demand for their softwood pulp in Asia, especially in the gritty paper factories of Indonesia. There, in a tropical archipelago of 200 million-plus people, a savage currency depreciation has dried up demand for dollar-priced imports.

"Anyone who was aware of how trade relationships work could see this coming," says Marilyn Culpepper, a Monroe County industrial-development specialist. "It's like ripples in the water."

More like waves pounding the beach. Asia's economic woes are rocking companies, cities, and countries world-wide. Though the global economy remains stable, the pain emanating from Asia reaches nearly every corner of the world. Reduced demand from Asia has struck family-run New Zealand dairies and European petro-chemical giants. Fishermen in Alaska and the Falkland islands are struggling to keep afloat as their major buyers in Asia content themselves with cheaper fish fare processed closer to home.

Source: The Wall Street Journal

In our integrated world economy, a recession in one part of the world can spread internationally like ripples on water. Asian recessions in 1998 reduced exports from the rest of the world, decreasing aggregate demand with a multiplier effect.

aggregate demand, *MV*. In other words, total spending rises because an increase in the interest rate leads people to spend money faster than before. So Al's decision to increase spending and reduce savings really does raise aggregate demand.

The size of the aggregate demand multiplier depends on two factors. First, how much does the initial increase in spending (and decrease in saving) raise the real interest rate? When Al reduces saving by $100, the supply of loans shifts leftward by $100. The size of the increase in the interest rate depends upon the elasticity of demand for loans (roughly, the shape of the demand curve), with larger increases in the interest rate reflecting a more inelastic (roughly, steeper) demand for loans. Second, how much does the velocity of money increase when the interest rate rises? The larger the increase in the interest rate, and the larger the response of velocity to that increase, the larger the aggregate-demand multiplier.

This same reasoning applies to any exogenous change in spending. An increase in investment, government spending, or net exports also raises aggregate demand. The ultimate change in aggregate demand resulting from such an increase in spending can exceed that original increase.

Review Questions

14. Zach decides to take $300 out of his bank account and buy the latest interactive game machine. Explain (a) a common *fallacy* about the effects of this spending on aggregate demand, (b) why the reasoning in part (a) is fallacious, and (c) the true effects on aggregate demand of Zach's spending.

15. How is the size of the aggregate demand multiplier affected by the responsiveness of velocity to a change in the nominal interest rate?

Thinking Exercise

16. Suppose the government decides to raise military spending by $25 billion, and to pay for this increase in spending by raising taxes. Explain how this change affects aggregate demand, and the factors that affect the *size* of the total response of aggregate demand.

The Great Depression

CASE STUDIES

The Great Depression, which lasted from 1929 through most of the 1930s, was the biggest recession in U.S. history. Real GDP per capita fell 30 percent from 1929 until 1933 and then rose slowly, reaching its 1929 level again only in 1940. The rise from 1933 to 1940 was interrupted by another recession in 1937 to 1938. Analysts customarily date the beginning of the Great Depression at the stock-market crash of October 1929, particularly October 24 (Black Thursday) and October 29 (Black Tuesday). Many people lost fortunes in the crash; some even committed suicide as a result. As much as some people suffered from the stock market crash, the coming depression would be far worse and affect more people. Deflation (negative inflation) occurred as the price level fell by more than 20 percent.[5] By 1933, nominal GDP was only 56 percent of its 1929 level.

The unemployment rate in the United States rose to almost 25 percent in 1933 and 1934; roughly one out of every four workers was unemployed. In September 1932, *Fortune* magazine estimated that 34 million people (28 percent of the U.S. population) had no incomes at all.[6]

A multiplier effect magnified the decline, as discussed in the last section. People without jobs or other incomes could not pay taxes or rents; landlords who could not collect rents could not pay taxes; cities that could not collect taxes could not pay for social programs or schools. People without incomes could not buy much, and many businesses closed.[7]

It is important not to let statistics hide the impact of the depression on people's lives—the depression caused considerable misery. That misery highlights the importance of economic models to analyze these events and help guide policies to prevent their recurrence. The issues in these chapters have great, direct effects on people's lives.

What Caused the Great Depression?

In 1933, the U.S. economy produced only about two-thirds as many goods as it produced in 1929, even though most of the same people, equipment, and technology remained available for production. Why did output fall so much? Although the stock market crash marks the beginning of the Great Depression, the crash did not *cause* the

---

[5] It fell 3.0 percent in 1930 and 8.7 percent in 1931 as the depression deepened, and it continued to fall until 1934.

[6] Cited in Paul Johnson, *Modern Times* (New York: Harper & Row, 1983), p. 247.

[7] Big retail stores did not suffer as badly as industry. James Thurber noted that they reduced prices and that anyone who could earn money could get bargains at these stores.

depression. After all, many recessions have occurred without major stock market crashes, and many stock market crashes (such as the crash of October 19, 1987) have occurred without recessions soon following.

Economists generally agree that the Great Depression cannot be explained with the basic model discussed in earlier chapters. Most economists believe that the sticky-price or sticky-wage models discussed in this chapter and the previous one play a major role in the explanation.

Economists generally interpret the Great Depression as the result of a huge fall in aggregate demand, but they disagree about the reasons for that fall. Perhaps the most prominent view, developed by Milton Friedman and Anna J. Schwartz in a famous study, holds that the main cause of the depression was a fall in the money supply. The M2 measure of the money supply fell by almost one-third from 1929 to 1933. Although the Federal Reserve increased the monetary base slightly during that period as the economy slid into the Great Depression, more than 9,000 banks stopped operating. People lost over $1 billion in deposits in those banks, making them poorer than before, though the loss was small compared to the $85 billion people lost in the stock market over the same period. Bank failures increased the currency–deposit ratio, which reduced the money multiplier (discussed in Chapter 29), causing M2 to fall. According to this view, this fall in the money supply reduced aggregate demand. Banking problems were related to the stock market crash. Because stock prices fell, many borrowers could not repay their loans on time, or even make scheduled interest payments. Consequently, most banks faced the liquidity problems discussed in Chapter 29. A banking panic occurred as depositors tried to withdraw their money. Many banks, lacking sufficient reserves to cover these withdrawals, closed down. Although most banks reopened later and most people recovered most of their deposits, many people lost their money for several years, and some lost it permanently.

Another prominent view holds that an exogenous fall in spending on consumption and investment reduced aggregate demand, causing the depression. Consumption spending may have fallen because people lost money in the stock market or because consumer confidence declined and people decided to increase savings and curtail spending. Some economists see unexpected deflation as a major factor, since it redistributed wealth from borrowers to lenders. Note, however, that this redistribution would reduce aggregate demand only if lenders tend to save more and spend less than borrowers.[8]

Finally, investment spending may have fallen because bank failures interfered with firms borrowing money from people who saved it. The unexpected deflation bankrupted many firms that had borrowed money and pushed other firms to the brink of bankruptcy. It became risky for people to lend money to firms, because the threat of bankruptcy increased, worrying lenders that they would not be repaid in full. With lenders increasingly cautious about lending money, firms had trouble obtaining funds to finance their operations and investments, which may have reduced aggregate demand and contributed to the depression.

Whatever the reason for the fall in aggregate demand, the result was a huge fall in real GDP and the price level from 1929 to 1933. This fall was followed by a long movement back toward the full-employment level of output.

Many, though not all, economists believe that if the Federal Reserve had prevented the fall in the M2 measure of the money supply, the action would have avoided the Great Depression or reduced its severity. Milton Friedman and Anna J. Schwartz took this position in their important book, *A Monetary History of the United States*.[9] They argued that

---

[8] Some history books attribute the fall in aggregate demand to a fall in wages, claiming that workers spent less because they earned less. This claim embodies two fallacies. First, although the average *nominal* wage fell from 57 cents per hour in 1929 to 44 cents an hour in 1933, a larger percentage fall in the price level *raised* the average real wage, for those who remained employed. Second, the claim ignores the increase in profits to firms resulting from a fall in wages. Even if the real wage had fallen, the redistribution from workers to firms' owners would reduce aggregate demand only if workers tended to spend more of their income than owners.

[9] Milton Friedman and Anna J. Schwartz, *A Monetary History of the United States* (Princeton, N.J.: Princeton University Press, 1963).

every major change in the money supply in U.S. history has led to changes in real GDP in the short run and the price level in the long run, regardless of why the money supply changed. As a result, a fall in M2 by one-third, the largest fall in U.S. history, should be expected to bring about the biggest depression in U.S. history. Friedman and Schwartz argued that if the Federal Reserve had increased the monetary base to keep M2 from falling, the Great Depression would have been, at most, a mild recession. Even if aggregate demand had fallen for some reason unrelated to the fall in M2, a stable money supply would have prevented aggregate demand from falling enough to cause a depression.[10]

International Comparisons

The Great Depression was a worldwide event. As the price level fell in the United States, international trade transmitted deflation to other countries on the gold standard. The depression became deeper in the United States, Canada, and Germany than in most other countries.

One way for economists to learn about the effects of government policies on the economy is to compare results in countries with different policies. From 1929 to 1933, countries with the biggest deflations also had the biggest recessions. Researchers have identified three groups of countries to compare. First, many countries, such as the United States and Germany, operated on the gold standard. These countries had deflations and major recessions from 1929 to 1933. Second, some countries, such as China and Spain, had no deflations because they were not on the gold standard. These countries had no major recessions.

Third, some countries stopped their deflations by abandoning the gold standard in 1931.[11] These countries put early ends to their recessions. For example, Great Britain went off the gold standard in September 1931, and its real GDP stopped falling. Figure 15a shows the results. From 1929 to 1933, aggregate demand fell in the United States, and the economy moved along the short-run aggregate supply curve, AS^{SR} from Point A to Point B to Point C, with falling prices and falling real GDP. In Great Britain, aggregate demand fell between 1929 and 1931, then stayed about constant from 1931 to 1933, so the price level and real GDP fell from 1929 to 1931 in Great Britain (from Point A to Point B in Panel (b) of the figure). As the British economy adjusted toward the long-run equilibrium, prices fell further and real GDP increased (from Point B to Point C) back to the level associated with the long-run aggregate supply curve, AS^{LR}.

Sweden also abandoned the gold standard in 1931, immediately ending its deflation. Prices and the money supply remained about constant for a year, then rose slowly for the next few years. Real GDP in Sweden fell 9.1 percent in 1931, almost as much as the 11.5 percent fall in U.S. real GDP. However, after Sweden stopped its deflation in 1932, Swedish real GDP fell only 3.2 percent, while U.S. real GDP fell another 18.7 percent.[12] By 1934, Swedish real GDP was back to its 1929 level, while U.S. real GDP remained at only ¾ of its 1929 level. These episodes suggest that the United States might have been able to end the Great Depression earlier if it had raised the monetary base to keep M1 and M2 from falling and to stop the deflation.

Some people have suggested that the Hawley-Smoot Act of 1930, which raised tariffs significantly, made the depression much worse than it otherwise would have been.

---

[10]Some economists claim that an increase in the money supply would not have helped in this situation. They say that in certain situations with low nominal interest rates, as in the Great Depression, people would be unwilling to spend increases in the money supply, so those increases would not raise aggregate demand. Instead, they argue, an increase in M would simply reduce velocity, V, so that aggregate demand, MV, would not increase.

[11]As Chapter 29 explained, the gold standard restricted growth rates of the money supply. In the early 1930s, these growth rates were low enough to cause deflation. Abandoning the gold standard gave governments the ability to raise money growth to prevent deflation.

[12]Why did Swedish real GDP not *rise*? Perhaps because depressions in other countries reduced the demand for Sweden's exports. This would have caused aggregate demand in Sweden to continue to fall, but by less than had Sweden remained on the gold standard and continued to endure deflation as in the United States, Germany, and other countries.

Figure 15 | An International Comparison of the Great Depression

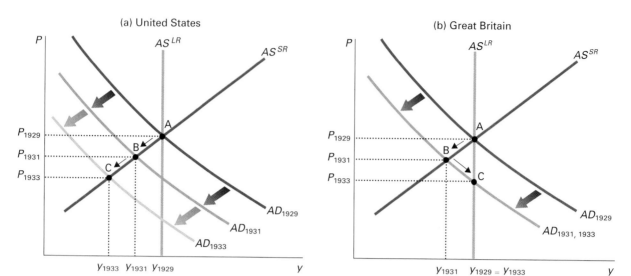

Panel (a): From 1929 to 1931, and from 1931 to 1933, the price level and real GDP fell in the United States. Panel (b): From 1929 to 1931, the price level and real GDP fell in Great Britain, but that country then abandoned the gold standard, and real GDP increased as the price level fell.

Economists generally agree that tariffs reduce economic efficiency, but most doubt that the Hawley-Smoot Act played a major role in causing the Great Depression. Its main role may have been to help spread the depression to European countries, many of which also increased their tariffs.

In the United States, the Great Depression helped Franklin Roosevelt win election over President Herbert Hoover in 1932, leading to the New Deal, Roosevelt's policies to fight the depression.[13] Real GDP started rising slowly in 1934.

The famous book by John Maynard Keynes, *The General Theory of Employment, Interest, and Money,* was published in 1936, when real GDP in the United States was still below its 1929 level. The book received immediate attention for its theory of why recessions occur and how to cure and prevent episodes like the Great Depression. Keynes's General Theory became the dominant influence on the development of macroeconomics over the next 40 years.

Credit Controls in 1980[14]

On March 14, 1980, President Carter imposed credit controls on the U.S. economy to try to reduce inflation, which had reached 12.4 percent in 1979. These credit controls subjected lenders to special regulations that effectively worked like a tax on loans.[15] They were intended to lower inflation by reducing the amount of money that consumers and businesses borrowed and spent on consumption and investment. That is, they were intended to reduce aggregate demand, and they succeeded.

---

[13] President Hoover, who had come into office in early 1929, had followed some policies to raise aggregate demand, such as cutting taxes and raising government spending (mainly for transfer payments), leading to a government budget deficit of almost 3 percent of GDP in 1931.

[14] This discussion is based on Stacey L. Schreft, "Credit Controls, 1980," *Economic Review* 76 no. 6 (November/December 1990), published by the Federal Reserve Bank of Richmond. Figure 16 comes from that paper.

[15] These controls included, for example, a special deposit requirement on lenders for certain types of consumer credit that required lenders to hold non-interest-bearing deposits at the Fed equal to 15 percent of their loans.

Figure 16 | Effects of Credit Controls in 1980

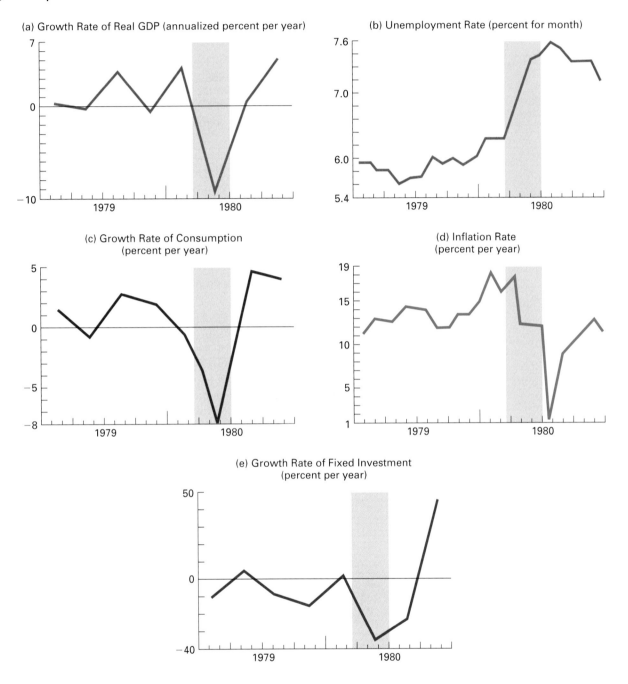

(a) Growth Rate of Real GDP (annualized percent per year)

(b) Unemployment Rate (percent for month)

(c) Growth Rate of Consumption
(percent per year)

(d) Inflation Rate
(percent per year)

(e) Growth Rate of Fixed Investment
(percent per year)

The controls led some banks to stop accepting new credit-card applications and others to tighten requirements to get credit cards, raise annual fees for credit cards, raise interest rates on the cards, and raise minimum required monthly payments. Although other controls on consumer borrowing were mainly symbolic, the publicity and confusion generated by the credit controls caused a large fall in consumer spending. Total bank loans fell 5 percent in April 1980 alone, and retail sales fell at the fastest rate in 29 years. Figure 16 shows growth rates of consumption, investment, and real GDP, as well as the unemployment rate and inflation rate. The shaded area indicates the period of credit controls.

The credit controls led to steep falls in consumption and investment spending, reducing aggregate demand, real GDP, and the rate of inflation and raising the unemployment rate. Although the growth rate of the monetary base did not change much, the growth rates of M1 and M2 fell because the money multiplier fell as banks reduced lending. In this way, the credit policy caused reductions in M1 and M2 as well as a fall in aggregate demand. This fact shows why economists must analyze data cautiously, without drawing hasty conclusions about cause and effect. One could easily look at the graph and conclude, falsely, that the fall in the money-growth rate *caused* the fall in consumption and investment that reduced real GDP. In fact, the fall in the money-growth rate was a *result* of the decrease in borrowing and spending, due to the credit controls; it did not *cause* that fall in spending.

Recession of 1982

In October 1979, the new chairman of the Federal Reserve Board, Paul Volcker, announced that the Fed would change its operating procedures to increase its attention to the money supply and to reduce inflation. The Federal Reserve did just that, with some help from a fall in velocity. The Fed quickly reduced the growth rate of the monetary base from almost 8.0 percent per year in 1980 to about 4.5 percent per year in 1981, before letting it gradually rise in 1982. The growth rate of M1, however, changed little.[16] The velocity of M1 had been growing steadily since 1960, and it suddenly started falling in 1982 for reasons that economists do not yet fully understand.[17]

The combination of a fall in the growth rate of the money supply and lower velocity reduced aggregate demand. Figure 17 shows the results. Inflation was 12.4 percent in 1979, 11.6 percent in 1980, and 8.5 percent in 1981. It suddenly fell to 3.8 percent in 1982, as the economy entered a recession, and to 3.7 percent in 1983. Real GDP fell more than 3.0 percent from fall 1981 to fall 1982, reaching 1.6 percent below its 1979 level. The unemployment rate rose from 5.8 percent in 1979 to more than 10.0 percent in the last half of 1982. The 1982 recession was the largest in the United States since the Great Depression. (Figure 9e shows the Phillips Curve for this period.)

Output in this graph is measured by industrial production; the money supply is measured by the monetary base. M1 also fell in 1981 prior to the 1982 recession.

Figure 17 | Money, Output, and Prices in the 1982 Recession

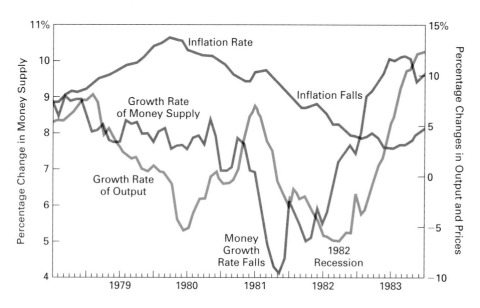

---

[16]The growth rate of M2 did not fall, but its velocity fell.

[17]The nominal interest rate fell, which helped to reduce velocity, but velocity fell by more than economists expected based on that fall in the nominal interest rate.

Recessions and Expected Inflation

Some economists believe that the short-run Phillips Curve does *not* shift quickly when expectations change. Instead, they argue, policies to reduce inflation cause a recession *even if* people expect inflation to fall. These economists cite the 1982 recession as evidence. That recession occurred after the Federal Reserve announced publicly that it would try to reduce inflation. People expected inflation to fall in 1982, argue these economists, but a recession occurred anyway. If the change in expectations had shifted the short-run Phillips Curve—if only unexpected inflation could affect real GDP—then, these economists say, the 1982 recession would not have happened.

Other economists argue that people did not expect inflation to fall despite the Federal Reserve's public announcement in October 1979. They argue that people pay attention to actions and may not believe announcements. After all, this was not the first time the government announced that it would fight inflation. Politicians and government officials (including Federal Reserve policymakers) make many announcements and people would be foolish to believe all of them. Whether a fully expected fall in inflation causes a recession remains a topic of controversy among economists.

Recession of 1990 to 1991

Economists disagree about the causes of the U.S. recession in 1990–1991. According to one view, that recession resulted from tight monetary policy, which reduced aggregate demand. Figure 18 shows the growth rate of real GDP in the United States from 1985–94, and the growth rate of M1 that had occurred 1½ years earlier. (The lag appears because changes in GDP tend to be more closely related to previous changes in M1 than

IN THE NEWS

Fed foresees slow growth in economy

More jobless the cost of curbing inflation

Source: Washington Post

Many economists believe that policies to reduce inflation also create a recession. However, others believe that those policies can avoid a recession if they also reduce expected inflation, shifting the short-run Phillips Curve.

IN THE NEWS

Busy factories revive fears of inflation

So the Fed, which has been trying since March to hold off inflation by raising interest rates, will likely push rates higher. The goal: dampen demand for loans, which would discourage spending. Then businesses would have to hold off on some price increases.

Job growth revives fears of inflation

If anyone out there knows when U.S. businesses will stop creating more than 10,000 jobs a day, please call Alan Greenspan.

The Federal Reserve chairman has been pushing up interest rates for a year, to slow the economy and head off what he fears is an onrushing wave of inflation.

Sources: USA Today

Fast growth of real GDP and falling unemployment in 1988-1989, led the Federal Reserve to conclude that the economy was moving upward along a short-run Phillips Curve. To prevent rising inflation, the Fed tightened monetary policy. Although the Fed may have been correct, its policy reaction might have caused the 1990 recession.

Figure 18 | Output and Money Growth in the 1990–1991 Recession

IN THE NEWS

Economy climbs while inflation slides

WASHINGTON—The economy exploded at a 4.2% annual rate in the first quarter while inflation fell to early 1950s levels, the Commerce Department said.

The data highlight the dilemma facing the Federal Reserve. Central bankers remain convinced that, at some point, the economy can't grow at its current pace without triggering inflation. Fed officials have stressed that their job is to pre-empt inflation before waiting for signs to emerge, not to wait for prices to escalate.

Source: The Wall Street Journal

Does fast growth of real GDP necessarily trigger inflation?

to current changes in M1.) The figure shows that large decreases in the growth rate of the money supply preceded the recession, and may have caused it.

Some economists believe that the 1990–91 recession resulted at least partly from two other factors. First, banks and other financial intermediaries became less willing to lend, partly because government regulators began stricter oversight of risky loans.[18] This decrease in lending may have contributed to a fall in aggregate demand by reducing investment. Second, Iraq's invasion of Kuwait in August 1990 suddenly raised the world price of oil substantially (though temporarily). This increase in the price of imported oil may have reduced aggregate supply, and the associated increase in uncertainty about future oil prices may have reduced investment and aggregate demand.

The U.S. Recovery of the 1990s

In recent years, the U.S. economy has experienced rapid growth, with real GDP rising at 3 percent per year from 1992 to 1998, and unemployment falling from 7.5 percent in 1992 to 4.5 percent in 1998. One remarkable feature of the 1990s has been the *combination* of low inflation, as shown in Figure 19, with rapid growth in real GDP and low unemployment. Many commentators have questioned whether this combination is consistent with economic theory—doesn't the Phillips Curve show that low unemployment goes with *high* inflation, while low inflation, as in the 1990s, occurs with high unemployment?

Of course, the commentators are wrong: Economic theory does not imply that inflation and unemployment move inversely. Prominent economic models predict that inflation and unemployment tend to move in opposite directions in the *short run*, given expected inflation, in response to changes in aggregate *demand*. However, falling unemployment

---

[18] The increased strictness of government regulation began after the federal government spent about $150 billion when savings and loan associations went bankrupt in the 1980s, as mentioned in the discussion of deposit insurance in Chapter 29.

Figure 19 | U.S. Inflation, 1980-1998

may occur with low inflation (as in the 1990s) as the economy returns to a long-run equilibrium, as in the movement from Point D to Point E in Figure 10. Similarly, unemployment may fall as real GDP rises and the price level falls, as in the movement from Point B to Point C in Figure 17 of the previous chapter. Moreover, changes in aggregate *supply* can lead to falling unemployment with low inflation. Figure 20 shows the effects of an

Figure 20 | Increase in Aggregate Supply Raises Real GDP and Reduces the Price Level

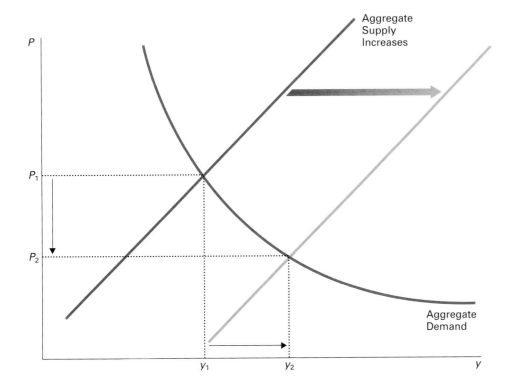

increase in aggregate supply, perhaps due to advances in technology and falling prices of imported inputs such as crude oil (which occurred in the 1990s). The increase in aggregate supply raises real GDP, reducing unemployment (by Okun's Law), as it reduces the price level.

Asian Recessions in the Late 1990s

Several Asian countries experienced severe economic crises in the late 1990s. Recessions, banking crises, and exchange-rate crises hit Japan, South Korea, Malaysia, Indonesia, and Thailand in 1997 and 1998. Along with recessions, these countries experienced bank failures, stock market crashes, devaluations of their currencies on foreign exchange markets, and corporate bankruptcies.

Economists do not yet understand fully the causes of the Asian crisis. However, they generally agree that banking crises played a key role. The banking crises grew from the problems with deposit insurance discussed in Chapter 29. Deposit insurance, or implicit promises of such insurance from the government as in most of the Asian countries, affected the incentives of banks. Deposit insurance encouraged banks to make risky loans and investments, with high chances of default. Governments of some countries encouraged lending to certain firms and industries, sometimes for political reasons and sometimes to encourage growth in certain parts of the economy, which added to the risky loans. Eventually, banks took big losses as many borrowers became unable to repay their loans. Banks became unable to extend additional loans, and many firms faced bankruptcy. Stock markets crashed. Some banks became insolvent, and closed. Decreases in lending reduced investment; decreases in wealth and financial panics reduced consumption spending. Aggregate demand decreased, and the economies fell into recessions. Concerns increased that governments would ignite inflation by loosening monetary policy to raise aggregate demand. Increases in expected inflation caused currency depreciation on foreign exchange markets.

The concept of moral hazard plays a key role in understanding the Asian crisis. *Moral hazard* refers to an effect of your actions on someone's incentives when you cannot monitor that person's actions. For example, when you pay someone $10 per hour to do a job for you, you may create an incentive for that person to work slowly, to raise the total payment. Moral hazard arises when someone can reap the rewards from their actions when things go well but do not suffer the full consequences when things go badly. When an insurance policy provides reimbursement if a car is stolen, that policy reduces owners' incentives to prevent theft. Similarly, when the government provides deposit insurance, it reduces banks' incentives to avoid risky loans and investments. If banks are lucky with their risks, they earn high profits; if they are unlucky, their losses are limited because the government bails them out with deposit insurance. That is why deposit insurance, without sufficient government regulation of banks, creates the possibility of a financial crisis. Moral hazard from deposit insurance contributed to the savings and loan crisis in the United States in the 1980s, and to the Asian crisis of 1997–1998.

Moral hazard also played other roles in the Asian crisis. The International Monetary Fund (IMF) provided loans to several of these countries to lessen the impact of the crisis, as the IMF had done in earlier years with other countries. Many economists became concerned that the moral hazard problems created by IMF assistance would reduce the incentives of governments to avoid the conditions that lead to such crises. An additional concern involves the moral hazard effect on incentives of major U.S. banks and corporations that lend to these countries. Do these lenders count on IMF bailouts to reduce their risks?

By late 1998, policymakers around the world were concerned about the spread of the Asian recessions internationally. The Federal Reserve, the Bank of Canada, the Bank of England, and other central banks loosened monetary policy to try to raise aggregate demand and prevent a world recession.

I N   T H E   N E W S

G7 nations try to halt slide to depression

Fear of a meltdown in world stock markets and a decline into a 1930s-style economic depression has pushed the world's leading finance ministers into making an unprecedentedly strong demand for an urgent and coordinated response to the current turmoil. The

Group of Seven industrialised nations is calling for immediate interest rate cuts and a rapid move towards the creation of a new international authority that would act to avert any future economic collapse.

In an effort to halt the panic that set in on world

stock markets last week, Gordon Brown, the Chancellor of the Exchequer, said that the world's major powers were now co-operating to boost international demand, restructure financial systems and provide help for the victims of the world financial crisis.

Source: The Times (London)

As the 1998 Asian financial crises and recessions threatened to spread internationally, the G7 industrial countries (the United States, Canada, Japan, England, Germany, France, and Italy) began policies to raise aggregate demand.

Review Questions

18. How did credit controls in 1980 affect aggregate demand? What happened to the U.S. economy?

19. (a) What is moral hazard and what role did it play in the Asian financial crises of the late 1990s? (b) How does a banking-system crisis reduce aggregate demand, as in those Asian countries?

20. How did the stock market crash of 1929 contribute to the banking crisis in the Great Depression, and how did that crisis contribute to the change in the money supply?

Thinking Exercises

21. Draw a graph of aggregate demand and supply and use it to interpret (a) the Great Depression (b) the U.S. recession of 1982, (c) the U.S. economic expansion in the 1990s, and (d) the Asian recessions of the late 1990s.

22. Cite two hypotheses about the causes of the fall in aggregate demand that caused the Great Depression. What evidence could help determine which hypothesis is correct?

Conclusion

Money and Interest Rates in the Short Run

Because the price level is sticky, Federal Reserve open market operations affect the real interest rate in the short run. An open market purchase lowers the real interest rate in the short run, while it increases the money supply. An open market sale raises the real interest rate in the short run, while it reduces the money supply. These short-run effects on the real interest rate vanish in the long run as the price level adjusts to its new equilibrium level.

Phillips Curves

The short-run Phillips Curve describes a statistical relationship between inflation and unemployment. Unemployment falls temporarily when inflation rises, and it rises temporarily when inflation falls. Eventually, the economy returns to the natural rate of unemployment and produces the full-employment level of output, so the long-run Phillips Curve is a vertical line at the natural rate of unemployment. Evidence indicates that the short-run Phillips Curve shifts over time, perhaps in response to changes in people's expectations for inflation.

Three Theories of Aggregate Supply

The sticky-price model states that the aggregate supply curve slopes upward because nominal prices of many goods and services are sticky in the short run, creating a sticky overall price level, as well. Nominal prices may be sticky due to menu costs. When prices of individual products eventually differ sufficiently from their equilibrium levels, firms pay the menu costs and adjust prices. At that point, the economy moves from its short-run equilibrium to a new long-run equilibrium.

The sticky-wage models states that the aggregate supply curve slopes upward because nominal wages are sticky in the short run. Nominal wages may be sticky due to employment contracts. The economy moves from its short-run equilibrium toward a new long-run equilibrium when wages change as new employment contracts eventually replace old contracts.

The imperfect-information theory asserts that the short-run aggregate supply curve slopes upward because sellers mistake nominal price changes for relative price changes. When the nominal price of a product falls, its sellers falsely believe that its relative price has decreased, so they cut production. The short-run aggregate supply curve shifts and the economy moves to a new long-run equilibrium when sellers eventually realize that they have made a mistake.

All three models imply that the long-run aggregate supply curve is vertical at the full-employment level of output. They differ in their interpretations of the causes of short-run unemployment. The sticky-price model implies that unemployed people cannot find jobs, even by offering to work for reduced wages, because firms cannot sell the additional products that those workers would produce. The sticky-wage theory implies that unemployment occurs because the real wage exceeds its equilibrium level. The incomplete information model implies that unemployed workers could find jobs by offering to work at reduced wages.

The Aggregate Demand Multiplier

An exogenous $100 increase in spending can raise aggregate demand by more or less than $100, due to the aggregate demand multiplier. The logic behind the multiplier—and a common fallacy—illustrates the importance of looking at indirect effects as well as direct effects when applying economic analysis. An exogenous $100 increase in spending may raise aggregate demand by more than $100, because it raises the interest rate and, therefore, raises the velocity of money.

Case Studies

Many economists believe that the Great Depression resulted from a large decrease in the money supply from 1929 to 1933 that reduced aggregate demand. Some economists believe that the Great Depression resulted from an exogenous fall in spending on consumption and investment. Redistributions of income due to an unexpected fall in the price level may have contributed to the fall in aggregate demand by causing some business firms to go bankrupt and inhibiting others from borrowing money to finance operations and new investments.

Many countries around the world suffered from the Great Depression. However, the depression ended earlier in countries that left the gold standard and adopted monetary policies to prevent deflation than in other countries. Credit controls imposed by the U.S. government in 1980 reduced aggregate demand by decreasing consumption spending. This fall in aggregate demand reduced real GDP. Most economists believe the 1982 recession in the United States resulted mainly from tight Federal Reserve monetary policies. The Fed adopted these policies to reduce inflation from 13.5 percent per year in 1979 to 3.2 percent per year in 1983. Monetary policy may also have helped cause the U.S. recession in 1990 and 1991.

Moral hazard problems at banks, created by government deposit insurance, led to financial crises in several Asian nations in 1997–1998. These nations experienced bank failures, bankruptcies of firms, currency depreciation, and stock market crashes, as decreases in aggregate demand drove the economies into recessions. Policymakers around the world became concerned about the spread of the recessions internationally, and began taking steps to raise aggregate demand and prevent a world recession.

Key Terms

| short-run Phillips Curve | natural rate of unemployment | long-run Phillips Curve | aggregate demand multiplier |

Q u e s t i o n s   a n d   P r o b l e m s

23. Use the framework in this chapter to explain why a city's real GDP may rise and its unemployment may fall if it hosts the Olympics or some other major event.

24. Suppose that aggregate demand rises. Explain what happens in the short run and the long run (and why) according to the:
    (a) Sticky-price model
    (b) Sticky-wage model
    (c) Incomplete information model

25. Use the model of aggregate demand and supply to explain the 1982 recession.

26. Use the model of aggregate demand and supply to help explain how a recession in one country can spread to other countries.

27. Why does unemployment return to its natural rate in long-run equilibrium?

28. According to the sticky-wage model, are real wages likely to rise or fall in a recession?

29. The GDP deflator in the United States fell 18 percent from 1920 to 1921 and another 8 percent from 1921 to 1922. Meanwhile, per-capita real GDP fell 11 percent from 1920 to 1921 and then rose 13 percent from 1921 to 1922. Explain, using aggregate supply and demand curves, what happened.

30. Great Britain had high inflation during and after World War I. The price level doubled from 1914 to 1918 and then rose 40 percent from 1918 to 1920. Then the British government decided to reduce the price level back to about its prewar level. From 1920 to 1921, the GDP deflator fell 11 percent, while real GDP fell 6 percent. The next year, the price level fell another 17 percent, and real GDP increased. Use the aggregate demand/aggregate supply framework to explain what happened.

31. Use aggregate supply and aggregate demand curves to discuss the short-run and long-run effects of:
    (a) An exogenous increase in consumer savings
    (b) An earthquake
    (c) An increase in government spending for defense, paid for by a tax increase
    (d) An increase in the government budget deficit caused by a tax cut without any cut in government spending

I n q u i r i e s   f o r   F u r t h e r   T h o u g h t

32. Some economists argue that it is incorrect to interpret the data in Figure 11 as a shifting Phillips Curve. They argue that economists see in that figure only what they *want* to see (downward sloping Phillips Curves), and that by grouping consecutive years together differently, we could produce *any* results—even upward-sloping Phillips Curves.
    (a) Get annual data on inflation and unemployment from the Web site for this book. Can you find a way to group consecutive years together that makes Phillips Curves appear to slope upward rather than downward?
    (b) What do you conclude about Phillips Curves from this evidence?

33. Consider the Asian countries that were subject to recessions in the late 1990s due to banking crises. What kinds of policies should these countries adopt? Why? How might other countries avoid their fates?

34. If you could guide U.S. economic policies, what would you do to try to avoid recessions?

35. Should the government follow policies that raise inflation permanently to reduce unemployment temporarily? Should they reduce inflation permanently if doing so raises unemployment temporarily?

36. Suppose you are an economic advisor for a country with high inflation. The President of that country wants to know if he can reduce inflation without causing a recession. What advice can you suggest for this country?

37. Find data on the Internet or in your library to graph Phillips Curves for other countries. What do you find?

MACROECONOMIC POLICIES

CHAPTER 32

MONETARY POLICY

In this Chapter. . .

Main Points to Understand

▶ Two fundamentally different views about government macroeconomic policy are reflected in the activist view, advocating discretionary policies, and the laissez-faire view, advocating policy rules.

▶ Monetary policy can try to offset changes in aggregate demand caused by changes in underlying conditions to stabilize real GDP and unemployment.

▶ Three main problems with activist, discretionary policies concern lags, information problems, and the effects of policies on expectations and incentives.

Thinking Skills to Develop

▶ Raise new questions about appropriate policies.

▶ Recognize the bases for legitimate disagreements about appropriate policies.

Not many people discuss monetary policy around the dinner table. Even news reports spend much less time reporting on monetary policy than on the latest political scandals or daily fluctuations in the stock market. Yet monetary policy has a more dramatic impact on your life than most of the issues discussed more frequently in the news. It determines whether you live in a country with stable prices or suffer through hyperinflation. It affects interest rates and redistributes income and wealth. In the short run, most economists believe, monetary policy affects the economy's output of goods and services, job opportunities for millions of workers, and unemployment. The Federal Reserve is one of the most powerful agencies in the world, perhaps with more impact on your life than the Supreme Court, but how much do you know of its policies? How many of its members can you name? (See the Web pages for this book for the answer.)

If you were in charge of the Federal Reserve or the central bank of another country, how would you make decisions?[1] How would you decide what the Fed should do this week? How would you decide whether to raise the money supply through open market purchases and by how much to raise it? How would you choose long-term goals for your policies to accomplish these decisions? What would those goals be? How would you decide whether to fight a possible recession if your actions would risk raising inflation?

---

[1]Chapter 29 discussed the Federal Reserve System and its main tools of monetary policy: open market operations, discount-window lending, reserve requirements, and other bank regulations.

If you had been in charge of designing the new monetary system for Europe, would you have chosen a single money, the Euro, for the nations of Europe? How would you have chosen operating procedures for the new European Central Bank? If you were an advisor to the British or Swiss governments, would you have advised joining the new system or remaining outside it (as these nations decided to do)? If you were a member of Congress in charge of redesigning U.S. monetary policy, would you want laws requiring the Fed to follow particular policies? Would you want to keep the Federal Reserve System at all or replace it with another system?

TWO VIEWS OF MACROECONOMIC POLICIES

Monetary policy is one of the two main types of government macroeconomic policies. (Fiscal policy, the second main type of macroeconomic policy, is discussed in the next chapter.)

> **Monetary policy** refers to changes in the nominal money supply through open market operations or other actions of a nation's central bank.

The Federal Reserve conducts monetary policy in the United States. Other countries have their own central banks, such as the Bank of Japan, the Bank of England, and the Bank of Mexico, which conduct those nations' monetary policies. Members of the European Union have created a new European Central Bank to operate European monetary policy for their new currency, the Euro.

Just as we often classify people's political views according to categories of liberal or conservative, views about the proper role of government economic policy fit into two categories: the *activist view* and the *laissez-faire view.* These categories don't fit everyone perfectly (just as the labels *liberal* and *conservative* don't), but they provide a useful contrast between two general views of government policy.

Activist View

Some economists take an activist view of policy.

> An **activist view** of policy maintains that the economy often operates inefficiently on its own and that government macroeconomic policies can improve its efficiency.

According to this view, changes in aggregate demand and supply often reduce output below its full-employment level and raise unemployment above its natural rate. Government macroeconomic policies can stabilize the economy—that is, prevent or reduce the business cycle fluctuations—by preventing or offsetting these changes in aggregate demand and supply.

Suppose, for example, that a decrease in investment demand reduces aggregate demand from AD_1 to AD_2 as in Figure 1. The Fed could *undo* this decrease in aggregate demand by raising the money supply. The increase in the money supply would raise the aggregate demand curve *back* to AD_1. To pursue this policy, the Fed would *loosen* monetary policy when it detected signs of declining real GDP and price level. The Fed, like most other central banks, usually describes its monetary policies in terms of effects on interest rates rather than effects on the money supply.[2]

---

[2]Chapters 29 and 31 discussed the effects of open market operations on the federal funds rate and other interest rates.

Figure 1 | An Activist View of Government Policy

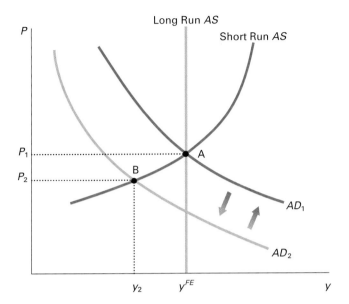

If aggregate demand were to fall from AD_1 to AD_2, an activist government policy might raise the money supply or government spending to try to raise aggregate demand back to AD_1.

> A **looser monetary policy** increases the growth rate of the money supply, decreasing the federal funds rate.

The Fed might loosen monetary policy by conducting open market purchases, lowering the discount rate, or reducing reserve requirements at banks. A loose policy is sometimes called *expansionary* policy because (by raising aggregate demand) it tends to expand real GDP.

Similarly, the Fed would *tighten* monetary policy, to decrease aggregate demand, when it believes that aggregate demand has increased beyond AD_1 in Figure 1. The tighter monetary policy is intended to bring aggregate demand back down to AD_1, preventing a short-run increase in real GDP but also preventing an increase in the price level.[3]

> A **tighter monetary policy** reduces the growth rate of the money supply, raising the federal funds rate.

The Fed might tighten monetary policy by conducting open market sales (or reducing the rate at which it conducts open market purchases), raising the discount rate, or raising reserve requirements at banks.

The Fed follows a *countercyclical* monetary policy if it loosens monetary policy to raise aggregate demand at times of low real GDP (relative to trend) and tightens monetary policy to reduce aggregate demand at times of high real GDP (relative to trend).

Figure 2 uses short-run Phillips Curves to describe countercyclical monetary policy. Many economists view the short-run Phillips Curve (discussed in the last chapter) as a short-run tradeoff between inflation and unemployment. They believe policy makers can *temporarily* choose any combination of inflation and unemployment on the short-run Phillips Curve, such as Point A, with high inflation and low unemployment, or Point B, with moderate inflation and unemployment, or Point C, with low inflation and high

IN THE NEWS

Most short-term interest rates rise amid talk Fed might be tightening its policy somewhat

NEW YORK—Most short-term interest rates rose amid speculation that the Federal Reserve may be tightening credit slightly in an effort to combat inflation.

Source: The Wall Street Journal

Changes in monetary policy have almost instant effects on financial markets.

[3]More precisely, the Fed would tighten monetary policy if it detected a rise in aggregate demand that seemed too rapid relative to its *long-run trend* associated with long-run economic growth. In other words, both aggregate demand and aggregate supply increase with long-run economic growth. The Fed would tighten policy if aggregate demand were to begin rising *faster* than aggregate supply.

Figure 2 | Conventional View of Inflation–Unemployment Tradeoff

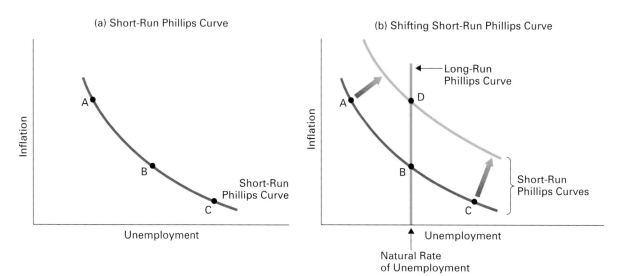

(a) Short-Run Phillips Curve

(b) Shifting Short-Run Phillips Curve

unemployment. However, if policy makers choose a combination of inflation and unemployment that lies *off* the *long-run* Phillips Curve (such as Point A or Point C), then the economy remains only temporarily at that point. Eventually, the short-run Phillips Curve shifts as in Figure 2b, so that the long run equilibrium occurs along the economy's long-run Phillips Curve, with unemployment returning to its natural rate.

If the Fed follows a countercyclical monetary policy, it loosens policy at times of high unemployment and low inflation, as at Point C in Figure 2. The Fed may try to move the economy upward and to the left *along* the short-run Phillips Curve, moving the economy from Point C to Point B. Although the policy increases inflation, it reduces unemployment. Similarly, the Fed may tighten monetary policy at times of high inflation and low unemployment, as at Point A in Figure 2. The Fed may try to move the economy downward and to the right along the short-run Phillips Curve from Point A to Point B. Although the policy raises unemployment, it reduces inflation.

The Fed must carefully avoid overreacting. Suppose that a fall in consumer spending or business investment spending causes a fall in aggregate demand. Real GDP falls and unemployment rises, as the economy moves from Point B to Point C in Figure 2. As a result, the Fed loosens monetary policy to try to increase aggregate demand and bring the economy back to Point B. The policy reduces unemployment and raises inflation. If the Fed loosens monetary policy too much, however, the economy moves past Point B to Point A, with even lower unemployment (temporarily) but higher inflation. In the long run, this overreaction may leave the economy at Point D, with the natural rate of unemployment but higher inflation than before the policy change.

Similarly, suppose that a rise in aggregate demand takes the economy from Point B to Point A in Figure 2, reducing unemployment but raising inflation. A tight monetary policy could bring the economy back to Point B. However, if the Fed overreacts by tightening too much, it creates a recession as the economy moves to Point C. The Fed faced this problem in 1989 and again in 1994 to 1995. In 1989, the Fed believed that U.S. aggregate demand was rapidly rising, so it tightened monetary policy to help prevent inflation from increasing. The tight monetary policy contributed to the 1990 to 1991 recession. Similarly, the Fed tightened monetary policy in 1994 and early 1995 because it interpreted rapid growth of real GDP as an increase in aggregate demand, and the Fed wanted to prevent inflation from rising. In this case, the Fed did not overreact, and the economy continued to grow without either a recession or an increase in inflation.

Goals of Activist Monetary Policy

As the discussion of Figure 2 indicates, monetary policy-making involves weighing the costs of low GDP and high unemployment against the costs of high inflation. Should the Fed follow policies to reduce unemployment temporarily even if the result is permanently higher inflation? Should the Fed follow policies to reduce inflation even if it creates a recession with a temporary rise in unemployment?

Economists need more statistical evidence on the effects of monetary policy to reach full agreement on its consequences. Their opinions differ on issues such as the size of the effects of monetary policy on real GDP, and the duration of those effects. Opinions also differ about the size of the short-run tradeoff between inflation and unemployment (the slope of the short-run Phillips Curve) and the duration of the tradeoff (the time before the short-run Phillips Curve shifts and unemployment returns to its natural rate). In addition, opinions differ regarding the costs of high inflation and the costs of low real GDP and high unemployment. These differences amount to disagreements over the best countercyclical monetary policy, that is, how loose or how tight the Fed should set policy in any given situation, and when it should change its policy.

As a result of these uncertainties and disagreements, advocates of activist monetary policy sometimes disagree about the best policy for the Fed to pursue. Most proponents of activist monetary policy argue that the Federal Reserve should focus on both inflation and real GDP or unemployment. Many economists advocate goals that compromise between pursuit of steady, low inflation and stable real GDP. In practice, the Federal Reserve itself usually states its goals only vaguely. Most Fed-watchers believe that the Fed compromises between these goals as it formulates policies.

Laissez-Faire View

While many economists take an activist view of economic policy, many others take a laissez-faire (hands-off) view:

> A **laissez-faire view** of policy maintains that the economy usually operates efficiently on its own and that even when it does not, active government policies will more likely aggravate inefficiencies and create new inefficiencies than alleviate problems.

Proponents of the laissez-faire view usually advocate a small role for government in the economy along with little government interference with individual freedom to make voluntary trades. Whenever possible, government policies should conform to a set of rules announced in advance rather than basing decisions on the discretion of government officials. For example, a rule might require the Federal Reserve to keep the growth rate of M1 between 2 percent and 4 percent per year; another rule might require the government to balance its budget each year.

Why do supporters of the laissez-faire view oppose activist policies? Don't they care about rising unemployment and falling real GDP when aggregate demand falls as in Figure 1? Why shouldn't government policy try to raise aggregate demand back to its original level to eliminate the rise in unemployment and fall in real GDP? Proponents of the laissez-faire view respond by arguing that activist policies usually do more harm than good. They argue that general *rules*, rather than discretionary judgment of policymakers, should govern policy.

Rules or Discretion?

Should the Federal Reserve act at its own discretion, that is, base its daily actions on its judgment of the economic situation, or should it follow a policy rule? Most proponents of activist monetary policy advocate *discretionary policy*. With discretionary policy, a group of experts, such as the people in the Federal Reserve System, watch the economy on a daily basis and use their best judgment and discretion about the most appropriate policy actions.

> **Discretionary policy** means that policy makers choose policy actions (such as open-market operations) on a daily basis, based on their own best judgments and discretion.

Most central banks around the world, including the Fed, operate in this way.

Proponents of the laissez-faire view, on the other hand, generally favor policy rules.[4]

> A **policy rule** is a specific statement of the policy actions that an agency will follow in the future.

For example, a policy rule might say that each month, the Fed will conduct open market operations to raise M1 at a constant rate of 3 percent per year. This example illustrates a *simple* policy rule.

> A **simple policy rule** requires a particular policy regardless of economic circumstances.

> A **contingent policy rule** states specifically how policies will depend on particular economic circumstances.

A contingent policy rule takes the form "if conditions are x, then policy will be y." For example, a contingent policy rule might state something like:

> Each month, the Fed will look at the most recent unemployment rate. If the unemployment rate is below 5 percent, the Fed will conduct open market operations to raise M1 at a constant rate of 3 percent per year. If the unemployment rate is 5 percent or higher, the Fed will conduct open market operations to raise M1 at a constant rate of 5 percent per year.

Contingent policy rules can specify any number of conditions and involve any level of complication.

The choice of a policy rule raises some of the same issues as the choice of a discretionary policy. What goals should monetary policy pursue? What kinds of actions would best achieve those goals? What kind of policy rule would best promote those actions? Should Congress or the Federal Reserve choose the policy rule? What happens if policymakers choose actions that violate the rule? When and how can the rule be changed? Advocates of policy rules advance three main arguments about the superiority of rules to discretion, The next section discusses those arguments.

Review Questions

1. Use a graph to help explain how a central bank can use monetary policy to stabilize real GDP.

---

[4]Questions of rules versus discretion in economic policy have analogies in criminal law. Should a judge have discretion to choose the punishment for a convicted criminal, or should the law set rules specifying punishments? The U.S. legal system sets rules for determining issues such as admissibility of evidence, but uses a combination of rules and discretion for determining punishments for various crimes. Like a legal system, a system of economic policy can be governed by either rules or discretion.

2. Use the economic analysis in this chapter to explain this newspaper headline: "Federal Reserve lowers interest rates to fight recession."

3. What is discretionary monetary policy?

4. What is a policy rule? What is the difference between a simple rule and a contingent rule?

Thinking Exercise

5. Suppose that the Fed raises the growth rate of the money supply from 3 percent per year to 6 percent per year and that people expect this new policy to last for many years. Explain the likely short-run and long-run effects of this policy change on real GDP, unemployment, the price level, the rate of inflation, the real interest rate, and the nominal interest rate.

Advocates of policy rules cite three main problems with discretionary policies. They see discretionary policy as inferior to rules because:

1. Lags complicate the effects of policies, reducing the effectiveness of discretionary policies and raising the dangers of overreaction.

2. The Fed lacks enough information to follow good discretionary policies.

3. Discretionary policies affect people's incentives in ways that hinder the economy's performance.

THREE PROBLEMS WITH DISCRETIONARY POLICY

First Problem: Lags

The first problem with discretionary policies involves lags in their implementation and effects. Any government agency, including the Fed, needs time to react to economic changes. Furthermore, the Fed gathers the economic data that tracks the economy with a lag. Try as it may, the Fed's information is never as fully up to date as it would like. These two factors create a lag in policy implementation.

The second type of lag involves the delay between a Fed policy action and its effects on the economy. Changes in the money supply take time to affect aggregate demand, real GDP, and prices. Evidence suggests that these lags are long, variable, and unpredictable. These lags make it difficult for the Fed to know when, and by how much, to act. For example, the Fed may want to loosen monetary policy to help bring the economy out of a recession, but lags might delay the effects of current actions until next year, when the recession is over and loose monetary policy only adds to inflation.

To see why lags matter, think about turning on the water to take a shower. You turn on the hot water along with the cold water, but the hot water takes time to reach the shower head; a lag separates the time when you turn on the faucet and the time when hot water arrives. After a minute, if the water feels too cold, you may turn on more hot water, but you may not have waited long enough for the hot water to arrive at the shower head. If you turn up the hot water, the shower may become too hot after a few minutes. The lag—the length of time hot water takes to arrive at the shower—may change from day to day depending on the outside temperature, how many other people in the building are using hot water, and so on. This may make it difficult to get the right water temperature. You may be better off with a simple rule such as "turn up the hot and cold water each halfway regardless of the water temperature for the first several minutes."

Remember lags, or you might get burned.

IN THE NEWS

Why the Fed's efforts to forestall inflation have thus far failed

Delayed reaction
It pushed up interest
rates, but maybe not
enough; Risk of
recession grows

Why has the Fed's anti-inflation campaign failed?

In part, the answer lies in the long and unpredictable lags that always separate Fed actions from desired results.

Source: The Wall Street Journal

A decade ago, when the Fed was trying to reduce inflation while avoiding a recession, its efforts were frustrated by unpredictable lags .

EXAMPLES

The Fed is aware of the policy problems created by lags, and it tries to minimize those problems. For example, in 1994 the Fed saw signs that inflation would soon rise. Although inflation was not yet increasing, the Fed began tightening monetary policy so that, after a lag, the tight policy would prevent inflation from rising in the future. This policy sparked controversy. Critics argued that the Fed should not tighten monetary policy because inflation was not rising and, in their view, was not likely to rise. The Fed defended its policy on the grounds that real GDP was rising very rapidly and that, based on historical experiences, inflation would soon increase. Because monetary policy affects the economy with a lag, argued the Fed, it could not wait for inflation to rise before tightening monetary policy. Similarly, the Fed reduced the funds rate in September 1998 mainly to reduce the chance that recessions in Asia would spread to the United States, rather than because it saw clear signs that the U.S. economy was entering a recession yet. The Fed, taking lags into account, tries to act preemptively before problems begin.

Second Problem: Lack of Information

The second problem with discretionary policy comes from policy makers' lack of enough information about the economy. Policy makers need two types of important information that they do not have. First, they don't have enough information about current changes in the economy. Second, they don't have enough information about how their policy actions will affect the economy.

Information about the Economy

Usually neither policy makers nor economists know whether a current change in GDP occurs because of a change in aggregate demand or a change in aggregate supply, nor do they know if the change will be temporary or permanent. Economists even disagree about causes of many *past* economic changes, including the Great Depression. Without good knowledge of current changes in the economy, the Fed lacks sufficient information to conduct good discretionary monetary policy.

Economist Milton Friedman has argued that the problems of lags and insufficient information have led the Fed's discretionary policies to *deepen* recessions and to raise

IN THE NEWS

Fed cuts short-term rates by 0.25 point

First cut since January '96 is a pre-emptive strike
to stave off recession

WASHINGTON—The Federal Reserve cut interest rates for the first time since January 1996 in a preemptive strike against recession that reflects a sudden reversal in the central bank's outlook for the economy and new worries about a credit crunch.

The Fed trimmed its key short-term interest rate by ¼ percentage point to 5.25%, saying it sought to "cushion the effects on prospective growth in the United States of increasing weakness in foreign economies" and offset what it termed "less accommodative financial conditions domestically."

Source: The Wall Street Journal

IN THE NEWS

The gloom factor

Fears of a recession are beginning to nip
at the economy's heels
While people are spending, some firms retrench
as Asian crisis hits home

The fact that hardly any economists are forecasting an imminent end to the boom isn't very comforting. "Nobody has a good record of predicting when a recession comes," says Milton Friedman, the Nobel-laureate economist. "If you look at the historical record, the first quarters of most recessions have been regarded by most commentators at the time as a continuation of prosperity."

After all, transcripts of Fed deliberations show that Mr. Greenspan himself told fellow policy makers in October 1990 that the U.S. hadn't slipped into a recession; the official arbiters later decided that the downturn had begun that July.

Source: The Wall Street Journal

inflation. When a fall in aggregate demand or supply raises unemployment, the Fed usually loosens monetary policy to help reduce unemployment and raise real GDP. The Fed often responds too vigorously, however, partly because it lacks sufficient information about the economy and partly because its policies affect the economy only after a lag. After the lag, when the effects of Fed policy appear, unemployment falls below its natural rate and inflation rises. However, unemployment does not remain permanently below its natural rate; it eventually begins to rise back toward its natural rate. This rise in unemployment creates political pressures for the Fed to loosen monetary policy even further. Consequently, unemployment falls in the short run again, but only at the cost of even higher inflation than before. As people begin to adjust to ever-higher rates of inflation, the Fed can keep unemployment below its natural rate only by continually accelerating money growth. Eventually, inflation rises enough that people become more concerned with price increases than with unemployment. At that point, political pressure leads the Fed to tighten monetary policy, raising unemployment above its natural rate and causing a recession. The more inflation rises, the deeper will be the recession when the Fed eventually acts to stop inflation.

Figure 3 shows Friedman's argument in terms of short-run Phillips Curves. When a fall in aggregate demand moves the economy from Point A to Point B, raising unemployment, the Fed overreacts (partly because of lags and information problems) and moves the economy to Point C, reducing unemployment and raising inflation. However, when the short-run Phillips Curve shifts from Curve 1 to Curve 2 and unemployment begins to rise again toward Point D, the Fed reacts again by loosening monetary policy, moving the economy to Point E. This cycle may repeat, as the economy moves toward Point F, but loose Fed policy takes it to Point G. Eventually, people become concerned about inflation. As the short-run Phillips Curve shifts again and the economy heads toward Point H, the Fed tightens policy and takes the economy to Point I, reducing inflation, but at the cost of a big recession.[5]

IN THE NEWS

Economists see jobless decline without inflation

A key question:
How low can the
unemployment rate
safely go?

No one, including the Fed, has enough knowledge of the economy to answer questions like this one. As a result, monetary policy sometimes underreacts and sometimes overreacts.

Source: New York Times

---

[5] Friedman, a winner of the Nobel Memorial Prize in Economic Science, is often called a *monetarist* due to his view that changes in the money supply are the most important causes of business cycles, and due to his view that the Fed should follow a policy rule of keeping the growth rate of M1 or M2 at a constant rate of about 3 percent per year.

A fall in aggregate demand takes the economy from Point A to Point B. The Fed loosens monetary policy, but because of lags and information problems, it may overreact, taking the economy to Point C. In the long run, the economy moves from Point C as the short-run Phillips Curve shifts. The Fed may react to the rise in unemployment by loosening policy again, taking the economy to Point E. This cycle repeats, and the economy moves to Point F and then Point G. Finally, as the economy moves toward Point H in the long run, pressures to reduce inflation lead the Fed to tighten policy and reduce inflation at the expense of a recession (Point I).

Figure 3 | When Monetary Policy Overreacts

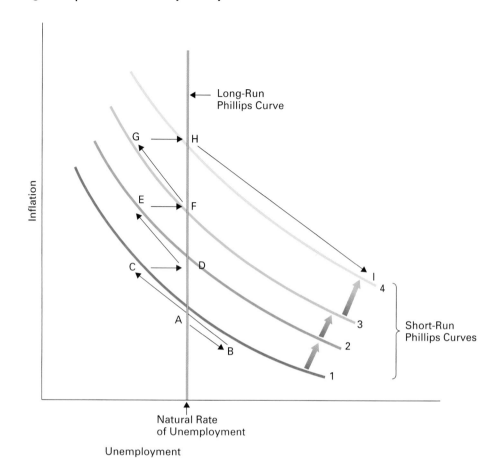

Information about the Effects of Policies

Policy makers lack a second type of information concerning the effects of their policies. Economists have constructed intricate mathematical models of the economy on computers to forecast the effects of changes in policies. The computer models use data from the past to try to predict effects of current policy changes. These models face an important problem, though: The effects of current policy changes may differ from the effects of past policy changes if people's expectations have changed. This problem leads to the Lucas critique of econometric policy evaluation.

> The **Lucas critique** says that people do not always respond the same way to a change in economic conditions or government policies, because their responses depend partly on their expectations about the future, and those expectations can change.

People's expectations about the future depend partly on their past experiences. The past responses of government policy to changes in underlying conditions affect how people expect the government to respond in the future. Therefore, past responses affect the results of current policies. For example, if the Fed has usually tightened monetary policy in the past when inflation rose by more than 2 percentage points over a 6-month period, then people may expect the same response in the future. The effects of a tight Fed policy under these conditions, when people *expect* it, may differ considerably from its effects when people expect a different policy.

The Lucas critique complicates efforts to predict the effects of a particular policy, because those effects depend on people's expectations, which change with circumstances. Then consequently, past experience does not necessarily provide a reliable guide to the effects of future policy changes. This complicates efforts of economists to obtain evidence on the effects of policies. This complication also limits the abilities of computer models to predict the effects of government policies in a reliable way. Obviously, it also complicates discretionary policymaking.

Public Information about Policy

Discretionary policy can add uncertainty to the economy. Firms and investors find it hard to predict what Fed officials will do in various situations. In contrast, a credible policy rule could reduce economic uncertainty.

> A **credible policy rule** is a rule that people believe policymakers will follow, perhaps because policymakers have incentives to follow the rule.

Some policy rules are more credible than others. The credibility of a rule increases as incentives rise for policymakers to follow that rule. A rule for monetary policy might be credible if Congress passed a law specifying a certain policy, and created mechanisms to ensure enforcement of that rule. Alternatively, policymakers themselves can try to commit to a rule.

> A policy maker makes a **commitment to a policy rule** by doing something to guarantee its implementation.

People sometimes say that a person "burned his bridges behind him" when he has done something that makes it hard to reverse some action. This phrase has its origins in war, when a general for an invading army might burn bridges after the army crosses them to prevent soldiers from retreating during a battle; burning bridges commits the army to either fight or surrender. Burning bridges increases the incentive to fight hard for the current goal; it is a method of promoting commitment. Commitment is more difficult for economic policymakers than for soldiers, but some degree of commitment may be possible through actions and public statements of policymakers.

Without a credible policy rule, people have difficulty forming expectations about policy. In a letter to the editor of *The Wall Street Journal,* Nobel Prize winning economist Milton Friedman wrote:

> I know, or can find out, what monetary actions have been: open market purchases and sales and discount rates at Federal Reserve Banks. I know also the federal funds rate and rates of growth of various monetary aggregates. What I do not know is the policy that produced those actions.
>
> The closest I can come to an official specification of current monetary policy is that it is to take those actions that the monetary authorities, in light of all evidence available, judge will best promote price stability and full employment— i.e., to do the right thing at the right time. But that surely is not a "policy." It is simply an expression of good intentions and an injunction to "trust us."
>
> I hasten to add that the present situation is not unique. On the contrary, it has persisted for nearly the entire . . . life of the Federal Reserve System. The only exception was from the outbreak of World War II to 1951, when the Fed followed an announced policy of pegging interest rates on federal government securities. For the rest, the Fed has consistently resorted to statements of good intentions . . . It has claimed credit for good results and blamed forces beyond its control—generally fiscal policy—for any bad outcomes.[6]

---

[6]"The Fed Has No Clothes," *The Wall Street Journal,* April 15, 1988, p. 28.

This third problem of information arises because discretionary policy creates uncertainty when the public lacks enough information about the Fed's policy to form accurate predictions of its future actions. This problem highlights an important benefit of rules over discretion.

Third Problem: Effects on Incentives

The third problem with discretionary policy is that it affects expectations, incentives, and behavior in ways that hinder economic performance. This leads to an important result:

> A credible rule for actions can lead to better results than even the best case-by-case (discretionary) actions.

The easiest way to understand this result is to consider an example from outside economics, in which this result is well known: Rules for dealing with terrorists.

EXAMPLE: DEALING WITH TERRORISTS

Suppose that you are a government official in charge of dealing with terrorist threats. Terrorists may take hostages and offer to trade their freedom for things like cash or armaments. A *credible* policy rule never to deal with terrorists gives them little incentive to take hostages. Terrorists will know that taking hostages has no benefits.

However, incentives are totally different without a credible policy rule against dealing with terrorists. If your policy calls for discretionary responses to terrorism—for doing whatever seems best in a particular case—then terrorists may expect hostages to be good bargaining chips. They may see at least a chance of gains by taking hostages. Consequently, terrorists are more likely to take hostages if you rely on discretionary policy than if you set a credible rule not to deal with them.

Time Consistency

The best discretionary decisions may differ from the best rules. In that case, a credible rule produces better results than discretion. To see why, consider the terrorist example. Suppose that you are a discretionary policy maker, and terrorists take hostages. You can either deal with the terrorists to try to save the hostages, or take a hard line on terrorism by not dealing with them and trying to discourage future hostage-taking. Sometimes the benefits of dealing with the terrorists and saving the hostages may exceed the costs of creating a bad precedent. In that case, you benefit by dealing with the terrorists to save the hostages. However, you would benefit from having a credible rule *not* to deal with terrorists because that rule would remove terrorists' incentives to take hostages in the first place.[7] A credible rule produces better results than discretionary policy when that policy is not *time consistent*.

> In a **time consistent policy,** the best case-by-case decisions are the same as the decisions suggested by the best policy rule.

> In a **time inconsistent policy,** the best case-by-case decisions differ from the decisions that the best policy rule would suggest.

---

[7]This statement assumes that terrorists' behavior responds to incentives. Evidence and general agreement among experts suggest that it does.

Time inconsistency occurs when a choice that *currently* seems best for today and tomorrow no longer seems best when tomorrow comes, even if no new information emerges. Consider an example of giving in to some temptation. You may sometimes benefit by committing to a rule that prevents you from giving in to temptation at the last minute, *even though* you may want to give in when the time comes. In fact, you benefit precisely *because* you want to prevent yourself from giving in at the future date.

Application to Taxes

High taxes on income from capital would discourage investment, but after someone had *already* invested in new capital equipment, the government could gain revenue by placing a very high tax on income from that capital equipment. If investors know that the government *could* do this, they have little incentive to invest. By reducing investment, expectations of a high tax actually *reduce* government tax revenue. Policy makers can raise government tax revenue by committing to a credible policy *not* to place high taxes on capital in the future. In this way, a credible commitment to a policy rule of low taxes on capital encourages investment, and provides higher revenue than even the best discretionary policy.

Application to Monetary Policy

Proponents of the laissez-faire view of policy argue that discretionary monetary policy has an inflationary bias.

Suppose the Fed follows discretionary policy. When inflation is low, and people expect low inflation to continue, the Fed has an incentive to loosen monetary policy, because the benefits of a (temporary) fall in employment may exceed the small costs of a slight increase in inflation. The Fed wants to move the economy from Point B to Point A in Figure 2. However, sophisticated business people and investors recognize the Fed's incentive for looser policy. As a result, they begin to expect inflation. This rise in expected inflation raises the short-run Phillips Curve, as in Figure 2b. This creates a problem for the Fed. If it loosens policy, it moves the economy to Point D, creating the inflation that people expected, without reducing unemployment. If it does *not* loosen policy, it prevents inflation, but unemployment *rises* temporarily above its natural rate. (The economy would move to a point below and to the right of Point D, along the higher short-run Phillips Curve.)

Discretionary policy, therefore, creates a problem for the Fed, because it allows inflationary expectations to increase. When expected inflation rises, the Fed must create the inflation that people expect simply *to prevent a rise* in unemployment. To prevent unemployment, the Fed has an incentive to respond to a rise in *expected* inflation by loosening policy to *create* the inflation that people expect. As a result, discretionary policy has an inflationary bias.

If the Fed could follow a credible rule, however, it could choose a rule that would create low inflation. A credible rule would affect expectations: it would lead people to expect low inflation. As a result, the Fed would not face the problem discussed above. With both actual and expected inflation remaining low, unemployment equals its natural rate, so the credible rule would produce better economic results than discretionary policy.

Can Credible Policy Rules Shift Short-Run Phillips Curves?

Suppose an economy has high inflation, as at Point H in Figure 3. Can the Fed reduce inflation without causing a recession? Suppose an economy is in a recession, as at Point C in Figure 2 or Point I in Figure 3. Can the Fed end a recession quickly without raising inflation?

Some economists argue that a *credible* change in monetary policy can reduce inflation without affecting unemployment or real GDP. The idea is that a credible change in policy leads people to change their expectations of inflation. The change in expectations shifts the short-run Phillips Curve (as described in the last chapter). This change allows inflation to fall without any rise in unemployment. Some economists argue that

IN THE NEWS

Economics aside, the Fed is not likely to risk its credibility by responding to political pressures, market participants said.

Source: New York Times

The Fed knows that it would benefit from credibility in its announced policies.

a government can make its policy credible by committing to a policy rule or by taking unusual and dramatic actions that would indicate a major change in policy, showing people that policy makers are not following "business as usual."

A credible policy rule could take the form of a law or a constitutional amendment stating a required policy, although even these measures leave the possibility of loopholes or simple disobedience. Unusual and dramatic actions might include major changes in fiscal policy, such as balancing a government budget that previously had run big deficits, making big changes in taxes or government regulations, and so on. History offers only a few good examples of major policy changes of the kind that may affect expectations. For example, at the end of the German hyperinflation in 1923, the central bank was separated from the government so the government could not force it to print money to finance budget deficits, as it had done during the period of hyperinflation.

Other economists argue, however, that even credible changes in policy cannot achieve these results, citing other historical experiences. For example, when Margaret Thatcher became prime minister of Great Britain in 1979, she promised to reduce inflation. Inflation fell, but Britain had a major recession. Similarly, when Alan Greenspan became Chairman of the Board of Governors of the Federal Reserve System, he stated that he would follow policies to reduce inflation. He did, and U.S. inflation fell, but the country suffered a major recession in 1982. Some economists argue that Thatcher and Greenspan made credible promises, and that these experiences show that policy makers cannot avoid the short-run Phillips Curve simply by adopting credible policies. Other economists argue that few people really believed these announcements of policy changes, so the changes in policy lacked credibility. Lacking credibility, tighter monetary policies created recessions. According to this argument, the recessions could have been avoided if both countries had been following formal, credible rules for monetary policy rather than discretionary policies.

Review Questions

6. What does it mean to say that a policy rule is credible?

7. Why do lags create difficulties for discretionary monetary policy?

8. Why can policy rules produce better results than case-by-case, discretionary policy making?

9. Why do information problems create difficulties for discretionary monetary policy?

10. Explain the Lucas critique.

Thinking Exercises

11. Explain why discretionary monetary policy has an inflationary bias.

12. Discuss this statement from a study by the Congressional Budget Office: "Inflation could be reduced relatively painlessly by lowering inflationary expectations."

TARGETS OF MONETARY POLICY

Once a society has chosen the goals for its monetary policy and decided whether to employ rules or use discretionary policy, it must choose a method for achieving those goals. If it decides on rules for monetary policy, it must decide *which* rules; if it decides on discretion, policy makers must decide *which* economic indicators they will use to guide their policy actions.

When economic signs point in different directions, the Fed may not know which way to turn.

Targeting the Federal Funds Rate

In recent years, the Federal Reserve has conducted discretionary monetary policy with an *informal* rule devoted to keeping the nominal federal funds interest rate at a *target* level. (The Fed targets the *nominal* federal funds rate, because it cannot affect the real rate in the long run.) Recall that the federal funds rate is the interest rate that banks charge each other for short-term loans of reserves. The Fed can control the federal funds rate by raising the supply of bank reserves when demand for them rises and reducing the supply when demand falls. An increase in the demand for bank reserves would ordinarily raise the equilibrium federal funds rate, but the Fed can prevent a rise by increasing the supply of reserves through open market purchases (i.e., loose monetary policy), as in Figure 4. The Fed can stabilize the federal funds interest rate by changing the supply of bank reserves to offset changes in the demand.

Targeting the Foreign Exchange Rate

The monetary policies of many nations are focused on the foreign exchange rates of their currencies. When a country chooses monetary policy to keep its exchange rate fixed, it maintains a fixed exchange-rate system.

> In a **fixed (or pegged) exchange-rate system**, the government buys or sells the country's currency in foreign exchange markets in whatever amounts are necessary to keep its exchange rate fixed (pegged) to some foreign currency.

Other countries maintain floating exchange-rate systems.

> In a **floating (or flexible) exchange-rate system**, the government does not actively trade in foreign exchange markets to try to influence exchange rates.

Figure 4 | Stabilizing the Federal Funds Rate

An increase in the demand for reserves by banks would raise the federal funds rate from i_1 to i_2, but the Fed can keep this rate at i_1 through an appropriate increase in the supply of reserves.

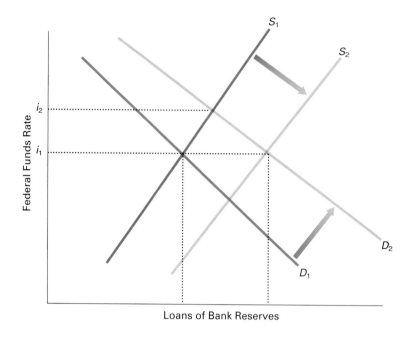

Some countries operate in-between, hybrid systems.

> A **managed-float exchange-rate system** combines elements of the other two systems; the government sometimes trades in foreign exchange markets to try to influence the exchange rate without trying to maintain a fixed rate.

Systems of Fixed Exchange Rates

The gold standard of the 19th century was one type of fixed exchange-rate system. Each country on the gold standard fixed the nominal price of gold in its currency by acting as a residual buyer or seller of gold. Because the law of one price applies to gold, this policy fixed the country's exchange rate. For example, suppose that the United States fixes the dollar price of gold at $35 per ounce, while the British government fixes the pound price of gold at £7 per ounce. Arbitrage (the law of one price) implies that the price of gold must be the same in both countries, so £7 must equal $35, implying that £1 is worth $5. The gold standard keeps the exchange rate between two countries fixed as long as each country maintains its policy of fixing the price of gold.

The gold standard evolved, and in 1944, it led to the Bretton Woods System of fixed exchange rates. The Bretton Woods agreement set the U.S. dollar price of gold and required other countries to keep their own exchange rates fixed against the dollar. For example, the British pound exchange rate was fixed at $4.80 per pound, and the Japanese yen exchange rate was fixed at 0.278¢ per yen (or ¥360 per dollar). To keep its exchange rate fixed, each country's government would sell as much of its own currency as people wanted to buy at the fixed exchange rate and buy as much as people wanted to sell. When a country sold its own money and bought U.S. dollars on the foreign exchange market, it was said to have a *balance-of-payments surplus*. When it bought its own money by selling U.S. dollars on the foreign exchange market, it was said to have a *balance-of-payments deficit*.

Under the Bretton Woods System of fixed exchange rates, governments bought and sold their own money for U.S. dollars rather than buying and selling gold, as they would under a gold standard. Whenever a government bought its own currency (with dollars) on the foreign exchange market, its money supply fell. Whenever it sold its own currency (for dollars), its money supply increased. In this way, the requirement that a government fix its exchange rate dictated the extent to which it could change its money supply, just as a requirement that you drive at 30 miles per hour would dictate the extent to which you press the accelerator pedal in a car. While a country fixed its exchange rate to the U.S. dollar, it could not use monetary policy to pursue other goals.

Devaluations

For many reasons, governments did not like the constraint that the fixed exchange rate system placed on their monetary policies. They frequently wanted to increase their money supplies more rapidly (or sometimes more slowly) than was dictated by fixed exchange rates. Countries that tried to increase their money supplies more rapidly experienced balance of payments deficits. A country with a large balance of payments deficit risked exhausting its supply of U.S. dollars to sell, which would prevent it from continuing to fix its exchange rate. This prospect often led to devaluations.

> A **devaluation** of a currency occurs when a country that fixes its exchange rate at a certain level changes that level so that its money loses value in terms of foreign money (that is, the exchange rate rises).

In the long run, a devaluation raises nominal prices of all goods and services along with the nominal money supply, without affecting relative prices, real GDP, or employment. A devaluation works like a currency reform in reverse. To see why, imagine that a country decides to add a zero to every unit of its money. A 1 peso bill becomes a 10 peso bill; a 10 peso bill becomes a 100 peso bill, and so on. The foreign exchange rate must also change. If 1 peso was originally worth $1.00, the devaluation reduces its value to only $0.10 (so that 10 pesos are worth $1.00). This currency reform in reverse, which would amount to a huge inflation that would raise prices by a factor of 10, is the same as a devaluation.

Short-Run Effects of Devaluation

In the short run, however, a devaluation can have real effects with sticky nominal prices or nominal wages. With sticky prices in the short run, a devaluation lowers the foreign-currency prices of domestically produced products and raises the domestic-currency

IN THE NEWS

Import prices start rising in response to ruble's fall

St. Petersburg Governor Vladimir Yakovlev's promise last Wednesday not to allow price rises on foodstuffs and consumer goods has wilted before the power of market mechanisms.

One week after the government allowed the ruble to devalue, consumers are starting to feel the effects, with shops around the city hiking prices on imported goods.

On Monday, most shops and kiosks interviewed by The St. Petersburg Times said that prices for imported goods had already risen by between 10 percent and 25 percent.

Source: St. Petersburg Times

IN THE NEWS

Yen's rally might bring Japan pain, not gain

Anxiety about the effects of yen surge on profits spurs Nikkei sell-off

A strong yen makes Japanese-made products more expensive overseas, cuts exporters' yen-dominated earnings, and tends to shrink the trade surplus.

Clinton hails dollar's fall against the yen

Says tumble could help manufacturers in U.S., boosting their exports

Although some investors worry the sharp decline in the value of the dollar against the Japanese yen portends tough times for the economy, President Clinton praised the development, saying it "coud be a good thing."

Speaking briefly to reporters before a late afternoon meeting with advisers, Mr. Clinton said that "the yen got too weak," causing a flood of cheaper Japanese imports into the U.S.

Source: The Wall Street Journal

prices of foreign products. For example, suppose that a country devalues its money from 10 francs per dollar to 12 francs per dollar. A product that sells for 100 francs cost foreigners $10.00 before the devaluation, but it costs only $8.33 after the devaluation; a foreign product that sells for $100 cost 1,000 francs before the devaluation, but it costs 1,200 francs after the devaluation. These price changes may lead people to buy more domestically produced goods and buy fewer foreign goods, reducing imports, raising exports, and possibly affecting the country's employment and real GDP.

Just as unexpected inflation can redistribute income, creating winners and losers, devaluations usually redistribute income. Losers include workers whose nominal wages are fixed in the short run. By raising prices of imported products, a devaluation reduces their real wages. People whose savings or pensions are fixed in nominal units of the domestic currency also lose real income from the devaluation. Winners include owners of some firms that increase their exports as a result of the devaluation, while paying the same nominal wages and lower real wages. Indeed, countries with fixed exchange rates sometimes devalue their currencies specifically to try to increase competitiveness of their goods in world markets, intentionally creating these winners and losers.

As a whole, however, a devaluation makes a country poorer than before, because it increases the cost of foreign goods and services. In the short run, a country cannot trade its products for as many foreign products after a devaluation as before. In the long run (after prices and wages fully adjust), the devaluation does not affect relative prices or boost a country's international competitiveness, although the effects of the redistribution of income may linger.

When speculators believe that a country might devalue its money, they try to avoid losses or make profits by selling that currency and buying others instead. This speculation can create a balance-of-payments crisis, in which people rapidly sell a country's money, forcing the country's government to spend a large amount of resources to continue to fix the exchange rate. Balance-of-payments crises usually result in devaluations, because governments are unwilling to spend the resources needed to continue to fix their exchange rates.

For example, in late 1994, speculators began to expect that the government of Mexico would devalue the peso. As a result, speculators tried to sell pesos and buy other currencies, such as U.S. dollars. This raised the amount of pesos that Mexico's central bank had to buy (with U.S. dollars) to maintain a fixed exchange rate. Mexico spent billions of dollars in this effort. Finally, rather than lose more dollars, Mexico devalued the peso. More recently, Russia devalued its ruble in 1998, abandoning a fixed exchange rate system and adopting a floating rate system, though it imposed many regulations and controls on trades. Several Asian countries, including Indonesia, South Korea, the Philippines, Thailand, and Malaysia experienced financial crises and devalued their currencies in late 1997 and early 1998, as Figure 5 shows.

A government may try to maintain a fixed exchange rate by increasing regulations and controls that obstruct efforts to sell the country's money. Although these regulations and controls reduce the losses that the government incurs to keep the exchange rate fixed, they can also cause large economic inefficiencies. Also, they seldom prevent devaluation in the long run.

Currency Boards

Some countries have added credibility to their monetary policies by replacing their central banks with currency boards. A currency board, like a central bank, buys or sells currencies on foreign exchange markets to keep the exchange rate fixed. However, a currency board has only one goal—keeping the exchange rate fixed—and has political independence and a sufficient level of assets (reserves) to meet that goal.

> A **currency board** is an institution whose sole purpose is to keep a foreign exchange rate fixed by acting as a residual buyer or seller of the country's money at that price.

Figure 5 | Asian Crisis: 1997–1998: Exchange Rates against U.S. Dollar

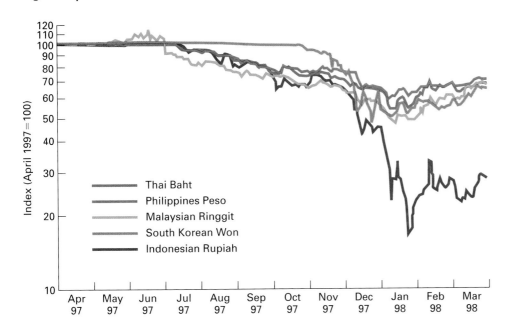

IN THE NEWS

Asian currencies tumble against dollar

Ringgit, Rupiah and Baht hit record lows

Companies and investors scrambled for dollars Monday as the Malaysian ringgit, the Indonesian rupiah, the Thai baht and the Philippine peso dropped to record lows against the U.S. currency.

Source: The Wall Street Journal

The reserves of the currency board must be large enough to fund any conceivable purchase of domestic money to maintain the designated fixed exchange rate.

Hong Kong has had a currency board since 1984. More recently, Argentina, Estonia, and Lithuania have created currency boards. A currency board disciplines monetary policy, adding credibility at the cost of flexibility to pursue other goals. Some economists believe that currency boards represent an attractive alternative for countries that suffer from high inflation or low credibility in their monetary policies.[8]

Which Exchange-Rate System Is Best?

Until the third quarter of the 20th century, most countries had fixed exchange rates. Then continuing balance-of-payments crises and devaluations led many countries to switch to floating exchange rates or hybrid systems. European countries have alternated between floating exchange-rate systems and managed-float systems.

Several European countries are now in the process of changing to an entirely new monetary system with a new money, the *Euro,* replacing their national currencies and a new European Central Bank to set combined monetary policy. When several nations share the same money, they have a *common currency.* A common currency has two main advantages over a pegged exchange rate system: People don't have to exchange currencies when they import goods and services, and the common currency system provides *credibility* by eliminating the risk that one of the countries may devalue its currency.

Economists disagree about the relative merits of fixed exchange rates and flexible exchange rates. Some argue for a floating exchange rate system, because it allows a government to choose its monetary policy without the restriction of keeping a fixed exchange rate. This frees a country to use monetary policy to pursue low inflation or other goals. With a fixed exchange rate, in contrast, a country cannot use monetary policy for these goals. While a country with a fixed exchange rate has the same long-run inflation rate as the country to which it fixes the exchange rate, a floating

Several European countries will soon share a common currency, the Euro.

---

[8] In 1998, international financier George Soros advocated a currency board for Russia.

IN THE NEWS

11 nations taking next pivotal step toward the Euro

Key meeting in Brussels
European governments likely to yield individual control over exchange rates

FRANKFURT—Nearly 50 years after European leaders dreamed of uniting their nations to prevent another world war, 11 countries led by Germany and France are soon to surrender a central pillar of national sovereignty: control over their currencies.

Despite some remaining feuding and recrimination, leaders from all but 4 of the 15 nations in the European Union are expected to approve final plans next weekend for the introduction of a single European currency on Jan. 1.

Financial institutions and a few big companies will shift in 1999 to Euro-based electronic transactions, although the actual bills and coins will not be used until 2002.

Source: New York Times

---

exchange-rate system allows the country to choose its own inflation rate and monetary policies. In addition, governments do not need to spend resources to keep their exchange rates fixed under a floating-rate system, freeing resources for other uses.

Perhaps the strongest argument for floating exchange rates centers on avoiding the balance-of-payments crises that seem inevitably to occur under fixed exchange-rate systems. These crises disrupt international trade and financial flows, often cause governments to lose billions of dollars to speculators, and sometimes lead governments to adopt economically inefficient restrictions on international trade.

Other economists argue for a fixed exchange-rate system as much more convenient than a floating-rate system. Information costs fall, because the exchange rate does not change every day. As a result, people and business firms can plan more easily. This stability helps to promote international trade. In contrast, the constant change in a floating exchange-rate system creates uncertainty that may hinder international trade. A fixed-rate system also imposes discipline on governments by preventing them from raising their money supplies rapidly and creating high inflation. This fosters international cooperation in setting policies.

Advocates of fixed exchange rates argue that exchange rates change too often and by too much under a floating exchange-rate system. Speculation causes large, unpredictable changes in exchange rates. Because prices are sticky in the short run, these changes affect relative prices between domestic and foreign goods. The resulting overvaluations or undervaluations cause economic inefficiencies and may affect a country's exports, imports, real GDP, and employment. Evidence shows that the relative prices of foreign goods in terms of domestic goods varies much less under a fixed exchange-rate system than under a floating exchange-rate system. A fixed exchange-rate system can avoid the problems of overvaluation and undervaluation of currencies if countries follow appropriate monetary and fiscal policies to avoid balance-of-payments crises. Proponents of floating exchange rates respond that countries with fixed exchange rates have seldom followed the necessary policies to prevent balance-of-payments crises.

IN THE NEWS

Malaysia imposes sweeping currency control

Ringgit trades abroad end; moves show emergence of capital restrictions

Malaysian Prime Minister Mahathir Mohamad announced sweeping currency controls, including an immediate end to trading the Malaysian ringgit abroad, to shelter the economy from the Asian economic crisis.

The new policy, announced Tuesday, is further evidence that capital controls, long scorned as anathema to economic development, are gaining credence as Asia's financial turmoil enters its second year.

Source: The Wall Street Journal

Banking Regulations

Chapter 29 discussed the important dual role of banks in the economy: They help to create money, and they act as intermediaries in the loan market. As a result, issues involving monetary policy and loan markets, including interest rates, savings, and investment, become intertwined. Because of these connections, bank regulation is one important component of monetary policy.

The importance of good bank-regulation policy is one key lesson from the 1997–1998 economic crises in Japan, South Korea, and other Asian countries. Banks in those countries made many bad loans to firms that are unlikely to repay. Some of these loans resulted from the moral hazard problems discussed in the previous chapter; others resulted from government policies that specifically encouraged those loans.

When the public became aware of the size of the bad loans in the banking systems of these countries, a financial crisis erupted in 1997, triggering currency devaluations and recessions. Devaluation of the Russian ruble in 1998 and other changes in Russian monetary policies also resulted from a banking crisis: Russian banks had extended large quantities of loans that were unlikely to be repaid. The Central Bank of Russia responded to the crisis by announcing that it would print money to subsidize those banks to save them from bankruptcy.

Alternative Monetary Institutions

A key long-run monetary policy issue concerns the *institutions* of policy. Should the Federal Reserve act as an independent agency of the government, as it does now, or should Congress or the president control the Fed more directly? What powers should the Fed have? Should the Federal Reserve exist at all? Similar questions arise in other countries. Should all the countries of Europe use the same money and have one European Central Bank rather than different moneys and different central banks? If so, how should that central bank be organized and who should control it? Should the law allow private firms such as banks to print their own money, as they did during part of the 19th century? Should people be free to use whichever money they want as long as someone else is willing to accept it? Should the government involve itself in the money business at all, or should it leave money to private producers in free markets like most other businesses?

IN THE NEWS

Japanese tell U.S. that their banks are in big trouble

WASHINGTON—Japan's top financial officials told their American counterparts this weekend that their country's banking system was acutely short of capital, with the top 19 banks in deeper trouble than Tokyo has ever before admitted, according to officials familiar with the discussions.

Source: New York Times

Institutions of monetary policy could be designed to help implement policy rules, to help policy makers exercise discretion with minimal political interference, or to strengthen political control over monetary policy. Some economists argue that a monetary policy rule should be written into an explicit law, perhaps even as a constitutional amendment. This change would help to make the rule credible and guarantee adherence. Other economists argue for maximum independence of the Fed from political pressures or control. They argue that political pressures generally focus on short-run goals, while monetary policy must take long-run goals into account. Independence, according to this argument, allows the Fed to pursue the best discretionary policies.

Federal Reserve Independence

The Federal Reserve is an independent agency of the federal government, as an earlier chapter explained. This status is supposed to free its officials from political influence so they can follow the best policies without political pressures. The Fed has faced many challenges to its independence, such as proposals in Congress to require it to report to Congress or the executive branch of the federal government, or to operate under the supervision of the General Accounting Office. (It currently escapes such control.) As an earlier chapter explained, the president of the United States appoints 7 of the 12 Federal Reserve governors, while the others are Federal Reserve Bank presidents, who are appointed by the boards of directors of those banks. The Board of Governors of the Fed appoints three of the nine members of those boards of directors, but the majority, six members, are elected by private banks in each Federal Reserve Bank's district.

Some critics have argued that this procedure is undemocratic and gives too much power to private banks. For example:

> The Federal Reserve Board is indefensible in theory and indispensable in practice. Twelve unelected people have their collective finger on the second most important button in America: the one that controls the money supply,

IN THE NEWS

Battle with White House never ends

The Federal Reserve Board's sweeping power over the economy—and the board's independence—has inevitably produced conflict with the White House.

That's true because, while a president can influence the economy by pushing through Congress measures like tax cuts or spending programs, what

ultimately happens to the economy depends to an enormous extent on what the Federal Reserve does with its day-to-day control over the nation's money supply.

Congress, hoping to influence future policy, pushes measures to curb Fed's independence

Fed cuts lending rates amid political pressure

Sources: Rochester Democrat and Chronicle, The Wall Street Journal, and New York Times

Political pressures on the Fed.

the biggest controllable factor in the equation of our economy. . . . Their decisions are made in secret and kept secret for 6 weeks. Their budget is also secret. They probably affect your life more than the Supreme Court. How many of them can you even name?[9]

Some people have proposed changes in the Fed's status, such as submission to increased control by the president or Congress; regular audits of Fed operations by the General Accounting Office; legal requirements that the Fed announce its policy decisions right away rather than 6 weeks after making them to limit secrecy; a requirement to announce its plans annually for the coming year; or a requirement to follow some specific, and perhaps very detailed, policies set by the president, Congress, or both.

More Radical Changes

Some economists favor more radical changes in monetary institutions. For example, some favor establishing a gold standard under which the Fed's main task would be to buy and sell gold to keep its nominal price fixed, as described earlier in this chapter and in Chapter 29.[10] Another radical proposal would privatize the money business; the government would stop supplying money and let private firms (banks or anyone else) print pieces of paper that people could exchange as money. Each issuing firm would put its own name on its money so people could distinguish it from other issuers' money. This idea, usually called *free banking*, would free people to choose whatever money they wanted to use, so that competition among suppliers of money could produce a currency with good properties, such as a low rate of inflation. Some proposals would let anyone issue money, providing that they back it 100 percent with gold. Another proposed reform, commonly suggested for countries that want to reduce inflation from high levels and keep it low, would establish a currency board.

Gold Standard

A gold standard is a special case of a commodity standard; the other historically important type of commodity standard is the silver standard. An earlier chapter explained the two main kinds of gold standards. In a pure gold standard, people trade gold coins as money. In a gold exchange standard, people trade paper money that is backed by gold.

The key feature of a gold exchange standard is the government's choice of a nominal money supply to keep the nominal price of gold at some fixed level, such as $350 per ounce. If something in the economy changes to reduce the price of gold below $350 per ounce, then the government increases the money supply, raising nominal prices until gold sells for $350 again. If something changes to raise the price of gold above $350 per ounce, then the government decreases the money supply, reducing nominal prices until gold sells for $350 again. The government can keep the price of gold at $350 per ounce at all times by announcing that it will act as a residual buyer and seller of gold. Precisely, it guarantees to:

1. Buy as much gold as anyone wants to sell at the price of $350 per ounce.

2. Sell as much gold as anyone wants to buy at that price.

The government buys gold by printing as much new money as it needs to pay for the purchases; it sells gold out of its storage facilities, destroying the money that it receives in payment. In this way, the money supply rises automatically whenever the government buys gold and falls whenever the government sells gold.

---

[9] Michael Kinsley, "TRB from Washington," *New Republic,* October 30, 1989, p. 4.

[10] In 1989, a Federal Reserve governor and several other people recommended to the former Soviet Union that it adopt a gold standard as part of its economic reforms. It did not follow this advice.

Because people can always buy gold from the government for $350 per ounce, they will never pay more to another seller. Because people can always sell gold to the government for $350 per ounce, they will never accept less from another buyer. In this way, the government can fix the nominal price of gold at $350.

While the government fixes the nominal price of gold, conditions of supply and demand determine its relative price. For example, the relative price of televisions in terms of gold might be 1 ounce of gold per television. With a nominal price of gold at $350 per ounce, the nominal price of a television is $350 per set. If the relative price of televisions in terms of gold falls (perhaps due to an increase in the supply of televisions) from 1 ounce of gold per television to 9/10 of an ounce of gold per television, then the nominal price of televisions falls from $350 to $315 per set, while the nominal price of gold remains at $350 per ounce. If the relative price of gold in terms of other goods and services does not change much over time, then the price level does not change much over time. Indeed, inflation averaged about zero under the gold standard of the 19th century, with varying episodes of positive and negative inflation roughly averaging out over the century.

The government has little or no discretion in monetary policy under a gold standard. It must keep the money supply at the level that guarantees the fixed nominal price of gold. If the government, or a central bank such as the Federal Reserve, were to try to raise the money supply through open market purchases, the increase in the money supply would raise the price level, which would raise the nominal price of gold above $350 per ounce. To maintain the fixed price, the government would have to reduce the money supply again. (This adjustment happens automatically if the government destroys the money that it collects in payment for gold sales.) Similarly, if the government were to try to lower the money supply through open market sales, the price level would fall, reducing the nominal price of gold below $350 per ounce. To maintain the fixed price, the government would have to raise the money supply again, which happens automatically if the government prints new money whenever it buys gold at $350 per ounce.

Debate on Free Banking

Free banking removes the government from any role in the money industry. History offers only a few cases in which governments have allowed free banking. Scotland had a form of free banking from 1716 to 1845, as did the United States in the first half of the 19th century.

Advocates of free banking argue that it removes the government almost entirely from the money business and ends political control of the money supply. It allows competition in which issuers of money can experiment with different types of products, and consumers (users of money) can choose what they prefer. Competition would encourage a high-quality money with stable and predictable purchasing power, along with innovation in the monetary and financial-payments systems.

Opponents of free banking argue that competition among private issuers' moneys would not work very well for two reasons. First, convenience dictates that people use only one kind of money instead of many different kinds. Use of many kinds of money at once would create confusion, space problems in cash registers, and costs to people who use time and resources to find out the values of the different moneys and exchange them. These problems have motivated European countries to try to adopt one money for all of Europe to replace the many national forms of money currently issued there.

Second, after a bank has printed money and some people have decided to use it, the bank then has an incentive to print *more* money. While this would create inflation, the bank could collect the inflation tax. Critics argue that banks could not easily commit to avoid this practice. Advocates of free banking respond that an offending bank's reputation would suffer, eliminating its incentive to exploit this opportunity, because a loss in reputation would hurt the bank's future profits. However, this incentive may not be strong enough to prevent some banks from inflating their currencies. Incentives to avoid inflation would be particularly weak for banks with poor financial conditions, for which reputation becomes less important.

These issues may soon arise in a new way, as governments of the world decide on policies related to electronic money for use on the Internet, or *e-money*. Will governments allow anyone to issue e-money without regulations? Will governments attempt to regulate issuance and uses of e-money? If so, what regulations will they choose and with what effects? Will people start using e-money for ordinary purchases *off* the Internet? What will be the consequences? How will government policy makers respond? How will the use of e-money affect the ability of the Fed to conduct monetary policy? These are some of the new monetary-policy questions that the world may face in coming years.

Incentives of Central Banks

While economists disagree about the best monetary-policy choices, they generally agree that central banks, like all government institutions, respond to incentives. The individual officials at the Fed may act from the best intentions, but they always operate under strong political pressures, despite the Fed's official independence. Changes in the Fed's organization, or the potential loss of its independence, would affect their incentives.

Some economists have suggested reducing the Fed's incentive to create inflation by requiring it to hold assets that lose value when inflation rises, and gain value when inflation falls. For example, the law could require the Fed to borrow money by selling bonds that are indexed to inflation, and lend money (buy bonds) without indexing to inflation. With these assets, the Fed would lose from an unexpected increase in inflation.[11]

A related proposal would force the government to replace its current, unindexed debt with indexed debt, so the federal government would not gain from inflation. Still another proposal would tie the salaries of Fed officials to inflation so that an increase in inflation would automatically reduce their salaries.

The value of these ideas depends on whether the Fed currently has an inappropriately strong incentive to produce inflation. Some economists believe it does, as the argument about the inflationary bias of discretionary policy demonstrated, but other economists believe that the Fed should emphasize inflation less and focus more on short-run changes in real GDP and unemployment.

Review Questions

13. How do Federal Reserve policy actions affect the federal funds rate? What actions does the Fed take to reduce this rate?

14. How can monetary policy maintain a fixed foreign exchange rate?

15. What is a devaluation? What happens during and after a devaluation?

Thinking Exercises

16. Discuss arguments in favor of fixed and floating exchange-rate systems.

17. After nations of Europe adopt a common currency, the Euro, what will determine the nominal supply of money held by people living in France?

---

[11]Although the Fed gives its profit back to the Treasury Department each year, the Fed gains from higher revenues because it can raise its spending on things that benefit its employees. As a result, this proposal would give the Fed an incentive to reduce inflation and keep it low.

Conclusion

Two Views of Macroeconomic Policies

Monetary and fiscal policies are the two main types of government macroeconomic policies. *Monetary policy* refers to changes in the nominal money supply through open market operations, changes in the discount rate or discount window lending policy, reserve requirement changes, or other policy actions of central banks. The Federal Reserve System conducts monetary policy in the United States.

Some economists hold an activist view about the proper role of government economic policy, believing that government policy actions can help to reduce inefficiencies in the economy. According to this view, the government should use monetary and fiscal policies to help stabilize real GDP, reducing economically inefficient fluctuations that move unemployment from its natural rate. The Fed can use monetary policy to *undo* the effects of changes in aggregate demand caused by changes in underlying conditions. The Fed can loosen monetary policy during a recession, to raise aggregate demand and therefore raise real GDP and reduce unemployment at the cost of raising inflation. The Fed can tighten monetary policy to reduce aggregate demand when inflation rises. In each case, the Fed must take care not to overreact. Most advocates of an active monetary policy favor *discretionary* policy, in which policy makers exercise their best judgment about policy actions on an ongoing basis.

Other economists hold a laissez-faire view of policy, believing that the economy usually operates efficiently on its own and that, even when it does not, active government policies usually aggravate inefficiencies and create new inefficiencies. According to this view, the economy operates best when the government plays a small role restricted to enforcing property rights and following a general set of rules for its monetary and fiscal actions.

Three Problems with Discretionary Policy

Proponents of the laissez-faire view argue for policy rules—specific statements of the policy actions that an agency will follow in the future—advancing three arguments. First, lags in the implementation and effects of policies reduce benefits of discretionary policies and create dangers of overreaction. Second, economists lack sufficient information about the economy's operation to improve its performance with activist policies.

Lack of sufficient information, combined with lags, may lead well-intentioned discretionary policies to increase the severity of business cycles and recessions. In addition, policy makers lack sufficient information about the effects of policies, partly because the effects depend on people's expectations, which change over time. The Lucas critique says that people do not always respond in the same way to a change in government policies, because changes in those policies can change their expectations, obscuring predictions about the effects of policies. These information problems create difficulties for discretionary policy making.

Third, credible rules can change incentives in ways that enhance economic efficiency. Discretionary policies affect expectations and incentives, creating an inflationary bias.

Targets of Monetary Policy

The Federal Reserve, like many other central banks, targets an interest rate (the federal funds rate) in its monetary policy. Central banks in many countries target exchange rates. Systems of fixed exchange rates require monetary policy to adjust the money supply to maintain the fixed exchange rate. Fixed exchange-rate systems are subject to problems of devaluations. Monetary policy includes decisions about the exchange-rate system, banking regulations, and the institutions for implementing policies.

Key Terms

monetary policy
activist view of policy
loose monetary policy
tight monetary policy
laissez-faire view of policy
discretionary policy

policy rule
simple policy rule
contingent policy
  rule
Lucas critique
credible policy rule

commitment to a policy
  rule
time consistent policy
time inconsistent policy
fixed (pegged)
  exchange rate system

floating (flexible) exchange
  rate system
managed-float exchange
  rate system
devaluation
currency board

Questions and Problems

18. Explain and contrast the activist and laissez-faire views of the role of government policy.

19. What factors influence the incentives of a central bank in its choice of monetary policy?

20. Argue the case for policy rules rather than discretion; argue the case for discretionary policy rather than rules.

21. Discuss this statement: "Improvements in computer models of the economy will increase the ability of policy makers to conduct effective discretionary monetary policy, but it will not improve the performance of policy rules."

22. How is monetary policy likely to differ between a country with a central bank that is partly independent of politics (as in the United States) and a country whose central bank is subject to more government control?

23. Discuss arguments for and against free banking. How might the creation of electronic money, or *e-money*, be similar to free banking?

24. What is a currency board, and what are its advantages and disadvantages?

25. What would happen if the United States were to abolish the Federal Reserve System and replace it with some form of free banking and privately issued money? What incentives would banks face in choosing their own monetary policies?

26. Suppose that the United States adopted a gold standard and set the nominal price of gold at $350 per ounce. Discuss the effects of the following changes:
    (a) Large gold discoveries in Russia that tend to reduce the world price of gold
    (b) Increase in the rate of technical progress and economic growth.

27. Discuss this statement: "Increased integration of the world economy, particularly international financial markets, reduces the effectiveness of monetary policy, because the Fed can no longer affect the interest rate."

Inquiries for Further Thought

28. Do you agree more with the activist view of policy or the laissez-faire view? Why?

29. Which guides monetary policy better: rules or discretion?
    (a) If you think that rules are better, what rule best promotes appropriate goals? Should the rule be part of a constitutional amendment?
    (b) If you think that discretionary policy is better than rules, who should get the discretion? How should they exercise that discretion?

30. What policy advice would you have given Asian nations facing financial crises, devaluations, and recessions in 1998?

31. If you were chairman of the Board of Governors of the Federal Reserve System, what specific data would you look at to decide when and by how much to raise or lower the federal funds rate? Be as specific as you can.

32. What incentives guide the Fed's actions? How could they be changed? How should they be changed? Should the Fed be independent of government control? Should the Federal Reserve maintain secrecy about its operations and the minutes of its meetings? Is the Federal Reserve System an undemocratic institution? Does the Fed respond to political pressures? How?

33. Should the United States adopt one of the more radical changes in monetary institutions discussed in this chapter? Why or why not?

34. How will electronic money work? How much will it be used 25 years from now? What will determine the nominal money supply? What will determine the price level? Will the government still be able to conduct effective monetary policy? Explain.

FISCAL POLICY

I n 1998, the government of China announced a plan to raise government spending by $1 trillion. This policy sought to shield China from the recessions that had hit other Asian countries. By raising government spending, China sought to raise aggregate demand through *fiscal policy*.

Nearly four decades earlier, the United States had used a different kind of fiscal policy to raise real GDP. Under President Kennedy, the United States raised aggregate demand by cutting taxes. Two decades later, under President Reagan, the United States again cut taxes. This time the architects of the tax cut intended to raise real GDP by raising aggregate supply.

Only a few years ago, in 1993, the U.S. federal government spent a quarter of a trillion dollars more than it collected in taxes—it had a *budget deficit* of more than $250 billion. Since then, the deficit has fallen rapidly. In 1998, President Clinton announced the first federal budget *surplus* in nearly three decades: the government collected more tax revenue than it spent that year.

The emergence of a government budget surplus after decades of deficits ignited strong debate over government *fiscal* policy. How should the government use the surplus money? Should it cut taxes? Should it pay back some of the money it had borrowed in previous decades? (That is, should it pay off part of its *debt*?) Which policies would help prevent world economic turmoil from causing a recession in the United States? What policies would best promote long-run economic growth?

Looming over these debates was the potential for huge future social security deficits. The social security issue raised key questions. How should the government measure its surplus or deficit? Does the surplus or deficit, as measured, have any real meaning at all? How will our current policies affect the lives of your generation and future generations? The magnitude of the money involved staggers the imagination. The U.S. federal government has a debt of several trillion dollars. Even today, with prominent reports on these issues in daily news and public discussions, few people realize the full extent to which government budget policies will affect their lives in the coming decades.

THE GOVERNMENT BUDGET IN THE UNITED STATES

Fiscal policy involves the government budget:

> **Fiscal policy** refers to government actions that affect total government spending, tax rates and revenues, and the government budget surplus or deficit.

Federal, state, and local governments in the United States collected over $2.8 trillion in tax revenues in fiscal year 1998.[1] They spent slightly less: $2.7 trillion. The combined government budget *surplus* (excess of tax revenue over spending) amounted to about $200 billion (according to the usual measure of the surplus, which a later section of this chapter criticizes). Total government spending took 32.6 percent of GDP, and people paid 34.4 percent of GDP in taxes.

People paid $1.7 trillion in taxes to the federal government (20.5 percent of GDP), which spent just slightly less (19.9 percent of GDP), for a federal budget surplus of $71 billion. The 1998 U.S. federal government budget surplus, the first in almost 3 decades, consisted of an *off-budget* surplus of $99 billion, reflecting mainly an excess of social security tax revenue over social security payments in 1998, and an *on-budget* deficit of $28 billion. As discussed later in this chapter, some analysts view the on-budget deficit

Figure 1 | Federal Government Revenues and Expenditures, 1998

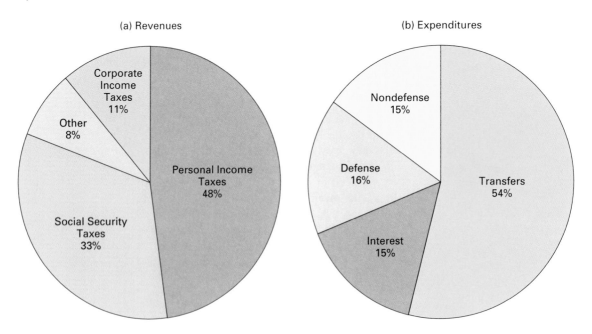

(a) Revenues

Corporate Income Taxes 11%

Other 8%

Personal Income Taxes 48%

Social Security Taxes 33%

(b) Expenditures

Nondefense 15%

Defense 16%

Interest 15%

Transfers 54%

[1]A fiscal year is an annual accounting period. The federal government's 1998 fiscal year began October 1, 1997 and ended September 30, 1998.

Figure 2 | Government Revenue as a Percentage of GDP

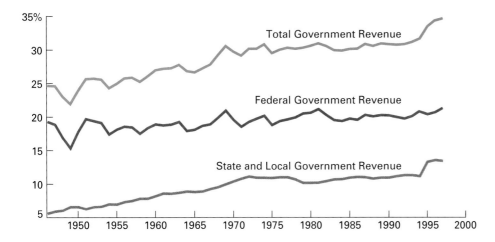

as the best indicator of the budget situation, because the off-budget surplus reflects money that the government will need in the future to meet its social security obligations.

Figure 1 shows where the federal government gets its money and how it spends money. In 1998, about 48 percent of its revenues came from personal income taxes; another 33 percent came from social security taxes. More than half of the federal government's spending covers transfer payments (mainly social security, medicare, and medicaid), 16 percent goes for defense, 15 percent goes to pay interest on its debt, and 15 percent pays for nondefense purchases of goods and services.

Figure 2 shows how government revenue has risen as a fraction of GDP in the second half of the 20th century. The fastest increase has occurred at the state-and-local government level, although the figure also shows an upward trend in federal government revenue as a fraction of GDP.

Figure 3 shows how government *spending* has risen as a fraction of GDP in the second half of the 20th century. Overall, government spending experienced a substantial increase. Figure 4 shows that the government developed a large budget deficit in the fourth quarter of the century, but that deficit has now vanished.

Figure 5 shows that increased spending on transfer payments has been the main factor behind increases in government spending in the last half-century. Decreases in government spending on national defense are the main factor behind decreases in government spending, as a fraction of GDP, in the last decade.

Latest Data Available
See the Web site for this book for the latest, up-to-date data on U.S. fiscal policy (along with other U.S. and international economic data).

Figure 3 | Government Spending as a Percentage of GDP

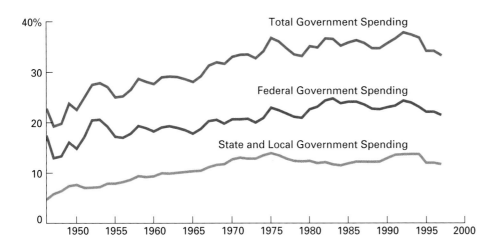

Figure 4 | **Government Spending and Tax Revenues as a Percentage of GDP**

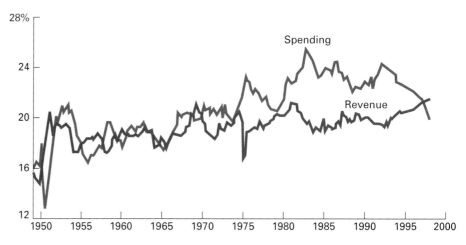

(a) Federal Government Spending

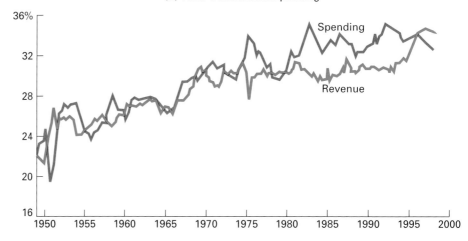

(b) Total Government Spending

Debt, Deficits, and Surpluses

The government runs a *budget surplus* when it collects more tax revenue than it spends. It runs a *budget deficit* when its spending exceeds its tax revenue. It has a *balanced budget* when its tax revenue equals its spending.

> The government **budget surplus** equals tax revenue minus (smaller) government spending.

> The government **budget deficit** (a negative surplus) equals government spending minus (smaller) tax revenue.

> The government has a **balanced budget** when tax revenue equals government spending.

Figure 5 | Components of Federal Government Spending (Percentage of GDP)

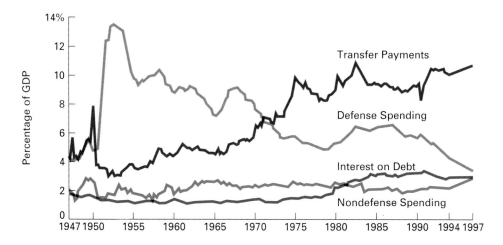

Figure 6 shows budget deficits and surpluses in the United States. A later section of this chapter discusses challenges to the usual measures of these deficits and surpluses.

When the government has a budget *deficit,* it must either borrow money or print money to spend in excess of its tax revenue.[2] The U.S. government, like governments of most developed countries, has generally *borrowed* money to finance its past deficits. However, some countries have printed money to finance budget deficits, as Russia did in the early 1990s and began doing again in 1998. The government *debt* (sometimes called the *national debt)* equals the amount of money the government currently owes due to its past borrowing.

> The **government debt** is the amount of money the government owes because it has borrowed money in the past.

Figure 6 | Government Budget Deficits as a Percentage of GDP

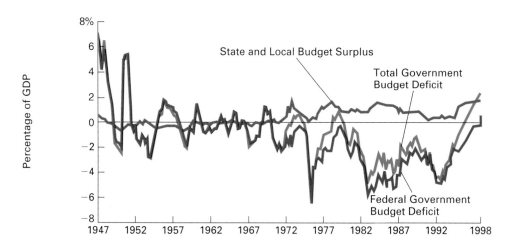

[2]A common mistake involves thinking that borrowing or printing money *eliminates* the deficit, but that is not true. The government has a budget deficit when it borrows or prints money to spend in excess of its income to *finance* its deficit. The amount of money it borrows or prints is the size of the deficit.

To whom does the government owe this money? It owes debts mostly to people and business firms in the United States. The government borrows money by selling government bonds—I.O.U.s that promise to repay money at future dates. People lend money to the government when they buy these bonds. People and businesses in the United States own most U.S. government bonds, so most of the government debt is money owed to them.

A budget deficit increases the government debt as the government borrows more money. A budget surplus reduces the government debt as it uses the surplus to repay part of its debt. Deficits and surpluses are *flow* variables, measured in dollars *per year*. In contrast, the debt is a *stock* variable, measured in dollars.

A government budget deficit raises the government's debt, and a surplus reduces its debt.

Figure 7 shows U.S. government debt as a fraction of GDP. Figure 8 shows the government's predictions about its *future* debt in the 21st century. The government predicts big increases in its debt as the baby-boom generation retires and begins collecting social security, creating large increases in government spending and budget deficits starting between 2010 and 2020. A later section of this chapter discusses social security.

Review Questions

1. State the approximate size of each variable in *dollars* and also as a share of GDP.
   (a) total government spending in the United States
   (b) total government tax revenue in the United States
   (c) federal government spending in the United States
   (d) federal government tax revenue in the United States

Figure 7 | U.S. Government Debt as a Percentage of GDP

Source: Congressional Budget Office

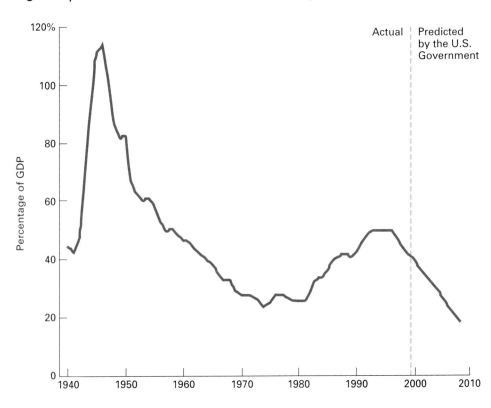

Figure 8 | Predicted U.S. Government Debt in the 21st Century

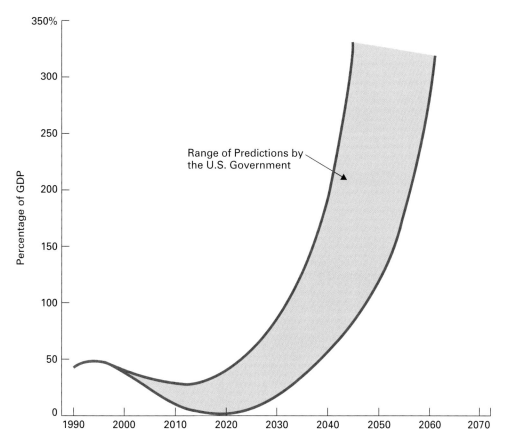

Range of Predictions by the U.S. Government

Source: Congressional Budget Office

2. Roughly how much money *per person* do units of government in the United States spend and collect in taxes?

3. What is the difference between the government's budget deficit and the government's debt? How does one affect the other? What is a government budget surplus?

Transfer payments take more than 40 cents out of every dollar of *total* (federal, state, and local) government spending in the United States. Purchases of goods and services take about half of total government spending. (The remainder of government spending covers interest payments on the government debt.) Transfer payments and government purchases of goods and services have different effects on the economy, and the effects of government purchases depend on what the government buys.

EFFECTS OF FISCAL POLICY: CHANGES IN GOVERNMENT SPENDING

Effects of Transfer Payments

Transfer payments are payments of money by the government to people. Social security is the largest transfer-payment program. Unemployment compensation payments are also transfer payments. When the government taxes one person to provide transfer payments to someone else, it redistributes income.

Transfer payments can affect demands and supplies for various goods and services. They raise demands for goods purchased by people who receive transfers, and they decrease demands for goods bought by people who pay the taxes to finance transfer payments. Aggregate demand rises if the government transfers money *from* people who *save* most of each dollar *to* people who *spend* most of each dollar. However, those transfers also reduce the supply of loans, raising the real interest rate and decreasing savings and investment.

Transfer payments, and taxes to pay for them, also affect supplies of goods, and they may affect aggregate supply. For example, the opportunity to receive social security encourages people to retire at an earlier age. It also gives them incentives to avoid actions that would reduce their payments, such as taking part-time jobs. Consequently, the social security program reduces labor supply, which decreases aggregate supply.[3]

Changes in taxes to pay for transfer payments can also affect aggregate supply. Taxes can affect aggregate supply by affecting equilibrium employment, as Chapter 26 explains. Taxes can also affect aggregate supply by affecting equilibrium investment, which affects the economy's capital stock. Because advances in technology result from investments in research and development, increases in taxes that reduce these investments may slow the growth of technology.

Effects of Government Purchases

Government purchases of goods and services directly affect aggregate demand; aggregate demand equals $C + I + G + NEX$, where G represents government purchases of goods and services (but does not include transfer payments). The effects of increases in government spending on the economy depend on several conditions:

1. What the government buys, including:
   a. How well government spending substitutes for private spending
   b. How productive the government spending is

2. How the government pays for its spending

Substitution between Government Purchases and Private Spending

Government spending can substitute for (or replace) private spending. Suppose (for now) that the government raises taxes when it raises spending, so the budget deficit does not increase. Assume that the government boosts its purchases of goods that substitute very well for spending that people already do on their own. This increase in government spending leaves aggregate demand unaffected because a fall in consumption (C) or investment (I) offsets the rise in government purchases (G). On the other hand, if the government raises spending on goods that substitute poorly for spending that people already do on their own, then aggregate demand rises. The following examples explain why.

EXAMPLE: LUNCH PROGRAM

Suppose that the government starts a free lunch program in which it buys your lunch for you. To keep the example simple, suppose that it buys exactly the same food that you would have bought for yourself, and it raises your taxes to pay for this program. (Ignore the salaries of government bureaucrats who run the program.)

This program has no effect on aggregate demand. You go through the cafeteria line and get your food, but you don't have to pay the cashier. Instead, you have to pay the tax collector, and the tax collector pays the cashier. This government program has almost

If the government buys your lunch and taxes you to pay for it, the economic effects are small—you pay the tax collector instead of the cashier, and then the tax collector pays the cashier.

---

[3]See the related discussion of tax cuts in Chapter 26.

[4]This ignores the fact that the increase in your taxes may change your incentives to work, consume, save, or invest, depending on what tax the government raises.

no effect on anything.[4] It only introduces an intermediary—the tax collector—between you and the cashier. Government spending *(G)* rises, but private consumption spending *(C)* falls, so $C + I + G + NEX$ does not change. The important feature of this example is the assumption that government spending substitutes very well (perfectly, in fact) for private spending, because the government buys exactly the same food that you would have bought for yourself.[5] The next example will consider government spending that substitutes poorly for private spending.

EXAMPLE: GOVERNMENT SPENDING ON DEFENSE

Suppose that the government raises spending on national defense, raising taxes to pay for the spending increase. Government spending on national defense is *not* a good substitute for private spending. As a result, people don't reduce their private consumption spending as in the lunch example; instead, they pay the higher taxes partly by reducing their savings. (In the lunch example, in contrast, people paid the higher taxes by reducing their private spending on lunches.) Consequently, private consumption falls by less than government spending rises. Therefore aggregate demand increases.

Types of Government Purchases
Most government purchases of goods and services fall somewhere between these two extremes; they do not substitute perfectly for private spending, as in the lunch example, but they substitute better than the spending in the national-defense example. Public schools, for example, substitute partially for spending on private schooling. (Government spending on schools exceeds $200 billion.) Government spending for police services (about $30 billion) substitutes partially for private spending to fight crime (locks and security systems on houses and businesses, private police or security guards, and so on). Government spending on natural resources, national parks, and recreation (over $100 billion) substitutes partially for private spending on recreation. Government spending for highways substitutes partially for private spending on replacement of cars, and construction of private roads or alternative transportation methods such as airlines and trains. Even government spending for courts substitutes partially for private spending on private courts and arbitration services.

Government spending on monuments, like spending on national defense (but unlike spending on lunch programs), substitutes poorly for private spending. Consequently, changes in this kind of government spending affect aggregate demand.

IN THE NEWS

China to Prime Economic Pump with Mammoth Building Outlay

BEIJING—China's leaders plan to spend $1 trillion on a huge range of public works projects in the next three years, in an ambitious effort to stop the Asian financial crisis from derailing the country's economic growth.

Huang Qifan, deputy secretary general of the Communist Party in Shanghai, said in an interview that the leadership had decided that spending money on an enormous crop of public works projects was needed to keep China's economic growth rate at 8 percent.

Source: New York Times

China uses fiscal policy by increasing government spending to raise aggregate demand.

---

[5] If the government bought different food than you would have bought for yourself, the government spending might not substitute very well for your own private spending. You might continue to buy some food for yourself. In that case, private spending on consumption would not fall by as much as government spending rises, so aggregate demand would rise.

Figure 9 uses the basic model from Chapter 26 to show the long-run effects of an increase in government purchases, financed by an increase in taxes. The figure applies to the case in which government purchases do *not* substitute well for private spending. The increases in government purchases and taxes do not affect the economy's technology, but they may affect real GDP by changing equilibrium employment.

Taxes to Pay for Government Spending

As Chapter 26 explained, taxes create a difference between before-tax wages and after-tax wages. A tax increase lowers after-tax wages, which affects workers in two ways. First, a fall in the after-tax wage can make people want to *reduce* their work hours. As the after-tax wage falls, the opportunity cost of leisure time also falls, leading people to expand leisure time and reduce time at work. In this way, a tax increase tends to reduce equilibrium employment and real GDP.

Second, a fall in the after-tax wage can make people want to *increase* their work hours. As the after-tax wage falls, people become poorer, leading them to choose less leisure time and more time at work. In this way, a tax increase tends to raise equilibrium employment and real GDP.

These conflicting forces imply that an increase in taxes can either reduce or increase equilibrium employment. For example, if you work 40 hours per week and earn $10 per hour, you earn $400 per week. If your after-tax wage were to fall to $8 per hour, you might decide to work fewer hours per week, because the hourly benefit of working has fallen. Alternatively, you might decide to increase your work time to 50 hours per week, to keep your weekly income at $400. Figure 9 shows the former case, in which an increase in taxes reduces equilibrium employment and real GDP.

Figure 10 uses the model of aggregate demand and supply to show the short-run effects of an increase in government purchases, financed by an increase in taxes. Like Figure 9, this figure applies to the case in which government purchases do *not* substitute well for private spending. The increase in government purchases raises aggregate demand. Aggregate supply falls if the tax increase reduces equilibrium employment, and rises if the tax increase raises equilibrium employment. Figure 10 shows the intermediate case in which aggregate supply remains unchanged, and the increase

As chapter 26 explained, an increase in taxes on labor income distorts incentives, and can reduce the equilibrium quantity of labor. The fall in equilibrium labor from l_0 to l_1 reduces long-run real GDP from y_0 to y_1.

When an increase in government purchases substitutes poorly for private spending, people pay part of the tax increase by reducing consumption, and part by reducing savings. This fall in savings decreases the supply of loans, reducing equilibrium investment and raising the equilibrium real interest rate. The fall in equilibrium investment reduces the economy's future capital stock, further reducing long-run equilibrium real GDP. The rise in the real interest rate raises the nominal interest rate, increasing the velocity of money, and raising the price level, since $P = MV/y$.

This figure shows that the long-run effects of an increase in government purchases (and taxes) differ from the short-run effects. In the short run, the increase in velocity raises aggregate demand, raising the real GDP along with the price level. In the long run, as this figure shows, the increase in government purchases, and taxes, lowers real GDP. (This conclusion could be reversed if government purchases are sufficiently productive, as discussed in a later section of this chapter.)

Figure 9 | Long-Run Effects of an Increase in Government Purchases and Taxes

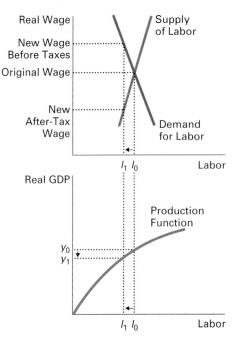

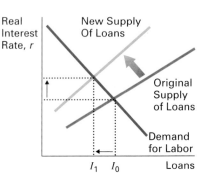

Figure 10 | An Activist View of Government Policy

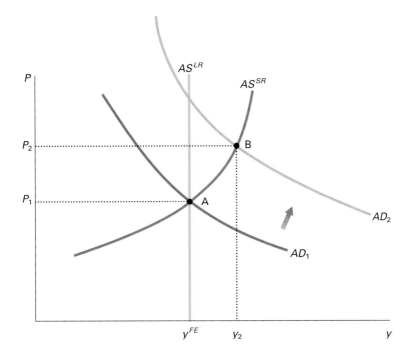

If government purchases do not substitute well for private spending, an increase in government spending raises aggregate demand from AD_1 to AD_2. If the rise in taxes and government spending does not affect aggregate supply, then the economy moves from Point A to Point B in the short run.

in government purchases raises real GDP and the price level in the short run as the economy moves from Point A to Point B.

Productivity of Government Spending

Some government spending helps private firms to produce goods. Government spending on infrastructure (transportation and communication systems, including roads, bridges, airports, mass transit, waterways, and so on) lowers private firms' costs of producing, distributing, and selling goods and services. Government spending on police and fire services, courts, hospitals, and education can also enhance productivity and reduce firms' costs of production.

An increase in government spending on productive goods or services can raise aggregate supply as well as aggregate demand. If the government spending substitutes very well for private spending (for example, if an increase in public police protection leads firms to reduce spending on their own security guards), then the increase in government spending does not have a big effect on either aggregate demand or aggregate supply.[6] If the government spending on goods and services does not substitute well for private spending, however, then it can affect both aggregate demand and aggregate supply, raising the productivity of labor and privately-owned capital.

EXAMPLE

Suppose that the government raises spending to repair bridges and roads. This outlay adds to aggregate demand; G rises while C and I do not fall, because this spending does not substitute well for private spending. This government spending also adds to aggregate supply, as improved roads and bridges allow firms to obtain inputs for production and distribute output to consumers faster and at lower cost than before.

---

[6]In the extreme case, in which a $1,000 increase in government spending for police leads to a $1,000 fall in private spending on security guards, the change has no effect on aggregate demand or supply.

Summary of the Effects of Changes in Government Spending

An increase in government purchases paid for by higher taxes has several effects. First, it raises aggregate demand if the government spending does not substitute well for private spending. (It has little effect on aggregate demand if they are good substitutes.) The increase in aggregate demand tends to raise real GDP (in the short run) and the price level.

Second, the increase in taxes may reduce aggregate supply if the rise in tax rates reduces the incentive to work. This fall in aggregate supply tends to reduce real GDP and raise the price level. (These effects would be reversed if the tax increase induced people to work more than before, rather than less.) In the intermediate case in which real GDP remains unchanged, the increase in government purchases leaves fewer goods and services available for other uses, so it reduces private consumption and investment.

Third, in the long run, an increase in government purchases on infrastructure may enhance productivity at private firms, tending to raise aggregate supply. Recall, however, that a tax increase (to finance the government spending) tends to reduce private investment. As a result, an increase in government purchases on infrastructure, financed by a tax increase, raises long-run aggregate supply only if the increase in government investment exceeds the fall in private investment; otherwise, it reduces long-run aggregate supply.[7]

Review Questions

4. How can transfer payments, and taxes to pay for them, affect aggregate demand and aggregate supply?

5. Why do the effects of government purchases depend on what the government buys? Explain specifically and give at least two examples.

6. Explain how a change in government purchases can affect aggregate supply.

Thinking Exercises

7. Suppose the government raises spending on national defense, and pays for the increased spending by raising taxes. Why does private consumption fall by *less* than the rise in government spending?

8. Explain how a decrease in income-tax rates affects equilibrium employment.

Borrowing to Pay for Government Spending

The effects of an increase in government spending depend on how the government pays for that spending. So far, the discussion has considered the case in which the government raises taxes to pay for a spending increase. Suppose instead that the government raises spending *without* raising taxes, so it runs a budget deficit, borrowing the money to finance the increase in spending.

The increase in government borrowing raises the government debt: it will owe more money in the future than it would have owed without the spending increase. Consequently, the government must either raise taxes in the future to repay its increased debt, with interest, or reduce its future spending. We now consider the case in which the government will respond to its increased future debt by raising future taxes. The effects of this increase in *future* taxes may differ from the effects of an increase in *current* taxes; that is, the *time path of taxes* may affect the economy.

---

[7]The relative productivity of government investment and private investment also influences the result.

Time Path of Taxes

Budget deficits and surpluses affect the time path of tax revenues. In other words, the government can cut taxes *this year* (and raise borrowing to pay for its spending) if it raises taxes *next year* to repay what it borrowed. To do this, the government must raise the *discounted present value* of future tax revenue by the amount of money it borrows this year.

EXAMPLE

Suppose that the government will spend $100 this year and $100 next year, and the nominal interest rate is 10 percent per year. The discounted present value of government spending is:

$$\$100 + \frac{\$100}{1.10} = \$191$$

where $1 + i = 1.10$.

Consider three possible time paths of taxes:

1. The government could balance its budget each year by collecting $100 in taxes both this year and next year. This policy would give it tax receipts with a discounted present value of $191, the same as the discounted present value of spending.

2. The government could collect no taxes this year and $210 in taxes next year.[8] The government would have a $100 deficit this year, which it would finance by borrowing $100. Next year the government would collect $210 in taxes to give it a $100 budget surplus. It would use $100 to pay for next year's spending and the other $110 to repay its loan with interest.

3. The government could collect $191 in taxes this year and no taxes next year. It would then have a $91 surplus this year and a $100 deficit next year. The government would use $100 for current spending and save $91, earning 10 percent interest. This would give the government $100 for next year's spending.

The government could also choose some other time path for taxes. For example, it could collect $80 in taxes this year, running a $20 budget deficit, then collect $122 in taxes next year to pay for its $100 in future spending and use $22 to repay its $20 debt with 10 percent interest.

Choosing the Time Path of Taxes

The time path of taxes affects the economy in two ways. First, the timing of tax receipts affects the size of the economic inefficiency caused by taxes. Second, it alters aggregate demand and aggregate supply, affecting real GDP and price level.

EXPLANATION

Taxes create economic inefficiencies because they affect incentives. Figure 11 shows how taxes drive a wedge between the price including tax that buyers pay, P_B, and the after-tax price that sellers receive, P_S. The difference, P_B minus P_S, is the per-unit tax. For example, with a 5 percent sales tax, buyers pay $10.50 for a good, sellers receive $10.00

---

[8]The discounted present value of this tax revenue is $210/1.1, or $191.

after taxes, and the government get $0.50 in taxes; P_B is $10.50, P_S is $10.00, and the per-unit tax is $0.50. Because buyers pay a higher price (including tax) than sellers keep (after taxes), the equilibrium quantity is Q_1 (instead of Q_0, the equilibrium quantity without any tax). Since buyers must pay P_B, they want to buy only Q_1 instead of Q_0, and since sellers keep only P_S for each good they sell, they want to sell Q_1 instead of Q_0. The tax reduces the equilibrium quantity bought and sold. This causes economic inefficiency, because it leads some people to forgo mutually advantageous trades (purchases and sales) because they can avoid the tax by not trading.

Each time the tax rate doubles, the amount of economic inefficiency more than doubles—it roughly quadruples. In fact, the economic inefficiency from a tax is roughly proportional to the tax rate squared. Raising a tax from 5 cents per unit to 10 cents per unit doubles the tax rate, but it raises the economic inefficiency about four times (5 cents squared gives 25, while 10 cents squared gives 100, which is four times larger). These relationships imply a greater benefit—less inefficiency—from a 5-cent tax for 2 years than a 10-cent tax for 1 year.[9] A 5-cent tax for 2 years also causes less economic inefficiency than an 8-cent tax for 1 year and a 2-cent tax for the other year.[10] In other words, the time path of taxes affects economic efficiency.

Analogy

Think about an analogy. The amount of gasoline a car burns per mile depends on its speed. Doubling speed *more* than doubles gasoline use. You could drive a car 80 miles by going 40 miles per hour for 2 hours. Alternatively, you could go the same distance at the same *average* speed by driving 20 miles per hour for one hour and 60 miles per hour for a second hour. However, you use less gasoline if you keep the constant speed of 40 miles per hour rather than varying between 20 and 60 miles per hour. Raising the *variation* in your speed raises the total amount of gasoline burned.

Similarly, the government could keep income taxes constant over time at 20 percent of income or vary the tax rate between 10 percent in some years and 30 percent in other

---

Figure 11 | Taxes Cause Economic Inefficiency

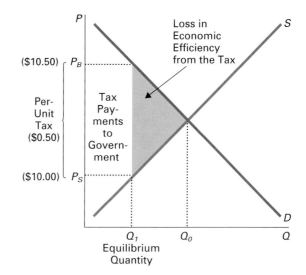

---

[9] Imposing a 5-cent tax for 2 years causes an efficiency loss proportional to $0.25 for 2 years, so the total loss is proportional to $0.50. Imposing a 10-cent tax for 1 year causes an efficiency loss proportional to $1.00.

[10] A 5-cent tax causes inefficiency proportional to 25 each year for 2 years, so the inefficiency is proportional to ($0.25)(2) = $0.50. An 8-cent tax causes inefficiency proportional to 64, and a 2-cent tax causes inefficiency proportional to 4, so an 8-cent tax for 1 year and a 2-cent tax for the other year cause an inefficiency proportional to 64 + 4 = 68, which is larger than the inefficiency from a 5-cent tax for 2 years.

years. However, economic inefficiency is like gasoline burned. Even if this variation in taxes produced the same tax revenue for the government, an increase in the *variance* of taxes from one year to the next would raise the economic inefficiency caused by the tax.

Timing of Taxes and Aggregate Demand

The government's budget deficit rises if it cuts tax revenue without cutting spending. As an earlier chapter explained, the increase in government borrowing raises the demand for loans. Taxes fall, so people's after-tax income rises. The supply of loans increases to the extent that people save some of this extra after-tax income. However, if people spend on consumption at least *part* of the income from the tax cut, two results occur. First, the supply of loans increases by less than the demand for loans, raising the equilibrium interest rate. Second, the increase in consumption spending raises aggregate demand.

The government can attempt to stabilize aggregate demand by choosing a time path of taxes that helps *undo* changes in aggregate demand that result from changes in underlying conditions. When aggregate demand falls, the government can reduce taxes to raise aggregate demand. For example, suppose that a change in underlying conditions (such as an increase in consumer patience) reduces consumption spending, and therefore aggregate demand, from AD_2 to AD_1 as in Figure 12. By cutting taxes, the government can help raise aggregate demand back to AD_2. Similarly, when aggregate demand rises due to variations in underlying conditions, the government can raise taxes to reduce aggregate demand.

Timing of Taxes and Aggregate Supply

Changes in the time path of taxes also affect aggregate supply. A cut in the income tax rate raises the after-tax wage and increases the incentive to work. This change raises the equilibrium input of labor, raising total employment, hours worked per person, and real GDP. Economic analysis that emphasizes the incentive effects of taxes and government regulations on aggregate supply is often called *supply-side economics*. This perspective became popular in public discussions with the election of President Ronald Reagan in 1980. Although some supply-side arguments remain controversial, others receive wide agreement among economists. Their implications for government policy amount largely to emphasizing on the incentive effects of taxes and regulations when thinking about policies.

Because a tax cut can increase both aggregate demand and aggregate supply, it can potentially raise real GDP with little effect on the price level, as Figure 12 shows. Whether the price level rises or falls depends on whether aggregate supply increases by more or less than aggregate demand.

IN THE NEWS

Japan ready to cut taxes

TOKYO—Japanese leaders Friday signaled their readiness for a permanent tax cut to jump start the country's moribund economy, a day after announcing a long-awaited plan to deal with Japan's banking crisis.

Source: USA Today

Japan uses fiscal policy by cutting taxes to raise aggregate demand.

Figure 12 | Tax Cuts and Aggregate Supply and Demand

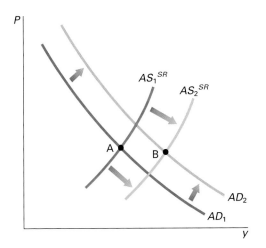

Case Studies: The Kennedy and Reagan Tax Cuts

Tax cuts proposed by President John Kennedy were enacted in 1964 and 1965, after Kennedy's assassination. Tax cuts proposed by President Ronald Reagan in 1980 took effect over the years from 1982–84. Both the Kennedy and Reagan tax cuts were followed by unusually long periods before the next recessions, which occurred in 1970 and 1990, respectively. Economists advising the government in the 1960s argued that the tax cuts helped the economy to grow during that decade by raising aggregate demand. Those advisors generally considered themselves as Keynesian economists, and they regarded the sticky-price or sticky-wage model as the best model of the economy. Economists advising the government in the 1980s, in contrast, argued that the tax cuts of that decade helped the economy to grow by raising aggregate supply. Those advisors generally regarded themselves as supply-side economists, with diverse views but a common emphasis on the effects of tax rates on incentives to work, save, and invest.

Before the Kennedy tax cuts, the top marginal federal income tax rate stood at 91 percent, although this tax rate applied only to incomes over $1 million per year in today's dollars.[11] The Kennedy tax cuts reduced taxes by about $11.5 billion in 1965. Economists at the time estimated the aggregate demand multiplier (discussed in Chapter 30) at between 1.3 and 2.0, so they expected the tax cut to increase real GDP by about $15 billion to $23 billion, through an increase in aggregate demand. GDP actually exceeded its trend rate of growth by about $28 billion.[12] If $15 billion to $23 billion of that increase in real GDP resulted from a rise in aggregate demand due to the tax cut, the remaining $5 billion to $13 billion may have resulted from an increase in aggregate supply, also caused by the tax cut.[13]

Nearly two decades later, by 1981, federal income tax rates had risen again, mainly because of bracket creep, which occurred when inflation automatically raised taxes.[14] The Reagan tax cut once again reduced federal income taxes. One study estimated that the increase in aggregate demand from the Reagan tax cut raised GDP by 3.2 percent in 1983 to 1984 and by 2.7 percent in 1985, while the increase in aggregate supply from the tax cut raised GDP by about half of this amount.[15]

Laffer Curve

Higher tax rates usually mean larger tax payments and more tax revenue for the government, but not always. The Laffer Curve shows the relationship between the marginal tax rate and the government's tax revenue.

The Laffer Curve in Figure 13 shows that the government collects no tax revenue at either a zero or a very high tax rate. If the income tax rate were 100 percent, for example, people would probably stop working for pay; without any income to tax, the government would not collect any tax revenue. At a very high tax rate (say, at Point B

---

[11]Chapter 26 discussed the difference between average tax rates and marginal tax rates.

[12]See Lawrence Lindsey, *The Growth Experiment* (New York: Basic Books, 1990). Lindsey later became a governor of the Federal Reserve System.

[13]Some economists, such as Lindsey, argue that the supply-side effects were larger than this estimate; other economists think they were smaller.

[14]To see how inflation pushes people into higher tax brackets, suppose that you are single and you earn $20,000 per year. Inflation doubles all prices and your pretax salary also doubles to $40,000. Before taxes, you have kept up with inflation. Everything costs twice as much as before, but you now earn twice as much. After taxes, however, you may have fallen behind. Suppose that you must pay a 15 percent tax on all income under $20,000 and 28 percent on all income above $20,000. Before inflation, your taxes were $3,000 (15 percent of $20,000) leaving after-tax income of $17,000. After inflation, your taxes are $8,600 ($3,000 on your first $20,000 of income and $5,600 on the rest) leaving after-tax income of $31,400. Your after-tax income did not double; it did not rise from $17,000 to $34,000. Instead, your taxes more than doubled, from $3,000 to $8,600, and your after-tax income rose from $17,000 to $31,400. The purchasing power of your after-tax income fell. This bracket creep results from inflation combined with unindexed tax rates. Starting in 1984, federal income taxes in the United States became indexed to inflation to prevent bracket creep; the tax tables now change automatically so that, if your salary keeps up with inflation before taxes, it also keeps up with inflation after federal income taxes.

[15]Lindsey, *Growth Experiment.*

Figure 13 | The Laffer Curve

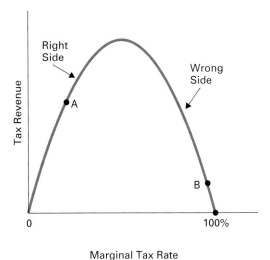

in the figure), the government would collect little tax revenue. In that case, the economy is said to be on the *wrong side of the Laffer Curve,* and the government could increase its tax revenue by reducing the tax rate.

In the early 1980s, some economists claimed that the U.S. economy was on the wrong side of the Laffer Curve and that the Reagan tax cuts would raise the government's tax revenue. Most believed, however, that the economy was on the rising (left) portion of the Laffer Curve, so that a cut in tax rates would reduce tax revenue. On balance, experience supported the majority. If the tax cut had not raised real GDP, evidence suggests that the federal government would have lost about $115 billion in tax revenue each year.[16] An increase in GDP raises the tax base, however, which helps to mitigate the fall in tax revenue. Evidence suggests that the increase in aggregate demand due to the Reagan tax cuts added about $40 billion annually to federal tax revenues, while the increase in aggregate supply from the tax cuts added about $20 billion. In addition, the decrease in tax rates raised government tax revenue by about $20 billion per year by reducing people's use of legal methods of tax avoidance.[17] While the direct effect of the tax cut may have reduced tax revenue by $115 billion per year, these three factors indirectly raised tax revenue by about $80 billion per year, so that the government had a net loss of about $35 billion annually in revenue from the tax cuts.[18]

Automatic Changes in Government Budget Deficits with GDP

Lags in the implementation of fiscal policy create difficulties for government attempts to stabilize aggregate demand through explicit changes in taxes or government spending.

---

[16] This is the estimate for 1985 from Lindsey, *Growth Experiment.*

[17] People use legal methods of tax avoidance when they choose investments that lower their taxes, even if those investments pay lower returns than others would. For example, one investment of $1,000 might return $100 of taxable income at the end of the year. If the marginal tax rate is 40 percent, people pay $40 in taxes and keep $60 for themselves. Another investment of $1,000 might pay back only $70, but in nontaxable income. If the tax rate is 40 percent, people choose the second investment, and the government gets zero tax revenue from this investment income. If the government cuts the tax rate to 25 percent, however, people choose the first investment, and they pay $25 in taxes and keep $75 for themselves. The lower tax rate leads people to change their behavior in ways that raise the government's tax revenue. (Notice that the government's revenue from a tax on investment can rise from a cut in the tax rate, even though the total amount of investment does not change. This result occurs because the type of investment changes.)

[18] Some evidence supports the claim that the tax cuts in the highest tax brackets actually raised tax revenue, so the economy was on the wrong side of the Laffer Curve for some taxes, though not for most.

However, fiscal policy can work *automatically,* without the need for explicit action by the government, through the use of automatic stabilizers.

> An **automatic stabilizer** is a feature of government policy that automatically changes taxes or spending to try to reduce fluctuations in real GDP, without any explicit actions of the government.

When aggregate demand falls, reducing real GDP, tax payments automatically fall, because people pay taxes on reduced incomes. The fall in tax payments partly offsets the fall in income. As a result, consumption spending and aggregate demand fall by less than they would if tax payments were unchanged. Similarly, when aggregate demand rises, the increase in real GDP automatically raises tax payments. Consequently, consumption spending and aggregate demand rise less than they otherwise would rise. In this way, the tax system serves as an automatic stabilizer, dampening variations in aggregate demand and real GDP.

How big is this effect? Suppose that a fall in aggregate demand reduces GDP by 1 percent. This reduces tax payments (and raises the federal government budget deficit) by about $30 billion. To see why, recall that GDP is close to $8 trillion, so a 1 percent rise in GDP amounts to an increase of about $80 billion. On average, the marginal tax rate in the United States lies between one-third and one-half, so a rise of $80 billion in GDP raises government tax revenue by between one-third and one-half of this amount, or about $30 billion. As a result, after-tax income falls by only $50 billion rather than $80 billion.

Review Questions

9. How can the government change the time path of taxes without changing its spending?

10. How does a change in the time path of taxes affect aggregate demand? How does it affect aggregate supply?

11. What is the Laffer Curve? What does it mean to be on the wrong side of the Laffer Curve?

Thinking Exercises

12. Which raises aggregate demand by a larger amount: (a) an increase in government spending financed by higher taxes, or (b) an increase in government spending without a tax increase, which raises the budget deficit as the government raises its borrowing? Explain.

13. Explain why the time path of taxes affects the level of economic inefficiency caused by taxes.

MEASURING GOVERNMENT DEBT, DEFICITS, AND SURPLUSES

Figures 6 and 7 showed the standard measures of the government's debt and the budget deficit as a percentage of GDP. However, important issues arise in measuring the debt and deficit. The first issue concerns ownership of the debt. Although the government debt in 1998 was about 5.6 trillion, the government owed part of this debt to the Social Security Trust Fund, the Federal Reserve, and other government agencies. In that sense, the government owed part of this debt to *itself*. The amount of money the government owes to other people—the government debt owned by people and business firms—is called the *privately held government debt.*

Government statistics show that the privately held government debt is about $3.8 trillion. However, that statistic raises a second measurement issue. The official government debt statistics ignore two large government liabilities: pensions for government employees, and social security benefits that the government has promised to pay in the future.

Pensions: About $1 Trillion

The official government debt figures do not include pensions that the government owes to its employees and former employees. Some of the money that the government has promised to pay as pensions is *funded:* Money has been put aside and invested to help pay the future pensions. However, about $1 trillion of the government's pension liabilities are *unfunded:* the government has no money saved or invested to cover these payments.

This $1 trillion unfunded pension debt raises the federal government's total debt from $3.8 trillion to about $4.8 trillion. This adjusted debt equals almost $18,000 for each person in the country.

Social Security: About $4 Trillion

The official government debt statistics also omit money that the government has promised to pay for social security benefits in the future. Rough estimates place the discounted present value of these payments between $3 trillion and $5 trillion. Some economists argue that the government debt statistics should include *all* liabilities of the government, regardless of type. Including the discounted present value of future social security payments raises the government's debt from $4.8 trillion to somewhere around $8 trillion: about $30,000 for every person in the country.

Other economists argue that government promises to repay loans in the future differ from government promises of future social security payments. The government can change its promises of future social security payments simply by changing the law. Many people, they argue, *expect* the government to reduce social security payments in the future, possible by raising the age at which people qualify for benefits. In contrast, the government would encounter serious legal problems if it failed to repay its explicit debt. This issue of measuring the government debt remains controversial.

Do Deficit Statistics Have *Any* Meaning?

The logic that suggests including unfunded pensions and social security obligations in government debt statistics can be extended to assets as well as liabilities. The government also owns assets such as land, mineral rights, capital equipment, and military hardware. The government collects income from some of these assets, such as lease payments on land. Perhaps the most important asset the government owns is its ability to collect taxes.

Economist Laurence J. Kotlikoff has argued that the usual measurement of the deficit, even with the corrections discussed so far, is an arbitrary and misleading guide to fiscal policy—like "driving in Los Angeles with a map of New York."[19] He argues that when the government takes money from people, it arbitrarily calls some of it *taxes* and the rest *borrowing.* When it pays money to people, it arbitrarily calls some of these payments *spending on transfer payments* and some of it *principal plus interest on the debt.* Since the *spending* and *taxes* labels are both arbitrary, their difference, the deficit, is also an arbitrary

---

[19] He suggests an entirely new way to measure fiscal policy based on its effects on people born in different years. See Laurence J. Kotlikoff, *Generational Accounting* (New York: Free Press, 1992).

figure. The pattern of taxes and government spending has important effects, however, and can affect different people (and different generations) in different ways. Kotlikoff proposes alternative statistics that measure the way government spending and taxes redistribute income from one generation to another. His proposal compares expected taxes with expected government spending for each age group. It estimates the discounted present value of *lifetime* tax payments net of lifetime receipts from the government, assuming that current government policies continue. These statistics are intended to show which age groups win and lose from the government's current fiscal policy. The main problem with the generational accounting measure centers on its need to make assumptions about future fiscal policies.

EXAMPLE

Consider social security. When the government collects money from people for social security, it labels the receipts a *social security tax*. When it makes social security payments to people, it labels this outlay *spending on transfer payments*. The government could just as well call such a payment a *loan*, though. The government could say that it borrows money from people when it collects social security taxes, and it repays the loan when it pays social security benefits. This arbitrary change in language changes the measured deficit, making the deficit a meaningless figure. Its size depends on the arbitrary language that describes what the government actually does. The government program, however, *does* redistribute income across generations. Kotlikoff proposes a way to measure that redistribution.

If this idea seems strange, consider what the government of France once did. It passed a law *requiring* people to lend money to the government. Was this a tax or a loan? If you call it a loan, you would say that the French government had a budget deficit and that its debt increased. If you call it a tax, then you would say that the program did not affect the deficit or the debt. Kotlikoff argues that this question of language has no right answer, so the measured budget deficit and debt are virtually meaningless. Nevertheless, an economist could calculate which generations pay the money to the government and which generations will pay future taxes so that the government can repay these "loans" in the future. Consequently, one can calculate the way this program redistributes wealth across generations, using assumptions about future tax policies. Issues about the best way to measure fiscal policies remain controversial.

Social Security Surplus

The $71 billion budget surplus that the U.S. federal government reported in 1998 had two parts: an *off-budget* surplus of $99 billion, reflecting mainly an excess of social security tax revenue over social security payments, and an *on-budget* deficit of $28 billion. Interpreting these numbers requires understanding the basics of the social security system.

When the government began the social security program, it began collecting social security taxes from working people and using that money to pay social security benefits to retired people. The system was *pay-as-you-go*: current taxes finance current payments. When retirees paid social security taxes during their working years, the government did not save and invest their money for them so that it could pay them social security benefits when they retired. Instead, the government distributed their money as social security payments to people who were already retired.

Recently, social security tax revenues have exceeded payments of social security benefits: a social security *surplus* has emerged. The government uses the money from this surplus to buy government bonds that it puts in the social security *trust fund*. In that sense, the government is currently saving and investing the social security surplus. However, when the social security trust fund buys government bonds, it *lends* money to the rest of the government. In 1998, the treasury department borrowed $99 billion in this way. If we count this as government borrowing rather than tax revenue, then the government had a deficit of $28 billion. This is the government's *on-budget* deficit. In contrast, the *overall* $71 billion surplus ignores this borrowing; it includes the $99 billion as part of overall tax revenue, and compares overall tax revenue with overall spending. Which is a better measure of fiscal policy? Most economists agree that no *single* number can adequately describe the government's budget situation.

Unless changes in social security soon occur, two problems will arise in the future, as the social security surplus turns into a deficit. First, when social security payments begin to exceed social security tax revenues, the government will need to use the money in the social security trust fund to cover payments. Because the government has already borrowed and spent that money, however, the overall government budget deficit will begin rising at that time. Second, the social security trust fund will not be large enough to finance future payments, because the discounted present value of expected future social security payments exceeds the discounted present value of expected future social security taxes. Both problems reflect demographic changes. The baby-boom generation (resulting from a large number of births between the end of World War II and 1960) will retire around the years 2020 to 2030, reducing social security tax revenues and raising social security payments. In 1998, the U.S. had about 3.4 workers for every social security recipient. By 2030, the U.S. is likely to have only about 2 workers per retired person. This change will have at least one of the following consequences:

1. Social security taxes will rise by about 33 percent to 50 percent.[20]

2. Social security payments will be cut by about one-third to one-half, perhaps by paying less per month, and perhaps by raising the age of eligibility.

3. The government will change its spending and taxing policies so that the social security system accumulates a larger trust fund, big enough to continue the same level of payments without higher taxes.

4. The government will make major changes in the social security program, perhaps privatizing it.[21]

All statistics on future social security problems are only rough estimates. The actual numbers will depend on issues such as overall economic growth over the next several decades, increases in life expectancy, and many other factors than are difficult to predict.

Review Questions

14. What are the main problems in measuring the size of the government debt?

15. Why does the U.S. social security system currently run a surplus? What happens to that surplus?

16. What main problems will the social security system cause in the future?

Thinking Exercise

17. Discuss the following claim: "The social security trust fund is an accounting fiction."

---

[20]Social security taxes, not including the part of the tax to cover Medicare, are currently 12.4 percent of salaries up to a certain level ($68,400 in 1998). This 12.4 percent figure includes both the employer and employee shares of the tax. A 33 percent *rise* in the tax means an increase in the tax rate from 12.4 percent to 16.5 percent (*not* an increase to 45.4 percent).

[21]Many people have advanced proposals to privatize social security. Most involve eliminating social security taxes; eliminating social security benefits entirely for people who are currently young; using general tax revenues to pay social security benefits to people who are already retired or who will retire within a decade or two; and requiring all workers to save for retirement in a government-approved manner with tax benefits for saving.

FUNDAMENTAL ISSUES OF FISCAL POLICY

Fiscal policy involves deeper issues than simply whether the government should change taxes or spending to affect aggregate demand or supply. Two fundamental types of issues underlie the main controversies and debates about fiscal policy. First, what are the proper roles of government spending and taxes in the economy? What is the optimal size of government? What are the appropriate levels of government spending, tax revenues, and budget surpluses or deficits? Second, should the government use discretionary fiscal policy to try to stabilize the economy, or should fiscal policy be guided by formal rules? What kinds of fiscal policy rules, if any, are appropriate? For example, should a rule, perhaps encoded in a constitutional amendment, require the government to balance its budget each year or to limit its taxation, its debt, or its spending?

The previous chapter discussed activist and laissez-faire views of monetary policy. Those categories also apply to fiscal policy. Economists who hold a laissez-faire view of fiscal policy tend to favor a smaller role for government spending and taxes than those who hold an activist view. Proponents of a laissez-faire view generally favor low levels of government spending and low tax rates, and they usually believe that the government should base spending and tax rates only on the merits of the programs involved and not on efforts to stabilize real GDP. Some proponents of the laissez-faire view, but not all, favor formal rules for fiscal policy, such as a balanced-budget rule or a limit on government spending as a fraction of GDP.

Proponents of an activist view of fiscal policy generally favor higher levels of government spending and higher tax rates, particularly on people with relatively high incomes. They also tend to believe that the government should vary its total spending and tax rates to try to stabilize real GDP and unemployment by offsetting, at least somewhat, other changes in aggregate demand. Most activists favor discretionary fiscal policies in addition to the automatic stabilizers discussed earlier.

Rules versus Discretion in Fiscal Policy

The three main arguments for fiscal policy rules echo the arguments for monetary policy rules:

1. Two kinds of lags complicate fiscal policies—lags in implementing policies (actual changes in tax rates or government spending) and lags in the effects of fiscal policies on the economy.[22] These lags make it difficult to improve economic performance with discretionary fiscal policy.

2. Economists and the government lack sufficient information about the economy to conduct good discretionary fiscal policy. They lack relevant information about both underlying economic conditions (including current and near-future conditions) and the likely effects of fiscal policies.

3. Credible rules for fiscal policy can improve economic performance by changing people's incentives.[23] Credible policy rules affect incentives and behavior in ways that discretionary policy cannot; rules can improve economic performance as compared to even the best discretionary policies.

The main argument for discretionary fiscal policy criticizes the inflexibility of rules. New situations might arise that call for new policy actions, and policy rules might prevent the best actions in certain situations. For example, the sticky-price model of aggregate supply

---

[22] In fact, implementing a change in fiscal policy usually takes longer than implementing a change in monetary policy.

[23] See the example of high taxes on capital in the previous chapter.

and aggregate demand from earlier chapters implies that the government can help to fight a recession by raising spending and reducing taxes, which would increase private consumption and investment spending. A policy rule that requires the government to balance its budget might prevent these actions. Because no policy rule can take into account all situations that might arise in the future, any policy rule might limit the ability of policy makers to choose the best actions in the future.

Connections between Fiscal and Monetary Policy

Some countries' governments require their central banks to print whatever money their governments need to finance budget deficits. In the United States, however, the Federal Reserve chooses monetary policy (subject to political pressures) without a requirement to finance budget deficits. The U.S. government must borrow money (sell bonds) to finance its budget deficit. It cannot directly force the Fed to print more money.

Fiscal policy can still affect monetary policy in several ways, though. For example, a government budget deficit may raise expectations of future inflation. This change raises the current nominal interest rate and velocity of money, which raises the equilibrium price level, creating temporary inflation. The new conditions may also change the incentives of the Federal Reserve. High levels of government debt may raise the incentive to create inflation to reduce the real value of this debt. High levels of debt and high budget deficits may raise political pressures on the Fed to increase the growth rate of the money supply.

Commitment and Policy Credibility

Fiscal policy, like monetary policy, can be discretionary or subject to rules. The government has had difficulty committing to policy rules in the past, though. For example, Congress passed a law in the 1980s that required a balanced budget (or surplus) by the year 1991. However, when the time came for lower deficits, the government exploited loopholes that allowed deficits to continue. Eventually, Congress changed the law and continued running deficits. Some people proposed a constitutional amendment to require a balanced government budget, arguing that such a rule is easier to enforce than a law that Congress can repeal by majority vote. When Congress voted down such an amendment in 1995, some opponents argued that it would remove the flexibility of discretionary fiscal policy, prohibiting the government from running deficits during recessions to raise aggregate demand. Others argued that enforcement of such a rule would ultimately prove an impossible task. Ultimately, the government eliminated its budget deficit (by the standard measure) in 1998. The government achieved this goal through a combination of reductions in the rate of growth of government spending, particularly military spending, and increases in tax revenue resulting from rapid growth in real GDP in the 1990s.

Fiscal policies can affect long-run economic growth by changing national savings.

> **National savings** equals private savings plus government savings.

FISCAL POLICIES AND ECONOMIC GROWTH

The government saves when it has a budget surplus; a budget deficit amounts to negative savings. Private savings equals disposable income (income after taxes, $y - T$) minus consumption spending (C). For the country as a whole, income is GDP, so disposable income is GDP minus taxes. This gives private savings as:

$$\text{Private savings} = y - T - C$$

Government savings equals the budget surplus, or tax revenue minus government spending, $T - G$. Adding private savings and government savings gives national savings:

$$\text{National savings} = (y - T - C) + (T - G)$$

$$= y - G - C$$

Chapter 24 explained that:

$$y = C + I + G + NEX$$

where NEX is net exports, which equals domestic lending to people in foreign countries. Subtracting G and C from both sides shows that national savings equals investment plus net exports:

$$\text{National savings} = I + NEX$$

This equation shows two uses for national savings:

1. Investment in the nation's economy (I)

2. Lending (investing) in foreign countries (NEX).

Investment in the nation's economy adds to its future capital stock and production, so it adds to economic growth. Investment in foreign economies (NEX) adds to the nation's future income, as foreigners pay interest or dividends on the investments. (It also adds to the foreign capital stock and promotes world economic growth.)

Deficits and National Savings

Many economists blamed government budget deficits for low rates of saving in the United States in the last quarter of the 20th century. To see why, suppose that the government cuts taxes by $100 per person without changing its spending. The government budget deficit rises by $100 per person, reducing national savings by that amount. If people save all the money they receive from the tax cut, then national savings, rises back to its original level. However, if people spend at least part of the money they receive from this tax cut, national savings falls. Because savings is essential for long-run economic growth, budget deficits could reduce growth.

Figure 14 shows national savings in the United States as a percentage of people's after-tax income. Despite reductions in the government budget deficit in recent years, the U.S. savings rate has continued its two-decade fall. Clearly, many other factors besides the government budget affect savings.

The social security program, like government budget deficits, reduces national savings. People expect to receive social security payments when they retire, so they save less than they would without the social security system. Therefore, this system reduces private savings. If the government were to save all of the money that people pay in social security taxes, then this increase in government savings would offset a fall in private savings, and the social security system would not affect national savings. (People would save less, but the government would save more.) However, the government has operated social security as a pay-as-you-go system rather than saving revenue from social security taxes. Consequently, most economists believe it has reduced overall national savings and long-run economic growth.

Current tax policies also discourage saving, and some economists favor policy changes that would reduce or eliminate the negative effects of taxes on saving. One proposal would replace the income tax with a consumption tax. This change would free people from paying income tax on money they save; government would tax only money they spend.

Figure 14 | Savings as a Percentage of Income in the United States

Many economists believe that a consumption tax would be more economically efficient than an income tax and, by encouraging savings, would raise long-run economic growth. Other proposals create various tax incentives for certain types of saving.

Taxes and Aggregate Supply

Some economists argue that the most important effects of taxes work on aggregate supply rather than aggregate demand. They argue that high taxes reduce savings, investment, and long-run economic growth. According to this view, a tax cut raises economic growth, even if the government does not reduce spending, that is, even if the tax cut raises the budget deficit. A reduction in marginal tax rates can raise aggregate supply by raising the incentive to work. It can also raise future aggregate supply by raising the incentives to save and invest, by raising the expected after-tax returns from investments.

Incentives and Rent Seeking

Some economists argue that discretionary fiscal policies reduce long-run economic growth in other ways. Discretionary changes in taxes create uncertainty, which reduces investment in physical and human capital, and slows technical progress by reducing investment in research and development. Discretionary changes in government spending can also create economic inefficiencies if the government spending is not justified solely by its own costs and benefits. According to this argument, government should choose its level of spending on each program (schools, roads, defense, and so on) based on those costs and benefits, and avoid spending more or less than this level in attempts to stabilize aggregate demand.

Discretionary government policies also reduce economic efficiency by encouraging *rent seeking*.

> **Rent seeking** is the use of time, money, and other resources to try to get government benefits (spending, tax changes, or regulations targeted to some special-interest group).

Rent seeking results from the very *possibility* that the government will take discretionary policy actions with benefits or harm to various special groups. Rent seeking is economically inefficient, because the resources devoted to rent seeking have an opportunity cost: they could be used to *produce* goods and services rather than redistributing them. Investing those resources in physical capital, human capital, or research and development would raise real GDP, raising the size of the economic pie rather than funding the fight about its division. Could credible policy rules reduce rent seeking? How could the government credibly commit to policy rules? Would such rules create inefficiencies by limiting policy flexibility? These are some of the fundamental issues of fiscal policy that will underlie the more immediate issues of taxes, spending, government debt, and social security reform in the coming years.

Review Questions

18. Cite arguments for rules to govern fiscal policy. Cite arguments for discretion.

19. Explain why government budget deficits may reduce national savings.

20. Explain why the social security system may reduce national savings.

21. What is rent seeking and why is it economically inefficient?

Thinking Exercise

22. Explain how the following fiscal policies may affect long-run economic growth:
    (a) An increase in government purchases for national defense, financed through an increase in income taxes
    (b) An increase in social security taxes to meet future obligations to pay social security benefits
    (c) A cut in income taxes, financed by an increase in government borrowing

Conclusion

The Government Budget in the United States

Fiscal policy refers to government actions that affect total government spending, tax rates and revenues, and the government budget deficit or surplus. Total government spending and tax payments in the United States amount to about one-third of GDP. The government runs a budget surplus when it collects more tax revenue than it spends. It runs a budget deficit when it spends more than it collects in tax revenue. It has a balanced budget when its tax revenue equals its spending. The government debt (national debt) equals the amount of money the government currently owes due to its past borrowing. A government budget deficit increases the government debt as the government borrows more money. A government budget surplus reduces the debt as government repays part of it.

Effects of Fiscal Policy: Changes in Government Spending

Transfer payments redistribute income, and affect the economy in two ways. First, people differ in their spending decisions, so redistribution may change the composition of spending, as well as aggregate demand. Second, transfer payments, (and the taxes to finance them) affect incentives, altering aggregate supply.

The effects of government purchases of goods and services depend on what the government buys. If government purchases substitute well for private spending, then changes in government purchases have little effect on aggregate demand, as in the lunch-program example. If, however, government purchases substitute poorly for private spending, then increases in government purchases raise aggregate demand, as in the defense spending example. Government spending may enhance productivity and raise aggregate supply when it does not substitute closely for similar, private spending.

Changes in taxes to finance changes in government purchases also affect the economy. A tax cut may raise or reduce equilibrium employment and real GDP, depending on how workers respond to an increase in after-tax wages. The government also affects the economy by its decision to run budget surpluses or deficits. These decisions involve choices about the time path of taxes. The government can raise economic efficiency by preventing unnecessary variations in taxes over time. However, the government can try to stabilize real GDP with fiscal policy by cutting taxes below their long-run average level when real GDP falls and raising taxes above their long-run average level when real GDP rises. Automatic stabilizers function by making these changes without direct action by the government.

Measuring Government Debt, Deficits, and Surpluses

The standard measures of government debt and the budget deficit are misleading. First, the government owes some of its debt to itself. The measure of *privately held* government debt corrects this problem. Second, the official statistics on government debt omit two large liabilities: future pensions for government employees, and social security payments that the government has promised to pay in the future. Controversies surround the measurement of the government's debt and deficit.

Social security presents two problems. The overall government surplus that emerged in 1998 includes the current social security surplus. When the current social security surplus turns into a deficit within the next 20 years, the overall government budget surplus will turn into an overall deficit. Second, the discounted present value of expected future social security taxes is less than the discounted present value of promised benefit payments, requiring either an increase in taxes or a reduction in benefits.

Fundamental Issues of Fiscal Policy

Fundamental issues of fiscal policy involve the proper roles of government spending and taxes, the optimal size of government, and issues of whether government policies should be guided by rules or discretion. The activist and laissez-faire views of monetary policy also apply to fiscal policy. Other basic issues include the effects of fiscal policy on national savings and long-run economic growth, and on inefficiencies from rent seeking.

Key Terms

fiscal policy
budget surplus
budget deficit

balanced budget
government debt
automatic stabilizer

privately held government debt
national savings
rent seeking

Questions and Problems

23. Suppose that Congress decides to build a giant pyramid in Washington, D.C., as a way to provide jobs for construction workers and stimulate the economy. Assume also that the government raises personal income taxes to pay for the additional spending. How is this project likely to affect total employment? How will it affect employment in different industries, real GDP, and the price level?

24. Summarize the effects on aggregate demand and supply of:
    (a) An increase in government spending financed by increased taxes

    (b) An increase in government spending financed by government borrowing

25. Explain the argument that the government's budget deficit or surplus is poorly measured and nearly meaningless.

26. Discuss this statement: "Large government budget deficits raise interest rates. To keep interest rates from rising, a country with rising budget deficits should loosen monetary policy." In your answer, distinguish between real and nominal interest rates, and between the short run and the long run.

27. Discuss this statement: "The government could reduce unemployment to almost zero by guaranteeing a government job to anyone who is unemployed. The people could work to clean up city streets and national parks and do other useful tasks, and everyone would benefit."

28. How are increases in government budget surpluses likely to affect:

    (a) Aggregate demand and supply?

    (b) Real GDP and employment in the short run?

    (c) Long-run economic growth?

Inquiries for Further Thought

29. Look on the Internet or in a library for information on the government budget and the economy over the last decade. Using this information, discuss (in as much detail as possible) the factors that caused the government budget deficit to vanish and turn into a surplus.

30. If the government continues to run a budget surplus (by the usual measure), what should it do with that surplus?

31. Should the government change the social security program? If so, how? If not, how should it deal with future deficits in that program?

32. Should the government exercise discretionary fiscal policy? What principles should guide the government's fiscal policy? Why?

33. What economic effects would result if the government repaid the national debt? Should it?

34. What, if anything, could the government do to reduce economic inefficiencies from rent seeking?

ADVANCED TOPICS IN MACROECONOMICS

FINANCIAL MARKETS

Every day, television news reports, newspapers, and business magazines are filled with news about stock markets and other financial markets. Despite all this information, financial markets mystify most people. This chapter provides the basic knowledge necessary to understand these news reports and to construct informed opinions about financial matters. You can refer back to this chapter to find the background you will need for your personal and business decisions in the future.

FINANCIAL ASSETS AND MARKETS

Earlier chapters have explained how asset markets play important roles in macroeconomics. The loans market played a key role in the basic macroeconomic model developed in Chapters 25–26. Chapter 28 discussed exchange rates and their connections with inflation. Chapter 29 discussed the dual role of financial intermediaries in the money market and loans market and the problems created by that dual role. Chapter 31 discussed the role of the loans market in some recent recessions, and Chapter 32 explained how financial markets and interest rates play key roles in monetary policy

Financial markets are sets of formal or informal trading arrangements for *financial assets.*

A **financial asset** is a right to collect some series of payments in the future.

The **rate of return** on a financial asset is the income the owner receives from the asset over some period of time, plus the increase in its value during that period, all as a percentage of the original value of the asset:

$$\text{Rate of return} = \frac{\text{Interest (or other) payments} + \text{Increase in asset price}}{\text{Beginning-of-period asset price}}$$

Suppose that General Television stock sells for $50 in October 1999 and for $52 one year later. Also suppose that each share of stock pays its owner $1 in dividends during that year. The rate of return on this stock is:

$$\text{Rate of return} = \frac{\$1 + (\$52 - \$50)}{\$50} = \frac{\$3}{\$50} = \frac{\$6}{\$100} = 6 \text{ percent per year}$$

Many types of assets are traded on financial markets. The most common are debt and equity.

Debt is a borrower's promise to pay.

When you borrow money, you incur a debt. Similarly, a business firm or government unit incurs a debt when it borrows money. Debt is the borrower's promise to repay a loan; it is an IOU. People can buy and sell these IOUs on financial markets. Trade in debt refers to buying and selling the rights to collect money that borrowers will repay. Government bonds, corporate bonds, and Treasury bills are types of debt traded on financial markets.

Equities (shares of stock) represent legal rights of ownership to part of a firm.

A firm's stockholders own that firm. They own its assets and liabilities, including its equipment and buildings, and legal rights to its brand names. They must pay its debts and meet its other legal obligations. A corporation's stockholders have *limited liability*, however, meaning that they cannot lose more than the value of their stock. (They cannot be required to pay a firm's debts out of their own personal funds.) A firm's stockholders choose its board of directors, who choose the firm's top management. If you own some shares of stock, you can take part in the stockholder votes through which these decisions are made.

Other common types of financial assets include futures contracts and options.

Futures contracts are agreements to buy or sell goods at some future date at a price set today.

You might buy 5,000 bushels of corn or 5,000 shares of General Motors stock to be delivered and paid for next July, at a price set today.

Options are legal rights, but not obligations, to buy or sell a certain amount of goods or assets in the future at a price set today.

The term *option* refers to the choice that such a contract gives to its owner. Suppose that you own an option to buy 100 shares of American Express stock at a price of $25 per share some time within the next 4 months. You can choose whether to buy that stock at the preset price of $25. Similarly, if you own an option to sell 500 shares of Xerox stock at a price of $50 per share some time within the next 2 months, you can choose whether or not to sell at that price. When people buy and sell options, they trade these rights to buy or sell at preset prices.

These assets change hands in two kinds of markets. Primary markets handle transactions where issuers sell financial assets for the first time, as when a firm issues new stock or new bonds to accumulate money to fund some investment. In secondary markets, investors (people or firms) buy and resell previously issued assets. Most financial-market trades occur on secondary markets such as the New York Stock Exchange.

Functions of Financial Markets

Financial markets promote economic efficiency in several ways. The most basic function of financial markets is to allow people to trade current goods for future goods by lending, and to trade future goods for current goods by borrowing. Financial markets allow people to borrow money to buy houses or cars, to invest in new capital, to modernize factories or start new businesses, and to finance development of new products.

Financial markets also pool resources: they allow thousands of people to pool small amounts of savings into one large sum of money to lend, giving them the highest possible return on their savings.

Financial markets allow people to reduce risks. Just as a person buys fire insurance to reduce the risk of losses in a fire, financial markets allow people to trade risks so as to reduce each person's total risk through *diversification*. People can gain from trading risks just as they gain from trading their labor services in the basic gains-from-trade examples of Chapters 1 and 3.

Financial markets help to channel the economy's resources into their most valuable uses. Chapter 7 explained how Adam Smith's metaphor of the "invisible hand" applies to the loan market as it guides the economy's response to "now or later" choices of consumers. When current resources become more valuable relative to future resources, financial markets respond with a higher interest rate, which gives consumers incentives to conserve current resources by saving and lending. Similarly, financial markets guide business firms as they judge whether to undertake risky investments: prices of financial assets reflect the willingness of savers to accept risks, and they provide incentives to businesses to undertake only the risks that consumers find worthwhile.

Because financial markets play critical roles in the economy's decisions about undertaking investments in new capital, and allocating risks, financial markets are essential for any modern economy. They are also critical for economic development of poor countries. As the 1997–1998 experiences of many Asian countries illustrate, problems in financial markets can rebound throughout the economy and may contribute to inflation and recessions.

The future is uncertain, so people's future plans rely on their *expectations*.

RISK AND INSURANCE

Expectations

An expectation is a guess about the future. A rational guess (or rational expectation) about some future variable, such as the score of a future ball game or the future price of a financial asset, is its expected value.

> The **expected value** of a variable is an average of every possible value for that variable, weighted by the chance of that value occurring.

The expected value is also called the *mean*. You can calculate an expected value in three steps:

1. Write down each possible value of the variable.

2. Multiply each value by its chance of occurring.

3. Add the answers from Step 2.

EXAMPLE 1

Suppose that you estimate a one-half chance that the rate of return on an investment will be 5 percent and a one-half chance that it will be 15 percent. The expected value of the rate of return (or the expected return, for short) is:

$$(1/2)(5\%) + (1/2)(15\%) = 10 \text{ percent}$$

EXAMPLE 2

Suppose that you lend someone $100. You estimate a 95 percent chance that the borrower will repay the loan and a 5 percent chance of default. Your expected payback is:

$$(95/100)(\$100) + (5/100)(\$0) = \$95$$

EXAMPLE 3

Suppose that you lend someone $100 for 1 year and charge 10 percent interest. The borrower owes you $110 at the end of the year. Suppose the chance that the borrower will repay you is 95 percent, and the chance that the borrower will *default* on the loan (fail to repay) is 5 percent. As a result, your expected payback is:

$$(95/100)(\$110) + (5/100)(\$0) = \$104.50$$

Notice that this loan has the same expected payback as a loan with 4½ percent interest and *no* chance of default.

Risk

Uncertainty about the future creates risks. A situation is risky for you when several things could happen, and some are better for you than others. The amount of risk you face depends on how much better or worse some of these possible outcomes are. Economists have developed a formal mathematical model of risk, but the basic ideas can be understood with examples. These examples introduce important ideas, and later discussions will refer back to them.

EXAMPLE 4

If you know for sure that your income next year will be $20,000, then your income is not risky. However, if you face a one-half chance that you will earn $30,000 and a one-half chance that you will earn $10,000, you have a risky income. If you face a one-half chance of earning $40,000 and a one-half chance of earning zero, you have an even riskier income. Notice that your expected income is the same in all three cases.

EXAMPLE 5 (PORTFOLIO RISK 1)

Suppose that you bet $10 that Team A will win a football game. If Team A wins, you win $10; if Team B wins, you lose $10. (If they tie, the bet is canceled.) The bet creates risky income. If you *also* bet $10 on Team B to win, then you can be sure of winning one bet and losing the other. Your betting income is no longer risky; you have hedged your bets. Although no sports fan would place opposing bets like this, the example shows how combining two risky investments (or bets) can reduce overall risk (to zero, in this case).

EXAMPLE 6 (PORTFOLIO RISK 2)

Larry lends someone $100 for 1 year and charges 10 percent interest. The chance that the borrower will repay Larry is 95 percent, and the chance of default is 5 percent. As a result, Larry's expected payback is $104.50 (as in Example 3).

Barb also has $100 to lend, but she lends $1 at 10 percent interest to each of 100 different people. Each loan has a 5 percent chance of default. Also, the chance that any one borrower will default is unrelated to whether any other borrowers default. Because Barb lends to a large number of separate borrowers, and each has a 5 percent chance of default, about 95 of the borrowers will repay their loans (each paying Barb $1.10) and about 5 of them will default. As a result, Barb will almost certainly collect about $104.50. Her expected payoff is the same as Larry's, but her risk is lower than Larry's. (Larry will either collect $110 or collect nothing at all.) Barb faces less risk because she *diversified* her loans. Diversification means spreading risks over many separate investments rather than "putting all your eggs in one basket" as Larry did. This example shows how diversification can reduce risk.

EXAMPLE 7 (PORTFOLIO RISK 3)

You have $100 to lend for 1 year at 10 percent interest. You could lend it all to Dave, who will repay the loan next year unless he loses his job making Silly Putty. There is a 5 percent chance that a new firm, Crazy Putty, will cut into Silly Putty's sales. If that happens, Dave will lose his job and he will default on the loan. Therefore, if you lend $100 to Dave, you have a 95 percent of collecting $110 next year and a 5 percent chance of collecting nothing.

Alternatively, you could lend $50 to Dave and $50 to Jay, who works for Crazy Putty. With these loans, you face three possible outcomes:

1. You take a 5 percent chance that Crazy Putty will put Silly Putty out of business. In this case, Dave will lose his job and default on the loan, but Jay will keep his job and repay the loan. You collect $55 from Jay and nothing from Dave.

2. You take a 5 percent chance that Crazy Putty will fail and go out of business. In this case, Dave will keep his job and repay the loan, but Jay will lose his job and default on the loan. You collect $55 from Dave and nothing from Jay.

3. You face a 90 percent chance that Crazy Putty will succeed but Silly Putty will remain in business. In this case, *both* David and Jay will repay their loans, so you collect $55 from each, for a total of $110.

You reduce your risk by lending to Dave *and* Jay rather than lending only to one of them. If you lend only to one, you face a 95 percent chance that you will collect $110 and a 5 percent chance that you will collect nothing. However, if you lend to both, you face a 90 percent chance of collecting $110 and a 10 percent chance of collecting $55. You have the same expected payback of $104.50 in either case, but a lower risk with two borrowers instead of one. Like the football-bet example, this example shows how you can reduce risk by choosing investments (bets or loans) that move out of step with each other. You can reduce your risk by choosing combinations of investments so that *some* investments have high payoffs in situations where others have low payoffs.

Diversification

The previous examples show how people can reduce the risks of their investments by diversifying.

> **Diversification** refers to the practice of spreading risks by choosing many unrelated investments or investments whose payoffs are out of step.[1]

Diversification restates the old adage, "Don't put all your eggs in one basket." This is good advice for reducing investment risk.

Insurance

Insurance is an investment specifically designed to move out of step with other investments. If you buy insurance against auto theft, the insurance company pays you only if you are robbed. If you are robbed, your investment in a car has a low payoff (because the robber takes it). However, your payoff from insurance is high in this case. On the other hand, if you are not robbed, your payoff from the car is higher but your payoff from insurance is low. In other words, your payoffs from investments in the car and in insurance move *out of step*. In the same way, you can insure against losing a bet on a football game by making another bet on the opposing team, as in Example 5. While a person who bets on a football game would not want this insurance, the logic applies to the more common situations in which people want to avoid risk through some form of insurance or diversification.[2] In Example 7, by lending money to Jay, you can partially insure against the chance that Dave will default.

Risk Aversion

People tend to be risk averse in most real-life situations.

> A **risk averse** person prefers less risk to more risk.

> A **risk neutral** person does not care about risk, only about expected return.[3]

People are usually willing to pay to reduce risk; they accept comparatively low expected returns on investments with correspondingly low risk. Risk averse people buy insurance

---

[1] In technical terms, the payoffs are negatively correlated with one another.

[2] Most people do want this insurance, so they choose not to bet on the game.

[3] A person who likes risk is said to be a *risk preferrer*.

and diversify their investments. Later sections will show that risky financial assets have higher expected returns than less risky assets; the risky assets must pay higher expected returns to get anyone to buy them.

Review Questions

1. What is a financial asset? What is its rate of return?

2. What are debts? Equities? Futures contracts? Options?

Thinking Exercises

3. If a stock price has a 4/10 chance of being at $5 next year, a 1/2 chance of being at $10, and a 1/10 chance of being at $80, what is the expected value of the stock price?

4. What is diversification? Explain how combining two risky investments can reduce overall risk.

Debt is a borrower's promise to repay a loan. When a business firm borrows money from you for 20 years, it gives you a security or I.O.U.—a written promise to repay the loan when the debt *matures* after 20 years. Before the debt matures, you can sell it to another buyer on a *secondary market*. Buying and selling debt means buying and selling the right to collect repayment on a loan.

DEBT INSTRUMENTS: BOND MARKETS AND MONEY MARKETS

Bond Markets

> A **bond** is long-term debt security, typically a loan lasting 10 years or more.

Corporate bonds are issued by corporations, government bonds by the federal government, and municipal bonds by state and local governments.[4]

Most bonds pledge to make interest payments each year called *coupon payments.*

> **Coupon payments** are payments of interest that borrowers make to bondholders.

Suppose that Walt Disney Corporation borrows money for 10 years by issuing and selling a $10,000 bond. If you pay $8,000 for the bond, you lend $8,000 to Disney for 10 years and earn $2,000 in interest when Disney repays the loan. The bond's *face value*— the money that Disney will repay in 10 years—is $10,000. The bond may also carry 5 percent coupons, which means that Disney pays you $500 every year (5 percent of $10,000). You receive these coupon payments in addition to the $10,000 repayment of the debt when the bond matures after 10 years. Some bonds, called *zero-coupon bonds,* have no coupons; they pay bondholders only at maturity.

---

[4]You may be familiar with bond issues for public schools. A vote of the community is usually required to allow a school system to borrow money by issuing bonds.

Markets for Short-Term Loans

Many kinds of short-term financial assets are available to investors. The government borrows money for several months by selling I.O.U.s called *Treasury bills,* and for longer periods by selling Treasury notes.

> **Treasury bills** (or **T-bills**) are short-term debt securities issued by the government, mostly for 3-month and 6-month loans. **Treasury notes** are similar I.O.U.s for loans of 1 year to 10 years.

A business firm can borrow money for a short period by issuing commercial paper.

> **Commercial paper** is short-term debt security (usually with a 30-day maturity) issued by a private firm.

Markets for loans of 1 year or less are sometimes called *money markets.* To simplify the discussion, the term *bond* will include these short-term assets as well as long-term assets for the remainder of this chapter.

Default Risk

The examples detailed earlier illustrated the risk of default on a loan.

> A borrower who fails to repay a loan in full **defaults.**

Note that a borrower can default by repaying some, but not all, of the loan.

The risk of default affects interest rates. Lenders demand higher interest rates to borrowers with higher chances of defaulting to compensate for that risk.

> The **risk-free interest rate** is the interest rate on a loan with no chance of default.

The interest rate on a risky loan includes a risk premium.

> A **risk premium** is an extra payment that compensates investors for risk.

The interest rate on a risky loan is the sum of the risk-free rate and a risk premium:

Interest rate on a risky loan = Risk-free interest rate + Risk premium

Riskier assets pay higher risk premiums. An increase in the risk of an asset raises its risk premium. By trading risky assets, people can buy and sell risks in financial markets. The equilibrium of supply and demand in the market for risk determines the equilibrium risk premium.

IN THE NEWS

Russia's creditors face payback of only 10%–30%

MOSCOW—Foreign investors may have to satisfy themselves with a third—or less—of what Russia owes them at the end of negotiations with the Kremlin on its domestic debt.

After the collapse of the Soviet Union, the Russian Federation assumed responsibility for about $90 billion of the Soviet Union's debts to foreign governments.

Russia already defaulted on part of that debt when it made only half of its $816.5 million payment due to the Paris Club last month.

Source: USA Today

Many countries have defaulted on debt. Recently, Russia defaulted on some debt that had been issued by the previous Soviet government. Many investors are concerned that additional defaults will soon occur.

EXAMPLE

Earlier, Example 3 considered a $100 loan at 10 percent interest to someone with a 5 percent chance of defaulting. In that example, the expected payback on the loan was $104.50, giving an expected rate of return on the loan of 4½ percent per year.

Suppose that a safe borrower (one who will not default) is willing to pay you 4½ percent interest for a 1-year, $100 loan. Another person, who has a 5 percent chance of defaulting on a loan, also wants to borrow $100 from you for 1 year. If you were risk neutral (caring only about the expected return on your investment), you would be indifferent between lending to the safe borrower at 4½ percent interest and lending to the risky borrower at a 10 percent interest rate. If the equilibrium interest rate on safe loans is 4½ percent per year, then the equilibrium interest rate on loans with a 5 percent chance of default is 10 percent per year.[5] This example shows that even a risk-neutral lender charges higher interest rates to riskier borrowers. Because most lenders are risk averse, risk premiums and risky bonds pay even higher interest rates than this example indicates.

Bond Prices and Yields to Maturity

The price of a bond is the discounted present value (DPV) of its expected payments. An increase in the interest rate reduces the DPV of expected future payments, decreasing the price of bonds. For example, if the interest rate is 5 percent per year, the DPV of the $100 to be paid 1 year from now is $100/1.05, or $95.24. If the interest rate rises to 10 percent per year, the DPV falls to $100/1.10, or $90.91. For a bond with no chance of default, investors use the risk-free interest rate to calculate discounted present value. For a bond with a chance of default, investors use a higher interest rate to compensate for that chance.

EXAMPLES[6]

Example 1
A typical Treasury bill pays $10,000 after 3 months. (It makes no coupon payments.) If you pay $9,750 for this T-bill, you loan the government $9,750. When the T-bill matures in 3 months, it pays $10,000, so you get (roughly) a 2½ percent interest rate on the loan. This rate equals roughly a 10 percent annualized (per year) return on your investment, because you could reinvest your money in this way four times during 1 year, earning 2½ percent each time, for a total return of about 10 percent.[7] The equilibrium price of the T-bill is $9,750 if (and only if) the equilibrium nominal annual interest rate on T-bills is about 10 percent.

Example 2
Suppose that the nominal interest rate is 8 percent per year and people expect it to remain constant in the future. The price of a 20-year, $1,000 zero-coupon bond is $215, because the discounted present value of $1,000 to be paid 20 years in the future is:

$$\$1,000/(1 + i)^{20}$$

This equals (about) $215 if i is 0.08 (8 percent) per year.

Example 3
The price of a 20-year, $1,000 bond with 5 percent (or $50) annual interest (coupon) payment is:

$$\frac{\$50}{1 + i} + \frac{\$50}{(1 + i)^2} + \frac{\$50}{(1 + i)^3} + \ldots + \frac{\$50}{(1 + i)^{20}} + \frac{\$1,000}{(1 + i)^{20}}$$

This series sums to about $705 if the nominal interest rate is 8 percent per year.

---

[5]If the interest rate on these risky loans were lower than 10 percent, no one would lend to the risky borrowers. If the interest rate on these risky loans were higher than 10 percent, all lenders would try to lend to the risky borrowers instead of the safe borrowers, and this competition would drive the interest rate down to 10 percent.

[6]Many assets have features that complicate these calculations. For example, corporate bonds typically pay interest twice per year rather than once.

[7]This figure is not exact because it ignores compound interest, or interest earned on earlier interest income.

Holding Period Yields and Capital Gains

Another important measure of the rate of return on a bond is its holding period yield.

> The **holding period yield** on a bond is the rate of return it would provide over some specified period of time (perhaps less than the time until the bond matures).

EXAMPLE

Suppose that an asset pays $10 in interest in June 2002 and $110 when it matures in June 2003. Suppose the interest rate is 10 percent per year and there is no risk of default. The price of the asset in June 2001 equals the discounted present value, at that date, of its future payments:

$$\$10/1.10 + \$110/1.10^2 = \$100$$

so the price of the asset is $100 in June 2001.

Now suppose that the interest rate unexpectedly falls in June 2002 to 5 percent per year. The price of the asset in June 2002 equals the discounted present value, at that date, of its future payments:

$$\$110.00/1.05 = \$104.76$$

so the price of the asset in June 2002 is $104.76. The increase in the value of this asset, from $100.00 in June 2001 to $104.76 in June 2002, is called a *capital gain*.

> A **capital gain** (or **capital loss**) is an increase (or decrease) in the value of an asset.

If you bought the asset for $100 in June 2001, then you gain $14.76 in June 2002: you collect $10.00 in interest and you obtain $4.76 in capital gains because the value of your asset rises by that amount. You collect that $4.76 in cash if you *realize* your capital gain by selling the asset. Whether or not you sell the asset, your wealth rises by $14.76, and your holding period yield from 2001 to 2002 is:

$$\frac{\$14.76}{\$100.00} = 0.1476 = 14.76 \text{ percent per year}$$

Bonds generate capital gains when their prices rise. Bond prices can rise for two reasons. First, the price of a bond rises as its maturity date gets closer. An earlier example showed the price of a zero-coupon bond, 20 years before maturity when it pays $1,000, was about $215 (given an 8 percent annual interest rate). The bond price rises over time as the maturity date gets closer. Five years before the bond's maturity, its price would be:

$$\$1,000/(1 + i)^5$$

This amount equals about $681 if the interest rate remains at 8 percent per year. Therefore the bond generates a capital gain of $466 ($681 minus $215) over its first 15 years.

Changes in interest rates also affect bond prices. The previous example showed that the price of a bond rises—giving the bondholder a capital gain—if the nominal interest rate falls. An interest rate increase raises the denominator in the formula for discounted present value, reducing bond prices because those prices are the discounted present values of the future payments that bonds provide to their owners.

Default Risk and Yields

Debt securities issued by the U.S. federal government are almost completely safe from default. In contrast, all private firms have some chance of going bankrupt and defaulting on their debt, or *partially* defaulting by failing to repay full amounts on time while avoiding bankruptcy in a legal sense. Some governments also have chances of defaulting (or partially defaulting) on their bonds. For example, in 1998, the government of Russia failed to make payments on some of its bonds.

Two private firms, Standard & Poor's Corporation and Moody's Investors Services, Inc., rate bonds based on their chances of default. The best bonds, rated AAA or Aaa, have the lowest chances of default, followed by bonds rated AA or Aa, A, BBB or Baa, and so on, down to C (the riskiest bonds). Because of these risk differences, yields to maturity on Baa bonds exceed yields on Aaa bonds, which exceed yields on government bonds. The differences reflect increasing risks of default. While bonds rated below Baa often carry the pejorative label *junk bonds*, they provide an important source of finance for many small, startup firms. The long-distance telephone company, MCI, for example, was initially financed with junk bonds.[8]

Term Structure of Interest Rates

The term structure of interest rates is the relationship between interest rates on short-term loans and those on longer-term loans. Long-term interest rates are averages of the many short-term interest rates that people expect during the period of the long-term loan.

EXAMPLE

Suppose that you want to borrow $100 for 2 years. You could borrow $100 for 1 year, and then take out another 1-year loan next year to pay off the first loan. Suppose you can borrow $100 now for 1 year at an interest rate of 8 percent per year, so you will owe $108 at the end of the year. Suppose also that you believe you can borrow $108 next year for 1 year at an interest rate of 12 percent. You can use this $108 to pay off the first loan, then after 2 years you will owe $120.96 (= $108.00 plus 12 percent interest on that amount, which is $15.96).

As an alternative, you can take out a 2-year loan now. If the interest rate on a 2-year loan is 9.9818 percent per year, then at the end of 2 years you will owe:

$$(\$100)(1 + 0.099818)^2 = \$120.96$$

At this interest rate, you would owe the same amount at the end of 2 years whether you (a) take out a 1-year loan now, then take out another 1-year loan a year from now, or (b) take out a 2-year loan now. If the interest rate on 2-year loans were lower than 9.9818 percent per year, people would try to make a profit by borrowing for 2 years and lending the money for 1 year now and lending the proceeds again next year for 1 year. This activity would raise the demand for 2-year loans, and the interest rate on these loans would also rise. If the interest rate on 2-year loans were higher than 9.9818 percent per year, people would try to make a profit by borrowing now for 1 year and lending the money for 2 years, borrowing again next year to repay the first loan. This activity would

---

[8]Before the 1980s, firms encountered difficulty selling bonds rated below Baa. (In language to be discussed later in this chapter, investment banks would not underwrite bonds rated below Baa.) In 1977, Michael Milken of the firm Drexel Burnham Lambert (later sentenced to prison for violating certain federal laws governing financial markets) started helping firms to sell junk bonds by helping them to find buyers, that is, lenders willing to accept high chances of default for sufficiently high interest rates. Junk bonds helped firms with high default risk to borrow. They also became very controversial because of their use in takeovers, as discussed later in the chapter.

Figure 1 | Flat and Rising Term Structures

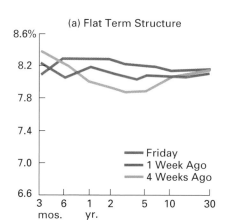

(a) Flat Term Structure

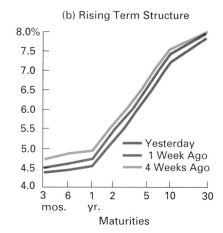

(b) Rising Term Structure

raise the supply of 2-year loans and lower their interest rate. In equilibrium, the interest rate on 2-year loans would be 9.9818 percent per year, a weighted average of the two interest rates on 1-year loans: 8 percent and 12 percent.

This example shows that if people expect short-term interest rates to rise in the future, the long-term interest rate is higher than the short-term interest rate. In the example, the short-term rate is the rate on 1-year loans and the long-term rate is the rate on 2-year loans. People expect the short-term interest rate to rise from 8 percent now to 12 percent in the future, so the long-term interest rate of 9.9818 percent per year exceeds the current short-term rate.

Figure 1 graphs the term structure of interest rates. When long-term interest rates are above short-term rates, the term structure rises. When long-term rates are below short-term rates, the term structure falls. Equal long-term and short-term rates give a flat term structure.

Reading Bond Quotes in the Financial Pages

Most bonds are traded over the counter (by telephone or computer links) among bond dealers. Figure 2 shows how to read bond tables from the financial pages of a newspaper like *The Wall Street Journal*.

Figure 3 shows quotes for various short-term interest rates, including:

▶ *Treasury bill rate*. The interest rate on Treasury bills

▶ *Commercial paper rate*. The interest rate that firms pay for short-term loans in the form of commercial paper

▶ *Federal funds rate*. The interest rate that banks charge other banks for overnight loans

▶ *Prime rate*. The interest rate banks charge their best customers for loans[9]

▶ *Federal Reserve discount rate*. The interest rate that Federal Reserve banks charge commercial banks for loans

[9]Sometimes, though, banks lend to very good customers at interest rates below their prime rates.

Figure 2 | Financial Page Quotes for Bonds and T-Bills

(a)

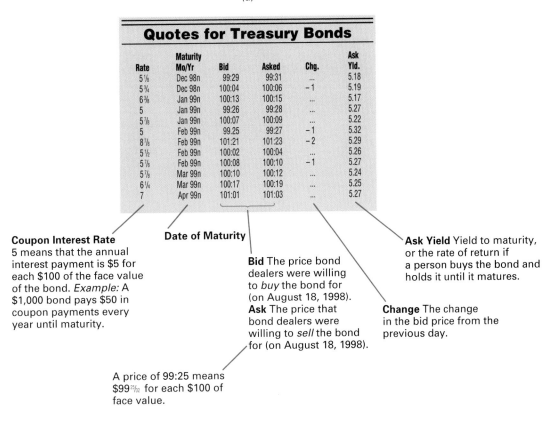

Quotes for Treasury Bonds

Rate	Maturity Mo/Yr	Bid	Asked	Chg.	Ask Yld.
5⅛	Dec 98n	99:29	99:31	...	5.18
5¾	Dec 98n	100:04	100:06	−1	5.19
6⅜	Jan 99n	100:13	100:15	...	5.17
5	Jan 99n	99:26	99:28	...	5.27
5⅞	Jan 99n	100:07	100:09	...	5.22
5	Feb 99n	99.25	99:27	−1	5.32
8⅞	Feb 99n	101:21	101:23	−2	5.29
5½	Feb 99n	100:02	100:04	...	5.26
5⅞	Feb 99n	100:08	100:10	−1	5.27
5⅞	Mar 99n	100:10	100:12	...	5.24
6¼	Mar 99n	100:17	100:19	...	5.25
7	Apr 99n	101:01	101:03	...	5.27

Coupon Interest Rate
5 means that the annual interest payment is $5 for each $100 of the face value of the bond. *Example:* A $1,000 bond pays $50 in coupon payments every year until maturity.

Date of Maturity

Bid The price bond dealers were willing to *buy* the bond for (on August 18, 1998).
Ask The price that bond dealers were willing to *sell* the bond for (on August 18, 1998).

A price of 99:25 means $99²⁵⁄₃₂ for each $100 of face value.

Ask Yield Yield to maturity, or the rate of return if a person buys the bond and holds it until it matures.

Change The change in the bid price from the previous day.

(b)

Quotes for Treasury Bills

Maturity	Days to Mat.	Bid	Asked	Chg.	Ask Yld.
Feb 11 '99	177	4.95	4.94	+0.02	5.13
Feb 18 '99	184	4.97	4.96	+0.04	5.16
Mar 04 '99	198	4.97	4.95	+0.02	5.15
Apr 01 '99	226	4.95	4.93	+0.02	5.13
Apr 29 '99	254	4.99	4.97	+0.03	5.18
May 27 '99	282	4.99	4.97	+0.01	5.20
Jun 24 '99	310	4.97	4.95	+0.01	5.19
Jul 22 '99	338	4.98	4.97	+0.01	5.22
Aug 19 '99	366	4.97	4.96	−0.01	5.23

Date of maturity.

Days to maturity measured from the current date.

The price a dealer will pay to buy the T-bill.

Price a dealer will accept to sell the T-bill.

Change in bid price from previous day.

Yields to maturity.

Source: The Wall Street Journal, August 18, 1998, p. C18.

Figure 3 | Quotes for Current Interest Rates

Source: The Wall Street Journal, July 30, 1998, pp. C1, C21.

Notice that tax-exempt bonds pay lower interest rates than treasury bonds. Investors are willing to accept lower interest rates on tax-exempt bonds because they don't have to pay taxes on the interest income from them.

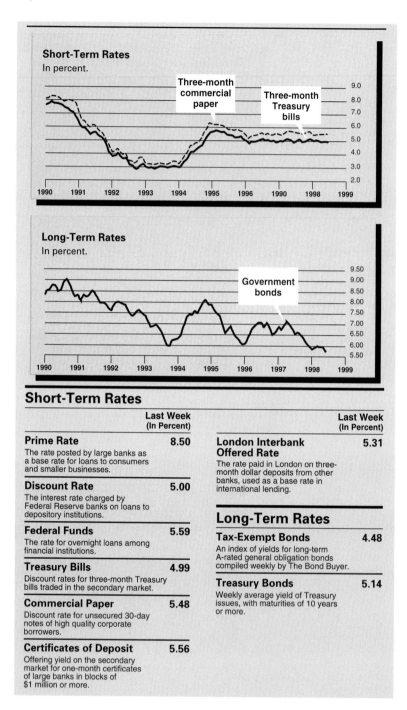

Short-Term Rates

	Last Week (In Percent)		Last Week (In Percent)
Prime Rate	8.50	**London Interbank Offered Rate**	5.31
The rate posted by large banks as a base rate for loans to consumers and smaller businesses.		The rate paid in London on three-month dollar deposits from other banks, used as a base rate in international lending.	
Discount Rate	5.00		
The interest rate charged by Federal Reserve banks on loans to depository institutions.		**Long-Term Rates**	
Federal Funds	5.59	**Tax-Exempt Bonds**	4.48
The rate for overnight loans among financial institutions.		An index of yields for long-term A-rated general obligation bonds compiled weekly by The Bond Buyer.	
Treasury Bills	4.99		
Discount rates for three-month Treasury bills traded in the secondary market.		**Treasury Bonds**	5.14
Commercial Paper	5.48	Weekly average yield of Treasury issues, with maturities of 10 years or more.	
Discount rate for unsecured 30-day notes of high quality corporate borrowers.			
Certificates of Deposit	5.56		
Offering yield on the secondary market for one-month certificates of large banks in blocks of $1 million or more.			

Review Questions

5. Name some types of debt.

6. Explain why default risk affects the interest rate on a loan.

7. What is a capital gain? Why do bondholders receive capital gains if interest rates fall?

8. Governments of many developing countries have borrowed money by issuing bonds. In some cases, recessions or other economic problems in countries with large debt burdens have drastically reduced the prices of their bonds. Why would such problems cause bond prices to fall?

9. Suppose that a change in monetary policy leads people to expect inflation to rise over the next several years. (a) How would this change affect bond prices? (b) Would it be more likely to cause a rising or falling term structure of interest rates?

STOCKS AND STOCK MARKETS

A share of stock, as discussed earlier, represents a legal right of partial ownership in a company. A firm's stockholders own that firm. Stockholders earn income through dividends and capital gains on their shares.

> **Dividends** are cash payments that firms make to stockholders, usually every quarter (four times per year).

The rate of return, or holding period yield, on a share of stock is:

$$\text{Rate of return} = \frac{\text{Dividend} + \text{Increase in stock price}}{\text{Beginning-of-period stock price}}$$

where the increase in the stock price shows the capital gain on the share.

Firms pay part of their profits to stockholders as dividends, and keep part as retained earnings. They spend retained earnings to pay for investments in equipment, research, and expansion. Retained earnings increase the price of stock and generate capital gains for reasons discussed in a later section.

How Firms Issue Stock

A firm can raise money to finance new investments by borrowing from a bank, issuing bonds or commercial paper, or issuing new shares of stock. Most of the money that firms raise from external sources (as opposed to retained earnings) comes from bank loans. About one-third comes from issuing bonds and commercial paper, and only about 2 percent comes from issuing new stock. Firms often sell newly-issued stock to investment banking companies, which find buyers for the stock. Sometimes, investment bankers underwrite stock issues—they buy the stock themselves and then resell it. This practice helps the firm that issues the stock by eliminating the risk that buyers will not be willing to pay much for it. Investment bankers, of course, charge fees for their services.

Firms that have never issued stock are called *privately held firms. Publicly held firms* are companies that have issued stock that trades on a stock exchange When a privately held firm issues stock, it *goes public,* becoming a publicly held firm. Its first sale of stock is called an *initial public offering (IPO).* After the IPO, owners of the stock can trade it on stock exchanges. Financial pages of newspapers regularly announce IPOs.

Dividends or Retained Earnings?
A firm's stockholders want it to retain earning, rather than paying profits as dividends, only if they expect to gain sufficiently from those retained earnings. Stockholders benefit from retained earnings when they generate higher *future* profits and dividends. If an increase in the discounted present value of expected future dividends raises the current price of the stock, then stockholders benefit through a capital gain.

An Economic Puzzle

On average, IPOs appear to be underpriced. Their prices on the primary market (when people buy shares from underwriters) average about 10 to 15 percent below their eventual selling prices in the first trades on the stock exchange. Economists have not yet succeeded in explaining why. A key question is why more people don't try to profit by buying predictably underpriced IPOs.

Reading Stock Tables

The New York Stock Exchange (NYSE) is a firm that operates the world's largest equities market. The American Stock Exchange (AMEX) operates another large U.S. stock market, and smaller, regional exchanges also trade shares of stock in the United States, such as the Pacific Exchange, the Philadelphia Exchange, the Boston Exchange, and the Midwest Exchange. Important foreign stock exchanges are in Tokyo, London, Toronto, Montreal, Brussels, Hong Kong, Mexico, Paris, Amsterdam, Milan, Stockholm, Sydney, and Switzerland.

Figure 4 shows how to read stock market quotations. Look first at the table for the New York Stock Exchange. It lists abbreviated company names, for example, CampblSoup for the Campbell Soup Company. To the right of the name is the company's trading symbol, CPB. These abbreviations show up in many summaries of stock prices, such as those on the Financial News Network on television or many Internet sites. To the left of the company's name, the quote lists the highest price (Hi) and lowest price (Lo) for one share of the company's stock during the previous year (52 weeks).[10] The price of one share of Campbell Soup stock varied between 44\%6 ($44.06 per share) and 60\%6 ($60.19) in the year before this quote appeared.

The second column from the right, labeled *Close*, shows the price of the stock when the market closed at 4 P.M. eastern standard time. Campbell Soup closed at $48.75 per share of stock. The last column, labeled *Net Chg*, shows the change in the stock's closing price from the previous day; the price of Campbell Soup stock rose $0.25 from the previous day. (It had closed at $48.50 the previous day.)

Just to the left of the closing price the quote lists the high (Hi) and low (Lo) prices for the day's trading. During that day, the price of Campbell's stock varied from $46.69 to $49.50 per share. Moving further to the left, the column labeled *Vol 100s* shows the volume of trading in the stock in hundreds of shares; traders exchanged 683,800 shares of Campbell Soup stock.

Further to the left appear three columns labeled *Div, Yld %,* and *PE*. The first of these shows the annual dividend per share, $0.84 for Campbell Soup. Dividing this dividend by the stock price ($48.75) gives 0.017, or 1.7 percent per year. This figure shows the rate of return on the stock from dividends only, ignoring capital gains or losses. The column labeled *PE* shows the stock's price–earnings ratio, the stock price divided by the firm's earnings per share. To calculate the price–earnings ratio, begin by dividing the company's accounting profit by the total number of shares of stock it has issued to find earnings (or profits) per share of stock. Divide the stock price by earnings per share to get the price–earnings (PE) ratio. Campbell Soup had a PE ratio of 34, so the price of one share of stock was 34 times the amount of earnings (profit) per share of stock. In other words, the Campbell Soup Company earned profits of $1 for each $34 of its stock. Quotes for the American Stock Exchange and the NASDAQ market are similar to the New York Stock Exchange table, as is the Foreign Markets table in Figure 5.[11]

The Dow Jones Industrial Average (DJIA) index is an average of the prices of 30 industrial stocks. The Standard & Poor's 500 (S&P 500) index is an average of the prices of 500 stocks.[12] Figure 6 shows stock market indexes for major foreign exchanges. The Nikkei Average, an average of 225 stock prices on the Tokyo Stock Exchange, resembles the Dow Jones Industrial Average or the S&P 500 in the United States. Other important stock indexes include the TSE 300 Index for the Toronto exchange and the Financial Times 100-share index for the London exchange. Many Internet sites and newspapers, such as the *Financial Times* of London, report stock

---

[10] The symbols to the left of these 52-week highs are footnotes that this chapter will ignore.

[11] More details on foreign stocks are available in foreign newspapers or in publications such as the *Financial Times* of London, or on a variety of Internet sites. See the Web site for this book for additional information.

[12] The Wilshire 5,000 is an even broader average, including the prices of almost all stocks of U.S. firms.

Figure 4 | Sample Stock Market Quotations, New York Stock Exchange

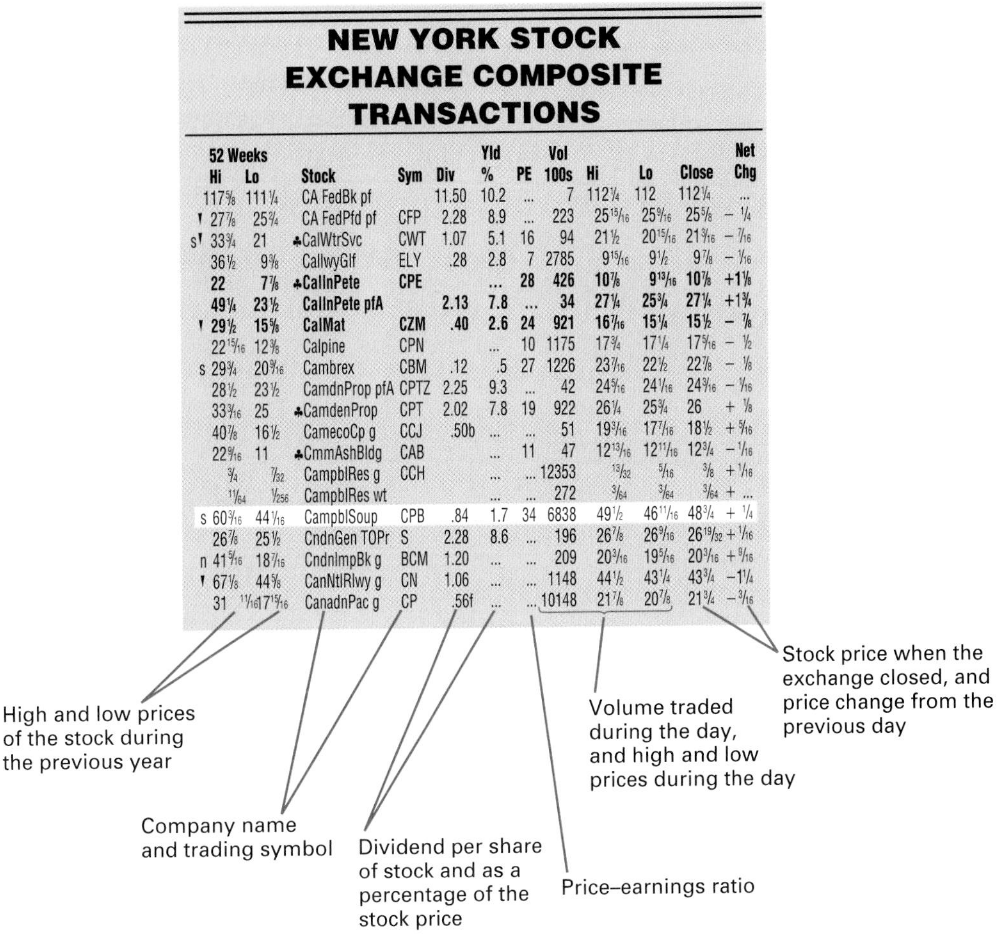

NEW YORK STOCK EXCHANGE COMPOSITE TRANSACTIONS

52 Weeks Hi	52 Weeks Lo	Stock	Sym	Div	Yld %	PE	Vol 100s	Hi	Lo	Close	Net Chg
117 5/8	111 1/4	CA FedBk pf		11.50	10.2	...	7	112 1/4	112	112 1/4	...
▼ 27 7/8	25 3/4	CA FedPfd pf	CFP	2.28	8.9	...	223	25 15/16	25 9/16	25 5/8	− 1/4
s▼ 33 3/4	21	♣CalWtrSvc	CWT	1.07	5.1	16	94	21 1/2	20 15/16	21 3/16	− 7/16
36 1/2	9 3/8	CallwyGlf	ELY	.28	2.8	7	2785	9 15/16	9 1/2	9 7/8	− 1/16
22	**7 7/8**	**♣CallnPete**	**CPE**		**...**	**28**	**426**	**10 7/8**	**9 13/16**	**10 7/8**	**+1 1/8**
49 1/4	**23 1/2**	**CallnPete pfA**		**2.13**	**7.8**	**...**	**34**	**27 1/4**	**25 3/4**	**27 1/4**	**+1 3/4**
▼ **29 1/2**	**15 5/8**	**CalMat**	**CZM**	**.40**	**2.6**	**24**	**921**	**16 7/16**	**15 1/4**	**15 1/2**	**− 7/8**
22 15/16	12 3/8	Calpine	CPN		...	10	1175	17 3/4	17 1/4	17 5/16	− 1/2
s 29 3/4	20 9/16	Cambrex	CBM	.12	.5	27	1226	23 7/16	22 1/2	22 7/8	− 1/8
28 1/2	23 1/2	CamdnProp pfA	CPTZ	2.25	9.3	...	42	24 5/16	24 1/16	24 3/16	− 1/16
33 3/16	25	♣CamdenProp	CPT	2.02	7.8	19	922	26 1/4	25 3/4	26	+ 1/8
40 7/8	16 1/2	CamecoCp g	CCJ	.50b	...	...	51	19 3/16	17 7/16	18 1/2	+ 5/16
22 9/16	11	♣CmmAshBldg	CAB		...	11	47	12 13/16	12 11/16	12 3/4	− 1/16
3/4	7/32	CampblRes g	CCH		...	...	12353	13/32	5/16	3/8	+ 1/16
11/64	1/256	CampblRes wt			...	...	272	3/64	3/64	3/64	+ ...
s 60 3/16	44 1/16	CampblSoup	CPB	.84	1.7	34	6838	49 1/2	46 11/16	48 3/4	+ 1/4
26 7/8	25 1/2	CndnGen TOPr	S	2.28	8.6	...	196	26 7/8	26 9/16	26 19/32	+ 1/16
n 41 5/16	18 7/16	CndnlmpBk g	BCM	1.20	...	...	209	20 3/16	19 5/16	20 3/16	+ 9/16
▼ 67 1/8	44 5/8	CanNtlRlwy g	CN	1.06	...	...	1148	44 1/2	43 1/4	43 3/4	−1 1/4
31 11/16	17 15/16	CanadnPac g	CP	.56f	...	...	10148	21 7/8	20 7/8	21 3/4	− 3/16

High and low prices of the stock during the previous year
Company name and trading symbol
Dividend per share of stock and as a percentage of the stock price
Price–earnings ratio
Volume traded during the day, and high and low prices during the day
Stock price when the exchange closed, and price change from the previous day

Source: The Wall Street Journal, September 11, 1998, p. C4.

market indexes for stock exchanges around the world. Some also report stock-price indexes measured in alternative currencies. For example, you can compute a stock-price index for Japanese stocks measured in either Japanese yen or U.S. dollars by converting yen prices to dollars using foreign exchange rates. Most U.S. investors are mainly interested in the dollar values of their stocks, while most investors in Japan are mainly interested in the yen values of their stocks. People who do business in other countries may be interested in both.

Mechanics of Stock Market Trades

People buy stocks through stockbrokers, who place orders to buy or to sell stocks either through their firms' New York offices or through other stock exchange members. Members of the New York Stock Exchange own seats on the NYSE; these seats can be bought and sold, sometimes at prices over $1 million each. Specialists at the New York Stock Exchange assume responsibility for trading in each stock; they match orders to buy a particular stock at some price with orders to sell it at the same price. Besides over 400 specialists, about 200 floor traders buy and sell stocks on the NYSE for their own profit. Floor traders are not allowed to trade stocks for other people.

Figure 5 | Sample Stock Market Quotations, Other Markets

AMERICAN STOCK EXCHANGE COMPOSITE TRANSACTIONS

	52 Weeks Hi	Lo	Stock	Sym	Div	Yld %	PE	Vol 100s	Hi	Lo	Close	Net Chg
	23 3/8	9 7/8	♣DiaMetMnl B	DMMB		...	...	10	12 5/8	11 59/64	12 5/8	+ 3/8
	10 3/4	1 9/16	DgtPwr	DPW		...	7	223	2 1/16	1 15/16	2 1/16	+ 1/8
▼	16 3/4	4	♣Diodes	DIO		...	5	471	4	3 7/8	4	− 1/8
n	14 3/4	6 13/16	DriversfCpRes	HIR		...	9	25	9 1/8	8 7/8	8 7/8	− 1/16
▼	16 15/16	10 5/8	Dixon Ti	DXT		...	10	13	10 3/4	10 1/2	10 1/2	− 1/4
▼	**50**	**38 3/4**	**DoleFd ACES**	**DLA**	**2.75**	**7.4**	**...**	**573**	**39 1/2**	**37**	**37**	**+ 3 1/4**
	15 1/8	11	♣DrewInd	DW		...	10	105	12	11 7/8	12	...
	10 15/16	8 7/8	♣DreyfMuninc	DMF	.58	6.0	...	100	9 3/4	9 11/16	9 11/16	− 1/16
	10 13/16	9 1/2	♣DreyfCalMn	DCM	.56	5.4	...	27	10 7/16	10 3/16	10 7/16	+ 3/16
	11 1/4	9 3/4	♣DreyfNYMun	DNM	.56	5.5	...	24	10 1/8	10	10 1/8	+ 1/16
n▼	25 5/8	24 7/8	EBS CapTr pf		.38p	...	...	21	25	24 3/4	24 3/4	− 1/2
n	15 1/4	9 3/4	EFC Bcp	EFC		...	...	84	10 3/4	10 3/8	10 1/2	− 1/2
▼	8	5 1/2	EtzLavud A			...	...	13	5 5/8	5 1/16	5 1/16	− 7/16
	6 1/8	1 7/16	EXX Inc A	EXXA		...	16	56	1 13/16	1 3/4	1 3/4	− 3/16

NASDAQ NATIONAL MARKET ISSUES

	52 Weeks Hi	Lo	Stock	Sym	Div	Yld %	PE	Vol 100s	Hi	Lo	Close	Net Chg
	4 31/32	1 19/32	♣JMAR Tch	JMAR		...	17	522	1 11/16	1 5/8	1 43/64	− 1/64
	15/16	1/16	♣JMAR Tch wt	JMARW		...	...	73	5/16	5/16	5/16	+ 1/32
	1 7/8	5/8	JMC Gp	JMCG		...	12	56	7/8	27/32	7/8	...
	27 5/8	7 3/4	JPM Co	JPMX		...	17	203	8 3/8	7 3/4	8 1/8	− 1/4
n	5 1/8	2 7/16	JPS Pack	JPSP		...	...	222	4	3 11/16	4	+ 1/8
n▼	**14 1/2**	**5 1/4**	**JPS Textile**	**JPST**		**...**	**...**	**82**	**5 1/4**	**4 3/4**	**4 3/4**	**− 1/2**
	46 1/2	22 3/4	JackHenry	JKHY	.26	.6	40	1655	44 3/4	42 1/2	44 1/8	− 5/8
	8	2 1/4	JacoElec	JACO	stk	...	12	1018	4	3 5/8	3 5/8	...
	15 3/4	**8 5/8**	**JacobsnStr**	**JCBS**		**...**	**10**	**171**	**9**	**8 11/16**	**8 11/16**	**− 13/16**
	65 1/4	**36 1/2**	**JacorComm**	**JCOR**		**...**	**dd**	**17313**	**52 7/8**	**47 7/8**	**50**	**− 4 1/8**
	8 1/4	**3 1/2**	**JacorComm wt**	**JCORZ**		**...**	**...**	**797**	**5 1/4**	**4 1/2**	**5**	**− 5/8**
	3 1/4	**1 3/8**	**JacoComm wt02**	**JCORM**		**...**	**...**	**5**	**1 3/4**	**1 3/4**	**1 3/4**	**− 5/16**
sx	26	15 53/64	JamsRvrBksh	JRBK	.40	2.2	15	26	17 13/16	17 13/16	17 13/16	− 1/16
	13 1/8	9 1/4	JamesonInns	JAMS	.92	9.7	22	313	9 3/4	9 7/16	9 7/16	...

FOREIGN MARKETS

Americas

	CLOSE	NET CHG.
MONTREAL in Canadian dollars		
Bio Pha	31.35	+ 0.50
Bombrdr B	18.60	+ 0.65
Cambior	7.40	− 0.10
Cascades	9.50	− 0.05
Celanese	20.05	− 0.60
Donohue A	30.35	− 0.15
NatBk Cda	23.70	+ 0.10
Power Corp	30.75	− 0.10
Provigo	11.00	+ 0.70
Quebecr B	31.00	+ 0.10
Quebecr P	28.85	+ 0.05
SNC-Lavalin	10.20	− 0.10
Teleglobe	39.95	+ 0.35
Videotron	19.25	− 0.35
TORONTO in Canadian dollars		
Abitibl C	17.10	+ .35
AirCanada	8.60	+ .20
Stelco A	9.35	+ .05
TIPS	35.25	+ .85
Talisman	32.95	− .25
Teck B f	13.15	+ .20
Telus Corp	32.00	+ .45
ThomCor	39.15	+ 1.90
TorDmBk	50.20	+ 1.10
TorstarBf	19.10	− .15
TrAlt corp	22.20	+ 1.20
TrCan PL	23.75	+ .20
Trilon A	10.80	...
Trimac	9.50	+ .60
TrizecHaf	31.25	+ .55
Wcoast E	28.95	+ .25
Weston	48.05	− .15
MEXICO CITY in pesos		
Alfa A	25.35	− 0.15
Apasco A	34.30	− 0.70
Banacci B	13.60	− 0.60
Bimbo A	16.50	+ 0.02
Cemex B	30.65	− 0.85

	CLOSE	NET CHG.
BRUSSELS in Belgian francs		
Arbed	3620	− .90
BarcoNV	9770	+ 40
Bekaert	26100	− 300
CBR	3465	+ 65
Delhaize	3020	+ 20
Electrabel	11775	− 175
Fortis	10375	− 75
Gevaert	2390	− 60
GIB	2005	+ 5
Kredietbank	3060	− 55
Petrofina	13675	− 75
Solvay	2675	− 20
Tractebel	5960	− 150
FRANKFURT in marks		
Adidas Salmn	212.00	− 12.00
Allianz	600.10	− 4.90
BASF	77.15	+ 0.65
Bayer	74.00	− 0.20
Beiersdorf	110.00	...

Source: The Wall Street Journal, August 18, 1998, pp. C12; September 11, 1998, pp. C9, C12.

Figure 6 | Foreign Stock Market Indexes

Source: The Wall Street Journal,
September 11, 1998, p. C14.

Stock Market Indexes

EXCHANGE	INDEX	9/10/98 CLOSE		NET CHG		PCT CHG		YTD NET CHG		YTD PCT CHG
Argentina	Merval Index	301.73	–	46.38	–	13.32	–	385.77	–	56.11
Australia	All Ordinaries	2526.30	–	16.20	–	0.64	–	90.20	–	3.45
Belgium	Bel-20 Index	3204.93	–	100.80	–	3.05	+	786.51	+	32.52
Brazil	Sao Paulo Bovespa	4760.00	–	895.00	–	15.83	–	5436.00	–	53.32
Britain	London FT 100-share	5136.60	–	174.70	–	3.29	+	1.10	+	0.02
Britain	London FT 250-share	4751.80	–	59.90	–	1.24	–	35.80	–	0.75
Canada	Toronto 300 Comp.	5796.77	–	75.66	–	1.29	–	902.67	–	13.47
Chile	Santiago IPSA	55.21	–	4.39	–	7.37	–	44.79	–	44.79
China	Dow Jones China 88	132.57	+	2.74	+	2.11	–	24.99	–	15.86
China	Dow Jones Shanghai	158.57	+	3.30	+	2.13	–	3.75	–	2.31
China	Dow Jones Shenzhen	157.43	+	3.17	+	2.05	–	15.84	–	9.14
Europe	DJ Stoxx (ECU)	250.71	–	11.51	–	4.39	+	14.92	+	6.33
Europe	DJ Stoxx 50 (ECU)	2914.00	–	147.69	–	4.82	+	280.37	+	10.65
Euro Zone	DJ Euro Stoxx (ECU)	264.57	–	12.77	–	4.60	+	34.71	+	15.10
Euro Zone	DJ Euro Stoxx 50 (ECU)	2903.71	–	147.78	–	4.84	+	371.72	+	14.68
France	Paris CAC 40	3589.35	–	172.78	–	4.59	+	590.44	+	19.69
Germany	Frankfurt DAX	4747.33	–	293.54	–	5.82	+	497.64	+	11.71
Germany	Frankfurt Xetra DAX	4744.05	–	214.39	–	4.32	+	519.75	+	12.30
Hong Kong	Hang Seng	7849.96	–	55.49	–	0.70	–	2872.80	–	26.79
India	Bombay Sensex	3108.67	+	11.55	+	0.37	–	550.31	–	15.04
Italy	Milan MIBtel	19719.00	–	1101.0	–	5.29	+	2913.0	+	17.33
Japan	Tokyo Nikkei 225	14666.03	–	89.51	–	0.61	–	592.71	–	3.88
Japan	Tokyo Nikkei 300	217.49	–	1.15	–	0.53	–	19.39	–	8.19
Japan	Tokyo Topix Index	1109.91	–	6.10	–	0.55	–	65.12	–	5.54
Mexico	I.P.C. All-Share	2856.10	–	311.16	–	9.82	–	2373.25	–	45.38
Netherlands	Amsterdam AEX	1021.31	–	55.28	–	5.13	+	107.64	+	11.78
Singapore	Straits Times	865.00	–	20.46	–	2.31	–	664.84	–	43.46
South Africa	Johannesburg Gold	1015.20	+	63.10	+	6.63	+	213.00	+	26.55
South Korea	Composite	338.95	+	9.73	+	2.96	+	37.36	–	9.93
Spain	Madrid General Index	710.35	–	47.63	–	6.28	+	77.80	+	12.30
Sweden	Stockholm General	3020.70	–	88.03	–	2.83	+	84.94	+	2.89
Switzerland	Zurich Swiss Market	6502.30	–	300.10	–	4.41	+	236.80	+	3.78
Taiwan	Weighted Index	6803.83	–	90.74	–	1.32	–	1383.44	–	16.90

na-Not available

A buyer pays a slightly higher price for a stock than the seller receives. The difference is the bid–ask spread. Buyers pay the (higher) bid price and sellers receive the (lower) ask price. The difference covers the broker's cost of buying or selling the stock. Stockbrokers also charge commissions to place orders; some also charge for investment advice.

Profiting from Stock Price Predictions

If you could accurately predict changes in stock prices, you could become a billionaire. Suppose you expect the price of Gap Incorporated stock to rise by 10 percent over the next month. You could buy shares of Gap stock now and resell it next month for a 10-percent gain in one month. (With a 10-percent monthly return, you would more than triple your money in a year.)

Suppose you expect the price of Sony Corporation stock to *fall* by 10 percent over the next week. You can profit from this by selling your Sony stock today, before the price falls, and buying it back next week after the price has fallen. You profit because you earn more from selling the stock than you will spend next week to buy back the stock.

Suppose you expect the price of Sony stock to fall, but you don't own any Sony stock to sell. In this case, you can profit by *selling short* the stock: you borrow the stock from a broker and sell it. Next week, after the stock price has fallen, you buy the stock to repay the loan. For example, you might borrow 1000 shares of Sony stock and sell them today for $80 per share, collecting $80,000. Next week, you must buy 1000 shares to repay the loan. If the price has fallen by 10 percent, to $72 per share, you spend only $72,000 to buy the stock and repay your loan, leaving you with a profit of $8,000 (minus brokerage commission and other fees).

Many people study the stock market daily, seeking opportunities for profits. When *many* investors buy a stock because they expect its price to rise over the next month, the increase in demand for that stock raises its price *today*. The current stock price rises until it equals (approximately) the expected future price of the stock. To see why, suppose (falsely) that the current price remained below the expected future price. In that case, investors would have an incentive to *increase* their current purchases of the stock, to increase their profits. Their actions raise the current price still further. In equilibrium, the current stock price equals (approximately) the expected future price.

Similarly, when *many* investors sell a stock because they expect its price to fall over the next week, their actions reduce the stock price *today*. The current stock price falls until it equals (approximately) the expected future price.

EXAMPLE

Suppose that investors expect the price of Nike stock to rise from its current level of $40 per share to $50 per share by next month. They will try to profit by buying Nike stock now, before the price rises. Their actions raise current demand for Nike stock, immediately raising its price to $50. The investors who gain from this price increase are those who *already* owned Nike stock before investors started predicting the price increase, or those who were able to buy it *before* its price rose to $50.

Why must the stock price rise all the way to $50 today? To see why, suppose (falsely) that it rises only to $48. Investors would then expect to earn additional profits of $2 per share by buying additional shares of Nike stock today. Their actions would increase the price further. Only when today's price equals $50 would investors stop seeking to buy additional shares of the stock. As a result, the price rises today to $50 per share.

Equilibrium Stock Prices and Returns

When people expect the price of a particular stock to rise in the future, their attempts to profit by buying it today raise its current price. When people expect the price of a particular stock to fall in the future, their attempts to profit by selling it today reduce its current price. These actions of profit-seeking investors change the current price of a stock until it equals (approximately) its expected future price.

> A stock's price rises or falls each day until most investors do not predict future increases or decreases.

Economists say a variable follows a *random walk* if its changes are unpredictable. Evidence shows that stock prices are approximately random walks.

> Stock prices are (approximately) random walks.

Although investors know that stock prices will change in the future, they view the prices as (roughly) equally likely to rise or fall (aside from the slow upward drift discussed below). The logical reasoning leading to the conclusion that stock prices follow random walks is often called the *efficient markets theory*.

IN THE NEWS

The concept is embedded in the ancient joke: "But where are the *customers'* yachts?"

The editors of this magazine have never found the random walk theory persuasive. We know lots of investors who own yachts.

Source: Forbes

Not everyone believes the efficient markets theory.

> The **efficient markets theory** is the logical reasoning leading to the conclusion that stock prices follow (approximate) random walks.

With a few well-known exceptions, evidence strongly supports the efficient markets theory.

Stock prices reflect all publicly available information: any information that is relevant for future stock prices and is generally available to investors. Stock prices change rapidly to reflect such new information immediately after it becomes generally available. As a result, it is impossible to use publicly available information to predict changes in stock prices.

Drift in Stock Prices

Stock prices are approximately, but not exactly, random walks. The current equilibrium price of a stock does not exactly equal its expected future price, because owning stocks has an opportunity cost. For every dollar you invest in stocks, you sacrifice the interest you could have earned on other investments (T-bills, for example). People invest in stocks because they expect rates of return high enough to compensate for this opportunity cost.

For example, suppose that the interest rate is 7 percent per year. If investors expect a stock price to be $107 next year, then they might be willing to pay only $100 for the stock this year. Their expected capital gain on the stock is about 7 percent per year, so equilibrium stock prices rise predictably. Stock prices have risen, on average, about 7 percent per year over the last half century. This trend leads a rational investor to expect a stock selling for $10.00 today to sell for about $10.01 after 1 week, giving a $0.01 capital gain during the week.

For this reason, today's stock price does not exactly equal the expected stock price next week or next year, but it is a close approximation. A stock price follows a random walk with a drift. The drift is the slow, average upward movement of overall stock prices.

Implications

The fact that stock prices follow random walks has several implications. First, investors cannot expect to *beat the market* (earning a higher rate of return than average) by using past changes in stock prices to predict future changes. Because the history of a stock's price (including any trends in its price) is public information, the current price already reflects that history. Evidence confirms that so-called *technical analysis* (which looks at historical data for patterns) cannot help investors raise their profits in the stock market. However, technical analysts do earn money by selling their predictions to other people!

Second, *fundamental analysis* of a stock (efforts to predict a future stock price by examining public data such as that in an annual report about a firm's profits, sales, and costs) is unlikely to help most investors. This information is publicly available, so it is already reflected in current stock prices. The main exception applies to a person with special knowledge that is not available to everyone. A person armed with special knowledge may interpret public information better than most other investors, and may earn higher returns as a result of this special knowledge.

Third, a person with *inside information* about a firm's prospects—information unavailable to most investors—can earn high returns by buying or selling stocks before that information becomes public and affects the price of the stock. However, trading based on inside information is illegal in many cases.

What About My Uncle, Who Can Beat the Market?

Most people know someone who claims to *beat the market*—to earn higher returns than a well-diversified investor would earn. Unless that person has inside information, or special knowledge that enables a more accurate interpretation of information, that person

If You're So Smart, Why Aren't You Rich?
Many people have a difficult time accepting the efficient markets theory, the evidence that stock prices follow an approximate random walk, and the implication that publicly available information is not useful for beating the market. However, it is fair to ask them, "If you're so smart, why aren't you rich?" If people could effectively predict stock prices, they could become rich. Rather than working as investment advisors, they would be vacationing on their yachts.

Be careful to avoid common mistakes in thinking about these issues. One common mistake is to neglect selection bias (discussed in Chapter 2). Technical analysts who beat the market by chance are more able to attract customers and stay in business longer than other analysts. As a result, those technical analysts who remain in business tend to be the ones who happened to be lucky in their past predictions. This fact means that the past performance of technical analysts *who remain in business* is better than the *average* performance of technical analysts (some of whom have gone out of business).

may have earned high returns in the past purely by luck. Luck plays a bigger role in investment success than many people may think. If one million people invest in the stock market, a few hundred of them will very likely get rich simply by chance. (In fact, the chance that none of them get rich is quite low.) Perhaps most of the million investors begin trading with a great deal of confidence in their ability to choose good investments. The few hundred people who get rich will (incorrectly) interpret their success as the result of their ability, confirming their self-confidence. They will be even more certain than before that they know how to beat the market. Other people are likely to believe them, since the few hundred people who lost money in the stock market won't go around talking about it. (If they did, people might view them as rather stupid.)

If you flip a coin, the chance that you will flip 10 heads in a row is almost 1 out of 1,000. Because stock prices are close to random walks (with equal chances of rising or falling), think of stock prices as rising if you flip heads and falling if you flip tails. If 1 million people flip coins, about 1,000 of them will flip 10 heads in a row. (About 122 of them will flip heads 13 times in a row!) Picking 10 winning stocks in 10 tries looks impressive, but 1,000 out of every 1 million investors will do it by chance. People sometimes ridicule the efficient markets theory by telling the fable of an efficient-markets believer who wouldn't pick up a $20 bill lying on the sidewalk because he was convinced that it couldn't really be there. Considerable evidence indicates that the efficient markets theory closely approximates reality, though.[13] On the other hand, the efficient markets theory is only a model—only an approximation to real life.[14]

Ex-Dividend Stock Prices

Stock prices do change predictably immediately after stocks pay dividends. To see why, suppose that a firm will pay a $5 dividend to the owner of a share of its stock as of 3 P.M. eastern time on March 1. The stock becomes less valuable at 4 P.M. than it was at 2 P.M. because if you buy the stock at 2 P.M. you will collect the dividend, but if you buy it at 4 P.M., you are too late—the previous owner gets the dividend. This difference makes the stock worth about $5 less at 4 P.M. than it was at 2 P.M. All investors know this, so they all expect the stock price to fall $5 just after 3 P.M., when the dividend is paid. This predictable change in the price of a stock does not create any profit opportunities for investors.

Level of Stock Prices

Ultimately, stocks are valuable because they pay dividends (or they will do so at some time in the future).

> The **fundamental price** of a stock is the discounted present value of its expected future dividends.

The present value of expected future dividends is:[15]

$$\text{DPV of expected future dividends}$$
$$= \frac{d_1}{1 + i} + \frac{d_2}{(1 + i)^2} + \frac{d_3}{(1 + i)^3} + \dots \text{ forever}$$

---

[13] The efficient markets theory says that most people cannot beat the market except by luck, but it doesn't deny that people sometimes gets lucky. Someone who sees a $20 bill should not stubbornly refuse to realize that gains are possible simply by luck!

[14] For example, the model ignores the fact that if stock prices always reflected all publicly available information, investors would lose incentives to collect relevant information.

[15] This simplified formula assumes that firms pay dividends once every year at the end of the year, rather than every quarter.

where d_1, d_2, and so on, are the expected dividends after 1 year, 2 years, and so on, and i is the interest rate.

This equation gives the stock's fundamental price. In fact, the fundamental price also equals:[16]

Fundamental stock price at beginning of 2000

$$= \frac{d_{2001}}{1 + i} + \frac{\text{Fundamental stock price at beginning of 2002}}{1 + i}$$

The fundamental price of the stock rises whenever expected future dividends change. For example, suppose investors alter their beliefs about dividends to be paid 5 years from now. An increase in expected future dividends raises d_5, which increases the current fundamental price of the stock. Stock prices of firms selling condoms rose immediately after basketball star Magic Johnson reported in 1991 that he had contracted HIV, which causes AIDS. Investors expected this news to raise the future profits and dividends of condom makers.

Stocks Are Risky

Stocks are risky investments. The expected rate of return on a stock equals the risk-free rate of return plus a risk premium:

Expected rate of return on stocks = Risk-free interest rate + Risk premium

Stock prices vary substantially every day; changes of more than 1 percent per day are fairly common. (If the DJIA is 8,000, a 1 percent change is a change of 80 points.)[17] The biggest daily change in recent U.S. history was the stock market crash on Black Monday, October 19, 1987, when the DJIA fell over 22 percent.[18] More recently, it fell by 6.4 percent in one day in August, 1998. Despite these decreases, stock prices have risen dramatically over the past two decades.

Price volatility alone, however, does not make stocks risky. Instead, a stock's risk reflects the amount of uncertainty it adds to the *overall wealth* of a typical investor.

A stock is risky if owning it adds uncertainty to an average investor's wealth.

A stock can have large variability in its price without being risky, if its return moves out of step with the returns on other stocks. Stocks whose prices move *in step* with those of other stocks expose investors to more risk than stocks that move *out of step* with other stocks.[19] Stocks that move out of step can have the opposite effect, reducing the uncertainty of an investor's overall wealth. Risky stocks pay higher risk premiums than less risky stocks; they pay higher average rates of return to induce investors to accept the risk of owning them.

EXAMPLE

If this summer brings a lot of rain, Umbrellas Unlimited will earn a $1 million profit and its stock price will rise, while Picnic Supplies Incorporated will suffer a $1 million

IN THE NEWS

Stock prices plunge around the world as investors fear higher interest rates

*By Douglas R. Sease
Staff Reporter of
The Wall Street Journal*

Stock prices fell around the world on fears of rising interest rates.

Source: The Wall Street Journal

An increase in interest rates reduces fundamental stock prices.

---

[16] If you are mathematically inclined, you might be able to prove the equivalence of these two equations for the stock's fundamental value are equivalent. (*Hint:* Use the first equation to write the fundamental value in both 2000 and 2001, then substitute both into the second equation and try to prove the truth of the second equation.)

[17] An increase of 1 percent per day is a very large change. If such a trend were to continue for a full year, a stock selling for $1 at the beginning of the year would sell for over $37 at the end of the year, a 3,600 percent annual increase in price!

[18] It had also fallen 17 percent in the 6 weeks before the crash, so stock prices fell almost 40 percent in 6 weeks.

[19] That is, stocks whose price changes are positively correlated with those for other stocks are riskier than stocks with changes uncorrelated or negatively correlated with other stocks.

Table 1 | Annual Rates of Return, 1926–1998

Asset	Nominal Rate of Return	Real Rate of Return
Common stock	11.4%	8.3%
Corporate bonds	5.2	2.1
Government bonds	4.8	1.7
1-month Treasury bills	3.5	0.4

Source: Center for Research in Securities Prices, University of Chicago, and author's calculations.

loss and its stock price will fall. If the weather is good, the opposite will occur. Forecasters project a one-half chance of good weather and a one-half chance of a lot of rain.

If you own stock only in Umbrellas Unlimited, your wealth depends on the uncertain weather. The same is true if you own stock only in Picnic Supplies Unlimited. If you invest in both stocks, however, you reduce your risk. In fact, if you invest equally in the two stocks, you may have no risk; one of your stocks will rise in value, and the other will fall, whatever the weather. (You still gain from the upward drift in stock prices, which implies that the rise in one stock price will exceed the fall in the other price.) When you already own stock in either company, investing in the other stock reduces uncertainty in your wealth because the two stocks move out of step.

A stock's risk to an average investor depends on whether that stock moves in step or out of step with all of that investor's other investments. Risky stocks—those that move in step with other investments—pay higher rates of return on average than less risky stocks, which move out of step with other investments.

IN THE NEWS

Unlike October dives, this stock market fall is due to fundamentals

Basic correction

As profits fall and rates rise, many buyers stand
aside and look for the bottom
A 250-point drop in 3 weeks

By Douglas R. Sease and Craig Torres —Staff Reporters of The Wall Street Journal

Reality is suddenly battering Wall Street.

Now, the raw essentials—earnings and interest rates—are driving the market. And as earnings fall and interest rates rise, the fundamentals are driving the market steadily lower.

Yields on long-term Treasury bonds have risen steeply.

Meantime, economic data continues to paint a gloomy picture of what lies ahead.

Recession or not, a slower economy means lower corporate earnings. And although investors were prepared for some deterioration in fourth-quarter profits, they didn't anticipate the flood of disappointing earnings announcements they have been seeing in recent weeks.

Source: The Wall Street Journal

Changes in fundamentals affect stock prices.

Tradeoffs between Risk and Expected Return

From 1926 to 1998, the average nominal rate of return on the stock market exceeded 11 percent per year. The average *real* rate of return on the stock market exceeded 8 percent per year. Over this same period, the average real return on long-term government bonds was less than 2 percent per year, and the average real return on Treasury bills was less than ½ percent per year. See Table 1.

Do Stock Prices Equal Their Fundamental Prices?

Economists cannot observe the fundamental prices of stocks, because those fundamental prices depend on investor's expectations. Nevertheless, economists can estimate fundamental prices, and evidence suggests that stock prices do *not* always equal their fundamental prices. Daily changes in stock prices are often larger than changes in estimated fundamental prices. For example, most economists doubt that fundamental prices changed much on the day in 1987 when stock prices fell by 22 percent. Similarly, large increases in stock prices in the 1990s most likely exceeded increases in fundamental prices.

Most economists believe that stock prices are more volatile than their fundamental prices for two reasons.

First, stock prices may exhibit *bubbles*. A bubble occurs when people bid up the price of an asset simply because they believe that other people will be willing to pay *even more* for the asset at a future date! Federal Reserve Chairman Alan Greenspan alluded to this idea in 1998 in expressing his belief that stock prices in the late 1990s reflected "irrational exuberance" of investors.

Bubbles can burst, sending prices into sudden falls. Many economists believe that major stock market crashes, such as the 1987 crash, reflect bursting bubbles.

Second, stock prices may also move away from their fundamental prices if some investors are sufficiently irrational or poorly informed about factors affecting the value of a stock. If enough investors believe that Digmore Mining Company stock is a good deal, they may buy it and drive up its price above its fundamental value. Actions of uninformed investors may also raise the volatility of stock prices on a daily basis.

IN THE NEWS

Dow dives 512.61, or 6.4 percent

NEW YORK—The Dow industrials fell more than 500 points on Monday as stocks wiped out what little remained of this year's once-robust gains and plunged toward the first bear market since 1990.

Less than two months after peaking above 9,300, the Dow Jones industrial average of 30 major American companies fell 512.61 points or 6.4 percent to 7,539.07, a loss of 4.7 percent for the year and its lowest level since November.

The Dow's 512-point loss surpassed the 508 lost in the "Black Monday" crash of Oct. 19, 1987, but it was well short of the 22.6 percent lost on that day.

While there were more discouraging developments among the laundry list of overseas troubles that have been rocking the market since mid-July, analysts attributed Monday's heavy selling to emotions more than the latest news.

Source: New York Times

Speculation can create bubbles in stock prices, and sometimes bubbles burst.

OTHER
FINANCIAL
ASSETS

Mutual Funds

A mutual fund is a firm that pools money from many small investors to buy and manage a portfolio of financial assets. It then pays the earnings back to the investors. Because a mutual fund buys many assets at once, it incurs lower transactions costs than individual investors through volume discounts on commissions. A mutual fund can also fully diversify its investments, so an individual investor can achieve automatic diversification just by owning shares in the mutual fund.

In an open-end fund, people can buy or sell shares whenever they want at a price near the value of the mutual fund's assets.[20] Most open-end mutual funds are no-load funds, funds that charge no commissions for buying and selling shares. Shareholders do pay fees to cover the wages and other costs of the funds' managers.[21]

Some mutual funds own stocks, some own bonds, some own both, and some money-market mutual funds own only short-term debt securities. Prices of mutual funds are reported in financial pages of newspapers and on the Internet, and many financial magazines also rate the performance of various mutual funds.

Futures Markets

A **futures market** is a market for trading contracts for future delivery of a good or asset.

In a futures market, you may agree today to buy or sell a certain amount of a good or asset in the future at a price set today.[22] You may buy wheat futures, contracting for 5,000 bushels of wheat to be delivered next March 1 at a price of $3.50 per bushel. Like most other people who buy these futures, you do not want 5,000 bushels of wheat, but you believe that the price of wheat will rise, giving you a chance to profit. To gain this profit, you lock in the $3.50 price today. If you are right and the price rises by March 1, you buy the wheat for $3.50 per bushel and simultaneously sell it at the higher future price without ever actually seeing any wheat.

Futures markets allow people to place bets on whether a price will rise or fall. For example, if wheat sells for $4.00 per bushel on March 1, then you earn a profit of $0.50 per bushel. On the other hand, if the price of wheat falls to $3.00 per bushel by March 1, you are stuck paying $3.50 for wheat that you can sell for only $3.00, so you lose $0.50 per bushel. When you buy futures, you are betting that the price of the good will rise, and you are said to *go long* in the good.

If you think that the price of a good will fall, you can sell futures. If you think that the price of silver will fall, you might agree to deliver 5,000 troy ounces next December 1 to someone who has agreed to pay you $4.00 per ounce. If the price of silver falls to $3.00 per ounce by December 1, you can buy the silver you have agreed to deliver for $3.00 per ounce and sell it for $4.00 per ounce, earning a profit of $1.00 per ounce. On the other hand, if the price of silver rises to $5.00 per ounce, you lose

---

[20] If you want to increase your investment in the mutual fund, you send your money and the mutual fund buys more assets. If you want to withdraw money, you redeem shares; the mutual fund sells some of its assets and sends you the money.

[21] Less common closed-end funds issue fixed numbers of shares when they begin operations. People can then buy and sell shares in such a fund, but the share price is not necessarily equal to the value of the financial assets it owns. In fact, closed-end mutual funds sell, on average, for less than the values of their assets. (The value of all the parts of the fund—the assets the mutual fund owns—are worth more than the mutual fund itself!) This apparently means that investors in such closed-end mutual funds would gain if the funds were converted to open-end funds. The fact that this conversion does not happen is an example of a situation in which a firm's managers fail to act in the interest of the firm's owners.

[22] This discussion ignores slight differences between futures markets and forward markets.

money; you must pay $5.00 per ounce for something that you have already agreed to sell for only $4.00 per ounce. When you sell futures in a good, you are said to *go short* in it.

Trading Futures

Traders buy and sell futures in commodities like soybeans, barley, pork bellies, cocoa, orange juice, and heating oil in organized futures markets like the Chicago Mercantile Exchange (CME); the Chicago Board of Trade (CBT); the Commodity Exchange (COMEX) in New York; the Coffee, Sugar, and Cocoa Exchange (NYCSCE), and many other exchanges. You can also buy and sell futures in financial assets like Treasury bills, government bonds, and many foreign currencies (like the Japanese yen). Some of these futures trade on other exchanges, like the Financial Instrument Exchange (FINEX), a division of the New York Cotton Exchange, and the International Monetary Market (IMM), a division of the CME in Chicago.

You can even buy or sell futures in stock indexes. For example, you can buy futures on the S&P 500 if you expect the index to rise, or you can sell futures on the S&P 500 if you expect it to fall. Futures exchanges also offer contracts on the Nikkei index of Japanese stock prices. Figure 7 shows how to read a futures table in a newspaper or on the Internet.

Options

Traders buy and sell two kinds of option contracts: call options (rights to buy) and put options (rights to sell).

> A **call option** is a legal right to buy some underlying asset during some specified period of time at some preset strike price.

If you own a call option, you have the choice (or option) of deciding whether to exercise it, that is, to buy the underlying asset. If you do not choose to exercise your right to buy, you let the option expire.

> A **put option** is a legal right to sell some underlying asset during some specified period of time at some preset strike price.

If you own a put option, you can decide whether to exercise it by selling the underlying asset or let it expire.

You can buy (go long) or sell (go short) in either kind of option. You need not own an option to sell one; you can simply have a broker issue the option contract and sell it for you. If you buy an option, you have the right to decide whether to exercise it. If you sell an option, the person who buys it from you has the right to decide whether to exercise it.

If you buy a call option, you are betting that the price of the underlying asset will rise. If you buy a put option, you are betting that it will fall. When you buy an option, your potential profits are unlimited, while your potential loss is limited to the price of the option contract.

If you sell a call option, you are betting that the price of the underlying asset will fall. If you sell a put option, you are betting that it will rise. When you sell an option, your potential profits are limited, but your potential loss may be unlimited. For example, if you sell a call option, nothing limits how high the price of the underlying asset may rise, so your possible loss has no limit.[23]

R#95402 STORE COUPON·9 EXPIRES: 8/13/94

PAY ONLY 1.99

ORAL·B ADVANTAGE
Straight or angle toothbrush.

Sale Price Without Coupon 2.24
•Children's Toothbrush, Sesame Street or novelty - With Coupon 1.24

Cannot be combined with other CVS coupons. Sales tax charged where required. Limit one per customer.

25¢ COUPON CVS 25¢ COUPON

A simple call option with strike price $1.99.

---

[23]However, you can limit your potential loss by combining two option positions.

Because options are rights to trade other assets, they are examples of *derivative securities*—assets whose values derive from prices of other assets. Futures markets in assets are also derivative securities.

Figure 7 | Sample Futures Contract Prices

Source: The Wall Street Journal,
September 11, 1998, p. C16.

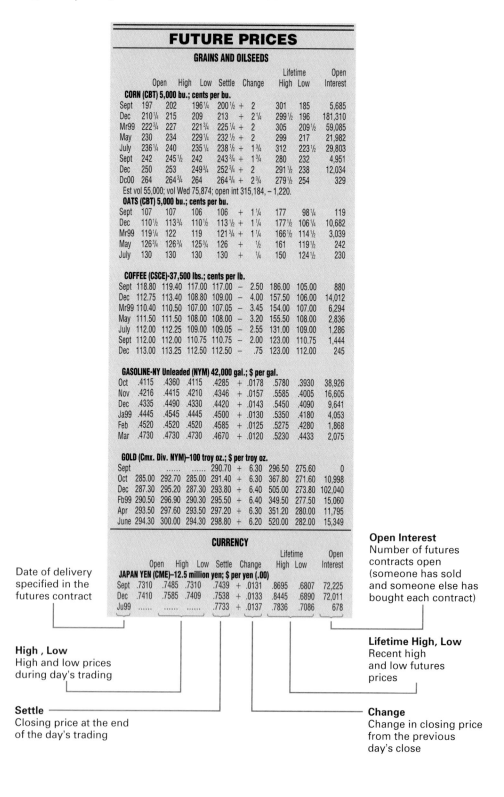

EXPLANATION AND EXAMPLES

Suppose that you buy a call option on stock in Levi Strauss & Company. The call option costs you $300, and it gives you the right to buy up to 100 shares of Levi stock before next March at $110 per share. Suppose that the price of Levi stock is currently $104 per share. If the stock price stays below $110 until March, you simply let the option expire; you don't buy Levi stock for $110, and you lose the $300 you paid for the call option. You cannot lose more than the money you paid for the option. If the price of Levi stock rises to $115 by March, you exercise the option; you buy Levi stock for $110 per share, and you can sell it for $115 per share, so you gain $5 per share on 100 shares, a profit of $500. Since you paid $300 for the option, your net profit is $200. Your potential profit is unlimited because the potential price of Levi stock could rise without limit; for every $1 increase in the price of Levi stock above $110, your profit rises by $100.

Suppose that you buy a put option on stock in the Boeing Corporation. The put option costs you $200 and gives you the right to sell 100 shares of Boeing stock before next February at a price of $45 per share. If the price of Boeing stock at the end of January exceeds $45 per share, you let the option expire and you lose the $200 you paid for it. If the stock price is below $45 per share, you exercise the put option. For example, if the stock price falls to $40 per share, you buy 100 shares of Boeing stock for $40 per share and exercise your option to sell it for $45 per share. You collect $500, a $300 profit (since you paid $200 to buy the option). As the stock price falls, your profit rises.

Trading Options

People can buy and sell options on stocks, bonds, and Treasury bills; options on foreign currencies and commodities like cattle and sugar; options on stock-price indexes like the S&P 500; and even options on futures contracts. Option contracts trade on the Chicago Board Options Exchange (CBOE) and other organized markets. Figure 8 shows how to read price tables for options.

Options are like bets; the seller of the option bets one way and the buyer bets the other way. The price of an option depends on what people believe might happen to the price of the underlying asset in the future. Paradoxically, an increase in uncertainty about the value of the underlying asset *raises* the value of an option to buy or sell that asset. To see why, consider a call option on Microsoft stock. Suppose that people become *less* certain about the future price of the stock—the chance rises that the price will either rise or fall by a lot. This raises the value of a call option on Microsoft stock because it

Figure 8 | Sample Option Contract Prices

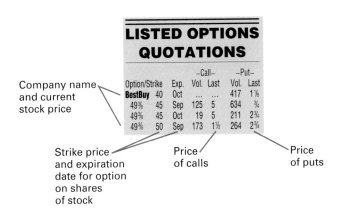

Source: The Wall Street Journal, September 11, 1998, p. C13.

Investment Advice

The best investment advice is fairly simple.

Rule 1: Diversify your investments. The best and easiest way to diversify is to invest in a mutual fund that diversifies for you. Many no-load mutual funds charge low fees and provide very effective diversification—probably better than you can do on your own, and with lower transactions costs. As an alternative, you can invest on your own; choosing five or ten stocks at random usually provides a fairly high degree of diversification.

Rule 2: Buy and hold. Don't keep changing your investments. You probably won't do much better, and you might do worse than a buy-and-hold strategy. Every time you buy and sell assets, you pay commissions and other transactions costs. You can also use your time in much more valuable ways than continually following your investments. Unless you have some inside information about a firm, you are unlikely to beat the market, anyway. Take transactions costs (fees, commissions, bid–ask spreads, and the value of your time) into account.

Rule 3: Consider stocks, despite the risk. For long-term investments, remember that the average rate of return on a diversified portfolio of stocks has been much higher in the past than the average rates of return on bonds or Treasury bills. Stocks are riskier than most other investments, but they may be worth the risk, especially if you plan to hold them for a long time.

Rule 4: Plan around taxes. Some investments, such as individual retirement accounts, pay tax-deferred returns; you don't have to pay taxes on them until you take income from them in the future, for example, when you retire. Unless you think that taxes are going to be much higher then, you can gain by deferring taxes. The discounted present value of your taxes is lower if you pay them in the future than if you pay them now. (In other words, you gain the annual interest on the money you will owe in taxes.) Also, remember to focus on the after-tax, real return on your investments. Taxes and transactions costs can have big effects on the rate of return you get.

Rule 5: Remember a penny saved is no longer a penny earned. It was close in Ben Franklin's day, but today taxes are higher, so $1.00 saved is about $1.50 earned. (It is exactly

increases the chance that the option's owner will be able to profit by exercising the option. Increasing uncertainty has little effect on the investor's potential loss, however, which is limited to the cost of the option.

Review Questions

10. Discuss the claim that stock prices follow a random walk; discuss some of the implications of random-walk stock prices.

11. How large (roughly) are the average rates of return on stocks, bonds, and Treasury bills?

12. What are mutual funds? What are Treasury bill futures?

13. Suppose that you buy a call option on General Cinema stock. Under what conditions do you earn a profit? Under what conditions do you suffer a loss?

Thinking Exercises

14. The price of DullCo stock never changes by more than a few percent per year. The price of WildCorp stock is highly variable. Is WildCorp stock riskier than DullCo stock? Explain.

that much, if you are in the 33⅓ percent marginal tax bracket, including federal and state income taxes and social security tax.) If you buy a VCR for $200, you spend about $300 in before-tax income to pay for it. Every $67 you save is like earning $100 before taxes.

Rule 6: Don't waste your time and money with so-called *technical analysis* of stocks. Instead, you are probably better off spending time working toward a promotion, figuring out how to start your own business, writing the Great American Novel, producing a hot music video, or enjoying yourself.

Rule 7: Budget your time. Most people gain less from an hour spent following their investments closely than from an hour spent clipping coupons for the grocery store or driving to a distant store with low prices.

Rule 8: Diversify your investments in international markets. Stocks in different countries do not move completely in step. Consequently, you can reduce your risk through international diversification.

Rule 9: Don't pay a lot of money for investment advice. Don't put much extra faith in people with financial planning degrees or certifications. Most people who call themselves financial planners have little training, and most will recommend that you buy assets on which they earn commissions. No law prohibits conflicts of interest in this business! If you can, find a financial advisor who (a) will give you a list of customers who have stayed with that person for several years, (b) gets good recommendations from those customers, and (c) charges a flat fee or hourly rate instead of getting commissions from selling recommended assets.

Ask the financial planner what percentage of his or her revenues come from commissions (ask even "fee-only" advisors) and whether the advisor accepts any kind of payment (including free trips and gifts) from people selling specific financial assets. You can also ask outright: "How might your interests in this matter differ from mine?"

Finally, remember that the investment advice of financial advisors will not help you to beat the market. Roughly two-thirds of advisors' recommendations end up doing worse than the S&P 500. When an advisor generates an expected return higher than that of the S&P 500, it usually comes at the cost of higher risk, with higher returns in some years and lower returns in other years.

15. What affects the fundamental price of a stock? Why might stock prices deviate from their fundamental prices? Do economists have any way to tell if and when this happens? How?

OWNERSHIP AND CONTROL OF FIRMS

Stockholders in a firm own that firm. They collect its profits, that is, any revenue that remains after workers, suppliers of material inputs, bondholders, and so on, have been paid. Stockholders are residual income recipients—they receive the amount that remains (if anything) after the firm pays everyone else. Stockholders also have the right to make the firm's decisions and to hire and fire its managers.

Although stockholders have the right to control the firm's decisions, actual control is difficult in a big firm. One person or a few people may own and manage a small firm, as at many small retail stores and restaurants. The same people own and control these privately held firms. However, in publicly held corporations, which have issued stock, ownership is often distributed among many stockholders.[24] The stockholders do not

---

[24] Privately held firms can also be incorporated. This structure limits the liability of the owners. In a sole proprietorship or a partnership, the owners (usually) have unlimited liability; if the firm borrows money and goes bankrupt, the owners must repay the loans, or if someone sues the firm in court, the owners are legally responsible for paying any judgment. A corporation, however, becomes (legally) like a person; if the corporation borrows money, only the corporation is responsible for repaying the loan. If the corporation goes bankrupt, the owners do not have to use their own money to repay the loans. Similarly, the owners are not responsible for paying lawsuits against the firm. The only money the owners of a corporation can lose is the money they have already invested in the firm.

directly control the firm. Instead, they choose managers to run it for them. Stockholders vote—each share of stock usually gives its owner one vote—to choose the firm's board of directors, which then chooses managers who make the firm's operating decisions.

This arrangement can create a separation of ownership and control so that the owners do not fully control the firm's decisions. The managers' decisions may differ from those that the stockholders would have made; management decisions do not always serve the stockholders' best interests. Separation of ownership and control can allow the managers to make decisions that are best for themselves, even if the owners (the stockholders) lose. The managers might concentrate more on the firm's short-run profits and less on its long-run profits than owners would like, particularly if the managers do not expect to remain in their jobs for long tenures. They might simply work less hard than they would if they owned the firm.

The owners try to maintain control of a corporation in two ways. First, they monitor the managers—they watch what the managers do. Monitoring efforts confront two main problems. Managers usually have more information about details of the firm's operations and investment opportunities than owners have, which makes it hard for owners to judge whether managers are making the choices that maximize benefits to the owners. Also, monitoring takes time and resources, so each of many stockholders may prefer to wait for some other stockholders to monitor the managers rather than spending their own time and resources.

Owners also try to keep control of the firm by giving managers incentives to make the decisions that are best for the owners. They have devised many ways to do this, although none works perfectly. Rather than paying managers flat salaries, owners often increase managers' pay when the firm's profits rise. Owners might require managers to own shares of stock in the firm to make the managers part-owners and give them some of the same incentives as other owners. This requirement does not solve the problem completely, however. To see why, suppose that a manager must decide whether to spend $1 million of the firm's money on a new office building. Suppose that the new building would add $600,000 to the discounted present value of the firm's profits—$400,000 less than it costs. Stockholders would choose not to spend the money because the total value of the firm's stock—the value of the firm—would fall by $400,000. If the manager owns 0.1 percent of the firm's stock, this cost amounts to a personal loss of only $400. The manager may want a new office, however, and may be willing to pay more than $400 to get it. Consequently, the manager may spend the $1 million even though the owners would have chosen not to do so.

Another problem arises in linking managers' pay to a firm's profits: Managers do not like risk. As a manager's ownership of stock in the firm rises, the manager's wealth becomes less diversified. This reduces the manager's incentive to choose risky investments for the firm—even risky investments that other owners with diversified investments would want the firm to choose. As a result, profit-based compensation is not a perfect solution to the problems caused by separation of ownership and control; in fact, no arrangement perfectly solves the problem.

Takeovers

If managers make decisions that fail to maximize the value of a firm's stock, the stockholders have an incentive to replace them. If the owners don't replace the managers, someone who notices this situation may buy enough stock in the firm to take control of it and then try to profit by replacing the managers or by taking other actions to change their incentives and improve the firm's performance.

> A **takeover** occurs when one person, a group of people, or another company buys enough stock in a firm to guarantee a majority vote at stockholder meetings.

> A **leveraged buyout (LBO)** is a form of takeover financed by extensive borrowing, often pledging the assets of the takeover target as collateral for the loans.

> A **merger** occurs when two firms voluntarily combine to form a single organization.

In a *hostile takeover,* the top managers of the target firm oppose the takeover, usually for fear that they will lose their jobs, which often happens. They may try to convince stockholders not to sell their stock to the would-be acquirers. They may try to use legal tricks to prevent a takeover by delaying it and imposing expenses on the potential acquirers. In some U.S. states, managers are partly protected from takeovers by antitakeover laws that add costly requirements to take over a firm. These laws tend to protect entrenched managers at the expense of stockholders.

Managers may invoke other tricks to make a takeover so expensive that no one will try. They may institute *poison pills,* provisions that raise the cost of a takeover by allowing old stockholders to buy new shares of stock at low prices if someone begins a hostile takeover. Managers may pay *greenmail,* a bribe to the acquirers to get them to abandon the takeover. Managers might establish *golden parachute* clauses in their employment contracts to pay themselves (very well, usually) if they lose their jobs in a takeover. (Despite the appearance of unfairness, golden parachutes can make top managers more willing to accept a takeover that would benefit stockholders, rather than to fight it.)

Fear of a takeover (as well as fear of being fired and replaced by the current owners) helps to give managers some incentive to act in the interests of the stockholders. A friendly takeover occurs when current managers of a firm support the takeover. (In such a case, obviously, the top managers do not expect to be replaced.) A friendly takeover can raise a firm's stock value by improving the efficiency of its operations. They can also help managers to fend off other takeovers that are not so friendly (and in which the managers might be replaced). Sometimes, managers look for *white knights*—people or firms friendly to the current managers and willing to take over the firms to preempt hostile takeovers.

Are Mergers and Takeovers Socially Wasteful?

Takeovers raise economic efficiency. Measures of productivity show that takeover targets usually have low productivity levels that improve after the takeovers. The number of managers and overhead spending usually fall after a takeover, although employment, wages, and production do not. Stock prices of takeover targets usually rise and stay high long after the takeovers. Also, the stock prices of the acquiring firms do not fall, so total stock market values—the discounted present values of expected future dividends—rise because of takeovers. Investors clearly expect firms to become more profitable after being taken over (usually including replacement of the old managers).[25]

People sometimes complain that mergers, takeovers, and leveraged buyouts harm the economy by wasting large amounts of money. These critics incorrectly believe that the money a company spends to take over another company is money that could have paid for something else, such as health care for the poor. This view is misleading. Suppose that Company A buys Company B for $100 million, that is, it buys most of the stock in Company B from that firm's previous stockholders. Company A then has less money to spend, but the previous stockholders of Company B have the money. The money does not just disappear! (The same is true if you buy stock on the New York Stock Exchange—you have less money than before, but the person who sold you the stock has

---

[25]Evidence also suggests that the increase in profitability does not result from an increase in monopoly power. However, some of the gains in stock-market value may occur because of reductions in wages paid to workers, rather than increases in productivity.

more.) Spending money for a takeover does not reduce the amount of other goods that society can afford; it does not reduce the amount of goods that society can produce.

Note one qualification to this result, though. The takeover may consume resources such as lawyers' time, preventing use of those resources in some more valuable way. Those resources are the true social cost of takeovers. Still, remember that takeovers raise the total value of stock in the firms involved by raising economic efficiency, so takeovers add to the economy's wealth.

Sometimes people say that the individuals involved in finance, takeovers, mergers, and similar activities don't produce anything useful (like cars or food), and that their activities cause problems for the economy. This argument ignores the value of services. Accountants and people in the insurance industry don't make tangible goods, either, but they provide valuable services. Without their work, production of tangible goods would be lower, not higher. Similarly, people involved in takeovers and mergers increase efficiency in the economy through their actions. The increase in total stock-market value from takeovers is a rough measure of the value of their production. (Their actions are really more valuable than this measure suggests, because the mere threat of takeovers also improves incentives for managers.)

Stockholders versus Bondholders

Stockholders and bondholders in the same firm often have different incentives and want the firm to make different decisions. One important area of disagreement concerns the riskiness of the firm's investments. Stockholders prefer riskier investments than bondholders want for a simple reason: If a firm makes a risky investment, it might win big or lose big. If it wins big, the stockholders get the benefits (profits), while the bondholders get only their usual interest payments. Bondholders usually do not gain if the risky investment succeeds. On the other hand, if the investment is a big loser, the firm may go bankrupt and bondholders may lose the chance for repayment in full. Bondholders view stockholders as saying "Heads, I win; tails, you lose" when they choose risky investments for a firm. For this reason, bondholders dislike risky investments and stockholders like them.[26]

To help protect their interests, bondholders often insist on bond covenants, special conditions in debt contracts that limit the risks the firm can take. Bond covenants help to protect bondholders from increases in risk. Conflict arises between bondholders and stockholders in many other areas, and many of the features of debt contracts and corporate law help resolve those conflicts and provide incentives for economically efficient decisions.

R e v i e w   Q u e s t i o n s

16. Explain the issue of separation of ownership and control.

17. What is a takeover? How and why does a takeover typically affect the stock price of the takeover target?

T h i n k i n g   E x e r c i s e s

18. Greedyblood Corporation spends $1 billion on a hostile takeover of the Goodfrus Corporation. Is this money a loss to society that it could have put to a more useful purpose? Explain.

19. What creates a conflict of interest between stockholders and bondholders?

---

[26] Stockholders like risky investments as long as they generate expected rates of return high enough to justify the risk.

Conclusion

The financial industry operates around the world, 24 hours per day, in a very competitive environment. Financial markets often innovate by creating new securities, sometimes very complicated assets, that help investors and add to economic efficiency.

Financial Assets and Markets

A financial asset is a right to collect some payment or series of payments in the future. Its rate of return is the income the asset pays, plus the increase in its price, all as a percentage of the original asset price. Financial markets increase opportunities for people and improve the economy's efficiency by helping people to borrow and lend, to diversify risk, and to direct resources toward their most economically efficient uses.

Risk and Insurance

Most people are risk averse; they dislike risk enough that they are willing to accept reduced expected rates of return in order to reduce risk. Therefore, risky assets must pay higher expected rates of return than safer assets pay. People try to reduce their risks by diversifying their investments, that is, by choosing investments whose returns move out of step with each other.

Debt Investments: Bond Markets and Money Markets

A debt is a borrower's promise to repay a loan. Bonds, Treasury bills, and commercial paper are examples of debt securities. The price of a bond is the discounted present value of its expected future payments. The discounted-present-value calculation uses a higher interest rate for bonds with higher risks of default.

Stocks and Stock Markets

Shares of stock are certificates that represent part-ownership in a corporation. The return on stock consists of dividends and capital gains. The fundamental price of a stock is the discounted present value of its expected future dividends. The discounted present value calculation uses a higher interest rate for a riskier stock. The risk of a stock depends on how much uncertainty it adds to the overall wealth of investors, which depends on whether its rate of return moves in step or out of step with other investments. Stock prices are approximately random walks; they rise slowly over time, but big changes in stock prices are not predictable with publicly available information. Stocks are riskier than bonds, but they pay much higher expected rates of return.

Other Financial Assets

A mutual fund pools investors' money to buy a diversified set of financial assets. These funds provide easy and cheap ways for individual investors to diversify. A futures market is a market for future delivery of a good or an asset. A call option is a legal right to buy an asset during some specified period of time at a preset price. A put option is a similar right to sell. Option and futures contracts allow investors to bet on a wide variety of financial events and to hedge a wide variety of risks.

Ownership and Control of Firms

Stockholders own a corporation, but they do not completely control it; they hire managers to make decisions for them, creating a separation of ownership and control. Managers' interests are not the same as stockholders' interests, so stockholders use a variety of methods to alter managers' incentives to encourage decisions that benefit the owners. If a firm has managers whose decisions differ substantially from the decisions that the owners would make, it may become the target of a takeover. A takeover raises the efficiency of the acquired firm and raises its stock market value. Managers usually oppose hostile takeovers because they are likely to lose their jobs. They have developed many ways to try to fight hostile takeovers.

Interests of bondholders and stockholders also conflict. Bondholders want the firm to make decisions that reduce its chance of bankruptcy and default, which raises the value of its bonds. Bondholders want the firm to choose less risky investments than stockholders want, even though the less risky investments pay lower expected rates of return.

Key Terms

financial asset	coupon payment	holding period yield	futures market
rate of return	Treasury bill (T-bill)	capital gain (or capital	call option
expected value	Treasury note	loss)	put option
diversification	commercial paper	dividends	takeover
risk averse	default	efficient markets theory	leveraged buyout (LBO)
risk neutral	risk-free interest rate	stock fundamental	merger
bond	risk premium	price	

Questions and Problems

20. Why do stock prices almost follow random walks? Why *almost?*

21. Suppose that a company discovers a new product that is likely to double its profits next year. What would happen to its stock price? How does your answer relate to the idea that stock prices follow random walks?

22. How would you expect reductions in government defense spending to affect the prices of stock in firms that make military equipment? What if the cuts in defense spending were already expected by investors?

23. Explain why diversifying your investments reduces your risk. Does diversification always reduce your expected profit?

Inquiries for Further Thought

24. If investment advisors are so smart, why aren't they rich? Why do they sell advice to others or write books about investing rather than earning high profits for their own benefit or for charitable contributions?

25. Why do financial markets offer so many different kinds of assets? What functions (if any) do they perform? What good (if any) do they do?

26. What are the incentives of a stockbroker? Why not compensate a broker by paying a fraction of your winnings if you win, and ask the broker to pay part of your losses if you lose? Why not pay doctors in a similar way?

27. Do you think that bubbles or fads move stock prices? Do stock prices usually equal their fundamental values?

28. Why do people work for firms? Why doesn't everyone work for himself or herself as a separate, private contractor or consultant, perhaps doing the same work?

29. Why can't you buy insurance against low grades in college?

CHAPTER 35

INTERNATIONAL TRADE

In this Chapter. . .

Main Points to Understand

▶ International trade creates winners and losers, but a country *as a whole* gains from international trade.

▶ A country has a trade deficit, and a current account deficit, when it spends more than its income (paying by borrowing from other countries).

▶ Restrictions on international trade create deadweight social losses.

Thinking Skills to Develop

▶ Understand the gains from international trade.

▶ Understand the causes and effects of trade deficits and surpluses.

▶ Recognize fallacious arguments about trade restrictions.

International trade conjures up images of romance and danger in foreign lands, of spices from China, tea from India, oranges from Morocco, fashions from France and Italy, and the latest consumer electronics from Japan, of established business opportunities in the European Union and entrepreneurial opportunities in developing economies. It also evokes fears of competition from foreign sellers and worries over future prospects for local jobs and family economic security.

Most of the 6 billion people in the world earn wages far below those of a typical American worker. As advances in technology, transportation, and communication create a more integrated world economy, American firms and workers will face increased competition from firms and workers in other countries. How will this competition affect the American economy and your future standard of living? Can American workers expect to earn the high incomes to which they have become accustomed when workers in other countries are willing to work for lower wages? Will American wages fall to world levels as international trade expands? What would be the consequences of shutting off the nation from the rest of the world economy? Why does the United States have a trade deficit? Is this deficit a sign that America cannot compete in the world marketplace? This chapter addresses the reasons for international trade and its economic consequences.

SCOPE OF INTERNATIONAL TRADE

International trade promotes economic efficiency; the ability to buy from foreign sellers helps consumers, and the ability to sell to foreign buyers helps producers. International trade adds to the competition facing domestic producers; it allows countries to specialize in the goods and services they can produce at lowest cost, and it helps to spread modern technology around the world, raising world output and economic growth.

Trade has two components: exports and imports.

> **Exports** are sales of goods and services to people in other countries.
> **Imports** are purchases of goods and services from people in other countries.

The United States exports about one-eighth of all goods and services that it produces, that is, U.S. exports are about 12 percent of GDP. People in the United States also import about one-eighth of everything they buy.[1] Figure 1 shows that the United States currently imports and exports a higher fraction of its GDP than it has in the past. Figure 2 shows that international trade is even more important for relatively small developed countries such as Italy and Canada than for large countries such as the United States and Japan.[2]

Figure 1 | U.S. Exports and Imports as a Percentage of GDP

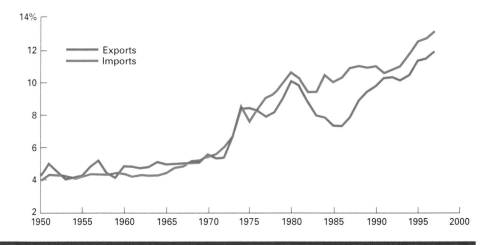

Figure 2 | International Trade as a Percentage of GDP for Selected Countries

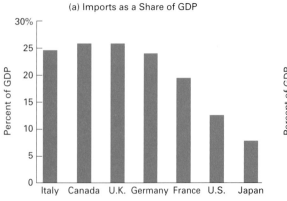
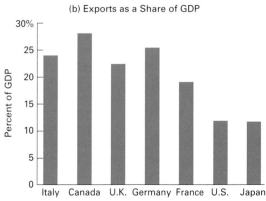

---

[1]The phrase "a country trades" means that people, business firms, or the government in that country trade. Many imports are inputs in the production of other products rather than final products themselves.

[2]*Small* and *large* refer to the relative sizes of economies (measured by total GDP), not to land areas.

A country has a trade surplus if it exports more than it imports; a country has a trade deficit if it imports more than it exports.

> A country's **balance of international trade** equals its exports minus its imports. When the balance is positive (exports exceed imports), the country has a **trade surplus;** when the balance is negative (imports exceed exports), it has a **trade deficit.**

As Figure 3 shows, the United States had a trade surplus through most of the third quarter of the 20th century, but it experienced a trade deficit throughout the final quarter of the century. Figure 4 breaks down the main categories of U.S. exports and imports.

News reports about trade deficits can create confusion, because they report two different measures of the balance of trade. The *merchandise trade balance* refers to trade in goods only (not services). It includes international trade in food, industrial supplies, machinery and equipment, automobiles, and other consumer and industrial goods. The *balance of trade on goods and services* covers both goods *and* services, such as travel, transportation, and financial services.

The balance of trade is another name for a country's net exports, NEX.

Figure 3 | U.S. Balance of Trade on Goods and Services

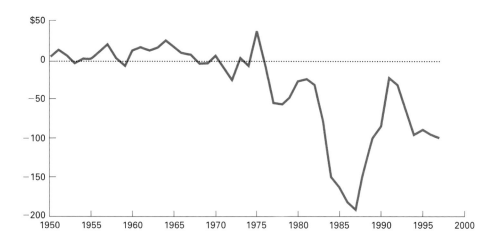

Figure 4 | Categories of U.S. Imports and Exports in 1997 ($ billions)

Total exports of merchandise and services	$932
Merchandise (excluding military goods)	678
Foods, beverages, feeds	51
Industrial supplies and materials	158
Capital goods (excluding autos)	294
Automobiles and parts	73
Nonfood consumer goods	77
Other exports	24
Services	253
Travel	74
Transportation	50
Royalties and license fees	30
Other services	99
Total imports of merchandise and services	$1,045
Merchandise (excluding miiltary goods)	877
Foods, beverages, feeds	40
Industrial supplies and materials	217
Capital goods (excluding autos)	254
Automobiles and parts	141
Nonfood consumer goods	193
Other imports	32
Services	168
Travel	52
Transportation	47
Royalties and license fees	8
Other services	61

Source: Survey of Current Business.

Figure 5 shows that Canada and Japan are the two biggest trading partners of the United States, accounting for about one-third of all U.S. international trade. Mexico, the United Kingdom, Germany, South Korea, and Taiwan are also major U.S. trading partners. As Figure 6 shows, the United States is Japan's single biggest trading partner, despite rapid growth in Japanese trade with other Asian nations.

Figure 5 | U.S. Trading Partners

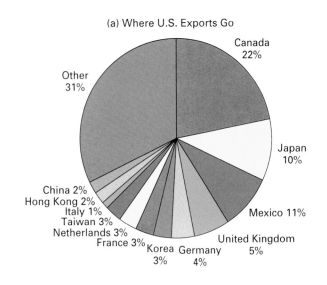

(a) Where U.S. Exports Go

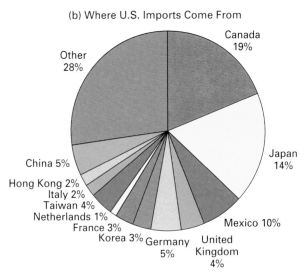

(b) Where U.S. Imports Come From

Figure 6 | Japan's Trading Partners

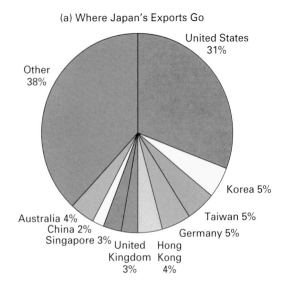

(a) Where Japan's Exports Go

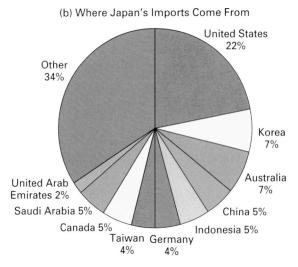

(b) Where Japan's Imports Come From

International trade works like a good technology. When the U.S. loads wheat on a boat and ships it to Japan, and boats come back filled with television sets, international trade works like a technology that turns wheat into television sets. (Recall the fable in Chapter 3 about making cars from grain.)

People gain from international trade for the same reason that they gain from an improvement in technology. Of course, some people also lose from an improvement in technology. (Producers of horse-drawn carriages lost business when changes in technology led to mass production of cars.) The gains to the winners (car makers and buyers who chose cars over carriages) exceed the losses to the losers, however. Similarly, domestic car manufacturers lose when people buy foreign cars. However, while some people lose from international trade, the gains to the winners exceed the losses to the losers, just as when technology improves. That is why international trade is economically efficient.

COMPARATIVE ADVANTAGE AND THE GAINS FROM TRADE

Principle of Comparative Advantage

Trade promotes economic efficiency, because costs of production differ across countries. A country gains from trade when it exports goods in which it has a comparative advantage. As Chapter 3 explained:

> A country has a **comparative advantage** in making a product when it can produce that product at a lower opportunity cost than other countries can.

Countries gain from international trade by concentrating resources on activities that they do best. Each country produces more of the products in which it has a comparative advantage, and each produces less of other products. This raises world output and allows people to consume more of every product than they could consume without trade, a result sometimes called the *law of comparative advantage.*

EXAMPLE

Table 1 shows the hypothetical costs of producing one music video or one computer program in the United States and in Japan. The costs are measured in the number of person-days each country takes to produce one unit of each good. U.S. producers take 1 person-day of work to produce a music video; Japanese producers take 4 person-days. On the other hand, U.S. programmers take 3 person-days to write a computer program; Japanese programmers take only 2 person-days. Notice that in the United States, the cost of writing a computer program is three times the cost of producing a music video; in Japan, it is one-half the cost of a music video. The United States has a comparative advantage in music videos, because it can produce them at a lower opportunity cost than Japan can; Japan has a comparative advantage in computer programming, because the opportunity cost of computer programming is lower there than in the United States.

Table 1 | Costs of Production: Amount of Labor Time Needed to Produce 1 Unit of a Product

	United States	Japan
One music video	1 person-day	4 person-days
One computer program	3 person-days	2 person-days

Table 2 | Total World Output With and Without International Trade

	United States	Japan	World
(A) OUTPUT WITHOUT TRADE			
Music videos	24	12	36
Computer programs	12	6	18
(B) OUTPUT WITH TRADE			
Music videos	60	0	60
Computer programs	0	30	30

Note: People in each country work 60 million person-days, and buyers in each country want exactly twice as many music videos as computer programs.

These countries can gain from international trade. Suppose that each country has 60 million person-days available for work (writing computer programs or producing music videos), and that people in each country want twice as many music videos as computer programs.[3] Table 2 summarizes the results. Without international trade, Japan would spend 48 million person-days to produce 12 million music videos. Japan would spend its other 12 million person-days writing 6 million computer programs (generating twice as many music videos as computer programs, the combination that people want to buy). The United States would spend 24 million person-days to produce 24 million music videos and the other 36 million person-days writing 12 million computer programs. World output (in the United States and Japan together) would total 36 million music videos and 18 million computer programs.

With international trade, the United States would spend all 60 million person-days producing music videos, and Japan would spend all 60 million person-days working on computer programs. Total world output would rise to 60 million music videos (all produced in the United States) and 30 million computer programs (all produced in Japan). International trade would raise world output of both products. That is why international trade resembles an improvement in technology. Although no one works harder than without trade, the world produces more output. World output rises because international trade raises economic efficiency.

In real life, the United States appears to have a comparative advantage in farm products and high-tech equipment. Specific products include aircraft, computers, medicines, organic chemicals, and wheat. The United States appears to have a comparative disadvantage in goods such as auto parts, electronic components, inorganic chemicals, semiconductors, and televisions. Evidence suggests that the United States has a comparative advantage in products that use relatively large quantities of land or skilled labor as inputs. It has a comparative disadvantage in products that use relatively large amounts of unskilled labor or capital equipment.

---

[3]This means that music videos and computer programs are (perfect) complements.

Review Questions

1. What is the balance of international trade?

2. Which countries are the biggest trading partners of the United States?

3. What is comparative advantage? What is the law of comparative advantage?

4. Explain why international trade resembles a good technology.

Thinking Exercises

5. Use the data in Table 1 to calculate (a) the opportunity cost of producing music videos in the United States, (b) the opportunity cost of producing computer programs in the United States, (c) the opportunity costs of producing each good in Japan. (d) Use your answers to Questions 5a through 5c to explain why the United States has a comparative advantage in music videos and Japan has a comparative advantage in computer programs.

6. Suppose that the numbers in Table 1 change to:

Costs of Production: Labor Time to Produce 1 Unit

	United States	Japan
One music video	1 person-day	3 person-days
One computer program	2 person-days	4 person-days

Which country has a comparative advantage in which product?

7. Discuss the following claim: "Regardless of how unproductive a country is, it always has a comparative advantage in *some* product."

Production and Consumption Possibilities

Without international trade, each country is limited to consuming the goods that it can produce. International trade allows each country to increase its consumption of every good. How much does it gain? The answer depends on world equilibrium prices and the country's production possibilities frontier.

Chapter 3 explained that a country's production possibilities frontier (PPF) graphs the combinations of various goods that it can produce with its limited resources and technology. Without international trade, a country's PPF also shows its consumption possibilities. People can buy any combination of goods that the economy can produce, such as Points A, B, or C in Figure 7, but they cannot consume at points above the PPF, such as Points D or E.

International trade, however, allows people to buy more than their country can produce! To see why, look at Figure 8. The world price line shows opportunities for trading with other countries. Its slope (in absolute value) shows the world relative price of cars in terms of fabric. People can consume at any point on the world price line, such as Points B, D, or E. To consume at Point D, the country produces at Point B (30 million cars and 600 million yards of fabric), and then it trades along the world price line

GAINS FROM INTERNATIONAL TRADE: GRAPHICAL ANALYSIS

Figure 7
Production Possibilities Frontier

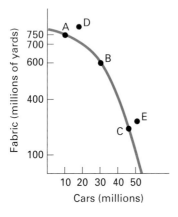

Figure 8
Consumption Possibilities with International Trade

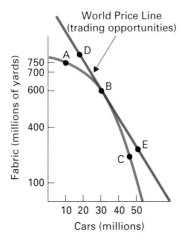

to Point D by exporting cars and importing fabric. The slope of the world price line (in absolute value) shows the amount of fabric the country can import for each car it exports. Similarly, if people in the country want to consume at Point E, they can produce at Point B, then export fabric and import cars. With international trade, people in each country can consume at any point on the world price line.

Slope of the World Price Line

The absolute value of the world price line's slope—the equilibrium relative price of the two goods—depends on world supply and demand.[4] Figure 9 summarizes equilibrium with international trade, as discussed in Chapter 7. If the United States does not trade with other countries, the equilibrium U.S. price is $12, and the equilibrium U.S. quantity is 20 units of fabric. If Mexico does not trade with other countries, its equilibrium price of fabric is $7, and its equilibrium quantity is 15 units. Without international trade, the difference in price between countries gives people an incentive to trade—to buy the good where its price is low, and to sell where its price is high.[5] With international trade, the equilibrium price is $10, and the world equilibrium quantity is 40 units. People in the United States buy 28 units of fabric, but U.S. firms produce and sell only 14 units, so the United States imports the other 14 units of fabric. Mexican firms produce and sell 26 units of fabric, while people in Mexico buy only 12, so Mexico exports 14 units of fabric; U.S. imports equal Mexican exports.

Winners and Losers: The Sizes of Gains from Trade

As chapters 7 and 9 explained, some people gain from international trade, and others lose. Figure 10 summarizes the sizes of these gains and losses.

1. Consumers in the importing country gain. International trade allows them to buy the good at a price of $10 instead of $12, so they gain consumer surplus equal to Areas A + B.

2. Producers in the importing country lose. They sell the good at a price of $10 instead of $12. These losers include the owners (stockholders) of firms that face additional foreign competition and workers at those firms. They lose producer surplus equal to Area A.

3. Producers in the exporting country gain. International trade allows them to charge a price of $10 instead of $7 and to increase sales. They gain producer surplus equal to Areas C + D.

4. Consumers in the exporting country lose. They pay $10 instead of $7 to buy the good, and they buy less than they would buy without trade, losing consumer surplus equal to Area C.

On net, the importing country gains Area B, and the exporting country gains Area D. The importing country experiences a net gain, because its consumers gain more (Areas A + B) than its producers lose (Area A). Its net gain is Area B. The exporting country experiences a net gain, because its producers gain more (Areas C + D) than its consumers

---

[4]Recall that the price in a supply/demand graph is always the relative price of the good. (See Chapter 4.) The $10 equilibrium price in Figure 9 takes as given the average level of other nominal prices. The equilibrium price would be $20 if other nominal prices were to double.

[5]As Chapter 7 explained, international trade equates relative prices across countries in situations with low transportation costs and transactions costs. High transportation and transactions costs can keep prices higher in some countries than in others. A Big Mac, for example, does not sell for the same price in all countries, or even in all cities within a country. Figure 9 ignores transportation costs and transactions costs.

Figure 9 | Equilibrium in World Markets

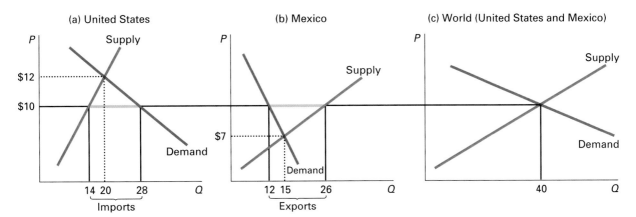

Without international trade, the equilibrium U.S. price is $12, and the United States produces and consumes 20 units of fabric. The equilibrium price is $7 in Mexico, and Mexico produces and consumes 15 units of fabric. With international trade, the world equilibrium price is $10 (that is, a unit of fabric sells for $10 in each country). The United States produces 14 units and consumes 28 units, so it imports 14 units. Mexico produces 26 units and consumes 12 units, so it exports 14 units. In equilibrium, Mexican exports of fabric equal U.S. imports. In Panel (c), world equilibrium occurs when the world quantity supplied equals the world quantity demanded.

Figure 10 | Measuring Gains from Trade

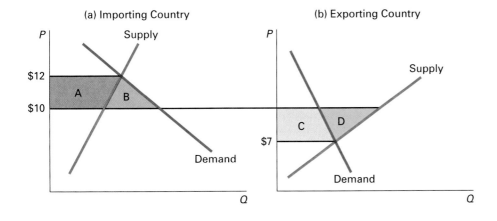

Without international trade, the equilibrium price is $12 in one country and $7 in the other. With international trade, the world equilibrium price is $10. (a) Consumers in the importing country gain Areas A + B from international trade, while producers there lose Area A; on net, the importing country gains Area B. (b) Consumers in the exporting country lose Area C from international trade, but producers there gain Areas C + D; on net, the exporting country gains Area D.

lose (Area C). Its net gain is Area D. The winners in each country gain enough that they could compensate the losers for their losses and still gain from international trade. In this sense, each country, and the world as a whole, gains from international trade. Areas B + D in Figure 10 show the world's net gain.

This result on the gains from international trade is one of the most famous results in economics. It implies that (on net) countries lose when they restrict international trade.

Production and Consumption Possibilities: Example

Figure 11 shows the PPFs for the United States and Japan for the example from Table 1. Each country has 60 million person-days available for work, so the United States can produce 60 million music videos and zero computer programs, or zero music videos and

Figure 11 | Trade Expands Consumption Opportunities

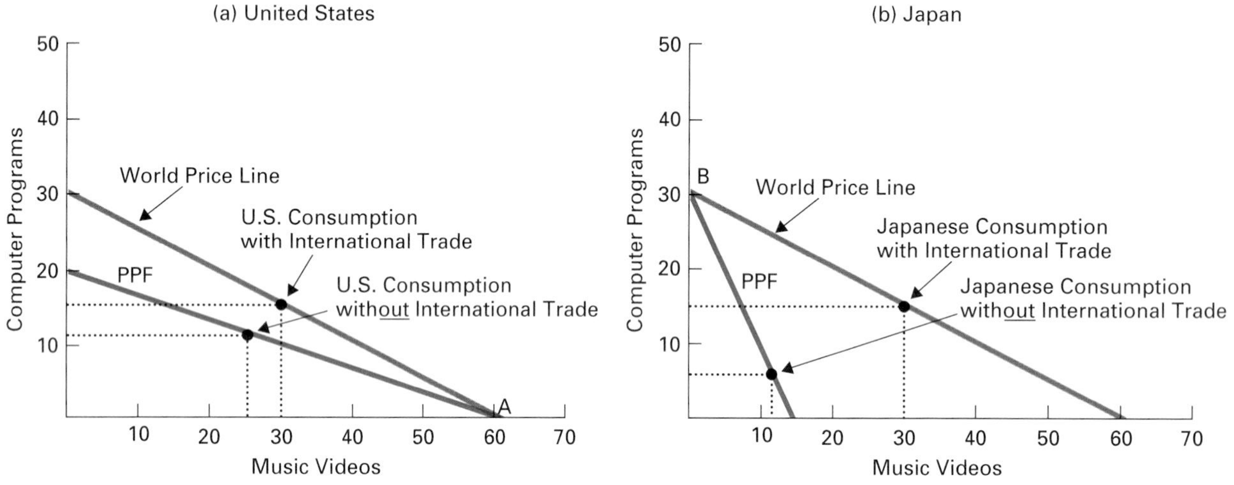

(a) Without international trade, the United States produces and consumes 24 million music videos and 12 million computer programs. With international trade, it produces 60 million music videos, exports 30 million, and imports 15 million computer programs, so the United States consumes 30 million music videos and 15 million computer programs. (b) Without international trade, Japan produces and consumes 12 million music videos and 6 million computer programs. With international trade, it produces 30 million computer programs, exports 15 million, and imports 30 million music videos, so Japan consumes 30 million music videos and 15 million computer programs.

20 million computer programs, or some combination along the PPF in Figure 11a. Japan can produce 15 million music videos and zero computer programs, or zero music videos and 30 million computer programs, or some combination along its PPF in Figure 11b.

Without international trade, people in the United States may consume 24 million music videos and 12 million computer programs, and people in Japan may consume 12 million music videos and 6 million computer programs.[6] With international trade, their opportunities depend on prices. Suppose that the world equilibrium relative price is one-half of a computer program per music video, that is, a computer program costs twice as much as a music video, as in Figure 12. This defines a slope for the world price line (in absolute value) of one-half, as in Figure 11, which shows consumption opportunities in each country. The United States produces at Point A, with 60 million music videos and no computer programs. It exports 30 million videos and imports 15 million computer programs, so people in the United States consume 30 million music videos and 15 million computer programs. Japan produces at Point B with 30 million computer programs and no music videos. It exports 15 million computer programs and imports 30 million music videos, so people in Japan consume 30 million music videos and 15 million computer programs. International trade, like an improvement in technology, allows everyone to consume more of every product.[7]

---

[6] The slopes of the PPFs show the relative prices of music videos and computer programs in the two countries without international trade. The relative price of computer programs in terms of music videos is 3 in the United States (equal to its opportunity cost); one computer program costs the same as 3 music videos. The relative price of computer programs in terms of music videos is ½ in Japan; one computer program costs half as much as one music video. Because music videos are relatively cheaper in the United States and computer programs are relatively cheaper in Japan, people in the United States may consume relatively more music videos, and people in Japan may consume relatively more computer programs.

[7] In this example, Japan gains more from international trade than does the United States. The division of the gains from international trade between the two countries depends on the world equilibrium relative price.

Figure 12 | World Equilibrium Relative Price

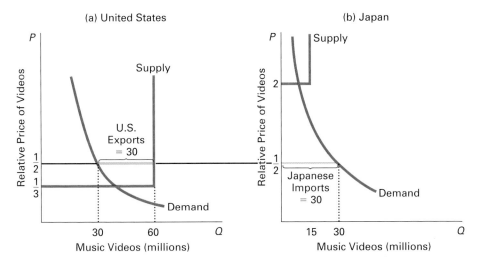

The world equilibrium relative price is one-half of a music video per computer program.

How Big Are the Gains from International Trade?

It is difficult to estimate precisely the total gains from international trade in real life, but evidence suggests that the gains are big. To see why, think about the gains from intercity trade (trade between cities in the same country). How much would your standard of living decline if you could not buy any products produced outside the city where you live? Most people would experience dramatic changes in lifestyle because each city would have to produce all of the food its people would eat, all of the materials for its housing, all of its consumer products, and so on. Most cities have few natural resources available as inputs into production of these goods. Most cities also lack sources of energy such as oil or natural gas. Trade between cities and between states clearly brings huge gains.[8]

Figure 10 may understate the gains from international trade in three ways. The economy benefits from (1) dynamic gains from trade, (2) extra gains from trade in industries with economies of scale, and (3) political gains from trade. None of these gains appear directly in the figure.

The gains shown in Figure 10 are often called the *static gains from international trade*. The benefits of international trade expand further if trade helps countries to increase their productivity. By increasing specialization, trade may raise the speed at which workers and firms improve productivity through experience. Also, the increase in competition from foreign sellers can increase incentives for firms to innovate. The benefits of increased productivity and innovation due to international trade are often called *dynamic gains from trade*. Some estimates suggest that dynamic gains from trade exceed the static gains.

In some industries, *economies of scale* reduce the average costs of producing products in large quantities. (Per-unit costs fall as the scale of operations increases.) International trade allows countries to specialize, perhaps further reducing the costs of production in these industries. This benefit adds to the gains from international trade. Increased specialization also reduces the cost of expanding the variety of sizes, colors, styles, and models available for a product. People gain from an increase in variety, because they can choose which style to buy, another addition to the gains from international trade.

IN THE NEWS

Trade accord would create winners and losers

Tariff reduction can be harmful to some American industries

"There will be winners and losers," says Frank Vibert, deputy director of the Institute of Economic Affairs in London. "But the momentum [toward economic integration] is unstoppable."

Indeed, the pact will force some countries and businesses to make difficult transitions. Workers in Sweden, Norway, and Finland might, under stiffer competition from cheap southern labor, have to forsake parts of their extensive social security systems. EFTA farmers will face competition from lower-cost producers in the EU.

Source: New York Times

Some people gain and others lose from international trade, though the gains to winners exceed the losses to losers.

---

[8]The gains from international trade in small countries, such as Hong Kong or Luxembourg, resemble the gains from intercity trade in large countries. People in large countries reap somewhat smaller gains from international trade than those in small countries, because they can trade with many other people within their own countries.

The *political gains from trade* refer to benefits of increased interdependencies among nations, which reinforces trust, improves communication and understanding, encourages cultural exchanges, and reduces chances of war. People are less willing to shoot other people when those other people are their customers. By encouraging economic interactions and interdependencies, increased international trade may generate many political and social benefits.

Review Questions

8. Why does international trade increase a country's consumption possibilities?

9. (a) What determines the slope of the world price line? (b) Why does the country in Figure 8 produce at Point B rather than Point A or Point C?

Thinking Exercises

10. How does international trade between two countries affect consumers and producers in each country? Draw a graph to show the sizes of the gains and losses from international trade to consumers and producers in each country.

11. Suppose that the numbers in Table 1 change to:

Costs of Production: Labor Time to Produce 1 Unit

	United States	Japan
One music video	6 person-days	1 person-day
One computer program	3 person-days	2 person-days

(a) Assume that each country has 60 million person-days available for work, as in the example in the text. Draw a production possibilities frontier for each country, and show how its consumption opportunities change if the world equilibrium relative price is *one computer program per music video*.

(b) Use your answer to help discuss whether a country gains or loses from international trade when the other country is more productive in *every* industry.

BALANCE OF TRADE AND THE CURRENT ACCOUNT

People gain from international trade in financial assets as well as trade in goods and services. Trade in financial assets allows countries to borrow and lend and to diversify investments to reduce risk. When a country lends money to other countries or invests in those countries, it creates a current account surplus.

> The **current account** measures the amount that a country lends to or borrows from other countries. A country has a **current account surplus** when it lends, and a **current account deficit** when it borrows.

The phrase "a country borrows" means that people, business firms, and units of government in one country borrow from people, business firms, and units of government in other countries.

A nation is a net debtor if it owes money on net to other countries because it has borrowed money in the past. A country to which other nations owe money is a net creditor.

Net debtor countries pay interest and make loan repayments to other countries. Net creditor countries earn income by collecting interest and repayments of past loans.

The balance of trade (or net exports, NEX) and current account are closely related. A country's current account surplus equals its trade balance surplus plus its net income from investments in other countries:

$$\text{Current account surplus} = \text{Trade balance surplus}$$

$$+ \text{ Net income from foreign investments and transfer payments}$$

In 1997, the United States exported goods and services worth $932 billion, and it imported goods and services worth $1,045 billion. U.S. GDP was $8,079 billion, so the United States exported about 12 percent (or about one-eighth) of the goods and services it produced. Because imports exceeded exports by $113 billion, the United States had a $113 billion trade deficit.[9] Other countries shipped more goods and services to the United States than it shipped to them. Other countries were willing to make those shipments, because the United States gave them financial assets in exchange (stocks, bonds, money, and other assets). In other words, the United States borrowed the money to pay for the excess of imports over exports; it borrowed to finance its trade deficit.

The United States also borrowed from other countries to make transfer payments, mainly foreign aid and gifts, to other countries. The United States gave $39 billion more to other countries as gifts and foreign aid—transfer payments to foreigners—than it received. At the same time, foreigners earned slightly more on their U.S. investments ($250 billion) than the United States earned on its investments in other countries ($236 billion), leaving net income from foreign investments of −$14 billion. On transfer payments and income on foreign investments combined, the United States paid other countries $53 billion more than it collected from them in 1997. This means that the United States owed these countries $53 billion more than it owed before that year. These countries hold U.S. financial assets that resemble IOUs from the United States. The United States owes goods and services to these countries in the future. They get these goods and services by spending the interest payments on the financial assets or selling the financial assets to buy goods from the United States.

U.S. borrowing from other countries exceeded the trade balance deficit by $53 billion:

1997 U.S. current account surplus	=	1997 U.S. trade balance surplus	+	1997 U.S. net income from foreign investments and transfer payments
−$166 billion	=	−$113 billion	+	−$53 billion

Note that a negative surplus represents a deficit; the United States had a $113 billion trade deficit and a $166 billion current account deficit. This means that the United States borrowed $166 billion from other countries.

Similarly, a country with a trade surplus lends to people in other countries. If Germany sells goods worth 20 billion Euros to other countries and imports goods worth only 16 billion Euros, then Germany lends 4 billion Euros to other countries. People in those countries receive only 16 billion Euros from German buyers, but spend 20 billion Euros, so they borrow the other 4 billion Euros to spend on German goods.

Causes of Current Account Deficits

A country has a current account deficit when it saves less than it invests. A country can invest more than it saves only by borrowing the extra money for investment from other

Advice

See the Web site (www.dryden.com) for this book for the latest statistics on international trade and other economic data. Because the government often revises its statistics as it obtains better estimates, the most recent data on the Internet may differ slightly from numbers in this book.

Don't memorize these data—use them to help learn concepts that you can apply to understand and analyze economic issues.

---

[9] In the equation, this result shows up as a negative number for the trade balance surplus.

Figure 13 | World Loan Market Equilibrium

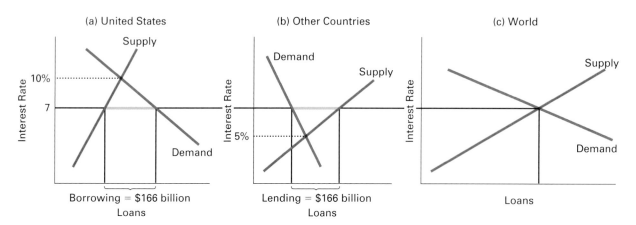

Without international borrowing and lending, the equilibrium interest rate in the United States is 10 percent per year. With international borrowing and lending, the world equilibrium interest rate is 7 percent per year and the United States borrows $166 billion from other countries (it has a $166 billion current account deficit).

countries. A country has a current account surplus when it saves more than it invests. A country can save more than it invests only by lending the extra savings to people in other countries.

Figure 13 shows three diagrams. Panel (a) shows the supply of loans and the demand for loans in the United States. Panel (b) shows the supply and demand for loans in other countries. Panel (c) shows the world supply and demand for loans. This graph resembles Figure 9, which showed exports and imports of goods. Figure 13, in contrast, shows exports and imports of loans. If the United States could not borrow from other countries in this example, the U.S. interest rate would be 10 percent per year and the foreign interest rate would be 5 percent per year. International borrowing and lending, however, gives a world real interest rate of 7 percent per year. The United States borrows $166 billion from foreign countries, so the U.S. current account deficit is $166 billion. Other countries lend $166 billion to the United States, so the rest of the world has a current account surplus of $166 billion.

The current account changes when the demand or supply of loans changes in any country. Most economists believe that U.S. government budget deficits are a main cause of U.S. current account deficits. Unless people save all the money they get from a tax cut, a government budget deficit raises the U.S. demand for loans more than the supply. Without international borrowing and lending, the deficit would raise the real interest rate in the United States. By borrowing and lending on international markets, however, the United States can meet part of its increased demand for loans. Borrowing from other countries raises the U.S. current account deficit.

The evidence on government budget deficits and current account deficits issue is mixed. U.S. current account deficits increased substantially in the mid-1980s, soon after government budget deficits increased, but the two deficits are not tightly linked in other periods. Figure 14 shows that the current account deficit appears to follow the budget deficit after a lag of about 2 years. The real U.S. government budget deficit has fallen in recent years and has recently become a surplus. If the relationship in the figure remains unaffected, a reduction in the U.S. current account deficit should soon follow.

Several other factors also affect the current account deficit. Tax policies affect supply and demand for loans by affecting investment demand. Changes in technology raise the demand for loans by increasing the demand for investment. Changes in people's tastes

**Figure 14 | Twin U.S. Deficits: Government Budget Deficit
and Current Account Deficit**

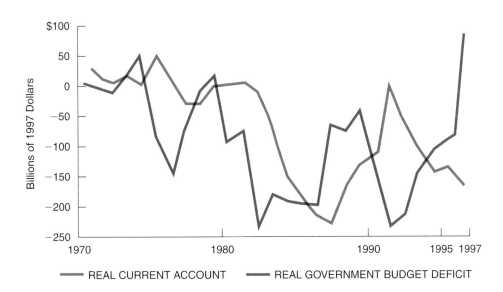

REAL CURRENT ACCOUNT   REAL GOVERNMENT BUDGET DEFICIT

The graph shows the real government budget deficit measured by increases in the real value of the privately-held federal government debt. The figure also shows the real U.S. current account deficit. A larger negative number indicates a larger deficit. Notice that the U.S. government had a real budget surplus in 1997, despite news reports of a small deficit, using a less accurate measure.

for spending or saving money, or changes in expected future incomes, affect saving and the supply of loans. These and other factors affect the current account by affecting the supply or demand for loans.

Effects of Current Account Deficits

Are trade deficits good or bad? The term *deficit* sounds bad, and people often express concern about trade deficits. Some people claim that exports are good because they create jobs and that imports are bad because they destroy jobs; they conclude that trade deficits reduce domestic employment.[10] Against this view, other people argue that imports are good because they allow a country to consume certain products without producing them, while exports require people to work at producing goods for other countries to enjoy.

Both arguments are misleading. Current account deficits and surpluses occur because people borrow from and lend to people in other countries. These loans are voluntary trades, and people expect to benefit from them. If you save your money and deposit it in a bank account, the bank lends that money to someone who wants to buy a car or start a business. International lending works the same way, but on a global scale. A country runs a current account deficit when it borrows; it trades away future products to get current products. Similarly, a country runs a current account surplus when it saves and lends; it trades current products to get future products.

Trade deficits may appear to reduce the total number of jobs available, but appearances can be misleading. Both imports and exports create local jobs. Jobs supported by

---

[10]This is the argument behind buy-American campaigns.

exports are easy to identify; jobs supported by imports are difficult to identify because they are spread throughout the economy. U.S. imports create American jobs by providing foreigners with dollars to spend on American products. (When foreign sellers do not spend those dollars, they lend the dollars to other people who spend them.) For the same reason, limiting purchases to American-made goods does not encourage American job creation. It simply changes the composition of those jobs, encouraging job creation in import-competing industries and discouraging it in exporting industries and other industries.

Review Questions

12. What are the dynamic gains from trade? What are the political gains from trade?

13. What is the current account? How is it related to the balance of trade?

14. What can cause a current account deficit?

Thinking Exercises

15. Are current account deficits necessarily bad for the economy?

16. Draw a graph to show the effects of a *fall* in the U.S. government budget deficit on the U.S. current account and the world equilibrium interest rate.

PROTECTIONISM

Governments often act to restrict international trade. Because restrictions on imports protect certain domestic firms from foreign competition, a government policy to restrict imports is often labeled *protectionism*.

Allowing free international trade usually enhances economic efficiency for the reasons discussed earlier in this chapter; protectionist policies almost always cause economic inefficiency. Some people gain and some people lose from restricting imports, but the losses to the losers (such as consumers) exceed the gains to the winners (mainly domestic firms protected from foreign competition). Trade restrictions help domestic firms to maintain high prices by limiting domestic supply. The restrictions prevent consumers from buying products from foreign competitors or impose special taxes on purchases from those foreign competitors. Trade restrictions tend to occur when the groups that stand to benefit have greater political influence than the groups that stand to lose.

Types of Trade Restrictions

The two most prominent forms of restrictions on international trade are tariffs and import quotas.

> A **tariff** is a tax on imports.

> An **import quota** is a direct limit on the number of imported goods of a certain type.

Exporters and consumers, like this shopkeeper in Tokyo, lose from protectionism.

The U.S. government has imposed tariffs in recent years on computers, ball bearings, and many other goods. It has set import quotas for steel, sugar, textiles, ice cream, and many other products. Japan has set quotas for imports of beef, oranges, and rice.

Other forms of trade restrictions include voluntary export restraints (VERs), which work like unofficial quotas in which the government of a country agrees "voluntarily" to limit its exports to another country. A country may agree to limit its exports to avert a threat of trade restrictions from another country.[11] In this way, the United States induced Japan to adopt voluntary export restraints on its cars starting in 1981. According to one estimate, this action raised the U.S. prices of Japanese cars by about $2,500 each and raised the U.S. prices of American cars by about $1,000 each. U.S. pressure led Japan to reduce its automobile exports further (to 1.65 million cars per year) in 1992. Under similar pressure, other countries have established VERs on a variety of other goods.

Another form of trade restriction, a local content requirement, creates a legal minimum fraction of a good's components (perhaps parts that represent one-half of a car's value) that must come from producers in the domestic country rather than from imports. Another form of protectionism, bureaucratic (red tape) protectionism, prevents foreign producers from legally selling their goods until they complete bureaucratic procedures designed to raise costs to foreign producers. Government regulations, sometimes disguised as health and safety regulations, also serve as trade restrictions. Suppose, for example, that foreign firms and domestic firms use different types of inputs in their products. The inputs may be identical in every important respect, but a government may ban the input used by foreign firms citing questionable health or safety threats. Governments have often restricted imports in this way.

Effects of Tariffs

Figure 15 shows the effects of a tariff that does not affect the world price of the good. For example, the United States buys only a small fraction of the world's tea, so a fall in its purchases of tea reduces the world demand—and the world price—by such a small amount that economists can ignore it in practice.

Suppose that the U.S. government puts a tariff on imports of tea. P^{US} is the price including tax (that is, including the tariff) that buyers pay for imported tea. Foreign sellers receive the after-tax world price P^W. The difference, $P^{US} - P^W$, is the per-unit tariff that the government collects.

As the tariff raises the U.S. price of tea above the world price, tea producers in the United States also raise their prices to P^{US}, so they benefit from the tariff, raising their production and sales from 10 to 15 units. Area A shows the gain to U.S. producers (the increase in their producer surplus) from the tariff. The tariff hurts American consumers, because it raises the U.S. price of tea.[12] Total sales of tea in the United States fall from 34 units (10 from U.S. firms and 24 imported from foreign firms) to 24 units. Imports fall from 24 to 9 units. American consumers lose Areas A, B, C, and D from the tariff. (These areas show the fall in consumer surplus.) The U.S. government gains Area C, because people pay the government $(P^{US} - P^W)$ for each of the 14 units they continue to import.

The loss to U.S. consumers—Areas A + B + C + D—exceeds the combined gain to the government and U.S. producers—Areas A + C. The difference, Areas B + D, shows the deadweight social loss from the tariff. While the tariff creates winners and losers, the losers lose more than the winners win. The deadweight social loss measures a loss to society as a whole from the economic inefficiency created by the tariff.

Tariffs and World Prices

When a country buys a large enough fraction of total world sales of a good, a tariff imposed by its government can actually reduce the world price of that good. This benefits the country that imposes the tariff by reducing the price it pays for imports. If this benefit exceeds the deadweight social loss from the tariff, the country can gain by

Some U.S. Trade Restrictions

Quotas restrict imports of foreign ice cream to about 1 teaspoonful per American per year, imports of foreign peanuts to about 2 per person per year, and imports of cheese to about 1 pound per person per year.

Tariffs on imports of low-priced watch parts have recently reached 151 percent; tariffs on some shoe imports have been 67 percent. The tariff on orange juice has been 40 percent; the tariff on mushrooms has been 25 percent. Tariffs have reached 41 percent on grapefruit juice, 20 percent on watermelon, 35 percent on dates, and 20 percent on yogurt. The tariff on imported brooms is 42 percent, and the government charges 25 percent for imported flashlights. Back in 1987, the United States imposed a 100 percent tariff on Japanese computers.

Source: James Bovard, *The Fair Trade Fraud* (New York: St. Martin's Press, 1991).

---

[11] The restriction is often voluntary in the same sense that a crime victim voluntarily gives up a wallet to a mugger.

[12] Even though the tariff applies only to imports, the increase in the price of imported goods reduces the foreign competition facing U.S. producers, so U.S. producers also raise their price. The price increase applies to tea produced anywhere, not just imported tea.

Figure 15 | Effects of a Tariff

Without a tariff, the United States produces 10 units, imports 24, and consumes 34. With a tariff, the U.S. price rises from P^W to P^{US}, U.S. production rises to 15 units, U.S. imports fall to 9, and U.S. consumption falls to 24. U.S. consumers lose Areas A + B + C + D from the tariff. U.S. producers gain Area A, and the U.S. government gains Area C in tariff (tax) revenue. The difference, Area B + D, is a deadweight social loss from the tariff.

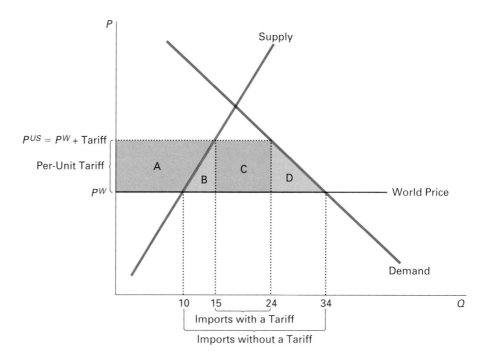

IN THE NEWS

Big tariff put on sweetener

BRUSSELS, Nov. 29 (Reuters)—The European Commission today imposed large duties on cut-price imports of the low-calorie sweetener aspartame from the United States and Japan to protect the only European producer of the product.

The duties, which will add 70 percent to the imported prices almost overnight, came just days before the final phase of talks on liberalizing trade were scheduled to begin here.

Source: New York Times

Another trade restriction.

imposing a tariff. The country's gain, though, comes at the expense of even bigger losses in foreign countries, that is, a substantial fall in world economic efficiency.

Although a country can sometimes gain at the expense of other countries, evidence indicates that countries usually lose on the whole when they impose tariffs. In most real-life situations, governments impose tariffs not because their countries stand to gain overall, but because the winners (firms that want to reduce foreign competition) have more political influence than the losers (such as consumers).

Tariffs can also provoke foreign retaliation. If the United States imposes tariffs on imports of a product from the European Union (EU), the EU may in turn impose tariffs on its imports of American products. In the end, all countries are likely to lose. Even if a country could gain from some tariff considered in isolation, it may lose when foreign political forces lead to retaliatory tariffs.

Effects of Nontariff Trade Restrictions

Import quotas have effects similar to those of tariffs, but with one main difference: the government collects no tax revenue from a quota. A quota simply limits the quantity of units imported. In Figure 15, a quota that limited U.S. imports to 9 units would produce the same effects as the tariff. The interpretation of the figure requires only a slight change. Area C represents a profit to the people who are legally allowed to import the 9 units of foreign goods, instead of a gain to the government. These importers profit, because they can buy those goods at the low world price, P^W, and resell them at the higher U.S. price, P^{US}; Area C shows the profits from these resales. Otherwise, a quota has the same effect as a tariff; the United States loses Area B + D from the import quota.

A voluntary export restraint (VER) has almost the same effect as a quota, with one difference: The people who gain Area C in Figure 15 are the foreign producers whom the foreign government allows to export the 9 units of the product. The effects of bureau-

IN THE NEWS

Hong Kong agrees to limit exports of textiles to U.S.

By Eduardo Lachica
Staff Reporter of The Wall
Street Journal

WASHINGTON—Hong Kong agreed to sharply curb the growth of its tex-tile and apparel exports to the U.S. through 1991.

"Obviously, we aren't happy about it, but like it or not there is a lot of protectionist pressure (in the U.S.) that forced us to make a realistic assessment of what we could get," said Hamish MacLeod, chief textile negotiator for Hong Kong.

Japanese quota extension pleases Detroit

But car-export limit is likely to hurt U.S. consumers

By Joseph B. White
Staff Reporter of The Wall
Street Journal

The Japanese government's decision to keep a cap on car exports to the U.S. pleased Detroit's auto makers, who will keep the benefit of trade restraint even though they may report record profits for 1988.

Detroit's gain, however, is likely to come at the expense of U.S. consumers. For them, Japan's decision announced yesterday to maintain a 2.3 million-car limit on annual exports to the U.S. means the most popular Japanese cars probably will remain expensive and in short supply.

"The impact of the quotas is quite heavy on the consumer," said a spokesman for Toyota Motor Corp.'s U.S. sales arm. "You're just making people pay more for products, and the extra money is going into Detroit's pocket, and ours."

Begun in 1981

The quotas were first established in 1981 as a device to give U.S. auto makers time to recover from the nation's deep recession. Detroit's Big Three, however, have earned near-record profits in the past 2 years, so the auto makers are using different arguments to press for continued quotas. Chief among them: the overall U.S. trade deficit is so bad that almost any measure is justified to reduce it.

Source: The Wall Street Journal

Trade restrictions imposed by the United States.

cratic restrictions are also similar to the effects of a tariff, since paying employees to handle the red tape is like paying a tax. The main difference is that the government does not collect the tariff revenue. Instead, Area C in Figure 15 represents spending by foreign firms to comply with the government's bureaucratic procedures.[13]

Scope of Protectionism

How much does protectionism cost? A recent study estimates that in 1990, protectionism cost U.S. consumers about $70 billion per year (about $270 per person each year).[14] Domestic producers gained about $35 billion from these restrictions, and they brought the government about $13 billion in revenue, so the net loss to the U.S. economy from

---

[13]Trade with some countries requires paying bribes to appropriate officials; the effects of these bribes resemble the effects of tariffs.

[14]See Gary Clyde Hufbauer and Kimberly Ann Elliott, *Measuring the Costs of Protection in the United States* (Washington, D.C.: Institute for International Economics, 1994).

Table 3 | Losses and Gains Due to Protectionism (1990 $ millions)

Protected Industry	Loss to American Consumers	Gain to American Producers	Gain to U.S. Government	Net Loss to U.S. Economy
Ceramics and tiles	$ 241	$ 63	$ 173	$ 5
Costume jewelry	103	46	51	5
Frozen concentrated orange juice	281	101	145	35
Glassware	266	162	95	9
Luggage	211	16	169	26
Rubber footwear	208	55	141	12
Women's footwear (excluding athletic shoes)	376	70	295	11
Apparel	21,158	9,901	3,545	7,712 (2,301)[a]
Textiles	3,274	1,749	632	894 (181)[a]
Canned tuna	73	31	31	10 (4)[a]
Machine tools	542	157	0	385 (35)[a]

[a]The first figure shows the net loss to the U.S. economy; the second figure (in parentheses) shows that loss after including the gains to foreign firms from U.S. protectionism.
Source: Gary Clyde Hufbauer and Kimberly Ann Elliott, *Measuring the Costs of Protection in the United States* (Washington, D.C.: Institute for International Economics, 1994).

protectionism was about $22 billion per year (about $85 per person each year). Table 3 summarizes the losses to consumers and gains to producers in certain industries.

Governments engage in less protectionism now than they did in the past. The average U.S. tariff rate in 1920 was 16 percent. It increased to 38 percent in 1922, partly because the government raised tariffs and partly because those rates rose automatically due to falling prices.[15] The Smoot-Hawley Act of 1930 and more increases in tariff rates due to falling prices raised the average U.S. tariff rate to 53 percent, though tariffs applied to only about one-third of U.S. imports.

In 1947, many countries signed the General Agreement on Tariffs and Trade (GATT) agreement to reduce trade restrictions. The GATT also established an international organization in Geneva, Switzerland, to assist trade negotiations and work to reduce restrictions on trade. The most recent round of international trade talks has renamed the GATT as the World Trade Organization (WTO).

The **World Trade Organization (WTO)** is an international organization and a series of related treaties that reduce trade restrictions.

The WTO has helped to reduce world protectionism in the last half of the 20th century. The United States reduced its tariffs to an average of about 25 percent, covering only about one-tenth of its imports, by 1960. Other countries also reduced trade restrictions. The Kennedy Round of trade talks in 1967 further reduced tariffs to an average of about 12 percent, covering only 7 percent of imports. The Tokyo Round in 1979 reduced U.S. tariff rates to 6 percent, covering only 4 percent of imports, with similar reductions in other countries.

The WTO now includes 132 countries. The latest agreement, the Uruguay Round,

---

[15] If a good costs $10 and the tariff is $2, then the tariff rate is 20 percent. If the price of the good falls to $5 and the tariff stays at $2, the tariff rate rises to 40 percent. Prices fell from 1920 to 1922, which automatically raised tariff rates.

emerged from 8 years of negotiations ending in 1994. In that agreement, the United States and the European Union agreed to cut tariffs on each others' goods in half (on average) and to cut tariffs on goods from other countries by a smaller amount. On average, the Uruguay Round reduced world tariffs by about one-third, and it requires countries to replace import quotas on many products with more visible tariffs. The agreement also included pioneering provisions on certain products, such as farm products and intellectual property (protection of patents, copyrights, and trademarks).[16] The agreement gave the WTO new powers to resolve trade disputes more quickly and at lower cost than previous arrangements allowed. Estimates suggest that the agreement will eventually raise U.S. real GDP by about $100 billion per year and world real GDP by about $300 billion.

Regional free trade agreements include the North American Free Trade Agreement (NAFTA) and the European Union (EU). NAFTA began with a 1989 agreement between Canada and the United States to eliminate most trade restrictions between the two countries. Its coverage was extended in 1993 to include Mexico, and it phases out most restrictions on trade with that country by 2004. In the coming years, NAFTA may expand to include other countries in the American continents, such as Chile. The EU established free trade among 15 nations of Europe and common policies toward non-EU countries. Four additional European nations have formed a European Free Trade Association (EFTA) to participate in free trade with EU countries.

The increasing economic integration of Europe has important consequences for the United States and other countries. About 400 million people live in EU and EFTA countries, roughly as many as in the United States and Japan combined. Free trade within Europe will help to raise European standards of living in the future. If trade restrictions between Europe and other countries remain low, the gains will be even larger, and most of the world will share those gains. If the European countries impose bigger trade barriers with countries outside the continent, however, the United States, Japan, and other countries could suffer. Some analysts are concerned that regional free trade agreements in Europe and North America will reduce the incentives for world free trade; other analysts see these agreements as steps toward that goal.

Review Questions

17. What are tariffs, import quotas, and voluntary export restraints?

18. What is the WTO? What is the NAFTA? What is the EU?

Thinking Exercise

19. Draw a graph to show the effects of *eliminating* a tariff. Who gains and who loses from eliminating a tariff? Show the sizes of these gains and losses on your graph.

Groups that favor trade restrictions (usually to benefit themselves) have advanced many arguments to justify their positions. Economists generally agree that these arguments are usually incorrect, and that legitimate arguments do not apply to most real-life cases of trade restrictions. This section considers some of the most common arguments for protectionism.

COMMON ARGUMENTS FOR PROTECTIONISM

---

[16] It failed to resolve trade disputes, however, on certain products such as movies, television shows, and music, as well as shipping and financial services.

Argument 1: Domestic Firms Need Trade Restrictions to Compete in World Markets

This argument is fallacious because every country has a comparative advantage in certain products. Domestic firms can profitably sell those products in world markets if they produce them. Firms that produce other products, those in which the country has no comparative advantage, fail to compete on world markets because their costs are higher than the costs of foreign firms. Losses at those firms, along with profits at firms producing the products at which the country has a comparative advantage, provide incentives to direct the nation's resources to their most economically efficient uses.

One form of this argument supports protection to bolster domestic competitiveness by claiming that domestic producers cannot compete on world markets because foreign countries pay lower wages in all industries. For this reason, the argument goes, no domestic producers in any industry can compete in world markets. Imagine what would happen if every domestic firm faced competition from foreign sellers who could charge lower prices based on lower costs. All domestic firms would lose most of their customers to foreign competitors. Domestic firms would lay off workers, and the demand for labor would fall. This would reduce wages until costs at some domestic firms fall to below the costs of their foreign competitors (adjusted for differences in productivity). These firms would produce the goods in which the domestic country has a comparative advantage. In summary, the level of wages adjusts so that (in equilibrium) firms in every country can compete in world markets.[17]

Argument 2: Trade Restrictions Protect Domestic Jobs

Trade restrictions save jobs in some industries, but they eliminate jobs in other industries. Suppose that the United States imposes a tariff on imports of foreign cars. This policy raises the price of cars in the United States and raises sales of American-made cars. The tariff creates jobs in the protected American car industry, but it destroys jobs in other industries for two reasons. First, American consumers spend more on cars than they would spend without the tariff, leaving them less income to spend on other products (movies, clothes, food, and so on). Sales of these other products fall, destroying jobs in those industries. Second, foreigners earn fewer dollars than they would earn without the tariff, because they sell fewer cars to U.S. buyers; this reduces their spending on American products and destroys jobs in various American industries. On net, trade restrictions have little effect on total employment.[18]

Note on Trade Deficits

What happens if foreigners do not spend the dollars they earn to buy American products? This creates a trade deficit for the United States. For example, in 1997 the United States imported $1,045 billion in goods and services from other countries and exported only $932 billion. Foreigners earned $1,045 billion by selling products in the United States (plus $53 billion from the United States in gifts, foreign aid, and net income on U.S. investments), but they spent only $932 billion of that money on American goods and services. The rest of the money—$166 billion—they loaned back to people in the United States and invested in U.S. assets (such as real estate and stocks). As a result, the Americans who borrowed this money or sold these assets acquired $166 billion for

Advice

Don't be confused by the fact that wages in the United States are higher than those in most other countries of the world. American firms can compete effectively in world markets, even when workers in many other countries earn lower wages in *every* industry, because productivity at American firms is substantially higher than productivity in those other countries. Differences in productivity result from differences in workers' education, skills, and experience, from differences in equipment per worker and in equipment quality, and from differences in technology.

[17] Wages in the United States are higher than those in most other countries of the world, but American firms nevertheless compete effectively in world markets, because productivity at American firms is substantially higher than the levels in most other countries.

[18] Much international trade occurs in intermediate products, which become inputs into production of other, final products. Restricting imports of intermediate products raises costs at domestic firms that use them as inputs. The cost increases reduce those firms' supplies of final products, reduce their equilibrium sales, and reduce employment at those firms.

their own spending. For this reason, a trade deficit does not necessarily affect total spending on American-made products. Foreigners spent $166 billion less on American products than Americans spent on foreign products and gave as gifts, but foreigners loaned that money back to Americans to spend.[19]

Argument 3: Trade Restrictions Raise Wages

Trade restrictions do not necessarily raise domestic wages. If a country has a comparative advantage in producing a product that requires a relatively large input of labor, then international trade tends to raise that country's wages. Trade restrictions tend to reduce its wages rather than raising them. In other cases, however, international trade can reduce wages, so restricting international trade can raise them. Even in these circumstances, however, restricting international trade reduces a country's *total* income.

While expanding international trade has benefited the United States as a whole, it has created winners and losers. Economists continue to gather and interpret evidence on the fall in wages of low-skilled U.S. workers that began in the early 1970s, and some evidence indicates that expansion of international trade has played a role (although most evidence attributes a much larger role to technological change). Trade restrictions by the United States would redistribute income, raising wages in certain industries at the expense of other people and reducing total U.S. income. Restrictions on international trade are probably a less efficient method of redistributing income than a simple program of taxing some people to fund payments to others.

Argument 4: Trade Restrictions Level the Playing Field

Some people argue for trade restrictions to keep a so-called "level playing field" in international trade. ("Other countries restrict imports, so we should, too.") International trade differs from a football game or a war, though. International trade, like all voluntary trade, occurs because both sides expect to gain, and both sides usually do. Trade restrictions reduce economic efficiency and redistribute income from domestic consumers to protected domestic producers, whether or not other countries impose their own trade restrictions.

Suppose that subsidies by the Korean government lead Korean firms to reduce the prices of goods they sell in the United States. Should the United States respond with trade restrictions to protect American firms that compete with those Korean firms? Notice that the Korean government's subsidies help American consumers, who can buy the Korean products at lower prices. The subsidies hurt American producers who compete with the Korean firms. Korean taxpayers lose, because they pay for the subsidies, while Korean firms benefit from the subsidies.

How large are these gains and losses? American consumers clearly gain more than American firms lose. To see why, notice that American firms must reduce prices to compete, but every dollar they lose by lowering prices is a gain to American buyers who pay those lower prices! In fact, American consumers gain even more, because they buy some Korean products at prices subsidized by Korean taxpayers. Therefore, the United States gains on net when a foreign government subsidizes its own producers that export to the U.S. market. Trade restrictions would prevent the domestic country from capturing those gains.[20]

---

[19]If foreigners did not lend the money back to Americans (and did not spend it on American products)—that is, if the foreigners simply kept the U.S. money—then the U.S. sellers would be in the enviable position of exporting pieces of paper (money) in return for goods and services that consumers want! Of course, most foreigners have little reason to keep U.S. money, so they do either spend it or lend it back to Americans.

[20]Sometimes people argue that a foreign government may subsidize its producers only long enough to drive domestic firms out of business, then eliminate the subsidies. Little evidence suggests that this scenario happens in real life. If domestic firms expect a foreign government to discontinue its subsidy in the future, they reduce production only temporarily and resume production when the subsidies stop. As a result, this argument provides little justification for trade restrictions.

Another version of the level playing field argument supports trade restrictions by claiming that foreign firms sometimes charge lower prices on exports than they charge for sales in their own countries. This practice, popularly called *dumping,* is illegal in the United States, and most countries restrict imports of goods from foreign firms that they find guilty of dumping. For example, in 1985, the United States required Japanese semiconductor producers to raise the prices they charged to American buyers.

Who gains and who loses from dumping? The answer resembles the case of foreign subsidies. Consumers benefit from low prices if a foreign firm dumps. Firms that compete with the foreign firm lose, because they must match its low prices or lose customers. However, domestic buyers gain every dollar that domestic firms lose by lowering their prices. In addition, buyers gain from the reduced price at which they purchase foreign products. Therefore dumping benefits domestic consumers more than it hurts domestic producers.[21] One study estimated that U.S. trade restrictions imposed in retaliation for dumping cost American consumers $2.6 billion per year and create a net annual loss to the U.S. economy of roughly $1 billion.

Argument 5: Temporary Trade Restrictions Help New Industries Get Started

Some people argue that infant industries—new industries that are not yet well-established—need protection from foreign competition until they recover high start-up costs. Without trade restrictions, the argument claims, these firms could not compete with foreign firms for the first few years, even though they could compete in the future. This argument suggests a need for temporary trade restrictions to give the new firms a chance to develop.

The main problem with this argument comes from the capital market. If investors foresee expected future profits high enough to justify the infant firms' losses for the first few years, then they would accept short-term losses in return for the prospects of future profits. If expected future profits are not high enough to compensate investors for losses in the first few years, then the infant industry is an economically inefficient use of the economy's resources. Efficiency would improve by diverting the resources to other industries. Because trade restrictions would allow infant firms to raise domestic prices high enough to profit in the short run, they essentially force buyers to subsidize infant industries by paying the high prices.

Argument 6: Trade Restrictions Help National Defense

Some people argue that free trade creates political danger, because it creates too much specialization. Suppose that a country has no comparative advantage in producing military equipment or some other product important for national defense. With free trade, the country may import these products rather than produce them. Proponents of the national-defense argument see a danger in this arrangement, because a country cannot rely on imports in wartime. (It might even fight the country from which it imports war materials.) This national-defense argument suggests that a country may benefit militarily (at the cost of some economic inefficiency) from trade restrictions in certain industries with critical importance to national defense. While this national-defense argument may apply to a few industries, it has little application to most real-life trade restrictions.

Argument 7: Strategic Trade Policy Can Move Other Nations toward Freer Trade

A strategic trade policy is a national policy to encourage other governments to reduce their trade restrictions. Strategic trade policies often involve threats to impose new trade

IN THE NEWS

Imported sweaters face duty

U.S. finds dumping by Far East makers

By Clyde H. Farnsworth
Special to the New York Times

WASHINGTON, April 23—In an action that could lead to higher prices for sweaters in the United States and increase trade tensions with nations in the Far East, the Commerce Department ruled today that Hong Kong, South Korea, and Taiwan were dumping sweaters on the American market and that importers should pay penalty duties.

Source: New York Times

Dumping can provide governments with an excuse for trade restrictions.

---

[21] Dumping is illegal in most countries, presumably, because domestic firms (who are harmed by dumping) have stronger political influence on this issue than domestic consumers have.

IN THE NEWS

U.S. tariff appears to backfire

Japan is retaliating for 63% charge on computer screens

By David E. Sanger
Special to the New York Times

TOKYO, Sept. 25—A month and a half after the United States imposed a 63 percent tariff on the most advanced screens for laptop and notebook computers, the Japanese have begun to retaliate.

Some companies have said they will stop sending the screens to the United States, and the Toshiba Corporation, one of the largest Japanese companies to make computers in the United States, has said it is moving its operations abroad to obtain the screens without paying the tariffs.

Thus, the retaliation will hurt the many American computer makers that rely on the Japanese screens and could lead to a loss of American jobs. The tariff was intended to protect a nascent sector of the American computer industry.

Canada puts levies on steel sheets of U.S., 5 nations

By John Urquhart
Staff Reporter of The Wall Street Journal

OTTAWA—Canada, in a retaliatory move, placed stiff antidumping levies on steel sheet imports from the U.S. and five other countries.

The case is one of three antidumping actions that were initiated by Canadian steel producers last year after the U.S. steel industry filed unfair trade complaints against steelmakers in Canada and 18 other countries.

Sources: New York Times,
The Wall Street Journal

Strategic trade policy may reduce foreign trade restrictions, but at the risk of causing a trade war.

restrictions unless other nations reduce their own restrictions. Some people believe that strategic trade policy can help to reduce worldwide trade restrictions. Others emphasize the potential danger from trade wars in which both countries raise restrictions with each other's exports, and every country loses.

Causes of Protectionism

Most restrictions on international trade result from political action by the interest groups who benefit from those restrictions. Trade restrictions, like many other government policies, create winners and losers. The winners, often relatively small, concentrated groups of people or firms, have strong incentives to lobby the government for policies that help them and to provide campaign contributions for cooperative politicians. Industry associations provide ready forums for groups to organize for effective political persuasion.

Losers from trade restrictions are usually members of large, diffuse groups who suffer relatively small per-person losses, giving each individual little incentive to spend the time and money to organize effective opposition to the trade restrictions. The losers may even be unaware of the effects of trade restrictions on the prices they pay. For these reasons, the groups that lose from trade restrictions often wield less political power than the groups that gain.

Restrictions on imports of children's pajamas may raise the price by $0.50 per pair, hardly noticeable to any one consumer. A firm selling 1 million pairs of pajamas, however, may earn an extra $500,000 from the import restrictions. The incentive for producers to lobby for restrictions is much stronger than the incentive for individual consumers to give the matter a second thought, let alone take the time to gather information, organize with other consumers, and lobby to eliminate the restrictions.

Transition to Free Trade

Eliminating trade restrictions creates losers as well as winners. Some firms lose sales, as buyers choose to import foreign products; other firms gain sales, as foreigners spend the dollars they earn from their exports. Because workers who lose their jobs need time to find new ones, the removal of trade barriers can cause short-term unemployment. Some people argue that the government should help workers who lose from the removal of trade restrictions, perhaps by providing increased unemployment compensation or job training. Some people argue that this adjustment assistance is not only fair, but that it also encourages free trade by easing the political process of removing trade restrictions. Other people argue against adjustment assistance, partly on the grounds that most changes in government policy help some people and hurt others, so they see nothing special about removing trade restrictions; these critics claim that the government could not possibly help everyone who is hurt by any change in government policies.

IN THE NEWS

As U.S. urges free markets, its trade barriers are many

By Keith Bradsher
Special to the New York Times

In comparison with Japan and America's other major trading partners, the United States is less protectionist—but many barriers to imports remain.

Quotas double the price of sugar in morning coffee and limit imports per American to no more than seven peanuts, a pound of dairy cheese, and a lick of ice cream each year. Fresh cream and milk are banned; frozen cream may be purchased only from New Zealand. And the Customs Service recently turned back a shipment of buttered croissants from France because it violated a quota on French butter shipments.

Imports of men's heavy and worsted wool suits are capped at 1.2 million, the equivalent of one for each male manager and professional every dozen years. The Commerce Department has imposed punitive duties on martial arts uniforms from Taiwan, awning window cranks from El Salvador, and the tiny pads for woodwind instrument keys from Italy after determining that they were being sold, or "dumped," at unfairly low prices.

Sprawling and Inconsistent

This sprawling and inconsistent collection of quotas, tariffs, and other barriers reflects lobbying by many industries, as well as the occasional national-security concern. The result has been higher prices for American consumers and fewer opportunities for millions of people in developing countries to escape poverty by growing crops or stitching clothes for people in wealthy countries.

Source: New York Times

Political forces, such as the relative political power of various groups, affect a country's trade policies.

Review Questions

20. Do some countries need trade restrictions to compete in world markets? Explain.

21. Do trade restrictions protect jobs? Explain.

22. Who loses and who gains if a foreign government subsidizes the exports of its country's producers?

23. What is a strategic trade policy? Cite one argument for and one argument against a strategic trade policy.

Conclusion

Scope of International Trade

International trade is an important and growing part of the world economy. Imports and exports each represent about one-eighth of U.S. GDP. Some countries have trade deficits, importing more than they export, while others have trade surpluses, exporting more than they import.

Comparative Advantage and the Gains from Trade

International trade, like a good technology, expands opportunities. International trade raises economic efficiency. Because all countries can share the gains from trade, it allows every country to consume more products than it can produce.

A country gains from trade by concentrating production on products in which it has a comparative advantage—a relatively low opportunity cost—and limiting production of goods in which it has a comparative disadvantage. It then exports the former products and imports the latter. This activity raises world output and consumption in every country.

Gains from International Trade: Graphical Analysis

Without international trade, each country's consumption is limited to what it can produce. International trade allows each country to consume more of *every* good than it can produce itself. Its consumption opportunities expand beyond its production possibilities frontier (PPF), because it can trade along a world price line, exporting some products and importing others. The slope of the world price line, in absolute value, gives the world relative price of the product on the horizontal axis of the graph. Equilibrium of world supply and demand determines the relative price.

Some individual people and firms gain from international trade, and others lose. When a country imports a good, its consumers gain because international trade reduces the good's price; firms whose products compete with the imported good lose. Consumers gain more than producers lose, however, so they could compensate the losers and still gain from international trade. Foreign exporters gain increases in sales, and foreign consumers lose because they pay a higher price for the good than they would pay without trade. Producers gain more than consumers lose, however, so on net both the importing country and the exporting country gain from trade.

Balance of Trade and the Current Account

A country runs a current account surplus if it lends money to other countries; a country that borrows experiences a current account deficit. A country's current account surplus equals its trade balance surplus plus its net income from past investments in other countries. A current account deficit results when a country saves less than it invests and borrows to finance the extra investment. A current account surplus results when a country saves more than it invests and lends the difference to people in other countries. Trade deficits are not good or bad per se; they each reflect underlying economic conditions.

Protectionism

Protectionism advocates government policies to restrict imports as protection for domestic producers from foreign competitors. Trade restrictions almost always hurt the country as a whole (ignoring the distribution of income), but they also create winners and losers. The two most prominent forms of restrictions on international trade are tariffs (taxes on imports) and import quotas (restrictions on the number of units of a particular product imported into a country). Other trade restrictions include voluntary export restraints, local content requirements, and bureaucratic (red tape) protectionism. Tariffs raise the domestic price of a product by taxing imported goods. Domestic producers benefit, but domestic consumers lose more than the producers gain. Other trade restrictions have similar effects. Trade restrictions may also provoke foreign retaliation.

The costs of protectionism are difficult to estimate. U.S. protectionism alone probably costs consumers about $70 billion per year (about $270 per person each year), while providing about a $35 billion gain to domestic producers and a $13 billion gain to the government. The U.S.

economy experiences a net loss from U.S. protectionism of about $22 billion per year (about $85 per person each year). Many countries have signed treaties to expand free international trade, and have joined the World Trade Organization (WTO). Other important agreements include the North American Free Trade Agreement (NAFTA), the European Union (EU), and the European Free Trade Association (EFTA).

Common Arguments for Protectionism

Some people argue fallaciously that domestic producers need trade restrictions to compete in world markets. In practice, the level of wages adjusts so that, in equilibrium, firms in every country can compete in world markets. Some people also claim that trade restrictions save jobs. While trade restrictions protect jobs in some industries, they eliminate jobs in other industries. Trade restrictions have little effect on overall employment.

Some people argue for trade restrictions to support high wages, because low foreign wages give cost advantages to foreign producers. In some circumstances, restrictions on international trade can keep wages higher than they would be with free trade, but even in these circumstances, restricting international trade reduces the economy's total income.

Trade restrictions are not necessary to level the playing field in international trade. International trade differs from a sporting contest or a war, because both sides win when they trade. (Everyone can gain from a voluntary trade.) Trade restrictions reduce economic efficiency and redistribute income from domestic consumers to protected domestic producers, whether or not other countries impose their own trade restrictions.

Another argument for trade restrictions urges temporary protection for infant industries with high start-up costs until they establish themselves. If investors expected future industry profits high enough to justify losses for a few years, however, they would willingly accept short-term losses in return for future profits; the industry would not need temporary protection from foreign competition. Trade restrictions essentially force buyers to subsidize economically inefficient industries.

Some people argue that trade restrictions are necessary to protect national defense. This argument may be important for a limited number of industries, but probably has little bearing on most real-life trade restrictions. Finally, some people argue that trade restrictions can help to provide leverage in bargaining with other countries to reduce their own restrictions. Such a strategic trade policy may invite further foreign retaliation and start a trade war, however, in which trade restrictions increase and every country loses.

Most real-life restrictions on international trade result from political action by the interest groups who benefit from those restrictions. The benefits of trade restrictions are usually concentrated in a small group of winners, who have an incentive to lobby for those restrictions, while the (larger) costs are spread out among many people, each of whom has little individual incentive to actively oppose the restrictions.

Key Terms

export

import

balance of international trade

trade surplus or deficit

comparative advantage

current account

current account surplus
  or deficit

tariff

import quota

World Trade
  Organization (WTO)

Questions and Problems

24. Make up a simple numerical example to show the gains from international trade.

25. Draw graphs like Figure 10 to show why the gains from trade are *larger* when trading countries are more different in the equilibrium relative prices that they would have in the absence of international trade.

26. Draw a graph to illustrate the effects of an import quota. Who gains and who loses from the quota? Show the sizes of the gains and losses on your graph. How large are the gains and losses to each country and to the world economy as a whole?

27. Consider the example from Figures 11 and 12, but suppose that the world equilibrium relative price of videos is *one* computer program per music video (that is, they have the same price).
   (a) Draw graphs like those in Figure 11 to show consumption opportunities in the United States and Japan if they trade.
   (b) Does the United States gain more from international trade if the relative price of music videos is one-half or one computer program? Explain why.

28. Suppose that the United States and Japan can produce either CD players or wheat. Each country has 60 person-days available for work. The table shows the labor required to produce each product:

Costs of Production: Labor Time to Produce 1 Unit

	United States	Japan
CD player (1 unit)	10 person-days	12 person-days
Wheat (1 ton)	1 person-day	2 person-days

(a) Draw (to scale) each country's production possibilities frontier (PPF).

(b) Which country has a comparative advantage in which product?

(c) Suppose that the world equilibrium price of a CD player is $80 and the world price of wheat is $10 per ton. What is the relative price of CD players in terms of wheat? Which country would produce which product at these prices?

(d) Add world price lines to your PPF graphs, and use those graphs to show why international trade allows each country to consume more than it could without trading.

Inquiries for Further Thought

29. What imported goods do you consume? What goods that you use have some imported parts (perhaps inside)?

30. Suppose that states in the United States could not trade with each other. What goods or services would you lose the opportunity to buy?
    (a) How much would your standard of living fall? (Be sure to think about inputs into production of goods that you buy.)
    (b) How much would your standard of living fall if governments were to prohibit international trade? How much would it rise if governments were to eliminate all restrictions and taxes on international trade?

31. What U.S. jobs depend on international trade?

32. When the U.S. government chooses its trade policies, should it take into account only the effects on people in the United States, or should it also consider the effects on people in other countries? For example, suppose that a policy would help the United States by $5 million and hurt people in other countries by $6 million. Should the government adopt that policy? What if it would hurt people in other countries by $60 million? What if the policy would hurt people in the United States by $5 million, but help people in other countries by $6 million or by $60 million?

33. Why would the government impose import quotas rather than levying tariffs? (It could collect revenue from tariffs, but the gains from quotas go to foreign sellers.)

34. The government of Italy subsidizes its steel industry. Italy also exports steel to the United States. How does Italy's subsidy affect U.S. consumers and steel producers? Some people say that the United States should impose an import quota or tariff in a case like this. (The U.S. government does set quotas in the form of voluntary export restraints.) Do you agree that Italian steel imports should face trade restrictions? If so, how big should they be, and who would gain and lose from the quota or tariff?

accounting profit–total revenue minus total cost as measured on accounting statements (p. 271)

activist view of policy–the view that the economy often operates inefficiently on its own and that government macroeconomic policies can improve its efficiency (p. 774)

adverse selection–a situation in which sellers have relevant information that buyers lack (or vice-versa) about some aspect of product quality (p. 459)

agent–the person hired to do something for a principal (p. 453)

aggregate demand curve–a graph showing the total amount of goods and services that people, firms, and the government would buy at each possible price level, given the nominal money supply and velocity (p. 723)

aggregate demand multiplier–the ratio of the ultimate increase in aggregate demand, due to an exogenous rise in spending, to that initial increase in spending (p. 754)

aggregate supply curve–a graph showing the total amount of goods and services that firms would produce and try to sell at each possible price level (p. 726)

antitrust law–legal prohibition of monopolies and cartels or monopoly-like behaviors (p. 338)

appreciation–an increase in the value of one money in terms of another (so that the price of foreign money falls) (p. 674)

arbitrage opportunity–a recognized price differential that exceeds the costs of arbitrage (p. 160)

arbitrage–buying a good at a place where its price is low and reselling it where its price is higher (p. 160)

area–a number that measures the size of some specific region in a graph (p. 39)

Arrow impossibility theorem–under very general conditions, voting can produce inconsistent results (in the sense that A can beat B in an election while B beats C, but A does not beat C) even if all voters make consistent choices (p. 528)

automatic stabilizer–a feature of government policy that automatically changes taxes or spending to try to

reduce fluctuations in real GDP, without any explicit actions of the government (p. 818)

average cost–total cost divided by the quantity produced (p. 264)

average fixed cost–total fixed cost divided by the quantity produced (p. 282)

average product of labor–total production divided by the number of hours worked (p. 576)

average revenue–total revenue divided by the quantity produced (p. 264)

average tax rate–a person's tax payment as a percentage of income (p. 520)

average total cost–total cost divided by the quantity produced (p. 283)

average variable cost–total variable cost divided by the quantity produced (p. 282)

backward-bending labor supply curve–a labor supply curve with a negatively sloped portion (p. 396)

balance of international trade–the value of a country's exports minus that of its imports (p. 869)

balanced budget–when tax receipts equal spending (p. 804)

bank reserves–the deposits that banks have *not* loaned (p. 695)

bank run–when many people try at the same time to withdraw their money from a bank that lacks sufficient reserves (p. 706)

banking panic–simultaneous runs on many banks (p. 706)

barriers to entry–a cost high enough to prevent potential competitors from entering an industry (p. 329)

best response–the action that maximizes a firm's profit, given the actions of rivals (p. 368, 377)

black market–a market for illegal transactions (p. 184)

bond–an IOU for a long-term debt, typically on a loan lasting 10 years or more (p. 837)

budget deficit–a negative surplus, or government spending minus (smaller) tax revenue (p. 804)

budget line–a graph of a person's possible choices (p. 236)

budget surplus–tax revenue minus (smaller) government spending (p. 804)

call option–a right to buy some underlying asset during some specified period of time at some preset strike price (p. 857)

capacity output–the level of output that minimizes average total cost (p. 283)

capital gain (or **capital loss**)–an increase (or decrease) in the value of an asset (p. 840)

capital–the stock of equipment, structures, inventories, human skills, and knowledge available to help produce goods and services (p. 556)

capture view of regulation–the assertion that regulatory agencies originally established to serve the general public interest end up serving the special interests of the industries they were intended to regulate (p. 510)

cartel–a group of firms that try to collude to act as a single monopoly (p. 334)

central bank–a bank for banks (p. 701)

change in demand–a change in the numbers in the demand schedule and a shift in the demand curve (p. 76)

change in quantity demanded–a movement along a demand curve due to a change in price (p. 77)

change in quantity supplied–a movement along a supply curve due to a change in price (p. 84)

change in supply–a change in the numbers in the supply schedule and a shift in the supply curve (p. 83)

commercial paper–a short-term debt security (usually with a 30-day maturity) issued by a private firm (p. 838)

commitment to a policy rule–an action by a policy maker to guarantee implementation of the rule (p. 783)

common resource–a resource that belongs to no one or to society as a whole (p. 480)

comparative advantage–the ability to produce a product at a lower opportunity cost than the costs that other countries would incur (p. 54, 871)

compensating differential–a difference in wages that offsets differences in nonpay features of jobs (p. 403)

complement–a good used in combination with another, so that a rise in the price of one decreases demand for the other (p. 79)

concentrated interest–a benefit limited to a small group of people or firms (p. 510)

constant costs–long-run average cost that does not change with the quantity of output (p. 265)

constant-cost industry–an industry with a perfectly elastic long-run market supply curve (p. 312)

consumer surplus–the benefit to a consumer of buying a good at the equilibrium price (p. 208)

consumption of a good–the amount that people use for their current benefit (wearing, eating, driving, or watching the good, for example) (p. 154)

consumption–spending by people on final goods and services for current use (p. 555)

contingent policy rule–a rule that states specifically how policies will depend on economic circumstances (p. 778)

correlation–a measure of how closely two variables are related (p. 28)

cost-benefit analysis–the process of identifying and comparing the costs and benefits of a regulation, tax, or other policy (p. 503)

coupon payment–an interest payment that a borrower makes to a bondholder (p. 837)

Cournot model–a model of oligopoly in which each firm believes that other firms will react to its decisions by changing their prices to maintain fixed levels of output and sales (p. 369)

credible policy rule–a rule that people believe policy makers will follow, perhaps because they have an incentive to follow it (p. 783)

cross-price elasticity of demand (or supply)–percentage change in the quantity demanded (or supplied) divided by the percentage change in the price of a related good (p. 112)

crowding out of private investment–a fall in equilibrium investment when government borrowing raises the real interest rate (p. 620)

currency board–an institution whose sole purpose is to keep a foreign exchange rate fixed by acting as a residual buyer or seller of the country's money at that price (p. 790)

currency reform–replacement of an old form of money with a new one, with automatic adjustment of all nominal values in existing contracts, such as nominal wages and nominal debts, to keep real values the same (p. 666)

currency–all the paper money and coins owned by people and business firms (p. 694)

current account deficit–net borrowing from other countries (p. 878)

current account surplus–net lending to other countries (p. 878)

current account–the amount that a country lends to or borrows from other countries (p. 878)

deadweight social loss–the consumer and producer surplus that people could get by eliminating an economic inefficiency (p. 218)

decrease in demand–a decrease in the quantity demanded at a given price and a leftward shift in the demand curve (p. 77)

decrease in supply–a decrease in the quantity supplied at a given price and a leftward shift in the supply curve (p. 84)

decreasing costs–long-run average cost that falls with an increase in output (p. 266)

default–failure to repay a loan in full (p. 838)

demand curve–a graph of the relation between the price of a good and the quantity demanded (p. 72)

demand deposit–a balance in a bank account that you can withdraw on demand by writing a check (p. 694)

depreciation–a fall in the value of a resource over time (p. 269)

depreciation–a fall in the value of one money in terms of another (so that the price of foreign money rises) (p. 674)

devaluation–a fall in the value of a currency on foreign exchange markets (an increase in the price of foreign currency in terms of domestic currency) (p. 789)

differentiated product–a product that buyers consider to be a good, but not perfect, substitute for another (p. 349)

diffuse interest–a benefit spread across many people (p. 510)

discounted present value (of a future amount of money)–the money you would need to save and invest today to end up with a specific amount of money in the future (p. 291)

discounted present value–the value today of a future payment of money (p. 597)

discretionary policy–choice of policy actions according to judgments of policymakers (p. 778)

disequilibrium–a situation in which the

quantity demanded does not equal the quantity supplied at the current price (p. 86)

distribution of prices–a situation in which some sellers charge higher prices than others charge (p. 448)

diversification–spreading risks across many different, unrelated investments (p. 450)

diversification–spreading risks by choosing many unrelated investments or investments whose payoffs are out of step (p. 836)

dividend–a regular cash payment from a firm to stockholders (p. 845)

economic cost–the sum of all opportunity costs, that is, all explicit and implicit costs (p. 270)

economic growth–a rise in real GDP per person (p. 627)

economic model–a description of logical thinking about an economic issue expressed in words, graphs, or mathematical symbols (p. 19)

economic profit–total revenue minus total economic cost (p. 271)

economically efficient change–a change in which the winners could compensate the losers by enough to make the change a Pareto improvement (p. 215)

economically efficient situation–a situation with no additional economically efficient changes to make (p. 215)

economically efficient–a situation that cannot be changed so that someone gains unless someone else loses (p. 57, 251)

economically inefficient situation–a situation with additional economically efficient changes yet to be made (p. 216)

economically inefficient–a situation that can be changed so that at least one person gains while no one else loses (p. 57)

economics–the study of people's choices and what happens to make everyone's choices compatible (p. 5)

effective labor input–labor input adjusted for knowledge and skills (p. 639)

efficiency wage–a wage above equilibrium intended to raise worker productivity (p. 413)

efficient markets theory–the argument that stock prices are random walks (p. 851)

egalitarianism–view that fairness requires equal results (p. 429)

elastic demand (or supply)–elasticity exceeding 1 (p. 103, 108)

elasticity of demand (or supply)–percentage change in the quantity demanded (or supplied) divided by the percentage change in price (p. 102, 108)

entrepreneur–a person who conceives and acts on a new business idea and takes the risk of its success or failure (p. 304)

entry–when a firm begins producing and selling an industry's product (p. 366)

equation of exchange–the equation $MV = Py$ (p. 583)

equilibrium price level–the price level that equates the quantity of money demanded with the quantity supplied (p. 663)

equilibrium price–the price at equilibrium (p. 86)

equilibrium quantity–the quantity at equilibrium (p. 86)

equilibrium rate of inflation–the growth rate of the equilibrium price level (p. 669)

equilibrium unemployment–unemployment that results from continuing changes in supplies and demands and the costs of searching for and matching jobs in labor markets (p. 586)

equilibrium–a situation in which the quantity supplied equals the quantity demanded (p. 86)

evidence–any set of facts that helps to convince people that a positive statement is true or false (p. 19)

excess capacity–the opportunity for a firm to reduce its average cost by raising its output (p. 356)

excess demand (shortage)–a situation in which the quantity demanded exceeds the quantity supplied (p. 87)

excess supply (surplus)–a situation in which the quantity supplied exceeds the quantity demanded (p. 88)

exchange rate–the price of foreign money (p. 673)

exhaustible resource–a resource that cannot be physically replenished and is depleted in production (p. 640)

exit–when a firm stops selling an industry's product (p. 306)

expected value–an average of every possible value that a variable can take, weighted by the chance of that value occurring (p. 833)

expected value–an average of numbers weighted by the probabilities (chances) that they will occur (p. 446)

export–a sale of goods or services to people in another country (p. 154, 556, 868)

externality–a difference between the private and social costs or benefits (p. 468)

fallacy of composition–false reasoning that what is true for one person must be true for the economy as a whole (p. 25)

federal funds rate–the interest rate that banks charge each other for short-term loans of reserves (p. 703)

Federal Reserve discount rate–the interest rate that the Fed charges banks for short-term loans (p. 703)

Federal Reserve System–an independent agency of the U.S. government that serves as the country's central bank (p. 701)

fiat money–paper money that is not backed by a commodity in the sense that people cannot trade it for a particular commodity at a fixed nominal price (p. 692)

financial asset–a right to collect some payment or series of payments in the future (p. 832)

financial intermediary–an organization that accumulates money from lenders (savers) and lends it to borrowers (spenders) (p. 705)

fiscal policy–government actions that change government spending, taxes, or both (p. 802)

fixed (or pegged) exchange rate system–system in which the government buys or sells the country's currency in whatever amounts are necessary to keep its exchange rate at a particular level (p. 787)

fixed cost–an unavoidable cost of a fixed input (p. 278)

fixed input–an input whose quantity a firm cannot change in the short run (p. 278)

fixed resource–a natural resource that cannot be replenished but is not depleted in production such as land (p. 639)

floating (or flexible) exchange rate system–system in which the government does not actively trade in foreign exchange markets to influence exchange rates (p. 787)

free entry or exit–entry or exit opportunities with no legal barriers (p. 306)

free-rider problem–the challenge of getting anyone to help pay for a public good when each individual can enjoy it freely if other people buy it (p. 491)

fundamental price–the discounted present value of a stock's expected future dividends (p. 852)

futures market–a market in which people buy and sell goods for future delivery (p. 172)

futures market–a market for trading contracts for future delivery of goods or assets (p. 856)

futures price–the price of a good for delivery at a future date (p. 172)

game theory–general theory of strategic behavior (p. 376)

GDP deflator–nominal GDP divided by real GDP (p. 551)

gold exchange standard–a system in which people trade paper money that is backed by gold stored in a warehouse (p. 692)

government budget deficit–the money that the government must borrow when it spends more money than it collects in taxes (p. 126, 170)

government budget deficit–government spending in excess of tax receipts (p. 601)

government debt–the amount of money the government owes because it has borrowed money in the past (p. 805)

government purchases–total spending on goods and services by federal, state, and local governments (p. 556)

gross domestic product (GDP)–the value of a country's production of final market goods and services during some time period (usually a year) (p. 549)

holding period yield–the rate of return a bond would provide over some specified period of time, perhaps less than the time until the bond matures (p. 840)

human capital–the skills, knowledge, and abilities of people (p. 401)

implicit cost–an opportunity cost that does not involve a direct payment (p. 270)

implicit labor contract–an informal agreement or understanding about the terms of employment (p. 412)

import quota–a government-imposed limit on the quantity of a good that can enter a country from foreign sources (p. 199, 882)

import–a purchase of goods or services from people in another country (p. 154, 557, 868)

income elasticity of demand–percentage change in quantity demanded divided by the percentage change in income (p. 112)

income–money received from all sources, measured as an amount per year (p. 78, 417)

increase in demand–an increase in the quantity demanded at a given price and a rightward shift in the demand curve (p. 76)

increase in supply–an increase in the quantity supplied at a given price and a rightward shift in the supply curve (p. 83)

increasing costs–long-run average cost that rises with an increase in output (p. 266)

increasing returns to scale–a situation in which average cost of production decreases as output rises (p. 331)

increasing-cost industry–an industry with an upward-sloping long-run market supply curve (p. 312)

indifference curve–a graph of combinations of goods between which a person is indifferent (p. 248)

inelastic demand (or supply)–elasticity less than 1 (p. 103, 108)

inferior good–a good whose demand falls if income rises (p. 78)

inflation tax–the loss that people suffer when inflation reduces the purchasing power of their assets (p. 681)

inflation–a continuing increase in the price level (the percentage increase in the average nominal price of goods and services) (p. 658)

interest rate–the price of a loan, expressed as a *percentage per year* of the amount loaned (p. 291, 597)

internalizing an externality–changing private costs or benefits so they equal social costs or benefits as a way to make people responsible for all the costs to other people of their own actions (p. 472)

isoquant–a–curve showing various technically efficient combinations of inputs that give the same amount of output (p. 296)

labor force–all the people who work in the market or who are looking for jobs in the market (p. 396)

labor turnover–the continuing flows of people into and out of the labor force, employment and unemployment, and various jobs (p. 406)

labor union–an organization of workers intended to improve the working conditions and pay of its members (p. 410)

laissez-faire view–the view that the economy usually operates efficiently on its own and, even when it does not, active government policies will more likely aggravate inefficiencies

and create new inefficiencies than alleviate problems (p. 777)

law of diminishing returns–the principle that raising the quantity of an input eventually reduces its marginal product, if the quantity of some other input remains fixed (p. 287, 577)

leveraged buyout (LBO)–a form of takeover financed by extensive borrowing, often pledging the assets of the takeover target as collateral for the loans (p. 863)

long run–a period of time over which people fully adjust their behavior to a change in conditions and over which a firm can change the quantities of all its inputs (p. 113, 261)

long-run demand (or supply)–the relation between the price of a good and the quantity demanded (or supplied) after people have fully adjusted to a price change (p. 113, 115)

long-run equilibrium–an equilibrium over a time long enough to allow firms to enter or exit the industry (p. 303, 307)

long-run Phillips Curve–a vertical line at the natural rate of unemployment (p. 746)

looser monetary policy–Fed actions that raise the growth rate of the money supply or decrease the federal funds rate (p. 713)

looser monetary policy–a policy that increases the growth rates of the monetary base and broader measures of the money supply, decreasing the federal funds rate (p. 775)

Lucas critique–the proposition that people do not always respond the same way to changes in economic conditions or government policies, because their responses depend partly on their expectations about the future, and those expectations can change (p. 782)

M1 money multiplier–the ratio of the M1 measure of the money supply to the monetary base (p. 698)

M1–a measure of the money supply that includes currency, demand deposits, other checkable deposits, and traveler's checks (p. 694)

M2–a measure of the money supply that combines M1 with balances in savings accounts, money market mutual funds, and similar accounts (p. 695)

managed-float exchange rate system–system in which the government sometimes trades in foreign

exchange markets to influence the exchange rate without maintaining a fixed rate (p. 788)

marginal benefit–the increase in total benefit from doing something a little more (p. 238)

marginal cost–the increase in total cost from doing something a little more (p. 240)

marginal product of labor–the *additional* production obtained from *increasing* labor a little, without changing the amounts of capital or natural resources (p. 576)

marginal rate of substitution–the largest amount of one good that you would be willing to trade away for an additional unit of another (p. 251, 254)

marginal revenue–the increase in total revenue from producing a little more of a good (p. 260)

marginal tax rate–the increase in a person's taxes when his income rises, expressed as a percentage of the increase in income (p. 520)

market demand curve–a graph of the relation between the price of a good and the market quantity demanded (p. 72)

market demand–demand for a good by all buyers, including the private sector and the government (p. 124)

market quantity demanded (at a given price)–the total amount of a good that all buyers in the economy would buy at that price (p. 72)

market quantity supplied (at some price)–the amount that all sellers in the economy would sell at that price (p. 82)

market supply curve–a graph of the relation between the price of a good and the market quantity supplied (p. 82)

markup (or profit margin)–price minus average cost (p. 303)

maximum legal price–(or price ceiling)–the highest price at which the government allows people to buy or sell a good (p. 180)

mean income–total income divided by the number of people (p. 418)

median income–the income level at which half of the population receive more income and half receive less (p. 418)

median voter–the voter whose views on a policy issue are in the middle of the spectrum, with half of the other voters on one side and half on the other side (p. 526)

median-voter theorem–the proposition that, under certain conditions, the equilibrium government policy chosen in political markets is the policy favored by the median voter (p. 526)

medium of exchange–an asset that sellers generally accept as payment for goods, services, and other assets (p. 690)

merger–when two firms voluntarily combine to form a single organization (p. 863)

minimum legal price (or price floor)–the lowest price at which the government allows people to buy or sell a good (p. 185)

misleading comparison–a comparison of two or more things that does not reflect their true differences (p. 26)

monetary base–a measure of the money supply that includes currency plus bank reserves (p. 696)

monetary policy–changes in a nation's nominal money supply through open market operations, changes in the discount rate or discount-window lending policy, or bank reserve requirement changes (p. 774)

monitoring–obtaining information about an agent's actions (perhaps by watching) (p. 455)

monopolistic competition–an industry in which (1) each firm sells a differentiated product; (2) enough firms compete that when one cuts its price, every other firm loses only a small quantity of its sales; and (3) the industry has free entry (p. 350)

monopoly–a firm that faces a downward-sloping demand curve for its product and makes decisions without considering the reactions of other firms (p. 321)

moral hazard–a situation in which a principal cannot observe the actions of an agent, who lacks an incentive to promote the best interests of the principal (p. 453)

Nash equilibrium–a situation in which each firm makes its best response, i.e., maximizes its profit, given the actions of rival firms (p. 368, 377)

national savings–private savings plus government savings (p. 823)

natural monopoly–an industry with increasing returns to scale over sufficiently large quantities (p. 331)

natural rate of unemployment–the unemployment rate that occurs when the economy produces the full-employment level of output (p. 745)

negative correlation–a relationship between variables that tend to move in opposite directions (inversely to one another) (p. 28)

negative externality–the result of a social cost of a good in excess of its private cost (p. 468)

negative slope–the shape of a curve that runs downward and to the right (p. 37)

net benefit (profit)–total benefit minus total cost (p. 240)

net exports, or the **balance of international trade**–exports minus imports (p. 557)

neutrality of money–the implication of an economic model that an increase in the nominal money supply raises nominal prices and wages but leaves real GDP, employment, and *relative* prices unaffected (p. 584)

nominal (money) wage–the wage rate measured in money (such as dollars, yen, or pesos (p. 400)

nominal GDP– GDP measured in money (dollars, yen, pesos, Euros, etc.) (p. 549)

nominal interest rate–the annual dollar interest payment on a loan expressed as a percentage of the dollar amount borrowed. (p. 606)

nominal money supply–the total amount of money in the economy, measured in monetary units such as dollars or yen (p. 582)

nominal money supply–the total dollar value of all paper money and coins in the economy (p. 658)

nominal price–the money price of a good (p. 94, 657)

nominal variable–a variable measured in terms of money, such as U.S. dollars, Mexican pesos, or Japanese yen (p. 657)

nominal wages–payments for labor services, measured in monetary units like dollars or yen (p. 584)

nonexcludable good–a good for which prohibitive costs prevent restricting access only to people who pay for it while excluding other people from obtaining it (p. 490)

nonprice rationing–a system for choosing who gets how many goods during a shortage (p. 180)

nonrival good–a good for which the quantity available to other people does not fall when someone consumes it (p. 490)

normal (accounting) profit–the level of accounting profit required for a zero economic profit (p. 308)

normal good–a good whose demand rises if income rises (p. 78)

normative statement–a statement that expresses a value judgment or says what should be; such a statement cannot be true or false (p. 18)

oligopoly–an industry in which (1) firms are not price takers (each faces a downward-sloping demand curve), and (2) each firm acts strategically, taking into account its competitors' likely reactions to its decisions and how it will be affected by those reactions (p. 365)

open market operation–a Federal Reserve purchase or sale of financial assets (p. 702)

opportunity cost–the value of whatever someone must sacrifice or give up to obtain something (p. 8)

optimal contract–an agreement that maximizes the principal's profit while providing an incentive for the agent to participate in the agreement (p. 453)

optimal taxation–a system of tax rates that minimizes the total deadweight social loss from taxes while raising a certain amount of revenue for the government (p. 518)

other-conditions fallacy–false reasoning that two events will always occur together in the future because they occurred together in the past (p. 26)

ownership–the right to make decisions about a scarce resource (p. 12)

Pareto improvement–a change in which at least one person gains and no one loses (p. 214)

payoff–amount that a player wins or loses in a particular game situation (p. 376)

perfect competition–competition among price-taking sellers (p. 303)

perfectly elastic demand (or supply)–infinite elasticity; demand (or supply) is a horizontal line (p. 103, 108)

perfectly inelastic demand (or supply)–elasticity equal to zero; demand (or supply) is a vertical line (p. 103, 108)

policy rule–a statement of what policy an agency will follow (p. 778)

positive correlation–a relationship between variables that tend to rise or fall together (p. 28)

positive externality–the result of a social benefit of a good in excess of its private benefit (p. 468)

positive externality–a situation in which the social benefit of an action exceeds its private benefit (p. 643)

positive slope–the shape of a curve that runs upward and to the right (p. 37)

positive statement–a statement of fact, of what is or what would be if something else were to happen; such a statement is either true or false (p. 18)

positive-sum game–an environment in which everyone can gain at the same time (p. 57)

post-hoc fallacy–false reasoning that, because one event happened before another, the first event must have caused the second event (p. 25)

price differential–a difference between the prices of identical goods in two locations (p. 160)

price discrimination–charging different prices to different buyers for the same good (p. 340)

price rigidity–slow adjustments of prices to changes in costs or demand (p. 367)

principal–a person who hires someone else to do something (p. 453)

private benefit–the benefit to people who buy and consume a good (p. 468)

private benefit–the benefit of production or investment to the people who produce a good or invest (p. 643)

private cost–the cost paid by a firm to produce and sell a good (p. 468)

private demand–demand for a good by people and businesses not owned or operated by the government (p. 124)

private ownership–a property right held by one person or a small group of people (p. 480)

privately held government debt–the amount of government debt owned by people and business firms outside the government (p. 819)

producer surplus–the benefit to a producer of selling a good at the equilibrium price (p. 211)

production function–a mathematical description of an economy's technology, showing the total production it can obtain from its inputs of labor, capital, and natural resources (p. 576)

production possibilities frontier (PPF)–a graph of the combinations of various goods that an economy can produce with its current resources and technology (p. 46)

profit–total revenue minus total cost (p. 260)

property right–a legal right to determine the use of a scarce resource or to sell the resource to someone else (p. 480)

public good–a nonrival and nonexcludable good (p. 491)

public-interest view of regulation–the assertion that government regulations serve the public interest (p. 510)

pure gold standard–a system in which people trade gold coins as money, and the economy includes no paper money (p. 692)

put option–a right to sell some underlying asset during some specified period of time at some preset strike price (p. 857)

quantity demanded (at a given price)–the amount that a person would buy at that price (p. 72)

quantity of money demanded–the amount of money that people would choose to own, given current conditions such as their income and wealth, the price level, the usefulness of money, and the costs and benefits of owning other assets (p. 661)

quantity supplied (at some price)–the amount that a seller would sell at that price (p. 81)

random walk–a price that is equally likely to rise or fall by the same amount, so, on average, people do not expect it to change (p. 174)

rate of job creation–the number of new workers hired each month (p. 587)

rate of job destruction–the number of people who quit or lose their jobs each month (p. 587)

rate of return–the income that an owner receives from an asset over some period of time plus the increase in its value during that period, all as a percentage of the original value of the asset (p. 832)

rational behavior–the actions of people when they do the best they can, based on their own values and information, under the circumstances they face (p. 24)

rational choice–the choice on your budget line that you most prefer (p. 237)

real GDP–GDP measured in the prices of a certain base year. (p. 549)

real interest rate–the interest rate *adjusted for inflation* (p. 606)

real variable–a variable that refers to a quantity of goods and services, often measured in base-year dollars (p. 657)

real wage–the wage rate adjusted for inflation, that is, measured in purchasing power units (p. 400)

real wages–wages measured in *base-year* dollars (p. 584)

recession–a period in which real GDP falls for two consecutive quarters (although the official National Bureau of Economic Research definition is more complex) (p. 560)

relative price–the opportunity cost of one good in terms of other goods (equal to one nominal price divided by another or divided by a price index) (p. 657)

relative price–the opportunity cost of the first good measured in units of the second good (p. 94)

renewable resource–a natural resource that can be replenished, such as trees (p. 639)

rent seeking–competition for favors from the government (p. 344)

rent seeking–the use of time, money, and other resources in pursuit of government benefits (spending, tax changes, or regulations targeted to some special-interest group) (p. 826)

required reserves–the reserves that the Fed requires banks to hold, based on their total deposits (p. 704)

reservation price–the highest price a person is willing to pay (if necessary) to acquire a good (p. 132)

risk averse–a preference for a less risky income, holding fixed its expected value (p. 452)

risk averse–a characteristic of a person who prefers less risk to more risk (p. 836)

risk neutral–an indifference toward risk (p. 452)

risk neutral–a characteristic of a person who does not care about risk, only about expected return (p. 836)

risk premium–an extra payment that compensates investors for risk (p. 838)

risk-free interest rate–the interest rate on a loan with no chance of default (p. 838)

rule of 72–a rule of thumb that a variable with a growth rate of X percent per year doubles after about $72/X$ years (p. 627)

search cost–the time and money cost of obtaining information about a price or a product (p. 446)

selection bias–use of data that are not typical, but are selected in a way that biases results (p. 27)

share of stock–legal right of ownership in a business firm, traded on a stock market (p. 173)

shift–a change in the position of a curve on a graph (p. 36)

short run–a period of time over which people cannot fully adjust their behavior to a change in conditions and a firm cannot vary the quantities of all its inputs (p. 277)

shortage–a situation in which quantity demanded exceeds quantity supplied at the current price (p. 87, 180)

short-run equilibrium–an equilibrium with a fixed number of firms (p. 303)

short-run Phillips Curve–a statistical relationship showing that unemployment falls temporarily when inflation rises, and unemployment rises temporarily when inflation falls (p. 745)

simple policy rule–a rule that requires a particular policy regardless of economic circumstances (p. 778)

slope–a number that shows the distance by which a curve goes up or down as it moves 1 unit to the right (p. 38)

social benefit–the total benefit of a good to everyone in society (p. 468)

social benefit–the benefit to everyone in society of private production or investment (p. 643)

social cost–the total cost of a good to everyone in society (p. 468)

special-interest view of regulation–the assertion that government regulations serve special-interest groups (p. 510)

speculation–buying a good when its price is low and storing it to sell in the future when its price might be higher (p. 162)

spot price–the price of a good for current delivery (p. 172)

statistical analysis–the use of mathematical probability theory to draw inferences in situations of uncertainty (p. 19)

statistical discrimination–involves making predictions about a person based on membership in a certain group (p. 434)

steady state–a long-run equilibrium with constant capital per person (p. 633)

sticky price–a price that takes time to adjust to its new equilibrium level following a change in conditions (also applies to the overall price level) (p. 723)

stock price–price of a share of stock (p. 173)

store of value–any good or asset that people can store while it maintains some or all of its value (p. 690)

substitute–a good that can replace another, so that a rise in the price of one increases demand for the other (p. 79)

sunk cost–a cost that you have already paid and cannot recover (p. 244)

supply curve–a graph of the relation between the price of a good and the quantity supplied (p. 82)

suppressed inflation–inflation that would occur without government controls on wages and prices, but that does not fully occur due to those controls (p. 684)

surplus–a situation in which quantity demanded is less than quantity supplied at the current price (p. 186)

takeover–when one person, a group of people, or another company buys enough stock in a firm to guarantee a majority vote at stockholder meetings (p. 862)

tariff–a tax on imports (p. 198, 882)

tax rate on income–the tax collected per dollar, as a percentage of income (p. 617)

tax rate–the per-unit tax on a good, expressed as a percentage of its price (p. 188)

technical efficiency–a situation in which an economy cannot produce more of one good without producing less of something else (p. 47)

technically efficient method of production–a method that does not waste any inputs, so the firm cannot produce the same amount of output using less of any input without using more of some other input (p. 259)

tie-in sale–a transaction in which a seller sells only to buyers who also agree to buy some other product (p. 182)

tighter monetary policy–Fed actions that reduce the growth rate of the money supply or raise the federal funds rate (p. 713)

tighter monetary policy–a policy that reduces the growth rates of the monetary base and broader measures of the money supply, increasing the federal funds rate (p. 775)

time consistent policy–policy in which the best discretionary decisions match the decisions suggested by the best rule (p. 784)

time cost–the time required to buy, prepare, and use a good (p. 133)

time inconsistent policy–policy in which the best discretionary decisions differ from the decisions suggested by the best rule (p. 784)

trade deficit–imports in excess of exports (p. 869)

trade surplus–exports in excess of imports (p. 869)

tragedy of the commons–overuse of a common resource relative to its economically efficient use (p. 481)

transactions costs–a cost of trading (buying and selling) (p. 475)

Treasury bill (T-bill)–a short-term debt security issued by the U.S. government, typically for a 3-month to 6-month loan (p. 838)

Treasury note–a debt security issued by the U.S. government, typically for a loan of 1 to 10 years (p. 838)

underemployed person–someone who wants a job that makes full use of his or her training and skills, but does not have one (p. 407)

unemployed person–someone who wants a job, but does not have one (p. 407)

unemployment rate–the fraction of unemployed people in the labor force. (p. 559)

unit of account–a measure for stating prices (p. 690)

unit-elastic demand (or supply)–elasticity equal to 1 (p. 103, 108)

utilitarianism–the view that justice results from maximizing the total amount of human happiness (p. 430)

utility–an abstract term for measuring human goals (such as happiness) (p. 239)

value of a firm–the discounted present value of the firm's expected future profits (p. 293)

value of the marginal product of an input–increase in the money value of a firm's output when it adds a little more of the input, keeping fixed the quantities of other inputs (p. 289)

value of the marginal product of labor–the increase in the money value of a firm's output when it employs a little more labor, keeping fixed quantities of other inputs (p. 397)

variable cost–an avoidable cost of a variable input (p. 278)

variable input–an input whose quantity a firm can change in the short run (p. 278)

variable–name of a set of numbers analyzed with a graph (ranged along the horizontal and vertical axes) or with mathematical methods (p. 32)

velocity of money–the average number of times per year that money is spent in the circular flow, equal to nominal GDP divided by the nominal money supply (p. 583)

wealth–the accumulated value of past savings, including human wealth (the value of education and skills) (p. 79)

World Trade Organization (WTO)–an international organization and a series of related treaties that reduce trade restrictions (p. 886)

zero-sum game–an environment in which one person's gain is another person's loss (p. 57)

Photo Credits

PP. 2, 5, 6 (margin), 7, 17, 45, 47, 48, 69, 70, 101, 114, 123, 132, 138, 153, 157, 179, 188, 207, 208, 235, 242, 257, 277, 278, 286, 301, 322, 342, 349, 351, 365, 366, 375, 376, 386, 387, 395, 404, 414, 417, 431, 445, 448, 455, 467, 469, 481, 490, 499, 501, 504, 525, 526, 529, 537, 547, 555, 556, 567, 571, 574, 578, 584, 595, 596, 603, 625, 640, 642, 667, 723, 754, 779, 787, 791, 801, 809, 855, 867, 882: © PhotoDisc

P. 6 (bottom) © Rob Crandall/Stock Connection

P. 23 © Looking Glass Studios, Inc. Used with permission.

P. 51 © Digital Stock

P. 79 © Roy Ooms/Masterfile

P. 106 © 1998 Don Couch Photography

P. 181 © SOVFOTO/TASS

P. 357 © 1998 Don Couch Photography

P. 572 Photo courtesy of University of Chicago.

P. 655 © UPI/Corbis-Bettman

P. 672 © Hulton Getty/Liaison Agency

P. 689 © Ken Reid/FPG International/PNI

P. 692 © Associated Press/European Union

P. 701 © Dennis Brack/Black Star/PNI

P. 707 © Associated Press/Misha Japaridze

P. 719 © Horace Bristol/Corbis Images

P. 739 © Keren Su/Stock, Boston/PNI

P. 773 © Dennis Brack/Black Star/PNI

P. 808 © Associated Press/Keith B. Srakocic

P. 831 Photo courtesy of the Chicago Board of Trade

"In the News" Credits

P. 9 © *New York Times,* April 25, 1993, p. F5.

P. 10 © *New York Times,* March 20, 1988, p. E6.

P. 15 *The Wall Street Journal,* April 9, 1991, p. A1, © Dow Jones & Company, Inc. All Rights Reserved Worldwide.

P. 28 © *New York Times,* December 1, 1987, p. C3.

P. 30 © *New York Times,* October 8, 1985, p. A14.

P. 78 *The Wall Street Journal,* May 11, 1993, p. B1, © Dow Jones & Company, Inc. All Rights Reserved Worldwide.

P. 79 © *The Rochester Democrat and Chronicle*

P. 80 © *New York Times,* April 16, 1991, p. A1.

P. 84 © *New York Times,* January 12, 1989.

P. 88 © *The Wall Street Journal,* © Dow Jones & Company, Inc. All Rights Reserved Worldwide.

P. 90 *The Wall Street Journal,* July 16, 1987, p. 31, © Dow Jones & Company, Inc. All Rights Reserved Worldwide.

P. 92 © *New York Times,* February 26, 1991.

P. 93 © *The Rochester Democrat and Chronicle*

P. 93 © *New York Times,* January 19, 1992, p. F8.

P. 107 © *Rochester Democrat and Chronicle,* May 27, 1989.

P. 116 *The Wall Street Journal,* July 29. 1980, p.1, © Dow Jones & Company, Inc. All Rights Reserved Worldwide.

P. 124 © *USA Today,* October 15, 1991, p. B1.

P. 127 *The Wall Street Journal,* January 25, 1993, p. C1, © Dow Jones & Company, Inc. All Rights Reserved Worldwide.

P. 130 *The Wall Street Journal,* March 11, 1988, p. 34, © Dow Jones & Company, Inc. All Rights Reserved Worldwide.

P. 131 *The Wall Street Journal,* October 28, 1986, © Dow Jones & Company, Inc. All Rights Reserved Worldwide.

P. 137 © *Economist,* May 8, 1993; and *Journal of Commerce,* May 16, 1994, p. 3A.

P. 138 © *The Economist*

P. 140 © *New York Times,* June 26, 1989, p. B1.

P. 141 *The Wall Street Journal,* September 22, 1988, © Dow Jones & Company, Inc. All Rights Reserved Worldwide.

P. 145 *The Wall Street Journal,* May 3, 1993, p. B1, © Dow Jones & Company, Inc. All Rights Reserved Worldwide.

P. 147 © *The Rochester Democrat and Chronicle,* January 31, 1993, p. 9F.

P. 147 *The Wall Street Journal,* June 25, 1986, p. 64, © Dow Jones & Company, Inc. All Rights Reserved Worldwide.

P. 148 © *The Rochester Democrat and Chronicle,* August 15, 1988.

P. 150 *The Wall Street Journal,* March 11, 1987, © Dow Jones & Company, Inc. All Rights Reserved Worldwide.

P. 151 *The Wall Street Journal,* May 13, 1988, p. 21R, © Dow Jones & Company, Inc. All Rights Reserved Worldwide.

P. 152 © *The Washington Post,* March 15, 1989, p. A26.

P. 157 © *The Rochester Democrat and Chronicle,* August 14, 1988.

P. 162 *The Wall Street Journal,* May 26, 1998, © Dow Jones & Company, Inc. All Rights Reserved Worldwide.

P. 165 *The Wall Street Journal,* February 10, 1989, © Dow Jones & Company, Inc. All Rights Reserved Worldwide.

P. 166 *The Wall Street Journal,* May 27, 1988, © Dow Jones & Company, Inc. All Rights Reserved Worldwide.

P. 170 *The Wall Street Journal,* July 12, 1993, p. C16, © Dow Jones & Company, Inc. All Rights Reserved Worldwide.

P. 173 © *The Rochester Democrat and Chronicle,* January 19, 1986, p. 17A.

P. 177 *The Wall Street Journal,* February 18, 1988, p. 34, © Dow Jones & Company, Inc. All Rights Reserved Worldwide.

P. 178 *The Wall Street Journal,* August 6, 1990, p. B1, © Dow Jones & Company, Inc. All Rights Reserved Worldwide.

P. 184 © *New York Times,* March 5, 1989, p. 3.

P. 185 © *New York Times International,* April 23, 1993.

P. 193 © *Montreal Gazette,* March 10, 1989, p. E1.

P. 196 "What Jane Austen Ate and Charles Dickens Knew," New York: Simon & Schuster, 1993.

P. 198 © *USA Today,* December 28, 1988.

P. 199 © *USA Today,* December 17, 1989, p. B1.

P. 200 © *New York Times,* December 6, 1988, p. D7.

P. 202 *The Wall Street Journal,* March 13, 1991, p. B3, © Dow Jones & Company, Inc. All Rights Reserved Worldwide.

P. 203 © *USA Today,* March 31, 1991, p. D1.

P. 229 © *Business Week*, June 5, 1989, p. 27.

P. 259 © *USA Today*, July 6, 1988, pp. B1–B2.

P. 259 *The Wall Street Journal*, June 28, 1988, p. 47, © Dow Jones & Company, Inc. All Rights Reserved Worldwide.

P. 267 © *Business Week*, March 27, 1989, p. 84.

P. 303 *The Wall Street Journal*, January 12, 1988, © Dow Jones & Company, Inc. All Rights Reserved Worldwide.

P. 304 © *San Francisco Chronicle*, February 10, 1989, p. C2; and *The Wall Street Journal*, June 10, 1988, p. R18, © Dow Jones & Company, Inc. All Rights Reserved Worldwide.

P. 305 *The Wall Street Journal*, June 3, 1988, p. 21, © Dow Jones & Company, Inc. All Rights Reserved Worldwide.

P. 306 *The Wall Street Journal*, April 24, 1987, © Dow Jones & Company, Inc. All Rights Reserved Worldwide.

P. 309 © *New York Times*, November 30, 1987, p. A1.

P. 315 *The Wall Street Journal*, June 10, 1988, p. R34, © Dow Jones & Company, Inc. All Rights Reserved Worldwide.

P. 319 *The Wall Street Journal*, September 29, 1988, p. 45, © Dow Jones & Company, Inc. All Rights Reserved Worldwide.

P. 322 © *New York Times*, December 11, 1988, p.1.

P. 332 © *Forbes*, May 23, 1994, p. 42.

P. 334 (margin) *The Wall Street Journal*, February 14, 1992, p. A2, © Dow Jones & Company, Inc. All Rights Reserved Worldwide.

P. 334 *The Wall Street Journal*, December 9, 1987, p. 6, © Dow Jones & Company, Inc. All Rights Reserved Worldwide.

P. 335 *The Wall Street Journal*, February 14, 1992, p. A2, © Dow Jones & Company, Inc. All Rights Reserved Worldwide.

P. 337 © *New York Times International*, September 15, 1993.

P. 337 *The Wall Street Journal*, June 17, 1987, p. 1, © Dow Jones & Company, Inc. All Rights Reserved Worldwide.

P. 338 *The Wall Street Journal*, March 24, 1993, © Dow Jones & Company, Inc. All Rights Reserved Worldwide.

P. 339 © *New York Times*, August 24, 1993.

P. 339 *The Wall Street Journal*, June 4, 1998, pp. A1, A11, © Dow Jones & Company, Inc. All Rights Reserved Worldwide.

P. 342 *The Wall Street Journal*, April 25, 1997, p. B1, © Dow Jones & Company, Inc. All Rights Reserved Worldwide.

P. 350 © *New York Times*, September 28, 1986, p. F1.

P. 363 *The Wall Street Journal*, August 23, 1989, p. B1, © Dow Jones & Company, Inc. All Rights Reserved Worldwide.

P. 366 © *New York Times*, May 15, 1987, p. 3.

P. 368 *The Wall Street Journal*, May 12, 1998, p. C1, © Dow Jones & Company, Inc. All Rights Reserved Worldwide.

P. 373 *The Wall Street Journal*, February 2, 1987, p. 25, © Dow Jones & Company, Inc. All Rights Reserved Worldwide.

P. 385 *The Wall Street Journal*, June 28, 1988, © Dow Jones & Company, Inc. All Rights Reserved Worldwide.

P. 389 *The Wall Street Journal*, November 17, 1988, p. A10, © Dow Jones & Company, Inc. All Rights Reserved Worldwide.

P. 390 © *Science'84*, October 1984.

P. 402 © *The Rochester Democrat & Chronicle*, September 25, 1989.

P. 404 (top) © *The Washington Post*

P. 404 (bottom) © *The New York Times*

P. 405 © *The Rochester Democrat and Chronicle*

P. 407 *The Wall Street Journal*, May 12, 1998, © Dow Jones & Company, Inc. All Rights Reserved Worldwide.

P. 426 © *U.S. News & World Report*, April 14, 1997, p. 68.

P. 427 © *Financial Times*, March 12–13, 1994, p. 3.

P. 428 *The Wall Street Journal*, January 2, 1998, © Dow Jones & Company, Inc. All Rights Reserved Worldwide.

P. 435 *The Wall Street Journal*, September 16, 1988, p. 27, © Dow Jones & Company, Inc. All Rights Reserved Worldwide.

P. 441 *The Wall Street Journal*, August 27, 1987, © Dow Jones & Company, Inc. All Rights Reserved Worldwide.

P. 442 *New York Times*, May 27, 1990.

P. 451 *The Wall Street Journal*, September, 1, 1989, p. C1, © Dow Jones & Company, Inc. All Rights Reserved Worldwide.

P. 454 *The Wall Street Journal*, February 9, 1989, © Dow Jones & Company, Inc. All Rights Reserved Worldwide.

P. 458 © *Washington Post*, March 12, 1993, p. F3.

P. 461 *The Wall Street Journal*, May 22, 1989, p. 89, © Dow Jones & Company, Inc. All Rights Reserved Worldwide.

P. 463 *The Wall Street Journal*, September 14, 1987, © Dow Jones & Company, Inc. All Rights Reserved Worldwide.

P. 471 *The Wall Street Journal*, September 4, 1997, p. B1, © Dow Jones & Company, Inc. All Rights Reserved Worldwide.

P. 473 © *Fort Worth Star-Telegram*, March 13, 1998, p. 23.

PP. 478, 479 © *New York Times*, March 17, 1989, p. A13.

P. 482 © *New York Times*, July 25, 1993, p. 13.

P. 485 © *New York Times*, August 20, 1991, p. C4.

P. 485 © *Financial Times*, May 16, 1994, p. 6.

P. 492 © *New York Times*, July 27, 1992, p. D3.

P. 493 © *New York Times*, February 18, 1987.

P. 511 © *Journal of Commerce*, November 21, 1994, p. 10A.

P. 514 (top) *The Wall Street Journal*, October 18, 1988, © Dow Jones & Company, Inc. All Rights Reserved Worldwide.

P. 514 (bottom) *The Wall Street Journal*, October 18, 1988, © Dow Jones & Company, Inc. All Rights Reserved Worldwide.

P. 515 © *New York Times*, April 22, 1988.

P. 516 *The Wall Street Journal*, © Dow Jones & Company, Inc. All Rights Reserved Worldwide.

P. 531 *The Wall Street Journal*, January 19, 1990, p. A16; *The Wall Street Journal*, January 10, 1991, p. A1, © Dow Jones & Company, Inc. All Rights Reserved Worldwide.

P. 534 *The Wall Street Journal*, October 27, 1988, p. B1, © Dow Jones & Company, Inc. All Rights Reserved Worldwide.

P. 536 © *The Rochester Democrat and Chronicle*, September 7, 1987, p. 12D.

P. 537 *The Wall Street Journal*, January 21, 1986, p. B1, © Dow Jones & Company, Inc. All Rights Reserved Worldwide.

P. 539 *The Wall Street Journal*, December 5, 1986, p. 33, © Dow Jones & Company, Inc. All Rights Reserved Worldwide.

P. 551 © *Investor's Business Daily*, June 26, 1998.

P. 560 (margin) © *International Herald Tribune*, June 6, 1998.

P. 560 (top) © *Reuters News*, October 15, 1998

P. 561 (margin) © *The Wall Street Journal*, May 12, 1998, © Dow Jones & Company, Inc. All Rights Reserved Worldwide.

P. 561 (bottom) © *CNBC*, September 3, 1998

P. 566 © *The Wall Street Journal*, January 9, 1998, p. A2, © Dow Jones & Company, Inc. All Rights Reserved Worldwide.

P. 569 © *The Wall Street Journal*, June 1, 1998, p. A4, © Dow Jones & Company, Inc. All Rights Reserved Worldwide.

P. 572 © *USA Today*, October 11, 1995, p. 2B.

P. 574 © *The Wall Street Journal*, June 15, 1998, p. C1, © Dow Jones & Company, Inc. All Rights Reserved Worldwide.

P. 581 © *New York Times*, September 6, 1998, p. A1.

P. 585 © *The Wall Street Journal*, July 17, 1998, p. A2, © Dow Jones & Company, Inc. All Rights Reserved Worldwide.

P. 586 © *PR Newswire*, September 8, 1998.

P. 587 © *USA Today*, September 4, 1998.

P. 599 © *Money Daily*, July 31, 1998.

P. 601 © *USA Today*, April 7, 1998, p. 1A.

P. 608 © *The Wall Street Journal*, February 22, 1990, p. C1, © Dow Jones & Company, Inc. All Rights Reserved Worldwide.

P. 613 © *USA Today*, July 1, 1998, p. 1B.

P. 614 © *USA Today*, June 14, 1990, p. 1B.

P. 621 © *The Wall Street Journal*, July 29, 1981, p. 46, © Dow Jones & Company, Inc. All Rights Reserved Worldwide.

P. 640 © *The Wall Street Journal*, May 1, 1989, p. A1, © Dow Jones & Company, Inc. All Rights Reserved Worldwide.

P. 644 © *New York Times*, September 24, 1987, p. A27.

P. 648 © *San Francisco Chronicle*

P. 649 © *New York Times*, May 22, 1988, p. F3.

P. 655 © *New York Times*, June 1, 1989, p. A7.

P. 656 © *New York Times*, June 18, 1988, p. A16.

P. 657 © *New York Times*, October 30, 1988, p. A3.

P. 666 © *The Wall Street Journal*, January 6, 1983, © Dow Jones & Company, Inc. All Rights Reserved Worldwide.

P. 668 (margin) © *USA Today*, December 31, 1986.

P. 668 (bottom) © *New York Times*, February 10, 1992, p. D5.

P. 672 © *The Wall Street Journal*, February 7, 1985, © Dow Jones & Company, Inc. All Rights Reserved Worldwide.

P. 673 © *The Wall Street Journal*, January 29, 1990, p. A10, © Dow Jones & Company, Inc. All Rights Reserved Worldwide.

P. 679 © *The Wall Street Journal*, June 14, 1988, p. A1, © Dow Jones & Company, Inc. All Rights Reserved Worldwide.

P. 680 © *Associated Press*, September 17, 1998.

P. 681 © *The Wall Street Journal*, August 2, 1993, p. A2, © Dow Jones & Company, Inc. All Rights Reserved Worldwide.

P. 683 (margin) © *USA Today*, May 20, 1988, pp. 1B–2B.

P. 683 (bottom) © *New York Times*, June 2, 1989, p. A2.

P. 684 © *New York Times*, July 6, 1989, p. A1.

P. 685 (margin) © *New York Times*, September 18, 1998, p. A1.

P. 685 (bottom) © *Associated Press*, September 16, 1998.

P. 694 © *Journal of Commerce*, March 9, 1994.

P. 703 © *The Wall Street Journal*, August 12, 1998, p. A4, © Dow Jones & Company, Inc. All Rights Reserved Worldwide.

P. 706 © *The Wall Street Journal*, August 31, 1998, p. A10, © Dow Jones & Company, Inc. All Rights Reserved Worldwide.

P. 707 (margin) © *The Wall Street Journal*, July 30, 1998, p. A13, © Dow Jones & Company, Inc. All Rights Reserved Worldwide.

P. 707 (bottom) © *New York Times*, January 8, 1989, p. B1.

P. 709 © *Newsweek*, May 21, 1990, p. 20.

P. 710 © *The Wall Street Journal*, May 8, 1989, p. A1, © Dow Jones & Company, Inc. All Rights Reserved Worldwide.

P. 712 © *The Wall Street Journal*, December 19, 1990, p. A2, © Dow Jones & Company, Inc. All Rights Reserved Worldwide.

P. 713 (margin) © *The Wall Street Journal*, May 21, 1992, p. A2, © Dow Jones & Company, Inc. All Rights Reserved Worldwide.

P. 713 (bottom) © *New York Times*, July 21, 1994, p. A1.

P. 720 © *Associated Press*, October 1, 1998.

P. 725 © *The Wall Street Journal*, September 2, 1998, p. A2, © Dow Jones & Company, Inc. All Rights Reserved Worldwide.

P. 730 © *International Herald Tribune*, June 23, 1998, p. 17.

P. 734 © *New York Times*, July 17, 1993, p. A1.

P. 735 © *The Asian Wall Street Journal*, April 22, 1991, p. 6., © Dow Jones & Company, Inc. All Rights Reserved Worldwide.

P. 742 © *MSNBC News*, October 8, 1998.

P. 744 © *The Wall Street Journal*, May 10, 1990, p. A1, © Dow Jones & Company, Inc. All Rights Reserved Worldwide.

P. 756 © *The Wall Street Journal*, May 1, 1998, p. A2, © Dow Jones & Company, Inc. All Rights Reserved Worldwide.

P. 763 (margin) © *The Washington Post*, July 21, 1989, p. 1.

P. 763 (bottom) © *USA Today*, December 15, 1988.

P. 764 © *The Wall Street Journal*, May 1, 1998, p. A2, © Dow Jones & Company, Inc. All Rights Reserved Worldwide.

P. 767 © *The Times* (London), October 5, 1998.

P. 775 © *The Wall Street Journal*, November 9, 1988, p. C23, © Dow Jones & Company, Inc. All Rights Reserved Worldwide.

P. 780 (margin) © *The Wall Street Journal*, March 20, 1989, p. A1, © Dow Jones & Company, Inc. All Rights Reserved Worldwide.

P. 780 (bottom) © *The Wall Street Journal*, September 30, 1998, p. A3, © Dow Jones & Company, Inc. All Rights Reserved Worldwide.

P. 781 (top) © *The Wall Street Journal,* July 31, 1998, p. A1, © Dow Jones & Company, Inc. All Rights Reserved Worldwide.

P. 781 © *New York Times,* September 20, 1987, p. 32.

P. 784 © *New York Times,* August 21, 1989, p. A25.

P. 789 © *St. Petersburg Times,* August 25, 1998, 393.

P. 790 © *The Wall Street Journal,* October 9, 1998, p. A8, © Dow Jones & Company, Inc. All Rights Reserved Worldwide.

P. 791 © *The Wall Street Journal,* January 6, 1998, p. A14, © Dow Jones & Company, Inc. All Rights Reserved Worldwide.

P. 792 © *New York Times,* April 26, 1998, p. A1.

P. 793 (top) © *The Wall Street Journal,* September 2, 1998, p. A10, © Dow Jones & Company, Inc. All Rights Reserved Worldwide.

P. 793 (margin) © *New York Times,* October 5, 1998.

P. 794 © *Rochester Democrat and Chronicle,* July 26, 1981, p. 3A.

P. 794 © *The Wall Street Journal,* October 21, 1989, © Dow Jones & Company, Inc. All Rights Reserved Worldwide.

P. 794 © *New York Times,* November 7, 1991, p. D8.

P. 809 © *New York Times,* March 6, 1998

P. 815 © *USA Today,* July 3, 1998

P. 838 © *USA Today,* September 30, 1998, p. 5B.

P. 843 © *The Wall Street Journal,* August 18, 1998, p. C18, © Dow Jones & Company, Inc. All Rights Reserved Worldwide.

P. 844 © *The Wall Street Journal,* July 30, 1998, pp. C1, C21, © Dow Jones & Company, Inc. All Rights Reserved Worldwide.

P. 847 © *The Wall Street Journal,* September 11, 1998, p. C4, © Dow Jones & Company, Inc. All Rights Reserved Worldwide.

P. 848 © *The Wall Street Journal,* September 11, 1998, p. C9, © Dow Jones & Company, Inc. All Rights Reserved Worldwide.

P. 849 © *The Wall Street Journal,* September 11, 1998, p. C14, © Dow Jones & Company, Inc. All Rights Reserved Worldwide.

P. 850 © *Forbes,* June 26, 1989, p. 178.

P. 853 © *The Wall Street Journal,* May 12, 1998, p. A38, © Dow Jones & Company, Inc. All Rights Reserved Worldwide.

P. 854 © *The Wall Street Journal,* January 26, 1990, p. A8, © Dow Jones & Company, Inc. All Rights Reserved Worldwide.

P. 855 © *New York Times,* August 31, 1998.

P. 858 © *The Wall Street Journal,* September 11, 1998, p. C16, © Dow Jones & Company, Inc. All Rights Reserved Worldwide.

P. 859 © *The Wall Street Journal,* September 11, 1998, p. C13, © Dow Jones & Company, Inc. All Rights Reserved Worldwide.

P. 877 © *New York Times,* November 29, 1990, p. D1.

P. 884 © *New York Times,* November 30, 1990, p. D6.

P. 885 (top) *The Wall Street Journal,* June 1, 1986, p. 30, © Dow Jones & Company, Inc. All Rights Reserved Worldwide.

P. 885 (bottom) *The Wall Street Journal,* January 11, 1989, p. A9, © Dow Jones & Company, Inc. All Rights Reserved Worldwide.

P. 890 © *New York Times,* April 24, 1990, p. D1.

P. 890 © *New York Times,* September 26, 1991, p. D1.

P. 891 ©*The Wall Street Journal,* February 1, 1993, p. A6, © Dow Jones & Company, Inc. All Rights Reserved Worldwide.

P. 892 © *New York Times,* February 7, 1992, p. A1.

Additional Credits (Cartoons, Figures, and Tables):

P. 90 *The Far Side.* 1987 FARWORKS, Inc. Distributed by Universal Press Syndicate. Reprinted with permission. All Rights Reserved.

P. 143 "Buying a $40,000 car made me a safer driver," by Sauers. From *The Wall Street Journal,* October 18, 1987. Reprinted by permission of Cartoon Features Syndicate.

P. 248 For Better or Worse © Lynn Johnston Prod., Inc. Reprinted with permission of Universal Press Syndicate. All Rights Reserved.

P. 340 "$200 for a loaf of bread! I told you never to go shopping in uniform!" From *The Wall Street Journal,* May 20, 1988. Reprinted by permission of Cartoon Features Syndicate.

P. 406 "He may be a highly paid anchorman, but I have the power to zap him anyway," From *The Wall Street Journal,* August 12, 1993. Reprinted by permission of Cartoon Features Syndicate.

P. 453 "Naughty or nice? You mean you'll just take my word for it?" From *The Wall Street Journal,* December 22, 1989. Reprinted by permission of Cartoon Feature Syndicate.

P. 457 "Since we took out that million-dollar insurance policy, I notice you don't remind me to use my seat belt anymore," by Hoest, November 22, 1988. Reprinted with special permission of King Features Syndicate.

P. 708 "Yeah, but who guarantees the federal government?" From *The Wall Street Journal,* August 15, 1986. Reprinted by permission of Cartoon Features Syndicate.

P. 726 "Whether the marriage lasts or not, we've certainly given the economy a boost." From *The Wall Street Journal,* October 25, 1988. Reprinted by permission of Cartoon Features Syndicate.

P. 733 ©*Richmond-Times Dispatch.* Reprinted by permission.

P. 883 James Bovard, *The Fair Trade Fraud,* New York: St. Martin's Press, 1991.